UNDERSTANDING MANAGEMENT

THIRD EDITION

UNDERSTANDING MANAGEMENT

THIRD EDITION

RICHARD L. DAFT
Vanderbilt University

DOROTHY MARCIC
Vanderbilt University

SOUTH-WESTERN
™
THOMSON LEARNING

Australia • Canada • Mexico • Singapore • Spain
United Kingdom • United States

SOUTH-WESTERN
THOMSON LEARNING

Publisher	Mike Roche	**Production Manager**	Serena Barnett Sipho
Senior Acquisitions Editor	John Weimeister	**Project Management**	Elm Street Publishing Services, Inc.
Market Strategist	Beverly Dunn		
Senior Developmental Editor	Tracy Morse	**Cover Printer**	R. R. Donnelley, Willard
Project Editors	Travis Tyre, Elaine Richards	**Compositor**	Graphic World
		Printer	R. R. Donnelley, Willard
Art Directors	Carol Kincaid, Burl Sloan		

For more information about our products,
contact us at:
Thomson Learning Academic Resource Center
1-800-423-0563

For permission to use material from this text,
contact us by:
Phone: 1-800-730-2214
Fax: 1-800-730-2215
Web: http://www.thomsonrights.com

Library of Congress Catalog Card Number: 00-30607
ISBN: 0-03-031816-5

Asia
Thomson Learning
60 Albert Street, #15-01
Albert Complex
Singapore 189969

Australia
Nelson Thomson Learning
102 Dodds Street
South Melbourne, Victoria 3205
Australia

Canada
Nelson Thomson Learning
1120 Birchmount Road
Toronto, Ontario M1K 5G4
Canada

Europe/Middle East/Africa
Thomson Learning
Berkshire House
168-173 High Holborn
London WC1 V7AA
United Kingdom

Latin America
Thomson Learning
Seneca, 53
Colonia Polanco
11560 Mexico D.F.
Mexico

Spain
Paraninfo Thomson Learning
Calle/Magallanes, 25
28015 Madrid, Spain

To the late Martin S. Geisel,
dean, mentor, and friend.
r.l.d.

For my father,
who has been the source of great learning for me in the last two years.
d.m.

PREFACE

TAKING THE LEAD

We are entering a new era, one unlike any before, and the major difference can be summed up in a word: change. The tremendous forces behind such change include the intensity of increased globalization; the movement of people around the world (with its accompanying multiculturalism); and perhaps most of all, the explosion of the information age, epitomized by e-commerce. *Understanding Management,* Third Edition, was developed to help students grasp these changes and cope with the emerging economies of the world, and it has particular relevance to those who are interested in understanding the value and dynamics of small- and medium-sized organizations. Unlike traditional management texts, this book does not rely on abstract theories and examples from corporations that are applicable only to top managers of billion-dollar companies. Rather, our vision is to appeal to students on a practical level and to provide insight and meaningful information for them to succeed in their futures of "working for a living." To this end, *Understanding Management* contains four distinctive elements, two of which are completely new to this edition:

1. **Management concepts** presented in each chapter and appendix are current and ongoing. They were selected for their relevance and appeal to students interested in real management issues and how problems are being addressed in local companies. These management concepts are especially applicable to readers with interests in small business management and entrepreneurship. In addition to the easy-to-understand writing style of the book, many practical examples and profiles are of real people involved in real business dilemmas.

2. **Case applications, boxed items, boldfaced key terms (with on-page definitions), exhibits, photo captions, and end-of-chapter materials** are heavily oriented toward middle management and explore supervisory issues being dealt with in smaller companies. *Understanding Management,* Third Edition, focuses on vivid illustrations of real organizations that affect people at every level, whatever the size of the company. In our view, this is not only the most interesting, up-to-date, and practical way to reinforce our vision of the book, but it is also a very effective way to help students identify with and fully comprehend the changing state of current management situations. Also, photo essays illustrate specific management concepts, and the carefully chosen photographs provide intimate glimpses into current management events and people, to give students a view of how a specific management concept looks and feels. Both the textual and the graphic portions of the textbook help students grasp the often abstract and sometimes distant world of management.

3. New to the third edition is an **emphasis on Internet businesses and e-commerce.** Every chapter contains examples of e-commerce and how it is affecting the world of business, locally, nationally, and globally. In keeping with the content and theme of the book, the focus is on small businesses and entrepreneurialism.

4. Also new is an intriguing **business novel (with exercises) called *Bottom Line.*** This unique addition to the ancillary package is a new novel about the current workplace that is not only a great read, but has opportunities for students to interact with the ideas and issues brought out in the story. More about this "novel" approach is explained later in the preface.

FOCUS ON THE FUTURE

The field of management is undergoing a revolution. Demands on today's managers go well beyond the techniques and ideas taught in traditional management courses. The old management paradigm assumed that the purpose of management was to control and limit people, enforce rules and regulations, seek stability and efficiency, design a top-down hierarchy to direct people, and achieve bottom-line results. However, the emerging paradigm recognizes that today's managers need different skills, ones that engage workers' hearts and minds, as well as their physical labor. This "new" management paradigm focuses on *leadership,* on harnessing everyone's creativity and enthusiasm, finding a shared vision and values, and sharing information and power. Teamwork, collaboration, participation, and learning are the guiding principles that help managers and employees navigate the difficult terrain of today's increasingly complex business environment. Managers now focus on developing—not controlling—people to adapt to extraordinary environmental shifts and achieve total corporate effectiveness.

But, the old has not, and perhaps should not, completely disappear from the business environment. Both paradigms—the new and the traditional—continue to guide management actions today. This book explores the new paradigm in a way that is interesting and valuable to students, yet it retains the best of traditional management ideas. We have included the most recent management thinking and research, as well as the traditional approaches that are being applied in contemporary organizations. The combination of established scholarship, new ideas, and real-life applications give students a taste of the energy, challenge, and adventure that are inherent in the dynamic field of management. In this way, *Understanding Management,* Third Edition, helps students gain both a respect for management concepts and the confidence to understand and master them.

Understanding Management, above all, is focused on the future: the future of business management principles, the future changes in store for the global marketplace, and the future success of students whose careers will take them into this exciting, ever-changing world. Our vision has been to provide a textbook that is better than any other at capturing the excitement of organizational management. We certainly hope you find our efforts worthwhile and stimulating.

ORGANIZATION

Understanding Management, Third Edition, is organized around the four management functions: planning, organizing, leading, and controlling. Its six parts encompass both management research and real-life characteristics of the manager's job. Using the challenging Whitbread sailing competition as a means to describe these concepts, each part opens with brief, exciting narratives designed to involve students' imagination and focus their attention on what is ahead. Here is a concise chronology of the book, with significant revisions for this edition described:

- **Part I: Managers in Learning Organizations**—Chapter 1 introduces the emerging management paradigm, the growing importance of leadership and new management competencies needed to thrive in today's business world. The chapter also explores the nature of management and the forces affecting contemporary organizations. The "learning organization" is introduced and examined as an extension of the historical development of management and organizations.
- **Part II: The Environment of Management**—Chapter 2 defines the business environment and corporate culture and the challenges of maintaining a unique identity and effective procedures in an increasingly global, multicultural environment. Chapters 3 and 4 delve into the details of managing in a global context and applying ethics and responsibility to management, to the corporation as a whole, and to society.

- **Part III: The Environment of Management**—Chapters 5 and 6 are complete revisions of previous material and describe managerial decision-making and information systems and technology. Keeping pace with rapid changes in these areas, these chapters include new or expanded material on such topics as intranets and extranets, geographic information systems, data mining, enterprise resource planning, and knowledge management. Recognizing that technologically-savvy companies are leading the information revolution, topics include online shopping, paperless office systems, Internet recruiting, and cross-cultural traps to avoid when building content on company Web sites. Trends toward empowerment and participation have been strengthened in these chapters. A brief discussion of personal decision-making styles has been added to give students a better understanding of how individual style differences affect managers and their decision making.

- **Part IV: Organizing**—These chapters describe dimensions of structural design, the design alternatives managers can use to achieve strategic objectives, structural designs for promoting innovation and change, the design and use of the human resource function, and the ways in which the managing of diverse employees can be significant to the organizing function. Chapters 7 and 8 explore the fundamentals of organizing in current environments. Chapter 9 provides current information on human resource management and examines the changing social contract between people and organizations and the ways this contract can affect the nature of careers and career management. Chapter 10 explores diversity in the workplace and emphasizes the challenges faced by minorities in business.

- **Part V: Leading**—This section is devoted to leadership and paves the way for discussions about motivating employees, communicating effectively, and managing teams. Chapters 11, 12, and 13 establish the foundations of organizational behavior with expanded topics on personality types, job satisfaction, organizational commitment, effects of stress, and person-job fit. Specific topics include symbolic leadership, job design for motivation, and using persuasion and influence. Chapter 14 explores the multifaceted issue of communication in the workplace. From the basics of the communication process to organizational hierarchies of communication to overcoming barriers to communication, this chapter shows the various approaches to communicating and their varying degrees of effectiveness. Chapter 15 defines teamwork, points out its inherent benefits and conflicts, and explores self-direction and accountability within teams.

- **Part VI: Controlling**—Chapter 16 describes the controlling function of management, including basic principles of total quality management (TQM), the design of control systems and information technology, and finally control techniques for successful operations management.

- **Appendixes**—Three appendixes include video cases, continuing cases, and a section on entrepreneurship and small business management. The latter explores various aspects of running a business, the entrepreneurial role, and topics such as the elements of a strong business plan, personality traits of entrepreneurs, and case studies of entrepreneurial firms and the environments entrepreneurs tend to create.

SPECIAL FEATURES

Another major goal of this book is to offer better ways of using the textbook medium to convey management knowledge to readers. We believe several special features do just that:

Chapter Outline and Objectives. Each chapter begins with a set of learning objectives and an outline of its contents to be used by students as an overview of what is to come and as a tool to evaluate whether they understand and have retained important points.

Management Problem/Solution. A real-life problem being faced by a real organization is profiled at the beginning of each chapter to heighten student interest and to focus on the scope of the chapter. Solutions are discussed in the Summary and Management Solution section at the end of each chapter.

Photo Essays. Photographs, accompanied by detailed captions, help describe management events and how they relate to the chapter material. Numerous full-color photos convey the vividness, immediacy, and concreteness of management events in today's very real business world.

Contemporary Examples. Every chapter contains numerous examples of management issues and incidents that demonstrate how specific management concepts have been applied in actual companies. Examples feature well-known companies such as McDonald's, General Electric, and Hewlett-Packard, as well as many lesser-known small and medium-sized companies, including a few not-for-profit organizations.

Exhibits. While many aspects and concepts of management are research-based, others tend to be abstract and theoretical. To enhance students' awareness of both kinds, chapter exhibits are included throughout the book. The exhibits consolidate key points, indicate relationships among theories and applications, and illustrate concepts in a colorful, concise, and graphically-appealing manner.

Boxed Items. Appearing in every chapter, these boxes graphically describe current management practices. *Leading the Revolution* focuses on Leadership and the emerging Learning Organization concept; *Manager's Shoptalk* addresses topics straight from the field of management; *Focus on . . .* boxes cover topics of diversity, cooperation, and entrepreneurship; and *Technology for Tomorrow* boxes describe specific technologies and how they are shaping the 21st century business environment. Companies profiled in these examples include Hewlett-Packard, Nissan Design International, the Girl Scouts of America, Lucent Technologies, Cisco Systems, and even the U.S. Army. Their purpose is to help students integrate topics with other concepts, so they can better understand and apply their ideas in assignments or in classroom discussion and interaction.

Glossaries. Gaining a solid grasp of management vocabulary is essential to understanding contemporary management. This book provides three ways to do this: (1) Key terms are bold-faced on the page; (2) Concise definitions of these terms are located directly across from them in the margin for easy review and follow up; (3) A comprehensive glossary containing all key terms and definitions appears at the end of the book for handy reference.

Chapter Summary and Discussion Questions. Each chapter closes with a summary of key points for students to review and retain. Discussion questions are a complementary learning tool to enable students to check their understanding of key issues, to think beyond basic concepts, and to determine areas that require further study.

Management in Practice Exercises. These end-of-chapter exercises provide self-tests for students and an opportunity to experience management issues in a personal way. Management Workbook activities are for individual work, while the Manager's Workshop exercises are designed for group effort. Exercises take the form of questionnaires, scenarios, and activities, and provide opportunities for students to work in teams. Additional Manager's Workbook and Workshop exercises can be found in the Study Guide/Workbook that accompanies this textbook.

Surf the Net. These Internet exercises involve students in the high-tech world of cyberspace. Students are given tools to explore the World Wide Web and are encouraged to research various topics related to each chapter and gain hands-on experience with the Internet to develop their management skills.

Case for Critical Analysis. Brief, but substantive, case studies appear at the end of each chapter to provide an opportunity for students to analyze and discuss relevant and current management issues and dilemmas. Some of the cases involve companies that students will readily recognize, while the identity of others has been disguised. Nevertheless, all cases are based on real management events and allow students to sharpen their diagnostic skills for management problem solving.

Video Cases. These cases found in Appendix A enhance class discussion and help students apply the management theories they have learned. The Instructor's Manual and accompanying Web site also provide detailed descriptions of each video, classroom activities, and discussion questions and answers.

SUPPLEMENTARY MATERIALS—LEADING BY EXAMPLE

The *Understanding Management,* Third Edition, ancillary package is loaded with powerful resources for students and instructors alike. Combining the latest technology with proven teaching tools, this innovative package enables students to put chapter concepts into action and gain valuable insight into real-world practices. In addition, an expansive collection of supplemental teaching material offers support to instructors—from the novice to the most seasoned professor.

Completely integrated with the text, this comprehensive package leads the market with these cutting-edge features:

- **New! The *Understanding Management* Web site**—Students and professors can access countless business and education resources. This easy-to-navigate site contains a wealth of *Management Topics.* Just follow the link to find topic-specific publication pages, trends and forecasts, business data, company profiles, general articles, tools, exercises and much more. Each topic site links instructors to teaching resources, bibliographies of articles related to text material, ideas on incorporating the Internet into the classroom, and more. In addition, the *Reading Room* links users to business journals, daily newspapers, magazines, and marketing publications from across the country and around the world. A *Syllabus Generator* is available to help professors quickly customize their course syllabi. Students will find the *Online Quizzing* section especially helpful, allowing them to take multiple quizzes. Comprised of approximately 15–20 questions per quiz, each quiz has True/False and multiple-choice questions that cover information presented in each chapter. A *Marketing Careers* section enables students to discover marketing careers and to locate currently-posted job opportunities in business. Many sites include extensive career information and guidance, such as interviewing techniques and résumé-writing. A *Time Management* section features advice and guidelines for students to effectively manage their study, work, and leisure time, including how to set priorities and avoid procrastinating on studying. The *Understanding Management* Web site includes so many resources for each chapter that it can be used as the foundation for a distance-learning course. Our interactive site helps students sharpen their surfing skills, while driving home key marketing concepts. Find it at:

  http://www.harcourtcollege.com/management

- **Instructor's Manual**—Designed to provide support for instructors new to the course, this innovative IM also features helpful materials for more experienced professors. *Lecture Outlines* offers information and examples not found in the text, such as annotated learning objectives, answers to chapter discussion questions, and teaching notes for the end-of-chapter cases and exercises. In addition, the video notes are available to help instructors integrate video segments directly into classroom discussion. Support materials include a video outline, references to concepts within the chapter that are discussed in the video, answers to video case discussion questions, and individual and group exercises. The Instructor's Manual is available for professors in an electronic format via the *Understanding Management* home page.

- **Test Bank and Computerized Test Bank**—The newest edition ExaMaster '99 is a cross-platform CD-ROM that works with the latest versions of Windows® and Windows NT® operating systems. *ExaMaster '99* includes online testing capabilities, a grade book, and much more. Scrutinized for accuracy, the Test Bank includes more than 2,000 True/False, multiple-choice, short-answer, and essay questions, which have been rated for difficulty. The Test Bank is available in printed form or in a Windows® format.

- **RequesTest and ON-Line Testing Service**—We make test planning quicker and easier than ever with this program. Instructors can order test masters by question number and criteria via a toll-free telephone number (available through your sales representative). Test masters will be mailed or faxed within 48 hours. Harcourt can provide instructors with software to install their own online testing program, allowing tests to be administered over network or individual terminals. This program offers instructors greater flexibility and convenience in grading and scoring test results.

- **Study Guide/Workbook**—Packed with additional applications, this learning supplement is an excellent resource for students. For each chapter of the text, the Study Guide includes chapter outlines; key term reviews; self tests comprised of multiple-choice, True/False, and short-answer questions; management applications; and a wealth of Manager's Workbook and Workshop exercises that can be assigned as homework or used in class. All of the Manager's Workbook and Manager's Workshop exercises from the main text are included in the Study Guide and Workbook, as well as many new additional ones.

- **New! Business Novel with Exercises**—*Bottom Line* by Dorothy Marcic is an intriguing, contemporary novel about murder, greed, and betrayal in the workplace. The heroine, Lenore, is the human resources director for Nelson Manufacturing—a small and well-run company—that is suddenly taken over by a greedy and profit-driven conglomerate.

  The novel shows the negative effects upon the workforce of a few common practices of modern management, such as indiscriminate cuts in personnel and budgets, the treatment of workers as cogs in a machine, egotism at the top, and an unrelenting obsession with the quarterly profit picture. *Bottom Line* synthesizes many true stories from a number of actual companies, and virtually all of the stories and people are real. *Bottom Line* is a morality tale of good versus evil in corporate America and is a unique and innovative addition to the case study approach of *Understanding Management*. A detailed *study guide* accompanies the novel and contains exercises that give students opportunities to interact with the issues brought out in the story.

- **Improved and updated! Acetates/Masters**—Using artwork from the text, as well as outside materials, the full-color acetates and masters are available separately and both include detailed teaching notes.

- **New and improved! Videos**—A complete set of videos featuring the management practices of actual companies and their executives supports the written video cases found in Appendix A. The videos have been updated for the third edition and include Hard Candy, Holigan Group, J. C. Penney, Southwest Airlines, Yahoo!, and more. Teaching notes for the video package can be found in the Instructor's Manual as well as on the home page of the *Understanding Management* Web site.

- **New! WebCT Course**—Delivered via the WebCT platform, this *Understanding Management* Online Course combines our market-leading textbook and ancillary package with the vast resources of the Internet and the convenience of anytime learning. WebCT facilitates the creation of sophisticated Web-based educational environments and provides a set of course design tools to help you manage course content. It also comes with a set of communication tools to facilitate online classroom collaboration and administrative tools for tracking and managing your students' progress.

Extremely user-friendly, the powerful customization features of the WebCT framework enable instructors to incorporate their own unique teaching styles and their students' individual needs into the course. Features include content keyed to *Understanding Management,* Third Edition; self-tests and online exams; Internet activities and links to related resources; a suggested course syllabus; student and instructor materials; free technical support for instructors; and much more. In addition, the text's PowerPoint Presentation Software also is integrated into the WebCT course.

Additionally, with a qualified adoption, We offer free access to a blank WebCT template. We will host any course for you (with no Thomson content) where you can input your original materials and use in your classroom.

- **New! WebCT Testing Service**—If testing is all you want, HCP will upload the computerized Test Bank into a course (with no publisher content). If you like, HCP will even host it for you on our server.

- **New! WebCT Student Manual**—Included with the *Understanding Management* Online Course, this unique manual offers a wealth of information for Web users, from novices to the most advanced. The manual provides general instruction about the World Wide Web for Internet beginners, while more experienced users can skip to the step-by-step information on how to use the WebCT's course tools.

- **New and improved! PowerPoint CD-ROM Presentation Software**—This innovative presentation tool enables instructors to customize their own multimedia classroom presentations. The package includes figures and tables from the text, as well as outside materials to supplement chapter concepts. Material is organized by chapter, and instructors can use the material as is or expand and modify it for individual classes. The software is available in PowerPoint 97, which allows instructors to simply click on links to move from the PowerPoint presentation to Web sites.

- **Discovering Your Management Career CD-ROM**—This CD-ROM titled "Discovering Your Management Career" contains three programs, each of which may be used in conjunction with your course. They are:

  1. *Discovering Your Management Career* helps students learn about and assess their compatibility in four major management career areas (1) Corporate Financial Management, (2) Marketing Management, (3) Retail Bank Management, and (4) Store Operations, which were selected not only to represent the diversity of management opportunities available, but also the number of jobs in these fields. For each career, students receive broad guidance and practical advice on everything from clarifying the depth of their interest in that management area to preparing and implementing an effective job search strategy.

  2. *Career Design* is a free student version of the landmark *Career Design* career planning software program. Based on the work of John Crystal, the major contributor to the most widely read career book of all time *What Color Is Your Parachute?* by Richard N. Bolles, *Career Design* has received worldwide coverage and praise from both the business and computer press, including *BusinessWeek, Fortune, The Wall Street Journal, The Financial Times, The London Times, PC Magazine,* and *PC Computing.* The student version provides general career exercises and a wealth of other resources.

  3. *Management at Sea* offers students a realistic and exciting view of management in action. Through commentary on actual footage from major sailing races, students learn how effective management can lead to better results. Sailing is a metaphor for this key management theme: If management can make a difference in a sport like sailing, it can clearly make a difference in the business world where a rapidly changing environment and intense

competition are norms, rather than exceptions. Footage of boat construction and race preparation is used to illustrate planning and organizing principles, while videos of sailing races demonstrate leading and controlling.

- **New! Performance Module**—In the real world, the bottom line is performance. Employees, managers, top-level executives, entire companies—everything—are evaluated on performance. This unique new module takes an in-depth look at performance issues. It provides insightful material to reinforce class discussions and gives students practice with performance issues.

- **Multicultural Diversity Module**—This module offers an inside look at the broad topic of cultural, ethnic, and gender diversity in today's workplace.

- **Quality Module**—This publication covers the history of the quality movement up to present practices and developments, spotlighting quality pioneers such as W. Edwards Deming, Joseph M. Juran, and Philip Crosby.

- **Management and the Natural Environment Module**—This module addresses issues of the natural environment with each functional management topic. The module includes a separate video, as well as instructor's notes.

ACKNOWLEDGMENTS

A gratifying experience for us has been working with the Fort Worth team of professionals at Harcourt College Publishers, who remain committed to the vision of producing a concise, market-leading management textbook. We are grateful to John Weimeister, senior acquisitions editor, whose enthusiasm, creative ideas, and vision kept the book's spirit alive. Tracy Morse, senior developmental editor, provided superb project coordination and offered excellent ideas and suggestions to help the team meet a demanding and sometimes arduous schedule. And last, but not least, we thank the project editors, whose overall attention to detail contributed greatly to the quality of the final book: Travis Tyre, who had an unending sense of patience as we worked together through the copyediting process, and Elaine Richards, who skillfully guided the book to completion.

We want to extend special appreciation to Linda Roberts at Vanderbilt, who provided excellent typing and additional assistance that allowed us time to write. We also wish to acknowledge an intellectual debt to colleagues Bruce Barry, Ray Friedman, Barry Gerhart, Tom Mahoney, Rich Oliver, David Owens, and Greg Stewart. Thanks also to the late dean Marty Geisel who always supported our various projects and maintained a positive scholarly atmosphere in the school.

Our heartfelt thanks goes to the departmental staff of Leadership and Organizations at Vanderbilt University. Ruby Fisher, Ida Reale, Joyce Barkesdale, Connie McGahey, and Marty Morrissey have helped so often with their unselfish efforts. Two department chairs who were most supportive: Joe Murphy, who never seemed to tire with solving our problems and Jim Guthrie, who showed a gift for clarifying issues and gathering resources for projects. Intellectual and emotional support were continuous from colleagues Mary Watson, John Maslyn, Janet Eyler,

Pat Arnold, Bonita Barger, Claire Smrekar, John Braxton, Phil Hallinger, Kassie Freeman, Bob Crowson, Ellen Goldring, Jacob Adams, and Michael McClendon. Dean Camilla Benbow has also been supportive of our intellectual pursuits. A special tribute goes to editorial associate Pat Lane, who provided truly outstanding help with this revision. She skillfully drafted materials for several cases and researched topics when new sources were lacking.

Enormous thanks go to our children—and grandchildren—who lived with stressed-out parents. Danielle, Amy, Roxanne, Solange, and Elizabeth are the joys of our lives, not to be outdone by the grandchildren B. J., Kaitlyn, Matthew, and Kaci.

Other people who made major contributions to this textbook are the management experts who provided advice, reviews, answers to our questions, and suggestions for changes, insertions, and clarifications. We want to thank these colleagues for their valuable feedback and suggestions: Hal Babson, Columbus State Community College; Kristin Backhaus, SUNY–New Paltz; Jan Beyer, University of Texas; Bonnie Chavez, Santa Barbara Community College; John Edwards, Southern Illinois University–Carbondale; Martin Lecker, Rockland Community College; Susan Leshnower, Midland College; Don Lisnerski, University of North Carolina–Ashville; Stephen Peters, Walla Walla Community College; Brian Porter, Hope College; Amit Shah, Frostburg State University; Jessica Simmons, University of Texas; and Kent Zimmerman, James Madison University.

ABOUT THE AUTHORS

Richard L. Daft, Ph.D., holds the Ralph Owen chair of management in the Owen School of Management at Vanderbilt University, where he specializes in the study of organization theory and leadership. Dr. Daft is a Fellow of the Academy of Management and has served on the editorial boards of *Academy of Management Journal, Administrative Science Quarterly,* and *Journal of Management Education.* He was associate editor-in-chief of *Organization Science* and served for three years as associate editor of *Administrative Science Quarterly.*

Professor Daft has authored or co-authored 11 books, including *Organization Theory and Design* (Southwestern College Publishing, 1998), *Management,* 5th Edition (Harcourt College Publishers, 2000), *Leadership: Theory and Practice* (The Dryden Press, 1999), and *What to Study: Generating and Developing Research Questions* (Sage, 1982). He recently published *Fusion Leadership: Unlocking the Subtle Forces That Change People and Organizations* (Berrett-Koehler, 1998, with Robert Lengel). He has also authored dozens of scholarly articles, papers, and chapters that have been published in *Academy of Management Review, Strategic Management Journal, Journal of Management, Accounting Organizations and Society, Management Science, MIS Quarterly, California Management Review,* and *Organizational Behavior Teaching Review.* Professor Daft has been awarded several government research grants to pursue studies in organization design, organizational innovation and change, strategy implementation, and organizational information processing.

Dr. Daft is also an active teacher and consultant and has taught management, leadership, organizational change, organizational theory, and organizational behavior. He has been involved in management development and consulting for many companies and government organizations, including American Banking Association, Bell Canada, National Transportation Research Board, NL Baroid, Nortel, TVA, Pratt & Whitney, State Farm Insurance, Tenneco, the United States Air Force, the U.S. Army, J. C. Bradford & Co., Central Parking System, Entergy Sales and Service, First American National Bank, and the Vanderbilt University Medical Center.

Dorothy Marcic, Ed.D. and, M.P.H., is a faculty member and director of graduate programs in human resource development at Vanderbilt University. Dr. Marcic is a former Fulbright Scholar at the University of Economics in Prague and the Czech Management Center, where she taught courses and did research in leadership, organizational behavior, and cross-cultural management. She also teaches courses at the Monterrey Institute of International Studies and the University of Economics in Prague and has taught courses or given presentations at the Helsinki School of Economics, Slovenian Management Center, College of Trade in Bulgaria, City University in Slovakia, Landegg Institute in Switzerland, the Swedish Management Association, Technion University in Israel, and the London School of Economics. Other international work includes projects at the Autonomous University in Guadalajara, Mexico, and a training program for the World Health Organization in Guatemala. She has served on the boards of the Organizational Behavior Teaching Society, the Health Administration Section of the American Public Health Association, and the Journal of Applied Business Research.

Dr. Marcic has authored 11 books, including *Organizational Behavior: Experiences and Cases* (Southwestern Publishing, 6th Edition, 2001), *Management International* (West Publishing, 1984) *Women and Men in Organizations* (George Washington University, 1984), and *Managing with the Wisdom of Love: Uncovering Virtue in People and Organizations* (Jossey-Bass, 1997), which was rated one of the top 10 business books of 1997 by *Management General*. In addition, she has had dozens of articles printed in such publications as *Journal of Management Development, International Quarterly of Community Health Education, Psychological Reports,* and *Executive Development.* She has recently been exploring how to use the arts in the teaching of leadership.

Professor Marcic has conducted hundreds of seminars on various business topics and consulted for executives at AT&T Bell Labs; the Governor and Cabinet of North Dakota; the U.S. Department of State; United Parcel Service; Aerial Beauty Supply Company; the U.S. Air Force; Slovak Management Assoc; Eurotel; Czech Ministry of Finance; the Cattaraugus Center; two arts organizations in the Twin Cities; and the Salt River-Pima Indian Tribe in Arizona.

Contents in Brief

CONTENTS

Focus on Diversity   81
Cross-Cultural
Communication

**Technology for
Tomorrow   82**
Cross-Cultural Web Traps

**Leading the
Revolution   91**
Shared Resources, Inc.

**Leading the
Revolution   95**
Exporting through the
Internet

**Leading the
Revolution   97**
Giving Workers the
Freedom to Learn

**Technology for
Tomorrow   110**
Firstuse.com

PART 3   Planning   136

**Manager's
Shoptalk   189**
Decision Biases to Avoid

**Leading the
Revolution   197**
Encouraging Wild Ideas

**Technology for
Tomorrow   201**
Broadcast.com

**Focus on
Collaboration   203**
Internet Etiquette

PART 4   Organizing   220

CHAPTER 9   HUMAN RESOURCE MANAGEMENT   288

CHAPTER 10   MANAGING DIVERSE EMPLOYEES   320

Leading the Revolution   333
Women Entrepreneurs

Focus on Diversity   344
The Strength of Diversity

PART 5   Leading   352

Leading the Revolution   365
Damark

Focus on Skills   366
Getting the Right Fit

Technology for Tomorrow 452
You.com

Leading the Revolution 458
The Friday Morning Appointment

Focus on Diversity 460
High Tech Connect L.L.C.

Focus on Diversity 473
Snowball.com

Technology for Tomorrow 478
VeriFone's Virtual World

PART 6 Controlling   500

UNDERSTANDING MANAGEMENT

THIRD EDITION

PART

1

MANAGERS IN LEARNING ORGANIZATIONS

The Whitbread Round the World Race, which began in 1973, is a punishing test of sailing skill. The most recent race (in 1997–1998) began in Southampton, England, and lasted nine months, through nine grueling legs and a total of 31,600 nautical miles. Boats chased each other—and the clock—from the northern to the southern hemisphere and back again. As a sporting challenge, it has been compared to scaling Mount Everest.

The Whitbread boats are finely tuned, high-tech machines. A dozen crew members per boat trains together for nearly half a year before finally hearing the starting signal. Each must draw on the skills they hone and the teamwork they develop. The skipper, whose experience and conceptual skills often mean the difference between success and failure, is in charge of coordinating the crew, processing information from the navigator on changing currents and wind conditions, and charting the course. He or she must also motivate the crew to perform at its best, even in the worst conditions, and to battle together through disasters and setbacks. All members know their roles and are counted on to perform flawlessly, especially when it counts. The ultimate goal of the crew? To endure the worst and beat the competition—to be the best professional sailors in the world—and capture the prized Volvo trophy. In Part One you will learn about leadership, the forces affecting contemporary organizations, the nature and history of management, and the new management skills needed to thrive in today's business world.

The Changing Paradigm of Management

LEARNING OBJECTIVES

After studying this chapter, you should be able to:

- Explain the management revolution and how it will affect you as a future manager

- Define 10 roles that managers perform in organizations

- Describe the new management paradigm and the issues managers must prepare for in the future

- Describe the learning organization and how it is designed through changes in leadership, structure, empowerment, information sharing, strategy, and culture

- Understand how historical forces influence the practice of management

- Identify and explain major developments in the history of management thought

- Describe the major components of the classical and humanistic management perspectives

- Discuss the quantitative management perspective

- Explain the concept of total quality management

MANAGEMENT PROBLEM

Chapter 1

AFTER READING one of the downsize-your-way-to-bliss books, Darwin Poe told a fellow CEO, "The guy who wrote this book is as dumb as dirt. He doesn't know a darn thing about running a company." Poe knew there had to be a better way than the widely practiced slash-and-burn method, and he was tested on his beliefs when he took over as CEO from distressed Tapistron International. Sitting in his office that first Monday, he stared at the financial statements in disbelief. With only $20,000 in the bank, he had a $60,000 payroll due at the end of the week, $7 million in debts, and no receivables. The company suffered from bloated operational expenses, low efficiency with its carpet-tufting machines, and a poor image with their customers. The previous management had done an Initial Public Offering

• *What management skills and techniques would turn Tapistron into a learning organization?*

(IPO), which earned them $13 million, then they sold 10 prototype machines at $1 million each but went through the $23 million and then some in the four years before Darwin arrived. The former president regularly took his whole family along on business trips, such as to England, where his children played tennis at Wimbledon. The plush executive offices had expensive artwork. A gardener was paid $600 a week. To complicate matters, Darwin was saddled with ineffective executives. The chairman, a handsome dreamer who had led the company into bankruptcy, had serious disagreements with Poe on financial policy. Even though his approach had gotten them into the current mess, the chairman was convinced that he alone was right.

Poe suspected the chairman of being less than he claimed to be and even of inflating his resume. Then the vice president of engineering and sales turned out to be no good at either one. Because he was on the road all the time, this executive let development languish to the point that the machines became highly inefficient. No improvements had been made on them since mid-1995. Also, sales were flat. Early on, 12 other executives had quit, sensing their fat-cat days were over. But this left a big hole in the small organization, and many of the remaining employees—mostly factory workers—had become alienated from management.

The company was sinking fast, and Darwin had meetings coming up with the Creditors Committee.[1]

Most students probably have never heard of Darwin Poe, but the management actions he and other managers perform every day are the keys to keeping Tapistron healthy, inspired, and productive. Poe's philosophy of creating effectiveness through people is increasingly important to all managers in companies in every industry. Today's companies are struggling to remain competitive in the face of increasingly tough global competition, uncertain environments, cutbacks in personnel and resources, and massive worldwide economic, political, and social shifts. The growing diversity of the workforce brings new challenges: maintaining a strong corporate culture while supporting diversity; balancing work and family concerns; coping with the conflict brought about by the demands of women and ethnic minorities for increased power and responsibility. Workers are asking that managers share rather than hoard power. Organizational structures are becoming flatter, with power and information pushed down and out among fewer layers and with teams of frontline workers playing new roles as decision makers.

Because of these changes, a revolution is taking place in the field of management. A new kind of leader is surfacing, one who can guide businesses through this turbulence—a strong leader who recognizes the complexity of today's world and realizes that there are no perfect answers.[2] The revolution asks managers to do more with less, to engage employees en-

tirely, to see change rather than stability as the nature of things, and to create vision and cultural values that allow people to create a truly collaborative workplace. This new management approach is very different from a traditional mind-set that emphasizes tight top-down control, employee separation and specialization, and management by impersonal measurements and analyses. Darwin Poe and Tapistron are excellent examples of a manager and company that are leading this revolution toward a new management paradigm, a.k.a. a new way of thinking.

Making a difference as a manager for today and tomorrow requires a different approach than it did yesterday. Successful departments and organizations don't just happen—they are *managed* to be that way. Managers in every organization today face major challenges and have the opportunity to make a difference.

Lee Iacocca made a difference at Chrysler Corporation when he rescued it from bankruptcy by reducing internal costs, developing new products, and gaining concessions from lenders, the union, and the government. Chad Holliday, executive vice president for DuPont, made a difference when he stuck to his decision to recruit local talent to head up DuPont in Japan, despite grumblings by several of the company's top managers. Since Akira Imamichi, who speaks little English, took the reins, earnings have been growing twice as fast, even as the Japanese economy has been in a rut. Chanut Piyaoui made a difference by altering the unsavory perception of Thailand hotels as "places of entertainment." With little initial capital, Chanut's vision and management skills created Thailand's leading hotel chain. Her Dusit Thani Group was ranked by *Asiamoney* magazine as one of the 100 best-managed companies in Asia.[3] These managers are not unusual. Every day, managers solve difficult problems, turn organizations around, and achieve astonishing performances. To be successful, every organization needs skilled managers.

This textbook introduces the process of management and explains the changing ways of thinking about and perceiving the world, ways that are becoming increasingly critical for managers of today and tomorrow. By the time you get to the end of the book, you will understand fundamental management skills for planning, organizing, leading, and controlling a department or an entire organization.

Throughout this chapter, we will define management and look at the ways in which roles and activities are changing for today's managers. By reviewing the actions of a few successful and some not-so-successful managers, you will learn more about the fundamentals of management. The chapter concludes with a discussion of the trend toward the learning organization, providing more detail about many of the challenges managers will face in the coming years.

■ THE DEFINITION OF MANAGEMENT

What do managers such as Lee Iacocca, Chad Holliday, and Darwin Poe have in common? They get things done through their organizations. One management scholar, Mary Parker Follett, described management as "the art of getting things done through people."[4] Peter Drucker, a noted management theorist, explains that managers give direction to their organizations, provide leadership, and decide how to use organizational resources to accomplish goals. Getting things done through people and other resources and providing direction and leadership are what managers do. These activities apply not just to top executives like Darwin Poe or Chanut Piyaoui, but are performed by successful managers on every level, whether they lead a cleaning crew, supervise a bottling plant, or direct the marketing efforts of Coca-Cola. Moreover, management often is considered universal because it uses organizational resources to accomplish goals and attain high performance in all types of profit and not-for-profit organizations. Thus, **management** is the attainment of organizational goals in an effective and efficient manner through planning, organizing, leading, and controlling organizational resources.

There are two important ideas in this definition: (1) the four functions of planning, organizing, leading, and controlling and (2) the attainment of organizational goals in an effective and efficient manner. Managers use a multitude of skills to perform these functions. Management's conceptual, human, and technical skills are discussed later in the chapter. Exhibit 1.1 illustrates the process of how managers use resources to attain organizational goals. Although some management theorists identify additional management functions, such as staffing, communicating, or decision making, those additional functions will be discussed as subsets of the four primary functions in Exhibit 1.1. Chapters of this book are devoted to the multiple activities and skills associated with each function, as well as to the environment, global competitiveness, and ethics, all of which influence how managers perform these functions. The next section begins with a brief overview of the four functions.

management
The attainment of organizational goals in an effective and efficient manner through planning, organizing, leading, and controlling organizational resources

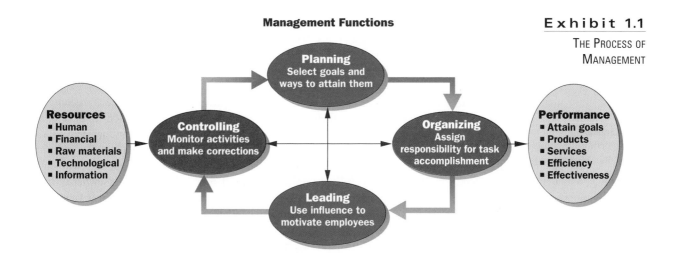

Management Functions

E x h i b i t 1.1
THE PROCESS OF MANAGEMENT

■ ORGANIZATIONAL PERFORMANCE

The other part of our definition of management is the attainment of organizational goals in an efficient and effective manner. Management is so important because organizations are so important. In an industrialized society where complex technologies dominate, organizations bring together knowledge, people, and raw materials to perform tasks no individual could do alone. Without organizations how could 17,000 airline flights a day be accomplished without an accident, electricity be produced from large dams or nuclear power generators, millions of automobiles be manufactured, or hundreds of films, videos, and compact discs be made available for our entertainment? Organizations pervade our society. Most college students will work in an organization—perhaps for Regal Cinemas, Federal Express, Standard Oil, or in some smaller entrepreneurial venture. College students already are members of organizations. These may include their university or junior college, the YMCA, churches, or fraternity or sorority. College students also deal with organizations every day when they renew a driver's license, are treated in a hospital emergency room, buy food from a supermarket, eat in a restaurant, or purchase new clothes. Managers are responsible for these organizations and for seeing that resources are used wisely to attain organizational goals.

Our formal definition of an **organization** is a social entity that is goal-directed and deliberately structured. Social entity means being made up of two or more people. Goal-directed means designed to achieve some outcome, such as make a profit (Boeing, Mack Trucks), win pay increases for members (AFL-CIO), meet spiritual needs (Methodist church), or provide social satisfaction (college sorority). Deliberately structured means that tasks are divided and responsibility for their performance is assigned to organization members. This definition applies to all organizations, including both profit and not-for-profit. Vickery Stoughton runs Toronto General Hospital and manages a $200 million budget. He endures intense public scrutiny, heavy government regulation, and daily crises of life and death. Hamilton Jordan, formerly President Carter's chief of staff, created a new organization called the Association of Tennis Professionals that has taken control of the professional tennis circuit. John and Marie Bouchard launched a small business called Wild Things that sells goods for outdoor activities. Small, offbeat, and not-for-profit organizations are more numerous than large, visible corporations—and just as important to society.

Based on our definition of management, the manager's responsibility is to coordinate resources in an effective and efficient manner to accomplish the organization's goals. Organizational **effectiveness** is the degree to which the organization achieves a stated goal. It means that the organization succeeds in accomplishing what it tries to do. Organizational effectiveness means providing a product or service that customers value. Organizational efficiency refers to the amount of resources used to achieve an organizational goal. It is based on how much raw materials, money, and people are necessary for producing a given volume of output. Efficiency can be calculated as the amount of resources used to produce a product or service.

Both efficiency and effectiveness can rank high within the same organization. For example, Nissan Motor Manufacturing's plant in Smyrna, Tennessee, was ranked as the most productive automaker in North America by the Harbour Report, which tracks productivity and efficiency at 40 auto-manufacturing facilities in the United States, Canada, and Mexico. According to consultant James Harbour, "That plant is lean, and its cars are designed for quality and to be assembled with a minimum number of workers." Nissan uses only 2.1 workers and produces more than 400 body panels an hour, about 25 percent better than the average at domestic auto plants. Likewise, management efforts to decentralize decision making and stay on top of technological developments enable Nucor Steel's Crawfordsville, Indiana, plant to produce a ton of flat-rolled steel in less than one worker-hour, compared with an average of four worker-hours elsewhere.[5] In addition to increasing efficiency, managers at Nissan and Nucor improved effectiveness, shown in better product quality, increased revenues, and higher profits.

organization
A social entity that is goal-directed and deliberately structured

effectiveness
The degree to which an organization achieves a stated goal

Managers in other organizations, especially service firms, are improving efficiency and effectiveness, too. Labor shortages in many parts of the United States have prompted managers to find laborsaving tricks. Burger King and Taco Bell restaurants let customers serve themselves drinks. Sleep Inn hotels have a washer and dryer installed behind the desk so that clerks can launder sheets and towels while waiting on customers.[6] Sometimes, however, management efforts to increase efficiency through severe cost-cutting can hurt organizational effectiveness. Delta Airlines has dramatically increased cost efficiency by cutting spending on personnel, food, cleaning, and maintenance. However, it has fallen to last place among major air carriers in on-time performance, and customer complaints about dirty planes and long lines at ticket counters have increased by more than 75 percent.[7]

The ultimate responsibility of managers is to achieve high **performance,** which is the attainment of organizational goals by using resources in an efficient and effective manner. One example of extraordinary performance in the entertainment industry is the Grateful Dead rock band. Whether managers are responsible for the organization as a whole, such as the Grateful Dead, or for a single department or division, their ultimate responsibility is performance.

BUSINESS AT THE GRATEFUL DEAD

News of Jerry Garcia's death in August 1995 stunned the music industry, and millions of Grateful Dead fans mourned the loss of a consummate artist whose words and music spanned generations. Few people remember the other side of Garcia—the leader who helped manage a successful business. Garcia rotated with each band member to share responsibility as chief financial and executive officer of Grateful Dead Productions (GDP). The carefully managed business behind the Grateful Dead was largely responsible for the group's financial success and its almost unmatched 29 years of performing the same program to sellout crowds.

Perhaps the service GDP's customers appreciated most was the band's ticketing business, which distributed nearly half of all Grateful Dead concert tickets directly to fans. The group listened to customers and gave them what they wanted. Most rock bands forbid tape-recording at concerts to prevent copyright infringement, yet the Dead would rope off a portion of the concert floor just for "tapeheads."

The band members jointly made major management decisions, but they empowered GDP's 60 or so employees to run the day-to-day business of the group. GDP employees, who earned good salaries and enjoyed extensive benefits, profit sharing, bonuses, and say-so, did everything from moving the band from concert to concert to handling catalog merchandising, a publishing company, and a nonprofit foundation. Employees felt like part of the business, and staff turnover was low in an industry known for its instability.

Management counts. The Grateful Dead successfully balanced control and delegation to run a thriving business and keep doing what they loved to do for nearly three decades. They created an organization with a powerful culture, a significant vision, and the motivation of human energy that set a great organization apart from the crowd.[8] ∎

■ MANAGEMENT SKILLS

A manager's job is complex and multidimensional and requires a range of skills. Although some management theorists propose a long list of skills, the necessary skills for managing a department or an organization can be summarized in three categories: conceptual, human, and technical.[9] As illustrated in Exhibit 1.2, the application of these skills changes as managers move up in the organization. Though the degree of each skill necessary at different levels of an organization may vary, all managers must possess skills in each of these important areas to perform effectively.

performance
The attainment of organizational goals by using resources in an efficient and effective manner

Exhibit 1.2

RELATIONSHIP OF CONCEPTUAL, HUMAN, AND TECHNICAL SKILLS TO MANAGEMENT LEVEL

Management Level

Top Managers

Middle Managers

First-Line Managers

Nonmanagers (Personnel)

Conceptual Skills   Human Skills   Technical Skills

■ MANAGEMENT TYPES

Managers use conceptual, human, and technical skills to perform the four management functions of planning, organizing, leading, and controlling in all organizations—large and small, manufacturing and service, profit and not-for-profit. But not all manager jobs are the same. Managers are responsible for different departments, work at different levels in the hierarchy, and meet different requirements for achieving high performance. For example, Mary Lee Bowen, a middle manager at Rubbermaid, is responsible for teams that create new home organization and bath accessories products. Phillip Knight is chief executive officer for Nike, world leader in sports shoe design and manufacturing.[10] Both are managers, and both must contribute to planning, organizing, leading, and controlling their organizations—but in different amounts and ways.

■ WHAT IS IT LIKE TO BE A MANAGER?

So far we have described how managers at various levels perform four basic functions that help ensure that organizational resources are used to attain high levels of performance. These tasks require conceptual, human, and technical skills. Unless someone has actually

Scott McNealy (left), chief executive of Sun Microsystems Inc., excels at human communication and skills. He works 80-hour weeks and maintains a heavy travel schedule but still finds time to enjoy activities such as this intramural squirt-gun war with employees. As a leader, McNealy is known for his humor and ability to raise a crowd to its feet.

performed managerial work, it is hard to understand exactly what managers do on an hour-by-hour, day-to-day basis. The manager's job is so diverse that a number of studies have been undertaken in an attempt to describe exactly what happens. The question of what managers actually do to plan, organize, lead, and control was addressed by Henry Mintzberg, who followed managers around and recorded all their activities.[11] He developed a description of managerial work that included three general characteristics and 10 roles. These characteristics and roles have been supported in subsequent research.[12]

MANAGER ACTIVITIES

One of the most interesting findings about managerial activities is how busy managers are and how hectic the average workday can be. For Hugh Murphy, operations manager of O'Hare International Airport, his managerial work involves tossing out litter left on windowsills one minute and making complex arrangements for an unexpected landing by Vice President Al Gore in Air Force Two the next. Then, after greeting the vice president, Murphy would zip back to his office, check his phone messages, return any urgent ones, then consult with computer technicians to make sure a critical malfunction of five security checkpoints had been corrected.

Managerial activity is characterized by variety, fragmentation, and brevity. The manager's involvement is so widespread and the tasks so voluminous that there is little time for quiet reflection. The average time spent on any one activity is less than nine minutes. Managers shift gears quickly. Significant crises are interspersed with trivial events in no predictable sequence. An example of two typical work hours in the life of a general manager, Janet Howard, follows. Note the frequent interruptions, as well as the brevity and variety of tasks.

7:30 A.M. Janet arrives at work and begins to plan her day.

7:37 A.M. A subordinate, Morgan Cook, stops in Janet's office to discuss a dinner party the previous night and to review the cost-benefit analysis for a proposed microcomputer.

7:45 A.M. Janet's secretary, Pat, motions for Janet to pick up the telephone. "Janet, they had serious water damage at the downtown office last night. A pipe broke, causing about $50,000 damage. Everything will be back in shape in three days. Thought you should know."

8:00 A.M. Pat brings in the mail. She also asks instructions for typing a report Janet gave her yesterday.

8:14 A.M. Janet gets a phone call from the accounting manager, who is returning a call from the day before. They talk about an accounting report.

8:25 A.M. A Mr. Nance is ushered in. Mr. Nance complains that a sales manager mistreats his employees and something must be done. Janet rearranges her schedule to investigate this claim.

9:00 A.M. Janet returns to the mail. One letter is from an irate customer. Janet dictates a helpful, restrained reply. Pat brings in phone messages.

9:15 A.M. Janet receives an urgent phone call from Larry Baldwin. They discuss lost business, unhappy subordinates, and a potential promotion.[13]

The manager performs a great deal of work at an unrelenting pace. Manager workloads are fast-paced, and they require great energy. The managers observed by Mintzberg processed 36 pieces of mail each day, attended eight meetings, and took a tour through the building or plant. As soon as a manager's daily calendar is set, unexpected disturbances erupt. New meetings are required. During time away from the office, executives catch up on work-related reading and paperwork.

At O'Hare, an unofficial count one Friday in October found operations manager Hugh Murphy interacting with more than 45 airport employees. In addition, he listened to complaints from local residents about airport noise, met with disgruntled executives of a French firm who built the airport's new $128 million people-mover system, attempted to soothe a Hispanic city alderman who complained that

manager's shoptalk

Do You Really Want to Be a Manager?

The first training course aspiring managers at FedEx take is called "Is Management for Me?" Because people entering the program ask this question first, those who complete it are better managers—happy with their jobs and capable of dealing with the stress and frustration of management in positive ways. Trent Cobb, an 18-year FedEx veteran who answered "yes" was eventually promoted to manager of international hub operations in Memphis. "The transition was good from day one," he says. "If you know at the outset how the change is going to affect you, it's much easier to handle."

There are a number of issues would-be managers should consider before deciding whether or not to pursue a career in management:

Increased workload. It isn't unusual for managers to work 70 to 80 hours a week, and some work even longer hours. A manager's job always starts before a shift begins and ends hours after the shift is over. Matt Scott, a software engineer promoted to management at Fore Systems, Inc., found himself frustrated by the increasing paperwork and crowded meeting schedule. Many new managers are surprised by how much of their time is taken up by meetings.

Unrelenting sense of obligation. A manager's work is never done. Nancy Carreon, an associate partner for an architectural firm, sometimes wakes up in the middle of the night thinking about something she needs to do—so she gets up and does it. Argues George Pollard, a senior human resources official at FedEx, "Managers are always on the clock. We're representatives of [the company] even when we're not at work."

Headache of responsibility for other people. A lot of people get into management because they like the idea of having power, but the reality is that many managers feel overwhelmed by the responsibility of supervising and disciplining others. As Mary Smith of FedEx says, "You

have to make hard decisions about people, decisions you might not like." Another manager referred to the feeling of constantly being pulled in 15 different directions. In addition, today's managers generally supervise large numbers of people who are spread over different locations and even different continents.

Getting caught in the middle. For many people, this is the most difficult aspect of management. Except for those in the top echelons, managers find themselves acting as a backstop, caught between upper management and the workforce. A computer software designer explains why she wanted out of management: "I didn't feel comfortable touting the company line in organizational policies and technical decisions I disagreed with. I found it very difficult to fire my team up on something I wasn't fired up about. It was very hard asking folks to do things I wouldn't like to do myself, like put in gobs of overtime or travel at the drop of a hat." Even when managers disagree with the decisions of top executives, they are responsible for implementing them.

For some people, the frustrations aren't worth it. One, who says "there wasn't a single day where I could say I enjoyed myself," left management after only six months. However, for others, management is a fulfilling and satisfying career choice and the emotional rewards can be great. One key to being happy as a manager may be carefully evaluating whether you can answer yes to the question, "Do I really want to be a manager?"

SOURCES: Heath Row, "Is Management for Me? That Is the Question," *Fast Company*, February–March 1998, pp. 50–52; Timothy D. Schellhardt, "Want to Be a Manager? Many People Say No, Calling Job Miserable," The *Wall Street Journal*, April 4, 1997, pp. A1, A4; Matt Murray, "A Software Engineer Becomes a Manager, with Many Regrets," The *Wall Street Journal*, May 14, 1997, pp. A1, A14; and Hal Lancaster, "Managing Your Career: Nancy Carreon Works Long, Hard Weeks. Does She Need To?" The *Wall Street Journal*, May 13, 1997, p. B1.

---

role
A set of expectations for a manager's behavior

Mexicana Airlines passengers were being singled out by overzealous tow-truck operators, toured the airport's new fire station, and visited the construction site for the new $20 million tower. Hugh Murphy's unrelenting pace is typical of managers.[14] In recent years, many managers' jobs have become even tougher. Management can be rewarding, but it can also be frustrating and stressful, as discussed in the Manager's Shoptalk section.

MANAGER ROLES

Mintzberg's observations and subsequent research indicate that diverse manager activities can be organized into 10 roles.[15] A **role** is a set of expectations for a manager's behavior. Exhibit 1.3 provides examples of each of the 10 roles. These roles are divided into three conceptual categories: informational (managing by information), interpersonal (managing through people), and decisional (managing through

John T. Chambers is the leader of Cisco Systems Inc., a San Jose, California, company with annual revenues of more than $8 billion. Cisco Systems is the global leader in networking for the Internet. In his interpersonal role as a leader, Chambers says that his vision is simple: "We can change the way people live and work, play and learn." This idealistic vision inspires and motivates Cisco's 13,000–plus employees. Here, Chambers attends a company picnic, demonstrating his emphasis on the value of employees.

E x h i b i t   1.3
TEN MANAGER ROLES

Category	Role	Activity
Informational	**Monitor**	Seek and receive information, scan periodicals and reports, maintain personal contacts
	Disseminator	Forward information to other organization members; send memos and reports, make phone calls
	Spokesperson	Transmit information to outsiders through speeches, reports, memos
Interpersonal	**Figurehead**	Perform ceremonial and symbolic duties such as greeting visitors and signing legal documents
	Leader	Direct and motivate subordinates; train, counsel, and communicate with subordinates
	Liaison	Maintain information links both inside and outside the organization; use mail, phone calls, meetings
Decisional	**Entrepreneur**	Initiate improvement projects; identify new ideas, delegate idea responsibility to others
	Disturbance handler	Take corrective action during disputes or crises; resolve conflicts among subordinates; adapt to environmental crises
	Resource allocator	Decide who gets resources; schedule, budget, and set priorities
	Negotiator	Represent department during negotiation of union contracts, sales, purchases, budgets; represent departmental interests

SOURCES: Adapted from Henry Mintzberg, *The Nature of Managerial Work* (New York: Harper & Row, 1973), pp. 92–93; and Henry Mintzberg, "Managerial Work: Analysis from Observation," *Management Science* 18(1971), pp. B97–B110.

action). Each role represents activities that managers undertake to ultimately accomplish the functions of planning, organizing, leading, and controlling. Although it is necessary to separate the components of the manager's job to understand the different roles and activities of a manager, it is important to remember that the real job of management cannot be practiced as a set of independent parts; all the roles interact in the real world of management. As Mintzberg says, "The manager who only communicates or only conceives never gets anything done, while the manager who only 'does' ends up doing it all alone."[16]

■ MANAGING IN SMALL BUSINESSES AND NOT-FOR-PROFIT ORGANIZATIONS

Small businesses are growing in importance. Hundreds of small businesses are opened every month by people who have found themselves squeezed out of corporations due to downsizing or who voluntarily leave the corporate world to seek a slower pace and a healthier balance between work and family life. Many small businesses are started by women and minorities who found limited opportunities for advancement in large corporations.

As even the smallest businesses become increasingly complicated due to globalization, government regulation, and customer demands for better quality at lower prices, managerial dexterity is critical to success. One survey on trends and future developments in small business found that nearly half of the respondents saw inadequate management skills as a threat to their companies, as compared to less than 25 percent in larger companies.[17]

One interesting finding is that managers in small businesses tend to emphasize roles differently from those of managers in large corporations. Managers in small companies often see their most important role as spokesperson, because they must promote the small, growing company to the outside world. The entrepreneurial role is also very important in small businesses, because managers must be creative and help their organizations develop new ideas in order to be competitive. Small-business managers tend to rank lower on the leader role and on information-processing roles compared with counterparts in large corporations.

Not-for-profit organizations also represent a major application of management talent. The Salvation Army, the Girl Scouts, universities, city governments, hospitals, public schools, symphonies, and art museums all require excellent management. Sometimes managers in not-for-profit organizations have been leaders in creating a sense of purpose that motivates employees; they empower workers to try new ideas, and they trim overlong vertical hierarchies.[18] We might expect managers in not-for-profit organizations to place more emphasis on the roles of figurehead (to deal with the public), leader (to motivate employees with fewer financial incentives), and resource allocator (to distribute government resources that often are assigned top down).

As the world of small and not-for-profit organizations becomes increasingly complex, managers should carefully integrate the three categories of roles: They must simultaneously manage by information, manage through people, and manage through action to keep their organizations healthy.

■ LEADING THE MANAGEMENT REVOLUTION

How do you learn to be a manager in an uncertain and rapidly changing world? How can a course in management or a college degree in business prepare you to face the challenges of the twenty-first century?

Management is both an art and a science. It is an art because many skills cannot be learned from a textbook. Management takes practice, just like golf, tennis, or skating. Management is a science because a growing body of knowledge and objective facts describes management and how to obtain organizational effectiveness. This knowledge can be conveyed through teaching and textbooks. Becoming a successful manager requires a blend of formal learning and practice, of art and science.

Students today will be leaders tomorrow, leading the management revolution that will change organizations in the twenty-first century.

TECHNOLOGY FOR TOMORROW

GROCERY DIRECT

Even a high-tech company has need for some low-tech work and personal connections. Johnny Bentley lugs groceries up apartment walk-ups, elevators, and around to back porches, politely asking customers, "How's the service working for you?" as he loads the refrigerator. Back to his van in six minutes flat, he continues on his 64 totes to 13 homes/businesses in downtown Boston.

Online grocery store Hannaford's HomeRuns is a leader in a new national trend: grocery direct. Each of the Web grocers has a different modus operandi. New Jersey's NetGrocer takes orders for nonperishable items (canned goods, cereal, bread) on its Web site and ships from its central warehouse via Federal Express. Peapod, in Skokie, Illinois, takes orders online, then sends employees to local grocery stores to fill and deliver. Boston's Streamline uses more of a "personal shopper" approach. New customers' cupboards are scanned with a bar coder to inventory a personal shopping list. Once a week, Streamline fills orders from its distribution center and delivers them to the customer's garage. This company will even bring along your requested Blockbuster video and your dry cleaning.

HomeRuns lets customers order via Web, fax, phone, or Newton notepad. In the early days of 1996, HomeRuns filled orders from its partner grocery store. In 1999 it moved to a new facility and has become its own wholesaler in some areas. Though other retailers are also trying direct services, the good thing for HomeRuns is that grocery shopping has to happen and it has to happen every week. Still, there are problems. Occasionally groceries get delivered to a neighbor, or a mailbox gets knocked down by the truck. And Boston's blizzard two years ago meant the whole city shut down under the 27 inches of snow. HomeRuns employees worked 16-hour shifts trying to fill the orders from the house-bound customers. It was the kind of bonding experience essential to successful start-ups.

So what is HomeRuns real service? President Tom Furber believes it is something new that meets an unarticulated need, more evident in our over-scheduled society. "We want to give them some time back."

SOURCES: Scott Kirsner, "Express Lane," *Wired*, May 1999, pp. 112–122; Tim McCollum, "End Your Internet Anxieties Now," *Nation's Business*, April 1999, pp. 17–26; Pierre M. Loewe and Mark S. Boncheck, "The Retail Revolution," *Management Review*, April 1999, pp. 38–44.

Exhibit 1.4
THE CHANGING PARADIGM OF MANAGEMENT

	Old Paradigm	New Paradigm
	Vertical Organization	Learning Organization
Forces on Organizations		
Markets	Local, domestic	Global
Workforce	Homogeneous	Diverse
Technology	Mechanical	Electronic
Values	Stability, efficiency	Change, chaos
Management Competencies		
Focus	Profits	Customers, employees
Leadership	Autocratic	Dispersed, empowering
Doing Work	By individuals	By teams
Relationships	Conflict, competition	Collaboration

One of the most important contributions that a textbook or a management course can make today is to define for students some of the forces that will affect their jobs as managers tomorrow.

■ THE CHANGING PARADIGM OF MANAGEMENT

The world of organizations and management is changing. Rapid environmental changes are causing fundamental transformations that have a dramatic impact on the manager's job. These transformations represent a shift from a traditional to a new paradigm, as outlined in Exhibit 1.4. A **paradigm** is a shared mind-set that represents a fundamental way of thinking about, perceiving, and understanding the world. Shifts in ways of thinking are occurring in our society, and these in turn impact organizations, causing shifts in management thinking and behavior.[19] The primary shift is from the traditional vertical organization to something called the **learning organization.** The shift to the learning organization is a result of a number of significant forces impacting today's organizations and managers.

FORCES ON ORGANIZATIONS

The most striking change now affecting organizations and management is globalization. Today, everyone is interconnected in the flow of information, money, or products, and interdependencies are increasing. Even the smallest companies are being affected by globalization. Taking a global approach has become a necessity for virtually every company and manager. Globalization brings a need for relentless innovation, greater concern for quality, rapid response, enhanced productivity, and new levels of customer service.[20]

Global competition has also triggered a need for new management approaches that emphasize empowerment of workers and involvement of employees. During the 1980s, for example, the success of Japanese firms encouraged U.S. companies to adopt more participatory management practices. A management perspective known as **Theory Z**

proposed a hybrid form of management that incorporates techniques from both Japanese and North American management practices. To briefly illustrate Theory Z, consider that traditional Japanese practices emphasize collective responsibility, informal control, and consensual decision making, whereas traditional North American practices encourage individual responsibility, formal control mechanisms, and individual decision making. Theory Z blends the two styles, retaining an emphasis on individual responsibility, but encouraging consensual decision making and more informal control methods.[21]

Today, managers have to understand cross-cultural patterns and often work with team members from many different countries. Diversity of the workforce has become a fact of life for all organizations, even those that do not operate globally. Most new entrants to the U.S. labor force are women and minorities (with half of these being first-generation immigrants), and the workforce in general is growing older, with the median age for U.S. workers now at 45.[22] Studies also project that Asian Americans, African Americans, and Hispanics will make up 85 percent of U.S. population growth and constitute about 30 percent of the total workforce in the twenty-first century.[23] Indeed, diversity is a real advantage in a global marketplace; employees who speak the language and understand the culture of international competitors, customers, and partners can provide a competitive advantage.

Another significant shift is that technology is electronic rather than mechanical, as the world is gradually shifting from a workforce that produces material things to one that primarily manages information. Success depends on the intellectual capacity of all employees. Information technology facilitates new ways of working, such as virtual teams and telecommuting, that challenge traditional methods of supervision and control. In addition, technology often leads to greater sharing of information and power throughout the organization.

In the face of such rapid transformations, organizations are learning to value change over stability. The fundamental paradigm during much of the twentieth century was that things could be stable and efficient. In con-

paradigm
A shared mind-set that represents a fundamental way of thinking about, perceiving, and understanding the world

learning organization
An organization in which everyone is engaged in identifying and solving problems, enabling the company to continuously experiment, improve, and increase its ability to grow, learn, and achieve its goals

Theory Z
A hybrid form of management that incorporates techniques from both Japanese and North American management practices

trast, the new paradigm is based on a recognition of change and chaos and that these are the natural order of things.[24] The science of **chaos theory** suggests that the world is characterized by randomness and uncertainty. Small events often have massive and far-reaching consequences. For example, a seemingly insignificant lawsuit against AT&T some years ago had far-reaching effects, resulting in the emergence of MCI, Sprint, and other long-distance carriers and ultimately creating a whole new world of telecommunications.

The change to the new paradigm of management means that managers now must rethink their approach to organizing, directing, and motivating workers. According to one consultant, many managers trained under the old paradigm complain that workers no longer play by the rules. The consultant's response: "Why should they play by the rules? The rules are dead."[25] Managers who have made a shift to the new paradigm are creating twenty-first century organizations by continuing to break the rules and embrace change. In this new environment, managers give up their command-and-control mind-set and rely on new skills and abilities. In Leading the Revolution box, The Learning Organization describes a paradigm shift that is taking place in the U.S. Army.

THE LEARNING ORGANIZATION

Traditionally, the most common organizational structure has been one in which activities are grouped by common function from the bottom to the top of the organization. The whole organization is coordinated and controlled through the vertical hierarchy, with decision-making authority residing with upper-level managers. Traditional organizations are characterized by routine, specialized jobs and standardized control procedures. These organizations are very effective in stable times. However, they often do not work well in fast-changing environments. In response, many companies are shifting to a new paradigm and becoming learning organizations.

In the new paradigm, the primary responsibility of managers is not to make decisions, but to create learning capability throughout the organization. Employees on the front lines routinely make decisions rather than passing them up the hierarchy for approval. There is no single model of the learning organization; it is a philosophy or attitude about what an organization is and the role of employees. Everyone in the organization participates in identifying and solving problems, enabling the organization to continuously experiment, improve, and increase its capability. In the learning organization, **top managers** are leaders who create a vision for the future that is widely understood and imprinted throughout the organization. Employees are empowered to identify and solve problems because they understand the vision and long-term goals of the organization.

The traditional top-down hierarchy is giving way to flatter organizations built around self-directed teams collaborating across levels and departments. Lower-level managers serve as team leaders, coaches, and facilitators. Monsanto, a large chemical company, achieved excellent results by tapping the power of teams. Teams of workers at Monsanto's chemical and nylon plant near Pensacola, Florida, were responsible for hiring, purchasing, making job assignments, and producing the product. Management was reduced from seven levels to four, and both profitability and safety increased.[26] However, even though layers of management are reduced, in learning organizations the job of the **middle manager** has a renewed vitality as a coordinator of teams and projects across levels, departments, and divisions. In addition, the growing trend toward telecommuting and virtual offices brings new challenges for managers.[27]

CHANGING ENVIRONMENT

The chaotic globalized economic environment has turned things upside down for many companies, which find themselves successful one day and in crisis the next. Everything is going along fine, and then suddenly the bottom drops out. Unexpected market forces devastated Digital Equipment Corporation, forcing managers to launch an internal revolution as a matter of survival. Behlen, a manufacturer of steel agricultural buildings, lost half its market for grain storage buildings almost overnight when the government stopped subsidizing grain storage.

chaos theory
A theory suggesting that the world is characterized by randomness and uncertainty and that small events can have massive and far-reaching consequences

top managers
Managers at the top of the organizational hierarchy who are responsible for the entire organization, its vision, and its culture

middle manager
A manager who works at the middle levels of the organization and is responsible for major departments

The Learning Organization
The Learning Organization
The Learning Organization

GUESS WHO'S SHIFTING PARADIGMS?

After crushing Iraq's regiments in a one-sided battle, the U.S. Army emerged as the world's premier land force. The army could rest on its laurels and prepare to succeed with a rigid, hierarchical structure. Maybe command and control are the way to go, with remote generals handing down orders to the field.

Nothing could be farther from the truth, however. At the prodding of General Gordon Sullivan, the army has gone through self-examination and self-renewal since the triumph of Desert Storm. Officers on every level are discussing change. The army's environment is highly variable. Since the Gulf War, troops have been sent on dozens of unrelated missions: feeding children in Somalia; purifying water for Rwandan refugees; fighting forest fires; chasing drug lords; and serving police duty in Haiti.

Meeting these demands requires a new way of thinking. Top army officers are choosing change over stability, dispersed control over top management control, transformational over autocratic leadership, and teams over individuals.

Everyone is involved. No other army is so egalitarian. In fact, delegations from other countries come to study the new army. In addition, several of America's most forward-thinking companies, including Motorola and General Electric, study the Army's National Training Center as a source of ideas about leadership and learning. The definitive model at the NTC—which applies to business as well as combat—is learning through failure. All personnel, from enlistees to brigadier generals, go through grueling maneuvers. For fourteen days, at every level, every fiber of the organization is stressed to the breaking point, and some of the fibers inevitably break. Those are the areas leaders hone in on during After Action Reviews—the crux of the learning experience, the place where hardship meets insight, where failure meets growth. The process encourages brutal honesty, enabling individuals and the group to become stronger. Day after day, After Action Reviews stress five key themes: (1) everyone needs to understand the big picture; (2) everyone needs to think all the time; (3) always put yourself in the shoes of an uncooperative opponent; (4) prepare yourself to the point where nothing can surprise you; and (5) put aside hierarchy, foster self-awareness and self-criticism, and learn to work as a team. Nowhere else do senior executives and junior people sit down together and examine how both parties overlooked vital information and made mistakes. Facilitators never lecture, yell, or criticize individual performance, and they continually reinforce the message that the exercise is not about success or failure but about what the experience allows each person to take away. This paradigm fosters continuous learning and growth.

The army continues to grow in technology, too, with new infrared equipment such as goggles and gun sights that enable soldiers to fight at night when the enemy is effectively blind. In the future, army elements will be connected by electronic mail, plus video pictures of battlefield conditions. The e-mail, as in corporations, will further erode the hierarchy and remove communication barriers between units and functions.

And the army believes in personal growth. Two-thirds of the army's officers have advanced degrees, including many with MBAs. The top generals have created brain trusts of dozens of junior officers and enlisted personnel who are challenged to solve the problems of future combat. Eventually lieutenants will see everything that a colonel can see, each person mastering a bigger picture than ever before. High-level officers are told they are preparing for leadership roles in a world that is violent, uncertain, complex, and ambiguous. They are creating a cohesive corporate mission that will be imprinted on every worker or soldier. Believe it or not, the army is way ahead of business in shifting to a paradigm that keeps everyone's eye on the future.

SOURCES: Lee Smith, "New Ideas from the Army (Really)," *Fortune*, September 19, 1994, 203–212; and Brian Smale, "Fight, Learn, Lead," *Fast Company*, August-September 1996, 65–70.

Companies such as LG&E Energy Company and Arizona Public Service Company face a crisis because of increasing deregulation and the growth of small, independent power producers.[28] When everything changes suddenly, managers face a seemingly impossible situation and have to create a new kind of company, one with which they have little experience or skill.

Many organizations succeed by developing centralized structure and control. These companies use a strict hierarchy to achieve efficiency and profitability. This works fine as long as the world is stable. But the world of the twenty-first century is one of chaos and rapid change. The emerging business world is asking far more of managers and requiring greater skills of them, which are what this book is about.

Some companies have taken up the challenge of reinventing themselves, of becoming more than status quo companies. For example, Disney's theme parks have become known for their people management and creative leadership. Johnsonville Foods and Saturn have moved to self-directed teams and a culture of employee empowerment. Motorola has achieved extraordinary quality. Federal Express achieves excellence by treating its people and customers well. Springfield Remanufacturing has led the way with open-book management, sharing all financial information with every employee. Rubbermaid has excelled by learning to create a flood of new products that are nearly always successful in the marketplace. These companies go beyond the norm to succeed in an increasingly difficult world.[29]

As we discussed earlier, we are currently experiencing a paradigm shift—the emergence of a new kind of organization and a new approach to management. Managers today face the ultimate paradox: (1) keeping everything running efficiently and profitably, while they are (2) changing everything.[30] It's no longer enough just to learn how to measure and control things. Success comes to those who become leaders, initiate change, and participate in and even create organizations with fewer managers and less hierarchy that are capable of changing quickly.

CREATING A LEARNING ORGANIZATION

The learning organization can be defined as one in which everyone is engaged in identifying and solving problems, enabling the organization to continuously experiment, change, improve, and thus increase its capacity to grow, learn, and achieve its purposes. The essential idea is problem solving, in contrast to the traditional organization designed for efficiency. In the learning organization all employees look for problems, such as understanding special customer needs. Employees also solve problems, which means putting things together in unique ways to meet a customer's needs.

Developing a learning organization means making specific changes in the areas of leadership, structure, empowerment, communications/ information sharing, participative strategy, and adaptive culture. These six characteristics are illustrated in Exhibit 1.5, and each is described in the following sections.

LEADERSHIP   Leadership is the only means through which a company can change into a learning organization. The traditional view of leaders who set goals, make decisions, and direct the troops reflects an individualistic view. Leadership in learning organizations requires something more. In learning organizations, managers learn to think in terms of

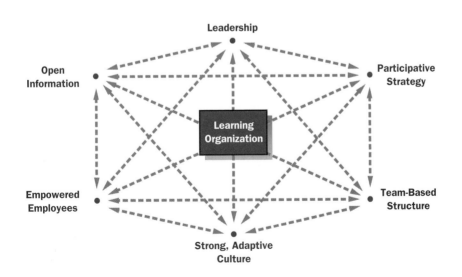

Exhibit 1.5

THE WEB OF INTERACTING ELEMENTS IN A LEARNING ORGANIZATION

"control with" rather than "control over" others. They "control with" others by building relationships based on a shared vision and shaping the culture that can help achieve it. Leaders help people see the whole system, facilitate teamwork, initiate change, and expand the capacity of people to shape the future.[31] Leaders who understand the learning organization can help other people build it.

One of the most important functions of a leader in a learning organization is to create a shared vision. The **shared vision** is a picture of an ideal future for the organization. The vision includes what the organization will look like, performance outcomes, and underlying values. A vision may be created by the leader or with employee participation, but this purpose must be widely understood and imprinted in people's minds. The vision represents desired long-term outcomes; hence, employees are free to identify and solve problems that help achieve that vision. Patricia Gallup, CEO of PC Connection, built a learning organization by spreading her vision of a company that is always thinking about what technology people will need in the future. Her vision, which includes the values of equality, employee empowerment, responsibility, and dedication to serving customers, has created a vibrant organization in which employees use their skills and creative energy to the fullest.[32] Because all employees understand the vision, they can carry it out without direct supervision from the top.

TEAM-BASED STRUCTURE   The learning organization breaks down the former vertical structure that separated managers and workers. Self-directed teams are the fundamental unit in a learning organization. These teams are made up of employees with different skills who rotate jobs to produce an entire product or service. They deal directly with customers and make changes and improvements as needed. Team members have the authority to make decisions about new ways of doing things. In learning organizations, bosses practically are eliminated, with team members taking responsibility for training, safety, scheduling vacations, and decisions about work methods, pay and reward systems, and coordination with other teams. Teams are discussed in detail in Chapter 15.

EMPLOYEE EMPOWERMENT   **Empowerment** means delegating to employees/subordinates decision-making authority, freedom, knowledge, autonomy, and skills; empowerment is a fundamental principle of learning organizations. Traditional management tries to limit employees, while empowerment expands their behavior. Empowerment may be reflected in self-directed work teams, quality circles, job enrichment, and employee participation groups.

GRANITE ROCK COMPANY

Granite Rock Co. of Watsonville, California, has been owned and operated by the Wilson/Woolpert family for more than 90 years, but was hit with big changes 10 years ago. The threat of absorption into a conglomerate was added to California's tightening industrial regulations, while customers were clamoring for high-quality materials and more responsive service. Computer technology to automate quarry work was new and expensive. Granite Rock would have to find new ways of doing business amid a host of changes and well-financed predators.

Bruce Woolpert, a joint CEO with brother Steve and eight-year veteran of Hewlett-Packard, wanted to be as efficient and customer-oriented as HP. First, he got maximum information flowing into the company. Instead of the industry standard of a dozen internal process controls, Granite Rock kept track of 100. Then, Bruce started asking customers to rate the company against competitors on "report cards."

Bruce went out and "benchmarked" within the company, identifying "best practices" by visiting cement plants and the quarry. Asking workers what they liked and disliked about their jobs and the company, he set up a model for two-way communication up and down the entire organization. He organized 100 highly focused quality teams of managers and hourly workers to analyze problems. Both groups also attended many seminars together. Merging the two groups to-

shared vision
A picture of an ideal future for the organization that includes what the organization will look like, performance outcomes, and underlying values

empowerment
The delegation of decision-making authority, freedom, knowledge, autonomy, and skills to subordinates; a fundamental principle of learning organizations

gether increased input and united the company's now 535 employees.

Technology and training have made Granite Rock the region's lowest-cost producer of crushed rock with annual sales of more than $110 million. Quality and service levels are high enough to allow charging a 6 percent premium and still increase market share. Granite Rock inspires fierce loyalty among workers. Former CEO Betsy Wilson Woolpert, Bruce's mother and daughter of founder Arthur Wilson, says, "Most Granite Rock people remain with us for their entire career. We like that and hope it can be maintained."[33] ∎

In learning organizations, people are a manager's primary source of strength, not a cost to be minimized. Companies that adopt this perspective believe in treating employees well by providing competitive wages, good working conditions, and opportunities for personal and professional development. In addition, they often provide a sense of employee ownership by sharing gains in productivity and profits.[34]

OPEN INFORMATION　A learning organization is flooded with information. To identify needs and solve problems, people have to be aware of what's going on. They must understand the whole organization as well as their part in it. Formal data about budgets, profits, and departmental expenses are available to everyone. As organizations work with ideas and information rather than products and things, information sharing reaches extraordinary levels. Like the oil in a car's engine, information is not allowed to get low. Leaders in learning organizations know that too much information is better than too little. Dave Duffield, CEO of PeopleSoft, Inc., puts it this way: "If people don't have total access to information, they have to guess at what they should be doing." Managers at PeopleSoft use information technology to create what they call an "infomacracy"—a transparent organization that provides open access to information for all its members. For example, unlike many software companies, which don't allow sales reps or account managers to see what's planned for future release, PeopleSoft lets anyone in the company tap into product development information. Employees have open access to all company databases as well as the ability to communicate electronically with any other person in the company.[35] In a learning organization, a manager's role is to give workers the information they need and the authority to act on it. The Technology for Tomorrow box describes how one leader has used this concept to create an unusual learning system.

PARTICIPATIVE STRATEGY　Strategy traditionally has been the responsibility of top executives. Strategy is seen as something that is formulated and imposed on the organization. Top managers think about how the company can best respond to competitors, cope with difficult environmental changes, and effectively use available resources. However, in learning organizations, strategy emerges bottom up as well as top down. Top executives shape a vision and direction that all employees support and believe in, but they do not control or direct strategy alone. Everyone helps. When all employees are committed to the vision, their accumulated actions contribute to the development of strategy. Since many employees in a learning organization are linked to customers, suppliers, and new technologies, they identify needs and solutions and participate directly in strategy making. Strategy in learning organizations also may emerge from partnerships with suppliers, customers, and even competitors. Learning organizations have permeable boundaries and often are linked with other companies, giving each organization greater access to information about new strategic needs and directions.[36]

STRONG, ADAPTIVE CULTURE　**Culture** is the set of key values, assumptions, beliefs, and norms shared by members of the organization. A strong, adaptive organizational culture is the foundation of a learning organization. Equality is one fundamental cultural value in a learning organization. The culture creates a sense of belonging, community, and caring that supports other elements, such as teamwork and participative strategy. Each person is valued

culture
The set of key values, assumptions, beliefs, and norms shared by members of an organization

TECHNOLOGY FOR TOMORROW

IDEALAB!

Traditional boundaries between departments are dropping in many companies, but one entrepreneur wants to break down boundaries *between* companies. When Bill Gross started idealab! in 1996, he wanted to offer an incubator environment for fledgling internet companies and had only two requirements for potential start-ups: the idea must be able to make money and it has to "break the mold."

Old Town Pasadena, California, hosts idealab!'s 10 incubator pods, which are small spaces in the warehouse. No walls separate different start-ups and people from any company can hear nearly everything other teams are talking about. If one resourceful employee overhears about a deal another group is brokering with Yahoo!, it is common for that person to walk over and join in, or at least find out how they closed the deal.

In the center is Gross's office, less than 15 feet from any CEO. Gross wants a "college" environment, with newer, freshmen start-ups learning from the more experienced, "senior" companies, those ready to move out on their own. Similar to a college, many graduates choose to stay near "home," with all of them less than a 30-minute drive. Just next door are eToys, GoTo.com, and the WeddingChannel.

Gross sees idealabs! future embodied in the type of company he is nurturing in three companies: NetZero, Free-PC, and GoTo.com, all of which give away services in order to provide ad space. For example, he unveiled his Free-PC idea at an industry trade show in 1999 and was immediately overwhelmed with news cameras and reporters. His plan was to give away 10,000 Compaq Presarios with two gigabytes of ads put into each hard drive.

Within a week, he had one million applications. Other successful companies he has helped launch include utility.com, which sells electricity to consumers; the free Internet service provider NetZero; and eWallet, which helps online shopping by storing billing information for customers.

Breaking down barriers, whether with new ideas or between traditional competitors, is Gross's key to success. He is now partnering with his graduate companies. For example, NetZero has agreed to be the free ISP for Free-PC. "I think I am the only one who thinks this way and that's great," he says. "The longer I have it alone out there, the better."

SOURCE: Lauren Barack, *Free Style, Business 2.0,* May 1999, pp. 125–126.

---

and the organization becomes a place for creating a web of relationships that allows people to be wholly engaged and to develop to their full potential. Activities that create status differences, such as executive dining rooms and assigned parking spaces, are discarded. The emphasis on treating everyone with care and respect creates a climate of safety and trust that allows experimentation, frequent mistakes, and failures that enable learning.

Another basic value is to question the status quo, a.k.a., the current way of doing things. The culture of a learning organization values risk-taking, improvement, and change. Constant questioning of assumptions opens the gates to creativity and improvement. The culture celebrates and rewards the creators of new ideas, products, and work processes.

Management philosophies and organizational forms change over time to meet new needs. This foundation of management understanding illustrates that the value of studying management lies not in learning current facts and research but in developing a perspective that will facilitate the broad, long-term view needed for management success.

■ MANAGEMENT AND ORGANIZATION

A historical perspective on management is important because it gives executives a way of thinking, a way of searching for patterns and understanding trends. A historical perspective provides a context or environment in which to interpret current problems. However, studying history does not mean merely arranging events in chronological order; it means developing an understanding of the impact of societal forces on organizations. Studying history is a way to achieve strategic thinking, see the big picture, and improve **conceptual skills.** We will start by examining how social, political, and economic forces have influenced organizations and the practice of management.[37]

Social forces are those aspects of a culture that guide and influence relationships among people. What do people value? What do people need? What are the standards of behavior among people? These forces shape what is known as the **social contract,** which refers to the unwritten, common rules and perceptions about relationships among people and between employees and management. Expressions such as "a man's as good as his word" and "a day's work for a day's pay" convey such perceptions.

A significant social force affecting organizations today is the changing attitudes, values, and demands of young, highly educated workers. With low unemployment and an aging population, companies are scrambling to attract "knowledge workers"—mostly young people who are smart, educated, creative, and computer literate. Rather than the organization having the power, the power has shifted to the worker, so that the worker can often make outrageous demands. Young college-educated workers don't just want a job; they want a job that's fun and that offers them opportunities for self-discovery and self-fulfillment as well as a top-notch salary.[38] Whereas in the past, many people expected to stay with one company for their entire careers, for today's workers, job-hopping is a way of life.

Political forces refer to the influence of political and legal institutions on people and organizations. Political forces include basic assumptions underlying the political system, such as the desirability of self-government, property rights, contract rights, the definition of justice, and the determination of innocence or guilt of a crime. The end of the Cold War and the spread of capitalism throughout the world are political forces that will dramatically affect business in coming years. Recent moves to establish a free market system in Eastern Europe underscore the growing interdependence among the world's countries. This interdependence requires managers to think in different ways. In addition, the empowerment of citizens throughout the world is a dramati-cally energetic political force. Power is being diffused both within and among countries as never before.[39] People are demanding empowerment, participation, and responsibility in all areas of their lives, including their work. Managers must learn to share rather than hoard power.

Economic forces pertain to the availability, production, and distribution of resources in a society. Governments, military agencies, churches, schools, and business organizations in every society require resources to achieve their goals, and economic forces influence the allocation of scarce resources. Resources may be human or material, fabricated or natural, physical or conceptual, but over time they are scarce and must be allocated among competing users.

Management practices and perspectives vary over time in response to these social, political, and economic forces in the larger society. Exhibit 1.6 illustrates the evolution of significant management perspectives over time, which have culminated with the learning organization. We will first look at the elements of a learning organization, and then examine each of the other management approaches in Exhibit 1.6.

Many students wonder why history matters to managers. A historical perspective provides a broader way of thinking, a way of searching for patterns and determining whether they recur across time periods. For example, certain management techniques that seem "modern," such as employee stock ownership programs, have repeatedly gained and lost popularity since the early twentieth century because of **historical forces.**[40]

A study of the past contributes to understanding both the present and the future. It is a way of learning: learning from the mistakes of others so as not to repeat them; learning from the successes of others so as to repeat them in the appropriate situation; and, most of all, learning to understand why things happen to improve things in the future. The remainder of this chapter will examine a number of management approaches that have led to the development of the learning organization.

---

conceptual skill
The cognitive ability to see the organization as a whole and the relationship among its parts

social forces
Those aspects of a culture that guide and influence relationships among people and their values, needs, and standards of behavior

social contract
The unwritten, common rules and perceptions about relationships among people and between employees and management

political forces
The influence of political and legal institutions on people and organizations

economic forces
The availability, production, and distribution of resources in a society that affect its competitiveness

historical forces
The effect of the past on the present and the future; the study of how learning from past mistakes and past successes can promote understanding of why thing_ happen and how they c improve

Exhibit 1.6

MANAGEMENT PERSPECTIVES OVER TIME

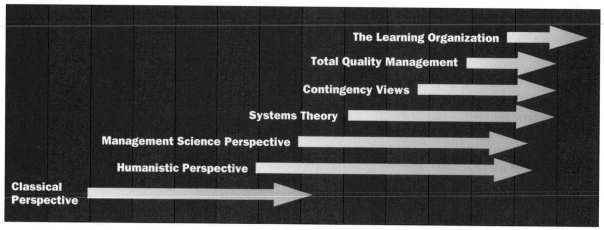

| The Learning Organization |
| Total Quality Management |
| Contingency Views |
| Systems Theory |
| Management Science Perspective |
| Humanistic Perspective |
| Classical Perspective |

1870 1880 1890 1900 1910 1920 1930 1940 1950 1960 1970 1980 1990 2000 2010

Frederick Winslow Taylor (1856–1915) Taylor's theory that labor productivity could be improved by scientifically determined management practices earned him the status as "father of scientific management."

classical perspective
A management perspective that emerged during the nineteenth and early-twentieth centuries that emphasized a rational, scientific approach to the study of management and sought to make organizations efficient operating machines

scientific management
A subfield of the classical management perspective that emphasized scientifically-determined changes in management practices as the solution to improving labor productivity

CLASSICAL PERSPECTIVE

The practice of management can be traced to 3000 B.C. to the first government organizations developed by the Sumerians and Egyptians, but the formal study of management is relatively recent.[41] The early study of management as we know it today began with what is now called the **classical perspective.**

The classical perspective on management emerged during the nineteenth and early twentieth centuries. The factory system that began to appear in the 1800s posed management challenges that earlier organizations had not encountered. Problems arose in tooling the plants, organizing managerial structure, training employees (many of them non-English-speaking immigrants), scheduling complex manufacturing operations, and dealing with increased labor dissatisfaction and resulting strikes.

In response to the myriad new problems facing management throughout industrial America, managers developed and tested solutions to the mounting challenges. The evolution of modern management, called the classical perspective, thus began. This perspective contains three subfields, each with a slightly different emphasis: scientific management, bureaucratic organizations, and administrative principles.[42]

SCIENTIFIC MANAGEMENT   The somewhat limited success of organizations in achieving improvements in labor productivity led a young engineer to suggest that the problem lay more in poor management practices than in labor. Frederick Winslow Taylor (1856–1915) insisted that management itself would have to change and, further, that the manner of change could be determined only by scientific study; hence, the label **scientific management** emerged. Taylor suggested that decisions based on rules of thumb and tradition be replaced with precise procedures developed after careful study of individual situations.[43]

Taylor's approach is illustrated by the unloading of iron from rail cars and reloading finished steel for the Bethlehem Steel plant in 1898. Taylor calculated that with correct movements, tools, and sequencing, each man was capable of loading 47.5 tons per day instead of the typical 12.5 tons. He also worked out an incentive system that paid each man $1.85 a day for meeting the new standard, an increase from the previous rate of $1.15. Productivity at Bethlehem Steel shot up overnight.

Although known as the "father of scientific management," Taylor was not alone in this area. Henry Gantt, an associate of Taylor's, developed the Gantt Chart—a bar graph that measures planned and completed work along each stage of production by time elapsed. Two other important pioneers in this area were the husband-and-wife team of Frank B. and Lillian M. Gilbreth. Frank B. Gilbreth (1868–1924) pioneered time and motion study and arrived at many of his management techniques independently of Taylor. He stressed efficiency and was known for his quest for the "one best way" to do work. Although Gilbreth is known for his early work with bricklayers, his work had great impact on medical surgery by drastically reducing the time patients spent on the operating table. Surgeons were able to save countless lives through the application of time and motion study. Lillian M. Gilbreth (1878–1972) was more interested in the human aspect of work. When her husband died at the age of 56, she had 12 children ages 2 to 19. The undaunted "first lady of management" went right on with her work. She presented a paper in place of her late husband, continued their seminars and consulting, lectured, and eventually became a professor at Purdue University.[44] She pioneered in the field of industrial psychology and made substantial contributions to human resource management.

The basic ideas of scientific management are shown in Exhibit 1.7. To use this approach, managers should develop standard methods for doing each job, select workers with the appropriate abilities, train workers in the standard methods, support workers and eliminate interruptions, and provide wage incentives.

Although scientific management improved productivity, its failure to deal with the social context and the needs of workers led to increased conflict between managers and employees. Under this system, workers often felt exploited. This was in sharp contrast to the harmony and cooperation that Taylor and his followers had envisioned.

BUREAUCRATIC ORGANIZATIONS A systematic approach developed in Europe that looked at the organization as a whole is the **bureaucratic organizations** approach, a subfield within the classical perspective. Max Weber (1864–1920), a German theorist, introduced

bureaucratic organizations
A subfield of the classical management perspective that emphasized management on an impersonal, rational basis through elements such as clearly defined authority and responsibility, formal record keeping, and separation of management and ownership

Frederick Taylor's *scientific management* techniques were expanded by automaker Henry Ford, who changed the work of heavy lifting and moving from human workers to machines. One of the first applications of the moving assembly line was the Magneto assembly operation at Ford's Highland Park plant in 1913. Magnetos moved from one worker to the next, cutting production times in half. The same principle was applied to total-car assembly, improving efficiency and reducing worker-hours required to produce a Model T Ford to less than two. Under this system, a Ford rolled off the assembly line every 10 seconds.

Exhibit 1.7

CHARACTERISTICS OF
SCIENTIFIC MANAGEMENT

General Approach
- Developed standard method for performing each job.
- Selected workers with appropriate abilities for each job.
- Trained workers in standard method.
- Supported workers by planning their work and eliminating interruptions.
- Provided wage incentives to workers for increased output.

Contributions
- Demonstrated the importance of compensation for performance.
- Initiated the careful study of tasks and jobs.
- Demonstrated the importance of personnel selection and training.

Criticisms
- Did not appreciate the social context of work and higher needs of workers.
- Did not acknowledge variance among individuals.
- Tended to regard workers as uninformed and ignored their ideas and suggestions.

Lillian M. Gilbreth (1878–1972); Frank B. Gilbreth (1868–1924)
Shown here using a "motion study" device, this husband-and-wife team contributed to the principles of *scientific management*. His development of time and motion studies and her work in industrial psychology pioneered many of today's management and human resource techniques.

bureaucracy
An organization managed on an impersonal, rational basis that depends on the legal power invested in the managerial position

most of the concepts on bureaucratic organizations.[45]

During the late 1800s, many European organizations were managed on a "personal," family-like basis. Employees were loyal to a single individual rather than to the organization or its mission. The dysfunctional consequence of this management practice was that resources were used to realize individual desires rather than organizational goals. Employees in effect owned the organization and used resources for their own gain rather than to serve customers. Weber envisioned organizations that would be managed on an impersonal,

rational basis. This form of organization was called a **bureaucracy**.

Weber believed that an organization based on rational authority would be more efficient and adaptable to change because continuity is related to formal structure and positions rather than to a particular person, who may leave or die. To Weber, rationality in organizations meant employee selection and advancement based on competence rather than on "whom you know." The organization relies on rules and written records for continuity. The manager depends not on his or her personality for successfully giving orders but on the legal power invested in the managerial position.

The term *bureaucracy* has taken on a negative meaning in today's organizations and is associated with endless rules and red tape. We have all been frustrated by waiting in long lines or following seemingly silly procedures. On the other hand, rules and other bureaucratic procedures provide a standard way of dealing with employees. Everyone gets equal treatment, and everyone knows what the rules are. This has enabled many organizations to become extremely efficient. Consider United Parcel Service (UPS), also called the "Brown Giant."

UNITED PARCEL SERVICE
www.ups.com

United Parcel Service took on the U.S. Postal Service at its own game—and won. UPS specializes in the delivery of small packages. Why has the Brown Giant been so successful? One important reason is the concept of bureaucracy. UPS is bound up in rules and regulations. There are safety rules for drivers, loaders, clerks, and managers. Strict dress codes are enforced—no beards; hair cannot touch the collar; mustaches must be trimmed evenly; and no sideburns. Rules specify cleanliness standards for buildings and other properties. No eating or drinking is permitted at employee desks. Every manager is given bound copies of policy books and expected to use them regularly.

UPS also has a well-defined division of labor. Each plant consists of specialized drivers, loaders, clerks, washers, sorters, and maintenance personnel. UPS thrives on written records. Daily worksheets specify performance goals and work output. Daily employee quotas and achievements are reported on a weekly and monthly basis.

Technical qualification is the criterion for hiring and promotion. The UPS policy book says the leader is expected to have the knowledge and capacity to justify the position of leadership. Favoritism is forbidden. The bureaucratic model works just fine at UPS, "the tightest ship in the shipping business."[46] ■

ADMINISTRATIVE PRINCIPLES Another major subfield within the classical perspective is known as the **administrative principles** approach. Whereas scientific management focused on the productivity of the individual worker, the administrative principles approach focused on the total organization. The contributors to this approach included Henri Fayol, Mary Parker Follett, and Chester I. Barnard.

Henri Fayol (1841–1925) was a French mining engineer who worked his way up to become head of a major mining group known as Comambault. Comambault survives today as part of Le Creusot-Loire, the largest mining and metallurgical group in central France. In his later years, Fayol wrote down his concepts

on administration, based largely on his own management experiences.[47]

In his most significant work, *General and Industrial Management,* Fayol discussed 14 general principles of management, several of which are part of management philosophy today. For example:

- *Unity of command.* Each subordinate receives orders from one—and only one—superior.

- *Division of work.* Managerial and technical work are amenable to specialization to produce more and better work with the same amount of effort.

- *Unity of direction.* Similar activities in an organization should be grouped together under one manager.

- *Scalar chain.* A chain of authority extends from the top to the bottom of the organization and should include every employee.

Fayol felt that these principles could be applied in any organizational setting. He also identified five basic functions or elements of management: planning, organizing, commanding, coordinating, and controlling. These functions underlie much of the general approach to today's management theory.

Mary Parker Follett (1868–1933) was trained in philosophy and political science at what today is Radcliffe College. She applied herself in many fields, including social psychology and management. She wrote of the importance of common superordinate goals for reducing conflict in organizations. Her work was popular with businesspeople of her day but was often overlooked by management scholars. Follett's ideas served as a contrast to scientific management and are reemerging as applicable for modern managers dealing with rapid changes in today's global environment. Her approach to leadership stressed the importance of people rather than engineering techniques. She offered the pithy admonition "Don't Hug Your Blueprints" and analyzed the dynamics of management-organization interactions. Follett addressed issues that are timely today, such as ethics, power, and how to lead in a way that encourages employees to

administrative principles
A subfield of the classical management perspective that focused on the total organization rather than the individual worker, delineating the management functions of planning, organizing, commanding, coordinating, and controlling

give their best. The concepts of empowerment, facilitating rather than controlling employees, and allowing employees to act depending on the authority of the situation opened new areas for theoretical study by Chester Barnard and others.[48] Harbor Sweets is one company Mary Parker Follet would have, no doubt, admired.

HARBOR SWEETS

Benneville Strohecker created Harbor Sweets candy company in his Salem, Massachusetts, basement in 1973. Today it is a $2.6 million business, and Strohecker is proud to have built a company that ignores convention. Increasingly, most of the workforce is part time, with flexible hours, and is composed of a diverse group of teenagers, old-agers, the handicapped, and immigrants from Laos to the Dominican Republic.

Strohecker pays his 150 employees similar to a McDonald's and with no benefits except paid vacation, but they are part of a company profit-sharing plan and receive discounted candy. In a seasonal business centered around holidays, summer layoffs are common.

If you think these workers feel like exploited stepchildren, think again. Harbor Sweets attracts smart, dedicated people who stay around. Strohecker

sums up the key to the company's success and the essence of his management style: "Trust still remains the most important ingredient in our recipes. But I believe it is not just being nice. Relying on trust is good business."

A lofty sentiment, and Strohecker means it. In an age of background checks and integrity profiles, he still "hires by gut." Trust extended to allowing employees to fill out their own time cards. Only recently, at the request of employees, were time clocks installed at Harbor Sweets.

On occasion, Strohecker has deviated from reliance on trust. He once brought in a consultant group to increase plant efficiency. What at first seemed prudent and reasonable turned out to be self-defeating, and the system was discarded. "The very fact that we were measuring is not the culture of Harbor Sweets," says Strohecker. Instead, he told his employees to work as hard as they could; they responded with many suggestions of their own, and the former sense of freedom was restored. A similar scenario evolved when a financial consultant wanted to present Strohecker some benefit options, but the boss suggested going directly to the employees. The astonished consultant was certain Strohecker had lost his mind and that the employees would plunder him. He was wrong on both counts. They decided on a package that was probably more conservative than even Strohecker would have chosen.

Some would say Strohecker's style is an anachronism, not likely to be duplicated elsewhere. But he is confident his company and its philosophy will survive without him, and though he remains CEO, he has turned over day-to-day management to chief operating officer Phyllis Leblanc, who bought the company from Strohecker in 1998.

"As long as we keep in mind that there's more to this company than making a lot of money, hiring faster people, or buying fancier equipment," he says, "I think our success will always be sweet."[49] ■

Mary Parker Follett (1868–1933)
Follett was a major contributor to the *administrative principles* approach to management. Her emphasis on worker participation and shared goals among managers was embraced by many businesspeople of the day and has been recently "rediscovered" by corporate America.

Chester I. Barnard (1886–1961) studied economics at Harvard but failed to receive a degree because he lacked a course in laboratory science. He went to work in the statistical department of AT&T and in 1927 became president of New Jersey Bell. One of Barnard's significant contributions was the concept of the informal organization. The informal organization occurs in all formal organizations and includes cliques and naturally occurring social groupings. Barnard argued that organizations are not machines and informal relationships are powerful forces that can help the organization if properly managed. Another significant contribution was the acceptance theory of authority, which states that people have free will and can choose whether to follow management orders. People typically follow orders because they perceive positive benefit to themselves, but they do have a choice. Managers should treat employees properly because their acceptance of authority may be critical to organization success in important situations.[50]

The overall classical perspective as an approach to management was very powerful and gave companies fundamental new skills for establishing high productivity and effective treatment of employees. Indeed, America surged ahead of the world in management techniques, and other countries, especially Japan, borrowed heavily from American ideas.

HUMANISTIC PERSPECTIVE

Mary Parker Follett and Chester Barnard were early advocates of a more **humanistic perspective** on management that emphasized the importance of understanding human behaviors, needs, and attitudes in the workplace as well as social interactions and group processes.[51] We will discuss three subfields based on the humanistic perspective: the human relations movement, the human resources perspective, and the behavioral sciences approach.

THE HUMAN RELATIONS MOVEMENT

America has always espoused the spirit of human equality. However, this spirit has not always been translated into practice when it comes to power sharing between managers and workers. The human relations school of

This 1914 photograph shows an initiation of a new arrival to a Nebraska planting camp. This ceremony was, of course, not part of the formal rules, but it illustrates the significance of the *informal organization* described by Barnard. Social values and behaviors were powerful forces that could help or hurt the planting organization, depending on how those forces were managed.

thought considers that truly effective control comes from within the individual worker rather than from strict, authoritarian control.[52] This school of thought recognized and directly responded to social pressures for enlightened treatment of employees. The early work on industrial psychology and personnel selection received little attention because of the prominence of scientific management. Then a series of studies at a Chicago electric company, which came to be known as the **Hawthorne studies,** changed all that.

Around 1895, a struggle began to develop between manufacturers of gas and electric lighting fixtures for control of the residential and industrial market.[53] By 1909 electric lighting had begun to win, but the increasingly efficient electric fixtures used less total power. The electric companies began a campaign to convince industrial users that they needed more light to get more productivity. When advertising did not work, the industry began using experimental tests to demonstrate their argument. Managers were skeptical about the results, so the Committee on Industrial Lighting (CIL) was set up to run the tests. To further add to the credibility of the tests, Thomas Edison was made honorary chairman of the CIL. In one test location—the Hawthorne plant of the Western Electric Company—some interesting events occurred.

humanistic perspective
A management perspective that emerged around the late nineteenth century that emphasized understanding human behavior, needs, and attitudes in the workplace

Hawthorne studies
A series of experiments on worker productivity begun in 1924 at the Hawthorne plant of Western Electric Company in Illinois; attributed employees' increased output to managers' better treatment of them during the study

The major part of this work involved four experimental and three control groups. In all, five different "tests" were conducted. These pointed to the importance of factors other than illumination in affecting productivity. To more carefully examine these factors, numerous other experiments were conducted.[54] The results of the most famous study, the first Relay Assembly Test Room (RATR) experiment, were extremely controversial. Under the guidance of two Harvard professors, Elton Mayo and Fritz Roethlisberger, the RATR studies lasted nearly six years (May 10, 1927, to May 4, 1933) and involved 24 separate experimental periods. So many factors were changed and so many unforeseen factors uncontrolled that scholars disagree on the factors that truly contributed to the general increase in performance over that period. Most early interpretations, however, agreed on one thing: Money was not the cause of the increased output.[55] However, recent reanalyses of the experiments have revealed that a number of factors were different for the workers involved, and some suggest that money may well have been the single most important factor.[56] An interview with one of the original participants revealed that just getting into the experimental group had meant a huge increase in income.[57]

These new data clearly show that money mattered a great deal at Hawthorne, but it was not recognized at the time of the experiments. Then it was felt that the factor that best explained increased output was "human relations." Employee output increased sharply when managers treated them in a positive manner. These findings were published and started a revolution in worker treatment for improving organizational productivity. To be historically accurate, money was probably the best explanation for increases in output, but at that time experimenters believed the explanation was human relations. Despite the inaccurate interpretation of the data, the findings provided the impetus for the **human relations movement.** That movement shaped management theory and practice for well over a quarter century, and the belief that human relations is the best approach for increasing productivity persists today. See the following Man-

ager's Shoptalk box for a number of management innovations that have become popular over the years.

THE HUMAN RESOURCES PERSPECTIVE

The human relations movement initially espoused a "dairy farm" view of management—contented cows give more milk, so satisfied workers will give more work. Gradually, views with deeper content began to emerge. The **human resources perspective** maintained an interest in worker participation and considerate leadership but shifted the emphasis to consider the daily tasks that people perform. The human resources perspective combines prescriptions for design of job tasks with theories of motivation.[58] In the human resources view, jobs should be designed so that tasks are not perceived as dehumanizing or demeaning but instead allow workers to use their full potential. Two of the best-known contributors to the human resources perspective were Abraham Maslow and Douglas McGregor.

Abraham Maslow (1908–1970), a practicing psychologist, observed that the problems of his patients usually stemmed from an inability to satisfy their needs. Thus, he generalized his work and suggested a hierarchy of needs. Maslow's hierarchy started with physiological needs and progressed to safety, belongingness, esteem, and, finally, self-actualization needs. His ideas are discussed in greater detail later in this book.

Douglas McGregor (1906–1964) had become frustrated with the early simplistic human relations notions while president of Antioch College in Ohio. He challenged both the classical perspective and the early human relations assumptions about human behavior. Based on his experiences as a manager and consultant, his training as a psychologist, and the work of Maslow, McGregor formulated his Theory X and Theory Y, which are explained in Exhibit 1.8. McGregor believed that the classical perspective was based on Theory X assumptions about workers. He also felt that a slightly modified version of Theory X fit early human relations ideas. In other words, human relations ideas did not go far enough.

human relations movement

A movement in management thinking and practice that emphasized satisfaction of employees' basic needs as the key to increased worker productivity

human resources perspective

A management perspective that suggests jobs should be designed to meet higher-level needs by allowing workers to use their full potential

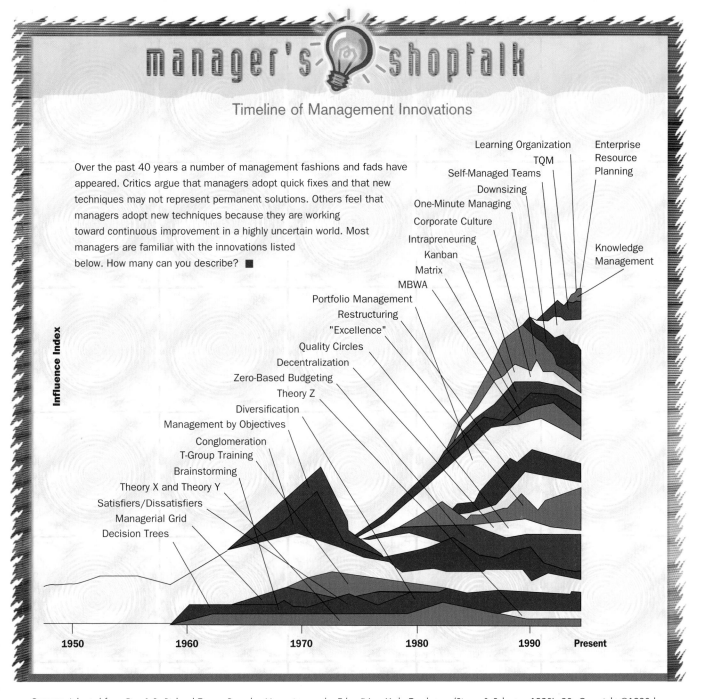

Timeline of Management Innovations

Over the past 40 years a number of management fashions and fads have appeared. Critics argue that managers adopt quick fixes and that new techniques may not represent permanent solutions. Others feel that managers adopt new techniques because they are working toward continuous improvement in a highly uncertain world. Most managers are familiar with the innovations listed below. How many can you describe? ■

Learning Organization
Enterprise Resource Planning
TQM
Self-Managed Teams
Downsizing
One-Minute Managing
Corporate Culture
Intrapreneuring
Knowledge Management
Kanban
Matrix
MBWA
Portfolio Management
Restructuring
"Excellence"
Quality Circles
Decentralization
Zero-Based Budgeting
Theory Z
Diversification
Management by Objectives
Conglomeration
T-Group Training
Brainstorming
Theory X and Theory Y
Satisfiers/Dissatisfiers
Managerial Grid
Decision Trees

Influence Index

1950   1960   1970   1980   1990   Present

SOURCE: Adapted from Fig. 1.3, Richard Tanner Pascale, *Managing on the Edge* (New York: Touchstone/Simon & Schuster, 1990), 20. Copyright ©1990 by Richard Pascale.

McGregor proposed Theory Y as a more realistic view of workers for guiding management thinking.

The point of Theory Y is that organizations can take advantage of the imagination and intellect of all their employees. Employees will exercise self-control and will contribute to organizational goals when given the opportunity. A few companies today still use Theory X management, but many are trying Theory Y techniques. The Danish company Oticon Holding A/S brings out the creativity and enthusiasm of its employees by operating from Theory Y assumptions.

Exhibit 1.8

THEORY X AND THEORY Y

Assumptions of Theory X

- The average human being has an inherent dislike of work and will avoid it if possible....
- Because of the human characteristic of dislike for work, most people must be coerced, controlled, directed, or threatened with punishment to get them to put forth adequate effort toward the achievement of organizational objectives....
- The average human being prefers to be directed, wishes to avoid responsibility, has relatively little ambition, wants security above all.

Assumptions of Theory Y

- The expenditure of physical and mental effort in work is as natural as play or rest. The average human being does not inherently dislike work....
- External control and the threat of punishment are not the only means for bringing about effort toward organizational objectives. A person will exercise self-direction and self-control in the service of objectives to which he or she is committed....
- The average human being learns, under proper conditions, not only to accept but to seek responsibility....
- The capacity to exercise a relatively high degree of imagination, ingenuity, and creativity in the solution of organizational problems is widely, not narrowly, distributed in the population.
- Under the conditions of modern industrial life, the intellectual potentialities of the average human being are only partially utilized.

SOURCE: Douglas McGregor, *The Human Side of Enterprise* (New York: McGraw-Hill, 1960), pp. 33–48.

OTICON HOLDING A/S
www.oticon.com

Lars Kolind, head of the Danish company Oticon Holding A/S, emphasizes that making hearing aids is not the core of what his company is about. "It's about something more fundamental," he says. "It's about the way people perceive work." At Oticon, there are no organization charts, no departments, no functions, no titles, and no permanent desks. Any vestiges of an organizational hierarchy have disappeared. All 150 employees have mobile workstations and are constantly forming and reforming into self-directed teams that work on specific projects. Their desks are wheeled caddies with room for hanging folders, a few binders, and maybe a family photo or two. Everyone has a mobile phone because employees are constantly on the move. Anyone with a compelling idea can become a project leader by competing to attract the people and resources needed to deliver results. Project teams make their own decisions and have almost complete freedom to run the project as they see fit. Kolind believed the formal organization was getting in the way of allowing employees to use their full potential and find joy in their work. He knew that breakthroughs in hearing aid technology required not only science but imagination. Oticon has been so successful at taking advantage of the imagination, creativity, and ability of its employees that it is the fastest-growing hearing aid producer in the world. Within the past eight years, Oticon has introduced at least 10 major product innovations, including the world's first digital hearing aid. Kolind thinks the organization of the future will liberate employees to grow personally and professionally and to become more creative and action-oriented. At Oticon, the future is now. Says Kolind, "We give people the freedom to do what they want."[59] ∎

THE BEHAVIORAL SCIENCES APPROACH The **behavioral sciences approach** develops theories about human behavior based on scientific methods and study. Behavioral science draws from sociology, psychology, anthropology, economics, and other disciplines to understand employee behavior and interaction in an organizational setting. The approach can be seen in practically every organization. When General Electric conducts research to determine the best set of tests, interviews, and employee profiles to use when selecting new employees, it is employing behavioral science techniques. Emery Air Freight has utilized reinforcement theory to improve the incentives given to workers and increase the performance of many of its operations. When Westinghouse trains new managers in the techniques of employee motivation, most of the theories and findings are rooted in behavioral science research.

In the behavioral sciences, economics and sociology have significantly influenced the way today's managers approach organizational strategy and structure. Psychology has influenced management approaches to motivation, communication, leadership, and the overall field of human resource management.

MANAGEMENT SCIENCE PERSPECTIVE

World War II caused many management changes. The massive and complicated problems associated with modern global warfare presented managerial decision makers with the need for more sophisticated tools than ever before. The **management science perspective** emerged to treat those problems. This view is distinguished for its application of mathematics, statistics, and other quantitative techniques to management decision making and problem solving. During World War II, groups of mathematicians, physicists, and other scientists were formed to solve military problems. Because those problems frequently involved moving massive amounts of materials and large numbers of people quickly and efficiently, the techniques had obvious applications to large-scale business firms.[60]

Operations research grew directly out of the World War II groups (called operational research teams in Great Britain and operations research teams in the United States).[61] It consists of mathematical model building and other applications of quantitative techniques to managerial problems.

Operations management refers to the field of management that specializes in the physical production of goods or services. Operations management specialists use quantitative techniques to solve manufacturing problems. Some of the commonly used methods are forecasting, inventory modeling, linear and nonlinear programming, queuing theory, scheduling, simulation, and break-even analysis.

Management information systems (MIS) is the most recent subfield of the management science perspective. These systems are designed to provide relevant information to managers in a timely and cost-efficient manner. The advent of the high-speed digital computer opened up the full potential of this area for management.

Many of today's organizations have departments of management science specialists to help solve quantitatively based problems. When Sears used computer models to minimize its inventory costs, it was applying a quantitative approach to management. When AT&T performed network analysis to speed up and control the construction of new facilities and switching systems, it was employing management science tools.

For example, the adoption of new information technology can have a significant impact on other parts of the organization, as described in the Focus on Collaboration box.

One specific technique used in many organizations is queuing theory. Queuing theory uses mathematics to calculate how to provide services that will minimize the waiting time of customers. Queuing theory has been used to analyze the traffic flow through the Lincoln Tunnel and to determine the number of toll booths and traffic officers for a toll road, and it was used to develop the single waiting line for tellers used in many banks.

TOTAL QUALITY MANAGEMENT

The quality movement in Japan emerged partly as a result of American influence after World

behavioral sciences approach
A subfield of the humanistic management perspective that applies social science to an organizational context, drawing from economics, psychology, sociology, and other disciplines

management science perspective
A management perspective that emerged after World War II and applied mathematics, statistics, and other quantitative techniques to managerial problems

management information systems
A recent subfield of the management science perspective that seeks to provide relevant information to managers in a timely and cost-efficient manner

FOCUS ON Collaboration   LDS HOSPITAL, UTAH

If you think the most highly computerized hospital in the United States is only about technology, think again. Salt Lake City's Latter Day Saints Hospital's 5,000 interlinked microcomputers whiz on as they immediately send captured medical data from 25 different clinical areas into electronic patient charts. Its computers are so highly evolved in artificial intelligence that they can override incorrect prescriptions, change intravenous drip rates, and automatically page nurses if a lab report looks abnormal.

The highly evolved and interconnected technology, though, is not enough. The LDS system works so well because of one thing: the doctors trust it and they trust each other. As someone said, all human transactions work better with trust, but speed without trust is impossible. That is why the LDS system is not necessarily exportable to its many visitors—some from as far away as Japan. So effective is the system that it can chillingly expose poor decision making and analyze medical outcomes statistically. Such information could be used in a "Big Brother" sense—the way some insurance companies do, in a punitive way, to the doctors. Because of so many bad experiences with technology, in order for the doctors to agree to sign on, the hospital had to promise never to use the data to evaluate individual physicians.

Trust and technology helped to save Betty Redocto from a transplant, and maybe even saved her life. With two previous clinics, she was told she had permanent liver damage, and either nothing could be done or (as the second clinic told her) the only possible solution was a liver transplant. So she took her medical files, filled with barely legible notes and prescription notations, to LDS. Just 24 hours after she was admitted, the computer-generated report of every patient having an adverse reaction to medication showed that Redocto had been overdosing on the antibiotic Macrodantin. An earlier doctor for years had given her the medication, which can induce hepatitis. LDS physicians took her off the drug and she recovered without a transplant.

Such a system can save lives, but, in the wrong hands and without trust, it can mean a disaster of breached confidentiality. LDS understands this. As physician David Classen says, punitive and prying uses of data are not helpful in the long run. "We make real-time information available to help doctors make medical decisions."

SOURCE: Katherine Eban Finkelstein, "The Computer Cure," *The New Republic*, Sept. 14 and 21, 1998, pp. 28–33.

War II. The ideas of W. Edwards Deming, known as the "father of the quality movement," were initially scoffed at in America, but the Japanese embraced his theories and modified them to help rebuild their industries into world powers.[62] Japanese companies achieved a significant departure from the American model by gradually shifting from an inspection-oriented approach to quality control toward an approach emphasizing employee involvement in the prevention of quality problems.[63]

During the 1980s and into the 1990s, **total quality management (TQM),** which focuses on managing the total organization to deliver high quality to customers, was at the forefront in helping managers deal with global competition. The approach infuses values of total quality throughout every activity within a company, with frontline workers intimately involved in the process. Four significant elements of total quality management are employee involvement, focus on the customer, benchmarking, and continuous improvement.

Employee involvement means that TQM requires companywide participation in quality control. All employees are focused on the customer; TQM companies find out what customers want and try to meet their needs and expectations. Benchmarking refers to a process whereby companies find out how others do something better than they do and then try to imitate or improve on it. Continuous improvement is the implementation of small, incremental improvements in all areas of the organization on an ongoing basis. TQM is not a quick fix, but companies such as Motorola, Procter & Gamble, Xerox, and Du Pont have achieved astonishing results in efficiency, quality, and customer satisfaction through total quality management.[64] TQM, which is still an important part of today's organizations, will be discussed in detail in Chapter 16.

total quality management (TQM)
A concept that focuses on managing the total organization in order to deliver total quality to customers and is characterized by employee involvement, focus on the customer, benchmarking, and continuous improvement

Summary and Management Solution

This chapter has described the emerging learning organization and examined the historical background leading up to this new approach to management. An understanding of the evolution of management helps present and future managers understand where we are now and continue to progress toward better management.

The three major perspectives on management that have evolved since the late 1800s are the classical perspective, the humanistic perspective, and the management science perspective. The most recent thinking about organizations has been brought about by the shift to a new management paradigm: the learning organization, which fully engages all employees in identifying and solving problems. The learning organization is characterized by visionary leadership, a team-based structure, participative strategy, a strong, adaptive culture, empowered employees, and open information. The learning organization represents a substantial departure from the traditional management hierarchy.

Today's managers put customers and employees ahead of profits. Leadership is widely dispersed and empowering, and most work is done by teams. Managers give employees opportunities for personal growth and self-fulfillment and emphasize collaboration over competition and conflict. The primary responsibility of managers is to create learning capability, and many companies are becoming learning organizations, such as Tapistron after Darwin Poe took over. You will recall that the company was in bankruptcy and sinking fast, with a suspicious chairman. With a little research, Poe found out the chairman's résumé was rather inflated. He had no MBA from Wharton, nor a Harvard Law degree. Soon the chairman was fired.

After that matter was settled, Poe spent two sleepless years turning the company around, cutting operating expenses down to about 25 percent in the first year, with help from one of his new recruits, long-time colleague Floyd Koegler, who became CFO. He brought in a new vice president of engineering, Rodney Hardeman, who invented a new system to improve the quality of their product, a computerized carpet tufting machine known as CYP, as well as the speed of the machines. By increasing efficiency of machines

already on the market from 40 percent to 75 percent, Tapistron's image changed from abysmal to glowing. Part of the success was because Darwin developed a sense of partnership with the factory workers, who had previously been treated with mostly contempt. Then, in 1998, despite a questionable future, Darwin took another risk, but one designed to create a closer sense of team spirit. He gave all plant employees a raise.

Darwin did something else that dramatically enhanced Tapistron's image. Against the advice of company lawyers, he decided to pay creditors 100 cents on the dollar, almost unheard of for Chapter 11 companies. When hearing of this, the company's Japanese rep said, "It's the only honorable thing to do" (O'Neill, 1997, p. 68).

Since then, Tapistron not only survived Chapter 11 (only 15 percent of companies survive Chapter 11), but it was named as one of the top Georgia companies (in one category 13th of the 100 best).

Darwin Poe was critical of many modern management practices. "Today's CEOs," he says, "are effectively absolute rulers. They can hire and fire at will and realize the financial and professional dreams of some, while denying or even destroying others. It is important that leaders of organizations regularly be reminded of the destructive consequences" of treating people with such disdain.

In February 1999, Darwin Poe died suddenly. Rodney Hardeman took over as president. Statistics show that more than 50 percent of small companies that lose their top leader do not survive. Once again, Tapistron is beating the odds as it continues to thrive.

Poe and Koegler's task is more challenging than that of a traditional manager's because it has less structure, more uncertainty, and greater reliance on leadership, human skills, and interpersonal roles. Creating learning organizations is the challenge for future managers.

SOURCES: Darwin Poe, his own personal communication, 1999; Floyd Koegler, personal communication, 1999; Frank O'Neill, "How Tapistron Emerged from Bankruptcy into a Seemingly Bright Future," *Focus,* Oct. 1997, pp. 67–68.

Discussion Questions

1. Assume you are a research engineer at a petrochemical company, collaborating with a marketing manager on a major product modification. You notice that every memo you receive from her has been copied to senior management. At every company function, she spends time talking to the big shots. You are also aware that sometimes when you are slaving away over the project, she is playing golf with senior managers. What is your evaluation of her behavior?

2. What do you think the text means by a management revolution? Do you expect to be a leader or follower in this revolution? Explain.

3. What similarities do you see among the four management functions of planning, organizing, leading, and controlling? Do you think these functions are related; that is, is a manager who performs well in one function likely to perform well in the others?

4. What is the difference between efficiency and effectiveness? Which is more important for performance? Can an organization succeed in both simultaneously?

5. What changes in management functions and skills occur as one is promoted from a nonmanagement to a management position? How can managers acquire the new skills?

6. If managerial work is characterized by variety, fragmentation, and brevity, how do managers perform basic management functions such as planning, which would seem to require reflection and analysis?

7. A college professor told her students, "The purpose of a management course is to teach students about management, not to teach them to be managers." Do you agree or disagree with this statement? Discuss.

8. Describe the characteristics of the new management paradigm. How do these characteristics compare to those of an organization in which you have worked? Would you like to work or manage in a learning organization? Discuss.

9. How could the teaching of management change to better prepare future managers to deal with workforce diversity? With empowerment? Do you think diversity and empowerment will have a substantial impact on organizations in the future? Explain.

10. A management professor once said that for successful management, studying the present was most important, studying the past was next, and studying the future was least important. Do you agree? Why?

11. Which of the six characteristics of learning organizations do you find most appealing? Which would be hardest for you to adopt?

12. Some experts believe that leadership is more important than ever in a learning organization. Do you agree? Explain.

13. What is the behavioral sciences approach? How does it differ from earlier approaches to management?

14. Why can an event such as the Hawthorne studies be a major turning point in the history of management even if the idea is later shown to be in error? Discuss.

15. Do you think management theory will ever be as precise as theories in the fields of physics, chemistry, or experimental psychology? Why or why not?

Management Exercises

Manager's Workbook

Management Aptitude Questionnaire

Rate each of the following questions according to this scale:

5. I always am like this.
4. I often am like this.
3. I sometimes am like this.
2. I rarely am like this.
1. I never am like this.

_____ **1.** When I have a number of tasks or homework to do, I set priorities and organize the work around the deadlines.   C

_____ **2.** Most people would describe me as a good listener.   H

_____ **3.** When I am deciding on a particular course of action for myself (such as hobbies to pursue, languages to study, which job to take, special projects to be involved in), I typically consider the long-term (3 years or more) implications of what I would choose to do.   C

_____ **4.** I prefer technical or quantitative courses rather than those involving literature, psychology, or sociology.   T

_____ **5.** When I have a serious disagreement with someone, I hang in there and talk it out until it is completely resolved.   H

_____ **6.** When I have a project or assignment, I really get into the details rather than the "big picture" issues.*   C

_____ **7.** I would rather sit in front of my computer than spend a lot of time with people.   T

_____ **8.** I try to include others in activities or when there are discussions.   H

_____ **9.** When I take a course, I relate what I am learning to other courses I have taken or concepts I have learned elsewhere.   C

_____ **10.** When somebody makes a mistake, I want to correct the person and let her or him know the proper answer or approach.*   H

_____ **11.** I think it is better to be efficient with my time when talking with someone, rather than worry about the other person's needs, so that I can get on with my real work.   T

_____ **12.** I know my long-term vision for career, family, and other activities and have thought it over carefully.   C

_____ **13.** When solving problems, I would much rather analyze some data or statistics than meet with a group of people.   T

_____ **14.** When I am working on a group project and someone doesn't pull a full share of the load, I am more likely to complain to my friends rather than confront the slacker.*   H

_____ **15.** Talking about ideas or concepts can get me really enthused and excited.   C

_____ **16.** The type of management course for which this book is used is really a waste of time.   T

_____ **17.** I think it is better to be polite and not to hurt people's feelings.*   H

_____ **18.** Data or things interest me more than people.   T

Scoring Key

*Add the total points for the following sections. Note that starred * items are reverse scored, as such:*

1. I always am like this.
2. I often am like this.
3. I sometimes am like this.
4. I rarely am like this.
5. I never am like this.

1, 3, 6, 9, 12, 15	Conceptual skills total score
2, 5, 8, 10, 14, 17	Human skills total score
4, 7, 11, 13, 16, 18	Technical skills total score

The above skills are three abilities needed to be a good manager. Ideally, a manager should be strong (though not necessarily equal) in all three. Anyone noticeably weaker in any of the skills should take courses and read to build up that skill. For further background on the three skills, please refer to the model on p. 8.

*reverse scoring item

Manager's Workshop

The Worst Manager

1. By yourself, think of two managers you have had—the best and the worst. Write down a few sentences to describe each.

   The best manager I ever had was . . .

The worst manager I ever had was . . .

2. Divide into groups of five to seven members. Share your experiences. Each group should choose a couple of examples to share with the whole group. Complete the table below as a group.

	Management principle followed or broken	Skills evident or missing	Lessons to be learned	Advice you would give managers
The best managers				
The worst managers				

1. What are the common problems managers have?

2. Prepare a list of "words of wisdom" you would give as a presentation to a group of managers. What are some basic principles they should use to be effective?

Management in Practice: Ethical Dilemma

The Supervisor

Karen Lowry, manager of a social service agency in a mid-sized city in Illinois, loved to see her employees learn and grow to their full potential. When a rare opening for a supervising clerk occurred, Karen quickly decided to give Charlotte Hines a shot at the job. Charlotte had been with the agency for 17 years and had shown herself to be a true leader. Charlotte worked hard at being a good supervisor, just as she had always worked hard at being a top-notch clerk. She paid attention to the human aspects of employee problems and introduced modern management techniques that strengthened the entire agency.

However, the Civil Service Board decided that a promotional exam should be given to find a permanent placement for the supervising clerk position. For the sake of fairness, the exam was an open competition—anyone, even a new employee, could sign up and take it. The board wanted the candidate with the highest score to get the job but allowed Karen, as manager of the agency, to have the final say.

Since she had accepted the provisional opening and proven herself on the job, Charlotte was upset that the entire clerical force was deemed qualified to take the test. When the results came back, she was devastated. Charlotte placed twelfth in the field of candidates, while one of her newly hired clerks placed first. The Civil Service Board, impressed by the new clerk's high score, is urging Karen to give her the permanent supervisory job. Karen wonders if it's fair to base her decision only on the test results.

What Do You Do?

1. Ignore the test. Charlotte has proven herself and deserves the job.

2. Give the job to the candidate with the highest score. You don't need to make enemies on the Civil Service Board, and, after all, it is an objective way to select a permanent placement.

3. Devise a more comprehensive set of selection criteria—including test results as well as supervisory experience, ability to motivate employees, and knowledge of agency procedures—that can be explained and justified to the board and to employees.

SOURCE: Based on Betty Harrigan, "Career Advice," *Working Woman*, July 1986, pp. 22–24.

Surf the Net

1. *The Learning Organization.* The learning organization guru, Peter Senge, is a senior lecturer at the Massachusetts Institute of Technology (MIT) and director of the Center for Organizational Learning at MIT's Sloan School of Management. Choose one of his articles, such as the one entitled "Learning Organizations," located at http://learning.mit.edu/res/kr/index.html. Be prepared to report in class your findings about the concept of learning organizations.

2. *Culture.* In the April–May 1998 issue of *Fast Company,* Dave Duffield, president and CEO of PeopleSoft, stated: "Our true core competency is our culture . . . That's what attracts people and keeps them here. It also helps sell customers. Customers want to work with companies that are competent, trustworthy, and fun. Winners like winners." Visit www.peoplesoft.com/en/corporate—info/people—culture/. After reading through the information provided about PeopleSoft's culture, select one of the following options to complete:

   OPTION 1: "I think I would fit in with the culture at PeopleSoft and would enjoy working there because of the following characteristics of its culture."

   OPTION 2: "I don't think I would enjoying working at PeopleSoft because of the following characteristics of its culture."

3. *Quality.* Provide information in response to the following questions: (a) What is the Malcolm Baldrige National Quality Award? (b) What criteria are used to evaluate the companies? (c) What organizations won the award last year? The sites below contain Malcolm Baldrige information.

   www.quality.nist.gov/

   http://www.asqc.org/abtquality/awards/baldrige.html

4. *Surfing skills.* To help you get the most out of the "Surf the Net" exercises throughout this text, visit one of the Web sites listed below. If you're new to the Internet, list three things you learned that will help you develop your "surfing" skills. If you're already a proficient surfer, list three items of information you learned that will help you enhance your level of proficiency.

   www.microsoft.com/magazine/guides/internet/

   www.zdnet.com/zdhelp/howto—help/websearch/search—1.html

   www.pbs.org/uti/begin.html

5. *Management career opportunities.* The Manager's Shoptalk section earlier in this chapter asked you to consider whether you really want to be a manager. To help you explore a future management career, access one of the online career Web sites, such as Career Mosaic or The Monster Board, accessible at www.100hot.com/jobs/

   Click on the "job search" feature. You will be asked to enter key search words or select a job title from a list provided. Choose a management career that you are interested in pursuing, such as "sales manager," "financial manager," "human resources manager," or any other field that you want to learn about, then click on the search button. The site will return job postings from many different companies. Select at least three, look at the information, and print out the job descriptions. Compile a list of the education and experience requirements as well as any information about the job that appeals to you. Your instructor may ask you to write a memo on what you found and why you think that a management career will or will not be a good choice for you.

6. *Management skills.* Option 1—Go online to search for past or present successful managers, such as Sam Walton (Wal-Mart founder); Dave Thomas (Wendy's Restaurants); Herb Kelleher (Southwest Airlines); or Jack Welch (CEO of General Electric). Identify examples of their conceptual, human, and technical skills.

   www.wal-mart.com/corporate/wm—story.shtml

   www.wendys.com/dave—history/meet—dave.html

   http://cgi.pathfinder.com/fortune/careers/1999/01/11/interview.html

   Option 2—Visit www.mgeneral.com. Find "Top Ten Management" section. What is said about effective manager skills?

Case for Critical Analysis

Electra-Quik

Barbara Russell, a manufacturing vice president, walked into the monthly companywide meeting with a light step and a hopefulness she hadn't felt in a long time. The company's new, dynamic CEO was going to announce a new era of empowerment at Electra-Quik, an 80-year-old publicly held company that had once been a leading manufacturer and retailer of electrical products and supplies. In recent years, the company experienced a host of problems: market share was declining in the face of increased foreign and domestic competition; new product ideas were few and far between; departments such as manufacturing and sales barely spoke to one another; morale was at an all-time low, and many employees were actively seeking other jobs. Everyone needed a dose of hope.

Martin Griffin, who had been hired to revive the failing company, briskly opened the meeting with a challenge: "As we face increasing competition, we need new ideas, new energy, new spirit to make this company great. And the source for this change is you—each one of you." He then went on to explain that under the new empowerment campaign, employees would be getting more information about how the company was run and would be able to work with their fellow employees in new and creative ways. Martin proclaimed a new era of trust and cooperation at Electra-Quik. Barbara felt the excitement stirring within her; but as she looked around the room, she saw many of the other employees, including her friend Harry, rolling their eyes. "Just another pile of corporate crap," Harry said later. "One minute they try downsizing, the next reengineering. Then they dabble in restructuring. Now Martin wants to push empowerment. Garbage like empowerment isn't a substitute for hard work and a little faith in the people who have been with this company for years. We made it great once, and we can do it again. Just get out of our way." Harry had been a manufacturing engineer with Electra-Quik for more than 20 years. Barbara knew he was extremely loyal to the company, but he—and a lot of others like him—were going to be an obstacle to the empowerment efforts.

Top management assigned selected managers to several problem-solving teams to come up with ideas for implementing the empowerment campaign. Barbara loved her assignment as team leader of the manufacturing team, working on ideas to improve how retail stores got the merchandise they needed when they needed it. The team thrived, and trust blossomed among the members. They even spent nights and weekends working to complete their report. They were proud of the ideas they had come up with, which they believed were innovative but easily achievable: permit a manager to follow a product from design through sales to customers; allow salespeople to refund up to $500 worth of merchandise on the spot; make information available to salespeople about future products; and swap sales and manufacturing personnel for short periods to let them get to know one another's jobs.

When the team presented their report to department heads, Martin Griffin was enthusiastic. But shortly into the meeting he had to excuse himself because of a late-breaking deal with a major hardware store chain. With Martin absent, the department heads rapidly formed a wall of resistance. The director of human resources complained that the ideas for personnel changes would destroy the carefully crafted job categories that had just been completed. The finance department argued that allowing salespeople to make $500 refunds would create a gold mine for unethical customers and salespeople. The legal department warned that providing information to salespeople about future products would invite industrial spying.

The team members were stunned. As Barbara mulled over the latest turn of events, she considered her options: keep her mouth shut; take a chance and confront Martin about her sincerity in making empowerment work; push slowly for reform and work for gradual support from the other teams; or look for another job and leave a company she really cared about. Barbara realized there would be no easy choices and no easy answers.

Questions

1. How might top management have done a better job changing Electra-Quik into a learning organization? What might they do now to get the empowerment process back on track?

2. Can you think of ways Barbara could have avoided the problems her team faced in the meeting with department heads?

3. If you were Barbara Russell, what would you do now? Why?

SOURCE: Based on Lawrence R. Rothstein, "The Empowerment Effort That Came Undone," *Harvard Business Review* (January–February 1995), 20-31.

Endnotes

1 Darwin Poe, personal communication, 1999; Floyd Koegler, personal communication, 1999; Frank O'Neill, "How Tapistron emerged from bankruptcy into a seemingly bright future," *Focus,* October, pp. 67–68, 1997.

2 Nicholas Imparato and Oren Harari, *Jumping the Curve: Innovation and Strategic Choice in an Age of Transition* (San Francisco: Jossey-Bass Publishers, 1994); Tom Broersma, "In Search of the Future," *Training and Development,* January 1995, 38–43; Rahul Jacob, "The Struggle to Create an Organization for the Twenty-First Century," *Fortune,* April 3, 1995, 90–99; and Charles Handy, *The Age of Paradox* (Boston: Harvard Business School Press, 1994).

3 Louis Kraar, "Iron Butterflies," *Fortune,* October 7, 1991, 143–154.

4 James A. F. Stoner and R. Edward Freeman, *Management,* 4th ed. (Englewood Cliffs, N.J.: Prentice-Hall, 1989).

5 Michael Davis, "Nissan Credits 'Good People' for Efficiency," *The Tennessean,* May 31, 1996, 1E, 4E; Wendy Zellner, Robert D. Hof, Richard Brandt, Stephen Baker, and David Greising, "Go-Go Goliaths," *Business Week,* February 13, 1995, 64–70.

6 David Wessell, "With Labor Scarce, Service Firms Strive to Raise Productivity," *The Wall Street Journal,* June 1, 1989, A1, A8.

7 Martha Brannigan and Eleena De Lisser, "Cost Cutting at Delta Raises the Stock Price But Lowers the Service," The *Wall Street Journal,* June 20, 1996, A1.

8 Esther Wachs Book, "Leadership for the Millennium," *Working Woman,* March 1998, pp. 29–34.

9 Robert L. Katz, "Skills of an Effective Administrator," *Harvard Business Review* 52 (September–October 1974), 90–102.

10 Eric Calonius, "Smart Moves by Quality Champs," *Fortune,* special 1991 issue—The New American Century, 24–28.

11 Henry Mintzberg, *The Nature of Managerial Work* (New York: Harper & Row, 1973); and Mintzberg, "Rounding Out the Manager's Job," *Sloan Management Review* (Fall 1994), 11–26.

12 Robert E. Kaplan, "Trade Routes: The Manager's Network of Relationships," *Organizational Dynamics* (Spring 1984), 37–52; Rosemary Stewart, "The Nature of Management: A Problem for Management Education," *Journal of Management Studies* 21 (1984), 323–330; John P. Kotter, "What Effective General Managers Really Do," *Harvard Business Review* (November–December 1982), 156–167; and Morgan W. McCall, Jr., Ann M. Morrison, and Robert L. Hannan, "Studies of Managerial Work: Results and Methods" (Technical Report No. 9, Center for Creative Leadership, Greensboro, N.C., 1978).

13 Based on Carol Saunders and Jack William Jones, "Temporal Sequences in Information Acquisition for Decision Making: A Focus on Source and Medium," *Academy of Management Review* 15 (1990), 29–46; Kotter, "What Effective General Managers Really Do"; and Mintzberg, "Managerial Work."

14 Lienert, "A Day in the Life."

15 Lance B. Kurke and Howard E. Aldrich, "Mintzberg Was Right!: A Replication and Extension of *The Nature of Managerial Work,*" *Management Science* 29 (1983), 975–984; and Colin P. Hales, "What Do Managers Do? A Critical Review of the Evidence," *Journal of Management Studies* 23 (1986), 88–115.

16 Mintzberg, "Rounding Out the Manager's Job."

17 Edward O. Welles, "There Are No Simple Businesses Anymore," *The State of Small Business,* 1995, 66–79.

18 John A. Byrne, "Profiting from the Nonprofits," *Business Week,* March 26, 1990, 66–74; and Michael Ryval, "Born-Again Bureaucrats," *Canadian Business,* November 1991, 64–71.

19 The following discussion is based on John A. Byrne, "Paradigms for Postmodern Managers," *Business Week/Reinventing America* (1992), 62–63; George Land and Beth Jarman, *Breakpoint and Beyond* (New York: Harper Business, 1992); Robert Barner, "Seven Changes That Will Challenge Managers—and Workers," *The Futurist,* March/ April, 1996, 33–42; and Lawrence Chimerine, "The New Realities in Business," *Management Review,* January 1997, 12–17.

20 Lawrence Chimerine, "The New Economic Realities in Business," *Management Review,* January 1997, 12–17; Steingraber, "The New Business Realities of the Twentieth Century," *Business Horizons,* November–December 1996, 2–5; and Koh Sera,

"Corporate Globalization: A New Trend," *Academy of Management Executive* 6, No. 1 (1992), 89–96.

21 For further information about Theory Z, see William G. Ouchi and Alfred M. Jaeger, "Type Z Organizations: Stability in the Midst of Mobility," *Academy of Management Review* 3 (1978), 308–314; and William G. Ouchi, *Theory Z: How American Business Can Meet the Japanese Challenge* (Reding, Mass.: Addison-Wesley, 1981).

22 Gilbert W. Fairholm, *Leadership and the Culture of Trust,* (Westport, Conn.: Praeger, 1994), 184; and Barner, "Seven Changes That Will Challenge Managers—and Workers."

23 Gilbert W. Fairholm, *Leadership and the Culture of Trust,* (Westport, Conn.: Praeger, 1994), 184.

24 Tetenbaum, "Shifting Paradigms: From Newton to Chaos."

25 Tetenbaum, "Shifting Paradigms: From Newton to Chaos."

26 Jeffrey Pfeffer, "Producing Sustainable Competitive Advantage through the Effective Management of People," *Academy of Management Executive* 9, No. 1 (1995), 55–72.

27 Mahlon Apgar, IV, "The Alternative Workplace: Changing How and Where People Work," *Harvard Business Review,* May–June 1998, 121–136; and Jenny C. McCune, "Telecommuting Revisited," *Management Review,* February 1998, 10–16.

28 John Huey, "Managing in the Midst of Chaos," *Fortune,* April 5, 1993, 38–48; Susan Greco, "The Decade-Long Overnight Success," *Inc.,* December 1994, 73–79; Agis Salpukas, "How a Staid Electric Company Becomes a Renegade," *The New York Times,* December 12, 1993, F10; Samuel M. DeMarie and Barbara W. Keats, "Deregulation, Reengineering, and Cultural Transformation at Arizona Public Service Company," *Organizational Dynamics* (winter 1995): 70–76.

29 John A. Byrne, "Management Meccas," *Business Week,* September 18, 1995, 122–132.

30 John Huey, Managing in the Midst of Chaos," *Fortune,* April 5, 1993, 38–48; and Toby J. Tetenbaum, "Shifting Paradigms: From Newton to Chaos." *Organizational Dynamics* (spring 1998), 21–32.

31 Peter M. Senge, "The Leader's New Work: Building Organizations," *Sloan Management Review* (fall 1990), 7–22.

32 Esther Wachs Book, "Leadership for the Millennium," *Working Woman,* March 1998, 29–34.

33 "The Concrete Intangibles," *Management Review,* May 1999, pp 30–33; "Granite Rock: A Family Operation Nears Its Centennial," *Stone Review,* October 1996, 6–7; David Franceschi, Quality Director, 1996; Edward Welles, "How're We Doing?" *Inc.,* May 1991, 80–83; John Case, "The Change Masters," *Inc.,* March 1992, 58–70.

34 Jeffrey Pfeffer, "Producing Sustainable Competitive Advantage through the Effective Management of People," *Academy of Management Executive* 9, no. 1 (1995), 55–69.

35 Paul Roberts, "We Are One Company, No Matter Where We Are," *Fast Company,* April–May 1998, 122–128.

36 Marc S. Gerstein, Robert B. Shaw, "Organizational Architectures for the Twenty-First Century," in David A. Nadler, Marc S. Gerstein, Robert B. Shaw, and Associates, eds., *Organizational Architecture: Designs for Changing Organizations* (San Francisco: Jossey-Bass, 1992), 263–274.

37 Daniel A. Wren, *The Evolution of Management Thought* (New York: Wiley, 1979), 6–8. Much of the discussion of these forces comes from Arthur M. Schlesinger, *Political and Social History of the United States, 1829–1925* (New York: Macmillan, 1925); and Homer C. Hockett, *Political and Social History of the United States, 1492–1828* (New York: Macmillan, 1925).

38 Nina Munk, "The New Organization Man," *Fortune,* March 16, 1998, 62–74.

39 Robin Wright and Doyle McManus, *Flashpoints: Promise and Peril in a New World* (New York: Alfred A. Knopf, 1991).

40 Wren, *Evolution of Management Thought,* 171; and George, *History of Management Thought,* 103–104.

41 Daniel A. Wren, "Management History: Issues and Ideas for Teaching and Research," *Journal of Management* 13 (1987), 339–350.

42 The following is based on Wren, *Evolution of Management Thought,* Chapters 4, 5; and Claude S. George, Jr., *The History of Management Thought* (Englewood Cliffs, N.J.: Prentice-Hall, 1968), Chapter 4.

43 Charles D. Wrege and Ann Marie Stoka, "Cooke Creates a Classic: The Story Behind F. W. Taylor's Principles of Scientific Management," *Academy of Management Review* (October 1978), 736–749; Robert Kanigel, *The One Best Way: Frederick Winslow Taylor and the Enigma of Efficiency* (New York: Viking, 1997); and Alan Farnham, "The Man Who Changed Work Forever," *Fortune,* July 21, 1997, 114.

44 Wren, *Evolution of Management Thought,* 171; and George, *History of Management Thought,* 103–104.

45 Max Weber, *General Economic History,* trans. Frank H. Knight (London: Allen & Unwin, 1927); Max Weber, *The Protestant Ethic and the Spirit of Capitalism,* trans. Talcott Parsons (New York: Scribner, 1930); and Max Weber, *The Theory of Social and Economic Organizations,* ed. and trans. A. M. Henderson and Talcott Parsons (New York: Free Press, 1947).

46 "UPS," *The Atlanta Journal and Constitution,* April 26, 1992, H1; Richard L. Daft, *Organizaiton Theory and Design,* 3d ed. (St. Paul, Minn.: West, 1989), 181–182; and Kathy Goode, Betty Hahn, and Cindy Seibert, "United Parcel Service: The Brown Giant" (unpublished manuscript, Texas A&M University, 1981).

47 Henri Fayol, *Industrial and General Administration,* trans. J. A. Coubrough (Geneva: International Management Institute, 1930); Henri Fayol, *General and Industrial Management,* trans. Constance Storrs (London: Pitman and Sons, 1949); and W. J. Arnold and the editors of *Business Week, Milestones in Management* (New York: McGraw-Hill, vol. I, 1965; vol. II, 1966).

48 Follett, *The New State;* Metcalf and Urwick, *Dynamic Administration* (London: Sir Isaac Pitman, 1941).

49 Source: "LeBlanc buys Harbor Sweets," *Candy Industry,* Nov. 1998, p. 12; Ben Strohehecker, "A Business Built on Trust," Guideposts, August 1996, pp. 6–9; Leslie Brokaw, "Like money for chocolate: Harbor Sweets," *Hemisphere,* Dec. 1995, pp. 35–38.

50 William B. Wolf, *How to Understand Management: An Introduction to Chester I. Barnard* (Los Angeles: Lucas Brothers, 1968); and David D. Van Fleet, "The Need-Hierarchy and Theories of Authority," *Human Relations* 9 (spring 1982), 111-118.

51 Gregory M. Bounds, Gregory H. Dobbins, and Oscar S. Fowler, *Management: A Total Quality Perspective* (Cincinnati: South-Western College Publishing, 1995), 52–53.

52 Curt Tausky, *Work Organizations: Major Theoretical Perspectives* (Itasca, Ill.: F. E. Peacock, 1978), 42.

53 Charles D. Wrege, "Solving Mayo's Mystery: The First Complete Account of the Origin of the Hawthorne Studies—The Forgotten Contributions of Charles E. Snow and Homer Hibarger" (paper presented to the Management History Division of the Academy of Management, August 1976).

54 Ronald G. Greenwood, Alfred A. Bolton, and Regina A. Greenwood, "Hawthorne a Half Century Later: Relay Assembly Participants Remember," *Journal of Management* 9 (fall/winter 1983), 217–231.

55 E. J. Roethlisberger, W. J. Dickson, and H. A. Wright, *Management and the Worker* (Cambridge, Mass.: Harvard University Press, 1939).

56 H. M. Parson, "What Happened at Hawthorne?" *Science* 183 (1974), 922–932; John G. Adair, "The Hawthorne Effect: A Reconsideration of the Methodological Artifact," *Journal of Applied Psychology* 69, No. 2 (1984), 334–345; and Gordon Diaper, "The Hawthorne Effect: A Fresh Examination," *Educational Studies* 16, no. 3 (1990), 261–268.

57 Greenwood, Bolton, and Greenwood, "Hawthorne a Half Century Later," 219–221.

58 Tausky, *Work Organizations: Major Theoretical Perspectives,* 55.

59 Polly LaBarre, "This Organization is Disorganization," *Fast Company,* June/July 1996, 110–113.

60 Mansel G. Blackford and K. Austin Kerr, *Business Enterprise in American History* (Boston: Houghton Mifflin, 1986), Chapters 10, 11; and Alex Groner and the editors of *American Heritage and Business Week, The American Heritage History of American Business and Industry* (New York: American Heritage Publishing, 1972), Chapter 9.

61 Larry M. Austin and James R. Burns, *Management Science* (New York: Macmillan, 1985).

62 Samuel Greengard, "25 Visionaries Who Shaped Today's Workplace," *Workforce,* January 1997, 50–59.

63 Mauro F. Guillen, "The Age of Eclecticism: Current Organizational Trends and the Evolution of Managerial Models," *Sloan Management Review* (fall 1994), 75–86.

64 Jeremy Main, "How to Steal the Best Ideas Around," *Fortune,* October 19, 1992, 102–106.

PART

2

THE ENVIRONMENT OF MANAGEMENT

During the Whitbread race, no other factor more profoundly affects the performance of crews and boats than the environment. Boats and crews suffer extremes in their external environment—blistering heat in the tropics, freezing rain and mammoth waves in the southern hemisphere's "roaring 40s" and "screaming 50s," and close calls (with hidden reefs and icebergs) in the North Atlantic. Several boats have hit whales, causing damage to the vessels' hulls and keels, and several more have been dismasted by buffeting winds. Crews pull together to overcome their obstacles. Forming such a strong group—a culture of cooperation and sharing—among diverse members from around the world is difficult in the best of circumstances, but here, the environment throws its worst at the crew, challenging them at every turn. When crews have setbacks that threaten to break their will, they take individual initiative to address and fix them, from repairing and replacing sails to diving into frigid waters to examine damage to a hull.

In Part Two you'll study the environment of management, the trend toward globalization, and the importance of managerial ethics and social responsibility.

The Environment and Corporate Culture

LEARNING OBJECTIVES

After studying this chapter, you should be able to:

- Describe the general and task environments and the dimensions of each

- Explain how organizations adapt to an uncertain environment and identify techniques managers use to influence and control the external environment

- Define corporate culture and give organizational examples

- Explain organizational symbols, stories, heroes, slogans, and ceremonies and their relationship to corporate culture

- Describe how corporate culture relates to the environment

- Define a symbolic leader and explain the tools a symbolic leader uses to change corporate culture

MANAGEMENT PROBLEM

AS THE HOLIDAYS arrive every year,

retailers battle for market share. None may be as

fierce as the Toy Wars, recently played out by old-timer Toys "R" Us

and the new kid on the block, eToys, which is one of the success stories of

Internet startup incubator idealab! (see Chapter 1). Although both companies started

around the same time in 1997, eToys had launched products and made distribution deals with

Yahoo! and America Online. Toys "R" Us Direct (Toys Direct), on the other hand, was still writing a

business plan. The Toys Direct team members were still performing their regular work for the company.

By 1999, eToys had built up a 100-person staff that was responsible for everything. In contrast, Toys "R" Us

• If you were Joel Anderson, what would you do to catch up and even overtake eToys? Would you spin

off Toys Direct from Toys "R" Us, like Barnes & Noble did with their e-commerce business? What

can you do to adapt to the e-commerce imperative that threatens the company's very existence?

Direct outsourced whatever it felt could be done cheaper and faster, including Web design and e-commerce

software. This meant it needed a staff of only 40—10 in Information Systems (IS) and 10 in order

fulfillment—all headed by Harvard-educated company vice president Joel Anderson. Losing

market share and having to close 90 of its 1,400 stores meant Toys "R" Us was in trouble.

Today, however, Web business is seen as the means for the company to get back on

track and regain its profitability. But, it still lags behind eToys in important

respects. More than twice as many Internet users visit eToys,

which continues to enjoy the early-bird advantage.

Because it ran its own warehouse from the start, eToys has always been able to carry the more conventionally popular toys, such as Barbie and Star Wars, while also offering more specialty items, such as Breyer horses.[1]

The environment for retail companies such as Toys "R" Us, as well as other companies operating in the information age, has changed dramatically since the early 1990s. Rapid advances in technology, increased competition, and growing customer demands mean companies constantly must adapt to the changing environment to remain competitive. The Internet has revolutionized communications and the transmission of data. Now, online firms around the world are waging war on a new level. But it isn't only high-tech firms that face environmental upheavals. Coke and Pepsi continue to do battle in the cola wars, with PepsiCo recently hauling Coca-Cola's Indian subsidiary into court, accusing Coke of illegal and unethical business practices in India.[2] The environment surprises many companies. In the 1980s, large companies like Sears, IBM, and General Motors were seriously damaged by competition they didn't anticipate. August Busch III, CEO of Anheuser-Busch, admits that his company was late in recognizing the threat of microbreweries: "If you had asked us 10 years ago whether there would be X-hundred little tiny breweries across this country who will end up with 3 percent of the market and 6 percent of the margin pool, we would have said no. . . . We were five years late in recognizing that they were going to take as much market as they did and five years late in recognizing we should have joined them."[3] Anheuser-Busch hasn't been seriously hurt by its tardiness, but consider the case of record store chains like Camelot Music, Record Giant, Wherehouse Entertainment, and Strawberries, each of which have filed for bankruptcy protection within the last few years. The whole nature of the record-selling business changed almost overnight when home electronics behemoth Best Buy started selling CDs for nearly half what they cost in traditional music stores. Today, electronics stores like Best Buy and Circuit City sell more CDs than Sam Goody's and other record retail chains.[4]

Government actions and red tape also can affect an organization's environment and foment a crisis. Deregulation of the electric utility industry will force a massive restructuring of power companies throughout the United States. Changes in Medicaid are hurting hospitals, such as La Rabida, on Chicago's South Side, which is dedicated to serving the poor.[5]

The study of management traditionally has focused on factors within the organization—a closed systems view—such as leading, motivating, and controlling employees, but globalization and the trend toward a borderless world affect companies in new ways. To be effective, managers must monitor and respond to the environment—an open systems view.

This chapter explores the external environment and how it affects the organization. We will also examine a major part of the organization's internal environment—corporate culture. Corporate culture is shaped by the external environment and is an important part of the context within which managers do their jobs.

■ THE EXTERNAL ENVIRONMENT

The world as we know it is undergoing tremendous and far-reaching change. This change can be better understood when components of the external environment are defined and examined.

The external **organizational environment** includes all elements existing outside the boundary of the organization that have the potential to affect the organization. The environment includes influential factors such as competitors, resources, technology, and economic conditions. Not included are those events so far removed from the organization that their impact is not, or only nominally, perceived. The organization's external environment can be further conceptualized as having two layers: general and task environments, as illustrated in Exhibit 2.1.

The **general environment** is the outer layer of the environment that is widely dispersed and affects organizations only indirectly. It includes social, demographic, and economic factors that influence all organizations more or

organizational environment
All elements existing outside the organization's boundaries that have the potential to affect the organization

general environment
The layer of the external environment that indirectly affects the organization

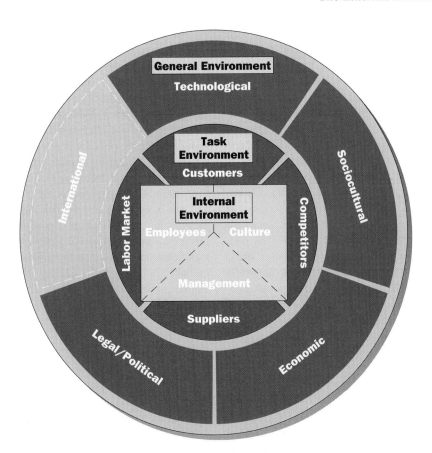

Exhibit 2.1

LOCATION OF THE
ORGANIZATION'S GENERAL,
TASK, AND INTERNAL
ENVIRONMENTS

less equally. Increases in the inflation rate or the percentage of dual-career couples in the workforce are part of the organization's general environment. These events do not directly change day-to-day operations, but they eventually do affect all organizations. The **task environment** is closer to the organization and includes the sectors that conduct day-to-day transactions with the organization and directly influence its basic operations and performance. It is generally considered to include competitors, suppliers, and customers.

The organization also has an **internal environment,** which includes the elements within the organization's boundaries. The internal environment is composed of current employees, management, and especially corporate culture that define employee behavior and determine how well the organization will adapt to external environmental factors.

As an open system, the organization draws resources from the external environment and releases goods and services back to it.

GENERAL ENVIRONMENT

The general environment represents the outer layer of the environment. These dimensions influence the organization over time but often are not involved in day-to-day transactions with it. The dimensions of the general environment include international, technological, sociocultural, economic, and legal-political.

INTERNATIONAL The **international dimension** of the external environment represents events originating in foreign countries as well as opportunities for American companies in other countries. Note in Exhibit 2.1 that the international dimension represents a context that influences all other aspects of the external environment. The international environment provides new competitors, customers, and suppliers and shapes social, technological, and economic trends, as well.

One study identified 136 U.S. industries— including automobiles, accounting services,

task environment
The layer of the external environment that directly influences the organization

internal environment
The environment within the organization's boundaries

international dimension
The portion of the external environment that represents events originating in foreign countries as well as opportunities for American companies in other countries

entertainment, consumer electronics, and publishing—that will have to compete on a global basis or disappear. The high-quality, low-priced automobiles from Japan and Korea have permanently changed the American automobile industry. Many companies have parts supplied from countries such as Mexico because of low-priced labor. A drop in the dollar's foreign exchange rate lowers the price of U.S. products overseas, increasing export competitiveness. A significant impact of globalization for U.S. business is that it has created an environment of disinflation. For example, companies find it more difficult now to raise prices than at virtually any time since World War II. Many companies have had to cut prices to remain competitive in the new global economy. Economic problems in other parts of the world now have a tremendous impact on U.S. companies. Companies such as Coca-Cola, which get a large percentage of sales from Asia, are feeling the pinch of the Asian economic crisis. Russia's economic woes also are affecting U.S. companies. For example, a small distributor of vitamins and sports supplements near Nashville, Tennessee, gets 20 percent of its sales from Russia. The economic turmoil in that country, however, has left U.S.A. Laboratories struggling to get paid and make up for lost orders.[6]

Today, every company must think internationally. Managers who are used to thinking only about the domestic environment must learn new rules to cope with goods, services, and ideas circulating around the globe. A better machine built in Oklahoma City will find buyers from Europe and Asia. Moreover, competitors in a global village come from all over. A company that does not export still will run into competitors in its own marketplace, including some from developing nations.

Perhaps the hardest lesson for managers in the United States to learn is that they do not know best. American decision makers know little about issues and competition in foreign countries, and their arrogance is a shortcut to failure. To counter this, Pall Corporation keeps a team of Ph.D.s traveling around the world gathering current information on markets and issues.[7]

The global environment represents an ever changing and uneven playing field compared with the domestic environment. Changes in the international domain can abruptly turn the domestic environment upside down. Consider, for example, the "peace dividend" brought on by the end of the Cold War and the fall of communism. Despite the need for periodic military action in areas such as the Persian Gulf or Bosnia, the peace dividend has increased demand for military cuts, pushing smaller defense contractors out of business and forcing large companies such as McDonnell Douglas, General Dynamics, and Lockheed Martin to convert a significant portion of their operations into non-military production.[8] Top industry scientists and engineers are switching to civilian developments like high-definition television and new areas of transportation such as electric cars.[9]

TECHNOLOGICAL The **technological dimension** includes scientific and technological advancements in a specific industry as well as in society at large. In recent years, the most striking advances have been in the computer industry. A greeting card that plays "Happy Birthday" today holds more computing power than anything available anywhere before 1950. Today's home video cameras wield more processing power than the old IBM 360, the wonder machine that launched the age of mainframe computers. Millions of households own personal computers (PCs) and have access to the Internet. Businesses, meanwhile, are demanding ever more sophisticated network technology to support the new global work environment. The retail industry has been impacted by changes in technology (see Comp-U-Card example).

COMP-U-CARD

www.netmarket.com
www.auto-by-tel.com

Walter A. Forbes, founder of Comp-U-Card, takes all this as a sign that his 25-year-old dream soon will be a reality. Since the early 1970s, Forbes has envisioned a day when shoppers will buy everything from Cuisinarts to Geo

technological dimension
The dimension of the general environment that includes scientific and technological advancements in the industry and society at large

Prizms via their home computers. Forbes recognized that with decreased leisure time, people wanted faster, easier ways to make smart purchasing decisions. So he built CUC International Inc., an operation of two dozen mail-order shopping, travel, auto, entertainment, and financial service clubs with some 68 million members. Now he's taking the next step to make his shopping-club powerhouse an Internet phenomenon. He recently opened netMarket, an electronic superstore offering 250,000 brand-name products, from perfume to furniture. Although online shopping malls have a troubled history, Forbes is betting that the convenience, comfort, and savings soon will change that. He predicts that within a few years Internet shopping habits will mimic those in the physical environment, where 80 percent of sales are concentrated in a handful of merchants. Whether Forbes's dream comes true remains to be seen, but it seems clear that Internet shopping will continue to grow.[10] ∎

Anyone who has ever bought a new car knows what an ordeal it can be fending off overly aggressive salespeople, haggling over prices, and sometimes driving away with the uncomfortable feeling that you've been had. The strain of car shopping, combined with a decrease in leisure time and a demand for convenience, have more and more people turning to the World Wide Web to shop for their dream car. Market researcher J. D. Power & Associates indicates that 16 percent of new-car buyers used the World Wide Web for shopping in 1997, and the number is expected to grow to 50 percent within a few years. Customers can compare prices, check the value of their trade-in, and ask for bids from on-line car-buying services such as Auto-By-Tel, Microsoft Car-Point, and AutoVantage. Daimler Chrysler and General Motors also are experimenting with Web sites to link online shoppers with dealers in a handful of regions.

The emerging "life sciences" industry, which brings together agriculture, biotechnol-

ogy, and pharmaceuticals, may soon produce grains that taste like meat and cotton that can produce its own color. These and other technological advances can change the rules of the game; thus, every organization must be ready to respond. Halsey Minor's CNET has worked hard to create the kind of adaptive, flexible company that can respond quickly to environmental changes.

CNET ONLINE

It's enough to make you click your mouse until your hand is stiff. As the cyberspace world grows, so new companies enter the revenue-rich field. CNET Online is a brash company trying to take on the most robust in the computer trade publication business. By offering technical support, technology news, game reviews, product reviews, and bulletin boards, and 190,000 shareware titles, founder and CEO 34-year-old Halsey Minor hoped to "gut" and siphon off advertising dollars from giant magazines such as *PC Magazine* and *InfoWorld.* In fact, he talked about eating them "for lunch."

Though online advertising is relatively new, CNET is making millions of dollars per year in advertising revenue from companies such as Hewlett-Packard, Intel, Apple, and IBM. It's still not enough to cover the cost of running a 100-employee business, but CNET has nothing to lose and everything to gain by gambling on the Internet. The reward of computer trade advertising for CNET is worth the fight. The U.S. market was $1.42 billion last year, and Ziff-David, publisher of *PC Magazine, Computer Shopper,* and some 20 other periodicals, took in almost 40 percent of that. One computer industry expert says this may be the year electronic media break the "stranglehold on the computer advertising market."

Minor seemed to understand early online potential, which others often saw as merely a dump of print advertising into cyberspace. CNET's innovative use of

TV/online has attracted a youthful audience, which also attracts solid advertisers.

Yet, the old standby magazines are still popular. Though CNET has grown and recently bought out Savvysearch Ltd for $22 million, it hasn't had any magazines for lunch. And the advertising industry hasn't changed much. In fact, lots of dot-com businesses are paying for space in print and on television.

Part of Minor's strategy involves tailoring his company to the needs of the fast-paced, rapidly changing external environment. He has done this so well that he can respond very quickly to conditions. Recently, in anticipation of his old rival ZDNet (Ziff-Davis) trying to acquire some companies, Minor bought three companies in three weeks.

Despite the predictions of some in the print media, Halsey Minor defied expectations and is not just still in business, but going strong. After years of hard work and success, one thing still eludes Halsey Minor. Most people don't know his company's name.[11] ∎

sociocultural dimension
The dimension of the general environment representing the demographic characteristics, norms, customs, and values of the population within which the organization operates

SOCIOCULTURAL

The **sociocultural dimension** of the general environment represents the demographic characteristics as well as the norms, customs, and values of the general population. Important sociocultural characteristics are geographical distribution and population density, age, and education levels. Today's demographic profiles are the foundation of tomorrow's workforce and consumers. Forecasters see increased globalization of both consumer markets and the labor supply, with increasing diversity both within organizations and consumer markets.[12] Consider the following key demographic trends in the United States:

1. Minorities, largely African Americans and Hispanics, will make up the majority of the U.S. population by the year 2050.

2. The population and the workforce continue to age with the baby boomers, and some analysts predict a coming shortage of skilled workers.

3. The United States will continue to receive a flood of immigrants, largely from Asia and Mexico. Approximately 15 percent of births in recent years were to foreign-born mothers.[13]

Blue Bird Bus Company has kept its keen eye on demographic changes and customer needs, doing so partially through the use of more sophisticated technology.

BLUE BIRD BUS COMPANY

Blue Bird Bus Company has been a family-run business with a firm hold on its leading position in the highly com-

MSNBC, the cable and online television news network, was begun by Microsoft Corp. and General Electric Co.'s NBC unit in recognition of the technological dimension of the company's general environment. MSNBC sees a high-tech future where TV and the Internet are combined. With high-tech appeal, NBC personalities such as Tom Brokaw, Katie Couric, and Jane Pauley allow MSNBC to draw the affluent 25–54 age group, viewers that advertisers covet. In the latter months of 1999, its primetime household viewership increased by 144 percent.

petitive school bus manufacturing business. Its recent sale to a large British firm will hopefully not change the culture much. A. Laurence Luce founded Blue Bird in 1932, and his sons George, Albert, and Joe assumed control in 1962. The sons learned their business and the value of a dollar from their Depression-era father. In an industry where flinty-eyed state and local school boards scrutinize bids for the lowest-cost producer, such lessons helped earn Blue Bird one sale in three in the U.S. market.

Still, the company had a dichotomy. Engineers at Blue Bird availed themselves of the latest computer-aided technology systems. On their way to lunch they passed by the company's ten "Beliefs of the Blue Bird Company," which opens with, "We will continue to build our companies on the foundations of Christianity and the free enterprise system."

The brothers saw the declining number of school-age children. Realizing the number of retirees with more disposable income would continue to increase, they began producing the Blue Bird Wander-lodges, or "Birds." These luxury vehicles contain amenities such as microwaves and satellite dishes, and are 31 to 40 feet long. Making up nearly half the company's profits, they are priced around $350,000 and have been sold to members of royalty around the world.

After George's death in 1991, the other brothers sold the company to Merrill Lynch, with the agreement that current management would stay on. Even without the Luces, the company still holds its place in innovation to customers. At Earth Day 1996, Blue Bird unveiled its new ultra-safe, ultra-low-emission school bus, featuring innovative application of alternative fuel, as well as sophisticated onboard electronics like sensors that alert the driver to activity on the bus's sides before driving away. It is said to be the safest heavy-duty vehicle ever made. Two years ago, the company dealt with low productivity caused by handwritten work-in-progress tickets that were slowing down the manufacturing process. So, the innovation-friendly company introduced bar coding. Whereas 200 daily orders on the factory line had had 100 items each, now 2000 orders a day have 10 each. This has resulted in machine operators' performances improving almost 100 percent. A. Laurence Luce would be proud.[14] ■

Demography also shapes society's norms and values. Recent sociocultural trends affecting many companies include the No Smoking movement, the anticholesterol and reduced fat fervor, the purchasing power of young children increase, and growing consumer diversity, with accompanying specialized markets for Hispanic groups and women over age 30. For example, the *Miami Herald* responded to changes in the sociocultural environment by launching a Spanish-language newspaper, *El Nuevo Herald*, with articles emphasizing Hispanic, Cuban, and Latin American news and sports.[15]

ECONOMIC The **economic dimension** represents the general economic health of the country or region in which the organization operates. Consumer purchasing power, the unemployment rate, and interest rates are part of the organization's economic environment. Because organizations today operate in a global environment, the economic dimension has become exceedingly complex and creates even more uncertainty for managers. The economies of countries are more closely tied together than ever before. Economic problems in Asia and Russia, for example, have a significant impact on U.S. companies and the stock market.

One significant recent trend in the economic environment is the frequency of mergers and acquisitions, and it is altering the corporate economic landscape. In the media industry, for example, Disney and ABC Television recently negotiated the biggest entertainment merger in history, and Westinghouse acquired CBS Television. In the toy industry, which once was made up of numerous small- to medium-sized companies, the three largest toy makers—Hasbro, Mattel, and Tyco—have

economic dimension
The dimension of the general environment representing the overall economic health of the country or region in which the organization functions

gobbled up at least a dozen smaller competitors within the past few years. The impact of these deals on employees can be overwhelming, creating uncertainty about future job security. The merger is just the beginning of employee uncertainty, because about half of the acquired companies are resold.[16]

LEGAL-POLITICAL The **legal-political dimension** includes government regulations at the local, state, and federal levels as well as political activities designed to influence company behavior. The U.S. political system encourages capitalism, and the government tries not to overregulate business. However, government laws do specify rules of the game. The federal government influences organizations through the Occupational Safety and Health Administration (OSHA), Environmental Protection Agency (EPA), and its fair trade practices, libel statutes that allow lawsuits against business, consumer protection legislation, product safety requirements, import and export restrictions, and information and labeling requirements. Although designed to solve problems, government actions often create problems for organizations. For example, with food imports on the rise—and expanding free-trade pacts paving the way for even more—U.S. food processors are facing increased competition. Imported beef from Canada, Mexico, and Argentina has hurt U.S. cattle farmers, and the National Farmers Union is opposing expanded trade agreements.[17]

Managers must recognize a variety of **pressure groups** that work within the legal-political framework to influence companies to behave in socially responsible ways. Automobile manufacturers, toy makers, and airlines have been targeted by Ralph Nader's Center for Responsive Law. Tobacco companies today are certainly feeling the far-reaching power of antismoking groups. Middle-aged activists who once protested the Vietnam War now battle to keep Wal-Mart from "destroying the quality of small-town life." Some groups have also attacked the giant retailer on environmental issues, which likely will be one of the strongest pressure points in the coming years. Environmental groups put pressure on the lumber industry in the Northwest in the early 1990s because of the industry's threat to the spotted owl, and Greenpeace has managed to make significant changes in the whaling, tuna fishing, and seal fur industries.[18]

TASK ENVIRONMENT

As described earlier, the task environment includes those sectors that have a direct working relationship with the organization, among them customers, competitors, suppliers, and the labor market.

CUSTOMERS Those individuals and organizations in the environment that acquire goods or services from the organization are **customers.** As recipients of the organization's output, customers are important because they determine the organization's success. Patients are the customers of hospitals, students the customers of schools, and travelers the customers of airlines. Companies such as AT&T, General Foods, and Beecham Products have designed special programs and advertising campaigns to court their older customers, who are, with the aging of baby boomers, becoming a larger percentage of their market.[19] To survive the competition with mass merchandisers such as Wal-Mart, small retailers have been forced to come up with new ways to win and keep customers. Baum's, in Morris, Illinois, was started in 1874 as a dry-goods store selling everything from fabrics to grain. Jim Baum, grandson of the founder, has survived by focusing his customer base; he now sells only large-size women's apparel and invests heavily in advertising and customer service efforts. One of Baum's most-appreciated touches is the comfortable bathrobe in the changing room; shoppers don't have to keep putting their street clothes on to venture onto the shopping floor to select another garment.[20] Sometimes the customer is another business. One of GTO's biggest customers was Sam's Club. Because Chuck Mitchell had created a culture of integrity at GTO, he felt obligated to hold Sam's Club to a standard of integrity as well, risking much, as you will read below.

GTO

When he was a 19-year-old daredevil, Chuck Mitchell almost forgot to open his

---

legal-political dimension
The dimension of the general environment that includes federal, state, and local government regulations and political activities designed to control company behavior

pressure group
An interest group that works within the legal-political framework to influence companies to behave in socially responsible ways

customers
Individuals and organizations in the environment that acquire goods or services from the organization

parachute because the scene he saw spread out below reminded him of a recurring dream he'd had at the age of 12. Chuck Mitchell took another daring leap into treacherous terrain more than 20 years later. After his friend and the founder of GTO, Inc., Lester M. Taub, suffered a fatal heart attack, Mitchell stepped in at the behest of the 16-member board. It didn't take a financial genius to know that GTO, a small company that manufactures automatic gate openers, was in trouble. Average monthly sales were $35,000 short of the break-even point. Most suppliers would send wares only on a COD basis. Morale was terrible on the shop floor. Taub had insisted that being a good manager meant he bicycled through the factory barking epithets at hapless workers, ordering them to work faster or scolding them for filing claims on the company's health insurance policy.

Chuck Mitchell had a powerful vision to transform GTO's culture. His opening speech to the employees amounted to a plea for help. "The bottom line," he said, "is that you've got to look within yourself and within the people around you to come up with answers." To Mitchell's way of thinking, the company's overriding inefficiency was its inability to tap into the inner reserves of its workers. One by one he trotted employees into his office. The more he listened, the more they talked. Linda Williams, who had quit several months earlier, returned to the company and suggested that GTO expand its product line and carry items made by other companies. Back then, out of the 15 products GTO added, only five were actually made there. Concerns over the company's minimal health insurance plan led Mitchell to change the policy, which doubled GTO's expenses. But "making people comfortable frees them to come up with ideas for making this business better," he says. "I need their help."

Mitchell also took other steps—some little and some big—to symbolize that he cared. Before he even negotiated a salary with GTO's board, he insisted that the company agree to put aside 5 percent of net profits in a profit-sharing plan. He went out and bought coffee and sugar, which Taub had neglected because he didn't consume it. He hired a roofer to fix the badly leaking roof. To promote a sense of ownership, he freely gave employees keys to the building and told them they can use GTO tools to repair their cars on weekends. He handed over a blank check when an employee needed to buy a part. Mitchell knows there's risk in such freedom. Yet he also knows that "any company in which there isn't trust is a company with one hand tied behind its back. . . . But to have that kind of trust, you need to make yourself vulnerable."

One thing Mitchell wouldn't be vulnerable to, though, was unethical practices of customers. As the diminutive David took on the proverbial Goliath, so did Mitchell take Sam's Club to court for allegedly sending back nondefective products (making money on the transaction); inappropriate cash discounts, and unauthorized credits—all totaling $515,000. Even though other vendors were said to have similar problems with Sam's Club, they were afraid of retribution—and losing business. In fact, Sam's Club did terminate their business relationship, but GTO managed to get new accounts with Home Depot. Finally, a few hours before the case was set for trial, Sam's Club offered Mitchell a $500,000 settlement. He had beaten the big guy.

GTO as a company and a culture has seen big changes. Sales have increased dramatically since 1989, when revenues of $1 million yielded a net loss of almost $500,000. By 1999, sales had gone up to $4.5 million. Today, the number of employees who submit substantive ideas for improvements has tripled. What matters most to Chuck Mitchell is that by now, GTO workers know that he cares, and they have started a culture to care about each other and the company.[21] ■

COMPETITORS   Other organizations in the same industry or type of business that provide goods or services to the same set of customers are referred to as **competitors.** Each industry is characterized by specific competitive issues. The recording industry differs from the steel industry and the pharmaceutical industry. Competition in the steel industry, especially from international producers, caused some companies to go bankrupt. Companies in the pharmaceutical industry are highly profitable because it is difficult for new firms to enter it. Despite the competitive wars being waged worldwide, competitors in some industries are finding that they can cooperate to achieve common goals. For example, Siemens AG of Germany, Toshiba Corporation of Japan, and IBM (an American corporation) joined together in a project called Triad to develop a revolutionary new memory chip.

SUPPLIERS   The raw materials that the organization uses to produce its output are provided by **suppliers.** A steel mill requires iron ore, machines, and financial resources. A small, private university may utilize hundreds of suppliers for paper, pencils, cafeteria food, computers, trucks, fuel, electricity, and textbooks. Large companies such as General Motors, Westinghouse, and Exxon depend on as many as 5,000 suppliers. However, many companies are now using fewer suppliers and trying to build good relationships with them so that they will receive high-quality parts at low prices. The relationship between manufacturers and suppliers has traditionally been an adversarial one, but many companies are finding that cooperation is the key to saving money, maintaining quality, and speeding products to market. Cooperation with suppliers is becoming the rule rather than the exception.

LABOR MARKET   The **labor market** refers to the people in the environment who can be hired to work for the organization. Every organization needs a supply of trained, qualified personnel. Unions, employee associations, and the availability of certain classes of employees can influence the organization's labor market. Two labor market factors having an impact on

organizations at present are: (1) the necessity for continuous investment in human resources through recruitment, education, and training to meet the competitive demands of the borderless world and (2) the effects of international trading blocs, automation, and shifting plant location upon labor dislocations, creating unused labor pools in some areas and labor shortages in others.[22]

SAS Institute, Inc., is in a business with an extremely tight labor market, where too many jobs go unfilled because of the shortage of high-tech professionals. Yet, it manages to have one of the lowest turnover rates in the field.

Working until midnight might make you seem dedicated, but SAS founder Jim Goodnight figured out long ago the productivity curve drops quickly after 5 P.M. And whereas his generation wanted a killer job and a killer salary, today's generation wants a killer life.

How does SAS help achieve the killer life? With 35-hour workweeks. Not only that, SAS has a 26,000-square-foot fitness center, "free snack" rooms, intramural sports, time for "mind-clearing" walks around the company lake, help with aging parents, plus an annual merit bonus. One result of these policies is a turnover rate of only 4 percent, while the industry average is 20 percent.

SAS Institute

Web master Alex Bost is hotly pursued by numerous high-tech companies who offer lucrative and tempting salaries, but she is fiercely loyal to her boss, James H. Goodnight, president and cofounder of SAS (Statistical Analysis Systems) Institute in Cary, North Carolina. As the mother of a three-year-old, Alex does not want to give up a work environment with on-site child care and lunch with her son every day in the company's inexpensive gourmet cafeteria, which also features live piano music.

Alex credits Goodnight for shaping a work environment that is not only personally rewarding but also professionally stimulating. An enormous 31 percent of revenues are put back into R&D, more than any other software

competitors
Other organizations in the same industry or type of business that provide goods or services to the same set of customers

suppliers
People and organizations who provide the raw materials the organization uses to produce its output

labor market
The people in the environment who can be hired by the organization

developer. Perhaps he values creativity so much because the beginnings of the company came from his own inventiveness. In the 1970s, Goodnight developed a software program to analyze agricultural data. This became the embryo for SAS, which now has over 30 different business decision modules that run on both PCs and mainframes.

Goodnight's vision of a worker-friendly culture is partly a result of his earlier negative experiences working with General Electric, where guards were everywhere and a cup of coffee required a long walk down to the vending machine. Even though his company sells sophisticated software for business decisions, though, he doesn't use one to decide on a new company benefit, but rather looks at the proposal and says, "This makes sense." He trusts his gut and follows the personal code of "If you do right by people, they'll do right by you."[23] ∎

∎ THE ORGANIZATION-ENVIRONMENT RELATIONSHIP

Why do organizations care so much about factors in the external environment? The reason is that the environment creates uncertainty for organization managers, and they must respond by designing the organization to adapt to the environment or to influence the environment.

ENVIRONMENTAL UNCERTAINTY

Organizations must manage environmental uncertainty to be effective. Uncertainty means that managers do not have sufficient information about environmental factors to understand and predict environmental needs and changes.[24] As indicated in Exhibit 2.2, environmental characteristics that influence uncertainty are the number of factors affecting the organization and the extent to which those factors change. A large multinational company like Northern Telecom has thousands of factors in the external environment that create

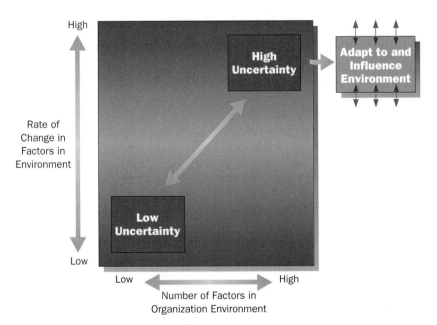

E x h i b i t 2.2

THE EXTERNAL ENVIRONMENT OF NORTHERN TELECOM (NORTEL NETWORKS)

SOURCES: William C. Symonds, J. B. Levine, N. Gross, and P. Coy, "High-Tech Star: Northern Telecom Is Challenging Even AT&T," *Business Week,* July 27, 1992, 54–58; Ian Austen, "Hooked on the Net," *Canadian Business,* June 26–July 10, 1998, 95–103; John Lorinc, "The Death of the Dream?" *Canadian Business,* October 1993, 36–50; Daniel Stoffman, "Mr. Clean," *Canadian Business,* June 1996, 59–65; and Jay Palmer, "A Comeback Coming?" *Barron's,* February 21, 1994, 12–13.

uncertainty for managers. When external factors change rapidly, the organization experiences very high uncertainty; examples are the electronics and aerospace industries. Firms must make efforts to adapt to these changes. When an organization deals with only a few external factors and these factors are relatively stable, such as for soft-drink bottlers or food processors, managers experience low uncertainty and may devote less attention to external issues.

Two basic strategies for coping with high environmental uncertainty are (1) to adapt the organization to changes in the environment and (2) to influence the environment to make it more compatible with organizational needs. Woods Memorial Hospital has adapted to the chaotic conditions of managed care.

WOODS MEMORIAL HOSPITAL

A woman lies barely conscious. Within moments, the hospital laboratory electronically sends blood sample results back to the emergency room; ultrasound images are sent to the radiologist, who sends a report to the surgeon's voice-mail box. Ninety minutes after the woman is rushed the hospital, she is on the operating table. Nothing extraordinary for high-tech health organizations. But this is rural, 72-bed Woods Memorial Hospital in Etowah, Tennessee (between Chatanooga and Knoxville), part of the group of small hospitals struggling to survive in the current chaotic health care environment.

When CEO Phil Campbell arrived a few years ago, the hospital was $200,000 short of making payroll and had a poor prognosis for survival. Inefficiency was ingrained everywhere, whether it was patient intake, blood work, or billing. Campbell's job became one of changing the culture toward efficiency.

Currently, Woods Memorial is thriving. Patient revenues have increased 75 percent. All because of the four-year-old transformation, focusing on cost containment through automation. Campbell's principles were "Improve Quality. Lower Costs. Increase Volume." He slashed prices on lab work, the hospital's largest profit center. But he knew the key was automation, so he persuaded a vendor to install a new UNIX-based system for one-fourth the going rate. Then he divided the whole medical staff into teams, each responsible for using its PC to search for waste in hospital services.

Computers now use a patient's ID number to instantly add charges so bills are always current, while food service can track every aspect of a patient's eating habits in order to serve preferred foods in desired quantities. Medicare logs are done automatically. Amazingly, not only has the hospital not raised rates in five years, but it has not added any clerical positions, even with the increase in billing due to the doubled patient load.

Woods Memorial's experience proves that even tiny organizations stuck in the downward spiral of an industry can reverse the trend—if they are willing to transform themselves.[25] ∎

ADAPTING TO THE ENVIRONMENT

If the organization faces increased uncertainty with respect to competition, customers, suppliers, or government regulation, managers can use several strategies to adapt to these changes, including boundary-spanning roles, increased planning and forecasting, a flexible structure, and mergers or joint ventures.

FLEXIBLE STRUCTURE   An organization's structure should enable it to effectively respond to shifts in the environment. Research has found that a loose, flexible structure works best when organizations experience uncertainty created by shifts in the external environment or by innovation within the organization, while a tight structure is most effective in a certain environment.[26] The term **organic structure** characterizes an organization that is free flowing, has few rules and regulations, encourages teamwork among employees, and decentralizes decision making to employees doing the job. This type of structure works best

organic structure
An organizational structure that is free flowing, has few rules and regulations, encourages employee teamwork, and decentralizes decision making to employees doing the job

"If businesses in America want to face the global challenges of a world economy," heard CEO Terry Murray at a business meeting, "they need to redesign work so it enhances both productivity and family life." Even though the Radcliffe Public Policy Center's Paula Rayman spoke with certainty, the Fleet Financial Group CEO was skeptical.

Fleet had grown from one bank in Rhode Island in the 1980s to 75 banks by the late 1990s. In order to remain "fighting trim," layoffs and extended hours were common. The company was anything but family-friendly. Turnover was running at 30 percent, costing hundreds of thousands of dollars each year.

Happy employees are more productive, noted Rayman, but unhappy employees end up being expensive. Murray's response: "Prove it! Prove that what's good for work and family is good for the bottom line." And he gave her a year and a budget to prove it.

Rayman and MIT professor Lotte Bailyn embarked on a project that put two Fleet units under a microscope—a 20-person group that had recently moved from Framingham, Massachusetts, to Boston and a Providence, Rhode Island, 35-employee group. Though the leaders feared ineffectual griping was probable, initial brainstorming sessions with employees uncovered their main concerns: how they knew if they were productive and how they balanced (or didn't balance) work and family. Small groups of employees further brainstormed solutions to both productivity and family issues.

How to prove this would work? Employees completed before-and-after questionnaires, as well as detailed diaries of work, productivity, and family. In the before responses, two-thirds were not satisfied with the work-family balance and some had severe conflicts at home that even caused stress-related physical illnesses.

The Framingham unit wanted to reduce the long commutes they were now experiencing, and they realized there was too much work piled on the underwriters, which resulted in backups and overtime. The team came up with ways to redistribute the work more equitably, including the hiring of two administrative assistants to write loan commitment letters. "The quality of our lives improved tremendously," said underwriter David Bengston. At the same time, the Providence group was feeling overloaded due to new accounting and computer systems, and many felt they were burning out. So, they asked for flextime and telecommuting to relieve pressure, as well as offering ways to streamline the workload itself. Half of the employees ended up telecommuting a few days a week and two-thirds went on flextime. An added bonus: the flexible environment required more communication, meaning they all learned more about what others were doing.

The final piece in making it work was a breakdown and analysis of the Providence computer network. Until now, the programmers at home were the only ones who could hook into their work, so manager Maria Barry told the employees, "Go home and we'll tell you when to come back."

Employees rated the experiment a success, flextime workers reported feeling more control over their jobs, productivity was up, and interviewed family members noted that loved ones worked fewer hours. Even skeptic CEO Murray now could see that it didn't matter how the work was completed. When employees were happy, results were better. "What impresses me is how enthusiastic our employees are," he says. "Morale is good, and the work is getting done."

SOURCE: Anne Cassidy, "Prove It!" *Working Mother*, January 2000, pp. 36–41.

when the environment changes rapidly. Dow Chemical and Star-Kist Foods set up "SWAT" teams that can swing into action if an unexpected disaster strikes. These teams include members from multiple departments who can provide the expertise needed for solving an immediate problem, such as a plant explosion. Organic organizations create many teams to handle changes in raw materials, new products, government regulations, or marketing. Fleet Financial Group found that flexible groups helped some important productivity problems, as described in the above Focus on Diversity segment.

A **mechanistic structure** is just the opposite, characterized by rigidly defined tasks, many rules and regulations, little teamwork, and centralized decision making. Although this is fine for a stable environment, few organizations today exist in a stable environment. Organizational structures are shifting toward the image of the networked structure of advanced, worldwide information systems—an organic web rather than a structured hierarchy.[27]

mechanistic structure
An organizational structure characterized by rigidly defined tasks, many rules and regulations, little teamwork, and centralized decision making

INFLUENCING THE ENVIRONMENT

The other major strategy for handling environmental uncertainty is to reach out and change those elements causing problems. Widely used techniques for changing the environment include advertising and public relations, political activity, and trade associations.

ADVERTISING AND PUBLIC RELATIONS

Advertising has become a highly successful way to manage demand for a company's products. Companies spend large amounts of money to influence consumer tastes. Hospitals have begun to advertise through billboards, newspapers, and radio commercials to promote special services. Increased competitiveness among CPA firms and law firms has caused them to start advertising for clients, a practice unheard of a decade ago. Advertising is an important way to reduce uncertainty about customers. For example, J.C. Penney and Sears have turned their low-priced, house-brand jeans into some of the hottest labels around with hip advertising campaigns that feature rock bands, Web sites, and edgy imagery targeted to teens.[28]

Public relations is similar to advertising, except that its goal is to influence public opinion about the company itself. Most companies care a great deal about their public image. Each year Fortune rates more than 300 companies to see which are the most and least admired in each of 32 industries. Public relations and a good public image are accomplished through advertising as well as speeches and press reports. Companies in the tobacco industry have launched an aggressive public relations campaign touting smokers' rights and freedom of choice in an effort to survive in this antismoking era.[29]

POLITICAL ACTIVITY   **Political activity** represents organizational attempts to influence government legislation and regulation. GM enlisted political bigwigs in its successful effort to settle a battle with the U.S. Transportation Department over the safety of certain of its pickup trucks. The settlement saved GM the cost of a $1 billion recall, basically allowing the company to buy its way out of the dispute by spending $51 million on safety programs over a five-year period.[30] Many corporations pay lobbyists to express their views to federal and state legislators. Foreign companies are becoming increasingly savvy in U.S. political maneuvering. For example, Japanese companies have placed former key U.S. political insiders on their payrolls as Washington lobbyists and advisers. Under pressure from U.S. companies about government-business collaboration in foreign countries, Washington has warmed to a technology policy that provides government policy support to critical technologies and industry study groups.[31]

TRADE ASSOCIATIONS   Most organizations join with others having similar interests; the result is a **trade association.** In this way, organizations work together to influence the environment, including federal legislation and regulation. The number and variety of trade associations is staggering. Although many students have heard of the National Rifle Association or the National Association of Manufacturers, few are aware that there is a National Academy of Nannies, a National Coil Coaters Association, or a National Association of Nameplate Manufacturers. One effective association is the National Tooling and Machining Association (NTMA). The NTMA

political activity
Organizational attempts, such as lobbying, to influence government legislation and regulation

trade association
An association made up of organizations with similar interests for the purpose of influencing the environment

Bell South's Lynn Holmes, executive director of governmental affairs in North Carolina, attempts to influence the environment through political activity. Holmes worked to get legislation passed that would open North Carolina's local market, enabling Bell South to boost earnings in newly competitive markets.

functions primarily as a center of knowledge. In a recent year, NTMA fielded 16,000 queries from members on everything from technical and marketing matters to taxes and labor problems. Since most tooling and machining companies are small, the association lobbies heavily on issues that affect small business, like taxes, health insurance, and government mandates. Recognizing that its members are competing with low-priced competitors in Europe and Japan, the NTMA provides statistics and information to help U.S. companies set competitive prices, and the association has recently committed itself to expanding ties with industry counterparts in Mexico and Canada.[32]

■ THE INTERNAL ENVIRONMENT: CORPORATE CULTURE

The internal environment within which managers work includes corporate culture, production technology, organization structure, and physical facilities. Of these, corporate culture has surfaced as extremely important to competitive advantage. The internal culture must fit the needs of the external environment and company strategy. When this fit occurs, highly committed employees create a high-performance organization that is tough to beat.[33]

Culture can be defined as the set of key values, beliefs, understandings, and norms shared by members of an organization.[34] The concept of culture helps managers understand the hidden, complex aspects of organizational life. Culture is a pattern of shared values and assumptions about how things are done within the organization. This pattern is learned by members as they cope with external and internal problems and taught to new members as the correct way to perceive, think, and feel. Culture can be analyzed at three levels, as illustrated in Exhibit 2.3, with each level becoming less obvious.[35] At the surface level are visible artifacts, which include such things as manner of dress, patterns of behavior, physical symbols, organizational ceremonies, and office layout. Visible artifacts are all the things one can see, hear, and observe by watching members of the organization. At a deeper level are the expressed values and beliefs, which are not observable but can be discerned from how people explain and justify what they do. These are values that members of the organization hold at a conscious level. They can be interpreted from the stories, language, and symbols organization members use to represent them. Some values become so deeply embedded in a culture that members are no longer consciously aware of them. These basic, underlying assumptions and beliefs are the essence of culture and subconsciously guide behavior and decisions. In some organizations, a basic assumption might be that people are essentially lazy and will shirk their duties whenever possible; thus, employees are closely supervised

culture
The set of key values, assumptions, beliefs, and norms shared by members of an organization

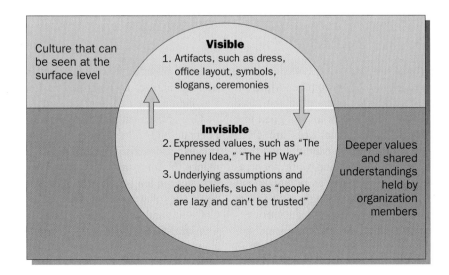

Exhibit 2.3
LEVELS OF CORPORATE CULTURE

Culture that can be seen at the surface level

Visible
1. Artifacts, such as dress, office layout, symbols, slogans, ceremonies

Invisible
2. Expressed values, such as "The Penney Idea," "The HP Way"
3. Underlying assumptions and deep beliefs, such as "people are lazy and can't be trusted"

Deeper values and shared understandings held by organization members

ST. LUKE'S

Integrity is not typically expected in advertising. A 1995 Gallup poll placed advertising near the bottom of ethical professions, with only Congresspeople and used-car salesmen ranking lower. A new advertising agency in London is out to change that. St. Luke's offers a completely new model of what it believes the industry must become: "honest, ethical advertising that represents a company's Total Role in Society (TRS)," which is an evaluation of the organization among the totality of its stakeholders: employees, customers, shareholders, the community, the environment, vendors, competitors, the families of employees, etc.

This is partly manifested in the corporate mission statement: "Profit Is Like Health; You Need It to Live, But It Is Not What You Live For." The founders' ideas of a company's TRS includes a company seeing itself as a force for social good, with the purpose to "benefit society," where profits are the requirement, but not the purpose, and where a company will have to be seen as a "trusted social citizen" before it will be able to sell or advertise productively. These ideas cannot be dismissed as naive when they are expressed by the fastest-growing advertising agency in London, with first-year revenues at $72 million. Though geared toward the future, some of the company's in-

spiration can be traced back thousands of years to Aristotle and the Gospel of St. Luke.

The agency preaches and practices a gospel of total ethics and common ownership. St. Luke's employees own all the company; every employee holds equal shares, from the person who answers the phone to the creative director.

St. Luke's was once the London office of Chiat/Day, the agency known for the Energizer bunny. When communications conglomerate Omnicom bought the struggling agency and announced plans to merge Chiat/Day with a larger agency, Andy Law, managing director, bought the London office and then called in all the employees to let them decide their own future. The employees' response was that they wanted to work for a company that embodied their own personal values. Further, they wanted a concrete mechanism for universal commitment and contribution.

The physical layout of St. Luke's reflects the company's cultural values. Employees have traded desks and personal work spaces for "brand rooms" large client-specific, glass-enclosed conference rooms where teams meet for each account to generate ideas and store work-in-progress. Between meetings and visits to clients, employees take a seat at any one of dozens of computers

that they share communally. Employees eat lunch together, play ping pong, or crawl out the window to enjoy a moment of sunshine on the rooftop. There are no trophies or awards lining the walls and shelves at St. Luke's. The company has never won any advertising awards for the simple reason that they refuse to enter any contests.

After only a year in business, St. Luke's was generating annual billings of around $72 million and was the fastest growing agency in London. In a recent survey asking London's art directors and copywriters where they would most like to work, tiny St. Luke's came in third. Law believes people want to work for a company they can be proud of, and he and his employees have created a distinctive culture at St. Luke's that emphasizes self-motivation, personal growth, and integrity in all actions. "We've created this company to live beyond us," says Law. "We're just renting resources. Remember that we're a collective here, everybody is equal. What's disappeared are ego and greed. . . ."

SOURCE: Andy Law, personal communication, 1998; Stevan Alburty, "The Ad Agency to End All Ad Agencies," *Fast Company*, December–January 1997, pp. 116–124.

and given little freedom, and colleagues are frequently suspicious of one another. More enlightened organizations operate on the basic assumption that people want to do a good job; in these organizations, employees are given more freedom and responsibility, and colleagues trust one another and work cooperatively. Basic assumptions in an organization's culture often begin with strongly held values espoused by a founder or early leader. For example, the founders of St. Luke's, a small advertising agency on the edge of London's Bloomsbury district, created a distinctive cul-

ture that provides the company with a competitive advantage, as described in Leading the Revolution: The Learning Organization.

One of the most important things leaders do is create and influence organizational culture because it has a significant impact on performance. In comparing 18 companies that have experienced long-term success with 18 similar companies that have not done so well, James C. Collins and Jerry I. Porras found the key determining factor in successful companies to be a culture in which employees share such a strong vision that they know in their hearts what is right for the company. Their book, *Built to Last: Successful Habits of Visionary Companies,* describes how companies such as Hewlett-Packard, Walt Disney, and Procter & Gamble have successfully adapted to a changing world without losing sight of the core values that guide the organization. Some companies put values in writing so they can be passed on to new generations of employees. Hewlett-Packard created a list of cultural concepts called "The HP Way." Companies known for their strong, distinctive cultures, such as Southwest Airlines, W.L. Gore, and Hewlett-Packard, regularly show up on *Fortune* magazine's list of the best companies to work for in America.[36]

The fundamental values that characterize cultures at these and other companies can be understood through the visible manifestations of symbols, stories, heroes, slogans, and ceremonies. Any company's culture can be interpreted by observing these factors. The slogan of St. Luke's—"Profit Is Like Health; You Need It to Live, But It Is Not What You Live For"—is described earlier in Leading the Revolution: The Learning Organization.

SYMBOLS

A **symbol** is an object, act, or event that conveys meaning. Symbols associated with corporate culture convey the organization's important values. For example, John Thomas, CEO of a mechanical contractor in Andover, Massachusetts, wanted to imprint the value of allowing mistakes and risk taking. He pulled a $450 mistake out of the dumpster, mounted it on a plaque, and named it the "No-Nuts Award" for the missing parts. The award is presented annually and symbolizes the freedom to make mistakes but not to make the same mistake twice.[37] The following open office layout at companies like St. Luke's and Nickelodeon—the most-watched cable network in the country—symbolizes a commitment to values of equality, having fun, and sharing ideas. Randall Larrimore, president of MasterBrand Industries, Inc., wanted to break down the vertical walls that isolated departments and develop a team culture. Faced with skeptical managers who felt incapable of lead-

Tom Loutzenheiser, technology president of software company Apexx Technology, appreciates the many positive attributes of the company's Boise, Idaho, location, including affordable housing, short commutes, and the opportunity to kayak on the Boise River just minutes away. Employees at Apexx also appreciate the company's corporate culture, which values the individual and believes in giving employees freedom, privacy, and responsibility. Apexx Technology's office layout reflects its cultural values by offering employees more personal space, offices with real windows, and solid walls that rise all the way to the ceiling. "It's not a cube farm," says employee Jennifer Bedford, reflecting her approval.

ing such a change process, Larrimore gave a motivational speech and then symbolized his message by giving each manager a copy of *Oh, the Places You'll Go,* by Dr. Seuss. The managers now proudly display the book as a symbol of their own pioneering efforts and achievements.[38]

STORIES

In organizations, a **story** is a narrative based on true events that is repeated frequently and shared among organizational (and related) employees. Stories are told, for example, to new employees to help keep the organization's primary values alive. Companies such as IBM, Royal Dutch/Shell, Coca-Cola, and U.S. West have sent managers to workshops to learn about how stories can communicate their company's significant values and promote change when and where needed.

One of Nordstrom's primary means of emphasizing the importance of customer service is through corporate storytelling. An example is the story about men's clothing salesman Van Mensah, who received a letter explaining that a customer had mistakenly washed his 12 new shirts in hot water, causing the shirts to shrink.

symbol
An object, act, or event that conveys significant meaning

story
In organizations, a narrative based on true events that is repeated frequently and shared by organizational employees

The customer wanted to know whether Mensah had any suggestions to help him out of his predicament. Mensah immediately called the customer in Sweden and informed him that a dozen new shirts—in the same size, style, and colors—were being mailed out that day, compliments of the company.[39] Likewise, for years, workers at U.S. Paper Mills Corporation told a story about the company's founder and principal stockholder, Walter Cloud. One morning, when Cloud saw a worker trying to unclog the drain of a blending vat using an extension pole, he quickly climbed over the edge of the vat and reached through the three-feet-deep slurry of paper fiber to unclog the drain with his hand. As he wiped the muck from his dress pants, Cloud asked the worker, "Now, what are you going to do the next time you need to unclog a drain?" By telling and retelling this story, workers at the mill now communicate the importance of jumping in to do whatever needs to be done.[40]

HEROES

A **hero** is a figure that exemplifies the deeds, character, and attributes of a strong culture. Heroes are role models for employees to follow. Sometimes heroes are real, such as Lee Iacocca, who by courage of conviction worked for $1 a year when he first came to Chrysler. Other times heroes are symbolic, such as the mythical sales representative at Robinson Jewelers who delivered a wedding ring directly to the church because the ring had been ordered late. The deeds of heroes are, by definition, out of the ordinary, but not unattainable by employees. Heroes show how to do the right thing in the organization. Companies with strong cultures take advantage of achievements that define heroes who uphold key values.

At Minnesota Mining and Manufacturing (3M), top managers keep alive heroes who developed unique projects. One hero (now a vice president) was fired early in his career for persisting with a new product, even after his boss told him, "That's a stupid idea. Stop!" After the worker was fired, he would not leave. He stayed in an unused office, working without a salary on the new product idea. Eventually he was rehired, the idea succeeded, and he was promoted to vice president. The lesson of this hero, a major element in 3M's culture, is to persist at what you believe in.[41]

SLOGANS

A **slogan** is a phrase or sentence that succinctly expresses a key corporate value. Many companies use a slogan or saying to convey special meaning to employees. H. Ross Perot of Electronic Data Systems established the philosophy of hiring the best people he could find and noted how difficult it was to find them. His motto was "Eagles don't flock. You gather them one at a time." At Sequins International, where 80 percent of the employees are Hispanic, words from W. Edwards Deming, "You don't have to please the boss; you have to please the customer," are embroidered in Spanish on the pockets of workers' jackets.[42] Cultural values can also be discerned in written public statements, such as corporate mission statements or other formal statements that express the core values of the organization. Eaton Corporation developed a philosophy statement called "Excellence through People," which includes a commitment to encouraging employee involvement in all decisions, regular face-to-face communication between executives and employees, promotion from within, and always focusing on the positive behavior of workers.

CEREMONIES

A **ceremony** is a planned activity or a special event conducted for the benefit of an audience. Managers hold ceremonies to provide dramatic examples of company values. Ceremonies are special occasions that reinforce valued principles and accomplishments, create a bond among people by allowing them to share an important event, and anoint and celebrate heroes.[43]

The value of a ceremony can be illustrated by the presentation of a major award. Mary Kay Cosmetics Company holds elaborate awards ceremonies that involve presenting gold and diamond pins, furs, and even pink Cadillacs to high-achieving sales consultants. The setting is typically a convention arena in

hero
A figure, real or not, that exemplifies the deeds, character, and attributes of a strong corporate culture

slogan
A phrase or sentence that succinctly expresses a key corporate value

ceremony
A planned activity or a special event conducted for the benefit of an audience to reinforce principles, create bonds, and celebrate heroes

front of a large, cheering audience, and everyone is dressed in glamorous evening clothes. The most successful consultants are introduced like award nominees in the entertainment industry. These ceremonies recognize and celebrate high-performing employees and emphasize the rewards of performance.[44]

In summary, organizational culture represents the values, understandings, and basic assumptions that employees share, and these values are signified by symbols, stories, heroes, slogans, and ceremonies. Managers help define important symbols, stories, and heroes to help shape the culture.

■ ENVIRONMENT AND CULTURE

As we've seen, an important influence on internal corporate culture is the external environment. Cultures can vary widely across organizations; however, organizations within the same industry may often reveal similar cultural characteristics because they are operating in similar environments.[45] The internal culture should embody the ideals required to succeed in the environment. If the external environment necessitates extraordinary customer service, the culture should encourage good service; if it calls for careful, technical decision making, cultural values should reinforce managerial decision making.

ADAPTIVE CULTURES

Research at Harvard on 207 U.S. firms illustrated the critical relationship between corporate culture and the external environment. The study found that a strong corporate culture alone did not ensure business success unless the culture encouraged healthy adaptation to the external environment. As illustrated in Exhibit 2.4, adaptive corporate cultures have different values and behavior from nonadaptive corporate cultures. In adaptive cultures, managers are concerned about customers and those internal people and processes that bring about useful change. In the nonadaptive corporate cultures, managers are concerned about themselves, and their values tend to discourage risk taking and change. Thus a strong culture alone is not enough, because an unhealthy culture may encourage the organization to march resolutely in the wrong direction. Healthy cultures help companies adapt to the environment.[46] Managers at McDonald's, for example,

	Adaptive Corporate Cultures	Unadaptive Corporate Cultures
Visible Behavior	Managers pay close attention to all their constituencies, especially customers, and initiate change when needed to serve their legitimate interests, even if it entails taking some risks.	Managers tend to behave somewhat insularly, politically, and bureaucratically. As a result, they do not change their strategies quickly to adjust to or take advantage of changes in their business environments.
Expressed Values	Managers care deeply about customers, stockholders, and employees. They also strongly value people and processes that can create useful change (e.g., leadership initiatives up and down the management hierarchy).	Managers care mainly about themselves, their immediate work group, or some product (or technology) associated with that work group. They value the orderly and risk-reducing management process much more highly than leadership initiatives.

Exhibit 2.4

ENVIRONMENTALLY ADAPTIVE VERSUS NONADAPTIVE CORPORATE CULTURES

SOURCE: John P. Kotter and James L. Heskett, *Corporate Culture and Performance* (New York, The Free Press, 1992), 51.

are struggling to transform a nonadaptive culture before it causes more damage to this giant of fast food.

McDonald's
www.mcdonalds.com

Ray Kroc, founder of McDonald's, once said, "I don't know what we'll be serving in the year 2000, but we'll be serving more of it than anybody." Since its founding through the early 1980s, McDonald's has changed with America's tastes, providing consumers with what they want before they even know they want it. Today, however, Kroc's bold claim doesn't seem so assured. Although McDonald's still has a 42 percent share of the U.S. fast-food market and continues to expand internationally, the company is slipping fast in its ability to recognize and shape popular trends. Its last successful new product was the Chicken McNugget, launched more than 15 years ago, and operating profits haven't even kept pace with inflation.

Some analysts and investors believe the widespread problems with McDonald's are due to the corporation's insular, arrogant culture. The average top executive at McDonald's started working at the company when Richard Nixon was president, and the company has been reluctant to bring in outside leaders to guide management as the environment changes. The board, as well, is made up of close-knit insiders who have done little to motivate change.

Now, McDonald's is embarking on an effort to reform. Management has been reorganized, and the new head of the domestic division, Jack M. Greenberg, has brought in at least a handful of new managers, including executives from Burger King, Boston Market, and General Electric. He's also dividing up the country into territories, creating smaller companies to recapture some of McDonald's entrepreneurial zeal. "We are not afraid to do things differently," Greenberg says. Managers are beginning to recognize that, even though Mc-Donald's is still the world's most successful restaurant company, it is far from achieving its potential. They are trying to turn McDonald's back to the healthy adaptive culture of the early years, when it was constantly in touch with the tastes of consumers.[47] ■

TYPES OF CULTURES

One way to think about corporate cultures was suggested by Jeffrey Sonnenfeld and included four types of culture—baseball team, club, academy, and fortress. Each culture has a somewhat different potential for supporting a healthy, successful company and has a different impact on the satisfaction and careers of employees.[48]

The *baseball team* culture emerges in an environmental situation with high-risk decision making and fast feedback from the environment. Decision makers quickly learn whether their decision was right or wrong. Talent, innovation, and performance are valued and rewarded. Top performers see themselves as "free agents," and companies scramble for their services. Performers with "low batting averages" are quickly dropped from the lineup. Baseball team cultures are found in fast-paced, high-risk companies involved in areas such as movie production, advertising, and software development where futures are bet on a new product or project. An example of organizations that best operate in the baseball club culture are e-commerce ventures, as described in the following Technology for Tomorrow section.

The *club* culture is characterized by loyalty, commitment, and fitting into the group. This stable, secure environment values age and experience, and it rewards seniority. As in the case of career military personnel, individuals start young and stay in. Club cultures promote from within, and members are expected to progress relatively slowly and prove their competence at each level. Individuals tend to be generalists and may have vast experience in a number of organizational functions. Top executives in commercial banks, for example, frequently began as tellers. While many club qualities contribute to flexibility within the organization, they can also contribute to the per-

TECHNOLOGY FOR TOMORROW
e-COMMERCE

Now you can see gory details of crime scenes without going to a slasher movie. Ex-banker Marshall Davidson wants his APB Online Web-based news service to be for crime what ESPN is for sports. And it looks as if he is succeeding. Within weeks of the site's launch in 1998, APB Online was attracting over one million hits per day. Viewers have choices between a graphic of Jon Benet's house in Boulder, breaking news on kidnapping or Mob trial cases, scans of convicted sex offenders registries, government documents on celebrities, etc.

Davidson got the idea for APB in 1995 when he saw the public's fascination with O. J. Simpson's trial. So, he found some partners, convinced a few venture capitalists, and wrote a business plan. The execution of his plan was more difficult. It required incredible coordination and precision to start the site in only 91 days. They went right to people they wanted to hire, often interviewing in coffee shops as they hunted for a headquarters, and buying everyone cell phones while they waited for telephone lines to be installed.

Healthshop.com was started on more of a shoe-string budget—only $7,500. So CEO Glenn Zweig thought up a cheap way to create buzz on the Web. In an almost bizarre way of life imitating art (in this case the movies, "The Truman Show" and EdTV), Healthshop provided round-the-clock broadcast of 29-year-old "Dani" as she exercised and dieted her way to top condition for her 1999 wedding. All-Herb.com's founder Ken Hakuta found his own way of getting more visibility online. He offered Seinfeld viewers free samples of St. John's Wort so they could cope with the emotional trauma of the sitcom's demise.

Wanting a Web site that felt more human, Amy Barnett and Bonnie Cohen call their online gift service "Violet," rather than "Cyber-something." Aiming at busy professionals who crave time, they allow buyers to enter characteristics of the gift-recipient and the budget, then Violet lists possibilities. Perhaps the perfect pair for such a venture, Barnett has a masters in electrical engineering and Cohen has years of retail experience. Barnett, in fact, managed software development and even built a chip. The new venture combines her two loves—computers and shopping. Now she and her partner have entered the intensely competitive e-commerce world, going up against Crate and Barrel and Amazon. Their current project is garnering expansion financing (Violet is currently self-financed) and hire a management team. Knowing the fast-paced, changing world they exist in, Barnett says, "We are acutely aware that we've got to get from here to there instantaneously."

Specializing in thoughtful, perfectly wrapped gifts accompanied by hand-written notes, Barnett and Cohen are looking for "chic." But they don't want the mass chic of Pottery Barn or the cheap chic of Target. Barnett notes, "We consider ourselves authentic chic."

Sources: Anne Stuart, "Can Crime Pay?" *CIO Web Business*, June 1, 1999, pp. 22–23; Marc Ballon, "Money Isn't Everything," *Inc.*, May 1999, p. 38; Evantheia Schibsted, "Nouveau Riche Media," *Business 2.0*, July 1999, pp. 25–26.

---

ception of a closed company, reluctant to change, as shown in the McDonald's example.

The *academy* culture also hires young recruits interested in a long-term association and a slow, steady, upward climb within the organization. Unlike the club culture, however, employees rarely move from one division to another. Each person enters a specific "track" and gains a high level of expertise in that area. Job and technical mastery are the bases for reward and advancement. Many long-established organizations such as universities, Coca-Cola, Ford, and GM maintain strong academy cultures. Although specialization provides job security, this culture may limit broad individual development and interdepart-mental collaboration, but it works very well in a stable environment.

The *fortress* culture may emerge in an environmental survival situation. Textile firms and savings and loan organizations are examples of former dominant industries that are now retrenching for survival. The fortress culture offers little job security or opportunity for professional growth while companies restructure and downsize to fit the new environment. This culture is perilous for employees but also offers tremendous turnaround opportunities for individual managers with confidence and a love of challenge. Those who succeed, such as Lee Iaccoca (Chrysler) or William Crouse (president of Ortho

Diagnostic Systems, Inc.) earn industry-wide and even national recognition.[49]

SHAPING CORPORATE CULTURE FOR THE TWENTY-FIRST CENTURY

CHANGING AND MERGING CORPORATE CULTURES

A corporation's culture may not always be in alignment with its needs and environment. Cultural values may reflect what seemed to work in the past. The difference between desired cultural norms and values and actual norms and values is called the **culture gap.**[50]

Culture gaps can be immense, especially in mergers and acquisitions.[51] Despite the popularity of mergers and acquisitions as a corporate strategy, many of them fail. Almost one-half of acquired companies are sold within five years, and some experts claim that 90 percent of mergers never live up to expectations.[52] One reason for failure is that although managers are able to integrate the acquired firm's financial systems and production technologies, they typically are unable to integrate the unwritten norms and values that have an even greater impact on a company's success.[53] These problems increase in scope and frequency with global companies and cross-cultural mergers and acquisitions. For example, investors cheered at the announcement of a merger between Upjohn Co. of Kalamazoo, Michigan, and Sweden's Pharmacia. The market value of the new Pharmacia & Upjohn, Inc. soared. Eight months later, however, there were clear signs that the merger was in trouble. Cost-cutting was behind schedule, earnings were low, key executives were jumping ship, and morale was lousy. Most agree it was due to the clash of cultures between the two companies. According to Magnus Lundberg, the ex-head of metabolic diseases at P&U, the merger "was like two different species meeting each other." Managers often forget that the human systems of a company are what make or break any change initiative.[54]

SYMBOLIC LEADERSHIP

One way managers change norms and values toward what is adaptive to the external environment or for smooth internal integration is through symbolic leadership. Managers can use symbols, stories, slogans, and ceremonies to change corporate culture. Managers literally must overcommunicate to ensure that employees understand the new culture values, and they must signal these values in actions as well as words.

A **symbolic leader** defines and uses signals and symbols to influence corporate culture. Symbolic leaders influence culture in the following manner:

1. The symbolic leader articulates a vision for the organizational culture that generates excitement and that employees can believe in. This means the leader defines and communicates central values that employees believe in and will rally around.

2. The symbolic leader heeds the day-to-day activities that reinforce the cultural vision. The symbolic leader makes sure that symbols, ceremonies, and slogans match the new values. Even more important, actions speak louder than words. Symbolic leaders "walk their talk."[55]

The reason symbolic leadership works is that executives are watched by employees.

culture gap

The difference between an organization's desired cultural norms and values and actual norms and values

symbolic leader

A manager who defines and uses signals and symbols to influence corporate culture

Symbolic leaders like Southwest Airlines' chairman, president, and CEO Herb Kelleher shape corporate culture by articulating a clear vision and expressing cultural values through deeds, actions, statements, and ceremonies. Kelleher plays many roles for his employees—inspirational leader, kindly uncle, cheerleader, and clown—to keep spirits high and build a culture where "kindness and the human spirit are nurtured." Through employee videos, Winning Spirit ceremonies, speeches, and everyday personal contact, Kelleher lets Southwest employees know they're the key to the company's success.

Employees learn what is valued most in a company by noting the attitudes and behaviors that managers pay attention to and reward, how they react to organizational crises, and whether the manager's own behavior matches the espoused values.[56] At Levi Strauss, for example, managers' bonus pay, which can be two-thirds of their total compensation, is tied explicitly to how well they follow the corporate aspirations in their daily work. Because leaders at Levi Strauss create linkages between stated values, training, everyday action, and appraisal and reward systems, employees rely on the aspirations as a standard of behavior. Some leaders fail to recognize how carefully they are watched by employees. One senior executive told a story of how employees always knew in advance when someone was about to be laid off in his company. He finally picked up on the pattern. Employees noticed that the executive always dressed in his favorite pink shirt and matching tie when layoffs were to be announced.

Symbolic leaders search for opportunities. They make public statements—including verbal, nonverbal, and written communications—to the organization as a whole. After articulating a vision, symbolic leaders change corporate culture through hundreds of small deeds, actions, statements, and ceremonies. A strong leader who articulated a clear vision accounted for the extraordinary success of Wal-Mart, Disney, Hewlett-Packard, and Levi Strauss. Harold Geneen, former CEO of ITT, captured his corporate value in a few words: "Search for the unshakeable facts." Herb Kelleher of Southwest Airlines has developed a strong, adaptive culture by sticking to the basics: "Do what your customer wants; be happy in your work."[57]

Scott Kohno, managing director of Chaix & Johnson, shocked and revitalized his 30 employees by hauling his desk from a comfortable executive office with 18-foot ceilings to the middle of the work floor. Kohno compared the move to the "difference between being on the basketball floor instead of the bleachers."

The increased contact with staff was soon matched by a supercharged employee energy level.[58]

Another story involving a desk illustrates Mars executives' concern for employees and began when Mr. Mars made a midsummer visit to a chocolate factory:

He went up to the third floor, where the biggest chocolate machines were placed. It was hotter than the hinges of hell. He asked the factory manager, "How come you don't have air conditioning up here?" The factory manager replied that it wasn't in his budget, and he darn well had to make the budget. While Mr. Mars allowed that was a fact, he nonetheless went over to the nearby phone and dialed the maintenance people downstairs and asked them to come up immediately. He said, "While we (he and the factory manager) stand here, would you please go downstairs and get all (the factory manager's) furniture and other things from his office and bring them up here? Sit them down next to the big chocolate machine up here, if you don't mind." Mr. Mars told him that once the factory had been air conditioned, he could move back to his office any time he wanted.[59]

Stories such as these are found in most companies and can be used to enhance the desired culture. The value of stories depends not on whether they are precisely true but whether they are repeated frequently and convey the correct values.

To summarize, symbolic leaders influence culture through the use of artifacts such as public statements, ceremonies, stories, heroes, symbols, and slogans. When cultural change is needed to adapt to the external environment or to bring about smoother internal integration, managers must become symbolic leaders and learn how to use speech, symbols, and stories to influence underlying cultural assumptions. Changing culture is not easy, but through their words—and particularly their actions—symbolic leaders let other organization members know what really counts in the company.

Summary and Management Solution

This chapter discussed several important ideas about internal and external organizational environments. Events in the external environment are considered important influences on organizational behavior and performance. The external environment consists of two layers: the task environment and the general environment. The task environment includes customers, competitors, suppliers, and the labor market. The general environment includes technological, sociocultural, economic, legal-political, and international dimensions. Management techniques for helping the organization adapt to the environment include boundary-spanning roles, forecasting and planning, a flexible structure, and mergers and joint ventures. Techniques managers can use to influence the external environment include advertising and public relations, political activities, and trade associations. Corporate culture, a major element of the internal environment, includes the key values, beliefs, understandings, and norms that organization members share. Organizational activities that illustrate corporate culture include symbols, stories, heroes, slogans, and ceremonies. For the organization to be effective, corporate culture should be aligned with the needs of the external environment.

Companies such as Toys "R" Us, described earlier in the chapter, operate in highly uncertain environments because of today's rapid technological change. Sometimes even decent plans by middle managers get torpedoed when upper management is unstable. Toys "R" Us endured a revolving-door approach with their top executives in 1999 that created lasting chaos for the whole company, including its fledgling Internet business. During this time, a new leader, Robert Moog replaced Anderson at Toys Direct in May 1999. Seeing how desperate the situation was and the intensity of the competition, Moog realized that the best strategy was to offer a price break on the toys. Since eToys and other upstarts were overtaking Toys Direct by offering toys below store prices, Moog realized there would be little incentive for customers to use Toy Direct. He pleaded with the Toys "R" Us executives to offer online discounts. But they soundly rebuffed him. The reason they gave: It would undercut the 700 franchises around the country, and further, could create resentment among store managers. Then, they fired Moog. Not long after that, Toys Direct announced a breakup with its online venture partner, Benchmark Capital. The problem was that Toys Direct was not willing to share any control with Benchmark and make it a real partner (i.e., more than an outsourcing service). Meanwhile, the Christmas season of 1999 proved that Toys Direct's online business remains in disarray, while eToys has become more nimble and powerful.

What are the reasons for Toys Direct problems? In part, chaos within the parent company and poor negotiation and communication skills with partners are certain contributors. Also, Toys "R" Us is getting away from its core competencies, what it knows best. Finally, though they got into e-commerce, there was no whole-hearted commitment to online success and were more concerned about cannibalizing its franchisee's sales. As CEO of Brainplay.com says, "If you're worried about what the Internet is going to do to your stores, you're not going to succeed." Analyst Selma Williams explains the advantage that online-only companies have. "From when we wake up in the morning until we go to bed at night, all our talents are focused on creating a great Web experience for our customers."

Four types of culture are baseball team, club, academy, and fortress, each of which suits a specific environment. Most companies in the software industry, including Intuit, have a baseball team culture. Strong cultures are effective when they enable the organization to adapt to changes in the external environment.

Symbolic leaders can strengthen or change corporate culture by (1) communicating a vision to employees and (2) reinforcing the vision with day-to-day public statements, ceremonies, slogans, symbols, and stories.

Discussion Questions

1. Some scientists predict major changes in the earth's climate, including a temperature rise of 8°F over the next 60 years. Should any companies be paying attention to this long-range environmental trend? Explain.

2. Would the task environment for a bank contain the same elements as that for a government welfare agency? Discuss.

3. What forces influence organizational uncertainty? Would such forces typically originate in the task environment or the general environment?

4. *In Search of Excellence,* by Peters and Waterman, argued that customers were the most important element in the external environment. Are there company situations for which this may not be true?

5. Caterpillar Corporation was thriving until the mid-1980s, when low oil prices, high interest rates, a worldwide recession, a soaring U.S. dollar, and Japanese competition stunned the giant equipment builder. Discuss the type of response Caterpillar's management might take.

6. Define corporate culture and explain its importance for managers.

7. Why are symbols important to a corporate culture? Do stories, heroes, slogans, and ceremonies also have symbolic value? Discuss.

8. Describe the cultural values of a company for which you have worked. Did those values fit the needs of the external environment? Of employees?

9. What type of environmental situation is associated with a baseball team culture? How does this culture differ from the academy culture?

10. Do you think a corporate culture with strong values is better for organizational effectiveness than a culture with weak values? Are there times when a strong culture might reduce effectiveness? Discuss.

Management Exercises

Manager's Workbook

What Is a Strong Corporate Culture?

Think about an organization with which you are familiar, such as your school or a company for which you have worked. Answer the questions below based on whether you agree that they describe the organization.

1. Virtually all managers and most employees can describe the company's values, purpose, and customer importance.

2. There is clarity among organization members about how their jobs contribute to organizational goals.

3. It is very seldom that a manager will act in a way contrary to the company's espoused values.

4. Warmth and support of other employees is a valued norm, even across departments.

5. The company and its managers value what's best for the company over the long term more than short-term results.

6. Leaders make it a point to develop and mentor others.

7. Recruiting is taken very seriously, with multiple interviews in an effort to find traits that fit the culture.

8. Recruits are given negative as well as positive information about the company so they can freely choose whether to join.

9. Employees are expected to acquire real knowledge and mastery—not political alliances—before they can be promoted.

10. Company values emphasize what the company must do well to succeed in a changing environment.

11. Conformity to company mission and values is more important than conformity to procedures and dress.

Disagree Strongly				Agree Strongly
1	2	3	4	5
1	2	3	4	5
1	2	3	4	5
1	2	3	4	5
1	2	3	4	5
1	2	3	4	5
1	2	3	4	5
1	2	3	4	5
1	2	3	4	5
1	2	3	4	5
1	2	3	4	5
1	2	3	4	5
1	2	3	4	5

12. You have heard stories about the company's leaders or "heroes" who helped make the company great.

13. Ceremonies and special events are used to recognize and reward individuals who contribute to the company in significant ways.

Total Score

Compute your score. If your total score is 52 or above, your organization has a strong culture, similar to a Procter & Gamble or Hewlett-Packard. A score from 26 to 51 suggests a culture of medium strength, which is positive for the organization, such as for American Airlines, Coca-Cola, and Citibank. A score of 25 or below indicates a weak culture, which is probably not helping the company adapt to the external environment or meet the needs of organization members. Discuss the pros and cons of a strong culture. Does a strong culture mean everyone has to be alike?

SOURCE: Adapted from Richard Pascale, "The Paradox of 'Corporate Culture': Reconciling Ourselves to Socialization," *California Management Review* 27 (2) (1985); and David A. Kolb, Joyce S. Osland, and Irwin M. Rubin, *Organizational Behavior: An Experiential Approach,* 6th ed. (Englewood Cliffs, N.J.: Prentice-Hall, 1995), pp. 346–347.

Manager's Workshop

Scavenger Hunt: Looking for the University's Culture

1. Divide into groups of four to seven members. These may be ad hoc or ongoing groups.

2. You are asked to find examples of the university's culture. Use 4″ × 6″ notecards. Put one symbol on each card, with the category listed at the top in capital letters. During a future class session, you will be asked to give a five-minute presentation of your findings to the class. You must find all four items from the required list and any four items from the elective list (except if you choose the cartoon option, then you need only two from the elective list).

3. Do NOT steal anything, and do not buy any item. Your group is limited to $7.00 to make copies or take photos.

What is needed for scavenger hunt?

Required list of symbols

1. Mission of university (teaching, research, service)

2. Customer/clients (students, researchers, business, community, country)

3. Locational information (e.g., city, county, state, U.S. or world map indicates local or cosmopolitan orientation)

4. Constituents (students, faculty, administrators, support staff, athletic teams, taxpayers, board of trustees)

Elective list (choose any four)

1. Leadership (representation, roles, administration or faculty or student)

2. The future of the university (short-term or long-term)

3. Inappropriate elements on campus (anything that is a mismatch between item and university culture)

4. Rules and policies (organizational policies on Americans With Disabilities Act, sexual harrassment, etc.)

5. Pranks or jokes (may be funny or hurtful masked as funny)

6. List of unique language to university and the meanings of words

7. Cartoons hung on faculty doors and bulletin boards. If you do this one, find enough of them to make comparisons between faculty levels and departments or schools. Are there different types of cartoons, for example, in the business school versus liberal arts? This one counts as three electives, since it is more time-consuming and requires more planning.

8. The value of a college education (technical skills, employability, increased income, life-long learning, intellectual heritage)

SOURCE: Adapted from Lizabeth A. Barclay and Kenneth M. York, "The Scavenger Hunt: Symbols of Organizational Culture," *Journal of Management Education,* Vol. 20 (1), Feb. 1996, pp. 125–128; Susan Rueschoff, "Scavenger Hunt," in Dorothy Marcic, *Instructor's Manual to Accompany Organizational Behavior: Experiences and Cases,* West Publishing, 1995; and Anand Narasimhan, Vanderbilt University.

Management in Practice: Ethical Dilemma

Watching Out for Larry

It was the end of the fourth quarter, and Holly Vasquez was completing the profitability statement for her division's regional manager. She was disturbed to see that, for the first time during her tenure as a sales manager for Wallog Computers, her group was not in the top 10 percent of the region. She had watched sales slip during the past year but hoped the fourth quarter might save their numbers. The company was under pressure from stockholders to increase sales. Vasquez was afraid that Wallog would be cutting staff and altering the "people culture" that had kept her there for the past 10 years.

As she entered the individual results in the spreadsheet, she saw her main problem: Larry Norris. After 27 years with the company, Norris had more career sales than anyone in the region, but, for the past three years, he had not even met his quota. Unlike some of her newer salespeople, Norris was uninformed on new products, and his old-style selling techniques didn't seem to be working. Vasquez had suggested he consult with the "new guys" on technical information and new sales techniques, but Norris was stubborn.

Vasquez knew she had the performance information to move him out of his position, but there was nowhere for him to go at Wallog. At 56, he was too young for retirement but too old to find a job elsewhere at his current salary. Not only was Larry Norris a friend, but also he was well liked in her department, and Vasquez wondered what effect his replacement would have on morale. She didn't want to fire him, but she couldn't risk her team's standing or her own reputation by protecting him anymore.

What do you do?

1. Fire Larry Norris and give him two-weeks' notice, a generous severance package, and all the help you can provide him in his job hunt.

2. Give him an ultimatum to meet his sales quota or else, and let him find the way. It is his responsibility to stay current and meet his quota.

3. Assign him to study the new products and the sales techniques of the top salespeople—then hope he improves and the others don't slip.

Surf the Net

1. *Sociocultural dimension of general environment.* As stated in this chapter, "Important sociocultural characteristics are geographical distribution and population density, age, and education levels. Today's demographic profiles are the foundation of tomorrow's workforce and consumers." Examine the demographic information available at

   http://www.census.gov/

   For example, among the wealth of information available at this site is a collection of statistics on social and economic conditions in the United States called the Statistical Abstract of the United States

   www.census.gov/statab/www/brief.html

   Find six statistics assigned by your instructor or chosen by you and be prepared to share your findings in the oral or written format assigned by your instructor.

2. *Competitors.* A sector of the task environment is competitors. Select an industry you're interested in researching and write a one- to two-page paper about the industry describing who the major players are and iden-

   tifying competitive information that would be useful for businesses operating in that industry. Try the following Web sites to gather your information.

   www.fuld.com/i3/index.html

   www.companiesonline.com/

   www.companysleuth.com/

   www.corporateinformation.com/

   businessdirectory.dowjones.com/

3. *Culture communicated through stories.* David M. Armstrong, CEO of Armstrong International, Inc., has authored three books for the purpose of communicating Armstrong's culture—its key values, beliefs, understandings, and norms shared by members of his organization—by storytelling. His books include *Managing by Storying Around; How to Turn Your Company's Parables into Profit;* and *Once Told, They're Gold.* Go to the Web site listed below and read the stories or watch the video clips that illustrate sample stories from each of his three books. If you choose a video, you will need the Quicktime movie player installed on your computer; the

player is available to download from the Armstrong Web site.

www.armintl.com/stories/david-bio.html

Visit www.mgeneral.com and go to "Fiscal Fairy Tales." Choose one fairy tale and write a short paper describing the cultural characteristics in that fairy tale, using concepts from the textook as well.

Case for Critical Analysis

Society of Equals

Ted Shelby doesn't make very many mistakes, but . . .

"Hey Stanley," says Ted Shelby, leaning in through the door, "you got a minute? I've just restructured my office. Come on and take a look. I've been implementing some great new concepts!"

Stanley is always interested in Ted Shelby's new ideas, for if there is anyone Stanley wants to do as well as, it is Edward W. Shelby IV. Stanley follows Ted back to his office and stops, nonplussed.

Restructured is right! Gone are Ted's size B (Junior Executive) walnut veneer desk and furniture, and his telephone table. In fact, the room is practically empty save for a large, round, stark white cafeteria table and the half-dozen padded vinyl swivel chairs that surround it.

"Isn't it a beauty! As far as I know, I'm the first executive in the plant to innovate this. The shape is the crucial factor here—no front or rear, no status problems. We can all sit there and communicate more effectively."

We? Communicate? Effectively? Well, it seems that Ted has been attending a series of Executive Development Seminars given by Dr. Faust. The theme of the seminars was (you guessed it) "participative management." Edward W. Shelby IV has always liked to think of himself as a truly democratic person.

"You see, Stanley," says Ted, managing his best sincere/intense attitude, "the main thing wrong with current mainstream management practice is that the principal communication channel is down-the-line oriented. We on the top send our messages down to you people, but we neglect the feedback potential. But just because we have more status and responsibility doesn't mean that we are necessarily" (Stanley duly noted the word, "necessarily") "better than the people below us. So, as I see the situation, what is needed is a two-way communication network: down-the-line and up-the-line."

"That's what the cafeteria table is for?" Stanley says.

"Yes!" says Ted. "We management people don't have all the answers, and I don't know why I never realized it before that seminar. Why . . . let's take an extreme example . . . the folks who run those machines out there. I'll bet that any one of them knows a thing or two that I've never thought of. So

I've transformed my office into a full-feedback communication net."

"That certainly is an innovation around here," says Stanley.

A few days later Stanley passed by Ted Shelby's office and was surprised that Ted's desk, furniture, and telephone table were back where they used to be.

Stanley, curious about the unrestructuring, went to Bonnie for enlightenment. "What happened," he asked, "to Shelby's round table?"

"That table we were supposed to sit around and input things?" she said. "All I know is, about two days after he had it put in, Mr. Drake came walking through here. He looked in that office, and then he sort of stopped and went back— and he looked in there for a long time. Then he came over to me, and you know how his face sort of gets red when he's really mad? Well, this time he was so mad that his face was absolutely white. And when he talked to me, I don't think he actually opened his mouth; and I could barely hear him, he was talking so low. And he said, 'Have that removed. Now. Have Mr. Shelby's furniture put back in his office. Have Mr. Shelby see me.'"

My, my. You would think Ted would have known better, wouldn't you? But then, by now you should have a pretty firm idea of just why it is those offices are set up as they are.

Questions

1. How would you characterize the culture in this company? What are the dominant values?

2. Why did Ted Shelby's change experiment fail? To what extent did Ted use the appropriate change tools to increase employee communication and participation?

3. What would you recommend Ted do to change his relationship with subordinates? Is it possible for a manager to change cultural values if the rest of the organization, especially top management, does not agree?

SOURCE: R. Richard Ritti and G. Ray Funkhouser, *The Ropes to Skip & The Ropes to Know,* 3d. ed. (New York: Wiley, 1987), pp. 176–177. Reprinted by permission of John Wiley & Sons, Inc.

Endnotes

1 George Anders, "Amazon, eToys Make Big, Opposing Bets: Which One Is Right?" *Wall Street Journal,* Dec. 2, 1999, pp. A1, A14; "Us vs. Them," *Advertising Age,* Aug. 30, 1999, p.18; Sari Kalin, "Whoever Sells the Most Toys Wins," *CIO Web Business,* Dec. 1, 1998, pp. 41–46.

2 Frances Cairncross, *The Death of Distance* (Boston, Mass.: Harvard Business School Press, 1997); Nikhil Deogun and Jonathan Karp, "Rivals Revive Cola Scuffle," *The Asian Wall Street Journal,* April 27, 1998, p. 12.

3 Gary Hamel, "Turning Your Business Upside Down," *Fortune,* June 23, 1997, pp. 87–88.

4 Tim Carvell, "The Crazy Record Business: These Prices Really Are Insane," *Fortune,* August 4, 1997, pp. 109–115.

5 Peter Coy and Gary McWilliams, "Electricity: The Power Shift Ahead," *Business Week,* December 2, 1996, pp. 78–82.

6 Ram Charan, "The Rules Have Changed," *Fortune,* March 16, 1998, pp. 159–162; and Lisa Benavides, "Handful of Tennessee Companies Feel a Pinch," *The Tennessean,* September 5, 1998, pp. 1E, 2E.

7 Richard I. Kirkland, Jr., "Entering a New Age of Boundless Competition," *Fortune,* March 14, 1988, pp. 40–48; and Kenichi Ohmae, "Managing in a Borderless World," *Harvard Business Review* (May–June 1989), pp. 152–161.

8 Nancy J. Perry, "The Arms Makers' Next Battle," *Fortune,* August 27, 1990, pp. 84–88.

9 Eric Schine, Amy Borrus, John Carey, and Geoffery Smith, "The Defense Whizzies Making It in Civvies," *Business Week,* September 7, 1992, pp. 88–90.

10 Larry Armstrong with Kathleen Kerwin, "Downloading Their Dream Cars," *Business Week,* March 9, 1998, pp. 93–94; and Susan Jackson, "Point, Click and Spend," *Business Week,* September 15, 1997, pp. 74–76.

11 Geoffrey Colvin, "What Media Revolution," *Fortune,* Oct. 25, 1999, p. 370; Geoffrey Colvin, "How to Be a Great eCEO," *Fortune,* May 24, 1999, 104–110; "Business Brief," *Wall Street Journal,* October 22, 1999, p. C17; Richard Rapaport, "CNET's Paper Chase," *Forbes ASAP,* June 3 1996, 62–66.

12 William B. Johnston, "Global Work Force 2000: The New World Labor Market," *Harvard Business Review* (March–April 1991), pp. 115–127.

13 Carol D'Amico, *Workforce 2020—Work and Workers in the 21st Century,* Hudson Institute, 1997.

14 Robb M. Stewart, "Big U.K. Bus Firm Pushes into U.S., Buying Blue Bird," *Wall Street Journal,* Sept. 2 1999, p. A11; Geoffrey Abdian, "A Bar-Coded Bird," *Automatic ID News,* Nov. 1997, pp. 36–39.

15 Nicholas Imparato and Oren Harari, *Jumping the Curve: Innovation and Strategic Choice in an Age of Transition* (San Francisco: Jossey-Bass, 1994), p. 121.

16 Joseph Pereira, "The Toy Industry, Too, Is Merging Like Crazy to Win Selling Power," *The Wall Street Journal,* October 28, 1994, pp. A1, A13.

17 Paul Magnusson and John Carey, with Elisabeth Malkin, "Eating Scared," *Business Week,* September 8, 1997, pp. 30–32.

18 Linda Himelstein and Laura Zinn, with Maria Mallory, John Carey, Richard S. Dunham, and Joan O'C. Hamilton, "Tobacco: Does It Have a Future?" *Business Week,* July 4, 1994, pp. 24–29.

19 Walecia Konrad and Gail DeGeorge, "U.S. Companies Go for the Gray," *Business Week,* April 3, 1989, pp. 64–67.

20 Jenny C. McCune, "In the Shadow of Wal-Mart," *Management Review,* December 1994, pp. 10–16.

21 Joshua Hyatt, "Payback," *Inc.,* April 1999, pp. 78–86; Joshua Hyatt, "Real-World Reengineering," *Inc.,* April 1995, pp. 40–53.

22 Michael R. Czinkota and Ilkka A. Ronkainen, "Global Marketing 2000: A Marketing Survival Guide," *Marketing Management* (Winter 1992), pp. 37–42.

23 Joanne Cole, "Sas Institute Inc. Uses Sanity as Strategy," *HR Focus,* May 1999, p. 6.

24 Robert B. Duncan, "Characteristics of Organizational Environment and Perceived Environmental Uncertainty," *Administrative Science Quarterly* 17 (1972), pp. 313–327.

25 Kelly Greene, "Government Aids Raid Hospital," *Wall Street Journal,* March 31, 1999, p. S1; Joshua Macht, "Critical Care," *Inc. Technology,* 1996 (2), pp. 61–65.

26 Tom Burns and G. M. Stalker, *The Management of Innovation* (London: Tavistock, 1961); J.C. Spender and Eric Kessler, "Managing the Uncertainties of Innovation: Extending Thompson (1967)," *Human Relations* 48 (1) (1995), pp. 35–56.

27 John Huey, "Waking up to the New Economy," *Fortune,* June 27, 1994, pp. 36–46.

28 Ellen Neuborne, "Look Who's Picking Levi's Pocket," *Business Week,* September 8, 1997, pp. 68–69.

29 John Carey, "Big Tobacco's Hidden War," *Business Week,* November 10, 1997, pp. 139–140.

30 Daniel Pearl and Gabriella Stern, "How GM Managed to Wring Pickup Pact and Keep on Truckin'," *The Wall Street Journal,* December 5, 1994, pp. A1, A8.

31 Edmund Faltermayer, "The Thaw in Washington," *Fortune* (The New American Century), 1991, pp. 46–51.

32 David Whitford, "Built by Association," *Inc.,* July 1994, pp. 71–75.

33 Andrew D. Brown and Ken Starkey, "The Effect of Organizational Culture on Communication and Information," *Journal of Management Studies* 31 (6) (November 1994), pp. 807–828.

34 Ralph H. Kilmann, Mary J. Saxton, and Roy Serpa, "Issues in Understanding and Changing Culture," *California Management Review* 28 (Winter 1986), pp. 87–94.

35 Based on Edgar H. Schein, *Organizational Culture and Leadership,* 2d ed. (San Francisco: Jossey-Bass, 1992), pp. 3–27.

36 Robert Levering and Milton Moskowitz, "The 100 Best Companies to Work For in America," *Fortune,* January 12, 1998, pp. 84–95.

37 "Make No Mistake," *Inc.,* June 1989, p. 115.

38 Patrick Flanagan, "The ABCs of Changing Corporate Culture," *Management Review,* July 1995, pp. 57–61.

39 Elizabeth Weil, "Every Leader Tells a Story," *Fast Company,* June–July 1998, pp. 38–39; and Robert Specter, "The Nordstom Way," *Corporate University Review,* May–June 1997, pp. 24–25, 60.

40 Gregory M. Bounds, Gregory H. Dobbins, and Oscar S. Fowler, *Management: A Total Quality Perspective* (Cincinnati: South-Western College Publishing, 1995), pp. 353–354.

41 Terrence E. Deal and Allan A. Kennedy, *Corporate Cultures: The Rites and Rituals of Corporate Life* (Reading, Mass.: AddisonWesley, 1982).

42 Barbara Ettorre, "Retooling People and Processes," *Management Review,* June 1995, pp. 19–23.

43 Harrison M. Trice and Janice M. Beyer, "Studying Organizational Cultures through Rites and Ceremonials," *Academy of Management Review* 9 (1984), pp. 653–669.

44 Alan Farnham, "Mary Kay's Lessons in Leadership," *Fortune,* September 20, 1993, pp. 68–77.

45 Jennifer A. Chatman and Karen A. Jehn, "Assessing the Relationship Between Industry Characteristics and Organizational Culture: How Different Can You Be?" *Academy of Management Journal* 37 (3) (1994), pp. 522–553.

46 John P. Kotter and James L. Heskett, *Corporate Culture and Performance* (New York: The Free Press, 1992).

47 David Leonhardt, "McDonald's: Can It Regain Its Golden Touch?" *Business Week,* March 9, 1998, pp. 70–77.

48 Jeffrey Sonnenfeld, *The Hero's Farewell: What Happens When CEOs Retire* (New York: Oxford University Press, 1988).

49 William A. Schiermann, "Organizational Change: Lessons from a Turnaround," *Management Review,* April 1992, pp. 34–37.

50 Ralph H. Kilmann, Mary J. Saxton, Roy Serpa, and Associates, *Gaining Control of the Corporate Culture* (San Francisco: Jossey-Bass, 1985).

51 Ralph Kilmann, "Corporate Culture," *Psychology Today,* April 1985, pp. 62–68.

52 Morty Lefkoe, "Why So Many Mergers Fail," *Fortune,* June 20, 1987, pp. 113–114.

53 Ibid.; and Afsaneh Nahavandi and Ali R. Malekzadeh, "Acculturation in Mergers and Acquisitions," *Academy of Management Review* 13 (1988), pp. 79–90.

54 Julia Flynn and Keith Naughton with Ariane Sains, "A Drug Giant's Allergic Reaction," *Business Week,* February 3, 1997, pp. 122–125.

55 Thomas J. Peters and Robert H. Waterman, Jr., *In Search of Excellence* (New York: Warner, 1988).

56 Deanne N. Den Hartog, Jaap J. Van Muijen, and Paul L. Koopman, "Linking Transformational Leadership and Organizational Culture," *The Journal of Leadership Studies* 3 (4) (1996), pp. 68–83; and Schein, "Organizational Culture."

57 "Southwest Airlines' Herb Kelleher: Unorthodoxy at Work," an interview with William G. Lee, *Management Review,* January 1995, pp. 9–12.

58 Ellyn E. Spragins, "Motivation: Out of the Frying Pan," *Inc.,* December 1991, p. 157.

59 Tom Peters and Nancy Austin, *A Passion for Excellence: The Leadership Difference* (New York: Random House, 1985), p. 278.

Managing in a Global Environment

LEARNING OBJECTIVES

After studying this chapter, you should be able to:

- Describe the emerging borderless world

- Define international management and explain how it differs from the management of domestic business operations

- Indicate how dissimilarities in the economic, sociocultural, and legal-political environments throughout the world can affect business operations

- Describe market entry strategies that businesses use to develop foreign markets

- Explain the challenges of managing in a global environment

MANAGEMENT PROBLEM

■ ■ ■ ■ ■ ■ ■ ■ ■ ■ ■

AS ONE OF HONG KONG'S most

Chapter

3

innovative entrepreneurs, Jimmy Lai has

applied his keen commercial instincts to creating Hong's

second-most popular newspaper, a leading clothing retailer, and a stable of

successful magazines. So, it seemed only natural that if anyone was going to triumph

on the Internet, it would be Jimmy Lai. In June 1999, Lai launched adM@rt, a groceries-to-

electronics firm, based on the highly-profitable San Francisco Webvan, one of the most closely

followed Internet companies. His first strategy was to blanket the city with delivery vans, while using

his *AppleDaily* newspaper to constantly promote with coupon discounts. This triggered a brutal

supermarket price war between the company and its two main competitors, who also happen to be the

• *If you were an advising Lai, what would your recommendations be? What should he have done differently?*

biggest advertisers for *Apple Daily*. adM@rt's advantages include being virtual in the world's

most-expensive retail-space city of six million inhabitants, using vans that are based in cheap

warehouse space, and being particularly skilled at using the shadowy import market to offer

cut-rate Coca-Cola and beer. Even with all of Jimmy Lai's experience, ingenuity, and networks,

he couldn't prevent the ordeals adM@rt would suffer. Needing 30,000 daily orders

to break even, adM@rt is taking in less than 4,000, losing $130,000 a day. Even

with its trendy @ sign, its Web site is a disaster. Not only did it break

down in the first few days, but it continues to regularly

crash. Most orders come by phone or fax,

■ ■ ■ ■ ■ ■ ■ ■ ■ ■ ■ ■ ■

both of which need more operators. Without prior grocery experience, inventory is meager and not consumer-friendly. Eveyone thought Jimmy Lai, of all people, would be able to re-program Hong Kong culture. Instead, his new company is hemorrhaging.[1]

Not only do foreign-local companies have problems imitating a U.S. business model overseas, but American companies have stumbled as well. Wal-Mart, a well-established company, faces enormous challenges in developing a successful international business and has lost millions of dollars making such mistakes as stocking footballs instead of soccer balls.[2] Other large, successful U.S. companies, including Federal Express and Nike, have found that "the rest of the world is not the United States of America," as one FedEx competitor put it. However, all of these companies recognize that international expansion is necessary, despite the risks. Companies such as McDonald's, IBM, Coca-Cola, Kellogg, General Motors, and Caterpillar Tractor all rely on international business for a substantial portion of sales and profits. These companies face special problems in trying to tailor their products and business management to the unique needs of foreign countries—but if they succeed, the whole world becomes their marketplace.

How important is international business to the study of management? If you are not think-ing international, you are not thinking business management. A dramatic example of how easy it is for business to cross national borders occurred during the Gulf War. When Iraq first attacked Kuwait, a shrewd Kuwaiti banker began faxing key records to a subsidiary in Bahrain. Even with transmissions being regularly interrupted due to the shooting, by the end of the day all of the bank's key records had been transferred. The next morning, the bank opened as a Bahrain institution, beyond the reach of the Iraqis and not subject to the U.S. freeze on Kuwaiti assets. Essentially, a bank was moved from one country to another via a fax machine.[3]

Rapid advances in technology and communications have made the international dimension an important part of the external environment (discussed in Chapter 2). Companies can locate different parts of the organization wherever it makes the most business sense—top leadership in one place, technical brainpower and production in other locales. For example, Samsung, the Korean electronics giant, moved its semiconductor manufacturing facilities to the Silicon Valley to be closer to the best scientific brains in the industry. Canada's Northern Telecom selected a location in southwest England as its world manufacturing center for a new fixed-access radio product. Siemens of Germany has moved its

Fuji Photo Film Co., Kodak's major competitor in the U.S. market, is operating in a global environment with international management. Headquartered in Japan, Fuji has purchased Wal-Mart's six wholesale photo labs (15 percent of the U.S. photo-processing market), and it opened a highly automated $300 million photographic paper plant in Greenwood, South Carolina, last year. Approximately 31 percent of Fuji's production is outside of Japan, up from 3.5 percent in 1987. Here, the Fuji blimp is part of a marketing campaign in France.

electronic ultrasound division to the United States, while the U.S. company DuPont shifted its electronic operations headquarters to Japan.[4]

If you think you are isolated from global influence, think again. Even if you do not budge from your hometown, your company may be purchased tomorrow by the English, Japanese, or Germans. People working for Firestone, Dr. Pepper, Pillsbury, Carnation, Shell Oil, and CBS Records already work for foreign bosses. Furthermore, most American machine tool companies have been foreign-owned for years.

All of this means that the environment for companies has become extremely complex and extremely competitive. Less-developed countries are challenging mature countries in a number of industries. India has become a major player in software development, and electronics manufacturing is rapidly leaving Japan for other countries in Asia.

This chapter introduces basic concepts about the global environment and international management. First, we consider the difficulty that managers have operating in an increasingly borderless world. We will address the economic, legal-political, and sociocultural challenges that face companies within the global business environment. Then we will discuss multinational corporations and touch upon the various types of strategies and techniques needed for entering and succeeding in foreign markets.

■ A BORDERLESS WORLD

Why do companies such as Wal-Mart, Federal Express, and Nike want to pursue a global strategy, despite failures and losses? They recognize that business is becoming a unified global field as trade barriers fall, communication becomes faster and cheaper, and consumer tastes in everything from clothing to cellular phones converge. Thomas Middelhoff of Germany's Bertelsmann AG, which purchased U.S. publisher Random House, put it this way: "There are no German and American companies. There are only successful and unsuccessful companies."[5]

Companies that think globally have a competitive edge. Consider Hong Kong's Johnson Electric Holdings Ltd., a $195 million producer of micromotors that power hair dryers, blenders, and automobile power windows and door locks. With factories in South China and a research and development lab in Hong Kong, Johnson is thousands of miles away from a leading automaker. Yet the company has cornered the market on electric gizmos for Detroit's Big Three by using new information technology. Via videoconferencing, Johnson design teams meet "face-to-face" for two hours each morning with their customers in the United States and Europe. The company's processes and procedures are so streamlined that Johnson can take a concept and deliver a prototype to the United States in six weeks.[6]

Additionally, for many companies, domestic markets are saturated. The only potential for significant growth lies overseas. Kimberly-Clark and Procter & Gamble, which spent years slugging it out in the now-flat U.S. diaper market, are targeting new markets in China, India, Israel, Russia, and Brazil. The combined demand for steel in China, India, and Brazil is expected to grow 10 percent annually in the coming years—three times the U.S. rate. Nucor is opening a mini-mill in Thailand and partnering with a Brazilian company for a $700 million steel mill in northeastern Brazil. Other steel companies, such as LTV Corp. and North Star Steel, are moving into Asia, Europe, and Australia.[7]

The reality of today's borderless companies also means consumers can no longer tell from which country they're buying. Your Mercury Tracer may have come from Mexico, while a neighbor's Nissan may have been built in Tennessee. A Gap polo shirt may be made from cloth cut in the United States but sewn in Honduras. Eat an all-American Whopper and you've just purchased from a British company.[8]

Corporations can participate in the international arena on a variety of levels, and the process of globalization typically passes through four distinct stages.

1. In the domestic stage, market potential is limited to the home country, with all production and marketing facilities located at

home. Managers may be aware of the global environment and may want to consider foreign involvement.

2. In the international stage, exports increase, and the company usually adopts a multidomestic approach, probably using an international division to deal with the marketing of products in several countries individually.

3. In the multinational stage, the company has marketing and production facilities located in many countries, with more than one-third of its sales outside the home country. Companies typically have a single home country, although they may opt for a bi-national approach, whereby two parent companies in separate countries maintain ownership and control. Examples are Unilever and the Royal Dutch/Shell Group, both of which are based in the United Kingdom and the Netherlands.

4. Finally, the global (or stateless) stage of corporate international development transcends any single home country. These corporations operate in true global fashion, making sales and acquiring resources in whatever country offers the best opportunities and lowest cost. At this stage, ownership, control, and top management tend to be dispersed among several nationalities.[9]

As the number of "stateless" corporations increases, the awareness of national borders decreases, as reflected by the frequency of foreign participation at the management level. Up-and-coming managers are expected to know a second or third language and to have international experience. The need for global managers with cross-cultural sensitivity is intensifying, as discussed in Focus on Diversity. Corporations around the world want the best and brightest candidates for global management, and young managers who want their careers to move forward recognize the importance of global experience. According to Harvard Business School professor Christopher Bartlett, author of *Managing across Borders,* people should try to get global exposure when they're young in order to start building skills and networks that will grow throughout their careers.[10] Consider the makeup of global companies in today's environment. Nestlé (Switzerland) personifies the stateless corporation with 98 percent of sales and 96 percent of employees outside the home country. Nestlé's CEO is German-born Helmut Maucher, and half of the company's general managers are non-Swiss. Maucher puts strong faith in regional managers who are native to the region and know the local culture. The combination of strong brands and autonomous regional

Today's companies operate in a borderless world. Procter & Gamble sales in Southeast Asia are only 3 percent of its worldwide sales, but those numbers are increasing. Shoppers are purchasing P&G's diaper products, Pampers, in Malaysia.

CROSS-CULTURAL COMMUNICATION

American managers are often at a disadvantage when doing business overseas. Part of this involves a lack of foreign language skills, but inexperience in dealing with other cultures and less-than-ideal living conditions are culprits as well. Consequently, many mistakes get made that could otherwise be easily avoided.

The manager's attitude is arguably the most important factor in success. Seeing differences as new and interesting is more productive than being critical. Those who go abroad with a sense of "wonder" about the new culture are better off than those with a judgmental view. These lead to no-win "Us versus Them" outcomes, which never sit well with the locals.

Although every culture has its own way of communicating, here are some basic principles to follow when engaging in international business relations:

1. Always show respect and listen carefully. Don't be in a hurry to finish the "business." Many cultures value the social component of these interactions.

2. Try to gain an appreciation for the differences between Hofsede's "masculine and feminine" cultures. American masculine business behaviors include high achievement and acquisition of material goods and efficiency, while other, more feminine cultures value relationships, leisure time with family, and developing a sense of community. Don't mistake this more feminine approach for a lack of motivation. Similarly, cultures that value "being and inner spiritual development" rather than compulsively "doing," are not necessarily inferior.

3. Try hard not to feel that your (American) way is the best way.

4. Emphasize points of agreement.

5. When there are disagreements, discern the perceived definitions of words. Often the problem may be a misunderstanding caused by a subtle difference in meaning.

6. Save face and "give" face as well, which can be a way of showing honor to others.

7. Don't go it alone. Take someone who knows the culture or language better than you. If you are discussing in English and the others "know" the language, you might be surprised by how much is missed, taken out of context, or misunderstood completely. Investing in an excellent translator is a wise move.

8. Don't assume the other country views leadership the same as you do. Many cultures interpret "empowerment" as something akin to anarchy or the result of an ineffectual manager.

9. Don't lose your temper. Patience and calmness will have the greatest effect in most cases.

10. Don't embarrass anyone (or even confront them with criticism) in front of others. Even if you meant a deprecating remark as a "joke," it likely won't be taken that way.

11. Remember, you are talking to a person not a country, so eliminate stereotypes.

12. Avoid clique-building and try to interact with the locals as much as possible. Often, Americans tend to keep together in social settings, which is not a welcoming sign to "outsiders."

13. Always show respect. It is one of the few actions that knows no boundaries.

14. Leave the common American task-oriented, fast-paced style at home.

15. Be sensitive to the difference between the North American low-context culture—where employees are encouraged to be self-reliant—and high-context cultures (much of Asia, Africa, South America), where workers expect warmly supportive relationships with their American supervisors and coworkers.

16. When you go to less-traveled locations (e.g., Eastern Europe), learn to tolerate a high degree of unpredictability with people and amenities. Calmly go without or have alternatives for what you may consider basic requirements (i.e., comfortable toilet paper, hotel towels, running water, or working thermostats). Avoid complaining to business clients. Just remember you are a guest and should act with the grace that goes along with that role.

SOURCES: Cornelius Grove, "Easing Overseas Workers into the U.S. Business Environment," *HR Focus,* Oct. 1999, Vol. 76 (10), p. 9; Hari Bedi, "A Little Respect Can Bridge the Divide," *Asian Business,* Jan. 1997, p. 50; Lorna Wright, "Building Cultural Competence," *Canadian Business Review,* Spring 1996, pp. 29–33; Lisa Miller, "Why Business Travel Is Such Hard Work," *Wall Street Journal,* Oct. 30, 1996, p. B1; Dorothy Marcic, "Challenges and Opportunities of Teaching Management in a Post-Socialist Society," *Executive Development,* Vol. 8 (5), 1995, pp. 26–31; Geert Hofstede, "Motivation, Leadership and Organization: Do American Theories Apply Abroad?" *Organizational Dynamics,* Summer 1980, pp. 42–63; Linda Beamer, "Learning Intercultural Communication Competence," *Journal of Business Communication,* Vol. 29 (3), 1992, pp. 285–302; Rosemary Neale and Richard Mindel, "Rigging Up Mulicultural Teamworking," *Personnel Management,* January 1992, pp. 36–39.

TECHNOLOGY FOR TOMORROW

CROSS-CULTURAL WEB TRAPS

Approximately 1.5 billion people speak either Mandarin, Arabic, or Hindi as their first or only language. So how does the World Wide Web, then, create sites that users with sketchy English can navigate? The World Wide Web is a valuable resource for companies hoping to expand in international markets. However, there are inherent problems with producing a Web site that can easily reach potential customers in more than 100 countries. Most Web site content is provided in English, the most widely spoken language in the world; however, to many people English is a second language, and they miss many of its nuances. As a result, mis-communications constantly occur. Web site developers should avoid terms that don't translate well and can be easily misunderstood, such as slang, euphemisms, cliches, proverbs, and military terminology. Even when graphics are used, problems occur. The thumbs up sign, for example, communicates approval or encouragement to Americans and Europeans, but in middle eastern countries, it is an obscene gesture.

Experts are recommending that companies localize their Web sites (as much as possible) and focus on select target markets, allowing surfers to access links in their own language. Webtrans (webtrans.com), Weblations (weblations.com), International Communications (intl.com), and Logos Corp. (logos-ca.com) will take a Web site and manually translate the entire site, including graphics. Browser add-ons also are available (try globalink.com) to translate sites written in German, Italian, Spanish, or French into English (or vice versa). As good Web sites become more important, they must communicate the right messages with clarity, simplicity, and cultural awareness.

SOURCES: Art Jahnke, "Power Play," *CIO Web Business,* July 1, 1999, pp. 23–42; Rick Borelli, "A Worldwide Language TRAP," *Management Review,* October 1997, pp. 52–54.

---

managers has made Nestlé the largest branded food company in Mexico, Brazil, Chile, and Thailand, and the company is on its way to becoming the leader in Vietnam and China as well. U.S. firms also show a growing international flavor. The global media giant News Corporation, owner of Fox Broadcasting Company, is run by Rupert Murdoch, who was born in Australia, educated in Britain, and is now an American citizen. At British firm ICI, 40 percent of the top 170 executives are non-British. Meanwhile, German companies such as Hoechst and BASF rely on local managers to run foreign operations.[11]

■ THE INTERNATIONAL BUSINESS ENVIRONMENT

International management is the management of business operations conducted in more than one country. The fundamental tasks of business management, including the financing, production, and distribution of products and services, do not change in any substantive way when a firm transacts business across international borders. The basic management functions of planning, organizing, leading, and controlling are the same whether a company operates domestically or internationally. However, managers will experience greater difficulties and risks when performing these management functions on an international scale. For example

- Wal-Mart has encountered difficulties in translating the warehouse club concept to Hong Kong. As a young accountant eyed a four-pound jar of peanut butter, he said, "The price is right, but where would I put it?"[12]

- When Coors Beer tried to translate a slogan with the phrase "Turn It Loose" into Spanish, it came out as "Drink Coors and Get Diarrhea." Budweiser goofed when its Spanish ad promoted Bud Lite as "Filling, less delicious."

- Nike ran a commercial with people from various countries supposedly saying "Just Do It" in foreign languages, but a Samburu tribesman was actually saying, "I don't want these; give me big shoes."

- United Airlines discovered that even colors can doom a product. The airline handed out white carnations when it started flying from

international management
The management of business operations conducted in more than one country

Hong Kong, only to discover that to many Asians such flowers represent death and bad luck.[13]

Although these examples may seem humorous, there's nothing funny about them to managers trying to operate in a competitive global environment. Companies seeking to expand their international presence on the Internet also can run into cross-cultural problems, as discussed in Technology for Tomorrow.

What should managers of emerging global companies look for in order to avoid obvious international mistakes? When they are comparing one country with another, the economic, legal-political, and sociocultural sectors present the greatest difficulties, and several key factors are important to understand.

■ THE ECONOMIC ENVIRONMENT

The economic environment represents the economic conditions in the country where the international organization operates. This part of the environment includes such factors as economic development; infrastructure; resource and product markets; exchange rates; and inflation, interest rates, and economic growth.

ECONOMIC DEVELOPMENT

Economic development differs widely among the countries and regions of the world. Countries can be categorized as either "developing" or "developed." The developing countries are referred to as less-developed countries (LDCs). The criterion traditionally used to classify countries as developed or developing is per capita income—the income generated by the nation's production of goods and services divided by its total population. The developing countries have low per capita incomes. LDCs generally are located in Asia, Africa, and South America. Developed countries include North America, Europe, and Japan. Today, developing countries in Southeast Asia, Latin America, and Eastern Europe are driving global growth.[14] Poverty is still the prevailing state in many places in the so-called Third World. Australia's Opportunity International is

working toward improving economic conditions in these countries.

OPPORTUNITY INTERNATIONAL

You think your life is hard? Compare it to lumberman Lescek in Poland, who borrowed $1,000 to buy a heat ventilator system to dry wood in an abandoned railroad car he had begged. When he became so successful he was able to take on more wood, the power company would not supply him with extra electricity, so he burned his scrap wood and dust.

Lescek is one of many entrepreneurs around the world who are given small loans by an Australian nonprofit organization called Opportunity International (OI). Whether it is in Poland, Russia, Bangladesh, India or Philippines, OI has a payback rate of 95 percent and a chance to see whole communities rise from poverty. Patterned after Muhammad Yunnus's Gramine Bank started in Bangladesh, OI gives loans to groups of entrepreneurs, so they are all responsible for one another's loans. That makes them more committed not only to paying back the money, but also to helping their fellow lendees.

A $100 loan to Jennie Lee in Manila helped her buy a sewing machine and enhance her rag business. She became treasurer of her 50-member women's cooperative of rag-makers, whose meetings start with a prayer and cover topics such as cooperation, communication, self-discipline, confrontation, leadership, and the like.

In the third-world countries served by Opportunity International, success is not defined by the size of a bank account or an IPO, but rather by "making a better life for one's children."[15] No wonder their payback rate is so high. ■

Most international business firms are headquartered in the wealthier, economically advanced countries. However, smart companies are investing heavily in Asia, Eastern Europe, and Latin America. Despite the economic convulsions that have rocked Southeast Asia, large Western companies such as Ford, Procter & Gamble, and Coca-Cola continue to see Asia as the big market of the future. Ford, for example, currently generates only 1 percent of its worldwide sales in Southeast Asia, but expects it to expand to 10 percent within the next five years.[16] Although they face risks and challenges today, these companies stand to reap huge benefits in the future. In China, Malaysia, and Brazil, for example, most of the population still is nearly 10 years away from their peak buying years.

INFRASTRUCTURE

A country's physical facilities that support economic activities make up its **infrastructure,** which includes transportation facilities such as airports, highways, and railroads; energy-producing facilities such as utilities and power plants; and communication facilities such as telephone lines and radio stations. Companies operating in LDCs must contend with lower levels of technology and perplexing logistical, distribution, and communication problems. Mike Mazzola, an executive for Reuters Ltd., found that in Mexico, getting a telephone installed could take up to a year. Even after he got one, he often had to dial several times before the call would go through. Undeveloped infrastructures represent opportunities for some

infrastructure
A country's physical facilities, such as highways and airports, that support economic activities

firms, such as United Technologies Corporation, based in Hartford, Connecticut, whose businesses include jet engines, air conditioning and heating systems, and elevators. As countries such as China, Russia, and Vietnam open their markets, new buildings need elevators and air and heat systems; opening remote regions for commerce requires more jet engines and helicopters.[17] One way companies can work globally with less infrastructure is through the Internet. What is necessary, though, is adequate phone lines and enough computers. Tips for entrepreneurs who want to use the Internet are described next.

RESOURCE AND PRODUCT MARKETS

When operating in another country, company managers must evaluate the market demand for their products. If market demand is high, managers may choose to export products to that country. To develop plants, however, resource markets for providing needed raw materials and labor must also be available. For example, the greatest challenge for McDonald's, which now sells Big Macs on every continent except Antarctica, is to obtain supplies of everything from potatoes to hamburger buns to plastic straws. At McDonald's in Cracow, the burgers come from a Polish plant, which is partly owned by Chicago-based OSI Industries; the onions come from Fresno, Cal-

Projects such as Beijing's fourth ring road, Shenzhen's subway, and the Three Gorges dam project (shown here) are examples of ongoing megaprojects in China. Analysts expect the Chinese government to boost its spending by 20 percent on public works and other projects to improve the infrastructure in China.

ifornia; the buns come from a production and distribution center near Moscow; and the potatoes come from a plant in Aldrup, Germany. McDonald's tries to contract with local suppliers when possible. In Thailand, McDonald's actually helped farmers cultivate Idaho russet potatoes of sufficient quality to produce their golden french fries.[18]

EXCHANGE RATES

The **exchange rate** is the rate at which one country's currency is exchanged for another country's. Changes in the exchange rate can have major implications for the profitability of international operations that exchange millions of dollars into other currencies every day.[19] For example, assume that the American dollar is exchanged for eight French francs. If the dollar increases in value to ten francs, U.S. goods will be more expensive in France because it will take more francs to buy a dollar's worth of U.S. goods. It will be more difficult to export American goods to France, and profits will be slim. If the dollar drops to a value of six francs, on the other hand, U.S. goods will be cheaper in France and can be exported at a profit.

■ THE LEGAL-POLITICAL ENVIRONMENT

Businesses must deal with unfamiliar political systems when they go international, as well as with more government supervision and regulation. Government officials and the general public often view foreign companies as outsiders or even intruders and are suspicious of their impact on economic independence and political sovereignty. Some of the major legal-political concerns affecting international business are political risk, political instability, and laws and regulations.

POLITICAL RISK

A company's **political risk** is defined as its risk of loss of assets, earning power, or managerial control due to politically based events or actions by host governments.[20] Political risk includes government takeovers of property and acts of violence directed against a firm's properties or employees. Because such acts are not uncommon, companies must formulate special plans and programs to guard against unexpected losses. For example, Hercules, Inc., a large chemical company, has increased the number of security guards at several of its European plants. Some companies actually buy political risk insurance, especially as they move into high-risk areas such as Eastern Europe, China, and Brazil. Political risk analysis has emerged as a critical component of environmental assessment for multinational organizations.[21]

POLITICAL INSTABILITY

Another frequently cited problem for international companies is political instability, which includes riots, revolutions, civil disorders, and frequent changes in government. Political instability increases uncertainty. Civil wars and large-scale violence have occurred in Indonesia, Malaysia, Thailand, Sri Lanka (Ceylon), and Myanmar (Burma) in recent decades. Companies moving into former Soviet republics face continued instability because of changing government personnel and political philosophies, as described below in the case of Ispat Steel.

ISPAT STEEL

Little did Ispat Steel realize when they bought the newly privatized Kazakastani steel plant Karmet that they would get the KGB in the bargain. It took months of negotiations for the KGB spooks to leave their electronically sophisticated offices, and the plant manager is still not sure they are all gone. Despite Ispat's success with manufacturing in eight countries around the world—in North and Central America, Europe, and Asia—and despite its being the only truly global steel producer in the world, it still faced monumental problems when it entered the murky, post-communist world.

As a manufacturer of tin cans and refrigerators, Karmet has become a

exchange rate
The rate at which one country's currency is exchanged for another country's

political risk
A company's risk of loss of assets, earning power, or managerial control due to politically based events or actions by host governments

metaphor for the problems that Western companies have encountered while doing business in the former Soviet Union. Here on the edge of Siberia, hundreds of workers report to work drunk and the largest customer (former Soviet Union) is broke. Chechen gunmen have been threatening suppliers, trying to extort bribes from customers, and has reportedly murdered one of the recent directors.

Karmet's success is desperately needed in this otherwise shrinking economy; it is a company down to 50 percent production with 10 layers of management still in place. At the same time Karmet has been loitering near death, its directors built lavish guest houses and spas, spending $1 million on armchairs alone.

Ispat faces a tough road. It must cut back one-third of its bloated 38,000 workforce, and this will occur partly by implementing a new discipline code. About 100 workers a week are fired for drunkenness and for cheating (e.g., performing a side job on company time). Ispat took on enormous debt and has paid out millions in back pay and notes to suppliers. To change workers, Ispat has started intensive courses in capitalism, from understanding market forces to generating profits.

The biggest problem is the dearth of orders. Two-thirds go to China, and any further increase is thwarted by shipping bottlenecks from different size rail tracks. With the nearest waterway half a continent away, geographical expansion to other countries is expensive. To ward off disaster, Ispat is considering going into consumer goods, trying to buy coal and steel mines and looking for foreign investors. Citizens are not happy. Though unable to manage these industries themselves, they nonetheless feel their resources have been "given away" to foreigners.[22] ■

Although most companies would prefer to do business in stable countries, some of the greatest growth opportunities lie in areas char-

acterized by instability. The greatest threat of violence is in countries experiencing political, ethnic, or religious upheaval. In China, for example, political winds have shifted rapidly, and often dangerously. Yet it is the largest potential market in the world for the goods and services of developed countries, and Xerox, AT&T, Motorola, and Kodak are busy making deals there.

U.S. firms or companies linked to the United States often are subject to major threats in countries characterized by political instability. Peruvian revolutionaries have targeted Pizza Hut and Kentucky Fried Chicken. Sixteen foreign managers were murdered in Russia in one recent year, and others working there often hire bodyguards. Even in countries that seem safe, such as Spain and Great Britain, terrorists have bombed tourist attractions.[23]

LAWS AND REGULATIONS

Government laws and regulations differ from country to country and make manufacturing and sales a true challenge for international firms. Host governments have myriad laws concerning libel statutes, consumer protection, information and labeling, employment and safety, and wages. International companies must learn these rules and regulations and abide by them. For example, French law forbids the use of children in advertising, and Germany prohibits the use of competitive claims.[24] In Mexico City, government inspectors made a surprise visit to Wal-Mart's Supercenter and charged that more than 10,000 of the store's items were improperly labeled or lacked instructions in Spanish. Likewise, Santa Clara, California-based Synergy Semiconductors found its partnership efforts in what used to be East Germany complicated by German labor laws.[25]

The most visible changes in legal-political factors grow out of international trade agreements and the emerging international trade alliance system. Consider, for example, the impact of the General Agreement on Tariffs and Trade (GATT), the European Union (EU), and the North American Free Trade Agreement (NAFTA).

GENERAL AGREEMENT ON TARIFFS AND TRADE (GATT)

GATT, signed by 23 nations in 1947, started as a set of rules to ensure nondiscrimination, clear procedures, the negotiation of disputes, and the participation of lesser developed countries in international trade. Today, more than 100 member countries abide by the rules of GATT. The primary tools GATT uses to increase trade are tariff concessions, through which member countries agree to limit the level of tariffs they will impose on imports from other GATT members, and the **most favored nation** clause, which calls for each member country to grant to every other member country the most favorable treatment it accords to any country with respect to imports and exports.[26]

GATT has sponsored various rounds of international trade negotiations aimed at reducing trade restrictions. Most recently, the Uruguay Round (the first to be named for a developing country) involved 125 countries and cut more tariffs than ever before. The Round's multilateral trade agreement, which took effect January 1, 1995, is the most comprehensive pact since the original 1947 agreement. Most experts believe the potential benefits for each country far outweigh the temporary costs. The goal of GATT negotiations is to encourage closer relationships among member nations and to help the global marketplace operate more efficiently. The Uruguay Round also boldly moved the world closer to global free trade by calling for the establishment of the World Trade Organization (WTO). The WTO represents the maturation of GATT into a permanent global institution that can monitor international trade and has legal authority to arbitrate disputes on some 400 trade issues.[27]

EUROPEAN UNION (EU)

Formed in 1958 to improve economic and social conditions among its members, the European Economic Community, now called the European Union (EU), has expanded to a 15-nation alliance illustrated in Exhibit 3.1. Countries in Central and Eastern Europe hope economic and political conditions there will

Despite the political risk, political instability, and the local laws and regulations of countries such as Morocco, The Coca-Cola Company earns about 80 percent of its profits from markets outside North America. The soft drink company was named in a recent *Fortune* magazine survey as the number one company in the world in product quality, attracting and developing new talent, and overall global effectiveness.

stabilize enough for them to begin joining soon.[28]

In the early 1980s, Europeans initiated steps to create a powerful single market system called Europe '92. The initiative called for creation of open markets for Europe's 340 million consumers. Europe '92 consisted of 282 directives proposing dramatic reform and deregulation in such areas as banking, insurance, health, safety standards, airlines, telecommunications, auto sales, social policy, and monetary union.

Initially opposed and later embraced by European industry, the increased competition and economies of scale within Europe will enable companies to grow large and efficient, becoming more competitive in U.S. and other world markets. Some observers fear that the EU will become a trade barrier, creating a "fortress Europe" that will be difficult to penetrate by companies in other nations.

The most significant aspect is the EU's monetary revolution and the introduction of the **euro.** The euro is the single European currency that will eventually replace 15 national currencies and unify a huge marketplace, creating a competitive $6.4 trillion economy second only to the United States. In 1999, 11 countries—Germany, France, Spain, Italy, Ireland, the Netherlands, Austria, Belgium, Finland, Portugal, and Luxembourg—formed the

most favored nation
A term describing a GATT clause that calls for member countries to grant other member countries the most favorable treatment they accord any country concerning imports and exports

euro
The single European currency that will replace 15 national currencies

Exhibit 3.1

THE FIFTEEN NATIONS
WITHIN THE EU

core group setting the exchange rates for adopting the single European currency, with the United Kingdom, Denmark, Greece, and Sweden expected to join later. The goal is to have the euro replace all national currencies by mid-2002.[29] The implications of a single European currency are enormous within as well as outside Europe. As it replaces European domestic currencies, the euro will affect legal contracts, financial management, sales and marketing tactics, manufacturing, distribution, payroll, pensions, training, taxes, and information management systems. Every corporation that does business in or with EU countries will feel the impact.[30] In addition, economic union is likely to speed deregulation, which has al-

ready reordered Europe's corporate and competitive landscape.

There still is much opposition to the idea of economic and monetary union, but success seems likely. Although building alliances among countries is difficult, the benefits of doing so are overcoming divisions and disagreements. Canada, Mexico, and the United States have established what is expected to be an equally powerful alliance.

NORTH AMERICAN FREE TRADE AGREEMENT (NAFTA)

The North American Free Trade Agreement, which went into effect on January 1, 1994, merged the United States, Canada, and Mexico into a megamarket with more than 360 million consumers. The agreement breaks down tariffs and trade restrictions on most agricultural and manufactured products for a 15-year period. The treaty builds upon the 1989 U.S.–Canada agreement and is expected to spur growth and investment, increase exports, and expand jobs in all three nations.[31]

NAFTA has spurred the entry of small businesses into the global arena. Jeff Victor, general manager of Treatment Products, Ltd., which makes car cleaners and waxes, credits NAFTA for his surging export volume. Prior to the pact, Mexican tariffs as high as 20 percent made it impossible for the Chicago-based company to expand its presence south of the border. Similarly, StoneHeart, Inc., of Cheney, Washington, began selling its scooters for people with leg or foot injuries to a distributor in Canada.[32] Although many groups in the United States opposed the agreement, warning of job loss and the potential for industrial "ghost towns," results so far have been positive. Ross Perot once warned of a "giant sucking sound" as Mexico inhaled jobs from America, but today that sound seems to be only an echo. Interviews with workers in various St. Louis area companies recently found not a single person who knew of a colleague, friend, or relative out of work because of international trade.[33] Although criticism of NAFTA continues, many people believe there are important benefits. Experts stress that NAFTA will enable companies in all three countries to compete more effectively with rival Asian and European companies.[34]

TRADE ALLIANCES: PROMISE OR PITFALL?

The creation of trading blocs is an increasingly popular part of international business. Plans are underway for the Southeast Asian Nations (ASEAN) free trade agreement, and the future will likely see the creation of a new trade alliance in Central and South America. These developments will provide cheaper Mexican watermelons in the United States, more Israeli shoes in Central Europe, and more Colombian roses in Venezuela. These agreements entail a new future for international companies and pose a range of new questions for international managers.

- Will the creation of multiple trade blocs lead to economic warfare among them?
- Will trade blocs gradually evolve into three powerful trading blocs composed of the American hemisphere, Europe (from Ireland across the former Soviet Union), and the "yen bloc" encompassing the Pacific Rim? Will the expansion of global, stateless corporations bypass trading zones and provide economic balance among them?[35]

Only the future will provide answers to these questions. International managers and global corporations will both shape and be shaped by these important trends.

■ THE SOCIOCULTURAL ENVIRONMENT

A nation's culture includes the shared knowledge, beliefs, and values, as well as the common modes of behavior and ways of thinking, among members of a society. Cultural factors are more perplexing than political and economic factors in foreign countries. Culture is intangible, pervasive, and difficult to learn. It is absolutely imperative that international businesses comprehend the significance of local cultures and deal with them effectively.

SOCIAL VALUES

Research done by Geert Hofstede on 116,000 IBM employees in 40 countries identified four dimensions of national value systems that influence organizational and employee working relationships.[36] Examples of how countries rate on the four dimensions are shown in Exhibit 3.2.

1. *Power distance.* High **power distance** means that people accept inequality in power among institutions, organizations, and people. Low power distance means that people expect equality in power. Countries that value high power distance are Malaysia, the Philippines, and Panama. Countries that value low power distance are Denmark, Austria, and Israel.

power distance
The degree to which people accept inequality in power among institutions, organizations, and people

Exhibit 3.2

RANK ORDERINGS OF TEN COUNTRIES ALONG FOUR DIMENSIONS OF NATIONAL VALUE SYSTEMS

Country	Power Distance[a]	Uncertainty Avoidance[b]	Individualism[c]	Masculinity[d]
Australia	7	7	2	5
Costa Rica	8 (tie)	2 (tie)	10	9
France	3	2 (tie)	4	7
West Germany	8 (tie)	5	5	3
India	2	9	6	6
Japan	5	1	7	1
Mexico	1	4	8	2
Sweden	10	10	3	10
Thailand	4	6	9	8
United States	6	8	1	4

[a] 1=highest power distance
10=lowest power distance
[b] 1=highest uncertainty avoidance
10=lowest uncertainty avoidance
[c] 1=highest individualism
10=highest collectivisim
[d] 1=highest masculinity
10=highest femininity

SOURCES: From Dorothy Marcic, *Organizational Behavior and Cases*, 4th ed. (St. Paul, Minn.: West, 1995). Based on Geert Hofstede, *Culture's Consequences* (London: Sage Publications, 1984); and *Cultures and Organizations: Software of the Mind* (New York: McGraw-Hill, 1991).

uncertainty avoidance
A value characterized by people's intolerance for uncertainty and ambiguity and resulting support for beliefs that promise certainty and conformity

individualism
A preference for a loosely knit social framework in which individuals are expected to take care of themselves

collectivism
A preference for a tightly knit social framework in which individuals look after one another and organizations protect their members' interests

masculinity
A cultural preference for achievement, heroism, assertiveness, work centrality, and material success

femininity
A cultural preference for cooperation, group decision making, and quality of life

2. *Uncertainty avoidance.* High **uncertainty avoidance** means that members of a society feel uncomfortable with uncertainty and ambiguity and thus support beliefs that promise certainty and conformity. Low uncertainty avoidance means that people have high tolerance for the unstructured, the unclear, and the unpredictable. High uncertainty avoidance countries include Greece, Portugal, and Uruguay. Countries with low uncertainty avoidance values are Singapore and Jamaica.

3. *Individualism and collectivism.* **Individualism** reflects a value for a loosely knit social framework in which individuals are expected to take care of themselves. **Collectivism** means a preference for a tightly knit social framework in which individuals look after one another and organizations protect their members' interests. Countries with individualist values include the United States, Canada, Great Britain, and Australia. Countries with collectivist values are Guatemala, Ecuador, and Panama. Individualist companies of North America doing business with collectivist countries can pro-

duce conflicts, as described in Leading the Revolution: Leadership.

4. *Masculinity/femininity.* **Masculinity** stands for preference for achievement, heroism, assertiveness, work centrality (with resultant high stress), and material success. **Femininity** reflects the values of relationships, cooperation, group decision making, and quality of life. Societies with strong masculine values are Japan, Austria, Mexico, and Germany. Countries with feminine values are Sweden, Norway, Denmark, and the former Yugoslavia. Both men and women subscribe to the dominant value in masculine and feminine cultures.

Social values influence organizational functioning and management styles. For example, organizations in France and Latin and Mediterranean countries tend to be hierarchical bureaucracies. Germany and other central European countries have organizations that strive to be impersonal, well-oiled machines. In India, Asia, and Africa, organizations are viewed as large families. Effective management styles differ in each country, depending on cultural characteristics.[37]

SHARED RESOURCES, INC.

High-tech companies still need people—smart and skilled people. Shared Resource, Inc., a Columbus, Ohio-based builder of computer systems with only 53 employees, discovered it had to go—literally—to the ends of the earth to get those smart people.

In order to find qualified workers in Columbus's tight labor market (unemployment is 2.6 percent), founder Maria Tray tried everything, including *paying* people just to send in their résumés. Tray couldn't hire fast enough, so she was forced to turn away business. Another local entrepreneur, from India, suggested she try his homeland. Tray first placed an ad in the English-language paper, *The Hindi,* and winnowed through the 350 résumés of respondents.

In January 1999, she and her husband boarded a plane and ended up in Madras (now Chennai), whose population is more than six million. For four solid days, Tray interviewed 51 candidates, who were amazed that an American employer would come over to India to personally recruit. Some of the most technically able candidates failed on another count: During the interview they neither talked to nor looked at Tray, but instead focused on her husband or the Indian recruiter. Because many of her stateside clients are women, Tray knew she had to find employees who were able to work with females. "I get plenty of that here [being marginalized as a woman]," she noted. "I don't have to go looking for it."

Another problem she had was getting the eastern Indians to talk about their positive qualities, something Americans have learned to do well. In India, as in other collectivist countries, such talk seems boastful, so the recruits were shy. Finally, she offered the job to eight and six accepted. Her total cost (including air fare for the six to Columbus) was less than half of the usual $15,000 per hire she would pay for a U.S. headhunter to do the whole job.

But that was not all. She arranged for work permits and visas, acquired a block of apartments in a suburban complex, plotted locations of Indian restaurants and grocery stores, and assigned her American employees as cultural guides for the arriving families.

With all that, Tray knows recruiting abroad is fraught with risks. Although she has asked each employee to commit to her for three years, the workers are free to go anywhere they want, since the United States does not support indentured servitude.

Would she do it again? For now, she has hired a headhunter to find applicants closer to home. But she still has a stack of résumés from Chennai.

Source: Timothy Aeppel, "A Passage to India Eases a Worker Scarcity in Ohio," *The Wall Street Journal,* Oct. 5, 1999, pp. B1, B20.

OTHER CULTURAL CHARACTERISTICS

Other cultural characteristics that influence international organizations are language, religion, attitudes, social organization, and education. Some countries, such as India, are characterized by linguistic pluralism, meaning that several languages exist there. Other countries rely heavily on spoken versus written language. Religion includes sacred objects, philosophical attitudes toward life, taboos, and rituals. Attitudes toward achievement, work, and time can all affect organizational productivity. An attitude called **ethnocentrism** refers to people who tend to regard their own culture as superior, which often results in the downgrading of other cultures. Ethnocentrism within a country makes it difficult for foreign firms to operate there. Social organization includes status systems, kinship and families, social institutions, and opportunities for social mobility. Education influences the literacy level, the availability of qualified employees, and the predominance of primary or secondary degrees.

Managers in international companies have found that cultural differences cannot be ignored if international operations are to succeed. For example, Coke withdrew its two-liter bottle from the Spanish market after discovering that compartments of Spanish refrigerators were too small for it.[38] McDonald's hasn't even tried to market Egg McMuffins in Brazil because of the deeply ingrained tradition of eating breakfast at home. On the other hand, Kellogg introduced breakfast cereal into Brazil through carefully chosen advertising. Although the traditional breakfast is coffee and a roll, many Brazilians have been won over to the American breakfast and now start their day with Kellogg's Sucrilhos (Frosted Flakes) and Crokinhos (Cocoa Krispies).[39] Organizations that recognize and manage cultural differences report major successes.

When people from different countries work together on a project, managers may find that

ethnocentrism
The tendency to regard one's own group or culture as superior to those of others

culture provides more barriers than any other factor to successful collaboration. Consider the Mercedes-Benz plant in Vance, Alabama.

MERCEDES-BENZ
www.mercedes-benz.com

"Here we have created—what's that American phrase of yours?—a melting-pot of styles," says Andreas Renschler, CEO of the Mercedes-Benz plant that sits along Interstate 20 in western Alabama. But he admits that creating it wasn't easy.

For his management team, the native German carefully selected executives from all of the major U.S. and Japanese automakers, originally choosing a perfectly balanced team of four Germans and four Americans. Today, there are six top executives, three of whom are German, two American, and one Canadian. The group was sequestered in Stuttgart, Germany, for a year to finalize the plans for the new U.S. plant. Cultures clashed repeatedly, but a rigid time frame forced the group to negotiate until its members reached compromises. The biggest disagreements were over issues of image and decorum. The Germans were accustomed to private offices and hallways, but the Americans argued for a more open environment. Renschler, at first uncomfortable with the idea of casual attire, eventually embraced the casual "team wear," including sweaters with the Mercedes logo worn by all executives and employees at the plant. However, for months, when executives arrived from Germany, managers at the Alabama plant would quickly don suit coats and ties.

The group also argued over building design and management styles. While the Germans wanted separate structures for the different assembly lines, the Americans felt that separation would work against the team concept of the plant. Eventually, the group decided on an operation that combines the precision of German industrial engineering with an American-style environment of open communications between managers and workers. Most of the team leaders are Alabama natives. Trained in Germany, they were paired with German families for socializing and acculturation. Although some initially found it difficult to adapt to the direct style of German trainers, most eventually came to like the style because it helped them learn faster. Difficulties continued at the plant itself, however. "The Germans are very blunt. . . ." said one worker. "You don't get politeness out of them about work." Most of the Alabama workers found their bosses to be rigid, formal, even humorless, while the Germans regarded the Americans as lax, too talkative, and somewhat superficial.

Some German executives at Daimler-Benz headquarters derided the American workers, saying "They'll never be able to do it." However, Renschler points out that within a few weeks, Germans and Americans were easily calling upon each other for help when the line was behind schedule. The Vance factory has proved successful, and the Mercedes M-Class sport utility vehicle is a hit in the marketplace. Renschler isn't surprised by the success. "We've shown that we can work with another culture."[40] Indeed, learning to do so proved useful in the German company's recent merger with Chrysler Corporation. ■

■ GETTING STARTED INTERNATIONALLY

Small and medium-sized companies have a couple of ways to become involved internationally. One is to seek cheaper sources of supply offshore, or outsourcing. Another is to develop markets for finished products outside their home country, which may include exporting, licensing, and direct investing through joint ventures or subsidiaries. These are called **market entry strategies,** because they represent alternative ways to sell products and services in foreign markets. Most firms begin

market entry strategy
An organizational strategy for entering a foreign market

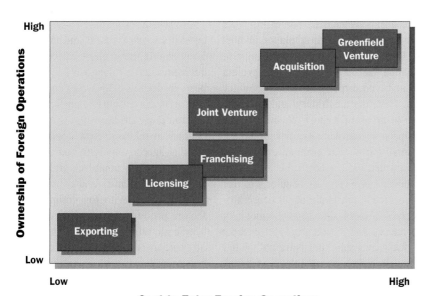

E x h i b i t 3.3
STRATEGIES FOR ENTERING
INTERNATIONAL MARKETS

with exporting and work up to direct investment. Exhibit 3.3 shows the strategies companies can use to enter foreign markets.

OUTSOURCING

Global outsourcing, sometimes called global sourcing, means engaging in the international division of labor so that manufacturing can be done in countries with the cheapest sources of labor and supplies. A company may take away a contract from a domestic supplier and place it with a company in the Far East, 8,000 miles away. With advances in telecommunications, service providers can outsource as well. For example, Citibank taps low-cost skilled labor in India, Hong Kong, Australia, and Singapore to manage data and develop products for its global financial services. M. W. Kellogg, a Houston-based company that builds power and chemical plants around the world, farms out the detailed architectural-engineering work to a partner in Mexico.[41]

A unique variation is the Maquiladora industry along the Texas-Mexico border. In the beginning, twin plants were set up, with the U.S. plant manufacturing components with sophisticated machinery and the Mexican plant assembling components using cheap labor. With increasing sophistication in Mexico, new factories with sophisticated equipment are be-

ing built farther south of the border, with assembled products imported into the United States at highly competitive prices. The Blue Bird Corporation, a bus manufacturer based in Macon, Georgia, is building a plant in Mexico. The auto industry took advantage of the Maquiladora industry throughout the 1980s to combat the Japanese price challenge. By 1992, more than 100,000 Mexicans were employed by U.S. auto companies in towns such as Hermosillo, giving the area the nickname "Detroit South." The low-cost, high-quality Mexican workforce has also attracted manufacturers from other countries, firms such as Nissan, Renault, and Volkswagen.[42] Asian companies in particular are fast establishing Maquiladoras in Mexican border towns, with more than 30 Japanese companies already assembling there.

EXPORTING

With **exporting,** the corporation maintains its production facilities within the home nation and transfers its products for sale in foreign countries.[43] Exporting enables a country to market its products in other countries at modest resource cost and with limited risk. Exporting does entail numerous problems based on physical distances, government regulations, foreign currencies, and cultural differences,

global outsourcing
Engaging in the international division of labor so as to obtain the cheapest sources of labor and supplies regardless of country; also called global sourcing

exporting
An entry strategy in which the organization maintains its production facilities within its home country and transfers its products for sale in foreign markets

but it is less expensive than committing the firm's own capital to building plants in host countries. For example, a high-tech equipment supplier called Gerber Scientific Inc. prefers not to get involved directly in foreign country operations. Because machinery and machine tools are hot areas of export, executives are happy to ship overseas. U.S. exports are on the rise, and small to mid-size companies are benefiting. Multiplex Co., a St. Louis manufacturer of beverage-dispensing equipment for fast-food service, exports about 40 percent of its products. National Graphics, a specialty coater of papers and films, ships 60 percent of its products overseas, and National's CEO believes exports helped to save the company.[44]

A form of exporting to less-developed countries is called **countertrade,** which is the barter of products for products rather than the sale of products for currency. Many less-developed countries have products to exchange but have no foreign currency. An estimated 20 percent of world trade is countertrade.

Exporting to other countries from the U.S. is a major economic factor. Small companies are increasingly using exports to expand their businesses, often through the Internet, as described in Leading the Revolution: Leadership.

LICENSING

With **licensing,** a corporation (the licensor) in one country makes certain resources available to companies in another country (the licensee).

These resources include technology, managerial skills, and/or patent and trademark rights. They enable the licensee to produce and market a product similar to what the licensor has been producing. This arrangement gives the licensor an opportunity to participate in the production and sale of products outside its home country at relatively low cost. Hasbro has licensing agreements with companies in several Latin American countries and Japan. Hasbro builds brand identity and consumer awareness by contracting with toy companies to manufacture products locally. Heineken, which has been called the world's first truly global brand of beer, usually begins by exporting to help boost familiarity with its product; if the market looks enticing enough, Heineken then licenses its brands to a local brewer.

Franchising is a form of licensing in which the franchisor provides foreign franchisees with a complete package of material and services, including equipment, products, product ingredients, trademark and trade name rights, managerial advice, and a standardized operating system. Some of the best-known international franchisors are the fast-food chains. Kentucky Fried Chicken, Burger King, Wendy's, and McDonald's outlets are found in almost every large city in the world. The story is often told of the Japanese child visiting Los Angeles who excitedly pointed out to his parents, "They have McDonald's in America."

Licensing and franchising offer a business firm relatively easy access to international

countertrade
The barter of products for other products rather than their sale for currency

licensing
An entry strategy in which an organization in one country makes certain resources available to companies in another in order to participate in the production and sale of its products abroad

franchising
A form of licensing in which an organization provides its foreign franchisees with a complete assortment of materials and services

Daewoo Campus Advisers at U.S. universities? Through exporting, Korea's Daewoo Motor Co. hopes to sell 30,000 vehicles in its first year in the U.S. market. The Campus Advisers, a group of 2,000 college students at some 200 campuses, will run Daewoo events and direct potential buyers to the nearest Daewoo sales showroom.

LEADING THE REVOLUTION:

EXPORTING THROUGH THE INTERNET

Thinking of starting a business? Then you better also think about exporting. Small companies, such as 100-employee Springfield, Missouri's International Dehydrated Foods, often make up to half their revenues by selling overseas. Going against conventional wisdom, being small can be an advantage. Daniel Oberer says "Foreign customers know when they call on the phone, they can get one of the top two people within a few minutes, without going through layers of bureaucracy."

The value of exports has increased 100-fold since 1977, from $100 billion to $1 trillion. Imports now account for 25 percent of the U.S. gross domestic product. But the biggest change for small businesses in exporting is the Internet. And in order to take on the big guys, some small firms are starting their own trading networks, such as Washington, D.C.-based The Trade Compass Web, which provides international trade information, custom regulations, shipping schedules, and the like. It also has become an international hub for small import-export firms, where they can develop business relationships, get advice about doing business in various countries, and even do business online through their new section called Caravan. President Browning Rockwell believes the Internet has made global aspiration possible to the smallest firm. Larger e-commerce companies, such as auctioneer eBay, have made going global easy for any venture. "The Internet is leveling the playing field," says Kathleen Doyle, who is in the art gallery business. "We've had many international buyers," she said. "But this gives us horsepower."

SOURCES: Lorrie Grant, "Going, Going, Gone.com," *USA Today,* May 17, 1999, pp. B1–B2; Tim McCollum, "E-Commerce Takes Off," *Nation's Business,* Oct. 1998, pp. 34–37; James Worsham, "Markets at Risk," *Nation's Business,* Aug. 1998, pp. 13–20.

---

markets at low cost, but they limit its participation in and control over the development of those markets.

A **joint venture** is currently a popular risk- and cost-sharing approach that many companies are taking to expand in a global market. It is typically set up in the host country to develop new products, build facilities, or set up sales and distribution networks. A partnership is often the fastest, cheapest, and least risky way to get into the global game. In its quest to become the dominant brand in an expanded European market, Heineken Breweries is teaming up with smaller rivals in Hungary, Poland, and Switzerland. In Asia, Heineken has entered into a joint venture with Singapore's Asia Pacific Breweries, makers of Tiger Beer.

The other choice is to have a **wholly owned foreign affiliate,** over which the company has complete control. Direct acquisition of an affiliate may provide cost savings over exporting by shortening distribution channels and reducing storage and transportation costs. Local managers also have heightened awareness of economic, cultural, and political conditions. For example, General Electric purchased Hungarian bulbmaker Tungsram in 1990. By 1994 the company was turning a profit, and quality was so good that GE shifted all European lightbulb production there.[45]

■ MANAGING IN A GLOBAL ENVIRONMENT

Managing in a foreign country is particularly challenging. Before undertaking a foreign assignment, managers must understand that they will face great personal challenges. Managers working in foreign countries must be sensitive to cultural subtleties and understand that the ways to provide proper leadership, decision making, motivation, and control vary in different cultures. When companies operate internationally, the need for personal learning and growth is critical.

PERSONAL CHALLENGES FOR GLOBAL MANAGERS

Managers will be most successful in foreign assignments if they are culturally flexible and easily adapt to new situations and ways of doing things. A tendency to be ethnocentric—to believe that your own country's cultural values and ways of doing things are superior—is a natural human condition. Managers can learn

joint venture
A currently popular risk- and cost-sharing approach that many companies are taking to expand in a global market

wholly owned foreign affiliate
A foreign subsidiary over which an organization has complete control

to break down those prejudices and appreciate another culture. As one Swedish executive of a large multinational corporation put it, "We Swedes are so content with . . . the Swedish way, that we forget that 99 percent of the rest of the world isn't Swedish."[46] Managers working in foreign countries may never come to understand the local culture like a native; the key is to be sensitive to cultural differences and understand that other ways of thinking and doing are also valid.

Most managers in foreign assignments face a period of homesickness, loneliness, and culture shock from being suddenly immersed in a culture with completely different languages, foods, values, beliefs, and ways of doing things. **Culture shock** refers to the frustration and anxiety that result from being subjected to new and unfamiliar cues about what to do and how to do it. Even simple, daily events can become sources of stress.[47]

Properly preparing managers to work in foreign cultures is essential. Some companies try to give future managers exposure to foreign cultures early in their careers. American Express Company's Travel-Related Services unit gives American business-school students summer jobs in which they work outside the United States for up to 10 weeks. Colgate-Palmolive selects 15 recent graduates each year and then provides up to 24 months of training prior to multiple overseas job stints.[48]

MANAGING CROSS-CULTURALLY

Effective international managers understand their own cultural values and assumptions and can interpret the culture of the country and organization in which they are working. They develop the sensitivity required to avoid making costly cultural blunders.[49] The following examples illustrate how cultural differences can be significant for foreign managers.

LEADING   In relationship-oriented societies such as those in Asia, the Arab world, and Latin America, leaders should use a warm, personalized approach with employees. One of the greatest difficulties American leaders have had doing business in China, for example, is failing to recognize that to the Chinese any

relationship is a personal relationship.[50] Managers are expected to have periodic social visits with workers, inquiring about morale and health. Leaders should be especially careful about criticizing others. To Asians, Africans, Arabs, and Latin Americans, the loss of self-respect brings dishonor to themselves and their families. One researcher tells of a Dutch doctor managing a company clinic who had what he considered a "frank discussion" with a Chinese subordinate. The subordinate, who perceived the doctor as a father figure, took the criticism as a "savage indictment" and committed suicide.[51] Though this is an extreme example, the principle of "losing face" is highly important in some cultures.

DECISION MAKING   In America, mid-level managers may discuss a problem and give the boss a recommendation. German managers, on the other hand, expect the boss to issue specific instructions. In Mexico, employees often don't understand participatory decision making. American managers doing business there have been advised to rarely explain a decision, lest workers perceive this as a sign of weakness.[52] In contrast, managers in Arab and African nations are expected to use consultative decision making in the extreme.

MOTIVATING   Motivation must fit the incentives within the culture. In Japan, employees are motivated to satisfy the company. A financial bonus for star performance would be humiliating to employees from Japan, China, or the former Yugoslavia. An American executive in Japan offered a holiday trip to the top salesperson, but employees were not interested. After he realized that Japanese are motivated in groups, he changed the reward to a trip for everyone if together they achieved the sales target. They did. Managers in Latin America, Africa, and the Middle East must show respect for employees as individuals with needs and interests outside of work.[53]

CONTROLLING   When things go wrong, managers in foreign countries often are unable to rid themselves of employees who do not perform at acceptable standards. In Europe, Mexico, and Indonesia, to hire and fire on per-

culture shock
The frustration, anxiety, and stress that result from being subjected to new and unfamiliar cues about what to do and how to do it

GIVING WORKERS THE FREEDOM TO LEARN

AES Corporation, a producer of electrical power with headquarters in Arlington, Virginia, has become a learning organization by handing power to workers on the front lines. Lots of companies talk about pushing power and responsibility to lower levels, but few have pushed as far as AES. With nearly 6,000 employees (or more than 30,000, counting those working in joint ventures), AES has never established departments for human resources, operations, purchasing, or legal affairs. Fewer than 30 people work at headquarters. All functions (even finance) are handled by decentralized teams that include coal handlers and maintenance workers. For example, two control room operators led the team that raised $350 million to finance a joint venture in Northern Ireland. Teams seek advice from managers or anyone else who may have helpful ideas, but they make their own decisions.

AES disperses power and information so widely because its managers believe this is the only way to keep people thinking and learning. According to cofounder and CEO Dennie Bakke, "If all information about finance goes to the finance department and all information about legal matters goes to the legal de-

partment, it's impossible to get well-rounded people who can think about the whole world." AES needs people to think about the whole world as it continues its rapid international expansion. The company opened its first plant in 1986. Today, it owns or has an interest in 82 power plants in the United States, Argentina, China, Brazil, Hungary, and other countries. The company has revenues of about $835 million and profits of $125 million. AES also believes in being a good corporate citizen in the countries in which it operates. It has planted 52 million trees in Guatemala, funded medical care in Kazakhstan, organized food banks in Argentina, and built schools in China. Although the company's social responsibility emphasis used to be on environmentalism, it has shifted gears to try to meet the needs of each specific country.

Bakke and cofounder and chairman Roger Sant believe AES has been able to expand so rapidly because giving people on the front lines the power to make decisions has made AES faster and nimbler than competitors. Oscar Prieto, a chemical engineer picked to lead AES's expansion into Brazil, agrees. He'd worked at AES only two years when

he was given the challenging assignment, but he'd experienced the power of empowerment and believed it could work crossculturally. He chose Carlos Baldi, a 34-year-old engineer, to manage the plant in Santa Branca, a small facility near São Paulo that had previously been run as a top-heavy bureaucracy. After agreeing on shared goals and expectations, Prieto turned the plant over to Baldi and told him to run it as he saw fit. Now Baldi operates the same way with his people—he gives advice, not approval.

"Power to the people" doesn't always translate so well to other countries, however. For example, managers in Northern Ireland are having a hard time giving up control and operating the AES way. Yet, Bakke and Sant are committed to expanding AES's bottom-up system around the world. The company's mission statement declares that work should be "fun, fulfilling, and exciting." At AES, that means giving workers freedom, challenge, and opportunities to think, learn, grow, and achieve.

SOURCE: Alex Markels, "Power to the People," *Fast Company*, February–March 1998, pp. 155–165.

formance seems unnaturally brutal. Workers are protected by strong labor laws and union rules.

In foreign cultures, managers also should not control the wrong things. A Sears manager in Hong Kong insisted that employees come to work on time instead of 15 minutes late. The employees did exactly as they were told, but they also left on time instead of working into the evening as they had previously. A lot of work was left unfinished. The manager eventually told the employees to go back to their old ways. His attempt at control had a negative effect.

GLOBAL LEARNING

Managing across borders calls for organizations to learn across borders. One reason

Japanese companies have been so successful internationally is that their culture encourages learning and adaptability. In Asia generally, teaching and learning are highly regarded, and the role of managers is seen as one of teaching or facilitating—of helping those around them to learn.[54] It is partly this emphasis on continuous learning that has helped Matsushita Electric master markets and diverse cultures in 38 countries, from Malaysia to Brazil, from Austria to China, from Iran to Tanzania. One of Matsushita's top lessons for going global is to be a good corporate citizen in every country, respecting cultures, customs, and languages. In countries with Muslim religious practices, for example, Matsushita provides special prayer rooms and allows two prayer sessions per shift.[55] AES Corporation, an American corporation that encourages continuous learning by giving freedom and power to front-line workers, is now trying to expand its business model internationally, as described in Leading the Revolution: The Learning Organization.

Some cross-cultural differences are described in the following poem:

An Asian View of Cultural Differences

We live in time. You live in space.
We are always at rest. You are always on the move.

We are passive. You are aggressive.
We like to contemplate. You like to act.

We accept the world as it is. You try to change the world according to your blueprint.

We live in peace with nature. You try to impose your will in her.

Religion is our first love. Technology is your passion.
We delight to think about the meaning of life. You delight in physics.

We believe in freedom of silence. You believe in freedom of speech.
We lapse into meditation. You strive for articulation.

We marry first, then love. You love first, then marry.
Our marriage is the beginning of a love affair. Your marriage is the happy end of a romance.
It is an indissoluble bond. It is a contract.

Our love is mute. Your love is vocal.
We try to conceal it from the world. You delight in showing it to others.

Self-denial is the secret to our survival. Self-assertiveness is the key to your success.

We are taught from the cradle to want less and less. You are urged every day to want more and more.

We glorify austerity and renunciation. You emphasize gracious living and enjoyment.

In the sunset years of life we renounce the world and prepare for the hereafter. You retire to enjoy the fruits of your labor.[56]

Summary and Management Solution

This chapter has emphasized the growing importance of having an international perspective in management. Business in the global arena involves special risks and difficulties because of complicated economic, legal-political, and sociocultural forces. Moreover, the global environment changes rapidly, as illustrated by the emergence of the European Union, the North American Free Trade Agreement, and the shift in Eastern Europe to democratic forms of government. Major alternatives for serving foreign markets are exporting, licensing, franchising, joint ventures, or wholly owned subsidiaries.

International markets provide many opportunities but are also fraught with difficulty, as adM@rt discovered. Jimmy Lai did not consider the difference in culture from Webvan's site in California, where harried dual-income couples like to have groceries delivered, to Hong Kong, where entire families are crowded into one-bedroom concrete boxes and where languishing in shops and malls is not only a favorite, but a necessary, pastime. Hong Kong is still a face-to-face shopping culture, where people still insist on "squeezing the melons." Underestimating cultural differences is a major problem in exporting business models from one culture to another.

Further, even though adM@rt saves money in retail space, it expends it in transport costs, as its fleet of vans grew from 200 to 400. Most of adM@rt's current business comes from wholesaling Coca-Cola, which does not provide the profit margins needed. To top it off, Lai's aggressive actions that triggered the price war so enraged the two main competitors/biggest advertisers that they pulled their large, revenue-generating ads out of Lai's *Apple Daily*.

Lai's best strategy now seems to pull out of the online grocery business before he loses even more. Some of his problems started from day one and have only become virtually insurmountable now. First of all, going into a business that used two core competencies he lacked (Internet and groceries) was a mistake. He should have either not done it, or worked in a strategic alliance with a more experienced partner. Next, he underestimated the complications of running a Web business and needed more resources and expertise on the Web site itself. Having it break down in the first days—and never getting it to work adequately afterwards—was the death knell to his Internet business. Finally, going head–to–head in fierce battle with his two best advertisers was a strategic mistake. For a virtual company owner, Lai is suffering pain all too real.

SOURCE: "Van @ttack," *The Economist,* Sept. 18, 1999, pp. 69–70.

Discussion Questions

1. Why do you think international businesses traditionally prefer to operate in industrialized countries? Discuss.

2. What considerations in recent years have led international businesses to expand their activities into less-developed countries?

3. What policies or actions would you recommend to an entrepreneurial business wanting to do business in Europe?

4. What steps could a company take to avoid making product design and marketing mistakes when introducing new products into a foreign country?

5. What does it mean to say that the world is becoming "borderless"? That large companies are "stateless"?

6. What might managers do to avoid making mistakes concerning control and decision making when operating in a foreign culture?

7. What is meant by the cultural values of individualism and masculinity/femininity? How might these values affect organization design and management processes?

8. How do you think trade alliances such as NAFTA and the EU may affect you as a future manager?

Management Exercises

Manager's Workbook

State of the World Test

Student: See the solutions section on p. 576 to check your responses.

How aware are you of the rest of the planet? If you will be working internationally, the better you know about the world, the more successful you are likely to be.

1. Six countries contain one-half the total population of the world. What are the six countries?

   1.   4.
   2.   5.
   3.   6.

2. Another nineteen countries account for 25 percent of the world's people. What are those countries?

   1.   7.
   2.   8.
   3.   9.
   4.   10.
   5.   11.
   6.   12.

   13.   17.
   14.   18.
   15.   19.
   16.

3. The ten most commonly spoken first languages are:

   1.   6.
   2.   7.
   3.   8.
   4.   9.
   5.   10.

4. How many languages are there in the world that have at least one million speakers?
   a. 73
   b. 123
   c. 223

5. How many nations were there in 1992?
   a. 288
   b. 188
   c. 88

6. Which nation is home to the largest number of commercial banks?

7. Which nation is home to the most transnational corporations?

8. Between 1970 and 1986, global agricultural (plant and livestock) production
   a. declined substantially.
   b. declined slightly.
   c. remained about the same.
   d. increased slightly.
   e. increased substantially.

9. Between 1970 and 1985, the number of people in the world suffering from malnutrition
   a. declined.
   b. remained about the same.
   c. increased.

10. Let one dot represent all the firepower used in World War II: This would be the equivalent of 200 Hiroshima-sized A-bombs. How many dots would you need to represent the firepower held in the combined U.S. and the former USSR before it dissolved?
    a. 60
    b. 600
    c. 6,000
    d. 60,000

11. Between 1960 and 1987, the world spent approximately $10 trillion on health care. How much did the world spend on military?
    a. $7 trillion
    b. $10 trillion
    c. $17 trillion
    d. $25 trillion

12. According to the United Nations, what percentage of the world's work (paid and unpaid) is done by women?
    a. 1/3
    b. 1/2
    c. 2/3
    d. 3/4

13. According to the United Nations, what percentage of the world's income is earned by women?
    a. 1/10
    b. 3/10
    c. 5/10
    d. 7/10

14. The nations of Africa, Asia, Latin America, and the Middle East, often referred to as the Third World, contain about 78 percent of the world's population. What percentage of the world's monetary income do they possess?
    a. 10 percent
    b. 20 percent
    c. 30 percent
    d. 40 percent

15. Americans constitute approximately 5 percent of the world's population. What percentage of the world's resources do Americans consume?
    a. 15 percent
    b. 25 percent
    c. 35 percent
    d. 45 percent

SOURCE: United Nations Web site, 1999; Jan Drum, Steve Hughes, and George Otere, "State-of-the-World Test," in *Global Winners*, Yarmouth, Maine: Intercultural Press, 1994, pp. 9–12.

Manager's Workshop

Global Economy Scavenger Hunt

In order to get a perspective on the pervasiveness of the global economy, you will be asked to find a number of things and bring them back to class.

1. Divide into teams of four to six members.

2. Each team is to bring items to a future class from the list below.

3. On the day in class, each team will give a short, two-minute presentation on the items that were the most difficult to find or the most interesting.

4. How many countries did your team get items from? How many for the entire class?

List for scavenger hunt:

1. Locate brochures of Annual Reports of four multinational corporations.

2. Gather evidence from three local businesses to show that they do business internationally.

3. Locate a retail store that sells only products listing them as "Made in America."

4. Find 10 toys or games that originate in other countries.

5. Find five toys or games that have components from one country and were assembled in another—or show how they were otherwise developed in more than one country.

6. List food items from 25 different countries.

7. List articles of clothing from 15 different countries.

8. List books sold in your town from authors of 12 different countries. Where were the books published? Who translated them?

9. List 12 films in the past five years that starred someone from another country.

10. List five films in the past five years that had multinational crews and locations. Include at least one that was co-produced by two or more countries.

11. Gather descriptions of interviews from five foreigners (not from your team or the class), in which they were asked to list six things they like about the United States and six things they don't like.

12. Create a list of eight places where a language other than English is displayed (on a bulletin board, poster, etc.).

13. Find two maps of the world drawn before 1900.

14. List five items in your town that were manufactured in another country and were not being made in that country six years ago.

SOURCE: Adapted from Jan Drum, Steve Hughes, and George Otere, "Global Scavenger Hunt," in *Global Winners,* Yarmouth, Maine: Intercultural Press, 1994, pp. 21–23.

Management in Practice: Ethical Dilemma

Quality or Closing

On the way home from the launch party celebrating Plaxcor Metals' entrance into the international arena, Donald Fields should have been smiling. He was part of the team that had closed the deal to sell component parts to Asian Business Machine, after his company had spent millions trying to break into this lucrative market. There were several more deals riding on the successful outcome of the first international venture.

The expansion into new markets was critical to Plaxcor's survival. As President Leslie Hanson had put it, "If we aren't global within five years, we may as well close up shop." Fields was tense because of news he learned tonight: intense bidding for the first sale and several last-minute changes requested by the customer had forced Plaxcor to heavily modify its production process. The production manager had confided that "the product is a mess but still better than most of the competition." He went on to assure him that, although well below normal standards, the variability would "probably not cause any problems" and could be worked out after a few more orders.

Fields had spent the last few months selling Plaxcor on its quality reputation. He knew they could probably get by with the first runs and meet the opening deadline. He was afraid that telling the customer of the potential problems or extending the deadline would risk not only this deal but pending projects as well. But he knew if problems arose with the products, Plaxcor's future in the Asian market would be bleak. Donald Fields wasn't sure Plaxcor could afford to gamble its entrance in the international market on a substandard product.

What Do You Do?

1. Ask the customer for an extension of the deadline and bring the products up to standard.

2. Gamble on the first runs and hope the products don't fail.

3. Inform the customer of the problem and let the customer make the decision.

Surf the Net

1. *Languages on the Web.* According to a recent Fortune Global 500 listing, Hewlett-Packard was ranked as the 47th largest company in the world based on sales revenues. Visit Hewlett-Packard's home page at www.hp.com to see how this multinational company provides information for its many customers throughout the world. Check out the links to its pages for countries in the Americas, Asia, and Europe. Compare how other Global 500 companies in the computers and office equipment industry provide access to information for their non-English-speaking customers, for example, IBM (www.ibm.com) and Fujitsu (www.fujitsu.com). Choose the Web site you thought was most effective in providing multilanguage access and explain your choice.

2. *Exchange Rates.* Visit a Web site, such as the CNN Financial Network listed below, to find currency exchange rates.

   http://cnnfn.com/markets/currencies

   If the Web site provides a currency converter, determine how much $100 in U.S. currency is worth in each of the following currencies:

Chilean Peso

Japanese Yen

Euro

United Kingdom Pound

If no currency converter is available, simply list the exchange rate per U.S. dollar for each of the above currencies.

3. *The Multinational Corporation.* To become more knowledgeable about the largest companies in the world, check out the Fortune Global 500 listing available at http://pathfinder.com/fortune/global500/500list.html

   Answer the following questions:
   (a) What countries are represented in the top ten?
   (b) Which country has the most companies represented in the top ten?
   (c) Select three industries of interest to you and identify the top three companies and their home countries in each industry.
   (d) After looking over the information available at this Web site, identify one fact that was particularly interesting to you.

Case for Critical Analysis

Unocal Corporation

Unocal Corporation seems an unlikely candidate for a high-risk global rampage. Consumers everywhere recognize the ubiquitous 76 logo of this quintessential California oil company. They know it as the nation's 11th largest petroleum retailer, with a prestigious downtown headquarters and important role as a Los Angeles civic booster. Casting aside its reputation as a conservative company with tightly defined domestic markets and focused petroleum interests in California, Unocal has rapidly transformed itself into an international company with major investments in some of the world's least-developed economies. It has also become a prominent topic among political activists, human-rights groups, and President Clinton's foreign policy team. Some observers say that Unocal will become a casualty of its high-risk policies.

Immediately after becoming chairman of Unocal in 1995, Roger Beach began to sell off domestic retail assets and eliminate exploration and refining activities in the United States. Resources shifted to unlikely places where few other major oil producers had risked operations—places such as Myanmar (more commonly known as Burma), Turkmenistan, Uzbekistan, and the strife-ridden Balkans. Beach turned up the heat on company investments in Indonesian oil fields, launched full-service energy subsidiaries through government alliances in Thailand, broadened holdings in Malaysia, and began negotiations for an integrated refining/retailing enterprise in Pakistan. Nearly 40 percent of Unocal's exploration and extraction budget was thrown into these emerging markets, much of it pinpointed for very high risk locations in the former Soviet republics and the Persian subcontinent.

Why take these risks? Beach answers that Unocal was unable to compete head-to-head with the oil industry giants for capital markets and decided to create an extremely attractive strategic package of full-service energy production in countries grasping to develop infrastructure. "What every government likes about Unocal's strategy is one-stop shopping; one group able to take the whole project from development to the marketing end," Beach said. "We have become partners in their development and as important to them as they are to us." The Unocal strategy defies normal industry trends based on distributing huge capital investments to tie up oil reserves and mineral rights, then cutting deals for operations. Instead, Unocal comes in the front door with packaged energy services ranging from turning the first spade of dirt on exploration to delivering power to the end user, and that proposal includes oil, gas, or electric power generation.

Beach sees far less risk than industry analysts perceive in the emerging markets. The dangers of war, political upheaval, and currency fluctuations are clear and present, yet the company says it has hedged against these threats by diversifying investments. By 2000, it intends to have reached its goal of establishing nearly 80 percent of its exploration and production capabilities in these underdeveloped areas, and by the end of 1996, it had almost totally abandoned domestic exploration, having sold off nearly $3 billion in assets and oil-field holdings in California. However, according to Beach, success will depend on creating a globally managed company capable of understanding and participating in foreign-market environments. Consequently, in 1996, he initiated a major transformation in Unocal's management systems, beginning by relocating its headquarters from its stately downtown offices to a small, highly efficient suite near the Los Angeles International Airport. Mid-level managers were either repositioned in regional offices, such as Singapore, Istanbul, or Jakarta, or they left the company. The executive core, which had been distinctly Los Angeles in character, gained a multicultural character, representing Eastern European and Asian group alliances. Subsidiaries in Jakarta, Thailand, and Burma took on local names and corporate identities, shedding their American profiles, and Unocal's many foreign alliances have made it part of the communities in which it operates.

In Thailand, Unocal has worked on the country's privatization plan to convert its Petroleum Authority of Thailand (PTT) operations into privately owned and operated international oil services. Unocal and the PTT have begun to build pipelines in the Gulf of Thailand linking Unocal's hydrocarbon fields in the nation's rugged peninsula, and a joint venture in Malaysia has begun to open regional energy markets from Burma to the Philippines. Surface evaluations have hailed this consortium as a master stroke of strategy; however, related activities have exposed Unocal to strong criticism. Unocal became the largest single U.S. investor in Burma as part of the expansion, but Burma's military government has languished in political and economic isolation

as a result of U.S. legislation aimed at boycotting the country for its unacceptable human-rights practices. Political activists in more than a dozen U.S. states have won passage of legislation barring imports from Burma and outlawing private investments there by U.S. firms. Municipal governments in five states have passed boycott laws as well, and Unocal, together with PepsiCo and several other American companies operating in Burma, have become major targets for international pressure groups. PepsiCo bowed to the pressure and recently moved out of Burma, but Unocal has flatly refused to budge.

The company's insistence on remaining in Burma, however, is not a vote in support of the country's human-rights record. Indeed, Unocal would find it difficult to withdraw, because it has formed an equity agreement with the giant French petrochemical company Total, which also has substantial pipeline investments with Unocal in the Persian Gulf and southern Asia. Unocal's contracts with Total make it a de facto partner of the French government. Moreover, Unocal has invested in public and private interests in Burma that spread to five other major Southeast Asian states. But a Unocal representative cites the importance of the company's role in helping the nation's development. "To withdraw and isolate Burma would have no effect. Questionable human-rights leadership and political practices would continue and perhaps proliferate," she said. "On the other hand, our strength and the fact that we can provide meaningful jobs and ethical international business encourages changes for the good. Even if every American firm vacated, firms from other nations would welcome the chance to develop Burma without American competition."

That position doesn't relieve the political or financial risk to Unocal. Ethics and U.S. policies aside, Burma lacks a strong track record for keeping its promises. As a closed military state, self-isolated for ideological reasons since the end of World War II, it has few friends anywhere in the world. For years, it was linked to the Soviet Union for aid and military support, and Burma backed insurgent forces in several neighboring civil conflicts. These situations did not endear the government to potential regional economic allies. However, the country is strategically positioned within the Southeast Asian theater, and it has attracted consideration, with much controversy, for membership in ASEAN.

Unocal holds a rather exposed position in the country, as it does in Uzbekistan, Turkmenistan, and the Balkans. An American company without the legal or political support of its home government can expect little help should the host government decide to freeze its assets, bar currency repatriation, or resort to outright expropriation. Meanwhile, Unocal has tied up several billion dollars in the region while maintaining no safety net at home. Indeed, it faces potentially costly threats from home, and if the company is pushed to the wall by legislation, the chairman says, he will take Unocal out of U.S. control.

Questions

1. What market entry strategies has Unocal used, based on the activities described in the case? Would you classify Unocal as a multinational corporation (MNC)? Why or why not?

2. Identify and discuss the various types of risks faced by Unocal in emerging markets (consider the economic,

legal-political, and sociocultural environment). Which risks seem most threatening to the company?

3. What do you think of the Unocal representative's statement that "to withdraw and isolate Burma would have no effect" regarding that country's poor human-rights record? Do you believe U.S. companies should stay in such countries in the hope of improving the ethical climate? Discuss.

SOURCE: David H. Holt, "Unocal Corporation," from *International Management: Text and Cases,* pp. 143–145, Copyright 1998 by Harcourt, Inc., reprinted by permission of the publisher.

Endnotes

1 "Van @ttack," *The Economist,* Sept. 18, 1999, pp. 69–70.

2 Jonathan Friedland and Louise Lee, "The Wal-Mart Way Sometimes Gets Lost in Translation Overseas," The *Wall Street Journal,* October 8, 1997, pp. A1, A12.

3 Murray Weidenbaum, "American Isolationism versus the Global Economy," in *International Business 97/98, Annual Editions,* Fred Maidment, ed. (Guilford, Conn.: Dushkin Publishing Group, 1997), pp. 12–15.

4 Nilly Ostro-Landau and Hugh D. Menzies, "The New World Economics Order," in *International Business 97/98, Annual Editions,* Fred Maidment, ed. (Guilford, Conn.: Dushkin Publishing Group, 1997), pp. 24–30; and Weidenbaum, "American Isolationism versus the Global Economy."

5 Joseph B. White, "There Are No German or U.S. Companies, Only Successful Ones," The *Wall Street Journal,* May 7, 1998, p. A1.

6 Pete Engardio, with Robert D. Hof, Elisabeth Malkin, Neil Gross, and Karen Lowry Miller, "High-Tech Jobs All Over the Map," *Business Week/21st Century Capitalism,* November 18, 1994, pp. 112–117.

7 Raju Narisetti and Jonathan Friedland, "Diaper Wars of P&G and Kimberly-Clark Now

Heat Up in Brazil," The *Wall Street Journal,* June 4, 1997.

8 Richard L. Daft, *Management,* 3d ed. (Fort Worth, Texas: The Dryden Press, 1994), p. 80; James L. Gibson, John M. Ivancevich, and James H. Donnelly, Jr., *Organizations,* 8th ed. (Burr Ridge, Ill.: Irwin, 1994), pp. 54–55.

9 Nancy J. Adler, *International Dimensions of Organizational Behavior* (Boston: PWS-Kent, 1991), pp. 7–8.

10 Eric Matson, "How to Globalize Yourself," *Fast Company,* April–May 1997, pp. 133–139; and Gunnar Beeth, "Multicultural Managers Wanted," *Management Review,* May 1997, pp. 17–21.

11 Holstein et al., "The Stateless Corporation"; and John A. Byrne and Kathleen Kerwin, with Amy Cortese and Paula Dwyer, "Borderless Management," *Business Week,* May 23, 1994, pp. 24–26.

12 Carla Rapoport, with Justin Martin, "Retailers Go Global," *Fortune,* February 20, 1995, pp. 102–108.

13 "Slogans Often Lose Something in Translation," *The New Mexican,* July 3, 1994, pp. F1, F2.

14 Louis S. Richman, "Global Growth Is on a Tear," in *International Business 97/98, Annual Editions,* Fred Maidment, ed. (Guilford, Conn.: Dushkin Publishing Group, 1997), pp. 6–11.

15 Thomas J. Suddes, "Fantastic Voyage," *Success,* October 1997, pp. 46–48.

16 Ronald Henkoff, "Asia: Why Business Is Still Bullish," *Fortune,* October 27, 1997, pp. 139–142.

17 Jennifer Farley, "Negotiating the Border," *American Way,* July 1, 1994, pp. 48–51.

18 Kathleen Deveny, "McWorld?" *Business Week,* October 13, 1986, pp. 78–86; and Andrew E. Serwer, "McDonald's Conquers the World," *Fortune,* October 17, 1994, pp. 103–116.

19 Bruce Kogut, "Designing Global Strategies: Profiting from Operational Flexibility," *Sloan Management Review* 27 (Fall 1985), pp. 27–38.

20 Mark Fitzpatrick, "The Definition and Assessment of Political Risk in International Business: A Review of the Literature," *Academy of Management Review* 8 (1983), pp. 249–254.

21 Frederick Stapenhurst, "A Political Risk Analysis in North American Multinationals: An Empirical Review and Assessment," *The International Executive,* March–April, 1995, pp. 127–145.

22 Don Sull, Matthew Hayward, and Gita Piramal, "Spinning Steel into Gold: The Case of Ispat Steel International NV," *European Business Journal,* Vol. 17 (4), Aug. 1999, pp. 368–381.

23 Michael R. Czinkota, Ilkka A. Ronkainen, Michael H. Moffett, and Eugene O. Moynihan, *Global Business* (Fort Worth, Texas: The Dryden Press, 1995).

24 Laura B. Pincus and James A. Belohlav, "Legal Issues in Multinational Business: To Play the Game, You Have to Know the Rules," *Academy of Management Executive* 10 (3) (1996), pp. 52–61; and Rick Borelli, "A Worldwide Language TRAP," *Management Review,* October 1997, pp. 52–54.

25 Ed Fishbein, "Kultur Klash," *World Trade,* March 1995, pp. 53–56.

26 Czinkota et al., *Global Business,* 151; and Robert D. Gatewood, Robert R. Taylor, and O. C. Ferrell, *Management* (Burr Ridge, Ill.: Irwin, 1995), pp. 131–132.

27 Salil S. Pitroda, "From GATT to WTO: The Institutionalization of World Trade," *Harvard International Review,* Spring 1995, pp. 46–47, 66–67; and David H. Holt, *International Management: Text and Cases* (Fort Worth, Texas: The Dryden Press, 1998).

28 Mark M. Nelson, "Extra Accommodations," The *Wall Street Journal,* September 30, 1994, pp. R13, R14.

29 Thane Peterson, "The Euro," *Business Week,* April 27, 1998, pp. 90–94.

30 Lynda Radosevich, "New Money," *CIO Enterprise,* Section 2, April 15, 1998, pp. 54–58.

31 Barbara Rudolph, "Megamarket," *Time,* August 10, 1992, pp. 43–44.

32 Amy Barrett, "It's a Small (Business) World," *Business Week,* April 17, 1995, pp. 96–101.

33 Robert S. Greenberger, "As U.S. Exports Rise, More Workers Benefit and Favor Free Trade," The *Wall Street Journal,* September 10, 1997, pp. A1, A10.

34 Amy Borrus, "A Free-Trade Milestone, with Many More Miles to Go," *Business Week,* August 24, 1992, pp. 30–31.

35 Keith Bradsher, "As Global Talks Stall, Regional Trade Pacts Multiply," *The New York Times,* August 23, 1992, p. F5.

36 Geert Hofstede, "The Cultural Relativity of the Quality of Life Concept," *Academy of Management Review* 9 (1984), pp. 389–398.

37 Ellen F. Jackofsky, John W. Slocum, Jr., and Sara J. McQuaid, "Cultural Values and the CEO: Alluring Companions?" *Academy of Management Executive* 2 (1988), pp. 39–49.

38 Orla Sheehan, "Managing a Multinational Corporation: Tomorrow's Decision Makers Speak Out," *Fortune,* August 24, 1992, p. 233.

39 Richard Gibson and Matt Moffett, "Why You Won't Find Any Egg McMuffins for Breakfast in Brazil," The *Wall Street Journal,* October 23, 1997, pp. A1, A8.

40 Douglas A. Blackmon, "A Factory in Alabama is the Merger in Microcosm," The *Wall Street Journal,* May 8, 1998, p. B1; and Justin Martin, "Mercedes: Made in Alabama," *Fortune,* July 7, 1997, pp. 150–158.

41 Engardio et al., "High-Tech Jobs All Over the Map."

42 Gary Jacobson, "The Boom on Mexico's Border," *Management Review* (July 1988), pp. 21–25.

43 Jean Kerr, "Export Strategies," *Small Business Reports* (May 1989), pp. 20–25.

44 Greenberger, "As U.S. Exports Rise, More Workers Benefit."

45 Karen Lowry Miller, with Bill Javetski, Peggy Simpson, and Tim Smart, "Europe: The Push East," *Business Week,* November 7, 1994, pp. 48–49.

46 Robert T. Moran and John R. Riesenberger, *The Global Challenge* (London: McGraw-Hill, 1994), p. 260.

47 Gibson et al., *Organizations,* p. 83.

48 Joann S. Lublin, "Younger Managers Learn Global Skills," The *Wall Street Journal,* March 31, 1992, p. B1.

49 Moran and Riesenberger, *The Global Challenge,* pp. 251–262.

50 Valerie Frazee, "Keeping Up on Chinese Culture," *Global Workforce,* October 1996, pp. 16–17.

51 Fons Trompenaars, *Riding the Waves of Culture: Understanding Diversity in Global Business* (Burr Ridge, Ill.: Irwin, 1994).

52 Randall S. Schuler, Susan E. Jackson, Ellen Jackofsky, and John W. Slocum, Jr., "Managing Human Resources in Mexico: A Cultural Understanding," *Business Horizons,* May–June 1996, pp. 55–61.

53 Caudron, "Lessons from HR Overseas."

54 Moran and Riesenberger, *The Global Challenge,* p. 255; and Caudron, "Lessons from HR Overseas."

55 Brenton R. Schlender, "Matsushita Shows How to Go Global," *Fortune,* July 11, 1994, pp. 159–166.

56 Indochinese Materials Center.

4

Managerial Ethics and Corporate Social Responsibility

LEARNING OBJECTIVES

After studying this chapter, you should be able to:

- Define ethics and explain how ethical behavior relates to behavior governed by law and free choice

- Explain the utilitarian, individualism, moral-rights, and justice approaches for evaluating ethical behavior

- Describe how both individual and organizational factors shape ethical decision making

- Define corporate social responsibility and how to evaluate it along with economic, legal, ethical, and discretionary criteria

- Describe four corporate responses to social demands

- Explain the concept of stakeholder and identify important stakeholders for organizations

- Describe structures that managers can use to improve the ethics of their organizations and social responsiveness

MANAGEMENT PROBLEM

WHAT HAPPENS WHEN technology

Chapter

4

outstrips legal contracts? Freelance writers

Stewart Wolpin, Ron Goldberg, and Mark Fleischmann were tired of

publications republishing their articles on the Web without compensation. When

the authors had written the articles, their contracts had not covered Internet usage. They

didn't question this because none of them knew their work might become content in a Webzine.

In order to retaliate against those who unfairly re-used their materials, the three decided to launch

their own Web site, e/Town, to offer news, research, and opinionated reviews of electronics equipment—

VCRs, pagers, DVD players, camcorders, and rear-projection TVs—which they hoped would be a cross between

• If you were Wolpin, Goldberg, or Fleischmann, what would you do? Do you think it is ethical to accept

corporate sponsorship on a site like e/Town? Would you change your policy to include corporate sponsorship

if that meant you could survive? Are there other means of generating enough income to remain solvent?[1]

"Siskel & Ebert" and "Car Talk." When giving recommendations, they knew they had to be completely

reliable and show absolutely no favoritism toward any company. So, they decided to reject corporate

sponsorship of the site, remain "pure," and avoid any kind of unethical temptations or appearances

that might give the impression of preferential reviews or treatment of "sponsored" products.

By early 1999, they had indeed become known as a reliable source of information,

installed a buyer's guide (to search past articles), and had an

enormously successful consumer-electronics message board.

But when they looked at their own bank

accounts and their meager freelance salaries, they knew that neither the design awards they were winning nor the heavy traffic of 350,000 hits a month would ensure their success, or even survival.

The situation at e/Town illustrates how difficult ethical issues can be and symbolizes the growing importance of discussing ethics and social responsibility. Corporations are rushing to adopt codes of ethics and develop socially responsible policies: Ethics consultants are doing a land-office business. Unfortunately, the trend is necessary. In recent years, numerous companies, including Prudential Insurance, Archer-Daniels-Midland, and Centennial Technology, have been charged with major breaches of ethical or legal standards, including price fixing and insider trading. By the end of 1999, Columbia/HCA, the largest hospital company in the United States, was still under federal investigation for possibly inflating the seriousness of patient illnesses to get larger Medicare and Medicaid payments. It comes as no surprise that in a Gallup poll asking about the perceived trustworthiness of six American institutions, only the U.S. government scored lower.[2]

On the other hand, there is positive news to report. Breadsmith's franchisees provide bread for charity events and disaster victims in their areas, donate all leftovers to food banks, and sponsor at least four charity events a year. Glaxo Wellcome has proposed a plan to slash the price of the AIDS drug AZT for pregnant women in developing nations by as much as 75 percent. Several major manufacturers, including DuPont, Electrolux, S. C. Johnson, and British Petroleum, are embracing environmental goals and developing eco-friendly products. And the Eastman Kodak Company took an unprecedented step several years ago by tying a percentage of a manager's pay to factors such as how well he or she treats employees.[3]

This chapter expands on the ideas about environment, corporate culture, and the international environment discussed in Chapters 2 and 3. It focuses on specific ethical values and examines corporate relationships and social responsibility. Also discussed are fundamental approaches that help managers think through ethical issues and better understand ethical approaches that build a solid foundation for decision making.

The Gap Inc. AIDS Walk reflects the company's commitment to a social responsibility approach to the communities in which it does business. Gap Inc. encourages employees to become involved in volunteer activities, and its Community Action Program, which allows headquarters employees to take paid time off to do so, has involved nearly half of all eligible workers. Gap Inc. also gives approximately 1 percent of pretax profits to organizations addressing social issues, strengthening the company's reputation as a socially responsible business.

may benefit the organization as a whole but reduce the individual freedom of employees? Or should products that fail to meet tough Food and Drug Administration (FDA) standards be exported to other countries where government standards are lower, which would benefit the company but potentially harm world citizens? Sometimes ethical decisions entail a conflict between two groups. For example, should the potential for local health problems resulting from the effluents of a company take precedence over the jobs it creates as the town's leading employer?

Managers faced with these kinds of tough ethical choices often benefit from a normative approach—one based on norms and values—to guide their decision making. Normative ethics uses several approaches to describe values for guiding ethical decision making. Four of these that are relevant to managers are the utilitarian approach, individualism approach, moral-rights approach, and justice approach.[8]

UTILITARIAN APPROACH

The **utilitarian approach,** espoused by the nineteenth-century philosophers Jeremy Bentham and John Stuart Mill, holds that moral behavior produces the greatest good for the greatest number. Under this approach, a decision maker is expected to consider the effect of each decision alternative on all parties and select the one that optimizes the satisfaction for the greatest number of people. Because actual computations can be very complex, simplifying them is considered appropriate. For example, a simple economic frame of reference could be used by calculating dollar costs and dollar benefits. Also, a decision could be made that considers only the people who are directly affected by the decision, not those who are indirectly affected. When GM chose to continue operations at its Arlington, Texas, plant while shutting down its Ypsilanti, Michigan, plant, managers justified the decision as producing the greater good for the corporation as a whole. The utilitarian ethic is cited as the basis for the recent trend among companies to police employee personal habits such as alcohol and tobacco consumption on the job, and in some cases after hours as well, because such behavior affects the entire workplace.[9]

The utilitarian ethic was the basis for the state of Oregon's decision to extend Medicaid to 400,000 previously ineligible recipients by refusing to pay for high-cost, high-risk procedures such as liver transplants and bone-marrow transplants. Although a few people needing these procedures have died because the state would not pay, many people have benefited from medical services they would otherwise have had to go without.[10] Critics of the utilitarian ethic fear a developing tendency toward a "Big Brother" approach and question whether the common good is squeezing the life out of the individual. Critics also claim that the Oregon decision does not fully take into account the concept of justice toward the unfortunate victims of life-threatening diseases.[11]

INDIVIDUALISM APPROACH

The **individualism approach** contends that acts are moral when they promote the individual's best long-term interests. Individual self-direction is paramount, and external forces that restrict self-direction should be severely limited.[12] Individuals calculate the best long-term advantage to themselves as a measure of a decision's goodness. The action that is intended to produce a greater ratio of good to bad for the individual compared with other alternatives is the right one to perform. In theory, with everyone pursuing self-direction, the greater good is ultimately served because people learn to accommodate each other in their own long-term interest. Individualism is believed to lead to honesty and integrity because that works best in the long run. Lying and cheating for immediate self-interest just causes business associates to lie and cheat in return. Thus, individualism ultimately leads to behavior toward others that fits standards of behavior people want toward themselves.[13] One value of understanding this approach is to recognize short-term variations if they are proposed. People might argue for short-term self-interest based on individualism, but that misses the point. Because individualism is easily misinterpreted to support immediate

utilitarian approach
The ethical concept that moral behaviors produce the greatest good for the greatest number

individualism approach
The ethical concept that acts are moral when they promote the individual's best long-term interests, which ultimately leads to the greater good

self-gain, it is not popular in the highly organized and group-oriented society of today. Individualism is closest to the domain of free choice (see Exhibit 4.1).

MORAL-RIGHTS APPROACH

The **moral-rights approach** asserts that human beings have fundamental rights and liberties that cannot be taken away by an individual's decision. Thus an ethically correct decision is one that best maintains the rights of those people affected by it.

Moral rights that could be considered during decision making are

1. *The right of free consent.* Individuals are to be treated only as they knowingly and freely consent to be treated.

2. *The right to privacy.* Individuals can choose to do as they please away from work and have control of information about their private life.

3. *The right of freedom of conscience.* Individuals may refrain from carrying out any order that violates their moral or religious norms.

4. *The right of free speech.* Individuals may criticize truthfully the ethics or legality of actions of others.

5. *The right to due process.* Individuals have a right to an impartial hearing and fair treatment.

6. *The right to life and safety.* Individuals have a right to live without endangerment or violation of their health and safety.

To make ethical decisions, managers need to avoid interfering with the fundamental rights of others. Thus a decision to eavesdrop on employees violates their right to privacy. Sexual harassment is unethical because it violates the right to freedom of conscience. The right of free speech would support whistleblowers who call attention to illegal or inappropriate actions within a company.

JUSTICE APPROACH

The **justice approach** holds that moral decisions must be based on standards of equity, fairness, and impartiality. Three types of justice should be of concern to managers. **Distributive justice** requires that different treatment of people not be based on arbitrary characteristics. Individuals who are similar in respects relevant to a decision should be treated similarly. Thus men and women should not receive different salaries if they are performing the same job. However, people who differ in a substantive way, such as job skills or job responsibility, can be treated differently

moral-rights approach
The ethical concept that moral decisions are those that best maintain the rights of those people affected by them

justice approach
The ethical concept that moral decisions must be based on standards of equity, fairness, and impartiality

distributive justice
The concept that different treatment of people should not be based on arbitrary characteristics; in cases of substantive differences, people can be treated differently in proportion to the differences among them

Critics say the forest products industry has behaved unethically for years, according to the moral-rights approach, by violating the rights to life and safety of the employees. At Georgia Pacific, the Atlanta-based company with more than 47,000 employees, you weren't considered a "mill guy" unless you were missing a few fingers. Due to a corporate makeover, safety now comes first. By changing attitudes and behavior regarding safety, G-P now records injuries of 0.7 per 100 workers annually, which according to OSHA is about one-third the injury rate at the average bank.

in proportion to the differences in skills or responsibility among them. This difference should have a clear relationship to organizational goals and tasks.

Procedural justice requires that rules be administered fairly. Rules should be clearly stated and be consistently and impartially enforced. **Compensatory justice** argues that individuals should be compensated for the cost of their injuries by the party responsible. Moreover, individuals should not be held responsible for matters over which they have no control.

The justice approach is closest to the thinking underlying the domain of law, because it assumes that justice is applied through rules and regulations. This theory does not require complex calculations such as those demanded by a utilitarian approach, nor does it justify self-interest as the individualism approach does. Managers are expected to define attributes on which different treatment of employees is acceptable. Questions such as how minority workers should be compensated for past discrimination are extremely difficult. However, this approach does justify as ethical behavior efforts to correct past wrongs, playing fair under the rules, and insisting on job-relevant differences as the basis for different levels of pay or promotion opportunities. Most of the laws guiding human resource management (Chapter 9) are based on the justice approach.

These are general principles that managers can recognize as useful in making ethical decisions. However, understanding the approaches is only a first step; managers still have to consider how to apply them.[14] The challenge of applying ethical approaches is illustrated by decisions facing companies in the insurance industry.

NORTHWESTERN MUTUAL LIFE INSURANCE COMPANY
www.nml.com

When 72-year-old Pok Dong Kim, a Korean-born U.S. citizen, applied for a $10,000 life insurance policy, she and her family never expected the application to be rejected. Yet, a month later, a letter arrived from Northwestern Mutual Life Insurance Co. stating that Kim "did not meet our language requirements for the ability to understand English." Although the company has now dropped the requirement, the family has sued Northwestern for national-origin discrimination.

Insurance companies increasingly are coming under attack for alleged discrimination against minorities and women. Companies often have U.S. citizens with foreign surnames investigated closely, arguing that they could later sue their way out of insurance contracts on grounds that they didn't understand English. In addition, GEICO contends that auto accident rates are 35 percent higher for noncitizens, and until recently the company sold insurance only to U.S. citizens. Insurance companies have also turned down applicants with histories of emergency room visits symptomatic of domestic abuse, prompting outcry from women's organizations.

The companies say they are just making careful business decisions in the best interest of their clients. A manager at GEICO responded to the recent ruling against them by saying, "Now rates have to go up for everybody." Kenney Shipley of the Florida Insurance Department believes there often may be valid reasons for rejecting applications based on race or gender issues. "But," he adds, "we as a society have to say whether or not it's acceptable."[15] ■

Consider for a moment how you think the various ethics approaches support or discredit the actions of insurance companies regarding women and minorities.

■ FACTORS AFFECTING ETHICAL CHOICES

When managers are accused of lying, cheating, or stealing, the blame is usually placed on the individual or on the company situation. Most people believe that individuals make ethical choices because of individual integrity, which is true, but it is not the whole story. Ethical or unethical business practices usually

procedural justice
The concept that rules should be clearly stated and consistently and impartially enforced

compensatory justice
The concept that individuals should be compensated for the cost of their injuries by the party responsible and also that individuals should not be held responsible for matters over which they have no control

reflect the values, attitudes, beliefs, and behavior patterns of the organizational culture; thus, ethics is as much an organizational as a personal issue.[16] Let's examine how both the manager and the organization shape ethical decision making.[17]

THE MANAGER

Managers bring specific personality and behavioral traits to the job. Personal needs, family influence, and religious background all shape a manager's value system. Specific personality characteristics, such as ego strength, self-confidence, and a strong sense of independence, may enable managers to make ethical decisions.

One person whose self-confidence has propelled his business hopes to ultimately help people lead more moral lives is Rabbi Presler, explained in the example below.

TORAH-FAX

Forget the idea of a quiet religious life. "The clergy today are swamped," similar to an overburdened corporate CEO, says Rabbi Berhard Presler, founder of Torah-Fax, a research and support operation that ministers to over 400 rabbis, representing about 15 percent of all U.S. Jewish congregations. For $400 per year, subscribers get twice-monthly sermons tied to the Hebrew Bible, plus two to three additional news-driven sermons drawn from Presler's network of authors and scholars. Presler offers more personal service as well, using his 50,000-item database. Need a blessing for a set of twins? Just call 800-TORAH-FX.

Some people don't like the idea of a technology-driven rabbi, from whom they want originality, feeling, and his own beliefs. Presler agrees and says the sermons are meant to be resource tools and should not be read word-for-word.

He must be doing something right, because Torah-Fax is growing by 75 subscribers a year, going to 35 states and 12 foreign countries, and its profitable revenue base tops $200,000 per year. But Presler has his eyes on a new market: Christian clergy, to whom he is offering his newest project, "Bible-Fax," aimed at the 400,000 churches in this country. Because the message of sermons is often universal, he has commis-

Exhibit 4.2

THREE LEVELS OF PERSONAL
MORAL DEVELOPMENT

Level 1: Preconventional

Follows rules to avoid punishment. Acts in own interest. Obedience for its own sake.

Level 2: Conventional

Lives up to expectations of others. Fulfills duties and obligations of social system. Upholds laws.

Level 3: Postconventional

Follows self-chosen principles of justice and right. Aware that people hold different values and seeks creative solutions to ethical dilemmas. Balances concern for individual with concern for common good.

Leadership Style:	Autocratic/coercive	Guiding/encouraging, team oriented	Transforming, or servant leadership
Employee Behavior:	Task accomplishment	Work group collaboration	Empowered employees, full participation

SOURCES: Based on L. Kohlberg, "Moral Stages and Moralization: The Cognitive-Developmental Approach," in *Moral Development and Behavior: Theory, Research, and Social Issues*, ed. T. Lickona (New York: Holt, Rinehart, and Winston, 1976) 31–53; and Jill W. Graham, "Leadership, Moral Development and Citizenship Behavior," *Business Ethics Quarterly* 5 (1) (January 1995), 43–54.

sioned an interfaith group to retool his database into a more Christian perspective. Even with the competition of over a dozen similar Christian-based services, Presler's optimism keeps him looking for common ground. It's a proof of his own faith.[18] ■

One important personal trait is the stage of moral development.[19] A simplified version of one model of personal moral development is shown in Exhibit 4.2. At the *preconventional level,* individuals are concerned with external rewards and punishments, and they obey authority to avoid detrimental personal consequences. In an organizational context, this level may be associated with managers who use an autocratic or coercive leadership style, with employees oriented toward dependable accomplishment of specific tasks. At level two, called the *conventional level,* people learn to conform to the expectations of good behavior as defined by colleagues, family, friends, and society. Meeting social and interpersonal obligations is important. Work group collaboration is the preferred manner for accomplishment of organizational goals, and managers use a leadership style that encourages interpersonal relationships and cooperation. At the *postconventional*, or *principled level,* individuals are guided by an internal set of values and standards and will even disobey rules or laws that violate these principles. Internal values become more important than the expectations of significant others. For example, when the USS *Indianapolis* sank after being torpedoed during World War II, one Navy pilot disobeyed orders and risked his life to save men who were being picked off by sharks. The pilot was operating from the highest level of moral development in attempting the rescue despite a direct order from superiors. When managers operate from this highest level of development, they use transformative or servant leadership, focusing on the needs of followers and encouraging others to think for themselves and to engage in higher levels of moral reasoning. Employees are empowered and given opportunities for constructive participation in governance of the organization.

The great majority of managers operate at level two. A few have not advanced beyond level one. Only about 20 percent of American adults reach the level-three stage of moral development. People at level three are able to act in an independent, ethical manner regardless of expectations from others inside or outside the organization. Managers at level three of moral development will make ethical decisions whatever the organizational consequences for them. Focus on Ethics lists some general guidelines to follow for making ethical decisions.

One interesting study indicates that most researchers have failed to account for the different ways in which women view social reality and develop psychologically, and thus consistently have classified women as being stuck at lower levels of development. Researcher Carol Gilligan has suggested that the moral domain be enlarged to include responsibility and care in relationships. Women may, in general, perceive moral complexities more astutely than men and make moral decisions based not on a set of absolute rights and wrongs but on principles of not causing harm to others.[20] Women's sense of integrity seems to be entwined with an ethic of care; hence, they may be ideally suited for the servant leadership needed in today's organizations.

One reason higher levels of ethical conduct are increasingly important is the impact of globalization on organizational ethics and corporate culture. As discussed in Chapter 3, globalization has complicated ethical issues for today's managers. American managers need to develop sensitivity and openness to other systems, as well as mature ethical judgment to work out differences. For example, although tolerance for bribery is waning, it is still an accepted way of doing business in many countries. Foreign managers sometimes resent the "holier-than-thou" attitudes of Americans and the stereotypical belief that all foreign managers are corrupt.[21] It is not always easy to resolve international issues. There are, however, increasing calls for the development of global standards for ethical business conduct, which may help managers negotiate the difficult terrain of international ethics. Organizations such as the Caux Round Table are trying to "identify the transcultural values that we can all salute."[22]

THE ORGANIZATION

The values adopted within the organization are important, especially when we understand that most people are at the level-two stage of moral development, which means they believe their duty is to fulfill obligations and expectations of others. Research has shown that the values of an organization or department strongly influence employee behavior and decision making.[23] In particular, corporate culture serves to let employees know what beliefs and behaviors the company supports and those it will not tolerate. For example, an investigation of thefts and kickbacks in the oil business found that the cause was the historical acceptance of thefts and kickbacks. Employees were socialized into those values and adopted them as

appropriate. In most companies, employees believe that if they do not go along with the ethical values expressed, their jobs will be in jeopardy or they will not fit in.[24]

Culture can be examined to see the kinds of ethical signals given to employees. Exhibit 4.3 indicates questions to ask to understand the cultural system. Heroes provide role models that can either support or refute ethical decision making. Founder Sam Walton stood for integrity at Wal-Mart, and his values are ingrained in the organizational culture. With respect to company rituals, high ethical standards are affirmed and communicated through public awards and ceremonies. Myths and stories can reinforce heroic ethical behavior. For example, a story at Johnson & Johnson describes its reaction to the cyanide poisoning of

FOCUS ON Ethics

GUIDELINES FOR ETHICAL DECISION MAKING

If Mike Wallace and a "60 Minutes" crew were waiting on your doorstep one morning, would you feel comfortable justifying your actions to the camera? One young manager, when confronted with ethical dilemmas, gives them the "60 Minutes" test. Others say they use such criteria as whether they would be proud to tell their parents or grandparents about their decision or whether they could sleep well at night and face themselves in the mirror in the morning. Managers often rely on their own personal integrity in making ethical decisions. But knowing what to do is not always easy. As a future manager, you will almost surely face ethical dilemmas one day. The following guidelines will not tell you exactly what to do, but, taken in the context of the text discussion, they will help you evaluate the situation more clearly by examining your own values and those of your organization. The answers to these questions will force you to think hard about the social and ethical consequences of your behavior.

1. Is the problem/dilemma really what it appears to be? If you are not sure, find out.

2. Is the action you are considering legal? Ethical? If you are not sure, find out.

3. If you do it, how will you feel about yourself?

4. Do you understand the position of those who oppose the action you are considering? Is it reasonable?

5. Who does the action benefit? Harm? How much? How long?

6. Would you be willing to allow everyone to do what you are considering doing?

7. Have you sought the opinion of others who are knowledgeable on the subject and who would be objective?

8. Would your action be embarrassing to you if it were made known to your family, friends, coworkers, or superiors?

There are no correct answers to these questions. Yet, if you determine that an action is potentially harmful to someone or would be embarrassing to you, or if you do not know the ethical or legal consequences, these guidelines will help you clarify whether the action is socially responsible.

1. Identify the organization's heroes. What values do they represent? Given an ambiguous ethical dilemma, what decision would they make and why?

2. What are some important organizational rituals? How do they encourage or discourage ethical behavior? Who gets the awards, people of integrity or individuals who use unethical methods to attain success?

3. What are the ethical messages sent to new entrants into the organization—must they obey authority at all costs or is questioning authority acceptable or even desirable?

4. Does analysis of organizational stories and myths reveal individuals who stand up for what's right, or is conformity the valued characteristic? Do people get fired or promoted in these stories?

5. Does language exist for discussing ethical concerns? Is this language routinely incorporated and encouraged in business decision making?

6. What informal socialization processes exist, and what norms for ethical/unethical behavior do they promote?

SOURCES: Linda Klebe Trevino, "A Cultural Perspective on Changing and Developing Organizational Ethics," in *Research in Organizational Change and Development*, ed. R. Woodman and W. Pasmore (Greenwich, Conn.: JAI Press, 1990), 4.

Tylenol capsule users. After seven people in Chicago died, the capsules were removed from the market voluntarily, costing the company more than $100 million. This action was taken against the advice of external agencies—Federal Bureau of Investigation and FDA—but was necessary because of Johnson & Johnson's ethical standards.

Culture is not the only aspect of an organization that influences ethics, but it is a major force because it defines company values. Other aspects of the organization, such as explicit rules and policies, the reward system, the extent to which the company cares for its people, the selection system, emphasis on legal and professional standards, and leadership and decision processes, can also have an impact on ethical values and manager decision making.[25] At Levi Strauss, for example, the selection system is aimed at promoting diversity of background and thought among workers, a set of "corporate aspirations" written by top management is to guide all major decisions, and one-third of a manager's raise can depend on how well he or she toes the values line.[26]

■ WHAT IS SOCIAL RESPONSIBILITY?

Now let's turn to the issue of social responsibility. In one sense, the concept of corporate

social responsibility, like ethics, is easy to understand: it means distinguishing right from wrong and doing right. It means being a good corporate citizen. The formal definition of social responsibility is management's obligation to make choices and take actions that will contribute to the welfare and interests of society as well as the organization.[27] One organization that practices social responsibility is Bagel Works, as described below.

BAGEL WORKS INC.

Each December employees in Keene, New Hampshire's Bagel Works have a contest with winners. But instead of door prizes or bonuses for themselves, the workers vote on selecting five local charities that will win a year's worth of financial support, promotional space at the nine locations, and—of course—free bagels.

Founders Richard French and Jennifer Pearl started the elections because they wanted a business based on values. Other benefits they discovered were improved community relations, enhanced marketing, and increased morale for the 140 employees, who also live with an "open-book management" style and environmental awareness.

It's a great idea, but does it help business? French and Pearl say it does not

social responsibility
The obligation of organization management to make decisions and take actions that will enhance the welfare and interests of society as well as the organization

matter to them, for their intentions were to be socially conscious. Still, they admit the kind of employees they can recruit and retain are higher quality, not a small thing in a tight labor market.

And, even if they don't care about business effects, French admits it does help with sales. Based on responses of shoppers, he says, "it absolutely relates to customer loyalty."[28] ■

As straightforward as the above definition seems, social responsibility can be a difficult concept to grasp, because different people have different beliefs as to which actions improve society's welfare.[29] To make matters worse, social responsibility covers a range of issues, many of which are ambiguous with respect to right or wrong. For example, if a bank deposits the money from a trust fund into a low-interest account for 90 days, from which it makes a substantial profit, has it been unethical? How about two companies engaging in intense competition, such as that between Cleveland Electric Illuminating Co. and Cleveland Public Power? Is it socially responsible for the stronger corporation to drive the weaker one into bankruptcy? Or consider companies such as A. H. Robins, maker of the Dalkon shield; Manville Corporation, maker of asbestos; Eastern Airlines; or Texaco, the oil company, all of which declared bankruptcy—which is perfectly legal—to avoid mounting financial obligations to suppliers, labor unions, or competitors. These examples contain moral, legal, and economic considerations that make socially responsible behavior hard to define. A company's environmental impact must also be taken into consideration.

■ ORGANIZATIONAL STAKEHOLDERS

One reason for the difficulty understanding social responsibility is that managers must confront the question "responsibility to whom?" The organization's environment consists of several sectors in both the task and general environment. From a social responsibility perspective, enlightened organizations view the internal and external environment as a variety of stakeholders.

A **stakeholder** is any group within or outside the organization that has a stake in the organization's performance. Each stakeholder has a different criterion of responsiveness, because it has a different interest in the organization.[30] For example, Wal-Mart uses aggressive bargaining tactics with suppliers so that it is able to provide low prices for customers. Some stakeholders see this as socially responsible behavior because it benefits customers and forces suppliers to be more efficient. Others, however, argue that the aggressive tactics are an abuse of power and may prevent suppliers from even paying their own employees a decent wage.[31]

Investors and shareholders, employees, customers, and suppliers are considered primary stakeholders, without whom the organization cannot survive. Their interests are served by managerial efficiency; that is, by using resources to achieve profits. Employees expect work satisfaction, pay, and good supervision. Customers are concerned with decisions about the quality, safety, and availability of goods and services. When any primary stakeholder group becomes seriously dissatisfied, the organization's viability is threatened.[32]

Other important stakeholders are the government and the community. Most corporations exist only under the proper charter and licenses and operate within the limits of safety laws, environmental protection requirements, and other laws and regulations in the government sector. The community includes local government, the natural and physical environments, and the quality of life provided for residents. Special-interest groups, still another stakeholder, may include trade associations, political action committees, professional associations, and consumerists. Socially responsible organizations consider the effects of their actions upon all stakeholders.

Enlightened corporations invest in a number of philanthropic causes that benefit stakeholders. Marriott Corp. tries to help build healthy communities through its "Pathways to Independence Program," which targets welfare recipients. The program candidates are put through dozens of hours of rigorous training and then "graduated" to a job in the company.[33] This example describes how urban entrepreneur José de Jesus Legaspi is helping to rebuild communities in Los Angeles.

stakeholder
Any group within or outside the organization that has a stake in the organization's performance

HELPING BUILD HEALTHY COMMUNITIES

Marketing consultant and real estate developer José de Jesus Legaspi drives more than 250 miles a day in his Toyota Land Cruiser, stopping frequently to get out and walk the streets of southcentral and east Los Angeles. Some people might see the areas as symbols of urban decay, but Legaspi knows better. Using his knowledge of the Hispanic community and his street smarts, the Mexican-born marketing consultant and real estate developer has brought new life to an amazing variety of retail outlets in the area, including a series of Blockbuster Video stores, a retailer of high-end electronics, and a thriving chain of charbroiled chicken restaurants. In the process, Legaspi has helped to transform decaying urban areas left for dead in the early 1980s.

Legaspi says his vision is built on customer focus, not do-gooder social consciousness. He wants to bring goods and services to the Hispanic community, and he believes Hispanic customers provide loyalty and a strong income base. He is quick to point out that there are more than 22 million Hispanics in the United States—a $220 billion unserved market. Many successful retail chains ask him, "Why won't they buy from us?" The answer "it isn't the competition and it isn't the customer. It's always, always, *you*," says Legaspi. One recent example was Thrifty Drug Stores, which had trouble remaining profitable in areas with high concentrations of Hispanics. Legaspi pointed out that these were areas with many recently arrived immigrants—people who had no bank accounts or credit cards. But, they were bringing in steady paychecks, so he suggested setting up in-store check-cashing machines and allowing customers to pay utility bills there. After the chain followed Legaspi's advice, Thrifty's sales went up by 20 percent.[34] ∎

Today, special interest groups continue to be one of the largest stakeholder concerns that companies encounter. Environmental responsibility has become a primary issue as both business and the public acknowledge the damage that has been done to our natural environment.

■ THE NATURAL ENVIRONMENT

When the first Earth Day celebration was held in 1970, environmentalists were considered by most business leaders to be an extremist fringe group, and few managers felt the need to respond to environmental concerns.[35] Today, the world has changed dramatically. Environmental issues have become a hot topic among business leaders, and large corporations as well as small businesses are targeting marketing efforts to woo the environmentally conscious consumer. Jeffrey Hollender built his small business, Seventh Heaven, by targeting the "green" consumer with environmentally friendly products.[36] Companies such as Aveda and John Paul Mitchell are responding to growing concerns for animal welfare by not testing on animals.

RETRIEVA FABRIC

Next time you take a sip of a soft drink from that plastic two-liter bottle, consider that someday it may end up as a T-shirt on your back. That's thanks to CEO Linda Bavaro, whose Global Green, Inc. made fabric out of plastic thread from the melted bottles.

Linda and her husband started the Norcross, Georgia, company in 1992 when she learned that recycled bottles could be turned into fabric that feels like a soft cotton blend. After much research, she located a mill that could produce it and took out a trademark on Retrieva fiber.

Hunting for large companies that had recycling as a priority and needed fabrics, she made her first call to Disney. Timing was important, for the managers were planning an in-house environmental exposition and they ordered 37,000 T-shirts. Even though the shirts were 15 percent more expensive than regular cotton, the company felt their commitment to the environment warranted it. Because of the shirt's popularity with

As part of its "Project Earth" program, A&P Stores urges customers to take an Earth Pledge and get involved in efforts to improve the natural environment. A&P adopted the turtle and frog, which are disappearing all over the world, as the company's mascots to roll out a new program aimed at building environmental awareness. The company contributes directly to conservation efforts through its Energy Conservation System, which monitors and adjusts operating equipment to ensure maximum energy efficiency.

employees, the next year Disney ordered baseball caps for workers.

Disney ordered more, too. The company was concerned about the wastefulness of its uniforms, which were disposed of in landfills. To be able to produce a uniform made of material that could be recycled again and again was intriguing. Turner Broadcasting System, Inc. gave Global Green more business, by developing a line of retail-sale Retrieva clothes based on its "Captain Planet" TV show.

But trouble brewed in the recycling bin. Some of the bigger competitors of Global Green were not so happy that the small company had the trademark on such a great fiber. Bavaro turned down an offer from a large chemical firm to buy the company, and when subcontracting factories did not follow her orders, she had to fold the company by 1999. Still, she furthered an important trend. Her vision and focus brought her to the attention of political leaders and large nonchemical companies who use her as a top advisor.

Now, thanks to companies like Global Green, those ugly bottles may someday become attractive clothing.[37] ■

The ranks of environmentally conscious consumers are growing, as revealed by a recent study conducted by the New York-based research firm Roper Starch Worldwide, Inc. Roper divides consumers into five categories.[38]

- *True-Blue Greens.* Making up 14 percent of the population, up from 11 percent in 1990, they make buying decisions and change their personal behavior to help the natural environment.

- *Greenback Greens.* These are 6 percent of the population who aren't usually willing to make substantial changes in their purchasing behavior, but they support environmental causes and often vote for proenvironment political candidates.

- *Sprouts.* This group shot up from 26 percent in 1990 to 35 percent and make a few environmentally friendly purchases. Occasionally, they become involved in environmental causes.

- *Grousers.* This is the 13 percent who only grudgingly acknowledge environmental mandates.

- *Basic Browns.* These 32 percent are the least environmentally active and generally do not recycle or support governmental regulation designed to help the natural environment.

Although the apathetic Basic Brown group is large, its ranks are thinning. Most observers agree that the direction of society is toward a greater concern for the natural environment and all living things and that managers must be ready for the next "green" wave.[39] Some companies, including Amoco, Southern California Edison, and Ciba-Geigy, have even begun working collaboratively with environmental groups to determine the best practices for saving the environment. Southern California Edison was intimately involved with the Desert Protection Act, which set aside 7.5 million acres for 70 separate wilderness areas. SCE worked closely with the National Park and Conservation Association, the Sierra Club, and other stakeholders to work out compromises that would preserve the wilderness area without disrupting SCE's existing infrastructure of pipelines, power lines, and telephone lines. Although some adversity still exists between business and environmental groups, there is an increasing emphasis on cooperation.[40] The Natural Step, an international environmental coalition that now has national organizations in Sweden, Australia, the United States, Canada, Japan, and the United Kingdom, is a leader in promoting the idea of cooperation rather than conflict to solve our environmental problems. As founder Karl-Henrik Robèrt describes the process: "First we educate business leaders, politicians, and scientists . . . then we ask them for advice. Instead of telling them what to do, we say, 'How could this be applied in your world?' This sparks creativity and enthusiasm into the process instead of defense mechanisms."[41] One CEO became educated on environmental needs and is now trying to help companies see the light, as described below.

INTERFACE INC.

"I am a plunderer of the earth," said successful CEO Ray Anderson. "Someday people like me may be put in jail." This realization came to him after his previously prosperous company went into a tailspin, putting him in a funk. During this dark time, he came across the book *The Ecology of Commerce,* which described the accumulation of toxins for succeeding generations and rate at which natural resources were being depleted. Images of his carpet factory inhaling hydrocarbons and discharging toxins gave him nightmares about his grandchildren's future. "It was a spear in my chest," he said.

What started from that point was a new mission: zero pollution and zero oil use, using an old model—nature. Since the goal of business is to economize, why not use nature's economical, no-waste method? Great idea, but how to do it? Anderson got Interface employees and consultants enthused and let them figure out solutions, offering bonuses to winners. The results included a new tufting method that used 10 percent less nylon; old fibers "combed" rather than melted for recycling; "leasing" all carpets to make recycling easier; substituting some yarns with flax and hemp; treating "used" water and sending it on for gold-course irrigation; and so on. These might sound small, but put together they have saved Interface an incredible $77 million since 1995. And how about ecology for employees? In a notoriously bad industry, Interface's mill is odor-free, soundproofed, bathed in three stories of sunlit

windows and landscaped with wild grasses and black-eyed Susans.

Anderson's goal of 100 percent sustainability is not met yet, but they are working on it (see more on Anderson and Interface on p. 129).[42] ∎

Let's look at criteria that can be used to evaluate a company's social performance.

∎ EVALUATING CORPORATE SOCIAL PERFORMANCE

One model for evaluating corporate social performance is presented in Exhibit 4.4. The model indicates that total corporate social responsibility can be subdivided into four criteria—economic, legal, ethical, and discretionary responsibilities.[43] The responsibilities are ordered from bottom to top based on their relative magnitude and the frequency with which managers deal with each issue.

Note the similarity between the categories in Exhibit 4.4 on following page and those in Exhibit 4.1. In both cases, ethical issues are located between the areas of legal and freely discretionary responsibilities. Exhibit 4.4 also has an economic category, because profits are a major reason for the existence of corporations.

ECONOMIC RESPONSIBILITIES

The first criterion of social responsibility is economic responsibility. The business institution is, above all, the basic economic unit of society. Its responsibility is to produce the goods and services that society wants and to maximize profits for its owners and shareholders. Economic responsibility, carried to the extreme, is called the profit-maximizing view, advocated by Nobel economist Milton Friedman. This view argues that the corporation should be operated on a profit-oriented basis, with its sole mission to increase its profits so long as it stays within the rules of the game.[44]

The purely profit-maximizing view is no longer considered an adequate criterion of performance in Canada, the United States, and Europe. This approach means that economic gain is the only social responsibility and can lead companies into trouble. A notorious example

E x h i b i t   4.4

CRITERIA OF CORPORATE
SOCIAL PERFORMANCE

Total Corporate Social Responsibility

Discretionary Responsibility
Contribute to the community and quality of life.

Ethical Responsibility
Be ethical. Do what is right. Avoid harm.

Legal Responsibility
Obey the law.

Economic Responsibility
Be profitable.

SOURCES: Archie B. Carroll, "A Three-Dimensional Conceptual Model of Corporate Performance," *Academy of Management Review* 4 (1979), 499; and "The Pyramid of Corporate Social Responsibility: Toward the Moral Management of Corporate Stakeholders," *Business Horizons* 34 (July–August 1991), 42.

was the attempt by Salomon Brothers to corner the Treasury securities market. Corporate greed, fostered by former chairman John Gutfreund's "win-at-all-costs" culture, resulted in mistakes that led to record penalties of $280 million.[45]

LEGAL RESPONSIBILITIES

All modern societies lay down ground rules, laws, and regulations that businesses are expected to follow. Legal responsibility defines what society deems as important with respect to appropriate corporate behavior.[46] Businesses are expected to fulfill their economic goals within the legal framework. Legal requirements are imposed by local town councils, state legislators, and federal regulatory agencies. Organizations that knowingly break the law are poor performers in this category. American Caster Corporation was caught by the L.A. Toxic Waste Strike Force and forced to send a letter to the residents of Los Angeles that stated, ". . . while you read this ad our President and Vice President are serving time in jail. . . take the legal alternative and protect our environment."

ETHICAL RESPONSIBILITIES

Ethical responsibility includes behaviors that are not necessarily codified into law and may not serve the corporation's direct economic interests. Unethical behavior occurs when decisions enable an individual or company to gain at the expense of society. One area that has recently been called into question concerns Internet sites for children set up by companies such as Kellogg, Nabisco, and Frito-Lay. Watchdog groups charge that these companies are acting unethically by using games and other forms of entertainment designed to gather marketing data from children as young as four years old.[47]

On the other hand, Microboard Processing Inc. and other firms provide an example of ethical action through its hiring of high-risk employees, from former welfare recipients with little job experience to felons and former drug addicts. CEO Craig T. Hoekenga sees one of his responsibilities to be helping people turn their lives around (see Leading the Revolution: The Learning Organization).

Having trouble hiring in this tight labor market? How about a convicted murderer? An unemployed welfare mother? Or a homeless person? Several companies are finding such workers, if selected properly, can be a boon for business.

Craig T. Hoekenga's Connecticut-based Microboard Processing Inc. (MPI) has discovered the secret of getting results from employees most other companies shun. By hiring and training high-risk hires such as murderers and welfare mothers, trusting them to do well, and giving them a new chance in life, Hoekenga sees the appreciation of the employees show up in higher productivity and loyalty. Profits are rising in his 240-person firm, and sales have nearly doubled over last year.

Oakland's Tucker Technology was growing faster than it could hire, until CEO Frank Tucker realized all the human resources he needed were hanging out on the street corner. Since much of his service is entry-level work, he found he could easily train these "street people" to pull fiber-optic cables through building walls. His pay of $23 per hour allowed these former drifters to build solid lives for themselves.

After getting his MBA at Stern School of Business and New York University, A. J. Wasserstein returned home to Waterbuy Connecticut. While his friends went off to Wall Street or plush office parks, Wasserstein borrowed $70,000 from his family and purchased a dilapidated brick building in the inner city of Waterbury, starting a file-storage company. Why here? Because it offered two important items: low cost and location, being right near the interstate. When he placed an ad for a customer representative, he got 25 eager applicants, inner-city people who were finding it hard to get other work. Sound risky? Archives Management has swelled to 25 employees with $2.6 million revenues.

Still, it's not always easy. Hoekenga has had to fire workers who just wouldn't work or who refused to kick their drug habits. Even with that, he says 70 percent of the high-risk hires turn out to become productive workers within six months.

Hoekenga's motivation goes deeper than profit maximization. As he says, "Businessmen have a unique opportunity to help people who haven't been as fortunate."

SOURCES: Christopher Gaggiano, "Insider Trading," *Inc.*, May 1999, pp. 83–84; Joshua Macht, "By the Numbers," *Inc.*, May 1999, pp. 53–54; Jeffrey A. Tannenbaum, "Making Risky Hires into Valued Workers," *Wall Street Journal*, June 19, 1997, pp. B1–B2.

DISCRETIONARY RESPONSIBILITIES

Discretionary responsibility is purely voluntary and guided by a company's desire to make social contributions not mandated by economics, law, or ethics. Discretionary activities include generous philanthropic contributions that offer no payback to the company and are not expected. An example of discretionary behavior occurred when Pittsburgh Brewing Company helped laid-off steelworkers by establishing and contributing to food banks in the Pittsburgh area. Discretionary responsibility is the highest criterion of social responsibility, because it goes beyond societal expectations to contribute to the community's welfare.

■ CORPORATE ACTIONS TOWARD SOCIAL DEMANDS

Confronted with a specific social demand, how might a corporation respond? If a stakeholder such as the local government places a demand on the company, what types of corporate action might be taken?

OBSTRUCTIVE

Companies that adopt **obstructive responses** deny all responsibility, claim that evidence of wrongdoing is misleading or distorted, and place obstacles to delay investigation. During the Watergate years, such obstruction was labeled *stonewalling*. A. H. Robins Company reportedly used obstructive actions when it received warnings about its Dalkon shield, an intrauterine device. The company built a wall around itself. It stood against all evidence and insisted to the public that the product was safe and effective. The company spared no effort to resist investigation. As word about injuries caused by the Dalkon shield kept pouring in, one attorney was told to search the files and destroy all papers pertaining to the product.[48] More recently, during class-action suits, the tobacco industry was accused of using obstructive measures by hiding the facts of their own research that indicated health hazards of smoking.

DEFENSIVE

The **defensive response** means that the company admits to some errors of omission or

discretionary responsibility
Organizational responsibility that is voluntary and guided by the organization's desire to make social contributions not mandated by economics, law, or ethics

obstructive response
A response to social demands in which the organization denies responsibility, claims that evidence of misconduct is misleading or distorted, and attempts to obstruct investigation

defensive response
A response to social demands in which the organization admits to some errors of commission or omission but does not act in an obstructive manner

commission. The company cuts its losses by defending itself but is not obstructive. Defensive managers generally believe that "these things happen, but they are nobody's fault." Goodyear adopted a defensive strategy by deciding to keep its South Africa plants open and provided an intelligent argument for why that was the proper action.

ACCOMMODATIVE

An **accommodative response** means that the company accepts social responsibility for its actions, although it may do so in response to external pressure. Firms that adopt this action try to meet economic, legal, and ethical responsibilities. If outside forces apply pressure, managers agree to curtail ethically questionable activities. Companies often will hire an ethics consultant to help them clean up their act and improve their public image. Both KPMG Peat Marwick and Arthur Andersen & Co. have started ethics consulting units and the field is a booming business.[49] Exxon's decision to clean up the oil spill in Prince William Sound was an accommodative decision based largely on the public's outcry.

PROACTIVE

The **proactive response** means that firms take the lead in social issues. They seek to learn what is in the public interest and respond without coaxing or pressure from stakeholders. One example of proactive behavior is the Potlatch Corporation. Potlatch makes milk cartons and came up with the idea of printing photographs of missing children on them. The company reported that within days after the Alta-Dena Dairy of Los Angeles placed a missing-kids carton in grocery stores, one of the youngsters returned home.[50] Another proactive response is corporate philanthropy. Many companies, including Miller Brewing, Coca-Cola, and Westinghouse, make generous donations to universities, United Way, and other charitable groups as a way of reaching out and improving society.

Obstructiveness tends to occur in firms whose actions are based solely on economic considerations. Defensive organizations are willing to work within the letter of the law. Accommodative organizations respond to ethical pressures. Proactive organizations use discretionary responsibilities to enhance community welfare.

Beech-Nut Nutrition Corporation was accused of unethical and socially irresponsible behavior. How would you evaluate its response?

BEECH-NUT NUTRITION CORPORATION
www.beech-nut.com

To Beech-Nut, feeding babies is a sacred trust. Bottles of fruit juice say "100 percent fruit juice." Yet Beech-Nut was found to have adulterated its best-selling line of apple juice products. A member of the research department became suspicious that the concentrate acquired from suppliers contained nothing more than sugar water and chemicals. When he voiced his concerns, top management accused the employee of not being a team player and wrote in his annual performance review that his judgment was "colored by naiveté and impractical ideals." The top managers were not hardened criminals trying to swindle customers. They were honest and well respected but under great financial pressure. The cheap concentrate from the new supplier saved millions of dollars, and managers simply did not want to recognize that they were receiving a poor product. Beech-Nut was running on a shoestring, and enormous financial pressure forced managers to stay with the low-cost supplier.

Beech-Nut learned its lesson the hard way after an FDA investigation. Had the company admitted its error, payment of a fine would have closed the issue. But management stonewalled, and Beech-Nut found itself in the middle of a nightmare as the case changed from civil to criminal. The company's strategy was to stall investigations and avoid publicity until it could unload the diluted apple juice. After two years and two criminal trials, Beech-Nut's two top executives were sentenced to one year and a day in prison and fined $100,000. The total cost to the company, including fines, legal expenses, and lost sales, was an estimated $25 million.[51] ■

accommodative response
A response to social demands in which the organization accepts—often under pressure—social responsibility for its actions to comply with the public interest

proactive response
A response to social demands in which the organization seeks to learn what is in its constituencies' interest and to respond without pressure from them

■ MANAGING COMPANY ETHICS AND SOCIAL RESPONSIBILITY

Many managers are concerned with improving the ethical climate and social responsiveness of their companies. They do not want to be surprised or be forced into an obstructionist or defensive position. As one expert on the topic of ethics said, "Management is responsible for creating and sustaining conditions in which people are likely to behave themselves."[52] Management methods for helping organizations be more responsible include leadership by example, codes of ethics, ethical structures, and supporting whistle-blowers.

LEADERSHIP BY EXAMPLE

In a study of ethics policy and practice in successful, ethical companies, such as Boeing, Chemical Bank, General Mills, GTE, Xerox, Johnson & Johnson, and Hewlett-Packard, no point emerged more clearly than the crucial role of top managers.[53] Leaders set the tone for an organization's ethics through their own actions. Leaders make a commitment to ethical values and help others throughout the organization embody and reflect those values.[54] The chief executive officer and senior managers need to be openly and strongly committed to ethical conduct. They must give constant leadership in renewing the ethical values of the organization. They must be active in communicating that commitment in speeches, directives, company publications, and especially in actions. The company "grapevine" quickly communicates situations in which top managers chose an expedient action over an ethical one, and subsequent pronouncements of commitment to ethics by top executives count for very little.[55] Top managers set the tone of the organization most clearly by their behavior.

CODE OF ETHICS

A **code of ethics** is a formal statement of the company's values concerning ethics and social issues; it communicates to employees what the company stands for. Codes of ethics tend to exist in two types: principle-based statements and policy-based statements. Principle-based statements are designed to affect corporate culture; they define fundamental values and contain general language about company responsibilities, quality of products, and treatment of employees. General statements of principle are often called *corporate credos.* Examples are GTE's "Vision and Values," Johnson & Johnson's "The Credo," and Hewlett-Packard's "The HP Way."[56]

Policy-based statements generally outline the procedures to be used in specific ethical situations. These situations include marketing practice, conflicts of interest, observance of laws, proprietary information, political gifts, and equal opportunities. Examples of policy-based statements are Boeing's "Business Conduct Guidelines," GTE's "Anti-Trust and Conflict of Interest Guidelines," and Norton's "Norton Policy on Business Ethics."[57]

Codes of ethics state the values or behaviors that are expected and those that will not be tolerated and are backed up by management's action. A recent study by the Center for Business Ethics found that 90 percent of Fortune 500 companies and almost half of all other companies now have codes of ethics. When top management supports and enforces these codes, including rewards for compliance and discipline for violation, ethics codes can uplift a company's ethical climate. When top management doesn't support them, ethics codes are worth little more than the paper on which they're written.[58] The code of ethics at McDonnell Douglas reflects the theme of the ethics program: "Always take the high road."

McDonnell Douglas
www.boeing.com

At McDonnell Douglas, a short version of the ethics code and an ethical decision-making checklist are printed on cards so that employees may carry them in a pocket or purse. The excerpt printed below indicates that McDonnell Douglas expects its employees to display ethical behavior above that required by law. Integrity and ethics exist in the individual or they do not exist at all. They must be upheld by individuals or they are not upheld at all. In order for integrity and ethics to be characteristics of McDonnell

code of ethics
A formal statement of the organization's values regarding ethics and social issues

Douglas, we who make up the Corporation must strive to be

- Honest and trustworthy in all our relationships
- Reliable in carrying out assignments and responsibilities
- Truthful and accurate in what we say and write
- Cooperative and constructive in all work undertaken
- Fair and considerate in our treatment of fellow employees, customers, and other persons
- Law abiding in all our activities
- Dedicated in service to our company and to improvement of the quality of life in the world in which we live

Integrity and high standards of ethics require hard work, courage, and difficult choices. Integrity and ethics may sometimes require us to forego business opportunities. In the long run, however, we will be better served by doing what is right rather than what is expedient.[59] ■

An area of growing concern for companies doing business internationally is developing ethics codes that focus on the issue of human rights. Responding to the public outcry against sweatshops, a New York nonprofit organization and a number of influential companies have proposed a set of global labor standards to deal with issues such as child labor, low wages, and unsafe working environments. The group has come up with a scheme called Social Accountability 8000 or SA 8000, which is designed to work like the ISO 9000 quality-auditing system of the International Standards Organization. The SA 8000 is the first auditable social standard in the world. Companies such as Avon and Toys "R" Us are certifying their factories and requiring their suppliers to do likewise.[60]

ETHICAL STRUCTURES

Ethical structures represent the various systems, positions, and programs a company can undertake to implement ethical behavior. An **ethics committee** is a group of executives appointed to oversee company ethics. The committee provides rulings on questionable ethical issues. The ethics committee assumes responsibility for disciplining wrongdoers, which is essential if the organization is to directly influence employee behavior. For example, Motorola has an Ethics Compliance Committee that is charged with interpreting, clarifying, and communicating the company's code of ethics and with adjudicating suspected code violations. An **ethics ombudsman** is an official given the responsibility of corporate conscience who hears and investigates ethical complaints and points out potential ethics failures to top management. Pitney Bowes has an ethics ombudsman and offers training seminars and a conduct guide on ethics for employees.

Many organizations today are setting up ethics departments with full-time staff. These offices, such as the one at Northrup Grumman, work as counseling centers rather than as police departments. They are charged with helping employees deal with day-to-day ethical problems or questions. A toll-free, confidential hot line allows employees to report questionable behavior as well as seek guidance regarding ethical dilemmas. The offices also provide training based on the organization's code of ethics or code of business conduct, so that employees can translate the values into daily behavior.[61] Training programs are an important supplement to a written code of ethics. Texas Instruments developed an eight-hour ethics training course for all employees. In addition, the company incorporates ethics into every course it offers. A computer-training class, for example, might include a discussion of the ethical issues of copying and distributing software. Starbucks Coffee uses new-employee training to begin instilling values such as taking personal responsibility, treating everyone with respect, and doing the right thing even if others disagree with you.[62]

A strong ethics program is important, but it is no guarantee against lapses. Dow Corning, whose faulty silicone breast implants shocked the business community, pioneered an ethics program that was looked upon as a model. Established in the mid-1970s, Dow's ambitious ethics program included the Business Conduct

ethics committee
A group of executives assigned to oversee the organization's ethics by ruling on questionable issues and disciplining violators

ethics ombudsman
An official given the responsibility of corporate conscience who hears and investigates ethics complaints and points out potential ethical failures to top management

committee, training programs, regular reviews and audits to monitor compliance, and reports to the Audit and Social Responsibility committee. What went wrong? The ethics program dealt with the overall environment, but specific programs such as product safety were handled through normal channels—in this case the Medical Device Business Board, which slowed further safety studies.[63] Dow Corning's problems sent a warning to other industries. It is not enough to have an impressive ethics program. The ethics program must be merged with day-to-day operations, encouraging ethical decisions to be made throughout the company. Here is one company using technology to increase ethical awareness and trust.

High-Tech Needs High Trust

Texas Instruments (TI) employees work in a rapidly changing environment where difficult decisions, often with no clear right or wrong answer, have to be made on a daily basis. It has found technology can help. In a company as large and complex as TI, maintaining high ethical standards requires more than lip service. Texas Instruments developed a code of ethics in 1961 but has now gone far beyond that initial step to hold the company and its employees to high standards of integrity. Currently, a staff of seven at TI's Dallas headquarters oversees ethics programs for the company's 60,000 employees worldwide. Carl Skooglund, ethics director, spends most of his time and his $700,000 annual budget on ethics awareness. In addition to regular newsletters and supplemental publications, weekly news articles are sent throughout the world on the company's electronic mail system. Topics include how to determine if a gift is acceptable, patent awards in other countries, the many faces of theft, and software copying. The company has also produced a series of more than 50 short videotapes on ethical dilemmas, which managers can use as a way to encourage discussion of ethical issues among employees.

Perhaps the most remarkable aspect of TI's ethics operation is how successfully the ethics office maintains direct dialog with a global workforce. Employees most frequently contact Skooglund's office through toll-free telephone lines, where anonymity is optional and confidentiality is guaranteed. Employees can also send a message to an ethics post office box, separate from the corporate mail system, or communicate through a secure e-mail address.

Skooglund says Texas Instruments stresses ethics for solid, strategic reasons: "We believe our reputation for integrity is every bit as important as the technology base we've developed." Investing in ethics has paid off for TI. Employees say they are proud to work for a company that holds them to the highest standards. Texas Instruments hasn't experienced the same legal troubles many other large defense contractors have, and the company has earned a string of awards for its ethics operation. So firm is TI's commitment to maintaining its integrity that it has often gone the extra mile. After delivering products to one of its contractors, TI discovered a slight technical variation that had an infinitesimal chance of causing problems in use. TI paid for the product to be recalled and adjusted. The company lost on the deal financially, but gained the undying trust of the contractor.[64] ■

WHISTLE-BLOWING

Employee disclosure of illegal, immoral, or illegitimate practices on the employer's part is called **whistle-blowing**.[65] No organization can rely exclusively on codes of conduct and ethical structures to prevent all unethical behavior. Holding organizations accountable depends to some degree on individuals who are willing to blow the whistle if they detect illegal, dangerous, or unethical activities. Whistle-blowers often report wrongdoing to outsiders, such as regulatory agencies, senators, or newspaper reporters. Some firms have instituted innovative programs to encourage and support internal whistle-blowing. For this to be an effective ethical safeguard, however, companies must view whistle-blowing as a benefit to the company and make dedicated efforts to protect whistle-blowers.[66]

whistle-blowing
The disclosure by an employee of illegal, immoral, or illegitimate practices by the organization

Starbucks Coffee has a proactive response to social issues with its funding of programs such as Pied Crow, a children's literary magazine distributed to more than 14,000 primary schools in Kenya. The magazine uses colorful stories and pictures to provide information on health and sanitation, environmental issues, starting a small business, and the prevention of AIDS. Starbucks is North America's leading corporate sponsor of CARE, the international aid and relief organization.

When there are no effective protective measures, whistle-blowers suffer. Although whistle-blowing has become widespread in recent years, it is still risky for employees, who can lose their jobs, be ostracized by coworkers, or be transferred to lower-level positions. For example, when Mark Jorgensen exposed fraud in the real-estate funds he managed for Prudential Insurance Company of America, he was shunned by his supervisor and coworkers, accused by company lawyers of breaking the law, and eventually dismissed.[67] Robert A. Bugai, who blew the whistle on unethical college marketing practices, warns that there are considerable costs involved—"mentally, financially, physically, emotionally, and spiritually."[68] It is not enough for top managers to encourage internal whistle-blowing. Managers can be trained to view whistle-blowing as a benefit rather than a threat, and systems can be set up to effectively protect employees who report illegal or unethical activities.

■ ETHICS AND THE MANAGEMENT REVOLUTION

Many of today's best companies realize that success can be measured in many ways, not all of which show up on the financial statement. However, the relationship of a corporation's ethics and social responsibility to its financial performance concerns both managers and management scholars and has generated a lively debate.[69] One concern of managers is whether good citizenship will hurt performance—after all, ethics programs cost money. A number of studies have been undertaken to determine whether heightened ethical and so-

cial responsiveness increases or decreases financial performance. Studies have provided varying results but generally have found that there is a small positive relationship between social responsibility and financial performance.[70] For example, James Burke, former CEO of Johnson & Johnson, put together a list of companies known for their high ethical standards, including J&J, Xerox, and Eastman Kodak. In the period from 1950 to 1990, Burke found that the market value of companies that made the list grew at 11.3 percent annually, almost double the 6.2 percent rate achieved by Dow Jones industrials as a group. In addition, the Domini Social Index, created in 1989 to track the stock performance of socially responsible companies, indicates that they perform as well as or better than companies that are not socially responsible. Although results from these studies are not proof, they do provide an indication that use of resources for ethics and social responsibility does not hurt companies.[71] Enlightened companies realize that integrity and trust are essential elements in sustaining successful and profitable business relationships. Although doing the right thing may not always be profitable in the short run, it develops a level of trust that money can't buy and that will ultimately benefit the company. McDonald's, for example, credits its strong community involvement for the fact that none of its 31 area restaurants was burned or looted during the 1992 Los Angeles riots.[72]

A related finding is that firms founded on spiritual values usually perform very well. These firms succeed because they have a clear mission, employees seldom have alcohol and drug problems, and a strong family

THE CORPORATION OF THE TWENTY-FIRST CENTURY

Ray Anderson spent most of his life as an environmental glutton. His company, Interface, Inc., an Atlanta-based business with 7,300 employees, turns petrochemicals into textiles. The petroleum the company uses took millions of years to make and is irreplaceable; the carpets that come from it last forever—and most of them end up in landfills after only a decade of use.

But Ray Anderson had a revelation when he came across a book called *The Ecology of Commerce,* by Paul Hawken. As he read about the breadth of toxins accumulating in humans from one generation to the next and the speed at which natural resources were being depleted, the captain of industrial capitalism thought of his grandchildren and wept. Today, Ray Anderson is becoming a radical environmentalist who makes the folks from Greenpeace look timid. He has embraced the concept of sustainability, which calls for mimicking nature—everything's waste is something else's food. Anderson's goal for Interface: create zero waste and consume zero oil while making a healthy profit. It took Anderson a year to convince the rest of his company (the largest maker of commercial carpeting and upholstery for office cubicles) that Interface could save the earth and still make money. Today, however, from the factory floor to the R&D lab, sustainability has become as important a consideration in every business decision as profitability.

Interface's performance shatters the idea that social responsibility and profits can't go hand in hand. From 1995 to 1996, sales grew from $800 million to $1 billion. During that time, the amount of raw materials used by the company dropped almost 20 percent per dollar of sales. That means, Anderson points out, "$200 million of sustainable business." Profits have been steadily increasing, and costs keep going down with reduced energy costs, reduced materials, and reduced waste. The company's latest innovation is an "Evergreen Lease," with building owners renting rather than buying carpet. Interface installs, maintains, replaces, carries away, and recycles carpet tiles as they wear out. The old tiles become new carpet. Interface also hopes to soon offer commercial hemp carpet, which can be composted completely when its use is over.

Interface still has a long way to go to reach its goals, but already air pollutants, landfill waste, and use of natural resources have dramatically decreased. The company's simple agenda for the twenty-first century has seven steps: (1) eliminate waste; (2) make emissions benign; (3) shift to renewable energy, gradually moving to solar power; (4) close the loop, using waste as a resource for new textiles; (5) make transportation efficient; (6) teach sustainability to customers, suppliers, and employees; and (7) redesign commerce to shift to cyclic capitalism. Ray Anderson wants to change the world, and ensure that his grandchildren will still have one.

www.interfaceinc.com

SOURCES: Charles Fishman, "I Want to Pioneer the Company of the Next Industrial Revolution," *Fast Company,* April–May 1998, pp. 136–142; Thomas Petzinger, Jr., "Business Achieves Greatest Efficiencies When at Its Greenest," The *Wall Street Journal,* July 11, 1997, p. B1; and Catherine Arnst with Stanley Reed, Gary McWilliams, and De'Ann Weimer, "When Green Begets Green," *Business Week,* November 10, 1997, pp. 98–106.

orientation exists. One of the largest and most successful companies is Chick-fil-A, Inc., which refuses to open on Sunday. The Sunday closing costs some sales and has gotten the chain frozen out of some shopping malls, but the policy helps attract excellent workers, and this offsets any disadvantages. When Tom Chappell, cofounder (with his wife Kate) of Tom's of Maine, became concerned about how to stick to his respect for humanity while keeping his company successful, he went to divinity school. In the writings of the great philosophers, Chappell says he learned that you don't have to sell your soul to make your numbers. Tom's of Maine, a highly successful maker of all-natural personal care products, thrives on spiritual values.[73]

Being ethical and socially responsible does not hurt a firm. Managers and companies can use their discretion to contribute to society's welfare and improve organizational performance at the same time. For Interface, Inc., profitability and social responsibility have become almost synonymous, as described in Leading the Revolution, "The Corporation of the Twenty-First Century." The public is tired of unethical and socially irresponsible business practices. Companies that make an uncompromising commitment to maintain integrity may well lead the way to a brighter future for both business and society.

Summary and Management Solution

Ethics and social responsibility are hot topics for today's managers. Ethical decisions and behavior are typically guided by a value system. Four value-based approaches that serve as criteria for ethical decision making are utilitarian, individualism, moral-rights, and justice. For an individual manager, the ability to make correct ethical choices will depend on both individual and organizational characteristics. An important individual characteristic is level of moral development. Corporate culture is an organizational characteristic that influences ethical behavior.

Corporate social responsibility concerns a company's values toward society. How can organizations be good corporate citizens? The model for evaluating social performance uses four criteria: economic, legal, ethical, and discretionary. Organizations may use four types of response to specific social pressures: obstructive, defensive, accommodative, and proactive. Evaluating corporate social behavior often requires assessing its impact on organizational stakeholders. Techniques for improving social responsiveness include leadership, codes of ethics, ethical structures, and whistle-blowing. Companies that are socially responsible perform as well as—and often better than—companies that are not socially responsible.

As seen in the management problem, despite its phenomenal Internet traffic, e/Town was not generating enough revenues to sustain. Rather than resorting to corporate sponsorship, which they deemed unethical, the founders hired a technology-based and experienced CEO, someone they knew and trusted. Robert Heiblim helped the group redirect its strategy toward e-commerce and helped them raise $3.5 million from private venture capitalists.

Starting in summer 1999, the site not only reviews and recommends electronics, it also has an interactive Q&A shipping engine that directly links surfers to retail sites. All this was done by Web builder extraordinaire, Organic, whose fee is a 5 percent stake in the company. Wolpin remarks, "When you think of books, you probably think of Amazon.com. When you think of electronics information and resources, we plan on your thinking of e/Town. And if you do, I guess we'll prove that living right is the best revenge."

Recall that e/Town started over the perceived misuse of intellectual property. As knowledge and information, not physical items, increasingly become the primary form of capital for companies, the legal as well as ethical complexities regarding ownership of information likely will increase.

SOURCE: Charles Pappas, "In E/Town We Trust," *Success,* May 1999, pp. 22–25.

Discussion Questions

1. Dr. Martin Luther King, Jr., said, "As long as there is poverty in the world, I can never be rich. . . . As long as diseases are rampant, I can never be healthy. . . . I can never be what I ought to be until you are what you ought to be." Discuss this quote with respect to the material in this chapter. Would this be true for corporations, too?

2. Environmentalists are trying to pass laws for oil spills that would remove all liability limits for the oil companies. This would punish corporations financially. Is this the best way to influence companies to be socially responsible?

3. Compare and contrast the utilitarian approach with the moral-rights approach to ethical decision making.

Which do you believe is the best for managers to follow? Why?

4. Imagine yourself in a situation of being encouraged to inflate your expense account. Do you think your choice would be most affected by your individual moral development or by the cultural values of the company for which you worked? Explain.

5. Is it socially responsible for organizations to undertake political activity or join with others in a trade association to influence the government? Discuss.

6. The criteria of corporate social responsibility suggest that economic responsibilities are of the greatest mag-

nitude, followed by legal, ethical, and discretionary responsibilities. How do these four types of responsibility relate to corporate responses to social demands? Discuss.

7. From where do managers derive ethical values? What can managers do to help define ethical standards for the corporation?

8. Have you ever experienced an ethical dilemma? Evaluate the dilemma with respect to its impact on other people.

9. Lincoln Electric considers customers and employees to be more important stakeholders than shareholders. Is it appropriate for management to define some stakeholders as more important than others? Should all stakeholders be considered equal?

10. Do you think a code of ethics combined with an ethics committee would be more effective than leadership for implementing ethical behavior? Discuss.

Management Exercises

Manager's Workbook

The spread of technology into the workplace has raised a variety of new ethical questions, and many old ones still linger. Compare your answers with those of other Americans surveyed.

Office Technology

1. Is it wrong to use company e-mail for personal reasons?
   Yes   No

2. Is it wrong to use office equipment to help your children or spouse do schoolwork?
   Yes   No

3. Is it wrong to play computer games on office equipment during the workday?
   Yes   No

4. Is it wrong to use office equipment to do Internet shopping?
   Yes   No

5. Is it unethical to blame an error you made on a technological glitch?
   Yes   No

6. Is it unethical to visit pornographic Web sites using office equipment?
   Yes   No

Gifts and Entertainment

7. What's the value at which a gift from a supplier or client becomes troubling?
   $25 $50 $100

8. Is a $50 gift to a boss unacceptable?
   Yes   No

9. Is a $50 gift *from* the boss unacceptable?
   Yes   No

10. Of gifts from suppliers: Is it OK to take a $200 pair of football tickets?
    Yes   No

11. Is it OK to take a $120 pair of theater tickets?
    Yes   No

12. Is it OK to take a $100 holiday food basket?
    Yes   No

13. Is it OK to take a $25 gift certificate?
    Yes   No

14. Can you accept a $75 prize won at a raffle at a supplier's conference?
    Yes   No

Truth and Lies

Students: See the solutions section on p. 576 to check your responses.

15. Due to on-the-job pressure, have you ever abused or lied about sick days?
    Yes   No

16. Due to on-the-job pressure, have you ever taken credit for someone else's work or idea?
    Yes   No

SOURCES: Ethics Officer Association, Belmont, Mass.; Ethical Leadership Group, Wilmette, Ill.; surveys sampled a cross-section of workers at large companies and nationwide; "The Wall Street Journal Workplace-Ethics Quiz," *The Wall Street Journal*; Oct. 21, 1999, pp. B1, B4.

Manager's Workshop

Ethics Investigation

Divide into groups of four to six members and choose a real ethical dilemma that members of some organization faced. Some examples include the Nestlé infant formula controversy, HB Fuller and glue-sniffing in Honduras, Kathy Lee Gifford and sweatshops, Silkwood, Nuremburg Trials, Valdez oil spill, CIA involvement in crack, Iran-Contra, trial behavior in the O.J. Simpson case, Whitewater, West Point honor code, sexual harassment cases in the Army or Navy, admission of women to the Virginia military academy, CEO salaries, Shell Oil in Nigeria, corporate downsizing, questionable political contributions, deception to consumers, Tobacco industry and teenage smokers, managed health care, globalization as a new kind of imperialism, politicians "bought" by PAC's and special interest groups, the NRA and national policy, violence in schools, and the like.

Your instructor will assign you one of the following two options, either A or B:

A. Debate

1. Prepare both sides of a debate on the "ethical" versus nonethical behaviors the company, person, or institution might have chosen. Back up your arguments with ethical theories and sound reasoning.

2. Your instructor will assign you to either write up the whole debate, or present both sides to the rest of the class.

B. Investigation

1. Consider that you have been hired as a consultant to a major ethics think tank. Conduct a thorough research on the subject and collect articles, which may include interviews, eyewitness reports, news magazines, editorials, and such. Try to find any movie or video clips that may be relevant, as well.

2. Write up a case study/report, keeping in mind the time frame and the historical context of this situation. Explicitly identify ethical issues and conflicts as they occur. Remember, the think tank is very concerned with these issues and wants you to particularly highlight them. Refer back to ethical concepts in the chapter and see which are relevant. In your case study, include what happened. What did the major "actors" do? How did they handle the dilemmas? Finally, describe how you would "rewrite the script" to make the behaviors more ethical. How would that change the outcome?

3. Develop an ethical "code of behavior" based on the events in your dilemma.

4. (optional) Be prepared to hand out copies of your case study and code of behavior to the rest of the class. Conduct a discussion. You may be asked to show the video clips, as well.

SOURCE: Copyright 1999 Dorothy Marcic; adapted from Karen L. Vinton and Melody M. Zajdel, "The Ethics Packet Assignment," *The Organizational Behavior Teaching Review,* Vol. 12 (2), pp. 108–110.

Management in Practice: Ethical Dilemma

Baby-Friendly Hospitals

Jason Rutledge sat in his office and wondered what to recommend in his report. As assistant administrator of 180-bed Babcock Memorial Hospital, he was charged with evaluating a proposal by a U.S. Committee for UNICEF group to become a "Baby-Friendly Hospital." Many U.S. hospitals tend to encourage bottle feeding through a combination of giving away free formula supplied by pharmaceutical companies, as well as employing underskilled staff, and this committee was appealing to hospitals to reverse the trend.

Their arguments were compelling. Breastfed babies cry less, and they are healthier, with reduced risk for ear infections, juvenile diabetes, allergies, dental caries, and Sudden Infant Death Syndrome. Every year, 200,000 U.S. children are hospitalized for diarrhea, most of which are bottle-fed babies. By six months, only 20 percent of mothers breastfeed. Though low-income mothers are 40 percent less likely to breastfeed as middle-income women, they feel a heavier burden with the $1,000 yearly cost of formula. Costs to HMOs and other insurers for basic health care are about 70 percent more for bottle-fed babies than those breastfed.

Still, Babcock Memorial was not an insurer nor even a parent. Jason's responsibilities were to help the hospital continue to trim unnecessary costs. Any help they could get was usually appreciated. Currently, formula companies were paying the hospital about $14,000 a year for formula, bottles, nipples, and feeders. If Babcock became a baby-friendly hospital, it would mean they would have to stop taking these "freebies" from the formula companies and would seriously start to encourage breastfeeding.

It was up to Jason to recommend either accepting the proposal or passing on it, and he realized what a difficult choice it was.

Questions:

1. Which of the normative approaches to ethical decision making is most relevant for Jason to use?

2. Give examples of the four decisions Jason would make using each of the four possible responses to social demands.

3. If you were Jason, what would you recommend?

SOURCES: Margaret Kyenkya-Isabirye, "UNICEF Launches Baby-Friendly Hospital Initiative," *Maternal and Child Nursing*, Vol. 17, 1992, pp. 177–179; "Baby-Friendly Expert Work Group in the United States: Blowing the Whistle," *Birth*, Vol. 22, June 1995, pp. 59–62; various hospital sources.

Surf the Net

1. *Social Responsibility.* The Global Business Responsibility Resource Center at http://www.bsr.org/resource-center/ states its mission is "to provide businesses with the information they need to understand and implement more responsible policies and practices, and to promote increased knowledge and collaboration among companies and between business and other sectors." Its goal is "to help companies achieve sustained commercial success in ways that honor high ethical standards and benefit people, communities, and the environment." After registering (free), select a topic and print out a report to submit to your instructor.

2. *Code of Ethics.* Use your search engine to find the codes of ethics for three organizations. One site that contains more than 850 codes of ethics is http://csep.iit.edu/codes/codes.html. Compare the three codes to determine the similarities and differences among them in terms of focus, approach, language, and emphases. Provide possible reasons for the similarities and differences you cited. How might you benefit as an employee working for an organization with a code of ethics compared to working for an organization without a code of ethics?

3. *Ethical Structures.* Lockheed Martin is one of the world's leading diversified technology companies. Government and commercial customers around the world purchase its advanced technology systems, products, and services. Its core businesses span aeronautics, electronics, energy, information and services, space, systems integration, and telecommunications. Lockheed Martin provides an excellent example of an organization with a variety of systems, positions, and programs to implement ethical behavior among its employees. Visit the Ethics option available at www.lockheed-martin.com/about/index.htm. Write a summary of the ethical structures at Lockheed Martin.

4. *Ethical Behaviors.* Visit www.mgeneral.com and see "Fiscal Fairy Tales." Find one that deals with unethical behavior. Write a paper on the unethical behaviors, using one or more of the models from this chapter.

Case for Critical Analysis

Colt 45 and the Ad Hoc Group Against Crime

The Ad Hoc Group Against Crime, a Kansas City organization, recently accepted a contribution from Colt 45—the group will get a 25-cent donation for every case of Colt 45 malt liquor sold through participating vendors. In accepting the money, Ad Hoc opened itself to an ethical dilemma that has hounded minority interest groups for decades. Violent crime hits many minority communities hard, and numerous studies have linked crime to alcohol consumption. Studies have also shown that although African Americans have higher rates of abstinence than whites, they still have higher death rates tied to alcohol abuse.

Ad Hoc's president, Alvin Brooks, says the group doesn't see this as encouraging sales of Colt 45. "We are saying to the alcohol companies: 'If you are taking something away from the community, you are going to have to give something back.'" Brooks also notes that Ad Hoc is not in a financial position to turn away viable fund-raising opportunities. Other minority interest groups have long accepted alcohol and tobacco funds for the same reason, and over the years a loyalty has developed—a loyalty that the alcohol and tobacco companies began actively courting decades ago. Studies have shown that billboards advertising tobacco products are placed in black communities four to five times more often than in predominantly white communities and that the number of liquor outlets in proportion to the population is much higher in inner-city neighborhoods.

A spokesperson for Colt 45 said the fund-raiser is simply a way for retailers to show their support for the community. In general, large alcohol and tobacco companies are reluctant to discuss their funding of minority causes. A Philip Morris representative, commenting that the contributions are important in keeping communities economically able to buy products, said, "Their vibrancy is our vibrancy."

Questions

1. Are companies such as Colt 45 and Philip Morris acting in an ethical and socially responsible way? What criteria of social responsibility are these companies following?

2. Is the Ad Hoc Group Against Crime being socially responsible by accepting this money? Should this group take a symbolic stand against alcohol?

3. Can you think of more socially responsible ways Colt 45 might contribute to minority communities?

SOURCE: Based on Mary Sanchez, "When Charity Taps 'Vice' for Money," *The Tennessean,* August 6, 1995, p. 2D.

Endnotes

1 Charles Pappas, "In E/Town We Trust," *Success,* May 1999, pp. 22–25.

2 Del Jones, "Doing the Wrong Thing: 48 Percent of Workers Admit to Unethical or Illegal Acts," *USA Today,* April 4, 1997, pp. 1A, 2A.

3 "Franchise Inc.," *Inc.,* November 1997, p. 121; Michael Waldholz, "AZT Prize Cut for Third World Mothers-to-Be," *The Wall Street Journal,* March 5, 1998, pp. B1, B12.

4 Gordon F. Shea, *Practical Ethics* (New York: American Management Association, 1988); and Linda K. Trevino, "Ethical Decision Making in Organizations; A Person-Situation Interactionist Model," *Academy of Management Review* 11 (1986), pp. 601–617.

5 Thomas M. Jones, "Ethical Decision Making by Individuals in Organizations: An Issue-Contingent Model," *Academy of Management Review* 16 (1991), pp. 366–395.

6 Rushworth M. Kidder, "The Three Great Domains of Human Action," *Christian Science Monitor,* January 30, 1990.

7 Jones, "Ethical Decision Making."

8 This discussion is based on Gerald F. Cavanagh, Dennis J. Moberg, and Manuel Velasquez, "The Ethics of Organizational Politics," *Academy of Management Review,* 6 (1981), pp. 363–374; Justin G. Longenecker, Joseph A. McKinney, and Carlos W. Moore, "Egoism and Independence: Entrepreneurial

Ethics," *Organizational Dynamics* (Winter 1988), pp. 64–72; and Carolyn Wiley, "The ABCs of Business Ethics: Definitions, Philosophies, and Implementation," *IM,* February 1995, pp. 22–27.

9 Zachary Schiller, Walecia Conrad, and Stephanie Anderson Forest, "If You Light Up on Sunday Don't Come in on Monday," *Business Week,* August 26, 1992, pp. 68–72.

10 Ron Winslow, "Rationing Care," *The Wall Street Journal,* November 13, 1989, p. R24.

11 Alan Wong and Eugene Beckman, "An Applied Ethical Analysis System in Business," *Journal of Business Ethics,* 11 (1992), pp. 173–178.

12 John Kekes, "Self-Direction: The Core of Ethical Individualism," *Organizations and Ethical Individualism,* ed. Konstanian Kolenda (New York: Praeger, 1988), pp. 1–18.

13 Tad Tulega, *Beyond the Bottom Line* (New York: Penguin Books, 1987).

14 Archie B. Carroll, "Principles of Business Ethics: Their Role in Decision Making and Initial Consensus," *Management Decisions,* 28 (8) (1990), pp. 20–24.

15 Catherine Yang, "Are Life Insurers Biased—Or Just Careful?" *Business Week,* October 16, 1995, pp. 82–85.

16 Lynn Sharp Paine, "Managing for Organizational Integrity," *Harvard Business Review* (March–April 1994), pp. 106–117.

17 This discussion is based on Trevino, "Ethical Decision Making in Organizations."

18 Dennis Berman, "Friday, the Rabbi Sold Sermons," *Business Week Enterprise,* Dec. 7, 1998, p. ENT 8.

19 L. Kohlberg, "Moral Stages and Moralization: The Cognitive-Developmental Approach," in *Moral Development and Behavior: Theory, Research, and Social Issues,* ed. T. Lickona (New York: Holt, Rinehart & Winston, 1976), pp. 31–83; and Jill W. Graham, "Leadership, Moral Development, and Citizenship Behavior," *Business Ethics Quarterly,* 5, (1) (January 1995), pp. 43–54.

20 Carol Gilligan, *In a Different Voice: Psychological Theory and Women's Development* (Cambridge, Mass.: Harvard University Press, 1982).

21 David Vogel, "Is U.S. Business Obsessed with Ethics?" *Across the Board,* November–December 1993, pp. 31–33.

22 Joe Skelly, "The Caux Round Table Principles for Business: The Rise of International Ethics," *Business Ethics,* March–April 1995 (Supplement), pp. 2–5.

23 James Weber, "Influences Upon Organizational Ethical Subclimates: A Multi-

Departmental Analysis of a Single Firm," *Organizational Science,* 6 (5) (September–October 1995), pp. 509–523.

24 This discussion is based on Linda Klebe Trevino, "A Cultural Perspective on Changing and Developing Organizational Ethics," in *Research and Organizational Change and Development,* ed. R. Woodman and W. Pasmore (Greenwich, Conn.: JAI Press, 1990), p. 4.

25 Ibid.; John B. Cullen, Bart Victor, and Carroll Stephens, "An Ethical Weather Report: Assessing the Organization's Ethical Climate," *Organizational Dynamics* (Autumn 1989), pp. 50–62.

26 Russell Mitchell with Michael Oneal, "Managing by Values," *Business Week,* August 1, 1994, pp. 46–52.

27 Eugene W. Szwajkowski, "The Myths and Realities of Research on Organizational Misconduct," in *Research in Corporate Social Performance and Policy,* ed. James E. Post (Greenwich, Conn.: JAI Press, 1986), Vol. 9, pp. 103–122.

28 Robin D. Schatz, "The Two Bottom Lines: Profits and People," *Business Week Enterprise,* Dec. 7, 1998, pp. Ent 4–6.

29 Douglas S. Sherwin, "The Ethical Roots of the Business System," *Harvard Business Review* 61 (November-December 1983), pp. 183–192.

30 Thomas Donaldson and Lee E. Preston, "The Stakeholder Theory of the Corporation: Concepts, Evidence, and Implications," *Academy of Management Review* 20 (1) (1995), pp. 65–91.

31 Jeffrey S. Harrison and Caron H. St. John, "Managing and Partnering with External Stakeholders," *Academy of Management Executive* 10 (2) (1996), pp. 46–60.

32 Max B. E. Clarkson, "A Stakeholder Framework for Analyzing and Evaluating Corporate Social Performance," *Academy of Management Review* 20 (1) (1995), pp. 92–117.

33 Jim Collins, "The Foundation for Doing Good," *Inc.,* December 1997, pp. 41–42.

34 Susan Beck, "It Takes Customers to Rebuild the City," *Fast Company,* December–January 1997, pp. 44–45.

35 Mark A. Cohen, "Management and the Environment," *The Owen Manager,* 15(1) (1993), pp. 2–6.

36 Laura M. Litvan, "Going 'Green' in the 90s," *Nation's Business,* February 1995, pp. 30–32.

37 Linda Bavaro, personal communication, Nov. 1999; Laura Litvan, "Going 'Green' in the 90s," *Nation's Business,* February 1995, pp. 30–32.

38 Based on Litvan, "Going 'Green' in the 90s", p. 31.

39 Mark Starik, *Management and the Natural Environment* (Fort Worth, Texas: The Dryden Press, 1994), p. 1.

40 Gail Dutton, "Green Partnerships," *Management Review,* January 1996, pp. 24–28.

41 "The Natural Step to Sustainability," *Wingspread Journal,* the quarterly publication of The Johnson Foundation, Inc., Spring 1997.

42 "Interface Practices Holistic Environmentalism," *Buildings,* Feb. 1999, p. 48; Warren Cohen, "Outlook 1999: Ray Anderson," *U.S. News & World Report,* Jan. 4, 1999, p. 51.

43 Archie B. Carroll, "A Three-Dimensional Conceptual Model of Corporate Performance," *Academy of Management Review* 4 (1979), pp. 497–505.

44 Milton Friedman and Rose Friedman, *Free to Choose* (New York: Harcourt Brace Jovanovich, 1979).

45 Bruce Hager, "What's Behind Business' Sudden Fervor for Ethics?" *Business Week,* September 23, 1991, p. 65.

46 Eugene W. Szwajkowski, "Organizational Illegality: Theoretical Integration and Illustrative Application," *Academy of Management Review* 10 (1985), pp. 558–567.

47 Denise Gellene, "Internet Marketing to Kids Is Seen As a Web of Deceit," *Los Angeles Times,* March 29, 1996, pp. A1, A20.

48 John Kenneth Galbraith, "Behind the Wall," *New York Review of Books,* April 10, 1986, pp. 11–13.

49 "Ethics for Hire," *Business Week,* July 15, 1996, pp. 26–28.

50 Milton R. Moskowitz, "Company Performance Roundup," *Business and Society Review* 53 (Spring 1985), pp. 74–77.

51 Chris Welles, "What Led Beech-Nut Down the Road to Disgrace," *Business Week,* February 22, 1988, pp. 124–128.

52 Saul W. Gellerman, "Managing Ethics from the Top Down," *Sloan Management Review* (Winter 1989), pp. 73–79.

53 "Corporate Ethics: A Prime Business Asset," The Business Roundtable, 200 Park Avenue, Suite 2222, New York, New York, 10166, February 1988.

54 E. Thomas Behr, "Acting from the Center," *Management Review,* March 1998, pp. 51–55; Patrick E. Murphy and George Enderle, "Managerial Ethical Leadership: Do Examples Matter?" *Business Ethics Quarterly,* 5 (1) (1995), pp. 117–128.

55 Joseph L. Badaracco, Jr., and Allen P. Webb, "Business Ethics: A View from the Trenches," *California Management Review,* 37 (2) (Winter 1995), pp. 8–28.

56 "Corporate Ethics."

57 Ibid.

58 Carolyn Wiley, "The ABCs of Business Ethics: Definitions, Philosophies, and Implementations," *IM,* January–February 1995, pp. 22–27.

59 Patrick E. Murphy, "Implementing Business Ethics," *Business Ethics 95/96,* 7th ed. (Guilford, Conn.: Dashkin Publishing, 1995), pp. 110–118.

60 Aaron Bernstein, "Sweatshop Police," *Business Week,* October 20, 1997, 39.

61 Beverly Geber, "The Right and Wrong of Ethics Offices," *Training,* October 1995, pp. 102–118.

62 Mark Henricks, "Ethics in Action," *Management Review,* January 1995, pp. 53–55; Jennifer Reese, "Starbucks: Inside the Coffee Cult," *Fortune,* December 9, 1996, pp. 190–200.

63 John A. Byrne, "The Best Laid Ethics Programs . . . ," *Business Week,* March 9, 1992, pp. 67–69.

64 Dorothy Marcic, *Managing with Wisdom and Love* (San Francisco: Jossey-Bass, 1997).

65 Marcia Parmarlee Miceli and Janet P. Near, "The Relationship among Beliefs, Organizational Positions, and Whistle-Blowing Status: A Discriminate Analysis," *Academy of Management Journal* 27(1984), pp. 687–705.

66 Marcia P. Miceli and Janet P. Near, "Whistleblowing: Reaping the Benefits," *Academy of Management Executive,* 8 (3) (1994), pp. 65–74.

67 Kurt Eichenwald, "He Told. He Suffered. Now He's a Hero." *The New York Times,* May 29, 1994, Section 3, 1.

68 Barbara Ettorre, "Whistleblowers: Who's the Real Bad Guy?" *Management Review,* May 1994, pp. 18–23.

69 Philip L. Cochran and Robert A. Wood, "Corporate Social Responsibility and Financial Performance," *Academy of Management Journal* 27 (1984), pp. 42–56.

70 Dale Kurschner, "5 Ways Ethical Business Creates Fatter Profits," *Business Ethics,* March–April 1996, pp. 20–23.

71 Louisa Wah, "Treading the Sacred Ground," *Management Review,* July–August 1998, pp. 18–22.

72 Edmund M. Burke, "Forget the Government, It's the Community That Can Shut You Down," *Business Ethics,* May–June 1997, pp. 11–13.

73 Roger Ricklefs, "Christian-Based Firms Find Following Principles Pays," *The Wall Street Journal,* December 8, 1989, p. B1; Jo David and Karen File; Tom Chappell, "The Soul of a Business," *Executive Female,* January–February 1994, pp. 38–77.

PART

3

PLANNING

Planning is a crucial task in successful racing. In a marathon such as the Whitbread, it is especially critical. The cost to enter a boat in the Whitbread averages $10 million, and the boat alone takes $2 million of that amount. Approximately $10,000 a week is needed to keep the boat, crew, and shore staff effectively supplied and ready. From the design of special hulls and sails that can carry less weight and gain greater speed to the delivery of equipment and supplies to ports and paring down costs, every detail along every leg of the race is plotted, planned, and reexamined. Why? Because the details make the difference. Racing strategy is determined before the race begins and reviewed before each leg. The navigator's skill in reading satellite weather forecasts and general ocean currents and plotting the course are sharpened when enhanced by state-of-the-art navigation software. Skippers use every available bit of this information to implement their strategy and gain an advantage. Quick decision making based on experience is also key to success. Every option must be determined and all decisions implemented—on the spot—based on general plans made long before. Crews that make the best judgments in these pressurized situations tend to leave the pack in their wake.

Part III discusses goal setting and planning, strategy formulation and implementation, and the importance of good managerial decision making.

Organizational Goal Setting and Planning

LEARNING OBJECTIVES

After studying this chapter, you should be able to:

- Define goals and plans and explain the relationship between them

- Explain the concept of organizational mission and how it influences goal setting and planning

- Describe the types of goals an organization should have and why they resemble a hierarchy

- Define the characteristics of effective goals

- Describe the four essential steps in the MBO process

- Explain the difference between single-use plans and standing plans

- Explain the new planning paradigm and its use in learning organizations

- Define the components of goal setting and strategic planning

"BIKING is a kind of cleansing of the

soul," says avid motorcyclist turned entrepreneur

Dave Hanlon, who with his wife and brother Dan decided to take on

the almighty Harley-Davidson, which owns about 40 percent of the street-bike

business. The Great Depression left Harley as King of the Road, and now Harleys are the

ultimate status symbol of bikers—the Cadillacs of bikes—and Harley owners join Harley clubs,

buy Harley clothes, even get Harley tattoos. Dan Hanlon had recently sold his biodegradable packaging

materials company, and his brother was bored with the trucking business. What better idea than to start a

company around their greatest passion—motorcycles. "Motorcyles are my release," says Dave. "I love to ride

• If you were one of the Hanlon brothers, what would you do? How would you get

financing and crucial core competencies to build the factory (both necessary steps in

their business plan)? Do you agree with their strategy to take on Harley-Davidson?

'em, fix 'em, beautify 'em." Adds Dan, "I like the feeling of the wind in my face and the freedom of the

open road. I like the smell of gasoline and oil." But loving motorcycles is not the same as knowing the

motorcycle business. Once they found that the name "Excelsior" was available, they committed

themselves to an arduous, capital-intensive endeavor of building a manufacturing plant from

scratch. Their resolve: to take on the $1.5 billion giant Harley-Davidson, which had

been unable to meet demand of its own product. The brothers had no

backers, no financing, no connections, and little cash.

Their first job was to create a business plan. Using their motorcycles as collateral, they took out a $40,000 loan and looked for serious financial backers. Even with their solid business background and enthusiasm, none of the hundreds of venture capitalists they contacted was willing to finance.[1]

The Hanlon brothers know that one of the primary responsibilities of leaders is to decide where they want the company to be in the future and how to get it there.

In some organizations, typically small ones, planning is informal. In others, managers follow a well-defined planning framework. The company establishes a basic mission and develops formal goals and strategic plans for carrying it out. Shell, IBM, Royal LaPaige, Mazda, and United Way undertake a strategic planning exercise each year—reviewing their missions, goals, and plans to meet environmental changes or the expectations of important stakeholders such as the community, owners, or stockholders.

Of the four management functions—planning, organizing, leading, and controlling—planning is the most fundamental. Everything else stems from planning. Yet planning also is the most controversial management function. Planning cannot address every event in an uncertain future. Planning cannot tame a turbulent environment. General Colin Powell offered this warning for managers: "No battle plan survives contact with the enemy." Consider the following comment by a noted authority on planning:

> Most corporate planning is like a ritual rain dance; it has no effect on the weather that follows, but it makes those who engage in it feel that they are in control. Most discussions of the role of models in planning are directed at improving the dancing, not the weather.[2] ∎

In this chapter, we're going to explore the process of planning and how it can help bring needed "rain." Special attention is given to goals and goal setting, for that is where planning starts. Also, the types of plans that organizations can use to achieve those goals are addressed, as well as new approaches to strate-

gic thinking and execution that emphasize the involvement of all employees. The chapter also covers the components of strategic management and presents a model of the strategic management process, as well as several models of strategy formulation. We will also discuss the tools managers use to implement their strategic plans. Finally, we'll look at management decision making and how information technology helps in that process.

Proper decision-making techniques are crucial to selecting the organization's goals, plans, and strategic options.

■ OVERVIEW OF GOALS AND PLANS

Goals and plans have become general concepts in our society. A **goal** is a desired future state that the organization attempts to realize.[3] Goals are important because organizations exist for a purpose and goals define and state that purpose. A **plan** is a blueprint for goal achievement and specifies the necessary resource allocations, schedules, tasks, and other actions. Goals specify future ends; plans specify today's means. The word **planning** usually incorporates both ideas; it means determining the organization's goals and defining the means for achieving them. Consider Germany's Volkswagen, where chief executive Ferdinand Piëch has set a goal to overtake Toyota Motor Company as the world's number three carmaker, with across-the-board brand recognition. To achieve this outcome, he wants to accomplish the following: purchase the Swedish truck maker Scania, which would add heavy trucks to the product line; buy Britain's Rolls Royce, to take VW into ultra-luxury cars; and design a V8-powered Volkswagen, to compete directly with Mercedes-Benz. To transform British Airways "from a British airline with a global reach to an airline of the world," CEO Bob Ayling is taking a four-pronged approach: Develop a marketing plan with universal appeal; help employees understand the global vision; benchmark off the mistakes others have made; and select the best partners for joint ventures overseas.[4]

Exhibit 5.1 illustrates the levels of goals and plans in an organization. The planning

goal
A desired future state that the organization attempts to realize

plan
A blueprint specifying the resource allocations, schedules, and other actions necessary for attaining goals

planning
The act of determining the organization's goals and the means for achieving them

process starts with a formal mission that defines the basic purpose of the organization, especially for external audiences. The mission is the basis for the strategic (company) level of goals and plans, which in turn shapes the tactical (divisional) level and the operational (departmental) level.[5] Planning at each level supports the other levels.

■ GOALS, PLANS, AND PERFORMANCE

The complexity of today's environment and uncertainty about the future overwhelm many managers and lead them to focus on operational issues and short-term results rather than long-term goals and plans. However, planning generally positively affects a company's performance.[6] In addition to improving financial and operational performance, developing explicit goals and plans at each level is important because of the external and internal messages they send. These messages go to both external and internal audiences and provide important benefits for the organization.[7]

LEGITIMACY

An organization's **mission** describes what the organization stands for and its reason for existence. It symbolizes legitimacy to external audiences such as investors, customers, and suppliers. The mission helps the local community to look on the company in a favorable light and, hence, accept its existence. A strong mission also has an impact on employees, enabling them to become committed to the organization because they can identify with its overall purpose and reason for existence. In *Fortune* magazine's study of the "100 Best Companies to Work for in America," a sense of purpose that employees could believe in and relate to was one of the top three traits cited by employees. For example, at Medtronic, a medical-products company, employees are inspired by the mission of "restoring patients to full life."[8]

SOURCE OF MOTIVATION AND COMMITMENT

Goals and plans help employees to identify with the organization and motivate them by

mission
The organization's reason for existence

reducing uncertainty and clarifying what they should accomplish. Lack of a clear goal can damage employee motivation and commitment.

Whereas a goal provides the "why" of an organization or subunit's existence, a plan tells the "how." A plan lets employees know what actions to undertake to achieve the goal. Etec uses planning not only to achieve its goals, but to help every employee become aligned with the company's mission.

Etec Systems, Inc., practically owns the market for pattern generation equipment—expensive machines that use lasers and electron beams to print intricate patterns onto silicon wafers. However, when Stephen Cooper took over as Etec's new president, the company was generating red ink at the rate of $1 million a month. What's worse, politicians and the press were pointing to Etec as a symbol of the decline of U.S. industry. Everyone thought Cooper was crazy when he announced a goal to generate $500 million in revenues by the year 2000. Four years later, Etec was being hailed as one of the most remarkable comebacks in Silicon Valley. Revenues increased by 75 percent and keep going up, while profits also are steadily growing. High-tech industries change so rapidly that many people think it's impossible to plan for the future. At Etec, managers spend most of their time dealing with short-term crises. Yet Cooper turned Etec around by getting back to the basics of planning: "When a company has a clear mission, and people know how their individual mission fits into the big picture, everyone paddles in the same direction," he says. The company is well on its way to reaching Cooper's audacious goal, thanks to a specific, step-by-step plan that helps employees maintain clarity in the face of rapid change. All 800 employees are intimately involved in planning. Cooper wants everyone to understand the mission and to understand how his or her work fits into the big picture. He sets stretch goals that prompt employees to reach for the stars. Each employee develops a personal list of goals and plans that correlate with those of the department and organization. Each person in the company, from shop-floor workers to the CEO, identifies five to seven key goals, creates metrics to track progress, and ranks each goal's importance rel-

ative to the others. However, Etec realizes that plans cannot be static. Each week, every employee meets briefly with a direct supervisor to review plans and work together on modifications. The end result of Etec's simple system is that every person in the organization knows what he or she should be doing, how important it is relative to other assignments, and how it relates to the goals of other employees. Etec's system thus enables the company's 800 employees to manage themselves. In a company moving as fast as Etec, says manager Phil Arnold, the system helps you to "keep your eye on the ball."[9]

GUIDES TO ACTION

Goals and plans provide a sense of direction. They focus attention on specific targets and direct employee efforts toward important outcomes. Hartford Technology Services Co., for example, set goals to establish a customer profile database, survey customer satisfaction, and secure service agreements with ten new customers.[10]

RATIONALE FOR DECISIONS

Through goal setting and planning, managers learn what the organization is trying to accomplish. They can make decisions to ensure that internal policies, roles, performance, structure, products, and expenditures will be made in accordance with desired outcomes. Decisions throughout the organization will be in alignment with the plan.

STANDARD OF PERFORMANCE

Because goals define desired outcomes for the organization, they also serve as performance criteria. They provide a standard of assessment. If an organization wishes to grow by 15 percent, and actual growth is 17 percent, managers will have exceeded their prescribed standard. Ed Woolard defined a goal at Du Pont of nurturing high-potential businesses while strengthening old-line businesses to produce an average return on equity of 16 percent. However, formerly fast-growing electronics businesses fell flat, and return on equity plunged to 8.3 percent. Du Pont did not meet its standard of performance for this goal.[11]

The overall planning process prevents managers from thinking merely in terms of day-to-day activities. When organizations drift away from goals and plans, they typically get into trouble. This occurred at Amex Life Assurance, an American Express subsidiary based in San Rafael, California. A new president implemented a strong planning system that illustrates the power of planning to improve organizational performance.

AMEX LIFE ASSURANCE

Sarah Nolan knew that the chairman of American Express was a self-professed maniac on quality. But when Nolan arrived as the new president of Amex Life Assurance, she found a paperwork assembly line that served customers at a snail's pace. A simple change of address took two days and sending out a new insurance policy took at least 10. Nolan's primary goal was to get everyone at Amex working together while keeping the focus on the customer. She sent five managers representing different specialties to an empty office park and told them to imagine they were setting up an entirely new business. Nolan gave the group only three rules to follow in their task of planning a new operation:

- Put the customer first.
- Don't copy anything we do here.
- Be ready to process applications yourselves in six months.

When the planning group returned, ten layers of personnel had been collapsed into three, each of which would deal directly with the public. Fewer employees were needed, so more than one-third were transferred to other divisions. Expenses were cut in half and profitability increased sixfold. Nolan used planning to help managers break out of their focus on day-to-day activities and reorient the company toward its strategic goal of customer satisfaction.[12] ∎

■ GOALS IN ORGANIZATIONS

Setting goals starts with top managers. The overall planning process begins with a mission statement and strategic goals for the organization as a whole.

ORGANIZATIONAL MISSION

At the top of the goal hierarchy is the mission—the organization's reason for existence. The mission describes the organization's values, aspirations, and reason for being. A well-defined mission is the basis for development of all subsequent goals and plans. Without a clear mission, goals and plans may be developed haphazardly and not take the organization in the direction it needs to go.

The formal **mission statement** is a broadly stated definition of basic business scope and operations that distinguishes the organization from others of a similar type.[13] The content of a mission statement often focuses on the market and customers and identifies desired fields of endeavor. Some mission statements describe company characteristics such as corporate values, product quality, location of facilities, and attitude toward employees. Mission statements often reveal the company's

mission statement
A broadly stated definition of the organization's basic business scope and operations that distinguishes it from similar types of organizations

"To be widely recognized for leadership and accomplishment as a food processing and marketing cooperative, by using all of our members' and employees' talents," is the mission statement of Pro-Fac Cooperative, an agricultural marketing cooperative that consists of over 600 members. The cooperative processes fruits, vegetables, and popcorn through its wholly-owned subsidiary, Agrilink Foods, in facilities across the United States. This mission statement, which promotes the talents of employees and introduces the annual report, seeks legitimacy with external audiences through recognition of Pro-Fac's leadership and accomplishments in food processing.

philosophy as well as purpose. One example is the mission statement for Fetzer Vineyards. Fetzer devised its three-sentence mission statement to express its commitment to ethical considerations as well as good business practices.

> We are an environmentally and socially conscious grower, producer, and marketer of wines of the highest quality and value.
>
> Working in harmony and with respect for the human spirit, we are committed to sharing information about the enjoyment of food and wine in a lifestyle of moderation and responsibility.
>
> We are dedicated to the continuous growth and development of our people and business.

Fetzer believes its social and environmental commitment contributes directly to the bottom line. For one thing, the statement fosters a positive image for Fetzer in the community. In addition, according to Andy Beckstoffer, one of Fetzer's outside growers, "It's good business to preserve your lands; it's good business to produce a healthy product." Providing employees with opportunities to develop their capabilities strengthens the organization as well. This simple statement makes clear to both employees and customers what Fetzer stands for.[14]

Such short, straightforward mission statements describe basic business activities and purposes as well as the values that guide the company. Another example of this type of mission statement is that of Lunar Productions, a Memphis, Tennessee, corporate-video producer with $800,000 in annual sales. Lunar's president, Geordy Wells, is a spiritual man who wanted to reflect Lunar's commitment to honest, ethical business practices:

> Honor God in all we do.
>
> Provide excellent and affordable corporate-video, audio/visual, and broadcast production services to our valued clients.
>
> Communicate with our clients and fellow employees as effectively as we communicate with our audiences.
>
> Make a fair profit.[15]

Because of mission statements such as those of Fetzer Vineyards and Lunar Productions, employees as well as customers, suppliers, and stockholders know the company's stated purpose and values. One company that learned through failure to pay attention to its mission is Jostens Inc.

JOSTENS INC.

You might have one of their products on your finger, but you probably don't own any of their software. That's because Minneapolis-based Jostens Inc. forgot what business it was in. Somehow the well-known class ring and yearbook maker's planning and strategy went haywire in 1989, when it launched Jostens Learning Corporation. It's 34-year record of continually increasing sales and earnings crashed in 1993 when the bubble burst.

Planners thought the move would capitalize on their excellent distribution channels. Why not expand into educational software, right? They bought up their biggest competitor and owned 60 percent of the market. Foolproof strategy, so it seemed.

But the planners neglected to consider the needs of their customers. Jostens integrated learning software linked all computers to a file system, which required a high start-up cost for schools. Modular step-by-step integration was offered by competitors. By 1993, Jostens had run up a $12 million loss.

Their lack of thoughtful planning and attention to mission was a recipe for disaster. Jostens Learning Corporation, that cost $54 million in 1994, was sold in June 1995. But late 1995 stock prices were up 40 percent from the previous year. Jostens could have avoided this mistake by looking more carefully at its own mission and core competencies. Simply having a distribution system in schools was not enough. They knew virtually nothing about computers and software and should have realized their lack of expertise.

After the sale of Jostens Learning in 1995, the company reevaluated its mission and decided to focus on strengths with rings, yearbooks, and graduation products. The new vision: to become the company that helps people "celebrate life's important moments," both in the workplace and through schools. It must be working, because sales have climbed steadily, increasing 16 percent by 1999.[16] ■

GOALS AND PLANS

Broad statements describing where the organization wants to be in the future are called **strategic goals.** They pertain to the organization as a whole rather than to specific divisions or departments. **Strategic plans** define the action steps by which the company intends to attain strategic goals. The strategic plan is the blueprint that defines the organizational activities and resource allocations—in the form of cash, personnel, space, and facilities—required for meeting these targets. Strategic planning tends to be long term and may define organizational action steps from two to five years in the future. The purpose of strategic plans is to turn organizational goals into realities within that time period.

The results that major divisions and departments within the organization intend to

strategic goals
Broad statements about the organization's direction and future that pertain to the organization as a whole rather than to specific divisions or departments

strategic plans
The action steps by which an organization intends to attain its strategic goals

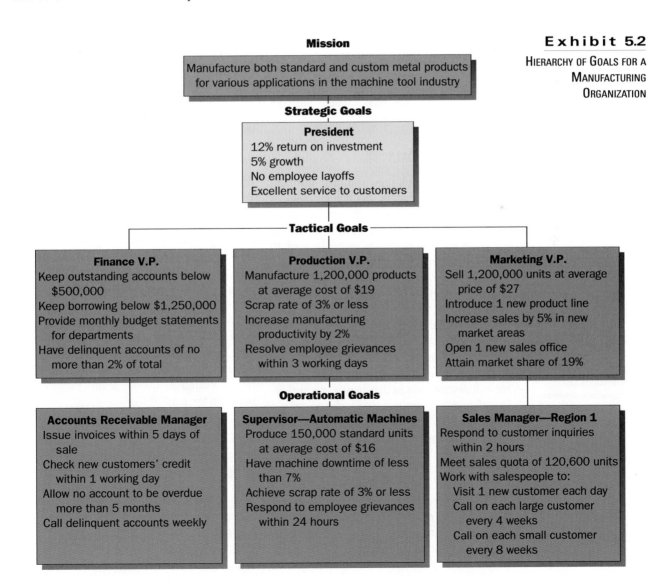

Exhibit 5.2

HIERARCHY OF GOALS FOR A MANUFACTURING ORGANIZATION

achieve are defined as **tactical goals. Tactical plans** are designed to help execute major strategic plans and to accomplish a specific part of the company's strategy. Tactical plans typically have a shorter time horizon than strategic plans—over the next year or so.

The specific results expected from departments, work groups, and individuals are the **operational goals.** They are precise and measurable. "Process 150 sales applications each week," "achieve 90 percent of deliveries on time," "reduce overtime by 10 percent next month," and "develop two new elective courses in accounting" are examples of operational goals. **Operational plans** are developed at the lower levels of the organization to specify action steps toward achieving operational goals and to support tactical plans. The operational plan is the department manager's tool for daily and weekly operations. Goals are stated in quantitative terms, and the department plan describes how goals will be achieved.

HIERARCHY OF GOALS

Effectively designed organizational goals fit into a hierarchy; that is, the achievement of goals at low levels permits the attainment of high-level goals. This is called a means-ends chain because low-level goals lead to accomplishment of high-level goals. Operational goals lead to the achievement of tactical goals, which in turn lead to the attainment of strategic goals. Strategic goals are traditionally considered the responsibility of top management, tactical goals that of middle management, and operational goals that of first-line supervisors and workers. However, as we will discuss later in the chapter, the shrinking of middle management combined with a new emphasis on employee empowerment have led to a greater involvement of all employees in goal setting and planning at each level.

An example of a goal hierarchy is illustrated in the preceding Exhibit 5.2. Note how the strategic goal of "excellent service to customers" translates into "Open one new sales office" and "Respond to customer inquiries within two hours" at lower management levels.

■ CRITERIA FOR EFFECTIVE GOALS

To make sure that goal-setting benefits the organization, certain characteristics and guidelines should be adopted. The characteristics of goals and the goal-setting process must pertain to organizational goals at the strategic, tactical, and operational levels.

SPECIFIC AND MEASURABLE   When possible, goals should be expressed in quantitative terms, such as increasing profits by 2 percent, decreasing scrap by 1 percent, or increasing average teacher effectiveness ratings from 3.5 to 3.7 percent. A team at Sealed Air Corporation, a manufacturer of packaging materials, was motivated by a goal to reduce by two hours the average time needed to change machine settings. The team was spurred to keep going when members could see that their earliest efforts reduced changeover time by a significant amount.[17] Not all goals can be expressed in numerical terms, but vague goals have little motivating power for employees. By necessity, goals are qualitative as well as quantitative, especially at the top of the organization. The important point is that the goals be precisely defined and allow for measurable progress. For example, Liisa Joronen, chairman of SOL Cleaning Service, believes in giving teams the right to set their own performance goals; however, she's a stickler for accountability. "The more we free our people from rules," she says, "the more we need good measurements." Every time SOL lands a contract, the salesperson works at the new customer's site along with the SOL team that will do the future cleaning. Together they establish performance goals. Every month, customers rate the team's performance based on the goals.[18]

COVER KEY RESULT AREAS   Goals cannot be set for every aspect of employee behavior or organizational performance; if they were, their sheer number would render them meaningless. Instead, managers should identify a few key result areas—perhaps up to four or five for any organizational department or job. Key result areas are those activities that contribute most to company performance.[19]

tactical goals
Goals that define the outcomes that major divisions and departments must achieve in order for the organization to reach its overall goals

tactical plans
Plans designed to help execute major strategic plans and to accomplish a specific part of the company's strategy

operational goals
Specific, measurable results expected from departments, work groups, and individuals within the organization

operational plans
Plans developed at the organization's lower levels that specify action steps toward achieving operational goals and that support tactical planning activities

Robert Hershey, partner in charge of KPMG Peat Marwick's World-Class Finance Practice, recommends that companies as a whole track no more than 20 key result areas in four distinct categories: financial indicators; customer-related indicators; process-related indicators; and future-value indicators (including human resources).[20]

CHALLENGING BUT REALISTIC   Goals should be challenging but not unreasonably difficult. One newly hired manager discovered that his staff would have to work 100-hour weeks to accomplish everything expected of them. When goals are unrealistic, they set employees up for failure and lead to decreasing employee morale.[21] However, if goals are too easy, employees may not feel motivated. Tom Peters, coauthor of *In Search of Excellence,* believes that the best quality programs start with extremely ambitious goals, called *stretch goals*, that challenge employees to meet high standards. Companies such as Rubbermaid and 3M bring out the best in their employees by making goals ever more challenging. The CEO of 3M has decreed that 30 percent of sales must come from products introduced in the past four years; the old standard was 25 percent.[22] Managers should, however, make sure that goals are set within the existing resource base, not beyond the time, equipment, and financial resources of departments.

DEFINED TIME PERIOD   Goals should specify the time period over which they will be achieved. A time period is a deadline stating the date on which goal attainment will be measured. A goal of setting up a customer database could have a deadline such as June 30, 2000. If a strategic goal involves a two- to three-year time horizon, specific dates for achieving parts of it can be set up. For example, strategic sales goals could be established on a three-year time horizon, with a $100 million target in year one, a $129 million target in year two, and a $165 million target in year three.

LINKED TO REWARDS   The ultimate impact of goals depends on the extent to which salary increases, promotions, and awards are based on goal achievement. People who attain goals should be rewarded. Rewards give meaning and significance to goals and help commit employees to achieving goals. Failure to attain goals often is due to factors outside the control of the employees. For example, failure to achieve a financial goal may be associated with a drop in market demand due to industry recession; thus, an employee could not be expected to reach it. Nevertheless, a reward may be appropriate if the employee partially achieved goals under difficult circumstances.[23]

■ PLANNING TYPES AND MODELS

Once strategic, tactical, and operational goals have been determined, managers may select a planning approach most appropriate for their situation. Critical to successful planning are flexibility and adaptability to changing environments. Managers use a number of planning approaches. Among the most popular are management by objectives, single-use plans, standing plans, and contingency (or scenario) plans.

MANAGEMENT BY OBJECTIVES

Management by objectives (MBO) is a method whereby managers and employees define goals for every department, project, and person and use them to monitor subsequent performance.[24] A model of the essential steps of the MBO process is presented in Exhibit 5.3. Four major activities must occur in order for MBO to be successful:[25]

1. *Set goals*. This is the most difficult step in MBO. Setting goals involves employees at all levels and looks beyond day-to-day activities to answer the question "What are we trying to accomplish?" A good goal should be concrete and realistic, provide a specific target and time frame, and assign responsibility. Goals may be quantitative or qualitative, depending on whether outcomes are measurable. Quantitative goals are described in numerical terms, such as "Salesperson Jones will obtain 16 new accounts in December." Qualitative goals use statements such as "Marketing will reduce complaints by improving customer service next

management by objectives (MBO)
A method of management whereby managers and employees define goals for every department, project, and person and use them to monitor subsequent performance

Exhibit 5.3

MODEL OF THE MBO PROCESS

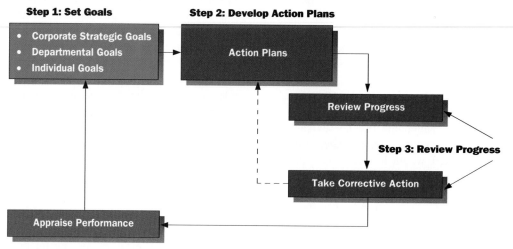

Step 1: Set Goals
- Corporate Strategic Goals
- Departmental Goals
- Individual Goals

Step 2: Develop Action Plans

Action Plans

Review Progress

Step 3: Review Progress

Take Corrective Action

Appraise Performance

Step 4: Appraise Overall Performance

year." Goals should be jointly derived. Mutual agreement between employee and supervisor creates the strongest commitment to achieving goals. In the case of teams, all team members may participate in setting goals.

2. *Develop action plans.* An action plan defines the course of action needed to achieve the stated goals. Action plans are made for both individuals and departments.

3. *Review progress.* A periodic progress review is important to ensure that action plans are working. These reviews can occur informally between managers and subordinates, where the organization may wish to conduct three-, six-, or nine-month reviews during the year. This periodic checkup allows managers and employees to see whether they are on target or whether corrective action is necessary. Managers and employees should not be locked into predefined behavior and must be willing to take whatever steps are necessary to produce meaningful results. The point of MBO is to achieve goals. The action plan can be changed whenever goals are not being met.

4. *Appraise overall performance.* The final step in MBO is to carefully evaluate

whether annual goals have been achieved for both individuals and departments. Success or failure to achieve goals can become part of the performance appraisal system and the designation of salary increases and other rewards. The appraisal of departmental and overall corporate performance shapes goals for the next year. The MBO cycle repeats itself on an annual basis.

BENEFITS AND PROBLEMS WITH MBO

Many companies, such as Intel, Tenneco, Black & Decker, and Du Pont, have adopted MBO, and most managers believe that MBO is an effective management tool.[26] Managers believe they are better oriented toward goal achievement when MBO is used. Like any system, MBO achieves benefits when used properly but results in problems when used improperly. Benefits and problems are summarized in Exhibit 5.4.

The benefits of the MBO process can be many. Corporate goals are more likely to be achieved when they focus manager and employee efforts. Performance is improved because employees are committed to attaining the goal, are motivated because they help decide what is expected, and are free to be resourceful. Goals at lower levels are aligned

Benefits of MBO	Problems with MBO
1. Manager and employee efforts are focused on activities that will lead to goal attainment.	1. Constant change prevents MBO from taking hold.
2. Performance can be improved at all company levels.	2. An environment of poor employer–employee relations reduces MBO effectiveness.
3. Employees are motivated.	3. Strategic goals may be displaced by operational goals.
4. Departmental and individual goals are aligned with company goals.	4. Mechanistic organizations and values that discourage participation can harm the MBO process.
	5. Too much paperwork saps MBO energy.

with and enable the attainment of goals at top management levels.

Problems with MBO occur when the company faces rapid change. The environment and internal activities must have some stability for performance to be measured and compared against goals. When new goals must be set every few months, there is no time for action plans and appraisal to take effect. Also, poor employer-employee relations reduce effectiveness because there is an element of distrust between managers and workers. Sometimes goal "displacement" occurs if employees focus exclusively on their operational goals to the detriment of other teams or departments. Overemphasis on operational goals can harm the attainment of overall goals. Another problem arises in mechanistic organizations characterized by rigidly defined tasks and rules that may not be compatible with MBO's emphasis on mutual determination of goals by employee and supervisor. In addition, when participation is discouraged, employees will lack the training and values to jointly set goals with employers. Finally, if MBO becomes a process of filling out annual paperwork rather than energizing employees to achieve goals, it becomes an empty exercise. Once the paperwork is completed, employees forget about the goals, perhaps even resenting the paperwork in the first place.

SINGLE-USE AND STANDING PLANS

Single-use plans are developed to achieve a set of goals that are not likely to be repeated in the future. **Standing plans** are ongoing plans that are used to provide guidance for tasks performed repeatedly within the organization. Exhibit 5.5 outlines the major types of single-use and standing plans. Single-use plans typically include both programs and projects. The primary standing plans are organizational policies, rules, and procedures. Standing plans generally pertain to such matters as employee illness, absences, smoking, discipline, hiring, and dismissal. Many companies are discovering a need to develop standing plans regarding the use of e-mail, as discussed in Focus on Ethics.

QUALITY PLANNING AND THE SHEWHART CYCLE

Many companies have instituted standing plans for quality improvement, often based on W. Edwards Deming's 14 points of quality management. Employees are encouraged to participate in the continuous improvement of product and service quality. Total quality management (introduced in Chapter 1) is discussed in greater detail in Chapter 16. These companies often use the **Shewhart Cycle** of continuous improvement (sometimes called the PDCA Cycle—Plan, Do, Check, Act), as illustrated in Exhibit 5.6. First, managers plan a test or change in a specific process, then they conduct the test or carry out the change, check the results, and finally act to improve the process based upon what they've learned. A number of cycle iterations may be needed before satisfactory results are achieved. The cycle repeats itself continuously. Planning is an

single-use plans
Plans that are developed to achieve a set of goals that are unlikely to be repeated in the future

standing plans
Ongoing plans used to provide guidance for tasks performed repeatedly within the organization

Shewhart cycle
A planning cycle used in companies that have instituted quality management; also called the PDCA Cycle—plan, do, check, act

Single-Use Plans	Standing Plans
Program	**Policy**
• Plans for attaining a one-time organizational goal	• Broad in scope—a general guide to action
• Major undertaking that may take several years to complete	• Based on organization's overall goals/strategic plan
• Large in scope; may be associated with several projects	• Defines boundaries within which to make decisions
Examples: Boeing's 777 aircraft NASA space station	**Examples:** Drug-free workplace policies Sexual harassment policies Continuous Improvement Shewhart Cycle
Project	**Rule**
• Also a set of plans for attaining a one-time goal	• Narrow in scope
• Smaller in scope and complexity than a program; shorter time horizon	• Describes how a specific action is to be performed
• Often one part of a larger program	• May apply to specific setting
Examples: Development of a rocket booster for NASA space station Development of external shell for NASA space station	**Example:** No-smoking rule in areas of plant where hazardous materials are stored
	Procedure
	• Sometimes called a standard operating procedure
	• Defines a precise series of steps to attain certain goals
	Examples: Procedures for issuing refunds Procedures for handling employee grievances

ongoing activity, and everyone in the organization can learn from experience to help the company improve.[27] An interesting variation of this cycle is used by the U.S. Army at its National Training Center and increasingly is being adopted by corporations.

U.S. ARMY
www.army.mil

At the National Training Center just south of Death Valley, U.S. Army troops engage in a simulated battle: the "enemy" has sent unmanned aerial vehicles (UAVs) to gather targeting data. When troops fire upon the UAVs, they reveal their location to attack helicopters hovering just behind a nearby ridge. After the exercise, unit members and their superiors hold "After-Action Reviews" to review battle plans, discuss what worked and what didn't, and talk about how to do things better. General William Hertzog suggested that inexpensive decoy UAVs might be just the thing to make a distracted enemy reveal his location. The observation amounts to a "lesson learned" for the entire army.

The army's "lessons-learned" system is a process of identifying and reducing mistakes, of innovating, and of continuously learning from experience. The system has led to lessons such as how to prevent problems leading to friendly fire casualties in the Gulf War and how to

FOCUS ON Ethics

REGULATING E-MAIL IN THE WORKPLACE

Top executives around the globe are discovering that casual e-mail messages can come back to haunt them—in court. Messages dashed off years ago by Bill Gates became digital "smoking guns" in the Justice Department's antitrust case against Microsoft. Authorities studied electronic messages by Gates and other top leaders at Microsoft for evidence that the company was out to crush competitors and monopolize access to the Internet.

"E-mail discovery" has companies scrambling to figure out how to avoid getting tripped up by the informal, candid, and sometimes inflammatory messages this new means of communication can foster. People have a tendency to put things in e-mail messages that they wouldn't consider writing in a paper document. Morgan Stanley Dean Witter & Co., for example, recently agreed to settle a discrimination suit based largely on e-mailed jokes that played on stereotypes about African American speech patterns. The growing use of e-mail has made it easier than ever to win lawsuits involving everything from sexual harassment to stolen trade secrets. Yet companies are just beginning to recognize their e-mail vulnerability. In a 1997 survey, barely half of the companies polled had written policies governing the use of e-mail, and only about a quarter of those actually enforced the policies. Some worry that monitoring e-mail will trigger complaints of Big Brother in the workplace, while others worry primarily that regulating e-mail stifles creativity.

A few companies are ahead of the game in developing strict e-mail policies. At Prudential Insurance Company, employees are prohibited from using company e-mail to share jokes, photographs, or any kind of nonbusiness information. Merrill Lynch requires all employees to sign off on the company's e-mail policy. Further, some companies are turning to software to help police e-mail. Citibank, Lockheed Martin, and General Electric, for example, have installed electronic shredding programs on thousands of laptops in the field. Hughes Hubbard & Reed LLP, a New York law firm, is developing software called MailCop that uses artificial intelligence to warn workers when they have written or received e-mail that may violate company rules. As problems with electronic mail—and lawsuits—continue to grow, more and more companies are likely to develop strict policies regulating e-mail in the workplace.

SOURCE: Marcia Stepanek, with Steve Hamm, "When the Devil Is in the E-mails," *Business Week*, June 8, 1998, pp. 72–74.

---

avoid minefields and booby traps in Bosnia. The army stockpiles lessons learned and disseminates them throughout the combat force. In Bosnia, a new list of lessons was distributed every 72 hours. The lessons are based not only on simulated battles, but also on real-life experiences of soldiers in the field. The Center for Army Lessons Learned (CALL) sends experts into the field to observe after-action reviews, interview soldiers, and read intelligence reports. In 1994, CALL compiled 26 lessons for replacement troops in Haiti, who actually confronted 23 of those scenarios within their first few months of deployment.

The army has come to depend greatly on its lessons-learned system for organizational learning and continuous improvement. A case study by the Harvard Business School concluded that the system enables the army to minimize mistakes and sustain successes efficiently. The lessons-learned system is now getting some attention from corporate America. Black & Veatch, an engineering company based in Kansas City, Missouri, and Steelcase Inc., an office furniture manufacturer in Grand Rapids, Michigan, are among the companies adapting the lessons-learned system to create a process of continuous learning and improvement.[28] ∎

CONTINGENCY PLANS

When organizations are operating in a highly uncertain environment or dealing with long

Exhibit 5.6

THE SHEWHART CYCLE OF
CONTINUOUS IMPROVEMENT

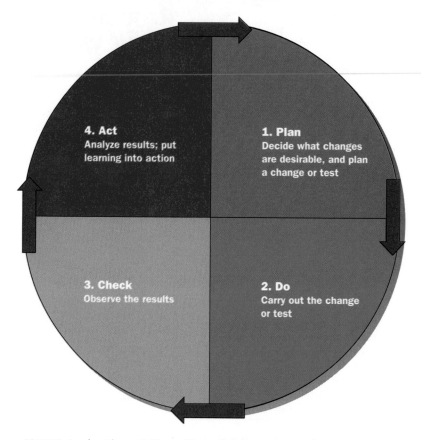

4. Act
Analyze results; put
learning into action

1. Plan
Decide what changes
are desirable, and plan
a change or test

3. Check
Observe the results

2. Do
Carry out the change
or test

SOURCE: Based on Thomas F. Rienzo, "Planning Deming Management for Service Organizations," *Business Horizons,* 36 (3) (May–June 1993), pp. 19–29.

time horizons, sometimes planning can seem like a waste of time. In fact, strict plans may even hinder rather than help an organization's performance in the face of rapid technological, social, economic, or other environmental change. In these cases, managers can develop multiple future scenarios to help them form more flexible plans. **Contingency plans,** sometimes referred to as *scenarios,* define company responses to be taken in the case of emergencies, setbacks, or unexpected conditions. To develop contingency plans, planners identify uncontrollable factors, such as recession, inflation, technological developments, or safety accidents. To minimize the impact of these potential factors, a planning team can forecast the worst-case scenarios. For example, if sales fall 20 percent and prices drop

8 percent, what will the company do? Contingency plans can then be defined for possible layoffs, emergency budgets, and sales efforts.[29]

Royal Dutch/Shell Oil has used scenario planning since the 1970s and has been consistently better in its oil forecasts than other major oil companies. Several years ago, contingency planning was used at Shell for dealing with a potential drop in oil prices that could be catastrophic. Oil was $28 a barrel and rising, but the planning group challenged Shell managers to consider what they would do in the unlikely event that oil suddenly dropped to $15 a barrel. As it turned out, the price of oil did drop to $15 a barrel within a few months, and Shell executives were ready because they had developed contingency plans.[30]

contingency plans
Plans that define company
responses to specific
situations, such as
emergencies, setbacks, or
unexpected conditions; also
called *scenarios*

■ PLANNING TIME HORIZON

Organizational goals and plans are associated with specific time horizons. The time horizons are long term, intermediate term, and short term, as illustrated in Exhibit 5.7. *Long-term planning* includes strategic goals and plans and may extend as far as five years into the future. *Intermediate-term planning* includes tactical goals and has a time horizon of from one to two years. *Short-term planning* includes operational goals for specific departments and individuals and has a time horizon of one year or less.

One of the major problems in companies today is the emphasis on *short-term results*. Long-term planning is difficult because the world is so uncertain. Moreover, the financial community, including stock analysts and mutual-fund managers, push companies for strong financial results in the short term. This pressure fits the natural inclination of many results-oriented managers, who are concerned with outcomes for today and next week—not next year, and certainly not five years out. These pressures tend to reward short-term performance and undercut long-range planning. For example, a Tennessee manufacturer of temperature control devices badly needed new plants and facilities that required massive expenditures. The managers' bonuses were calculated on profits for a one-year period. In this case, the pressures for short-term results took precedence, and the managers did not invest money in new facilities because short-term profits would suffer.

Focusing too heavily on short-term profitability as a goal has handicapped many U.S. and other Western businesses competing internationally. Japanese companies, by contrast, often take a long-term view and have multiple goals, giving equal weight to market share, profitability, and innovation.[31] Consider Matsushita Electric, the world's largest producer of consumer electronics, VCRs, color televisions, and video cameras. Sixty years ago, Konosuke Matsushita foresaw the day when the United States would provide both major markets and manufacturing centers for his company's small appliances. In 1932 he announced an ambitious 250-year plan for the company, perhaps an all-time record for long-range planning.[32] Long-term planning need not resort to such extremes. Today, senior executives are redirecting Matsushita into four areas where future growth is expected: semiconductors, factory automation, office automation, and audiovisual products. These products generate only 13 percent of sales but are expected to do well in the twenty-first century and so today are receiving 70 percent of the company's research expenditures.[33]

THE NEW PLANNING PARADIGM

Today, some companies are taking decentralized planning even further and involving workers at every level of the organization in the planning process. In this new paradigm, a **decentralized planning staff**—made up of middle managers and other planners—works with a **planning task force** of line managers and

decentralized planning staff
A group of planning specialists assigned to major departments and divisions to help managers develop their own strategic plans

planning task force
A temporary group consisting of line managers responsible for developing strategic plans

Exhibit 5.7
PLANNING TIME HORIZON

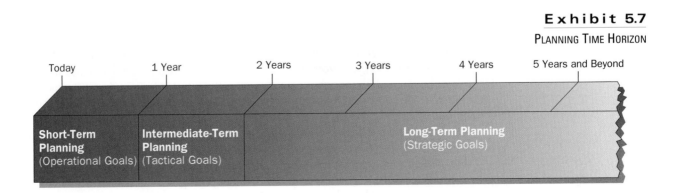

frontline workers to develop dynamic plans that meet the organization's needs. In a complex and competitive business environment, traditional planning done by a select few no longer works. Strategic thinking and execution become the expectation of every employee.[34] For an example of a company that is finding hidden sources of ideas and innovation by involving all its workers in planning, consider Springfield Remanufacturing.

SPRINGFIELD REMANUFACTURING CORPORATION

Jack Stack, chairman and CEO of Springfield Remanufacturing Corp. (SRC), believes companies can thrive by tapping into people's universal desire to win. SRC, which began as a division of International Harvester, is a business Stack calls tough, loud, and dirty—a place "where people work with plugs in their ears and leave the factory every day covered in grease." Stack has built a highly successful company based on the philosophy that "the best, most efficient, most profitable way to operate a business is to give everybody a voice in how the company is run and a stake in the financial outcome, good or bad."

Stack involves every employee in the planning process and uses a bonus system based on hitting the plan's targets. SRC's planning officially kicks off when Stack and other top executives meet with the sales and marketing managers of SRC's 15 divisions in a formal two-day event. But before that meeting, the sales and marketing managers have done their homework by meeting with managers, supervisors, and frontline workers throughout their divisions. If a manager's plan is beyond the plant's capacity, the workers suggest workable alternatives. By the time managers present their plans to the top brass, everyone in the various divisions has had a say and has thus developed a sense of ownership in the plan.

All employees have access to the company's financial data and can compare performance to the plan. SRC has invested heavily in financial education for all workers—everyone learns what's at risk and what's to be gained, and everyone knows how to make a difference. Kevin Dotson, an ex-Marine who works in the Heavy Duty warehouse, says he learns something new about the financial statements every time he goes to a meeting. "It's not like you have just one meeting and learn everything. . . . But you do understand the lines on the statement that you actually affect. That's how you see how you can be more efficient or how we as a small team within a large team can improve so the next group can take the handoff more smoothly. We all have different jobs, but we're all pulling for the same goals."[35] ■

Planning comes alive when employees are involved in setting goals and determining the means to reach them. Learning organizations follow six rules of planning.

START WITH A STRONG MISSION   Employee commitment and involvement are critical to helping companies compete in today's rapidly changing world. A compelling mission often serves to increase employee commitment and motivation as well as provide a guide for planning and decision making.[36] In a six-year study of exceptional companies that have stood the test of time, including Wal-Mart, 3M, General Electric, and Johnson & Johnson, James C. Collins and Jerry Porras identified a number of timeless fundamentals that helped make these companies great. They found one of the key factors to be that these companies were guided by a "core ideology"—values and a sense of purpose that go beyond just making money and that provide a guide for behavior. For example, a lot of the faith Johnson & Johnson executives place in decentralized managers can be traced to the well-known Johnson & Johnson Credo, a code of ethics that tells managers what to care about and in what order. Interestingly, in this complex $15 billion organization that has never lost money since going public in 1944, the Credo puts profits dead last on the list of things managers should care about.[37]

SET STRETCH GOALS   Stretch goals are highly ambitious goals that are so clear, compelling, and imaginative that they fuel progress. When shifting to a learning organization, top managers can set stretch goals to compel employees to think in new ways. Motorola used stretch goals to improve quality. Leaders first set a goal of a tenfold increase in quality over a two-year period. After this goal was met, they set a new stretch goal of a hundredfold improvement in quality over four years.[38]

CREATE AN ENVIRONMENT THAT ENCOURAGES LEARNING   A basic value in learning organizations is to question the status quo. Constant questioning opens the gates to creativity and learning. Companies such as Nucor Steel encourage and reward constant experimentation and risk taking. So much worker experimentation is going on that Larry Roos, manager of the Crawfordsville, Indiana, plant, says "Half the time I don't know who's doing what out there." Although an environment of rampant experimentation can lead to failures, more importantly it leads to flexibility, learning, and improving.[39]

MAKE CONTINUOUS IMPROVEMENT A WAY OF LIFE   Involving everyone in planning encourages employees to continuously learn and grow, thus helping the organization improve its capability. No plan is set in stone because people are constantly learning and improving. Highly successful companies such as 3M often make their best moves through constant experimentation and improvement. 3M encourages its employees to try just about anything and gives them 15 percent of their work time to do so.

■ THINKING STRATEGICALLY

The story of Fuji and Kodak illustrates the importance of strategic planning. When CEO George Fisher took over at Kodak in late 1993, he recognized that the ailing company needed a strategy overhaul. Although conditions have greatly improved for Kodak since that time, the company seems to be out of touch with customers and struggling still to develop a strategic direction for the future. Meanwhile, Fuji's managers have formulated and implemented strategies that have led to significant growth and increased market share for the Japanese company.

Blessed with a powerhouse brand name, Kodak was rich, proud, and much admired by consumers. But things haven't been so bright at Kodak lately. Earnings have dropped, the stock took a nosedive, and the company announced its eighth round of layoffs since the mid-1980s. Meanwhile, Kodak's biggest competitor, Japan's Fuji Photo Film Co., is gradually gaining market share, and its stock price has been on a rapid climb. Fuji is already on the brink of overtaking Kodak on a global basis, particularly in Asia, where film sales are growing at about 20 percent a year. Moreover, the Japanese company is creeping up on Kodak's U.S. market at a rate of about 2 percent a year. For the first time in its 118-year history, Kodak can no longer take its home market for granted. In addition to film sales, the two companies are competing in film processing, the manufacture of photographic paper for sale to big photo-processing labs and small retail developers, and digital photography—areas in which Fuji also is gaining an edge. Fuji's current slogan, "You can see the future from here," plays on the desire to differentiate the company from Kodak's nostalgic approach. For Kodak, the future isn't looking too rosy. As one analyst said, if current trends hold, "Kodak will go from being Coke to being Pepsi."[40]

Every organization is concerned with strategy. Hershey developed a new strategy of being a fierce product innovator to compete with Mars in the candy wars. Hershey has scored big with the introduction of products such as Hugs, a white-chocolate version of the Hershey's Kiss, and NutRageous, a candy bar.[41] Strategic blunders can hurt a company. Sears suffered in the 1980s by losing sight of what business it was in and what customers it wanted to serve. When Alfred C. Martinez became CEO, he disposed of nonretail assets, closed the catalog division, renovated dowdy stores, upgraded women's apparel, and launched a new, forward-thinking ad campaign. His strategy led to a major turnaround at the department store giant.

Every organization must think strategically and the restaurant industry is no exception. ". . . if we aren't seen trying to keep one step ahead, then we'll just end up in the wilderness," states Philip Britten, chef and restauranteur. His restaurant, The Capital, is located just around the corner from Harrods. Over the years, Britten's strategic management has taken his menu through various stages, from classic French haute cuisine to current passions for spices on seafood dishes.

changes and trends are occurring in the competitive environment? Who are our customers? What products or services should we offer? How can we offer those products and services most efficiently?" Answers to these questions help managers make choices about how to position their organization in the environment with respect to rival companies.[43] Superior organizational performance is not a matter of luck. It is determined by the choices managers make. Top executives use strategic management to define an overall direction for the organization, which is the firm's grand strategy, which can be accomplished through growth, stability or retrenchment. One small Montreal-based company used growth through diversification to become a global player.

BOMBARDIER
www.bombardier.com

When CEO Laurent Beaudoin took the reins of Bombardier in 1966 at the age of 27, the company's annual sales of the Ski-Doo snowmobile totaled some $15 million. Today, sales of snowmobiles top $400 million. But Bombardier also is a global force in three industries: aerospace, transportation, and consumer products. Beaudoin turned Bombardier into a premier worldwide manufacturer of transportation equipment by pursuing a strategy of acquiring a string of nearly bankrupt companies and melding them into a competitive whole. Bombardier still makes Ski-Doo snowmobiles, along with Sea-Doo personal watercraft, but today these products account for only 17 percent of sales.

Bombardier's frantic diversification began in 1973, when the energy crisis wiped out all but four of the 100 snowmobile manufacturers. Beaudoin's first key deal was a contract to make subway cars for Montreal. Today, Bombardier is building 680 highly automated subway cars for New York City for nearly $1 billion, as well as Amtrak's first high-speed trains, which will carry passengers from Boston to Washington at 150 miles per hour.

Now, Sears is positioning itself for growth, particularly through opening a chain of freestanding hardware stores.

The first part of this chapter provided an overview of the types of goals and plans that organizations use. In this part of the chapter, we will explore strategic management, which is considered one specific type of planning. Strategic planning in for-profit business organizations typically pertains to competitive actions in the marketplace. In not-for-profit organizations such as the Red Cross, strategic planning pertains to events in the external environment. Strategic thinking means to take the long-term view and to see the big picture, including the organization and the competitive environment, and to consider how they fit together. Understanding the strategy concept, the levels of strategy, and strategy formulation versus implementation is an important start toward strategic thinking.

WHAT IS STRATEGIC MANAGEMENT?

Strategic management is the set of decisions and actions used to formulate and implement strategies that will provide a competitively superior fit between the organization and its environment so as to achieve organizational goals.[42] Managers ask questions such as "What

Beaudoin's next strategic push was into aerospace. Government-owned Canadair was drowning in debt and had only one viable product, a large business jet. Beaudoin admits "we knew nothing about aerospace," but he knew his company's manufacturing know-how was among the best in the world, and he saw a chance to move into two niches in which his company could excel—business jets and regional aircraft. After acquiring Canadair, Beaudoin snatched up three other ailing plane makers to round out the product line: Boeing's de Havilland unit, business-jet pioneer Lear-jet, and Short Brothers, Northern Ireland's biggest employer.

With 43 percent of sales coming from the United States and Mexico, 41 percent from Europe, 10 percent from Canada, and 6 percent from Asia and the rest of the world, Montreal's Bombardier is one of today's most thoroughly international companies. Although Bombardier has experienced some recent setbacks, many investors believe Beaudoin's continued pursuit of a growth strategy will pull the company out of its stall. To fuel new growth, Beaudoin is counting on a host of new products, including the Global Express, a top-of-the-line executive jet to rival Gulfstream; the electric-powered Neighborhood Vehicle, a souped-up golf cart targeted at gated or retirement communities; and an unmanned hovering aircraft designed to detect buried land mines.[44] ■

PURPOSE OF STRATEGY

Within the overall grand strategy of an organization, executives define an explicit strategy, which is the plan of action that describes resource allocation and activities for dealing with the environment and attaining the organization's goals. The essence of strategy is choosing to perform different activities or to execute activities differently than competitors do.[45] For example, Dell Computer succeeded by bypassing the middleman and selling computers directly to the consumer. Today, Dell is finding that electronic commerce is a natural extension of its direct sales approach, as described below. Strategy necessarily changes over time to fit environmental conditions, but to remain competitive, companies develop strategies that focus on core competencies, develop synergy, and create value for customers.

DELL COMPUTER
www.dell.com

For years, Michael Dell has put up with skeptics predicting that direct sales of PCs would never capture more than 15 percent of the market. Today, direct buyers make up a third of the market, and the percentage is growing. Suddenly, everyone wants to be in Dell's position.

Now, the company that invented direct selling of PCs is taking the concept a step further. Dell has become an Internet phenomenon, selling $1 million worth of computers a day on its Web site, and electronic sales are growing 20 percent a month. Dell is making buying over the Internet even more attractive by customizing Web pages for its biggest buyers, including Eastman Chemical, Monsanto, and Wells Fargo, and by developing a new feature that can dash off a digital configuration to customers within five minutes of placing an order. Taking advantage of the Internet is just one more way for Dell to get more bang for its buck—in contrast to the 700 sales reps needed to take orders over the phone, Dell has only 30 people managing Web sales.

Dell's simple secret for turning a classically low-margin mail-order operation into a high-profit business is speed. A custom order placed with Dell at 9 A.M. on Monday can be on a delivery truck by 9 P.M. on Tuesday. The company has spent years developing a core competence in speedy delivery by squeezing time lags and inefficiencies out of the manufacturing and assembly process. Now Dell has applied the same brutal standards to the supply chain. Good relationships with key suppliers and precise coordination mean that sometimes Dell can receive parts in fifteen minutes that could take two days to reach IBM or Gateway. Dell also achieves synergy by turning to logistics specialists, such as Caliber Logistics, Inc., to manage supply chains. Speed has enabled Dell to slash inventories and parts costs so low that it can underprice rivals by 10 to 15 percent. Combine all that with electronic sales—the ultimate in low-cost, fast-paced business—and Dell is tough to beat. Now Michael Dell is looking for the next breakthrough. Dell is moving gradually into the $10 billion network server business, exploring ways to combine its PC knowledge with better networking service.

Competitors, having watched as more and more customers turned to Dell, are trying to imitate the company's way of doing business. "In the ideal world," said a Hewlett-Packard marketer, "your customer wants to buy a PC, you source all the parts that day, ship it that day, and get it to the customer that day. . . . Michael Dell is probably as close to that as anybody."[46] ■

CORE COMPETENCE   A company's core competence is something the organization does especially well in comparison to its competitors. A core competence represents a competitive advantage because the company acquires expertise that competitors do not have. A core competence may be in the area of superior research and development, mastery of a technology, manufacturing efficiency, or customer service.[47] Or it may be in excellent service to customers and suppliers and streamlined distribution systems that result in lower prices for customers. Amgen, a pharmaceuticals company with a 68 percent average annual return over the past decade, succeeds with a core competence of high-quality scientific research. Unlike most drug companies, which start with a disease and work backward, Amgen starts with brilliant science and then finds unique uses for it. For example, the recent discovery of a gene that may hold the key to fighting obesity is the kind of science that could really pay off.[48]

SYNERGY   When organizational parts interact to produce a joint effect that is greater than the sum of the parts acting alone, synergy occurs. The organization may attain a special advantage with respect to cost, market power, technology, or management skill. When properly managed, synergy can create additional value with existing resources, providing a big boost to the bottom line. Rupert Murdoch's News Corp., for example, is trying to develop synergy between publishing and the movie/television business. News Corp.'s Harper-Collins found renewed life after years of losses by bringing out books tied to corporate sibling Twentieth Century Fox's blockbuster *Titanic*, *The Simpsons*, *Ally McBeal*, *King of the Hill*, and *The X-Files* movie.[49] Synergy also can be obtained by good relations between suppliers and customers and by strong alliances among companies. Erie Bolt, a small Erie, Pennsylvania, company, teamed up with 14 other area companies to give itself more muscle in tackling competitive markets. Team members share equipment, customer lists, and other information that enables these small companies to go after more business than they ever could have without the team approach.[50] Hammond Enterprises, a seven-employee firm in Marietta, Georgia, designs and produces promotional caps, mugs, and T-shirts for major corporations such as Coca-Cola and Lockheed Martin. Synergy develops because Hammond relieves the corporate giants of the hassle of research, paperwork, and design of logo-bearing promotional items, enabling the corporations to obtain the items at less cost than if they produced the items themselves.[51]

VALUE CREATION   Exploiting core competencies and attaining synergy help companies create value for their customers. **Value** can be defined as the combination of benefits received and costs paid by the customer.[52] A product that is low in cost but does not provide benefits is not a good value. For example, People Express Airlines initially made a splash with ultra-low prices, but travelers couldn't tolerate the airline's consistently late takeoffs at any

value
The combined benefit to the customer of cost and quality

price.[53] Delivering value to the customer should be at the heart of strategy. Giving a product away free is one way to deliver value, as Platinum Entertainment does.

PLATINUM ENTERTAINMENT

When's the last time you went to a music store and got free CDs—as many as you wanted? That's essentially the strategy of "Best of" compilations maker Platinum Entertainment, which has posted its entire 15,000-song catalog on the Web for free downloads. Platinum promises to pay royalties to artists and hopes to make money by selling advertisements on its site.

Music industry experts are wondering how Platinum will make money by giving away its music. But e-commerce expert Aram Sinreich believes the company may be creating the future of the music business, by getting names and addresses and matching those with musical tastes. "It sounds like they are building a tremendous marketing tool," he says, and a powerful database as well.

Other companies are doing similar things, though not as drastically free. Lycos is forming an all-encompassing site with content, downloads, and commerce, and it claims to be the "most comprehensive online music destination."

Still, it is hard to beat Platinum's all-free site and its management doesn't understand what the cacophony is all about. "In radio, they give the music away and the artist doesn't get paid," says executive Steven Devick. "Here we're giving the music away, and we're paying the artist."[54] ∎

STRATEGY FORMULATION VERSUS IMPLEMENTATION

The final aspect of strategic management involves the stages of formulation and implementation. Strategy formulation includes the planning and decision making that lead to the establishment of the firm's goals and the development of a specific strategic plan.[55] Strategy formulation may include assessing the external environment and internal problems and integrating the results into goals and strategy. This is in contrast to strategy implementation, which is the use of managerial and organizational tools to direct resources toward accomplishing strategic results.[56] Strategy implementation is the administration and execution of the strategic plan. Managers may use persuasion, new equipment, changes in organization structure, or a reward system to ensure that employees and resources are used to make formulated strategy a reality.

■ THE STRATEGIC MANAGEMENT PROCESS

The overall strategic management process is illustrated in Exhibit 5.8. It begins when executives evaluate their current position with respect to mission, goals, and strategies. They then scan the organization's internal and external environments and identify strategic factors that may require change. Internal or external events may indicate a need to redefine the mission or goals or to formulate a new strategy at either the corporate, business, or functional level. The final stage in the strategic management process is implementation of the new strategy.

SITUATION ANALYSIS

Situation analysis typically includes a search for SWOT—strengths, weaknesses, opportunities, and threats—that affect organizational performance. Situation analysis is important to all companies but is crucial to those considering globalization because of the diverse environments in which they will operate. External information about opportunities and threats may be obtained from a variety of sources, including customers, government reports, professional journals, suppliers, bankers, friends in other organizations, consultants, or association meetings. Many firms hire special scanning organizations to provide them with newspaper clippings and analyses of relevant domestic and global trends. Some firms use more subtle techniques to learn about competitors, such as asking potential recruits about

Exhibit 5.8

THE STRATEGIC MANAGEMENT PROCESS

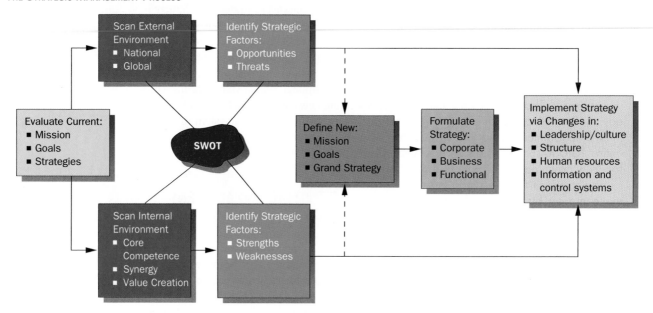

their visits to other companies, hiring people away from competitors, debriefing former employees or customers of competitors, taking plant tours posing as "innocent" visitors, and even buying the garbage of competitors.[57]

Executives acquire information about internal strengths and weaknesses from a variety of reports, including budgets, financial ratios, profit and loss statements, and surveys of employee attitudes and satisfaction. Managers spend 80 percent of their time giving and receiving information. Through frequent face-to-face discussions and meetings with people at all levels of the hierarchy, executives build an understanding of the company's internal strengths and weaknesses.

INTERNAL STRENGTHS AND WEAKNESSES
Strengths are positive internal characteristics that the organization can exploit to achieve its strategic performance goals. *Weaknesses* are internal characteristics that may inhibit or restrict the organization's performance. The information sought typically pertains to specific functions such as marketing, finance, production, and R&D. Internal analysis also examines

overall organization structure, management competence and quality, and human resource characteristics. Based on their understanding of these areas, managers can determine their strengths or weaknesses vis-à-vis other companies. For example, Marriott Corporation has been able to grow rapidly because of its financial strength. It has a strong financial base, enjoys an excellent reputation with creditors, and has always been able to acquire financing needed to support its strategy of constructing hotels in new locations.[58]

EXTERNAL OPPORTUNITIES AND THREATS
Threats are characteristics of the external environment that may prevent the organization from achieving its strategic goals. *Opportunities* are characteristics of the external environment that have the potential to help the organization achieve or exceed its strategic goals. Executives evaluate the external environment with information about nine sectors discussed earlier. The task environment sectors are the most relevant to strategic behavior and include the behavior of competitors, customers, suppliers, and the labor supply. The general

Most e-commerce start-ups go searching for funders and hope they find enough money. But garden.com had to turn investors away after raising the first $10.5 million. The founding triumvate, Lisa and Cliff Staples plus friend Jamie O'Neill, quit their jobs at Trilogy Software after only 10 weeks of work and had no idea they would ultimately be so successful.

The morning after their unemployment the three gathered in the recently purchased home of the newly married Staples and used a whiteboard to brainstorm a strategy for the perfect Internet business. Four months later, they were still living off their credit cards and eating peanut butter and jelly sandwiches.

By 1999 they had 550,000 members, a list that grows 300 percent a year in the fast-growing American hobby—gardening. What's the secret they have that others have missed? A customer-focused and market-driven method of establishing marketing channels. They knew they had to distinguish between *supply chain* (how the product moves from producer to end user) and *marketing channel* (how producer conceives product and end user receives it), to produce a "distribution chain based around customer's needs."

When this is done, certain companies become superbrands and make it difficult for others to even compete with them. For example, Wal-Mart has not only great prices, but the warm and fuzzy feeling that Sam is somehow behind it all. Garden.com's founders knew the pitfalls of being too egotistical, thinking they already knew what customers wanted, and getting distracted by logistics and benchmarking.

They searched for a fragmented market, which could be consolidated before attracting any potential competitor. They needed repeat business and knew they had to build trust and a sense of community, which meant an unending flow of content on their Web. Customers would then flock to their site as coffee drinkers do to Starbucks. They needed some product that people would be willing to pay a premium for, if they got superior service. Apparel was a no-go as well, since they realized consumers had little need for sophisticated information. How about seeds online? they asked themselves, finding that gardening is a $40 billion-a-year market. It has what they wanted: highly fragmented consumer industry with no one business having more than one percent of the market; gar-

deners are educated and affluent, willing to pay premium depending on information and service.

They set up focus groups that continue to this day, endlessly seeking customers needs, also receiving about 1,500 e-mails a day. Customer Solutions members are on the phone seven days a week from 7 A.M. to midnight. Plus they have signed on 75 strategic supply partners, but not until they visited each one and determined the quality level. Garden.com's brand has become a seal of approval for its suppliers.

But the heart of their e-commerce success currently is their focus on newly registered customers, what they are like and what they want. They have never lost sight of their original strategy of customer focus while establishing marketing channels. The founders are techie MBA's who have plenty of energy and vision. As one supplier says, "They get the power of the Internet, which few people do."

SOURCE: Edward O. Welles, "The Perfect Internet Business," *Inc.*, August 1999, pp. 71–78.

environment contains those sectors that have an indirect influence on the organization but nevertheless must be understood and incorporated into strategic behavior. The general environment includes technological developments, the economy, legal-political and international events, and sociocultural changes. Additional areas that might reveal opportunities or threats include pressure groups, interest groups, creditors, natural resources, and potentially competitive industries. The founders of Garden.com looked to a fast-growing industry and potential customers to determine its opportunity, as described in Leading the Revolution: The Learning Organization.

An example of how external analysis can uncover a threat occurred in Kellogg Company's cereal business. Scanning the environment revealed that Kellogg's once formidable share of the U.S. cold-cereal market had dropped nearly 10 percent. Information from the competitor and customer sectors indicated that major rivals were stepping up new-product innovations and cutting prices. In addition, private-label versions of such standbys as cornflakes were cutting into Kellogg's sales. Kellogg executives used knowledge of this threat as a basis for a strategic response. As a first step, the company boosted national advertising to build its brand names.[59]

■ BUSINESS-LEVEL STRATEGY

Now we turn to strategy formulation within the strategic business unit, in which the concern is how to compete. The same three generic strategies—growth, stability, and retrenchment—apply at the business level, but they are accomplished through competitive actions rather than the acquisition or divestment of business divisions. One model for formulating strategy is Porter's competitive strategies, which provides a framework for business unit competitive action.

PORTER'S COMPETITIVE FORCES AND STRATEGIES

Michael E. Porter studied a number of business organizations and proposed that business-level strategies are the result of five competitive forces in the company's environment.[60]

1. *Potential new entrants*. Capital requirements and economies of scale are examples of two potential barriers to entry that can keep out new competitors. It is far more costly to enter the automobile industry, for example, than to start a specialized mail-order business.

2. *Bargaining power of buyers*. Informed customers become empowered customers. As advertising and buyer information educate customers about the full range of price and product options available in the marketplace, their influence over a company increases. This is especially true when a company relies on one or two large, powerful customers for the majority of its sales.

3. *Bargaining power of suppliers*. The concentration of suppliers and the availability of substitute suppliers are significant factors in determining supplier power. The sole supplier of engines to a manufacturer of small airplanes will have great power. Other factors include whether a supplier can survive without a particular purchaser, or whether the purchaser can threaten to self-manufacture the needed supplies.

4. *Threat of substitute products*. The power of alternatives and substitutes for a company's product may be affected by cost changes or trends such as increased health consciousness that will deflect buyer loyalty to companies. Companies in the sugar industry suffered from the growth of sugar substitutes; manufacturers of aerosol spray cans lost business as environmentally conscious consumers chose other products.

5. *Rivalry among competitors*. The scrambling and jockeying for position is often exemplified by what Porter called the "advertising slugfest." A famous example of competitive rivalry is the battle between Pepsi and Coke. Rivalry between Federal Express and United Parcel Service is becoming almost as fierce as the two companies grapple for dominance of the express delivery business. After UPS rolled out an 8:30 A.M. delivery, FedEx introduced its new First Overnight service, promising "earliest morning delivery." When Federal Express introduced FedEx Ship, offering a free PC-based system that lets even the smallest customers order pickups, print shipping labels, and track delivery without ever using a telephone, UPS fired back by unveiling a new alliance to enable customers to book orders through online services.[61]

COMPETITIVE STRATEGIES   In finding its competitive edge within these five forces, Porter suggests that a company can adopt one of three strategies: differentiation, cost leadership, and focus. The three organizational characteristics typically associated with each strategy are

1. *Differentiation*. The differentiation strategy involves an attempt to distinguish the firm's products or services from others in the industry. The organization may use advertising, distinctive product features, exceptional service, or new technology to achieve a product perceived as unique. The differentiation strategy can be profitable because customers are loyal and will pay high prices for the product. Examples of products that have benefited from a differentiation strategy include Mercedes-Benz automobiles, Maytag appliances, and Tylenol, all of which are perceived as distinctive in their markets. Companies that

Merck's business-level strategy of competing through product innovation has Merck researchers Amy Cheung and Thomas Rano using advanced technology to produce new compounds in less time than ever before. Merck spends $1.3 billion on R&D and has reduced by months its processes of drug discovery, development, and testing.

pursue a differentiation strategy typically need strong marketing abilities, a creative flair, and a reputation for leadership.[62]

A differentiation strategy can reduce rivalry with competitors if buyers are loyal to a company's brand. For example, successful differentiation reduces the bargaining power of large buyers because other products are less attractive, and this also helps the firm fight off threats of substitute products. Differentiation also erects entry barriers in the form of customer loyalty that a new entrant into the market would have difficulty overcoming.

2. *Cost Leadership*. With a cost leadership strategy, the organization aggressively seeks efficient facilities, pursues cost reductions, and uses tight cost controls to produce products more efficiently than competitors. A low-cost position means that the company can undercut prices of competitors and still offer comparable quality and earn a reasonable profit. Scottish Inns and Motel 6 are low-priced alternatives to Holiday Inn and Ramada Inn. WestJet Airlines Ltd., in Canada, is using a cost-leadership strategy to compete successfully against major carriers such as Air Canada and Canadian Airlines. Chairman and CEO Clive Beddoe analyzed U.S. discount carriers such as Southwest Airlines and saw an opportunity to reap the same kind of rewards in the Canadian market.[63] Dell Computer, described in the example earlier in the chapter, has used a cost-leadership strategy to gain a competitive edge over larger companies.

TECHNOLOGY FOR TOMORROW

PILLS.COM

Tired of waiting in line at your local pharmacy? Or maybe you have questions for the pharmacist that are too embarrassing to ask. Three new start-ups are banking on these to build their success. Going after the potentially lucrative online prescription and medication market, each of them has a different strategy and hopes to be the big winner. And big it could be. Last year, Americans spent over $200 billion on prescription and nonprescription drugs.

Drugstore.com, Soma.com, and PlanetRx and are all scrambling to establish themselves before the traditional drugstores start moving on the Web. They are in a complex business, regulated state by state, and are developing partnerships with insurance companies and prescription plans, hoping to convince consumers that they are trustworthy and that their product is more convenient. Yet each has developed a distinct strategy, manifested in how they use technology.

Drugstore.com hypes its broad array of health and beauty products, as well as detailed information on its medications. Soma.com is the only one to sell class two pharmaceuticals, which are potentially addictive, such as the narcotic painkiller Percocet. PlanetRx's distinction is its original content, including an extensive online library on almost any health topic with advice and treatment options. But none of these will last if its IT infrastructure cannot support the kind of serious business they are in. If some incorrect information is dispensed on Garden.com (also described in this chapter), the worst that may happen is a languishing plant, but in the pharmaceutical business, the wrong blood pressure pills could be lethal.

Drugstore.com had a different IT strategy than either Soma.com or PlanetRx, both of which developed their marketing and distribution capabilities either before or while they worked out their technology. But with Drugstore.com, the strategy was to develop IT before the other parts, so they hired a technology leader first and later found a partner to fill prescriptions. Alyse Terhune of GartnerGroup Inc. agrees with this sequence, saying that the technology strategy is so crucial, it must come first. "You can outsource the grunt work, but you should never really outsource the strategy," he says. Other IT leaders, such as Ron Shevlin of Forrester Research Inc, believes a CIO at startup is not necessary, since CIOs are used to dealing with large companies and managers who are clueless about technology. Since with Internet startups, everyone understands the business *is* the computer, there is no need for a separate IT leader.

Only time will tell which of the strategies is the best.

SOURCE: Sari Kalin, "Choose Your Medicine," *CIO Web Business*, June 1, 1999, pp. 30–38.

Being a low-cost producer provides a successful strategy to defend against the five competitive forces. For example, the most efficient, low-cost company is in the best position to succeed in a price war while still making a profit. Likewise, the low-cost producer is protected from powerful customers and suppliers, because customers cannot find lower prices elsewhere, and other buyers would have less slack for price negotiation with suppliers. If substitute products or potential new entrants occur, the low-cost producer is better positioned than higher-cost rivals to prevent loss of market share. The low price acts as a barrier against new entrants and substitute products.[64]

3. *Focus*. With a focus strategy, the organization concentrates on a specific regional market or buyer group. The company will use either a differentiation or low-cost approach, but only for a narrow target market.

Enterprise Rent-A-Car has made its mark by focusing on a market the major companies such as Hertz and Avis don't even play in—the low-budget insurance replacement market. Drivers whose cars have been wrecked or stolen have one less thing to worry about when Enterprise delivers a car right to their driveway. By using a focus strategy, Enterprise has been able to grow rapidly.[65] Three online start-ups are focusing on people who buy medications and want lots of information, and each company has its own brand of focus as explained in Technology for Tomorrow.

Managers think carefully about which strategy will provide their company with its competitive advantage. Gibson Guitar Corp., famous in the music world for its innovative, high-quality products, found that switching to a low-cost strategy to compete against Japanese rivals such as Yamaha and Ibanez actually hurt the company. When managers realized people wanted Gibson products because of their reputation, not their price, they went back to a differentiation strategy and invested in new technology and marketing.[66] In his studies, Porter found that some businesses did not consciously adopt one of these three strategies and were stuck with no strategic advantage. Without a strategic advantage, businesses earned below-average profits compared with those that used differentiation, cost leadership, or focus strategies.

COOPERATIVE STRATEGIES

So far, we have been discussing strategies that are based on how to compete with other companies. An alternative approach to strategy emphasizes collaboration. In some situations, companies can achieve competitive advantages by cooperating with other firms rather than competing. Cooperative strategies are becoming increasingly popular as firms in all industries join with other organizations to promote innovation, expand markets, and pursue joint goals. Partnering was once a strategy adopted primarily by small firms that needed greater marketing muscle or international access. Today, however, it has become a way of life for most companies, large and small. The question is no longer whether to collaborate, but rather where, how much, and with whom to collaborate.[67] Competition and cooperation often exist at the same time. In New York City, Time Warner refused to carry Fox's 24-hour news channel on its New York City cable systems. The two companies engaged in all-out war that included court lawsuits and front-page headlines. This conflict, however, masked a simple fact: The two companies can't live without each other. Fox and Time Warner are wedded to one another in separate business deals around the world. They will never let the local competition in New York upset their larger cooperation on a global scale.[68] A new Internet company has staked its success on the ability to collaborate with local governments to reach mutually beneficial goals—that is, to help constituents interact more effectively with their governments, including paying taxes and other bills.

GOVWORKS.COM

Moving out of an apartment and finding a two-year-old unpaid parking ticket would not generally be an uplifting experience. Most people would panic, then hurry to City Hall to pay the bill before a warrant was issued. Not Kaleil Isaza Tuzman. The Harvard grad Goldman Sachs employee saw it as a business opportunity. So he started a company that allows taxpayers to pay online for parking tickets, as well as utility bills, real estate taxes, business licenses, special events permits—and get frequent flier miles and rebates in the process. And that's not all, people can bid in government auctions, search the GovJobs page for help-wanted ads, watch presidential campaign videos, and read government calendars of events. With a bent toward social responsibility, the site allows donations to local charities as well as involvement in community discussions. In 2000 they were linked with 3,500 local municipalities. GovWorks makes money in three ways: (1) a percentage on bills paid and classifieds, (2) corporate sponsorship, and (3) a cut on partner-offered special promotions. And considering that the 80,000 local governments collect $4 trillion annually from their constituents, the potential market is huge.

It all started in 1998 in New York City, as a means to trim public bureaucracy and revolutionize government's relationship to its constituents, when Tuzman and high school buddy Tom Herman, a Bates psychology grad and then-Web architect at TVisions, dreamed up the idea. They saw the Internet as the perfect medium to improve government services, which almost exclusively involve the transfer of information and money. So they quit their promising jobs, found an office in New York City, and managed to enthuse venture capitalists to the tune of $19 million. In February 1999 they started hiring and by January 2000 had 130 mostly 20- and 30-something employees, who work 18 hours a day, seven days a week for modest wages and stock options.

One of the people who came on board as vice president of marketing was former Saatchi & Saatchi account executive David Camp, who was impressed with the company's midwestern ethos. "It's authentic," he says. "It's American. It's about the populace."

Tom Herman had wanted to be a doctor and even worked for two years in the Jamaican Ministry of Health as a Health Education Officer. Finally, he decided to forgo graduate school after he realized how much he loved Web design. When he and Tuzman talked about starting the company, he was ready. "I have nothing to lose," he said. "I can support myself frugally for the next year, and the worst that will happen is that we fail. In either case, fail or succeed, this is the best education I could possibly get." The vision and hard work have led to success, but it took its toll. Herman recalls returning from an overnight 36-hour trip to visit government officials in Buenos Aires, Argentina, and finding overflowing voicemails and hundreds of e-mails, which were all urgent and had to be answered quickly, in between showers and changes. "I'm so overwhelmed," he says. "There is no way to do what needs to done and I'm too busy to hire and train people." So goes Internet start-up success.[69] ■

Mutual dependencies and partnerships have become a fact of life, but the degree of collaboration varies. Organizations can choose to build cooperative relationships in many ways, such as through preferred suppliers, joint ventures, mergers and acquisitions, or strategic business partnering, as fast-growing, high-tech Cisco does.

CISCO SYSTEMS

Cisco Systems is transforming itself into a learning organization through strategic partnerships. The pioneer of *Internetworking*, Cisco is first or second in all but one of the seven major equipment markets in which it competes. The company is one of the fastest growing companies in Silicon Valley and one of the hottest stocks of the decade. Cisco has achieved its status primarily through strategic relationships.

Cisco Systems was founded in 1984 by a husband-and-wife team who devised a means to connect incompatible computer networks at Stanford University. A series of mergers and acquisitions with start-up companies such as Crescendo Communications, a maker of hubs, and StrataCom, a maker of frame relay devices and switches, turned Cisco into a full-service provider of networking equipment and garnered the technological know-how to keep it on the cutting edge. Just as important, Cisco has developed numerous strategic partnerships with other high-tech companies. The company partners with Hewlett-Packard, for example, to develop and sell Internet-based corporate computing systems built with each other's products. Cisco is working with Microsoft to create industry standards for network security. A strategic alliance with MCI means Cisco will deliver premium Internet services via MCI's data-networking infrastructure. Now, Cisco is working with the two giants of computing—Microsoft and Intel—in a joint project called the Networked Multimedia Lab. On the ground floor of the world headquarters of Cisco Systems is a series of rooms in which customers explore how the Internet can deliver voice, video, and interactive multimedia with the clarity and reliability of conventional telephone and cable TV networks.

Cisco CEO John T. Chambers considers picking the right strategic partners to be a key element of his company's strategy. He targets partners who are aggressive, technologically strong, and very customer-focused. Chambers believes his company's partnership with Microsoft and Intel symbolizes that the three will form a triumvirate that will plot the course of the digital revolution. Although that remains to be seen, so far Cisco is playing all its cards right. "We've always known networking is too complex for any one company to tackle—even for MCI, HP, Microsoft, or Intel," says Chambers. "They know it now too. It's better to partner than to compete because . . . it grows the pie bigger for everybody faster."[70] ■

A still higher degree of collaboration is reflected in joint ventures, which are separate entities created with two or more active firms as sponsors. For example, MTV Networks was originally created as a joint venture of Warner Communications and American Express in the late 1970s. In a joint venture, organizations share the risks and costs associated with the new venture. It is estimated that the rate of joint venture formation between U.S. and international companies has been growing by 27 percent annually since 1985. Texas Instruments and Hitachi, for example, formed an international joint venture to produce memory chips. Merck has put together major ventures with such competitors as Johnson & Johnson and AB Astra of Sweden.[71] Mergers and acquisitions represent the ultimate in collaborative relationships. U.S. business is in the midst of the biggest merger and acquisition boom in its history. In 1997 alone, more than 11,000 deals totaled some $908 billion, 47 percent more than the total in 1996, which was itself a record year.[72] The U.S. pharmaceuticals company Upjohn merged with Sweden's Pharmacia. Boeing acquired McDonnell Douglas to form the industry's largest company, and Citicorp and Travelers Group have announced a $70 billion merger that will create a megabank with $700 billion in assets. The two organizations shared a desire to create a fully integrated financial services giant and recognized the synergies they could achieve by merging. Citicorp gains a stronger U.S. direct-sales force to market Citi checking accounts, mutual funds, and credit cards, while Travelers gains greater access to international markets. Reflecting the emphasis on collaboration, John S. Reed of Citicorp and Sanford I. Weill of Travelers will serve as co-CEOs of the new financial services behemoth.[73]

Today's companies simultaneously embrace both competition and cooperation. Few companies can go it alone under a constant onslaught of international competition, changing technology, and new regulations. In this new environment, businesses choose a combination of competitive and cooperative strategies that add to their overall sustainable advantage.[74]

■ PUTTING STRATEGY INTO ACTION

The final step in the strategic management process is implementation—which is how strategy is put into action. Some people argue that strategy implementation is the most difficult and important part of strategic management.[75] No matter how creative the formulated strategy, the organization will not benefit if it is incorrectly implemented. In today's competitive environment, there is an increasing recognition of the need for more dynamic approaches to formulating as well as implementing strategies. Strategy is not a static, analytical process; it requires vision, intuition, and employee participation.[76] Many organizations are abandoning central planning departments, and strategy is becoming an everyday part of the job for workers at all levels. Strategy implementation involves using several tools—parts of the firm that can be adjusted to put strategy into action. Once a new strategy is selected, it is implemented through changes in leadership, information and control systems, and human resources.[77]

LEADERSHIP

Leadership is the ability to influence organization members to adopt the behaviors needed for strategy implementation. Leadership includes persuasion, motivation, and changes in corporate values and culture. Managers seeking to implement a new strategy may make speeches to employees, issue edicts, build coalitions, and persuade middle managers to go along with their vision for the corporation.

If leaders let other employees participate during strategy formulation, implementation will be easier because managers and employees will already understand and be committed to the new strategy. In essence, leadership is used to motivate employees to adopt new behaviors and, for some strategies, to infuse new values and attitudes.

For example, Jürgen Schrempp is using leadership to instill a new culture of responsibility and entrepreneurism at DaimlerChrysler. Whereas previous Daimler chairmen managed from a distance, Schrempp communicates directly with his managers in meetings that can run into the night, fueled by beer and cigars. He personally visits clients and takes an active role in labor negotiations. Schrempp's leadership has turned the formerly stodgy company into an innovative, fast-moving organization.[78]

INFORMATION AND CONTROL SYSTEMS

Information and control systems include reward systems, pay incentives, budgets for allocating resources, information systems, and the organization's rules, policies, and procedures. Changes in these systems represent major tools for putting strategy into action. For example, resources can be reassigned from research and development to marketing if a new strategy requires increased advertising but no product innovations. Managers and employees must be rewarded for adhering to the new strategy and making it a success.[79]

At ConAgra, maker of Healthy Choice and Banquet brands, CEO Philip B. Fletcher instituted top-down cost controls in the corporation's 60 operating units and developed new systems for pooling resources to reduce purchasing, warehousing, and transportation costs. To ensure that managers embraced the new strategy of cooperation and efficiency, Fletcher tied 25 percent of their bonuses directly to savings targets. Division heads saved $100 million in the first fiscal year. Fletcher also made changes in information systems by introducing a computerized network to track how much suppliers charge each ConAgra unit.[80] As another example, Outback Steakhouse built one of the nation's hottest restaurant chains by giving managers a significant ownership stake, including 10 percent of their restaurant's cash flow and shares of company stock. Outback's incentive program, believed to be unique among casual-restaurant chains, helped founders Chris Sullivan, Robert Basham, and Timothy Gannon move in only six years from their modest goal of five restaurants to more than 200 Outbacks, with revenues of $544 million.[81]

HUMAN RESOURCES

The organization's *human resources* are its employees. The human resource function recruits, selects, trains, transfers, promotes, and lays off employees to achieve strategic goals. For example, training employees can help them understand the purpose and importance of a new strategy or help them develop the necessary specific skills and behaviors. Sometimes employees may have to be let go and replaced. One newspaper shifted its strategy from an evening to a morning paper to compete with a large newspaper from a nearby city. The new strategy fostered resentment and resistance among department heads. In order to implement it, 80 percent of the department heads had to be let go because they refused to cooperate. New people were recruited and placed in those positions, and the morning newspaper strategy was a resounding success.[82]

Mannie Jackson revived the Harlem Globetrotters, an organization on the brink of bankruptcy and irrelevancy, by recruiting new players who could recapture the glory the Globetrotters enjoyed in the 1960s and 1970s. Jackson rates potential players on their skill, charisma, punctuality, and attitude. He wants only top athletes who can promote the Globetrotter brand and are willing to be role models.[83]

IMPLEMENTING GLOBAL STRATEGIES

The difficulty of implementing strategy is greater when a company goes global. In the international arena, flexibility and superb communication emerge as mandatory leadership skills. Likewise, structural design must merge successfully with foreign cultures as well as link foreign operations to the home country. Information and control systems must fit the needs and incentives within local cultures. In a country such as Japan or China, financial bonuses for star performance would be humiliating to an individual, whereas group motivation and reward are acceptable. As in North America, control is typically created through timetables and budgets and by monitoring progress toward desired goals. Finally, the recruitment, training, transfer, promotion, and layoff of international human resources create an array of problems not confronted in North America. Labor laws, guaranteed jobs, and cultural traditions of keeping unproductive employees on the job provide special problems for strategy implementation. Strategy implementation must receive even more attention in the international domain than in the domestic realm.

In summary, strategy implementation is essential for effective strategic management. Managers implement strategy through the tools of leadership, structural design, information and control systems, and human resources. Without effective implementation, even the most creative strategy will fail.

Summary and Management Solution

This chapter focused on organizational planning. Organizational planning involves defining goals and developing a plan with which to achieve them. An organization exists for a single, overriding purpose known as its mission—the basis for strategic goals and plans. Goals within the organization are defined in a hierarchical fashion, beginning with strategic goals followed by tactical and operational goals. Plans are defined similarly, with strategic, tactical, and operational plans used to achieve the goals. Other goal concepts include characteristics of effective goals and goal-setting behavior.

Several types of plans were described, including strategic, tactical, operational, single-use, standing, and contingency plans, as well as management by objectives. The Shewhart or PDCA Cycle is used by many companies that have instituted quality management. In the Shewhart Cycle, planning is continuous and everyone can learn and help the company improve. Long-term, intermediate-term, and short-term plans have time horizons of from five years down to six months.

Strategic management begins with an evaluation of the organization's current mission, goals, and strategy. This evaluation is followed by situation analysis (called SWOT analysis), which examines opportunities and threats in the external environment as well as strengths and weaknesses within the organization. Situation analysis leads to the formulation of explicit strategic plans, which then must be implemented.

Strategy formulation includes grand strategies of growth, stability, retrenchment, and global. One approach to business-level strategy is Porter's competitive forces and strategies. An alternative approach to strategic thought emphasizes cooperation rather than competition. Cooperative strategies include preferred supplier arrangements, strategic business partnering, joint ventures, and mergers and acquisitions. Most of today's companies choose a mix of competitive and cooperative strategies. Once business strategies have been formulated, functional strategies for supporting them can be developed.

Even the most creative strategies have no value if they cannot be translated into action. Organizational tools used for strategy implementation are leadership, information and control systems, and human resources.

In the opening case, Excelsior motorcycle company founders Dave and Dan Hanlon had a great idea, but no money and no luck with venture capitalists. To get financing, the brothers looked to a group who would understand them: CEOs and founders of marketing or manufacturing companies, looking for their names in annual reports, calling them on the phone and telling their story. Within a few months, they had raised $15 million. The next problem was gaining core competencies. Their enthusiasm convinced two Triumph Motorcycle executives to jump ship. The new and experienced marketing director quickly lined up 35 national dealers, and they got a 30-year veteran of accounting to head up the finance department. By 1997, they had their business plan in gear and were starting to make prototypes, getting a lot of interest. Their new Super-X was to be Harley-like, with a difference.

The brothers still face a tough road. Harley increased their own production, so demand for other brands of bikes was reduced. Then Excelsior was not able to produce at the rate of its business plan. Losses have been increasing. Until the company can rev up production to about 3,000 units a year, it will continue to lose money. In 1998, losses were about $6 million, and in 1999 they totaled about $23 million, which has resulted in layoffs of 45 percent of their factory workers. On the same day, a whole new management team was installed.

New marketing head Gary "Jet Ski" Johnson now says it is "not smart" for the company to go head to head with Harley and they would be happy with just three percent of the fast-growing cruiser bike business. As for the family,

they continue moving ahead with the business plan. Dave Hanlon sees the current problems as another challenge. "We are upbeat," he says.

SOURCES: Eric Torbenson, "Belle Pain, Minn., Motorbike Maker Cuts Workforce by 45 Percent," *St. Paul Pioneer Press,* Sept. 3, 1999; David Edwards, "Inside Excelsior-Henderson," *Cycle World,* Sept. 1999, Vol. 38 (9), pp. 48–49; Eric Torbenson, "Minnesota-Based Motorcycle Firm Executive Seeks to Motivate Sales Force," *St. Paul Pioneer Press,* Oct. 10, 1999; David Edwards, "Growing Pains Hit Excelsior," *Cycle World,* July 1999, Vol. 38 (7), p. 28; and Marc Ballon, "Born to Be Wild," *Inc.,* Nov. 1997, pp. 41–53.

Discussion Questions

1. If you were either Attorney General or head of INS (Immigration and Naturalization Service), what type of planning would you have used to help respond in the Elían Gonzales case?

2. Write a brief mission statement for a local business. Try to capture the purpose and values of a small organization in a written statement.

3. What strategies could the college or university at which you are taking this management course adopt to compete for students in the marketplace? Would these strategies depend on the school's goals?

4. If you were a top manager of a small real estate sales agency, how would you use MBO? Give examples of goals you might set for managers and sales agents.

5. A new business venture has to develop a comprehensive business plan to borrow money to get started. Companies such as Federal Express, Nike, and Rolm Corporation say they did not follow the original plan very closely. Does that mean that developing the plan was a waste of time for these eventually successful companies?

6. A famous management theorist proposed that the time horizons for all strategic plans are becoming shorter because of the rapid changes in the external environments of organizations. Do you agree? Would the planning time horizon for IBM or Ford Motor Company be shorter than it was 20 years ago?

7. What are the characteristics of effective goals? Is it better to have no goals at all or goals that do not meet these criteria?

8. Assume Southern University decides to raise its admission standards and initiate a business fair to which local townspeople will be invited. What types of plans would it use to carry out these two activities?

9. Assume you are the general manager of a local hotel and have formulated a strategy of renting banquet facilities to corporations for big events. At a monthly management meeting, your sales manager informs the head of food operations that a big reception in one week will require converting a large hall from a meeting room to a banquet facility in only 60 minutes—a difficult, but doable operation that will require precise planning and extra help. The food operations manager is furious about not being informed earlier. What is wrong here?

10. Perform a situation (SWOT) analysis for the university you attend. Do you think university administrators consider these factors when devising their strategy?

11. What is meant by the core competence and synergy components of strategy? Give examples.

12. Using Porter's competitive strategies, how would you describe the strategies of Wal-Mart, Bloomingdale's, and Kmart? Do any of these companies also use cooperative strategies? Discuss.

Management Exercises

Manager's Workbook

Goal Setting

Consider goals for yourself regarding doing well in this course. What do you need to do in order to get a good grade? Goals should be according to the "Criteria for Effective Goals" in the chapter on pp. 146–147. In addition, you need a system to monitor your progress, such as the following table, which shows the types of goals you may choose to select for yourself.

GOALS		**CLASS WEEKS**		
	First week (from now)	**Second week**	**Third week**	**Fourth week**
1. 100 percent attendance				
2. Class notes				
3. Read assigned chapters				
4. Outline chapters				
5. Define vocabulary words				
6. Answer end of chapter questions				
7. Complete "Workbook" assignments				
8. Class participation				
9.				
10.				

Your instructor may ask you to turn in your monitor sheets at the end of the course.

1. According to goal-setting theory, using and monitoring goals is supposed to help performance. Did you do better as a result of your goals?

2. What did you learn from this that could help you in other classes?

Copyright 1996 by Dorothy Marcic. SOURCE: Nancy C. Morey, "Applying goal setting in the classroom," *The Organizational Behavior Teaching Review,* Vol. 11 (4), 1986–87, pp. 53–59.

Manager's Workshop

Outcome Designed Problem Solving

A. Think of a problem you are currently trying to solve. Consider either your work or personal life. Answer the following questions to yourself and then in groups of four to six members (have an even number of people in each group):

1. What's the reason this is a problem?

2. What caused the problem?

3. Who or what can be blamed?

4. What are the blocks keeping me from solving this problem?

5. What is the likelihood that I can solve the problem?

B. Now consider the same problem, but do as the instructions indicate below.

Divide your group into teams of two. With your partner, take turns being the manager and the employee with the problem. The manager asks the employee the following questions:

1. What would you rather have than this problem? Come up with a desired outcome.

2. How will you know when you have reached your desired outcome? List examples of what you would see, measure, hear, etc.

3. What advantage would this outcome be for you? What could you lose? Is it worth the risk?

4. Explain what the first step would be to work toward your outcome. Now, as a class discuss the differences in the two different problem-solving approaches.

Bob Bostrom reports that when groups do the problem-based discussions, they become deenergized and even depressed. But when groups engage in the outcome-based discussions, enthusiasm and positive attitudes prevail, increasing the likelihood of an enduring solution being achieved.

Management in Practice: Ethical Dilemma

Repair or Replace?

After only a few months in sales at ComputerSource, a full-service computer business, Sam Nolan realized there were serious problems in the software department. Most of the complaints from customers were related to the incorrect selection or installation of the software needed to meet their needs. He discussed the problem with his sales manager, who was part owner and partner with the head of service for ComputerSource. They both were aware of the problem, but they were facing an industrywide shortage of qualified software engineers.

Nolan received an urgent call from Katherine Perry, operations manager for Ross & Lindsey, a fast-growing financial management firm that was becoming one of his best accounts. She was calling to report that they were having daily network problems that were interfering with her staff's productivity and morale. She needed an immediate solution to the problem. Like many firms, Ross & Lindsey had a hodgepodge of computer equipment and software on their network. They had bought from a series of vendors, with a patchwork approach to problems.

Nolan realized it would take an expert software engineer days or weeks of work to fix all the bugs in their existing system, which ComputerSource could not afford. A costlier alternative was to recommend a system upgrade, replacing the older hardware and loading a newer software version on the entire network. Perry had already confided that she had pushed her bosses as far as they wanted to go on computer expenditures this year, but Nolan knew she was desperate. He didn't want to risk losing her business, but he didn't trust the software engineers to fix the problems. He was also pretty sure Perry would face the same dilemma at any computer retailer in town.

What Do You Do?

1. Gamble on the service department to fix their existing system, within the limits of their budget and their frustration. If it doesn't work, it is their problem.

2. Recommend a system upgrade to correct the problem, even though it will cost the clients more than they want to pay and may jeopardize future sales.

3. Confide in the clients about your perception of the problem, give them the chance to make an informed choice, and risk having them take their business elsewhere.

Surf the Net

1. *Organizational Mission.* As stated in the text, one of the top three traits employees cited in *Fortune* magazine's study of the "100 Best Companies to Work for in America" was a sense of purpose that employees could believe in and relate to. Find three examples of mission statements that you can contribute during a class discussion of mission. If corporate missions are available at a company's Web site, you can usually find them under the "About" option. For example at TDIndustries' home page, click on "About TDIndustries." Listed below are some companies that appeared in the Top 100 of the January 10, 2000, edition of *Fortune*'s "100 Best Companies to Work for in America." You may prefer to find mission statements for other organizations in which you have an interest.

   www.containerstore.com (Container Store, ranked #1)

   www.tdindustries.com/ (TDIndustries, ranked #4)

   www.hp.com/abouthp/hpway.html (Hewlett-Packard, ranked #43)

   www.synovus.com/infocntr/philosophies.html (Synovus Financial, ranked #5)

2. *Schedules.* Managers must plan for their personal schedules, as well as oversee planning for their areas of responsibility. Among the personal scheduling tools available on the Internet are online calendars. Try one of the following such tools and write a review concerning its effectiveness and usefulness. Your review should include a brief description of how the online calendar works, its main features, and the advantages and disadvantages of using such a planning tool.

   www.when.com

   www.digital.daytimer.com

   www.anyday.com

3. *Shewhart Cycle.* Use a search engine to find information for a report on Walter A. Shewhart and the Shewhart Cycle. In your report, provide a brief biographical sketch of Shewhart as well as information to supplement what the text provides on his continuous improvement model. Two possible sites are listed below:

   www.miep.org/mqc/news/otm/march—96/toolbox.html

   www.asqc.org/about/history/shewhart.html

Case for Critical Analysis

Starbucks Coffee

Beginning with nine Seattle stores in 1987, Starbucks CEO Howard Schultz has exported the company's chic cafes throughout the country. Service is anything but fast, and the price of a cup of coffee could make the Dunkin' Donuts crowd faint, but each week almost two million Americans hit Starbucks to sip skinny lattes or no-whip mochas.

Despite a slowdown in sales from established stores, Starbucks is pursuing rapid expansion. It made its first acquisition in 1994, buying The Coffee Connection Inc., a 23-store Boston rival. With more than 400 stores in place, Schultz plans to open 200 more within a year and has announced plans to team up with foreign partners to open stores in Asia and Europe. In addition, Starbucks has entered into a venture with PepsiCo to develop a new bottled coffee drink. Schultz's strategies are risky, but some analysts think Starbucks has the flexibility and management strength to succeed.

Many managers at Starbucks have years of experience from such companies as Burger King, Taco Bell, Wendy's,

and Blockbuster. Schultz believes a CEO should "hire people smarter than you are and get out of their way." Equally crucial to the success of Starbucks are the "baristas" who prepare coffee drinks. Starbucks recruits its workers from colleges and community groups and gives them 24 hours of training in coffee making and lore—a key to creating the company's hip image and quality service. To maintain quality control, Starbucks roasts all its coffee in-house. The company also has turned down lucrative alternatives such as franchising and supermarket distribution.

A computer network links the expanding Starbucks empire, and Schultz hired a top information-technology specialist from McDonald's to design a point-of-sale system to enable managers to track sales. Every night, computers from all 400-plus stores send information to headquarters in Seattle so that executives can spot regional buying trends.

For Schultz, a man who has already changed America's coffee-drinking habits, the risks Starbucks is taking are just another challenge.

Questions

1. Which of Porter's competitive strategies is Starbucks using?

2. Discuss how Schultz is using leadership, structure, information and control systems, and human resources to implement strategy at Starbucks.

3. What challenges may Schultz face in trying to expand Starbucks internationally?

SOURCES: Dori Jones Yang, "The Starbucks Enterprise Shifts into Warp Speed," *Business Week,* October 24, 1994, p. 76; and Michael Treacy, "You Need a Value Discipline—But Which One?" *Fortune,* April 17, 1995, p. 195.

Endnotes

1 Eric Torbenson, "Belle Pain, Minn., Motorbike Maker Cuts Workforce by 45%," *St. Paul Pioneer Press,* Sept 3, 1999; David Edwards, "Inside Excelsior-Henderson," *Cycle World,* Sept. 1999, Vol. 38 (9), pp. 48–49; Eric Torbenson, "Minnesota-Based Motorcycle Firm Executive Seeks to Motivate Sales Force," *St. Paul Pioneer Press,* Oct. 10, 1999; David Edwards, "Growing Pains Hit Excelsior," *Cycle World,* July 1999, Vol. 38 (7), p. 28; Marc Ballon, "Born to be wild," *Inc.,* Nov. 1997, pp. 41–53.

2 Russell L. Ackoff, "On the Use of Models in Corporate Planning," *Strategic Management Journal* 2 (1981), pp. 353–359; and Oren Harari, "Good/Bad News about Strategy," *Management Review,* July 1995, pp. 29–31.

3 Amitai Etzioni, *Modern Organizations* (Englewood Cliffs, N.J.: Prentice-Hall, 1984), p. 6.

4 David Woodruff, "Is VW Revving Too High?" *Business Week,* March 30, 1998, pp. 48–49; and Ronald B. Lieber, "Flying High, Going Global," *Fortune,* July 7, 1997, pp. 195–197.

5 Max D. Richards, *Setting Strategic Goals and Objectives,* 2d ed. (St. Paul, Minn.: West, 1986).

6 C. Chet Miller and Laura B. Cardinal, "Strategic Planning and Firm Performance: A Synthesis of More than Two Decades of Research," *Academy of Management Journal* 37 (6) (1994), pp. 1649–1685.

7 This discussion is based on Herbert A. Simon, "On the Concept of Organizational Goals," *Administrative Science Quarterly* 9 (1964), pp. 1–22.

8 Ronald B. Lieber, "Why Employees Love These Companies," *Fortune,* January 12, 1998, pp. 72–74.

9 Eric Matson, "The Discipline of High-Tech Leaders," *Fast Company,* April–May 1997, pp. 34–36.

9 Steven L. Marks, "Say When," *Inc.,* February 1995, pp. 19–20.

10 David Pearson, "Breaking Away," *CIO,* Section 1, May 1, 1998, pp. 34–46.

11 Joseph Weber, "Du Pont's Trailblazer Wants to Get Out of the Woods," *Business Week,* August 31, 1992, pp. 70–71.

12 Frank Rose, "Now Quality Means Service Too," *Fortune,* April 22, 1991, pp. 99–108.

13 John A. Pearce II and Fred David, "Corporate Mission Statements: The Bottom Line," *Academy of Management Executive* (1987), pp. 109–116; and Alan Farnham, "Brushing Up Your Vision Thing," *Fortune,* May 1, 1995, p. 129.

14 Miriam Schulman, "Winery with a Mission," *Issues in Ethics,* Spring 1996, pp. 14–15.

15 Sharon Nelton, "Put Your Purpose in Writing," *Nation's Business,* February 1994, pp. 61–64.

16 "Jostens Inc., Disclosure Incorporated, 1999; Kenneth Labich, "Why Companies Fail," *Fortune,* Nov. 14, 1995, pp. 52–68; and Neal St. Anthony, "'Dutch Auction' Is Jostens Ploy to Bolster Its Stock in the Long Term," *Minneapolis Star-Tribune,* Aug. 13, 1995, p. 1D.

17 Mark Fischetti, "Team Doctors, Report to ER!" *Fast Company,* February/March 1998, pp. 170–177.

18 Gina Imperato, "Dirty Business, Bright Ideas," *Fast Company,* February/March, 1997, pp. 89–93.

19 John O. Alexander, "Toward Real Performance: The Circuit-Breaker Technique," *Supervisory Management* (April 1989), pp. 5–12.

20 Cathy Lazere, "All Together Now," *CFO,* February 1998, pp. 29–36.

21 Joy Riggs, "Empowering Workers by Setting Goals," *Nation's Business,* January 1995, p. 6.

22 A. J. Vogl, "Noble Survivors," *Across the Board,* June 1994, pp. 25–30; and Rahul Jacob, "Corporate Reputations," *Fortune,* March 6, 1995, pp. 54–67.

23 Edwin A. Locke, Garp P. Latham, and Miriam Erez, "The Determinants of Goal Commitment," *Academy of Management Review* 13 (1988), pp. 23–39.

24 George S. Odiorne, "MBO: A Backward Glance," *Business Horizons* 21 (October 1978), pp. 14–24.

25 Jan P. Muczyk and Bernard C. Reimann, "MBO as a Complement to Effective Leadership," *The Academy of Management Executive,* 3 (1989), pp. 131–138.

26 John Ivancevich, J. Timothy McMahon, J. William Streidl, and Andrew D. Szilagyi, "Goal Setting: The Tenneco Approach to Personnel Development and Management Effectiveness," *Organizational Dynamics* (Winter 1978), pp. 48–80.

27 Gregory M. Bounds, Gregory H. Dobbins, and Oscar S. Fowler, *Management: A Total Quality Perspective* (Cincinnati: South-Western College Publishing, 1995), pp. 219–220.

28 Thomas E. Ricks, "Army Devises System to Decide What Does, and Does Not, Work," *The Wall Street Journal,* May 23, 1997, pp. A1, A10.

29 "Corporate Planning: Drafting a Blueprint for Success," *Small Business Report* (August 1987), pp. 40–44.

30 Paul J. H. Schoemaker, "Scenario Planning: A Tool for Strategic Thinking," *Sloan Management Review* (Winter 1995), pp. 25–40; Arie P. de Geus, "Planning as Learning," *Harvard Business Review* (March–April 1988), pp. 70–74.

31 Peter Doyle, "Setting Business Objectives and Measuring Performance," *Journal of General Management,* 20 (2) (Winter 1994), pp. 1–19.

32 Anne B. Fisher, "Is Long-Range Planning Worth It?" *Fortune,* April 23, 1990, pp. 281–284.

33 Andrew Tanzer, "We Do Not Take a Short-Term View," *Forbes,* July 13, 1987, pp. 372–374.

34 Milton Leontiodes, *Strategies for Diversification and Change* (Boston: Little, Brown, 1980), p. 63; and Dan E. Schendel and Charles W. Hofer, eds. *Strategic Management: A New View of Business Policy and Planning* (Boston: Little, Brown, 1979), p. 11–14.

35 Jay Finegan, "Everything According to Plan," *Inc.,* March 1995, pp. 78–85.

36 Gerald E. Ledford, Jr., Jon R. Wendenhof, and James T. Strahley, "Realizing a Corporate Philosophy," *Organizational Dynamics* (Winter 1995), pp. 5–18.

37 James C. Collins and Jerry I. Porras, "Building a Visionary Company," *California Management Review,* 37 (2) (Winter 1995), pp. 80–100.

38 See Kenneth R. Thompson, Wayne A. Hockwarter, and Nicholas J. Mathys, "Stretch Targets: What Makes Them Effective?" *Academy of Management Executive,* 11 (3) (August 1997), p. 48.

39 Edward O. Welles, "Bootstrapping for Billions," *Inc.,* September 1994, pp. 78–83.

40 Edward W. Desmond, "What's Ailing Kodak? Fuji," *Fortune,* October 27, 1997, 1985–192.

41 Bill Saporito, "The Eclipse of Mars," *Fortune,* November 28, 1994, 82–92.

42 John E. Prescott, "Environments as Moderators of the Relationship between Strategy and Performance," *Academy of Management Journal* 29 (1986), 329–346; John A. Pearce II and Richard B. Robinson, Jr., *Strategic Management: Strategy, Formulation, and Implementation,* 2d ed. (Homewood, Ill.: Irwin, 1985); and David J. Teece, "Economic Analysis and Strategic Management," *California Management Review* 26 (spring 1984), 87–110.

43 Markides, "Strategic Innovation."

44 William C. Symonds, with Farah Nayeri, Geri Smith, and Ted Plafker, "Bombardier's Blitz," *Business Week,* February 6, 1995, 62–66; and Joseph Weber, with Wendy Zellner and Geri Smith. "Loud Noises at Bombardier," *Business Week,* January 26, 1998, 94–95.

45 Michael E. Porter, "What Is Strategy?" *Harvard Business Review,* November–December 1996, 61–78.

46 Gary McWilliams, "Whirlwind on the Web," *Business Week,* April 7, 1997, pp. 132–136.

47 Arthur A. Thompson, Jr., and A. J. Strickland III, *Strategic Management: Concepts and Cases,* 6th ed. (Homewood, Ill.: Irwin, 1992).

48 Carl Long and Mary Vickers-Koch, "Using Core Capabilities to Create Competitive Advantage," *Organizational Dynamics* 24, no. 1 (summer 1995), 7–22; and Ronald B. Lieber, "Smart Science," *Fortune,* June 23, 1997, 73.

49 Michael Goold and Andrew Campbell, "Desperately Seeking Synergy," *Harvard Business Review,* September–October 1998, 131–143; and Jill Hamburg, "Synergy or Bust," *Working Woman,* September 1998, 15.

50 John S. DeMott, "Company Alliances for Market Muscle," *Nation's Business,* February 1994, 52–53.

51 Bradford McKee, "Ties That Bind Large and Small," *Nation's Business,* February 1992, 24–26.

52 Gregory M. Bounds, Gregory H. Dobbins, and Oscar S. Fowler, *Management: A Total Quality Perspective* (Cincinnati: South-Western College Publishing, 1995), 244.

53 Michael Treacy, "You Need a Value Discipline—But Which One?" *Fortune,* April 17, 1995, 195.

54 Eileen Fitzpatrick, "Web Music Sector Gains Ground," *Billboard,* No. 20, 1999, pp. 1, 125.

55 Milton Leontiades, "The Confusing Words of Business Policy," *Academy of Management Review* 7 (1982), 45–48.

56 Lawrence G. Hrebiniak and William E. Joyce, *Implementing Strategy* (New York: Macmillan, 1984)

57 James E. Svarko, "Analyzing the Competition," *Small Business Reports* (January 1989), 21–28; and Brian Dumaine, "Corporate Spies Snoop to Conquer," *Fortune,* November 7, 1988, 68–76.

58 Steve Swartz, "Basic Bedrooms: How Marriott Changes Hotel Design to Tap Mid-Priced Market," *The Wall Street Journal,* September 18, 1985, 1.

59 James B. Treece with Greg Burns, "The Nervous Faces around Kellogg's Breakfast Table," *Business Week,* July 18, 1994, 33.

60 Michael E. Porter, "From Competitive Advantage to Corporate Strategy," *Harvard Business Review* (May–June 1987), 43–59.

61 David Greising, "Watch Out for Flying Packages," *Business Week,* November 14, 1994, 40.

62 Thomas L. Wheelen and J. David Hunger, *Strategic Management and Business Policy* (Reading, Mass.: Addison-Wesley, 1989).

63 Peter Verburg, "The Little Airline That Could," *Canadian Business,* April, 1997, 34–40.

64 Thompson and Strickland, *Strategic Management.*

65 Greg Burns, "It Only Hertz When Enterprise Laughs," *Business Week,* December 12, 1994, 44.

66 Joshua Rosenbaum, "Guitar Maker Looks for a New Key," *The Wall Street Journal,* February 11, 1998, B1, B5.

67 Based on John Burton, "Composite Strategy: The Combination of Collaboration and Competition," *Journal of General Management* 21, No. 1 (autumn 1995), 1–23; and Roberta Maynard, "Striking the Right Match," *Nation's Business,* May 1996, 18–28.

68 Elizabeth Jensen and Eben Shapiro, "Time Warner's Fight with News Corp. Belies Mutual Dependence," *The Wall Street Journal,* October 28, 1996, A1, A6.

69 "Deals and Dealmakers," *The Wall Street Journal,* Dec. 7, 1999, p. C24; Vanessa Richardson, "GovWorks Receives VC Vote," *Red Herring,* Nov. 8, 1999; Andrew McMains, "Fallon N.Y. Wins $40 Million GovWorks," *Adweek,* Sept. 6, 1999, p. 2; Whit Clay, "Govworks.com Raises over $18 Million in Second Round of Financing," *The Hearst Corporation News,* Nov. 3, 1999; Susan Herman, personal communication, Jan. 2000.

70 Brent Schlender, "Computing's Next Superpower," *Fortune,* May 12, 1997, pp. 88–101.

71 Stratford Sherman, "Are Strategic Alliances Working?" *Fortune,* September 21, 1992, 77–78; and David Lei, "Strategies for Global Competition," *Long-Range Planning* 22 (1989), 102–109.

72 James Aley and Matt Siegel, "The Fallout from Merger Mania," *Fortune,* March 2, 1998, 26–27.

73 William Glasgall with John Rossant and Thane Peterson, "Citigroup: Just the Start?" *Business Week,* April 20, 1998, 34–37; and Leah Nathans Spiro, with Debra Sparks, Andreas Mandel-Campbell, Brian Bremmer, and Owen Ullmann, "The 'Coca-Cola of Personal Finance,'" *Business Week,* April 20, 1998, 37–38.

74 Burton, "Composite Strategy: The Combination of Collaboration and Competition."

75 L. J. Bourgeois III and David R. Brodwin, "Strategic Implementation: Five Approaches to an Elusive Phenomenon," *Strategic Management Journal* 5 (1984), 241–264; Anil K. Gupta and V. Govindarajan, "Business Unit Strategy, Managerial Characteristics, and Business Unit Effectiveness at Strategy Implementation," *Academy of Management Journal* (1984), 25–41; and Jeffrey G. Covin, Dennis P. Slevin, and Randall L. Schultz, "Implementing Strategic Missions: Effective Strategic, Structural, and Tactical Choices," *Journal of Management Studies* 31, no. 4 (1994), 481–505.

76 Rainer Feurer and Kazem Chaharbaghi, "Dynamic Strategy Formulation and Alignment," *Journal of General Management* 20, no. 3 (spring 1995), 76–90; and Henry Mintzberg, *The Rise and Fall of Strategic Planning* (Toronto: Maxwell Macmillan Canada, 1994).

77 Jay R. Galbraith and Robert K. Kazanjiian, *Strategy Implementation: Structure, Systems and Process,* 2d ed. (St. Paul, Minn.: West, 1986); and Paul C. Nutt, "Selecting Tactics to Implement Strategic Plans," *Strategic Management Journal* 10 (1989), 145–161.

78 Alex Taylor III, "Neutron Jurgen Ignites a Revolution at Daimler-Benz," *Fortune,* November 10, 1997, 144-152.

79 Gupta and Govindarajan, "Business Unit Strategy"; and Bourgeois and Brodwin, "Strategic Implementation."

80 Greg Burns, "How a New Boss Got ConAgra Cooking Again," *Business Week,* July 25, 1994, 72–73.

81 Jay Finegan, "Unconventional Wisdom," *Inc.,* December 1994, 44–59.

82 James E. Skivington and Richard L. Daft, "A Study of Organizational 'Framework' and 'Process Modalities for the Implementation of Business-Level Strategies" (unpublished manuscript, Texas A&M University, 1987).

83 Roger Thurow, "A Sports Icon Regains Its Footing by Using the Moves of the Past," *The Wall Street Journal,* January 21, 1998, A1, A10.

6

Managerial Decision Making

LEARNING OBJECTIVES

After studying this chapter, you should be able to:

- Explain why decision making is an important component of good management

- Explain the difference between programmed and nonprogrammed decisions and the decision characteristics of risk, uncertainty, and ambiguity

- Describe the classical, administrative, and political models of decision making and their applications

- Identify the six steps used in managerial decision making

- Explain four personal decision styles used by managers

- Discuss the advantages and disadvantages of participative decision making

- Identify guidelines for improving decision-making effectiveness in organizations

- Describe the importance of information technology for organizations and the attributes of quality information

- Explain how networks are transforming the way companies operate and the services they offer

- Identify different types of information systems

- Tell how information systems support daily operations and decision making

- Summarize the impact of information technology on competitive strategy

TIME is always an important commodity

and never more so than for Mike & Ally, a small

business specializing in purse, bath, and tabletop design and

manufacturing. Founders Allison Rosson and Michael Nash, plus nine employees,

were spread too thin. Ally and Mike were putting in 60-hour workweeks, while only giving

themselves $25,000 (annual) salaries. They kept up with all the paperwork and performed the duties

of controller, production coordinator, and marketing manager. With a 500-person customer base, 100

items in their line, and $250,000 in sales, they were still writing their invoices by hand. They had been

postponing the inevitable—going digital and computerizing their systems—until Saks and Bloomingdale's (their

main customers) insisted that they exchange data electronically for order processing, shipping, and invoicing.

• *If you were Ally or Mike, what would you do? Would you shut down to computerize? Would*

you hire an in-house person? How would you decide what kind of system you needed?

But, such a change could not have come at a worse time. Right in the middle of their busiest season—

with Christmas orders needing to be shipped quickly—they had to make some important decisions

about when and how to digitize. There was no time to hesitate. If they shut down for a week, the

change would be easier on them, but they would miss shipping deadlines for about

40 customers, which would result in a loss of $40,000 in revenue. Then came

the question of whether they should hire someone in-house

to handle the new system or outsource it.[1]

Managers often are referred to as *decision makers,* and Mike & Ally had some really important decisions to make. Although their decisions often are strategic, managers must make decisions about every other aspect of the organization, including structure, control systems, responses to the environment, and human resources. Managers scout for problems, make decisions about solutions, and monitor the consequences to see whether additional decisions are required. Good decision making is a vital part of good management, and it is defined by how well managers solve problems, allocate resources, and accomplish the organization's goals. If Mike & Ally make the wrong decision, it could be disastrous for their small company.

Consider the case of Encyclopedia Britannica. For most of its 230-year history this near-national treasure was viewed as an illustrious repository of cultural and historical knowledge. Generations of students and librarians relied on this 32-volume collection of encyclopedias to research everything from the Aleutian Islands to the history of zydeco. But all of that was before CD-ROMs and the Internet. Suddenly, the Britannica was destined to fade into history. The company was slow to discover electronic media, and it practically handed over the market to upstarts, such as Microsoft's Encarta. Britannica managers blundered in 1993 when they sold the company's Compton unit, a CD-ROM pioneer now being used by millions of consumers. Even when Britannica finally introduced a CD-ROM, it was priced at a staggering $1,200, while Microsoft was giving away its Encarta free with software packages.

Recently, Swiss-based financier Jacob Safra bought Britannica and hopes to usher the company into the digital age. He believes Britannica can once again be the leader in quality, but good decisions have to be made about how to use the company's venerable name to compete with Encarta, Compton's, IBM's joint venture with World Book, and the numerous free or low-cost information options available on the Internet.[2]

Recognizing the problem was easy: The venerable company was collapsing because of an ossified management culture dominated by book salesmen. Years of squabbling over new product development was hindering the move into electronic media. One of the first decisions Jacob Safra made was to bring in a new management team. The team set about reviving the faltering company. Because Britannica was so far behind in the world of electronic media, the new management decided to rush out a series of new products and price them to compete with Encarta and the others.

The new Britannica products included a revamped, graphics-intensive CD-ROM package, a complete online subscription service (www.eb.com), and a new Internet search engine (www.eblast.com), filtering out marginal Web pages and offering consumers what Britannica editors think are the most useful sites. To lure users, Britannica implemented a multimillion-dollar advertising campaign. In addition, to exploit Britannica's wealth of information, the company develops CD-ROMs on subjects ranging from Shakespeare to Black history. The original 32-volume set remains available to those who like the feel of a book in their hands, but Safra decided to do away with the 500-person direct-to-home sales force and strike deals with 300 bookstores and superchains instead. Managers are now in the process of evaluating feedback to determine whether new decisions need to be made.

Decision making is not easy. It must be done amid ever-changing factors, unclear information, and often conflicting points of view. For example, during the 1997 Teamster's strike against United Parcel Service, UPS found itself in the middle of a public relations disaster because of a faulty decision. Executives failed to understand the seriousness of the strike, expecting it to last only a day or two. Thus, they decided not to appoint a single UPS spokesperson to handle the media. With as many as a dozen human resources executives answering questions from the press, UPS was unable to tell a clear, unified story, contributing to a loss of public sympathy for the company.[3] The top U.S. toymakers Mattel and Hasbro passed up the idea of the Teenage Mutant Ninja Turtles in the late 1980s, and the action figures went on to sell millions. Coca-Cola pumped some $30 million into developing the BreakMate, a miniature soda fountain, but the product flopped in the marketplace. Now, Break-Mate fountains gather dust in storage sheds.[4]

The business world is full of evidence of good decisions and poor ones. Andy Grove, CEO of Intel Corporation, decided to get out of the DRAM memory-chip business in the mid-1980s and focus relentlessly on microprocessors. The decision was a risky one, and many Intel executives opposed it, but it set Intel on a course to becoming one of the richest and most powerful companies in the world. Now, some observers believe Intel missed a chance for a second wave of tremendous growth by failing to build simple, fast, inexpensive chips for non-PC devices such as smart identification cards, Internet-ready telephones, handheld computers, digital cameras, video game players, computers on car dashboards, and other consumer gadgets. As industry watchers talk about the "convergence" of computing and consumer electronics, some warn that Intel's decision to focus on ever-more-powerful processors for PCs will ultimately hurt the company.[5]

Strategic planning was covered in the previous chapters. Now we'll move to the decision process that underlies strategic planning. Plans and strategies are arrived at through decision making; the better the decision making, the better the plan. First we will examine decision characteristics. Then we will look at decision-making models and the steps executives should take when making important decisions. We will also examine participative decision making and discuss techniques for improving decision making in organizations.

■ TYPES OF DECISIONS AND PROBLEMS

A **decision** is a determination made from available choices and alternatives. For example, an accounting manager's selection among Bill, Nancy, and Joan for the position of junior auditor is a decision. Many people assume that the choosing is the bulk of decision making, but it is only a part.

Decision making is the process of identifying problems and opportunities and then resolving them.[6] Decision making involves mental and physical effort before *and* after the actual choosing. For instance, the selection of Bill, Nancy, or Joan requires the accounting manager first to ascertain whether a new junior auditor is needed, then determine the availability of potential job candidates, interview the candidates in order to gain necessary information, select a candidate, make the offer, and follow up with the integration of the new employee into the organizational setting. All of these go into ensuring the decision's success.

PROGRAMMED AND NONPROGRAMMED DECISIONS

Management decisions typically fall into one of two categories: (1) programmed and (2) nonprogrammed. **Programmed decisions** involve situations that have occurred often enough to enable decision rules to be developed and applied in the future, and thus are made in response to recurring organizational problems.[7] The decision to reorder paper and other office supplies when inventories drop to a pre-determined level is a programmed decision. Others concern the skills required to fill certain jobs, determine the reorder point for diminishing inventory, report exceptions for expenditures of 10 percent or more over the budget, and select freight routes for product deliveries. Once managers formulate decision rules, subordinates and others can make the decision, freeing managers for other tasks.

Nonprogrammed decisions are made in response to situations that are unique, poorly defined, largely unstructured, or involve important consequences for the organization. Many nonprogrammed decisions require strategic planning, because uncertainty is great and decisions are complex. Decisions to build a new factory, develop a new product or service, enter a new geographical market, or relocate headquarters to another city are all nonprogrammed decisions. When AT&T's new CEO C. Michael Armstrong decided to sell two unrelated business units and buy Teleport Communications, a local phone company, he made a

decision
A determination made from available choices and alternatives

decision making
The process of identifying problems and opportunities and then resolving them

programmed decision
A decision made in response to a situation that has occurred often enough to enable decision rules to be developed and applied in the future

nonprogrammed decision
A decision made in response to a situation that is unique, poorly defined, largely unstructured, or involve important consequences for the organization

nonprogrammed decision. Armstrong and other top managers had to analyze complex problems, evaluate alternatives, and make a decision about how to revive the struggling company. Armstrong's decisions have improved both employee morale and AT&T's flagging stock price.[8] The following example examines a sector that is struggling with issues about how it should proceed on the Internet and shows how nonprogrammed decisions may produce different results from varying decision makers.

GOSPELCOM.NET AND iBELIEVE

Should religion be in e-commerce? Can religion on the Web substitute for real-world worship? While theologians and laypersons debate the sticky questions, two religious organizations have gotten dot-com fever and opened up heavily trafficked sites.

Gospelcom.net is the Web's busiest Bible site and the home of 147 evangelical Christian groups. But while the dot-com image conjures up visions of dollar signs for many people, Gospelcom has a strict rule: no online fundraising. The organization's founders made other early decisions that have led directly to the site's success: putting a fully searchable Bible on the Web in English, German, French, Norwegian, and six other languages and calling it the Bible Gateway. By working with other evangelical groups, Gospelcom was able to expand its site and geographical reach, helping people hook up offline. Asks leader Richard M. DeVos, "How else can you reach so many people at that price?"

Another Christian startup, iBelieve, is taking another approach to building a cyberspace community. Former manager for Anderson Consulting, Jef Fite speaks of "content, community and commerce," and wants iBelieve to become a full-service portal like AOL or Yahoo!, to combine daily inspirations with church, local, and world news and weather.

While iBelieve easily mixes commerce with prayer, Gospelcom is inching its way toward revenue production.

Without breaking its rule against fundraising, Gospelcom is developing partnerships with Christian stores to develop e-commerce pages on its site. "Methods change," says Rev. Billy Zeoli, "But our motive never changes."[9] ■

CERTAINTY, RISK, UNCERTAINTY, AND AMBIGUITY

One primary difference between programmed and nonprogrammed decisions relates to the degree of certainty or uncertainty managers deal with in making the decision. In a perfect world, managers would have all the information they need to make their decisions. But, some things are unknowable. Some decisions will simply fail to solve the problem and not attain the desired outcome. To minimize risk and uncertainty, managers will attempt to obtain information about alternatives. Every decision situation can be placed on a scale according to the availability of information and the potential for failure. The four positions on the scale are certainty, risk, uncertainty, and ambiguity, as illustrated in Exhibit 6.1.

CERTAINTY **Certainty** accompanies situations in which all the information the decision maker needs is fully available and accessible,[10] such as information on operating conditions, resource costs or restraints, and the appropriate actions and possible outcomes. For example, if a company considers a $10,000 investment in new equipment that it knows for certain will yield $4,000 in cost savings per year over the next five years, managers can calculate a before-tax rate of return of about 40 percent. If managers compare this investment with one that will yield only $3,000 per year in cost savings, they can confidently select the 40 percent return. However, few decisions in the real world are without uncertainty and risk.

RISK **Risk** accompanies situations in which outcomes are subject to chance. Risk is lessened when a decision has clear-cut goals and enough information is available to allow the probability of a successful outcome to be estimated.[11] Statistical analysis might be used

certainty
Accompanies situations in which all the information the decision maker needs is fully available and accessible

risk
Accompanies situations in which outcomes are subject to chance

Peter Metcalf feels on top of the world since sales of his company's climbing equipment and backcountry skis have doubled to $20 million. As CEO of Salt Lake City, Utah-based Black Diamond Equipment, Ltd., Metcalf made a strategic nonprogrammed decision three years ago to relocate company headquarters from Ventura, California. Real estate prices in Ventura were sky-high, and Black Diamond faced strict regulations, high worker compensation costs, and rapidly rising health insurance premiums. Yet, relocation would be costly, and there were no guarantees it would pull the company out of its slump. After evaluating alternatives, Metcalf made a decision that proved to be right on target.

to calculate the probabilities of success or failure. Measuring risk incorporates the possibility that future events will render a decision unsuccessful. Some oil companies use a quantitative simulation approach to estimating hydrocarbon reserves. This enables oil executives to evaluate the variation in risk at each stage of exploration and production and make better decisions. McDonald's took a calculated risk and lost with the introduction of its Arch Deluxe sandwich line. McDonald's had information that indicated a line of sandwiches targeted toward adults would be successful, but the Arch Deluxe, which risked $100 million, flopped.[12]

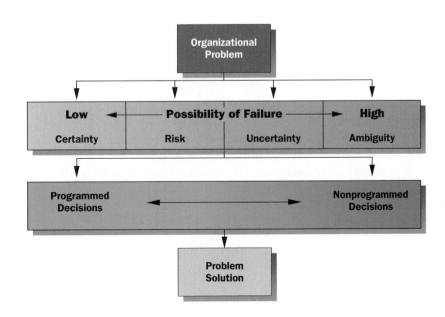

Exhibit 6.1

CONDITIONS THAT AFFECT
THE POSSIBILITY OF
DECISION FAILURE

UNCERTAINTY   **Uncertainty** enters into situations when managers know the goals they wish to achieve, but information about alternatives and future events is incomplete or unpredictable.[13] Uncertainty increases when managers do not have enough information to be clear about alternatives or to effectively estimate their risk. Factors that may affect a decision, such as price, production costs, volume, and future interest rates, are difficult to analyze and nearly impossible to predict. Managers often make assumptions to forge a decision, but the decision turns out to be wrong because the assumptions were incorrect. Managers must develop creative approaches to decision making and use their personal judgment to determine the best alternative.

Eastman Kodak faced great uncertainty in its decision to invest $500 million per year to develop digital photography products that the company hoped would fundamentally change the way people create, store, and view photographs. Microsoft faced uncertainty in deciding to commit major development costs to the Microsoft Network (MSN). At the time, it was not clear whether open networks, such as the Internet or proprietary networks such as MSN, would become the standard. When it became clear that open networks would prevail, Microsoft was able to cut its losses and reorient the MSN concept around the Internet.[14]

Many decisions made under uncertainty do not produce the desired results, but managers face uncertainty every day. They must find creative ways to cope with uncertainty in order to make effective decisions.

AMBIGUITY   **Ambiguity** is by far the most difficult decision situation. Ambiguity is present when unclear goals or unsolved problems prevail and alternatives are difficult to define and information about outcomes is unavailable, unstable, or unpredictable.[15] Ambiguity is what students feel when instructors put them in groups, tell them to complete a project, and give them no topic, direction, or guidelines. Ambiguity keeps managers from coming to grips with the issues, it creates conflicts over goals, and it confuses decision alternatives. When circumstances are rapidly changing, fuzzy information is barely avail-

able, and unclear linkages among decision elements are rife, ambiguity reigns.[16] Sometimes managers will arrive at a "solution" only to realize that they had not clearly defined the real problem.[17] Fortunately, most decisions are not characterized by ambiguity. But when they are, managers must conjure up goals and develop reasonable scenarios for decision alternatives, often in the absence of useful information. When reports surfaced several years ago that syringes and hypodermic needles had been found in cans of Pepsi, PepsiCo executives faced ambiguity squarely in the face.

PEPSI-COLA
www.pepsico.com

PepsiCo executives faced a truly ambiguous problem when reports surfaced that syringes and hypodermic needles had been found in Pepsi cans around the country. Before they could develop decision alternatives, executives first had to identify the problem—could needles have been put in Pepsi at the canning plants, or were the reports a hoax? Information was fuzzy and rapidly changing, but executives needed to make a decision quickly.

Pepsi's dilemma involved evidence of danger that might demand a product recall. But such evidence did not exist. A recall would be extremely costly for the company, but loss of consumer trust would be even more expensive in the long run. After carefully analyzing the situation, Pepsi's managers believed syringes could not appear in unopened cans of Pepsi. They decided not to issue a recall, but rather to respond with a massive public relations and education campaign to quickly and openly address consumer fears. PepsiCo's CEO Craig Weatherup himself took to the airwaves to explain how implausible it was that syringes could have been put into Pepsi cans at the plants. At one point, Weatherup appeared on ABC's *Nightline* with FDA Commissioner David Kessler, who did not believe there was evidence of nationwide tampering.

uncertainty
Accompanies situations in which managers know the goals they wish to achieve, but information about alternatives and future events is incomplete or unpredictable

ambiguity
Occurs when unclear goals or unsolved problems prevail and alternatives are difficult to define and information about outcomes is unavailable, unstable, or unpredictable

The company kept bottlers up to speed on fastbreaking developments, and bottlers were then to pass along the information to every level of the organization—from filling line operators to route salespeople. Nationwide ad campaigns explained the decision and assured consumers that there had been no injuries and not a single confirmed case of a needle found in an unopened can of Pepsi.

By allying itself with the FDA and responding quickly and openly to public fears, Pepsi weathered the syringe-scare crisis with little damage. Pepsi managers made the right decision, believing, based on careful internal analysis, that needles could not possibly have been put into cans at the plants. However, it was a decision that could have backfired if the company was unable to convince consumers that Pepsi products were truly safe.[18] ■

■ DECISION-MAKING MODELS

Decision-making approaches can be categorized into three types—the classical model, the administrative model, or the political model. Choosing the right model depends on the manager's personal preference, whether the decision is programmed or nonprogrammed, and on the degree of risk, uncertainty, or ambiguity.

CLASSICAL MODEL

The **classical model** of decision making is based on economic assumptions. This model has arisen within the management literature because managers are expected to make decisions that are economically sensible and in the organization's best economic interests. The assumptions underlying this model are:

1. The decision maker accomplishes goals that are known and agreed upon. Problems are precisely formulated and defined.
2. The decision maker strives for certainty by gathering complete information. All alter-

natives and the potential results of each are calculated.

3. Criteria for evaluating alternatives are known. The decision maker selects the alternative that will maximize the economic return to the organization.
4. The decision maker uses logic to assign values, order preferences, evaluate alternatives, and attain organizational goals.

The classical model of decision making is considered to be **normative,** which means it provides norms and guidelines on how to reach an ideal outcome. The classical model is most valuable when it (1) helps decision makers be more rational and (2) combats decisions based solely on intuition and personal preferences.[19] In recent years, this approach has seen increased application because of the numerous quantitative decision techniques that use computers. Quantitative techniques (see Appendix C) include decision trees, payoff matrices, break-even analysis, linear programming, forecasting, and operations research models. The use of computerized information systems and databases has increased the power of the classical approach.

In many respects, the classical model is an ideal; a fanciful notion about decision making unattainable in the real world. Its value is best seen when it is applied to programmed decisions and to decisions characterized by certainty or low risk, because relevant information is available and probabilities can be calculated. The classical approach in practice can be seen in this Canadian organization's scheduling of ambulance services.

URGENCES SANTÉ

Urgences Santé, a public agency responsible for coordinating ambulance service in the Montreal area, schedules vehicle time and working hours for approximately 80 ambulances and 700 technicians. Because Urgences Santé does not own its vehicles or hire technicians but rents these from private companies, agency managers wanted to optimize the schedule to avoid unnecessary rental costs.

classical model
A decision-making model based on economic assumptions in which managers make logical decisions based on the organization's economic interests

normative
Norms and guidelines on how to reach an ideal outcome

Two types of calls require ambulance service: (1) emergency calls from the public, which occur randomly and require immediate attention, and (2) calls from hospitals, which are concentrated in specific time periods and are generally not urgent. In addition, demand for ambulance service usually is higher in the winter, but more emergency calls on weekends occur during the summer months. Besides meeting shifting demand, a number of other restraints governed the design of a new schedule.

Urgences Santé applied mathematical formulations and techniques to first build seasonal workday schedules for each type of day (weekend/weekday), equitably assign workdays to the 15 or so private service companies, then build individual schedules for the 700 technicians. More than 85 percent of the individual schedules can now be created automatically. The new system has had two positive effects. First, the agency is able to meet demand while cutting rental hours per week by up to 110 hours, saving approximately $250,000 per year. Second, the quality of schedules for technicians has been dramatically improved, leading to a decrease in turnover.[20] ■

ADMINISTRATIVE MODEL

The **administrative model** of decision making focuses on organizational, rather than economic, factors that influence individual decisions. It describes how managers actually make decisions in difficult, nonprogrammed situations that involve uncertainty and ambiguity. Because many management decisions are not sufficiently programmable and do not lend themselves to stable quantification, managers are unable to make economically-rational decisions, even if they wanted to.[21]

BOUNDED RATIONALITY AND SATISFICING

The administrative model of decision making is based on the work of Herbert A. Simon, who proposed two instrumental concepts: bounded

rationality and satisficing. **Bounded rationality** means that people have limits, or boundaries, on their cognitive abilities and on how rational they can be in a given situation, such as when the organization is incredibly complex, and managers only have the time and ability to process a limited amount of information before making decisions.[22] In this situation, managers must **satisfice,** which means to choose the first alternative that satisfies criteria minimums. Rather than pursuing all alternatives and identifying a lasting solution that will maximize economic returns, managers opt for the first solution that appears to solve the problem, even when better solutions are presumed to exist. Also, the decision maker cannot justify the time and expense of obtaining complete information.[23]

An example of both bounded rationality and satisficing occurs when a junior executive on a business trip stains her blouse just before an important meeting. She will run to a nearby clothing store and buy the first satisfactory replacement she finds. Having neither the time nor the opportunity to explore all the blouses in town, she satisfices by choosing a blouse that will solve the immediate problem. In a similar fashion, managers generate alternatives for complex problems only until they find one they believe will work. For example, several years ago then-Disney chairman Ray Watson and chief operating officer Ron Miller attempted to thwart takeover attempts, but they had limited options. They satisficed with a quick decision to acquire Arivda Realty and Gibson Court Company. The acquisition of these companies had the potential to solve the problem at hand; thus, they looked no further for better alternatives.[24]

Because the administrative model relies on different assumptions than those of the classical model and focuses on organizational (not economic) factors, it is more realistic and is therefore more effective when applied to complex, nonprogrammed decisions. According to the administrative model:

1. Decision goals often are vague, conflicting, and lack consensus among managers. Man-

---

administrative model
A decision-making model that focuses on organizational factors and describes how managers actually make decisions in difficult, nonprogrammed situations

bounded rationality
The concept that people have limits, or boundaries, on their cognitive abilities and on how rational they can be in a given situation

satisfice
To choose the first alternative that satisfies criteria minimums, even when better solutions are presumed to exist

agers often are unaware of problems or opportunities that exist in the organization.

2. Rational procedures are not always used, and, when they are, they are confined to a simplistic view of the problem that does not capture the complexity of events. When rationality is underutilized in decision making, disaster can strike (see Industry.net).

3. The search for alternatives by managers is limited by human, informational, or resource factors.

4. Managers settle for a satisficing, rather than a maximizing, solution. This is partly because they have limited information and partly because they have only vague criteria for what constitutes a lasting, optimal solution.

INDUSTRY.NET

Founders and investors were so hyped during the early days of the Internet frenzy that the heady atmosphere they created short-circuited their ability to think through all the steps for making their business successful. The unprecedented success of a few startups making millions by being sold or going public with initial public offerings (IPOs) was just too much. Decision making and rationality got lost in dreams of a brave, new world.

Founded by entrepreneur Donald Jones, Industry.net published a business-to-business directory of distributors and manufacturers. Jones hired former Lotus development chief Jim Manzi as CEO and charged him with hurling Industry.net to the frontlines of online marketing. The company had already started to build a Web directory where engineers and manufacturers could look for ball bearings and the like from various vendors.

Manzi decided to grow the company quickly, at the same time that engineers were developing software to allow secure online ordering. Everything was going well. Five thousand paying customers allowed Industry.net to have 300 employees on the payroll. Then, it all

crashed. It had raised $25 million from venture capitalists, but the company was spending $3 million a month, and annual sales were only $10 million. Manzi, for all his techie smarts, never learned the entrepreneurial skill of "minding every penny," said director Raj Reddy.

The final blows came when the crucial software could not be developed in time. It was soon realized that the vision of the company lacked coherence, and poor decisions had been made by Jones, Manzi, and the venture capitalists. Perhaps the only real winner was H. Ross Perot, whose Perot Systems purchased Industry.net after it went bankrupt and slid into Chapter 11. It's still operational, but part of a big conglomerate, rather than the brash upstart it had hoped to be.[25] ∎

The administrative model is considered to be **descriptive,** meaning that it describes how managers actually make decisions in complex situations and does not impose a theoretical ideal on their decision making. The administrative model recognizes the human and environmental limitations that affect the rational decision-making process.

INTUITION   Another aspect of administrative decision making involves intuition. **Intuition** is the quick apprehension of a situation using past experience, not conscious planning or thought.[26] Intuitive decision making is not arbitrary or irrational, because it is based on years of practice and hands-on experience. This enables managers to quickly identify solutions without going through painstaking computations. In fact, Michael Ray and Rochelle Myers, in their book *Creativity in Business,* suggest that "intuition" is really "recognition." When people build up a wealth of experience and knowledge in a particular area, the right decision often comes quickly and effortlessly as a recognition of information that has been largely forgotten by the conscious mind. For example, actor and director Jodie Foster is known for making good intuitive decisions at

descriptive
An approach that describes how managers actually make complex decisions and does not impose a theoretical ideal on their decision making

intuition
The quick apprehension of a situation using past experience, not conscious planning or thought

her production company, Egg Pictures. Foster's movie career began at eight, and her manager-mother involved her in almost every decision about roles, script changes, and the like. "She understands Hollywood almost mathematically," said one producer.[27] Managers use their intuitive understanding to check the results of rational analysis. If the rational analysis does not agree with their intuition, managers may dig deeper into a problem before accepting a proposed alternative.[28]

POLITICAL MODEL

The third model of decision making is useful for making nonprogrammed decisions when conditions are uncertain, information is limited, and there is disagreement among managers about what goals to pursue or what course of action to take. Managers often engage in coalition building for making complex organizational decisions. A **coalition** is an informal alliance among managers who support a specific goal. Coalition building involves informal talks between a manager and other executives as he tries to persuade them to support a certain decision. When the outcomes are not predictable, managers gain support through discussion, negotiation, and bargaining. Without a coalition, a powerful individual or group could derail the decision-making process. Coalition building gives several managers an opportunity to contribute to decision making, enhancing their commitment to the alternative that is ultimately adopted.[29]

The political model closely resembles the real environment in which most managers and decision makers operate. Decisions are complex and involve many people, information is often ambiguous, and disagreement and conflict over problems and solutions are normal operating procedures. The basic assumptions of the political model are:

1. Organizations are made up of groups with diverse interests, goals, and values. Managers disagree about problem priorities and may not understand or share the goals and interests of other managers.

2. Information is ambiguous and incomplete. The attempt to be rational is limited by the complexity of many problems as well as personal and organizational constraints.

3. Managers do not have the time, resources, or mental capacity to identify all dimensions of the problem and process all relevant information. Managers talk to each other and exchange viewpoints to gather information and reduce ambiguity.

4. Managers engage in the push and pull of debate to decide goals and discuss alternatives. Decisions are the result of bargaining and discussion among coalition members.

Recent research into decision-making procedures has found that rational, classical procedures are associated with high performance for organizations in stable environments. Administrative and political decision-making procedures and intuition tend to be associated with high performance in unstable environments in which complex decisions are made rapidly.[30]

■ DECISION-MAKING STEPS

Whether a decision is programmed or nonprogrammed and regardless of managers' choice of the classical, administrative, or political model of decision making, six steps typically are associated with effective decision processes. These are summarized in Exhibit 6.2.

RECOGNITION OF DECISION REQUIREMENT

Managers confront problems or opportunities every day. A **problem** occurs when organizational accomplishment falls below established goals. An **opportunity** exists when managers recognize the possibility of enhancing performance beyond current levels.

Awareness of a problem or opportunity is the first step in the decision sequence and requires surveillance of the internal and external environment for issues that merit executive attention.[31] This resembles the military concept of gathering intelligence. Managers

coalition
An informal alliance among managers who support a specific goal

problem
A situation in which organizational accomplishment falls below established goals

opportunity
A situation in which managers recognize the possibility of enhancing performance beyond current levels

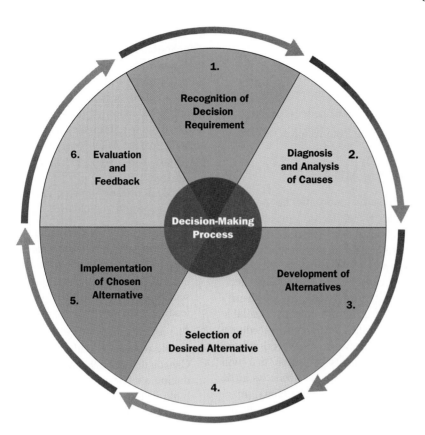

DIAGNOSIS AND ANALYSIS OF CAUSES

scan their environment and determine whether the organization is satisfactorily progressing toward its goals. Managers also take advantage of informal sources. They talk to other managers, gather opinions on how things are going, and seek advice on which problems should be tackled or which opportunities embraced.[32]

Some information comes from periodic accounting reports, MIS reports, and other sources that are designed to discover problems before they become too serious. For example, while reading a routine internal company report, Becky Roloff, a vice president for IDS Financial Services (now American Express Financial Advisors), noted a high level of employee turnover that was not being addressed by the company. Her discovery of the problem eventually led to a comprehensive redesign of the company, including better training programs, more emphasis on teamwork, and stronger efforts to hire minorities.[33]

DIAGNOSIS AND ANALYSIS OF CAUSES

Once a problem or opportunity has come to a manager's attention, the understanding of the situation should be refined. **Diagnosis** is the step in the decision-making process in which managers analyze underlying causal factors. Mistakes occur at this stage when alternatives are generated and implemented before root causes of the problem are explored.

Kepner and Tregoe have conducted extensive studies of manager decision making and recommend asking the following series of questions to specify underlying causes:

- What is the state of disequilibrium affecting us?
- When did it occur?

diagnosis
The step in the decision-making process in which managers analyze underlying causal factors

- Where did it occur?
- How did it occur?
- To whom did it occur?
- What is the urgency of the problem?
- What is the interconnectedness of events?
- What result came from which activity?[34]

DEVELOPMENT OF ALTERNATIVES

Once the problem or opportunity has been recognized and analyzed, decision makers begin to consider taking action. The next stage is to generate possible alternative solutions that will identify the needs of the situation and correct the underlying causes. For a programmed decision, feasible alternatives are easy to identify and, in fact, usually are already available within the organization's rules and procedures. Nonprogrammed decisions, however, require developing new courses of action that will meet the company's needs. For decisions made under conditions of high uncertainty, managers may develop only one or two custom solutions that will satisfice for handling the problem.

SELECTION OF DESIRED ALTERNATIVE

Once feasible alternatives have been developed, the most promising course of action must be chosen. The best choice is the one in which the solution (1) best fits the overall goals and values of the organization, (2) achieves the desired results, (3) uses the fewest resources, and (4) assumes the least amount of risk and uncertainty.[35] Because risk is inherent in most nonprogrammed decisions, managers try to gauge prospects for success. Under conditions of uncertainty, they often have to rely on their intuition and experience to estimate whether the course of action is likely to succeed. Basing choices on overall goals and values can also effectively guide selection of alternatives. **Risk propensity** refers to the willingness to undertake risk with the opportunity of gaining a positive result. The level of risk a manager is willing to accept will influence the analysis of cost and benefits to be derived from any decision. Consider the following situations. Which alternative would you choose? A person with a low risk propensity would tend to take assured moderate returns by going for a tie score, building a domestic plant, or pursuing a career as a physician. A risk taker would go for the victory, build a plant in a foreign country, or embark on an acting career. Manager's Shoptalk describes biases to avoid when selecting the desired alternative.

For each of the following decisions, which alternative would you choose?

1. In the final seconds of a game with the college's traditional rival, the coach of a college football team may choose a play that has a 95 percent chance of producing a tie score or one with a 30 percent chance of leading to victory or to sure defeat if it fails.

2. The president of a Canadian company must decide whether to build a new plant within Canada that has a 90 percent chance of producing a modest return on investment or to build it in a foreign country with an unstable political history. The latter alternative has a 40 percent chance of failing, but the returns would be enormous if it succeeded.

3. A college senior with considerable acting talent must choose a career. She has the opportunity to go on to medical school and become a physician, a career in which she has an 80 percent likelihood for success. But, she would rather be an actress and realizes that the opportunity for success is about 20 percent.

IMPLEMENTATION OF CHOSEN ALTERNATIVE

The **implementation** stage involves the use of managerial, administrative, and persuasive abilities to ensure that the chosen alternative is carried out. This is similar to strategic implementation described earlier in the book. The ultimate success of the chosen alternative depends on how it becomes action. Sometimes an alternative never becomes reality because managers lack the resources or energy to set it in motion. In an atmosphere of openness, implementation may involves discussion with the people affected by the decision, and

risk propensity
The willingness to undertake risk with the opportunity of gaining a positive result

implementation
The step in the decision-making process that involves using managerial, administrative, and persuasive abilities to ensure that a chosen alternative is carried out

manager's shoptalk

Decision Biases to Avoid

At a time when decision making is so important, many corporate executives do not know how to make a good choice among alternatives. They may rely on computer analyses or personal intuition without realizing that their own cognitive biases affect their judgment. The complexities of modern corporate life make good judgment more critical than ever. Many errors in judgment originate in the human mind's limited capacity and in the natural biases most managers display during decision making. Awareness of the six biases below can help managers make more enlightened choices:

1. Being influenced by initial impressions. When considering decisions, the mind often gives disproportionate weight to the first information it receives. These initial impressions, statistics, or estimates act as an anchor to our subsequent thoughts and judgments. Anchors can be as simple as a random comment by a colleague or a statistic read in a newspaper. Past events and trends also act as anchors. For example, in business, managers frequently look at the previous year's sales when estimating sales for the coming year. However, in rapidly changing environments, giving too much weight to the past can lead to poor forecasts and misguided decisions.

2. Justifying past decisions. Many people fall into the trap of making choices that justify their past decisions, even if those decisions no longer seem valid. For example, managers may invest tremendous time and energy into improving the performance of a problem employee whom they now realize should never have been hired in the first place. Another example is when investors continue to pour money into failing businesses hoping to turn things around. People are often unwilling to admit they made a mistake, so they continue to make flawed decisions in an effort to correct the past. This tendency to "throw good money after bad" is sometimes called escalating commitment.

3. Seeing what you want to see. People frequently look for information that supports their existing instinct or point of view and avoid information that contradicts it. This bias affects where managers look for information when considering decisions, as well as how they interpret the information they find. People tend to give too much weight to supporting information and too little to information that conflicts with their established viewpoints. It is important for managers to be honest with themselves about their motives and to examine all the evidence with equal rigor. Having a devil's advocate to argue against a decision can also help avoid this decision trap.

4. Perpetuating the status quo. Managers may base decisions on what has worked in the past and fail to explore new options, dig for additional information, or investigate new technologies. For example, Du Pont clung to its cash cow, nylon, despite growing evidence in the scientific community that a new product, polyester, was superior for tire cords. Celanese, a relatively small competitor, blew Du Pont out of the water by exploiting this new evidence, quickly capturing 75 percent of the tire market.

5. Being influenced by problem framing. The decision response of a manager can be influenced by the mere wording of a problem. For example, consider a manager faced with a decision about salvaging the cargo of three barges that sank off the coast of Alaska. If managers are given the option of approving (A) a plan that has a 100 percent chance of saving the cargo of one of the three barges, worth $200,000 or (B) a plan that has a one-third chance of saving the cargo of all three barges, worth $600,000 and a two-thirds chance of saving nothing, most managers choose option A. The same problem with a negative frame would give managers a choice of selecting (C) a plan that has a 100 percent chance of losing two of the three cargoes, worth $400,000 or (D) a plan that has a two-thirds chance of losing all three cargoes but a one-third chance of losing no cargo. With this framing, most managers choose option D. Because both problems are identical, the decision choice depends strictly on how the problem is framed.

6. Overconfidence. One of the interesting research findings on decision-making biases is that most people overestimate their ability to predict uncertain outcomes. Before making a decision, managers have unrealistic expectations of their ability to understand the risk and make the right choice. Overconfidence is greatest when answering questions of moderate to extreme difficulty. For example, when people were asked to define quantities about which they had little direct knowledge ("What was the dollar value of Canadian lumber exports in 1997?" "What was the amount of taxes collected by the U.S. Internal Revenue Service in 1990?"), they overestimated their accuracy. Evidence of overconfidence is illustrated in cases in which subjects were so certain of an answer that they assigned odds of 1,000 to 1 of being correct but in fact were correct only about 85 percent of the time. These findings are especially important for strategic decision making, in which uncertainty is high because managers may unrealistically expect that they can successfully predict outcomes and hence select the wrong alternative.

Sources: Based on John Hammond, Ralph L. Keeney, and Howard Raiffa, "The Hidden Traps in Decision Making," *Harvard Business Review*, September–October 1998, pp. 47–58; Oren Harari; "The Thomas Lawson Syndrome," *Management Review*, February 1994, pp. 58–61; and Gary Belsky, "Why Smart People Make Major Money Mistakes," *Money*, July 1995, pp. 76–85.

communication, motivation, and leadership skills come into play.

EVALUATION AND FEEDBACK

In the evaluation stage of the decision process, decision makers gather information that tells them how well the decision was implemented and whether it was effective in achieving its goals. Feedback is important because decision making is a continuous, never-ending process. Decision making is not completed when an executive or the board of directors votes yes or no. Feedback can precipitate a new decision cycle, or it can generate a new analysis of the problem, a new evaluation of alternatives, or selection of a new alternative. Feedback assesses whether a new decision needs to be made. An illustration of the overall decision-making process, including evaluation and feedback, can be seen in the experience of Tom's of Maine.

TOM'S OF MAINE
www.tomsofmaine.com

Tom's of Maine, known for its all-natural personal hygiene products, saw an opportunity to expand its line with a new natural deodorant. However, the opportunity quickly became a problem when the deodorant worked only half of the time with half of the customers who used it, and its all-recyclable plastic dials tended to break.

The problem of the failed deodorant led founder Tom Chappell and other managers to analyze and diagnose what went wrong. They finally determined that the company's product development process had run amok. Responsible from conception to launch of the product was the same group of merry product developers. They were so attached to the product that they failed to test it properly or consider potential problems. Managers considered several alternatives for solving the problem created by this "mutual admiration society." The decision to publicly admit the problem and recall the deodorant was an easy one for Chappell, who has always run his company on principles of fairness and honesty. Not only did the company apologize to its customers but it listened to their complaints and suggestions. Chappell himself answered calls and letters. Even though the recall cost the company $400,000 and led to a stream of negative publicity, it ultimately helped the company improve relationships with customers.

Evaluation and feedback also led the company to set up "acorn groups," cross-departmental teams that shepherd new products through the process. The teams were created to find problems—and new opportunities—that ordinarily would get missed. They pass on their ideas and findings to senior managers and the product-development team.

Tom's of Maine was able to turn a problem into an opportunity, due to evaluation and feedback. Not only did the disaster ultimately help the company solidify relationships with customers, but it also led to a formal mechanism for learning and sharing ideas, something the company did not have before.[36] ■

Strategic decisions always contain risk, but feedback and follow-up decisions can help get companies back on track. By learning from their decision-making mistakes, managers and companies can turn problems into opportunities.[37]

■ PERSONAL DECISION FRAMEWORK

Imagine you were a manager at Tom's of Maine, a local movie theater, or the public library. How would you go about making important decisions that shape the future of your department or company? So far, we have discussed a number of factors that affect how managers make decisions. Exhibit 6.3 illustrates the role of personal style in the decision-making process. Personal **decision style** refers to differences among people with respect to how they perceive problems and make decisions. Research has identified four major

decision style
Differences among people with respect to how they perceive problems and make decisions

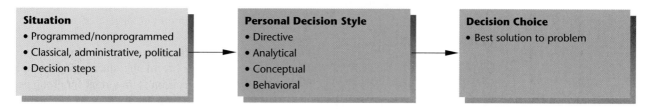

Situation	Personal Decision Style	Decision Choice
• Programmed/nonprogrammed • Classical, administrative, political • Decision steps	• Directive • Analytical • Conceptual • Behavioral	• Best solution to problem

decision styles: directive, analytical, conceptual, and behavioral.[38]

1. The *directive* style is used by people who prefer simple, clear-cut solutions to problems. Managers who use this style often make decisions quickly because they do not like to deal with a lot of information and may consider only one or two alternatives. People who prefer the directive style generally are efficient and rational and prefer to make decisions based on existing rules or procedures.

2. Managers with an *analytical* style, on the other hand, like to consider complex solutions based on as much data as they can gather. These individuals carefully consider alternatives and often base their decisions on objective, rational data from management control systems and other sources. They search for the best possible decision based on the information available.

3. People who tend toward a *conceptual* style also like to consider a broad amount of information. However, they are more socially inclined than those with an analytical style and like to talk to others about problems, alternatives, and solutions. Managers using a conceptual style consider many broad alternatives, rely on information from both people and systems, and like to solve problems creatively.

4. The *behavioral* style is often the style adopted by managers who display a deep concern for others as individuals. This type of manager enjoys talking one-on-one and understands the feelings of others and the effect a given decision might have upon

them. People with a behavioral style usually are concerned with the personal development of others and will tend to make decisions that help others achieve their goals.

Although most managers have a dominant decision style, frequently they will use several different styles or a combination of styles in making varied decisions. For example, a manager might use a directive style for deciding on which printing company to use for new business cards, yet shift to a more conceptual style when handling an interdepartmental conflict. The most effective managers are able to shift among styles to meet the needs of a situation. Being aware of one's dominant decision style can help a manager avoid making critical mistakes when his or her usual style may be inappropriate to the problem at hand.

■ INCREASING PARTICIPATION IN DECISION MAKING

While managers do make some decisions as individuals, decision makers more often are part of a group. Indeed, major decisions in the business world rarely are made by a single person. Effective decision making often depends on whether managers involve the right people in the right ways.[39] Today, many managers are including lower-level employees in the decision-making process whenever possible and finding that some decisions actually *require* the participation of subordinates. Most decisions are made through a committee, by a task force, with departmental participation, or via informal coalition. Participative decision making begins with the Vroom-Jago model, which identifies effective amounts of subordinate participation in making decisions.

VROOM-JAGO MODEL

Victor Vroom and Arthur Jago developed their model of participative decision making to provide guidance to practicing managers.[40] The **Vroom-Jago model** helps managers gauge the appropriate amount of participation usually needed from subordinates. It has three major components: leader participation styles, a set of diagnostic questions used to analyze a decision situation, and a series of decision rules.

LEADER PARTICIPATION STYLES   The model ranges from highly autocratic participation to highly democratic (see Exhibit 6.4). Autocratic leadership styles are represented by AI and AII, consulting styles by CI and CII, and a group decision by G. The five styles fall along a continuum, and the manager should select one style appropriate to the situation. If the situation warrants, the manager could make the decision alone (AI), share the problem with subordinates individually (CI), or let group members make the decision (G).

Vroom-Jago model
A model designed to help managers gauge the appropriate amount of subordinate participation in decision making

DIAGNOSTIC QUESTIONS   How does a manager decide which of the five decision styles to use? Eight diagnostic questions address the appropriate degree of participation.

1. *Quality Requirement (QR)*—How important is the quality of this decision? If a high-quality decision is important for group performance, the leader has to be actively involved.

2. *Commitment Requirement (CR)*—How important is subordinate commitment to the decision? If implementation requires that subordinates commit to the decision, leaders should involve the subordinates in the decision process.

3. *Leader's Information (LI)*—Do I have sufficient information to make a high-quality decision? If the leader does not have sufficient information or expertise, the leader should involve subordinates to obtain that information.

4. *Problem Structure (ST)*—Is the decision problem well structured? If the problem is ambiguous and poorly structured, the leader will need to interact with subordinates to clarify the problem and identify possible solutions.

Exhibit 6.4

FIVE LEADER DECISION STYLES

	Decision Style	Description
Highly Autocratic	AI	You solve the problem or make the decision yourself using information available to you at that time.
	AII	You obtain the necessary information from your subordinates and then decide on the solution to the problem yourself.
	CI	You share the problem with relevant subordinates individually, getting their ideas and suggestions without bringing them together as a group. Then you make the decision.
	CII	You share the problem with your subordinates as a group, collectively obtaining their ideas and suggestions. Then you make the decision.
Highly Democratic	G	You share a problem with your subordinates as a group. Your role is much like that of chairman. You do not try to influence the group to adopt "your" solution, and you are willing to accept and implement any solution that has the support of the entire group.

Note: A = autocratic; C = consultative; G = group

SOURCE: Reprinted from Victor H. Vroom and Arthur G. Jago, *The New Leadership: Managing Participation in Organizations* (Englewood Cliffs, N.J.: Prentice-Hall, 1988). Copyright 1987 by V. H. Vroom and A. G. Jago. Used with permission of the authors.

5. *Commitment Probability (CP)*—If I were to make the decision by myself, is it reasonably certain that my subordinates would be committed to the decision? If subordinates typically go along with whatever the leader decides, their involvement in the decision process will be less important.

6. *Goal Congruence (GC)*—Do subordinates share the organizational goals to be attained in solving this problem? If subordinates do not share the goals of the organization, the leader should not allow the group to make the decision alone.

7. *Subordinate Conflict (CO)*—Is conflict over preferred solutions likely to occur among subordinates? Disagreement among subordinates can be resolved by allowing their participation and discussion.

8. *Subordinate Information (SI)*—Do subordinates have enough information to make a high-quality decision? If subordinates have good information, then more responsibility for the decision can be delegated to them.

These questions seem detailed, but they quickly narrow the options available to managers and point to the appropriate level of group participation in the decision.

SELECTING A DECISION STYLE   The decision flowchart in Exhibit 6.5 allows a leader to

E x h i b i t   6.5

VROOM-JAGO DECISION TREE FOR DETERMINING AN APPROPRIATE DECISION-MAKING METHOD—GROUP PROBLEMS

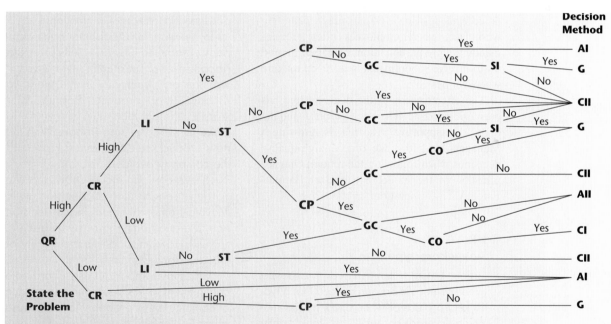

QR How important is the quality of this decision?

CR How important is subordinate commitment to the decision?

LI Do you have sufficient information to make a high-quality decision?

ST Is the problem well structured?

CP If you were to make the decision by yourself, is it reasonably certain that your subordinates would be committed to it?

GC Do subordinates share the organization goals to be attained in solving this problem?

CO Is conflict among subordinates over preferred solutions likely?

SI Do subordinates have sufficient information to make a high-quality decision?

adopt a participation style by answering the questions in sequence. The leader begins at the left side of the chart with question QR: How important is the quality of the decision? If the answer is high, then the leader proceeds to question CR: How important is subordinate commitment to the decision? If the answer is high, the next question is LI: Do I have sufficient information to make a high-quality decision? If the answer is yes, the leader proceeds to answer question CP because question ST is irrelevant if the leader has sufficient information to make a high-quality decision. Managers can quickly learn to use the basic model to adapt their leadership styles to fit their decision problem and the situation.

Several decision styles are equally acceptable in many situations. When this happens, Vroom and Jago note that the autocratic style saves time without reducing decision quality or acceptance. However, in today's changing workplace, where employees often are demanding more participation, managers should try to involve subordinates in decision making whenever possible.

The effectiveness of the decision tree has been criticized, but it serves a purpose, and the body of supportive research is growing.[41] Managers tend to make timely, high-quality decisions when following the model. One application of the model occurred at Barouh-Eaton Allen Corporation.

Ko-Rec-Type

www.korectype.com

Barouh-Eaton Allen started prospering when owner Vic Barouh noticed that a typist kept a piece of white chalk by her machine. To erase an error, she would lightly rub over it with the chalk. It took several passes, but the correction was neatly made. Barouh's company already made carbon paper, so he tried rubbing chalk on one side of a sheet of paper, putting the paper between the error and typewriter, and striking the same key. Most of the error disappeared under a thin coating of chalk dust. Thus, Ko-Rec-Type was born. Demand for the product was enormous, and the company prospered.

Then IBM invented the self-correcting typewriter. Within two days after IBM's announcement, nearly 40 people told Barouh that the company was in trouble. Nobody was going to buy Ko-Rec-Type again.

Barouh bought a self-correcting typewriter, took it to the plant, called everybody together, and told them what they had to do. To survive, the company had to learn to make this ribbon. They also had to learn to make the cartridge that held the ribbon, because cartridges could not be purchased on the market. They also had to learn to make the spools that held the tape. They had to learn to make the ink, the machine that puts on ink, injection molding to make the spools, and so on. It was an enormous challenge. Barouh got everyone involved regardless of position or education.

To everyone's astonishment, the company produced its first self-correcting ribbon in only six months. Moreover, it was the only company in the world to produce that product. Barouh later learned that it took IBM six years to make its self-correcting ribbon. With the new product, sales remained high, and the company avoided disaster.

The Vroom-Jago model shows that Vic Barouh used the correct decision style. Moving from left to right in the decision tree, the questions and answers are:

(QR) How important is the quality of this decision? Definitely high.

(CR) How important is subordinate commitment to the decision? Importance of commitment is probably low, because subordinates had a great deal of respect for Barouh and would do whatever he asked.

(LI) Did Barouh have sufficient information to make a high-quality decision? Definitely no.

(ST) Is the problem well structured? Definitely no. The remaining questions are not relevant because at this point the decision tree leads directly to the CII decision style. Barouh should have used a consultative decision style by having subordinates participate in problem discussions as a group—which he did.[42] ■

ADVANTAGES AND DISADVANTAGES OF PARTICIPATIVE DECISION MAKING

The Vroom-Jago model illustrates that managers can select the degree of group participation in decision making. Managers also can decide whether to bring people together to discuss problems and decision alternatives face-to-face or to consult one-on-one with each member. Research on the Vroom-Jago model indicates that bringing people together as a group leads to more effective decisions than having a manager consult with each member individually.[43]

Increasingly, in today's more empowered workplaces, involving lower-level workers in decision making is the rule rather than the exception. However, managers should remember that group (or participative) decision making has both advantages and disadvantages.

ADVANTAGES   Groups have an advantage over individuals because they bring together a broader perspective for defining the problem and diagnosing underlying causes and effects. In addition to enriching problem diagnoses, groups offer more knowledge and facts with which to identify potential solutions and produce more decision alternatives. Moreover, people who participate in decision making are more satisfied with the decision and more likely to support it, thereby facilitating implementation. Group discussion also can help reduce uncertainty for decision makers who may be unwilling to undertake a big risk by themselves. Finally, group discussion enhances member satisfaction and produces support for a possibly risky decision. Gordon Naylor learned early on in his business that involving the group in decisions and plans was the road to success.

HATTS OFF TREATMENT CENTER

Gordon Naylor began working with troubled teens when he returned from six years in Guyana and got a job as a family service worker in a residential treatment center based in Ontario, Canada. It didn't take long to realize how inadequate the services were and how much this was short-changing the youthful clients. The focus was clearly on the facility—not on the children and youth, who were being made to adapt to the institution, rather than the institution seeking to meet the needs of the child. Also, the most difficult and less desirable of the youth were constantly being moved around from one facility to another. Naylor could see that each move was taking a greater and greater toll on them. Yet, no one seemed to care what the long-term effects would be on their lives.

So, he decided to start his own business—this one would be devoted to caring—even though it was not the most practical time in his life, as his wife was pregnant with twins. But, with the forward thinking vision and drive of an entrepreneur, the Naylor family decided to open a for-profit four-bed treatment home called Hatts Off. In June 1985, they moved in, received their licenses and, in August, had their twins.

Of the first four residents, two had come from extremely abusive environments. "We operated on two fundamental principles that we've maintained to this day," says Naylor. "First, to remain committed to these young people and bring the necessary supports for success. Second, to create programs to meet the needs of residents on a case-by-case basis, 'recognizing that every person requires unique care and growth development plans.'"

By March of 2000, Hatts Off had grown to 107 residential beds, 150 employees, and a $8 million budget, despite having their state-regulated billing rates cut by the government.

Their formula for success?

(1) Take the worst kids—those that no other center wants—and provide an innovative program (It's the only place that shows improvements for those youth.)

(2) Have all staff discuss and consult on an equal basis with supervisors to

create the programs (This creates tremendous empowerment and innovation, as well as an open atmosphere more conducive to tackling the often-difficult problems.)

(3) Make sure budgets are well-attended and necessary services are provided (State regulations limit what can be charged for services.)

Despite the fact that Hatts Off cannot pay employees as much as the state institutions can, it has a staff turnover of only 10 percent, compared to the 40 percent industry average.

Naylor finds it exciting to create an environment where people can work and develop their potential. "When you empower staff," he says, "it is a joy to be a participant." People feel they're not being made to do things well; the things just get done "better than well." He talks passionately about this level of commitment from his employees. "When the Ministry of Education does their review, they always comment on the spirit of dedication our staff [has for] the children and youth. It makes you happy to go to work."[44] ■

DISADVANTAGES   Group decisions tend to be time-consuming. People must be consulted, and they must then jointly diagnose problems and discuss solutions. Moreover, groups may reach a compromise that is less than optimal for the organization. Another problem is group-think. **Groupthink** is a phenomenon in which people are so committed to a cohesive in-group that their reluctance to express contrary opinions overrides their motivation to realistically consider alternatives.[45] People do not want to disagree with one another; thus, the group loses the diversity of opinions essential to effective decision making. Another problem is that there may be no consensus or focus on decision responsibility, because the group rather than any individual makes the decision.

One example of the disadvantages of group decision making occurred when a coalition at Citibank refused to change the practice of "parking"—the bogus transfer of foreign ex-

change deposits to shift bank profits to countries with low tax rates. The line between illegal and legal activities was hazy, and groupthink appeared—people were unwilling to disagree with the current practice because group norms supported high profits and reduced taxes. Group members were willing to compromise their values, groupthink reduced dissent, and there was no clear focus of responsibility because everyone had agreed to the potentially illegal practice.[46]

■ IMPROVING DECISION-MAKING BREADTH AND CREATIVITY

Encouraging employee thinking and participation in solving problems can improve decision quality. Frontline workers who are in touch with the needs and concerns of customers can have a clearer insight into how to solve problems that directly concern those customers. In today's fast-changing world, decisions often must be made quickly, and an organization's ability to stimulate the creativity and innovative skills of its employees is becoming increasingly important. Competitive pressures are challenging managers to create environments that foster and support creative thinking and sharing of diverse opinions. In addition, the growing use of information technology is making it easier than ever to share information widely and decentralize decision making. An environment in which bosses make all the decisions and hand them down to frontline workers is becoming not only inappropriate, but inefficient.[47]

How can managers use the advantages of participation and overcome—or at least effectively deal with—the disadvantages? A number of techniques have been developed to help managers and groups make better decisions. Perhaps the best-known decision tool is **brainstorming.** Brainstorming involves a face-to-face, interactive group to spontaneously suggest problem-solving ideas.[48] Kodak encourages continuous brainstorming and has created a "humor room" where workers can relax and have creative brainstorming sessions. The room is filled with videotapes of comedi-

groupthink
A phenomenon in which members of a group are reluctant to express contrary opinions

brainstorming
A decision-making technique in which group members present spontaneous, problem-solving suggestions to promote free, flexible, and creative thinking

LEADING THE REVOLUTION:
ENCOURAGING WILD IDEAS

At IDEO Product Development, managers believe in heavy doses of fun and freedom to encourage creativity and learning. IDEO, the largest product design consulting firm in the United States, has contributed to the development of over 3,000 products, including Crest's Neat Squeeze toothpaste container, Levolor blinds, Nike sunglasses, and a recharger for General Motors electric vehicles. The company averages about 90 new products a year. Where do IDEO's employees, who work in a network of offices stretching from San Francisco to London to Tokyo, come up with so many creative ideas?

IDEO employees are continuously dreaming, experimenting, and sharing ideas. The culture values playfulness, risk-taking, and nonconformity, and a valued company slogan is "fail often to succeed sooner." A "brainstorm" or "brainstormer" is often called at the beginning of a new project or whenever a design team feels

stumped, and an invitation goes out by e-mail. Although participation is voluntary, people from a mix of disciplines gladly participate because they want the same participation from others regarding their own projects. Sometimes clients are involved in brainstorms, particularly at the beginning of a project. A project team typically calls several broad brainstorms during the early weeks of a project to generate a range of possible solutions. After that, brainstorms are used sporadically to get fresh ideas when the team gets stale or needs help with a specific problem.

IDEO managers create an environment that encourages brainstorming. The company's brainstorming rooms have whiteboard-covered walls and conference tables covered with butcher paper so people can doodle anywhere, anytime the mood strikes them. The "rules" are posted in several locations so everyone can see them: (1) defer judgment, (2)

build on the ideas of others, (3) one conversation at a time, (4) stay focused on the topic, and (5) encourage wild ideas. Criticism in any form, positive or negative, is discouraged. These rules tend to guide the interaction of employees outside the brainstorming sessions as well. At IDEO, brainstorming is a way of life. Although some people are naturally better at brainstorming than others, IDEO's designers point out that effective brainstorming skills develop over time. By encouraging and supporting brainstorming, IDEO managers help their employees, and their company, get smarter.

www.ideo.com

SOURCES: Tia O'Brien, "Encourage Wild Ideas," *Fast Company*, April–May 1996, pp. 82–88; and Robert I. Sutton and Andrew Hargadon, "Brainstorming Groups in Context: Effectiveness in a Product Design Firm," *Administrative Science Quarterly* 41 (1996), pp. 685–718.

ans, joke books, stress-reducing toys, and software for creative decision making.[49] Brainstorming encourages group members to freely suggest alternatives, whether or not they will be used. No critical comments of any kind are allowed until all suggestions have been listed. In the sessions, members are encouraged to think aloud, and freewheeling is welcomed. The more novel and unusual the idea, the better. The object is to promote free, flexible thinking and to enable group members to build on one another's creativity. A typical session begins with a warm-up where definitions of terms are addressed, then it proceeds through the freewheeling idea-generation stage and concludes with an evaluation of feasible ideas.[50] At IDEO Product Development, managers use brainstorming to foster creativity across the organization that has made the company the world's most celebrated design firm (see Leading the Revolution: The Learning Organization).

Another technique for better group decision making is to assign a **devil's advocate;** a role set up to challenge the assumptions and assertions made by the group.[51] The devil's advocate forces the group to rethink its approach to the problem and avoid reaching premature consensus or making unreasonable assumptions before proceeding with problem solutions. One management scholar has recommended that companies create "an institutionalized devil's advocate" by appointing teams to act as perpetual challengers of ideas and proposals. This forces managers and others to examine and explain the risks associated with a particular decision alternative.[52]

This approach is similar to **multiple advocacy,** a technique that involves several advocates and multiple points of view. Minority opinions and unpopular viewpoints are assigned to forceful representatives, who then debate the issues in front of the decision makers. Former president Bush was renowned

devil's advocate
A decision-making technique in which an individual is assigned to challenge the assumptions and assertions made by the group and prevent premature consensus

multiple advocacy
A decision-making technique that involves several advocates and presentation of multiple points of view, including minority and unpopular opinions

for using multiple advocacy in his decision making. The proposal for clean-air legislation in 1989 was a textbook case, because White House aides staged debates they called "Scheduled Train Wrecks" to help Bush think through the issue. These were live scrimmages with Bush asking questions back and forth during the debate. The result was a decision based on solid argument *for* and understanding *of* all perspectives.[53]

■ USING INFORMATION TECHNOLOGY FOR DECISION MAKING

Today, almost every company uses some form of information technology (IT). The strategic use of information technology may be one of the defining aspects of organizational success today. It is thus important to develop some understanding of the types of information technology systems and the changes IT brings to organizations. Managing information technology is all about managing change and uncertainty, particularly under time duress.

In order to understand the challenges managers and organizations face today, let us begin by developing an understanding of information technology and the attributes of quality information.

■ INFORMATION TECHNOLOGY

An organization's information technology consists of the hardware, software, telecommunications, database management, and other technologies it uses to store data and make them available in the form of information for organizational decision making. These technologies give the organization's managers and employees access to complex databases of customer and organizational information. The greater availability and lower costs of information technology pressure organizations to invest in new hardware, software, and other information-processing technologies lest they lose their market position.

By providing managers with more information more quickly than ever before, modern information technology improves efficiency and effectiveness at each stage of the strategic decision-making process. Whether through computer-aided manufacturing, information sharing with customers, or international inventory control, information technology aids operational processes and decision making. Consider the case of American Greetings Corporation, which sells greeting cards in about 35,000 retail locations in the United States. The company uses information technology to gather and analyze data to test the popularity of new card designs, automate production of cards, identify which kinds of cards will sell best at particular stores, fill orders, and report to retailers on the performance of American Greetings displays in their stores. For example, the company once had hundreds of workers filling orders by hand. Today, practically the entire order-filling process has been automated, enabling American Greetings to cut labor costs. By combining efficiency through automation with a precisely targeted and well-tested product line, American Greetings stays profitable and helps its customers, the retailers, to be profitable as well.[54] Even very small businesses can benefit from automation, as seen in this example.

DON HOLCOMBE

Time was when lesser-know artists had to wait for galleries to sell their work or else be consigned to an every-weekend-at-a-fair life where they personally exhibited their crafts. That was, until the Internet. Not only are big galleries moving online, but smaller, home-based artists are going on the Web and finding that their world is changing. Take former commercial artist and Navy electronic systems worker Don Holcombe, who took breaks from technology to paint "glyph" scenes on surfaces of rocks and stones. Soon, he realized his heart was in art, and so he began using technology to make a living at it. Over time, he learned the efficiency of automating all of his office chores of billing, accounting, and managing mailing lists. "It takes a tremendous amount of work to run a one-man show," he notes, "But the computer almost does the work of a second person."

His commercial art background helped him produce brochures of his artwork, but getting the word out was difficult. He distributes promotional materials on his Web site, responds to e-mails with glossy brochures, displays scanned glyphs, and even sells his works for anywhere from $95 to $6,500 to buyers all over the world. All from his home studio in Payson, Arizona. The thousands of dollars Holcombe invested in the computer, scanner, and other equipment was easily recouped by increased sales. One of his customers was popular radio personality Paul Harvey, who placed an $8,000 order. In his first year with the site, he got 1,500 hits, resulting in sales of 50 pieces of artwork. "Because of the technology," says Holcombe, "Things that used to seem impossible, now seem probable."[55] ∎

DATA VERSUS INFORMATION

The ability to generate more information with technology presents a serious challenge to information technicians, managers, and other users of information. They must sort through overwhelming amounts of data to identify only that information necessary for a particular purpose. Data are raw facts and figures that in and of themselves may not be useful. To be useful, data must be processed into finished information—that is, data that have been converted into a meaningful and useful context for specific users. An increasing challenge for managers is being able to effectively identify and access useful information. American Greetings, for example, might gather data about demographics in various parts of the country. These data are then translated into information; for example, stores in Florida require an enormous assortment of greeting cards directed at grandson, granddaughter, niece, and nephew, while stores in some other parts of the country might need a larger percentage of slightly irreverent, youth-oriented products.

The magnitude of the job of transforming data into useful information is reflected in organizations' introduction of the chief information officer (CIO) position (introduced in Chapter 5). CIOs are responsible for managing organizational databases and implementing new information technology. As they make decisions involving the adoption and management of new technologies, CIOs integrate old and new technology to support organizational decision making, operations, and communication. The purchase options in hardware, software, networking, and telecommunications products can be overwhelming to information officers. The enormous amount of data that combinations of this technology can produce is equally overwhelming. Despite these challenges, the CIO manages the infrastructure so that it will place the necessary information in the right place at the right time. Ideally, this means the CIO combines knowledge of IT with the ability to help managers and employees identify their information needs as well as ways the organization can use its IT capabilities in support of its strategy. Through a variety of technologies described in this chapter, the CIO can empower managers and employees to use shared information to meet customer needs in ways that in the past would have been impossible.

CHARACTERISTICS OF USEFUL INFORMATION

Organizations depend on high-quality information to develop strategic plans, identify problems, and interact with other organizations. Information is of high quality if it has characteristics that make it useful for these tasks. The characteristics of useful information fall into three broad categories, as illustrated in Exhibit 6.6.

1. *Time*—Information should be available and provided when needed, up-to-date, and related to the appropriate time period (past, present, or future).

2. *Content*—Useful information is error free, suited to the user's needs, complete, concise, relevant; that is, it excludes unnecessary data, and will be an accurate measure of performance.

E x h i b i t 6.6

CHARACTERISTICS OF HIGH-
QUALITY INFORMATION

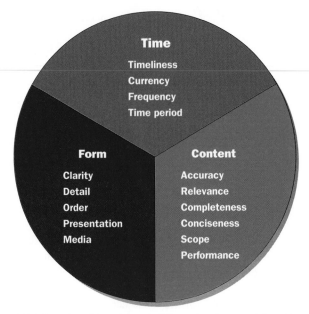

Time
Timeliness
Currency
Frequency
Time period

Form
Clarity
Detail
Order
Presentation
Media

Content
Accuracy
Relevance
Completeness
Conciseness
Scope
Performance

SOURCE: Adapted from James A. O'Brien, *Introduction to Information Systems,* 8th ed. (Burr Ridge, IL: Irwin, 1997), 284–285.

3. *Form*—The information should be provided in a user-friendly format at appropriate level of detail. The presentation should be ordered and will use words, numbers, and diagrams that are most helpful to the user. Also, useful information should be presented in the most appropriate medium (e.g., printed documents, video display, or sound).

Two entreprenuers who realized many people want information at a convenient time, with attractive content and a form they desire started a company to deliver just that (see Technology for Tomorrow).

COMPUTER NETWORKS

Modern information technology recognizes that most organizational activities involve groups of people—the organization's employees, suppliers, and customers. For these people to cooperate, agree on solutions to problems, and meet one another's needs, they must be able to share information. Thus, many companies use information technology that offers the ability for people to use their computers to share information.

Networks are systems that link people and departments within a particular building or across corporate offices. They may also allow company representatives to interact globally with one another and with customers. A network can be thought of as multiple brains connected to help expand the mindpower of the organization. Networks play a critical role in the shift to the learning organization because they expand the capacity for learning in fast-changing companies. They support the broad sharing of information that is an essential component of the learning organization. Networks empower workers, provide a geographical dispersion of the workforce, decentralize decision making, allow for team-based structures, and facilitate collaboration with other organizations.

In the past, when only large mainframe computers could handle complex tasks, employees typically used terminals to send data to the mainframe or to retrieve information. Employees could not use these systems to share information directly with one another.

TECHNOLOGY FOR TOMORROW

BROADCAST.com

Todd Wagner and Mark Cuban were just two guys at Indiana University who loved Hoosier basketball. After graduating and moving to Dallas, they were continually frustrated in their attempts to listen to Indiana basketball. So Todd, a lawyer, and Mark, a high-tech entrepreneur, decided to find a way that they, and others, could fill the needs of displaced fans who were passionate about their teams.

Their yearnings gave way to the start of AudioNet (changed to broadcast.com in 1999), which controls rights to play-by-play Internet broadcasts for almost 420 professional and college sports teams and has agreements with 385 radio and 40 TV stations. After their startup, their SportsWorld.com, a subsidiary of sorts of broadcast.com, began offering views of armchair quarterbacks. Other sites broadcast from stations devoted solely to the Grateful Dead and Jimmy Buffet, while Police Scanner.com lets people listen to drug

busts and hostage situations around the country. Their newer scuba show is already successful. "This is cable on steroids," says Todd. "This is not 50 or 500 channels. This is 5,000 channels."

What is the secret to broadcast .com's success in becoming the 11th busiest news-and-entertainment site on the Web? Besides hard work (or as Todd says, "This is not about business hours. It's about *waking* hours. You try and do as much as you can for as long as you can stay awake"), it was having a solid business plan and focused strategy, which has three parts and has remained constant throughout. First, broadcast .com is in the business of aggregating content, not producing it. Secondly, it reduces the barriers of time and place that traditional TV and radio have. Listeners can tune in to programs sent out from any location and at any time. And finally, Mark and Todd knew early on that recruiting a top-flight sales force was essential. About one-third of the 200 em-

ployees are in sales, a blind spot for most Web sites. Mark believes broadcast.com's core competency of sales will ensure its success.

And keeping that success means moving in Web-year speed, on to the broadcast.com "sprint." The two entrepreneurs don't even talk about enjoying the fruits of their labors. Even though they know the rest of the world is only now catching up with broadcast.com's vision of multimedia Internet, they are cautious with self-congratulations. "On the Web," says Mark, "the people who think they've won are the ones who lose." His partner agrees. "You can't even think about slowing down. You never know who's going to be gaining on you."

Sources: Richard Murphy, "Mark Cuban and Todd Wagner," *Success* (May 1999), pp. 55–59; Eric Ransdell, "How Do You Win on the Web?" *Fast Company* (Aug. 1998), pp. 152–165.

However, as personal computers became more sophisticated, organizations began linking them with cables and software, establishing networks for communication among employees. They created local area networks (LANs) by wiring together users at a single location and wide area networks (WANs) by using modems to link people at different locations via telephone.

As organizations created networks, they faced the challenge of how to enable different kinds of computers to communicate with one another. One solution has been to use a category of software called middleware, which mediates among myriad types of hardware and software. Even a single company may have many sizes and brands of computers and software, and middleware helps these varied components communicate on a network.

THE INTERNET, INTRANETS, AND EXTRANETS

Today, widespread use of the Internet offers another way to link people in networks. Unlike other kinds of networking, the Internet enables any computer with Internet capabilities to share information with others on the Internet. Government agencies, publishers, and other service providers offer access to a mind-boggling array of data and news stories. The Internet also provides a conduit for individuals to share information via e-mail and in discussion groups. Salestar, which markets software customized for telephone companies, uses the Internet to recruit employees. The company has found this to be the most cost-effective way to reach people with experience at phone companies.[56] Focus on Collaboration lists do's and don'ts for businesses using the Internet.

Internet, intranet, and *extranet* information technology advances provide companies with the ability to have employees dispersed geographically—working at home. Anne Britt is a mortgage banker, who converted a 10′ × 10′ storage closet into her home office. Anne works for Norwest from her home in Houston, Texas. Her computer, linking her to Norwest database information, a separate business line, and an answering service provide her with the ability to conduct business as if she were located at Norwest headquarters.

The wide accessibility of the Internet can also be its major downside for businesses, however. Most organizations want to limit access to certain details of their activities. Also, they need to protect employee privacy by not disclosing personal information about the employee. Consequently, many organizations use the technology of the Internet to create networks that may be used only by authorized persons. The software that limits access is called a **firewall.** One type of such network is an **intranet,** a network that uses Internet technology but limits access to all or some of the organization's employees. Ford Motor Company's intranet connects some 120,000 workstations at offices and factories around the world to thousands of Ford Web sites offering proprietary information such as market research, analyses of competitors' components, and product development. The product-development system, for example, which is updated hourly on the intranet, lets engineers, designers, and suppliers work from the same data, thus keeping the process moving and saving the company time and money.[57]

An **extranet** also uses Internet technology but links authorized users inside the company with certain outsiders such as customers or vendors. A recent survey of 2,500 businesses by ActivMedia, a marketing research company, found that 13 percent of the companies were using extranets and that number is growing fast.[58] One reason for this popularity is because they enable users at a variety of locations to utilize different computers and operating systems. Extranets are also an efficient network for international communication.

Extranets support the trend to specialize in core competencies (what the company does best) and to outsource other activities. For example, a manufacturing company would focus on developing and producing goods and let other organizations handle such activities as inventory management, payroll, and billing. With an extranet, it can be just as easy to share data with such a service provider as with an internal department, and the service provider has an incentive to keep up with the latest technology and regulations in its area of speciality. Here's how one company set up a small extranet.

PUCK PAGES

Can't afford expensive software or high-priced consultants to build an extranet? If you have groups of clients you regularly give information to, or if you want

firewall
Software that limits access by unauthorized users

intranet
A network that uses Internet technology to provide access to some or all of the organization's employees

extranet
A network that uses Internet technology to link authorized users inside the company with certain outsiders, including international ones, such as customers or vendors

FOCUS ON Collaboration

INTERNET ETIQUETTE

Throughout the 1970s and 1980s, the Internet and business were incompatible notions. However, over the past several years, the Internet has opened up more and more to commercial activity. Despite this increased commercial use, many Internet users still cherish the noncommercial culture of the past. Managers who wish to promote their business in cyberspace can avoid incurring the wrath of these users by following some basic rules of Internet etiquette:

1. Don't send mass electronic mailings. Businesses that send unsolicited e-mail to individuals or newsgroups do so at their own risk. Some users will respond immediately with vitriolic messages known as "flames." In some cases, the volume of incoming flames has overloaded the server of the offending company's Internet service provider, resulting in the cancellation of the company's account.

2. Provide information in a timely manner to those who request it. Sending e-mail about your company's products or services to people who have expressed an interest is an inexpensive, fast, and convenient way to reach potential new customers. In addition, certain newsgroups allow advertising by businesses.

3. Don't violate the sanctity of the chat room. Many users consider it especially offensive for businesses to post unrelated questions or comments in discussion areas such as chat rooms, newsgroups, and mailing lists. Businesses can participate in these areas when they have something pertinent to say about the subject matter under discus-

sion, but they should not use chat rooms to promote their products. It's okay, however, to give advice in areas in which you and your company can offer expertise.

4. Another acceptable approach is to "lurk" in a discussion area to become familiar with the subject matter and post any relevant messages. Read the group's frequently asked questions (FAQ) to understand what is acceptable.

5. Don't type entire messages in capital letters. This is the online equivalent of SHOUTING.

6. Keep messages short and to the point. Don't send potential customers files that take an excessively long time to download.

7. Don't overload your Web site with graphics. Although graphics are eye-catching, they can take a long time to appear on the user's computer screen, particularly for users with slower modems. The less frustration you create for Internet users, the better for your business.

Some veteran Internet users still grumble about the increasing commercialization of the Internet. However, they are outnumbered by those who believe in the potential of the Internet to bring about a better way of doing business. If businesses keep the rules of Internet etiquette in mind and conduct themselves with decorum, they will encounter less grumbling and more interest.

SOURCE: Tim McCollum, "Making the Internet Work for You," *Nation's Business* (March 1997), pp. 6–13.

---

your friends to read your annual Holiday Letter without you spending a fortune on postage, the answer is easy and relatively cheap. First, you need a Web page. Internet service providers (ISPs) offer them for nominal costs between $10 and $200 per month. Then, assign different URLs for the various locations within your site and voila!—your own extranet.

Think of your "Puck pages" (named after a dog) as unlisted numbers on the Internet. You give out the URL to only

those people you choose. And you can have some pages password-protected as well. The pages are not linked anywhere or listed in any publication, so the intended audience is limited.

Small businesses might use it to post company information only intended for vendors. Or a consulting company might make its PowerPoint presentations available to conference hosts, or handouts to workshop organizers (rather than mailing them over and over again to the various companies). Sensitive issues such as relevant strategies, potential markets, various business models the consulting company might share, could be password-protected. Or, you can do as one consultant-writer and post pictures of your dog for your nearest and dearest.[59] ■

GROUPWARE   To maximize their networks, organizations design systems to take on the characteristics of face-to-face interaction, allowing people to collaborate in real time. Several users who are scattered around the world can be hooked to a network, for example, and collaborate on a project almost as easily as if they were sitting around a conference table. The technology that makes this possible is a type of software called *groupware*, which displays a document on more than one user's screen and allows all the users to see changes or comments as they are made by one person. Thus, engineers in different locations can review and discuss a drawing, or a sales team can review and comment on a proposal or marketing literature. With groupware, participants can simultaneously share the information in the documents displayed and their own knowledge and ideas about the documents.

■ TYPES OF INFORMATION SYSTEMS

Most managers today appreciate the value of making information readily available in some kind of formal, computer-based information system. Such a system combines hardware, software, and human resources to support organizational information and communication needs. One way to distinguish among the many types of information systems is to focus on the functions they perform and the people they serve in an organization. There are three broad categories of information systems widely used today. *Operations information systems* support information-processing needs of a business's day-to-day operations as well as low-level operations management functions. *Management information systems* typically support the strategic decision-making needs of higher-level managers. *Other organizational support systems* include those designed to interpret

geographic data, those that clone expert decision-making models for use by nonexpert users, and broad-scale systems that support planning for the needs of the enterprise as a whole. Most organizational information systems combine aspects of several of these categories in an integrated information system to provide decision makers with more support than could be obtained through the use of an individual technology.

OPERATIONS INFORMATION SYSTEMS

A variety of systems, called operations information systems, support the information-processing needs related to a business's day-to-day operations. Transaction-processing systems (TPSs) record and process data resulting from business operations. They include information systems that record sales to customers, purchases from suppliers, inventory changes, and wages to employees. A TPS system collects data from these transactions and stores them in a database. Employees use information from the database to produce reports and other information, such as customer statements and employee paychecks. Most of an organization's reports are generated from these databases. Transaction-processing systems identify, collect, and organize the fundamental information from which an organization operates.

While a transaction-processing system keeps track of the size, type, and financial consequences of the organization's transactions, companies also need information about the quantity and quality of their production activities. Therefore, they may use process control systems to monitor and control ongoing physical processes. For example, petroleum refineries, pulp and paper mills, food manufacturing plants, and electric power plants use process control systems with special sensing devices that monitor and record physical phenomena such as temperature or pressure change. The system relays the measurements or sensor-detected data to a computer for processing; employees and operations managers can check the data to look for problems requiring action.

Office automation systems combine modern hardware and software such as word processors, desktop publishers, e-mail, and teleconferencing to handle the tasks of publishing and distributing information. Office automation systems also are used to transform manual accounting procedures to electronic media. Companies such as Wal-Mart, Chevron, and American Airlines send thousands of electronic payments a month to suppliers, eliminating the need for writing and mailing checks. These systems enable businesses to streamline office tasks, reduce errors, and improve customer service. In this way, office automation systems support the other kinds of information systems.

MANAGEMENT INFORMATION SYSTEMS

Until the 1960s, information systems were used primarily for transaction processing, accounting, and record keeping. Then the introduction of computers using silicon chip circuitry allowed for more processing power per dollar. As computer manufacturers promoted these systems and managers began visualizing ways in which the computers could help them make important decisions, management information systems were born. A management information system (MIS) is a computer-based system that provides information and support

for effective managerial decision making. The basic elements of a management information system are illustrated in Exhibit 6.7. The MIS is supported by the organization's operations information systems and by organizational databases (and frequently databases of external data, as well).

MISs typically support strategic decision-making needs of midlevel and top management. However, as technology becomes more widely accessible, more employees are wired into networks, and organizations push decision making downward in the hierarchy, these kinds of systems are seeing use at all levels of the organization.

When a production manager needs to make a decision about production scheduling, he or she may need data on the anticipated number of orders in the coming month, inventory levels, and availability of computers and personnel. The MIS can provide these data. In fact, information reporting systems, the most common form of MIS, provide managers and decision makers with reports that support day-to-day decision-making needs. These reports typically give managers prespecified information for use in making structured

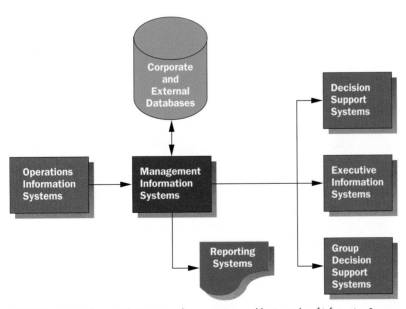

E x h i b i t   6.7
BASIC ELEMENTS OF MIS

SOURCE: Adapted from Ralph M. Stair and George W. Reynolds, *Principles of Information Systems: A Managerial Approach,* 4th ed. (Cambridge, MA.: Course Technology, 1999), 391.

decisions. For example, activity-based costing software, such as NetProphet, EasyABC Plus, and HyperABC, allows managers to see all the costs associated with producing and selling particular products. Managers can monitor the costs and identify which products are profitable, which should be discontinued, and so on. After Koehler Manufacturing Company, a small business in Marlboro, Massachusetts, installed activity-based costing software, managers discovered that Koehler's best-selling product line—lead-acid batteries—was devouring company profits. This gave management the information they needed to make better decisions about future products.[60]

Decision support systems (DSSs) are interactive, computer-based information systems that rely on decision models and specialized databases to support decision makers. With electronic spreadsheets and other decision support software, users can pose a series of what-if questions to test alternatives they are considering. Based on the assumptions used in the software or specified by the user, managers can explore various alternatives and receive tentative information to help them choose the alternative with the best outcome.

Executive information systems (EISs) are management information systems to facilitate strategic decision making at the highest level of management. These systems are typically based on software that provides easy access to large amounts of complex data and can analyze and present the data in a timely fashion. EISs provide top management with quick access to relevant internal and external information and, if designed properly, can help them diagnose problems as well as develop solutions.

A *group decision support system* (GDSS) is an interactive computer-based system that facilitates group decision making. Also called collaborative work systems, GDSSs are designed to allow team members to interact and at the same time take advantage of computer-based support data. Participating managers may sit around a conference table equipped with a computer terminal at each position or may sit thousands of miles apart and, through live television, use team conferencing to view one another and share data displays. Such a system may employ groupware or such Inter-

net technology as real-time discussion groups or live video or audio feeds.

A leader in the use of management information systems is retailing giant Wal-Mart. The company uses a massive database to make decisions about what to stock, how to price it, and when to reorder. The company sends store managers weekly reports of the 50 top items in terms of sales and profits. Store managers who want to boost their store's profitability can check whether they are properly promoting those 50 items. In addition, the department managers at each store keep track of which items are the top sellers in their department, then signal employees to take special care to ensure that those items are in stock. Department managers also carry scanners that allow them to check inventory levels of any item by scanning its bar code. If they run low on something, they can scan the bar code to obtain data on inventory levels at nearby stores. Back at headquarters, Wal-Mart managers and employees continuously analyze transactions data to identify relationships among purchases, looking for ways to cross-promote items that are typically purchased together.[61]

OTHER ORGANIZATIONAL SUPPORT SYSTEMS

Several other types of information systems may support either operations or management applications and are used at various levels of the organization. Among the most significant support systems are geographic information systems, expert systems, and enterprise resource planning systems.

GEOGRAPHIC INFORMATION SYSTEMS   A geographic information system (GIS) is a type of decision support system that provides users with layers of information expressed visually through maps. Users of such a system might combine maps with data to identify the areas with the greatest concentration of customers or the history of the most rainfall, for instance, or they might use a GIS to plan the most efficient routes to their customers, quickly modifying their plans as customers place or cancel orders. GISs support analytical decision making for business as well as for the management of defense troops, species management, emergency management, land use planning, redistricting, and demographics, among many other applications. In business, GISs often help perform distribution planning, site selection, trade area analysis, and regulatory compliance.[62] Exhibit 6.8 provides an example of the kind of information that can be retrieved with a GIS. This output from ArcView® software, the desktop GIS software from Environmental Systems Research Institute, shows a marketing view of the Atlanta, Georgia, market, providing a new and powerful context in which to perform comprehensive demographic, consumer, or product performance analysis. Such marketing views are created by integrating and visualizing both internal customer data and a variety of external GIS data sources. ArcView® can then be used to identify and target available customers from the lowest levels (i.e., household, block, group, sales territory) to the broadest of marketing levels (i.e., distribution market, national territory).

ENTERPRISE RESOURCE PLANNING (ERP) SYSTEMS   As managers have seen how access to data can improve their decisions, they have increasingly looked for ways to pull together various kinds of data to show how a decision about one area of the business will affect the other areas of the enterprise. Fortunately, as computing power has become more affordable, information systems have been able to address that desire by taking an increasingly broad view of the organization's activities. Today, a growing number of companies are setting up a broad-scale information system called enterprise resource planning (ERP). An ERP system collects, processes, and provides information about an organization's entire enterprise, including orders, product design, production, purchasing, inventory, distribution, human resources, receipt of payments, and forecasting of future demand. Such a system links these areas of activity into a network, as illustrated in Exhibit 6.9. When a salesperson takes an order, the ERP system checks to see

E x h i b i t   6.8

OUTPUT FROM ARCVIEW® GIS SOFTWARE

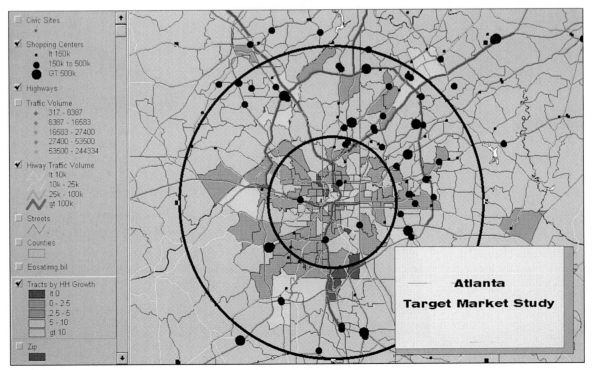

SOURCE: Reprinted courtesy of Environmental Systems Research Institute, Inc. ArcView® is a registered trademark of ESRI.

Exhibit 6.9

EXAMPLE OF ERP APPLICATIONS

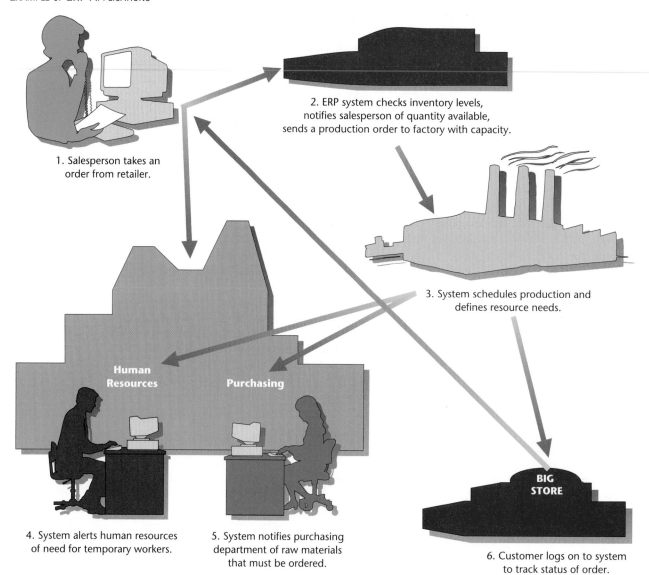

1. Salesperson takes an order from retailer.

2. ERP system checks inventory levels, notifies salesperson of quantity available, sends a production order to factory with capacity.

3. System schedules production and defines resource needs.

Human Resources

Purchasing

BIG STORE

4. System alerts human resources of need for temporary workers.

5. System notifies purchasing department of raw materials that must be ordered.

6. Customer logs on to system to track status of order.

Strategic Planning Group

7. Management uses ERP data to evaluate and adjust its strategic plan.

Source: Adapted from Gail Edmondson, "Silicon Valley on the Rhine," *Business Week*, November 3, 1997, 162–166.

how the order impacts inventory levels, scheduling, human resources, purchasing, and distribution. Executives can use this information to evaluate operations and adjust their plans as needed to meet changing conditions.

Given the massive computing power required to run such a system, the original ERP applications were for the largest companies with powerful mainframe computers. The leading ERP system, SAP's R/3, was designed to handle different currencies, languages, and legal systems, so multinational corporations can use it for the entire company. However, the growing use of networked PCs and the Internet have enabled SAP and other companies such as Oracle to offer versions of ERP that are suited for smaller organizations.

An enterprise resource planning system blurs the line dividing operations information systems from management information systems. By integrating data about all aspects of operations, ERP enables employees at every level to retrieve information to make decisions about their area of activity. A salesperson, for example, can enter an order and see what the real delivery date will be. An engineer can see how a decision about product design will affect production schedules and resource needs. Thus, the organization's ability to reap the benefits of ERP depends largely on how well it sets up organizational processes and delegates responsibility so that employees can use the information the system makes available. Hershey Foods, a $4 billion-a-year company known for its chocolate, is taking a careful approach to ensure that its ERP system will serve the needs of employees and managers.

HERSHEY FOODS CORPORATION
www.hersheys.com

Hershey Foods recently embarked on a three-year, $75 million project to install an ERP system that will integrate the best finance, logistics, and sales practices from multiple business divisions. The new system lets Hershey track all outstanding accounts with retailers, so the company can measure payment risks and set consistent credit terms across all Hershey's divisions, large and small. In the past, a supermarket chain might negotiate credit terms with the Ronzini pasta division, then wind up having to negotiate all over again with the chocolate division.

Managers plan to have 85 percent of the company's core processes running on ERP infrastructure by 2001. The process is not an easy one, however. As Rick Bentz, Hershey's vice president for information technology, says of the undertaking: "You think that a problem is solved and then you get farther down the road and find that it's not. It's two steps forward and one step back." However, managers know that a careful, adaptive approach is the best way to ensure that the company will reap the benefits of an ERP system. They also see the implementation of ERP as an opportunity to study business practices in each of Hershey's divisions, identifying and adopting the best practices for key activities such as demand forecasting companywide.[63] ∎

■ STRATEGIC USE OF INFORMATION TECHNOLOGY

Information technology is dramatically changing the processes and possibilities for doing business. Today, a minimum strategy for remaining competitive includes enabling employees, suppliers, and customers to share information over some type of computer network. Organizations adopt this technology because it allows them to improve operational efficiency and control, remain competitive in a rapidly changing environment, and tap into the knowledge of employees.

OPERATIONAL EFFICIENCY AND CONTROL

Many companies adopt information technology in an effort to speed work processes, cut costs, and improve coordination. In these ways, the appropriate use of technology can greatly increase an organization's efficiency.

Efficiency Through investment in information systems, a company can increase its operational efficiency and lower costs. This increased efficiency better enables a company to lock in customers and broaden market reach. EZRider, a Massachusetts-based retailer of snowboards, has seen numerous benefits of information technology. Whenever a salesperson keys in a purchase, the system makes a record of the amount of the sale, and at the end of the pay period, the computer system has already computed the salesperson's commission. Historical sales figures can be accessed to identify busy periods, then employees can be scheduled accordingly.

More and more companies are incorporating CIOs into high-level strategic decision making and appointing them to manage technological change within the organization. CIOs are even getting involved in high-level decisions regarding investment, product, and service. Using information technology, systems, and personnel in efficient ways is vital for today's organizations.

Improved Coordination and Flexibility Another benefit of information technology is the reduction of time and geographic barriers as global networks and mobile computing dissolve these restraints. Time and place are becoming less important variables. A management team can work throughout the day on a project in Switzerland and, while they sleep, a team in the United States can continue where the Swiss team left off. With e-mail and voice mail, managers no longer have to arrive at 4 A.M. to communicate with personnel abroad.

"Wired executives" are abandoning the confines of corporate offices and still staying on top of business. Increased mobility, through laptop computers, e-mail, cellular phones, voice mail, and faxes, have freed them to be wherever they are most needed and most productive. Improved flexibility means greater responsiveness to changing customer demands.

COMPETITIVE STRATEGY

Because of advances in information technology, organizations are competing in a new era. Amazon.com, the e-tailing giant, discovered a new way to offer its core product—books.

AMAZON.COM
www.amazon.com

Most of us think of bookstores as cozy old places where the floorboards creak and the stacks are jammed to the ceiling with bestsellers and obscure book titles side by side. Bookstores make us think of taking some time out during the day to browse and read, maybe even have a cup of coffee or tea if the store also has a café. Jeff Bezos understands this, but he knows that the average person does not have time to browse. He also understands how the Internet has changed commerce. So a few years ago, the former Wall Street fund manager decided to open a virtual bookstore. In order to be competitive, Bezos knew that he needed to offer three things that a "real" bookstore couldn't: convenience, low prices, and selection. Further, he knew that, in this new shopping arena, he had to get there first—before Barnes & Noble, for example—in order to get ahead.

With his Wall Street background, Bezos was able to secure the venture capital to start up Amazon, as he called his new business. Based in Seattle, he had a Web site designed that was attractive and simple to use. "We had to make it a destination," explains Bezos, "the way any enjoyable store is a destination." The site does not feature elaborate graphics or animation, but consumers can easily find just about any title they want. In addition, Amazon provides descriptions of its books as well as e-mail notification to regular customers of books they might like. Because Amazon acts as a clearinghouse instead of a warehouse (Amazon directs orders to distributors, who ship the books to Amazon, who then sends them to customers), the company does not have to hold a huge inventory and can thus offer books for prices as low as 40 percent off the list price. Finally, Amazon's selection is huge; the site initially went online with 1 million titles and now offers more than twice that number. Theoretically, customers should be able to get any book that still is in print.

Amazon has proved to be a huge success. Within a few years, sales reached $16 million. Browsing now means scrolling through titles on the computer screen instead of thumbing through them in the store. But Amazon customers still can sip that cup of coffee as they browse, and they may order at as leisurely a pace as they choose. The Internet has opened yet another door to do business.[64] ■

loyalty, improved service, better information gathering, and cost reduction.

Organizations may adopt IT to support planned strategic change, or access to new technology may inspire a change in the organization's structure or strategy. Changes in business strategy usually precede other organizational changes, including technology adoption. Sometimes, however, adoption of information technology is followed by restructuring of positions and processes. A common example today is the use of enterprise resource planning. As the technology becomes affordable at more companies, those managers want to reap the benefits of sharing information. However, widespread access to information is useful only if the organization's functions are integrated as well as the software modules. According to Bruce Richardson, a vice president at Advanced Manufacturing Research, a Boston consultant specializing in ERP, "About 80 percent of the benefits [of using ERP] come from what you change in your business. The software is just an enabler."[65]

In today's organizations, information processing systems shape their strategic competitive advantage, shortening the distance between customers and the organization. For example, UPS and Federal Express provide customers with the exact tracking location for packages. IT supports their strategy. Effective use of these systems leads to greater customer

Summary and Management Solution

This chapter made several important points about the process of organizational decision making. The study of decision making is important because it describes how managers make successful strategic and operational decisions. Managers must confront many types of decisions, including programmed and nonprogrammed, and these decisions differ according to the amount of risk, uncertainty, and ambiguity in the environment.

Three decision-making approaches (1) the classical model, (2) the administrative model, and (3) the political model were introduced. The classical model shows how managers make decisions that maximize economic efficiency. The administrative model describes how managers actually make nonprogrammed, uncertain decisions with skills that include intuition. The political model relates to making nonprogrammed decisions when conditions are uncertain, information is limited and ambiguous, and there is conflict among managers about what goals to pursue or what course of action to take. Managers have to engage in discussion and coalition building to reach agreement for decisions.

Decision making involves six basic steps: (1) problem recognition, (2) diagnosis of causes, (3) development of alternatives, (4) choice of an alternative, (5) implementation of the alternative, and (6) feedback and evaluation. Another factor affecting decision making is the manager's personal decision style. Four major decision styles are directive, analytical, conceptual, and behavioral. The chapter also explained the Vroom-Jago model, which managers can use to determine how much group participation a problem needs. As competitive pressures force today's organizations to shift toward forms of decision making that encourage creativity and sharing of diverse views, managers need to maximize the advantages of group decision making and overcome the disadvantages. Useful techniques include appointing a devil's advocate, providing multiple advocacy, and brainstorming, which can help managers and groups define problems and develop creative solutions.

Organizations are evolving into information cultures in which managers and employees alike can share information, and in which routine decision making can be automated through the use of expert models. Thanks to networks and communications technology, these emerging information cultures are not bound by physical space. Information technology (IT) allows companies to generate new services and products, but also creates demand for quality, low cost, and speedy delivery.

Modern information technology gathers huge amounts of data and transforms them into useful information for decision makers. The systems that use this technology should be designed to generate information with appropriate time, content, and form attributes. The array of information systems available and the multitude of data they produce can be overwhelming. Many organizations hire a chief information officer (CIO) to help manage decisions regarding investment and integration of old and new information system products. Often, the systems link employees and others in networks, including the Internet, intranets, and extranets.

Information systems often combine hardware, software, and human resources to organize information and make it readily available. Operations information systems, including transaction-processing systems, process control systems, and office automation systems support daily business operations and the needs of low-level managers. Management information systems, including information reporting systems, decision support systems, and executive information systems, typically support the decision-making needs of

middle- and upper-level managers. Other types of information systems, including expert systems, geographic information systems, and enterprise resource planning systems, may support either operations or management applications and are used at various levels of the organization.

Recall the case of Mike & Ally at the beginning of the chapter. Mike & Ally's accessory business needed to computerize in a hurry and the questions were whether to shut down, what kind of system to install, and who should run it. They decided not to lose the $40,000 in revenue, but instead to go digital on an as-needed basis, buying computers and software only when they would lose customers or business without it. Finding products that fit into that schedule and their budget was a challenge. They chose Intuit's Quick-Books because it was easy to learn. With their tight budget, they could not afford to hire an IT person, so it fell on them to learn and to outsource what they could. "Computerizing on a time shoestring," they called it. Things got better when they finally found a consultant who would give them unlimited telephone technical support for $400 a year and would come to their office for $60 per hour. It took six months to fully integrate the new system, but they are thankful for their slow and steady progression into the information age. Only now do they realize the benefits. Their customer base has tripled and sales have quadrupled, to about $1 million. Finally they have time for what they love—design.

Discussion Questions

1. You are a busy partner in a legal firm, and an experienced secretary complains of continued headaches, drowsiness, dry throat, and occasional spells of fatigue and flu. She tells you she believes air quality in the building is bad and would like something done. How would you respond?

2. Why is decision making considered a fundamental part of management effectiveness?

3. Explain the difference between risk and ambiguity. How might decision making differ for each situation?

4. Analyze three decisions you made over the past six months. Which of these were programmed and which were nonprogrammed?

5. Why are many decisions made by groups rather than by individuals?

6. The Vroom-Jago model describes five decision styles. How should a manager go about choosing which style to use?

7. What are the major differences between the administrative and political models of decision making?

8. What is meant by bounded rationality and satisficing? Why do managers not strive to find the economically best solution for many organizational decisions?

9. What techniques could you use to improve your own creativity and effectiveness in decision making?

10. Which of the six steps in the decision-making process do you think is most likely to be ignored by a manager? Explain.

11. Why is it important for managers to understand the difference between data and information?

12. Choose a business. In what ways would the role of a CIO be important?

13. What types of information technology do you use as a student on a regular basis? How might your life be different if you did not have this technology available to you?

14. How might the organizers of the upcoming Olympics use an extranet to get all the elements of the event up and running on schedule?

15. Choose a worldwide retail or restaurant chain. How might groupware be useful?

16. Do you think that a geographic information system would be beneficial to a smaller, specialty-type company? Why or why not?

Management Exercises

Manager's Workbook

What Is Your MIS Style?

Following are 14 statements. Circle the number that indicates how much you agree that each statement is characteristic of you. The questions refer to how you use information and make decisions.

	Disagree Strongly				Agree Strongly
1. I like to wait until all relevant information is examined before deciding something.	1	2	3	4	5
2. I prefer information that can be interpreted in several ways and leads to different but acceptable solutions.	1	2	3	4	5
3. I like to keep gathering data until an excellent solution emerges.	1	2	3	4	5
4. To make decisions, I often use information that means different things to different people.	1	2	3	4	5
5. I want just enough data to make a decision quickly.	1	2	3	4	5
6. I act on logical analysis of the situation rather than on my "gut feelings" about the best alternative.	1	2	3	4	5
7. I seek information sources or people that will provide me with many ideas and details.	1	2	3	4	5
8. I try to generate more than one satisfactory solution for the problem faced.	1	2	3	4	5
9. When reading something, I confine my thoughts to what is written rather than search for additional understanding.	1	2	3	4	5
10. When working on a project, I try to narrow, not broaden, the scope so it is clearly defined.	1	2	3	4	5
11. I typically acquire all possible information before making a final decision.	1	2	3	4	5
12. I like to work on something I've done before rather than take on a complicated problem.	1	2	3	4	5
13. I prefer clear, precise data.	1	2	3	4	5

	Disagree Strongly				Agree Strongly
14. When working on a project, I like to explore various options rather than maintain a narrow focus.	1	2	3	4	5

Total Score _____

Your information-processing style determines the extent to which you will benefit from computer-based information systems.

The odd-numbered questions pertain to the "amount of information" you like to use. A score of 28 or more suggests you prefer a large amount. A score of 14 or less indicates you like a small amount of information.

The even-numbered questions pertain to the "focus of information" you prefer. A score of 28 or more suggests you are comfortable with ambiguous, multifocused information, while a score of 14 or less suggests you like clear, unifocused data.

If you are a person who likes a large amount of information and clear, focused data, you will tend to make effective use of management information systems. You could be expected to benefit greatly from an EIS or MIS in your company. If you are a person who prefers a small amount of data and data that are multifocused, you would probably not get the information you need to make decisions through formal information systems. You probably won't utilize EIS or MIS to a great extent, preferring instead to get decision data from other convenient sources, including face-to-face discussions.

SOURCES: This questionnaire is adapted from Richard L. Daft and Norman B. Macintosh, "A Tentative Exploration into the Amount and Equivocality of Information Processing in Organizational Work Units," *Administrative Science Quarterly,* 26 (1981), pp. 207–224; and Dorothy Marcic, *Organizational Behavior: Experiences and Cases,* 4th ed. (St. Paul, Minn.: West, 1995).

Manager's Workshop

Decision Styles

Think of some recent decisions that have influenced your life. Choose two significant decisions that you made and two that other people made. Then fill out the following table. Use Exhibit 6.1 on decision conditions to choose which condition it was (column B). Decide how bounded rationality worked (column C), and use the information on decision biases to fill in column D. In groups of three to six members discuss your results. What did you learn about how you make decisions? How can you improve your decision-making style?

Column A	B	C	D	E
Your decisions	Decision condition relevant	Bounded rationality: Was there satisficing?	Which decision biases were working?	Outcomes—recommendations for improvement?
1.				
2.				
Decisions by others				
1.				
2.				

SOURCE: © Dorothy Marcic. Adapted from "Action Assignment" in Jennifer M. Howard and Lawrence M. Miller, *Team Management,* Miller Consulting Group, 1994, p. 205.

Manager's Workshop

Below are listed some situations that require a decision. In groups of three to six members, discuss which of the decision-making models (as discussed in the chapter) would be most relevant for each problem. Do not come up with the actual decision, but rather talk about which model is the best for that situation. Often we jump too quickly to solutions and spend too little time in the process of how to arrive at the best outcome.

Situation	Different variables	Which decision-making model is best?
1. Whether to quit your job	a. You are main breadwinner, have three school-aged children, you are in a difficult field; a new job—if you found it—would mean a move, unless you changed fields.	
	b. You are single and in a field where good jobs are plentiful.	
	c. You are married with no children, spouse with good job, and maybe you could find a decent job without moving.	
1. Whether to start a business	a. You have an inheritance of $50,000 and several ideas, but have not done reality check yet.	
	b. You have no money in bank and your family counts on your income, but you hate working for other people and you have some hot ideas.	
	c. You have a solid idea, some family friend who told you two years ago he would back you in a business, and a spouse who works and earns almost enough for expenses.	

© Dorothy Marcic.

Discussion Questions:

1. Do you often analyze the process of decision making before actually making the decision?

2. How can it be helpful to attend to the process?

3. What will you do next time you have an important decision to make?

Management in Practice: Ethical Dilemma

The Unhealthy Hospital

When Bruce Reid was hired as Blake Memorial Hospital's new CEO, the mandate had been clear: Improve the quality of care, and set the financial house in order.

As Reid struggled to finalize his budget for approval at next week's board meeting, his attention kept returning to one issue—the future of six off-site clinics. The clinics had been set up six years earlier to provide primary health care to the community's poorer neighborhoods. Although they provided a valuable service, they also diverted funds away from Blake's in-house services, many of which were underfunded. Cutting hospital personnel and freezing salaries could affect Blake's quality of care, which was already slipping. Eliminating the clinics, on the other hand, would save $256,000 without compromising Blake's internal operations.

However, there would be political consequences. Clara Bryant, the recently appointed commissioner of health services, repeatedly argued that the clinics were an essential service for the poor. Closing the clinics could jeopardize Blake's access to city funds. Dr. Susan Russell, the hospital's director of clinics, was equally vocal about Blake's responsibility to the community, although Dr. Winston Lee, chief of surgery, argued forcefully for closing the off-site clinics and having shuttle buses bring patients to the hospital weekly. Dr. Russell argued for an entirely new way of delivering health care—"A hospital is not a building," she said, "it's a service. And wherever the service is needed, that is where the hospital should be." In Blake's case, that meant funding more clinics. Russell wanted to create a network of neighborhood-based centers for all the surrounding poor and middle-income neighborhoods. Besides improving health care, the network would act as an inpatient referral system for hospital services. Reid considered the proposal: If a clinic network could tap the paying public and generate more in-patient business, it might be worth looking into. Blake's rival hospital, located on the affluent side of town, certainly wasn't doing anything that creative.

What Do You Do?

1. Close the clinics and save a quick $256,000, then move on to tackle the greater problems that threaten Blake's long-term future.

2. Gradually abandon the neighborhood altogether and open free-standing clinics in more affluent suburbs, at the same time opening a minihospital in the poor neighborhood for critical care.

3. Tighten internal efficiency to deal with immediate financial problems. Keep the clinics open for now, bring Clara Bryant into the decision-making process, and begin working with community groups to explore unmet health-care needs and develop innovative options for meeting them.

SOURCE: Based on Anthony R. Kovner, "The Case of the Unhealthy Hospital," *Harvard Business Review,* September–October 1991, pp. 12–25.

Surf the Net

1. *Creativity.* Your creativity can be a major asset in the decision-making process. Use your search engine to find Web sites related to creativity, such as www.tiac.net/users/seeker/brainlinks.html. Summarize your findings and present a three- to five-minute report in class about what you found that relates to creativity in the problem-solving/decision-making process.

2. Visit www.mgeneral.com and use the search feature to identify two leaders' "ezzays" about decision making. Compare and contrast their styles and relate those styles back to concepts in Chapter 6 of this book.

3. *Pushing Key Data to Decision Makers.* Go to www.pointcast.com, choose "What Is PointCast?," and learn how you can use it to stay informed. You can have personalized news and information from such sources as CNN, *The Wall Street Journal,* and *The New York Times* sent to your computer. Read how companies use PointCast's free suite of tools called the PointCast Intranet Broadcast Solution to deploy news broadcasts that keep employees competitive. Next, download and install the PointCast Network on your computer. PointCast replaces your screensaver with the latest headline news. Personalize your newscast by selecting which channels you receive as well as the type of information broadcast within each channel.

4. *Participative Decision Making.* Gather information from the Internet suitable to share in a small-group discussion on participative decision making. This exercise provides an opportunity for you to try a specialized search tool called "Ask Jeeves!" This search tool finds answers to natural-language questions such as "Who won Super Bowl XXV?" Go to www.ask.com and type in "What is participative decision making?" Select information from the links that "Ask Jeeves!" provides and be prepared to discuss your findings in class. One particularly interesting article on participative decision making is available at www.fed.org/leading_companies/oct98/tips.html.

Case for Critical Analysis

Greyhound Lines Inc.

Everyone agreed that Greyhound Lines had problems. The company was operating on paper-thin margins and could not afford to dispatch nearly empty vehicles or have buses and drivers on call to meet surges in demand. In the terminals, employees could be observed making fun of passengers, ignoring them, and handling their baggage haphazardly. To reduce operating costs and improve customer service, Greyhound's top executives put together a reorganization plan that called for massive cuts in personnel, routes, and services, along with the computerization of everything from passenger reservations to fleet scheduling.

However, middle managers disagreed with the plan. Many felt that huge workforce reductions would only exacerbate the company's real problem regarding customer services. Managers in computer programming urged a delay in introducing the computerized reservations system, called Trips, to work out bugs in the highly complex software. The human resources department pointed out that terminal workers often had less than a high school education and would need extensive training before they could be expected to use the system effectively. Terminal managers warned that many of Greyhound's low-income passengers didn't have credit cards or even telephones to use Trips. Despite the disagreements, executives rolled out the new system, emphasizing that the data they had studied showed that Trips would improve customer service, make ticket buying more convenient, and allow customers to reserve space on specific trips. A nightmare resulted. The time Greyhound operators spent responding to phone calls dramatically increased. Many callers couldn't even get through because of problems in the new switching mechanism. Most passengers arrived to buy their tickets and get on the bus just like they always had, but the computers were so swamped that it sometimes took 45 seconds to respond to a single keystroke and five minutes to print a ticket. The system crashed so often that agents frequently had to hand write tickets. Customers stood in long lines, were separated from their luggage, missed connections, and were left to sleep in terminals overnight. Discourtesy to customers increased as a downsized workforce struggled to cope with a system they were ill-trained to operate. Ridership plunged sharply, and regional rivals continued to pick off Greyhound's dissatisfied customers.

Questions

1. Was the decision facing Greyhound executives programmed or nonprogrammed?

2. Do you think they should have used the classical, administrative, or political model to make their decision? Which do you believe they used? Discuss.

3. Analyze the Greyhound case in terms of the six steps in the managerial decision making process. Do you think top executives paid adequate attention to all six steps? If you were a Greyhound executive, what would you do now and why?

SOURCE: Robert Tomsho, "How Greyhound Lines Re-Engineered Itself Right Into a Deep Hole," *The Wall Street Journal,* October 30, 1994, p. A1.

Endnotes

1 Teri Agins, "Forget the Clothes—Fashion Fortunes Turn on Heels and Purses," *The Wall Street Journal,* Vol. CCXXXIV (102), Nov. 23, 1999, pp. A1, A12; Allison Rossono, "Timing's Everything," *Inc.* Technology, No. 3, 1997, pp. 31–32.

2 Richard A. Melcher, "Dusting Off the Britannica," *Business Week,* October 21, 1997, pp. 143, 146.

3 Linda Grant, "How UPS Blew It," *Fortune,* September 29, 1997, pp. 29–30.

4 "Tickling a Child's Fancy," *The Tennessean,* February 6, 1997, pp. 1E, 4E.

5 Dean Takahashi, "How the Competition Got Ahead of Intel in Making Cheap Chips," *The Wall Street Journal,* February 12, 1998, p. A1.

6 Ronald A. Howard, "Decision Analysis: Practice and Promise," *Management Science* 34 (1988), pp. 679–695.

7 Herbert A. Simon, *The New Science of Management* (Englewood Cliffs, N.J.: Prentice-Hall, 1977), p. 47.

8 Henry Goldblatt, "AT&T Finally Has an Operator," *Fortune,* February 16, 1998, pp. 79–82.

9 Thomas E. Weber, "As Religion Spreads on Web, Will Ideal or Mammon Prevail?" *The Wall Street Journal,* Nov. 29, 1999, p. B1.

10 Samuel Eilon, "Structuring Unstructured Decisions"; and Philip A. Roussel, "Cutting Down the Guesswork in R&D," *Harvard Business Review,* 61 (September–October 1983), 154–160.

11 Samuel Eilon, "Structuring Unstructured Decisions," *Omega* 13 (1985), 369–377; and Max H. Bazerman, *Judgment in Managerial Decision Making* (New York: Wiley, 1986).

12 James G. March and Zur Shapira, "Managerial Perspectives on Risk and Risk Taking," *Management Science* 33 (1987), 1404–1418; and Inga Skromme Baird and Howard Thomas, "Toward a Contingency Model of Strategic Risk Taking," *Academy of Management Review* 10 (1985), 230–243.

13 J. G. Higgins, "Planning for Risk and Uncertainty in Oil Exploration," *Long Range Planning* 26, no. 1 (February 1993), 111–122; and Bruce Horovitz and Gary Strauss, "Fast-Food Icon Wants Shine Restored to Golden Arches," *USA Today,* May 1, 1998, 1B, 2B.

14 Hugh Courtney, Jane Kirkland, and Patrick Viguerie, "Strategy under Uncertainty," *Harvard Business Review* (November–December 1997), pp. 67–79.

15 Michael Masuch and Perry LaPotin, "Beyond Garbage Cans: An AI Model of Organizational Choice," *Administrative Science Quarterly,* 34 (1989), pp. 38–67.

16 David M. Schweiger, William R. Sandberg, and James W. Ragan, "Group Approaches for Improving Strategic Decision Making: A Comparative Analysis of Dialectical Inquiry, Devil's Advocacy, and Consensus," *Academy of Management Journal* 29 (1986), 51–71.

17 Michael Pacanowsky, "Team Tools for Wicked Problems," *Organizational Dynamics* 23, No. 3 (winter 1995), 36–51.

18 Michael J. McCarthy, "Pepsi Faces Problem in Trying to Contain Syringe Scare," *The Wall Street Journal,* June 17, 1993, p. B1.

19 Boris Blai, Jr., "Eight Steps to Successful Problem Solving," *Supervisory Management* (January 1986), pp. 7–9.

20 Jean Aubin, "Scheduling Ambulances," *Interfaces* 22 (March–April 1992), 1–10.

21 Herbert A. Simon, *Models of Man* (New York: Wiley, 1957), pp. 196–205.

22 James G. March and Herbert A. Simon, *Organizations* (New York: Wiley, 1958).

23 Herbert A. Simon, *Models of Man* (New York: Wiley, 1957), 196–205; and Herbert A. Simon, *Administrative Behavior,* 2d ed. (New York: Free Press, 1957).

24 John Taylor, "Project Fantasy: A Behind-the-Scenes Account of Disney's Desperate Battle against the Raiders," *Manhattan* (November 1984).

25 Sara Procknow, "Serious about the Web," *Industrial Distribution,* Vol. 88 (8), Aug 1999, pp. M16–M18; Peter Carbonara, "Freewheeling Expansion Ends in Free Fall," *Inc.,* March 1998, p. 23.

26 Weston H. Agor, "The Logic of Intuition: How Top Executives Make Important Decisions," *Organizational Dynamics,* 14 (Winter 1986), pp. 5–18.

27 Suzanna Andrews, "Calling the Shots," *Working Woman* (November 1995), pp. 30–35, 90.

28 Daniel J. Isenberg, "How Senior Managers Think," *Harvard Business Review,* 62 (November–December 1984), 80–90.

29 William B. Stevenson, Jon L. Pierce, and Lyman W. Porter, "The Concept of 'Coalition' in Organization Theory and Research," *Academy of Management Review* 10 (1985), pp. 256–268.

30 Nandini Rajagopalan, Abdul M. A. Rasheed, and Deepak K. Datta, "Strategic Decision Processes: Critical Review and Future Directions," *Journal of Management,* 19 (2) (1993), pp. 349–384; and Paul J. H. Schoemaker, "Strategic Decisions in Organizations: Rational and Behavioral Views," *Journal of Management Studies,* 30 (1) (January 1993), pp. 107–129.

31 Susan E. Jackson and Jane E. Dutton, "Discerning Threats and Opportunities," *Adminis-*

trative Science Quarterly, 33 (1988), pp. 370–387.

32 Richard L. Daft, Juhani Sormumen, and Don Parks, "Chief Executive Scanning, Environmental Characteristics, and Company Performance: An Empirical Study" (unpublished manuscript, Texas A&M University, 1988).

33 David Greising, "Rethinking IDS from the Bottom Up," *Business Week,* February 8, 1993, pp. 110–112.

34 C. Kepner and B. Tregoe, *The Rational Manager* (New York: McGraw-Hill, 1965).

35 Ralph L. Keeney, "Creativity in Decision-Making with Value-Focused Thinking," *Sloan Management Review* (Summer 1994), pp. 33–41.

36 McCune, "Making Lemonade."

37 Based on A. J. Rowe, J. D. Boulgaides, and M. R. McGrath, *Managerial Decision Making,* (Chicago: Science Research Associates, 1984); and Alan J. Rowe and Richard O. Mason *Managing with Style: A Guide to Understanding, Assessing, and Improving Your Decision Making,* (San Francisco: Jossey-Bass 1987).

38 Alan J. Rowe and Richard O. Mason, *Managing with Style: A Guide to Understanding, Assessing, and Improving Your Decision Making* (San Francisco: Jossey-Bass, 1987).

39 Victor H. Vroom, "A New Look at Managerial Decision Making," *Organizational Dynamics* (Spring 1972), pp. 66–80.

40 V. H. Vroom and Arthur G. Jago, *The New Leadership: Managing Participation in Organizations* (Englewood Cliffs, N.J.: Prentice-Hall, 1988).

41 Jennifer T. Ettling and Arthur G. Jago, "Participation under Conditions of Conflict: More on the Validity of the Vroom-Yetton Model," *Journal of Management Studies,* 25 (1988), pp. 73–83.

42 Tom Richman, "One Man's Family," *Inc.* (November 1983), pp. 151–156.

43 Ettling and Jago, "Participation under Conditions of Conflict."

44 "Hatts Off Specialized Services," 1999 (Gordon Naylor, personal communication, Jan. 2000.)

45 Brian Mullen, Tara Anthony, Eduardo Salas, and James E. Driskell, "Group Cohesiveness and Quality of Decision Making: An Integration of Tests of the Groupthink Hypothesis," *Small Group Research,* 25 (2) (May 1994), pp. 189–204.

46 Roy Rowan, "The Maverick Who Yelled Foul at Citibank," *Fortune,* January 10, 1983, pp. 46–56.

47 Thomas W. Malone, "Is Empowerment Just a Fad? Control, Decision Making, and IT," *Sloan Management Review* (Winter 1997), pp. 23–35.

48 Robert I. Sutton and Andrew Hargadon, "Brainstorming Groups in Context: Effectiveness in a Product Design Firm," *Administrative Science Quarterly* 41 (1996), pp. 685–718.

49 Robert Kreitner and Angelo Kinicki, *Organizational Behavior,* 3d ed. (Chicago: Irwin, 1995), p. 323.

50 A. Osborn, *Applied Imagination* (New York: Scribner, 1957).

51 David M. Schweiger and William R. Sandberg, "The Utilization of Individual Capabilities in Group Approaches to Strategic Decision-Making," *Strategic Management Journal,* 10 (1989), pp. 31–43.

52 Stern, "Why Good Managers Approve Bad Ideas."

53 Michael Duffy, "Mr. Consensus," *Time,* August 21, 1989, pp. 16–22.

54 Derek Slater, "Chain Commanders," *CIO Enterprise,* August 15, 1998, 29–30+.

55 Suzanne Muchnic, "Going Once, Going Twice in Cyberspace," *Los Angeles Times,* Feb. 23, 1999, p. 1; Gianna Jacobson, "Rock Steady: Technology Turns Home-Based Selling into an Art," *Selling Success,* May 1997, pp. 41–42.

56 Roberta Maynard, "Casting the Net for Job Seekers," *Nation's Business,* March 1997, 28–29.

57 Michael J. Major, "Working Smart: The University of Central Florida's Intranet-Based Administration Application," *CIO,* April 15, 1998, 80; and Mary J. Cronin, "Ford's Intranet Success," *Fortune,* March 30, 1998, 158.

58 Jenny C. McCune, "The In's and Out's of Extranets," *Management Review,* July/August 1998, 23–25; and Sari Kalin, "The Fast Lane," *CIO Web Business,* April 1, 1998, sec. 2, 28, 32–35.

59 Jim Sterne, "A Fine and Private Page," *Inc. Technology,* 1999, No. 4, pp. 144–145.

60 Srikumar S. Rao, "ABCs of Cost Control," *Inc. Technology,* 1997, no. 2, 79–81.

61 Christopher Palmeri, "Believe in Yourself, Believe in the Merchandise," *Continental,* December 1997, 49–51.

62 ESRI Map Book, vol. 10, "Creating a New World," Environmental Systems Research Institute, Inc., 1995.

63 Michael H. Martin, "Smart Managing: Best Practices, Careers, and Ideas," *Fortune,* February 2, 1998, 149–151.

64 Charles C. Mann, "Volume Business," *Inc. Technology,* 1997, No. 2, pp. 54–61.

65 Martin, "Smart Managing," 150.

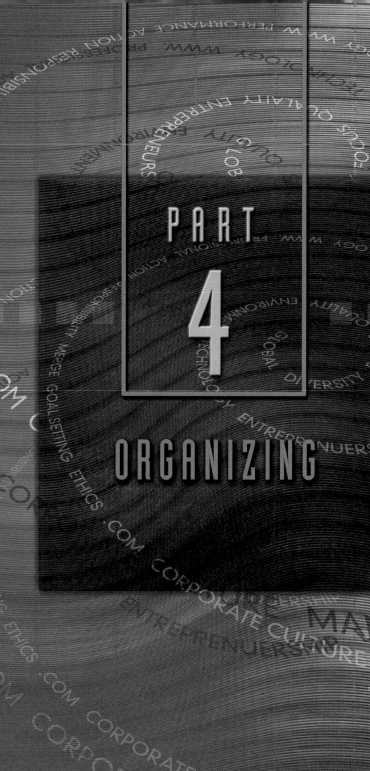

PART

4

ORGANIZING

Clear chains of command are vital to the success of any organization—even a sailboat crew. Authority and responsibility must flow throughout the crew, from the skipper to the navigator and watch leader to the trimmers and the riggers. Some boats have co-skippers who share duties and trade off when the particular demands of a race leg fit the particular strengths of the other. Regardless of the hierarchy, coordination is key to peak performance. All crew members must know their jobs well and, when called upon, must execute their tasks with precision. Selecting the right mix of crew members, training them to function as a well-oiled team, and preparing them for the challenges ahead are crucial tasks. In the best-functioning crews, members understand the overall strategy and goals. They do not just have a broad perspective on the whole race in general, but rather, they maintain a steady eye on each leg along the way. Throughout the race, they adapt to changing conditions, make decisions, and learn from their mistakes. Diverse crew members range in age from weathered, middle-aged veterans to ambitious, young newcomers. One boat, the *EF Education* from Sweden, had an all-female crew. But every successful crew has two things that bind them together—their love of sailing and a steadfast pride and determination to be the best.

Part IV introduces the elements of effective organizing and explores the necessary skills for developing competitive strategies, personnel recruiting, and creating and maintaining an effective workforce.

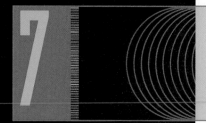

Fundamentals of Organizing

LEARNING OBJECTIVES

After studying this chapter, you should be able to:

- Explain the fundamental characteristics of organizing, including such concepts as work specialization, chain of command, line and staff, and task forces

- Explain when specific structural characteristics such as centralization and span of management should be used within organizations

- Explain the functional approach to structure

- Explain the divisional approach to structure

- Explain the contemporary team and network structures and why they are being adopted by organizations

MANAGEMENT PROBLEM

CompUSA **is on a deathwatch. The**

personal computer retailer has seen competition

and falling personal computer prices strangle its market share and

margins. Its 1998 poorly-timed purchase of the Tandy Computer chain made

matters even worse, and its strategy of sticking with a narrow product line, while others (i.e.,

Circuit City) focused on a broader range of electronic goods, has made it a has-been. Seeing the

handwriting on the wall, executives decided to create a new Web site for its e-commerce business. Its

existing CompUSA site had not done particularly well. Executives looked at other firms to see how they

had handled their Web business. CompUSA executives benchmarked the Web success of Dell Computer

and Amazon.com, as well as those that didn't do well, such as Toys "R" Us (see beginning of Chapter 2).

• *If you were Jim Halpin, what would you recommend for CompUSA? How would you structure the new Web site?*

CEO Jim Halpin and his executives had some tough decisions to make. When a company sets up a "click-

and-mortar" storefront (i.e., Web site), chances are it will compete with its "bricks-and-mortar" stores.

Often, both lose, as was the case with Toys "R" Us. CompUSA was deteriorating, and unless

severe changes occurred, the whole company would die. Intentionally setting up a snazzy Web site

meant possibly endangering its CompUSA stores, thus quickening the entire company's

demise. It came down to setting up a new Web site as part of CompUSA,

or turning the company into an entirely e-commerce business,

completely separate from its parent.[1]

Every firm wrestles with the problem of how to organize. Reorganization often is necessary to reflect a new strategy, changing market conditions, or innovative production technology. Companies throughout the world are restructuring to become leaner, more efficient, and more nimble in today's highly competitive global environment.

A growing number of companies operate as network or virtual organizations, limiting themselves to a few core activities and letting outside specialists handle the rest. Super Bakery, Inc., a Pittsburgh-based donut maker (majority-owned by former Pittsburgh Steelers running back Franco Harris) achieved a national presence in a highly competitive industry by using the network approach. Super Bakery concentrates on product development and outsources the selling, manufacturing, and shipping of its products to outside contractors.[2]

Each of these organizations is using fundamental concepts of organizing. **Organizing** is the deployment of organizational resources to achieve strategic goals. The deployment of resources is reflected in the organization's division of labor into specific departments and jobs, formal lines of authority, and mechanisms for coordinating diverse organization tasks.

Organizing is important because it follows from strategy. Strategy defines what to do; organizing defines how to do it. **Organization structure** is a tool that managers use to harness resources for getting things done. Part IV explains the variety of organizing principles and concepts used by managers. Chapters 7, 8, 9, and 10 introduce fundamental concepts that apply to all organizations and departments, describe how structural designs are tailored to an organization's situation, discuss how organizations can be structured to facilitate innovation and change, and examine how to maximize human resources within the organization's structure.

■ ORGANIZING THE VERTICAL STRUCTURE

The organizing process leads to the creation of organization structure, which defines how tasks are divided and resources deployed. Or-

ganization structure is defined as (1) the set of formal tasks assigned to individuals and departments; (2) formal reporting relationships, including lines of authority, decision responsibility, number of hierarchical levels, and span of managerial control; and (3) the design of systems to ensure effective coordination of employees across departments.[3]

The set of formal tasks and formal reporting relationships provides a framework for vertical control of the organization. The characteristics of vertical structure are portrayed in the **organization chart,** which is the visual representation of an organization's structure.

Exhibit 7.1 shows an organization chart for a soda bottling plant. The plant has four major departments—accounting, human resources, production, and marketing. The chart delineates the chain of command, indicates departmental tasks and how they fit together, and provides order and logic within the organization. Every employee has an appointed task, line of authority, and decision responsibility. Here are several important features of vertical structure.

WORK SPECIALIZATION

Organizations perform a wide variety of tasks. A fundamental principle is that work can be performed more efficiently if employees are allowed to specialize.[4] **Work specialization,** sometimes called division of labor, is the degree to which organizational tasks are subdivided into separate jobs. Work specialization in Exhibit 7.1 is illustrated by the separation of production tasks into bottling, high-quality control, and maintenance. Employees within each department perform only the tasks relevant to their specialized function. When work specialization is extensive, employees specialize in a single task. Jobs tend to be small, but they can be performed efficiently. Work specialization is readily visible on an automobile assembly line where each employee performs the same task over and over again. It would not be efficient to have a single employee build the entire automobile or even perform a large number of unrelated jobs.

Despite the apparent advantages of specialization, many organizations are moving away

---

organizing
The deployment of organizational resources to achieve strategic goals

organization structure
A management tool used to define how tasks are divided, deploy resources, and coordinate departments

organization chart
The visual representation of an organization's structure

work specialization
The degree to which organizational tasks are subdivided into individual jobs; also called *division of labor*

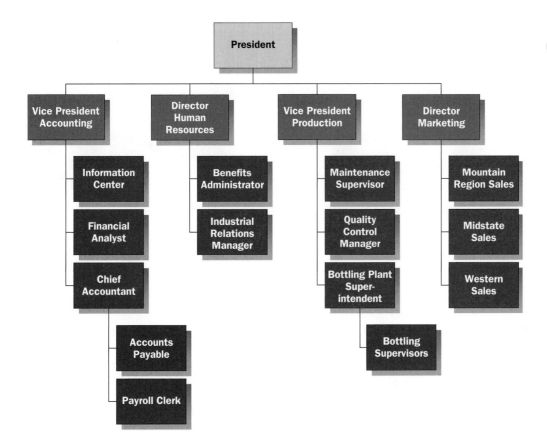

from this principle. With too much specialization, employees are isolated and perform only small, narrow, boring tasks. Many companies are enlarging jobs to provide greater challenges and assigning teams so employees can rotate among several jobs. At Sony Corporation's factory in Kohda, Japan, the assembly line for camcorders has been dismantled and replaced with small, four-person shops, where workers walk through a spiral line to assemble entire cameras themselves, doing everything from soldering to testing. U.S. companies are taking similar paths. Production increased 51 percent after Compaq Computer's Scotland and Texas plants switched from assembly lines to four-worker manufacturing teams.[5] The team approach to organization design will be discussed later in this chapter.

CHAIN OF COMMAND

The **chain of command** is an unbroken line of authority that links all persons in an organiza-

tion and defines who reports to whom. It has two underlying principles. Unity of command means that each employee is held accountable to only one supervisor. The scalar principle refers to a clearly defined line of authority in the organization that includes all employees. Authority and responsibility for different tasks should be distinct. In Exhibit 7.1, the payroll clerk reports to the chief accountant, who in turn reports to the vice president, who in turn reports to the company president.

AUTHORITY, RESPONSIBILITY, AND DELEGATION

The chain of command illustrates the authority structure of the organization. **Authority** is the formal and legitimate right of a manager to make decisions, issue orders, and allocate resources to achieve organizationally desired outcomes.

Three principles undergird organizational authority.

chain of command
An unbroken line of authority that links all individuals in the organization and defines who reports to whom

authority
The formal and legitimate right of a manager to make decisions, issue orders, and allocate resources to achieve organizationally desired outcomes

Organizing helps GTE remain competitive in the volatile, worldwide telecommunications industry. GTE Telephone Operations, the largest U.S.-based local telephone company, restructured from an organization based on functions and geographic regions to one focused on markets and customers. Employees at GTE's high-tech Network Operations Center (Dallas) continually monitor the company's telephone network to improve customer service, provide a more efficient network nationwide, and reduce overall costs.

responsibility
The duty to perform the task or activity an employee has been assigned

accountability
The degree to which people with authority and responsibility are subject to reporting and justifying task outcomes to those above them in the chain of command

delegation
The means by which managers transfer authority and responsibility to positions below them in the hierarchy

1. Authority is vested in organizational positions, not people. Managers have authority because of the positions they hold, and anyone in the same position would have the same authority.

2. Authority is accepted by subordinates. Although authority flows top down through the organization's hierarchy, subordinates comply because they believe that managers have a legitimate right to issue orders. The acceptance theory of authority argues that a manager has authority only if subordinates choose to accept his or her commands. If subordinates refuse to obey because the order is outside their zone of acceptance, a manager's authority disappears.[6] For example, Richard Ferris, the former chairman of United Airlines, resigned because few people accepted his strategy of acquiring hotels, a car rental company, and other organizations to build a travel empire. When key people refused to accept his direction, his authority was lost, and he resigned.

3. Authority flows down the vertical hierarchy. Positions at the top of the hierarchy are vested with more formal authority than are positions at the bottom.

Responsibility is the flip side of the authority coin. Responsibility is the duty to perform the task or activity an employee has been assigned. Typically, managers are assigned authority commensurate with responsibility. When managers have responsibility for task outcomes but little authority, the job is possible but difficult. They rely on persuasion and luck. When managers have authority exceeding responsibility, they may become tyrants, using authority toward frivolous outcomes.[7]

Accountability is the mechanism through which authority and responsibility are brought into alignment. Accountability is the degree to which people with authority and responsibility are subject to reporting and justifying task outcomes to those above them in the chain of command.[8] Subordinates must be aware that they are accountable for a task and accept the responsibility and authority for performing it. Accountability can be built into the organization structure. At Whirlpool, for example, incentive programs provide strict accountability. Performance of all managers is monitored, and bonus payments are tied to successful outcomes.

Another concept related to authority is **delegation.**[9] Delegation is the means by which managers transfer authority and responsibility to positions below them in the hierarchy. Most organizations today encourage managers to delegate authority to the lowest possible level to provide maximum flexibility to meet customer needs and adapt to the environment. Managers are encouraged to delegate authority, although they often find it difficult. Techniques for delegation are discussed in Leading the Revolution. The trend toward increased delegation begins in the chief executive's office in companies such as USX, PPG Industries, Johnsonville Foods, Ford, and General Electric. At Johnsonville, a committee of employees from the shop floor has been delegated authority to formulate the manufacturing budget.

HOW TO DELEGATE

The attempt by top management to decentralize decision making often gets bogged down because middle managers are unable to delegate. Managers may cling tightly to their decision-making and task responsibilities. Failure to delegate occurs for a number of reasons: Managers are most comfortable making familiar decisions; they feel they will lose personal status by delegating tasks; they believe they can do a better job themselves; or they have an aversion to risk—they will not take a chance on delegating because performance responsibility ultimately rests with them.

Yet decentralization offers an organization many advantages. Decisions are made at the right level, lower-level employees are motivated, and employees have the opportunity to develop decision-making skills. Overcoming barriers to delegation in order to gain these advantages is a major challenge. The following approach can help each manager delegate more effectively:

1. Delegate the whole task. A manager should delegate an entire task to one person rather than dividing it among several people. This gives the individual complete responsibility and increases his or her initiative while giving the manager some control over the results.

2. Select the right person. Not all employees have the same capabilities and degree of motivation. Managers must match talent to task if delegation is to be effective. They should identify subordinates who have made independent decisions in the past and have shown a desire for more responsibility.

3. Ensure that authority equals responsibility. Merely assigning a task is not effective delegation. Managers often load subordinates with increased responsibility but do not extend their decision-making range. In addition to having responsibility for completing a task, the worker must be given the authority to make decisions about how best to do the job.

4. Give thorough instruction. Successful delegation includes information on what, when, why, where, who, and how. The subordinate must clearly understand the task and the expected results. It is a good idea to write down all provisions discussed, including required resources and when and how the results will be reported.

5. Maintain feedback. Feedback means keeping open lines of communication with the subordinate to answer questions and provide advice, but without exerting too much control. Open lines of communication make it easier to trust subordinates. Feedback keeps the subordinate on the right track.

6. Evaluate and reward performance. Once the task is completed, the manager should evaluate results, not methods. When results do not meet expectations, the manager must assess the consequences. When they do meet expectations, the manager should reward employees for a job well done with praise, financial rewards when appropriate, and delegation of future assignments.

Are You a Positive Delegator?

Positive delegation is the way an organization implements decentralization. Do you help or hinder the decentralization process? If you answer yes to more than three of the following questions, you may have a problem delegating:

- I tend to be a perfectionist.
- My boss expects me to know all the details of my job.
- I don't have the time to explain clearly and concisely how a task should be accomplished.
- I often end up doing tasks myself.
- My subordinates typically are not as committed as I am.
- I get upset when other people don't do the task right.
- I really enjoy doing the details of my job to the best of my ability.
- I like to be in control of task outcomes.

Sources: Thomas R. Horton, "Delegation and Team Building: No Solo Acts Please," *Management Review*, September 1992, pp. 58–61; Andrew E. Schwartz, "The Why, What, and to Whom of Delegation," *Management Solutions* (June 1987), pp. 31–38; "Delegation," *Small Business Report* (June 1986), pp. 38–43; and Max E. Douglas, "How to Delegate Safely," *Training and Development Journal*, February 1987, p. 8.

An important distinction in many organizations is between line authority and staff authority, reflecting whether managers work in line or staff departments in the organization's structure. *Line departments* perform tasks that reflect the organization's primary goal and mission. In a manufacturing organization, line departments make and sell the product. *Staff departments* include all those that provide specialized skills to support line departments. Staff departments have an advisory relationship with line departments, and they typically include marketing, labor relations, research, accounting, and human resources.

Line authority means that people in management positions have formal authority to direct and control immediate subordinates. **Staff authority** is narrower and includes the right to

line authority
Authority in which individuals in management positions have the formal power to direct and control immediate subordinates

staff authority
Authority granted to staff specialists in their areas of expertise

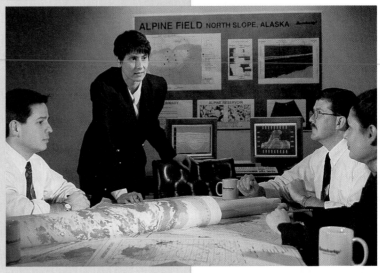

Diane Kerr, standing, is a senior staff geophysicist for Anadarko Petroleum Corporation, one of the world's largest independent oil exploration and production companies. Kerr uses her staff authority to help develop the Alpine Field on Alaska's North Slope. She considers new technology and the strength received from company partnerships to be her most valuable resources on this job. Diane's coworkers at Anadarko include, from left to right, Glenn Raney, Kevin Stacy, and Valerie Cadden.

advise, recommend, and counsel in the area of expertise of the staff specialists. Staff authority is a communication relationship; staff specialists advise managers in technical areas. The finance department of a manufacturing firm, for instance, would have staff authority to coordinate with line departments about which accounting forms to use to facilitate equipment purchases and standardize payroll services.

SPAN OF MANAGEMENT

The **span of management** is the number of employees reporting to a supervisor. Sometimes called the *span of control,* this characteristic of structure determines how closely a supervisor can monitor subordinates. Traditional views of organization design recommended a span of management of seven or so subordinates per manager. However, many lean organizations today have spans of management as high as 30, 40, and even higher. Research on the Lockheed Missile and Space Company and other manufacturing companies suggests that span of management can vary widely and that several factors influence it.[10] Generally, when supervisors must be closely involved with subordinates, the span would be small, and when supervisors need little involvement with subordinates, it can be large. The following factors are associated with less

supervisor involvement and thus larger spans of control:

1. Work performed by subordinates is stable and routine.
2. Subordinates perform similar work tasks.
3. Subordinates are concentrated in a single location.
4. Subordinates are highly trained and need little direction in performing tasks.
5. Rules and procedures defining task activities are available.
6. Support systems and personnel are available for the manager.
7. Little time is required in nonsupervisory activities, such as coordination with other departments or planning.
8. Personal preferences and styles of managers favor a large span.

The average span of control used in an organization determines whether the structure is tall or flat. A **tall structure** has an overall narrow span and more hierarchical levels. A **flat structure** has a wide span, is horizontally dispersed, and has fewer hierarchical levels.

The trend in recent years has been toward wider spans of control as a way to facilitate delegation.[11] Exhibit 7.2 illustrates how an international metals company was reorganized.

span of management
The number of employees who report to a supervisor; also called *span of control*

tall structure
A management structure characterized by an overall narrow span of management and a relatively large number of hierarchical levels

flat structure
A management structure characterized by an overall broad span of control and relatively few hierarchical levels

REORGANIZATION TO INCREASE SPAN OF MANAGEMENT FOR PRESIDENT OF AN INTERNATIONAL METALS COMPANY

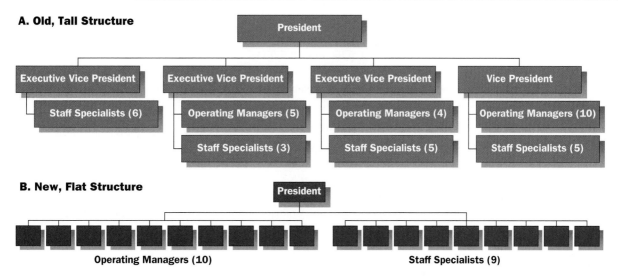

A. Old, Tall Structure

President

Executive Vice President — Staff Specialists (6)

Executive Vice President — Operating Managers (5), Staff Specialists (3)

Executive Vice President — Operating Managers (4), Staff Specialists (5)

Vice President — Operating Managers (10), Staff Specialists (5)

B. New, Flat Structure

President

Operating Managers (10)   Staff Specialists (9)

The multilevel set of managers shown in panel A was replaced with 10 operating managers and nine staff specialists reporting directly to the CEO, as shown in panel B. The CEO welcomed this wide span of 19 management subordinates because it fit his style; his management team was top quality and needed little supervision, and they were all located on the same floor of an office building.

CENTRALIZATION AND DECENTRALIZATION

Centralization and decentralization pertain to the hierarchical level at which decisions are made. **Centralization** means that decision authority is located near the top of the organization. With **decentralization,** decision authority is spread downward to lower organization levels.

In the United States and Canada, the trend over the past 30 years has been toward greater decentralization of organizations. Decentralization is believed to relieve the burden on top managers, make greater use of the skills and abilities of workers, ensure that decisions are made close to the action by well-informed people, and permit more rapid response to external changes.

However, this trend does not mean that every organization should decentralize all decisions. Managers should experiment and diagnose the organizational situation and select the decision-making level that will best meet the organization's needs. Advantages that typify centralization over decentralization include:

1. Greater change and uncertainty in the environment are usually associated with decentralization. Rapid change and uncertainty can create negative outcomes, such as during Operation Desert Shield when the highly decentralized U.S. Tactical Air Command deployed twice the number of squadrons previously expected for the first week while other centralized U.S. forces fell behind their deployment schedules.[12] Today, most companies feel greater uncertainty because of intense global competition; hence, many have decentralized.

2. The amount of centralization or decentralization should fit the firm's strategy. For example, Johnson & Johnson gives almost complete authority to its 180 operating companies to develop and market their own products. Decentralization fits the corporate strategy of empowerment that gets each

centralization
Refers to decision authority located near the top of organizational levels

decentralization
Refers to decision authority located at lower organizational levels

division close to customers so it can speedily adapt to consumer needs.[13] As new technology and competition changed the banking industry, BancOne Chairman John B. McCoy switched to centralization to cut costs, speed up decision making, and move faster with new products and services.[14]

3. In times of crisis or risk of company failure, authority may become centralized at the top.

In this example, Rick Lewandowski's company used a centralized technological system to decrease paperwork and increase productivity.

MDP CONSTRUCTION

We've all heard about the Pentagon's extravagant spending: $250 for a hammer, $600 for a toilet seat. You might think having the Pentagon as a client would be every small contractor's dream. But there are plenty of nightmares, says Rick Lewandowski of MDP Construction, Inc. Winning one of those government contracts means contending with a bureaucracy and dealing with loads of regulations, mountains of paperwork, and endless scheduling delays. Small contractors are at a distinct disadvantage; the paperwork alone can bury them.

MDP Construction has learned not only to compete but to thrive in this bureaucratic system by harnessing the power of information technology. "For the type of construction that we do," says Lewandowski, "we'd normally need maybe eight people in our office just to take care of the correspondence. We have four." Virtually every aspect of Lewandowski's business has been revamped by IT. Every piece of government-required paperwork has been scanned into MDP's network so that project supervisors equipped with laptops and modems can access any document they need directly from the construction site. Another benefit of computerization is the ability to coordinate logistics with improved speed and accuracy. A project-management program called SureTrak Project Manager allows MDP to track time lines for the myriad tasks involved in each construction project. Previously, supervisors had to chart all those steps manually, an arduous job considering many complex construction projects involve well over 1,000 tasks. With SureTrak, managers can oversee a larger number of projects, as well as quickly determine how one "simple" change requested by the client could end up adding months to the schedule. For example, when MDP was building a fire station at Peterson Air Force Base, the government wanted to make a mid-project change in wall color. Using SureTrak, Lewandowski was able to show that even this minor adjustment would lead to a delay of 12 weeks in completing the project. Such delays not only waste government dollars but also keep MDP workers idle and tie up company resources that could be used elsewhere.

Lewandowski admits it took some time for MDP's supervisors—all former painters and carpenters—to get the hang of continuously updating SureTrak. Today, however, supervisors in the field use SureTrak to manage their own individual budgets and make better economic decisions. The next step in Lewandowski's revolution is a company Web site that will not only improve internal communication but also smooth the process of exchanging information with the government. Overall, government officials have come to appreciate MDP's streamlined efficiency. For this small construction company, that translates into $12 million in revenues from government contracts.[15] ■

■ DEPARTMENTALIZATION

A fundamental characteristic of organization structure is **departmentalization,** which is the basis for grouping positions into departments and departments into the total organization. Managers make choices about how to use the chain of command to group people together to perform their work. There are five approaches to structural design that reflect different uses of the chain of command in departmentalization.

---

departmentalization
The fundamental principle by which individuals are grouped into departments and departments into total organizations

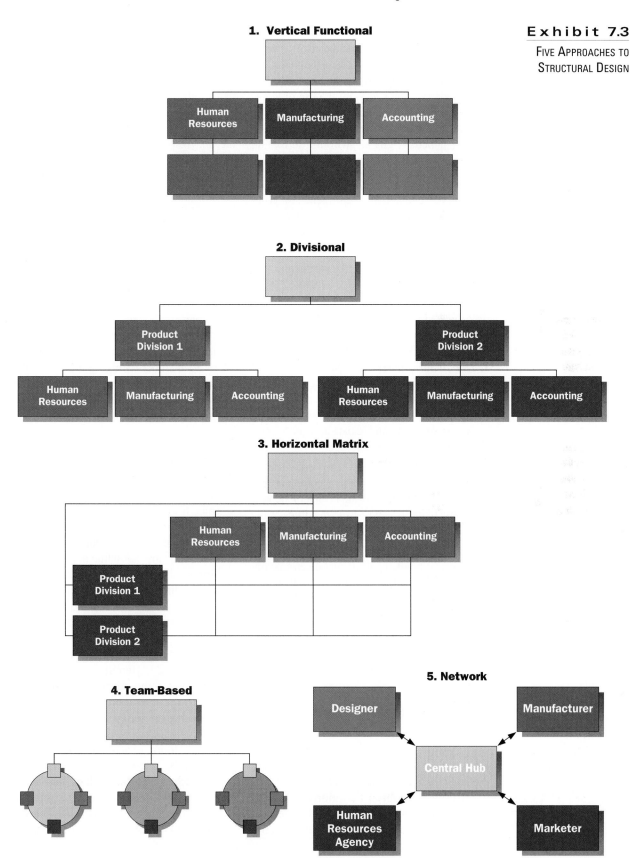

E x h i b i t 7.3

FIVE APPROACHES TO
STRUCTURAL DESIGN

1. Vertical Functional

Human Resources

Manufacturing

Accounting

2. Divisional

Product Division 1

Product Division 2

Human Resources

Manufacturing

Accounting

Human Resources

Manufacturing

Accounting

3. Horizontal Matrix

Human Resources

Manufacturing

Accounting

Product Division 1

Product Division 2

4. Team-Based

5. Network

Designer

Manufacturer

Central Hub

Human Resources Agency

Marketer

The functional, divisional, and matrix are traditional approaches that rely on the chain of command to define departmental groupings and reporting relationships along the hierarchy. Two contemporary approaches are the use of teams and networks. These newer approaches have emerged to meet organizational needs in a highly competitive global environment. Exhibit 7.3 shows five structural alternatives.

1. *Vertical functional approach.* People are grouped together in departments by common skills and work activities, such as in an engineering department and an accounting department.

2. *Divisional approach.* Departments are grouped together into separate, self-contained divisions based on a common product, program, or geographical region. Diverse skills, rather than similar skills, are the basis of departmentalization.

3. *Horizontal matrix approach.* Functional and divisional chains of command are implemented simultaneously and overlay one another in the same departments. Two chains of command exist, and some employees report to two bosses.

4. *Team-based approach.* The organization creates a series of teams to accomplish specific tasks and to coordinate major departments. Teams can exist from the office of the president all the way down to the shop floor.

5. *Network approach.* The organization becomes a small, central hub electronically connected to other organizations that perform vital functions. Departments are independent, contracting services to the central hub for a profit. Departments can be located anywhere in the world.[16]

■ NEW APPROACHES TO DEPARTMENTALIZATION

TEAM APPROACH

Probably the most widespread trend in departmentalization has been the effort by companies to implement team concepts. The vertical chain of command is a powerful means of con-

trol, but passing all decisions up the hierarchy takes too long and keeps responsibility at the top. Today, companies are trying to find ways to delegate authority, push responsibility to low levels, and create participative teams that engage the commitment of workers. This approach enables organizations to be more flexible and responsive in the competitive global environment.

Cross-functional teams consist of employees from various functional departments who are responsible for resolving mutual problems mutually. Team members typically still report to their functional departments, but they also report to the team, one member of whom may be the leader.

Some organizations create **permanent teams,** groups of employees who become a formal department. The permanent-team approach resembles the divisional approach described earlier, but teams are much smaller, with only 20 to 30 members bringing a functional specialty to the team. American Express Financial Advisors implemented such teams to improve internal communication and customer service.

AMERICAN EXPRESS FINANCIAL ADVISORS
www.americanexpress.com
American Express Financial Advisors sells financial products such as insurance, mutual funds, and investment certificates. But its redesign focuses on how the company sells these products, with teams of empowered workers focused on building relationships with customers. The reorganization came about because managers recognized environmental changes that could threaten client retention. Although AEFA was basking in the glow of 21 percent annual earnings growth, top managers believed stronger horizontal coordination was needed to keep the company successful and competitive. Today, frontline teams set up around core processes are the foundation of the organizational structure.

Leaders also recognized that stronger horizontal coordination was needed in the executive office, as well. Therefore, the position of general sales manager

cross-functional teams
Groups of employees from functional departments responsible for resolving mutual problems mutually.

permanent teams
Groups of employees who are permanently assigned to solve ongoing, mutual problems

was dropped, and those duties are now shared by seven senior executives. Each has a vertical responsibility, but each also "owns" a process that horizontally spans the organization—for example, client acquisition or account management. Although the organization retains some elements of a functional structure, emphasis is on horizontal collaboration and empowered teams, promoting better and faster communication within the company and with clients.[17] ∎

Many companies reorganize into permanent teams after going through a process called **reengineering.** Reengineering is the radical redesign of business processes to achieve dramatic improvements in cost, quality, service, and speed. Because the focus is on process rather than function, reengineering often leads to a shift away from a vertical structure to one emphasizing teamwork and empowerment.[18]

At Hallmark, reengineering led to a new team approach to greeting-card development. Hallmark used to be organized by functional departments and designed cards in a step-by-step process. Because of delays and rework, it sometimes took the company more than two years to produce a new card. Today, teams of artists, lithographers, writers, designers, and photographers work together, each empowered to develop and make decisions about cards for a particular holiday. Thanks to the power of teams, cycle time for getting new cards to market has been cut in half.[19]

The advantages and disadvantages of the team structure are summarized in Exhibit 7.4. Teams and reengineering are also important

concepts in structural design, which will be discussed later in the chapter.

NETWORK APPROACH

The most recent approach to departmentalization extends the idea of horizontal coordination and collaboration beyond the boundaries of the organization. The **network structure** means that the firm subcontracts many of its major functions to separate companies and coordinates their activities from a small headquarters organization.[20] The organization may be viewed as a central hub surrounded by a network of outside specialists. Rather than being housed under one roof, services such as accounting, design, manufacturing, and distribution are outsourced to separate organizations that are connected electronically to the central office.[21] The nature of the network structure means that subcontractors flow into and out of the system when needed. Much like building blocks, parts of the network can be added or taken away to meet changing needs.[22] A further development of the network is the virtual network organization, which is a continually evolving group of companies that unite temporarily to exploit specific opportunities or attain strategic advantages and then disband when objectives are met.[23] Data and information are shared electronically among participating companies. Unlike the network structure, in which the hub organization maintains control over work done by various subcontractors, in a virtual organization each independent company gives up some control to temporarily become part of a new, larger organizational system.

reengineering
Radically redesigning business processes to achieve dramatic improvements in cost, quality, service, and speed

network structure
An organization structure in which major functions are outsourced to discrete organizations and activities are coordinated by a central headquarters

Advantages	Disadvantages
• Some advantages of functional structure	• Dual loyalties and conflict
• Reduced barriers among departments, increased compromise	• Time and resources spent on meetings
• Less response time, quicker decisions	• Unplanned decentralization
• Better morale, enthusiasm from employee involvement	
• Reduced administrative overhead	

E x h i b i t 7.4
ADVANTAGES AND DISADVANTAGES OF TEAM STRUCTURE

The network approach makes it difficult to answer the question "Where is the organization?" A firm may contract out for expensive services such as training, transportation, legal, and engineering, and those functions will no longer be part of the organization. Today, a piece of ice hockey equipment may be designed in Scandinavia, engineered in the United States, manufactured in Korea, and distributed in Canada by a Japanese sales organization. These pieces are drawn together contractually and coordinated electronically, creating a new form of organization.

The network approach allows companies to concentrate on what they do best and outsource the rest. Nike, Reebok, and others have succeeded by focusing on their core strengths in design and marketing and contracting all their footwear manufacturing to outside suppliers. Computer firms such as Dell, Gateway, and CompuAdd either purchase their products ready-made or buy all the parts and handle only the final assembly. Sun Microsystems relies so heavily on outside manufacturers and distributors that its own employees never touch one of its computers.[24] Another computer firm thriving with a network approach is Monorail, described in Leading the Revolution: The Learning Organization.

Small entrepreneurial firms find they can save money and reach a larger market for their products by using outside manufacturers and distributors. For example, Tomima Edmark built TopsyTail, Inc. into an $80 million company with only two full-time employees. TopsyTail's production partners include a toolmaker, two injection molders, a package designer, a logo designer, freelance photographers, and a printer. The company also outsources packaging and shipping to three fulfillment houses, television commercials to a video production company, customer mailings to a mailing list firm, and publicity to a public relations firm. Four distributing companies sell TopsyTail products in the United States, Canada, Mexico, the Pacific Rim, Europe, and South Africa.[25]

ADVANTAGES AND DISADVANTAGES   The biggest advantage to the network structure seems to be competitiveness on a global scale.

Network organizations, even small ones, can be truly global. A network organization can draw on resources worldwide to achieve the best quality and price and can sell its products and services worldwide. A second advantage is workforce flexibility and challenge. Flexibility comes from the ability to hire whatever services are needed, such as engineering design or maintenance, and to change a few months later without constraints from owning plant, equipment, and facilities. The organization can continually redefine itself to fit new product and market opportunities. For those employees who are a permanent part of the organization, the challenge comes from greater job variety and job satisfaction from working within the lean structure. Finally, this structure is perhaps the leanest of all organization forms because little supervision is required. Large teams of staff specialists and administrators are not needed. A network organization may have only two or three levels of hierarchy compared with 10 or more in traditional organizations.[26]

One of the major disadvantages is lack of hands-on control.[27] Managers do not have all operations under one roof and must rely on contracts, coordination, negotiation, and electronic messages to hold things together. A problem of equal importance is the possibility of losing an organizational part. If a subcontractor fails to deliver, goes out of business, or has a plant burn down, the headquarters organization can be put out of business. Uncertainty is higher because necessary services are not under one roof and under direct management control. Finally, in this type of organization, employee loyalty can weaken. Employees may feel they can be replaced by contract services. Turnover increases because the emotional commitment between organization and employee is weak. The reality is that with changing products and markets, the organization sometimes needs to reshuffle its employees to meet goals.

THE HORIZONTAL ORGANIZATION

Many companies are recognizing that traditional vertical organization structures are ineffective in today's fast-shifting environment. Managers are working to transform their orga-

Monorail, Inc., a fast-growing startup based in Marietta, Georgia, is succeeding in a competitive industry based on the strength of partnerships. The company has no factories, no warehouses, no credit department, and no help desks or call centers. Yet it is already the 14th leading manufacturer of desktop PCs and is growing at a rate of 50 percent per quarter. Monorail concentrates on product design and marketing and outsources everything else to other organizations. The company was one of the first to offer a computer for less than $1,000, and has designed a remarkably compact PC that takes up only 20 percent of the desk space occupied by a traditional computer.

Monorail founders Doug Johns, David Hocker, and Nicholas Forlenza (all former Compaq managers) point out that relationships are the glue that holds their organization together. Consider how a typical Monorail transaction works. Retailer CompUSA orders a Monorail PC. The order is transmitted electronically through FedEx Logistics Services to one of Monorail's many contract manufacturers. The manufacturer assembles the PC from an inventory of Monorail parts and ships it via FedEx directly to the CompUSA outlet. Meanwhile, FedEx wires an invoice to SunTrust Bank in Atlanta, whose factoring department handles billing and credit approvals for Monorail. Monorail receives payment from Sun-Trust, which assumes the risk of collecting the funds from CompUSA. Whenever Monorail customers need technical help, they call a service center that is staffed and run by Sykes Enterprises, Inc., a call-center outsourcing company based in Tampa, Florida. There are only two things Monorail founders believe they can't outsource: world-class management expertise and a knack for partnerships. Monorail's business model depends on seamless integration with its two major partners, FedEx and SunTrust, which play a central role in Monorail's operations. In fact, the unique design feature of Monorail's product line—the compact dimensions of its PC—grew directly out of learning brought about by its partnership with FedEx. Monorail's founders wanted to design a PC that could fit easily into a standard FedEx box.

By using the network approach, Monorail has managed to be one of the leanest and meanest companies in the computer industry. When Doug Johns left Compaq, he was managing six million square feet of warehouse and office space. Now, at Monorail, his 50 employees work on a single leased floor of an office building near Atlanta. "We've got the shortest supply lines in the world," he says.

www.monorail.com

SOURCES: Heath Row, "This 'Virtual' Company is for Real," *Fast Company*, December–January, 1998, pp. 48–50; and Evan Ramstad, "A PC Maker's Low-Tech Formula: Start with the Box," *The Wall Street Journal*, December 29, 1997, pp. B1, B8.

nizations into more flexible systems that emphasize rapid response and customer focus. In general, the trend is toward breaking down barriers between departments, and many companies are moving toward horizontal structures based on work processes rather than departmental functions.[28] Regardless of the type of structure, all organizations need mechanisms for horizontal coordination.

THE NEED FOR COORDINATION

As organizations grow and evolve, two things happen. First, new positions and departments are added to deal with factors in the external environment or with new strategic needs. Raytheon established a new-products center to facilitate innovation in its various divisions. Korbel Champagne Cellars created a Department of Romance, Weddings, and Entertaining to enhance the linkage between romance and champagne consumption among potential customers. Exhibit 7.5 shows an ad for Korbel's Director of Romance that generated more than 800 applications.[29] CIOs may be brought in to manage the growing amount of technology-based information and help seize new competitive advantages. As companies add positions and departments to meet changing needs, they grow more complex, with hundreds of positions and departments performing incredibly diverse activities.

Second, senior managers have to find a way to tie all of these departments together. The formal chain of command and the supervision it provides is effective, but it is not enough. The organization needs systems to process information and enable communication among people in different departments and at different levels. Coordination refers to the high quality of collaboration across departments. Without coordination, a company's left hand

DIRECTOR OF ROMANCE

Korbel Champagne Cellars, California-based producer of America's best-selling premium champagne, seeks dynamic individual for one-of-a-kind corporate position as Director of Romance for the winery's Department of Romance, Weddings & Entertaining. Position involves:
- reporting to media on lighthearted romance surveys commissioned by Korbel
- researching the latest news and information on the romance front
- writing articles on romance-related subjects
- appearing on television and radio programs to discuss the subject of romance

Ideal candidate will have published books or articles on the subject of romance, possess a degree in a related field such as psychology and/or personify romance in some highly visible or glamorous way. Previous media experience preferred. Individuals and spokesperson search firm applicants welcome. No phone calls please. An equal opportunity employer. Send resume to:

FRANK DE FALCO
KORBEL CHAMPAGNE CELLARS
13250 RIVER ROAD
GUERNEVILLE, CA 95446

SOURCE: Courtesy of Korbel Champagne Cellars.

will not act in concert with the right hand, causing problems and conflicts. Coordination is required regardless of whether the organization has a functional, divisional, or team structure. Employees identify with their immediate department or team, taking its interest to heart, and may not want to compromise with other units for the good of the organization as a whole.

Without a major effort at coordination, an organization may be like Chrysler Corporation when Lee Iacocca took over:

What I found at Chrysler were 35 vice presidents, each with his own turf. . . . I couldn't believe, for example, that the guy running engineering departments wasn't in constant touch with his counterpart in manufacturing. But that's how it was. Everybody worked independently. I took one look at that system and I almost threw up. That's when I knew I was in really deep trouble.

I'd call in a guy from engineering, and he'd stand there dumbfounded when I'd explain to him that we had a design problem or some other hitch in the engineering-manufacturing relation-

ship. He might have the ability to invent a brilliant piece of engineering that would save us a lot of money. He might come up with a terrific new design. There was only one problem: He didn't know that the manufacturing people couldn't build it. Why? Because he had never talked to them about it. Nobody at Chrysler seemed to understand that interaction among the different functions in a company is absolutely critical. People in engineering and manufacturing almost have to be sleeping together. These guys weren't even flirting![30] ■

If one thing changed at Chrysler in the years before Iacocca retired, it was improved coordination. Cooperation among engineering, marketing, and manufacturing enabled the design and production of the stunning line of new LH automobiles in only three years, compared with the five years of development previously required.

In the international arena, coordination is especially important. How can managers ensure that needed coordination will take place in their company, both domestically and globally? Coordination is the outcome of

Exhibit 7.6
EVOLUTION OF ORGANIZATION STRUCTURES

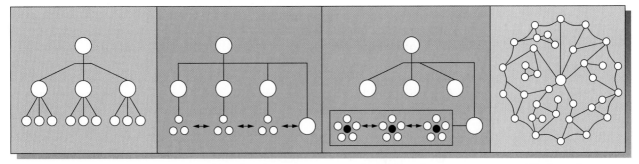

| Traditional Vertical Structure | Teams and Project Managers for Horizontal Coordination | Reengineering to Horizontal Processes | The Learning Organization |

information and cooperation. Managers can design systems and structures to promote horizontal coordination. Exhibit 7.6 illustrates the evolution of organizational structures, with a growing emphasis on horizontal coordination and communication.

The vertical **functional structure** began nearly a century ago and was the first to be widely used by large organizations. Although the structure is effective in stable environments, it does not provide the horizontal coordination needed in times of rapid change. Innovations such as teams, task forces, and project managers work within the vertical structure but provide a means to increase cross-functional communication and cooperation. The next stage involves reengineering to structure the organization around horizontal processes rather than vertical functions. The vertical hierarchy is flattened, with perhaps only a few senior executives in traditional support functions such as finance and human resources. Some organizations have taken a further step to the learning organization, doing away with all vestiges of an organizational hierarchy. Internet startup USWeb eliminated a great deal of hierarchy when it bought out other companies, choosing instead to let them operate as affiliates, as described below.

USWEB

Web design shop USWeb's strategy for success has been to buy other similar companies, realizing that Web designing is becoming more complicated all the time. A single vendor now needs to be able to do everything from nuts-and-bolts design to strategy implementation, offering assistance with marketing, technology, and branding. So, three-year-old USWeb went on a buying spree and acquired 1,200 employees in 44 locations and structured itself loosely, with the various locations being run not as tightly controlled divisions, but as affiliates.

Sometimes the site gets its own work. Other times, each affiliate is given work from the parent company's clients, according to the competencies of that affiliate, which then bills the client and passes along a percentage to the parent. Co-founder Sheldon Laube says, "If you hire an entire company, you buy teams of people that already know how to work together." USWeb relies on a sophisticated information system to keep every employee and teams competencies up to date on the database. "The system allows you to find out the expertise of any staff member anywhere in the world," states Laube.

Laube got practice with startups in college, when he launched several small businesses. Now he has a company that in a mere 1000 days has grown to $73 million in revenues. But how does he

functional structure
An organization structure in which positions are grouped into departments based on similar skills, expertise, and resource use

prevent this seemingly unwieldy setup to deteriorate into competing fiefdoms? By offering a strong shared structure—one name, network, and training program—while allowing each affiliate wide entrepreneurial latitude to respond to any business opportunity. Compensation favors the company's goal of collaboration. Any office that lands and services a client and uses another location gets to keep a larger percentage.

Lest you think these young entrepreneurs are happy with their success, here's their long-term goal: to become the General Electric of the Internet.[31] ■

TASK FORCES, TEAMS, AND PROJECT MANAGEMENT

When task forces (temporary team) and other teams work cooperatively, new-product projects sail smoothly through the design and development cycle.[32] To facilitate this, companies will use project managers to increase coordination between functional departments. A **project manager** is a person who is responsible for coordinating the activities of several departments for the completion of a specific project and will typically work on several projects at the same time.[33] The person is generally assigned on a full-time basis to achieve desired outcomes on products or projects, or both. The project manager position may have any number of titles (e.g., product manager, program manager, or branch manager), but a

project manager
A person responsible for coordinating the activities of several departments for the completion of a specific project

distinctive feature of the role is that the project manager is not a member of one of the departments being coordinated.

General Mills, Procter & Gamble, and General Foods all use product managers to coordinate their product lines. A manager is assigned to each line, such as Cheerios, Bisquick, and Hamburger Helper. Product managers set budget goals, marketing targets, and strategies and coordinates the participation of advertising, production, and sales personnel to implement the product strategy.

In some organizations, project managers are included on the organization chart, as illustrated in Exhibit 7.7. The project manager is drawn to one side of the chart to indicate authority over the project but not over the people assigned to it. Dashed lines to the project manager indicate responsibility for coordination and communication with assigned team members, but department managers retain line authority over functional employees.

TRADITIONAL VERSUS LEARNING ORGANIZATIONS

Recall that the purpose of structure is to organize resources to accomplish organizational goals. Elements of structure such as chain of command, centralization/decentralization, formal authority, teams, and coordination devices fit together to form an overall structural approach. In some organizations, the formal, vertical hierarchy is emphasized as the way to achieve control and coordination. In other

Exhibit 7.7

EXAMPLE OF PROJECT MANAGER RELATIONSHIPS TO OTHER DEPARTMENTS

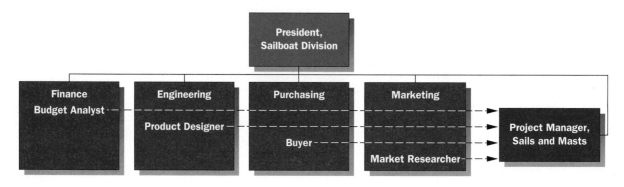

organizations, decision making is decentralized, cross-functional teams are implemented, and employees are given great freedom to pursue their tasks as they see fit.

The increasing shift toward more horizontal versus vertical structures reflects the trend toward greater employee empowerment, broad information sharing, and decentralized decision making. At the apex of this movement is a type of organization called the **learning organization.** Although there is no single view of what the learning organization looks like or operates like, it is an organization in which everyone is engaged in identifying and solving problems, which enables the company to continuously experiment, improve, and increase its ability to grow, learn, and achieve its goals. It is an attitude or philosophy about what an organization can become. Exhibit 7.8 compares characteristics of the learning organization with the traditional vertical organization.

In the traditional organization, the vertical structure predominates, with few task forces, teams, or project managers for horizontal coordination. Information is formally communicated up and down the organizational hierarchy and is not widely shared. In addition, jobs are broken down into narrow, specialized tasks, and employees generally have little say

over how they do their work. The culture is rigid and does not encourage risk taking and change, and decision making is centralized. At the opposite end of the scale is the learning organization. Everyone is actively engaged in identifying and solving problems and enabling the organization to continuously experiment, change, and improve, thus increasing its capacity to grow, learn, and achieve its purpose. The learning organization is characterized by a horizontal team-based structure, open information, decentralized decision making, empowered employees, and a strong adaptive culture.

TEAM-BASED STRUCTURE   In the learning organization, the vertical structure that created distance between the top and bottom of the organization is disbanded. Self-directed teams are a fundamental unit; made up of employees with different skills who rotate jobs to produce an entire product or service, and deal directly with customers, making changes and improvements as needed. Team members have the authority to make decisions about new ways of doing things. In learning organizations, bosses are practically eliminated, with team members taking responsibility for training, safety, scheduling vacations, and decisions about

learning organization
One in which everyone is engaged in identifying and solving problems, enabling the company to continuously experiment, improve, and increase its ability to grow, learn, and achieve its goals

E x h i b i t 7.8

Differences in Traditional versus Learning Organizations

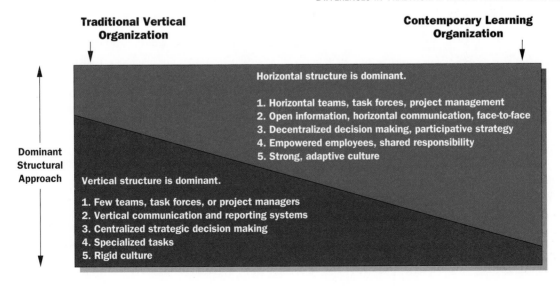

TECHNOLOGY FOR TOMORROW
THE STARTUP ECONOMY

Get ready to download "Tech Startup Legend 3.0" and change your attitude on what it takes to get a technology or Internet company going these days. Gone are the days when pimply faced college dropout geeks (such as Bill Gates) or other misfits (such as Steve Jobs) could work in their garages and change an entire industry and turn themselves into moguls of billion-dollar enterprises. Because the Internet spawned three new driving forces—a rising tide of capital, new platforms, and unbridled opportunity—the success formula of the 21st century entrepreneur is quite different. Breakthrough capabilities in commerce and communications are available through Internet-based platforms, the Web, MP# technology, and XML (Extensible Markup Language).

The new entrepreneurs are more like Jeff Bezos and Michael Dell, who both are now revered as cultural icons of the Internet society. Dell scoured the country for locations for a new factory, ending up with six possible sites. After talks with local officials, Dell told them they had 10 days to come up with a package. Most locations balked, saying it would take six or more months to get approvals from city councils, zoning boards, and so on. Dell's response: If you can't do it in 10 days, we don't want to be there. We are a fast company and need a fast city to help us respond to environmental changes. Nashville, Tennessee, won and the factory was up and running in 90 days.

So what's the magic for success in the startup economy? Six components: people, innovation, focus, customer choice, speed, and equity.

1. PEOPLE. After all the patent filings, venture capital, media coverage—and after nearly everything in sight has been marginalized—one thing left sacred and necessary is original thought and human intuition. Why is it that Jeff Bezos, a refugee from Wall Street, could command more market presence than giant Barnes & Noble? Or why did the two Stanford graduate students who started Yahoo! best the attempts of media conglomerate Time Warner's attempt to dominate the Internet? Because the best Internet startups have the best people, which includes employees, partners, and customers. So, first priority is to hire the best. Drugstore.com spent most of its startup time not on getting the best Web site, but on hiring the best people. Several Internet companies—Excite, CNET, TicketmasterOnline—were in serious trouble but had teams able to move them to a new level. Those teams also can help negotiate relationships with partners and go after the large customer base needed to succeed.

2. INNOVATION. Too many entrepreneurs fall into a common trap: put an e-commerce storefront on the same old business. In the startup economy the rule is: *different* not just *digital*. For example, Dell created a new business paradigm, building up e-commerce-oriented sales and customer service processes. But Compaq did more of what it had done off-line. Pre-Internet startups tended to be about technological innovation, while post-Internet startups are more about the *application* of the technology. Amazon is not merely a bookseller, though it seemed that way at first. Through endless networking, partnerships, and joint ventures, it has created a new kind of retailer. In the old way, you might think of a new business process, or mull over whether to lower prices. In e-commerce, you have no cushion left to decide. If you think about it and you can, well, then you *must.* Or someone else will.

3. FOCUS. Before, the focus might have been what you sell. Now it is the experience of the customer. Though perfecting the one-click order and intuitive topic-related searches (every book you look at has a list of other similar books, and you can keep clicking indefinitely), Amazon's focus is "customer ecstasy."

4. CUSTOMER CHOICE. While sites devoted to one manufacturer only (such as Sony's CD site) languish, Web sites like compare.com and Cdnow.com let consumers choose from the best selections and prices—and that is why they are successful. Dell and Gateway do so well because they let the customer order *exactly* what they want and have it delivered almost immediately, rather than relying on choices of what is in stock already or waiting months to order something different.

5. SPEED. If you're not first with a new product or technological application, then you must spend your time explaining what you do. A good team can compete in the global marketplace and look for the "lowest viscosity" market opportunities and partners. Look for leverage. When things can change completely on the Web in six months, it doesn't make sense to spend three months negotiating a complicated contract with a partner or vendor. And don't make the common mistake of assuming you know what the customer wants. Get feedback and then move—fast. Speed wins.

6. EQUITY. Stock ownership motivates people to work hard and it also helps attract the best and the brightest. But startup stocks have the potential to increase exponentially.

Startups have become the *state* of business itself. And perhaps the greatest irony of the information economy is that *human initiative* has become the most potent force of all.

SOURCES: J. Neil Weintraut and Jeffrey Davis, "The Startup Economy," *Business 2.0,* July 1999, pp. 61–68; Joanna Ettinger, personal communication, November 1999; Gary Hamel and Jeff Sampler, "E-Corporation: Building a New Industrial Order," *Fortune,* Dec. 7, 1998, pp. 81–92.

work methods, pay and reward systems, and coordination with other teams.

The learning organization increases collaboration within and between organizations, such as virtual teams, alliances, and concepts such as the network organization. In Technology for Tomorrow, we see how Internet start-ups have influenced the way many companies are focusing on the way they organize, but particularly how important a high-performing team is.

OPEN INFORMATION In a learning organization, information is widely shared. To identify needs and solve problems, people have to be aware of what's going on. They must understand the whole organization as well as their part in it. Formal data about budgets, profits, and departmental expenses are available to everyone. This approach, called open-book management, allows every employee to look freely at the books and exchange information with anyone in the company. At PeopleSoft, everyone has access to all company information, including product development information and financial data. Employees have open access to all company databases as well as the ability to communicate electronically with any other person in the company.[34]

Electronic communication is essential to information sharing in today's learning organization. However, the learning organization also emphasizes the importance of getting people communicating face-to-face, with the emphasis on listening. Some companies are "dialoguing" to get people away from groups of 30 or 40 and communicating deeply and honestly. The concepts of open communication and information sharing will be discussed in greater detail later.

DECENTRALIZED DECISION MAKING AND PARTICIPATIVE STRATEGY In traditional organizations, decisions are passed up the hierarchy for approval. In a learning organization, the people closest to the problem are given the authority and responsibility for decision making. Because people at all levels are intimately involved in making decisions, this allows strategy to emerge bottom up as well as top down. In traditional vertical organizations,

top executives are responsible for strategy because only they have the big picture, knowledge, and expertise to direct the corporation. In the learning organization, leaders still influence overall vision and direction, but they do not control or direct strategy alone. Everyone helps. Information is gathered by employees who work directly with customers, suppliers, and other organizations. Perhaps thousands of people are in touch with the environment, providing data about external changes in technology and customer needs. They are the ones to identify needs and solutions, passing these ideas into the organization for discussion.[35]

Participative strategy relies on an experimental mind-set. People are encouraged to try new things, and failure is accepted. Problems and decisions are a series of learning opportunities. Ralph Stayer, CEO of Johnsonville Foods, did not make the decision to accept an invitation to make products to be sold under a grocery store chain's own label. He turned the decision over to employees, who met in teams for an entire day to investigate every aspect of this opportunity. The employees determined it would be beneficial to the company. In this example, they decided strategy. Strategy in learning organizations also may emerge from partnerships with suppliers, customers, and even competitors. Learning organizations have permeable boundaries and often are linked with other companies, giving each organization greater access to information about new strategic needs and directions.[36]

EMPOWERED EMPLOYEES AND SHARED RESPONSIBILITY Learning organizations empower employees to an extraordinary degree, giving them the authority and responsibility to use their own discretion and ability to achieve an outcome. **Empowerment** means delegating decision-making authority, freedom, knowledge, autonomy, and skills to subordinates, which is a fundamental principle of learning organizations. Rather than dividing jobs into rigidly defined, specialized tasks, learning organizations allow people the freedom and opportunity to react quickly to changing conditions. There are few rules and procedures, and knowledge and control of tasks are located with workers rather than top

empowerment
The delegation of decision-making authority, freedom, knowledge, autonomy, and skills to subordinates; a fundamental principle of learning organizations

managers. Individuals are encouraged to experiment, learn, and solve problems within the team. How do companies implement empowerment? It starts by promoting the decentralization of decision making and broader worker participation. There are very few rules for teams at SEI Investments. Teams have as few as two members or as many as 30, and the various teams are structured differently. The teams themselves make the decisions about what roles each worker plays, how the team will operate, when it's time to disband, and so forth. The company's CEO calls it "fluid leadership."[37]

In learning organizations, people are considered a primary source of strength, not a cost to be minimized. Firms that adopt this perspective often employ the following practices: Treat employees well. Provide employment security and good wages. Provide a sense of employee ownership by sharing gains in productivity and profits. Commit to education for growth and development for all members. Help employees become world-renowned experts. Cross-train to help people acquire multiple skills. Promote from within.[38]

STRONG, ADAPTIVE CULTURE   *Corporate culture* is the set of key values, beliefs, understandings, and norms shared by members of the organization. The culture is the foundation of a learning organization. The culture of a learning organization is strong and typically includes strong values in the following three areas:

1. *The whole is more important than the part*, and boundaries between parts are minimized.[39] People in the learning organization are aware of the whole system and how parts fit together, and information and ideas are openly shared. The move toward a "boundaryless organization" means reducing barriers among departments, divisions, and external organizations. The free flow of ideas and information allows coordinated action to occur in an uncertain and changing environment.

2. *The culture is egalitarian.* The culture of a learning organization creates a sense of community, compassion, and caring for one another. People count. Every person has value. The learning organization becomes a place for creating a web of relationships that nurtures and develops each person to his or her maximum potential. Executive perks such as private dining rooms or reserved parking spots are eliminated. Everyone gets the same amount of vacation regardless of position and may share in stock options or performance bonuses. This people-orientation provides safety for experimentation, frequent mistakes, and failures that enable learning. People are treated with respect and therefore tend to contribute their best to the company.

3. *The culture values improvement and adaptation.* A basic value is to question the status quo, the current way of doing things. Can we do this any better? Why do we do this job that way? Constant questioning of assumptions and challenging the status quo open the gates to creativity and improvement. The organization learns to do things faster and to improve everything on an ongoing basis. An adaptive culture means that people care about important stakeholders, including employees, customers, and stockholders. Managers pay close attention to stakeholders and initiate change when needed. The culture also celebrates and

In the past two years, over 300 software engineers have immigrated to Barbados from all over the world. Doug Mellinger, CEO of PRT, a custom-software engineering company, has created a high-tech nation, an *egalitarian culture* on a tropical island. Workers are provided with their own state-of-the-art computer platforms, and they work directly with managers who can teach and challenge them while working on projects considered "the good stuff." On the island, bills are paid for employees, transportation is free, and their savings pile up in the bank. Mellinger likes to say, "I don't want them to have to think about anything but having fun and writing killer code."

rewards the creators of new ideas, products, and work processes.

The learning organization is always moving forward. Although no company represents a perfect example of a learning organization, one excellent example is Chaparral Steel, which has been called a learning laboratory.

CHAPARRAL STEEL
www.chaparralsteel.com

The tenth-largest U.S. steel producer, Chaparral Steel has won international recognition for high quality and productivity. Chaparral produces 1,100 tons of steel each year compared to the U.S. average of 350 tons. Started nearly 20 years ago, it has become an experimental laboratory for the latest techniques of learning organizations.

What makes Chaparral so effective? Managers articulate a clear vision—to lead the world in the low-cost, safe production of high-quality steel—along with the cultural values of egalitarianism and respect for the individual. Everyone participates. Everyone is empowered to solve problems. When a cooling hose burst, a group of operators—a welder, a foreman, and a buyer—all responded because they saw the problem. There is no assumption that other people are expected to do a job. Since employees know the vision and values, supervisors do not micromanage. Chaparral has few supervisors, and only two levels of hierarchy separate the CEO from operators in the rolling mill.

Employees are rewarded for learning new skills and for performance. Ideas are contributed by just about everyone. Employees are paid a salary rather than an hourly wage—hence, everyone acts like an owner and a manager. People are also rewarded with bonuses from company profits, which are shared with everyone, including janitors and secretaries.

All employees contribute to sharing information and knowledge. A steel plant is deliberately held to fewer than 1,000 employees so that people can communicate easily. An employee experimenting with new equipment will tell other people how it works. Employees who visit a competitor's plant will explain to others what they learned. There are no staff people and no boundaries among departments because there are few departments. Everyone is considered a salesperson and is free to communicate with customers and potential customers. There is no research and development department because employees on the line are responsible for innovation in new techniques and products. To reinforce continuous learning, employees are encouraged to attend school, and many are teachers of other employees in formal classes. The culture values ideas that benefit the whole company rather than individual ownership of ideas, so new knowledge is shared liberally.

Experimentation is rampant. The cultural value is: If you have an idea, try it. First-level managers can authorize thousands of dollars for employee experiments. Everyone is encouraged to push beyond current knowledge. This involves risk, which is another cultural value. Employees tolerate, even welcome, risk on a production line that is very expensive to shut down.

Strategy emerges from employee contacts outside the organization. Employees travel constantly, scanning for new ideas at trade shows and other companies. Teams of employees that include vice presidents and shop people travel together to investigate a new technology.

Chaparral is so good at what it does that it welcomes competitors to visit the plant. A competitor can be shown everything Chaparral does and yet take away nothing, because a learning organization is created by leadership, culture, and empowered people. Most other steelmakers have been unable to achieve this, because they don't have the commitment or the vision.[40] ∎

Chaparral Steel is becoming a true learning organization. The leadership provides a flat, team-based design, a shared vision, and an attitude of serving employees. The culture stresses egalitarian values, providing support for risk taking. There are no boundaries separating departments. People are empowered to the point where no one has to take orders if he or she feels the order is wrong. The strategy emerges through the experiences of employees who work with customers and new technologies. Chaparral is flooded with information from experiments and travel, which is liberally shared.

FACTORS AFFECTING STRUCTURE

How do managers know whether to design a structure that emphasizes the formal, vertical hierarchy or one with an emphasis on horizontal communication and collaboration? The answer lies in the contingency factors that influence organization structure. Recall from Chapter 1 that contingency pertains to those factors on which structure depends. Research on organization structure shows that the emphasis given to a rigid or flexible structure depends on the contingency factors of strategy, environment, and production technology. The right structure is designed to "fit" the contingency factors as illustrated in Exhibit 7.9. Let us look at the relationship between each contingency factor and organization structure in more detail to see how structure should be designed.

CONTINGENCY FACTOR: STRATEGIC GOALS
There are several strategies that business firms adopt. Two strategies are differentiation and cost leadership.[41] With a differentiation strategy, the organization attempts to develop innovative products unique to the market. With a cost leadership strategy, the organization strives for internal efficiency. The strategies of cost leadership versus differentiation typically require different structural approaches, so managers try to pick strategies and structures that are congruent.

Exhibit 7.10 shows a simplified continuum that illustrates how structural approaches are associated with strategic goals. The pure functional structure is appropriate for achieving internal efficiency goals. The vertical functional structure uses task specialization and a strict chain of command to gain efficient use of scarce resources, but it does not enable the organization to be flexible or innovative. In contrast, the learning organization is appropriate when the primary goal is innovation and flexibility. Each team is small, is able to be responsive, and has the people and resources necessary for performing its task. The flexible horizontal structure enables organizations to differentiate themselves and respond quickly to the demands of a shifting environment but at the expense of efficient resource use. Changing strategy and environmental conditions also shape structure in government organizations. For example, under financial pressure to cut costs and political pressure to keep customers happy, Departments of Motor Vehicles in some states farm out DMV business whenever possible, moving toward a network structure. In Illinois and Oregon, auto dealers register new cars on site when they're sold.[42] See the following example for how Lands' End online learned to structure itself according to its strategy of better-quality customer service.

Exhibit 7.9

CONTINGENCY FACTORS THAT INFLUENCE ORGANIZATION STRUCTURE

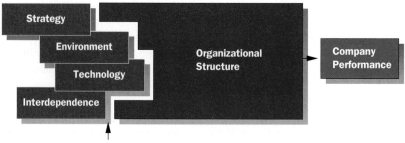

Contingency Factors

The right mix of vertical/horizontal structure fits the contingency factors.

RELATIONSHIP OF STRATEGIC GOALS TO STRUCTURAL APPROACH

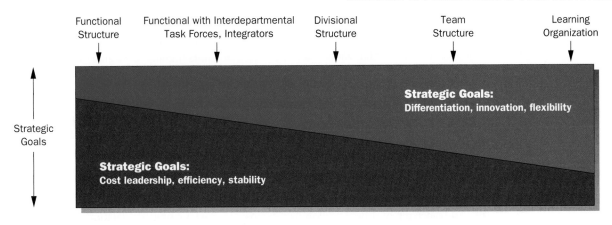

LANDS' END

www.landsend.com

Why don't more people buy clothes online? How many women, for instance, would buy a swimsuit off the Internet? Most want to see what it looks like on *their* particular body, not the model's perfect body, right? One company has figured out a creative way to solve this problem.

The real innovation in clothing online has come not from Silicon Valley, but from a small town in the midwest. Dodgeville, Wisconsin, is home to catalog-retailer Lands' End, which sells more clothing online than anyone else. By the end of 1999, Lands' End had doubled its Internet sales, to 10 percent of its total sales.

What Lands' End has done is realize the power of Web sites. Rather than having a digital version of their normal catalog, as most online retailers seem to, Lands' End makes use of the computer age by letting visitors assemble outfits. Men can see how various combinations of clothing look, both casual or dressy, while the Oxford Express offers hundreds of dress-shirt options. Women can create their own figure with a 3-D model builder that lets them see what a partic-ular swim suit, dress, or slacks would look like on their own body. More than 100,000 women built models in the first six months.

At any time, shoppers can click and connect to a live customer-service rep, either on phone or online. In 1999, about 27,000 visitors sent e-mails to its "Specialty Shoppers" mailbox. Within three hours, each question gets a personalized response.

What makes Lands' End so unique is how they use the Internet to continue designing their business to be customer-focused. They were an early innovator in mail order, with other companies regularly visiting the difficult-to-reach northern Wisconsin location to benchmark their own business processes of order taking and fulfillment.

And while other sites may give you a digital busy signal and not download when they are swamped, Lands' End even manages to fully operate its total customer services during the peak Christmas season, when it sometimes gets 10,000 visits an hour. It may not be from the Silicon valley geeks, but it still shows the power of innovation and competence, in both customer service and organization structure.[43] ∎

Exhibit 7.10 also illustrates how other forms of structure—decentralized with horizontal coordination, divisional, and team—represent intermediate steps on the organization's path to efficiency and/or innovation. The functional structure with horizontal teams and integrating managers provides greater coordination and flexibility than the pure functional structure. The **divisional structure** promotes differentiation because each division can focus on specific products and customers, although divisions tend to be larger and less flexible than small teams. Exhibit 7.10 does not include all possible structures, but it illustrates how structures can be used to facilitate the strategic goals of cost leadership or differentiation. For example, Polaroid changed its structure as it changed its strategy.

POLAROID

www.polaroid.com

Polaroid president I. M. Booth used a scale similar to the one in Exhibit 7.10 to describe his efforts to tear down internal barriers, decentralize decisions, and achieve coordination across functional departments. He defined a structural scale of 1 to 10. A 10 is a structure made up of autonomous teams, each with its own marketing, engineering, and management people. A 1 is a totally functional structure, with a single manufacturing division for the whole company, a single marketing division, and so on. Booth claims that Polaroid was a 1 for many years. Its departments were uncoordinated, and little things were being neglected. Booth's goal was to break up Polaroid's vertical functional structure by creating separate divisions for three businesses: magnetics, consumer products, and industrial photography products. Booth felt that the right amount of flexibility and innovation would put Polaroid at a 6 or 7 on the structural scale, and he planned to continue pushing until it neared the high end of the scale.[44] ■

divisional structure
An organization structure in which departments are grouped based on similar organizational outputs

CONTINGENCY FACTOR: THE ENVIRONMENT
Environmental uncertainty means that decision makers have difficulty acquiring good information and predicting external changes. Uncertainty occurs when the external environment is rapidly changing and complex. An uncertain environment causes three things to happen within an organization.

1. Increased differences occur among departments.
2. The organization needs increased coordination to keep departments working together.
3. The organization must adapt to change.

The contingency relationship between environmental uncertainty and structural approach is illustrated in Exhibit 7.11. When the external environment is more stable, the organization should have a traditional structure that emphasizes vertical control. There is little need for change, flexibility, or intense coordination. The structure can emphasize specialization, centralized decision making, and wide spans of control. When environmental uncertainty is high, a horizontal structure that emphasizes lateral relationships such as teams and task forces is appropriate. Vertical structure characteristics such as specialization, centralization, and formalized procedures should be downplayed. In an uncertain environment, the organization figures things out as it goes along, departments must cooperate, and decisions should be decentralized to the teams and task forces working on specific problems.

CONTINGENCY FACTOR: MANUFACTURING AND SERVICE TECHNOLOGIES
Technology includes the knowledge, tools, techniques, and activities used to transform organizational inputs into outputs.[45] Technology includes machinery, employee skills, and work procedures. A useful way to think about technology is as "work flow." The production work flow may be to produce steel castings, television programs, or computer software.

Production technology is significant because it has direct influence on the organization structure. Structure must be designed to fit the technology as well as to accommodate the external environment. Technologies vary

STRUCTURE

	Vertical	Horizontal
ENVIRONMENT Uncertain (Unstable)	**Incorrect Fit:** Vertical structure in uncertain environment **Structure too tight**	**Correct Fit:** Horizontal structure in uncertain environment
Certain (Stable)	**Correct Fit:** Vertical structure in certain environment	**Incorrect Fit:** Horizontal structure in certain environment **Structure too loose**

between manufacturing and service organizations. In the following paragraphs, we discuss each characteristic of technology and the structure that best fits it.

WOODWARD'S MANUFACTURING TECHNOLOGY

The most influential research into the relationship between manufacturing technology and organization structure was conducted by Joan Woodward, a British industrial sociologist.[46] She gathered data from 100 British firms to determine whether basic structural characteristics, such as administrative overhead, span of control, centralization, and **formalization,** were different across firms. She found that manufacturing firms could be categorized according to three basic types of work flow technology:

1. *Small batch and unit production.* Small batch production firms produce goods in batches of one or a few products designed to customer specification. Each customer orders a unique product. This technology also is used to make large, one-of-a-kind products, such as computer-controlled machines. Small batch manufacturing is close to traditional skilled-craft work, because human beings are a large part of the process; they run machines to make the product. Examples of items produced through small batch manufacturing include custom clothing, special-order machine tools, space capsules, satellites, and submarines.

2. *Large batch and mass production.* Mass production technology is distinguished by standardized production runs. A large volume of products is produced, and all customers receive the same product. Standard products go into inventory for sale as customers need them. This technology makes greater use of machines than does small batch production. Machines are designed to do most of the physical work, and employees complement the machinery. Examples of mass production are automobile assembly lines and the large batch techniques used to produce computers, tobacco products, and textiles.

3. *Continuous process production.* In continuous process production, the entire work flow is mechanized. This is the most sophisticated and complex form of production technology. Because the process runs continuously, there is no starting and stopping. Human operators are not part of actual production because machinery does all of the work. Human operators simply read dials, fix machines that break down, and manage the production process. Examples of continuous process technologies are chemical plants, distilleries, petroleum refineries, and nuclear power plants.

The difference among the three manufacturing technologies is called technical complexity. **Technical complexity** means the degree to which machinery is involved in the production to the exclusion of people. With a

formalization
The written documentation used to direct and control employees

technical complexity
The degree to which machinery is involved in the production to the exclusion of people

complex technology, employees are hardly needed except to monitor the machines.

The structural characteristics associated with each type of manufacturing technology are illustrated in Exhibit 7.12. Note that formalization and centralization are high for mass production technology and low for continuous process. Unlike small batch and continuous process, standardized mass production machinery requires centralized decision making and well-defined rules and procedures. The administrative ratio and the percentage of indirect labor required also increase with technological complexity. Because the production process is nonroutine, closer supervision is needed. More indirect labor in the form of maintenance people is required because of the machinery's complexity; thus, the indirect/direct labor ratio is high. Span of control for first-line supervisors is greatest for mass production. On an assembly line, jobs are so routinized that a supervisor can handle an average of 48 employees. The number of employees per supervisor in small batch and continuous process production is lower because closer supervision is needed. Overall, small batch and continuous process firms have somewhat loose, flexible structures, and mass production firms have tight, vertical structures.

The important conclusion about manufacturing technology was described by Woodward as follows: "Different technologies impose different kinds of demands on individuals and organizations, and these demands have to be met through an appropriate structure."[47] Woodward found that the relationship between structure and technology was directly related to company performance. Low-performing firms tended to deviate from the preferred structural form, often adopting a structure appropriate for another type of technology.

FLEXIBLE MANUFACTURING   The most recent development in manufacturing technology is called flexible manufacturing, which uses computers to automate and integrate manufacturing components such as robots, machines, product design, and engineering analysis. Companies such as Deere, General Motors, Intel, and Illinois Tool Works use flexible manufacturing in a single manufacturing plant to do small batch and mass production operations at the same time. Bar codes enable machines to make instantaneous changes—such as putting a larger screw in a different location—as different batches flow down the automated assembly line. Sunrise Medical uses flexible manufacturing to make wheelchairs tailored to an individual customer's exact specifications.[48] Taken to its ultimate, flexible manufacturing allows for mass customization, producing products in large batches but with each product tailored to customer specification. Levi Strauss

Exhibit 7.12

RELATIONSHIP BETWEEN MANUFACTURING TECHNOLOGY AND ORGANIZATION STRUCTURE

	Manufacturing Technology		
	Small Batch	Mass Production	Continuous Process
Technical Complexity of Production Technology	Low	Medium	High
Organization structure:			
Formalization	Low	High	Low
Centralization	Low	High	Low
Top administrator ratio	Low	Medium	High
Indirect/direct labor ratio	1/9	1/4	1/1
Supervisor span of control	23	48	15
Communication:			
Written (vertical)	Low	High	Low
Verbal (horizontal)	High	Low	High
Overall structure	Flexible	Rigid	Flexible

SOURCE: Based on Joan Woodward, *Industrial Organizations: Theory and Practice* (Longon: Oxford University Press, 1965).

has experimented with mass producing custom-made jeans through its Personal Pair program. At Custom Foot stores, customers browse through the store, mixing and matching design components such as style, color, and leather type. A high-tech electronic scanner measures the customer's foot, and the complete order is zapped by modem to Custom Foot's headquarters in Florence, Italy. Shoes generally are ready in about three weeks and often cost slightly less than many premium brands sold off the shelf.[49] Flexible manufacturing and mass customization are considered to be at a higher level of technical complexity than the three manufacturing technologies studied by Woodward. The structures associated with the new technology tend to have few rules, decentralization, a small ratio of administrators to workers, face-to-face horizontal communication, and a team-oriented, flexible approach.[50]

SERVICE TECHNOLOGY   Service organizations are becoming increasingly important in North America. Since 1982, more employees have been employed in service organizations than in manufacturing organizations. Thus, new research has been undertaken to understand the structural characteristics of service organizations. Service technology can be defined as follows:

1. *Intangible output.* The output of a service firm is intangible. Services are perishable and, unlike physical products, cannot be stored in inventory. The service is either consumed immediately or lost forever. Manufactured products are produced at one point in time and can be stored until sold at another time.

2. *Direct contact with customers.* Employees and customers interact directly to provide and purchase the service. Production and consumption are simultaneous. Service firm employees have direct contact with customers. In a manufacturing firm, technical employees are separated from customers, and hence no direct interactions occur.[51]

The output of service organizations is frequently intangible; that of manufacturing organizations is tangible. Examples of service firms include consulting companies, law firms,

brokerage houses, airlines, hotels, advertising firms, public relations firms, amusement parks, and educational organizations. Service technology also characterizes many departments in large corporations, even manufacturing firms. In a manufacturing organization such as Ford Motor Company, the legal, human resources, finance, and market research departments provide service. Thus, the structure and design of each of these departments reflect its own service technology rather than the manufacturing plant's technology. Service technology concepts therefore can be used to structure both service organizations and the many large service departments within manufacturing organizations.

One distinct feature of service technology that directly influences structure is the need for employees to be close to the customer.[52] Structural characteristics are similar to those for continuous manufacturing technology. Service firms tend to be flexible, informal, and decentralized. Horizontal communication is high because employees must share information and resources to serve customers and solve problems. Some Taco Bell restaurants operate with no manager on the premises. Self-directed teams manage inventory, schedule work, order supplies, and train new employees. Services also are dispersed; hence each unit is often small and located geographically close to customers. For example, banks, hotels, fast-food franchises, and physician's offices disperse their facilities into regional and local offices.

Although service firms in general tend to be more flexible and decentralized, some, such as McDonald's, develop set rules and procedures for customer service. When services can be standardized, a tight, centralized structure can be very effective, as revealed by the Marriott Corporation.

MARRIOTT CORPORATION
www.marriott.com
Marriott Corporation's success has come from two strategies: Put hotels where the customers are and provide excellent service. Putting hotels where the customers are means building hotels downtown and at airports. Convention centers, such as Atlantic City, are another target.

Marriott also searches for new niches. The Courtyard is a new type of garden apartment hotel aimed at the moderate-priced segment of the market. Courtyards are scattered around major metropolitan areas.

At Marriott, the hotel itself is the main service, and a mind-boggling system is used to make the right impression every time. Top managers make no apologies for the tightly centralized system of policies, procedures, and controls for operational details. Room attendants have 66 things to do in cleaning a room, from dusting the tops of pictures (number 7) to keeping the telephone book and Bibles in a neat condition (number 37). President Bill Marriott says, "The more the system works like the Army, the better." The cooks have 6,000 recipes available to them, and they are not allowed to deviate. One rule for chefs says, "Deviations from the standard written specifications may not be made without prior approval and written consent of the vice president of food and beverages."

Marriott Corporation plans to add new hotels each year. It routinizes the service and builds luxury into the physical structure to ensure that guests are treated the same way every time. One recent program is First 10, which focuses on making a lasting impression of great service on customers during the first 10 minutes of their hotel stay. Marriott was rated as one of the five best-managed companies, and Bill Marriott and four executive vice presidents spend half the year on the road visiting company facilities. The close, personal supervision and careful reading of customer suggestions help Bill Marriott give business travelers the service they expect and deserve.[53] ■

The managers at Marriott designed the structure and procedures to fit a service where work can be broken down into a series of explicit steps for employees to follow in serving customers. The many rules and procedures, centralized decision making, and refined division of labor provide a structure that is suited to the underlying technology. However, this structure would not work in a service such as a doctor's office, where new problems are encountered every day and employees must develop creative solutions for solving problems and serving customers.

Summary and Management Solution

This chapter introduced a number of important organizing concepts. Fundamental characteristics of organization structure include work specialization, chain of command, authority and responsibility, span of management, and centralization and decentralization. These dimensions of organization represent the vertical hierarchy and indicate how authority and responsibility are distributed along the hierarchy.

The other major concept is departmentalization, which describes how organization employees are grouped. Two traditional approaches are functional and divisional; contemporary approaches are team and network structures. The functional approach groups employees by common skills and tasks. The opposite structure is divisional, which groups people by organizational output so that each division has a mix of functional skills and tasks. The two chains of command in a domestic organization typically are functional and product division. The team approach uses permanent teams and cross-functional teams to achieve better coordination and employee commitment than is possible with a pure functional structure. The network approach represents the newest form of organization structure. With the network approach, a firm concentrates on what it does best and subcontracts other functions to separate organizations that are connected to the headquarters electronically. Each organization form has advantages and disadvantages and can be used by managers to meet the needs of the competitive situation.

As organizations grow, they add new departments, functions, and hierarchical levels. A major problem confronting management is how to tie the whole organization together. Structural characteristics such as chain of command, work specialization, and departmentalization are valuable organization concepts but often are not sufficient to coordinate far-flung departments. Horizontal coordination mechanisms provide coordination across departments and include reengineering, task forces, teams, and project managers.

There is an increasing shift toward more horizontal versus vertical structures, which reflects the trend toward greater employee involvement and participation. At the apex of this movement is a type of organization called the learning organization. The learning organization is characterized by a horizontal structure, open information, decentralized decision making, empowered employees, and a strong, adaptive culture. Contingency factors of strategy, environment, and production technology influence the correct structural approach. When a firm's strategy is to differentiate the firm's product from competitors, a flexible structural approach using teams, decentralization, and empowered employees is appropriate. When environmental uncertainty is high, horizontal coordination is important, and the organization should have a looser, flexible structure, such as in a learning organization.

Another factor that influences structure is technology. For manufacturing firms, small batch, continuous process, and flexible manufacturing technologies tend to be structured loosely, whereas a tighter vertical structure is appropriate for mass production. Service technologies are people oriented, and firms are located geographically close to dispersed customers. Some services can be broken down into explicit steps where employees follow objective, standardized procedures for serving customers and solving problems, and these may be controlled with a vertical structure. However, in general, services tend to have more flexible, horizontal structures, with decentralized decision making.

Recall the case of CompUSA and its decision to start a new Web site? CEO Jim Halpin and his executives decided they needed a new image and a new name for its e-commerce business. Wholly-owned subsidiary Cozone.com would not conjure up ideas—in fact, CompUSA is not even mentioned on the Cozone Home Page—and had different personnel and goals. Having a new unit steers them away from sticky state-tax situations where CompUSA might have a location.

For CEO of Cozone they hired Stephen Polley. He took advice of Harvard professor Clayton Christensen, who says that large corporations can avoid failure only if their e-commerce subsidiaries are allowed to attack the parent. They are offering a wide range of electronic goods, in addition to computers and plan to have top-quality customer service. Role models were limited. Dell computers only sells computers and Amazon, while considered the gold standard, had no real need for customer technical assistance. Of all the sites they researched, financial services companies did the best of selling, explaining, and servicing. So they hired Fidelity Investments Web developer Lang Joen, with the result of having a superior Web site. Whereas competitors tend to have little more than an online catalog, Cozone's site is crammed full of information and includes an extensive download site for software. The most popular part of Cozone's site is its computer-generated brunette advisor "Jill" (already getting fan mail), who guides customers through a series of questions.

But the final question is: With all that help from friendly and competent technical advisors, why would anyone even want to go to a CompUSA store? That is the real question companies are struggling with. Success for Cozone can only spell more disaster for CompUSA.

SOURCE: Julie Creswell, "CompUSA Is Killing Itself—On Purpose," *Fortune*, Dec. 20, 1999, pp. 279–280.

Discussion Questions

1. Sonny Holt, manager of Electronics Assembly, asked Hector Cruz, his senior technician, to handle things in the department while Sonny worked on the budget. Sonny needed peace and quiet for at least a week to complete his figures. After 10 days, Sonny discovered that Hector had hired a senior secretary, not realizing that Sonny had promised interviews to two other people. Evaluate Sonny's approach to delegation.

2. Many experts note that organizations have been making greater use of teams in recent years. What factors might account for this trend?

3. Contrast centralization with span of management. Would you expect these characteristics to affect each other in organizations? Why?

4. An organizational consultant was heard to say, "Some aspect of functional structure appears in every organization." Do you agree? Explain.

5. The divisional structure is often considered almost the opposite of a functional structure. Do you agree? Briefly explain the major differences in these two approaches to departmentalization.

6. What is the network approach to structure? Is the use of authority and responsibility different compared with other forms of departmentalization? Explain.

7. Why are divisional structures frequently used in large corporations?

8. Carnival Cruise Lines provides pleasure cruises to the masses. Carnival has several ships and works on high volume/low price rather than offering luxury cruises. What would you predict about the organization structure of a Carnival Cruise ship?

9. Why is structure different depending on whether a firm's strategy is low cost or differentiation?

10. The chapter suggested that structure should be designed to fit strategy. Some theorists argue that strategy should be designed to fit the organization's structure. With which theory do you agree? Explain.

11. What is the difference between a task force and a project manager? Which would be more effective in achieving coordination?

12. Discuss why an organization in an uncertain environment requires more horizontal relationships than one in a certain environment.

13. Why are empowered employees, open information, and cultural values of minimal boundaries and equality important in a learning organization as opposed to a traditional, vertical organization?

14. What is the difference between manufacturing and service technology? How would you classify a university, a local discount store, a nursery school? How would you expect the structure of a service organization to differ from that of a manufacturing organization?

15. Flexible manufacturing systems combine elements of both small batch and mass production. What effect might this new form of technology have on organization structure? Explain.

Management Exercises

Manager's Workbook

Loose versus Tight Organization Structure

Interview an employee at your university, such as a department head or secretary. Have the employee answer the following thirteen questions about his or her job and organizational conditions.

	Disagree Strongly				Agree Strongly
1. Your work would be considered routine.	1	2	3	4	5
2. There is a clearly known way to do the major tasks you encounter.	1	2	3	4	5
3. Your work has high variety and frequent exceptions.	1	2	3	4	5
4. Communications from above consist of information and advice rather than instructions and directions.	1	2	3	4	5
5. You have the support of peers and supervisor to do your job well.	1	2	3	4	5
6. You seldom exchange ideas or information with people doing other kinds of jobs.	1	2	3	4	5
7. Decisions relevant to your work are made above you and passed down.	1	2	3	4	5
8. People at your level frequently have to figure out for themselves what their jobs are for the day.	1	2	3	4	5
9. Lines of authority are clear and precisely defined.	1	2	3	4	5

10. Leadership tends to be democratic rather than autocratic in style.	1	2	3	4	5
11. Job descriptions are written and up-to-date for each job.	1	2	3	4	5
12. People understand each other's jobs and often do different tasks.	1	2	3	4	5
13. A manual of policies and procedures is available to use when a problem arises.	1	2	3	4	5

Total Score _____

A score of 52 or above suggests that the employee is working in a "loosely structured" organization. The score reflects a flexible structure that is often associated with uncertain environments and small-batch technology. People working in this structure feel empowered. Many organizations today are moving in the direction of flexible structures and empowerment.

A score of 26 or below suggests a "tight structure." This structure utilizes traditional control and functional specialization, which often occurs in a certain environment, a stable organization, and routine or mass-production technology. People in this structure may feel controlled and constrained.

Discuss the pros and cons of loose versus tight structure. Does the structure of the employee you interviewed fit the nature of the organization's environment, strategic goals, and technology? How might you redesign the structure to make the work organization more effective?

Manager's Workshop

You and Organization Structure

In order to better understand the importance of organization structure in your life, do the following assignment in groups of four to six members.

Select one of the following situations to organize:

a. the registration process at your university or college
b. a new fast-food franchise
c. a sports rental in an ocean resort area, such as jet-ski, etc.
d. a bakery

Background

Organization is a way of gaining some power against an unreliable environment. The environment provides the organization with inputs, which include raw materials, human resources, and financial resources. There is a service or product to produce that involves technology. The output goes to clients, a group that must be nurtured. The complexities of the environment and the technology determine the complexity of the organization.

Planning your organization:

1. Write down the mission or purpose of the organization in a few sentences.

2. What are the specific things to be done to accomplish the mission?

3. Based on the specifics in problem 2, develop an organization chart. Each position in the chart will perform a specific task or is responsible for a certain outcome.

4. Add duties to each job position in the chart. These will be the job descriptions.

5. How can you make sure people in each position will work together?

6. What level of skill and abilities is required at each position and level in order to hire the right persons?

7. Make a list of the decisions that would have to be made as you developed your organization.

8. Who is responsible for customer satisfaction? How will you know if the needs of customers are met?

9. How will information flow within the organization?

SOURCE: Adapted by Dorothy Marcic from "Organizing," in Donald D. White and H. William Vroman, *Action in Organizations,* 2nd ed. Boston: Allyn and Bacon, p. 154.

Management in Practice: Ethical Dilemma

Caught in the Middle

Tom Harrington loved his job as an assistant high-quality control officer for Rockingham Toys. After six months of unemployment, he was anxious to make a good impression on his boss, Frank Golopolus. One of the responsibilities of his boss was ensuring that new product lines met federal safety guidelines. Rockingham had made several manufacturing changes over the past year. Golopolus and the rest of the high-quality control team had been working 60-hour weeks to troubleshoot the new production process.

While sorting incoming mail during the past weeks, Harrington had become aware of numerous changes in product safety guidelines that he knew would impact the new Rockingham toys. Golopolus was taking no action to implement new guidelines, and he didn't seem to understand or care about them. Harrington, who avoided the questions he received from the floor to cover for his boss, was beginning to wonder if Rockingham would have time to make changes with the Christmas season rapidly approaching.

Harrington knew it was not his job to order the changes, and he didn't want to alienate Golopolus by interfering, but he was beginning to worry what might happen if he didn't act. Rockingham had a fine product safety reputation and was rarely challenged on matters of quality. He felt loyalty to Golopolus for giving him a job, but he worried Golopolus was in over his head.

What Do You Do?

1. Prepare a memo to Golopolus, summarizing the new safety guidelines that affect the Rockingham product line and recommending implementation.

2. Mind your own business. You do not have authority to monitor the federal regulations. Besides, you've been unemployed and need this job.

3. Send copies of the reports anonymously to the operations manager, who is Golopolus's boss.

SOURCE: Based on Doug Wallace, "The Man Who Knew Too Much," *What Would You Do? Business Ethics,* vol. II (March–April 1993), pp. 7–8.

Surf the Net

1. *Examples of Organizational Structure.* Visit the Web sites for several companies to find two examples of organization charts or organizational structure descriptors that you can print out and bring to class. These examples can be analyzed by you and your classmates to determine what approach to structure the organization has used. For example, does the chart or description illustrate the functional, divisional, matrix, contemporary team, or network approach to structure?

   Two examples are listed below. When you're looking for a company's organizational structure, you can often find it under a heading such as "Company Overview," "About Us," "Corporate Profile," or other such descriptors. Sometimes, the organizational structure is verbally described (as the Microsoft example below), and other times, a literal organization chart is provided (as the Xerox example below).

   www.xerox.com/factbook/1998/orgchart.htm

   www.microsoft.com/presspass/cpOrg.htm

2. *Divisional Structure.* Examine the divisional structure illustrated by PepsiCo. Visit www.pepsico.com, select "Corporate Information" and then "Corporate Structure." Write a brief summary describing the PepsiCo divisions and examples of products in each division.

3. Option 1—*The Virtual Network.* After reading the information in this chapter's Learning Organization box on the virtual computer company, Monorail, Inc., visit the company's Web site at www.monorail.com. Write a two- to three-paragraph description of your impressions of this company from a consumer perspective. If you hadn't had the textbook background before going to the site, would you have known this is a virtual company? What clues did you get from the Web site alone that this is a virtual company? Also list reasons why you would or would not consider purchasing a computer made by one of this company's contract manufacturers.

   Option 2—Revisit www.mgeneral.com and surf through it. How might a site like this one become part of a virtual network or virtual community?

Case for Critical Analysis

Tucker Company

In 1978 the Tucker Company underwent an extensive re-organization that divided the company into three major divisions. These new divisions represented Tucker's three principal product lines. Mr. Harnett, Tucker's president, explained the basis for the new organization in a memo to the board of directors as follows:

The diversity of our products requires that we reorganize along our major product lines. Toward this end I have established three new divisions: commercial jet engines, military jet engines, and utility turbines. Each division will be headed by a new vice president who will report directly to me. I believe that this new approach will enhance our performance through the commitment of individual managers. It should also help us to identify unprofitable areas where the special attention of management may be required.

For the most part, each division will be able to operate independently. That is, each will have its own engineering, manufacturing, accounting departments, etc. In some cases, however, it will be necessary for a division to utilize the services of other divisions or departments. This is necessary because the complete servicing with individual divisional staffs would result in unjustifiable additional staffing and facilities.

The old companywide laboratory was one such service department. Functionally, it continued to support all of the major divisions. Administratively, however, the manager of the laboratory reported to the manager of manufacturing in the military jet engine division.

From the time the new organization was initiated until February 1988, when the laboratory manager Mr. Garfield retired, there was little evidence of interdepartmental or interdivisional conflict. His replacement, Mr. Hodge, unlike Mr. Garfield, was always eager to gain the attention of management. Many of Hodge's peers perceived him as an empire builder who was interested in his own advancement rather than the company's well-being. After about six months in the new position, Hodge became involved in several interdepartmental conflicts over work that was being conducted in his laboratory.

Historically, the engineering departments had used the laboratory as a testing facility to determine the properties of materials selected by the design engineers. Hodge felt that the laboratory should be more involved in the selection of these materials and in the design of experiments and subsequent evaluations of the experimental data. Hodge discussed this with Mr. Franklin of the engineering department of the utility turbine division. Franklin offered to consult with Hodge but stated that the final responsibility for the selection of materials was charged to his department.

In the months that followed, Hodge and Franklin had several disagreements over the implementation of the results. Franklin told Hodge that, because of his position at the testing lab, he was unable to appreciate the detailed design considerations that affected the final decision on materials selection. Hodge claimed that Franklin lacked the materials expertise that he, as a metallurgist, had.

Franklin also noted that the handling of his requests, which had been prompt under Garfield's management, was taking longer and longer under Hodge's management. Hodge explained that military jet engine divisional problems had to be assigned first priority because of his administrative reporting structure. He also said that if he were more involved in Franklin's problems, he could perhaps appreciate when a true sense of urgency existed and could revise priorities.

The tensions between Franklin and Hodge reached a peak when one of Franklin's critical projects failed to receive the scheduling that he considered necessary. Franklin phoned Hodge to discuss the need for a schedule change. Hodge suggested that they have a meeting to review the need for the work. Franklin then told Hodge that this was not a matter of his concern and that his function was merely to perform the tests as requested. He further stated that he was not satisfied with the low-priority rating that his division's work received. Hodge reminded Franklin that when Hodge had suggested a means for resolving this problem, Franklin was not receptive. At this point, Franklin lost his temper and hung up on Hodge.

Questions

1. Sketch out a simple organization chart showing Tucker Company's three divisions, including the location of the laboratory. Why would the laboratory be located in the military jet engine division?

2. Analyze the conflict between Mr. Hodge and Mr. Franklin. Do you think the conflict is based on personalities or on the way in which the organization is structured?

3. Sketch out a new organization chart showing how you would restructure Tucker Company so that the laboratory would provide equal services to all divisions. What advantages and disadvantages do you see in the new structure compared to the previous one?

SOURCE: Reprinted with permission of Macmillan Publishing Company from "The Laboratory," *Organizational Behavior: Readings and Cases,* 2d ed., pp. 385–387, by L. Katz, prepared under the supervision of Theodore T. Herbert. Copyright 1981 by Theodore T. Herbert.

Endnotes

1 Julie Creswell, "CompUSA Is Killing Itself—On Purpose," *Fortune,* Dec. 20, 1999, pp. 279–280.

2 Tim R. V. Davis and Bruce L. Darling, "How Virtual Corporations Manage the Performance of Contractors: The Super Bakery Case," *Organizational Dynamics* 26, no. 1 (summer 1995), 70–75.

3 John Child, *Organization: A Guide to Problems and Practice,* 2d ed. (London: Harper & Row, 1984).

4 Adam Smith, *The Wealth of Nations* (New York: Modern Library, 1937).

5 Michael Williams, "Some Plants Tear Out Long Assembly Lines, Switch to Craft Work," *The Wall Street Journal,* October 24, 1994, A1, A6.

6 C. I. Barnard, *The Functions of the Executive* (Cambridge, Mass.: Harvard University Press, 1938).

7 Thomas A. Stewart, "CEOs See Clout Shifting," *Fortune,* November 6, 1989, 66.

8 Michael G. O'Loughlin, "What Is Bureaucratic Accountability and How Can We Measure It?" *Administration & Society* 22, no. 3 (November 1990), 275–302.

9 Carrie R. Leana, "Predictors and Consequences of Delegation," *Academy of Management Journal* 29 (1986), 754–774.

10 Paul D. Collins and Frank Hull, "Technology and Span of Control: Woodward Revisited," *Journal of Management Studies* 23 (March 1986), 143–164; David D. Van Fleet and Arthur G. Bedeian, "A History of the Span of Management," *Academy of Management Review* 2 (1977), 356–372; and C. W. Barkdull, "Span of Control—A Method of Evaluation," *Michigan Business Review* 15 (May 1963), 25–32.

11 Brian Bumaine, "What the Leaders of Tomorrow See," *Fortune,* July 3, 1989, 48–62.

12 James Kitfield, "Superior Command," *Government Executive,* October 1993, 18–23.

13 Brian O'Reilly, "J&J Is on a Roll," *Fortune,* December 26, 1994, 178–191; and Joseph Weber, "A Big Company That Works," *Business Week,* May 4, 1992, 124–132.

14 Saul Hansell, "Banc One Lives Up to Its Name," *The New York Times,* May 12, 1995, C1, C4.

15 Christopher Caggiano, "Thriving on Bureaucracy," *Inc. Technology,* 1997, no. 1, 63-66.

16 Raymond E. Miles, "Adapting to Technology and Competition: A New Industrial Relation System for the Twenty-First Century," *California Management Review* (winter 1989), 9–28.

17 Rahul Jacob, "The Struggle to Create an Organization for the 21st Century," *Fortune,* April 3, 1995, 90–99.

18 Michael Hammer with Steven Stanton, "The Art of Change," *Success,* April 1995, 44A–44H; and Byrne, "The Horizontal Corporation."

19 John Hillkirk, "Challenging Status Quo Now in Vogue," *USA Today,* November 9, 1993; and Thomas A. Stewart, "The Search for the Organization of Tomorrow," *Fortune,* May 18, 1992, 92–98.

20 Raymond E. Miles and Charles C. Snow, "The New Network Firm: A Spherical Structure Built on a Human Investment Philosophy," *Organizational Dynamics,* (spring 1995), 5–18; and Raymond E. Miles, Charles C. Snow, John A. Matthews, Grant Miles, and Henry J. Coleman, Jr., "Organizing in the KNowledge Age: Anticipating the Cellular Form," *Academy of Management Executive* 11, no. 4 (1997), 7–24.

21 Raymond E. Miles and Charles C. Snow, "Organizations: New Concepts for New Forms," *California Management Review* 28 (spring 1986), 62–73; and "Now, The Post-Industrial Corporation," *Business Week,* March 3, 1986, 64–74.

22 Gregory G. Dess, Abdul M. A. Rasheed, Kevin J. McLaughlin, and Richard L. Priem, "The New Corporate Architecture," *Academy of Management Executive* 9, no. 3 (1995), 7–20.

23 John Byrne, "The Virtual Corporation," *Business Week,* February 8, 1993, 99–103; and Dess et al., "The New Corporate Architecture."

24 Gianni Lorenzoni and Charles Baden-Fuller, "Creating a Strategic Center to Manage a Web of Partners," *California Management Review* 37, no. 3 (spring 1995), 146–163; Shawn Tully, "You'll Never Guess Who Really Makes . . . ," *Fortune,* October 3, 1994, 124–128; and G. Pascal Zachary, "High-Tech Firms Find It's Good to Line Up Outside Contractors," *The Wall Street Journal,* July 29, 1992, A1, A5.

25 Echo Montgomery Garrett, "Innovation + Outsourcing = Big Success," *Management Review,* September 1994, 17–20; and Tom Field, "The Personal Touch," *CIO,* August 1, 1998, 18.

26 Miles, "Adapting to Technology and Competition," and Miles and Snow, "The New Network Firm."

27 Dess et al., "The New Corporate Architecture."

28 Laurie P. O'Leary, "Curing the Monday BLues: A U.S. Navy Guide for Structuring Cross-Functional Teams," *National Productivity Review,* spring 1996, 43–51; and Alan Hurwitz, "Organizational Structures for the 'New World Order,' " *Business Horizons,* May–June 1996, 5–14.

29 Bruce Buursma, "Wanted: Romance Executive," *Chicago Tribune,* July 19, 1989.

30 Lee Iacocca with William Novak, *Iacocca: An Autobiography* (New York: Phantom Books, 1984), 152–153.

31 William R. Pape, "Little Giant," *Inc. Tech* 1999, No. 1, pp. 27–28.

32 Barbara Ettorre, "Simplicity Cuts a New Pattern," *Management Review* (December 1993), 25–29; and Joyce Hoffman, ed., *Reflections,* vol. 10 (1989), 12–15.

33 Paul R. Lawrence and Jay W. Lorsch, "New Managerial Job: The Integrator," *Harvard Business Review* (November-December 1967), 142–151.

34 Paul Roberts, "We Are One Company, No Matter Where We Are," *Fast Company,* April–May 1998, 122–128.

35 C. Nevis, A. J. DiBella, and J. M. Gould, "Understanding Organizations as Learning Systems," *Sloan Management Review,* Winter 1995), 73–85; and G. Hamel, "Strategy as Revolution," *Harvard Business Review,* July–August 1996, pp. 69–82.

36 Marc S. Gerstein and Robert B. Shaw, "Organizational Architectures for the Twenty-First Century," in David A. Nadler, Marc S. Berstein, Robert B. Shaw and Associates, eds., *Organizational Architecture: Designs for Changing Organizations* (San Francisco: Jossey-Bass, 1992); pp. 263–274.

37 Scott Kirsner, "Every Day, It's a New Place," *Fast Company,* April–May 1998; pp. 130–134.

38 Jeffrey Pfeffer, "Producing Sustainable Competitive Advantage through the Effective Management of People," *Academy of Management Executive* 9, no. 1 (1995), pp. 55–69.

39 Mary Anne Devanna and Noel Tichy, "Creating the Competitive Organization of the Twenty-First Century: The Boundaryless Corporation," *Human Resource Management* 29 (winter 1990), pp. 55–471.

40 Dorothy Leonard-Barton, "The Factory as a Learning Laboratory," *Sloan Management Review* (fall 1992), pp. 23–38.

41 Michael E. Porter, *Competitive Strategy* (New York: Free Press, 1980), pp. 36–46.

42 Pam Black, "Finally, Human Rights for Motorists," *Business Week,* May 1, 1995, 45.

43 Daniel Roth, "10 Companies That Get It," *Fortune,* Nov. 8, 1999, pp. 115–117; Jules Abend, "Lands' End Uses Internet to Expand Sales, Personalize Customer Service," *Bobbin,* June 1999, pp. 10–13.

44 Clem Morgello, "Booth: Creating a New Polaroid," *Dun's Business Month,* August 1985, pp. 51–52.

45 Denise M. Rousseau and Robert A. Cooke, "Technology and Structure: The Concrete, Abstract, and Activity Systems of Organizations," *Journal of Management* 10 (1984), pp. 345–361.

46 Joan Woodward, *Industrial Organizations: Theory and Practice* (London: Oxford University Press, 1965); and Joan Woodward, *Management and Technology* (London: Her Majesty's Stationery Office, 1958).

47 Woodward, *Industrial Organizations,* vi.

48 Barrier, "Re-engineering Your Company."

49 Justin Martin, "Give 'Em *Exactly* What They Want," *Fortune,* November 10, 1997, 283, 285.

50 R. Parthasarthy and S. B. Sethi, "The Impact of Flexible Automation on Business Strategy and Organizational Structure," *Academy of Management Review* 17 (1992), pp. 86–111.

51 Peter K. Mills and Thomas Kurk, "A Preliminary Investigation into the Influence of Customer-Firm Interface on Information Processing and Task Activity in Service Organizations," *Journal of Management* 12 (1986), pp. 91–104.

52 Richard B. Chase and David A. Tansik, "The Customer Contact Model for Organization Design," *Management Science* 29 (1983), pp. 1037–1050.

53 Maryfran Johnson, "Marriott Rests on RS/6000," *Computerworld,* October 5, 1992, 6; and Thomas Moore, "Marriott Grabs for More Rooms," *Fortune,* October 31, 1983, pp. 107–122.

8

Change and Development

LEARNING OBJECTIVES

After studying this chapter, you should be able to:

- Define organizational change and explain the forces for change

- Describe the sequence of four change activities that must be performed in order for change to be successful

- Explain the techniques managers can use to facilitate the initiation of change in organizations, including idea champions and new-venture teams

- Define sources of resistance to change

- Explain force field analysis and other implementation tactics that can be used to overcome resistance to change

- Explain the difference among technology, product, structure, and culture/people changes

- Explain the change process—bottom up, top down, horizontal—associated with each type of change

- Define organizational development and large-group interventions

MANAGEMENT PROBLEM

■ ■ ■ ■ ■ ■ ■ ■ ■ ■

A SMALL FIRM that designs and

furnishes hotel interiors, Midwest Contract

Furnishings, Inc., faced a crisis that left employees reeling. The

company's biggest customer, Renaissance Hotels International, was sold to Mar-

riott International, which was unlikely to need Midwest's services. Even though Midwest had

only 20 employees and had been in business for only five years, it had landed a showcase project in

Orlando that brought it to the attention of Renaissance. So, for two years, Midwest had been focusing

much of its energies on serving the huge Renaissance account. Now, since Marriott did most of that kind of

work in-house, Midwest faced the loss of at least 80 percent of its revenues. Midwest owner Christopher

• *If you were Christopher Cogan, how would you handle this situation? What approaches*

can/should he take to help employees adapt to the changes he has in mind for Midwest?

Cogan needed to reshape his company immediately, and he needed the full commitment of employees to do it.

However, everyone—including Cogan—was devastated by the loss of the Renaissance account. "I wanted to

crawl under a rock and not show up for work for a couple of months," he said. Employees were fearful

of losing their jobs and didn't feel very motivated to come to work either. Cogan pushed aside his

own fears and developed a plan for taking Midwest in a new direction. Then he asked

himself a tough question: How could he implement the changes in such a way

that employees would be motivated to help the company

emerge from this crisis?[1]

■ ■ ■ ■ ■ ■ ■ ■ ■ ■ ■ ■ ■

Christopher Cogan and Midwest Contract Furnishings are not alone. Every organization goes through periods of change that cause stress and uncertainty. Sometimes, changes are brought about by forces outside the organization, as in the case at Midwest. Other times, managers within the company want to initiate major changes, but don't know how. Lack of innovation from within is widely recognized as one of the critical problems facing business today in the United States and Canada. To be successful, organizations must embrace many types of change. Businesses must develop improved production technologies, create new products that meet changing needs of the marketplace, implement new administrative systems, and upgrade the skills of employees. Companies such as Westinghouse, Black & Decker, and Merck implement all of these changes and more.

How important is organizational change? Consider this: The parents of today's college students grew up without digital cameras, e-mail, personal computers, VCRs, electronic games, CDs, cellular phones, video stores, or laser checkout systems in supermarkets. Companies that produce the new products have prospered, but many companies caught with outdated products and technologies have failed. Today's successful companies are constantly striving to come up with new products and services. For example, automakers such as Daimler-Chrysler, General Motors, and Toyota invest heavily to develop fuel-cell power systems that could make today's noisy, polluting piston engines obsolete. Colt's Manufacturing is working on a computerized "smart gun" that can be fired only by the owner. Pharmaceutical companies around the world are searching for new drugs and vaccines to fight diseases such as AIDS and cancer. Organizations that change successfully, such as General Electric, Hewlett-Packard, and Motorola, are both profitable and admired.

Organizational change is defined as the adoption of a new idea or behavior by an organization.[2] In this chapter, we will look at how organizations can be designed to respond to the environment through internal change and development. First we will examine the basic forces for organizational change. Then we will

organizational change
The adoption of a new idea or behavior by an organization

look closely at how managers facilitate two change requirements: initiation and implementation. Finally, we will discuss the four major types of change—technology, new product, structure, and culture/people—and how the organization can be designed to facilitate each.

■ THE LEARNING ORGANIZATION

In today's highly complex world, organizations need to continuously adapt to new situations if they are to survive and prosper. The current trend is toward development of the learning organization, which is the epitome of continuous organizational change and growth. As we have discussed in previous chapters, the learning organization engages everyone in problem solving and continuous improvement based on the lessons of experience.[3]

The interacting systems that make up the learning organization resemble a web in which each element responds to and influences every other element toward change. For example, leadership provides vision for development of new strategies and serves as a crucial support function for empowerment of employees and the extent of openness in information sharing. Empowerment liberates employees but also places upon them the added responsibilities of working collaboratively, initiating changes, and participating in strategy to benefit the entire organization. Redefining culture demands the rethinking of roles, processes, and values, and the breaking down of barriers that have separated departments so that everyone shares information and works together. Information sharing requires adjustments on the part of managers for the inclusion of employees, suppliers, and customers, often necessitating cultural and structural changes. Strategy is likewise linked to structure and culture as the organization changes its fundamental way of doing business and allows change initiatives to flow bottom up as well as top down. The horizontal structure, which replaces the familiar hierarchical pyramid, incorporates empowerment and information sharing and relies on employees as team members and managers as facilitators.

The learning organization simultaneously embraces two types of planned change: *operational* change, based on organizational efforts to improve basic work and organizational processes in different areas of the business, and *transformational* change, which involves redesign and renewal of the total organization.[4]

■ MODEL OF PLANNED ORGANIZATIONAL CHANGE

Change can be managed. By observing external trends, patterns, and needs, managers use planned change to help the organization adapt to external problems and opportunities.[5] When organizations are caught flat-footed, failing to anticipate or respond to new needs, management is at fault.

An overall model for planned change is presented in Exhibit 8.1. Four events make up the change sequence: (1) internal and external forces for change exist; (2) organization managers monitor these forces and become aware of a need for change; and (3) the perceived need triggers the initiation of change, which (4) is then implemented. How each of these activities is handled depends on the organization and styles of managers.

We now turn to a brief discussion of the specific activities associated with the first two events—forces for change and the perceived need for the organization to respond.

FORCES FOR CHANGE

Forces for organizational change exist both in the external environment and within the organization.

ENVIRONMENTAL FORCES   As described in Chapters 2 and 3, external forces originate in all environmental sectors, including customers, competitors, technology, economic forces, and the international arena. For example, many North American companies have been blindsided by global competition. Consider General Electric, which built a new factory to produce microwave ovens. As GE's plans were being made, Yun Soo Chu was working 80 hours per week for Samsung in Korea to perfect a microwave oven. About the time the GE plant came on stream, Samsung started exporting thousands of microwaves to the United States at one-third the cost of GE microwaves. Today, Samsung has 25 percent of the U.S. market, and GE is one of its best customers. GE closed its microwave plant, preferring to buy the cheaper Samsung ovens to sell under the GE label.[6]

INTERNAL FORCES   Internal forces for change arise from internal activities and decisions. If top managers select a goal of rapid company growth, internal actions will have to be changed to meet that growth. New departments or technologies will be created. Senior

management at General Motors, frustrated by poor internal efficiency, designed the Saturn manufacturing plant to solve this internal need. Demands by employees, labor unions, and production inefficiencies all can generate a force to which management must respond with change.

NEED FOR CHANGE

As indicated in Exhibit 8.1, external or internal forces translate into a perceived need for change within the organization.[7] Managers sense a need for change when there is a **performance gap**—a disparity between existing and desired performance levels. The performance gap may occur because current procedures are not up to standard or because a new idea or technology could improve current performance. Managers try to establish a sense of urgency so that others will understand the need for change. Sometimes a crisis, like the one at Midwest, provides an unquestioned sense of urgency. In many cases, however, there is no obvious crisis and managers have to recognize and then make others aware of the need for change.[8] Management's responsibility is to monitor threats and opportunities in the external environment as well as strengths and weaknesses within the organization to determine whether a need for change exists. Looking at the weaknesses of an entire industry can alert the smart entrepreneur to opportunities in the environment where others have found only failure, as this example illustrates.

EASYEVERYTHING CAFÉ

It was a great idea. It just didn't work. Cybercafés, where people can drink coffee, cogitate on the world's problems, and get online. Historically, most cybercafés go bottom up before the coffee beans are roasted because of cash-burning strategies of expensive equipment purchases accompanied by marginal visitors and revenue. As Nick Rosen, former co-owner of one of London's cybercafés, says, "Nobody's been able to work out how to make them very profitable."

Until now, that is. Former cheap-seat airline entrepreneur Stellios Haji-Ioannou, who is all of 32 years old, thinks he can shake up this industry the way he did with airlines. His London easyEverything café may be the busiest in the world, with 5,000 visitors each day to the 380-seat facility. Some days it's so busy that it looks like a nightclub; even bouncers manage the long lines outside.

Mr. Haji-Ioannou saw early on that in order for his cybercafé to be successful, he had to run it like one of his jets. That is, it had to be speedy, almost full, aggressively advertised, and with as many cafés running on maximum hours each day. In order to fill the around-the-clock capacity, cheaper prices are offered during off-peak hours, with the best deals available from midnight to 6 A.M. He plans to open four more in England and calculates that, with even a 60 percent capacity, he would have 10 million visitors per year. Now he sells franchises to Eastern Europe.

Even if computers and Internet access become so cheap it hurts his business, Mr. Haji-Ioannou is not worried. He will merely keep moving east, where technology lags further behind.[9] ∎

Managers in every company must be alert to problems and opportunities, because the perceived need for change is what sets the stage for subsequent actions that create a new product or technology. Big problems are easy to spot. Sensitive monitoring systems are needed to detect gradual changes that can fool managers into thinking their company is doing fine. An organization may be in greater danger when the environment changes slowly, because managers may fail to trigger an organizational response. Failing to use planned change to meet small needs can place the organization in hot water, as this excerpt illustrates:

When frogs are placed in a boiling pail of water, they jump out—they don't want to boil to death. However, when frogs are placed in a cold pail of water, and the pail is placed on a stove with the

performance gap
A disparity between existing and desired performance levels

heat turned very low, over time the frogs will boil to death.[10] ■

■ INITIATING CHANGE

After the *need* for change has been perceived and communicated, the next part of the change process is to actually initiate change, a truly critical aspect of change management. This is where the ideas that solve perceived needs are developed. Responses that an organization can make are to search for or create a change to adopt.

SEARCH

Search is the process of learning about current developments inside or outside the organization that can be used to meet the perceived need for change. Search typically uncovers existing knowledge that can be applied or adopted within the organization. Managers talk to friends and colleagues, read professional reports, or hire consultants to learn about ideas used elsewhere.

Many needs, however, cannot be resolved through existing knowledge and require that the organization develop a new response. Initiating a new response means that managers must design the organization so as to facilitate creativity of both individuals and departments, encourage innovative people to initiate new ideas, or create new-venture departments. These techniques have been adopted by such corporations as GE and Apple with great success.

CREATIVITY

Creativity involves generating novel ideas that have the potential to meet perceived needs or respond to opportunities. Creativity is the essential first step in innovation, which is vital to long-term organizational success.[11] People noted for their creativity include Edwin Land, who invented the Polaroid camera; Frederick Smith, who came up with the idea for Federal Express's overnight delivery service during an undergraduate class at Yale; and Swiss engineer George de Mestral, who created Velcro after noticing the tiny hooks on the burrs caught on his wool socks. Each of these people saw unique opportunities and sought creative solutions to familiar problems.

Everyone has the capacity to be creative. Characteristics of highly creative people are illustrated in the left-hand column of Exhibit 8.2. Creative people often are known for originality, open-mindedness, curiosity, a focused approach to problem solving, persistence, a relaxed and playful attitude, and receptivity to new ideas.[12]

Creativity can also be designed into organizations. Companies—or departments within companies—can be organized specifically for generating creative ideas and initiating changes. Most companies want highly creative employees and often seek to hire them. However, all employees have potential for creativity. Another responsibility of managers is to create a work environment that allows creativity to flourish.[13]

The characteristics of creative organizations correspond to those of individuals, as illustrated in the right-hand column of Exhibit 8.2. Creative organizations are loosely structured. People find themselves in a situation of ambiguity, assignments are vague, territories overlap, tasks are abstractly defined, and much

search
The process of learning about current developments inside or outside the organization that can be used to meet a perceived need for change

creativity
Generating novel ideas that have the potential to meet perceived needs or respond to opportunities

CEO Robert Benmosche is initiating change at Metropolitan Life Insurance Co. His search discovered the need to change the company that had operated as a mutual company since 1915 and led to a plan to go public, or "demutualize." Employees play an intrinsic role in his plan, which includes energizing the company culture. Benmosche is known to be at his best when mixing with the troops, as he does in the photo taken at a corporate retreat in Puerto Rico. Recently, he spent four hours at a conference center encouraging the creativity of some 40 branch managers to find solutions for company problems. Benmosche has boosted productivity per MetLife sales agent from $19,000 to $23,000, while sales practice and service complaints are down 50 percent from their peak in 1994.

The Creative Individual	The Creative Organization or Department

1. Conceptual fluency
   Open-mindedness
	1. Open channels of communication
	   Contact with outside sources
	   Overlapping territories
	   Suggestion systems, brainstorming, group
	   techniques

2. Originality	2. Assignment of nonspecialists to problems
	   Eccentricity allowed
	   Use of teams

3. Less authority
   Independence
	3. Decentralization, loosely defined positions, loose
	   control
	   Acceptance of mistakes
	   Risk-taking norms

4. Playfulness
   Undisciplined exploration
   Curiosity
	4. Freedom to choose and pursue problems
	   Not a tight ship, playful culture
	   Freedom to discuss ideas, long time horizon

5. Persistence
   Commitment
   Focused approach
	5. Resources allocated to creative personnel and
	   projects without immediate payoff
	   Reward system encourages innovation
	   Absolution of peripheral responsibilities

SOURCE: James Brian Quinn, "Managing Innovation: Controlled Chaos," *Harvard Business Review,* 63 (May–June 1985), 73–84.

work is done through teams.[14] Creative organizations have an internal culture of playfulness, freedom, challenge, and grass-roots participation.[15] They harness all potential sources of new ideas from within. Many participative management programs are born out of the desire to enhance creativity for initiating changes. People are not stuck to the rhythm of routine jobs.

The most creative companies embrace risk and encourage employees to make mistakes. Jim Read, president of the Read Corporation, says, "When my employees make mistakes trying to improve something, I give them a round of applause. No mistakes mean no new products. If they ever become afraid to make one, my company is doomed."[16]

Open channels of communication, overlapping jobs, discretionary resources, decentralization, and freedom of the employees to choose problems and make mistakes can generate unexpected benefits for companies. Creative organizational conditions—see right column of Exhibit 8.2—enable more than 200 new products a year to bubble up from 3M's research labs.

The same creative conditions enabled the project team working on the NASA/Jet Propul-

sion Laboratory's Mars Pathfinder to find better, faster, and cheaper ways of doing things. When the Pathfinder landed on July 4, 1997, millions watched as the Sojourner rover explored the rocky planet for clues to the evolution of Mars and hints to whether life could have existed there. The project took only 44 months from start to touchdown, compared to the seven years it had taken to complete the 1976 Viking mission to Mars. In addition to saving time and money, the Pathfinder team achieved innovative engineering feats and scientific breakthroughs by fostering conditions that allowed creativity to flourish. The team set ambitious goals, made a commitment to extensive communication and information sharing, and encouraged eccentricity and diverse perspectives.[17] Leading the Revolution: Leadership describes a unique approach to sparking creativity by teaming up people who have dramatically different perspectives.

IDEA CHAMPIONS AND NEW-VENTURE TEAMS

If creative conditions are successful, new ideas will be generated that must be carried forward for acceptance and implementation. This is where idea champions come in. An **idea champion** is a person who sees the need for and champions productive change within the organization. For example, Bonnie McKeever of Federal Express championed the idea of a coalition of companies to combat mounting medical fees. Wendy Black of Best Western International championed the idea of coordinating the corporate mailings (to the company's 2,800 hoteliers) into a single packet every two weeks after learning that some hotels received three mailings a day from various departments. Her idea saved $600,000 every year for five years, just in postage.[18]

Change does not occur by itself. Personal energy and effort are required to successfully promote a new idea. Champions are passionately committed to a new product or idea despite its potential for rejection by others, including management.

Championing an idea successfully requires four roles within organizations. Sometimes one individual may play two or more of the roles, but successful innovation in most companies involves an interplay of different people, with each adopting a single role.

The *inventor* develops a new idea and understands its technical value but has neither the ability nor the interest to promote it for acceptance within the organization.

idea champion
A person who sees the need for productive change and champions it within the organization

Technological creativity is not new to Charles Schwab. The company's Pockterm, a chunky hand-held device that downloads stock quotes, dates back to 1982. But Schwab's latest creative venture is **www.schwab.com,** which invented a new kind of brokerage and reshaped the firm. Schwab.com is responsible for more than $4 billion worth of security trades each week. It was designed by Hyo Yeon and Arun Bordoloi (of Razorfish), who gave the site a consistent look and easy navigation.

Leadership *Leadership*
Leadership *Leadership* LEADING THE REVOLUTION:
Leadership
MAKING CREATIVE SPARKS FLY

Jerry Hirshberg argues that sometimes the right person for the job is two people. Hirshberg's world-renowned design studio, Nissan Design International, hires people in what he calls divergent pairs—people who see the world in totally different ways. Consider Tom Semple and Allan Flowers. Semple searches for "artistic intuition" when he starts to work on the design of a new car. He likes to clear away all traces of earlier projects, start with a blank piece of paper, and invent entirely new forms. Flowers, on the other hand, worries about nuts and bolts. He conducts a methodical assessment of components and materials, schedules and priorities. Semple and Flowers are one of about two dozen odd

couples creating the vehicles of the future at NDI. Teaming people with widely different perspectives produces what Hirshberg calls "creative abrasion," a kind of friction that produces wildly creative sparks. Those sparks have been flying at NDI for more than 20 years, producing such trendsetting innovations as the Nissan Pathfinder and the Infiniti series.

Hirshberg's ideas about hiring in divergent pairs began by accident. After Nissan recruited him from General Motors in the late 1970s to create its first design studio in the United States, he needed to find great designers to work with him. Semple and Flowers agreed to join the firm—but that's about the only thing they did agree on. "They were spectacu-

larly gifted but utterly different," Hirshberg says. "They were from different solar systems." However, Hirshberg noticed that the creative tension between the two spawned a vitality that quickly began paying off in good ideas. Today, hiring in divergent pairs has become an organizing principle of NDI, which has grown to about 50 design professionals. Whereas one divergent pair sets off sparks, Hirshberg believes that 25 such pairs create an organization with unlimited potential for creativity.

Source: Katharine Mieszkowski, "Opposites Attract," *Fast Company,* December–January 1998, pp. 42–44.

The *champion* believes in the idea, confronts the organizational realities of costs and benefits, and gains the political and financial support needed to bring it to reality.

The *sponsor* is a high-level manager who approves the idea, protects it, and removes major organizational barriers to acceptance.

The *critic* counterbalances the zeal of the champion by challenging the concept and providing reality checks with hard-nosed criteria. The critic prevents people in the other roles from adopting a bad idea.[19]

Managers (sponsors, as well as critics) can directly influence whether champions will flourish. When Texas Instruments studied 50 of its new-product introductions, a surprising fact emerged: Without exception, every new product that had failed lacked a zealous champion. And most of the new products that succeeded had one. Managers at Texas Instruments made an immediate decision: No new product would be approved unless someone championed it.

A recent idea for facilitating corporate innovation is known as a new-venture team. A **new-venture team** is a unit separate from the rest of the organization, responsible for developing and initiating a major innovation.[20] New-venture teams give free reign to the creativity of members because their separate facilities and location provide freedom from other organizational rules and procedures. These teams typically are small, loosely structured, and flexible, reflecting the characteristics of creative organizations (see Exhibit 8.2). Peter Drucker advises organizations that wish to innovate to use a separate team or department:

> For the existing business to be capable of innovation, it has to create a structure that allows people to be entrepreneurial. . . . This means, first, that the entrepreneurial, the new, has to be organized separately from the old and the existing. Whenever we have tried to make an existing unit the carrier of the entrepreneurial project, we have failed.[21] ∎

Under the new-venture team concept, employees no longer report through the normal structure.[22] New-venture teams are kept small and separate to guard against bureaucratic intrusion. 3M utilizes action teams to create new products. The action team concept allows individuals with new product ideas to recruit team members from anywhere in the company. These people may end up running the newly created division if the idea is successful.[23]

One variation of new-venture teams is the **new-venture fund** that provides resources from which individuals and groups can draw to develop new ideas, products, or businesses. For example, Lockheed-Martin employees can take two years of unpaid leave to explore new ideas, using the company's labs and paying company rates for health insurance. When an idea is successful, Lockheed-Martin's venture-capital group invests about $250,000 in the startup company. One successful startup is Genase, which creates and sells an enzyme that "stonewashes" denim.[24]

∎ IMPLEMENTING CHANGE

Creative culture, idea champions, and new-venture teams are ways to facilitate the initiation of new ideas. The other step to be managed in the change process is implementation. A new, creative idea will not benefit the organization until it is in place and being fully utilized. One frustration for managers is that employees often seem to resist change for no apparent reason. To effectively manage the implementation process, managers should be aware of the reasons for employee resistance and be prepared to use techniques for obtaining employee cooperation. Major, corporate-wide changes can be particularly difficult, as seen in Focus on Collaboration.

RESISTANCE TO CHANGE

Idea champions often discover that other employees are unenthusiastic about their new ideas. Members of a new-venture group may be surprised when managers in the regular organization do not support or approve their innovations. Managers and employees not involved in an innovation often seem to prefer the status quo. Employees appear to resist

new-venture team
A unit separate from the mainstream of the organization that is responsible for developing and initiating innovations

new-venture fund
A fund that provides resources from which individuals and groups draw to develop new ideas, products, or businesses

FOCUS ON Collaboration — LANDS' END

Employees are not always receptive to change. A combination of factors can lead to rejection of, or even outright rebellion against, management's new and better ideas. Successful companies have learned to create an environment of collaboration when bringing change.

Lands' End, Inc., of Dodgeville, Wisconsin, began as a small mail-order business specializing in sailing gear. Employees enjoyed the family-like atmosphere and uncomplicated work environment. By 1994, the company had mushroomed into a $1 billion company with several overseas outlets and had passed giant L. L. Bean as number one in specialty catalog sales in the United States.

Such success encouraged founder and chairman Gary Comer to embark on a dramatic management experiment incorporating many of today's trends—teams, 401k plans, peer reviews, and the elimination of guards and time clocks. Comer brought in top talent, including former L. L. Bean executive William T. End as CEO, to implement the changes.

But employees balked. Weekly production meetings became a nuisance to workers. "We spent so much time in meetings that we were getting away from the basic stuff of taking care of business," says one employee. Even a much-ballyhooed new mission statement seemed pushy. One long-time employee complained that "we don't need anything hanging over our heads or anyone telling us to do something we're already doing."

Confusion and frustration reigned at Lands' End and was reflected in an earnings drop of 17 percent. By the end of December 1994, End was forced out, and a new CEO initiated a return to the familiar "Lands' End Way" of doing things. Teams were disbanded and many of the once-promising initiatives were shelved as workers embraced what was familiar and uncomplicated.

The inability of people to adapt to change is not new. Neither is the failure of management to sufficiently lay the groundwork to prepare employees for change. Harvard professor John P. Kotter established an eight-step plan for implementing change that can provide a greater potential for successful transformation of a company:

1. Establish a sense of urgency through careful examination of the market and identification of opportunities and potential crises.

2. Form a powerful coalition of managers able to lead the change.

3. Create a vision to direct the change and the strategies for achieving that vision.

4. Communicate the vision throughout the organization.

5. Empower others to act on the vision by removing barriers, changing systems, and encouraging risk taking.

6. Plan for visible, short-term performance improvements and create those improvements.

7. Consolidate improvements, reassess changes, and make necessary adjustments in the new programs.

8. Articulate the relationship between new behaviors and organizational success.

Major change efforts can be messy and full of surprises, but following these guidelines can break down resistance and mean the difference between success and failure.

SOURCES: Gregory A. Patterson, "Lands' End Kicks Out Modern New Managers, Rejecting a Makeover," *The Wall Street Journal*, April 3, 1995, A1, A6; and John P. Kotter, "Leading Changes: Why Transformation Efforts Fail," *Harvard Business Review* (March–April 1995), pp. 59–67.

---

change for several reasons and understanding them helps managers implement change more effectively.

SELF-INTEREST Employees typically resist a change they believe will take away something of value. A proposed change in job design, structure, or technology may lead to a perceived loss of power, prestige, pay, or company benefits. The fear of personal loss is perhaps the biggest obstacle to organizational change.[25] When Mesa Oil Corporation tried to buy Phillips Petroleum, Phillips employees started a campaign to prevent the takeover. Employees believed that Mesa would not treat them well and that they would lose financial benefits. Their resistance to change was so effective that the merger failed to take place. Sometimes top managers miss the boat on an important change because they let their own self-interest blind them to new opportunities in the marketplace, as top record companies learned (see example).

MP3

College students nowadays are likely to download their favorite songs off the Internet and put them on writeable CDs. Web sales of music are likely to be $1.6 billion by 2002.

Now the sales are with CDs, but the real promise is with a new technology called MP3, which lets Web users compress songs and download onto their computer's hard drive, storing many with fewer bytes.

Though record-store sales are dominated by the Big Five Studios (Sony, TimeWarner, BMG, Holdings, and Polygram), net sales are being run by new upstarts such as MP3.com, Inc. and Emusic.com, as well as smaller but established labels such as Public Enemy and Chuck D. In fact, the top studios have dismissed MP3 and are afraid of its potential threat, but are working behind the scenes to develop technology that won't make pirating so easy.

In the meantime, brash companies such as Atomic Pop and Listen.com are signing hip artists to sweet deals. Whereas an artist makes about $1.50 per record, the online deals offer $3 to $5 per record sold.

What MP3 offers could just revolutionize the way music is sold. Music can be bought more customized and the availability is much wider, appealing to more individualized tastes. And even though the big companies see MP3 as a threat, what they don't realize is that many downloaders go out and buy the actual CD. Take customer Brian Crissie. Even with the download, he still wants the words, the pictures, the liner, the photos. "I want to have it, just to have it," he says.[26] ■

LACK OF UNDERSTANDING AND TRUST Employees often do not understand the intended purpose of a change. Sometimes they distrust the intentions—or perceived intentions—behind it. If previous working relationships with an idea champion have been negative, resistance may occur. One manager had a habit of initiating a change in the financial reporting system about every 12 months and then losing interest and not following through. After the third time, employees no longer went along with the change because they did not trust the manager's intention to follow through to their benefit.

UNCERTAINTY   Uncertainty occurs when there is a lack of information about future events. It represents a fear of the unknown. Uncertainty is especially threatening for employees who have a low tolerance for change and fear the novel and unusual. They do not know how a change will affect them and worry about whether they will be able to meet the demands of a new procedure or technology.[27] Entrepreneurs also face a great deal of uncertainty. Many fail because they do not understand what it takes to be an entrepreneur. Want to reduce your own uncertainty about whether you should start your own business? Read on for ideas about your potential as an entrepreneur.

ENTREPRENEUR INTERNSHIP PROGRAM
First, look honestly at yourself in light of the skills the U.S. Small Business Administration lists as essential to being an entrepreneur: (a) *drive:* the willingness to spend the long, necessary hours and high stress required; (b) *multiple thinking skills:* analytical, creative, original, and critical—being able to see the big picture and develop a tight strategy to achieve it; (c) *people skills:* ability to motivate employees, negotiate with vendors, persuade lenders, and sell to customers.

If you have those skills and still are not certain entrepreneurialism is right for you, or you want to affirm the choice you made to be an entrepreneur, become part of the national Entrepreneurship Internship Program that is run in about 800 university undergraduate and graduate programs. In one program, Andrea Torres works with the president of Nature Technology to develop new business plans. In another,

Brooke Connover works a few doors away from the CEO at Xodiac in Lincoln, Nebraska, assisting the executive team. Other interns scout out sales accounts worth $1 million, line up multi-million-dollar venture capitalists, and work hand-in-hand with managers in high-tech startups. For more information, contact the Kauffman Foundation at www.emfk.org and click on "programs/partners" and then "Kauffman Entrepreneur Internship Program."

The program has been wonderfully successful. Of the 15 students in last year's University of Nebraska group, four have already started their own businesses.[28] ■

DIFFERENT ASSESSMENTS AND GOALS

Another reason for resistance to change is that people who will be affected by innovation may assess the situation differently than would an idea champion or new-venture group. Often *critics* voice legitimate disagreements over the proposed benefits of change. Managers in each department pursue different goals, and an innovation may detract from performance and goal achievement for some departments. For example, if marketing gets the new product it wants for its customers, the cost of manufacturing may increase, and the manufacturing superintendent thus will resist. Resistance may call attention to problems with the innovation itself. At a consumer products company in Racine, Wisconsin, middle managers resisted the introduction of a new employee program that turned out to be a bad idea, but the managers truly believed that the program would do more harm than good. One manager bluntly told his boss, "I've been here longer than you, and I'll be here after you've gone, so don't tell me what really counts at this company."[29]

These reasons for resistance are legitimate in the eyes of employees affected by the change. The best procedure for managers is not to ignore resistance but to diagnose the reasons and design strategies that will be acceptable. Strategies for overcoming resistance to change typically involve two approaches: analyzing resistance through the force field

technique and using selective implementation tactics.

FORCE FIELD ANALYSIS

Force field analysis grew from the work of Kurt Lewin, who proposed that change was a result of the competition between driving and restraining forces.[30] When a change is introduced, some forces drive it and other forces resist it. To implement a change, management should analyze the change forces. By selectively removing forces that restrain change, the driving forces will be strong enough to enable implementation, as illustrated by the move from A to B in Exhibit 8.3. As restraining forces are reduced or removed, behavior will shift to incorporate the desired changes.

Just-in-time (JIT) inventory control systems schedule materials to arrive at a company just as they are needed on the production line. In an Ohio manufacturing company, management's analysis showed that the driving forces associated with the implementation of JIT were (1) the large cost savings from reduced inventories, (2) savings from needing fewer workers to handle the inventory, and (3) a quicker, more competitive market response for the company. Restraining forces discovered by managers were (1) a freight system that was too slow to deliver inventory on time, (2) a facility layout that emphasized inventory maintenance over new deliveries, (3) worker skills inappropriate for handling rapid inventory deployment, and (4) union resistance to loss of jobs. The driving forces were not sufficient to overcome the restraining forces.

To shift the behavior to JIT, managers attacked the restraining forces. An analysis of the freight system showed that delivery by truck provided the flexibility and quickness needed to schedule inventory arrival at a specific time each day. The problem with facility layout was met by adding four new loading docks. Inappropriate worker skills were attacked with a training program to instruct workers in JIT methods and in assembling products with un-inspected parts. Union resistance was overcome by agreeing to reassign workers no longer needed for maintaining

force field analysis
The process of determining which forces drive and which resist a proposed change

Exhibit 8.3

USING FORCE FIELD ANALYSIS TO CHANGE FROM TRADITIONAL TO JUST-IN-TIME INVENTORY SYSTEM

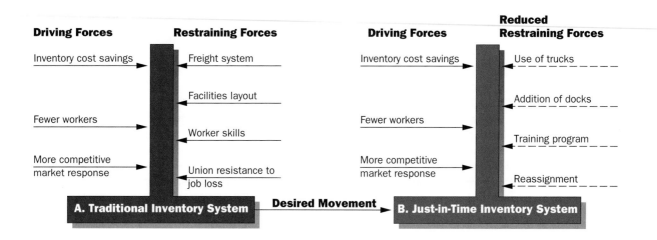

inventory to jobs in another plant. With the restraining forces reduced, the driving forces were sufficient to allow the JIT system to be implemented.

IMPLEMENTATION TACTICS

The other approach to managing implementation is to adopt specific tactics to overcome employee resistance. For example, resistance to change may be overcome by educating employees or inviting them to participate in implementing the change. Methods for dealing with resistance to change have been studied by researchers. The following five tactics, summarized in Exhibit 8.4, have seen successful results.[31]

COMMUNICATION AND EDUCATION

Communication and education are used when solid information about the change is needed by users and others who may resist implementation. Education is especially important when the change involves new technical knowledge or users are unfamiliar with the idea. Canadian Airlines International spent a year and a half preparing and training employees before changing its entire reservations, airport, cargo, and financial systems as part of a new "Service Quality" strategy. Smooth implementation resulted from this intensive training and communications effort, which involved 50,000 tasks, 12,000 people, and 26 classrooms around the world.[32]

PARTICIPATION

Participation involves users and potential resisters in designing the change. This approach is time-consuming, but it pays off because users understand and become committed to the change. Participation also helps managers determine potential problems and understand the differences in perceptions of change among employees.[33] When General Motors tried to implement a new management appraisal system for supervisors in its Adrian, Michigan, plant, it met with immediate resistance. Rebuffed by the lack of cooperation, top managers proceeded more slowly, involving supervisors in the design of the new appraisal system. Through participation in system design, managers understood what the new approach was all about and dropped their resistance to it.

NEGOTIATION

Negotiation is a more formal means of achieving cooperation. Negotiation uses formal bargaining to win acceptance and approval of a desired change. General

Approach	When to Use
Communication, education	• Change is technical. • Users need accurate information and analysis to understand change.
Participation	• Users need to feel involved. • Design requires information from others. • Users have power to resist.
Negotiation	• Group has power over implementation. • Group will lose out in the change.
Coercion	• A crisis exists. • Initiators clearly have power. • Other implementation techniques have failed.
Top management support	• Change involves multiple departments or reallocation of resources. • Users doubt legitimacy of change.

SOURCE: Based on J. P. Kotter and L. A. Schlesinger, "Choosing Strategies for Change," *Harvard Business Review, 57* (March–April 1979), 106–114.

Motors, General Electric, and other companies that have strong unions frequently must formally negotiate change with the unions. The change may become part of the union contract reflecting the agreement of both parties.

COERCION   Coercion is the exertion of formal power in order to force employees to change. Resisters are told to accept the change or lose rewards or even their jobs. In most cases, this approach is ineffective because employees will feel like victims, grow angry toward managers and the proposed changes, and may even sabotage the changes. However, coercion may be necessary in crisis situations when a rapid response is urgent. When middle managers at TRW, Inc.'s Valve Division in Cleveland refused to go along with a new employee involvement program, top management reassigned several first-line supervisors and managers. The new jobs did not involve supervisory responsibility. Further, other TRW managers were told that future pay increases depended on their adoption of the new procedures. Coercive techniques had to be used in this case—as a last resort—because of continued resistance to change.[34]

TOP MANAGEMENT SUPPORT   The visible support of top management also helps overcome resistance to change. Top management support symbolizes to all employees that the change is important for the organization. Top management support is especially important when a change involves multiple departments or when resources are being reallocated among departments. Without top management support, these changes can get bogged down in squabbling among departments. Moreover, when top managers fail to support a project, they can inadvertently undercut it by issuing contradictory orders. At Flying Tiger Lines, the airborne freight hauler implemented a new layout of offices so that two agents rather than four could handle each shipment. Right after the switch was begun, top management ordered another layout. The newest one was not as efficient, but it was supported by top management. This example (and the following one on General Stair Corporation) illustrates how smart implementation techniques can smooth the change process.

GENERAL STAIR CORPORATION
General Stair Corp., a maker of prefabricated stairs and railings, was facing increased competition, and its profit and market share were declining. The company found itself dealing with a constant

Herman Wright, PruCare of Austin's director of sales and marketing, shown here with his sales and service staff, knows that top management support is essential to overcoming resistance to change. In PruCare's thrust toward customer satisfaction, Wright used the implementation tactics of communication and participation. He communicated his desire to build customer relationships based on trust and then pushed responsibility down to everyone in the organization: "We stopped telling people what to do and started listening."

price war. Founder Saby Behar wanted to find a way to keep his customers less focused on price. To distinguish his company from the competition, Behar decided General Stair should start offering a money-back delivery guarantee, something he knew his customers (who often worked on 30 or more buildings at a time) would appreciate. However, managers and other employees were aghast at the suggestion. Workers weren't sure they could meet the requirements for such a guarantee and were concerned that it might require more overtime. Managers worried about the cost of upgrading communications systems to keep field reps in touch with headquarters, builders, and the contractors.

Implementation of the change involved several steps. To combat the initial resistance among his managers, Behar held several meetings explaining his reasons for making the change and answering their questions. This at least got people talking about whether and how such a guarantee could actually work. Next, managers brought in the rest of the employees to discuss the proposed change and how to put it into action. Managers knew they had to revamp communications, but discussions with employees led them to realize other systems, such as distribution and compensation, needed to change as well. In addition, rather than a complete money-back guarantee, the group eventually settled on a fine of $50 per day for late deliveries. Although the company already had a good on-time delivery record, employees were trained in new procedures that would help assure consistent performance.

Because top management involved employees from the early stages, the changes went smoothly. Labor costs were slashed by 30 percent, even though employees were earning up to 60 percent more money because of a new piece-rate system. Productivity was up 300 percent. And, within the first year, the company had to pay out only a few $50 vouchers for late deliveries. General Stair's market share and profits were once again healthy.[35] ■

■ TYPES OF PLANNED CHANGE

Now that we have explored how the initiation and implementation of change can be carried out, let us look at the different types of change that occur in organizations. Two issues will be addressed: (1) the parts of the organization that can be changed and (2) how managers can apply initiation and implementation ideas to each type of change.

Exhibit 8.5 shows the types of organizational change. Organizations may innovate in one or more areas, depending on internal and external forces for change. In the rapidly changing toy industry, a manufacturer has to introduce new products frequently. In a mature, competitive industry, production technology changes are adopted to improve efficiency. In the model, the arrows show that a change in one part may affect other parts of the organization. For instance, a new product may require changes in technology, and a new technology may require new people skills or a new structure. When Shenandoah Life Insurance Company computerized processing and claims operations, the structure had to be decentralized, employees required intensive training, and a more participative culture was needed. Related changes were required for the new technology to increase efficiency.

TECHNOLOGY CHANGES

A **technology change** is related to the organization's production process—how the organization does its work. Technology changes are designed to make the production of a product or service more efficient. For example, the adoption of robotics to improve production efficiency at General Motors is an example of a technology change, as is the adoption of laser-scanning checkout systems at supermarkets. At IBM's manufacturing plant in Charlotte, North Carolina, an automated mini-load storage and retrieval system was installed to handle production parts. This change provided an efficient method for handling small-parts inventory and changed the technology of the IBM plant. Another change many companies now face is e-commerce. Technology for Tomorrow describes how one company created a successful Web site.

How can managers encourage technology change? The general rule is that technology change is bottom up.[36] The bottom-up approach means that ideas are initiated at lower

technology change
A change that pertains to the organization's production process

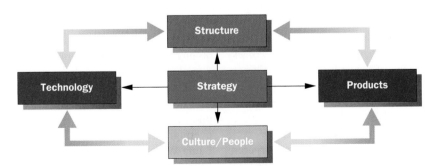

E x h i b i t 8.5
TYPES OF ORGANIZATIONAL CHANGE

TECHNOLOGY FOR TOMORROW
BRINGING THE COMPANY ONLINE

Bringing a business into the e-commerce age may mean some fundamental changes. One thing that needs adequate and competent attention is preparing or upgrading the company's Web page. Here are some suggestions from the experts: If you want your small business to do business online, there are five basic steps to follow.

1. Build a Web site that displays merchandise and will take orders electronically. You can purchase from a myriad selection of Web site templates offered by various software developers. But beware, mistakes are often made. Avoid making your site cluttered, having lengthy and frustrating downloads; distracting and conflicting colors, leaving visitors aimless without knowing how to get to the next page or back to Home. If you don't want to do it yourself, you can find many Web designers, at whatever budget you have. Increasingly, companies in other countries such as India (see www.NetEcho.com) are designing reasonably priced Web pages. There are also companies that systematize order taking and get you set up accepting credit cards.

2. Choose a name. It might be your company name, followed by dot-com. Or it might be related to what you do. One furniture company considered using "ForMyHome.com," or "Furniture.com," which it declined because someone else owned the domain name and would only sell it for $1 million. So, if you think up a good name, rush as fast as you can to the register of Internet names, Network Solutions Inc, which has already given out 5 million names. By the way, the dot-coms are considered more desirable than the dot-net names.

3. Find someone to "host" your site, which can cost as little as $100 per year if you are using a site from your Internet provider to $60 to $80 per month if you have your own site. But make sure your server will attend to technical problems in net speed. Visitors will quickly learn to avoid your site if it is too frequently down.

4. Advertise your site. Some companies offer—for a small fee—to list your site on up to 400 Internet search engines.

5. Keep your site current with frequent—even daily—updates. When writing content and articles for your site, choose a folksy, down-to-earth tone, treating Web visitors as confidants. That's what's made Garden.com (see Chapter 5) so popular and beloved by its readers. Give information, but write it in a more conversational tone. Avoid humor, because something spoken funny may offend people when in print. And remember, you have about three sentences to catch attention before your site is discarded with one simple "click."

SOURCES: Joelle Tessler, "Small Investment, Big Results," *The Wall Street Journal*, Nov. 22, 1999, p. R16; Nick Wingfield, "The Name of the Game," *The Wall Street Journal*, Nov. 22, 1999, p. R14; Megan Doscher, "Decisions, Decisions," *The Wall Street Journal*, Nov. 22, 1999, p. R54; Lee Gomes, "(Not) Made in America," *The Wall Street Journal*, Nov. 22, 1999, p. R66; "Jennifer L. Rewick, "Elements of Cyberstyle," *The Wall Street Journal*, Nov. 22, 1999, p. R64.

organization levels and channeled upward for approval. Lower-level technical experts act as idea champions—they invent and champion technological changes. Employees at lower levels understand the technology and have the expertise needed to propose changes. For example, at Dana Corporation's Elizabethtown, Kentucky, plant, two workers came up with an idea to automatically load steel sheets into a forming press. This technology change saves the auto parts maker $250,000 a year.[37]

A loose, flexible, decentralized structure provides employees with the freedom and opportunity to initiate continuous improvements. A rigid, centralized, standardized structure stifles technology innovation. Anything managers can do to involve the grass roots of the organization—the people who are experts in their parts of the production process—will increase technology change. Great Harvest Bread Company encourages bottom-up change among its franchisees by giving them almost complete freedom to run their businesses. This freedom inspires new and better ways of doing things that quickly spread to other stores by phone, fax, and e-mail. "Innovation happens overnight in our company," says cofounder Laura Wakeman.[38]

A top-down approach to technology change usually does not work.[39] Top managers are not close to the production process and lack expertise in technological developments.

Mandating technology change from the top produces fewer rather than more technology innovations. The spark for a creative new idea comes from people close to the technology. The rationale behind Motorola's "participative management program," Data General's "pride teams," and Honeywell's "positive action teams" is to encourage new technology ideas from people at lower levels of the organization.

NEW-PRODUCT CHANGES

A **product change** is a change in the organization's product or service output. New-product innovations have major implications for an organization, because they often are an outcome of a new strategy and may define a new market.[40] In addition, product life cycles are getting shorter, so that companies need to continuously come up with innovative ideas for new products and services that meet needs in the marketplace. Product innovation is the primary way in which many organizations adapt to changes in markets, technologies, and competition.[41] Examples of new products include Frappuccino, a bottled drink from Starbuck's; Apple Computer's new iMac; and Gillette's MACH3, triple-bladed razor.

Introducing a new product is not easy, but hundreds of new products are introduced every day. Even though the cost of successfully launching a new product is $20 million to $50 million, approximately 25,000 new products appeared in 1997 alone. The majority of those products will fail in the marketplace—the most optimistic estimate is that one in five launches will succeed, while the most pessimistic forecast is for one out of 671. Consider such flops as Gerber's "Singles" meals for adults, which looked like jars of baby food, or Nestea's launch of a yellowish carbonated beverage called Tea Whiz.[42] Product development is a risky, high-stakes game for organizations. Companies that successfully develop new products usually have the following characteristics:

1. Marketing people have a good understanding of customer needs.

2. Technical specialists are aware of recent technological developments and make effective use of new technology.

3. Members from key departments—research, manufacturing, marketing—cooperate in the development of the new product.[43]

These findings mean that the ideas for new products typically originate at the lower levels of the organization just as they do for technology changes. The difference is that new-product ideas flow horizontally among departments. Product innovation requires expertise from several departments simultaneously. A new-product failure is often the result of failed cooperation.[44]

One approach to successful new-product innovation is called the **horizontal linkage model,** illustrated in Exhibit 8.6, which shows that research, manufacturing, and marketing must simultaneously develop new products. People from these departments meet frequently in teams and task forces to share ideas and solve problems. Research people inform marketing of new technical developments to learn whether they will be useful to customers. Marketing people pass customer complaints to research to use in the design of new products. Manufacturing informs other departments whether a product idea can be manufactured within cost limits. When the horizontal linkage model is used, the decision to develop a new product is a joint one.

Today's increasingly sophisticated consumer is demanding an ever increasing role in product development and marketing. Empowerment in today's competitive environment goes beyond employees to include suppliers and customers in the product development process. Entire industries, like automakers, are actively soliciting consumer feedback for new products and are including consumer participation from the beginning of the design process. Marketing departments have been surveying customers for years to determine what they want and need. A new approach is to actually observe customers using products or services in their normal, everyday routines in order to gather information about unarticulated customer desires. For example, after visiting the homes of customers, Kimberly-Clark recognized the emotional appeal of pull-on diapers and invented Huggies Pull-Ups. By the time competitors caught on, the company was

product change
A change in the organization's product or service output

horizontal linkage model
An approach to product change that emphasizes shared development of innovations among several departments

Exhibit 8.6

HORIZONTAL LINKAGE
MODEL FOR NEW-PRODUCT
INNOVATION

selling $400 million worth of the product annually.[45] This type of consumer research requires creative interaction among many departments, which is characteristic of the horizontal linkage model.

Horizontal linkages are being adopted in the computer industry to overcome new-product problems. For example, at Convergent Technologies, Workslate, a portable computer, received accolades when it was introduced. One year later, Workslate was dead. Production problems with the new product had not been worked out. Marketing people had not fully analyzed customer needs. The idea had been pushed through without sufficient consultation among research, manufacturing, and marketing. IBM PC Company changed its approach to new-product development to reduce development time. New products are now created by teams of workers from research, design, procurement, logistics, marketing, and manufacturing—all working side-by-side in one location rather than being spread out across the country as they were before.[46] Developing a radically new process for manufacturing and marketing a new product can shake up an industry, as iUniverse hopes to do.

iUNIVERSE AND MELISSE SHAPIRO

For all the budding authors who don't have the clout of an Anne Rice or Tom Clancy and have enough rejection letters to wallpaper their apartment, there is another alternative to getting your book published. New company iUniverse is reinventing book publishing—by leveraging the Internet's technology as a medium for production, marketing, and distribution—and thereby making it easier for worthy but unknown authors to get their books published. Under the

old model, an author either had to have a big name or a surefire hit that would make a lot of money. With iUniverse's Internet technology, they have changed the economic picture so they can make money on sales of hundreds, rather than millions, of books.

Not only is a new product developed, or at least a new twist on an old product, but developer iUniverse is one of the dot-com companies who are helping to completely redefine industries and forcing traditional firms to rethink strategies, philosophy, and customer relationships.

With print-on-demand technology to publish books for new and out-of-print authors, iUniverse lists the books on its Web site as well as with online booksellers. iUniverse has simplified the entire book publishing chain into multiple channels taking four to six weeks, through the use of a system for content management, a complex e-commerce back end, and integrated publishing technologies. By next year, CEO Richard Tam expects the cycle time to be reduced to two weeks. By this time, the book is ready digitally, but is not produced until an order is placed.

The company, which recently sold a stake to Barnes & Noble, is an Internet business with products and services spanning both Internet and traditional bookstores, and it sells to large book chains as well as directly to customers. It generated 1,000 titles in its first year and had 3,000 by the end of 1999, placing it among the top five publishers. Tam has high expectations. "We expect to be the largest title producer in this country," he says.

And, if even that is too much bureaucracy for you, follow the lead of Melisse Shapiro, who found dead ends with every publisher she contacted. Rather than going the small-press route, she set up her own Web site and sold digital copies of her book as a downloadable text document. Then she had 3,000 copies made through a small printer and used Amazon to sell more. But realizing she needed more visibility, she started sending free review copies to Web sites and asked for links. "For three months I spent six hours a day, six days a week working in the Internet . . . following links to more links to more links."

After the success she earned online, she got a lucrative book deal from Pocket Books and has climbed to the top of the charts at both Barnes & Noble and Amazon. How did she get the deal? A young editor was cruising the Internet and was interested in fresh approaches. Hers definitely fit the bill.[47] ■

Innovation is becoming a major strategic weapon in the global marketplace. One example of innovation is the use of **time-based competition,** which means delivering products and services faster than competitors, giving companies a significant strategic advantage. For example, Hewlett-Packard reduced the time to develop a new printer from 4.5 years to 22 months. Lenscrafters jumped from 3 to 300 stores based on its ability to provide high-quality eyeglasses in one hour. Dillard's department stores went to an automatic reorder system that replenishes stocks in 12 days rather than 30, providing retail goods to customers more quickly.[48] Sprinting to market with a new product requires a parallel approach, or simultaneous linkage among departments. This is similar to a rugby match wherein players run together, passing the ball back and forth as they move downfield. The teamwork required for the horizontal linkage model is a major component of using rapid innovation to beat the competition with speed.[49]

STRUCTURAL CHANGES

Structural changes involve the hierarchy of authority, goals, structural characteristics, administrative procedures, and management systems.[50] Almost any change in how the organization is managed falls under the category of structural change. For example, IBM's change from a functional to a product structure was a structural change.

Successful structural change is accomplished through a top-down approach, which is distinct from a technology change (bottom up) and new products (horizontal).[51] Structural change is top down because the expertise for administrative improvements originates at the middle and upper levels of the organization. The champions for structural change are middle and top managers. Lower-level technical specialists have little interest or expertise in administrative procedures. If organization structure causes negative consequences for lower-level employees, complaints and dissatisfaction alert managers to a problem. Employee dissatisfaction is an internal force for change. The need for change is perceived by higher managers, who then take the initiative to propose and implement it.

The top-down process does not mean that coercion is the best implementation tactic. Implementation tactics include education, participation, and negotiation with employees. Unless there is an emergency, managers should not force structural change on employees. They may hit a resistance wall, and the change will fail. This is exactly what happened at the company for which Mary Kay Ash worked before she started her own cosmetics business. The owner learned that even a top-down change in commission rate needs to incorporate education and participation to succeed:

I worked for a company whose owner decided to revise the commission schedule paid to his sales managers. . . . To an audience of 50 sales managers he announced that the 2 percent override they were presently earning on their units' sales production was to be reduced to 1 percent. "However," he said,

time-based competition
A strategy of competition based on the ability to deliver products and services faster than competitors

structural change
Any change in the way the organization is designed and managed

"in lieu of that 1 percent, you will receive a very nice gift for each new person you recruit and train."

At that point a sales manager stood up and let him have it with both barrels. "How dare you do this to us? Why, even 2 percent wasn't enough. But cutting our overrides in half and offering us a crummy gift for appeasement insults our intelligence." With that she stormed out of the room. And every other sales manager for that state followed her—all 50 of them. In one fell swoop the owner had lost his entire sales organization in that region—the best in the country. I had never seen such an overwhelming rejection of a change of this kind in my entire life![52] ■

■ CULTURE/PEOPLE CHANGES

A **culture/people change** refers to a change in values, norms, attitudes, beliefs, and behaviors of employees. Changes in culture and people pertain to how employees think; these are changes in mind-set rather than technology, structure, or products. People change pertains to just a few employees, such as when a handful of middle managers is sent to a training course to improve their leadership skills. Culture change pertains to the organization as a whole, such as when Union Pacific Railroad changed its basic mind-set by becoming less bureaucratic and focusing employees on customer service and quality through teamwork and employee participation.[53] Training is the most frequently used tool for changing the organization's mind-set. A company may offer training programs to large blocks of employees on subjects such as teamwork, listening skills, quality circles, and participative management. Training programs will be discussed further in Chapter 9 on human resource management.

Another major approach to changing people and culture is organizational development. This has evolved as a separate field devoted to large-scale organizational change.

ORGANIZATIONAL DEVELOPMENT

Organizational development (OD) is the application of behavioral science knowledge to improve an organization's health and effectiveness by coping with environmental changes, improving internal relationships, and increasing problem-solving capabilities.[54]

The following are three types of current problems that OD can help managers address.

1. *Mergers/acquisitions.* The disappointing financial results of many mergers and acquisitions are caused by the failure of executives to determine whether the administrative style and corporate culture of the two companies "fit." Executives may concentrate on potential synergies in technology, products, marketing, and control systems but fail to recognize that two firms may have widely different values, beliefs, and practices. These differences create stress and anxiety for employees, and these negative emotions affect future performance. Cultural differences should be evaluated during the acquisition process, and OD experts can be used to smooth the integration process.

2. *Organizational decline/revitalization.* Organizations undergoing a period of decline and revitalization experience a variety of problems, including a low level of trust, lack of innovation, high turnover, and high levels of conflict and stress. The period of transition requires opposite behaviors, including confronting stress, creating open communication, and fostering creative innovation to emerge with high levels of productivity. OD techniques can contribute greatly to cultural revitalization by managing conflicts, fostering commitment, and facilitating communication.

3. *Conflict management.* Conflict can occur at any time and place within a healthy organization. For example, a product team for the introduction of a new software package was formed at a computer company. Made up of strong-willed individuals, the team made little progress because members would not agree on project goals. At a manufacturing firm, salespeople promised delivery dates to customers that were in conflict with shop supervisor priorities for assembling customer orders. In a publishing company, two managers disliked each other intensely. They argued at meetings, lobbied politically

---

culture/people change
A change in employees' values, norms, attitudes, beliefs, and behavior

organizational development (OD)
The application of behavioral science knowledge to improve an organization's health and effectiveness by coping with environmental changes, improving internal relationships, and increasing problem-solving capabilities

against each other, and hurt the achievement of both departments. Organizational development efforts can help solve these kinds of conflicts.[55]

Organizational development can be used to solve the types of problems just described and many others. However, to be truly valuable to companies and employees, organizational development practitioners go beyond looking at ways to solve specific problems. Instead, they become involved in broader issues that contribute to improving organizational life, such as encouraging a sense of community, pushing for an organizational climate of openness and trust, and making sure the company provides employees with opportunities for personal growth and development.[56] Specialized techniques have been developed to help meet OD goals.

OD ACTIVITIES

A number of OD activities have emerged in recent years. Some of the most popular and effective are **team-building activities,** which enhance the cohesiveness and success of organizational groups and teams. For example, a series of OD exercises can be used with members of cross-departmental teams to help them learn to act and function as a team. An OD expert can work with team members to increase their communication skills, facilitate their ability to confront one another, and accept common goals.

Survey-feedback activities begin with a questionnaire distributed to employees on values, climate, participation, leadership, and group cohesion within their organization.[57] After the survey is completed, an OD consultant meets with groups of employees to provide feedback about their responses and the problems identified.[58] Employees are engaged in problem solving based on the data.

The **large-group intervention** approach brings together participants from all parts of the organization, who often are key stakeholders from outside the organization, to discuss problems or opportunities and make plans for change. A large-group intervention might involve 50 to 500 people and may last several days. The idea is to include everyone who has a stake in the change, gather perspectives from all parts of the system, and enable people to create a collective future through sustained, guided conversation and dialogue.[59]

Large-group interventions reflect a significant shift in the approach to organizational change from earlier OD concepts and approaches. Exhibit 8.7 lists the primary differences between the traditional OD model and the large-scale intervention model of organizational change. In the newer approach, the focus is on the entire system, which takes into account the organization's interaction with its environment. The source of information for discussion is expanded to include customers, suppliers, community members, even competitors, and this information is shared widely so that everyone has the same picture of the organization and its environment. The acceleration of change when the entire system is involved can be remarkable. In addition, learning occurs across all parts of the organization simultaneously, rather than in individuals, small groups, or business units. The end result is that the large-group approach offers greater possibilities for fundamental, radical transformation of the entire culture, whereas the traditional approach creates incremental change in a few individuals or small groups at a time.

Large-group interventions represent a significant shift in the way leaders think about change and reflect an increasing awareness of the importance of dealing with the entire system, including external stakeholders, in any significant change effort.

OD STEPS

Organizational development experts acknowledge that corporate culture and human behavior are relatively stable and that companywide changes require major effort. The theory underlying organizational development proposes three distinct steps for achieving behavioral and attitudinal change: (1) unfreezing, (2) changing, and (3) refreezing.[60]

In the first step, called **unfreezing,** participants become aware of problems and then increase their willingness to change. This step is often associated with diagnosis—from an outside **change agent,** who gathers and analyzes data through personal interviews, questionnaires, and observations of meetings. The diagnosis helps determine the extent of organizational problems and helps unfreeze managers by making them aware of problems in their behavior.

---

team-building activities
OD interventions that enhance the cohesiveness of departments by helping members learn to function as a team

survey-feedback activities
OD interventions in which questionnaires on organizational climate and other factors are distributed among employees and the results reported back to them

large-group intervention
OD approach that brings together participants from all parts of the organization, who often are key stakeholders from outside the organization, to discuss problems or opportunities and make plans for change

unfreezing
OD diagnosis in which participants become aware of problems and increase their willingness to change

change agent
OD specialist who performs a systematic diagnosis of the organization and identifies work-related problems

Exhibit 8.7

OD Approaches to
Culture Change

	Traditional Organizational Development Model	Large-Group Intervention Model
Focus for action:	Specific problem or group	Entire system
Information Source: Distribution:	Organization Limited	Organization and environment Widely shared
Time frame:	Gradual	Fast
Learning:	Individual, small group	Whole organization

Change process:	Incremental change	Rapid transformation

SOURCE: Adapted from Barbara Benedict Bunker and Billie T. Alban, "Conclusion: What Makes Large Group Interventions Effective," *The Journal of Applied Behavioral Science,* 28 (4) (December 1992), 579–591.

The second step, **changing,** occurs when individuals experiment with new behavior and learn new skills to be used in the workplace. This is sometimes known as intervention, during which the change agent implements a specific plan for training managers and employees.

The third step, **refreezing,** occurs when the impact of new behaviors is evaluated and reinforced by individuals who have newly-acquired attitudes or values and are rewarded for them by the organization. The change agent supplies new data that show positive changes in performance. Senior executives can reward positive behavioral changes by employees. Managers and employees also participate in refresher courses to maintain and reinforce the new behaviors.

The spirit of what OD tries to accomplish with culture/people change is illustrated by General Electric's Work Out Program, which provides an excellent example of the large-group intervention approach.

General Electric
www.ge.com

The Work Out program is one of the ways in which Jack Welch has reshaped General Electric for renewed productivity and growth. The program was created out of Welch's desire to reach and motivate 300,000 employees and his insistence that the people on the front lines, where change had to happen, be empowered to create the change.

GE's Work Out began in large-scale off-site meetings facilitated by a combination of top leaders, outside consultants, and human resources specialists. In each business unit, the basic pattern was the same. Hourly and salaried workers came together from many different parts of the organization in an informal three-day meeting to discuss and solve problems. Gradually, the Work Out events began to include external stakeholders such as suppliers and customers as well as employees. Today, GE's Work Out is not an event, but a process of how work is done and problems are solved.

Seven steps comprise the format: (1) choose a work process or problem for discussion; (2) select an appropriate cross-functional team, to include external stakeholders; (3) assign a champion to follow through on recommendations; (4) meet for several days and come up with recommendations to improve processes or solve problems; (5) meet with leaders, who are required to respond to recommendations on the spot; (6) hold additional meetings as needed to pursue the

changing
OD intervention in which individuals experiment with new workplace behavior and learn new skills

refreezing
OD reinforcement in which individuals acquire a desired new skill or attitude for which they are rewarded by the organization

recommendations; (7) start the process all over again with a new process or problem.

GE's Work Out process not only solves problems and improves productivity for the company but also gives employees the experience of openly and honestly interacting with one another without regard to vertical or horizontal boundaries. By doing so, the process has helped to create what Welch calls a "culture of boundarylessness" that is critical for continuous learning and improvement.[61] ∎

Summary and Management Solution

Change is inevitable in organizations. This chapter discussed the techniques available for managing the change process. The trend today is toward the learning organization, which embraces continuous learning and change. Managers should think of change as having four elements—the forces for change, the perceived need for change, the initiation of change, and the implementation of change. Forces for change can originate either within or outside the firm, and managers are responsible for monitoring events that may require a planned organizational response. Techniques for initiating changes include designing the organization for creativity, encouraging change agents, and establishing new-venture teams. The final step is implementation. Force field analysis is one technique for diagnosing restraining forces, which often can be removed. Managers also should draw on the implementation tactics of communication, participation, negotiation, coercion, or top management support.

At Midwest Contract Furnishings, discussed in the chapter opening, a crisis caused by the loss of a major customer made managers and employees acutely aware of a need for change. Today, teams of workers regularly look for ways to cut costs or do things better. Midwest's new business approach,

Hotel Co-op, an online source for hotel products, is up and running smoothly. In addition, the company has won several major new contracts, including two projects for Marriott. Because Cogan carefully managed the change process, Midwest weathered the crisis and has even begun hiring new people.

This chapter also discussed specific types of change. Technology changes are accomplished through a bottom-up approach that utilizes experts close to the technology. Successful new-product introduction requires horizontal linkage among marketing, research and development, manufacturing, and perhaps other departments. Structural changes tend to be initiated in a top-down fashion, because upper managers are the administrative experts and champion these ideas for approval and implementation. Culture/people change pertains to the skills, behaviors, and attitudes of employees. Organizational development is an important approach to changes in people's mind-set and corporate culture. The OD process entails three steps—unfreezing (diagnosis of the problem), the actual change (intervention), and refreezing (reinforcement of new attitudes and behaviors). Popular OD techniques include team building, survey feedback, and large-group interventions.

Discussion Questions

1. A manager of an international chemical company said that very few new products in her company were successful. What would you advise the manager to do to help increase the company's success rate?

2. What are internal and external forces for change? Which force do you think is the major cause of organizational change?

3. Carefully planned change often is assumed to be effective. Do you think unplanned change can sometimes be beneficial to an organization? Discuss.

4. Why do organizations experience resistance to change? What techniques can managers use to overcome resistance?

5. Explain force field analysis. Analyze the driving and restraining forces for a change with which you have been associated.

6. Define the roles associated with an idea champion. Why are idea champions so essential to the initiation of change?

7. To what extent would changes in technology affect products and vice versa? Compare the process for changing technology and that for product change.

8. Given that structural change is often made top down, should coercive implementation techniques be used?

9. Do the underlying values of organizational development differ from assumptions associated with other types of change? Discuss.

10. How do large-group interventions differ from OD techniques such as team-building and survey feedback?

Management Exercises

Manager's Workbook

Personal Change

Think of a situation where you wanted to (or had to) change and successfully executed the change. Then, think of another time when your attempt to change was unsuccessful. Referring to Exhibit 8.1 in the chapter, answer the following questions:

	When change was successful	When change was not successful
1. Describe the situation		
2. What was the motive or need to change?		
3. How did you feel initially about the change?		
4. What were sources of resistance?		
5. How did you get beyond the resistance? What *worked* in the process of changing?		
6. What did you learn about yourself in the process of change?		
7. What have you learned about change? About motivating others to change?		

Manager's Workshop

An Ancient Tale

1. Read the introduction and case study and answer the questions.

2. In groups of three to four discuss your answers.

3. Groups report to the whole class and the instructor leads a discussion on the issues raised.

Introduction

To understand, analyze, and improve organizations, we must carefully think through the issue of who is responsible for what activities in different organizational settings. Often we hold responsible someone who has no control over the outcome, or we fail to teach or train someone who could make the vital difference.

To explore this issue, the following exercise could be conducted on either an individual or group basis. It provides an opportunity to see how different individuals assign responsibility for an event. It is also a good opportunity to discuss the concept of organizational boundaries (what is the organization, who is in or out, etc.).

Case Study

Read the short story and respond quickly to the first three questions. Then take a little more time on questions four through six. Then, discuss in groups the results, criteria, and implications.

Long ago in an ancient kingdom there lived a princess who was very young and very beautiful. The princess, recently married, lived in a large and luxurious castle with her husband, a powerful and wealthy lord. The young princess was not content, however, to sit and eat strawberries by herself while her husband took frequent and long journeys to neighboring kingdoms. She felt neglected and soon became quite unhappy. One day, while she was alone in the castle gardens, a handsome vagabond rode out of the forest bordering the castle. He spied the beautiful princess, quickly won her heart, and carried her away with him.

Following a day of dalliance, the young princess found herself ruthlessly abandoned by the vagabond. She then discovered that the only way back to the castle led through the bewitched forest of the wicked sorcerer. Fearing to venture into the forest alone, she sought out her kind and wise godfather. She explained her plight, begged the forgiveness of the godfather, and asked his assistance in returning home before her husband returned. The godfather, however, surprised and shocked at her behavior, refused forgiveness and denied her any assistance. Discouraged but still determined, the princess disguised her identity and sought the help of the most noble of all the kingdom's knights. After hearing the sad story, the knight pledged his unfailing aid—for a modest fee. But alas, the princess had no money and the knight rode away to save other damsels.

The beautiful princess had no one else from whom she might seek help, and decided to brave the great peril alone. She followed the safest path she knew, but when she was almost through the forest, the wicked sorcerer spied her and caused her to be devoured by the fire-breathing dragon.

1. Who was inside the organization and who was outside? Where were the boundaries?

2. Who is most responsible for the death of the beautiful princess?

3. Who is second most responsible? Least responsible?

4. What criteria did you employ to reach your decisions for problems 2 and 3?

5. What interventions would you suggest to prevent a recurrence?

6. What are the implications for *organizational development and change?*

Character	Most responsible	Next most responsible	Least responsible
Princess			
Husband			
Vagabond			
Godfather			
Knight			
Sorcerer			

Check one character in each column.

Additional Manager's Workbook and Workshop Exercises can be found in the Study Guide/Workbook that accompanies this textbook.

Surf the Net

1. *The Learning Organization.* Released in March 1999, the learning organization guru, Peter Senge, authored *The Dance of Change: The Challenges of Sustaining Momentum in Learning Organizations.* Use your search engine to find a book review of this work and write a summary of your findings. One place to find book reviews is www.amazon.com.

2. *New-Venture Team.* Xerox Corporation's Palo Alto Research Center (PARC) was mentioned in the text as an example of an organization with new-venture teams. Visit PARC at www.parc.xerox.com/parc-go.html to find answers to the following questions: (a) What are the strategic themes of PARC's research agenda? (b) Which one of PARC's inventions (available under the "History" section) do you think is most useful, and why? (c) Which one of the current PARC projects did you find most intriguing, and why?

3. *Survey Feedback.* One of the OD activities mentioned in the chapter is survey feedback. One leading company in the field of employee attitude surveys is Stanard and Associates, Chicago, Illinois. Go to their Web site at www5.interaccess.com/stanard to learn more about the attitude survey instrument and to respond to the survey questions online so you can see how the procedure would work in an organizational setting. If your instructor asks you to do so, you may also want to print out the sample survey to refer to during the classroom discussion on this topic.

4. *Changes.* Visit www.mgeneral.com. Search for "Girl Power," "Fred Smith," Craig Kielburger, and also choose one other from "FindFire." Write a report describing how these four leaders affected change.

Case for Critical Analysis

Southern Discomfort

Jim Malesckowski remembers the call of two weeks ago as if he just put down the telephone receiver. "I just read your analysis and I want you to get down to Mexico right away," Jack Ripon, his boss and chief executive officer, had blurted in his ear. "You know we can't make the plant in Oconomo work anymore—the costs are just too high. So go down there, check out what our operational costs would be if we move, and report back to me in a week."

At that moment, Jim felt as if a shiv had been stuck in his side, just below the rib cage. As president of the Wisconsin Specialty Products Division of Lamprey, Inc., he knew quite well the challenge of dealing with high-cost labor in a third-generation, unionized U.S. manufacturing plant. And although he had done the analysis that led to his boss's knee-jerk response, the call still stunned him. There were 520 people who made a living at Lamprey's Oconomo facility, and if it closed, most of them wouldn't have a journeyman's prayer of finding another job in the town of 9,000 people.

Instead of the $16-per-hour average wage paid at the Oconomo plant, the wages paid to the Mexican workers—who lived in a town without sanitation and with an unbelievably toxic effluent from industrial pollution—would amount to about $1.60 an hour on average. That's a savings of nearly $15 million a year for Lamprey, to be offset in part

by increased costs for training, transportation, and other matters.

After two days of talking with Mexican government representatives and managers of other companies in the town, Jim had enough information to develop a set of comparative figures of production and shipping costs. On the way home, he started to outline the report, knowing full well that unless some miracle occurred, he would be ushering in a blizzard of pink slips for people he had come to appreciate.

The plant in Oconomo had been in operation since 1921, making special apparel for persons suffering from injuries and other medical conditions. Jim had often talked with employees who would recount stories about their fathers or grandfathers working in the same Lamprey company plant—the last of the original manufacturing operations in town.

But friendship aside, competitors had already edged past Lamprey in terms of price and were dangerously close to overtaking it in product quality. Although both Jim and the plant manager had tried to convince the union to accept lower wages, union leaders resisted. In fact, on one occasion when Jim and the plant manager tried to discuss a cell-manufacturing approach, which would cross-train employees to perform up to three different jobs, local union leaders could barely restrain their anger. Yet probing beyond the fray, Jim sensed the fear that lurked under the gruff exterior of the union reps. He sensed their vulnerability, but could not break through the reactionary bark that protected it.

A week has passed and Jim just submitted his report to his boss. Although he didn't specifically bring up the point, it was apparent that Lamprey could put its investment dollars in a bank and receive a better return than what its Oconomo operation is currently producing.

Tomorrow, he'll discuss the report with the CEO. Jim doesn't want to be responsible for the plant's dismantling, an act he personally believes would be wrong as long as there's a chance its costs can be lowered. "But Ripon's right," he says to himself. "The costs are too high, the union's unwilling to cooperate, and the company needs to make a better return on its investment if it's to continue at all. It sounds right but feels wrong. What should I do?"

Questions

1. Assume you want to lead the change to save the Oconomo plant. How would you proceed, using the four stages of the change process described in the chapter—forces, need, initiation, and implementation?

2. What is the primary type of change needed—technology, product, structure, or people/culture? To what extent will the primary change have secondary effects on other types of change at the Oconomo factory?

3. What techniques would you use to overcome union resistance and implement change?

SOURCE: Doug Wallace, "What Would You Do?" *Business Ethics,* March/April 1996, pp. 52–53. Reprinted with permission.

Endnotes

1 Michael Barrier, "Managing Workers in Times of Change," *Nation's Business,* May 1998, pp. 31, 34.

2 Richard L. Daft, "Bureaucratic vs. Nonbureaucratic Structure in the Process of Innovation and Change," in *Perspectives in Organizational Sociology: Theory and Research,* ed. Samuel B. Bacharach (Greenwich, Conn.: JAI Press, 1982), pp. 129–166.

3 Don Hellriegel and John W. Slocum, Jr., *Management,* 7th ed. (South-Western, 1996).

4 Tom Broersma, "In Search of the Future," *Training and Development,* January 1995, pp. 38–43.

5 Andre L. Delbecq and Peter K. Mills, "Managerial Practices That Enhance Innovation," *Organizational Dynamics,* 14 (Summer 1985), pp. 24–34.

6 Ira Magaziner and Mark Tatinkin, *The Silent War: Inside the Global Business Battles Shaping America's Future* (New York: Random House, 1989).

7 A. H. Van de Ven, H. Angle, and M. S. Poole, *Research on the Management of Innovation* (Cambridge, Mass.: Ballinger, 1989).

8 John P. Kotter, *Leading Change* (Boston: Harvard University Press, 1996), pp. 20–25.

9 Stephanie Gruner, "An Entrepreneur Courts Café Society (Cyber Version)," *Wall Street Journal*, Sept. 24, 1999, pp. B1, B4.

10 Attributed to Gregory Bateson in Andrew H. Van de Ven, "Central Problems in the Management of Innovation," *Management Science,* 32 (1986), p. 595.

11 Teresa M. Amabile, "Motivating Creativity in Organizations: On Doing What You Love and Loving What You Do," *California Management Review,* 40 (1) (Fall 1997), pp. 39–58.

12 Gordon Vessels, "The Creative Process: An Open-Systems Conceptualization," *Journal of Creative Behavior,* 16 (1982), pp. 185–196; and Pearlman, "A Theoretical Model."

13 Robert J. Sternberg, Linda A. O'Hara, and Todd I. Lubart, "Creativity as Investment," *California Management Review,* 40 (1) (Fall 1997), pp. 8–21; and Ken Lizotte, "A Creative State of Mind," *Management Review,* May 1998, pp. 15–17.

14 Marsha Sinetar, "Entrepreneurs, Chaos, and Creativity—Can Creative People Really Survive Large Company Structure?" *Sloan Management Review,* 6 (Winter 1985), pp. 57–62.

15 Cynthia Browne, "Jest for Success," *Moonbeams,* August 1989, pp. 3–5.

16 "Hands On: A Manager's Notebook," *Inc.,* January 1989, p. 106.

17 Price Pritchett and Brian Muirhead, *The Mars Pathfinder Approach to "Faster-Better-Cheaper"* (Dallas: Pritchett & Associates, Inc., 1998).

18 Katy Koontz, "How to Stand Out from the Crowd," *Working Woman,* January 1988, pp. 74–76.

19 Harold L. Angle and Andrew H. Van de Ven, "Suggestions for Managing the Innovation Journey," in *Research in the Management of Innovation: The Minnesota Studies,* ed. A. H. Van de Ven, H. L. Angle, and Marshall Scott Poole (Cambridge, Mass.: Ballinger/Harper & Row, 1989).

20 C. K. Bart, "New Venture Units: Use Them Wisely to Manage Innovation," *Sloan Management Review* (Summer 1988), pp. 35–43.

21 Peter F. Drucker, *Innovation and Entrepreneurship* (New York: Harper & Row, 1985).

22 Michael Tushman and David Nadler, "Organizing for Innovation," *California Management Review,* 28 (Spring 1986), pp. 74–92.

23 Russell Mitchell, "Masters of Innovation: How 3M Keeps Its New Products Coming," *Business Week,* April 10, 1989, pp. 58–63.

24 Phaedra Hise, "New Recruitment Strategy: Ask Your Best Employees to Leave," *Inc.,* July 1997, p. 2.29 Gregory A. Patterson, "Lands' End Kicks Out Modern New Managers, Rejecting a Makeover," *The Wall Street Journal,* April 3, 1995, pp. A1, A6; and John P. Kotter, "Leading Changes: Why Transformation Efforts Fail," *Harvard Business Review* (March–April 1995), pp. 59–67.

25 J. P. Kotter and L. A. Schlesinger, "Choosing Strategies for Change," *Harvard Business Review,* 57 (March–April 1979), pp. 106–114.

26 Roger O. Crockett, "Computer Files Lately?" *Business Week e-Biz,* Sept 27, 999, pp. EB 16–17.

27 G. Zaltman and Robert B. Duncan, *Strategies for Planned Change* (New York: Wiley Interscience, 1977).

28 Dennis McCafferty, "Who Wants to Be a Millionaire?" *USA Weekend*, Dec. 3-5, 1999, p. 6.

29 Leonard M. Apcar, "Middle Managers and Supervisors Resist Moves to More Participatory Management," *The Wall Street Journal,* September 16, 1985, p. 25.

30 Kurt Lewin, *Field Theory in Social Science: Selected Theoretical Papers* (New York: Harper & Brothers, 1951).

31 Paul C. Nutt, "Tactics of Implementation," *Academy of Management Journal,* 29 (1986), pp. 230–261.

32 Rob Muller, "Training for Change," *Canadian Business Review* (Spring 1995), pp. 16–19.

33 Taggart F. Frost, "Creating a Teamwork-Based Culture within a Manufacturing Setting," *IM,* May–June 1994, pp. 17–20.

34 Apcar, "Middle Managers."

35 J. Hyatt, "Guaranteed Growth," *Inc.,* Sept. 1995, pp. 69–78.

36 Tom Burns and G.M. Stalker, *The Management of Innovation* (London: Tavistock Publications, 1961).

37 Richard Teitelbaum, "How to Harness Gray Matter," *Fortune,* June 9, 1997, p. 168.

38 Thomas Petzinger, Jr., "The Front Lines: Bread Store Chain Tells Its Franchisees: Do Your Own Thing," *The Wall Street Journal,* November 21, 1997, p. B1.

39 Richard L. Daft, "A Dual-Core Model of Organizational Innovation," *Academy of Management Journal,* 21 (1978), pp. 193–210.

40 Harold J. Leavitt, "Applied Organizational Change in Industry: Structural, Technical, and Human Approaches," in *New Perspectives in Organization Research,* ed. W. W. Cooper, H. J. Leavitt, and M. W. Shelly II (New York: Wiley, 1964), pp. 55–74.

41 Glenn Rifkin, "Competing through Innovation: The Case of Broderbund," *Strategy & Business,* 11 (Second Quarter) 1998, pp. 48–58.

42 Paul Lukas, "The Ghastliest Product Launches," Fortune, March 16, 1998, p. 44; and Robert McMath, *What Were They Thinking? Marketing Lessons I've Learned from Over 80,000 New-Product Innovations and Idiocies* (New York: Times Business, 1998).

43 Andrew H. Van de Ven, "Central Problems in the Management of Innovation," *Management Science,* 32 (1986), pp. 590–607.

44 Arnold O. Putnam, "A Redesign for Engineering," *Harvard Business Review,* 63 (May–June 1985), pp. 139–144.

45 Dorothy Leonard and Jeffrey F. Rayport, "Spark Innovation through Empathic Design," *Harvard Business Review,* November–December 1997, pp. 102–113.

46 Ira Sager, "The Man Who's Rebooting IBM's PC Business," *Business Week,* July 24, 1995, pp. 68–72.

47 Glenn McDonald, "Novel Idea," *Business 2.0,* Dec. 1999, pp. 266–267; Rebecca Quick, "Barnes & Noble gets stake in Web publisher," *Wall Street Journal,* Nov. 2, 1999, p. B11.

48 Susan Caminiti, "A Quiet Superstar Rises in Retailing," *Fortune,* October 23, 1989, pp. 167–174.

49 Brian Dumaine, "How Managers Can Succeed through Speed," *Fortune,* February 13, 1989, pp. 54–59.

50 Fariborz Damanpour, "The Adoption of Technological, Administrative, and Ancillary Innovations: Impact of Organizational Factors," *Journal of Management,* 13 (1987), pp. 675–688.

51 Daft, "Bureaucratic vs. Nonbureaucratic Structure."

52 Mary Kay Ash, *Mary Kay on People Management* (New York: Warner, 1984), p. 75.

53 E. H. Schein, "Organizational Culture," *American Psychologist 45* (Feb. 1990), pp. 109–119, and A. Kupfer, "An Outsider Fires Up a Railroad," *Fortune,* Dec. 18, 1989, pp. 133–146.

54 M. Sashkin and W. W. Burke, "Organization Development in the 1980s," *General Management,* 13 (1987), pp. 393–417.

55 Robert M. Fulmer and Roderick Gilkey, "Blending Corporate Families: Management and Organization Development in a Postmerger Environment," *The Academy of Management Executive,* 2 (1988), pp. 275–283.

56 W. Warner Burke, "The New Agenda for Organizational Development," *Organizational Dynamics,* Summer 1997, pp. 7–19.

57 David A. Nadler, *Feedback and Organizational Development: Using Data-Based Methods* (Reading, Mass.: Addison-Wesley, 1977).

58 Wendell L. French and Cecil H. Bell, Jr., *Organization Development: Behavioral Science Interventions for Organization Improvement,* 3d ed. (Englewood Cliffs, N.J.: Prentice-Hall, 1984).

59 This discussion is based on Kathleen D. Dannemiller and Robert W. Jacobs, "Changing the Way Organizations Change: A Revolution of Common Sense," *The Journal of Applied Behavioral Science,* 28 (4) (December 1992), pp. 480–498; and Barbara Benedict Bunker and Billie T. Alban, "Conclusion: What Makes Large Group Interventions Effective?" *The Journal of Applied Behavioral Science* 28, no. 4 (December 1992), pp. 570–591.

60 Kurt Lewin, "Frontiers in Group Dynamics: Concepts, Method, and Reality in Social Science," *Human Relations,* 1 (1947), pp. 5–41; and Huse and Cummings, *Organization Development.*

61 J. Quinn, "What a Work-Out!" Performance, November 1994, pp. 58–63; and B. B. Bunker and B. T. Alban, "Conclusion: What Makes Large Group Interventions Effective?" *The Journal of Applied Behavioral Science,* 28 (4) (December 1992), pp. 572–591.

9

Human Resource Management

LEARNING OBJECTIVES

After studying this chapter, you should be able to:

- Explain the role of human resource management in organizational strategic planning

- Describe federal legislation and societal trends that influence human resource management

- Explain what the changing social contract between organizations and employees means for workers and human resource managers

- Explain how organizations determine their future staffing needs through human resource planning

- Describe the tools managers use to recruit and select employees

- Describe how organizations develop an effective workforce through training and performance appraisal

- Explain how organizations maintain a workforce through the administration of wages and salaries, benefits, and terminations

MANAGEMENT PROBLEM

JIM McCANN took over as president of

Chapter

9

800-Flowers when the company was burdened by

debt and had less than $1 million in annual revenues. To effectively

meet floral delivery needs of customers in this international, e-commerce-based

business, 800-Flowers needed dedicated order takers and customer service representatives.

Yet it was in these departments that employee enthusiasm was lowest and turnover was highest. The

problem was compounded by the seasonal ebb and flow of the floral business, which meant that the

company needed around 2,400 employees during peak seasons, such as Valentine's Day or Mother's Day, and

only 900 workers during slow periods. To regain competitiveness, McCann needed a strategy to deal with this

• *How can McCann find and keep a core group of high-quality employees and cope with seasonal demands for additional*

workers? Can human resource management be part of the strategy to restore 800-Flowers to competitiveness?

fluctuating demand for workers. In addition, to build and maintain a reputation for high-quality service, the

company needed to retain good employees in the high-pressure order-taking and customer service

departments.[1] Jim McCann's problem at 800-Flowers illustrates the need for managing human

resources. McCann and his management team must develop the company's ability to recruit,

train, and keep high-quality year-round (and seasonal) employees. Without effective

human resource management, company growth will be restricted and

performance will continue to suffer.

The term **human resource management (HRM)** refers to activities undertaken to attract, develop, and maintain an effective workforce within an organization. General Electric, Hewlett-Packard, and others have become famous for their human resource management philosophy, which is the foundation of their success. HRM is equally important for not-for-profit organizations. For example, the Catholic Church must address the crisis of the sharply declining number of priests. Unless the church can find ways to attract and keep priests, a mere 17,000 priests will be serving 75 million U.S. Catholics by the year 2005.[2]

Over the past decade, human resource management has shed its old "personnel" image and gained recognition as a vital player in corporate strategy. Research has found that effective human resource management has a positive impact on organizational performance, including higher employee productivity and stronger financial performance.[3] Small businesses in particular report that finding and keeping good workers is the biggest problem they face.[4] Especially in today's tight labor market, the ability to attract and retain high-quality employees can be a powerful strategic weapon. With unemployment in the early 2000s at a 25-year low, many businesses had to develop creative ways to attract and keep workers. Steve Jacobus moved his company, Olson Warehouse & Distribution, from the suburbs to inner-city Milwaukee in order to tap into the larger pool of unemployed workers. To keep talented workers at Booz, Allen & Hamilton Inc., the New York consulting firm recently started a job rotation plan to help employees cope with a consultant's grueling schedule.[5]

Despite its importance, many managers still do not understand the value of human resources activities. In addition, company employees often do not understand the full range of HRM functions. For example, at Transamerica surveys indicated employees were not aware of the full range of human resource services or their access to those services. Effective education about HRM functions is essential.[6]

Human resource management consists of three parts. First, all managers are human resource managers. For example, at IBM line managers use surveys, career planning, performance appraisal, and compensation to encourage commitment. Second, employees are viewed as assets. Employees, not buildings and machinery, give a company a competitive advantage. Third, human resource management is a matching process, integrating the

human resource management (HRM)
Activities undertaken to attract, develop, and maintain an effective workforce within an organization

Exhibit 9.1
HUMAN RESOURCE MANAGEMENT GOALS

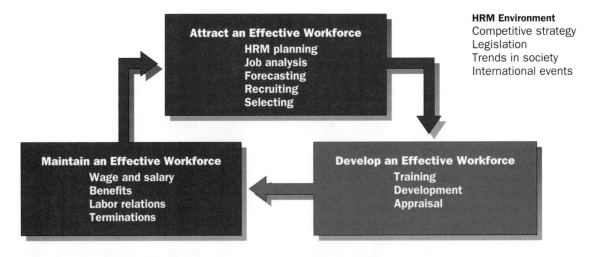

HRM Environment
Competitive strategy
Legislation
Trends in society
International events

Attract an Effective Workforce
HRM planning
Job analysis
Forecasting
Recruiting
Selecting

Develop an Effective Workforce
Training
Development
Appraisal

Maintain an Effective Workforce
Wage and salary
Benefits
Labor relations
Terminations

organization's goals with the needs of employees. Employees should receive satisfaction equal to that of the company.

■ THE STRATEGIC ROLE OF HRM

There are three primary goals of HRM (see Exhibit 9.1). These goals pertain to the organizational environment and encompass competitive strategy, federal legislation, and societal trends. Their purposes are to attract an effective workforce to the organization, develop the workforce to its potential, and maintain the workforce over the long term.[7] Achieving these goals requires skills in planning, training, performance appraisal, wage and salary administration, benefit programs, and even termination. Most organizations employ human resource professionals to perform these functions. Human resource *specialists* focus on one of the HRM areas, such as recruitment of employees or administration of wage or benefit programs. Human resource *generalists* have responsibility in more than one HRM area.

■ ENVIRONMENTAL INFLUENCES ON HRM

"Our strength is the quality of our people," and "Our people are our most important resource." These often-repeated statements by executives emphasize the importance of HRM. Human resource managers must find, recruit, train, nurture, and retain the best people. Human resource programs are designed to fit organizational needs, core values, and strategic goals. HRM is more important today than ever before.[8] A mix of economic, demographic, and social factors has led to an excessively tight labor market in most areas of the United States, making recruiting more of a challenge. In order to hire enough workers, some firms have tried hiring people who are considered a more difficult group by some employers. But in a tight labor market, businesses need to be more creative in hiring, in order to have the manpower necessary to pursue their strategies. Perhaps no company does recruiting better than McDonald's, a company for which 1 out of every 8 Americans has worked.

McDonald's
www.mcdonalds.com

The fast-food business is known for high turnover, so recruiting is a never-ending job. However, McDonald's has some unique recruiting strategies that help the company lure a larger number of job applicants than most other fast-food restaurants. McDonald's emphasizes alternative labor sources. It has long been one of the nation's largest employers of young people, and the company makes effective use of internal recruiting to move some of these workers into management jobs rather than losing them after they graduate from school. In addition, two highly successful programs target groups that have proven to be loyal workers: older people and people who have physical or mental challenges.

A program called ReHIREment has recruited more than 40,000 older employees to serve McDonald's customers. Each older person is assigned a "buddy" who works alongside the new employee for the training period. Older workers appreciate McDonald's flexibility in scheduling and they are able to set the number of hours they work so as not to jeopardize Social Security benefits. The McJobs program was founded to assist in recruiting employees with physical or mental disabilities. Each recruit is paired with a job coach, who may be a specially trained McDonald's worker or a state agency counselor, for a period of six to eight weeks. So far, more than 9,000 workers have gone through the McJobs program. As a result of these two innovative recruiting programs, an entire pool of workers that often goes untapped is now successfully working for McDonald's rather than its competitors.[9] ■

In addition, years of downsizing, restructuring, and reengineering have produced decreased morale among employees, and a tenuous loyalty to employers has become the norm. In this environment, more managers are recognizing the value of paying attention to human resources issues. Without the proper personnel, the brightest idea or management trend—whether teams, quality circles, telecommuting, or flexible compensation—is doomed to failure. In addition, when employees don't feel valued, usually they are not willing to give their best to the company and often leave to find a more supportive work environment. For these reasons, it is important that human resource executives be involved in competitive strategy. Human resource executives also interpret federal legislation and respond to the changing nature of careers and work relationships.

COMPETITIVE STRATEGY

HRM helps companies find the right mix of people and skills they need to meet organizational goals. HRM contributes directly to the bottom line by appreciating the organization's greatest assets—its people—and how they meet strategic goals. Judy Lyles of DET Distributing Company in Nashville, Tennessee, which delivers for Adolph Coors and Miller Brewing Company, reports that when her boss hired her as human resources manager, he said: "Any good manager will tell you that a company's greatest asset is its employees, but employees show up as a liability on a profit-and-loss statement. Yet our trucks are an asset. So, we've got all these mechanics to work on the fleet, but we don't have anyone working on our greatest asset, which is our people." Lyles sees herself as the human mechanic and head cheerleader for DET workers. She considers the human resources department not just as the keeper of the rules but as the "keeper of workers' hearts—the keeper of why they want to come to work every day."[10]

The human resource management function has changed enormously over the years. In the 1920s, HRM was a low-level position charged with ensuring that procedures were developed for hiring and firing employees and with implementing benefit plans. By the 1950s unions were a major force, and the HRM manager was elevated to a senior position as chief negotiator. During the 1980s, unions began to decline, and top HRM managers became directly involved in corporate strategic management.[11]

Exhibit 9.2 illustrates the interdependence between company and human resource strategy. Human resource strategy is designed to provide the correct mix of employees and skills needed to meet competitive conditions. The Louis Harris Laborforce 2000 survey of 400 American-based corporations found that the top strategic issues of concern to managers were to become more competitive on a global basis, to cut costs and improve efficiency, and to improve quality, productivity, and customer service. An organization's competitive strategy may also include mergers and acquisitions, reengineering, or the acquisition of automated production technology.[12] All of these strategic decisions determine the company's need for skills and employees. It is the role of HRM strategy to include the correct employee composition to implement the organization's competitive strategy.

Today more than ever, strategic decisions are related to human resource considerations. For example, the shift to the learning organization, where everyone is engaged in making decisions and solving problems, requires a different mix of workers and skills than what is needed in a traditional vertical organization where most decisions are made by top managers. Learning companies look for people who are open-minded, curious, and willing to break the rules. One staffing director at a computer company that emphasizes autonomy, informality, and learning reports that "we look for people's passions, what they've done with their lives; the guy who took a year off after his MBA to play the violin or travel the world."[13]

As another example, the introduction of flexible manufacturing systems, such as those discussed in Chapter 7, have dramatically changed the need for workforce skill. These new machines require a highly skilled workforce, including interpersonal skills and the ability to work as a team. To make the strategic change to automated technology, the HRM department must upgrade the skills of shop

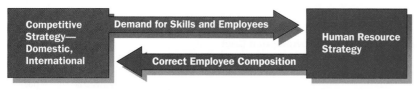

SOURCE: Adapted from Cynthia A. Lengnick-Hall and Mark L. Lengnick-Hall, "Strategic Human Resources Management: A Review of the Literature and a Proposed Typology," *Academy of Management Review,* 13 (1988), 454–470.

Exhibit 9.2

INTERDEPENDENCE OF ORGANIZATIONAL AND HUMAN RESOURCE STRATEGY

machine operators and recruit new employees who have human skills as well as technical skills.[14] Chrysler spent a million hours training workers, many without a high school education, to run its highly automated Detroit plant using self-directed work teams. As aging factory workers retire, the company is recruiting workers with more education to replace them. Today, most companies want workers who can learn new skills quickly and require less supervision.[15]

FEDERAL LEGISLATION

Over the past 30 years, several federal laws have been passed to ensure equal employment opportunity (EEO). Some of the most significant legislation and executive orders are summarized in Exhibit 9.3. The point of the laws is to stop discriminatory practices that are unfair to specific groups and to define enforcement agencies for these laws. EEO legislation attempts to balance the pay given to men and women; provide employment opportunities without regard to race, religion, national origin, and sex; ensure fair treatment for employees of all ages; and avoid discrimination against disabled individuals.

The Equal Employment Opportunity Commission (EEOC) created by the Civil Rights Act of 1964 initiates investigations in response to complaints concerning discrimination. The EEOC is the major agency involved with employment discrimination. **Discrimination** occurs when some applicants are hired or promoted based on criteria that are not job relevant. For example, refusing to hire a black applicant for a job he is qualified to fill or paying a woman a lower wage than a man for the

same work are discriminatory acts. When discrimination is found, remedies include providing back pay and taking **affirmative action.** Affirmative action requires that an employer take positive steps to guarantee equal employment opportunities for people within protected groups. An affirmative action plan is a formal document that can be reviewed by employees and enforcement agencies. The goal of organizational affirmative action is to reduce or eliminate internal inequities among affected employee groups.

However, in recent years, the perception of affirmative action as a means for "leveling the playing field" has been replaced by complaints of the program as a way of imposing quotas. Even the intended beneficiaries of affirmative action are divided on the need for continuation. For example, a 1995 poll revealed that 49 percent of women favor continuation of affirmative action while 41 percent oppose it.[16]

Failure to comply with equal employment opportunity legislation can result in substantial fines and penalties for employers. For example, Shoney's was accused of discrimination against black employees and job applicants. The class-action suit charged that company policy conspired to limit the number of black employees working in public areas of the restaurant. In 1992 the company agreed to pay $105 million to victims of its hiring, promotion, and firing policies, dating back to 1985.[17] Suits for discriminatory practices can cover a broad range of employee complaints.

One thing concerning human resource legislation is clear: The scope of equal employment opportunity legislation is increasing at federal, state, and municipal levels. The working rights and conditions of women, minorities, older

discrimination
The hiring or promoting of applicants based on criteria that are not job relevant

affirmative action
A policy requiring employers to take positive steps to guarantee equal employment opportunities for people within protected groups

Exhibit 9.3

MAJOR FEDERAL LAWS
RELATED TO HUMAN
RESOURCE MANAGEMENT

Federal Law	Year	Provisions
Equal Opportunity/Discrimination Laws		
Civil Rights Act	1991	Provides for possible compensatory and punitive damages plus traditional back pay for cases of intentional discrimination brought under Title VII of the 1964 Civil Rights Act. Shifts the burden of proof to the employer.
Americans With Disabilities Act	1990	Prohibits discrimination against qualified individuals by employers on the basis of disability and demands that "reasonable accommodations" be provided for the disabled to allow performance of duties.
Vocational Rehabilitation Act	1973	Prohibits discrimination based on physical or mental disability and requires that employees be informed about affirmative action plans.
Age Discrimination in Employment Act (ADEA)	1967 (amended 1978, 1986)	Prohibits age discrimination and restricts mandatory retirement.
Civil Rights Act, Title VII	1964	Prohibits discrimination in employment on the basis of race, religion, color, sex, or national origin.
Compensation/Benefits Laws		
Family and Medical Leave Act	1993	Requires employers to provide up to 12 weeks unpaid leave for childbirth, adoption, or family emergencies.
Equal Pay Act	1963	Prohibits sex differences in pay for substantially equal work.
Health/Safety Laws		
Consolidated Omnibus Budget Reconciliation Act (COBRA)	1985	Requires continued health insurance coverage (paid by employee) following termination.
Occupational Safety and Health Act (OSHA)	1970	Establishes mandatory safety and health standards in organizations.

employees, and the disabled will receive increasing legislative attention in the future. Also, most cases in the past have concerned low-level jobs, but increasing attention is being given to equal employment opportunity in upper-level management positions.

■ THE CHANGING NATURE OF CAREERS

One issue of growing concern to organizations and human resource managers is the changing nature of careers. HRM can benefit employees and organizations by responding to recent changes in the relationship between employers and employees and new ways of working, such as telecommuting and job sharing.

THE CHANGING SOCIAL CONTRACT

In the old social contract between organization and employee, the employee could contribute ability, education, loyalty, and commitment and expect in return the company would provide wages and benefits, work, advancement, and training throughout the employee's working life. But the volatile changes in the environment have disrupted this contract. Many organizations have been downsized, eliminating many employees. Employees who are left may feel little stability. In a fast-moving company, a person is hired and assigned to a project. The project changes over time, as do the person's tasks. Then the person is assigned to another project and then to still another. These new projects require working with different groups and leaders and schedules. Workers often have no place to call their own.[18] Careers no longer progress up a vertical hierarchy but move across jobs horizontally. People succeed only if the organization succeeds, and they may lose their jobs. Particularly in learning organizations, everyone is expected to be a self-motivated worker who has excellent interpersonal relationships and is continuously acquiring new skills.

Exhibit 9.4 lists some elements of the new social contract. The new contract is based on the concept of employability rather than lifetime employment. Individuals manage their own careers; the organization no longer takes care of them or guarantees employment. Companies agree to pay somewhat higher wages and invest in creative training and development opportunities so that people will be more employable when the company no longer needs their services. Employees take more responsibility and control in their jobs, becoming partners in business improvement rather than cogs in a machine. In return, the organization provides challenging work assignments as well as information and resources to enable workers to continuously learn new skills. The new contract can provide many opportunities for employees to be more involved and express new aspects of themselves.

However, many employees are not prepared for new levels of cooperation or responsibility on the job. Employment insecurity is stressful for most employees, and it is harder than it was in the past to gain an employee's full commitment and enthusiasm. In addition, one study found that while most workers today feel they are contributing to the success of their company, they are increasingly skeptical that their hard work is being fully recognized.[19] Some companies are discovering they went overboard with downsizing efforts in the 1990s and are now finding it difficult to keep good

	New Contract	**Old Contract**
Employee	Employability, personal responsibility	Job security
	Partner in business improvement	A cog in the machine
	Learning	Knowing
Employer	Continuous learning, lateral career movement, incentive compensation	Traditional compensation package
	Creative development opportunities	Standard training programs
	Challenging assignments	Routine jobs
	Information and resources	Limited information

E x h i b i t 9.4
THE CHANGING SOCIAL CONTACT

SOURCE: Based on Louisa Wah, "The New Workplace Paradox," *Management Review*, January 1998, 7; and Douglas T. Hall and Jonathan E. Moss, "The New Protean Career Contract: Helping Organizations and Employees Adapt," *Organizational Dynamics* (winter 1998), 22–37.

workers because employee trust has been destroyed. Many employees feel little loyalty to their employers. To respond to these problems, HRM departments can help organizations develop a mix of training, career development opportunities, compensation packages, and rewards and incentives. They can provide career information and assessment, combined with career coaching, to help employees determine new career directions.[20]

NEW WAYS OF WORKING

America's largest employer is a temporary agency, Manpower, Inc. More companies are turning to interim or contingency workers to save money and avoid layoffs in the future. People in these temporary jobs do everything from typing to becoming the temporary CEO. In addition, organizational transformation is taking place on a global scale.[21] Not since the advent of mass production and modern organizations has a redefinition of work and career been so profound. In the new image, each person must take care of herself or himself.

Companies undergoing rapid change no longer offer certain employment. Instead, it's the individual's responsibility to maintain life-long employability. The employer's obligation is to provide opportunity for self-improvement. It is up to the individual, however, to take charge of his or her own career.

Career paths in this new century will be a mix of the old and the new. There still will be traditional managers in traditional hierarchies, but many careers will be less linear and less secure than before. People can look for niches that suit their talents and ways of working that suit their needs. One of the biggest trends is telecommuting. **Telecommuting** means using computers and telecommunications equipment to do work without going to an office. The U.S. Department of Transportation has predicted that the number of telecommuters will increase to 15 million workers by the year 2002.[22] These "virtual" workers and managers live wherever they want, untethered to any office or city. At PeopleSoft, for example, all 6,000 employees work from remote locations at some time during their employment. Weekly meetings sometimes are conducted in person and

telecommuting
Using computers and telecommunications equipment to perform work from home or another remote location

sometimes online. AT&T has 35,000 telecommuters, who e-mail a list of weekly goals on Monday and follow up on Friday.[23] Entrepreneurs are increasingly using telecommuting to work from their homes, as described below.

HOME-BASED BUSINESSES

Not long ago, magazines for entrepreneurs advertised audio tapes with office sounds to play while talking on the phone. That way, instead of the client hearing the doorbell ring or the dog bark, the sounds would be typewriters (remember them?) and distant phone rings. Back then it was an embarrassment to be working from home. Other tactics people used were putting "Suite Number 201" after their street address, renting post office boxes, adding "and Associates" after the surname, and having a recorded message that said, "All our lines are currently occupied."

Things have changed. In Mountain View, California, one-third of new Chamber of Commerce members are home-based businesses. One example is advertiser Mike Ball, who got tired of being an employee and did not want the burden of renting office space, hiring a secretary, production assistant, art director and account executive—all employees whose salary he would have to meet each payday. No thanks.

Instead, he set up shop as The Advertising Group in a spare bedroom and runs his virtual company alone by subcontracting work out to similar home-based entrepreneurs. His mode of communication to them and to clients is e-mail, fax, and his corporate Web site.

As researcher and consultant to libraries and Fortune 100 companies, Mary Ellen Bates's Washington, D.C. operation is first-class and high tech. If you call her, you will never get a busy signal, but will always roll over to voice mail. She has a professional Web site and makes light of home realities. When talking with a client and her dog barks, she chuckles, "Oh, that's my only office mate." The client will often say something like, "I've always wanted to do that. How do you like working from home?" Just fine, thanks.[24] ■

The advent of teams is another significant trend in careers. People who used to work alone on the shop floor, in the advertising department, or in middle management are now part of teams and charged with succeeding as a group. Each member of the team acts like a manager, becoming responsible for high-quality standards, scheduling, and even hiring and firing other team workers. At an empowered Frito-Lay plant in Lubbock, Texas, the number of managers dropped from 38 to 13 while the hourly workforce grew by more than 20 percent to about 220.[25] With less supervision the plant has improved quality, productivity, and profits. But people on the teams lose some of their autonomy and must develop excellent skills of communication and a positive attitude. They also must learn several jobs; they won't be doing just one thing.

Sometimes, people looking for a new career direction decide to start their own businesses. Often, employees who are laid off during company downsizing do not want to return. Other people never want to join a large corporation, preferring the challenge and autonomy of running their own businesses. People who become freelancers or virtual workers often can create their own enterprise, hiring their own employees to provide services to larger companies. As corporations try to reduce costs, they *outsource,* or hire outside services to meet their needs. Entrepreneurship is challenging and exciting, and if you fit the criteria described in Appendix C, this may be an effective career path for you.

Within the context of new trends in careers and working relationships, human resource managers must achieve the three primary goals described earlier in this chapter: attracting, developing, and maintaining an effective workforce for the organization. Let us now review some of the established techniques for accomplishing these goals.

ATTRACTING AN EFFECTIVE WORKFORCE

The first goal of HRM is to attract individuals who show signs of becoming valued, produc-tive, and satisfied employees. The first step in attracting an effective workforce involves human resource planning, in which managers or HRM professionals predict the need for new employees based on the types of vacancies that exist, as illustrated in Exhibit 9.5. The second step is to use recruiting procedures to communicate with potential applicants. The third step is to select from the applicants those persons believed to be the best potential contributors to the organization. Finally, the new employee is welcomed into the organization.

HUMAN RESOURCE PLANNING

Human resource planning is the forecasting of human resource needs and the projected matching of individuals with expected vacancies. Human resource planning begins with several questions:

- What new technologies are emerging, and how will these affect the work system?
- What is the volume of the business likely to be in the next five to ten years?
- What is the turnover rate, and how much, if any, is avoidable?

The responses to these questions are used to formulate specific questions pertaining to HRM activities, such as the following:

human resource planning
The forecasting of human resource needs and the projected matching of individuals with expected job vacancies

When Betty Ford launched City Boxers, an online retailer of hand-tailored boxer shorts, the product filled an attractive niche geared toward the Net's large male audience. Its continued success is due in part, according to Ford, because the virtual world allows shoppers to "make their decision on what the boxer shorts will look like, not on who's selling them," which she says helps minority entrepreneurs like herself.

Exhibit 9.5

ATTRACTING AN EFFECTIVE WORKFORCE

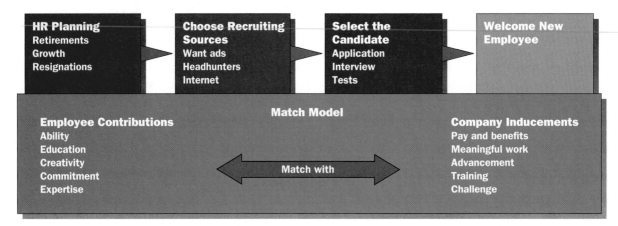

Answers to these questions help define the direction for the organization's HRM strategy. For example, if forecasting suggests that there will be a strong need for more technically trained individuals, the organization can (1) define the jobs and skills needed in some detail, (2) hire and train recruiters to look for the specified skills, and/or (3) provide new training for existing employees. By anticipating future HRM needs, the organization can prepare itself to meet competitive challenges more effectively than organizations that react to problems only as they arise.

One of the most successful applications of human resource planning is the Tennessee Valley Authority's development of an eight-step system.

TVA

www.tva.com

In the confusion and uncertainty following a period of reorganization and downsizing, a crucial role for HRM is balancing the need for future workforce planning with the creation of a climate of stability for the remaining workers. TVA created an eight-step plan that can serve as a model for companies in assessing future HR needs and formulating actions to meet those needs. The first step is laying the groundwork for later implementation of the program by creating planning and oversight teams within each business unit. Step two involves assessing processes and functions that can be benchmarked. Step three involves the projection of skills and employee numbers (demand data) necessary to reach goals within each business unit. Once these numbers are in place, step four involves projection of the current employee numbers (supply data) over the "planning horizon" without new hires and taking into consideration the normal attrition of staff through death, retirement, resignation, and so forth. Comparison of the difference between supply and demand (step five) gives the "future gap" or "surplus situation." This knowledge enables HR to develop strategies and operational plans (step six). Step seven involves communication of the action plan to employees. The final step is to periodically evaluate and update the plan as the organization's needs change.

- How many senior managers will we need during this time period?

- What types of engineers will we need, and how many?

- Are persons with adequate computer skills available for meeting our projected needs?

- How many administrative personnel—technicians, secretaries—will we need to support the additional managers and engineers?[26]

Although, in a small organization, developing demand and supply data could be handled with a pad and a calculator, TVA uses a sophisticated automated system to update and revise the plan as needed to meet new competitive situations. Determining skills-gap and surplus information (step five) helped TVA develop a workforce plan to implement cross-organizational placement and retraining as alternatives to further employee cutbacks in the individual business units, thereby providing a greater sense of stability for workers. If needs change and TVA faces a demand for additional employees, this process will enable the company to recruit workers with the skills needed to help meet organizational goals.[27] ■

RECRUITING

Recruiting refers to the activities or practices involved in seeking out applicants and applying selection procedures to determine qualifications for specific positions. Many organizations use *internal recruiting,* or "promote-from-within" policies, to fill their high-level positions.[28] At Mellon Bank, for example, current employees are given preference when a position opens. Open positions are listed in Mellon's career opportunity bulletins, which are distributed to employees. Internal recruiting has several advantages: (1) it is less costly than an external search; (2) it generates higher employee commitment, development, and satisfaction; and (3) it offers opportunities for career advancement to employees rather than outsiders.

Frequently, however, *external recruiting*—recruiting newcomers from outside the organization—is advantageous. Advertising, state employment services, private employment agencies ("headhunters"), job fairs, and employee referrals are sources for outside applicants. Some employers even provide cash awards for employees who submit names of people who subsequently accept employment, because referral is one of the cheapest and most reliable methods for external recruiting.[29]

REALISTIC JOB PREVIEWS One approach to enhancing recruiting effectiveness is called a realistic job preview. A **realistic job preview (RJP)** gives applicants all pertinent and realistic information—positive and negative—about the job and the organization.[30] RJPs enhance employee satisfaction and

recruiting
The activities or practices involved in seeking out applicants and applying selection procedures to determine qualifications for specific positions

realistic job preview (RJP)
A recruiting approach that gives applicants all pertinent and realistic information about the job and the organization

Craig Johnson (standing, with some of his recruits) is the founder of Venture Law Group, a firm that redefined what a law firm can do by seizing a unique niche for itself. The firm helps launch successful startup companies using services that include external recruiting. Joseph Grundfest, a Stanford University professor, called Johnson with a vague glimmer of a business idea. Johnson recognized the elements of a successful startup and used his expertise to get the business off the ground. "What we needed was somebody who could act as a coach and a team builder, who could bring to the table the right mix of people early on," comments Grundfest, who compares Johnson's role in Silicon Valley to that of a talent agent in Hollywood.

reduce turnover, because they facilitate matching individuals, jobs, and organizations. Individuals have a better basis on which to determine their suitability to the organization and "self-select" into or out of positions based on full information. When employees choose positions without RJPs, unmet expectations may cause initial job dissatisfaction and increased turnover. For example, Linda McDermott left a good position in an accounting firm to become an executive vice president of a new management consulting company. She was told she would have a major role in helping the business grow. As it turned out, her boss relegated her to administrative duties, so she quit after a few months, causing the company to initiate another lengthy search and sidetracking her career for a year or two.[31]

LEGAL CONSIDERATIONS   Organizations must ensure that their recruiting practices conform to the law. EEO laws stipulate that recruiting and hiring decisions cannot discriminate on the basis of race, national origin, religion, or sex. *Affirmative action* refers to the use of goals, timetables, or other methods in recruiting to promote the hiring, development, and retention of "protected groups"—persons historically underrepresented in the workplace.

NEW APPROACHES TO RECRUITING   Today's tight labor market has motivated human resource managers to acquire new tools for recruiting. The World Wide Web enables companies to cast a wide net in search of employees. This approach is increasingly used by both large and small companies and has taken on new shapes, as described in Technology for Tomorrow.

Another innovative approach involves turning to nontraditional sources of employees. Arte Nathan, vice president for human resources at Mirage Resorts in Las Vegas, seeks out nonviolent first offenders sentenced to boot camp rather than prison. Nathan works closely with parole officers and other court representatives to identify graduates who will make good employees. United Parcel Service recruits welfare recipients and arranges transportation and on-the-job assistance that will keep them working. A test program in Philadelphia showed that UPS retained 88 percent of its welfare employees and saw no decline in productivity.[32] Cisco Systems methods of recruiting allow the company to gain an edge.

CISCO SYSTEMS
www.cisco.com

For Cisco Systems, effective recruiting has become a powerful strategic weapon. The company's rapid growth has meant doubling its workforce while hiring only the highest-caliber workers. Cisco's human resources team identified exactly the kind of people they wanted and then figured out the best methods to recruit them. A key element: the World Wide Web.

Cisco still uses newspaper classifieds sections, but in an unusual way. Rather than listing specific job openings, the company runs ads featuring an Internet address and an invitation to apply for employment. Cisco's Web site has become a turbo-charged recruiting tool. The site allows the company to post hundreds of job openings with specific information about each one. The company also advertises its site in cyberspace, which helps to reach a self-selected set of candidates (people who can easily navigate the Internet) from around the globe. Want a job? Search by keyword and match your skills to their job openings. File a résumé or fill out a résumé form online using their résumé builder program. And, the site will pair you up with a volunteer "friend" inside the company. This friend will teach you about Cisco, introduce you to important people, and lead you through the hiring process.

The real power of Cisco's Web site is that it targets "passive" job-seekers—people who are happy and successful in their current jobs. Cisco advertises its site at places where its "kind of people" are likely to hang out. The company has linked to the Dilbert Web page, for instance, which attracts programmers.

TECHNOLOGY FOR TOMORROW
VIRTUAL RECRUITING

It's a tough recruiting world out there for entrepreneurs. Low unemployment, in many places reaching a "full-employment economy," means a difficult time hiring necessary employees for the small-business owner.

Enter the information age and the Internet. A number of other small businesses have sprung up to meet this need by offering recruiting services online. Advantages include a more inexpensive way to reach a wider audience and the ease of operation by filling out a simpler form and e-mailing it—all good for the entrepreneur. The Monster Board reports that over 70 percent of its business comes from small companies. Places to start include careermag.com, careermosaic.com, cweb.com, jobcenter.com, monster.com, and occ.com.

Some individuals who are looking for jobs are taking matters into their own hands. They are designing snazzy résumés and posting them on the Web, then paying to have them listed in the various search engines. And unless you think this is limited to techies, a recent survey showed that 65 percent of online job seekers are in nontechnical fields.

But, suppose you have a virtual company, with employees spread all over the map. How do you interview for key players, let's say the CIO (Chief Information Officer), who needs to meet as many employees as possible? Verifone

developed a committee comprised of three IS staffers, a manager from another department, and the CEO. This committee was responsible for updating job description, deciding on a recruiting firm, sorting through résumés, conducting interviews, and finally polling those who had talked with the candidates.

But none of the employees worked in the same place. So they had to communicate via fax, e-mail, and teleconferencing, which was very important in early meetings to set the committee's tone and for members to feel comfortable with one another. As trust built, e-mails became more substantive. The whole process is not unlike managing a globally diverse think tank. Each person's viewpoint was influenced by their geography and culture, and each one left meetings with often very divergent views.

In order to achieve consensus through the remote interactions, CEO William Pape had all members rank every candidate after each step and each meeting, that is, after receiving résumés, after interviews, after committee meetings. He also asked them to list what they thought were important characteristics of a new CIO and had the group discuss each person's list.

That was half the problem. The other half was communicating with candidates. On the first round, conference

calls were made, so that each member could ask questions and all could hear the answers. On the final round, at least one committee member was present with the candidate for the call. Even though these candidates were seasoned IS professionals, many of them were uncomfortable being interviewed virtually, so the interview process in itself became a selection criteria. If someone could not handle that process, how could they be CIO of a virtual company? One previous hire, who lasted only a few months, had no idea how important face-to-face interactions were for him.

Finally, a new director was hired, but then the committee continued working to help her assimilate and had to figure out ways to simulate mentoring, building bonds with others, and just plain learn the ropes. Pape asked team members to be the new director's "buddies" and to help her in any way possible.

Virtual recruiting is new, but with the explosion of companies whose employees are often linked mainly through modem lines, it will only become more important. And those firms that do it well will have a competitive advantage.

Sources: Jerry Useem, "For Sale Online: You," *Fortune*, July 5, 1999, pp. 67–78; William R. Pape, "Hiring Blind," *Inc. Technology*, 1997 no. 4, pp. 31–32.

Competitors also provide potential employees. Because many prospects visit Cisco's Web site from their jobs, Cisco can tell where they work and pull some sneaky tricks. For instance, anyone who visits the site from arch-rival 3Com is greeted with the following message: "Welcome to Cisco. Would you like a job?"[33] ■

SELECTING

The next step for managers is to select desired employees from the pool of recruited applicants. In the **selection** process, employers attempt to determine the skills, abilities, and other attributes a person needs to perform a particular job, and they assess the applicant's characteristics in an attempt to determine the right "fit" between job and applicant.

selection
The process of determining the skills, abilities, and other attributes a person needs to perform a particular job

JOB DESCRIPTIONS   A good place to start in making a selection decision is the **job description.** Human resource professionals or line managers who make selection decisions may have little direct experience with the job to be filled. If these persons are to make a good match between job and candidate, they should read the job description before they review applications.

A job description typically lists job duties as well as desirable qualifications for a particular job. For internal recruiting, companies may come up with lists of skills and abilities they want candidates to have. Financial officers are tracked on their development and moved into other positions to help them acquire needed skills. Many companies believe that by developing talent internally, they will rarely have to recruit top managers from outside the company.

SELECTION DEVICES   Several devices are used for assessing applicant qualifications. The application form, interview, paper-and-pencil test, and assessment center are the most common. Human resource professionals may use a combination of these devices to obtain a valid prediction of employee job performance. **Validity** refers to the relationship between one's score on a selection device and one's future job performance. A valid selection procedure will provide high scores that correspond to subsequent high job performance.

Application Form   The **application form** is used to collect information about the applicant's education, previous job experience, and other background characteristics. Research in the life insurance industry shows that biographical information inventories can validly predict future job success.[34]

Questions that are irrelevant to job success are to be avoided. In line with affirmative action, the application form should not ask questions that will create an adverse impact on "protected groups." For example, employers should not ask whether the applicant rents or owns his or her own home because (1) an applicant's response might adversely affect his or her chances at the job, (2) minorities and women may be less likely to own a home, and

(3) home ownership is probably unrelated to job performance. On the other hand, the CPA exam is relevant to job performance in a CPA firm; thus, it is appropriate to ask whether an applicant for employment has passed the CPA exam even if only one-half of all female or minority applicants have done so versus nine-tenths of male applicants.

Interview   The interview is used in the hiring process in almost every job category in virtually every organization. The interview serves as a two-way communication channel that allows both the organization and the applicant to collect information that would otherwise be difficult to obtain.

Although widely used, the interview as generally practiced is not a valid predictor of later job performance. Interviews are more likely to test how well someone interviews than how well they will actually perform on the job. Most interviews follow a rather predictable series of steps, and candidates can prepare and practice their answers. Less predictable interviews help give a better idea of how a person actually will perform.[35] In Focus on Skills, several ideas for effective interviewing are discussed, as well as some unusual interview experiences.

Paper-and-Pencil Test   Many companies use **paper-and-pencil tests** such as intelligence tests, aptitude and ability tests, and personality inventories, particularly those shown to be valid predictors.[36] Many companies today are particularly interested in personality inventories that measure such characteristics as openness to learning, initiative, responsibility, creativity, and emotional stability. One of the newest types of testing is an emotional intelligence quotient scale, designed by Multi-Health Systems in Toronto. The idea is that measuring a candidate's emotional intelligence, including such things as self-awareness, ability to empathize with others, and the capacity to build positive relationships, can give clues as to how well the person will do in his or her professional as well as personal life. Both the U.S. Air Force and Canada Life, a large insurance company, have used the EQ test.[37]

job description
A listing of duties as well as desirable qualifications for a particular job

validity
The relationship between an applicant's score on a selection device and his or her future job performance

application form
A device for collecting information about an applicant's education, previous job experience, and other background characteristics

paper-and-pencil test
A written test designed to measure a particular attribute such as intelligence or aptitude

THE RIGHT WAY TO INTERVIEW A JOB APPLICANT

A so-so interview usually nets a so-so employee. Many hiring mistakes can be prevented during the interview. The following techniques will ensure a successful interview:

1. KNOW WHAT YOU WANT. Before the interview, prepare questions based on your knowledge of the job to be filled. If you do not have a thorough knowledge of the job, read a job description. If possible, call one or more jobholders, and ask them about the job duties and what is required to succeed. Another idea is to make up a list of traits and qualifications for the ideal candidate. Be specific about what it will take to get the job done.

2. PREPARE A ROAD MAP. Develop questions that will reveal whether the candidate has the correct background and qualifications. The questions should focus on previous experiences that are relevant to the current job. If the job requires creativity and innovation, ask a question such as "What do you do differently from other sales reps?"

3. USE OPEN-ENDED QUESTIONS IN WHICH THE RIGHT ANSWER IS NOT OBVIOUS. Ask the applicant to give specific examples of previous work experiences. For example, don't ask, "Are you a hard worker?" or "Tell me about yourself." Instead ask, "Can you give me examples from your previous work history that reflect your level of motivation?" or "How did you go about getting your current job?"

4. DO NOT ASK QUESTIONS THAT ARE NOT RELEVANT TO THE JOB. This is particularly important when the irrelevant questions might adversely affect minorities or women. Questions that are considered objectionable are the same as those considered objectionable on application forms.

5. LISTEN; DON'T TALK. You should spend most of the interview listening. If you talk too much, the focus will shift to you, and you may miss important cues. One expert actually recommends laying out all your questions right at the beginning of the interview and following up with only brief reminders. This forces you to sit back and listen and also gives you a chance to watch a candidate's behavior and body language.

6. ALLOW ENOUGH TIME SO THAT THE INTERVIEW WILL NOT BE RUSHED. Leave time for the candidate to ask questions about the job. The types of questions the candidate asks can be an important clue to his or her interest in the job. Try to delay forming an opinion about the applicant until after the entire interview has been completed.

7. AVOID RELIANCE ON YOUR MEMORY. Request the applicant's permission to take notes; then do so unobtrusively during the interview or immediately after. If several applicants are interviewed, notes are essential for remembering what they said and the impressions they made.

Even a well-planned interview may be disrupted by the unexpected. Robert Half asked vice presidents and human resource directors at 100 major American corporations to describe the most unusual thing that they were aware of ever happening during a job interview. A few of their responses about applicants were:

- "Wore a Walkman and said she could listen to me and the music at the same time."

- "Announced she hadn't had lunch and proceeded to eat a hamburger and french fries in the interviewer's office."

- "Wore a jogging suit to interview for a position as a vice president."

- "He said he was so well-qualified that if he didn't get the job, it would prove that the company's management was incompetent."

- "A balding candidate abruptly excused himself. He returned to the office a few minutes later wearing a hairpiece."

- "Not only did he ignore the 'No Smoking' sign in my office, he lit up the wrong end of several filter-tip cigarettes."

- "She chewed bubble gum and constantly blew bubbles."

- "Job applicant challenged the interviewer to arm wrestle."

- "He stretched out on the floor to fill out the job application."

- "He interrupted to telephone his therapist for advice on answering specific interview questions."

- "He dozed off and started snoring during the interview."

- "He said that if he were hired, he would demonstrate his loyalty by having the corporate logo tattooed on his forearm."

SOURCES: James M. Jenks and Brian L. P. Zevnik, "ABCs of Job Interviewing," *Harvard Business Review* (July–August 1989), pp. 38–42; Dr. Pierre Mornell, "Zero Defect Hiring," *Inc.*, March 1998, pp. 75–83; and Martha H. Peak, "What Color Is Your Bumbershoot?" Reprinted by permission of publisher from *Management Review* (October 1989), p. 63, ©1989. American Management Association, New York. All rights reserved.

Assessment Centers   First developed by psychologists at AT&T, **assessment centers** are used to select individuals with high potential for managerial careers by such organizations as AT&T, IBM, General Electric, and JCPenney.[38] Assessment centers present a series of managerial situations to groups of applicants over, say, a two- or three-day period. One technique is the "in-basket" simulation, which requires the applicant to play the role of a manager who must decide how to respond to ten memos in his or her in-basket within a two-

hour period. Panels of two or three trained judges observe the applicant's decisions and assess the extent to which they reflect interpersonal, communication, and problem-solving skills.

■ DEVELOPING AN EFFECTIVE WORKFORCE

Following selection, the major goal of HRM is to develop employees into an effective work-

assessment center
An approach for selecting individuals with high managerial potential based on their performance on a series of simulated managerial tasks

Dillard's, one of the most successful retail chains in the United States, takes advantage of information technology for training and developing an effective workforce. Interactive software programs use touch-screen technology to teach computerized transaction processing to new sales associates. The system eliminates the need for one-on-one training and allows employees to learn at their own pace. Dillard's further develops the skills of sales associates through training programs regularly broadcast over the company's private satellite network. The high-tech approach allows employees to instantaneously receive the latest information on products and key company developments.

We have developed our own proprietary interactive software programs that use touch-screen technology to teach transaction processing to our sales associates. They can learn at their own pace, and the system eliminates the need for one-on-one training by another staff member.

force. Development includes training and performance appraisal.

TRAINING AND DEVELOPMENT

Training and development represent a planned effort by an organization to facilitate the learning of job-related behaviors by employees. Some authors distinguish the two forms of intervention by noting that the term *training* usually refers to teaching low-level or technical employees how to do their present jobs, whereas *development* refers to teaching managers and professionals the skills needed for both present and future jobs. For simplicity, we will refer to both interventions as *training*.

Organizations spend nearly $100 billion each year on training. Training may occur in a variety of forms. The most common method is on-the-job training. In **on-the-job training (OJT)**, an experienced employee is asked to take a new employee "under his or her wing" and show the newcomer how to perform job duties. OJT has many advantages, such as few out-of-pocket costs for training facilities, materials, or instructor fees and easy transfer of learning back to the job. The learning site is the work site.

Other frequently used training methods include:

- *Orientation training,* in which newcomers are introduced to the organization's "culture," standards, and goals.
- *Classroom training,* including lectures, films, audiovisual techniques, and simulations.
- *Programmed and computer-assisted instruction,* in which the employee works at his or her own pace to learn material from a text that includes exercises and quizzes to enhance learning.
- *Conference and case discussion groups,* in which participants analyze cases or discuss topics assisted by a training leader.

Companies, as well as employees, are increasingly appreciating the importance of training programs. Workers are not only expected to have skills related to specific tasks but also to demonstrate the ability to think critically and solve problems. Also, most companies are increasing training budgets and experimenting with a variety of new training approaches. One of the most popular is "cross-training," which teaches employees multiple skills so they can perform a number of different jobs, thus providing variety for employees and enabling companies to quickly adjust to changes in staffing needs. Another approach, "integrative learning," uses team exercises to establish and reinforce effective teamwork habits.[39]

PROMOTION FROM WITHIN   Promotion from within helps companies retain and develop productive employees. It provides challenging assignments, prescribes new responsibilities, and helps employees grow by developing their abilities.

One approach to promotion from within is *job posting,* which means that positions are announced on bulletin boards or in company publications as openings occur. Interested employees notify the human resources department, which then helps make the fit between employees and positions.

Another approach is the *employee resource chart,* which is designed to identify likely successors for each management position. The chart looks like a typical organization chart with every employee listed. Every key position includes the names of top candidates to move into that position when it becomes vacant. Candidates are rated on a five-point scale reflecting whether they are ready for immediate promotion or need additional experience. These charts show the potential flow of employees up through the hierarchy and provide motivation to employees who have an opportunity for promotion.

PERFORMANCE APPRAISAL

Performance appraisal is another important technique for developing an effective workforce. Performance appraisal comprises the steps of observing and assessing employee performance, recording the assessment, and providing feedback to the employee. Managers use performance appraisal to describe and evaluate the performances of employees. During performance appraisal, skillful managers give

on-the-job training (OJT)
Training in which an experienced employee "adopts" a new employee to teach him or her how to perform job duties

performance appraisal
The process of observing and evaluating an employee's performance, recording the assessment, and providing feedback to the employee

feedback and praise concerning the acceptable elements of the employee's performance. They also describe performance areas that need improvement. Employees can use this information to change their job performance.

Performance appraisal can also reward high performers with merit pay, recognition, and other rewards. However, the most recent thinking is that linking performance appraisal to rewards has unintended consequences. The idea is that performance appraisal should be ongoing, not something that is done once a year as part of a consideration of raises. Kelly Allan, senior associate of Kelly Allen Associates, Ltd., a consulting firm based in Columbus, Ohio, puts it this way: "A raise is a transaction about how much money you or I can get. Feedback is a conversation about how much meaning you and I can create." At Allan's company, associates meet weekly to discuss performance on their current projects. The firm schedules formal sessions monthly or quarterly to discuss the past, present, and future of each person's work. These conversations never include discussions of pay, which are considered separately.[40]

Generally, HRM professionals concentrate on two things to make performance appraisal a positive force in their organization: (1) the accurate assessment of performance through the development and application of assessment systems such as rating scales, and (2) training managers to effectively use the performance appraisal interview, so managers can provide feedback that will reinforce good performance and motivate employee development.

ASSESSING PERFORMANCE ACCURATELY   To obtain an accurate performance rating, managers must acknowledge that jobs are multidimensional and performance thus may be multidimensional as well. For example, a sports broadcaster may perform well on the job-knowledge dimension; that is, she or he may be able to report facts and figures about the players and describe which rule applies when there is a questionable play on the field. But the same sports broadcaster may not communicate well and be unable to express the information in a colorful, interesting way to an audience or other broadcasters.

If performance is to be rated accurately, the performance appraisal system should require the rater—usually the supervisor—to assess each relevant performance dimension. A multidimensional form increases the usefulness of the performance appraisal and facilitates employee growth and development.

A recent trend in performance appraisal is called **360-degree feedback,** a process that uses multiple raters, including self-rating, as a

360-degree feedback
A process that uses multiple raters, including self-rating, to appraise employee performance and guide development

To rehearse for the complex and rapidly changing real world, the United States Army puts everyone from PFCs to brigadier generals through maneuvers that stress them to the breaking point and then subjects them to a rigorous performance appraisal in public. The army is way ahead of most corporations in designing a bottom-up process that allows subordinates to appraise the performance of their bosses. In the After Action Review process, a colonel may question the actions of a subordinate, but junior officers can question the judgment of superiors as well. In this photo, a captain leads his tank platoon in a review following a mock battle at Fort Polk, Louisiana.

LEADING THE REVOLUTION:
CON-WAY'S TEAM IMPROVEMENT REVIEW

Most work in companies that are shifting to a learning organization is performed by empowered teams of workers. Yet performance reviews in many cases are handled the same way they always have been—in one-on-one sessions between a manager and the individuals who report directly to him or her. The Information Systems department at Con-Way Transportation Services knew there had to be a better way.

Now, teams in Con-Way's IS department evaluate themselves through a process called the Team Improvement Review (TIR). The department wanted to avoid the terms "performance review" or "appraisal" because they conjure up the old image of a boss judging a subordinate. The TIR process takes a more positive approach by having teams look at what

they're doing that's working, what they're doing that's not working, and ways to improve. The TIR process has three core features. First, it separates feedback sessions from salary reviews. Debbie Blanchard, a senior systems analyst, points out that people are much more open when they know that whatever they say is not going to affect their own or another team member's salary. The TIR also guarantees that feedback takes place in a "safe" environment. Managers usually are not present for sessions; instead, the team brings in a neutral facilitator to lead the discussions. Last, the TIR provides a formal process about once every three months by which team members can offer feedback. Prior to a session, participants rate team performance on a 1 to 5 scale for 31 different cri-

teria. In the group meeting, people discuss the team's overall performance as well as individual performance in the context of the team. One technique for making individual reviews easier is called the Round Robin. Each team member creates two columns on a sheet of paper, one headed "Strengths" and the other headed "Something to Work On." People almost always list something that other team members believe they need to improve, so it gives the team an opportunity to coach the individual rather than criticize.

www.con-way.com

SOURCE: Gina Imperato, "How to Give Good Feedback," *Fast Company*, September 1998, pp. 144–156.

---

way to increase awareness of strengths and weaknesses and guide employee development. Members of the appraisal group may include supervisors, coworkers, and customers, as well as the individual, thus providing appraisal of the employee from a variety of perspectives.[41] With the advent of empowered teams and learning organizations, the appraisal and feedback process is changing. Parkview Medical Center in Pueblo, Colorado, did away with its top-down performance appraisal process. There's still an annual review, but it consists of employees telling managers what they can do to help the worker better perform his or her job. The review process is called APOP (Annual Piece of Paper) because the only form used is a piece of paper signed and dated by both parties that records that the conversation occurred. There are no scores, written reviews, or lists of goals for the coming year. Performance feedback is handled on a daily basis between employees and managers, not once a year in an appraisal meeting.[42] Another innov-

ative approach to performance appraisal is presented in Leading the Revolution: The Learning Organization.

Although we would like to believe that every manager carefully assesses performances of employees, researchers have identified several rating problems.[43] For example, **halo error** occurs when an employee receives the same rating on all dimensions even if his or her performance is good on some dimensions and poor on others. **Homogeneity** occurs when a rater gives all employees a similar rating even if their performances are not equally good.

One approach to overcoming management performance evaluation errors is to use a behavior-based rating technique, such as the behaviorally anchored rating scale. The **behaviorally anchored rating scale (BARS)** is developed from critical incidents pertaining to job performance. Each job performance scale is anchored with specific behavioral statements that describe varying degrees of performance. By relating employee performance to

halo error
A type of rating error that occurs when an employee receives the same rating on all dimensions regardless of his or her performance on individual ones

homogeneity
A type of rating error that occurs when a rater gives all employees a similar rating regardless of their individual performances

behaviorally anchored rating scale (BARS)
A rating technique that relates an employee's performance to specific job-related incidents

Exhibit 9.6

EXAMPLE OF A BEHAVIORALLY ANCHORED RATING SCALE

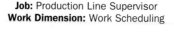

Job: Production Line Supervisor
Work Dimension: Work Scheduling

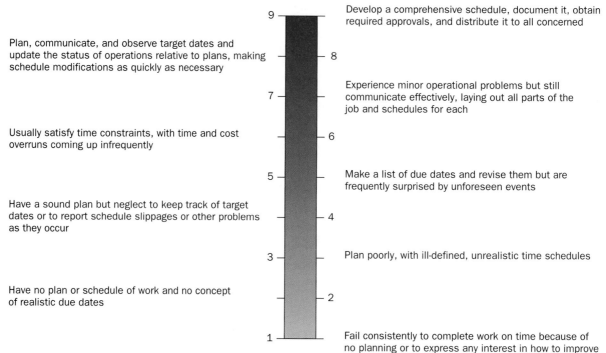

9 — Develop a comprehensive schedule, document it, obtain required approvals, and distribute it to all concerned

Plan, communicate, and observe target dates and update the status of operations relative to plans, making schedule modifications as quickly as necessary — 8

7 — Experience minor operational problems but still communicate effectively, laying out all parts of the job and schedules for each

Usually satisfy time constraints, with time and cost overruns coming up infrequently — 6

5 — Make a list of due dates and revise them but are frequently surprised by unforeseen events

Have a sound plan but neglect to keep track of target dates or to report schedule slippages or other problems as they occur — 4

3 — Plan poorly, with ill-defined, unrealistic time schedules

Have no plan or schedule of work and no concept of realistic due dates — 2

1 — Fail consistently to complete work on time because of no planning or to express any interest in how to improve

SOURCE: Based on J. P. Campbell, M. D. Dunnette, R. D. Arvey, and L. V. Hellervik, "The Development and Evaluation of Behaviorally Based Rating Scales," *Journal of Applied Psychology, 57* (1973), 15–22; and Francine Alexander, "Performance Appraisals," *Small Business Reports* (March 1989), 20–29.

specific incidents, raters can more accurately evaluate an employee's performance.[44]

Exhibit 9.6 illustrates the BARS method for evaluating a production line supervisor. The production supervisor's job can be broken down into several dimensions, such as equipment maintenance, employee training, or work scheduling. A behaviorally anchored rating scale should be developed for each dimension. The dimension in Exhibit 9.6 is work scheduling. Good performance is represented by a 7, 8, or 9 on the scale and unacceptable performance as a 1, 2, or 3. If a production supervisor's job has eight dimensions, the total performance evaluation will be the sum of the scores for each of eight scales.[45]

compensation
Monetary payments (wages, salaries) and nonmonetary goods/commodities (benefits, vacations) used to reward employees

■ MAINTAINING AN EFFECTIVE WORKFORCE

Now we turn to the topic of how managers and HRM professionals maintain a workforce that has been recruited and developed. Maintenance of the current workforce involves compensation, wage and salary structure, benefits, and occasional terminations.

COMPENSATION

The term **compensation** refers to (1) all monetary payments and (2) all goods or commodities used in lieu of money to reward employees.[46] An organization's compensation structure includes wages and/or salaries and benefits such as health insurance, paid vacations, or employee fitness centers. Developing an effective compensation system is an important part of human resource management because it helps to attract and retain talented workers. In addition, a company's compensation system has an impact on strategic performance.[47] Human resource managers design the pay and benefits systems to fit company strategy and to provide compensation equity.

WAGE AND SALARY SYSTEMS   Ideally, management's strategy for the organization should be a critical determinant of the features and operations of the pay system.[48] For example, managers may have the goal of maintaining or improving profitability or market share by stimulating employee performance. Thus, they should design and use a merit pay system rather than a system based on other criteria such as seniority. As another example, managers may have the goal of attracting and retaining desirable employees. Here they can use a pay survey to determine competitive wages in comparable companies and adjust pay rates to meet or exceed the going rates.

Skill-based pay systems are becoming increasingly popular in both large and small companies, including Nortel, au Bon Pain, and Quaker Oats. Employees with higher skill levels receive higher pay than those with lower skill levels. At Quaker Oats pet food plant in Topeka, Kansas, for example, employees start at $8.75 per hour but can reach a top hourly rate of $14.50 when they master a series of skills.[49] Also called *competency-based pay,* skill-based pay systems encourage employees to develop their skills and competencies, thus making them more valuable to the organization as well as more employable if they leave their present job. Thus, these systems work well within the context of the changing nature of careers and working relationships discussed earlier in this chapter. In addition, skill-based pay helps the organization be more flexible and adaptable to changing needs from the environment.

Another approach to establishing wage or salary rates, which has been widely used in the past, is *job-based pay.* With job-based pay, compensation is linked to the specific tasks that an employee performs. Although job-based pay systems still are used by some companies, they do present some problems. For one thing, job-based pay may fail to reward the type of learning behavior needed for the organization to adapt and survive in today's rapidly changing environment. In addition, these systems reinforce an emphasis on organizational hierarchy and centralized decision making and control, which are inconsistent with the growing emphasis on employee participation and increased responsibility.[50]

COMPENSATION EQUITY   Whether the organization uses job-based pay or skill-based pay, managers strive to maintain a sense of fairness and equity within the pay structure and thereby fortify employee morale. **Job evaluation** refers to the process of determining the value or worth of jobs within an organization through an examination of job content. Job evaluation techniques enable managers to compare similar and dissimilar jobs and to determine internally equitable pay rates—that is, pay rates that employees believe are fair compared with those for other jobs in the organization. Managers also may want to provide income security so that their employees need not be overly concerned with the financial consequences of disability or retirement.

INCENTIVE PAY   Another approach increasingly used is *incentive pay,* which links some portion of an employee's pay beyond base wage or salary to job performance. Incentives are aligned with the behaviors needed to help the organization achieve its strategic goals. Employees have an incentive to make the company more efficient and profitable because if goals are not met, no bonuses are paid. Duke Power Company gives cash awards to employees in 30 different business units based on the company's achieving its targeted return on equity and the business unit realizing its goals.[51] Incentive pay systems may also be designed as a form of profit sharing to reward employees when the company meets its overall profitability goals.

job evaluation
The process of determining the value of jobs within an organization through an examination of job content

DESIGNING A WAGE AND SALARY STRUCTURE

Large organizations typically employ HRM compensation specialists to establish and maintain a pay structure. They may also hire outside consultants, such as the Hay Group or PAQ (Position Analysis Questionnaire) Associates, whose pay systems have been adopted by many companies and government organizations. The majority of large public- and private-sector U.S. employers use some formal process of job evaluation.[52]

The most commonly used job evaluation system is the **point system.**[53] First, compensation specialists must ensure that job descriptions are complete, up-to-date, and accurate. Next, top managers select compensable job factors (such as skill, effort, and responsibility) and decide how each factor will be weighed in establishing job worth. These factors are described in a point manual, which is used to assign point values to each job. For example, the characteristic of "responsibility" could receive from 0 to 5 points depending on whether job responsibility is "routine work performed under close supervision" (0 points) or "complete discretion with errors having extreme consequences to the organization and public safety" (5 points).

The compensation specialist then compares each job factor in a given job description to that specified in the point manual. This process is repeated until the job has been evaluated on all factors. Then the compensation specialist evaluates a second job and repeats the process until all jobs have been evaluated.

The job evaluation process can establish an internal hierarchy of job worth. However, to determine competitive market pay rates, most organizations obtain one or more pay surveys. **Pay surveys** show what other organizations pay incumbents in jobs that match a sample of "key" jobs selected by the organization. Pay surveys are available from many sources, including consulting firms and the U.S. Bureau of Labor Statistics.

The compensation specialist then compares the survey pay rates for key jobs with their job evaluation points by plotting them on a graph as illustrated in Exhibit 9.7. The **pay-trend line** shows the relationship between pay and total point values. The compensation specialist can use the pay-trend line to determine the pay values of all jobs for which point values have been calculated. Ranges of pay for each job class are established, enabling a newcomer or low performer to be paid less than other people in the same job class. The organization must then specify how individuals in the same

point system
A job evaluation system that assigns a predetermined point value to each compensable job factor in order to determine the worth of a given job

pay surveys
Studies of what other companies pay employees in jobs that correspond to a sample of key positions selected by the organization

pay-trend line
A graph that shows the relationship between pay and total job point values for determining the worth of a given job

Exhibit 9.7

PAY-TREND LINE

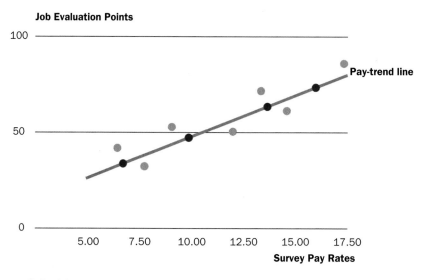

● Key jobs on which pay-trend line is based
● Other jobs placed on pay-trend line to determine pay rate

job class can advance from the low to the high end of the range. For example, the organization can reward merit, seniority, or a combination of both.

BENEFITS

Good human resource managers know that a compensation package requires more than money. Equally important is the benefits package, which has become a central rather than a "fringe" part of the compensation structure. A U.S. Chamber of Commerce survey has revealed that benefits in general compose more than one-third of labor costs and in some industries nearly two-thirds.[54]

Some benefits are required by law, such as social security, unemployment compensation, and workers' compensation. In addition, companies with 50 or more employees are required by the Family and Medical Leave Act of 1993 to give up to twelve weeks of unpaid leave for such things as the birth or adoption of a child, the serious illness of a spouse or family member, or an employee's serious illness. Other types of benefits, such as health insurance, vacations, and such things as on-site fitness centers are not required by law but are provided by organizations to maintain an effective workforce.

One reason that benefits make up such a large portion of compensation is that health-care costs have increased so quickly. Because employers frequently include health insurance as a benefit, these costs require benefit management. Between 1983 and 1993, annual corporate spending on health care tripled to $225 billion.[55]

Organizations that want to provide cost-effective benefits should be sensitive to changes in employee lifestyles. Two decades ago, benefits were based on the assumption that the typical worker was a married man with a dependent wife and two school-age children. The benefits packages provided life insurance coverage for the worker, health insurance coverage for all family members, and no assistance with child-care expenses. But today fewer than 10 percent of American workers fit the description of the so-called typical worker.[56] Increased workforce diversity means that far more workers are single; in addition, both spouses in most families are working. These workers are not likely to value the traditional benefits package. In response, some companies are establishing *cafeteria-plan benefits packages* that allow employees to select the benefits of greatest value to them.[57] Other companies use surveys to determine which combination of fixed benefits is most desirable. The benefits packages provided by large companies attempt to meet the needs of all employees.

Sometimes companies need to offer benefits to the whole family when it comes to relocation. Here, two small businesses got started based on this need.

IMPACT GROUP AND RELONETWORKS

Clinical psychologist and Employee-Assistance-Program-trainer Marilyn Herring saw a business opportunity when so many of her clients reported the ordeals of corporate relocation. As a teen, Herring herself had endured a traumatic move and knew of what these people spoke. Sixteen months later and $380,000 poorer, she had mortgaged her house and had developed a superb self-help program called Momentum.

Her cold calls to executives were unsuccessful when she tried to sell the program, so she wangled her way in to a corporate relocation convention. Unfortunately, no vendors were allowed to set up booths. For three days she wore a cheesy sports visor touting "Momentum," along with her business suits and a black lace cocktail dress. At the end of the convention, a Johnson & Johnson executive asked her what it was and exclaimed, "we've been looking for something like that." Such was the birth of the Impact Group.

Her initial program's success has led to the development of other products, such as spousal employment help, outplacement firms for downsizees, and corporate recruiting. "We use each product to build a product," says Herring. Rather than outsourcing as other similar firms do, Herring keeps all 110 employees under one roof, so they can talk together a lot and learn what clients are saying, keeping an ear open for any vague need they express.

As a management trainee, Brian Boettcher was asked to supervise a relocation for 200 people and learned three things: moving sucks, and when lots of people move, the suck rate increases exponentially. And—that companies need lots of help.

With that one experience, Boettcher became enough of an expert to launch ReloNetworks in 1999, which is described as a "hand-holding, arrangement-making, bumpy-road-smoothing service" geared toward corporations reshuffling employees to the San Francisco Bay area. When soon-to-be Bay residents arrive, a ReloNetworks employee meets them at the airport and then spends a couple of days showing them preselected real estate, introducing them to school principals, showing them supermarkets and hospitals. After the trip, that same person is available to answer questions via e-mail or cell phone.

Other entrepreneurs in the information business hoard their knowledge, but not Boettcher. He figured all the data he had amassed on communities, housing, attractions, and so on, was good for everyone and he would help them even if they weren't clients. So it all is available on the Web site, at www.relonetworks.com. Is it working? ReloNetworks site had 8,000 visitors a month within six months. There is even an online bookstore, with every kind of book on the Bay area, such as culture, adventures, single life, and schools. Boettcher's generosity has paid off. ReloNetworks has 25 major clients, some of them so impressed by the wealth of information on the Web, they decided to hire the company.

Technology has played another role, too. Boettcher wanted visitors to the Web site to do more than research. He wanted them to *do* something, so he partnered with Homefair.com in order to offer a menu of interactive tools, such as

a salary calculator to see how much they would need to earn in the Bay area to maintain their current standard of living (hint: a lot!).

So, here are two entrepreneurs who turned someone else's headache into a chance to build their own dream.[58] ■

TERMINATION

Despite the best efforts of line managers and HRM professionals, the organization will lose employees. Some will retire, others will depart voluntarily for other jobs, and still others will be forced out through mergers and cutbacks or for poor performance. The value of termination for maintaining an effective workforce is twofold. First, employees who are poor performers can be dismissed. Productive employees often resent disruptive, low-performing employees who are allowed to stay with the company and receive pay and benefits comparable to theirs. Second, employers can use exit interviews. An **exit interview** is an interview conducted with departing employees to determine why they are leaving.[59] The value of the exit interview is to provide an excellent and inexpensive tool for learning about pockets of dissatisfaction within the organization and hence for reducing future turnover.

When companies experience downsizing through mergers or because of global competition, often a large number of managers and workers are terminated at the same time. In these cases, enlightened companies try to find a smooth transition for departing employees. When General Electric laid off 900 employees in three gradual steps, it also set up a reemployment center to assist employees in finding new jobs or in learning new skills. It provided counseling in how to write a résumé and conduct a job search. An additional step General Electric took was to place an advertisement in local newspapers saying that these employees were available.[60]

To avoid massive layoffs, Chevron set up a special program to rematch and train employees to job-hop to other units. A petroleum engineer might be trained to fill in for a chemical engineering position. Employees scheduled for termination were generally given a six-month grace

exit interview
An interview conducted with departing employees to determine the reasons for their leaving/termination

period to find an intracompany job. The company also provided training and job-hunting assistance for employees who couldn't find an intracompany job or who chose to leave rather than move to a different unit. In addition, an educational assistance program reimbursed 75 percent of tuition, books, and fees for up to two years after termination for former employees who took courses that would enhance their opportunities for finding a job outside the company.[61] By showing genuine concern in helping place laid-off employees, a company communicates the value of human resources and helps maintain a positive corporate culture as shown below.

HUNT TRACTOR

Imagine you get laid off, and your employer hires a grief counselor to help you deal with the trauma.

Then imagine a company that never lays off anyone. Construction-equipment dealership Hunt Tractor's president, Frank Miske, Jr., says he doesn't even "fantasize" about axing workers. "We don't lay people off because we don't want to lose them. Besides that, it's not morally right to lay them off because loyal employees

built this company," which has been profitable since it began in 1969.

Hunt Tractor belongs to a rare group of businesses that have never laid off anyone. During down times, chairman Roy Hunt keeps workers busy with painting, roofing, building renovation, training, machine repairs, and tidying up. What does the company see as the benefits? High rates of retention of its highly skilled workers, increased productivity, lower recruiting costs, superior customers service due to extremely loyal and satisfied employees, and costs savings because of lower turnover and absenteeism. Not a bad deal.

Roy Hunt knows all too well the difficulties of layoffs and then rehiring later when business picks up. "Our people are not robots," he says. "You can't just take somebody from off the street and expect them to do the job." He gets tired of reading all the headlines about cold and uncaring companies that eliminate thousands of jobs at will. "Our business isn't run like that," he adds. "I'd like to dispel the notion that we're all only interested in the bottom line."[62] ■

Summary and Management Solution

All managers are responsible for human resources, and most organizations have a human resource department that works with line managers to ensure a productive workforce. The human resource department is responsible for interpreting and responding to the large human resource environment. The HR department must be part of the organization's competitive strategy, implement procedures to reflect federal and state legislation, and respond to changes in working relationships and career directions. The old social contract of the employee being loyal to the company and the company taking care of the employee until retirement no longer holds. Employees are responsible for managing their own careers. While many people still follow a traditional management career path, others look for new opportunities as telecommuters, team players, and entrepreneurs.

The HR department strives to achieve three goals for the organization. Goals of human resource departments are (1) to attract an effective workforce through human resource planning, recruiting, and employee selection; (2) to develop an effective workforce (i.e., introduce new hires to the organization and to their jobs through orientation and training programs and evaluate them through performance appraisal programs); and (3) to maintain an effective workforce. Human resource managers retain employees with wage and salary systems, benefits packages, and termination procedures.

At e-commerce 800-Flowers, Jim McCann used a new approach to training that helped him motivate workers, reduce bureaucracy, and adjust to fluctuating labor demands. 800-Flowers cross-trains employees so they can switch to different jobs as departmental needs change. Employees in the fast-paced order-taking and customer service departments traditionally burn out quickly, so as a reward for their hard work they may be transferred to one of the company's retail stores or to a job in headquarters. During the peak season, regular order takers become supervisors to train and assist temporary workers. Switching jobs helps keep employee enthusiasm high and revitalizes the business as employees bring fresh perspectives to each new job they do. To symbolize their cross-training in what McCann calls the "Reebok System," each participant gets a new pair of sneakers. The Reebok System has helped McCann turn the debt-ridden company into a blockbuster with more than $100 million in revenues. Effec-

tively managing human resources enables 800-Flowers to do more with fewer workers, retain quality employees, and be more responsive and efficient in satisfying customers. And to further enhance customer satisfaction in what is becoming a highly competitive e-commerce business, 800-Flowers was one of the first companies to institute a program that allows customers to "chat" online with a service representative.

SOURCES: Erik Sherman, "How It Click Off the Customer," *Computerworld*, Vol. 33 (42), Oct. 18, 1999, p. 48; Mike Campbell, "Floral Website Ends Online Stress," *Bank Marketing*, Vol. 31 (4), April 1999, p. 8; Jenny C. McCune, "On the Train Gang," *Management Review*, October 1994, pp. 57–60.

Discussion Questions

1. It is the year 2010. In your company, central planning has given way to frontline decision making, and bureaucracy has given way to teamwork. Shop floor workers use computers and robots. There is a labor shortage for many job openings, and the few applicants lack skills to work in teams, make decisions, or use sophisticated technology. As vice president of human resource management since 1990, what did you do to prepare for this problem?

2. If you were asked to advise a private company about its equal employment opportunity responsibilities, what two points would you emphasize as most important? Why?

3. How can the human resource activities of planning, recruiting, performance appraisal, and compensation be related to corporate strategy?

4. Recall your own job experience. What human resource management activities described in this chapter were performed for the job you filled? Which ones were absent?

5. How might the changing social contract affect the ways human resource departments recruit, develop, and retain workers?

6. How "valid" do you think the information obtained from a personal interview versus a paper-and-pencil test versus an assessment center would be for predicting effective job performance for a college professor? An assembly-line worker in a team-oriented plant? Discuss.

7. What techniques can managers adopt to improve their recruiting and interviewing practices?

8. How does affirmative action differ from equal employment opportunity in recruiting and selection?

9. How can exit interviews be used to maintain an effective workforce?

10. Describe the procedure used to build a wage and salary structure for an organization.

Management Exercises

Manager's Workbook

Want Ads

1. Find 10 want ads for jobs. Five should be from a local newspaper and five from a professional journal (there are many available in the university's library). Choose a selection of jobs from professional, technical, clerical and manual labor.

2. Prepare a report, with ads attached, to turn in to your instructor answering the following questions:

   a. What differences in the way the ads are worded or designed do you notice between the journal and newspaper?

   b. Write a short paragraph for each ad, indicating the strengths and weaknesses of the ad itself (not the job). Look at qualities such as: ability to gain interest of job seeker, adequate information, ease of contact to company, etc.

   c. What type of ad grabbed your interest the most?

d. If you were hired as a consultant to the companies that placed those ads, what would you recommend

to them in order to make their job advertisements more effective?

e. Write an advertisement for your dream job.

Manager's Workshop

Hiring and Evaluating Using Core Competencies

1. Form groups of four to seven members. Develop a list of "core competencies" for the job of student in this course. (Or alternately, you may choose a job in one of the group members' organizations.) List the core competencies below.

    1.   5.
    2.   6.
    3.   7.
    4.   8.

2. Which of the above are the most important four?

    1.   3.
    2.   4.

3. What questions would you ask a potential student to determine if that person could be successful in this class, based on the four most important core competencies as listed in problem 2? (interviewing process)

1.
2.
3.
4.

4. What learning experiences would you develop to enhance those core competencies? (training and development process)

    1.
    2.
    3.
    4.

5. How would you evaluate or measure the success of a student in this class, based on the four core competencies? (performance evaluation process)

    1.
    2.
    3.
    4.

Management in Practice: Ethical Dilemma

A Conflict of Responsibilities

As director of human resources, Tess Danville was asked to negotiate a severance deal with Terry Winston, the Midwest regional sales manager for Cyn-Com Systems. Winston's problems with drugs and alcohol had become severe enough to precipitate his dismissal. His customers were devoted to him, but top management was reluctant to continue gambling on his reliability. Lives depended on his work as the salesman and installer of Cyn-Com's respiratory diagnostic technology. Winston had been warned twice to clean up his act, but had not succeeded. Only his unique blend of technical knowledge and high-powered sales ability had saved him before.

But now the vice president of sales asked Danville to offer Winston the option of resigning rather than be fired if he would sign a noncompete agreement and agree to go into rehabilitation. Cyn-Com would also extend a guarantee of

confidentiality on the abuse issue and a good work reference as thanks for the millions of dollars of business that Winston had brought to Cyn-Com. Winston agreed to take the deal. After his departure, a series of near disasters was uncovered as a result of Winston's mismanagement. Some of his maneuvers to cover up his mistakes bordered on fraud.

Today Danville received a message to call the human resources director at a cardiopulmonary technology company to give a personal reference on Terry Winston. From the area code, Danville could see that he was not in violation of the noncompete agreement. She had also heard that Winston had completed a 30-day treatment program as promised. Danville knew she was expected to honor the confidentiality agreement, but she also knew that if his shady dealings had been discovered before his departure, he would have been fired without any agreement. Now she was being asked to give Winston a reference for another medical sales position.

What Do You Do?

1. Honor the agreement, trusting Winston's rehabilitation is complete on all levels and that he is now ready for a responsible position. Give a good recommendation.

2. Contact the vice president of sales and ask him to release you from the agreement or to give the reference himself. After all, he made the agreement. You don't want to lie.

3. Without mentioning specifics, give Winston such an unenthusiastic reference that you hope the other human resources director can read between the lines and believe that Winston will be a poor choice.

Surf the Net

1. *Equal Employment Opportunity.* Andrea Kingston, a small business owner with 35 employees, has hired you as a human resources consultant. One area you are working on is making sure your client is in compliance with the federal laws related to her employees. The first step in the process is educating Andrea on what is required of her because her level of knowledge in this area is very minimal. Go to "Small Business Information" at the U.S. Equal Employment Opportunity Commission's home page (www.eeoc.gov) to gather information for Andrea. Write an outline of the information you will cover in that meeting.

2. *Recruiting.* Option 1—Just as you get impressions about companies based on how you are treated when you visit their human resources departments to inquire about job openings or to ask for a job application form, you also get impressions based on how companies present themselves on the Internet. Go to several online human resources departments at companies you might like to work for someday, or check out those listed below, and record your impressions—things you liked and didn't like—as you conduct your on-line job search:

   Federal Express (http://www.fedex.com/us/careers)

   Intel (www.intel.com/intel/oppty/index.htm)

   Cisco Systems (www.cisco.com/jobs)

   Option 2—Surf www.mgeneral.com to find its supersite (listed at bottom of home page). Then click "Careers." List 15 sources for a job search and career information you found there.

3. *Benefits.* The Employee Benefit Research Institute (EBRI) at www.ebri.org/ebrilinks.htm provides access to a number of sites that deal with benefits issues. Assuming the human resources consultant role described in problem 1, prepare a recommended benefits checklist for Andrea so that she can compare her current benefits package with the benefits appropriate for a small business to offer its employees.

Case for Critical Analysis

Waterway Industries

Waterway Industries was founded in the early 1960s as a small manufacturer of high-quality canoes. Based in Lake Placid, New York, the company quickly gained a solid reputation throughout the Northeast and began building a customer base in the Pacific Northwest as well. By the early 1980s, Waterway was comfortably ensconced in the canoe market nationwide. Although earnings growth was fairly steady up until 1990, CEO Cyrus Maher was persuaded by a friend to venture into kayaks. After Waterway began selling its own line of compact, inexpensive kayaks in 1992, Maher quickly learned that the decision was a good one. Most of Waterway's existing canoe customers placed sizable kayak orders, and a number of private-label companies also began contacting Maher about making kayaks for their companies. When Lee Carter was hired to establish a formal marketing department at Waterway, things really took off. Carter began bringing in so many large orders that the company had to contract with other manufacturers to keep up.

For the most part, Waterway's 45 or so employees adjusted well to the faster pace at the company. The expanded business didn't seem to change the company's relaxed, informal working atmosphere. Most employees were outdoor enthusiasts, and on days when the weather was good Maher knew that the building would be almost empty by 4:00 P.M. He also knew, however, that employees enjoyed their jobs, got their work completed on time, and were always speaking out with new ideas and suggestions. However, Lee Carter, unlike other employees, seemed totally focused on her work. She traveled constantly and worked so hard that she barely had time to get to know the rest of the staff. She came in on weekends to catch up on paperwork. She had even missed the Waterway picnic, along with two of her direct reports, because the three were on the road trying to nail down a large order. Maher likes the dedication but wonders if this approach could eventually have a negative effect on the company's culture.

Turnover at Waterway has always been low, and Maher believes most employees are happy working at the company. However, within the past year, both of Waterway's designers have approached Maher to request salary adjustments. Each suggested they would be interested in equity in the company, whereby they would receive a share of the profits if their designs did well. Maher's response was to give the senior designer a modest pay raise and extra vacation and to increase the bonuses for both designers. Both seemed satisfied with the new arrangement. Waterway's CFO, on the other hand, recently left the company to take a position with a power boat manufacturer after Maher twice refused his request for a redesigned compensation package to include equity. Now, on a trip to the cafeteria to get a cup of coffee, Maher has just overheard Lee Carter discussing a possible job opportunity with another company. He is well aware of the lucrative packages being offered to sales and marketing managers in the sporting goods industry, and he doesn't want to lose

Carter. Even though he suspects she will eventually leave the company anyway, especially if the market for kayaks falls flat, he would like to find a way to recognize her hard work and keep her at Waterway for at least a few more years.

Maher has asked you, the company's sole human resource manager, for advice about changing the company's compensation system. In the past, he has handled things informally, giving employees annual salary increases and bonuses, and dealing with employees one-on-one (as he did with the designers) when they have concerns about their current compensation. Now, Maher is wondering if his company has grown to the point where he needs to establish some kind of formal compensation system that can recognize employees who make outstanding contributions to the company's success.

Questions

1. What impact, positive or negative, do you think a formal compensation system might have on Waterway?

2. What type of compensation approach would you suggest Maher implement?

3. How can nonfinancial incentives play a role in helping Waterway retain aggressive, ambitious employees like Lee Carter?

SOURCE: Based on Robert D. Nicoson, "Growing Pains," *Harvard Business Review,* July–August 1996, pp. 20–36.

Endnotes

1 Erik Sherman, "How It Click off the Customer," *Computerworld*, Vol. 33 (42), Oct. 18, 1999, p. 48; Mike Campbell, "Floral Website Ends Online Stress," *Bank Marketing*, Vol. 31 (4), April 1999, p. 8.

2 R. Gustav Niebuhr, "Mass Shortage: Catholic Church Faces Crisis as Priests Quit and Recruiting Falls," *The Wall Street Journal,* November 13, 1990, pp. A1, A13.

3 Mark A. Huselid, Susan E. Jackson, and Randall S. Schuler, "Technical and Strategic Human Resource Management Effectiveness as Determinants of Firm Performance," *Academy of Management Journal,* 40 (1) (1997), pp. 171–188.

4 Dale D. Buss, "Help Wanted Desperately," *Nation's Business,* April 1996, pp. 16–23.

5 Buss, "Help Wanted Desperately,"; and Aaron Bernstein, "We Want You to Stay. Really," *Business Week,* June 22, 1998, pp. 67–72.

6 David E. Bowen and Edward E. Lawler III, "Total Quality-Oriented Human Resource Management," *Organizational Dynamics* (Spring 1992), pp. 29–41.

7 Cynthia D. Fisher, "Current and Recurrent Challenges in HRM," *Journal of Management,* 15 (1989), pp. 157–180.

8 See Dave Ulrich, "A New Mandate for Human Resources," *Harvard Business Review,* January–February 1998, pp. 124–134.

9 Gillian Flynn, "Can't Get This Big without HR Deluxe," *Personnel Journal,* December 1996, pp. 47–53.

10 Jennifer J. Laabs, "It's OK to Focus on Heart and Soul," *Workforce,* January 1997, pp. 60–69.

11 Cynthia A. Lengnick-Hall and Mark L. Lengnick-Hall, "Strategic Human Resources Management: A Review of the Literature and a Proposed Typology," *Academy of Management Review,* 13 (1988), pp. 454–470.

12 Philip H. Mirvis, "Human Resource Management: Leaders, Laggards, and Followers," *Academy of Management Executive,* 11 (2) (1997), pp. 43–56.

13 Peter Carbonara, "Hire for Attitude, Train for Skill," *Fast Company,* August–September 1996, pp. 73–81.

14 Randall S. Schuler and Susan E. Jackson, "Linking Competitive Strategies with Human Resource Management Practices," *The Academy of Management Executive* 1 (1987), pp. 207–219.

15 Neal Templin, "Auto Plants, Hiring Again, Are Demanding Higher-Skilled Labor," *The Wall Street Journal,* March 11, 1994, pp. A1, A4.

16 Joanne L. Symons, "Is Affirmative Action in America's Interest?" *Executive Female,* May–June 1995, p. 52.

17 Deidre A. Depke, "Picking Up the Tab for Bias at Shoney's," *Business Week,* November 6, 1992, p. 50.

18 Charles F. Falk and Kathleen A. Carlson, "Newer Patterns in Management for the Post-Social Contract Era," *Midwest Management Society Proceedings* (1995), pp. 45–52.

19 Louisa Wah, "The New Workplace Paradox," *Management Review,* January 1998, p. 7.

20 Douglas T. Hall and Jonathan E. Moss, "The New Protean Career Contract: Helping Organizations and Employees Adapt," *Organizational Dynamics* (Winter 1998), pp. 22–37.

21 Hall and Moss, "The New Protean Career Contract."

22 Richard W. Judy and Carol D'Amico, *Workforce 2020: Work and Workers in the 21st Century* (Indianapolis, Ind.: The Hudson Institute, 1997); Jenny C. McCune, "Telecommuting Revisited," *Management Review,* February 1998, pp. 10–16.

23 Carol A. L. Dannhauser, "The Invisible Worker," *Working Woman,* November 1998, p. 38.

24 John Grossman, "Meetings at 9, I'll Be the One in Slippers," *Inc.,* Vol 20 (7), May 19, 1998, pp. 47–48.

25 Wendy Zellner, "Team Player: No More 'Same-ol'-same-ol'," *Business Week,* October 17, 1994, pp. 95–96.

26 Dennis J. Kravetz, *The Human Resources Revolution* (San Francisco, Calif.: Jossey-Bass, 1989).

27 David E. Ripley, "How to Determine Future Workforce Needs," *Personnel Journal,* January 1995, pp. 83–89.

28 Brian Dumaine, "The New Art of Hiring Smart," *Fortune,* August 17, 1987, pp. 78–81.

29 P. Farish, "HRM Update: Referral Results," *Personnel Administrator,* 31 (1986), p. 22.

30 J. P. Wanous, *Organizational Entry* (Reading, Mass.: Addison-Wesley, 1980).

31 Larry Reibstein, "Crushed Hopes: When a New Job Proves to Be Something Different," *The Wall Street Journal,* June 10, 1987, p. 25.

32 Thomas Love, "Smart Tactics for Finding Workers," *Nation's Business,* January 1998, p. 20.

33 Patricia Nakache, "Cisco's Recruiting Edge," *Fortune,* September 29, 1997, pp. 275–276.

34 P. W. Thayer, "Somethings Old, Somethings New," *Personnel Psychology* 30 (1977), pp. 513–524.

35 Pierre Mornell, "Zero Defect Hiring," *Inc.,* March 1998, pp. 75–83.

36 A. Brown, "Employment Tests: Issues without Clear Answers," *Personnel Administrator,* 30 (1985), pp. 43–56.

37 Lorie Parch, "Testing . . . 1, 2, 3," *Working Woman,* October 1997, pp. 74–78.

38 "Assessment Centers: Identifying Leadership through Testing," *Small Business Report* (June 1987), pp. 22–24.

39 Pfeffer, "Producing Sustainable Competitive Advantage."

40 Gina Imperato, "How to Give Good Feedback," *Fast Company,* September 1998, pp. 144–156.

41 Brian O'Reilly, "360 Feedback Can Change Your Life," *Fortune,* October 17, 1994, pp. 93–100.

42 Imperato, "How to Give Good Feedback."

43 V. R. Buzzotta, "Improve Your Performance Appraisals," *Management Review* (August 1988), pp. 40–43.

44 Ibid.

45 Francine Alexander, "Performance Appraisals," *Small Business Reports* (March 1989), pp. 20–29.

46 Richard I. Henderson, *Compensation Management: Rewarding Performance,* 4th ed. (Reston, Va.: Reston, 1985).

47 E. Montemayor, "Congruence Between Pay Policy and Competitive Strategy in High-Performing Firms," *Journal of Management,* 22 (6) (1996), pp. 889–908.

48 Renée F. Broderick and George T. Milkovich, "Pay Planning, Organization Strategy, Structure and 'Fit': A Prescriptive Model of Pay" (August 1985).

49 L. Wiener, "No New Skills? No Raise," *U.S. News and World Report,* October 26, 1992, p. 78.

50 R. J. Greene, "Person-Focused Pay: Should It Replace Job-Based Pay?" *Compensation and Benefits Management,* 9 (4) (1993), pp. 46–55.

51 Don Hellriegel, Susan E. Jackson, and John W. Slocum, Jr., *Management,* 8th edition, (Cincinnati: South-Western College Publishing, 1999), p. 417.

52 L. R. Burgess, *Wage and Salary Administration* (Columbus, Ohio: Merrill, 1984).

53 D. Doverspike, A. M. Carlisi, G. V. Barrett, and R. A. Alexander, "Generalizability Analysis of a Point-Method Job Evaluation Instrument," *Journal of Applied Psychology,* 68 (1983), pp. 476–483.

54 U.S. Chamber of Commerce, Employee Benefits 1983 (Washington, D.C.: U.S. Chamber of Commerce, 1984).

55 Christopher Farrell, Paul Magnusson, and Wendy Zellner, "The Scary Math of New Hires," *Business Week,* February 22, 1993, pp. 70–71.

56 J. A. Haslinger, "Flexible Compensation: Getting a Return on Benefit Dollars," *Personnel Administrator,* 30 (1985), pp. 39–46, 224.

57 Robert S. Catapano-Friedman, "Cafeteria Plans: New Menu for the '90s," *Management Review* (November 1991), pp. 25–29.

58 Leigh Buchanan, "Transplant Operation," *Inc. Tech 1999*, No. 4, pp. 96–97.

59 "Exit Interviews: An Overlooked Information Source," *Small Business Report* (July 1986), pp. 52–55.

60 Yvette Debow, "GE: Easing the Pain of Layoffs," *Management Review,* September 1997, pp. 15–18.

61 Gillian Flynn, "New Skills Equal New Opportunities," *Personnel Journal,* June 1996, pp. 77–79.

62 Greg Jaffe, "After the Ax Falls, a Plant's Workers Find Good News in the Bad," *Wall Street Journal*, November 30, 1999, pp. A1, A6.

10

Managing Diverse Employees

LEARNING OBJECTIVES

After studying this chapter, you should be able to:

• Explain the dimensions of employee diversity and why ethnorelativism is the appropriate attitude for today's corporations

• Discuss the changing workplace and the management activities required for a culturally diverse workforce

• Understand the daily challenges minority employees face

• Explain affirmative action and why the glass ceiling and other factors have kept it from being more successful

• Describe how to change the corporate culture, structure, and policies and how to use diversity awareness training to meet the needs of diverse employees

• Explain the importance of addressing sexual harassment in the workplace

• Describe benefits that accrue to companies that value diversity

LORNE PRINCE, an African American,

started his business at age 25 with great hopes. He

wanted his Accokeek, Maryland, company to bring its new shrink-

wrapped e-commerce software to market. But after losing three government contract

bids totaling $1.2 million, and seeing his sales stuck at $200,000 per year, he realized he did not have

enough capital to bear the hefty costs necessary for the product's development. There was no mystery why.

He was losing to "certified" companies. Even though the Small Business Administration (SBA) gives

• If you were Prince, what would you do? Would you hire extra staff to help with the paperwork? Would you

forget the certification and be content with the $200,000 per year? Would you find some other solution?

an edge to minority business owners in competing for government contracts, the company has to go through the

certification process to even get in the game. And when Prince had looked at the four-inch high stack of

paperwork he would have to complete, he realized it was a matter of spending 14 hours a day building

the business or doing paperwork. The fact that most certification applications are sent back to the

entrepreneur for more information didn't make him feel more positive about the

process. He rejected the paperwork, and now four years later, he found

himself uncertified and unable to compete and grow.

Prince is not alone in his problems with minority issues and business.[1] Take the case of another company. After paying $275,000 to settle a class-action lawsuit alleging racial discrimination at one of its facilities, Chicago's R. R. Donnelley & Sons initiated a company-wide diversity training program. Since 1993, Donnelley has spent millions on diversity training, believing it would promote understanding and defuse tensions between workers of diverse backgrounds. However, the program backfired, leading to even more charges of discrimination and harassment. Employees say the diversity program is nothing but window dressing and that top managers have failed to address the real concerns of minority employees. They point out, for example, that black employment actually fell from 8 percent to 6.6 percent in the two years after the program began. There were so few minority workers at Donnelley that some were asked to attend training sessions multiple times in order to ensure diverse participation. One employee, who spoke out in a diversity session about how hard it was to work in a place that was insensitive to women and minorities, claims she was later denied a customer service position because she was "too direct and too honest." Although a group of minority employees asked for a review of hiring and compensation policies, the group charged that company officials failed to include the request in a list of issues to be addressed by the corporate diversity council.[2]

For diversity efforts to be successful, they have to be integrated into the organization's culture and strategy. Now, managers at R. R. Donnelley & Sons understand that supporting diversity means linking diversity training to concrete hiring and promotion goals for minorities. The first step the company took was to retain a consultant to examine hiring, pay, and promotion policies, a step minority employees had earlier requested. In addition, R. R. Donnelley is undergoing an overall culture change effort that includes diversity and inclusion initiatives. The company is on the right track, but only time will tell if managers can make the necessary changes in culture, structure, and policies to help the organization reap the benefits of a diverse workforce.

Of course, R. R. Donnelley & Sons is not the only company to have faced difficulties with diversity issues. Today, diversity in the population, the workforce, and the marketplace is a fact of life no manager can afford to ignore. All managers face daily challenges of managing employee diversity, the most common of which are recruiting, training, and fully utilizing workers who reflect the broad spectrum of society in all areas—gender, race, age, disability, ethnicity, religion, sexual orientation, education, and economic level.

American Express, Monsanto, Avon, Hoechst Celanese, Hewlett-Packard and others foster diversity and enforce this value in day-to-day recruitment and promotion decisions. They have established programs for increasing diversity that teach current employees to value ethnic, racial, and gender differences, and they direct their recruiting efforts toward, and provide for, development training for females and minorities.

American companies are beginning to reflect the U.S. image as a melting pot, but with a difference. In the past, the United States was a place where people of different national origins, ethnicities, races, and religions came together and blended to resemble one another. Opportunities for advancement were limited to those workers who fit easily into the mainstream of the larger culture. Some immigrants chose desperate measures to fit in, such as abandoning their native language, changing their last name, and sacrificing their own unique cultures. In essence, everyone in workplace organizations was encouraged to share similar beliefs, values, and lifestyles despite differences in gender, race, and ethnicity.[3]

Now, organizations are recognizing that everyone is not the same and that their differences have value in the workplace.[4] Rather than expecting all employees to adopt similar attitudes and values, companies are learning that diversity enables them to compete globally and to acquire rich sources of new talent. Although diversity in North America has been a reality for some time, genuine efforts to accept and manage diverse people began only in recent years.

This chapter introduces the topic of diversity, its causes and consequences. Ways to deal with workforce diversity are discussed, and organizational responses to diversity are explored. Further, the benefits of successfully maintaining a diverse workforce are examined.

■ VALUING DIVERSITY

At 3Com Corporation's sprawling modem factory near Chicago, 65 different national flags are displayed, each representing the origin of at least one person who has worked at the plant. The 1,200 employees at 3Com speak more than 20 different languages, including Tagalog, Gujarati, and Chinese. Most instructions are in the form of big color-coded drawings that hang over each workstation to illustrate the procedure to be followed. At Rotoflow, a small southern California factory that manufactures giant turbines used in the natural gas industry, president Frank Van Gogh counts 30 nationalities among only 200 employees.[5] Such astonishing diversity is becoming typical in many companies.

Most managers, from any ethnic background, are ill-prepared to handle these multicultural differences. Many Americans attended segregated schools, lived in racially unmixed neighborhoods, and were unexposed to people substantially different from themselves.[6] A typical manager, schooled in traditional management training, easily could make the following mistakes.[7]

- To reward a Vietnamese employee's high performance, her manager promoted her, placing her at the same level as her husband, who also worked at the factory. Rather than being pleased, the worker became upset and declined the promotion because Vietnamese husbands are expected to have a higher status than their wives.

- A manager, believing that a friendly pat on the arm or back would make workers feel good, took every chance to touch his subordinates. His Asian employees hated being touched and thus started avoiding him, and several asked for transfers.

- A manager declined a gift offered by a new employee, an immigrant who wanted to show gratitude for her job. He was concerned about ethics and explained the company's policy about not accepting gifts. The employee was so insulted, she quit.

These issues related to cultural diversity are difficult and real. But before discussing how companies handle them, let's define diversity and explore people's attitudes toward it.

In college, Ken Chenault spent endless hours arguing that the Afro-American cause was best served in the long run by rising to power within the Establishment instead of assailing it from the outside. Today he is president and chief operating officer of American Express Co., a $19 billion company that he and CEO Harvey Golub helped bring back from the brink. Together they raised earnings per share by 12 percent to 15 percent annually while maintaining a return to equity of 20 percent. Chenault has been conspicuous at AmEx not only for his accomplishments but also for the workforce diversity he brings to the company. Minorities at AmEx now make up 17 percent of the company's managers. "His ambition is to become the best CEO, not the best African-American CEO," says John Utendahl, founder and CEO of Utendahl Capital Partners, Wall Street's largest black-owned investment bank.

DIMENSIONS OF DIVERSITY

Workforce diversity refers to the hiring and inclusion of people with different human qualities or who belong to different cultural groups. From the perspective of individuals, diversity means being inclusive with people who are different in terms of age, ethnicity, gender, or race.

Several important dimensions of diversity are illustrated in Exhibit 10.1. This "diversity wheel" shows the multiple combinations of traits that define diversity. The inside wheel represents primary dimensions of diversity, which include inborn differences or differences that have an impact throughout one's life. Primary dimensions are core elements through which people shape their self-image and worldview. These dimensions include age, race, ethnicity, gender, mental or physical abilities, and sexual orientation. Turn the wheel, and these primary characteristics match up with various secondary dimensions of diversity.

Secondary dimensions can be acquired or changed throughout one's lifetime, and they tend to have less impact than those of the core. Nevertheless, they do have an affect on a person's self-definition, worldview, and on how the person is viewed by others. Vietnam veterans, for example, may have been affected profoundly by their military experience and may be perceived differently from other people. Also, an employee living in a public housing project will certainly be perceived differently from one who lives in an affluent neighborhood. Secondary dimensions such as work style, communication style, and educational or skill level are particularly relevant in the organizational setting.[8] The challenge for today's managers is to recognize that each person can bring value and strengths to the workplace based on his or her own unique combination of diversity characteristics.

ATTITUDES TOWARD DIVERSITY

Valuing diversity by welcoming, recognizing, and cultivating differences among people so they can develop their unique talents and be effective organizational members is difficult to achieve. **Ethnocentrism** is the tendency to regard one's own group or culture as superior to other groups and cultures. Ethnocentrism is a natural tendency among most people,[9] but it makes valuing diversity difficult. Historically in the business world, ethnocentrism has tended to reflect the values, behaviors, and assumptions of a rather homogeneous, white, middle-class, male workforce.[10] Indeed, most theories of management presume that workers share similar values, beliefs, motivations, and attitudes about work and life in general. As Focus on Collaboration points out, this supposition has always been false, even when the environment is composed of workers who share the same cultural background, in this case male and female. These theories presume there is one set of behaviors that best helps an organization to be productive and effective and therefore should be adopted by all employees,[11] but it also why managers can cause problems (i.e., touching Asian employees or not understanding the meaning of a gift from an immigrant).

Ethnocentric viewpoints and a standard set of cultural practices produce a **monoculture**, a culture that accepts only one way of doing things and one set of values and beliefs, which can cause problems for minority employees. People of color, women, gay people, the disabled, the elderly, and other diverse employees may feel undue pressure to conform, may be victims of stereotyping attitudes, and may be presumed deficient because they are different.

---

workforce diversity
Hiring and being inclusive with people who have different human qualities and/or belong to different cultural groups

ethnocentrism
The tendency to regard one's own group or culture as superior to those of others

monoculture
A culture that accepts only one way of doing things and one set of values and beliefs

---

E x h i b i t   10.1

THE DIVERSITY WHEEL

SOURCE: Marilyn Loden, *Implementing Diversity* (Homewood, IL: Irwin, 1996). Used with permission.

FOCUS ON Collaboration

DO WOMEN AND MEN COMMUNICATE DIFFERENTLY?

In recent years, researchers and writers have captured the public imagination with descriptions of gender differences in communication and moral development. Carol Gilligan's *In a Different Voice* describes how women's sense of morality and right versus wrong is different (though not necessarily better or worse) than men's. In decision making, then, men are more concerned with abstract concepts, rules, and hierarchy, while women focus on connections with other human beings and the quality of relationships. Similarly, Deborah Tannen's *You Just Don't Understand* identified the tendency for women to be more relationship oriented. Hence, they tend to be better communicators and try to be supportive and inclusive without offending others. Men, on the other hand, have a more competitive communication style that is outcome oriented. In relationships, women often want to share and process, while men want to give advice and offer solutions.

It should be pointed out that no one is ever purely a "male" or "female" style. However, the following chart shows some basic gender differences in communication.

Male style	Female style
EMPHASIS IS ON	**EMPHASIS IS ON**
Superiority or uniqueness	Understanding
Work accomplishments	Personal needs of self or others
Content	Process
Asking directly for needs	Hinting about needs
Acting businesslike with others at work	Making others feel comfortable and included
Raising voice	Speaking politely
Rules, procedures, and techniques to solve problems	Relying on the strength of relationships to resolve issues
Showing power with position in organization	Showing power with respect to others
Negotiates to win, competitively	Negotiates collaboratively, considers relationships

Gilligan found that the differences begin early in life. Young boys tend to play games with elaborate rules and a lot of competition; when there is a problem, the rules are used to solve it. Girls, on the other hand, play games that are more relationship oriented and have few rules, being designed to make other players feel included. When they have problems, girls often end the game rather than jeopardize the friendship. Gilligan believes adult male and female style differences are based on these early divergent approaches.

As to where these differences come from, the debate over whether boys and girls are born different or socialized to be different rages on. As shown in the following chart from an actual kindergarten class, girls are often taught different values, motivations, and attitudes at an early age and carry these into adulthood.

Chart of Kindergarten Awards

BOYS	GIRLS
Very best thinker	All-around sweetheart
Most eager learner	Sweetest personality
Most imaginative	Cutest personality
Most enthusiastic	Best sharer
Most scientific	Best artist
Best friend	Biggest heart
Mr. Personality	Best manners
Hardest worker	Best helper
Best sense of humor	Most creative

SOURCES: Alice F. Stuhlmacher and Amy E. Walters, "Gender Differences in Negotiation Outcome: A Meta Analysis," *Personnel Psychology*, 52 (3) (Autumn 1999), pp. 653–677; Carol Gilligan, *In a Different Voice* (Cambridge, Mass.: Harvard University Press, 1982); Deborah Tannen, *You Just Don't Understand* (New York: Morrow Books, 1990); Nancy Langton, "Gender Difference in Communication," in *Organizational Behavior: Experiences and Cases*, ed. Dorothy Marcic, 4th ed. (St. Paul, Minn.: West, 1995), p. 265–268; and Kathleen Deveny, "Chart of Kindergarten Awards," *The Wall Street Journal*, December 5, 1994, p. B1.

White, heterosexual men, many of whom themselves do not fit the notions of the "ideal" employee, may also feel uncomfortable with the monoculture and resent stereotypes that label all white males as racists and sexists. Valuing diversity means ensuring that all people are given equal opportunities in the workplace.[12]

The goal for organizations seeking cultural diversity is pluralism rather than a monoculture and ethnorelativism rather than ethnocentrism. **Ethnorelativism** is the acceptance of groups and subcultures as being inherently equal. **Pluralism** in the workplace means that the organization accommodates several subcultures. Movement toward pluralism seeks to fully integrate into the organization the employees who otherwise would feel isolated and ignored. As the workforce changes, organizations will come to resemble a global village.

Most organizations must undertake conscious efforts to shift from a monoculture perspective to one of pluralism. Employees in a monoculture may not be aware of culture differences, or they may have acquired negative stereotypes toward other cultural values and assume that their own culture is superior. Through effective training, employees can be helped to accept different ways of thinking and behaving, the first step away from narrow, ethnocentric thinking. Ultimately, employees are able to integrate diverse cultures and make appropriate judgments about appropriateness, goodness, badness, and morality. Cultural differences are accepted as essential, natural, and joyful, enabling an organization to enjoy true pluralism and take advantage of diverse human resources.[13]

UNUM Life Insurance Company of America has made a firm commitment to break out of monoculture thinking. Senior managers, most of whom were white males, began meeting regularly with representatives of minority groups and were shocked to hear how "out of place" many minorities felt in the workplace. Since then, UNUM has implemented a widespread diversity program, including a three-day diversity workshop to help employees develop "cultural competence," a newsletter covering diversity topics, and "Lunch and Learn" talks that help employees understand different cultures and perspectives. Most importantly, a diversity board made up of members from each minority group represented at the company meets monthly with UNUM's president to discuss systematic changes in policies and procedures to encourage and support diversity.[14] By helping all employees develop greater sensitivity and acceptance of cultural differences, beginning with senior managers, UNUM moves away from an ethnocentric attitude and is able to accept and integrate people from diverse backgrounds.

■ THE CHANGING WORKPLACE

The importance of cultural diversity and employee attitudes that welcome cultural differences will result from the inevitable changes taking place in the workplace, in our society, and in the economic environment. These changes include globalization and the changing workforce.[15] In previous chapters, we've discussed the impact and intensity of global competition on business in North America. About 70 percent of all U.S. businesses are engaged directly in competition with companies overseas. Companies that succeed in this environment need to adopt radical new ways of doing business, with sensitivity toward the needs of different cultural practices. Southern California is an Anglo-Afro-Latino-Asian ethnic mix. Approximately 18 car companies, especially those from Japan and Germany, have established design centers in Los Angeles and enjoy the diverse values of this multicultural proving ground.[16]

The single biggest challenge facing companies is the changing composition of the workforce. The average worker is older, and many more women, people of color, and immigrants are members of the workforce. Indeed, immigration accounted for nearly half of the increase in the labor force in the 1990s, and immigrants likely will constitute an increasing share of workers in the twenty-first century.[17] Studies also project that Asian Americans, African Americans, and Hispanics will make up 85 percent of U.S. population growth and constitute about 30 percent of the total workforce.[18] So far, the ability of organizations to manage diversity has not kept pace with the changing workforce, and this lag has created a number of significant challenges for minority workers and managers. Some small companies, such as Lopez Negrete Communications, have capitalized on the difficulties of multiculturalism and are helping large companies to understand the issues (see the following example).

ethnorelativism
The acceptance of groups and subcultures as being inherently equal

pluralism
The organization accommodates several subcultures, including employees who would otherwise feel isolated and ignored

TECHNOLOGY FOR TOMORROW
LEVELING THE PLAYING FIELD

Betty Ford is used to having customers approach the white sales clerk at her company, Mailbox Haven, and assume he is the manager of her suburban Seattle package-delivery business. Ford, who is African American, deals constantly with a subtle racism that still pervades much of American society. Ford says other customers have been more blatant—she recalls one who warned her, "I'm going to watch you wrap my package." Although Ford's business is thriving, she's selling out to focus all her energy on her new business, City Boxers, an online retailer of hand-tailored boxer shorts.

Ford isn't the only person who appreciates the "color-blindness" of the Internet. Many other minority entrepreneurs are bypassing the real-life racial tensions of the workplace by doing business on the World Wide Web, where they can succeed or not based on their own merits. Roosevelt Gist, a 51-year-old former car salesman, launched an online forum for buying, selling, and researching cars. His site attracts 40,000 visitors a month and collects about $200,000 a year in advertising revenue. Gist recalls his days working at a large Virginia dealership, where white customers would frequently ask to speak to another salesman when Gist approached them.

Working in the anonymity of cyberspace has psychological benefits for minority entrepreneurs, but there are other advantages, too. Launching and running an online business is much less expensive than starting a traditional business, and getting previously hard-to-get financing is a lot easier. While the online world of business is no answer to the real problem of racism, it does level the playing field for minority entrepreneurs.

www.cityboxers.com

SOURCE: Roger O. Crockett, "Invisible—And Loving It," *Business Week,* October 5, 1998, pp. 124, 128.

LOPEZ NEGRETE COMMUNICATIONS

"He quit his job? Oh boy," was Alex Lopez Negrete's mother's not-exactly-thrilled response when she heard her son left his job as head of a successful advertising agency to start his own company. Lopez Negrete, a Mexican immigrant, now in his 30's always knew what he wanted to do. And when he came to America, he did as many new immigrants, he relished his own culture. And that is part of the secret of his success.

Over 90 percent of his advertising business is based on helping clients market more effectively to the growing Hispanic market. And companies are finally taking note of the tremendous buying power of African and Hispanic markets. He has learned a lot from big clients and small, and he especially urges small business owners to adopt a multicultural strategy. "It's not just advertising," he says, "but a whole way to thinking and doing business that becomes "in-language" and "in-culture." Some tips he has learned are (1) Don't use stereotyped portrayals of ethnic groups—this will drive away your intended ethnic market; (2) Don't skimp on ads to an ethnic market—this will turn off potential customers who may feel one-down; (3) If your Spanish is less-than-perfect, hire someone to do the voice-overs in your commercials—this will help increase your credibility.

Lopez Negrete is doing very well, in part because the marketplace has changed and awakened to reality. As fellow entrepreneur African American Byron Lewis says, "Diversity represents an opportunity to increase profits for many advertisers."[19] ■

Technology for Tomorrow describes how the Internet is leveling the playing field for many minority entrepreneurs.

CHALLENGES MINORITIES FACE

The one-best-way approach leads to a mind-set that views difference as deficiency or dysfunction. Many career women and minorities feel that no matter how many college degrees they earn, how many hours they work, how they dress, or how much effort and enthusiasm they invest, they are never perceived as "having the right stuff." A recent Gallup poll found that 45 percent of blacks surveyed believe that blacks are treated less fairly on the job than whites.[20] A Hispanic executive discussing the animosity he experienced in one job, said, "The fact that I graduated first in my class didn't make as much difference as the fact that I looked different."[21] This dilemma often is difficult for ethnocentric white males to understand because most are not intentionally racist and sexist. Many men feel extremely uncomfortable with the prevailing attitudes and stereotypes, but don't know how to change them. These attitudes are deeply rooted in our society as well as in our organizations.

Another problem is that many minority workers feel they have to become bicultural in order to succeed. **Biculturalism** refers to the sociocultural skills and attitudes used by racial minorities as they move back and forth between the dominant culture and their own ethnic or racial culture.[22] Research on differences between whites and blacks has focused on issues of biculturalism and how it affects access to information, level of respect and appreciation, and relation to superiors and subordinates. In general, African Americans and other racial minorities, feel less accepted in their organizations, perceive themselves to have less discretion on their jobs, receive lower ratings on job performance, experience lower levels of job satisfaction, and reach career plateaus earlier than whites.

Racism in the workplace often shows up in subtle ways—the disregard by a subordinate for an assigned chore; a lack of urgency in completing an important assignment; the ignoring of comments or suggestions made at a meeting. Black managers often struggle daily with the problem of delegating authority and responsibility to employees who show them little respect. They find themselves striving to adopt behaviors and attitudes that will help them be successful in the white-dominated corporate world while at the same time maintaining their ties to the black community and culture.

Other minority groups struggle with biculturalism as well. J. D. Hokoyama started a nonprofit organization, Leadership Education for Asian Pacifics, Inc., to teach Asian Americans how to be bicultural. Asian Americans who aspire to management positions are often frustrated by the stereotype that they are hard workers but not executive material because they are too quiet or not assertive enough. Hokoyama's workshops alert Asian Americans to the ways in which their communication style may hold them back in the American workplace. Participants are taught to use more eye contact, start more sentences with "I," and use more assertive body language. Many Asian Americans are offended by the implication that they should abandon their cultural values to succeed. Hokoyama, however, looks at this as a way to help more Asian Americans adjust their style so they can move into management positions.[23] Often, the workshops offered by Leadership Education for Asian Pacifics, Inc., are perceived as being a sad commentary on the opportunities for minorities in America's organizations. Culturally sensitive managers can work to remove these barriers.

MANAGEMENT ACTIVITIES FOR A DIVERSE WORKFORCE

Exhibit 10.2 illustrates the management activities required for dealing with a culturally diverse workforce. Consider the increased career involvement of women. It is estimated that by the year 2020, women will comprise fully half of the total U.S. workforce.[24] This change represents an enormous opportunity to organizations, but it also means that organizations must deal with issues such as work-family conflicts, dual-career couples, and sexual harassment. Since seven of 10 women in the labor force have children, organizations should prepare to take more of the responsibility for child care.

By 2020, people of African, Asian, and Hispanic descent are expected to make up about 35 percent of the U.S. population. Already more than 30 percent of New York City's residents are foreign born. Miami is two-thirds Hispanic American; Detroit is two-thirds African American; and San Francisco is one-third Asian American.[25] Whereas in previous generations most foreign-born immigrants came from Western Europe, 84 percent of recent immigrants have come from Asia and

biculturalism
The sociocultural skills and attitudes used by racial minorities to move back and forth between the dominant culture and their own ethnic or racial culture

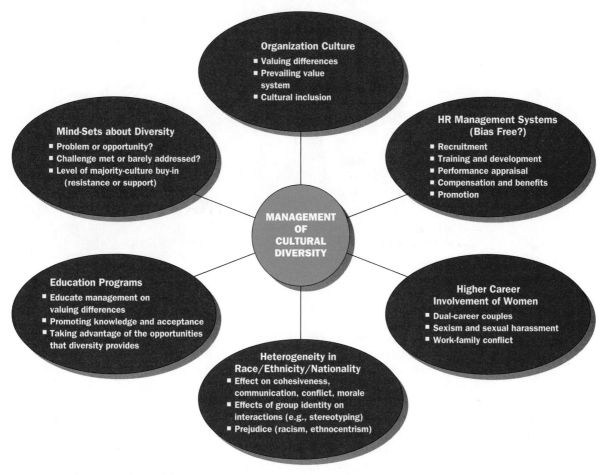

Organization Culture
- Valuing differences
- Prevailing value system
- Cultural inclusion

Mind-Sets about Diversity
- Problem or opportunity?
- Challenge met or barely addressed?
- Level of majority-culture buy-in (resistance or support)

HR Management Systems (Bias Free?)
- Recruitment
- Training and development
- Performance appraisal
- Compensation and benefits
- Promotion

MANAGEMENT OF CULTURAL DIVERSITY

Education Programs
- Educate management on valuing differences
- Promoting knowledge and acceptance
- Taking advantage of the opportunities that diversity provides

Higher Career Involvement of Women
- Dual-career couples
- Sexism and sexual harassment
- Work-family conflict

Heterogeneity in Race/Ethnicity/Nationality
- Effect on cohesiveness, communication, conflict, morale
- Effects of group identity on interactions (e.g., stereotyping)
- Prejudice (racism, ethnocentrism)

SOURCE: Taylor H. Cox and Stacy Blake, "Managing Cultural Diversity: Implications for Organizational Competitiveness," *Academy of Management Executive,* 5 (3) (1991), 45–56.

Latin America.[26] They come to the United States with diverse backgrounds and often without adequate skills for communicating in English. So, service-economy organizations must not only provide a prejudice-free workplace by effectively dealing with the issues of race, ethnicity, and nationality, but also develop sufficient educational programs to help immigrants acquire necessary technical and customer service skills.

Top managers can help shape organizational values and employee mind-sets about cultural differences, and training programs can promote knowledge and acceptance. Allstate Insurance Company actually rates its managers on how well they handle diversity.

ALLSTATE INSURANCE COMPANY
www.allstate.com

Allstate Insurance doesn't just talk about the importance of diversity; it actually tracks support for diversity at every level of management. As the largest property insurer of African Americans and Hispanics, Allstate made diversity a priority

At AT&T, former Chairman Robert Allen helped shape organizational values to meet the company's goal of creating "a work environment that sets the world-class standard for valuing diversity." Pictured here are representatives of AT&T's seven caucuses that represent African-American, Latino, Native American, Asian, gay, female, and disabled employees.

in 1993. The company already had a working affirmative action program and had tried several approaches to diversity training. However, Jerry Choate, CEO, and Carlton Yearwood, director of Allstate's diversity team, believed the company needed a way to track its success on supporting diversity. Its new system gives top executives feedback that they can use continually to make the workplace more comfortable and satisfying for all employees. Today, Allstate surveys all 50,000 workers each quarter on how well they are meeting their commitments to employees and customers, including recruiting, developing, and promoting employees regardless of race or gender. A "diversity index" probes how well workers feel their managers "walk the talk" about bias-free service, respect for the individual, and promotion of a culturally sensitive workplace. Performance on these indexes determines 25 percent of a manager's bonus pay.

Overall, Allstate is doing pretty well on the diversity index. Some 21 percent of executives and managers are minorities, compared to a national average of around 10 percent. An African American who worked his way up through the system holds the company's top sales position. Allstate believes the tracking system contributes to a more productive work environment, where all employees feel valued.[27] ■

■ AFFIRMATIVE ACTION

Since 1964, civil legislation has prohibited discrimination in hiring based on race, religion, sex, or national origin. These policies were designed to facilitate recruitment, retention, and promotion of minorities and women and have been fairly successful in opening the doors of organizations to women and minorities. However, women and minorities are still not acquiring top management posts.

CURRENT DEBATES ABOUT AFFIRMATIVE ACTION

Affirmative action was developed in response to conditions 30 years ago when adult white males dominated the workforce, and economic conditions were stable and improving. Because of widespread discrimination, legal and social coercion were necessary to bring women, people of color, immigrants, and other minorities into the economic system.[28] Many companies have since been actively recruiting women and minorities, to comply with affirmative action guidelines. Companies often succeeded in identifying a few select individuals who were recruited, trained, and given special consideration. These people carried great expectations and pressure. They were highly visible role models for the newly recruited groups. It was generally expected that these individuals would march right to the top of the corporate ladder.

Within a few years, though, it became clear that few of these people would actually reach the top. Management typically was frustrated and upset because of the money poured into the affirmative action programs. The individuals were disillusioned about how difficult it was to achieve and felt frustrated and alienated. Managers were unhappy with the program failures and may have doubted the qualifications of people they recruited. Did their hires deserve the jobs at all? Were women and minority candidates to blame for the failure of the affirmative action program? Should companies be required to meet federally mandated minority-hiring targets?

Today, more than half the U.S. workforce consists of women and minorities, and international competition is rapidly changing the face of the economy, but problems still persist. Outspoken opponents of affirmative action have brought the debate into the public consciousness. Affirmative action is hotly debated in the states, Congress, the Supreme Court, and corporate America. Politically conservative leaders (typically Republicans) continue to make statements strongly opposing racial hiring preferences, and affirmative action hiring and college admissions practices have been dismantled in several states. President Bill Clinton recently ordered an internal review of affirmative action—for the first time since its inception—which signaled a less-than-firm commitment on the part of politically liberal leaders (typically Democrats).[29] Even the intended beneficiaries of affirmative action programs often disagree as to their value, and some believe these programs do more harm than good. One reason for this may be the "stigma of incompetence" that often is associated with affirmative action hires. One study found that both managers and students consistently rated affirmative action hires and fellow students as less competent and that managers often recommended lower salary increases relative to non-affirmative action hires.[30]

While it is rare to hear or see blatant expressions of racism and sexism in corporate America today, many minorities believe a more subtle but just as dangerous form has replaced them. While many whites believe racial discrimination has passed and that blacks are pushing too hard and moving too fast, the "new racists" often see affirmative action programs as unfair.[31] In addition, top managers often find it hard to understand just how white and male their corporate culture is and how forbidding it seems to those who are obviously different.[32] The affirmative action cycle fails when women, people of color, and immigrants are brought into a monoculture system, and the burden of adaptation falls on the candidates coming through the system rather than on the organization itself. Part of the reason for the failure of affirmative action may be attributed to what is called the "glass ceiling."

THE GLASS CEILING

The **glass ceiling** is an invisible barrier that separates women and minorities from top management positions. They can "look up through the ceiling" and see top management, but the prevailing attitudes and obstacles against their advancement are invisible. A recent study suggested the additional existence of "glass walls," which serve as invisible barriers to important lateral movement within the organization. Glass walls bar experience in areas such as line supervisor positions that would enable women and minorities to advance vertically.[33]

Evidence of the glass ceiling is the distribution of women and minorities, who are clustered at the bottom levels of the corporate hierarchy. A recent study shows that 97 percent of the top managers in the United States are white, and at

glass ceiling
Invisible barrier that separates women and minorities from top management positions

Exhibit 10.3

THE WAGE GAP

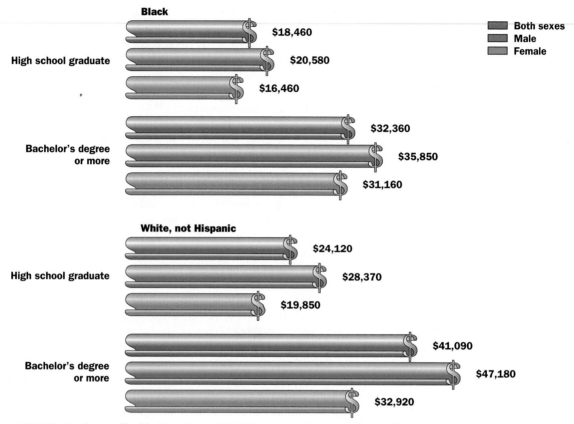

SOURCE: *Population Profile of the United States 1995,* U.S. Department of Commerce, Bureau of the Census, July 1995.

least 95 percent of them are male.[34] Women and minorities also earn substantially less. As shown in Exhibit 10.3, black, male employees earn 24 percent to 27 percent less than their white counterparts earn, even when educational levels are similar. Women earn considerably less than their male peers, with black women earning the least. As women move up the career ladder, the wage gap widens; at the level of vice president, a woman's average salary is 42 percent less than her male counterpart.[35]

In particular, women who leave the corporate world to care for young children have a difficult time moving up the hierarchy when they return. One term used to describe this is the "mommy track," which implies that women's commitment to their children limits

their commitment to the company or impairs their ability to handle the rigors of corporate management. These women risk being treated as beginners when they return, no matter how vast their skills and experience, and they continue to lag behind in salary, title, and responsibility.[36] In *Leading the Revolution*, some women are taking the situation into their own hands and starting their own companies.

Another current issue related to the glass ceiling involves homosexuals in the workplace. Many gay men and lesbians believe they are not accepted and are at risk of losing their jobs or chances for advancement. Thus, gays and lesbians often fabricate heterosexual identities to keep their jobs or avoid running into the glass ceiling.

WOMEN ENTREPRENEURS

Can you hear the sound of the stampede? It's the sound of eight million women starting their own businesses. While half of them were top-level executives who wanted to prove they could do something extraordinary, almost one-fourth say it was because they experienced a glass ceiling at their former jobs, where they were unable to reach their desired potential. But the potential they are creating is exploding into the economy. One out of five U.S. employees works for a female-owned firm, while the number of female-led companies has more than doubled in the past 10 years. Now, these organizations account for one-third of all businesses and earn annually about $2.5 trillion. Minority women are becoming entrepreneurs at even faster rates. And businesses started by women are more likely to stay in business than those started by a male.

What are the trends? (1) Women used to start service businesses, but now there is more variety. (2) Women are finding it easier to get credit. Gone are the days when the husband had to cosign the loan. (3) Women of all ages are starting businesses and 50 percent of them started their firms before age 35.

What's needed? (1) Networking and lots of it, especially outside your normal interactions; (2) Strong vision and stay true to it; (3) Hard work and

keep at it; (4) Creativity and keep experimenting; (5) Willingness to try new approaches. For example, when Oregonian Barbara Todd started her catalog-based business, she needed only $50,000—one-tenth of the normal—for startup costs. Instead of buying wholesale and selling through the catalog, she charged each client $5,000 to list products in her catalog. (6) Seeing the opportunities and keep looking. Eloise Blackmon started her Gary, Indiana, F&B Transport company when she saw the difficulty people were having getting off welfare because they lacked transportation. Now her vans deliver 100 adults and children to work and day care. Her clients, she says, "are dedicated and want to work." They just needed some help. (7) Seeing employees as resources and use them. Patty Dominic's PDQ personnel services was growing so fast she had a cash flow problem and could not meet payroll. So, she brought her employees together and told them the truth. The next day a woman brought in a check for $5,000 as a loan and other women offered services of their husbands, who were investment bankers, CPAs, and management consultants. They helped her put together a sound business plan and to secure financing. (8) Value yourself and your product. New Orleans cab driver Jacquelyn

Hughes Mooney's hobby was sewing decorative pillows. She gave up her secure income to push her pillows full time at craft fairs and did so well, she went on to designer quilts, with some selling for as much as $6,000 to celebrities such as Oprah Winfrey and Bryant Gumbel. After a woman complained about spending two hundred dollars on a quilt, Mooney realized how important it is for women to place value on their work. "No one else will think my work is significant until I do," she says of her company named Rhythm and Hughes.

For these women, a real attractive quality about starting their businesses was the chance to be their own boss and to be able to build their own vision. As biotech entrepreneur Nancy Levy said, "I like to create things, grow things . . . I took a huge risk." Her husband asked her why she was doing this, putting so much on the line. Her answer, "I like to create things."

SOURCES: Paulette Thomas, "Closing the Gender Gap," *The Wall Street Journal*, May 24, 1999, p. R12; Steven J. Stark, "Breaking In," *Success*, January 1999, p. 39; Sharon Nelton, "Women's Firms Thrive," *Nation's Business*, Aug. 1998, pp. 37–40; Amanda Walmac, "The Entrepreneurial Era Reality Check," *Working Woman*, July/Aug. 1998, pp. 31–36; Elain Pofeldt, "Self-Made Woman," *Success*, June 1997, pp. 37–46.

Why does the glass ceiling persist? The most frequent explanation is the monoculture that exists at top levels. Here, corporate culture tends to revolve around white, heterosexual, American males, who tend to hire and promote in kind. Compatibility in thought and behavior also plays an important role at higher levels of organizations.[37] For example, in a survey of women who have managed to break through the glass ceiling, fully 96 percent said adapting to a predominantly white male culture was an important factor in their success.[38]

Another reason for the persistent glass ceiling is the relegation of women and minorities to less visible positions and projects so that their work fails to come to the attention of top executives. Male middle managers may assume that a woman's family life will interfere with her work or that minorities lack the competence for important assignments. As a result, women and minorities often believe that they must work harder and perform at higher levels than their white male counterparts just to be noticed, recognized, and treated with respect, much less accepted and promoted.

NEW RESPONSES TO CULTURAL DIVERSITY

How can managers prepare their organizations to accommodate diversity? First, organization leaders and managers must come to terms with diversity, attitudes toward race, and understanding of gender issues and be encouraged to consider education, background, and personality differences as important factors. Another type of diversity is age. In the new workplace, younger workers are often more technically skilled than older ones. This can create additional tensions as organizations try to manage and utilize the skills of younger workers, sometimes teenagers, as in the following example.

POKÉMON DOT-COMS

When our parents were young, there weren't many teenage, self-made millionaires. If kids had jobs, they delivered newspapers, bagged groceries, or made fries at the local fast-food joint. Success was achieved more often in coins than dollars. Now, a growing number are turning Internet hobbies into money-making businesses. Leading the pack are the Pokémon groupies, often 14- to 16-year-olds who are later wooed by lucrative advertisement deals on the sites and grownups who want a piece of the action.

The thousands of Pokémon Web sites offer chat rooms, message boards, endless trivia about the "pocket monsters," and news of new games, like a candymaker's deal to make Poké Gum.

Bomby Kitchpanich (www.pokec.com), a freshman in Alaska, started his site because he wanted to praise Squirtle's powers and help others to defeat Rhydon. Started in February 1999, the site got only a few hits a week. By November, the hits were coming several thousand times a day with running ads from American Express and Qualcomm.

Bomby did it for fun. "I never intended to make money off it," he says. "But if you put in an hour every day for eight months, you can get something pretty big." Still, some of the young entrepreneurs are lured into business deals they scarcely understand. Sometimes parents step in, as when Bomby Kitchpanich's father hired a lawyer to oversee the sale of his Web site.

Even sites started by kids don't stay amateur for long if they are any good. Many of them compete for visitors and agree to be part of a rankings system developed by grownup Scott Smith (who encourages links back to his own site). He says the rankings have brought out the worst in Pokémon masters, with many cheating by visiting their own sites over and over. Mr. Smith is working to develop a new, cheatproof system.

Sixteen-year-old Richard Cao spends a lot of time on his site (www.psypoke.com) updating the content. His reason would make any business professor wax proudly: It's critical to bring new material every day, so that frequent visitors will not be disappointed, which can cause traffic to drop off.[39] ■

Once a vision for a diverse workplace has been created and defined, the organization can analyze and assess the current culture and systems within the organization. This assessment is followed by a willingness to change the status quo in order to modify current systems and ways of thinking. Throughout this process, people need support in dealing with the many challenges and inevitable conflicts they will face. Training and support are important for the people in pioneering roles. Finally, managers should not de-emphasize affirmative action programs, because these are critical for giving minorities and women access to jobs in the organization.

Once managers accept the need for developing a truly diverse workplace, action can begin. A program to implement such change involves three major steps: (1) building a corporate culture that values diversity; (2) changing structures, policies, and systems to support diversity; and (3) providing diversity awareness training. Managers can start by actively using symbols for the new values, for instance, like celebrating the promotion of minorities. Executives must lead the way in changing from a white male monoculture to a multiculture in which differences among people are valued. For the programs and individual efforts to succeed, top management must provide critical support and be held accountable for encouraging and increasing diversity awareness and training.

CHANGING THE CORPORATE CULTURE

To accomplish meaningful, productive, and positive change in the corporate culture, managers can examine the unwritten rules and assumptions. What are the myths about minorities? What are the values that exemplify the existing culture? Are unwritten rules communicated from one person to another in a way that excludes women and minorities? Other steps include (1) using surveys, interviews, and focus groups to identify how minorities and women are affected by the company's culture; (2) setting up structured networks of people of color, women, and other minority groups to explore workplace issues and recommend changes to senior management.

Many companies have discovered that people will choose companies that are accepting, inviting, friendly, and helpful to them in meeting personal goals.[40] Successful companies carefully assess their cultures and make changes from the top down because the key to productivity is a loyal, trained, capable workforce. These new cultural values are bringing the exclusionary practices of the past to an end.

Texaco learned this the hard way a few years ago when they paid more than $175 million to settle a racial discrimination suit. Following a public scandal related to the suit, which included reports of executives using racial slurs, top managers greatly expanded the company's diversity efforts. Prior to the suit, Texaco's diversity program was a routine workshop giving top executives practical tips for managing a diverse workforce. Today, all 20,000 Texaco employees are required to attend a two-day diversity "learning experience"

When corporate cultures are not conducive to including women and minorities in important decision-making processes or enabling them to move up the corporate hierarchy, the talents of employees will be underutilized, and the corporation will be less competitive. Women like Susannah Swihart, chief financial officer and vice chairman of BankBoston Corp. ($71.4 billion in assets) are becoming more common. In 1995, only 10 women held the CFO post at a Fortune 500 company, but there are now about 23 women holding that position—a 130 percent increase.

that includes experiencing exclusionary tactics. One employee leaves the room while the others form a circle, hold hands and stand shoulder to shoulder. When the person returns to the room, the people in the circle totally ignore him or her, all the while laughing and joking among themselves.[41] Texaco also uses a number of other exercises to develop the sensitivity of employees to others as well as their skills for interacting with diverse coworkers. These programs are part of a widespread culture change effort at Texaco. Exhibit 10.4 outlines major components of Texaco's initiatives that go far beyond a few workshops to value diversity.

CHANGING STRUCTURES AND POLICIES

Leading companies are now changing structures and policies to facilitate the recruitment and career advancement of diverse employee groups.

RECRUITMENT   A good way to revitalize the recruiting process is for the company to examine employee demographics, the composition of the labor pool in the area, and the composition of the customer base. Managers then can work toward a workforce composition

Recruitment and Hiring
- Ask search firms to identify wider arrays of candidates
- Enhance the interviewing, selection, and hiring skills of managers
- Expand college recruitment at historically minority colleges

Identifying and Developing Talent
- From a partnership with INROADS, a nationwide internship program that targets minority students for management careers
- Establish a mentoring process
- Refine the company's global succession planning system to improve identification of talent
- Improve the selection and development of managers and leaders to help ensure that they are capable of maximizing team performance

Ensuring Fair Treatment
- Conduct extensive diversity training
- Implement an alternative dispute resolution process
- Include women and minorities on all human resources committees throughout the company

Holding Managers Accountable
- Link managers' compensation to their success in creating "openness and inclusion in the workplace"
- Implement 360-degree feedback for all managers and supervisors
- Redesign the company's employee attitude survey and begin using it annually to monitor employee attitudes

Improve Relationships with External Stakeholders
- Broaden the company's base of vendors and suppliers to incorporate more minority- and women-owned businesses
- Increase banking, investment, and insurance business with minority- and women-owned firms
- Add more independent, minority retailers and increase the number of minority managers in company-owned gas stations and Xpress Lube outlets

SOURCES: Don Hellriegel, Susan E. Jackson, and John W. Slocum, Jr., *Management*, 8th ed. (Cincinnati, OH; South-Western College Publishing, 1999). Used with permission. Originally adapted from V. C. Smith, "Texaco Outlines Comprehensive Initiatives," *Human Resource Executive*, February 1997, 13; A. Bryant, "How Much Has Texaco Changed? A Mixed Report Card on Anti-Bias Efforts," *New York Times*, November 2, 1997, 3–1, 3–16, 3–17; and "Texaco's Workforce Diversity Plan," as reprinted in *Workforce*, March 1997 (suppl.).

that reflects the labor pool and the customer base. Moreover, the company can examine several dimensions of diversity beyond race and gender (e.g., age, ethnicity, physical abilities, and sexual orientation). For example, because workers age 55 and over are the fastest growing segment of America's labor force, concern about age discrimination is an increasingly important issue.[42]

For many organizations, a new approach to recruitment will mean recruiting more effectively than in the past. Making better use of formal recruiting strategies, offering intern-ship programs to give people opportunities, and developing creative ways to draw upon previously unused labor markets are typical steps being taken.

CAREER ADVANCEMENT The successful advancement of diverse group members means that organizations must find ways to eliminate the glass ceiling. One of the most successful structures to accomplish this is the mentoring relationship. A mentor is a higher ranking, senior organizational member committed to providing upward mobility and support to a protégé's professional career.[43] Mentoring provides minorities and women direct training and inside information on the norms and expectations of the organization. A mentor also acts as a friend or counselor, enabling the employee to feel more confident and capable.

Research indicates that women and minorities are less likely than white men to develop mentoring relationships.[44] Reasons may be that women often do not seek mentors because they feel job competency is enough to succeed, or they may fear that initiating a mentoring relationship could be misunderstood as a romantic overture or perceived as a way to compensate for incompetence. Also, male mentors may feel uncomfortable with minority male protégés. Their backgrounds and interests may differ, leaving them with nothing but work in common. Male mentors may stereotype women as mothers, wives, or sisters rather than as executive material. The few minorities and women who have reached the upper ranks often are overwhelmed with mentoring requests from people like themselves, and they may feel uncomfortable in highly visible minority-minority or female-female mentoring relationships, which isolate them from the white male status quo.

The solution is for organizations to overcome these barriers to mentoring. When organizations can institutionalize the value of white males actively seeking women and minority protégés, the benefits will mean that women and minorities will be steered into pivotal jobs and positions critical to advancement. Mentoring programs also are consistent with the Civil Rights Act of 1991 that requires the diversification of middle and upper management.

ACCOMMODATING SPECIAL NEEDS   People outside the legally protected classes previously mentioned may often have special needs that top managers are unaware of. If, for instance, a number of lower level employees entering the organization are single parents, the company can reassess job scheduling and opportunities for child care. If a substantial labor pool is non-English-speaking, training materials and information packets can be provided in another language.

Often, both parents in the family work, so the company could provide structures to deal with child care, maternity or paternity leave, flexible work schedules, home-based employment, and perhaps part-time employment or seasonal hours that reflect the school year. The key to attracting and keeping elderly or disabled workers may include long-term-care insurance and special health or life benefits. Alternative work scheduling also may be important for these groups of workers.

In the United States, racial/ethnic minorities and immigrants have fewer educational opportunities than most other groups. Many companies have started working with high schools to provide fundamental skills in literacy and arithmetic, or they provide these skills within the company to upgrade employees to appropriate educational levels. The movement toward increasing educational services for employees can be expected to increase for immigrants and the economically disadvantaged in the years to come. In this example, one entrepreneur took accommodating special needs to a new and creative level when he hired gang members and criminals.

JOHN PARK'S ATHLETE'S FOOT FRANCHISE

Korean immigrant John Park saw a business advantage where others saw only trouble. When the 23-year-old started his first Athlete's Foot franchise four years ago in one of the most violent neighborhoods in Chicago, an early job applicant was a member of one of the area's infamous gangs, Gangster Disciples. Park hired Eric Lymore, not totally believing his bravado about what a good salesman he would be.

Was he ever wrong. Despite the fact that the other salespeople felt pushed aside, Park encouraged the early success of Lymore and learned that gang members can have real leadership and selling skills. With Lymore's success came nine more franchises (all in rough areas), and Lymore is the star salesman. Park's labor force is filled with former gang members and drug dealers, and 90 percent of his sales force has criminal records. Park has learned not to ask questions about what they do on their own time, or what needs they have.

"From 9:30 A.M. to 6 P.M. [you're on] my time," he tells them.

In the early days, he tended to hire "nicer" salespeople, but they often complained about the neighborhood and customers. He has since learned to hire salespeople who are loud, vocal, and outgoing, because they interact better with customers. Sometimes he hires right out of prison and gets something intangible— someone with real "street" currency and clout. Yet, with prudence, none of the former criminals is allowed to work the cash register. Another advantage, Park has never been held up. The gangs know these stores are off limits.

Park has rewritten the book on success in the inner city for Athlete's Foot, which had previously shunned urban markets. And Park has provided a new way of life for his employees. Lymore and Park have become associates and friends, as Park depends more and more on his colleagues' judgment. And Lymore, well, is starting to appreciate the rewards of living clean.[45] ■

DIVERSITY AWARENESS TRAINING

Many organizations are providing special training, called **diversity awareness training,** to help employees become aware of their own cultural boundaries, prejudices, and stereotypes, so they can learn to work and live together. Working or living in a multicultural context requires interaction skills that transcend the skills effective in one's own ingroup.[46] Diversity awareness programs help people learn how to handle conflict in a constructive manner, which tends to reduce stress and negative energy in diverse work teams.

People vary in their sensitivity and openness to other cultures. Exhibit 10.5 shows a model of six stages of diversity awareness. The continuum ranges from a total lack of awareness to a complete understanding and acceptance of others' differences. This model is useful in assessing "the openness to change" of participants. People at different stages may require different kinds of training. A basic aim of awareness training is to help people recog-

nize that hidden and overt biases direct their thinking about specific individuals and groups. If people can come away from a training session recognizing that they prejudge people and that this needs to be consciously addressed in communications with and treatment of others, an important goal of diversity awareness training has been reached.

The point of this training is to help people be more flexible in their communications with others, to treat each person as an individual, and not to rely on stereotypes. Effective programs move people toward being open in their relationships with others. For example, if you were a part of such a program, it would help you develop an explicit awareness of your own cultural values, your own cultural boundaries, and your own cultural behaviors. Then you would be provided the same information about other groups, and you would be given the opportunity to learn about and communicate with people from other groups. One of the most important elements in diversity training is to bring together people of differing perspectives so that they can engage in learning new interpersonal communication skills with one another.

■ DEFINING NEW RELATIONSHIPS IN ORGANIZATIONS

One outcome of diversity training and awareness is an increased incidence of close personal relationships in the workplace, which can have both positive and negative results for employees as well as the organization. Two issues of concern are emotional intimacy and sexual harassment.

EMOTIONAL INTIMACY

Close relationships between men and women generally have been discouraged in companies for fear that they disrupt the balance of power and threaten organizational stability.[47] This opinion grew out of the assumption that organizations are designed for rationality and efficiency, which were best achieved in a nonemotional environment.

A recent study of friendships in organizations sheds interesting light on this issue. Man-

diversity awareness training
Special training designed to provide awareness of personal prejudices and stereotypes

E x h i b i t   10.5

STAGES OF DIVERSITY AWARENESS

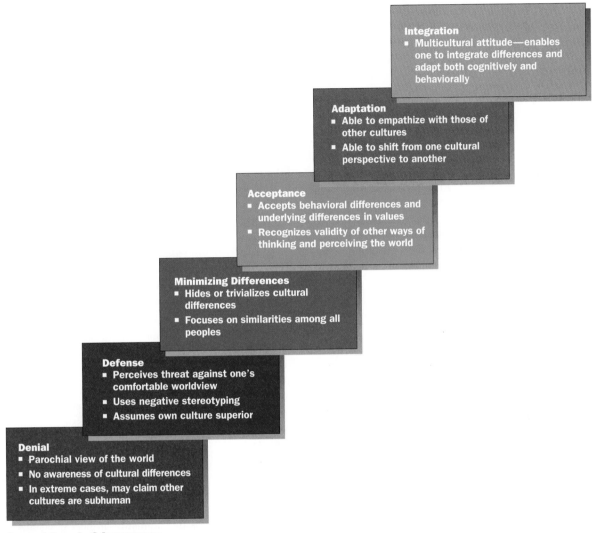

Highest Level of Awareness

Integration
- Multicultural attitude—enables one to integrate differences and adapt both cognitively and behaviorally

Adaptation
- Able to empathize with those of other cultures
- Able to shift from one cultural perspective to another

Acceptance
- Accepts behavioral differences and underlying differences in values
- Recognizes validity of other ways of thinking and perceiving the world

Minimizing Differences
- Hides or trivializes cultural differences
- Focuses on similarities among all peoples

Defense
- Perceives threat against one's comfortable worldview
- Uses negative stereotyping
- Assumes own culture superior

Denial
- Parochial view of the world
- No awareness of cultural differences
- In extreme cases, may claim other cultures are subhuman

Lowest Level of Awareness

SOURCE: Based on M. Bennett, "A Developmental Approach to Training for Intercultural Sensitivity," *International Journal of Intercultural Relations,* 10 (1986), 179–196.

agers and workers responded to a survey about emotionally intimate relationships with both male and female coworkers. Many men and women reported having close relationships with an opposite-sex coworker. Called "nonromantic love relationships," the friendships resulted in trust, respect, constructive feedback, and support in achieving work goals. Intimate friendships did not necessarily become romantic, and they affected each person's job and career in a positive way. Rather than causing problems, nonromantic love relationships, according to the study, affected work teams in a positive manner because conflict was reduced. Indeed, men reported somewhat greater benefit than women from these relationships, perhaps because the men had fewer close relationships outside the workplace upon which to depend.[48]

However, when such relationships *do* become romantic or sexual in nature, real problems can result. Office romance is on the rise, with more than 30 percent of employees reporting they have been involved with a coworker at some time in their careers. Not all office romances lead to trouble, but usually they create difficulties for managers. Such relationships are disruptive to productivity and distracting to other workers. According to Dorothy Light, president of Alden Enterprises, a consulting business in Minneapolis, office romance is the biggest productivity disrupter next to mergers and downsizing and results in jealousy, intrigue, or embarrassment, and other workers may spend time gossiping about such entanglements.[49] There is a growing recognition that companies cannot ban office romancing, but it is an important issue that needs to be managed carefully.

Romances that arise between a supervisor and a subordinate require the most attention from managers. These relationships often lead to morale problems among other staff members, complaints of favoritism, and questions about the supervisor's intentions or judgment. Although few companies have written policies about workplace romance in general, 70 percent of companies recently surveyed have policies prohibiting romantic relationships between a superior and a subordinate.[50] Some companies emphasize that a manager can become romantically involved with a subordinate only if he or she is no longer supervising the subordinate. If a manager wants to pursue a relationship with a subordinate, the companies request a transfer to another job within or outside the company. In these companies, the onus is on the manager rather than the subordinate to take action.[51] The most difficult part of any office romance is often when and how it comes to an end. Failed relationships occasionally have led to sexual harassment claims—one of the most troubling people-issues faced by managers.

SEXUAL HARASSMENT

While psychological closeness between men and women in the workplace may be a positive experience, sexual harassment is not. Sexual harassment is illegal. Sexual harassment in the workplace is a form of discrimination and is a violation of Title VII of the 1964 Civil Rights Act. Sexual harassment in the classroom is a violation of Title VIII of the Education Amendment of 1972. As defined and categorized by one university, the forms of sexual harassment are:

- *Generalized.* This form involves sexual remarks and actions that are not intended to lead to sexual activity but are directed toward a coworker based solely on gender.

- *Inappropriate/offensive.* Although not sexually threatening, this form causes discomfort for a coworker whose reaction in avoiding the harasser may limit his or her freedom and ability to function in the workplace.

- *Solicitation with promise of reward.* This action treads a fine line as an attempt to "purchase" sex, with the potential for criminal prosecution.

- *Coercion with threat of punishment.* The harasser coerces a coworker into sexual activity by using the threat of power (through recommendations, grades, promotions, and so on) to jeopardize the victim's career.

- *Sexual crimes and misdemeanors.* The highest level of sexual harassment, these acts would, if reported to the police, be considered felony crimes and misdemeanors.[52]

Ever since the Anita Hill/Clarence Thomas confrontation on national television nearly a decade ago, the number of sexual harassment claims filed annually in the United States has more than doubled. Nearly 16,000 claims were filed in 1997 alone.[53] During that year, Mitsubishi Motor Corp. agreed to pay $9.5 million to settle with 27 female employees who claimed they were regularly groped and grabbed by male coworkers at the company's factory in Normal, Illinois. Some women said they had to agree to sex to win jobs. Mitsubishi has since sent the factory's 4,000 workers through an eight-hour course in sexual harassment awareness and has created a special unit to investigate all sexual harassment claims.[54]

Recently, a decision handed down by the U.S. Supreme Court broadened the definition of sexual harassment to include same sex harassment as well as harassment of men by female coworkers. In the suit that prompted the Court's decision, a male oil-rig worker claimed he was singled out by other members of the all-male crew for crude sex play, unwanted touching, and threats of rape.[55] Eight men, former employees of Jenny Craig Inc., have sued the company charging that female bosses made lewd comments or that they were denied promotions because of their sex. A male worker at a hot tub manufacturer won a $1 million court decision after claiming that his female boss made sexual overtures to him almost daily. These are among a growing number of men urging recognition that sexual harassment is not just a woman's problem.[56]

Because the corporate world is dominated by a male culture, however, sexual harassment affects women to a much greater extent. Women who are moving up the corporate hierarchy by entering male-dominated industries report a high frequency of harassment. Surveys report an increase in sexual harassment programs, but female employees also report a lack of prompt and just action by executives to incidents of sexual harassment. However, companies are discovering that "an ounce of prevention really is worth a pound of cure." Top executives are seeking to address problems of harassment through company diversity programs, revised complaint systems and grievance procedures, written policy statements, workshops, lectures, and role-playing exercises to increase employee sensitivity and awareness to the issue.[57]

■ GLOBAL DIVERSITY

Globalization is a reality for today's companies. A recent report from the Hudson Institute, Workforce 2020, states "The rest of the world matters to a degree that it never did in the past."[58] Even small companies that do not do business in other countries are affected by global diversity issues. However, large multinational companies that hire employees in many countries face tremendous challenges because they must apply diversity management across a broader stage than North America. Managers must develop new skills and awareness to handle the unique challenges of global diversity: cross-cultural understanding, the ability to build networks, and the understanding of geopolitical forces. Two significant aspects of global diversity programs involve employee selection and training and the understanding of the communication context.

The children in this Avezzano, Italy, school share cultures and learn firsthand the dynamics of global diversity. The school was established by Texas Instruments for the families of U.S. and Japanese employees involved in TI's six-nation team that is building Europe's largest semiconductor. Such efforts, along with Minority Procurement programs, demonstrate TI's commitment to a diverse, multinational corporate environment.

SELECTION AND TRAINING

Expatriates are employees who live and work in a country other than their own. Careful screening, selection, and training of employees to serve overseas increase the potential for corporate global success. Human resource managers consider global skills in the selection process. In addition, expatriates receive cross-cultural training that develops language skills and cultural and historical orientation. Career-path counseling often is available.[59] General Motors has a variety of exchange programs that provide opportunities for its employees around the world to learn about different cultures. According to Cindy Gier, diversity manager at GM Powertrain Division, such experiences "expose people to cultures other than their own, providing them with new insights while changing their perceptions of the world and equipping them with global management skills."[60]

Equally important, however, is honest self-analysis by overseas candidates and their families. Before seeking or accepting an assignment in another country, a candidate should ask himself or herself such questions as the following:

- Is your spouse interrupting his or her own career path to support your career? Is that acceptable to both of you?

- Is family separation for long periods involved?

- Can you initiate social contacts in a foreign culture?

- Can you adjust well to different environments and changes in personal comfort or quality of living, such as the lack of television, gasoline at $5 per gallon, limited hot water, varied cuisine, national phone strikes, and *warm* beer?

- Can you manage your future reentry into the job market by networking and maintaining contacts in your home country?[61]

Employees working overseas must adjust to all of these conditions. Managers going global may find that their own management "style" needs adjustment to succeed in a foreign country. One aspect of this adjustment is learning the communication context of a foreign location.

COMMUNICATION DIFFERENCES

People from some cultures tend to pay more attention to the social context (social setting, nonverbal behavior, social status) of their verbal communication than Americans do. For example, General Norman Schwarzkopf soon realized that social context was of considerable importance to leaders of Saudi Arabia. During the initial buildup for the Persian Gulf War, he suppressed his own tendency toward impatience and devoted hours to "philosophizing" with members of the Saudi royal family. Schwarzkopf realized it was their way of making decisions.[62]

In a **high-context culture**, people are sensitive to circumstances surrounding social exchanges. People in this group (typically Asian, Arab, and Greek) use communication primarily to build personal social relationships; meaning is derived from context—setting, status, nonverbal behavior—more than from explicit words; relationships and trust are more important than business; and the welfare and harmony of the group are valued. In a **low-context culture,** people (typically European, Scandinavian, and North American) use communication primarily to exchange facts and information; meaning is derived primarily from words; business transactions are more important than building relationships and trust; and individual welfare and achievement are more important than the group.[63]

To understand how differences in cultural context affect communications, consider the U.S. expression "The squeaky wheel gets the oil." It means that the loudest person will get the most attention, and attention is assumed to be favorable. Equivalent sayings in China and Japan are "Quacking ducks get shot" and "The nail that sticks up gets hammered down," respectively. Standing out as an individual in these cultures clearly merits unfavorable attention.

Even within North America, cultural subgroups vary in the extent to which context counts, explaining why differences among groups make successful communication difficult. White females, Native Americans, and African Americans all tend to prefer higher context communication than do white males. A high-context interaction requires more time because a relationship has to be developed, and

expatriates
Employees who live and work in a country other than their own

high-context culture
A culture in which communication is used to enhance personal relationships

low-context culture
A culture in which communication is used to exchange facts and information

For Michele Luna, president of Atlas Headwear, Inc., a Phoenix company that manufactures military and sports hats, managing diversity is just good business. Luna has built a diverse management team that includes Freddy Torres, left, and Alfredo Luna, her husband. Ninety-four percent of the employees are Asian and Hispanic, and many of them are immigrants. Bilingual employees help bridge the communication gap with employees who do not speak English, and weekly meetings are held to facilitate mutual understanding among workers. For Luna, rising revenues and a committed workforce reflect the benefits of valuing diversity.

trust and friendship must be established. Furthermore, most male managers and most people doing the hiring in organizations are from low-context cultures, which conflicts with people entering the organization from a background in a higher context culture. Overcoming these differences in communication is a major goal of diversity awareness training.

■ BENEFITS OF VALUING DIVERSITY

As a rule, organizations have not been highly successful in managing women and minorities, as evidenced by higher turnover rates, higher absenteeism, lower job satisfaction, and general frustration over career development for these groups. Moreover, the fact that women and minorities are clustered at lower organization levels indicates they are not progressing as far as they might and are not developing their full potential.[64]

Diversity in the workplace is inevitable and provides many benefits for organizations. Organizations need internal diversity to help them meet the needs of an increasingly diverse marketplace. With the growing diversity of the U.S. population, African American, Asian American, and Hispanic members are becoming major market niches, and more and more

companies want to pursue them. Avon Company and Maybelline are successfully marketing cosmetics to African Americans and Hispanics by hiring representatives of these minority groups as marketing managers.

Another benefit is the opportunity to develop employee and organizational potential. This produces *higher morale*—because people feel valued for what they bring to the organization—and *better relationships* at work—because people acquire the skills to recognize, understand, and accept cultural differences. Clearly, the benefits are having positive effects on many organizations' bottom line.

In terms of better recruiting, companies that treat women and racial/ethnic minorities well will be able to acquire the best employees. Retaining these employees produces a qualified, trained workforce for the future. Demographic research suggests that the labor market is slowly tightening, and organizations that boast a healthy environment for women and minorities will be in the best competitive position to attract and retain scarce employees. When women and minorities experience prejudice and nonacceptance, reduced individual and organizational productivity occurs because people do not feel valued and are not willing to take risks for the organization. Minority employees often leave the company out of frustration when they feel their opportunities for career advancement are blocked.

Finally, diversity within the organization provides a broader and deeper base of experience for problem solving, creativity, and innovation. For example, research shows that heterogeneous teams produce more innovative solutions to problems than do homogeneous teams. One reason is that people with diverse backgrounds bring different perspectives to problem solving. Also, when given an active role, minority employees can help organiza-

tions grow and improve by challenging basic assumptions about how the organization works. African Americans, women, Hispanics, Native Americans, Asian Americans, and others outside the mainstream of corporate America can help managers and organizations break out of status quo thinking.[65]

Diversity is essential to the learning organization, in which teams of workers that cross functional boundaries are engaged regularly in identifying and solving problems. Employees in learning organizations are encouraged to

FOCUS ON Diversity   THE STRENGTH OF DIVERSITY

Creating a diverse, inclusive workforce is a continuous process at Hewlett-Packard, where managers see diversity as an opportunity to tap a broad range of human potential and use it to keep learning, changing, and growing. H-P's commitment to diversity began years before equal employment opportunity or affirmative action guidelines required it. It is an outgrowth of the company's founding values of treating each employee with dignity and respect.

However, after a survey revealed that many women and employees of color did not feel they had equal opportunities at Hewlett-Packard, company managers involved all employees in a complete examination of H-P's work environment. By involving all employees, managers avoided the problem of issuing a "diversity directive" that did not have the support of line managers. In addition, participation ensured that the real needs of employees were addressed. Today, Hewlett-Packard's diversity strategy recognizes many aspects of diversity, including race, gender, culture, age, economic status, sexual orientation, and physical ability. The emphasis on employee involvement has continued, with the formation of employee network groups that represent various minority groups in the organization. Workers also are involved in discussing diversity issues at coffee talks, task forces, diversity councils, conferences, and regular team meetings. Supporting diversity is ingrained in the culture at H-P. Managers and other workers are encouraged to challenge norms and biases and address inappropriate language or behavior. Often, those who do so are rewarded by the company for being "diversity champions."

Another key to a successful diversity program at Hewlett-Packard is ensuring management leadership and involvement. Senior managers representing all of H-P's businesses develop and drive diversity initiatives worldwide. However, top managers then cascade responsibility and accountability for diversity success to all managers and employees through performance plans and evaluations. Diversity objectives are of major importance in staffing activities and decisions. When hiring new people, a diverse interviewing team is considered equally as important as a diverse slate of candidates. This helps to ensure that minority candidates have equal opportunities to move into higher management positions. In addition, H-P sponsors a unique mentoring program to make sure "supporting diversity" is more than talk. The program matches minority employees with higher-level managers, who are evaluated on their protégé's progress. Many participants in the program move into higher-level jobs in the company. The company also supports and funds a number of other employee development and job enrichment opportunities and assignments for minority employees. As a learning organization, Hewlett-Packard is continually striving to create an environment where everyone feels valued and included.

www.hewlett-packard.com

Source: Michael L. Wheeler, "Global Diversity: Reality, Opportunity, and Challenge," *Business Week*, December 1, 1997, Special Advertising Section.

think, express divergent opinions, and be creative in order to help the organization learn and change; a diverse mix of employees is a real plus in this environment. One study found that companies that rate highly on creativity and innovation have a higher percentage of women and nonwhite male employees than less innovative companies.[66] Hewlett-Packard, a company long known for innovation, makes a strong commitment to diversity, as discussed in Focus on Diversity. As one senior executive said, "In a country seeking competitive advantage in a global economy, the goal of managing diversity is to develop our capacity to accept, incorporate, and empower the diverse human talents of the most diverse nation on earth. It is our reality. We need to make it our strength."[67]

Summary and Management Solution

Several important ideas pertain to workforce diversity, which means hiring and being inclusive with people who have different human qualities and/or belong to different cultural groups. Dimensions of diversity are both primary, such as age, gender, and race; and secondary, such as education, marital status, and income. Ethnocentric attitudes generally produce a monoculture that accepts only one way of doing things and one set of values and beliefs, thereby excluding nontraditional employees from full participation. Minority employees face several significant challenges in the workplace.

Acceptance of workforce diversity is becoming especially important because of sociocultural changes and the changing workforce. Diversity in the workplace reflects diversity in the larger environment. Innovative companies are initiating a variety of programs to take advantage of the diverse workforce.

Affirmative action programs have been successful in gaining employment for women and minorities, but the glass ceiling has kept many women and minorities from obtaining top management positions. The Civil Rights Act of 1991 amends and strengthens the Civil Rights Act of 1964.

Breaking down the glass ceiling ultimately means changing the corporate culture within organizations; changing internal structures and policies toward employees, including accommodating special needs; and providing diversity awareness training to help people become aware of their own cultural boundaries and prejudices. This training also helps employees learn to communicate with people from other cultural contexts.

The increased diversity in organizations has provided opportunities for emotional intimacy and friendship between men and women that are beneficial to all parties. However, when these relationships become romantic or sexual, they can present problems for managers. Increasing diversity also means that organizations must develop programs to deal with global as well as domestic diversity and with potential conflicts, such as sexual harassment, that arise.

Valuing diversity has many benefits, such as developing employees to their full potential and allowing successful interaction with diverse clients in the marketplace. Diversity also provides a broader and deeper base of experience for problem solving, creativity, and innovation.

Technology is helping some diverse entrepreneurs to succeed. Recall the case at the beginning where entrepreneur Lorne Prince had to decide whether to go for government certification and how to do so. Prince decided to do some research and see what resources were available to help him. By surfing the Internet, he discovered EZCertify.com, which sells a CD-Rom that automates the process of applying for two kinds of SBA certification.

He spent a few hours learning the program and typing in data, which the software inserted in all necessary places, eliminating the redundancy of the process. The program told him exactly what documents he would need, such as W2 forms, company bylaws, articles of incorporation, and the like. Within two weeks he mailed in the package to the SBA and has already planned for what he will do with the first government contract cash. "We'll unleash our software ideas," he says.

Discussion Questions

1. If you were a senior manager at a company such as R. R. Donnelley, Allstate Insurance, or Texaco, how would you address the challenges faced by minority employees?

2. Some people argue that social class is a major source of cultural differences, yet social class is not listed as a primary or secondary dimension in Exhibit 10.1. Discuss reasons for this.

3. Have you been associated with an organization that made assumptions associated with a monoculture? Describe the culture.

4. Do you think any organization can successfully resist diversity today? Discuss.

5. What is the glass ceiling, and why do you think it has proved to be such a barrier to women and minorities?

6. In preparing an organization to accept diversity, do you think it is more important to change the corporate culture or to change structures and policies? Explain.

7. If a North American corporation could choose either high-context or low-context communications, which do you think would be best for the company's long-term health? Discuss.

8. What do you think the impact on an organization would be for diversity within its own country versus international diversity? Discuss.

9. Many single people meet and date people from the office because the organization provides a context within which to know and trust another person. How do you think this practice affects the potential for emotional intimacy? Sexual harassment?

10. How might diversity within the organization ultimately lead to better problem solving and greater creativity?

Management Exercises

Manager's Workbook

Women and Work Quiz

How well do you know the status of women in the workplace? Test yourself below:

_____ 1. Women account for 40 percent on the total U.S. workforce.   T   F

_____ 2. By 2006, women will account for 50 percent of the total growth in the labor force.   T   F

_____ 3. Of divorced women, 75 percent percent are in the labor force, while 52 percent of married women work.   T   F

_____ 4. The largest occupational group for women is secretaries, while the second largest is cashiers.   T   F

_____ 5. About four million women hold more than one job.   T   F

_____ 6. In families with a working wife, the median income is $68,000, while a family without a wife in the paid labor force is $40,000.   T   F

_____ 7. Over the age of 65, 14 percent of women live below the poverty line, while only 7 percent of men do.   T   F

_____ 8. The number of working women has doubled since 1970—from 30 million to 60 million.   T   F

_____ 9. Overall, women earn 80 cents on the dollar compared to men.   T   F

_____10. The highest weekly earnings for women come from which group, lawyers, engineers, or physicians?   T   F

Answers: 1. False, 46 percent; 2. False, 59 percent; 3. False, divorced 75 percent, married 63 percent; 4. True; 5. True; 6. False, working wife $60,000, other is $34,000; 7. True; 8. True; 9. False, 74 cents; 10. lawyers.

SOURCE: Adapted from Department of Labor, *Facts on Working Women,* 1998.

Management in Practice: Ethical Dilemma

Promotion or Not?

You are the president of CrownCutters, Inc. You have worked closely with Bill Smith for several years now. In many situations, he has served as your de facto right-hand person.

Due to a retirement, you have an opening in the position of executive vice president. Bill is the natural choice—and this is obvious to the other mid- and senior-level managers at CrownCutters. Bill is popular with most of the managers in the company. Of course, he also has his share of detractors.

Prior to announcing the appointment of Bill Smith, you receive a memo from Jane Jones, your controller. Jane's memo indicates that she was subjected to sporadic sexual harassment by Bill starting 10 years ago when she first joined the company and was working for him. Her memo indicates that the harassment essentially stopped six years ago when she moved to a position in which Bill was no longer her superior. She requests that this information be kept totally confidential.

You have never heard of any allegations like this about Bill before.

What Do You Do?

1. Move ahead with the promotion because, even if true, this is an isolated incident that is a part of Bill's past and is not his current behavior.

2. Stop the promotion because Bill is not the type of person who should help lead the company and shape its values.

3. Put the promotion on hold until you can discuss the situation extensively with Bill and Jane, although this means the accusation probably will become public knowledge.

SOURCE: This case was provided by Professor David Scheffman, Owen Graduate School of Management, Vanderbilt University, Nashville, Tennessee.

Surf the Net

1. *The Glass Ceiling.* In order to learn more about the glass ceiling, visit www.ilr.cornell.edu/library/e_archive/glassceiling. You will need to have the Acrobat Reader, available as a free download from this site, installed on your computer. Select the "Recommendations of the Glass Ceiling Commission," and answer these two questions: (a) What was the mission of the Glass Ceiling Commission? (b) What are the eight recommendations the Commission made for business?

2. *Diversity Awareness Training.* Access a search engine and key in the words "diversity awareness training," then compare the content and focus of three to four different training programs in this area. Recommend the training program you think would do the best job of improving the diversity awareness of employees. Sample sites are:

   www.adl.org/frames/front_awod.html

   chrissy-jackson.com/diversity.html

   www.corcommunications.com

   www.dnai.com/~mail/daw.html

3. *Sexual Harassment.* Go to www.capstn.com and find the sexual harassment quiz prepared by Capstone Communications. Take the quiz, print out a copy after you have selected your answers, and bring the completed quiz to class. Your instructor may wish to use this quiz to determine how well the class understands sexual harassment.

Case for Critical Analysis

Draper Manufacturing

You have just been hired as a diversity consultant by Draper Manufacturing. Ralph Draper, chairman and CEO, and other top managers feel a need to resolve some racial issues that have been growing over the past several years at their plant in Nashville, Tennessee. Draper Manufacturing is a small, family-owned company that manufactures mattresses. It employs 90 people full-time, including African Americans, Asians, and Hispanics, with 75 percent of the workforce being female. The company also occasionally hires part-time workers, most of whom are Hispanic women. Most of these part-timers are hired for periods of a few months at a time, when production is falling behind schedule.

To begin your orientation to the company, Draper has asked his production manager, Wallace Burns, to take you around the plant. As Burns points out the various areas responsible for each stage of the production process, you overhear several different languages being spoken. In the shipping and receiving department, you notice that most workers are black men. Burns confirms that 90 percent of the workers in shipping and receiving are African American and points out that the manager of that department, Adam Fox, is also African American.

Later in the afternoon you attend a regular meeting of top managers to meet everyone and get a feel for the organizational culture. Draper introduces you as a diversity consultant and notes that several of his managers have expressed concerns about festering racial tensions in the company. He notes that "Each of the minority groups sticks together. The blacks and Orientals rarely mix, and most of the Mexicans stick together and speak only in Spanish. It seems that some of our workers are just downright lazy sometimes. We keep falling behind in our production schedule and having to hire part-time workers, but then we generally have to fire two or three of those a month for goofing off on the job." He closes his introduction by saying that you

have been hired to help the company solve their growing diversity problems.

Draper then turns toward the management committee's routine daily business. The others present are the general manager, human resources manager (the only woman), sales manager, quality control manager, plant manager (Wallace Burns), and shipping and receiving manager (Adam Fox, the only nonwhite manager). Soon an angry debate begins between Fox and the sales manager. The sales manager says that orders are not being shipped on time, and several complaints have been received about the quality of the product. Fox argues that he needs more workers in shipping and receiving to do the job right, and he adds that the quality of incoming supplies is lousy. While this debate continues, the other managers remain silent and seem quite uncomfortable. Finally, the quality control manager attempts to calm things down with a joke about his wife. Most of the men in the group laugh loudly, and the conversation shifts to other topics on the agenda.

Questions

1. What suggestions would you make to Draper's managers to help them move toward successfully managing diversity issues?

2. If you were the shipping and receiving or human resources manager, how do you think you would feel about working at Draper? What are some of the challenges you might face at this company?

3. Based on the information in the case, at what stage of diversity awareness (Exhibit 10.5 on p. 339) do managers at Draper Manufacturing seem to be? Discuss.

SOURCE: Based on "Northern Industries," a case prepared by Rae Andre of Northeastern University.

Endnotes

1 Ilan Mochari, "3-2-1 Contract," *Inc. Tech,* No. 4 (1999), p. 140.

2 Alex Markels, "A Diversity Program Can Prove Divisive," *The Wall Street Journal,* January 30, 1997, pp. B1, B2.

3 M. Fine, F. Johnson, and M. S. Ryan, "Cultural Diversity in the Workforce," *Public Personnel Management,* 19 (1990), pp. 305–319.

4 Taylor H. Cox, "Managing Cultural Diversity: Implications for Organizational Competitiveness," *Academy of Management Executive,* 5 (3) (1991), pp. 45–56; and Faye Rice, "How to Make Diversity Pay," *Fortune,* August 8, 1994, pp. 78–86.

5 Timothy Aeppel, "A 3Com Factory Hires a Lot of Immigrants, Gets Mix of Languages," *The Wall Street Journal,* March 30, 1998, p. A1.

6 Lennie Copeland, "Valuing Diversity, Part I: Making the Most of Cultural Differences at the Workplace," *Personnel,* June 1988, pp. 52–60.

7 D. Farid Elashmawi, "Culture Clashes: Barriers to Business," *Managing Diversity,* 2 (11) (August 1993), pp. 1–3.

8 Frances J. Milliken and Luis I. Martins, "Searching for Common Threads: Understanding the Multiple Effects of Diversity in Organizational Groups," *Academy of Management Review,* 21 (2) (1996), pp. 402–433.

9 G. Haight, "Managing Diversity," *Across the Board,* 27 (3) (1990), pp. 22–29.

10 Songer, "Workforce Diversity," *B&E Review,* April–June 1991, pp. 3–6.

11 Robert Doktor, Rosalie Tung, and Mary Ann von Glinow, "Future Directions for Management Theory Development," *Academy of Management Review,* 16 (1991), pp. 362–365.

12 Renee Blank and Sandra Slipp, "The White Male: An Endangered Species?" *Management Review,* September 1994, pp. 27–32.

13 M. Bennett, "A Developmental Approach to Training for Intercultural Sensitivity," *International Journal of Intercultural Relations,* 10 (1986), pp. 179–196.

14 Jenny C. McCune, "Diversity Training: A Competitive Weapon," *Management Review,* June 1996, pp. 25–28.

15 C. Keen, "Human Resource Management Issues in the '90s," *Vital Speeches,* 56 (24) (1990), pp. 752–754.

16 Kurt Anderson, "California Dreamin'," *Time,* September 23, 1991, pp. 38–42.

17 Richard W. Judy and Carol D'Amico, *Workforce 2020: Work and Workers in the 21st Century* (Indianapolis, IN: Hudson Institute, 1997).

18 Gilbert W. Fairholm, *Leadership and the Culture of Trust* (Westport, Conn.: Praeger, 1994), p. 184.

19 Chris Sandlund, "There's a New Face to America," *Success,* April 1999, pp. 38–45.

20 Judy Rosener, *America's Competitive Secret: Women Managers* (New York: Oxford University Press, 1997), pp. 33–34.

21 Ann Morrison, *The New Leaders: Guidelines on Leadership Diversity in America* (San Francisco: Jossey-Bass, 1992), p. 37.

22 Robert Hooijberg and Nancy DeTomaso, "Leadership In and Of Demographically Diverse Organizations," *Leadership Quarterly,* 7 (1) (1996), pp. 1–19.

23 Vivian Louie, "For Asian-Americans, A Way to Fight a Maddening Stereotype," *The New York Times,* 8 August 1993, p. 9.

24 Judy and D'Amico, *Workforce 2020.*

25 Copeland, "Valuing Diversity, Part I: Making the Most of Cultural Differences at the Workplace"; and Judy and D'Amico, *Workforce 2020.*

26 S. Hutchins, Jr., "Preparing for Diversity: The Year 2000," *Quality Process,* 22 (10) (1989), pp. 66–68.

27 Leon E. Wynter, "Allstate Rates Managers on Handling Diversity," *The Wall Street Journal* (Business and Race column), October 1, 1997, p. B1.

28 Nicholas Lemann, "Taking Affirmative Action Apart," *The New York Times Magazine,* July 11, 1995, pp. 36–43.

29 Catherine Yang, Maria Mallory, and Alice Cuneo, "A 'Race-Neutral' Helping Hand?" *Business Week,* February 27, 1995, pp. 120–121.

30 Madeline E. Heilman, Caryn J. Block, and Peter Stathatos, "The Affirmative Action Stigma of Incompetence: Effects of Performance Information Ambiguity," *Academy of Management Journal,* 40, (1) (1997), pp. 603–625.

31 Arthur P. Brief, Robert T. Buttram, Robin M. Reizenstein, S. Douglas Pugh, Jodi D. Callahan, Richard L. McCline, and Joel B. Vaslow, "Beyond Good Intentions: The Next Steps Toward Racial Equality in the American Workplace," *Academy of Management Executive,* 11 (4) (1997), pp. 59–72.

32 B. Geber, "Managing Diversity," *Training,* 27 (7) (1990), pp. 23–30.

33 Ida L. Castro, "Q: Should Women Be Worried About the Glass Ceiling in the Workplace?" *Insight,* February 10, 1997, pp. 24–27.

34 Nelton, "Nurturing Diversity."

35 C. Soloman, "Careers under Glass," *Personnel Journal,* 69 (4) (1990), pp. 96–105.

36 Deborah L. Jacobs, "Back from the Mommy Track," *The New York Times,* October 9, 1994, pp. F1, F6.

37 Soloman, "Careers under Glass."

38 Belle Rose Ragins, Bickley Townsend, and Mary Mattis, "Gender Gap in the Executive Suite: CEOs and Female Executives Report on Breaking the Glass Ceiling," *Academy of Management Executive,* 12 (1) (1998), pp. 28–42.

39 Thomas E. Weber, "When Adults Crash Pokemon Party, Kids Grow Up at Net Speed," *Wall Street Journal,* Oct. 25, 1999, p. B1.

40 Geber, "Managing Diversity."

41 Hanna Rosin, "Cultural Revolution at Texaco," *The New Republic,* February 2, 1998, pp. 15–18.

42 Loden and Rosener, *Workforce America!* (Homewood, IL: Business One Irwin, 1991); and Genevieve Capowski, "Ageism: The New Diversity Issue," *Management Review,* October 1994, pp. 10–15.

43 B. Ragins, "Barriers to Mentoring: The Female Manager's Dilemma," *Human Relations,* 42 (1) (1989), pp. 1–22.

44 Mary Zey, "A Mentor for All," *Personnel Journal,* January 1988, pp. 46–51.

45 Dan Morse, "Where Gang Members Are Shoe Salesmen: A novel Franchise," *Wall Street Journal,* Feb. 19, 1999, pp. A1,A6.

46 J. Black and M. Mendenhall, "Cross-Cultural Training Effectiveness: A Review and a Theoretical Framework for Future Research," *Academy of Management Review,* 15 (1990), pp. 113–136.

47 E. G. Collins, "Managers and Lovers," *Harvard Business Review,* 61 (1983), pp. 142–153.

48 Sharon A. Lobel, Robert E. Quinn, Lynda St. Clair, and Andrea Warfield, "Love without Sex: The Impact of Psychological Intimacy between Men and Women at Work," *Organizational Dynamics* (summer 1994), pp. 5–16.

49 Carol Hymowitz, "Drawing the Line on Budding Romances in Your Workplace," *The Wall Street Journal* (Managing Your Career column), November 18, 1997, p. B1.

50 William C. Symonds with Steve Hamm and Gail DeGeorge, "Sex on the Job," *Business Week,* February 16, 1998, pp. 30–31.

51 Carol Hymowitz and Ellen Joan Pollock, "The One Clear Line in Interoffice Romance Has Become Blurred," *The Wall Street Journal,* February 4, 1998, pp. A1, A8.

52 "Sexual Harassment: Vanderbilt University Policy" (Nashville: Vanderbilt University, 1993).

53 Jack Corcoran, "Of Nice and Men," *Success,* June 1998, pp. 65–67.

54 De'Ann Weimer with Emily Thornton, "Slow Healing at Mitsubishi," *Business Week,* September 22, 1997, p. 74.

55 Corcoran, "Of Nice and Men."

56 Barbara Carton, "At Jenny Craig, Men Are Ones Who Claim Sex Discrimination," *The Wall Street Journal,* November 29, 1994, pp. A1, A11.

57 Jennifer J. Laabs, "Sexual Harassment: HR Puts Its Questions on the Line," *Personnel Journal,* February 1995, pp. 35–45.

58 Judy and D'Amico, *Workforce 2020.*

59 Joann S. Lublin, "Companies Use Cross-Cultural Training to Help Their Employees Adjust Abroad," *The Wall Street Journal,* August 4, 1992, pp. B1, B9.

60 Michael L. Wheeler, "Global Diversity: Reality, Opportunity, and Challenge," *Business Week,* December 1, 1997, Special Advertising Section.

61 Gilbert Fuchsberg, "As Costs of Overseas Assignments Climb, Firms Select Expatriates More Carefully," *The Wall Street Journal,* January 9, 1992, pp. B3, B4.

62 Brian Dumaine, "Management Lessons from the General," *Fortune,* November 2, 1992, p. 143.

63 J. Kennedy and A. Everest, "Put Diversity in Context," *Personnel Journal,* September 1991, pp. 50–54.

64 Cox, "Managing Cultural Diversity."

65 Gail Robinson and Kathleen Dechant, "Building a Business Case for Diversity," *Academy of Management Executive,* 11 (3) (1997), pp. 21–31.

66 Taylor H. Cox, *Cultural Diversity in Organizations* (San Francisco: Berrett-Koehler, 1994).

67 Thomas, "From Affirmative Action to Affirming Diversity.

PART

5

LEADING

What does it take to lead and motivate groups of individuals to perform at their best? The nine skippers of the Whitbread race know. While their personalities may vary from crusty and abrasive, to determined and driven, to energetic and likable, their crews know, too. The best are worthy of piloting $2 million boats around the world—each with a dozen people's lives in their hands. Personal expertise as a sailor, confidence in their own abilities, competitiveness to win, intensity, and, above all, professionalism are characteristics they share. Despite the stresses of long and physically uncomfortable voyages, one Dutch crew aboard the *BrunelSunenergy* dubbed itself the "Happy Crew" and exhibited good humor, drive, spirit, and nerve. Christine Guillou, the skipper of the all-female crew of *EF Education,* said, "It was a great experience, especially discovering . . . what you can do with a good team and good spirit." Winning skipper, Paul Cayard of *EF Language,* praises his crew and their professionalism, saying that "maximizing the use of every minute . . . and my team's mentality being the same was the key factor."

In Part V, you'll learn about behavior in organizations—the ways leadership, motivation, and communication can be powerful influences on performance—and the importance of teamwork in today's competitive world.

Foundations of Behavior in Organizations

LEARNING OBJECTIVES

After studying this chapter, you should be able to:

• Define attitudes, including their major components, and explain their relationship to behavior

• Discuss the importance of work-related attitudes

• Identify major personality traits and describe how personality can influence workplace attitudes and behaviors

• Summarize the steps in the perception process and perceptual biases

• Explain how people learn in general and in terms of individual learning styles

• Discuss the effects of stress and how individuals differ in their responses to stress

• Identify ways organizations and individuals can manage stress

THE COMMON MYTH that dot-coms

are an easy ticket to riches is more fiction than

reality, a fact borne out by a growing number of startups. Many

companies are being afflicted with post-IPO blues, such as at Beyond.com,

which began by focusing on selling software through online downloads. After going

public in 1998, the company decided to switch its focus from the consumer market to big-ticket

customers in government and corporations. Suddenly the free-spirited thinkers who knew how to

market Pokémon were not being valued as much as the buttondown types. Then, people started leaving.

• If you were Mark Breier, what would you do to solve the diverse problems of staggering losses and employee listlessness?

What kinds of personality traits and problem-solving styles are needed for a manager wrestling with these problems?

Morale sagged. CEO Mark Breier held pep rallies to get everyone enthused, and he succeeded—for a few

hours anyway. The focus on goals was unclear, and the vision was ahead of the day-to-day realities.

By 1999, losses were staggering, totaling nearly $100 million. The company decided to be brash

and go nude—well, practically—when an executive appeared on CNBC in his boxer shorts

to show how easy—and undressed—the whole process of online downloading is.

It didn't work. Employees continued to quit or complain, as operating

margins grew thinner. Breier felt he needed to eliminate

the whiners.[1]

People differ in many ways. At work, these differences influence how they set goals and how they handle challenges. The personalities and attitudes of managers can also profoundly affect the workplace, as Mark Breier's story illustrates. People are an organization's most valuable resource; they also can be the source of the most difficult problems. People problems can be particularly challenging because of the complex and unique qualities they bring to the workplace. Three core leadership skills are needed to effectively identify and evaluate people problems: (1) diagnosing, or gaining insight into the situation a manager is trying to influence; (2) adapting individual behavior and resources to meet the needs of the situation; and (3) communicating in a way that others can understand and accept. Thus, managers need insight about individual differences to understand what a behavioral situation is now and what it may become in the future.

To handle this responsibility, managers must understand the principles of organizational behavior; that is, the ways in which individuals and groups tend to act in the organizational environment. By increasing their knowledge of individual differences in the areas of attitudes, personality, perception, learning, and stress management, managers can understand and lead employees and colleagues through many workplace challenges.

■ ORGANIZATIONAL BEHAVIOR

Organizational behavior, commonly called OB, is an interdisciplinary field dedicated to the study of human attitudes, behavior, and performance in organizations. OB draws concepts from many disciplines, including psychology, sociology, cultural anthropology, industrial engineering, economics, ethics, and vocational counseling, as well as the discipline of management. The concepts and principles of organizational behavior are important to managers because in every organization human beings ultimately make the decisions that control how the organization will acquire and use resources. Those people may cooperate with, compete with, support, or undermine one another. Their beliefs and feelings about themselves, their coworkers, and the organization shape what they do and how well they do it. People can distract the organization from its strategy by engaging in conflict and misunderstandings, or they can pool their diverse talents and perspectives to accomplish much more as a group than they could ever do as individuals.

By understanding what causes people to behave as they do, managers can exercise leadership to achieve positive outcomes. They can foster behaviors such as **organizational citizenship;** that is, work behavior that goes beyond job requirements and contributes as needed to the organization's success. An employee demonstrates organizational citizenship by being helpful to coworkers and customers, doing extra work when necessary, and looking for ways to improve products and procedures. Managers can encourage organizational citizenship by applying their knowledge of human behavior in many ways, such as selecting people with positive attitudes and personalities, helping them see how they can contribute, and enabling them to learn from and cope with workplace challenges.

ATTITUDES

Managers observe that some people show up at work eager to get started, whereas others appear to wish they were elsewhere. Some employees tackle problems with the expectation that they and their coworkers will cooperate to find a solution; others grumble or panic. These different kinds of behavior partly reflect variations in employee attitudes. Defined formally, an **attitude** is an evaluation that predisposes a person to act in a certain way. A person who has the attitude "I love my work; it's challenging and fun" probably will tackle work-related problems cheerfully, while one who comes to work with the attitude "I hate my job" is not likely to exhibit much enthusiasm or commitment to solving problems.

COMPONENTS OF ATTITUDES

Behavioral scientists consider attitudes to have three components: cognitions (thoughts), affect (feelings), and behavior.[2] The cognitive component of an attitude includes the beliefs,

---

organizational behavior
An interdisciplinary field dedicated to the study of how individuals and groups tend to act in organizations

organizational citizenship
Work behavior that goes beyond job requirements and contributes as needed to the organization's success

attitude
A cognitive and affective evaluation that predisposes a person to act in a certain way

Exhibit 11.1

COMPONENTS OF AN
ATTITUDE

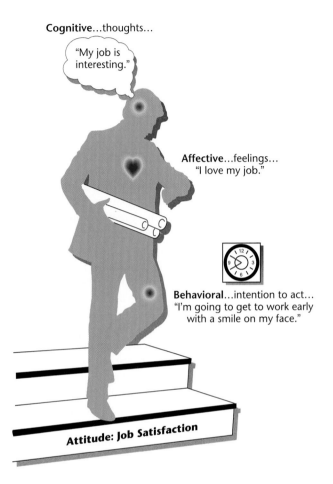

Cognitive...thoughts...

"My job is interesting."

Affective...feelings...
"I love my job."

Behavioral...intention to act...
"I'm going to get to work early
with a smile on my face."

Attitude: Job Satisfaction

opinions, and information the person has about the object of the attitude, such as knowledge of what a job entails and opinions about personal abilities. The affective component is the person's emotions or feelings about the object of the attitude, such as enjoying or hating a job. The behavioral component of an attitude is the person's intention to behave toward the object of the attitude in a certain way. Exhibit 11.1 illustrates the three components of a positive attitude toward one's job.

Too often, managers think only of the cognitive component, but other components are just as important. When people feel strongly about something, the affective component may predispose them to act, no matter what someone does to change their opinions. For example, if an employee is passionate about a new idea, that employee may go to great lengths to implement it. Likewise, an employee who is furious about being asked to work overtime

on his birthday may fail to cooperate, lash out at coworkers, or even quit, despite well-intentioned arguments from the manager about the need to meet deadlines. In these cases, effective leadership is needed to address the affective component (emotions) associated with the attitude. Are employees so excited that their judgment may be clouded, or so discouraged that they have given up trying? If nothing else, the manager probably needs to be aware of situations that involve strong emotions and give employees a chance to vent their feelings safely.

Recognizing components of attitudes also is useful for managers when they want to change an attitude. As a general rule, altering one component of an attitude can contribute to an overall change in attitude. Suppose a manager concludes that some employees think he should make all the decisions that affect the department, but he wants employees to assume more decision-making responsibility. To change the underlying attitude, the manager would consider whether to educate employees about the areas in which they can make good decisions (changing the cognitive component), build enthusiasm with pep talks about the satisfaction of employee empowerment (changing the affective component), or simply insist that employees make their own decisions (behavioral component) with the expectation that once they experience the advantages of decision-making authority, they will begin to like it.

WORK-RELATED ATTITUDES

The attitudes of most interest to managers are those related to work, especially attitudes that influence how well employees perform. To lead employees effectively, managers logically seek to cultivate the kinds of attitudes that are associated with high performance. Two attitudes that are believed to relate to high performance are satisfaction with one's job and commitment to the organization.

JOB SATISFACTION   A positive attitude toward one's job is called **job satisfaction.** In general, people experience this attitude when their work matches their needs and interests, when working conditions and rewards (such as pay) are satisfactory, and when the employees

job satisfaction
A positive attitude toward one's job

like their coworkers. In the Emergent Solutions Group of PricewaterhouseCoopers, a gathering of talented programmers and systems designers are developing an advanced computer system that models complex human behavior, such as the way people interact in stores. Here, employees often labor long hours, motivated by the excitement of working on ground-breaking technology. Their attitude toward participation in pioneering work supports a high degree of job satisfaction.[3]

Many managers believe job satisfaction is important because they believe satisfied employees will do better work. But, research has shown that the link between satisfaction and performance is generally small and is affected by other factors.[4] The importance of satisfaction varies according to the amount of control the employee has; an employee doing routine tasks may produce about the same output no matter how he or she feels about the job. But, there are reasons managers should care about job satisfaction. When unemployment rates are low and workers can easily find jobs elsewhere, managers want their productive employees to be happy enough to stay with the organization. In addition, as human beings, managers may simply want employees to feel good about their work, and they will more often prefer to work with people who have a positive outlook.

Set designer Anne Larlab's job satisfaction is high. One of a new breed of global workers, her attitude toward work takes her anywhere for an interesting job. After graduating from college, Larlab went to London on a student visa to assist a famous set designer. Here, she is in Thailand apprenticing on a major motion picture, working 14-hour days, and living out of a hotel and three suitcases. E-mail is her only address. For Larlab, it's worth it. Exposure to new cultures brings invaluable research for her design work. She displays her attitude with a one-word comment in her journal: "Wow!"

ORGANIZATIONAL COMMITMENT   Another important attitude is **organizational commitment,** which is loyalty to and heavy involvement in the organization. An employee with a high degree of organizational commitment is likely to say "we" when talking about the organization. Such a person tries to contribute to the organization's success and wishes to remain with the organization. One company taking a personal interest in employees—and being dependent on their loyalty—is described next.

PC CONNECTION

Avid backpackers Patricia Gallup and David Hall met some years ago when they both served as support crew to endurance hikers on the Appalachian Trail. There they learned to put themselves in other people's shoes and to work together to find solutions.

Hall asked Gallup to join his Marlow, New Hampshire-based broadcasting and recording equipment family business, Audio Accessories, which sold through a catalog, shipped via UPS, and answered questions over the telephone. They had trouble trying to buy a computer for Audio Accessories and were overwhelmed by the technical knowledge needed to make the purchase and the lack of any company ready to help give technical information. Like all good entrepreneurs, they immediately saw the light and knew there was a need for a firm that could not only sell technology and computers to relative neophytes, but could also serve as a source of valuable information.

Back then almost no retailers sold computers. But would people do so over the telephone? They figured they could make customers comfortable because of the experience gained from the years of ordering hiking supplies via phone. "After all," Gallup said, "We knew how we wanted to be treated."

So they invested their entire savings of $8,000 and started off with 12 products. It took three days after catalogs arrived for people to start calling and they haven't stopped since. Crucial factors in their success were the decisions to: (1) lightning fast delivery (anything ordered in the evening up to 2:45 A.M. is delivered the next business day, or even that same day); and (2) give free technical advice at any time, even if someone bought the product elsewhere, for they knew this would bring them customers—and it did. But perhaps even more important has been their employee loyalty, which they have nurtured carefully by treating employees respectfully.

Being so isolated, they had to find ways to attract employees, including buying studded snow tires and ice-breaker windshield wipers for them. Having their headquarters in a remote area has turned into an advantage. "Everyone dreams about being able to live and work in a magical rural town like Marlow," says Gallup.[5] ■

Most managers want to enjoy the benefits of loyal, committed employees, including low turnover and willingness to do more than the job's basic requirements. Organizational commitment has become especially important in recent years, because a tight labor market has forced employers to compete harder to attract and keep good workers in many fields. Adding to the challenge have been past downsizing and restructuring that have made many employees distrustful of their employers. As shown in Exhibit 11.2, a survey of 450,000 employees found that although most executives believe employees respect management, the attitudes of the employees are in fact quite different.[6] The percentage of workers who say management is respected by employees has been steadily declining since 1991. In the most recent available year of the survey (1997), about 50 percent of employees reported that management generally is respected, as compared with about 70 percent of top managers who believed that. Managers can take action to promote organizational commitment by keeping employees informed, giving them a say in decisions, providing the necessary training and other resources that enable them to succeed, treating them fairly, and offering rewards they

organizational commitment
Loyalty to, and heavy involvement in, one's organization

E x h i b i t 11.2

CHANGING ATTITUDES:
EMPLOYEES' RESPECT FOR
MANAGEMENT

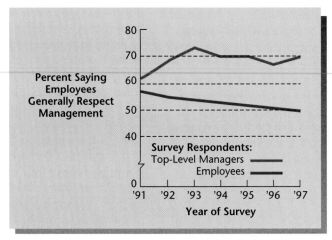

SOURCE: Adapted from Aaron Bernstein, "We Want You to Stay. Really," *Business Week*, June 22, 1998, 67–68+ (citing data from an annual survey of 450,000 employees and managers by the International Survey Research Corporation).

value. Microsoft keeps turnover for its technical support staff exceedingly low by fostering organizational commitment.

MICROSOFT
www.microsoft.com

Ever had trouble calling technical support for help with your computer? In many large, high-tech companies this is likely due to their difficulty in keeping their help desks well staffed. Listening to problems all day eventually wears a person down, and the reality is that help-desk help is hard to keep. In addition, technical support people often feel the help-desk position is a dead-end job; consequently, the average turnover rate for help-desk engineers is 65 percent.

Microsoft, however, beats the odds. Turnover rate for technical support staff is just 7 percent, in large part because Microsoft goes to great lengths to foster organizational commitment. In hiring support engineers, it looks for people with intelligence and drive, not just technical skills. Then the company provides them with an ample amount of training that allows them to grow and feel that they're constantly learning. Microsoft

not only provides instructions about the company's products but offers training in areas such as customer satisfaction, customer relations, handling sensitive customer issues, and even communications skills such as writing or developing effective presentations.

Microsoft also offers technical support people a variety of career paths so they can see that their training is leading them somewhere. For example, there's a management path for engineers whose goal is to become managers and a technical path for those who want to specialize in one area, such as operating systems or end-user applications. A mentoring path gives engineers a chance to take on the added responsibility of helping other support staff solve problems. Other career paths are a training path and a product-preparation path. Managers play a big role in helping keep support staff committed by actively listening to them and understanding their career development concerns.[7] ∎

CONFLICTS AMONG ATTITUDES

Sometimes a person may discover that his or her attitudes conflict with one another or are not reflected in his or her behavior. For example, a person's high level of organizational commitment may conflict with that person's commitment to family members. If employees routinely work evenings and weekends, their long hours and dedication to the job may conflict with their belief that family ties are important. This can create a state of **cognitive dissonance,** a psychological discomfort that occurs when individuals recognize inconsistencies in their own attitudes and behaviors.[8] The theory of cognitive dissonance, developed by social psychologist Leon Festinger in the 1950s, says that people want to behave in accordance with their attitudes and usually will take corrective action to alleviate the dissonance and achieve balance.

In the case of working overtime, a person who feels in control of her hours might restructure her responsibilities so that she has time for both work and family. In contrast, another individual who is unable to restructure his workload might change his attitude toward his employer, reducing his organizational commitment. He might resolve his dissonance by saying he loves his children but has to work long hours because his unreasonable employer demands it.

■ PERSONALITY

In the workplace, we find people whose behavior is consistently pleasant or aggressive or stubborn in a variety of situations. To explain that behavior, we may say, "He has a pleasant personality" or "She has an aggressive personality." An individual's **personality** is the set of characteristics supporting a relatively stable pattern of behavior in response to ideas, objects, or people in the environment. Understanding an individual's personality can help managers predict how that person will act in a particular situation.

PERSONALITY TRAITS

In common usage, people think of personality in terms of traits, or relatively stable characteristics of a person. Researchers have examined thousands of traits over the years and distilled their findings into five personality factors (see

Exhibit 11.3).[9] Called the **Big Five personality factors,** they describe the degrees of extroversion, agreeableness, conscientiousness, emotional stability, and openness to experience individuals display.

1. *Extroversion.* The degree to which a person is sociable, talkative, assertive, and comfortable with interpersonal relationships

2. *Agreeableness.* The degree to which a person is able to get along with others by being good-natured, cooperative, forgiving, understanding, and trusting

3. *Conscientiousness.* The degree to which a person is focused on a few goals, thus behaving in ways that are responsible, dependable, persistent, and achievement oriented

4. *Emotional stability.* The degree to which a person is calm, enthusiastic, and secure, rather than tense, nervous, depressed, moody, or insecure

5. *Openness to experience.* The degree to which a person has a broad range of interests and is imaginative, creative, artistically sensitive, and willing to consider new ideas

As the exhibit shows, these factors represent a continuum. That is, any individual may manifest a low, moderate, or high degree of each quality. A person with an extremely high degree of agreeableness would likely be described as warm, friendly, and good natured, while one at the opposite extreme might be described as cold, rude, or hard to get along with. In general, having a moderate-to-high degree of each of the personality factors is considered desirable for a wide range of employees. In addition, certain factors may be particularly important for specific kinds of work.

When Stacey Kanzler was watching coverage of disaster relief for the flood-stricken Midwest, she was amazed to see that sandbags were filled by hand. She applied her experience in working at an earth-moving business to develop the idea for a machine that could automate the work, eventually turning the idea into a $2 million company. In the case of FUBU The Collection, its four founders showed extraordinary conscientiousness. They sought financing at over 20 banks, but none were interested in backing a company selling

cognitive dissonance
A condition in which two attitudes or a behavior and an attitude conflict

personality
The set of characteristics supporting a relatively stable pattern of behavior in response to ideas, objects, or people in the environment

Big Five personality factors
Traits that describe the degrees of extroversion, agreeableness, conscientiousness, emotional stability, and openness to experience individuals display

E x h i b i t 11.3

THE "BIG FIVE"
PERSONALITY FACTORS

A person may have a low, moderate, or high degree of each of these factors:

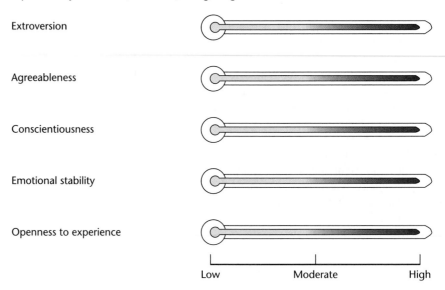

Extroversion

Agreeableness

Conscientiousness

Emotional stability

Openness to experience

Low   Moderate   High

---

urban fashions and owned by four young black men. Still they persisted, and one owner mortgaged his home. With publicity from rap artist LL Cool J, the company eventually began bringing in millions of dollars in revenues.[10]

Despite the logic and even the validity of the Big Five personality factors, they can be difficult to measure precisely. Furthermore, applying the principles in an international context cannot be done, because research has been mostly limited to subjects in the United States.

ATTITUDES AND BEHAVIORS INFLUENCED BY PERSONALITY

An individual's personality influences a wide variety of work-related attitudes and behaviors. Among those of particular interest to managers are locus of control, authoritarianism, machiavellianism, and problem-solving styles.

Locus of control defines the tendency of individuals to place the primary responsibility for their success or failure either within themselves (internally) or on outside forces (externally).[11] When people believe that their own actions strongly influence what happens to them and feel in control of their fate, they have a high *internal* locus of control. When they be-

lieve that events in their lives occur because of chance, luck, or outside people or events and may feel helpless to change things, they have a high *external* locus of control. Gail Lieberman, chief financial officer at Thomson Financial & Professional Publishing Group, exhibits an internal locus of control when she says "People have asked me, 'How did you do it? Who helped you?' And I say, 'No one ever helped me. I did it myself.'"[12]

Research shows that people with an internal locus of control are easier to motivate; are better able to handle complex information and solve problems; and are oriented toward achievement, because they view rewards as results of their own behavior and initiative. But, they are independent and therefore more difficult to lead. On the other hand, people with an external locus of control are harder to motivate; are less involved in their jobs, and are more likely to blame others when faced with a poor performance evaluation. But they are generally more compliant and conforming and therefore easier to lead).[13]

Do you believe luck plays an important role in your life, or do you feel that you control your own fate? To find out more about your locus of control, read the instructions and complete the following questionnaire.

locus of control
The tendency to place the primary responsibility for one's success or failure either within oneself (internally) or on outside forces (externally)

With no boss worries, James Oxedine has a reasonable income, a home office with a view, and a high internal locus of control. He works as a free agent, helping neighborhoods, banks, and bureaucrats get along during revitalization projects in cities such as Spartanburg, South Carolina, and Atlanta, Georgia. Oxedine believes that being independent means never being bored.

E x h i b i t   11.4

MEASURING LOCUS OF CONTROL

The questionnaire below is designed to measure locus-of-control beliefs. Researchers using this questionnaire in a recent study of college students found a mean of 51.8 for men and 52.2 for women, with a standard deviation of 6 for each. The higher your score on this questionnaire, the more you tend to believe that you are generally responsible for what happens to you; in other words, higher scores are associated with internal locus of control. Low scores are associated with external locus of control. Scoring low indicates that you tend to believe that forces beyond your control, such as powerful other people, fate, or chance, are responsible for what happens to you.

For each of these ten questions, indicate the extent to which you agree or disagree using the following scale:

1. = strongly disagree   5. = slightly agree
2. = disagree   6. = agree
3. = slightly disagree   7. = strongly agree
4. = neither disagree nor agree

_____ 1. When I get what I want, it's usually because I worked hard for it.
_____ 2. When I make plans, I am almost certain to make them work.
_____ 3. I prefer games involving some luck over games requiring pure skill.
_____ 4. I can learn almost anything if I set my mind to it.
_____ 5. My major accomplishments are entirely due to my hard work and ability.
_____ 6. I usually don't set goals, because I have a hard time following through on them.
_____ 7. Competition discourages excellence.
_____ 8. Often people get ahead just by being lucky.
_____ 9. On any sort of exam or competition, I like to know how well I do relative to everyone else.
_____ 10. It's pointless to keep working on something that's too difficult for me.

To determine your score, reverse the values you selected for questions 3, 6, 7, 8, and 10 (1 = 7, 2 = 6, 3 = 5, 4 = 4, 5 = 3, 6 = 2, 7 =1). For example, if you strongly disagreed with the statement in question 3, you would have given it a value of 1. Change this value to a 7. Reverse the scores in a similar manner for questions 6, 7, 8, and 10. Now add the point values from all ten questions together.

Your score: _____

SOURCE: Adapted from J. M. Burger, *Personality: Theory and Research* (Belmont, Calif.: Wadsworth, 1986), pp. 400–401, cited in D. Hellriegel, J. W. Slocum, Jr., and R. W. Woodman, *Organizational Behavior,* 6th ed. (St. Paul, Minn.: West, 1992), 97–100.

Authoritarianism is the belief that differences in power, and status should exist within the organization.[14] Such individuals are preoccupied with power and toughness, generally obey the authority above them, adhere to conventional values, critically judge others, and oppose the use of subjective feelings.

Machiavellianism is characterized by the tendency to focus one's attention on acquiring power and manipulating others for purely personal gain. The concept is named for Niccolo Machiavelli, a sixteenth-century politician, who wrote *The Prince,* a treatise on the "proper" acquisition and use of power.[15] High Machs (those with high machiavellian predispositions) will be pragmatic, capable of lying to achieve personal goals, more likely to win in win-lose situations, and more likely to persuade than be persuaded.[16] In contrast, Kathryn Gould, general partner of Foundation Capital, shows a low Mach tendency when she says, "I suppose I could wield that kind of power, but I choose not to. I'd rather persuade people with my powers of reasoning than dictate to them from a higher position."[17]

Problem-Solving Styles describes the different ways that people gather and evaluate information for problem solving and decision making. Psychologist Carl Jung identified four functions (see Exhibit 11.5) related to this process: (1) sensation, (2) intuition, (3) thinking, and (4) feeling.[18] According to Jung, gathering information and evaluating information are separate activities. People gather information either by sensation or intuition (but not by both simultaneously). Sensation-oriented people work with known facts and hard data and prefer a routine and orderliness in gathering information. Intuitive-oriented people look for possibilities, work less with facts, and prefer solving new problems and using abstract concepts. Those who evaluate information by thinking or feeling represent the extremes in orientation. Thinking-type individuals base their judgments on impersonal analysis and use reason and logic rather than personal values or emotional aspects of the situation. Feeling-type individuals base their judgments more on personal feelings, such as harmony, and tend to make decisions that result in approval from others.

authoritarianism
The belief that differences in power and status should exist within the organization

machiavellianism
The tendency to focus one's attention on acquiring power and manipulating others for purely personal gain

Exhibit 11.5
FOUR PROBLEM-SOLVING STYLES

Personal Style	Action Tendencies	Likely Occupations
Sensation–thinking	• Emphasizes details, facts, certainty • Is decisive, applied thinker • Focuses on short-term, realistic goals • Develops rules and regulations for judging performance	• Accounting • Production • Computer programming • Market research • Engineering
Intuitive–thinking	• Prefers dealing with theoretical or technical problems • Is creative, progressive, perceptive thinker • Focuses on possibilities using impersonal analysis • Is able to consider a number of options and problems simultaneously	• Systems design • Systems analysis • Law • Middle/Top management • Teaching business, economics
Sensation–feeling	• Shows concern for current, real-life human problems • Is pragmatic, analytical, methodical, and conscientious • Emphasizes detailed facts about people rather than tasks • Focuses on structuring organizations for the benefit of people	• Directing supervisor • Counseling • Negotiating • Selling • Interviewing
Intuitive–feeling	• Avoids specifics • Is charismatic, participative, people oriented, and helpful • Focuses on general views, broad themes, and feelings • Decentralizes decision making, develops few rules and regulations	• Public relations • Advertising • Personnel • Politics • Customer services

Mark Johannson's job at Minneapolis-based Damark International is "patching up relationships," even though his title says director of leadership and team development. Most companies don't have such a position and wouldn't even understand it. "I used to wonder what exactly does he do and why is he here?" says Kurt Larsen, who learned the answer to that question a few months after he was hired and got help from Johannson on how to get along with his boss and subordinates.

The general-merchandising catalog company has been expanding into e-commerce and is hiring an even more diverse staff, so Johannson has his work cut out for him. With a Ph.D. in psychology, he does things such as counsel the 10 top executives on how to work together with more cooperation in a more synchronized way. But he does not go looking for problems, rather he waits for people to come to him. "It works better when it is self-initiated," he says. And what he hears remains confidential, for they are his "clients."

Recently he advised a very logical manager with a sensitive assignment on how to deal with another department's manager, who happened to be more emotional. He told the logical manager to "speak the emotional manager's language so he can hear you." The session took only ten minutes, but saved a lot more than in enhanced productivity. He also advises managers to quit taking the high road and leave their egos behind. One person took five sessions on ego with Johannson to get the idea in practice, but now he is working collaboratively with people he previously didn't get along with. His techniques include listening and letting the other person come up with the solution, brainstorming possible outcomes, and role-playing.

Because people conflicts at work are inevitable, the anger that results causes employees to become distracted from their work. So he compares his role to "helping people take pebbles out of their shoes. A pebble won't disable you but it hurts and slows your gait. Once you remove it, there's a lot of relief."

SOURCE: Carol Hymowitz, "Damark's Unique Post: A Manager Who Helps Work on Relationships," *The Wall Street Journal*, Sept. 7, 1999, p. B1.

PERSON-JOB FIT

Given the wide variation among personalities and among jobs, an important responsibility of managers is to try to match employee and job characteristics so that work is done by people who are well suited to do it. Managers must be clear about what they expect employees to do and have a sense of the kinds of people who would succeed at the work to be done. The extent to which a person's ability and personality match the requirements of a job is called **person-job fit.** When hiring and leading employees, managers should try to achieve person-job fit, so that employees are more likely to contribute and be satisfied.[19] Focus on Skills box gives tips to help managers put the right people in the right jobs.

An understanding of personality also is important when managers want to change the nature of the work, because such changes may affect person-job fit. How flexible are employees? Will they be likely to voice their questions and concerns? Will the new work structure require a level of responsibility with which the employees will be comfortable? Personality does not lend itself to change. When person-job fit is poor, the manager may have to restructure tasks or replace employees. Richard Tuck knows the importance of getting the right fit, as described below.

LANDER INTERNATIONAL

CEO and founder Richard Tuck is looking for the right kind of people for his highly successful information technology company. He might place an ad for a "Juggler Extraordinaire" or seek out driftwood artisans, concert trombonists, fish biologists, or golf putting-green designers, any of whom have become valuable employees in this firm, which specializes in placing information technology auditors in high-tech firms.

Tuck believes the foundation of Lander International's success is the level of enthusiasm in the employees. He actively seeks out people who are passionate about some activity or hobby or save-the-world project; plus he wants "fun" people, those who know what makes them happy and do what it takes to pursue their dreams. Executive recruiter

person-job fit
The extent to which a person's ability and personality match the requirements of a job

FOCUS ON Skills

GETTING THE RIGHT FIT

One of the most important parts of a manager's job is getting the right person-job fit. Bruce M. Hubby, chairman and founder of Professional Dynamic Programs, is a consultant who has designed surveys to help managers determine which candidates are right for which jobs. In the past two decades, he has helped more than 5,000 companies match people to jobs, and jobs to people. Here are some of his tips:

1. PEOPLE DO BEST WHEN THEY CAN USE THEIR NATURAL STRENGTHS. Look for the strongest traits in employees and create an environment that enhances them. When people act naturally, they are the most productive; when they are forced to act against their nature, they become stressed and less productive.

2. LEARN WHICH OF THE FOUR BASIC TRAITS IS MOST PROMINENT IN A PERSON. Hubby identifies dominance, extroversion, patience, and conformity as the four basic personality traits that describe most people. Dominant people are innovative and confident, and they like to be in control. Extro-

verted people are outgoing and social. Patient people know how to pace themselves; they are focused but adaptable. Conforming people have a strong sense of right and wrong; they are structured and quality oriented. Learning which basic trait is most prevalent (and how the other three factor in) will help managers determine who is right for a job.

3. RESIST THE URGE TO HIRE SOMEONE WHO IS EXACTLY LIKE YOU. We naturally gravitate toward people who are like us, so a manager may hire someone who has the same natural strengths or personality traits, even if those strengths and traits are not right for the job.

4. RESHAPE THE JOB, NOT THE PERSON. If an employee is struggling with a job because of poor person-job fit, it's much easier to reshape the job (or move the employee to another job) than it is to reshape the employee's personality. Usually, there's no need to let that worker go.

SOURCE: David Beardsley, "These Tests Will Give You Fits," *Fast Company*, November 1998, pp. 88, 90.

Jon Landis was in a slump after a 30-year career. Tuck's advice: spend more time on his art, sculpting furniture from salvaged wood. Sure enough, it gave Landis the deep sense of fulfillment needed to restore his professional achievements.

But how does Tuck find these people? He places unusual ads in newspapers, then leaves a voice-mail message asking the person to call back and leave a two-minute message about their deepest hopes, ambitions, or fondest dreams. If the person is not threatened by all of this and ends up with an interview, Tuck is quick to be honest about himself, sharing such information as taking five-week trips to visit rollercoasters around the world.

You might think such attitudes about work and employees don't fit in an information technology company. Think otherwise. From 1993 to 1997, Lander's revenues rose from $231,000 to over $2.5 million, which is a growth rate of almost 1,000 percent.

What about employees who just don't seem to fit? Tuck tries everything to keep valuable staff. When one single mother was overstressed by her recruiter job and quit, Tuck asked her why. She said she didn't like the job, to which Tuck answered, "OK, but why does that mean you have to quit?" And they worked out another job as office manager that required less travel. She's back and thriving.

Tuck learned the hard way that having the wrong people can be disastrous. An earlier incarnation of his company went bankrupt because he was too focused on hiring people with the right credentials. It was no fun and Tuck became depressed. Seeking out therapy he learned what made him happy and vowed to run his next company on those principles. It even shows with a friend he hired who was terminally ill and not wanting to do much. "So why are you dying now?" he asked. "All of us are going to die. Why not live to the fullest until you die?" He took the job.[20] ■

■ PERCEPTION

People often approach an assignment differently because one person "sees" the assignment differently from others. "Seeing" things differently is an inevitable outcome of **perception**—the process people use to make sense out of the environment by selecting, organizing, and interpreting information from the environment. Because of individual differences in what people perceive and how they organize and interpret it, perceptions vary among people and differ from objective reality. Recognizing the difference between what is perceived and what is real is a key element in diagnosing a situation.

Perception can be thought of as a step-by-step process. First, we observe information (sensory data) from the environment through our senses: taste, smell, hear, see, and touch. Next, our mind screens the data and selects only the items that it will process further. Third, we organize the selected data into meaningful patterns for interpretation and response. Most differences in perception among people at work are related to how they select and organize sensory data.

PERCEPTUAL SELECTIVITY

We all are aware of our environment, but not everything in it is equally important to our perception of it. We tune in to some data (e.g., a familiar voice off in the distance) and tune out other data (e.g., paper shuffling next to us). People are bombarded by so much sensory data that it is impossible to process it all. The brain's solution is to run the data through a perceptual filter that retains some parts (selective attention) and eliminates others. **Perceptual selectivity** is the process by which individuals screen and select various environmental stimuli to either catch their attention or not.

CHARACTERISTICS OF THE STIMULI   The following characteristics of environmental stimuli can enhance the chance it will be selected:

* *Contrast.* A loud noise in a quiet room or bold type on a white page
* *Novelty.* New or different stimuli than were previously perceived (e.g., a woman making a presentation that typically has been performed by a man)
* *Familiarity.* Known or familiar stimuli
* *Intensity.* Stimuli that is in some way more intense (e.g., something loud or bright)
* *Motion.* Moving objects
* *Repetition.* Repeated stimuli
* *Size.* Larger objects generally receive more attention than smaller ones

Employment interviews can show the influence of stimuli characteristics on the perceptual process. In evaluating a job applicant, interviewers may notice particular characteristics that are either novel or comfortingly familiar. In addition, if a candidate repeatedly refers to some qualification, the interviewer is likely to pay more attention to that piece of information.

CHARACTERISTICS OF THE PERCEIVER   Several characteristics of the perceiver also can influence the selection of sensory data. People tend to notice stimuli that:

* Satifies their *needs and motivations*
* Coincides with their *values and beliefs*
* Reinforces and validates their *personality*
* Teaches important concepts they need to be *learning*
* Occurs near the beginning of an event, or *primacy*
* Occurs near the end of an event, or *recency*

The impact of primacy on perceptual selectivity supports the old adage that first impressions are important (as in a job interview). Primacy causes people to form impressions quickly and pay less attention to later behavior that may even contradict the first impression. Unfortunately, early impressions can lead to perceptual errors.

APPLICATIONS OF PERCEPTUAL SELECTIVITY
Perceptual selectivity is a complex filtering process that determines which sensory data will receive attention. An obvious application of the concept is advertising, in which organizations want to use the factors that enhance perception in ads that grab attention. Columbia Sportswear, for example, wanted to distinguish

perception
The process people use to make sense of the environment by selecting, organizing, and interpreting information from the environment

perceptual selectivity
The process by which individuals screen and select various environmental stimuli

itself from its competitors, which invariably advertised by showing images of their high-tech gear worn by obviously fit models. Columbia, in contrast, began running a series of ads featuring the company's chairwoman, Gert Boyle, as a "tough mother," determined that her products would meet her high standards. The ploy worked; sales soon skyrocketed.[21]

PERCEPTUAL DISTORTIONS

Errors in perceptual judgment, called **perceptual distortions,** can arise from inaccuracies in any part of the perception process. Some types of errors are so common that managers should become familiar with them. Managers who recognize the following common perceptual distortions can better adjust their perceptions to more closely match objective reality.

Stereotyping is the tendency to assign an individual to a group or broad category (e.g., female, black, elderly, white, disabled) and then to attribute widely held generalizations about the group to the individual. Because stereotyping clouds individual differences, it prevents people from truly knowing those they classify in this way. In addition, negative stereotypes can prevent talented people from advancing in an organization and fully contributing their talents to the organization's success. The following example describes a woman who started a nonprofit company to help people overcome stereotypes and transform themselves through service to others.

CRUISE WITH A CAUSE

Radiologist Dr. Juliette Engel was not in the social-betterment business; that is, until she traveled to Russia in 1990 for a conference and was transformed. Russia was a country desperately in need of basic health care. Maternity clinics were appallingly lacking in basic sanitation. One hundred-fifty abandoned children packed into small orphanage quarters, often with no shoes and little food. Villages throughout the large country (Russia has 12 time zones) were without clinics, prenatal care, doctors, or basic services. So, Engel opened a maternity

clinic in Moscow. But that was not enough.

She quit her $250,000 job later that year and found herself in the tourism business after starting MiraMed International to help support the growing number of clinics. She hired relatively inexpensive and underused Russian tourist boats and set up "Cruise with a Cause" trips. Participants pay money to go on the 12-day river cruises. They stop along the way at clinics and orphanages, where they bring suitcases of school materials, aspirin, cough syrup, toothpaste and toothbrushes, clothing, and the like.

About 70 percent of the tourists are women over 40 years old, many of whom have never traveled before. At the end of the trip, there is a deep sense of fulfillment and of having touched the lives of others. And they overcome their stereotypes about Russian life. Many of them keep in touch with the orphanages and continue to make donations. MiraMed has expanded to conducting 17 tours in other countries, including Costa Rica and Nepal and has programs where volunteers spend summers teaching orphanage staff members to establish enterprise centers and teach computer and job skills to the orphans (aged 4–17).

Engel is clear about why she helps people serve others. Not only does her work make the world a better place, but also it fills the deeper needs of the participants to bring meaning to their own lives. "People can make a difference by being there and giving back," she says. Her business is about "the power of the individual to effect change."[22] ■

The halo effect occurs when the perceiver develops an overall impression of a person or situation based on one attribute, either favorable or unfavorable. The halo effect can play a significant role in performance appraisals. One person with an outstanding attendance record may be assessed as responsible, industrious, and highly productive, while another person

perceptual distortions
Errors in perceptual judgment that arise from inaccuracies in any part of the perception process

stereotyping
The tendency to assign an individual to a group or broad category and then attribute generalizations about the group to the individual

with less-than-average attendance may be assessed as a poor performer. Either assessment may be true, but it is the manager's job to be sure the assessment is based on complete information about all job-related attributes and not just his or her preferences for good attendance.

Projection is the tendency of perceivers to see their own personal traits in other people; that is, their judgments come from projecting their own needs, feelings, values, and attitudes onto the situation or person. For example, a manager who is achievement oriented may assume that her subordinates are as well. This may cause her to restructure jobs in her department to be less routine and more challenging, without regard for the actual satisfaction of her employees. Self-awareness and empathy are the best guards against these sorts of errors. *Empathy* means being able to put yourself in someone else's shoes and to recognize the feelings of others without them having to tell you.

Perceptual defense is the tendency of perceivers to protect themselves against ideas, objects, or people that are threatening. People perceive things that are satisfying and pleasant but tend to disregard things that are disturbing and unpleasant. They create "blind spots" so that negative sensory data do not hurt them. In the early years of her career, Darlene Mann, now a venture partner with Onset Ventures in Menlo Park, California, tried to help an entrepreneur by offering advice (but not funding). She later learned that he said she was overly critical and liked telling people what was wrong with their ideas. Mann's original response was anger based on the belief that the entrepreneur would not have said that about a man. She then reevaluated her reaction and concluded that she had been mistaken to offer advice the entrepreneur did not ask for.[23] By recognizing this perceptual blind spot, she developed a clearer picture of reality.

ATTRIBUTIONS

Attributions are judgments about what caused a person's behavior—something about the person or something about the situation. An internal attribution says characteristics of the person led to the behavior ("My boss yelled at me because he's impatient and doesn't listen").

An external attribution says something about the situation caused the person's behavior ("My boss yelled at me because I missed the deadline and the customer is upset"). Attributions help people decide how to handle a situation. A person who blames the boss's yelling on the boss's personality will view the boss as the problem and might cope by avoiding the boss. In contrast, someone who blames the yelling on the situation is more likely to prevent such situations in the future.

Three factors that influence whether an attribution will be external or internal are:

1. *Distinctiveness.* When the behavior is unusual for that person (in contrast to a person who typically displays the same kind of behavior). When the behavior is distinctive, the perceiver probably will make an external attribution.

2. *Consensus.* When other people tend to respond to similar situations in the same way. A person who has observed others handle a similar situation in the same way will likely make an external attribution; that is, it will seem that the situation produces the type of behavior observed.

3. *Consistency.* When the person being observed has a history of behaving in the same way. People generally make internal attributions about consistent behavior.

In addition to these general rules, people tend to have biases that they apply when making attributions. When evaluating others, we tend to underestimate the influence of external factors and overestimate the influence of internal factors. This tendency is called the **fundamental attribution error.** For example, when someone has been promoted to chief executive officer, people generally consider the characteristics of the person that allowed him or her to achieve the promotion. In reality, however, the selection of that person may have been heavily influenced by external factors, such as business conditions that created a need for someone with a strong financial or marketing background at that particular time.

Another bias that distorts attributions involves our own behavior. People tend to overestimate the contribution of internal factors to

projection
The tendency to see one's own personal traits in other people and to allow these traits to affect one's judgment of others

perceptual defense
The tendency of perceivers to protect themselves by disregarding threatening ideas, objects, or people

attributions
Judgments about what caused a person's behavior—either characteristics of the person or of the situation

fundamental attribution error
The tendency to underestimate the influence of external factors on another's behavior and to overestimate the influence of internal factors

their successes and overestimate the contribution of external factors to their failures. This tendency, called the **self-serving bias,** means people give themselves too much credit for what they do well and give external forces too much blame for the failures.

■ LEARNING

Years of schooling have conditioned many of us to think that learning is something students do in response to teachers in a classroom. With this view, in the managerial world of time deadlines and concrete action, learning seems remote—even irrelevant. However, today's successful managers need specific knowledge and skills as well as the ability to adapt to changes in the world around them. Managers have to learn.

Learning is a change in behavior or performance that occurs as the result of experience. Experience may take the form of observing others, reading or listening to sources of information, or experiencing the consequences of one's own behavior. This important way of adapting to events is linked to perception, because learning depends on the way a person perceives sensory data.

self-serving bias
The tendency to overestimate the contribution of internal factors to one's successes and the contribution of external factors to one's failures

learning
A change in behavior or performance as a result of experience

THE LEARNING PROCESS

One model of the learning process, shown in Exhibit 11.6 depicts learning as a four-stage cycle.[24] First, a person encounters a concrete experience. This is followed by thinking and reflective observation, which lead to abstract conceptualization and, in turn, to active experimentation. The results of the experimentation generate new experiences, and the cycle repeats.

The Best Buy chain of consumer electronics superstores owes its birth to the learning process of its founder, Richard M. Schulze. In the 1960s, Schulze built a stereo store called Sound of Music into a chain of nine stores in and near St. Paul, Minnesota. However, a tornado destroyed his largest and most profitable store, so he held a massive clearance sale in the parking lot. So many shoppers descended on the lot that they caused traffic to back up for two miles. Reflecting on this experience, Schulze decided there was great demand for a store featuring large selection and low prices, backed by heavy advertising. He tried out his idea by launching his first Best Buy superstore. Today there are more than 280 Best Buy outlets, and the chain's profits have reached billions of dollars.[25]

Exhibit 11.6
EXPERIENTIAL LEARNING
CYCLE

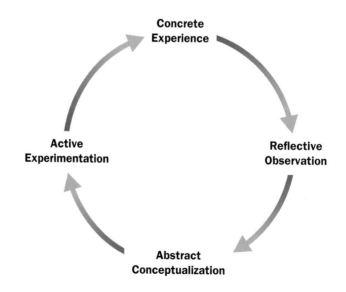

Learning Style Type	Dominant Learning Abilities	Learning Characteristics	Likely Occupations
Diverger	• Concrete experience • Reflective observation	• Is good at generating ideas, seeing a situation from multiple perspectives, and being aware of meaning and value • Tends to be interested in people, culture, and the arts	• Human resource management • Counseling • Organization development specialist
Assimilator	• Abstract conceptualization • Reflective observation	• Is good at inductive reasoning, creating theoretical models, and combining disparate observations into an integrated explanation • Tends to be less concerned with people than ideas and abstract concepts	• Research • Strategic planning
Converger	• Abstract conceptualization • Active experimentation	• Is good at decisiveness, practical application of ideas, and hypothetical deductive reasoning • Prefers dealing with technical tasks rather than interpersonal issues	• Engineering • Production
Accommodator	• Concrete experience • Active experimentation	• Is good at implementing decisions, carrying out plans, and getting involved in new experiences • Tends to be at ease with people but may be seen as impatient or pushy	• Marketing • Sales

LEARNING STYLES

Individuals develop personal learning styles that vary in terms of how much they emphasize each stage of the learning cycle. These differences occur because the learning process is directed by individual needs and goals.

To assess a person's strong and weak points as a learner in the learning cycle, questionnaires and other tools have been developed to measure the relative emphasis people place on concrete experiences, reflective observations, abstract conceptualizations, and active experimentations. Not many people have totally balanced profiles, but the key to effective learning is gaining competence in each of the four stages when needed.

Researchers have identified four fundamental learning styles (shown in Exhibit 11.7).[26] Managers can use their understanding of these styles to grasp how they approach problems and issues, what learning strengths and weaknesses they have, and how they react to employees or coworkers who have different learning styles.

CONTINUOUS LEARNING

To thrive or even to survive in today's fast-changing business climate, individuals and organizations must be continuous learners. For the individuals in the organization, continuous learning means learning from classes, reading, and talking to others, as well as looking for the lessons in life's experiences. For organizations themselves, continuous learning involves the processes and systems that enable its people to learn, share their growing knowledge, and apply it to their work. In such an organization, employees actively apply comments from customers, evaluate news about competitors, engage in training programs, and increase their knowledge in the organization's practices.

Embodying the spirit of continuous learning is Dr. Ben Carson, a respected pediatric neurosurgeon. Carson notes that the medical community has learned more about the human brain in the past two decades than it knew in total before that. He expects that pattern to repeat itself, as researchers gain knowledge at an exponential rate. This humbling realization of what he has yet to learn inspires Carson to keep his mind open to new information. When a patient improved as a result of another doctor's surgery, Carson contacts that doctor to see if he can learn anything that will help him when preparing his own surgery. He also builds on the knowledge gained from experience. For example, he found that patients were taking a long time to regain consciousness following a radical brain operation called a hemispherectomy. He evaluated the circumstances and revised how the procedure is performed so that the patient's brain stem would not be disturbed.[27]

Good managers can foster continuous learning by consciously asking employees, "What can we learn from this experience?" They can allow employees time to attend training and reflect on their experiences. They know that experience can be the best teacher, and they encourage employees to learn from mistakes, rather than foster a climate in which employees hide mistakes because they fear being punished.

■ STRESS AND STRESS MANAGEMENT

Just as organizations can support or discourage learning, many other organizational characteristics interact with individual differences to influence behavior in the organization. In every organization, these characteristics include **stress,** which is an individual's physiological/emotional response to physical or psychological demands in which uncertainty and a lack of personal control become evident and important outcomes are at stake.[28] These stimuli, called *stressors,* occur when a combination exists of frustration (perhaps caused by the inability to achieve a goal because of inadequate resources) and anxiety (a feeling of fear that heightens based on the degree of importance of the outcome).

People's responses to stressors vary according to their personality, the resources available to help them cope, and the context in which the stress occurs. Thus, a looming deadline will feel different depending on the degree to which you enjoy a challenge, the willingness of coworkers to team up and help each other succeed, and family members being understanding of your need to work extra hours.

When the level of stress is low relative to a person's coping resources, stress can be a positive force, stimulating desirable change and achievement. However, too much stress is associated with many negative consequences, including sleep disturbances, drug and alcohol abuse, headaches, ulcers, high blood pressure, and heart disease. People who are experiencing the ill effects of too much stress may withdraw from interactions with their coworkers, take time off for illnesses, and look for less stressful jobs elsewhere. They may become so irritable that they cannot work constructively with others; some employees may even explode in tantrums or violence. Clearly, too much stress is harmful to employees as well as the organization.

In biological terms, the stress response follows a pattern known as the **General Adaptation Syndrome (GAS),** a physiological response to a stressor that begins with an alarm response, continues to resistance, and will end in exhaustion when the stressor continues beyond a person's ability to cope (see Exhibit 11.8).[29]

TYPE A AND TYPE B BEHAVIOR

When researchers observed that some people seem to be more vulnerable than others to the ill effects of stress (in studies linking this to stress-related heart disease), they found two behavior patterns: (1) **Type A behavior** includes extreme competitiveness, impatience, aggressiveness, and devotion to work and (2) **Type B behavior** that exhibits less of all these behaviors. Type B people experience less conflict with others and have a more balanced, relaxed lifestyle, while Type A people tend to experience more stress-related illness.[30]

---

stress
A physiological/emotional response to physical or psychological demands in which uncertainty and a lack of personal control become evident and important outcomes are at stake

General Adaptation Syndrome (GAS)
A physiological response to a stressor that begins with an alarm response, continues to resistance, and will end in exhaustion when the stressor continues beyond a person's ability to cope

Type A behavior
Behavior pattern characterized by extreme competitiveness, impatience, aggressiveness, and devotion to work

Type B behavior
Behavior pattern that lacks every Type A characteristic and includes a more balanced, relaxed lifestyle

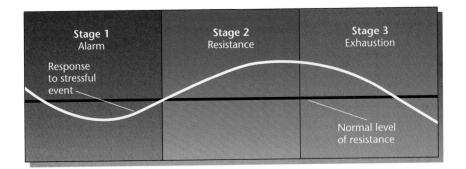

Exhibit 11.8

THE STRESS RESPONSE: GENERAL ADAPTATION SYNDROME

David L. House, chief executive of Bay Networks, exhibits many Type A characteristics. He proudly told a *Business Week* reporter that on one business trip he led seven meetings in nine hours, handled business on his car phone, and attended a dinner. At his former employer, Intel, coworkers gave him a T-shirt with the message "Captain Adrenaline," reflecting his high-energy, driven style. His drive and discipline carry over to activities outside the workplace. He schedules early-morning exercise five days a week, and his aggressive play at racquetball has reportedly caused several opponents to require stitches. House admits that his behavior has consequences and that his intense schedule is a reason for his two divorces.[31]

By pacing themselves and learning control and intelligent use of their natural high-energy tendencies, Type A individuals can be powerful forces for innovation and leadership within their organizations. However, many Type A personalities cause stress-related problems for themselves and sometimes for those around them. Type-B individuals typically live with less stress unless they are in high-stress situations. There are a number of factors that can cause stress in the workplace, even for people who are not naturally prone to high stress.

CAUSES OF WORK STRESS

Stressful jobs, to most people, are difficult, uncomfortable, exhausting, even frightening. Managers can better cope with their own stress and establish ways for the organization to help employees cope when they define the conditions that tend to produce work stress. One way to identify work stressors is to place them in four categories: demands associated with job tasks, physical conditions, roles (sets of expected behaviors), and interpersonal pressures and conflicts.

Task demands are stressors arising from the tasks required of a person holding a particular job. Some kinds of decisions are inherently stressful: those made under time pressure, those that have serious consequences, and those that must be made with incomplete information. For example, emergency room doctors are under tremendous stress as a result of the task demands of their jobs. They regularly have to make quick decisions, based on limited information, that may determine whether a patient lives or dies. Though not as extreme, other stresses can afflict managers, such as the responsibility of supervising or disciplining a large group of people, working long hours over a prolonged period of time, and unpredicted time-demands.

Physical demands are stressors associated with the work setting. An office with inadequate lighting or little privacy can cause stress, as can having to maneuver in a cramped workspace and too high or too low temperature for adequate comfort. Also, workspaces with safety and health hazards (greasy floors or polluted air) or work that involves repetitive motion (assembly line or extensive keyboard typing) may lead to injury, compounding stress in the environment.

Role demands are challenges associated with a role—that is, the set of behaviors expected of a person because of that person's position in the group. Some people encounter **role ambiguity,** in which they are uncertain about the behaviors expected of them.

role ambiguity
A stressor created by uncertainty about the behaviors expected of a person in a particular role

Although role ambiguity can be stressful, people who experience **role conflict** feel as if they are being torn apart by conflicting expectations. Role conflict occurs when an individual perceives incompatible demands from others. Managers often feel role conflict because the demands of their superiors conflict with those of the employees in their department. For example, they may be expected to support employees and provide them with opportunities to experiment and be creative, while at the same time top executives are demanding a consistent level of output that leaves little time for creativity and experimentation. In a company whose philosophy is "We're one big family," a manager who has to lay off employees would likely feel that this role conflicts with the expectation that she care about employees. These types of role conflict can create a high level of stress. Role conflict may also be experienced when a person's internalized values and beliefs collide with the expectations of others. A manager who believes in being honest and ethical in all his relationships, for instance, will experience stress when told by a superior to "fudge a little." This role conflict leaves the manager with the choice of either being disloyal to his superior or acting unethically.[32]

Interpersonal demands are stressors associated with relationships in the organization. In some cases interpersonal relationships can alleviate stress, but they also can contribute to stress when the individual feels pressure from the group. Interpersonal conflict occurs when two or more individuals perceive that their attitudes or goals are in opposition. A particularly challenging stressor is the personality clash. A personality clash occurs when two people simply cannot get along and do not see eye-to-eye on any issue. This type of conflict can be exceedingly difficult to resolve, and many managers have found that it is best to separate the two people so that they will not come easily in contact with one another.

STRESS MANAGEMENT

Organizations that want to challenge their employees and stay competitive in a fast-changing environment will never be stress-free, but they look for ways to reduce stressors and increase the coping skills of employees. They also can provide training to assist employees with stress-reducing strategies, and individuals can take the initiative to develop their knowledge and skills in stress management.

A variety of techniques help individuals manage their stress, like staying healthy: exercising regularly, getting plenty of rest, and eating a healthful diet. Organizations can support these good habits through wellness programs that, for example, provide access to nutrition counseling and exercise facilities. Relaxation and meditation also help people cope with stress. Organizations can support these stress management techniques by encouraging employees to take regular breaks and vacations. The time off is a valuable investment when it allows employees to approach their tasks with renewed energy and a fresh perspective when they return to work.

Nan K. Chase faced a challenge peculiar to business owners: taking time off for herself. Chase, a consultant and freelance writer, loved her work so much that she was neglecting her family life. She found the solution in her Jewish roots: the Sabbath, a weekly day of rest. She began organizing her time so that she could treat each Sabbath day as a minivacation, refusing even to discuss work with her husband. As a result, not only did Chase rejuvenate her family relationships, but her more focused work efforts allowed her to double her income within a year.[33]

role conflict
A stressor created by incompatible demands of different roles

Summary and Management Solution

The principles of organizational behavior describe how people as individuals and groups behave and affect the performance of the organization as a whole. Attitudes are evaluations that predispose people to behave in certain ways. Desirable work-related attitudes include job satisfaction and organizational commitment. Conflicts among attitudes create a state of cognitive dissonance, which people try to alleviate by shifting attitudes or behaviors. Personality, the set of characteristics that underlie a relatively stable pattern of behavior, contributes to shaping attitudes and behaviors. When an individual's personality and abilities match the requirements of a particular job, the individual and organization enjoy a good person-job fit.

Work-related attitudes and behaviors of particular interest to managers are locus of control, authoritarianism, machiavellianism, and problem-solving styles. Four problem-solving styles are sensation-thinking, intuitive-thinking, sensation-feeling, and intuitive-feeling. Mark Breier in the beginning case showed how Beyond.com was struggling with horrendous losses after having a successful IPO. They found that good ideas and generating enthusiasm are not enough. Those are skills exhibited by the personality types of "intuitive-thinking" and "intuitive-feeling." Also, they changed their strategy quickly and were seen as zigzagging, a common characteristic of the "openness to experience" type. One of their main problems now, "too many projects competing for resources," is also an "openness to experience" problem.

In a startup, lots of enthusiasm and broad vision are crucial, so the intuitive types are necessary. But once the business gets going and has to deal with day-to-day realities of market fluctuations, creating more efficiencies and keeping on track, then there needs to be a better balance with the sensing types, which offer more stability and detail orientation, as well as the conscientiousness, which is less prone to hasty and wild enthusiasm. Beyond.com will not survive in the long run unless it attends to its balance of personality traits and problem-solving styles.

This chapter also discussed the perception process. Individuals often make errors in perceptual judgment, called perceptual distortions. These include stereotyping, the halo effect, projection, and perceptual defense. Attributions are judgments individuals make about whether a person's behavior was caused by internal or external factors.

Learning is a change in behavior or performance that occurs as a result of experience. The learning process goes through a four-stage cycle, and individual learning styles differ. Four learning styles are Diverger, Assimilator, Converger, and Accommodator. Today's rapidly changing business environment requires a commitment to continuous learning by both individuals and organizations. Rapid changes in today's marketplace may create more than the need for ongoing learning, however. It may also create greater stress for many of today's workers. Stress is a response toward stimuli that place demands on the individual and have important outcomes. Physiologically, the stress response follows a pattern known as the General Adaptation Syndrome. The causes of work stress include task demands, physical demands, role demands, and interpersonal demands. Individuals and organizations can alleviate the negative effects of stress by engaging in a variety of techniques for stress management.

Discussion Questions

1. What are the three basic leadership skills that lie at the core of identifying and solving people problems? Why is it important for managers to develop these skills?

2. In what ways might the cognitive and affective components of attitude influence the behavior of employees who are faced with learning an entirely new set of computer-related skills in order to retain their jobs at a manufacturing facility?

3. What steps might managers at a company (about to be merged with another company) take to promote organizational commitment among employees?

4. Think about an important event in your life. Do you believe that the success or failure of the event was your responsibility (internal locus of control) or the responsibility of outside forces or people (external locus of control)? Has your belief changed since the event took

place? How does your locus of control affect the way you now view the event?

5. In the Big Five personality factors, extroversion is considered a "good" quality to have. Why might introversion be an equally positive quality?

6. Which type of problem-solving style do you prefer? Sensation-thinking, intuitive-thinking, sensation-feeling, or intuitive feeling? Describe briefly a decision you have made using this style.

7. Why is it important for managers to achieve person-job fit when they are hiring employees?

8. How might a design manager use a combination of novelty, familiarity, and repetition in the presentation

of a new product idea to the company's financial managers?

9. What characteristics of perceivers might influence the attendees of a human resources seminar on employee benefits (such as retirement planning, health care insurance, vacation, and the like)?

10. Describe a situation in which you learned how to do something—use a computer or ride a snowboard. In your description, identify the four stages of the learning cycle.

11. Do you think that a Type A person or a Type B person would be better suited to managing a health care facility? Why?

Management Exercises

Manager's Workbook

Your personality is what you are. You have similarities and differences from other people. The differences measured here are not better or worse, merely different. Complete and score the inventory below to find out your personality type.

Personality Inventory

For each item, circle either *a* or *b*. If you feel both *a* and *b* are true, decide which one is more like you, even if it is only slightly more true.

1. When making a decision, the most important considerations are
   a. rational thoughts, ideas and data.
   b. people's feelings and values.

2. When discussing a problem with colleagues, it is easy for me
   a. to see "the big picture."
   b. to grasp the specifics of the situation.

3. When I am working on an assignment, I tend to
   a. work steadily and consistently.
   b. work in bursts of energy with "down time" in between.

4. When I listen to someone talk on a subject, I usually try to
   a. relate it to my own experience and see if it fits.
   b. assess and analyze the message.

5. In work, I prefer spending a great deal of time on issues of

   a. ideas.
   b. people.

6. In meetings I am most often annoyed with people who
   a. come up with many sketchy ideas.
   b. lengthen meetings with many practical details.

7. I would rather work for an organization where
   a. my job was intellectually stimulating.
   b. I was committed to its goals and mission.

8. I would rather work for a boss who is
   a. full of new ideas.
   b. practical.

In the following, choose the word in each pair that appeals to you more:

9. *a.* social
   b. theoretical

10. *a.* ingenuity
    b. practicality

Scoring Key

Count one point for each item listed below that you circled in the inventory.

Score for S	Score for N
2b	2a
3a	3b
6a	6b
8b	8a
10b	10a

Total

Circle the one with more points: S or N

Score for T	Score for F
1a	1b
4b	4a
5a	5b
7a	7b
9b	9a

Total

Circle the one with more points: T or F

Your score is:

S or N _____   T or F _____

S = Sensation
N = Intuitive
T = Thinking
F = Feeling

(see Exhibit 11.5 on p. 364)

Manager's Workshop

Apply what you know about perceptual biases and rater errors.

Scully and Mulder have to speak with a number of informants about a UFO sighting that occurred in Flatbush, Kansas. The informants are all poor, middle-aged farmers who have little education and strong rural accents. It appears that they don't bathe very often, and they also happen to have poor dental hygiene (many in fact are missing their teeth). Listed below are a number of perceptual biases and rater errors and examples of how Scully and Mulder may be susceptible to each of them when interacting with these people or evaluating the quality of their stories. Match each of the biases with the example that best reflects that error.

	Primacy effect	Recency effect
Implicit personality theory	Projection	Stereotyping
Contrast effects	Leniency (too easy on some things)	Harshness (intensity)
Central tendency (seeing all things at same level)	Halo effect	Similar-to-me effect (familiarity)

1. At the beginning of her first interview, Scully discovers that the informant can't read and has very slow, drawn out speech, which leads her to conclude that the person is probably mentally disabled. She conducts the rest of her interview based on that assumption.

2. Scully is a Christian, and her religion is very important to her. As a result, she is very skeptical about the whole UFO phenomenon and thinks that others are as well. Her interview questions are often phrased to reflect her skepticism: "Do you think the light you saw might have been an airplane?" and "You don't really believe that what you saw was visitors from another planet, do you?"

3. Because Scully thinks that there is no such thing as UFOs, she has a tendency to invalidate the stories of all the farmers by finding flaws and inconsistencies in them.

4. Mulder has interviewed three people, all of whom fit the general description of the residents of this area. The fourth person who arrives is clean, well dressed, and very articulate. The difference is amazing and leads Mulder to put more weight on what this individual has to tell him.

5. On their way into town, Scully and Mulder nearly get into an accident with one of the local farmers. An argument ensues, and Mulder is tempted to arrest the man for obstruction of justice. When they meet later during one of the interview sessions, Mulder can't shake his negative impression of the guy and finds himself being very harsh.

6. At the conclusion of an interview that was going very well, an informant suddenly bursts into a medley of Broadway show tunes. Mulder is stunned by how nutty this person appears to be and forgets all the apparently rational things the individual has told him.

7. Because Mulder believes that UFOs are very real, he has a tendency to accept all of the stories of the farmers as being highly accurate and valid.

8. The Sheriff helped Mulder and Scully conduct the interviews. When it came time to evaluate them, however, he had a hard time distinguishing the good stories from the bad, so he classified them all as somewhat believable but flawed.

9. Scully thinks personal hygiene is extremely important; therefore, she concludes that if these people aren't very good at taking care of themselves, they are probably not very reliable as witnesses due to a lack of attention to detail.

10. One person whom Scully interviews is also a devout Christian, and she articulates many of the same concerns and skepticism that Scully has. Because of their obvious similarities, Scully is predisposed to like this woman and to believe her version of events.

11. Mulder thinks of farmers has having a strong work ethic and being very honest and forthright. Therefore, he is predisposed to believe everything that the informants tell him, even though the Sheriff has told him that one of the farmers is a known liar and a convicted criminal.

12. Mulder thinks that people who are hard working and make a lot of sacrifices are also generally honest. He therefore tends to believe the stories of the farmers who seem to be very hard working and self-sacrificing.

SOURCE: Courtney Hunt, Northern Illinois University. Used with permission.

Management in Practice: Ethical Dilemma

Should I Fudge the Numbers?

Sara MacIntosh recently joined MicroPhone, a large telecommunications company with headquarters in Denver, to take over the implementation of a massive customer service training project. The program was created by Kristin Cole, head of human resources and Sara's new boss. According to the grapevine, Kristin was hoping this project alone would give her the "star quality" she needed to earn a promotion she'd been longing for. Industry competition was heating up, and MicroPhone's strategy called for being the very best at customer service. That meant having the most highly trained people in the industry, especially those who would work directly with customers. Kristin had put together a crash team to develop the new training program, which called for an average of one full week of intense customer service training for each of 3,000 people and had a price tag in the neighborhood of $40 million. Kristin's team, made up of several staffers who already felt overwhelmed with their day-to-day workload, rushed to put the proposal together. It was scheduled to go to the board of directors next month.

Kristin knew she needed someone well qualified and dedicated to manage and implement the project, and Sara, with eight years of experience, a long list of accomplishments, and advanced degrees in finance and organizational behavior, was perfect for the job. When Sara agreed to come aboard, Kristin expressed great relief and confidence in Sara's ability to make the program work. However, during a thorough review of the proposal, Sara discovered some assumptions built into the formulas of the proposal that raised red flags. She approached Dan Sotal, the team's coordinator, about her concerns, but the more Dan tried to explain how the financial projections were derived, the more Sara realized that Kristin's proposal was seriously flawed. No matter how she tried to work them out, the most that could be squeezed out of the $40 million budget was 20 hours of training a week, not the 40 hours everyone expected for such a high price tag.

Sara knew that although the proposal had been largely developed before she came on board, it would bear her signature. As she carefully described the problems with the proposal to Kristin and outlined the potentially devastating consequences, Kristin impatiently tapped her pencil on the marble tabletop. Finally, she stood up, leaned forward, and interrupted Sara, quietly saying, "Sara, make the numbers work so that it adds up to forty hours and stays within the $40 million budget." Sara glanced up and replied, "I don't think it can be done unless we either change the number of employees who are to be trained or the cost figure. . . ." Kristin's smile froze on her face and her eyes began to snap as she again interrupted. "I don't think you understand what I'm saying. We have too much at stake here. Make the previous numbers work." Stunned, Sara belatedly began to realize that Kristin was ordering her to fudge the numbers. She felt an anxiety attack coming on as she wondered what she should do.

What Do You Do?

1. Make the previous numbers work. Kristin and the entire team have put massive amounts of time into the project and they all expect you to be a team player. You don't want to let them down. Besides, this is a great opportunity for you in a highly visible position.

2. Stick to your ethical principles and refuse to fudge the numbers. Tell Kristin you will work overtime to help develop an alternate proposal that stays within the budget by providing more training to employees who work directly with customers and fewer training hours for those who don't have direct customer contact.

3. Go to the team and tell them what you've been asked to do. If they refuse to support you, threaten to reveal the true numbers to the CEO and board members.

SOURCE: Adapted from Doug Wallace, "Fudge the Numbers or Leave," *Business Ethics,* May–June, 1996, pp. 58–59. Adapted with permission.

Surf the Net

1. *Authoritarianism.* The textbook example of authoritarianism is Carlson Companies, one of the largest privately held corporations in the United States, with operations in more than 140 countries and 147,000 people employed under its brands. Go to the corporate Web site at www.carlson.com and find information for the following items: (a) Name two brands of Carlson Companies not mentioned in the chapter. (b) Besides the fact that Curtis Carlson graduated from the University of Minnesota's School of Management, what other connection is there between the two?

2. *Perceptual Organization.* Using the keyword "perception" in your Web browser, locate interesting perceptual images. The following sites provide excellent examples. Select your favorite perceptual image; print it out, and bring it to class to contribute during a class discussion on this topic.

   valley.uml.edu/landrigan/illusion.html

   www.illusionworks.com

   www.exploratorium.edu/exhibits (NOTE: Many of the Exploratorium online exhibits at this site require plug-ins, such as Shockwave, RealAudio, or QuickTime)

3. *Learning Styles.* Many approaches exist for analyzing personal learning styles. For example, at www.hcc.hawaii. edu/intranet/committees/FacDevCom/guidebk/teachtip/lernstyle.htm, you can access a learning styles instrument that will categorize you as a visual, auditory, or tactile learner. Other sites at which you can get feedback on your learning styles are

   www.dc.peachnet.edu/

   ~jgutliph/Books/learning styles/the form.html

   www.fln.vcu.edu/Intensive/chronotope.html

   mumnt1.mid.muohio.edu/phy/inventory/invent.htm

   Choose and take an online learning styles instrument, print out the results, and submit a copy of both the instrument and the results to your instructor.

Case for Critical Analysis

Volkswagen's Ferdinand Piëch

While many of today's organizations are shifting toward more democratic, participative types of management, one is not: Volkswagen. In fact, Volkswagen's chief executive, Ferdinand Piëch, rules his realm with an iron hand. After a long executive career at such prestigious automakers as Audi and Porsche (Piëch's maternal grandfather was Ferdinand Porsche), Piëch took over as Volkswagen's CEO in 1993. He immediately centralized power in the organization, firing managers who questioned his ideas or who didn't follow his lead. He dove into engineering projects himself, proposing new projects, tinkering with designs. He presided over meetings with the demeanor of an autocrat, with the occasional result that "critical questions aren't asked, because people know things can rapidly get uncomfortable," notes one former executive.

Piëch had—and still has—a reason for ruling supreme over his company. He isn't satisfied that VW is Europe's leading mass-market auto manufacturer; he wants to turn it into the most powerful, most respected carmaker in the world. He won't settle for less. "We're trying to redefine the status game," explains Jens Neumann, a member of Volkswagen's management board and supporter of Piëch. After creating successes at both Porsche and Audi, such as the Quattro all-wheel drive, Piëch is intent on doing even more at VW. "He is the most brilliant and forward-looking CEO in the business today," claims an analyst for a major VW investor. Indeed, in the first five years at the wheel, Piëch turned around several languishing auto models, increased the company's lead in Europe, and created a comeback in the U.S. market. His most famous project perhaps is his reintroduction of the beloved VW Beetle. Despite warnings by market experts, Piëch pushed the bug ahead—redesigned so it's a little larger than its predecessor and with all the necessary technological bells and whistles—to a warm welcome from U.S. customers.

Perhaps one reason Piëch is so successful in his method of management is his extensive knowledge of and passion for the cars themselves. From his days as an automotive engineering student at Zurich's Swiss Federal Institute of Technology, through his stint at Porsche, where he helped create world-class race cars, to his development of Audi's Quattro and now the launch of the VW Beetle, Piëch has been found under the hood, tinkering. Thus, he knows his product and his customers and how to fit them together better than anyone else in the industry.

Critics charge that Piëch has too tight a hold over his company. "At VW, nothing happens without Piëch," notes a former colleague. One-person rule can result in massive mistakes. For instance, several years ago, Piëch pushed for the purchase of Rolls-Royce Motors from its parent, Vickers PLC. But in a botched deal, he lost the rights to the Rolls-Royce brand name, which actually belongs to Rolls-Royce PLC, the aerospace manufacturer. Critics also point out that Piëch's fanatical grip on VW has more to do with his personal insecurity than a philosophy of management. "He wants to prove that he has been underestimated for years," muses one former VW executive. But with Piëch in the lead, VW now is reporting over $2 billion a year in earnings, over 100 percent more than before he took the driver's seat.

Questions

1. What personality traits do you think Ferdinand Piëch exhibits? Do you think these contribute to a good person-job fit? Why or why not?

2. Hardly anyone would argue that Piëch is an authoritarian executive. Do you sense that he is machiavellian as well? Do you think these characteristics have a positive or negative impact on the way Volkswagen is run? Explain your answer.

3. Imagine that you are a manager at Volkswagen, and you are experiencing some cognitive dissonance about being asked to work long hours on one of Piëch's pet projects—a new car model whose success you have doubts about. How might you resolve your dissonance?

SOURCE: David Woodruff and Keith Naughton, "Hard-Driving Boss," *Business Week,* October 5, 1998, pp. 82–87.

Endnotes

1 George Anders, "Dot-com's Downside: Post-IPO, the Chore Is Making an Idea Pay," *Wall Street Journal,* Dec. 10, 1999, pp. A1, A10.

2 J. M. Olson and M. P. Zanna, "Attitudes and Attitude Change," *Annual Review of Psychology,* 44 (1993), pp. 117–154.

3 John A. Byrne, "Virtual Management," *Business Week,* September 21, 1998, p. 80–82.

4 C. Ostroff, "The Relationship between Satisfaction, Attitudes, and Performance: An Organizational Level Analysis," *Journal of Applied Psychology,* December 1992, pp. 963–974; and M. M. Petty, G. W. McGee.

5 Patricia Gallup, "You, Me and All Those Others Just Like Us," *State of Small Business, Inc.,* May, 1998, pp. 51–52.

6 Aaron Bernstein, "We Want You to Stay. Really," *Business Week,* June 22, 1998, pp. 67–68+.

7 John P. Mello, "Good Help Is Hard to Keep," Inside *Technology Training,* November 1998, pp. 20–22, 24.

8 For a discussion of cognitive dissonance theory, see Leon A. Festinger, *Theory of Cognitive Dissonance* (Stanford, California.: Stanford University Press, 1957).

9 See J. M. Digman, "Personality Structure: Emergence of the Five-Factor Model," *Annual Review of Psychology,* 41 (1990), pp. 417–440; M. R. Barrick and M. K. Mount, "Autonomy as a Moderator of the Relationship between the Big Five Personality Dimensions and Job Performance," *Journal of Applied Psychology,* February 1993, pp. 111–118; and J. S. Wiggins and A. L. Pincus, "Personality: Structure and Assess-

ment," *Annual Review of Psychology,* 43 (1992), pp. 473–605.

10 Debra Phillips, G. David Doran, Elaine W. Teague, and Laura Tiffany, "Young Millionaires," *Entrepreneur,* November 1998, pp. 118–126.

11 J. B. Rotter, "Generalized Expectancies for Internal versus External Control of Reinforcement," *Psychological Monographs,* 80 (609) (1966).

12 Julie C. Dalton, "More Room at the Top," *CFO,* August 1998, pp. 30–38.

13 See P. E. Spector, "Behavior in Organizations as a Function of Employee's Locus of Control," *Psychological Bulletin,* May 1982, pp. 482–497.

14 T. W. Adorno, E. Frenkel-Brunswick, D. J. Levinson, and R. N. Sanford, *The Authoritarian Personality* (New York: Harper & Row, 1950).

15 Niccolo Machiavelli, *The Prince,* trans. George Bull (Middlesex: Penguin, 1961).

16 R. G. Vleeming, "Machiavellianism: A Preliminary Review," *Psychological Reports,* February 1979, pp. 295–310.

17 Anna Muoio, "Women and Men, Work and Power," *Fast Company,* February/March 1998, pp. 71–72+.

18 Carl Jung, *Psychological Types* (London: Routledge and Kegan Paul, 1923).

19 Charles A. O'Reilly III, Jennifer Chatman, and David F. Caldwell, "People and Organizational Culture: A Profile Comparison Approach to Assessing Person-Organization Fit," *Academy of Management Journal,* 34 (3) 1991, pp. 487–516.

20 Samuel Fromartz, "The Right Staff," *Inc.,* Oct 20, 1999, pp. 125–131.

21 Stephanie Gruner, "Our Company, Ourselves," *Inc.,* April 1998, pp. 127–128.

22 "American Volunteers Bring Hope for the Future of Hundreds of Russian Orphans," *MiraMed Institute Newsletter,* Winter 2000, p. 1; Ed Fischbein, "Practicing Peaceful Medicine," *Hemispheres Magazine,* Nov. 1996, pp. 27–30.

23 Muoio, "Women and Men, Work and Power," p. 82.

24 David A. Kolb, "Management and the Learning Process," *California Management Review,* 18 (3) (Spring 1976), pp. 21–31.

25 De' Ann Weimer, "The Houdini of Consumer Electronics," *Business Week,* June 22, 1998, p. 88, 92.

26 See David A. Kolb, I. M. Rubin, and J. M. McIntyre, *Organizational Psychology: An Experimental Approach,* 3rd ed. (Englewood Cliffs, N. J.: Prentice Hall, 1984), pp. 27–54.

27 Chuck Salter, "This Is Brain Surgery," *Fast Company,* February/March 1998, pp. 147–150.

28 T. A. Beehr and R. S. Bhagat, *Human Stress and Cognition in Organizations: An Integrated Perspective* (New York: Wiley, 1985).

29 Hans Selye, *The Stress of Life* (New York: McGraw-Hill, 1976).

30 M. Friedman and R. Rosenman, *Type A Behavior and Your Heart* (New York: Knopf, 1974).

31 Andy Reinhardt, "Mr. House Finds His Fixer-Upper," *Business Week,* February 2, 1998, pp. 66–68.

32 Robert Kreitner and Angelo Kinicki, *Organizational Behavior,* 4th ed. (Boston, Mass.: Irwin/McGraw-Hill, 1998), p. 293.

33 Nan K. Chase, "The One-Day Rest Cure," *Inc.,* August 1998, p. 106.

Leadership in Organizations

LEARNING OBJECTIVES

After studying this chapter, you should be able to:

- Define leadership and explain its importance for organizations

- Identify personal characteristics associated with effective leaders

- Explain the five sources of power and how each causes different subordinate behavior

- Describe the leader behaviors of initiating structure and consideration and when they should be used

- Describe Hersey and Blanchard's situational theory and its application to subordinate participation

- Explain the path-goal model of leadership

- Explain how leadership fits the organizational situation and how organizational characteristics can substitute for leadership behaviors

- Describe transformational leadership and when it should be used

- Explain the role of leaders in learning organizations

MANAGEMENT PROBLEM

RIDING CAMELS and spending several *Chapter*

12

years in Africa and Asia working at orphanages

may not seem like ideal experiences for running an Internet company,

but Harvard MBA Gregory Slayton is not like the rest of us. After working at

McKinsey, he landed in Silicon Valley and ultimately started his own business. But the

backbreaking hours began to wreak havoc on his family. He worked late on his wife's birthday and

their anniversary, his employees were showing signs of burnout, and productivity was decreasing. He kept

telling himself, "It's going to be worth it, we're going to make millions." But he learned, "It is never worth it."

• *If you were Gregory Slayton, what would you do? How would you go about leading the failing company to success?*

After taking a six-month sabbatical, he wanted something new. With great enthusiasm, he took over

the helm at MySoftware, Inc., an Internet marketing services company. But the challenge was great. This

was a company whose revenue, gross margins, and stock price were all falling as fast as staff morale.

The senior vice president of sales, Joe Cortale, was ready to quit. Offices were located in a

nondescript strip mall. Despair hung in the air. His reaction normally would

have been to roll up his sleeves and burn the midnight oil trying

to turn around the ailing company.[1]

Gregory Slayton is a leader at one of today's thriving high-tech companies, and his leadership style may differ from another successful leader in a different situation. Contrast the leadership style of Warnaco CEO Linda Wachner with that of Jan Carlzon, president and CEO of Scandinavian Airline Systems Group (SAS). Wachner is known for her tough leadership style and "Do It Now" philosophy, which energizes the entire workforce to achieve her vision of becoming the Coca-Cola of the intimate apparel business. Carlzon, on the other hand, used caring and compassion, listening, and connecting to employees on a personal basis to turn SAS around in an era of brutal competition.[2] Carlzon and Wachner use very different leadership styles, and yet both are highly successful leaders who have helped their organizations thrive. Many styles of leadership can be effective, depending on the leader and the situation.

This chapter explores leadership, one of the most widely discussed and researched topics in management. We'll define leadership, explore the differences between a leader and a manager, and discuss the sources of leader power. We'll examine trait, behavioral, and contingency theories of leadership effectiveness, as well as new leadership styles such as transformational and charismatic approaches. A discussion of leadership for learning organizations closes the chapter.

■ THE NATURE OF LEADERSHIP

There is probably no topic more important to business success today than leadership. Three ideas about it stand out: (1) Leadership continues to evolve as the needs of organizations change; (2) Leadership occurs *among* people and involves the use of *influence;* and (3) Leadership is used to attain *goals*.[3] Influence means that the relationship among people is not passive. Moreover, influence is designed to achieve some end or goal. Thus, **leadership** is the ability to influence people toward the attainment of goals.

Leadership is reciprocal, occurring among people.[4] Leadership is a "people" activity, distinct from administrative paper shuffling or problem-solving activities. Leadership is dynamic and involves the use of power. Since not everyone is a born leader, some people have to learn to do it, as Pamela Barefoot did.

BLUE CRAB BAY CO.

What happens when the CEO of a small company does not feel like a leader? "I felt like I was in the back seat of the car and nobody was driving," says Pamela Barefoot, owner and CEO of specialty food and gift producer Blue Crab Bay Co.

From her home in 1985, Barefoot started selling gift baskets of Virginia products and saw sales go from $5,000 in her first year to $600,000 five years later. But rather than solve problems, the growth only created more. "I was scared because I didn't know what I was doing," she says. "I'd never run a company before. This company was growing so fast, and we were undercapitalized, and everything I had was on the line."

Hiring a consulting company to get her through the morass, Barefoot learned how to be a leader and keep her company successful. First, she learned to communicate, which involved writing a mission statement to describe her vision, and when she involved her employees in creating it, the results got better. Then she was taught the importance of communication during everyday work life. Barefoot now believes that once a company grows beyond five employees, everyone, especially the leader, needs to devote serious time to communication. "It seems as if every time we get upset here or something goes wrong, it's because we're not communicating. Somebody will say something and somebody else will hear it a different way," she says.

Barefoot has also learned the importance of making employees accountable, which engendered respect, built trust, and encouraged openness, integrity, and clarity of expression. Now, because of the greater sense of shared

leadership
The ability to influence people toward the attainment of goals

purpose and vision, any of her employees feels free to step in when there is a problem and tries to resolve it.

Finally, Barefoot has opened herself to learning, which she sees as vital to leaders. "In 1990, I didn't even know how to turn on a computer. I didn't know how to read a financial statement, and I'm not intimidated by that anymore."[5] ∎

LEADERSHIP VERSUS MANAGEMENT

Much has been written in recent years about the difference between management and leadership. Management and leadership are both important to organizations. Because management power comes from organizational structure, it promotes stability, order, and problem solving within the structure. Leadership power, on the other hand, comes from personal sources that are not as invested in the organization, such as personal interests, goals, and values. Leadership power promotes vision, creativity, and change in the organization. Exhibit 12.1 illustrates the difference in qualities between leaders and managers (although people can express a combination of qualities).

One of the major differences between the leader and the manager relates to their source of power and the level of compliance it engenders within followers. **Power** is the potential ability to influence the behavior of others. It represents the range of resources with which a leader can effect changes in employee behavior. Within organizations, there are typically five discernible sources of power: (1) legitimate, (2) reward, (3) coercive, (4) expert, and (5) referent.[6] Power can also come from a person's position in the organization, his/her real or perceived status, and personal characteristics.

POSITION POWER

The traditional manager's power comes from the position he or she holds within the organization, which includes the power to reward or punish subordinates to influence their behavior. Legitimate power, reward power, and coercive power are all forms of position power used by managers to change employee behavior.

power
The potential ability to influence the behavior of others

LEADER

MANAGER

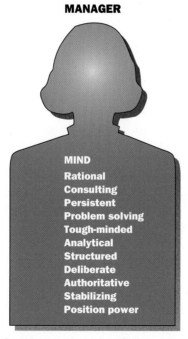

E x h i b i t **12.1**

LEADER VERSUS MANAGER
QUALITIES

SOUL
Visionary
Passionate
Creative
Flexible
Inspiring
Innovative
Courageous
Imaginative
Experimental
Initiates change
Personal power

MIND
Rational
Consulting
Persistent
Problem solving
Tough-minded
Analytical
Structured
Deliberate
Authoritative
Stabilizing
Position power

SOURCE: Genevieve Capowski, "Anatomy of a Leader: Where Are the Leaders of Tomorrow?" *Management Review*, March 1994, 12.

Legitimate power stems from a formal management position in an organization and the authority granted to it. Subordinates accept this as a legitimate source of power and comply with it.

Reward power stems from the authority to reward others. Managers can bestow formal rewards, such as pay increases or promotions, and may also use praise, attention, and recognition to influence behavior.

Coercive power is the opposite of reward power and stems from the authority to punish or to recommend punishment. Managers have coercive power when they have the right to fire or demote employees, criticize, withhold pay increases, give reprimands, make negative entries in employee files, and the like.

Different types of position power elicit different responses in followers.[7] Legitimate power and reward power are most likely to generate follower compliance. Compliance means that workers will obey orders and carry out instructions, although they may personally disagree with them and be unenthusiastic. Coercive power most often generates resistance, which may lead workers to deliberately avoid carrying out instructions or disobey orders.

Thomas C. Graham, chairman of AK Steel, is a believer in these types of position power. Unimpressed with new ideas about empowering workers, he prefers a military-style management, where cost cutting is rewarded and mistakes are quickly disciplined. His blunt views suggest that management in the steel industry has failed to push people and equipment hard enough. Graham's tough hierarchical approach has resulted in turnarounds for mills at LTV, U.S. Steel, and Washington Steel, but has also caused him to be ousted or passed over for promotion despite his successes.[8]

PERSONAL POWER

In contrast to the external sources of position power, personal power most often comes from internal sources, such as a person's special knowledge or personality characteristics. Personal power is the tool of the leader. Subordinates follow a leader because of the respect, admiration, or caring they feel for the individual and his or her ideas. Personal power is becoming increasingly important as more businesses are run by teams of workers who are less tolerant of authoritarian management.[9] Two types of personal power are expert power and referent power.

Expert power results from a leader's special knowledge or skills regarding the tasks performed by followers. When the leader is a true expert, subordinates tend to quickly go along with her recommendations.

Referent power results from leadership characteristics that command identification, respect, and admiration from subordinates who then desire to emulate the leader. When workers admire a supervisor because of the way she deals with them, the influence is based on referent power. Referent power depends on the leader's personal characteristics rather than on a formal title or position and is most visible in the area of charismatic leadership (discussed later in this chapter).

The most common follower response to expert power and referent power is *commitment*.[10] Commitment means that workers will share the leader's point of view and enthusiastically carry out instructions. Needless to say, commitment is preferred to compliance or resistance. It is particularly important when change is the desired outcome of a leader's instructions, because change carries risk or uncertainty. Commitment assists the follower in overcoming fear of change.

An example of expert power is Rachel Hubka, owner of Rachel's Bus Company (formerly Stewart Bus Company) in Chicago. When Rachel joined Stewart Bus Company as a dispatcher, she wanted to learn every job in the business. She mastered the complex routing systems, hired and trained drivers, developed and implemented a safety program, scrubbed floors, among numerous other tasks. After she bought the company, employees respected Rachel's leadership because of her intimate knowledge of the company's operations. Rachel also demonstrates referent power. She often hires people with marginal

legitimate power
Power that stems from a formal management position in an organization and the authority granted to it

reward power
Power that stems from the authority to reward others

coercive power
Power that stems from the authority to punish or recommend punishment

expert power
Power that stems from special knowledge or skills regarding the tasks performed by subordinates

referent power
Power that results from leadership characteristics that command identification, respect, and admiration from subordinates who then desire to emulate the leader

employment histories, gives them extensive training, and treats them like professionals. She is known as a great listener who is able to engage others in meaningful conversation. Rachel takes pride when employees leave her company to start their own businesses.[11]

EMPOWERMENT

A significant recent trend in corporate America is for top executives to *empower* subordinates. Fully 74 percent of executives in a survey claimed that they are more participatory, more concerned with consensus building, and more reliant on communication than in the past. Hoarding power is less common.

Empowering employees works because total power in the organization increases. Everyone has more say and hence contributes more to organizational goals. The goal of senior executives in many corporations today is not simply to wield power but also to give it away to people who can get jobs done.[12]

■ LEADERSHIP TRAITS

Early research efforts to understand leadership success focused on the leader's personal characteristics or **traits,** the distinguishing personal characteristics of a leader such as intelligence, values, and appearance. The ob-

jective was relatively simple: Find out what made people great, and select future leaders who exhibited the same traits or could be trained to. The research generally found only a weak relationship between personal traits and leader success.[13]

Additional research has studied personality traits, physical, social, and work-related characteristics. Exhibit 12.2 summarizes the physical, social, and personal leadership characteristics that have received the greatest research support.[14] However, these characteristics do not stand alone. The appropriateness of a trait or set of traits depends on the leadership situation. The same traits do not apply to every organization or situation.

Further studies have expanded the understanding of leadership to focus on the dynamics of the relationship between leaders and followers.

AUTOCRATIC VERSUS DEMOCRATIC LEADERS

An **autocratic leader** tends to centralize authority and rely on legitimate, reward, and coercive power. A **democratic leader** delegates authority to others, encourages participation, and relies on expert and referent power to influence subordinates.

Kurt Lewin and his associates were the first to study these traits at Iowa State University.[15]

traits
Distinguishing personal characteristics such as intelligence, values, and appearance

autocratic leader
A leader who tends to centralize authority and rely on legitimate, reward, and coercive power to manage subordinates

democratic leader
A leader who delegates authority to others, encourages participation, and relies on expert and referent power to manage subordinates

Exhibit 12.2
PERSONAL CHARACTERISTICS OF LEADERS

Physical characteristics	**Personality**	**Social characteristics**
Activity	Alertness	Ability to enlist cooperation
Energy	Originality, creativity	Cooperativeness
	Personal integrity, ethical conduct	Popularity, prestige
Social background	Self-confidence	Sociability, interpersonal skills
Mobility		Social participation
	Work-related characteristics	Tact, diplomacy
Intelligence and ability	Achievement drive, desire to excel	
Judgment, decisiveness	Drive for responsibility	
Knowledge	Responsibility in pursuit of goals	
Fluency of speech	Task orientation	

SOURCE: Adapted from Bernard M. Bass, *Stogdill's Handbook of Leadership,* rev. ed. (New York: Free Press, 1981), 75–76. This adaptation appeared in R. Albanese and D. D. Van Fleet, *Organizational Behavior: A Managerial Viewpoint* (Hinsdale, Ill.: The Dryden Press, 1983).

Exhibit 12.3

LEADERSHIP CONTINUUM

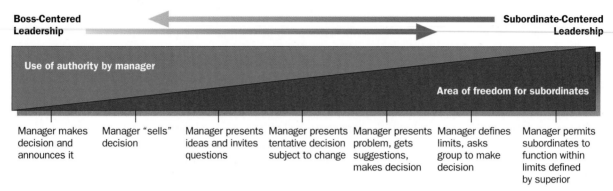

SOURCE: Reprinted by permission of *Harvard Business Review.* An exhibit from Robert Tannenbaum and Warren Schmidt, "How to Choose a Leadership Pattern" (May–June 1973). Copyright © 1973 by the president and Fellows of Harvard College, all rights reserved.

Their work compared autocratic and democratic leadership and showed that groups with autocratic leaders performed highly so long as the leader was present to supervise them, but would grow displeased with the style and allow feelings of hostility to frequently arise. Groups assigned to democratic leaders showed positive feelings rather than hostility and performed well even when the leader was absent.[16] The participative techniques and majority rule decision making characterized by democratic leadership explain why the empowerment of lower employees is a popular trend in companies today.

Later work by Tannenbaum and Schmidt indicated that leadership could be a continuum[17] reflecting different amounts of employee participation (see Exhibit 12.3) and that leaders may adjust their styles depending on the situation. Recall the Vroom-Jago model from p. 193, which assists the leader in determining the appropriate levels of subordinate participation in the decision-making process.

Tannenbaum and Schmidt suggested that the extent to which leadership is boss centered or subordinate centered depends on organizational circumstances. For example, if there is time pressure on a leader or if it takes too long for subordinates to learn how to make decisions, the leader will tend to use an autocratic style. When subordinates are able to learn decision-making skills readily, a participative style can be used. Another situational factor is the skill difference between subordinates and the leader. The greater the difference is, the more autocratic the leadership approach will be.[18]

For example, John B. McCoy built Banc One into the nation's seventh largest bank using a democratic leadership style. He let the chairmen of local banks run their own show and prided himself on having a friendly, informal relationship with employees throughout the company. However, when Banc One's profits and stock price took a sharp dive in late 1994, McCoy shifted to an autocratic style to try to get things back on track. He began issuing directives from headquarters, stripped local bank chiefs of much of their power, and toned down his gung-ho informality and bantering with employees. McCoy believes the organization's current situation demands a more autocratic style of leadership. In Technology for Tomorrow a school superintendent used participative leadership to launch a technological and educational revolution.

■ BEHAVIORAL APPROACHES

The autocratic and democratic styles suggest that it is the "behavior" of the leader rather

TECHNOLOGY FOR TOMORROW
HUNTERDON HIGH SCHOOL

According to Ray Farley, "Once you put people in charge of their own destiny and say, 'Here's where you need to go if you want to be ready for the future,' the rest just happens." Farley has turned some of the traditional power of a school superintendent over to teams of students, teachers, and parents. Now, they decide what gets taught, who gets hired, and what the school calendar looks like.

One of the most important outcomes of this participative leadership has been a technological revolution at Hunterdon High School. The school's team found a way to equip the school with PCs, video facilities, ISDN lines, fiber-optic cables—the works—for $40,000 per classroom.

Hunterdon also has a student-run FM radio station, a television studio, a telephone in every classroom, and a state-of-the-art instructional media center. Each classroom is linked to the school library, to the Internet, and to a host of other databases. The technology has led to a sort of virtual busing that links suburban, mostly white Hunterdon to four inner-city, mostly black New Jersey schools. Students at Hunterdon collaborate, for example, with their counterparts at Asbury Park to produce a poetry magazine in real time. With just a mouse-click, a teacher can drop in and participate in the teamwork going on. Now, Asbury Park is increasing its technological edge as well. According to

Dan Murphy, Asbury Park's principal, "One year ago we had two computers hooked up to the Internet. Right now, technicians are setting up 200 computers, providing them all with access. . . . And all of this is just the tip of the iceberg. It's unbelievable."

"Kids today live in a nanosecond world," Farley says. "You have to make available all the technology you can get your hands on. And then you have to do one more thing—you have to trust them."

www.hcrhs.hunterdon.k12.nj.us

SOURCE: Nicholas Morgan, "Fast Times at Hunterdon High," *Fast Company*, February/March 1998, pp. 42, 44.

---

than a personality trait that determines leadership effectiveness. Recent research has shifted from studying leader personality traits to focusing on the behaviors displayed by successful leaders, with interesting results.

OHIO STATE STUDIES

Researchers at Ohio State University surveyed hundreds of leaders to determine the many dimensions of leader behavior.[19] Two major behaviors were identified: *consideration* and *initiating structure.*

Consideration is the extent to which the leader is mindful of subordinates, respects other's ideas and feelings, and establishes mutual trust. Considerate leaders are friendly, open in their communication, focused on teamwork development, and oriented toward the welfare of subordinates.

Initiating structure is the extent to which the leader is task oriented and directs subordinate work activities toward goal attainment. Leaders with this style typically give instructions, spend time planning, emphasize deadlines, and provide explicit schedules of work activities.

Consideration and initiating structure are independent of each other, which means that a leader with a high degree of consideration may be either high or low on initiating structure. A leader may have any of four styles: (1) high initiating structure–low consideration, (2) high initiating structure–high consideration, (3) low initiating structure–low consideration, or (4) low initiating structure–high consideration. But, while the Ohio State research found that the high consideration–high initiating structure style achieved better performance and greater satisfaction than the other leader styles, the "high-high" style is not always the best in every situation.[20]

MICHIGAN STUDIES

Studies at the University of Michigan at about the same time compared the behavior of effective and ineffective supervisors.[21] The most effective supervisors were those who focused on the human needs of subordinates in order to "build effective work groups with high performance goals." The Michigan researchers used the term *employee-centered leaders* for leaders who established high performance goals and

consideration
The extent to which the leader is mindful of subordinates, respects other's ideas and feelings, and establishes mutual trust

initiating structure
The extent to which a leader is task oriented and directs a subordinate's work activities toward goal achievement

E x h i b i t 12.4

THE LEADERSHIP GRID®
FIGURE

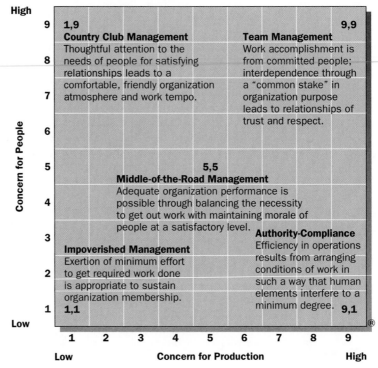

SOURCE: The Leadership Grid® Figure from Robert R. Blake and Anne Adams McCanse, *Leadership Dilemmas—Grid Solutions* (Houston: Gulf, 1991), 29. Copyright © 1991, by Scientific Methods, Inc. Reproduced by permission of the owners.

displayed supportive behavior toward subordinates. The less effective leaders were called *job-centered leaders;* these tended to be less concerned with goal achievement and human needs in favor of meeting schedules, keeping costs low, and achieving production efficiency.

THE LEADERSHIP GRID

Blake and Mouton of the University of Texas proposed a two-dimensional leadership theory of the leadership grid that builds on the work of the Ohio State and Michigan studies (see Exhibit 12.4).[22] Each axis on the grid is a 9-point scale, with 1 meaning low concern and 9 high concern.

Team management (9,9) often is considered the most effective style and is recommended for managers because organization members work together to accomplish tasks. *Country club management* (1,9) occurs when primary

emphasis is given to people rather than to work outputs. *Authority-compliance management* (9,1) occurs when efficiency in operations is the dominant orientation. *Middle-of-the-road management* (5,5) reflects a moderate amount of concern for both people and production. *Impoverished management* (1,1) means the absence of a management philosophy; managers exert little effort toward interpersonal relationships or work accomplishment.

■ CONTINGENCY APPROACHES

Developed by Fred Fiedler and his associates and incorporating the situational theory of Hersey and Blanchard, the path-goal theory presented by Evans and House, and the substitutes-for-leadership concept, several models of leadership, called **contingency approaches,** describe the relationship between leadership styles and specific situations.

contingency approaches
Models of leadership that describe the relationship between leadership styles and specific organizational situations

FIEDLER'S CONTINGENCY THEORY

The basic idea of Fiedler's contingency theory is simple: Match the leader's style with the situation most favorable for his or her success.[23] By diagnosing leadership style and the organizational situation, the correct fit can be arranged. Contingency theory expresses the extent to which the leader's style is relationship oriented or task oriented. A *relationship-oriented leader* is concerned with people, and a *task-oriented leader* is primarily motivated by task accomplishment.

Leadership style was measured with a questionnaire known as the least preferred coworker (LPC) scale. The **LPC scale** has a set of 16 bipolar adjectives along an eight-point scale. Examples of the bipolar adjectives used by Fiedler on the LPC scale follow:

open _ _ _ _ _ _ _ _ _ _ _ _ _ _ _ guarded
quarrelsome _ _ _ _ _ _ _ _ _ _ harmonious
efficient _ _ _ _ _ _ _ _ _ _ _ _ inefficient
self-assured _ _ _ _ _ _ _ _ _ _ _ hesitant
gloomy _ _ _ _ _ _ _ _ _ _ _ _ _ _ cheerful

When the leader describes the least preferred coworker using positive adjectives, he or she is considered relationship oriented; that is, a leader who cares about and is sensitive to other people's feelings. Conversely, if a leader uses negative adjectives to describe the least preferred coworker, he or she is considered task oriented; that is, a leader who sees other people in negative terms and places greater value on task activities than on people.

SITUATION   Leadership situations can be analyzed in terms of three elements: the quality of leader-member relationships, task structure, and position power.[24] Each of these elements can be described as either favorable or unfavorable for the leader.

1. *Leader-member relations* refers to group atmosphere and attitudes of the members toward and acceptance of the leader. When subordinates trust, respect, and have confidence in the leader, leader-member relations are considered good. When subordinates distrust, do not respect, and have little confidence in the leader, leader-member relations are poor.

2. *Task structure* refers to the extent to which tasks performed by the group are defined, involve specific procedures, and have clear, explicit goals. Routine, well-defined tasks, such as those of assembly line workers, have a high degree of structure. Creative, ill-defined tasks, such as research and development or strategic planning, have a low degree of task structure. When task structure is high, the situation is considered favorable to the leader; when low, the situation is less favorable.

3. *Position power* is the extent to which the leader has formal authority over subordinates. Position power is high when the leader has the power to plan and direct the work of subordinates, evaluate it, and reward or punish them. Position power is low when the leader has little authority over subordinates and cannot evaluate their work or reward them. When position power is high, the situation is considered favorable for the leader; when low, the situation is unfavorable.

One company that has good leader-member relations and is highly successful as a result, is Dollar General.

LPC scale
The "least preferred coworker" questionnaire designed to measure relationship-oriented leadership versus task-oriented leadership

Minoru Nakamura, president of the $16 billion Nissan North America, Inc., demonstrated high initiating structure–low consideration when he pushed aside five top executives and stepped in as head of Nissan's U.S. sales. Nakamura disbanded the sales department and folded it into Nissan North America. Using centralized authority, he stopped a $200 million brand advertising campaign, dropped two sporty cars from the Nissan line, trimmed customer and dealer cash incentives, and closed the Smyrna, Tennessee, Nissan factory on Fridays. Nakamura is using his leadership power in an attempt to overcome a $787 million sales loss by focusing on quality and long-term profits instead of U.S. sales volume.

DOLLAR GENERAL

Consider a retail chain located in small towns and poor urban areas. Stores are relatively small, plain, and simple, with tile floors and bright fluorescent lights, giving the feeling more of a 1950s Woolworth's or Ben Franklin than their competitor Wal-Mart. Most customers have family incomes below $25,000. Average sale is $8, and they like it that way, not wanting poor folks to spend too much in their stores.

Though this might not seem a recipe for success, Dollar General has defied conventional wisdom to become the most successful publicly held retail chain in the United States for five years running. And it's growing by a billion dollars a year. "Our strategy is to hire ordinary folks with moral integrity, give them a sense of mission, and then get out of their way. Good people in pursuit of mission need the least amount of policies and controls," owner Cal Turner, Jr. explained with the exuberance of a young boy hitting his first home run. "Values and mission are the greatest control factor for getting everyone to work towards common goals. It's the values that control them, not rules."

Turner really believes in the first sentence of the Dollar General's mission statement: "A better life for our customers." His compassion is not limited to customers. Employees are special, too. Prospective employees see a short video of Cal, Jr. describing just how Dollar General considers its workers "an honored and valued asset" of the organization. Each year the company pays out millions of dollars in employee bonuses tied to corporate performance.

Each of the 28 senior managers writes a development plan once a year and are evaluated by top management, including Turner, on their vision, their ability to work in teams to achieve their goals, and how well they know and work with their employees. If store supervisor Mary Schmidt's mother was in the hospital three months ago, the executive is expected to know the mother's name and condition.[25] ∎

CONTINGENCY THEORY Task-oriented leaders are more effective when the situation is either highly favorable (everyone gets along, the task is clear, and the leader has power) or highly unfavorable (structure and task direction is needed).

Relationship-oriented leaders perform better in situations of moderate (or intermediate) favorability because human relations skills, not the tasks, are more important in achieving high group performance. In these situations, the leader may be moderately well liked, have some power, and supervise jobs that contain some ambiguity. A leader with good interpersonal skills can create a positive group atmosphere that will improve relationships, clarify task structure, and establish position power. Fitting leader style to the situation can yield big dividends in profits and efficiency.[26]

Fiedler's research goes beyond the notion of leadership styles to show how styles fit the situation to improve organizational effectiveness. Yet, the model has been criticized. Using the LPC score as a measure of relationship- or task-oriented behavior seems simplistic, and how the model works over time is unclear. For example, if a task-oriented leader is matched with an unfavorable situation and is successful, the organizational situation is likely to improve and become more favorable to the leader. Thus, the leader might have to adjust his or her style or go to a new situation.

HERSEY AND BLANCHARD'S SITUATIONAL THEORY

The **situational theory** of leadership is an interesting extension of the leadership grid (see Exhibit 12.4). Hersey and Blanchard's improved approach focuses more attention on employee characteristics in determining appropriate leadership behavior. The point of Hersey and Blanchard is that subordinates vary in readiness level. People who are low in task readiness (i.e., too little ability or training) or are highly insecure require a different leadership style than those who are high in readiness and have good ability, skills, confidence, and willingness to work.[27]

The relationships between leader style and follower readiness are summarized in Exhibit

situational theory
A contingency approach to leadership that links the leader's behavioral style with the task readiness of subordinates

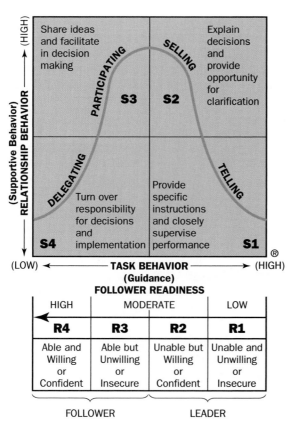

Exhibit 12.5

THE SITUATIONAL THEORY
OF LEADERSHIP

SOURCE: Paul Hersey, *Situational Selling* (Escondido, CA, Center for Leadership Studies, Inc., 1985) Copyrighted material. Used by permission. All rights reserved.

12.5. The upper part of the exhibit indicates style of leader, which is based on a combination of relationship behavior and task behavior. The bell-shaped curve is called a prescriptive curve, because it indicates when each leader style should be used. The four styles of telling (S1), selling (S2), participating (S3), and delegating (S4) depend on the readiness of followers, indicated in the lower part of the exhibit. R1 is low readiness and R4 represents high readiness. The telling style is for low-readiness subordinates, because people are unable and unwilling to take responsibility for their own task behavior. The selling and participating styles work for followers with moderate readiness, and delegating is appropriate for employees with high readiness.

This contingency model is easier to understand than Fiedler's model, but it incorporates only the characteristics of followers, not those of the situation. The leader should evaluate subordinates and adopt whichever style is needed. If one or more followers are at low levels of readiness, the leader must be very specific, telling them exactly what to do, how to do it, and when. For followers high in readiness, the leader provides a general goal and sufficient authority to do the task as the followers see fit. Leaders must carefully diagnose the readiness level of followers and then tell, sell, participate, or delegate.

PATH-GOAL THEORY

Another contingency approach to leadership is called the **path-goal theory.**[28] According to the path-goal theory, the leader's responsibility is to increase motivation in subordinates to attain personal and organizational goals. As illustrated in Exhibit 12.6, the leader increases

path-goal theory
A contingency approach to leadership specifying that the leader's responsibility is to increase a subordinate's motivation by clarifying the behaviors necessary for task accomplishment and rewards

Exhibit 12.6

LEADER ROLES IN THE PATH-GOAL MODEL

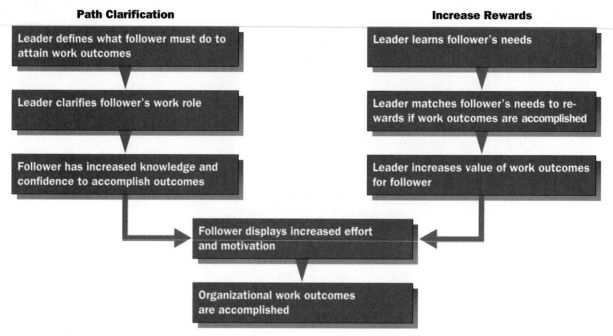

SOURCE: Based on Bernard M. Bass, "Leadership: Good, Better, Best," *Organizational Dynamics,* 13 (Winter 1985), 26–40.

subordinate's motivation by either (1) clarifying the paths to rewards or (2) increasing the rewards that the subordinate values and desires. Path clarification means that the leader helps subordinates identify and apply the behaviors that will lead to successful task accomplishment and organizational rewards. The leader's job is to increase personal payoffs to subordinates for goal attainment and to make the paths to these payoffs clear and easy to travel.[29]

Whereas the Fiedler theory described switching leaders as situations change, the path-goal theory has leaders switching their behaviors to match the situation.

LEADER BEHAVIOR The path-goal theory suggests a fourfold classification of leader behaviors.[30]

1. *Supportive leadership* is behavior that shows concern for the well-being and personal needs of subordinates. This behavior is open, friendly, and approachable, and the leader creates a team climate and treats subordinates as equals.

2. *Directive leadership* occurs when the leader directs subordinates in exactly what they are supposed to do. This behavior includes planning, making schedules, setting performance goals and behavior standards, and stressing adherence to rules and regulations.

3. *Participative leadership* applies to leaders who consult subordinates about decisions, ask for opinions and suggestions, encourage group decision making, and meet with subordinates in their workplaces.

4. *Achievement-oriented leadership* occurs when the leader sets clear and challenging goals for subordinates, stresses high-quality performance and improvement over current performance, shows confidence in subordinates, and assists them in learning how to achieve high goals.

SITUATIONAL CONTINGENCIES The two important situational contingencies in the path-goal theory are (1) the personal characteristics of group members and (2) the work environment. Personal characteristics of subordinates are similar to Hersey and Blanchard's readiness level and include such factors as ability, skills, needs, and motivations. For example, if an employee has a low level of ability or skill, the leader may need to provide additional training or coaching in order for the worker to improve performance. If a subordinate is self-centered, the leader must use rewards to motivate him or her. Subordinates who want clear direction and authority require a directive leader who will tell them exactly what to do. Craftworkers and professionals, however, may want more freedom and autonomy and work best under a participative leadership style.

The work environment contingencies include the degree of task structure, the nature of the formal authority system, and the work group itself. The task structure is similar to the same concept described in Fiedler's contingency theory; it includes the extent to which tasks are defined and have explicit job descriptions and work procedures. The formal authority system includes the amount of legitimate power used by managers and the extent to which policies and rules constrain behavior of employees. Work group characteristics are the educational level of subordinates and the quality of relationships among them.

USE OF REWARDS   As previously mentioned, the leader's responsibility is to clarify the path to rewards for subordinates or to increase the amount of rewards that enhance satisfaction and job performance. Exhibit 12.7 illustrates four examples of how leadership behavior is tailored to the situation.

Lorry Lokey, founder and president of San Francisco-based Business Wire, believes in holding on to valued employees, and he uses a participative style to understand the rewards that motivate highly skilled professionals. Business Wire was founded over 35 years ago to transmit corporate press releases to the news media, and Lokey attributes the success to highly committed long-time employees. After listening to what employees wanted, the company began (and continues) to offer a state-of-

"Nothing can quite compare with Marine Corps training and combat service to stretch your leadership skills," states Phillip Rooney, vice chairman of the building and maintenance service company, ServiceMaster. The colonel (Marine version of CEO) has absolute authority, but is trained in making "participative" decisions with the team. If a group, for instance, receives a humanitarian mission order, such as the one in the photo, the team determines the potential strengths and weaknesses, any information requirements, the targets, and key questions for clarification. The team draws the detailed mission plans and, if they are lucky, they will get a few hours sleep before they execute their plans.

the-art benefits package that helps keep his talented people from moving on.

Listening is Lokey's most important leadership skill. When one employee wanted to bring her baby to the office, he converted a spare conference room into a nursery. Today, the nursery is run like a cooperative, with parents bringing in toys and supplies and staffing it in a round-robin fashion.[31]

Using the model to specify precise relationships and make exact predictions about employee outcomes may be difficult, but the four types of leader behavior and the ideas for fitting them to situational contingencies provide a useful way for leaders to think about motivating subordinates.

SUBSTITUTES FOR LEADERSHIP

The contingency leadership approaches considered so far have focused on leader styles, subordinate natures, and situation characteristics. The final contingency approach suggests that situational variables can be so powerful that they actually substitute for or neutralize the need for leadership (see Exhibit 12.8).[32]

A **substitute** for leadership makes the leadership style unnecessary or redundant. For example, highly professional subordinates who know how to do their tasks do not need a leader who initiates structure for them and tells

substitute
A situational variable that makes a leadership style redundant or unnecessary

E x h i b i t 12.7

PATH-GOAL SITUATIONS AND PREFERRED LEADER BEHAVIORS

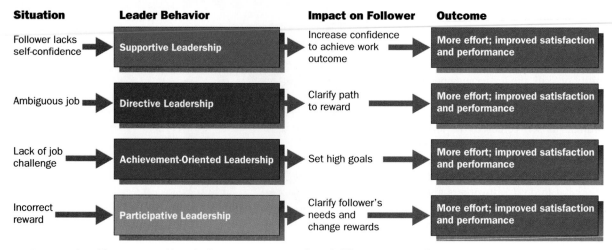

Situation	Leader Behavior	Impact on Follower	Outcome
Follower lacks self-confidence	Supportive Leadership	Increase confidence to achieve work outcome	More effort; improved satisfaction and performance
Ambiguous job	Directive Leadership	Clarify path to reward	More effort; improved satisfaction and performance
Lack of job challenge	Achievement-Oriented Leadership	Set high goals	More effort; improved satisfaction and performance
Incorrect reward	Participative Leadership	Clarify follower's needs and change rewards	More effort; improved satisfaction and performance

SOURCE: Adapted from Gary A. Yukl, *Leadership in Organizations* (Englewood Cliffs, N.J.: Prentice-Hall, 1981), 146–152.

neutralizer
A situational variable that counteracts a leadership style and prevents the leader from displaying directive behaviors

them what to do. A **neutralizer** counteracts the leadership style and prevents the leader from displaying certain behaviors. For example, if a leader has absolutely no position power or is physically removed from subordinates, the leader's ability to give directions to subordinates is greatly reduced.

The situations described in the exhibit help leaders avoid leadership overkill. Leaders should adopt a style that complements the organizational situation. For example, the work situation for bank tellers provides a high level of formalization, little flexibility, and a highly structured task. The head teller should not adopt a task-oriented style, because the organization already provides structure and direction. The head teller should concentrate on a people-oriented style.

E x h i b i t 12.8

SUBSTITUTES AND NEUTRALIZERS FOR LEADERSHIP

Variable		Task-Oriented Leadership	People-Oriented Leadership
Organizational variables:	Group cohesiveness	Substitutes for	Substitutes for
	Formalization	Substitutes for	No effect on
	Inflexibility	Neutralizes	No effect on
	Low positional power	Neutralizes	Neutralizes
	Physical separation	Neutralizes	Neutralizes
Task characteristics:	Highly structured task	Substitutes for	No effect on
	Automatic feedback	Substitutes for	No effect on
	Intrinsic satisfaction	No effect on	Substitutes for
Group characteristics:	Professionalism	Substitutes for	Substitutes for
	Training/experience	Substitutes for	No effect on
	Low value of rewards	Neutralizes	Neutralizes

■ NEW LEADERSHIP FOR LEARNING ORGANIZATIONS

Management includes the functions of leading, planning, organizing, and controlling. But recent work on leadership has begun to distinguish leadership as something more: a quality that inspires and motivates people beyond their normal levels of performance. Leadership is particularly important in companies trying to make the shift to a learning organization. Research has found that some leadership approaches are more effective than others for bringing about such change.

CHANGE LEADERSHIP

Two types of people can lead an organization through major changes and have a substantial impact on the organization. These types of leadership are best understood in comparison to transactional leadership.

The traditional management functions of a **transactional leader** are to clarify the role and task requirements of subordinates, initiate structure, provide appropriate rewards, and try to be considerate to and meet the social needs of subordinates.[33] The transactional leader's ability to satisfy subordinates may improve productivity. Transactional leaders are hardworking, tolerant, fair minded, and take pride in keeping things running smoothly and efficiently. Transactional leaders often stress the impersonal aspects of performance, such as plans, schedules, and budgets. They have a sense of commitment to the organization and conform to organizational norms and values.

The **charismatic leader** employs techniques that go beyond transactional leadership.[34] Charisma has been referred to as "a fire that ignites followers" and allows the charismatic leader to inspire and motivate people to do more than they would normally would despite perceived obstacles and personal sacrifice. Followers transcend their own self-interests for the sake of the department or organization. Such leaders tend to be less predictable than transactional leaders. They create an atmosphere of change, and they may be obsessed by visionary ideas that excite, stimu-late, and drive other people to work hard. Charismatic leaders have an emotional impact on subordinates. They stand for something, have a vision of the future, are able to communicate that vision to subordinates, and motivate them to realize it.[35] To find out if you're a charismatic leader, read Focus on Leadership.

Charismatic leaders include Mother Theresa and Martin Luther King, Jr., both positive examples, but charisma can also be used for self-serving purposes, deception, manipulation, and exploitation of others, such as with Adolf Hitler and Charles Manson, whose charismatic qualities remain strong to this day.

When charismatic leaders respond to organizational problems in terms of the needs of the entire group rather than their own emotional needs, they can have a powerful, positive influence on organizational performance.[36] Herb Kelleher, CEO of Southwest Airlines, is a contemporary example of such a business leader. Kelleher inspires his employees to break the rules, maintain their individuality, and have fun (see Kelleher Video Case in Appendix A). In general, leaders who genuinely love what they do exhibit a greater degree of charisma.

A **transformational leader** is similar to a charismatic leader, but is distinguished by a special ability to bring about innovation and change. Transformational leaders create significant change in both followers and the organization.[37] They have the ability to lead changes in the organization's mission, strategy, structure, and culture, as well as to promote innovation in products and technologies. Transformational leaders do not rely solely on tangible rules and incentives to control specific transactions with followers. They focus on intangible qualities such as vision, shared values, and ideas to build relationships, give larger meaning to diverse activities, and find common ground to enlist followers in the change process, as Corsair Communications' president did.[38]

CORSAIR COMMUNICATIONS

When Mary Ann Byrnes took over as president of Corsair Communications, she was faced with a group of complacent

---

transactional leader
A leader who clarifies a subordinate's role and task requirements, initiates structure, provides rewards, and displays consideration for subordinates

charismatic leader
A leader who has the ability to motivate subordinates to transcend their expected performance

transformational leader
A leader distinguished by a special ability to bring about innovation and change

FOCUS ON Leadership

ARE YOU A CHARISMATIC LEADER?

If you were the head of a major department in a corporation, how important would each of the following activities be to you? Answer yes or no to indicate whether you would strive to perform each activity.

1. Help subordinates clarify goals and how to reach them
2. Give people a sense of mission and overall purpose
3. Help get jobs out on time
4. Look for the new product or service opportunities
5. Use policies and procedures as guides for problem solving
6. Promote unconventional beliefs and values
7. Give monetary rewards in exchange for high performance from subordinates
8. Command respect from everyone in the department
9. Work alone to accomplish important tasks
10. Suggest new and unique ways of doing things
11. Give credit to people who do their jobs well
12. Inspire loyalty to yourself and to the organization
13. Establish procedures to help the department operate smoothly
14. Use ideas to motivate others
15. Set reasonable limits on new approaches
16. Demonstrate social nonconformity

The even-numbered items represent behaviors and activities of charismatic leaders. Charismatic leaders are personally involved in shaping ideas, goals, and direction of change. They use an intuitive approach to develop fresh ideas for old problems and seek new directions for the department or organization. The odd-numbered items are considered more traditional management activities, or what would be called transactional leadership. Managers respond to organizational problems in an impersonal way, make rational decisions, and coordinate and facilitate the work of others. If you answered yes to more even-numbered than odd-numbered items, you may be a potential charismatic leader.

SOURCES: Based on Bernard M. Bass, *Leadership and Performance beyond Expectations* (New York: Free Press, 1985); and Lawton R. Burns and Selwyn W. Becker, "Leadership and Managership," in *Health Care Management*, ed. S. Shortell and A. Kaluzny (New York: Wiley, 1986).

Co-chairmen of California Pizza Kitchen Inc. (CPK) restaurants, Rick Rosenfield and Larry Flax are leading their company through major changes. After PepsiCo Inc. bought 67 percent of CPK, the two leaders stayed on as co-CEOs, managing a Pepsi-financed expansion that tripled the company's size to 90 restaurants. When Pepsi sold its restaurant business, Rosenfield and Flax bought their chain back at a profit. Now the co-leaders are sharpening their transformational leadership skills as they execute their vision to add 15 outlets a year and introduce frozen supermarket pizzas. "We always believed we could surpass Pizza Hut [a $4.7 billion chain]," says Flax, "We still believe we will."

employees who were accustomed to working what one called a "10-percent-of-the-day kind of job." These government-contract engineers, all men, had spent most of their careers working for defense contractor TRW, which had just jettisoned them and their project. Byrnes needed to find a way to turn this uninterested group into a team of quick-thinking, fast-moving entrepreneurs. One of their technologies was useful to the military because it could identify such things as which particular Soviet submarine emitted a transmission. It also had significant commercial potential for inhibiting fraudulent cellular-telephone use, because no two cellular phones—like no two military devices—emit the same electronic fingerprint. When Byrnes was hired, Corsair already had a product (although it was far from perfected), a multimillion-dollar contract with a cellular carrier, and a group of first-rate engineers. Everything was in place to build the new business—except the glue that would hold it together.

Byrnes's first step was to visualize the kind of place she wanted Corsair to be and to instill enthusiasm throughout the company. She wanted to create a culture that communicated a sense of shared responsibility and destiny in which everyone pulled together to serve the customer and in which they would share in the success (or failure) of their collaborative efforts. She started by allowing workers to make the decisions they would have to live with. For example, Byrnes had to narrow a group of 60 engineers down to 30, so she allowed the engineers themselves to decide who would stay and who would go. Later, she let those who stayed select the new vice president of engineering. She set up cross-functional teams that work face-to-face with customers and began sharing all company information with employees. Today, Corsair is thriving, and most agree it is due to the leadership of Byrnes, who was promoted to CEO in 1999. Corsair's culture has become its major competitive weapon. By trusting her workers and not making all the decisions herself, Byrnes has created an environment that motivates the engineers and helps them to get the job done.[39] ∎

LEADING THE LEARNING ORGANIZATION

Leadership is the only means by which a company can change into a learning organization. The view of leaders who set goals, make decisions, and direct the troops reflects an individualistic approach. In learning organizations, managers learn to think in terms of "control with" rather than "control over" others. In order to control *with* others, leaders build relationships based on a shared vision and shape the culture that can help achieve it. In learning organizations, leaders help people see the whole system, facilitate teamwork, initiate change, and expand the capacity of people to shape the future.[40] Leaders in a learning organization have three distinct roles.

1. *Create a shared vision.* The shared vision is a picture of an ideal future for the organization. The vision includes what the organization will look like, performance outcomes, and underlying values. A vision may be created by the leader or with employee participation, but this purpose must be widely understood and imprinted in people's minds. The vision represents desired long-term outcomes; hence, employees are free to identify and solve problems that help achieve that vision.

2. *Design structure.* The leader puts in place an organization structure, including policies, strategies, and formats that support the learning organization. The learning organization takes advantage of horizontal relationships, including teams, task forces, and frequent meetings that involve cross-sections of employees. The structure works toward *boundarylessness*, with people reaching out to each other across departments rather than competing. The leader also helps people understand that reorganization is continuous, with people taking on new roles and learning new skills. At some learning organizations, all workers have mobile workstations because teams are continuously reorganizing as needed to

solve problems. Employees at Xerox Business Services (XBS) are constantly switching jobs and learning new skills to keep up with rapid change and growth. Chris Turner, XBS's "Chief Learning Person," says her main job is to "disturb the system" and turn the company's 15,000 workers into a community of inquirers and learners.[41]

3. *Servant leadership.* Learning organizations are built by **servant leaders** who devote themselves to others and to the organization's mission. Servant leadership operates from the premise that work exists for the development of the worker as much as the worker exists to do the work.[42] Servant leaders operate on two levels: for the fulfillment of the goals of their subordinates and needs and for the realization of the larger purpose or mission of their organization. Servant leaders give things away—power, ideas, information, recognition, credit for accomplishments—and truly value other people. They encourage participation, share power, enhance the self-worth of others, and unleash people's creativity, full commitment, and natural impulse to learn.[43] Frances Hesselbein, former CEO of the Girl Scouts, exhibits many of the qualities of a servant leader, as seen in The Girl Scout Way example. Servant leaders bring the follower's higher motives to the work and connect them to the organizational mission and goals. They are devoted to building the organization rather than acquiring things for themselves. The leader who wants to be a single actor, a hero seeking personal recognition and resources, cannot build a learning organization.

THE GIRL SCOUT WAY

Frances Hesselbein currently runs the Drucker Foundation, a small organization dedicated to sharing the leadership thinking of Peter Drucker. But she got her start more than 40 years ago as a volunteer Scout leader. She eventually rose to CEO of the Girl Scouts, inheriting a troubled organization of 680,000 people, only one percent of whom were paid employees. By the time she retired in 1990, Hesselbein had turned around declining membership, dramatically increased participation by minorities, and replaced a brittle hierarchy with one of the most vibrant organizations in the nonprofit or business world.

How did she do it? By developing a leadership philosophy that emphasizes helping other people meet their needs. Hesselbein describes how she works with others as a circle in which everyone is included. Business and nonprofit leaders learn from Hesselbein's leadership style. George Sparks, manager of Hewlett-Packard's measuring-equipment business, says the time he spent following Hesselbein around was the best two days of his career. As Sparks observed Hesselbein in action, he noted her ability to sense people's needs on an emotional level. Hesselbein listens carefully and then links people with matching needs and skills so that their personal needs are met at the same time they are serving the needs of the organization. She recognizes that the only way to achieve high performance is through the work of others, and she consistently treats people with care and respect. Hesselbein doesn't believe in forcing change on others. She draws her power from moral values, not from her position. For example, when she proposed that five-year-old girls from single-parent households be included as Girl Scout members (the minimum age was six), most of the councils opposed the plan. Even though the change was important because it would expand the reach of the Girl Scouts into the minority community, Hesselbein didn't impose the change. She began working with the few councils who agreed with her and let the others continue their own way. Within a year, two-thirds of the councils had adopted the new age limit.

Hesselbein says her definition of leadership was "very hard to arrive at, very painful. . . . [It] is not a basket of tricks or skills. It is the quality and character and courage of the person who is the leader. Its a matter of ethics and moral

servant leaders
Leaders who work to fulfill the needs and goals of subordinates, as well as to achieve the organization's larger mission

compass, the willingness to remain highly vulnerable." To Frances Hesselbein, leadership means serving others, helping employees meet their personal needs at the same time they serve the organization.[44] ■

Summary and Management Solution

This chapter covered the early research on leadership that focused on personal traits such as intelligence, energy, and appearance. Later, the focus of research shifted to leadership behaviors that are appropriate to the organizational situation. Behavioral approaches dominated the early work in this area; consideration and initiating structure were suggested as behaviors that lead work groups toward high performance. The Ohio State and Michigan approaches and the managerial grid are in this category. Contingency approaches include Fiedler's theory, Hersey and Blanchard's situational theory, the path-goal model, and the substitutes-for-leadership concept.

Leadership concepts have evolved from the transactional approach to charismatic and transformational leadership behaviors. Charismatic leadership is the ability to articulate a vision and motivate followers to make it a reality. Transformational leadership extends charismatic qualities to guide and foster dramatic organizational change. Leadership is particularly important in companies trying to make the shift to a learning organization. Leaders in learning organizations have three distinct roles: to create a shared vision; to design an appropriate horizontal structure to help achieve the vision; and to act as servant leaders. Servant leadership facilitates the growth, goals, and empowerment of followers first in order to liberate their best qualities in pursuing organizational goals.

Recall the case at the beginning of the chapter where Gregory Slayton took over the ailing MySoftware, Inc., whose vice president of sales was ready to quit. In a previous leadership role, Slayton overworked to the extent it was hurting his family life and was creating workers with severe burnout. So, this time he knew the answer lay elsewhere. He reasoned that when you own something, you take better care of it. So he made everyone, even the workers on the loading dock, significant shareholders. The vice president was so impressed, he decided to stay. Once the workers were owners, they started making serious improvements. Dock workers were among the first to initiate cost-saving practices, and Slayton turned over the budgeting process to department heads, making them responsible for profits and losses. He sees himself as an implementer whose successes come from new ideas developed by the employees he has encouraged. The ability to forge trusting relationships has been a key ingredient in the company's turnaround. And, he now discourages backbreaking hours, realizing burned out employees are less productive and often leave behind wrecked marriages and troubled children. Slayton has learned some important lessons as a leader and has turned an ailing company into one that is profitable in the process.

Discussion Questions

1. Rob Martin became manager of a forklift assembly plant and believed in participative management, even when one supervisor used Rob's delegation to replace two competent line managers with his own friends. What would you say to Rob about his leadership style in this situation?

2. Suggest some personal traits that you believe would be useful to a leader. Are these traits more valuable in some situations than in others?

3. What is the difference between trait theories and behavioral theories of leadership?

4. Suggest the sources of power that would be available to a leader of a student government organization. To be effective, should student leaders keep power to themselves or delegate power to other students?

5. Would you prefer working for a leader who has a consideration or an initiating-structure leadership style? Discuss the reasons for your answer.

6. Consider Fiedler's theory. How often do very favorable, intermediate, or very unfavorable situations occur in real life? Discuss.

7. What is transformational leadership? Differentiate between transformational leadership and transactional leadership. Give an example of each.

8. Some experts believe that leadership is more important than ever in a learning organization. Do you agree? Explain.

9. What is meant by "servant leadership"? Have you ever known a servant leader? Discuss.

10. Do you think leadership style is fixed and unchangeable for a leader or flexible and adaptable? Discuss.

11. Consider the leadership position of a senior partner in a law firm. What task, subordinate, and organizational factors might serve as substitutes for leadership in this situation?

Management Exercises

Manager's Workbook

T–P Leadership Questionnaire: An Assessment of Style

Some leaders deal with general directions, leaving details to subordinates. Other leaders focus on specific details with the expectation that subordinates will carry out orders. Depending on the situation, both approaches may be effective. The important issue is the ability to identify relevant dimensions of the situation and behave accordingly. Through this questionnaire, you can identify your relative emphasis on two dimensions of leadership: task orientation (T) and people orientation (P). These are not opposite approaches, and an individual can rate high or low on either or both.

Directions: The following items describe aspects of leadership behavior. Respond to each item according to the way you would most likely act if you were the leader of a work group. Circle whether you would most likely behave in the described way: always (A), frequently (F), occasionally (O), seldom (S), or never (N).

_____ 1. I would most likely act as the spokesperson of the group.   A F O S N

_____ 2. I would encourage overtime work.   A F O S N

_____ 3. I would allow members complete freedom in their work.   A F O S N

_____ 4. I would encourage the use of uniform procedures.   A F O S N

_____ 5. I would permit members to use their own judgment in solving problems.   A F O S N

_____ 6. I would stress being ahead of competing groups.   A F O S N

_____ 7. I would speak as a representative of the group.   A F O S N

_____ 8. I would needle members for greater effort.   A F O S N

_____ 9. I would try out my ideas in the group.   A F O S N

_____10. I would let members do their work the way they think best.   A F O S N

_____11. I would be working hard for a promotion.   A F O S N

_____12. I would tolerate postponement and uncertainty.   A F O S N

_____13. I would speak for the group if there were visitors present.   A F O S N

_____14. I would keep the work moving at a rapid pace.   A F O S N

_____15. I would turn the members loose on a job and let them go to it.   A F O S N

_____**16.** I would settle conflicts when they occur in the group.   A   F   O   S   N

_____**17.** I would get swamped by details.   A   F   O   S   N

_____**18.** I would represent the group at outside meetings.   A   F   O   S   N

_____**19.** I would be reluctant to allow the members any freedom of action.   A   F   O   S   N

_____**20.** I would decide what should be done and how it should be done.   A   F   O   S   N

_____**21.** I would push for increased production.   A   F   O   S   N

_____**22.** I would let some members have authority which I could keep.   A   F   O   S   N

_____**23.** Things would usually turn out as I had predicted.   A   F   O   S   N

_____**24.** I would allow the group a high degree of initiative.   A   F   O   S   N

_____**25.** I would assign group members to particular tasks.   A   F   O   S   N

_____**26.** I would be willing to make changes.   A   F   O   S   N

_____**27.** I would ask the members to work harder.   A   F   O   S   N

_____**28.** I would trust the group members to exercise good judgment.   A   F   O   S   N

_____**29.** I would schedule the work to be done.   A   F   O   S   N

_____**30.** I would refuse to explain my actions.   A   F   O   S   N

_____**31.** I would persuade others that my ideas are to their advantage.   A   F   O   S   N

_____**32.** I would permit the group to set its own pace.   A   F   O   S   N

_____**33.** I would urge the group to beat its previous record.   A   F   O   S   N

_____**34.** I would act without consulting the group.   A   F   O   S   N

_____**35.** I would ask that group members follow standard rules and regulations.   A   F   O   S   N

T _____ P_____

The T–P Leadership Questionnaire is scored as follows:

a. Circle the item number for items 8, 12, 17, 18, 19, 30, 34, and 35.

b. Write the number 1 in front of a circled item number if you responded S (seldom) or N (never) to that item.

c. Also write a number 1 in front of item numbers not circled if you responded A (always) or F (frequently).

d. Circle the number 1s that you have written in front of the following items: 3, 5, 8, 10, 15, 18, 19, 22, 24, 26, 28, 30, 32, 34, and 35.

e. Count the circled number 1s. This is your score for concern for people. Record the score in the blank following the letter P at the end of the questionnaire.

f. Count uncircled number 1s. This is your score for concern for task. Record this number in the blank following the letter T.

SOURCE: The T–P Leadership Questionnaire was adapted by J. B. Ritchie and P. Thompson in *Organization and People* (New York: West, 1984). Copyright 1969 by the American Educational Research Association. Adapted by permission of the publisher.

Manager's Workshop

Developing Meeting Leadership Roles

1. Divide the class into groups of six to eight students. Each group develops a list of desirable ("Do") and undesirable ("Do Not") behavioral roles for leading a meeting.

To run an effective meeting a leader must:

Do the following	Do not do the following

2. Each group develops a plan of action for a convenience store that is continually plagued by random cash drawer shortages.

   A participant from each group is selected to serve as the group meeting leader for each group during the decision making process to develop the action plans.

Plan of Action:

   a.

   b.

   c.

   d.

   e.

   f.

3. After 10 minutes, the group leader describes what it was like to serve as group leader. The group then provides feedback to the group leader, using the previously developed list of "Do" and "Do Not" group leadership roles.

4. Next, a new leader is selected to continue the development of the action plan. After 5 minutes, the steps described in step 3 are repeated for the new leader. This process continues until each group participant has had an opportunity to serve as group leader.

Discussion Questions

1. What is the difference between listing a desirable behavior and exhibiting it?

2. How can leaders learn to be more effective?

SOURCE: Adapted by Dorothy Marcic from Gerald Klein, Meeting Leadership. *Journal of Management Education*, Vol. 18 (3), 1994, pp. 375–379.

Management in Practice: Ethical Dilemma

Does Wage Reform Start at the Top?

Paula Smith has just been offered the opportunity of a lifetime. The chairman of the board of Resitronic Corporation has just called to ask her to take the job as director of the troubled audio equipment manufacturing subsidiary. The first question Smith asked was "Will the board give me the autonomy to turn this company around?" The answer was yes. Resitronic's problems were so severe that the board was desperate for change and ready to give Smith whatever it took to save the company.

Smith knows that cost cutting is the first place she needs to focus. Labor expenses are too high, and product quality and production times are below industry standards. She sees that labor and management at Resitronic are two armed camps, but she needs cooperation at all levels to achieve a turnaround. Smith is energized. She knows she finally has the autonomy to try out her theories about an empowered workforce. Smith knows she must ask managers and workers to take a serious pay cut, with the promise of incentives to share in any improvements they might make. She also knows that everyone will be looking at her own salary as an indication of whether she walks her talk.

Smith is torn. She realizes she faces a year or two of complete hell, with long hours, little time for her family or outside interests, bitter resistance in subordinates, and no guarantees of success. Even if she comes in at the current director's salary, she will be taking a cut in pay. But if she takes a bigger cut coming in, with the promise of bonuses and stock options tied to her own performance, she sends a strong message to the entire subsidiary that they rise or fall together. She wonders what might happen if she fails. Many influences on the audio equipment subsidiary are beyond her control. Resitronic itself is in trouble. From her current vantage point, Smith believes she can turn things around, but what will she discover when she gets inside? What if the board undercuts her? Doesn't she owe it to herself and her family to be compensated at the highest possible level for the stress and risk they will be enduring? Can she afford to risk her own security to send a message of commitment to the plan she is asking others to follow?

What Do You Do?

1. Take the same salary as the current director for one year. Circulate the information that although you are taking a cut to come to Resitronic, you are confident that you can make a difference. Build in pay incentive bonuses for the following years if the subsidiary succeeds.

2. Take a bigger cut in pay with generous incentive bonuses. Ask the board and the entire workforce to do the same. Open the books and let the whole company know exactly where they stand.

3. Ask for the same salary you are making now. You know you are going to be worth it, and you don't want to ask your family to suffer monetarily as well as in their quality of life during this transition.

Surf the Net

1. *Leadership Style.* Test your leadership style with a questionnaire available at www.leaderx.com. After you complete the assessment, select the "Submit to Tabulate Your Score" button, and receive a customized report on your leadership style. Print out your report so that you may evaluate it. Write a one- to two-paragraph statement regarding what you agree/disagree with in the report, whether anything surprised you in the report, and what you've learned from the report. Submit both the printout and your comments to your instructor.

2. *Leadership Training.* As stated at its Web site, Ninth House Network www.ninthhouse.com is the "only online learning network, Ninth House delivers personalized, interactive strategic business skills training to the desktop on demand." Further, Ninth House Network was "established to offer companies an innovative, entertaining, and cost-effective way for employees to develop business skills that will enable them to perform their jobs with greater confidence, competence, and efficiency." Through an innovative combination of proven training techniques, captivating storytelling, and universally adopted technology, the Ninth House Network provides business skills learning in areas that corporations consider most critical to their success, including leadership, communication, the basics of good business, managing, team building and project management. Download and watch the nearly three-minute video at this Web site (video player instructions are provided at the Web site) to become familiar with this leadership training tool.

3. *Leadership Research.* The Leadership-Development Web site offers insight and information on leadership for executives, CEOs, and other leaders. Visit the site at www.leadership-development.com, select a leadership topic of interest to you, and print out the information you can use during a small-group discussion of your topic.

4. *Leader Attitudes and Values.* Management General's site, www.mgeneral.com, has many "ezzays" by leaders. Find five "ezzays" that express varying points of view and write a report on what those leaders' attitudes, values, and behaviors are. Be prepared to discuss them in a small group in class.

Case for Critical Analysis

DGL International

When DGL International, a manufacturer of refinery equipment, brought in John Terrill to manage its Technical Services division, company executives informed him of the urgent situation. Technical Services, with 20 engineers, was the highest-paid, best-educated, and least-productive division in the company. The instructions to Terill: Turn it around. Terrill called a meeting of the engineers. He showed great concern for their personal welfare and asked point blank: "What's the problem? Why can't we produce? Why does this division have such turnover?"

Without hesitation, employees launched a hail of complaints. "I was hired as an engineer, not a pencil pusher." "We spend over half our time writing asinine reports in triplicate for top management, and no one reads the reports."

After a two-hour discussion, Terrill concluded he had to get top management off the backs of the engineers. He promised the engineers, "My job is to stay out of your way so you can do your work, and I'll try to keep top management off your backs too." He called for the day's reports and issued an order effective immediately that the originals be turned in daily to his office rather than mailed to headquarters. For three weeks, technical reports piled up on his desk. By month's end, the stack was nearly three feet high. During that time no one called for the reports. When other managers entered his office and saw the stack, they usually asked, "What's all this?" Terrill answered, "Technical reports." No one asked to read them.

Finally, at month's end, a secretary from finance called and asked for the monthly travel and expense report. Terrill responded, "Meet me in the president's office tomorrow morning."

The next morning the engineers cheered as Terrill walked through the department pushing a cart loaded with the enormous stack of reports. They knew the showdown had come.

Terrill entered the president's office and placed the stack of reports on his desk. The president and the other senior executives looked bewildered.

"This," Terrill announced, "is the reason for the lack of productivity in the Technical Services division. These are the reports you people require every month. The fact that they sat on my desk all month shows that no one reads this material. I suggest that the engineers' time could be used in a more productive manner, and that one brief monthly report from my office will satisfy the needs of other departments."

Questions

1. What leadership style did John Terrill use? What do you think was his primary source of power?

2. Based on the Hersey-Blanchard theory, should Terrill have been less participative? Should he have initiated more task structure for the engineers? Explain.

3. What leadership approach would you have taken in this situation?

Endnotes

1 Hal Lancaster, "Silicon Valley Hybrid: A Boss Who Makes Others' Ideas Pay Off," *The Wall Street Journal*, October 26, 1999, p. B1.

2 Charles Pappas, "The Top 20 Best-Paid Women in Corporate America," *Working Woman*, February 1998, pp. 26–39.

3 Gary Yukl, "Managerial Leadership: A Review of Theory and Research," *Journal of Management*, 15 (1989), pp. 251–289.

4 James M. Kouzes and Barry Z. Posner, "The Credibility Factor: What Followers Expect from Their Leaders," *Management Review*, January 1990, pp. 29–33.

5 Michael Barrier, "Leadership Skills Employees Respect," *Nation's Business*, January 1999, pp. 28–30.

6 J. R. P. French, Jr., and B. Raven, "The Bases of Social Power," in *Group Dynamics*, ed. D. Cartwright and Alvin F. Zander (Evanston, Ill.: Row, Peterson, 1960), pp. 607–623.

7 G. A. Yukl and T. Taber, "The Effective Use of Managerial Power," *Personnel* (March–April 1983), pp. 37–44.

8 Erle Norton, "Chairman of AK Steel Tries to Shake Off Tag of 'Operating Man,'" *The Wall Street Journal*, November 25, 1994, pp. A1, A5.

9 Jay A. Conger, "The Necessary Art of Persuasion," *Harvard Business Review,* May–June 1998, pp. 84–95.

10 Yukl and Taber, "The Effective Use of Managerial Power."

11 Michael E. McGill and John W. Slocum, Jr., "A Little Leadership, Please?" *Organizational Dynamics,* Winter 1998, pp. 39–49.

12 Thomas A. Stewart, "New Ways to Exercise Power," *Fortune,* November 6, 1989.

13 G. A. Yukl, *Leadership in Organizations* (Englewood Cliffs, N.J.: Prentice-Hall, 1981); and S. C. Kohs and K. W. Irle, "Prophesying Army Promotion," *Journal of Applied Psychology* 4 (1920), pp. 73–87.

14 R. Albanese and D. D. Van Fleet, *Organizational Behavior: A Managerial Viewpoint* (Hinsdale, Ill.: The Dryden Press, 1983).

15 K. Lewin, "Field Theory and Experiment in Social Psychology: Concepts and Methods," *American Journal of Sociology,* 44 (1939), pp. 868–896.

16 R. K. White and R. Lippitt, *Autocracy and Democracy: An Experimental Inquiry* (New York: Harper, 1960).

17 R. Tannenbaum and W. H. Schmidt, "How to Choose a Leadership Pattern," *Harvard Business Review,* 36 (1958), pp. 95–101.

18 F. A. Heller and G. A. Yukl, "Participation, Managerial Decision Making and Situational Variables," *Organizational Behavior and Human Performance,* 4 (1969), pp. 227–241.

19 C. A. Schriesheim and B. J. Bird, "Contributions of the Ohio State Studies to the Field of Leadership," *Journal of Management,* 5 (1979), pp. 135–145.

20 P. C. Nystrom, "Managers and the High-High Leader Myth," *Academy of Management Journal,* 21 (1978), pp. 325–331.

21 R. Likert, "From Production- and Employee-Centeredness to Systems 1–4," *Journal of Management,* 5 (1979), pp. 147–156.

22 Robert R. Blake and Jane S. Mouton, *The Managerial Grid III* (Houston: Gulf, 1985).

23 Fred E. Fiedler, *A Theory of Leadership Effectiveness* (New York: McGraw-Hill, 1967).

24 Fred E. Fiedler and M. M. Chemers, *Leadership and Effective Management* (Glenview, Ill.: Scott, Foresman, 1974).

25 Robert Berner, "Penny Pinchers Propel a Retail Star." *Wall Street Journal,* March 20, 1998, p. B6; C. Frederic Wiegold, "Shareholder Scorecard: The Quest for Shareholder Value." *Wall Street Journal,* Feb. 26, 1998, pp. R1–R17.

26 F. E. Fiedler, M. M. Chemers, and L. Mahar, *Improving Leadership Effectiveness: The Leader Match Concept* (New York: Wiley, 1976).

27 Paul Hersey and Kenneth H. Blanchard, *Management of Organizational Behavior: Utilizing Human Resources,* 4th ed. (Englewood Cliffs, N.J.: Prentice-Hall, 1982).

28 M. G. Evans, "The Effects of Supervisory Behavior on the Path-Goal Relationship," *Organizational Behavior and Human Performance,* 5 (1970), pp. 277–298.

29 Robert J. House, "A Path-Goal Theory of Leader Effectiveness," *Administrative Science Quarterly,* 16 (1971), pp. 321–338.

30 Robert J. House and Terrence R. Mitchell, "Path-Goal Theory of Leadership," *Journal of Contemporary Business,* (Autumn 1974), pp. 81–97.

31 Jill Andresky Fraser, "'Tis Better to Give and Receive," *Inc.,* February, 1995, pp. 84–90.

32 Jon P. Howell and Peter W. Dorfman, "Leadership and Substitutes for Leadership among Professional and Nonprofessional Workers," *Journal of Applied Behavioral Science,* 22 (1986), pp. 29–46.

33 The terms transactional and transformational come from James M. Burns, *Leadership* (New York: Harper & Row, 1978); and Bernard M. Bass, "Leadership: Good, Better,

Best," *Organizational Dynamics,* 13 (Winter 1985), pp. 26–40.

34 Katherine J. Klein and Robert J. House, "On Fire: Charismatic Leadership and Levels of Analysis," *Leadership Quarterly,* 6 (2) (1995), pp. 183–198.

35 Robert J. House, "Research Contrasting the Behavior and Effects of Reputed Charismatic vs. Reputed Non-Charismatic Leaders" (paper presented as part of a symposium, "Charismatic Leadership: Theory and Evidence," Academy of Management, San Diego, 1985).

36 Jennifer O'Connor, Michael D. Mumford, Timothy C. Clifton, Theodore L. Gessner, and Mary Shane Connelly, "Charismatic Leaders and Destructiveness: A Historiometric Study," *Leadership Quarterly,* 6 (4) (1995), pp. 529–555.

37 Badrinarayan Shankar Pawar and Kenneth K. Eastman, "The Nature and Implications of Contextual Influences on Transformational Leadership: A Conceptual Examination," *Academy of Management Review,* 22 (1) (1997), pp. 80–109.

38 Richard L. Daft and Robert H. Lengel, *Fusion Leadership: Unlocking the Subtle Forces That Change People and Organizations* (San Francisco: Berrett-Koehler, 1998).

39 "Corsair Communications," *Wall Street Journal,* Feb. 25, 1999; Alessandra Bianchi, "Mission Improbable," *Inc.* September 1996, pp. 69–75.

40 Peter M. Senge, "The Leader's New Work: Building Learning Organizations," *Sloan Management Review* (Fall 1990), pp. 7–22.

41 Scott Kirsner, "Every Day, It's a New Place," *Fast Company,* April–May 1998, pp. 130–134.

42 Daft and Lengel, *Fusion Leadership.*

43 Senge, "The Leader's New Work."

44 Stratford Sherman, "How Tomorrow's Best Leaders Are Learning Their Stuff," *Fortune,* September 27, 1995, pp. 90–102.

Motivation in Organizations

LEARNING OBJECTIVES

After studying this chapter, you should be able to:

- Define motivation and explain the difference between current approaches and traditional approaches to motivation

- Identify and describe content theories of motivation based on employee needs

- Identify and explain process theories of motivation

- Describe reinforcement theory and how it can be used to motivate employees

- Discuss major approaches to job design and how job design influences motivation

- Discuss how empowerment heightens employee motivation

MANAGEMENT PROBLEM

LEAVING THE FAMILIAR surroundings

Chapter 13

of Fargo, North Dakota, 27-year-old Great

Plains Software founder Doug Burgum headed off in 1983 to

Comdex, a megashowcase for the computer industry. Trying to capitalize on the

expected attention toward a software engineer from North Dakota, Burgum brought along

a rancher, who taught lasso skills at the booth. Burgum thought he had it made until he looked

at the program to see whether all five accounting software companies with which he was familiar had

made it to the convention. He was shocked to see there were 63 companies listed. He was devastated. How

• *If you were Burgum, what would you do to distinguish yourself in the marketplace? And how would*

you motivate your employees to give the kind of productivity you so badly need to be successful?

could he possibly beat those 63 competitors, when he was operating from America's flatlands? If he drove

prices down, it surely would kill the margins of his retailers, but running a never-ending race to have

the sexiest bells and whistles didn't interest him, either. He tried to keep costs down by not

overloading the payroll, but he discovered that nobody was answering the phone when

customers were calling in with questions. And when they did get an answer,

it was often a new person each time and the customer would

have to start from the beginning.[1]

The problem for Great Plains Software is that unmotivated employees don't do the maximum amount of work, which causes product quality to suffer, and the company loses its competitive edge. One secret for success for small and medium-sized businesses is having motivated and enthusiastic employees. The challenge for Great Plains Software and other companies is to keep employee motivation consistent with organizational goals. Motivation is a challenge for managers because motivation arises from within employees and typically differs for each employee. For example, Frances Blais sells World Book Encyclopedias. She is a top salesperson, but she does not care about the $50,000-plus commissions: "I'm not even thinking money when I'm selling. I'm really on a crusade to help children read well." In stark contrast, Rob Michaels gets sick to his stomach before he goes to work. Rob is a telephone salesperson who spends all day trying to get people to buy products they do not need, and the rejections are painful. His motivation is money; he earned $120,000 in the past year and cannot make nearly that much doing anything else.[2]

Rob is motivated by money; Frances by a desire to help children read. Each is motivated to perform, yet each has different reasons for performing. With such diverse motivations, it is a challenge for managers to motivate employees toward common organizational goals.

This chapter presents theories and models of employee motivation, beginning with several perspectives and models that describe employee needs and the processes associated with motivation. It also introduces two elements of motivation found in a growing number of contemporary organizations: (1) job design—the changing of the work structure itself and how it can affect employee satisfaction and productivity and (2) empowerment—where more authority and decision making power are delegated to subordinates to increase employee motivation.

■ THE CONCEPT OF MOTIVATION

Most of us get up in the morning, go to school or work, and behave in ways that are pre-

dictably our own. We respond to our environment and the people in it with little thought as to why we work hard, enjoy certain classes, or find some recreational activities so much fun. Yet all these behaviors are motivated by something. **Motivation** refers to the internal and external forces that arouse enthusiasm, desire, purpose, and persistence to pursue a certain course of action. Employee motivation affects productivity, and part of a manager's job is to channel motivation toward the accomplishment of organizational goals.[3] The study of motivation helps managers understand what prompts people to initiate action, what influences their choice of action, and why they persist in that action over time.

A simple model of human motivation is illustrated in Exhibit 13.1. People have basic needs, such as food, achievement, or monetary gain, that motivate specific behaviors they employ to fulfill the need. To the extent that the behavior is successful and the need satisfied, the person is rewarded. The reward also informs the person that the behavior was appropriate and can be used again in the future.

Intrinsic rewards are the satisfactions a person receives in the process of performing a particular action. The completion of a complex task may bestow a pleasant feeling of accomplishment, or solving a problem that benefits others may fulfill a personal mission. Frances Blais sells encyclopedias for the intrinsic reward of helping children read well. **Extrinsic rewards** are given by another person, typically a manager, and include promotions and pay increases. They originate externally, as a result of pleasing others. Rob Michaels, who hates his sales job, nevertheless is motivated by the extrinsic reward of high pay.

Motivation, as illustrated in the model, can lead to behaviors that reflect high performance within organizations. One recent study found that high employee motivation goes hand-in-hand with high organizational performance and profits.[4] Managers can use motivation theory to help satisfy the needs of employees and simultaneously encourage high work performance. Particularly in today's era of low unemployment, with many companies scrambling to find and keep qualified workers, managers are searching for the right combination

motivation
Internal and external forces that arouse enthusiasm, desire, purpose, and persistence; affects productivity and the company's ability to meet its organizational goals

intrinsic reward
The satisfactions received in the process of performing an action

extrinsic reward
Rewards given by another person for performing an action

Some employees at software developer SAS Institute in Cary, North Carolina, are motivated by the top quality day care that is available at $250 per month for their young children. Other SAS employees are motivated by 35-hour work weeks, free onsite medical clinic, and 12 holidays a year plus a paid week off between Christmas and New Year's. These extrinsic rewards help employees maintain a balance between work and personal life and have earned SAS third-place honors in *Fortune* magazine's list of the 100 best companies to work for in America.

of motivational techniques and rewards to keep workers happy and productive. Workers at many of today's leading companies say they are motivated by factors such as a fun, challenging work environment; flexibility that provides a balance between work and personal life; and the potential to learn, grow, and be creative in their jobs.[5]

■ FOUNDATIONS OF MOTIVATION

The manager's perspective on motivation dictates the use of rewards toward employees. Three distinct perspectives are (1) the traditional approach, (2) the human relations ap-

proach, and (3) the human resources approach,[6] with a recent theory representing another perspective called *contemporary approaches.*

TRADITIONAL APPROACH

The study of employee motivation really began with the work of Frederick Winslow Taylor on scientific management. Recall from Chapter 1 that scientific management pertains to the systematic analysis of an employee's job for the purpose of increasing efficiency. Economic rewards are provided to employees for high performance. The emphasis on pay evolved into the perception of workers as *economic* people— people who would work harder for higher pay.

E x h i b i t   13.1
A SIMPLE MODEL OF MOTIVATION

NEED Creates desire to fulfill needs (food, friendship, recognition, achievement) → **BEHAVIOR** Results in actions to fulfill needs → **REWARDS** Satisfy needs; intrinsic or extrinsic rewards

FEEDBACK Reward informs person whether behavior was appropriate and should be used again.

How to get the most motivated workforce has been a dilemma for decades. The Gallup Organization has developed a 12-item questionnaire to help examine this issue further. Interestingly, Gallup found in a study of over 100,000 employees in 24 organizations that the culture of the employee's workgroup was more in setting the standard for motivation and productivity than the culture of the whole company. The questionnaire contains:

- I know what is expected of me at work.
- I have the materials and equipment I need to do my work right.
- At work, I have the opportunity to do what I do best every day.
- In the last seven days, I have received recognition or praise for doing good work.
- My supervisor or someone at work seems to care about me as a person.

- There is someone at work who encourages my development.
- At work, my opinions seem to count.
- The mission/purpose of my company makes me feel my job is important.
- My associates (fellow employees) are committed to doing high-quality work.
- I have a best friend at work.
- In the last six months, someone at work has talked to me about my progress.
- This last year, I have had opportunities at work to learn and grow.

SOURCES: Marcus Buckingham and Curt Coffman, *First, Break the Rules*, (New York: Simon & Schuster, 1999); Curt Coffman and Jim Harter, "A Hard Look at Soft Numbers," www.divorcedoc.com/gallup.htm; "Are Your Employees Happy?" *CIO*, Jan 15, 1999, p. 46.

This approach led to the development of incentive pay systems, in which people were paid strictly on the quantity and quality of their work outputs.

HUMAN RELATIONS APPROACH

The economic man was gradually replaced by a more sociable employee in the minds of managers. Beginning with the landmark Hawthorne studies at a Western Electric plant, as described in Chapter 1, noneconomic rewards, such as congenial work groups who met social needs, seemed more important than money as a motivator of work behavior.[7] For the first time, workers were studied as people, and the concept of *social* man was born. These ideas are still relevant today. Focus on Collaboration describes how an employee's workgroup remains one of the most important variables in motivation.

HUMAN RESOURCE APPROACH

The human resource approach carries the concepts of economic man and social man farther to introduce the concept of the *whole person*. Human resource theory suggests that employees are complex and motivated by many factors. For example, the work by McGregor on Theory X and Theory Y (see Chapter 1) argued that people want to do a good job and that work is as natural and healthy as play. Proponents of the human resource approach believed that earlier approaches had tried to manipulate employees through economic or social rewards. By assuming that employees are competent and able to make major contributions, managers can enhance organizational performance. The human resource approach laid the groundwork for contemporary perspectives on employee motivation.

CONTEMPORARY APPROACHES

The category of contemporary approaches to employee motivation is comprised of three types of theories. **Content theories** stress the analysis of underlying human needs and provide insight into the needs of people in organizations to help managers understand how needs can be satisfied in the workplace.

content theories
Motivation theories emphasizing the needs that motivate people

Process theories concern the thought processes that influence behavior. They focus on how employees seek rewards in work circumstances. Reinforcement theories focus on employee learning of desired work behaviors. In Exhibit 13.1, content theories focus on the first arrow, process theories on the second, and reinforcement theories on the third.

■ CONTENT PERSPECTIVES ON MOTIVATION

The need for food, achievement, or monetary reward are among those that drive people to specific behaviors that attempt to fulfill those needs. An individual's needs are like a hidden catalog of the things he or she wants and will work to get. To the extent that managers understand worker needs, the organization's reward systems can be designed to meet them and reinforce employees for directing energies and priorities toward attainment of organizational goals.

HIERARCHY OF NEEDS THEORY

Probably the most famous content theory was developed by Abraham Maslow.[8] Maslow's **hierarchy of needs theory** proposes that humans are motivated by multiple needs and that these needs exist in a hierarchical order—

physiological, safety, belongingness, esteem, and self-actualization. See Exhibit 13.2.

1. *Physiological.* According to Maslow's theory, food, water, and sex are the most basic human physical needs. In the organizational setting, these are reflected in the needs for adequate heat, air, and salary necessary to ensure survival.

2. *Safety.* These are the needs for a safe and secure physical and emotional environment and freedom from threats—that is, for freedom from violence and for an orderly society. In an organizational workplace, safety needs reflect the needs for safe jobs, fringe benefits, and job security.

3. *Belongingness.* These needs reflect the desire to be accepted by one's peers, have friendships, be part of a group, and be loved. In the organization, these needs influence the desire for good relationships with coworkers, participation in a work group, and a positive relationship with supervisors.

4. *Esteem.* These needs relate to the desire for a positive self-image and to receive attention, recognition, and appreciation from others. Within organizations, esteem needs reflect a motivation for recognition, an increase in responsibility, high status, and credit for contributions to the organization.

process theories
Motivation theories emphasizing the thought processes that influence behavior

hierarchy of needs theory
A content theory that proposes a hierarchy of five categories of needs that motivate people—physiological, safety, belongingness, esteem, and self-actualization

E x h i b i t 13.2
MASLOW'S HIERARCHY OF NEEDS

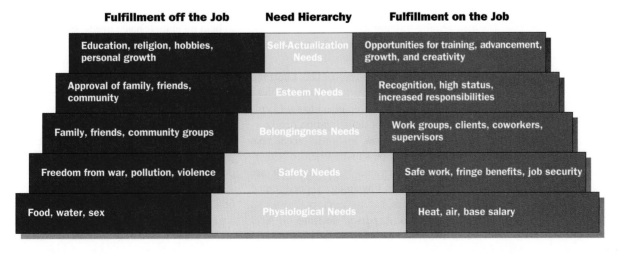

Fulfillment off the Job	Need Hierarchy	Fulfillment on the Job
Education, religion, hobbies, personal growth	Self-Actualization Needs	Opportunities for training, advancement, growth, and creativity
Approval of family, friends, community	Esteem Needs	Recognition, high status, increased responsibilities
Family, friends, community groups	Belongingness Needs	Work groups, clients, coworkers, supervisors
Freedom from war, pollution, violence	Safety Needs	Safe work, fringe benefits, job security
Food, water, sex	Physiological Needs	Heat, air, base salary

THE SOCIAL EXPERIMENT AT QUAD/GRAPHICS

Harry V. Quadracci, founder of the $600 million printing giant Quad/Graphics in Pewaukee, Wisconsin, has been called revolutionary because he wanted to help his employees, mostly high school graduates, "become something more than what they ever hoped to be." Quad/Graphics doesn't use organizational charts, strategic plans, or even budgets. Top executives run the company with a minimum of rules and a maximum of indoctrination with values. For example, Quadracci believed organizational charts limit people's responsibility, and thus their motivation and job satisfaction. At Quad/Graphics, if you see something that needs to be done, you do it. There is no separation between management and labor. There are supervisors, but they wear the same uniform as their charges and do the same work. People and relationships are highly valued.

Quadracci once said that all of business is an experiment: "You try something and if it works, it works. If it doesn't work, you try something else. Quad/Graphics is a social experiment because we've . . . just tried to experiment with the way we can interact in the workplace as individuals and as responsible citizens." Quad/Graphics managers may do things differently, but their approach has enabled the company to boast average annual growth rates near 40 percent in an industry that is struggling to maintain double-digit growth.

The Quad/Graphics system takes a lot of trust, but managers agree with Quadracci's belief that "if you trust your employees, they'll trust you, and they'll rise to your level of belief in them." Managers celebrate employee mistakes, particularly what Quadracci called "perfect failures." An example of a perfect failure is when two technicians spent a year and almost $800,000 developing a paper-folding machine that didn't work. The company celebrated after-

ward, and even gave the workers a bonus for having the courage to try. Quad/Graphics top managers believe that when employees are afraid to make mistakes, the business is doomed. This belief has made Quad/Graphics a certifiable success, racing ahead of its competitors. Managers continue to look for ways to give employees opportunities to grow financially and personally, to continue to "become something more than what they ever hoped to be."

He's also a risk taker and believes in doing things in his own unique way. Once he walked on a highwire across the company floor and wore pink shoes to the company's twenty-fifth anniversary celebration. Why? "Because I can," he replies.

SOURCES: Charles Tanowitz, "Production Profiles," *Publishers Weekly*, June 1998, pp. S16–S20; Peter Newcomb and Dolores Lataniotis, "Harry V. Quadracci," *Forbes*, Oct. 13, 1997, p. 310; "Harry V. Quadracci," an interview with Craig Cox, *Business Ethics*, May/June 1993, pp. 19–21.

5. *Self-actualization.* This involves the need for self-fulfillment, the highest need category. It concerns developing one's full potential, increasing one's competence, and becoming a better person. Self-actualization needs can be met in the organization when people have opportunities to grow, are allowed to be creative, and can acquire training to meet challenging assignments and to advance in their ambitions.

In Leading the Revolution: The Learning Organization, managers at Quad/Graphics have incorporated effective ideas to meet employees fulfill their self-actualization needs.

According to Maslow, low-order needs take priority—they must be satisfied before higher-order needs are activated—and the needs are satisfied in sequence: Physiological needs come before safety needs, safety needs before social needs, and so on. A person desiring physical

safety will devote his or her efforts to securing a safer environment and will not be concerned with esteem needs or self-actualization needs. Once a need is satisfied, it declines in importance and the next higher need is activated. At All Metro Health Care in Lynbrook, New York, CEO Irving Edwards set up a special "customer service" department for his home health aides to help meet their basic needs, such as applying for food stamps and finding transportation and child care. Three employees are available solely to help workers with these issues. Once these lower-level needs are met, employees desire to have higher-level needs met in the workplace, so Irving developed programs such as an award for caregiver of the year, essay contests with prizes, and special recognition for high scoring on quarterly training exercises.[9]

ERG THEORY Clayton Alderfer proposed a modification of Maslow's theory in an effort to simplify it and respond to criticisms of its lack of empirical verification.[10] His **ERG theory** identified three categories of needs:

1. *Existence.* These are the needs for physical well-being.
2. *Relatedness.* These pertain to the need for satisfactory relationships with others.
3. *Growth.* These focus on the development of human potential and the desire for personal growth and increased competence.

The ERG model and Maslow's need hierarchy are similar because both are in hierarchical form and presume that individuals move up the hierarchy one step at a time. However, Alderfer reduced the number of need categories to three and proposed that movement up the hierarchy is more complex, reflecting a **frustration-regression principle,** namely, that failure to meet a high-order need may trigger a regression to an already fulfilled lower-order need. Thus, a worker who cannot fulfill a need for personal growth may revert to a lower-order need and redirect his or her efforts toward making a lot of money. The ERG model therefore is less rigid than Maslow's need hierarchy, suggesting that individuals may move down as well as up the hierarchy, depending on their ability to satisfy needs.

Need hierarchy theory helps explain why organizations find ways to recognize employees and encourage their participation in decision making. Fine Host Corp., a food service company in Greenwich, Connecticut, regularly gives quality awards and posts the names of workers in company buildings to recognize their good work. Employees receive framed certificates when they complete training courses. According to president and CEO Richard Kerley, "Though there may be economic restraints on what we pay them, there are no restraints on the recognition we give them."[11] The importance of filling higher-level belongingness and esteem needs on the job was illustrated by a young manager who said, "If I had to tell you in one sentence why I am motivated by my job, it is because when I know what is going on and how I fit into the overall picture, it makes me feel important." Many companies are finding that "fun" is also a great, high-level motivator, particularly for today's young, well-educated, computer-savvy workers who are in high demand and can command high salaries wherever they go. At Vantage One Communications Group, a marketing firm in Cleveland, Ohio, employees regularly take breaks by playing foosball in the company's recreation room. Such diversions lighten up the daily routine and create a feeling of belongingness and community.

TWO-FACTOR THEORY

Frederick Herzberg developed another popular theory of motivation called the two-factor theory.[12] His findings suggested that the work characteristics associated with dissatisfaction were quite different from those pertaining to satisfaction, which prompted the notion that two factors influence work motivation.

The two-factor theory assumes a neutral area in which workers are neither satisfied nor dissatisfied, and this area is surrounded by two entirely separate dimensions that contribute to an employee's behavior at work. The first, called **hygiene factors,** involves the presence or absence of job dissatisfiers, such as working conditions, pay, company policies, and interpersonal relationships. When hygiene factors are poor, work is dissatisfying. However, good hygiene factors only remove the dissatisfaction; they do not in themselves cause people to become highly satisfied and motivated in their work.

The second set of factors does influence job satisfaction. **Motivators** are high-level needs that include achievement, recognition, responsibility, and opportunity for growth. Herzberg believed that when motivators are absent, workers are neutral toward work, but when motivators are present, workers are highly motivated and satisfied. Thus, hygiene factors and motivators represent two distinct factors that influence motivation.

By providing hygiene factors, managers can eliminate employee dissatisfaction but will not motivate workers to high achievement levels. On the other hand, recognition, challenge, and opportunities for personal growth are powerful motivators and will promote high satisfaction and performance. The manager's role

ERG theory
A simplification of Maslow's hierarchy that proposes three categories of needs: existence, relatedness, and growth

frustration-regression principle
The idea that failure to meet a high-order need may cause a regression to an already satisfied lower-order need

hygiene factors
Factors that involve the presence or absence of job dissatisfiers, including working conditions, pay, company policies, and interpersonal relationships

motivators
Factors that influence job satisfaction based on fulfillment of high-level needs such as achievement, recognition, responsibility, and opportunity for growth

is to remove dissatisfiers—that is, to provide hygiene factors sufficient to meet basic needs—and then use motivators to meet higher-level needs and propel employees toward greater achievement and satisfaction.

ACQUIRED NEEDS THEORY

The final content theory, known as acquired needs theory, was developed by David McClelland and proposes that certain types of needs are acquired during the individual's lifetime. In other words, people are not born with these needs but may learn them through their life experiences.[13] The three needs include (1) the need for *achievement*—a desire to accomplish something difficult, attain a high standard of success, master complex tasks, and surpass others; (2) the need for *affiliation*—a desire to form close personal relationships, avoid conflict, and establish warm friendships; and (3) the need for *power*—a desire to influence or control others, be responsible for others, and have authority over others. Early life experiences determine whether people acquire these needs. If children are encouraged to do things for themselves and receive reinforcement, they will acquire a need to achieve. If they are reinforced for forming warm human relationships, they will develop a need for affiliation. If they get satisfaction from controlling others, they will acquire a need for power.

In summary, content theories focus on people's underlying needs and categorize them in terms of how they motivate people to behave. The hierarchy of needs theory, the ERG theory, the two-factor theory, and the acquired needs theory all help managers understand what motivates people. In this way, managers can design work to meet needs and hence elicit appropriate and successful work behaviors. Looking at people's deeper and perhaps unnoticed need for achievement as well as need for esteem (from Maslow) can be a basis for social good, as Dorothy Balsis Thompson proved.

STREETLIGHTS

Can you motivate high performance from a group of former convicts, welfare recipients, and homeless people? Dorothy Balsis Thompson tried. After the 1992 Los Angeles riots, the 49-year-old producer of TV commercials wanted to help ease racial tensions. So, she quit her cushy job and invested all her savings to start Streetlights in an effort to combat the entertainment industry's lack of interest in fighting the frustration, unemployment, and violence of inner-city minority youth.

Initially, movie companies were reluctant to hire former gang members and thieves, but after seven years, she had placed 125 "graduates" as production assistants on such movies as *The Nutty Professor, The Truth about Cats and Dogs,* and *Liar Liar,* plus a long list of TV shows and commercials.

Thompson looks for deprived youth who want a chance to work. Many of them were gang leaders, such as Robert "Crazy Ace" Leon, an intensely tattooed convicted felon at the top of the gang hierarchy because of his social skills and flair for leadership. People like Ace want to "be somebody," and Thompson has capitalized on that ambition, using it for positive rather than violent outcomes.

Motivation for them is the chance to work in one of the world's most glamorous industries. Thompson requires their attendance at a six-week training program of set etiquette, film-crew hierarchy, work habits, and money management, with the goal of attaining vital self-confidence in the process.

Another Streetlight success story is Maurice "Moe" Freeman, who had previously lived with his welfare mother and had a minimum-wage warehouse job. He has since worked on *Dangerous Minds* and has worked with Whoopi Goldberg. He learned "success depends most on the strength of one's will." And then there's 27-year-old former gang member Robert Aragon, who spent seven Christmases in prison. These days he's hunkered down in the animation department of DreamWorks SKG studio. "So many guys like me end up dead or in prison," he says. "Instead I have a new apartment and a career that makes me happy to get up in the morning."

Thompson knows that a person without hope is dangerous. Streetlights motivates through bringing hope. "I used to dream about a good future," said Ace. "But I couldn't see it. Now I can see it."[14] ■

■ PROCESS PERSPECTIVES ON MOTIVATION

Process theories explain how workers select behavioral actions to meet their needs and determine whether their choices were successful. There are two basic process theories:

EQUITY THEORY

Equity theory is a process theory that focuses on the perceptions of individuals and of how individuals perceive they are being treated as compared with others. Developed by J. Stacy Adams, equity theory proposes that people are motivated to seek social equity in the rewards they expect for performance.[15] According to the theory, when people perceive their compensation to be equal to what others receive for similar contributions, they will believe that their treatment is fair and equitable. Also, peo-

ple evaluate equity by a ratio of inputs to outcomes. Inputs to a job include education, experience, effort, and ability. Outcomes from a job include pay, recognition, benefits, and promotions. The input-to-outcome ratio may be compared to another person in the work group or to a perceived group average. A **state of equity** exists whenever the ratio of one person's outcomes to inputs equals the ratio of another's outcomes to inputs.

Inequity occurs when the input/outcome ratios are out of balance, such as when a person with a high level of education or experience receives the same salary as a new, less-educated employee. Perceived inequity also occurs in the other direction. Thus, if an employee discovers she is making more money than other people who contribute the same inputs to the company, she may feel the need to correct the inequity by working harder, getting more education, or considering lower pay. Perceived inequity creates tensions within individuals that motivate them to bring equity into balance.[16] To achieve a balance, people typically will (1) *change inputs,* or increase or decrease their inputs to the organization; (2) *change outcomes,* or alter their outcome, such as by requesting a salary increase or a bigger office; (3) *distort perceptions,* which occurs when people who are unable to change their inputs or outcomes artificially increase the status attached to their

equity theory
A process theory that focuses on individuals' perceptions of how fairly they are treated relative to others

state of equity
A situation that exists when the ratio of one person's outcomes to inputs equals that of another's

At Georgia Pacific's Philomath, Oregon, sawmill, employees know they'll get a fair chance at any available job because their peers, such as Curtis Chilcote and Ben Garcia shown here, will make the selection. Georgia Pacific values its employees and fosters an environment in which workers feel secure, challenged, committed to common goals, and treated fairly in line with equity theory. Job openings are posted internally for 48 hours, and interested workers submit a bid to a volunteer committee made up of one salaried and four hourly workers. Crew members appreciate the system because it allows those closest to the job to make hiring and transfer decisions.

TECHNOLOGY FOR TOMORROW

WOMEN.com

Women are starting to believe, in large numbers, that they can be successful as entrepreneurs, and they are making an impact on the Internet as founders of startups. Whereas men often start more tools and research-oriented ventures, women tend to create consumer-oriented technology ventures. And not just little basement ventures, but big money dot-coms, such as Allyson Campa, who secured $8 million to start her online business gift site BravoGifts.com, Inc.

Two types of female entrepreneurs are emerging online. One is the over-35 group who is either tired of corporate America or just plain itching to get out on their own. Then there are the twenty-somethings with fresh MBAs and a couple years of experience working in other startups. These younger women "are not burdened with gender issues," says Margarita Quihuis, director of San Francisco's Women's Technology Cluster. "They haven't hit the [glass] ceilings and they feel they can do anything."

In addition, the number of women holding funding posts in venture capital firms has increased over 1,000 percent in five years—from six to a total of 70 currently. The lack of women in the white male-dominated ranks of venture capital has been one reason women have gotten only 4 percent of the $13 billion awarded in the United States per year. Forum for Women Entrepreneurs president Denise Brosseau believes that will change soon.

With the maturation of the Internet and technology companies comes a shift away from infrastructure and tools to more content and services, which are dependent on good customer relations and communications, where women excel.

Still, women entrepreneurs should not assume a general business background is enough. They still need to be grounded in technology and be able to see what changes are coming. The Internet is "not some kind of vanilla, generic business idea," says Jon Goodman of EC2 incubator. Internet consulting firm J Parker Co. head Jeannine Parker agrees, saying, "There's an intimidation factor, whether cultural or mythical, that math, science and technology is for boys. Women just have to get over that." And they seem to be doing just that these days.

SOURCE: Vicki Torres, "Changing Internet Opening New Doors to Women Entrepreneurs," *Los Angeles Times*, Oct. 27, 1999, p. 8.

---

jobs or distort the perceived rewards of others; (4) *leave the job,* which becomes a better alternative to suffering the inequities (being underpaid, overpaid, etc.). In their new jobs, they expect to find a more favorable balance of rewards. Smart managers try to keep balance in the state of equity and keep their workforces motivated.

EXPECTANCY THEORY

expectancy theory
A process theory proposing that motivation depends on individuals' expectations about their ability to perform tasks and receive desired rewards

E→P expectancy
The degree of expectation that putting effort into a given task will lead to high performance

Expectancy theory suggests that motivation depends on the expectations of individuals about their ability to perform tasks and receive desired rewards. Expectancy theory is associated with the work of Victor Vroom, although a number of scholars have made contributions in this area.[17] Expectancy theory is concerned not with identifying types of needs but with the thinking process that individuals use to achieve rewards. Consider Bill Bradley, a university student with a strong desire for a B in his accounting course. Bill has a C+ average and one more exam to take. Bill's motivation to study for that last exam will be influenced by (1) the expectation that hard study will lead to an A on the exam and (2) the expectation that an A on the exam will result in a B for the course. If Bill believes he cannot get an A on the exam or that receiving an A will not lead to a B for the course, he will not be motivated to study particularly hard. One reason more women are starting their own businesses these days is because they believe they can overcome inequities they perceive in the traditional workplace (see Technology for Tomorrow).

Expectancy theory is based on the relationship among the individual's effort, the individual's performance, and the desirability of outcomes associated with high performance. The keys to expectancy theory are the expectancies for the relationships among effort (E), performance (P), and outcomes (O) with the value of the outcomes to the individual.

E→P expectancy involves whether putting effort into a task will lead to high performance. For this expectancy to be high, the individual must have the ability, previous experience, and necessary machinery, tools, and opportunity to perform. For Bill Bradley to get a B in the accounting course, the E→P expectancy is high if Bill truly believes that with hard work, he can get an A on the final exam. If Bill believes he has neither the ability nor the opportunity to achieve high performance, the expectancy will be low, and so will be his motivation.

P→O expectancy involves whether successful performance will lead to the desired outcome. In the case of a person who is motivated to win a job-related award, this expectancy concerns the belief that high performance will truly lead to the award. If the P→O expectancy is high, the individual will be more highly motivated. If the expectancy is that high performance will not produce the desired outcome, motivation will be lower. If an A on the final exam is likely to produce a B in the accounting course, Bill Bradley's P→O expectancy will be high. Bill may talk to the professor to see whether an A will be sufficient to earn him the B in the course. If not, he will be less motivated to study hard for the final exam.

Valence is the value of outcomes, or attraction for outcomes, for the individual. If the outcomes that are available from high effort and good performance are not valued by employees, motivation will be low. Likewise, if outcomes have a high value, motivation will be higher.

One employee may want to be promoted to a position of increased responsibility, and another may have high valence for good relationships with peers. Consequently, the first person will be motivated to work hard for a promotion and the second for the opportunity for a team position that will keep him or her associated with a group.

The responsibility of managers is to help subordinates meet their needs and at the same time attain organizational goals. Managers must try to find a match between the skills and abilities of subordinates and the demands of the job. To increase motivation, managers can clarify the needs of individuals, define the outcomes available from the organization, and ensure that each individual has the ability and support (namely, time and equipment) needed to attain outcomes.

Some companies use expectancy theory principles by designing incentive systems that identify desired organizational outcomes and give everyone the same shot at getting the rewards. The trick is to design a system that fits with the abilities and needs of employees. Consider the following example from the restaurant industry.

KATZINGER'S DELICATESSEN

When Steve and Diane Warren, co-owners of Katzinger's Delicatessen in Columbus, Ohio, instituted open-book management, they hoped it would help them cut costs and save money. The Warrens trained employees in how to read the financials and told them Katzinger's would share the rewards with employees if financial performance improved. However, because most of their workers were young and mobile, not committed to a long-term career with the company, the vague long-range goals and rewards did not provide a high degree of motivation. Many of them felt that they could do little to improve overall performance and that doing so was the job of managers anyway. Thus, both E→P expectancy and P→O expectancy were low. The Warrens needed a simple, short-term goal as a way to energize their young workers. They proposed a simple plan: if workers would help reduce food costs to below 35 percent of sales without sacrificing food quality or service, they would be rewarded with half the savings.

Katzinger's workers were well trained and knew they had the skills and ability to meet the goal if they all worked together; thus, the E→P expectancy was high. Workers immediately began proposing ideas to reduce waste, such as matching perishable food orders more closely to expected sales. The P→O expectancy was also high because of the level of trust at the company; workers were highly motivated to cooperate to decrease food costs because they knew everyone would benefit from the savings. Because anyone could look at the financials, workers could actually track their progress toward

P→O expectancy
The degree of expectation that successful performance of a task will lead to the desired outcome

valence
The value or attraction an individual has for an outcome

reinforcement theory
A motivation theory emphasizing the relationship between behavior and its consequences for the purpose of teaching desired work behaviors

reinforcement
The appropriate application of rewards and punishments meant to modify on-the-job behaviors and cause certain behaviors to be repeated or inhibited

behavior modification
Reinforcement techniques used to modify human behavior

law of effect
The assumption that positively reinforced behavior tends to be repeated and unreinforced or negatively reinforced behavior tends to be inhibited

meeting the goal. At the end of the first month, food costs had fallen nearly 2 percent and employees took home about $40 each from the savings. Later monthly payouts were as high as $95 per employee. By the end of the year, food consistency and service had improved and Katzinger's had indeed reduced its food costs to below 35 percent of total sales, saving the company $30,000. The Warrens gladly distributed $15,000 of that amount to their workers for helping to meet the goal. Now, the Warrens are working out a similar plan to increase sales at Katzinger's.[18] ■

■ REINFORCEMENT PERSPECTIVE ON MOTIVATION

Reinforcement theory sidesteps the issues of employee needs and thinking processes of the content and process theories and simply looks at the relationship between behavior and its consequences. **Reinforcement** is the appropriate application of rewards and punishments

meant to modify on-the-job behaviors. The goal of reinforcement is to cause a certain behavior to be repeated or inhibited.

REINFORCEMENT TOOLS

Behavior modification is the name given to the set of reinforcement techniques used to modify human behavior.[19] The basic assumption underlying this concept is the **law of effect,** which states that behavior that is positively reinforced tends to be repeated, and behavior that is not reinforced tends not to be repeated. Four reinforcement tools are (1) positive reinforcement, (2) avoidance learning, (3) punishment, and (4) extinction. Each type of reinforcement is a consequence of either a pleasant or unpleasant event being applied or withdrawn as a result of a person's behavior (see Exhibit 13.3).

Positive reinforcement is the administration of a pleasant and rewarding consequence following a desired behavior. Immediate praise for an employee who arrives on time or does a little extra in his or her work is a good example. The pleasant consequence

Exhibit 13.3
CHANGING BEHAVIOR WITH REINFORCEMENT

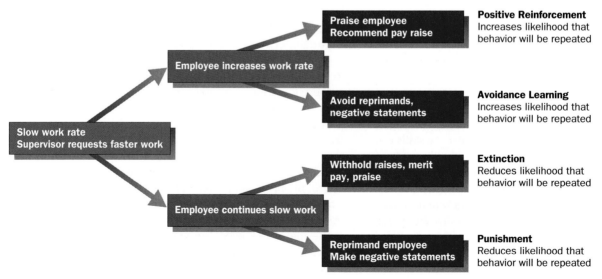

SOURCE: Based on Richard L. Daft and Richard M. Steers, *Organizations: A Micro/Macro Approach* (Glenview, Ill.: Scott, Foresman, 1986), 109.

will increase the likelihood of the excellent work behavior occurring again. Studies have shown that positive reinforcement (including both financial and nonfinancial awards, such as positive comments and the like) does help to improve organizational performance.

Avoidance learning is the removal of an unpleasant consequence following a desired behavior, also called *negative* reinforcement. The assumption is that employees will learn to do the right thing by avoiding unpleasant situations. Avoidance learning occurs when a supervisor stops criticizing or reprimanding an employee once the incorrect behavior has stopped.

Punishment means imposing unpleasant outcomes on an employee and typically occurs following undesirable behavior. For example, a supervisor may berate an employee for incorrectly performing a task. The supervisor expects that the negative outcome will serve as a punishment and reduce the likelihood of the behavior recurring. The use of punishment in organizations is controversial and often criticized because it fails to indicate the correct behavior. However, almost all managers report finding it necessary to occasionally impose forms of punishment, which range from verbal reprimands to employee suspensions or firings.[20]

Extinction is the withdrawal of a positive reward, meaning that behavior is no longer reinforced and hence is less likely to occur in the future. If a perpetually tardy employee fails to receive praise and pay raises, he or she will begin to realize that the behavior is not producing desired outcomes. The behavior will gradually disappear if it is continually nonreinforced.

Some executives use reinforcement theory very effectively to shape behavior. Jack Welch, chairman of General Electric, always made it a point to reinforce behavior. As an up-and-coming group executive, Welch reinforced purchasing agents by having someone telephone him whenever an agent got a price concession from a vendor. Welch would stop whatever he was doing and call the agent to say, "That's wonderful news; you just knocked a nickel a ton off the price of steel." He would also sit down and scribble out a congratulatory note to the agent. The effective use of positive reinforcement and the heightened motivation of purchasing employees marked Jack Welch as executive material in the organization.[21]

SCHEDULES OF REINFORCEMENT

A great deal of research into reinforcement theory suggests that the timing of reinforcement has an impact on the speed of employee learning. **Schedules of reinforcement** pertain to the frequency of reinforcement; that is, the frequency of the occurrence and the intervals between the occurrences. A reinforcement schedule can be selected to have maximum impact on job behavior. Five basic types of reinforcement schedules, as well as four types of partial reinforcement are:

In a **continuous reinforcement schedule,** every occurrence of the desired behavior is reinforced. This schedule can be very effective in the early stages of learning new types of behavior, because every attempt has a pleasant consequence.

In a **partial reinforcement schedule,** reinforcement is administered only after some occurrences of the correct behavior. However, in the real world of organizations, it is often impossible to reinforce every correct behavior. There are four types of partial reinforcement schedules: (1) the *fixed-interval schedule* in which employees are rewarded at specified time intervals, such as regular paychecks or quarterly bonuses; (2) the *fixed-ratio schedule* which provides reinforcement after a specified number of desired responses has occurred, such as when paying a field hand $1.50 for picking 10 pounds of peppers; (3) the *variable-interval schedule* in which reinforcement is administered at random times that cannot be predicted by the employee, such as when an unexpected inspection takes place and the supervisor commends employees on their good behavior; (4) the *variable-ratio schedule,*

schedules of reinforcement
The frequency of reinforcement; that is, the frequency of the occurrence and the intervals between the occurrences

continuous reinforcement schedule
A schedule in which every occurrence of the desired behavior is reinforced

partial reinforcement schedule
A schedule in which only some occurrences of the desired behavior are reinforced

Exhibit 13.4

SCHEDULES OF REINFORCEMENT

Schedule of Reinforcement	Nature of Reinforcement	Effect on Behavior When Applied	Effect on Behavior When Withdrawn	Example
Continuous	Reward given after each desired behavior	Leads to fast learning of new behavior	Rapid extinction	Praise
Fixed-interval	Reward given at fixed time intervals	Leads to average and irregular performance	Rapid extinction	Weekly paycheck
Fixed-ratio	Reward given at fixed amounts of output	Quickly leads to very high and stable performance	Rapid extinction	Piece-rate pay system
Variable-interval	Reward given at variable times	Leads to moderately high and stable performance	Slow extinction	Performance appraisal and awards given at random times each month
Variable-ratio	Reward given at variable amounts of output	Leads to very high performance	Slow extinction	Sales bonus tied to number of sales calls, with random checks

which is based on a random number of desired behaviors rather than on variable time periods. Reinforcement may occur sometimes after 5, 10, 15, or 20 displays of behavior. One example is the attraction of slot machines for gamblers. People anticipate that the machine will pay a jackpot after a certain number of plays, but the exact number of plays is variable. Schedules of reinforcement available to managers are illustrated in Exhibit 13.4.

Parsons Pine Products is an example of a small business that effectively uses reinforcement techniques. With only 75 employees, it is the world's largest manufacturer of slats for louvered doors and shutters. The plan that managers use includes:

- *Safety pay.* Every employee who goes for a month without a lost-time accident receives a bonus equal to four hours of pay.
- *Retro pay.* If the company saves money when its workers' compensation premiums go down because of a lower accident rate, the savings are distributed among employees.
- *Well pay.* Employees receive monthly well pay equal to eight hours of wages if they have been neither absent nor tardy.

- *Profit pay.* All company earnings above 4 percent after taxes go into a bonus pool, which is shared among employees.

The plan for reinforcing correct behaviors has been extraordinarily effective. Parsons's previous accident rate had been 86 percent above the state average; today it is 32 percent below it. Turnover and tardiness are minimal, and absenteeism has dropped to almost nothing. The plan works because the reinforcement schedules are strictly applied, with no exceptions.

Reinforcement also works at such organizations as Campbell Soup Co., Emery Air Freight, Michigan Bell, and General Electric, because managers reward appropriate behavior. They tell employees what they can do to receive reinforcement, tell them what they are doing wrong, distribute rewards equitably, tailor rewards to behaviors, and keep in mind that failure to reward deserving behavior has an equally powerful impact on employees.

Reward and punishment motivational practices dominate organizations, with as many as 94 percent of companies in the United States reporting that they use practices that reward performance or merit with pay.[22] However, despite the testimonies of numerous organizations that enjoy successful incentive programs, there is growing criticism of so-called carrot-and-stick methods.

MARSHALL INDUSTRIES

Everybody thought Rob Rodin was crazy when he decided to wipe out all individual incentives for his sales force at Marshall Industries, a large distributor of electronic components based in El Monte, California. He did away with all bonuses, commissions, vacations, and other awards and rewards. All salespeople would receive a base salary plus the opportunity for profit sharing, which would be the same percent of salary for everyone, based on the entire company's performance. Six years later, Rodin says productivity per person has tripled at the company, but still he gets questions and criticism about his decision.

Rodin is standing right in the middle of a big controversy in modern management. Do financial and other rewards really motivate the kind of behavior organizations want and need? A growing number of critics say no, arguing that carrot-and-stick approaches are a holdover from the Industrial Age and are inappropriate and ineffective in today's economy. Today's workplace demands innovation and creativity from everyone—behaviors that rarely are inspired by money or other financial incentives. Reasons for criticism of carrot-and-stick approaches include:

- *Extrinsic rewards diminish intrinsic rewards.* When people are motivated to seek an extrinsic reward, whether it is a bonus, an award, or the approval of a supervisor, generally they focus on the reward rather than on the work they do to achieve it. Thus, the intrinsic satisfaction people receive from performing their jobs actually declines. When people lack intrinsic rewards in their work, their performance stays just adequate to achieve the reward offered. In the worst case, employees may cover up mistakes, such as hiding an on-the-job accident in order to win a safety award.

- *Extrinsic rewards are temporary.* Offering outside incentives may ensure short-term success, but not long-term high performance. When employees are focused only on the reward, they lose interest in their work. Without personal interest, the potential for exploration, creativity, and innovation disappears. While the current deadline or goal may be met, better ways of working will not be discovered.

- *Extrinsic rewards assume people are driven by lower-level needs.* Rewards such as bonuses, pay increases, and even praise presume that the primary reason people initiate and persist in behavior is to satisfy lower-level needs. However, particularly among today's knowledge workers, behavior also is based on yearnings for self-expression, and on feelings of self-esteem and self-worth. Offers of an extrinsic reward do not encourage the myriad behaviors that are motivated by people's need to express themselves and realize their higher needs for growth and fulfillment.

As Rob Rodin discovered at Marshall Industries, today's organizations need employees who are motivated to think, experiment, and continuously search for ways to solve new problems. Alfie Kohn, one of the most vocal critics of carrot-and-stick approaches, offers the following advice to managers regarding how to pay employees: "Pay well, pay fairly, and then do everything you can to get money off people's minds." Indeed there is some evidence that money is not primarily what people work for. Managers should understand the limits of extrinsic motivators and work to satisfy a higher, as well as lower, needs of employees. To be motivated, employees need jobs that offer self-satisfaction in addition to a yearly pay raise.[23] ■

■ JOB DESIGN FOR MOTIVATION

A job in an organization is a unit of work that a single employee is responsible for performing.

A job could include writing tickets for parking violators in New York City or doing long-range planning for ABC television. Jobs are important because performance of their components may provide rewards that meet the needs of employees. An assembly line worker may install the same bolt over and over, whereas an emergency room physician may provide each trauma victim with a unique treatment package. Managers need to know what aspects of a job provide motivation as well as how to compensate for routine tasks that have little inherent satisfaction. Job design is the application of motivational theories to the structure of work for improving productivity and satisfaction. Approaches to **job design** are generally classified as job simplification, job rotation, job enlargement, and job enrichment.

JOB SIMPLIFICATION

Job simplification pursues task efficiency by reducing the number of tasks one person must do. Job simplification is based on principles drawn from scientific management and industrial engineering. Tasks are designed to be simple, repetitive, and standardized. As complexity is stripped from a job, the worker has more time to concentrate on doing more of the same routine task. Workers with low skill requirements can perform the job, and the organization achieves a high level of efficiency. Indeed, workers are interchangeable, because they need little training or skill and exercise little judgment. As a motivational technique, however, job simplification has failed. People

dislike routine and boring jobs and react in a number of negative ways, including sabotage, absenteeism, and unionization. Job simplification is compared with job rotation and job enlargement in Exhibit 13.5.

JOB ROTATION

Job rotation systematically moves employees from one job to another, thereby increasing the number of different tasks an employee performs without increasing the complexity of any one job. For example, an autoworker may install windshields one week and front bumpers the next. Job rotation still takes advantage of engineering efficiencies, but it provides variety and stimulation for employees. Although employees may find the new job interesting at first, the novelty soon wears off as the repetitive work is mastered.

JOB ENLARGEMENT

Job enlargement combines a series of tasks into one new, broader job. This is a response to the dissatisfaction of employees with oversimplified jobs. Instead of only one job, an employee may be responsible for three or four and will have more time to do them. Job enlargement provides job variety and a greater challenge for employees. At Maytag, jobs were enlarged when work was redesigned so that workers assembled an entire water pump rather than doing each part as it reached them on the assembly line. In the new assembly plants at General Motors, the assembly line is gone. In

job design
The application of motivational theories to the structure of work for improving productivity and satisfaction

job simplification
A job design whose purpose is to improve task efficiency by reducing the number of tasks a single person must perform

job rotation
A job design that systematically moves employees from one job to another to provide them with variety and stimulation

job enlargement
A job design that combines a series of tasks into one new, broader job to give employees variety and challenge

Exhibit 13.5
TYPES OF JOB DESIGN

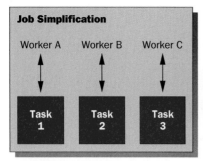

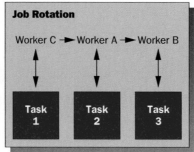

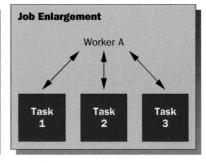

its place is a freewheeling, motorized carrier that transports each car independently through the assembly process. The carrier moves to a workstation, where it stops for a group of workers to perform a coordinated block of tasks, such as installing an engine and its accessories. Thus the workers perform an enlarged job on a stationary automobile, rather than a single task on a series of automobiles moving past them.

JOB ENRICHMENT

Recall the discussion of Maslow's need hierarchy and Herzberg's two-factor theory. Rather than just changing the number and frequency of tasks a worker performs, **job enrichment** incorporates high-level motivators into the work, including job responsibility, recognition, and opportunities for growth, learning, and achievement. In an enriched job, employees have control over the resources necessary for performing it, make decisions on how to do the work, experience personal growth, and set their own work pace. Many companies, including AT&T, Procter & Gamble, and Motorola, have undertaken job enrichment programs to increase the motivation and job satisfaction of employees.

Half-Price Books took job enrichment to the limit by basing its planning and expansion on satisfying valued employees managerial aspirations.

HALF-PRICE BOOKS

What's a CEO of a $50 million company doing driving a 1986 Volkswagen and earning only $50,000 per year? Sharon Wright, daughter of the founder of Dallas's Half-Price Books, is following in her late mother's footsteps by keeping costs low in order to make the business flourish.

Everything in the first store in 1972 was homemade or secondhand, and employees were hired for their eccentricities as well as love of books, meaning they were educated and often had gifts in display and promotion. Pat Anderson—Wright's mother—had a knack for pricing books low enough so that they fly off the shelves at a profit.

Half-Price Books has a number of unusual practices, perhaps the one that defies common business practice most was its stubborn refusal to grow intentionally through a systematic plan or analysis of optimum market conditions. Instead, the company opened new stores mostly to reward valuable employees who wanted to be managers. When Dallas became saturated with Half-Price stores, expansion took place in cities where employees had a desire to relocate. By 1999, Half-Price Books had 62 stores in 10 states. But she recognized that a business must create benefits that emanate outward and toward society and that there must be an organizing principle—simpler is better—to the firm. Hers? Providing a livelihood and career growth to friends and family. And finally, even though this seems contradictory to her rejection of systematic plans, she understood it is better to track information than it is to control people, who, when allowed to be playful, make a more successful business.

After Pat Anderson died in 1995, many employees assumed Wright would sell off the business and start to live the good life. But Sharon never thought of that. "Why would I want to sell?" she asks. "My family and friends all work here!"[24] ■

JOB CHARACTERISTICS MODEL

One significant approach to job design was developed by Richard Hackman and Greg Oldham.[25] Their **job characteristics model** consists of three major parts: core job dimensions, critical psychological states, and employee growth-need strength (see Exhibit 13.6). Hackman and Oldham's research concerned **work redesign,** in which jobs are altered to increase both the quality of work experience and productivity of employees.

CORE JOB DIMENSIONS
Hackman and Oldham identified five dimensions that determine a job's motivational potential:

---

job enrichment
A job design that incorporates achievement, recognition, and other high-level motivators into the work

job characteristics model
A model of job design that comprises core job dimensions, critical psychological states, and employee growth-need strength

work redesign
The altering of jobs to increase both the quality of employees' work experience and their productivity

Exhibit 13.6

THE JOB CHARACTERISTICS MODEL

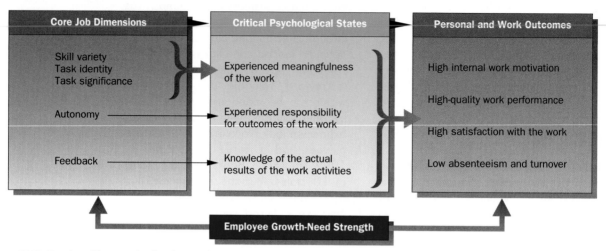

SOURCE: Adapted from J. Richard Hackman and G. R. Oldham, "Motivation through the Design of Work: Test of a Theory," *Organizational Behavior and Human Performance*, 16 (1976), 256.

1. *Skill variety* is the number of diverse activities that compose a job and the number of skills used to perform it. A routine, repetitious, assembly line job is low in variety, whereas an applied research position that entails working on new problems every day is high in variety.

2. *Task identity* is the degree to which an employee performs a total job with a recognizable beginning and ending. A chef who prepares an entire meal has more task identity than a worker on a cafeteria line who ladles mashed potatoes.

3. *Task significance* is the degree to which the job is perceived as important and having impact on the company or consumers. For instance, people who distribute penicillin and other medical supplies during times of emergencies would have higher task significance.

4. *Autonomy* is the degree to which the worker has freedom, discretion, and self-determination in planning and carrying out tasks. A house painter can determine how to paint the house; a paint sprayer on an assembly line has little autonomy.

5. *Feedback* is the extent to which doing the job provides information back to the employee about his or her performance. Jobs vary in their ability to let workers see the outcomes of their efforts. A football coach knows whether the team won or lost, but a basic research scientist may have to wait years to learn whether a research project was successful.

The job characteristics model says that the more these five core characteristics can be designed into the job, the more the employees will be motivated and the higher will be performance quality and satisfaction.

CRITICAL PSYCHOLOGICAL STATES   The model posits that core job dimensions are more rewarding when individuals experience three psychological states in response to job design. Skill variety, task identity, and task significance tend to influence the employee's psychological state of experienced meaningfulness of work. The work itself is satisfying and provides intrinsic rewards for the worker. The job characteristic of autonomy influences the worker's experienced responsibility. The

Workers at the Alexander Doll Company in Harlem manufacture Madame Alexander dolls, which cost from $40 to $600 a piece and have hand-painted faces and elaborate costumes. Employees work in teams of seven or eight, with each team being responsible for completing about 300 dolls or wardrobe assemblies a day. Their work provides skill variety because the costumes alone contain 20 or more separate items that have to go through as many as 30 production steps. Workers also experience task identity because each team performs the complete job of manufacturing dolls that are ready for consumers.

job characteristic of feedback provides the worker with knowledge of actual results. The employee thus knows how he or she is doing and can change work performance to increase desired outcomes.

PERSONAL AND WORK OUTCOMES The impact of the five job characteristics on the psychological states of experienced meaningfulness, responsibility, and knowledge of actual results leads to the personal and work outcomes of high work motivation, high work performance, high satisfaction, and low absenteeism and turnover.

EMPLOYEE GROWTH-NEED STRENGTH The final component of the job characteristics model is called employee growth-need strength, which means that people have different needs for growth and development. If a person wants to satisfy low-level needs, such as safety and belongingness, the job characteristics model has less effect. When a person has a high need for growth and development, including the desire for personal challenge, achievement, and challenging work, the model is especially effective. People with a high need to grow and expand their abilities respond very favorably to the application of the model and to improvements in core job dimensions.

■ EMPOWERMENT AND OTHER MOTIVATIONAL PROGRAMS

Despite the controversy over carrot-and-stick motivational practices, many organizations continue to use various types of incentive compensation as a way to motivate employees to higher levels of performance. Exhibit 13.7 shows several methods of incentive pay. These programs can be effective when used appropriately and combined with motivational ideas that provide employees with intrinsic rewards and meet higher-level needs. Effective organizations do not use incentive pay plans as the sole basis of motivation.

The newest trend in motivation is **empowerment,** the delegation of power or authority to subordinates in an organization. Increasing employee power heightens motivation for task accomplishment because people improve their own effectiveness when choosing how to do a task and using their creativity.[26] Most people come into an organization with the desire to do a good job, and empowerment releases the motivation that is already there.

Ralph Stayer, CEO of Johnsonville Foods, believes a manager's strongest power comes from committed and motivated employees: "Real power comes from giving it up to others who are in a better position to do things than

empowerment
The delegation of decision-making authority, freedom, knowledge, autonomy, and skills to subordinates; a fundamental principle of learning organizations

you are."[27] The manager who shares power with employees receives motivation and creativity in return.

To empower employees means to provide four elements that enable them to feel more free to accomplish their tasks:

1. *Information.* In companies where employees are fully empowered, no information is secret. At Com-Corp, every employee has access to all financial information, including executive salaries.

2. *Knowledge.* Employees have knowledge and skills to contribute to company goals. Companies use training programs to help employees acquire the knowledge and skills they need to contribute to organizational performance.

3. *Power.* Employees have the power to make substantive decisions. Empowered employees have the authority to directly influence work procedures and organizational performance, often through quality circles or self-directed work teams. At Compaq Computer, salespeople now work out of their homes and set their own schedules. The company provides a fully equipped networked computer so workers can share information with colleagues and access comprehensive databases. Under the new system, Compaq's sales force has set new records for productivity.[28]

4. *Rewards.* Employees are rewarded based on company performance, often shown in the company's bottom line. Johnsonville Foods instituted a "company performance share," a fixed percentage of pretax profits to be divided every six months among employees. Individual shares are based on a performance appraisal system designed and administered by a volunteer team of line workers.[29] Organizations may also use other motivational programs described in Exhibit 13.7 to tie employee efforts to company performance.

Many of today's organizations are implementing empowerment programs, but they are empowering workers to varying degrees. At some companies, empowerment means encouraging the ideas of workers while managers retain final authority for decisions; at others it means giving employees almost complete freedom and power to make decisions and exercise initiative and imagination.[30] An example of full empowerment is when self-directed teams

Exhibit 13.7

NEW MOTIVATIONAL COMPENSATION PROGRAMS

Program Name	Purpose
Pay for Performance	Rewards individual employees in proportion to their performance contributions. Also called merit pay.
Gain Sharing	Rewards all employees and managers within a business unit when predetermined performance targets are met. Encourages teamwork.
Employee Stock Ownership Plan (ESOP)	Gives employees part ownership of the organization, enabling them to share in improved profit performance.
Lump-Sum Bonuses	Rewards employees with a one-time cash payment based on performance.
Pay for Knowledge	Links employee salary with the number of task skills acquired. Workers are motivated to learn the skills for many jobs, thus increasing company flexibility and efficiency.
Flexible Work Schedule	Flextime allows workers to set their own hours. Job sharing allows two or more part-time workers to jointly cover one job. Telecommuting, sometimes called flex-place, allows employees to work from home or an alternate workspace.
Team-based Compensation	Rewards employees for behavior and activities that benefit the team, such as cooperation, listening, and empowering others.

are given the authority to hire, discipline, and dismiss team members and to set compensation rates. W. L. Gore and Associates have moved closer to this than most. The company operates with no titles, hierarchy, or any of the conventional structures associated with a company of its size. Gore's culture emphasizes teamwork, mutual support, freedom, intrinsic motivation, independent effort, and commitment to the total organization rather than to narrow jobs or departments. With empowerment, workers are motivated because they are intellectually challenged, provided with opportunities to use their minds and imaginations, and given the power to make decisions that affect their work. Research indicates that most people have a need for self-efficacy, which is the capacity to produce results or outcomes, to feel that they are effective.[31] By meeting higher-level needs, empowerment can provide powerful motivation.

Patagonia's mission statement and purpose meet higher-level needs and has proved how powerful empowerment can be for business. The outdoor clothing maker nearly went bankrupt in 1991 and mournfully laid off 120 of its 620 employees and then started on restructuring its way back to financial health.

But, Patagonia did not reduce budgets in two of its most expensive costs centers: R&D and its environmental grants program. When times are tough, the real values of a company become evident, and Patagonia stayed true. A deep commitment to the environment permeates the entire firm and is one of the important reasons it has such a loyal and productive workforce.

Employees get involved in environmental causes by recycling everything, going to activist conferences, reading extensive articles in company newsletters, and making phone calls during slow times to urge voters to support environmental proposals. Staff graphic artists donate their time and skills to groups that might need a membership design or logo. The children's designer proposed a new line of patchwork clothes that uses scraps from adult clothes cutting, which lessen waste. In addition, employees can take a two-month paid leave to work as volunteers for nonprofit environmental groups.

While the company keeps its pledge to environmental issues, it also works to stay profitable. "Not to hit our profit goals is as big a problem as falling in our social mission," says founder Yvon Chouinard. Part of their environmental awareness means they want to sell *fewer* goods, something not often seen in retail. For example, customer Leslie Barnes sent in a 10-year-old jacket and the company repaired the zipper for free. "After 10 years," she said, "You'd expect to buy another coat, but once the zipper was replaced, this parka was ready to go for another decade." So rather than wanting customers to buy another garment, Patagonia sees their long-lasting goods as lessening the environmental burden of manufacturing. Sure, it lessens their profit picture, but, as operations director Karyn Barsa says, they learned their lesson from the early nineties and now want to grow at a slow and sustainable rate.

Every business decision is made with the goals of profitability and environmentalism in mind and it has imbued the entire company with a high level of commitment and enthusiasm. Patagonia has achieved handsome profits by doing good through treating employees well and merging environmentalism into their business model.[32]

Summary and Management Solution

This chapter introduced a number of important ideas about the motivation of people in organizations. The content theories of motivation focus on the nature of underlying employee needs. Maslow's hierarchy of needs, Alderfer's ERG theory, Herzberg's two-factor theory, and McClelland's acquired needs theory all suggest that people are motivated to meet a range of needs. Process theories examine how people go about selecting rewards with which to meet needs. Equity theory says that people compare their contributions and outcomes with those of others and are motivated to maintain a feeling of equity. Expectancy theory suggests that people calculate the probability of achieving certain outcomes. Managers can increase motivation by treating employees fairly and by clarifying employee paths toward meeting their needs. Still another motivational approach is reinforcement theory, which says that employees learn to behave in certain ways based on the availability of reinforcements.

The application of motivational ideas is illustrated in job design and other motivational programs. Job design approaches include job simplification, job rotation, job enlargement, job enrichment, and the job characteristics model. Managers can change the structure of work to meet the high-level needs of employees. The recent trend toward empowerment motivates by giving employees more information and authority to make decisions in their work while connecting compensation to the results.

Recall from the beginning of the chapter that Doug Burgum's problem of trying to make a software company from North Dakota successful grew into despair when 63 other companies were offering the same type of accounting software. He needed to find a way to distinguish his company and a way to motivate employees to carry out the company's vision. The first problem was getting people to answer phones. Burgum believed he would go broke if he paid overtime for reps to stay long enough to get every call. So he came up with a daring idea—charge for calls, something none of his competitors were doing. But he figured they were used to getting charged to call their accountant and would be willing to pay if they got good service. He offered customers the opportunity to pay a fixed amount and get an unlimited amount of calls. Today those customers get a returned call within 30 minutes and their record of 249,020 straight calls within deadline is incredible. And Burgum rewards employees who deliver high-quality service with bonuses. Senior managers are taken on offsite strategy meetings with team-building events such as cattle roping and branding, fence-mending and rodeos. Because most of them don't have skills in these areas, they "learn how to work together without judging," says vice president of global sales Tim Eichorst. They pay attention to all the employees, making sure they are satisfied and engaged in challenging work, which has resulted in the low turnover rate of 6.2 percent. The industry average is 20 percent. Burgum's focus on people, culture, and motivation has resulted in revenues soaring to $135 million in 1999, at a growth rate of 37 percent per year over a five year period.

Discussion Questions

1. Low-paid service workers represent a motivational problem for many companies. Consider the ill-trained and poorly motivated X-ray machine operators trying to detect weapons in airports. How might these people be motivated to reduce boredom and increase their vigilance?

2. One small company recognizes an employee of the month, who is given a parking spot next to the president's space near the front door. What theories would explain the positive motivation associated with this policy?

3. One executive argues that managers have too much stability because of benefit and retirement plans. He rewards his managers for taking risks and has removed many guaranteed benefits. Would this approach motivate managers? Why?

4. Would you rather work for a supervisor high in need for achievement, need for affiliation, or need for power? Why? What are the advantages and disadvantages of each?

5. A survey of teachers found that two of the most important rewards were the belief that their work was impor-

tant and a feeling of accomplishment. Is this consistent with Hackman and Oldham's job characteristics model?

6. Many organizations use sales contests and motivational speakers to energize salespeople to overcome frequent rejections and turndowns. How would these devices help motivate salespeople?

7. What characteristics of individuals determine the extent to which work redesign will have a positive impact on work satisfaction and work effectiveness?

Management Exercises

Manager's Workbook

What Motivates You?

You are to indicate how important each characteristic is to you. Answer according to your feelings about the most recent job you had or about the job you currently hold. Circle the number on the scale that represents your feeling—1 (very unimportant) to 7 (very important).

When you have completed the questionnaire, score it as follows:

Rating for question 5 = ___, then divide by 1 = security.

Rating for questions 9 and 13 = ___, then divide by 2 = ___ social.

Rating for questions 1, 3, and 7 = ___. Divide by 3 = ___ esteem.

Rating for questions 4, 10, 11, and 12 = ___. Divide by 4 = ___ autonomy.

Rating for questions 2, 6, and 8 = ___. Divide by 3 + ___ self-actualization.

The instructor has national norm scores for presidents, vice presidents, and upper middle-level, lower middle-level, and lower-level managers with which you can compare your mean importance scores. How do your scores compare with the scores of managers working in organizations?

1. The feeling of self-esteem a person gets from being in that job　　　1　2　3　4　5　6　7

2. The opportunity for personal growth and development in that job　　　1　2　3　4　5　6　7

3. The prestige of the job inside the company (that is, regard received from others in the company)
　　　1　2　3　4　5　6　7

4. The opportunity for independent thought and action in that job　　　1　2　3　4　5　6　7

5. The feeling of security in that job
　　　1　2　3　4　5　6　7

6. The feeling of self-fulfillment a person gets from being in that position (that is, the feeling of being able to use one's own unique capabilities, realizing one's potential)
　　　1　2　3　4　5　6　7

7. The prestige of the job outside the company (that is, the regard received from others not in the company)
　　　1　2　3　4　5　6　7

8. The feeling of worthwhile accomplishment in that job
　　　1　2　3　4　5　6　7

9. The opportunity in that job to give help to other people
　　　1　2　3　4　5　6　7

10. The opportunity in that job for participation in the setting of goals　　　1　2　3　4　5　6　7

11. The opportunity in that job for participation in the determination of methods and procedures
　　　1　2　3　4　5　6　7

12. The authority connected with the job
　　　1　2　3　4　5　6　7

13. The opportunity to develop close friendships in the job
　　　1　2　3　4　5　6　7

SOURCE: Lyman W. Porter, *Organizational Patterns of Managerial Job Attitudes* (New York: American Foundation for Management Research, 1964), pp. 17, 19.

Manager's Workshop

Hey, That's Not Fair!

These six vignettes depict situations in which the Brady kids have perceived an unfair situation. For each vignette, identify the equity theory method (change inputs, change outcomes, distort perceptions, or leave the situation) that you feel the Brady kids should employ. Then, in groups of four to six discuss which method is most relevant for each situation.

1. Greg just found out that Tommy has been picked by the coach to be the new quarterback for the football team because his dad and the coach are old high school buddies. He is really bummed because that is the position he has been hoping to play ever since junior high.

2. Marcia was upset about being turned down for the job of emcee for the school talent show, but she was even more bothered by the fact that the director of the show made her wait for half an hour and was rude and inconsiderate when giving her feedback about her tryout performance. To top it off, she found out later the person chosen as emcee was the homecoming queen.

3. Jan studied about five hours for her geometry final, but her friend Sue only spent about 30 minutes cramming at the last minute. They just got back their test results today—much to Jan's surprise, she only got a B−, but Sue got an A!

4. Peter has been working really hard at the malt shop for the last six months, doing extra chores and helping out other employees when they needed it. The manager of the store just told him that he was going to give him a raise, but Peter is frustrated by the fact that it's only an extra 15¢ an hour. He thought he deserved more. Then yesterday he found out that the new guy hired just two months ago got the same raise.

5. Bobby and his friend Dennis just finished doing a bunch of yard work for Mr. Wilson. Bobby worked nonstop, rarely taking a break, but Dennis kept goofing off and playing around. In the end Mr. Wilson gave them both the same amount of money, which Bobby didn't think was right.

6. Cindy is upset because her science teacher selected three other people to compete in the upcoming science fair without first asking if anybody wanted to volunteer to participate in it.

SOURCE: Courtney Hunt, Northern Illinois University, "Must See TV: The Timelessness of Television as a Teaching Tool," presented at Academy of Management, August 2000. Used with permission.

Management in Practice: Ethical Dilemma

Compensation Showdown

When Suzanne Lebeau, human resources manager, received a call from Bert Wilkes, comptroller of Farley Glass Works, she anticipated hearing good news to share with the Wage and Bonus Committee. She had already seen numbers to indicate that the year-end bonus plan, which was instituted by her committee in lieu of the traditional guaranteed raises of the past, was going to exceed expectations. It was a real relief to her, because the plan, devised by a committee representing all levels of the workforce, had taken eleven months to complete. It had also been a real boost to morale at a low point in the company's history. Workers at the glass shower production plant were bringing new effort and energy to their jobs, and Lebeau wanted to see them rewarded.

She was shocked to see Wilkes's face so grim when she arrived for her meeting. "We have a serious problem, Suzanne," Wilkes said to open the meeting. "We ran the numbers from third quarter to project our end-of-the-year figures and discovered that the executive bonus objectives, which are based on net operating profit, would not be met if we paid out the employee bonuses first. The executive bonuses are a major source of their income. We can't ask them to do without their salary to ensure a bonus for the workers."

Lebeau felt her temper rising. After all their hard work, she was not going to sit by and watch the employees be disappointed because the accounting department had not structured the employee bonus plan to work with the executive plan. She was afraid they would undo all the good that the bonus plan had done in motivating the plant workers. They had kept their end of the bargain, and the company's high profits were common knowledge in the plant.

What Do You Do?

1. Ask to appear before the executive committee to argue that the year-end bonus plan for workers be honored. Executives could defer their bonuses until the problem in the structure of the compensation plan is resolved.

2. Go along with the comptroller. It isn't fair for the executives to lose so much money. Begin to prepare the workers to not expect much this first year of the plan.

3. Go to the board of directors and ask for a compromise plan that splits the bonuses between the executives and the workers.

SOURCE: Based on Doug Wallace, "Promises to Keep," *What Would You Do?* (reprinted from *Business Ethics*), Vol. II (July–August 1993), pp. 11–12. Reprinted with permission from *Business Ethics Magazine*, P.O. Box 8439, Minneapolis, MN 55408 (612) 879-0695.

Surf the Net

1. *Motivation.* Go to www.recognition-plus.com/motivati. htm and print out the page "Motivation: Fact vs. Fallacy." For each of the 10 points, think of a personal or work-related example that illustrates the point being made. If you disagree with any of the 10 points, be prepared to give your reasons during a class discussion on motivation.

2. *Employee Rewards and Recognition.* Bob Nelson, author of two best-selling books on motivation, *1001 Ways to Reward Employees* and *1001 Ways to Energize Employees* provides many excellent resources at his Web site (www.nelson-motivation.com). Check out the page titled "Bob Nelson's Guide to the Best Employee Rewards and Recognition Sites on the Web." After checking out several sites, write a one- to two-page summary of what you learned about rewarding and recognizing employees that you believe would be most useful for managers.

3. *Motivational Compensation Programs.* The Foundation for Economic Development (www.fed.org) provides a 10-question quiz that allows you to test your knowledge of employee ownership as a means of motivating employees. After completing and scoring the quiz, explore the links provided to learn more about employee ownership. In addition, check out the links on the main page that provide articles, case studies, and research on such topics as "Employee Motivation and Empowerment" and "Trends in Employee Ownership."

4. Visit www.mgeneral.com and find six unique ways to motivate described by leaders in their "ezzays."

Case for Critical Analysis

Bloomingdale's

Bloomingdale's is at the forefront of a quiet revolution sweeping department store retailing. Thousands of hourly sales employees are being converted to commission pay. Bloomingdale's hopes to use commissions to motivate employees to work harder, to attract better salespeople, and to enable them to earn more money. For example, under the old plan, a Bloomingdale's salesclerk in women's wear would earn about $16,000 a year, based on $7 per hour and 0.5 percent commission on $500,000 sales. Under the new plan, the annual pay would be $25,000 based on 5 percent commission on $500,000 sales.

John Palmerio, who works in the men's shoe salon, is enthusiastic about the changeover. His pay has increased an average of $175 per week. But in women's lingerie, employees are less enthusiastic. A target of $1,600 in sales per week is difficult to achieve but is necessary for salespeople to earn their previous salary and even to keep their jobs. In previous years, the practice of commission pay was limited to big-ticket items such as furniture, appliances, and men's suits, where extra sales skill pays off. The move into small-item purchases may not work as well, but Bloomingdale's and other stores are trying anyway.

One question is whether Bloomingdale's can create more customer-oriented salespeople when they work on commission. They may be reluctant to handle complaints, make returns, and clean shelves, preferring instead to chase customers. Moreover, it cost Bloomingdale's about $1 million per store to install the commission system because of training programs, computer changes, and increased pay in many departments. If the overall impact on service is negative, the increased efficiency may not seem worthwhile.

Questions

1. What theories about motivation underlie the switch from salary to commission pay?

2. Are high-level needs met under the commission system?

3. As a customer, would you prefer to shop where employees are motivated to make commissions?

SOURCES: Based on Francine Schwadel, "Chain Finds Incentives a Hard Sell," *The Wall Street Journal,* July 5, 1990, p. B4; and Amy Dunkin, "Now Salespeople Really Must Sell for Their Supper," *Business Week,* July 31, 1989, pp. 50–52.

Endnotes

1 Daintry Duffy, "Cultural Evolution," *CIO,* Jan. 15, 1999, pp. 44–50; Ronald B. Lieber, "Beating the Odds," *Fortune,* March 31, 1997, pp. 82–88.

2 David Silburt, "Secrets of the Super Sellers," *Canadian Business,* January 1987, pp. 54–59; "Meet the Savvy Supersalesmen," *Fortune,* February 4, 1985, pp. 56–62; Michael Brody, "Meet Today's Young American Worker," *Fortune,* November 11, 1985, pp. 90–98; and Tom Richman, "Meet the Masters. They Could Sell You Anything . . . ," *Inc.,* March 1985, pp. 79–86.

3 Jerry L. Gray and Frederick A. Starke, *Organizational Behavior: Concepts and Applications,* 4th ed. (New York: Macmillan, 1988), pp. 104–105.

4 Linda Grant, "Happy Workers, High Returns," *Fortune,* January 12, 1998, p. 81.

5 Anne Fisher, "The 100 Best Companies to Work for in America," *Fortune,* January 12, 1998, pp. 69–70.

6 Steers and Porter, *Motivation.*

7 J. F. Rothlisberger and W. J. Dickson, *Management and the Worker* (Cambridge, Mass.: Harvard University Press, 1939).

8 Abraham F. Maslow, "A Theory of Human Motivation," *Psychological Review,* 50 (1943), pp. 370–396.

9 Roberta Maynard, "How to Motivate Low-Wage Workers," *Nation's Business,* May 1997, pp. 35–39.

10 Clayton Alderfer, *Existence, Relatedness and Growth* (New York: Free Press, 1972).

11 Roberta Maynard, "How to Motivate Low-Wage Workers."

12 Frederick Herzberg, "One More Time: How Do You Motivate Employees?" *Harvard Business Review* (January–February 1968), pp. 53–62.

13 David C. McClelland, *Human Motivation* (Glenview, Ill.: Scott, Foresman, 1985).

14 Celest Fremon, "Off the Streets, onto Hollywood Sets," *Good Housekeeping,* Nov. 1998, p. 30.

15 J. Stacy Adams, "Injustice in Social Exchange," in *Advances in Experimental Social Psychology,* 2d ed., ed. L. Berkowitz (New York: Academic Press, 1965).

16 Ray V. Montagno, "The Effects of Comparison to Others and Primary Experience on Responses to Task Design," *Academy of Management Journal,* 28 (1985), pp. 491–498.

17 Victor H. Vroom, *Work and Motivation* (New York: Wiley, 1964); B. S. Gorgopoulos, G. M. Mahoney, and N. Jones, "A Path-Goal Approach to Productivity," *Journal of Applied Psychology,* 41 (1957), pp. 345–353.

18 Abby Livingston, "Gain-Sharing Encourages Productivity," *Nation's Business,* January 1998, pp. 21–22.

19 Alexander D. Stajkovic and Fred Luthans, "A Meta-Analysis of the Effects of Organizational Behavior Modification on Task Performance, 1975–95," *Academy of Management Journal,* October 1997, pp. 1122–1149; H. Richlin, Modern Behaviorism (San Francisco: Freeman, 1970); and B. F. Skinner, *Science and Human Behavior* (New York: Macmillan, 1953).

20 Kenneth D. Butterfield and Linda Klebe Trevino, "Punishment from the Manager's Perspective: A Grounded Investigation and Inductive Model," *Academy of Management Journal,* 39 (6) (December 1996), pp. 1479–1512; and Andrea Casey, "Voices from the Firing Line: Managers Discuss Punishment in the Workplace," *Academy of Management Executive,* 11 (3) (1997), pp. 93–94.

21 Tom Peters and Nancy Austin, *A Passion for Excellence: The Leadership Difference* (New York: Random House, 1985), p. 267.

22 "Creating Incentives for Hourly Workers," *Inc.*, July 1986, pp. 89–90.

23 Alfie Kohn, "Incentives Can Be Bad for Business," *Inc.*, January 1998, pp. 93–94.

24 Thomas Petzinger, Jr. "In Search of the New World (of Work)," *Fast Company*, April 1999, pp. 219–226.

25 J. Richard Hackman and Greg R. Oldham, *Work Redesign* (Reading, Mass.: Addison-Wesley, 1980).

26 Jay A. Conger and Rabindra N. Kanungo, "The Empowerment Process: Integrating Theory and Practice," *Academy of Management Review,* 13 (1988), pp. 471–482.

27 Thomas A. Stewart, "New Ways to Exercise Power," *Fortune,* 6 (November 1989), pp. 52–64.

28 Arno Penzias, "New Paths to Success," *Fortune,* June 12, 1995, pp. 90–94.

29 Ralph Stayer, "How I Learned to Let My Workers Lead," *Harvard Business Review,* November–December 1990, pp. 66–83.

30 This discussion is based on Robert C. Ford and Myron D. Fottler, "Empowerment: A Matter of Degree," *Academy of Management Executive,* 9 (3) (1995), pp. 21–31.

31 Jay A. Conger and Rabindra N. Kanungo, "The Empowerment Process: Integrating Theory and Practice," *Academy of Management Review,* 13 (1998), pp. 471–482.

32 Carol Hildebrand, "Turn Green," *CIO*, Aug. 15, 1999, pp. 94–101; Mindy Blodgett, "Fast Forward," *CIO*, Aug.15, 1999, pp. 46–58.

14

Communicating in Organizations

LEARNING OBJECTIVES

After studying this chapter, you should be able to:

- Explain why communication is essential for effective management and describe how nonverbal behavior and listening affect communication among people

- Explain how managers use communication to persuade and influence others

- Describe the concept of channel richness, and explain how communication channels influence the quality of communication among managers

- Explain the difference between formal and informal organizational communications and the importance of each for organization management

- Describe team communication and how structure influences communication outcomes

- Discuss how open communication and dialogue can enhance team spirit and effectiveness

- Describe barriers to organizational communication, and suggest ways to avoid or overcome them

MANAGEMENT PROBLEM

UMANG GUPTA **had a dream.**

Ever since moving from India to the United

States in 1980, he wanted to start his own computer company.

Realizing Silicon Valley was a good place for training, he first worked at IBM and

then moved to the startup Oracle, helping to write its business plan. But his dream persisted.

In 1984 he launched Gupta Corp, sparsely financed from fees of early customers, such as Lotus

Corporation. This is a riskier strategy than venture-capital financing, because it demands a lengthy

technological lead in order to withstand competition from later and better-financed rivals. But the strategy

• *If you were Gupta, what would you do now? What could you have done to*

prevent this fiasco? Who should he be communicating with and in what form?

worked—for a while anyway. Gupta's vision of creating software to manage databases brought in enough

revenue to peak at $400 million, allowing Gupta to have a net worth of $100 million "for a few days."

So convinced he was of his mission to change the world, he was going to push it as far as he could.

Because of the power of his mission, he was cramming as many meetings as he could each day—

none too thoughtfully planned. Then the bottom fell out. Powerful new well-financed

competitors piled into the market and Gupta Corp suffered through

seven quarters of losses. Stock prices plummeted.[1]

Umang Gupta believes in communication, but other demands get in the way. In today's intensely competitive environment, top managers at many companies are trying to improve communication. Jim Chesterton, CEO of A. W. Chesterton Co., holds quarterly meetings at which employees can ask him about anything and everything. Similarly, at Cisco Systems, every year during their birthday month employees get an invitation to a birthday breakfast with CEO John Chambers, where they can put their toughest questions directly to the top executive.[2] It isn't always easy when workers confront top managers with difficult questions or challenge them regarding management failings, but getting candid feedback from employees helps executives spot problems or recognize opportunities that might otherwise be missed.

These executives are interested in staying connected with employees and customers and with shaping company direction. To do so, they must be in touch; hence they excel at personal communications. Nonmanagers often are amazed at how much energy successful executives put into communication.

This chapter explains why these executives are effective communicators. First, we will see how managerial jobs require communication. Next, we will define communication and describe a model of the communication process. Then, we will consider the interpersonal aspects of communication, including communication channels, persuasion, and listening skills, that affect the ability of managers to communicate. Finally, with a look at the organization as a whole, we'll discuss formal and informal communications and how managers can overcome the barriers to effective communication that exist.

■ COMMUNICATION AND THE MANAGER'S JOB

How important is communication? Consider this: Managers spend at least 80 percent of every working day in direct communication with others. In other words, 48 minutes of every hour is spent in meetings, on the telephone, or talking informally while walking around. The other 20 percent of a typical manager's time is spent doing desk work, most of which is also communication in the form of reading and writing.[3] Exhibit 14.1 illustrates the crucial position of management in the information network. Managers gather important information from both inside and outside the organization and then distribute appropriate information to others who need it.

Communication permeates every management function. When managers perform the planning function, they gather information; write letters, memos, and reports; and then meet with other managers to explain the plan. When managers lead, they communicate to share a vision of what the organization can be and motivate employees to help achieve it. When managers organize, they gather information about the state of the organization and communicate a new structure to others. Communication skills are a fundamental part of every managerial activity.

WHAT IS COMMUNICATION?

A professor at Harvard once asked a class to define communication by drawing pictures. Most students drew a manager speaking or writing. Some placed "speech balloons" next to their characters; others showed pages flying from a typewriter. "No," the professor told the class, "none of you has captured the essence of communication." He went on to explain that communication means "to share"—not "to speak" or "to write."

Communication thus can be defined as the process by which information is exchanged and understood by two or more people, usually with the intent to motivate or influence behavior. Communication is not just sending information. This distinction between *sharing* and *proclaiming* is crucial for successful management. A manager who does not listen is like a used-car salesperson who claims, "I sold a car—they just did not buy it." Management communication is a two-way street that includes listening and other forms of feedback. Effective communication, in the words of one expert, is as follows:

communication
The process by which information is exchanged and understood by two or more people, usually with the intent to motivate or influence behavior

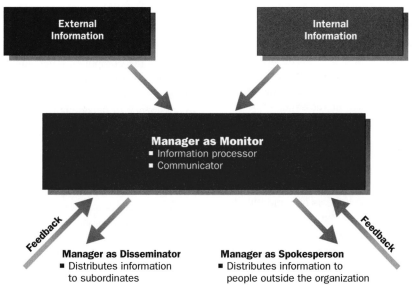

SOURCE: Adapted from Henry Mintzberg, *The Nature of Managerial Work* (New York: Harper & Row, 1973), p. 72.

When two people interact, they put themselves into each other's shoes, try to perceive the world as the other person perceives it, try to predict how the other will respond. Interaction involves reciprocal role-taking, the mutual employment of empathetic skills. The goal of interaction is the merger of self and other, a complete ability to anticipate, predict, and behave in accordance with the joint needs of self and other.[4] ■

It is the desire to share understanding that motivates executives to visit employees on the shop floor or eat breakfast with them. The things managers learn from direct communication with employees shape their understanding of the corporation.

THE COMMUNICATION PROCESS

Many people think communication is simple because they communicate without conscious thought or effort. However, communication usually is complex, and the opportunities for sending or receiving the wrong messages are innumerable. No doubt, you have heard someone say, "But that's not what I meant!" Have you ever received directions you thought were clear and yet still got lost? How often have you wasted time on misunderstood instructions?

To more fully understand the complexity of the communication process, note the key elements outlined in Exhibit 14.2. Two common elements in every communication situation are the sender and the receiver. The *sender* is anyone who wishes to convey an idea or concept to others, to seek information, or to express a thought or emotion. The *receiver* is the person to whom the message is sent. The sender **encodes** the idea by selecting symbols with which to compose a message. The **message** is the tangible formulation of the idea that is sent to the receiver. The message is sent through a **channel,** which is the communication carrier. The channel can be a formal report, a telephone call, or a face-to-face meeting. The receiver **decodes** the symbols to interpret the meaning of the message. Encoding and decoding are potential sources for communication errors, because knowledge, attitudes, and background act as filters and create "noise" when translating from symbols to meaning. Finally, **feedback** occurs when the receiver

encode
To select symbols with which to compose a message

message
The tangible formulation of an idea to be sent to a receiver

channel
The carrier of a communication

decode
To translate the symbols used in a message for the purpose of interpreting its meaning

feedback
A response by the receiver to the sender's communication

responds to the sender's communication with a return message. Without feedback, the communication is *one-way*; with feedback, it is *two-way*. Feedback is a powerful aid to communication effectiveness, because it enables the sender to determine whether the receiver correctly interpreted the message.

Managers who are effective communicators understand and use the circular nature of communication. For example, James Treybig of Tandem Computers, Inc., widened the open-door policy in order to communicate with employees. Treybig appears on a monthly television program broadcast over the company's in-house television station. Employees around the world watch the show and call in their questions and comments. The television is the channel through which Treybig sends his encoded message. Employees decode and interpret the message and encode their feedback, which is sent through the channel of the telephone hookup. The communication circuit is complete. At Graphic Solutions, a custom printer in Burr Ridge, Illinois, owners Suzanne Zaccone and her brother Bob maintain communication channels by meeting monthly with a few workers from each department. The questions and comments from workers range from daily workplace concerns to the company's long-range plans.[5] Jim Treybig and the Zaccones understand the elements of communication and have developed systems that work.

■ COMMUNICATING AMONG PEOPLE

The communication model in Exhibit 14.2 illustrates the components that must be mastered for effective communication. Communications can break down if sender and receiver do not encode or decode language in the same way.[6] The selection of communication channels can determine whether the message is distorted by noise and interference. The listening skills of both parties can determine whether a message is truly shared. Thus, for managers to be effective communicators, they must understand how interpersonal factors such as communication channels, nonverbal behavior, and listening all work to enhance or detract from communication.

COMMUNICATION CHANNELS

Managers have a choice of many channels through which to communicate to other managers or employees. A manager may discuss a problem face-to-face, use the telephone, send an electronic message, write a memo or letter, or put an item in a newsletter, depending on the nature of the message. Recent research has attempted to explain how managers select communication channels to enhance communication effectiveness.[7] The research has found that channels differ in their capacity to convey information. Just as a pipeline's physical char-

Exhibit 14.2

A MODEL OF THE COMMUNICATION PROCESS

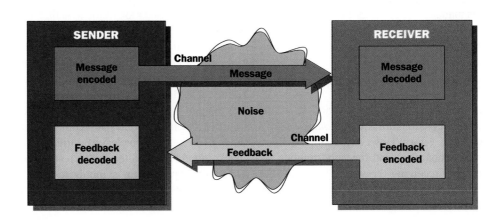

acteristics limit the kind and amount of liquid that can be pumped through it, a communication channel's physical characteristics limit the kind and amount of information that can be conveyed among managers. The channels available to managers can be classified into a hierarchy based on information richness. **Channel richness** is the amount of information that can be transmitted during a communication episode. The hierarchy of channel richness is illustrated in Exhibit 14.3.

The capacity of an information channel is influenced by three characteristics: (1) the ability to handle multiple cues simultaneously; (2) the ability to facilitate rapid, two-way feedback; and (3) the ability to establish a personal focus for the communication. Face-to-face discussion is the richest medium, because it permits direct experience, multiple information cues, immediate feedback, and personal focus. Face-to-face discussions facilitate the assimilation of broad cues and deep, emotional understanding of the situation. For example, Tony Burns, CEO of Ryder Systems, Inc., likes to handle things face-to-face: "You can look someone in the eyes, and you can tell by the look in his eyes or the inflection in his voice what the real problem or question or answer is."[8] Telephone conversations and inter-

active electronic media, such as voice mail and electronic mail, while increasing the speed of communication, lack the element of "being there." Eye contact, gaze, blush, posture, and body language cues are eliminated. In recognition of the need for channel richness, interactive communication is taking on the immediacy of "being there" through increased use of video conferencing. Written media that are personalized, such as memos, notes, and letters, can be personally focused, but they convey only the cues written on paper and are slow to provide feedback. Impersonal written media, including fliers, bulletins, and standard computer reports, are the lowest in richness. These channels are not focused on a single receiver, use limited information cues, and do not permit feedback.

It is important for managers to understand that each communication channel has advantages and disadvantages, and that each can be an effective means of communication in the appropriate circumstances.[9] Channel selection depends on whether the message is routine or nonroutine. *Nonroutine messages* typically are ambiguous, concern novel events, and impose great potential for misunderstanding. Nonroutine messages often are characterized by time pressure and surprise. Managers can

channel richness
The amount of information that can be transmitted during a communication episode

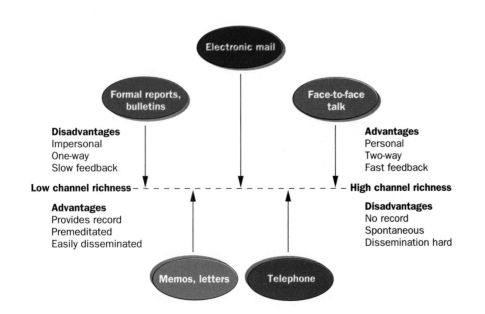

E x h i b i t   14.3
A CONTINUUM OF CHANNEL RICHNESS

communicate nonroutine messages effectively only by selecting rich channels. On the other hand, routine communications are simple and straightforward. *Routine messages* convey data or statistics or simply put into words what managers already agree on and understand. Routine messages can be efficiently communicated through a channel lower in richness. Written communications also should be used when the audience is widely dispersed or when the communication is "official" and a permanent record is required.[10]

Consider a CEO trying to work out a press release with public relations people about a plant explosion that injured 15 employees. If the press release must be ready in three hours, the communication is truly nonroutine and forces a rich information exchange. The group will meet face-to-face, brainstorm ideas, and provide rapid feedback to resolve disagreement and convey the correct information. If the CEO has three days to prepare the release, less information capacity is needed. The CEO and public relations people might begin developing the press release with an exchange of memos and telephone calls.

The key is to select a channel to fit the message. One successful manager who understands channel selection is Jack Welch, chairman and CEO of General Electric.

GENERAL ELECTRIC
www.ge.com

For more than 17 years, Jack Welch has led General Electric to one revenue and earnings record after another and helped increase the market share of GE from $12 billion in 1981 to about $280 billion today. Welch, a master at communication, spends more than half his time on what he calls "people issues." He has created a sense of informality and sharing that is rare for a huge company such as GE. His preferred form of communication typically is personal notes accompanied by a phone call. He is well known for dashing off handwritten notes to people throughout the company to congratulate them for a job well done or to explain a controversial decision. For ex-

ample, when Welch vetoed the idea of buying AT&T Universal Card, he sent a note to the manager at GE Capital who had spent hundreds of hours studying the proposed acquisition. He wanted her to know that despite his decision, he had been impressed with her analysis and presentation. There are no form letters or memos from Welch—not to employees, managers, top executives, or even board members. Everything is handled with personal notes, phone calls, or face-to-face communication.

Welch kicks off each year for GE with a session in Boca Raton, Florida, for the top 500 executives. The meeting gives Welch a chance to set the agenda for the year and to celebrate the company's newest heroes. Managers from the various businesses can exchange ideas with their counterparts. Informal chat sessions may last until 2 or 3 A.M., with Welch himself participating. His wrap-up talk at the end of the meeting is videotaped, translated into eight different languages, and dispatched to GE locations around the world, where managers use it to spark communication with their own teams about the issues GE will face in the coming year. Other formal means of communication are the Corporate Executive Council sessions held each quarter, at which GE's top 30 officers track progress and swap ideas. These meetings have earned descriptions from executives such as "food fights" or "free-for-alls" because all information—good and bad—is shared openly. At these sessions Welch gets unfiltered information.

One of the most important forms of communication for Welch is the informal, unscheduled communication in which he participates almost daily. Every week, there are unexpected visits to plants and offices, during which Welch talks directly with GE people at all levels. He regularly schedules impromptu luncheons with managers several layers below him to get their ideas and perspectives. Indeed, in an average year, Welch directly meets and talks with several thousand General Electric employees. He uses a metaphor of the company as an old-fashioned grocery store, where he can mentally roll up his sleeves, get behind the counter, and get to know employees and customers intimately.[11] ■

Jack Welch's communication skills have helped him wield enormous influence over the most far-flung, complex organization in American business. Leaders such as Welch understand that, in addition to the message content, the choice of communication channel can convey a symbolic meaning to the receiver. Welch's decision to communicate through personal notes, phone calls, and face-to-face meetings rather than by form letters and memos signals to employees that he cares about them as individuals.

PERSUASION AND INFLUENCE

Communication is used not only to convey information, but to persuade and influence people. Managers use communication to sell employees on the vision for the organization and influence them to behave in such a way as to accomplish the vision. While communication skills have always been important to managers, the ability to persuade and influence others is more critical today than ever before. The command-and-control mindset of managers telling workers what to do and how to do it is gone. Businesses are run largely by cross-functional teams who are actively involved in making decisions. Issuing directives is no longer an appropriate or effective way to get things done.[12] Therefore, managers should understand how communication can be used to persuade and influence others.

Managers can enrich their communication encounters by paying attention to the language they use as well as the channels of communication they select to convey their messages. To persuade and influence, managers connect with others on an emotional level by using symbols, metaphors, and stories to express their messages. David Armstrong, president of Armstrong International, wrote *Management by Storying Around* after he noticed the way people listened to his minister's stories each Sunday.[13] Even when people had heard a story many times, their attention perked up. Armstrong saw that people loved to hear stories and decided to use that to enhance his management and communication skills. He began using stories to replace rules and regulations. For example, he told a story about an executive traveling for the company who spent money just the way he did at home. This story gradually replaced Armstrong International's travel and entertainment expense rulebook. Stories eventually replaced the entire policy manual.

Using symbols and stories also helps managers make sense of a fast-changing environment in ways that members throughout the organization can understand. Managers help inspire desirable behaviors for change by tapping into the imaginations of their subordinates. If we think back to our early school years, we may remember that the most effective lessons often were couched in stories. Consider the meaning conveyed by a manager telling the following story: "Every morning in Africa, a gazelle wakes up. It knows it must outrun the fastest lion or it will be killed. Every morning in Africa, a lion wakes up. It knows it must run faster than the slowest gazelle or it will starve. It doesn't matter whether you're a lion or a gazelle—when the sun comes up, you'd better be running."[14]

Presenting hard facts and figures rarely has the same power as telling vivid stories. Evidence of the compatibility of stories with human thinking was demonstrated by a study at Stanford Business School.[15] The point was to convince MBA students that a company practiced a policy of avoiding layoffs. For some students, only a story was used. For others, statistical data were provided that showed little turnover compared to competitors. For other students, statistics and stories were combined, and yet other students were shown the company's official policy statements. Of all these approaches, the students presented with a vivid story alone were most convinced that the company truly practiced a policy of avoiding layoffs.

NONVERBAL COMMUNICATION

Managers also use symbols to communicate what is important. Managers are watched, and their behavior, appearance, actions, and attitudes are symbolic of what they value and expect of others.

Nonverbal communication refers to messages sent through human actions and behaviors rather than through words.[16] Although most nonverbal communication is unconscious or subconscious on our part, it represents a major portion of the messages we send and receive. Most managers are astonished to learn that words themselves carry little meaning. Major parts of the shared understanding from communication come from the nonverbal messages of facial expression, voice, mannerisms, posture, and dress.

Nonverbal communication occurs mostly face-to-face. One researcher found three sources of communication cues during face-to-face communication: the verbal, which are the actual spoken words; the vocal, which include the pitch, tone, and timbre of a person's voice; and facial expressions. According to this study, the relative weights of these three factors in message interpretation are as follows: verbal impact, 7 percent; vocal impact, 38 percent; and facial impact, 55 percent.[17]

This research strongly implies that "it's not what you say but how you say it." A manager's tone of voice or glint in the eye may signal something entirely different from his or her words. Nonverbal messages convey thoughts and feelings with greater force than do our most carefully selected words. Body language often communicates our real feelings eloquently. Thus, while the conscious mind may be formulating vocal messages such as "I'm happy" or "Congratulations on your promotion," the body language may be signaling true feelings through blushing, perspiring, glancing, crying, or avoiding eye contact. When the verbal and nonverbal messages are contradictory, the receiver may be confused and usually will give more weight to behavioral actions than to verbal messages.[18]

A manager's office also sends powerful nonverbal cues. For example, what do the following seating arrangements mean if used by your supervisor? (1) She stays behind her desk, and you sit in a straight chair on the opposite side. (2) The two of you sit in straight chairs away from her desk, perhaps at a table. (3) The two of you sit in a seating arrangement consisting of a sofa and easy chair. To most people, the first arrangement indicates "I'm the boss here" or "I'm in authority." The second arrangement indicates "This is serious business." The third indicates a more casual and friendly "Let's get to know each other."[19] Nonverbal messages can be a powerful asset to communication if they complement and support verbal messages. Managers should pay close attention to nonverbal behavior when communicating. They must learn to coordinate their verbal and nonverbal messages and at the same time be sensitive to what their peers, subordinates, and supervisors are saying nonverbally.

Nonverbal communication also includes graphics, such as pictures. Deb Edlhuber used the power of nonverbal pictures to build her Internet business.

PRAIRIE FRONTIER

Talk about making lemonade out of a lemon! When a tornado destroyed the woods on her family's Waukesha, Wisconsin, farm, Deb Edlhuber was entranced by the array of wildflowers that sprung up in areas previously lacking sunlight. She and her husband started photographing the flowers in all their bewildering glory, from the bottle gentian's ice blue starburst to swamp milkweed's butterfly-baiting clusters. Before they knew it, boxes of photos were cluttering their entire house. They decided to communicate all that beauty to others. So they started a business, selling the seeds of all those lovely flowers, becoming a wholesaler to garden centers. "It was meant to be a part-time thing," she now says.

That all changed when she bought her first PC and got a scanner in 1997, teaching herself how to build a Web page. She also signed on with Link-Exchange, which works with small companies who want to swap banner ads, and then the torrent of e-business started. "We had never advertised before," she says, "and I had no idea it would snowball like that."

---

nonverbal communication
Messages sent through human actions and behaviors rather than through words

What made her site so desirable were, of course, the pictures, which she had posted as patiently as she had photographed. Each one is exquisitely beautiful, alongside text describing the plant's name, how tall it grows, what months it blooms, how much sunlight it needs, and also what wildlife it attracts. When people saw the beautiful flowers, they wanted them and started placing orders ranging from $50 to $100.

Long since a full-time occupation, Edlhuber has expanded her business, adding to the Web site games and wildflower puzzles, as well as a slide show instructing how to build a prairie. One of the biggest draws is free musical greeting cards, of which 6,000 a day were sent in December.[20] ■

LISTENING

One of the most important tools of manager communication is listening, both to employees and customers. Most managers now recognize that important information flows from the bottom up, not the top down, and managers had

better be tuned in.[21] In the communication model on page 440, the listener is responsible for message reception, which is a vital link in the communication process. **Listening** is the skill of grasping both facts and feelings to interpret a message's genuine meaning. Only then can the manager provide the appropriate response. Listening requires attention, energy, and skill. Lt. General William G. Pagonis, who led the U.S. Army's 22nd Support Command for the Persian Gulf War, believes that one of the keys to effective leadership in war or business is to develop effective listening skills and put them into practice. He recalls a wise commanding officer once telling him, "Never pass up the opportunity to remain silent."[22]

Many people do not listen effectively. They concentrate on formulating what they are going to say next rather than on what is being said to them. Our listening efficiency, as measured by the amount of material understood and remembered by subjects 48 hours after listening to a 10-minute message, is, on average, no better than 25 percent.[23]

What constitutes good listening? Exhibit 14.4 gives ten keys to effective listening and illustrates a number of ways to distinguish a bad

listening
The skill of grasping facts and feelings to interpret a message's genuine meaning

E x h i b i t 14.4
TEN KEYS TO EFFECTIVE LISTENING

Keys	Poor Listener	Good Listener
1. Listen actively	Is passive, laid back	Asks questions, paraphrases what is said
2. Find areas of interest	Tunes out dry subjects	Looks for opportunities, new learning
3. Resist distractions	Is easily distracted	Fights or avoids distractions; tolerates bad habits; knows how to concentrate
4. Capitalize on the fact that thought is faster than speech	Tends to daydream with slow speakers	Challenges, anticipates, mentally summarizes; weighs the evidence; listens between the lines to tone of voice
5. Be responsive	Is minimally involved	Nods; shows interest, give and take, positive feedback
6. Judge content, not delivery	Tunes out if delivery is poor	Judges content; skips over delivery errors
7. Hold one's fire	Has preconceptions, starts to argue	Does not judge until comprehension is complete
8. Listen for ideas	Listens for facts	Listens to central themes
9. Work at listening	Shows no energy output; faked attention	Works hard, exhibits active body state, eye contact
10. Exercise one's mind	Resists difficult material in favor of light, recreational material	Uses heavier material as exercise for the mind

SOURCES: Adapted from Sherman K. Okum, "How to Be a Better Listener," *Nation's Business* (August 1975), 62; and Philip Morgan and Kent Baker, "Building a Professional Image: Improving Listening Behavior," *Supervisory Management* (November 1985), 34–38.

listener from a good listener. A good listener finds areas of interest, is flexible, works hard at listening, and uses thought speed to mentally summarize, weigh, and anticipate what the speaker says. Meetings with coffee growers in the Andean mountains, rebel guerrillas, or purchasing agents at coffee distributors has taught Karen Cebreros the importance of listening and creating trust.

ELAN ORGANIC COFFEES

When Karen Cebreros was diagnosed with a life-threatening heart ailment 10 years ago, she decided to do something radical with her life. The headstrong mother of two flew down to Peru and dropped in on her brother-in-law, who lived in a village that is a 16-hour bus ride and then a 10-hour hike from the airport. Seeing the impoverished village coffee growers cultivating the Andean earth with no chemical fertilizers or pesticides gave the former Xerox sales executive the jolt she needed. Her mind percolated with an idea: Since Americans were buying more organic foods, why not organic coffee?

So began her journey of learning and business development. She learned that most coffee is grown in open, highly sunned plantations with lots of pesticides. "Shade-grown" beans are cultivated, on the other hand, beneath tree canopies that help protect the crops without chemicals. It also creates superior-quality coffee. As she got more interested in organic foods, she changed her diet, added exercise, and healed her heart condition.

Meanwhile, she emptied her retirement fund and took out a home equity loan to raise the $100,000 needed to start Elan. Her skills in communication have paid off in several ways, including: organizing coffee farmers (in El Salvador, Guatemala, Colombia, Mexico, and Peru), whom she pays $1.40 per pound, compared to the eight cents they were paid previously; negotiating with rebel guerrillas who control coffee plantations; and working with large coffee distributors or chains such as Rainforest Café and Starbucks—all of which has help her sell $2 million per year of organic beans.

A true believer, Cebreros herself drinks three cups of caffeinated coffee each day. "I've pretty much dedicated my life to this," she says.[24] ∎

Merrill Lynch superbroker Richard F. Green explained the importance of listening to organizational success: "If you talk, you'll like me. If I talk, I'll like you—but if I do the talking, my business will not be served." Green builds long-term relationships with his clients by listening. Rick Pitino, coach of the Boston Celtics, also believes in the power of listening. His rule for improving your communication skills is to listen four times as much as you speak. Pitino tells a story of how, as coach of the University of Kentucky Wildcats, he failed to recruit a hot prospect because he spent the entire time talking, impressing the player and his family with the greatness of the Wildcats, the team's half-million-dollar weight room and private plane, and the thrill of playing before Kentucky's worshipful fans. Having learned his lesson, Pitino took a different approach with prospect Tony Delk, a player thought unlikely to choose the University of Kentucky. When he met with Delk and his parents, Pitino didn't do much talking. Instead he asked a lot of questions—what Delk wanted from a coach; what the parents wanted for their son in a college. For nearly an hour, Pitino only asked questions and listened to the answers. Not only did Pitino successfully recruit Delk, but four years later the star player helped lead Kentucky to its sixth national championship. It's a story Pitino says he likes to tell business groups because "it illustrates how important it is to listen to people."[25]

∎ ORGANIZATIONAL COMMUNICATION

Another aspect of management communication concerns the organization as a whole. Organizationwide communications typically flow in three directions—downward, upward, and horizontally. Managers are responsible for establishing and maintaining formal channels of communication in these three directions. Managers also use informal channels, which means they get out of their offices and mingle with employees.

FORMAL COMMUNICATION CHANNELS

Formal communication channels are those that flow within the chain of command or task responsibility defined by the organization. The three formal channels and the types of information conveyed in each are illustrated in Exhibit 14.5. Downward and upward communication are the primary forms of communication used in most traditional, vertically organized companies. The learning organization, in contrast, emphasizes horizontal communication, with people constantly sharing information across departments and levels. Electronic communications, such as e-mail, have made it easier than ever for information to flow in all directions. For example, when used appropriately and in the right organizational environment, e-mail can improve upward communication flow because employees can contact managers at any time to ask questions or offer ideas, without having to wait for a meeting. Suzanne Zaccone of Graphic Solutions prefers face-to-face communication with her 65 employees, but when she's on the road, she encourages them to communicate with her through electronic mail.[26]

Rykodisc, Inc., the largest independent record label in the United States, was started in 1983, but the four partners were spread all over the country—from Los Angeles to Salem, Massachusetts—and no one intended to move. The solution from the beginning was constant information sharing, and the company maintains an obsession with keeping every type of information constantly flowing among all employees, no matter where they're situated geographically, functionally, or hierarchically. All Rykodisc employees, from the mailroom clerk to the chief financial officer, write and circulate short weekly memos, so that everyone knows what everyone else in the company is doing. Armed with information, Rykodisc employees consistently outproduce larger competitors. The founders and department heads also hold weekly conference calls to talk about specific problems or opportunities.

At first, Rykodisc built its communications primarily around phone calls, faxes, and airline schedules, avoiding networks and e-mail because of a fear that less-personal communications might erode the sense of community. "Technology itself is a cool medium," says founder Dan Rose, "[but] the way we use it we make it a warm process." He's found that some employees are more comfortable leaving an e-mail message than walking into his office or calling him on the phone. Rose answers all internal e-mail personally and now corresponds regularly with some employees he'd had little interaction with before the company networked. Rykodisc knows that connection to the customer is a vital part of information flow, so its Web page allows customers to download art and music directly and easily. For a company intent on sharing information as broadly as possible, high technology is another tool to maintain a sense of community.[27]

DOWNWARD COMMUNICATION The most familiar and obvious flow of formal communication is **downward communication,** which refers to the messages and information sent from top management to subordinates in a downward direction. For example, Mike Olson, plant manager at Ryerson Midwest Coil Processing, holds monthly meetings to discuss financial data and performance analyses with all employees. He also uses other forms of communication. Because workers were continuously dropping expensive power tools, Olson hung price tags on the tools to show the replacement cost; workers solved the problem by finding a way to hook up the tools so they wouldn't be dropped. Olson's communication helps workers see how their actions affect the entire company and creates a climate of working together for solutions.[28]

Managers can communicate downward to employees in many ways. Some of the most common are through speeches, messages in company newsletters, electronic mail, information leaflets tucked into pay envelopes, material on bulletin boards, and policy and procedure manuals. At VeriFone Inc. (described

formal communication channels
Channels of communication that flow within the chain of command or task responsibility defined by the organization; traditional approach is upward/downward versus newer horizontal approach

downward communication
The flow of communication from top management downward to subordinates

Exhibit 14.5

DOWNWARD, UPWARD, AND HORIZONTAL COMMUNICATION IN ORGANIZATIONS

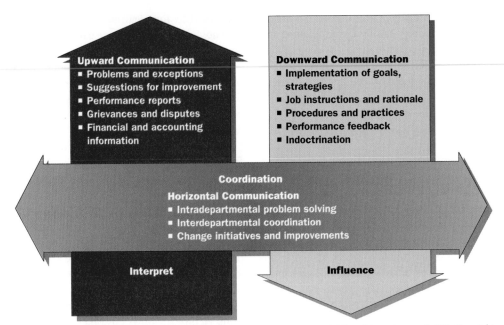

Upward Communication
- Problems and exceptions
- Suggestions for improvement
- Performance reports
- Grievances and disputes
- Financial and accounting information

Downward Communication
- Implementation of goals, strategies
- Job instructions and rationale
- Procedures and practices
- Performance feedback
- Indoctrination

Coordination
Horizontal Communication
- Intradepartmental problem solving
- Interdepartmental coordination
- Change initiatives and improvements

Interpret   Influence

SOURCE: Adapted from Richard L. Daft and Richard M. Steers, *Organizations: A Micro/Macro Approach*, 538. Copyright © 1986 by Scott, Foresman and Company. Used by permission.

later in this chapter), managers believe there's no such thing as giving employees too much information. They flood home mailboxes of employees with newsletters, total-compensation updates, benefit-program descriptions, and stock option plans. Since VeriFone is largely a "virtual" company in which geographical dispersion is the operating principle, the company also makes extensive use of electronic mail. CEO Hatim Tyabji distributes e-mail about leadership and invites employees to challenge him if he is not living up to his own precepts.[29] One Internet startup found it essential to be very clear with its downward communication to new employees.

STAMPS.COM

Buying stamps used to be boring. Sometimes you had to wait in long lines at the post office. But 20-something Jeffrey Green and two partners are out to change that. They started stamps.com to sell good old postage stamps online. With special software they provide, you can pay online with your credit card and print a bar-coded "stamp" directly

onto an envelope or adhesive label. Does it fill a need? Three years later they have over 100 employees and are growing so fast they are racing just to keep up.

How do they cope? By practicing good downward communication. "You have to hire people who are willing to jump right in the middle and start sprinting," says Green. "And you have to let them know that upfront. It's not the most nurturing environment, but if you slow down to teach everyone everything about the company before they start working, you fall behind."

Stanford University Professor Charles O'Reilley agrees, saying the important concept is not so much learning in organizations as it being less rigid and be willing to undo the way things were done before. "If you really want to be fast, you have to unlearn."

They had to change faster than they expected, moving from one temporary quarter to another every few months, as their staff kept ballooning to keep up with all the new business. "You can't imagine how big your company is going to be when you start off working with three guys in a room, and you don't even have your own offices," says Green.[30] ∎

Downward communication in an organization usually encompasses the following topics:

1. *Implementation of goals and strategies.* Communicating new strategies and goals provides information about specific targets and expected behaviors. It gives direction for lower levels of the organization. Example: "The new quality campaign is for real. We must improve product quality if we are to survive."

2. *Job instructions and rationale.* These are directives on how to do a specific task and how the job relates to other organizational activities. Example: "Purchasing should order the bricks now so the work crew can begin construction of the building in two weeks."

3. *Procedures and practices.* These are messages defining the organization's policies, rules, regulations, benefits, and structural arrangements. Example: "After your first 90 days of employment, you are eligible to enroll in our company-sponsored savings plan."

4. *Performance feedback.* These messages appraise how well individuals and departments are doing their jobs. Example: "Joe, your work on the computer network has greatly improved the efficiency of our ordering process."

5. *Indoctrination.* These messages are designed to motivate employees to adopt the company's mission and cultural values and to participate in special ceremonies, such as picnics and United Way campaigns. Example: "The company thinks of its employees as family and would like to invite everyone to attend the annual picnic and fair on March 3rd."

The major problem with downward communication is drop-off, the distortion or loss of message content. Although formal communi-cations are a powerful way to reach all employees, much information gets lost—25 percent or so each time a message is passed from one person to the next. In addition, the message can be distorted if it travels a great distance from its originating source to the ultimate receiver. A tragic example is the following:

A reporter was present at a hamlet burned down by the U.S. Army 1st Air Cavalry Division in 1967. Investigations showed that the order from the Division headquarters to the brigade was: "On no occasion must hamlets be burned down."

The brigade radioed the battalion: "Do not burn down any hamlets unless you are absolutely convinced that the Viet Cong are in them."

The battalion radioed the infantry company at the scene: "If you think there are any Viet Cong in the hamlet, burn it down."

The company commander ordered his troops: "Burn down that hamlet."[31] ∎

Information drop-off cannot be completely avoided, but the techniques described earlier can reduce it substantially. Using the right communication channel, consistency between verbal and nonverbal messages and active listening can maintain communication accuracy as it moves down the organization.

UPWARD COMMUNICATION   Formal **upward communication** includes messages that flow from the lower to the higher levels in the organization's hierarchy. Most organizations take pains to build in healthy channels for upward communication. Employees need to air grievances, report progress, and provide feedback on management initiatives. Coupling a healthy flow of upward and downward communication ensures that the communication circuit between managers and employees is complete.[32] Wild Oats Market became successful because the founders began to understand the importance of upward communication.

upward communication
The flow of messages from the lower to the higher levels in the organization's hierarchy

WILD OATS MARKET

From its beginnings, Wild Oats Market was offbeat, serving up health foods in a tiny market in Boulder, Colorado. Owners Libby Cook, Michael Gilliland, and Randy Clapp rang up sales and stocked the shelves themselves. It was easy back then to stay in touch with employees and customers. After four years, though, their success had exacted a price. With 11 stores scattered across three states they found themselves managing a corporation rather than a tiny market. Employees training and performance reviews had deteriorated. Back when they worked side by side with shelf stockers and produce clerks, they could gauge employee morale, important information for them. As Cook said, "In our business we need to keep our staff happy because they're the first line of defense when customers come into the store." But now they not only could not work alongside them, they couldn't even visit them all. The three owners knew they had to devise some means of knowing what was happening in each store, to get feedback from each worker, so they could prevent potential problems before customers shopped elsewhere.

Because Wild Oats staffers were known for their free-spirited attitudes, Cook, Gilliland, and Clapp developed a questionnaire to evaluate employee morale and satisfaction using potential measures of "awful," "remarkably bad," to "wonderful," and "terrific." Their "Happiness-Index" rated respondents' sentiments from "giddy" to "suicidal." Gilliland discovered that store managers were taking negative criticisms hard, even if they had a lot of "terrifics." To prevent this, he began reviewing the questionnaires to remove gratuitous or nonconstructive carping comments before going over them personally with each manager. The feedback has not only given a clear idea of workforce morale, but has also resulted in employee solutions to specific problems, such as employee participation in a stock option program and a $200 per worker wellness program allowance. Since the program began, turnover has dramatically decreased.

Communication and management practices at Wild Oats continue to be successful, for the company now operates 105 stores nationwide and is up to yearly revenues of over $500 million.[33] ∎

Here are five types of information communicated upward.

1. *Problems and exceptions.* These messages describe serious problems with and exceptions to routine performance in order to make senior managers aware of difficulties. Example: "The printer has been out of operation for two days, and it will be at least a week before a new one arrives."

2. *Suggestions for improvement.* These messages are ideas for improving task-related procedures to increase quality or efficiency. Example: "I think we should eliminate step two in the audit procedure because it takes a lot of time and produces no results."

3. *Performance reports.* These messages include periodic reports that inform management how individuals and departments are performing. Example: "We completed the audit report for Smith & Smith on schedule but are one week behind on the Jackson report."

4. *Grievances and disputes.* These messages are employee complaints and conflicts that travel up the hierarchy for a hearing and possible resolution. Example: "The manager of operations research cannot get the cooperation of the Lincoln plant for the study of machine utilization."

5. *Financial and accounting information.* These messages pertain to costs, accounts receivable, sales volume, anticipated profits, return on investment, and other matters of interest to senior managers. Example: "Costs are 2 percent over budget, but sales are 10 percent ahead of target, so the profit picture for the third quarter is excellent."

Many organizations make a great effort to facilitate upward communication. Mechanisms

Managers at the plumbing and air-conditioning contractor, TDIndustries, facilitate upward communication through their commitment to the philosophy of "servant leadership." Upward communication and active listening allow managers to respect the interests and heed the preferences of workers. Apprentices, such as those in the photo being taught to install plumbing systems, look forward to being part of the company's democratic system in addition to enjoying ownership of part of the 75 percent of the company's stock that is owned by lower-level employees.

include suggestion boxes, employee surveys, open-door policies, management information system reports, and face-to-face conversations between workers and executives.

William J. O'Brien, CEO of Hanover Insurance Company, points out: "The fundamental movement in business in the next 25 years will be in the dispersing of power, to give meaning and fulfillment to employees in a way that avoids chaos and disorder." Power sharing means inviting upward communication. At Pacific Gas & Electric, CEO Richard A. Clark keeps employee communication lines open with employee surveys, biannual video presentations, and monthly brown-bag lunches to hear questions and complaints.[34]

Despite these efforts, however, barriers to accurate upward communication exist. Managers may resist hearing about employee problems, or employees may not trust managers sufficiently to push information upward.[35] Innovative companies search for ways to ensure that information gets to top managers without distortion. IBM's respected Speak Up program consists of anonymous employee letters or e-mails regularly channeled to management for action. Top managers at Golden Corral, a restaurant chain with headquarters in Raleigh, North Carolina, spend at least one weekend a year in the trenches—cutting steaks, rolling silverware, setting tables, and taking out the trash. This gives managers a better understanding of the needs of both employees and customers. For example, while taking out the trash at the restaurant, executives discovered that the narrow dimensions of the trash disposal area made it almost impossible for two workers to lift the heavy cans into a large trash container. It was a situation that was not only inefficient but also ripe for employee injury—and one that managers would not have known about without the innovative program. By understanding the daily routines and challenges of waiters, chefs, and other employees at their restaurants, Golden Corral executives increase their awareness of how management actions affect others.[36]

HORIZONTAL COMMUNICATION Horizontal communication is the lateral or diagonal exchange of messages among peers or coworkers. It may occur within or across departments. The purpose of horizontal communication is not only to inform but also to request support and coordinate activities. Horizontal communication falls into one of three categories:

1. *Intradepartmental problem solving.* These messages take place among members of the same department and concern task accomplishment. Example: "Betty, can you help us figure out how to complete this medical expense report form?"

2. *Interdepartmental coordination.* Interdepartmental messages facilitate the

horizontal communication
The flow of communication laterally or diagonally among peers or coworkers

TECHNOLOGY FOR TOMORROW

YOU.com

Information and the communication of that information is the secret to success for many e-businesses. Maybe you have thought of starting a Web business, but were too intimidated by the technology. There are more and more services available for the novice, whether an experienced merchant, but new to the Internet, or a new startup. Here are some tips and available help for you.

TIPS

1. INVOLVE EVERYONE POSSIBLE IN THE DESIGN OF YOUR WEB PAGE: every department, anyone dealing with public relations, customer service, marketing, engineering, etc. Then the site will be more complete and you can move very, very fast when a new product is announced, because everyone will be on-board.

2. ANY DOCUMENTATION YOU HAVE, save it to your group's personal Web site, rather than in some file drawer. That makes it easily retrievable and accessible.

3. GIVE LOTS OF INFORMATION. Long-Islander Dan Harrison's poolandspa.com's original brick-and-mortar shop closed as his Internet business took off. It became a real Web site in 1994, offering 50,000 pool, hot tub, and spa products and services, as well as information on what to do if the pool turned green or spas were frothy. Now the site has 1,000 pages and generates a greatly increased revenue of $4 million per year. "We believe offering information gives us a competitive advantage. The more our customers have, the better it is for all of us," says Harrison.

4. OFFER CHAT ROOMS AND EXPERT IN-FORMATION. Visitors often want to chat and joint message boards, but they also want competent help with problems, so Harrison started offering, "Ask the Pool Guy," which receives 400 questions per day and is used as a means of building their marketing mailing list. But beware.

To do a chat room requires vigorous promotion of the chat community—another expense. So make sure the chat room will add to the value of your business.

5. BRING WELL-KNOWN SPEAKERS ON IN REAL-TIME. Garden.com (see Chapter 5) hosts chats with recognized garden experts, authors and consultants, who answer questions and discuss issues.

6. IF YOU SELL TECHNICAL PRODUCTS, consider offering registered customers private-password-protected access to quick turnaround technical assistance, which can save thousands of dollars spent on phone centers. If you sell software, offering online download can save lots of money in shipping costs. Large companies as Cisco Systems have saved millions this way.

7. DON'T BE DISCOURAGED even if you are a technophobe, such as novice 25-year-old Matthew Pickeny, who took HTML tutorials on AOL and now is a Net-preneur, developing and hosting Web sites. Or partner with a techie, as Blair Fuller did, whose Webcasting company now brings in $800,000 annually. The companies who do really well are those that redesign their strategies and structures to really leverage technology. And that's easier in small companies. Those gains were crucial for the success of 96 percent of the United States' fastest-growing firms.

8. AGAIN, FOCUS ON CONTENT. Pool-andspa's Harrison believes the resources he's poured into his Web site have paid off handsomely. If you need to buy a product and go to a search engine, you might find 10 or 12 sites and seven of those will offer the same price. "But," he adds, "if only one really explains to you what it is you are buying—whom are you going to buy from?"

SERVICES AVAILABLE

1. For help getting content on your Website, visit www.trellix.com; www.

quicksite.com; http://www.entrepreneur mag.com/resource.hts; or your own Internet service provider (ISP), many of whom are offering e-business solutions. For example, IBM has its own HomePage creator.

2. NEED TO CONVERT PAPER DOCUMENTS INTO HTML? See www.caere.com; or try to monk- and nun-based Electronic Scriptorium at www.electronicscriptorium.com, which keeps the monastic tradition, dating from the eleventh century, where monks supported themselves through manual labor, often copying manuscripts. In this case it is copying them to HTML.

3. DON'T KNOW WHERE TO START TO INITIATE CREDIT-CARD SALES? Try online-merchant.com or shoppingexpress.net.

4. WANT TO CHECK OUT ONLINE MALLS AND POSSIBLY JOIN ONE? See www.viaweb.com; www.virtualspin.com; or www.successmagazine.com.

5. HOW TO DO YOUR OWN ACCOUNT-ING? Try www.peachtree.com, which has a program to link your online orders to the accounting system.

6. HOW TO CUT SHIPPING COSTS? Visit www.upss.com

7. NEED TO NETWORK WITH OTHER NET-PRENEURS? Women visit Women in Computing (sss.awc-hq.org) or Webgr-rls (www.webgrrls.com); Web authors see HTML Writer's Guild (www.hwg.org); Internet professionals—marketing, sales, and graphics go to Association of Internet Professionals (www.association.org); startup entrepreneurs visit Information Technology Association of America (www.itaa.org).

SOURCES: Melissa Campanelli, "Content Is King," *Entrepreneur*, Oct. 1999, pp. 46–49; Monica Fuertes, "Tech for Dummies," *Business StartUp*, June 1999; David Haskin, "If I Had a Cyberhammer," *Business Week Enterprise*," March 29, 1999, pp. ENT8–ENT9; David Carnov, "Virtual Startup," *Success*, Jan. 1998, pp. 38–41.

accomplishment of joint projects or tasks. Example: "Bob, please contact marketing and production and arrange a meeting to discuss the specifications for the new subassembly. It looks like we may not be able to meet their requirements."

3. *Change initiatives and improvements.* These messages are designed to share information among teams and departments that can help the organization change, grow, and improve. Example: We are streamlining the company travel procedures and would like to discuss them with your department.

Some successful e-businesses use everyone in the company to help design the Web page (see Technology for Tomorrow).

Horizontal communication is particularly important in learning organizations, where teams of workers are continuously solving problems and searching for new ways of doing things. Many organizations have built-in horizontal communications in the form of task forces, committees, or even a matrix structure to encourage coordination. At Chicago's Northwestern Memorial Hospital, two doctors created a horizontal task force to solve a serious patient health problem.

NORTHWESTERN MEMORIAL HOSPITAL

We've all heard of it happening—a patient checks into the hospital for a routine procedure and ends up getting sicker instead of better. Hospital-borne infections afflict about two million patients—and kill nearly 100,000—each year. Greater antibiotic use only causes the germs to develop greater resistance. The infection epidemic is growing worse worldwide, but a task force at Northwestern Memorial Hospital has reversed the trend by breaking down communication barriers.

When a cancer patient became Northwestern's first victim of a new strain of deadly bacteria, infectious-disease specialists Lance Peterson and Gary Noskin realized it would take everyone's help to defeat the insidious enemy. As infection spread throughout the hospital, they launched a regular Monday morning meeting to plot countermoves. Although some physicians and staff members were offended at having their procedures questioned, the goal of preventing needless deaths overrode their concerns. Absolute candor was the rule at the Monday morning meetings, which involved not only doctors and nurses, but also lab technicians, pharmacists, computer technicians, and admissions representatives. One pharmacist, for example, recognized that antibiotics act as fertilizer for many bacteria, which encouraged physicians to decrease their use of antibiotics in favor of alternative treatments. Computer representatives and admissions people got together to develop software to identify which returning patients might pose a threat for bringing infection back into the hospital. Eventually, the task force even included maintenance staff when studies showed that a shortage of sinks was inhibiting hand-washing.

Increasing horizontal communication paid off at Northwestern, saving millions in annual medical costs and at least a few lives. Over three years, Northwestern's rate of hospital-borne infections plunged 22 percent. In the last fiscal year, such infections totaled 5.1 per 1,000 patients, roughly half the national average.[37] ■

INFORMAL COMMUNICATION CHANNELS

Informal communication channels exist outside the formally authorized channels and do not adhere to the organization's hierarchy of authority. Informal communications coexist with formal communications but may skip hierarchical levels, cutting across vertical chains of command to connect virtually anyone in the organization. For example, to improve communications at SafeCard Services of Jacksonville, Florida, Paul Kahn propped open the door to the executive wing, made the "executives-only" fitness center available to all employees, and began scheduling regular breakfasts and lunches for employees and managers to get together in a relaxed, informal atmosphere.

informal communication channels
Channels of communication that exist outside the formally authorized channels and often cut across vertical chains of command

Verifone goes beyond the normal boundaries to promote informal communication channels.

VERIFONE INC.

Talk about informal. Verifone Inc. not only allows employees to handle personal business at work, the company *encourages* it. For most firms, family-friendly means giving workers flexibility to handle spouse and kid matters *away* from the office. But Verifone's William R. Pape talks of the many studies showing the "correlation between strong family life and increased worker productivity." The typical response to that has been a plethora of programs, such as job-sharing, flextime, and on-site day care, all of which increases the segregation between work and home.

Verifone has learned that keeping employees close to family members not only helps them recruit the best talent, but keeps them more focused on their work and productivity. Because their company is spread out throughout North America and around the world, their various sites communicate regularly through e-mails, compensation updates, memos—and these are often done with family in mind. For example, company newsletters have a children's page. They even went one step further. Every spouse and child is given access via a unique ID to the company's intranet, where they can access general information sections and sections created especially for children, and they even subsidize home PCs. Online training is available to family members, who can learn programming languages or how to create a Web page.

Because employees are so spread out, their children cannot meet at company picnics, so Verifone has come up with other solutions to create a larger community. Children send e-mails, maps, photos and videos via the VeriPal pen-pal program—and they can participate in a new student exchange program, where kids from different areas stay in one another's homes.

People often ask if this family focus is abused. Pape says those who spend all their time socializing don't get work done and the results are obvious. But the most common form of abuse in the virtual office is *overwork*, when family members feel abandoned as the employee is hunkered over their home PC. Therefore Verifone monitors time stamps on e-mails to make sure workers are not chained to their computers and have enough family time.

The family integration has helped Verifone achieve one of the lowest turnover rates in the industry. As Pape says, "It becomes clear that supporting families isn't only the right thing to do morally; it is the right thing to do for business."[38] ■

An illustration of both formal and informal communications is given in Exhibit 14.6. Note how formal communications can be vertical or horizontal, depending on task assignments and coordination responsibilities. Other channels of informal communication include:

MANAGEMENT BY WANDERING AROUND
Management by wandering around (MBWA) was made famous by the books *In Search of Excellence* and *A Passion for Excellence*,[39] which describe executives who talk directly with employees to learn what is going on. MBWA works for managers at all levels. They mingle and develop positive relationships with employees and learn directly from them about their department, division, or organization. For example, the president of ARCO had a habit of visiting a district field office. Rather than schedule a big strategic meeting with the district supervisor, he would come in unannounced and chat with the lowest-level employees. In any organization, both upward and downward communication are enhanced with MBWA. Managers have a chance to describe key ideas and values to employees and in turn learn about the problems and issues confronting employees.

When managers fail to take advantage of MBWA, they become aloof and isolated from employees. For example, Peter Anderson, president of Ztel, Inc., a maker of television

Management by wandering around (MBWA)
Informal communication channel in which management "wanders around" to describe key ideas and values and to learn about problems

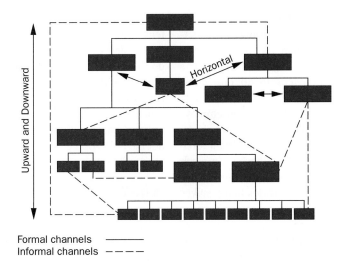

Upward and Downward

Horizontal

Formal channels ——————
Informal channels — — — —

switching systems, preferred not to personally communicate with employees. He managed at arm's length. As one manager said, "I don't know how many times I asked Peter to come to the lab, but he stayed in his office. He wasn't that visible to the troops." This formal management style contributed to Ztel's troubles and eventual bankruptcy.[40] Golden Corral modified MBWA to be Management by Working Around.

GOLDEN CORRAL RESTAURANT

It's too easy for managers to become far removed from the day-to-day operations of their business. The more layers of hierarchy between them means they have to rely on "surrogates"—sophisticated feedback, often from supervisors.

Golden Corral restaurant implemented a solution for this problem. One weekend a year, each of its 50 top managers work hands-on restaurant duties, so that the chain's decision makers will remember what the business is all about. For example, Chief Financial Officer Lamar Bell spent his weekend setting tables, cutting steaks and taking out the garbage.

A small-company competitive edge is their quick reaction to marketplace changes, resulting from the closer connection between front-line employees and top management. Now larger com-

panies are seeing the advantages and sending out senior managers to wait on customers. Even an operation with as few as three locations should start this practice, believes Professor Rollie Tillman, Jr. of University of North Carolina at Chapel Hill. Otherwise, he says, "you start getting too many pieces of paper to too much to keep track of."

In addition, Golden Corral sees more attention to human resources as the key to improved operations and holds "soft skills"—coaching, leadership, retention, etc.—training at its monthly meetings of managers. "Everybody talks about people being so important," says HR training director Rick Smith. "Yet district managers spend 95 percent of their time talking about operations issues." So their monthly meetings and the hands-on restaurant duties help them keep focused on people.

Bell has been working his yearly weekends for all the 11 years he has been with the company. He has learned a lot, including that store managers may be completing their paperwork at 2 A.M., after working a full day and night in the restaurant. Now he is more careful about the kinds of things he requests of them. "Those managers are serving the customers first," he says, "anything we require of them is secondary."[41] ∎

THE GRAPEVINE   The **grapevine** is an informal, person-to-person communication network of employees that is not officially sanctioned by the organization.[42] The grapevine links employees in all directions, ranging from the president through middle management, support staff, and line employees. The grapevine will always exist in an organization, but it can become a dominant force when formal channels are closed. In such cases, the grapevine is actually a service because the information it provides helps makes sense of an unclear or uncertain situation. Employees use grapevine rumors to fill in information gaps and clarify management decisions. The grapevine tends to be more active during periods of change, excitement, anxiety, and sagging economic conditions.

Research suggests that a few people are primarily responsible for the grapevine's success. In a *gossip chain*, a single individual conveys a piece of news to many other people. In a *cluster chain*, a few individuals each convey information to several others. Having only a few people conveying information may account for the accuracy of grapevines. If every person told one other person in sequence, distortions would be greater.

Surprising aspects of the grapevine are its accuracy and its relevance to the organization. About 80 percent of grapevine communications pertain to business-related topics rather than personal, vicious gossip. Moreover, from 70 to 90 percent of the details passed through a grapevine are accurate.[43] Many managers would like the grapevine to be destroyed because they consider its rumors to be untrue, malicious, and harmful to personnel. Typically this is not the case; however, managers should be aware that almost five of every six important messages are carried to some extent by the grapevine rather than through official channels. In a recent survey of 22,000 shift workers in varied industries, 55 percent said they get most of their information via the grapevine.[44] Smart managers accept and use the grapevine to their advantage, sharing information with people they know will spread it to others. They recognize who's connected to whom and which employees are key players in the informal spread of information. However, one interesting finding is that in today's workplace young people tend to participate in the grapevine much less than older workers. Young workers generally don't plan to stay with a company for more than a few years, so they are less involved in the rumor mill.[45] In all cases, but particularly in times of crisis, executives need to manage communications effectively so that the grapevine is not the only source of information.

■ COMMUNICATING IN TEAMS

Team members work together to accomplish tasks, and the team's communication structure influences both team performance and employee satisfaction. Three aspects of team communication are networks, open communication, and dialogue.

NETWORKS

Research into team communication has focused on two characteristics: the extent to which team communications are centralized and the nature of the team's task.[46] The relationship between these characteristics is illustrated in Exhibit 14.7. In a **centralized network,** team members must communicate through one individual to solve problems or make decisions. In a **decentralized network**, individuals can communicate freely with other team members. Members process information equally among themselves until all agree on a decision.[47]

In laboratory experiments, centralized communication networks achieved faster solutions for simple problems. Members could simply pass relevant information to a central person for a decision. Decentralized communications were slower for simple problems because information was passed among individuals until someone finally put the pieces together and solved the problem. However, for more complex problems, the decentralized communication network was faster. Because all necessary information was not restricted to one person, a pooling of information through widespread communications provided greater input into the decision. Similarly, the accuracy of problem solving was related to problem complexity.

grapevine
Informal, person-to-person communication network of employees that is not officially sanctioned by the organization

centralized network
A communication structure in which team members must communicate through one individual to solve problems or make decisions

decentralized network
A communication structure in which individuals can communicate freely with other team members

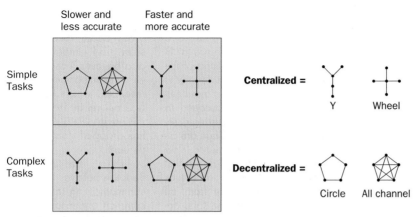

SOURCES: Adapted from A. Bavelas and D. Barrett, "An Experimental Approach to Organization Communication," *Personnel*, 27 (1951), 366–371; M. E. Shaw, *Group Dynamics: The Psychology of Small Group Behavior* (New York: McGraw-Hill, 1976); and E. M. Rogers and R. A. Rogers, *Communication in Organizations* (New York: Free Press, 1976).

The centralized networks made fewer errors on simple problems but more errors on complex ones. Decentralized networks were less accurate for simple problems but more accurate for complex ones.[48]

The implication for organizations is that in a highly competitive global environment, organizations use teams to deal with complex problems. When team activities are complex and difficult, all members should share information in a decentralized structure to solve problems. Teams need a free flow of communication in all directions.[49] At Microsoft, for example, teams hold "triage" meetings in the final months of a software development cycle. Everyone jumps in with their ideas and opinions and then "negotiates" to a decision.[50] However, teams who perform routine tasks spend less time processing information, and thus communications can be centralized. Data can be channeled to a supervisor for decisions, freeing workers to spend a greater percentage of time on task activities.

OPEN COMMUNICATION

A recent trend that reflects management's increased emphasis on empowering employees and enhancing team productivity is **open communication**, which refers to sharing all types of information throughout the company, across

functional and hierarchical levels. AES Corporation, a power producer, shares so much financial data with its 2,000 employees that it has declared them all insiders for stock-trading purposes.[51]

DIALOGUE

Another means of creating team spirit is through **dialogue,** or "stream of meaning," a communication process in which groups create a stream of shared meaning that enables them to understand each other and share a view of the world.[52] People may start out at polar opposites, but by talking openly to one another, they discover common ground, common issues, and shared goals on which they can build a better, cooperative future.

A useful way to describe dialogue is to contrast it with discussion. The intent of discussion, generally, is to deliver one's point of view and persuade others to adopt it. A discussion is often resolved by logic or "beating down" opponents. Dialogue, on the other hand, asks that participants suspend their attachments to a particular viewpoint so that a deeper level of listening, synthesis, and meaning can evolve from the group. A dialogue's focus is to reveal feelings and build common ground. One company even hired a psychologist to help employees engage in dialogue and cope with

open communication
A communication structure that allows sharing of all types of information throughout the company, across functional and hierarchical levels

dialogue
A communication process in which groups create a stream of shared meaning about each other and their views of the world

THE FRIDAY MORNING APPOINTMENT

From the outside, everything looked fine at NECX, the world's leading independent distributor of semiconductors and other computer products. The company was highly successful and growing fast—its workforce had swelled from 100 to 250 in just a few years. However, from the inside, Henry Bertolon, cofounder and CEO, could see that NECX was coming apart at the seams. "We'd have meetings that just melted down," he says. "Everyone would scream at each other and then leave."

Bertolon's first plan was to hire a management consultant to help solve the company's communication problems. However, most consultants he interviewed came in and told the company what its problems were rather than listening to managers and employees. So Bertolon took an unusual approach: he hired Wil Calmas, a Boston psychologist with an MBA, to be the organizational shrink. Calmas set up a one-day-a-week program to get people talking—and listening—to one another on a new and deeper level. The day begins at 8 A.M. with a 90-minute meeting of the company's top executives. There is never a formal agenda for the meetings—executives are encouraged to express fear, hostility, frustration, secret wishes, whatever feelings are affecting their lives and work. The early-morning meeting is just the first of a daylong series of dialogues among NECX employees from all ranks and departments. The sales department has become so adept at dialogue that they now meet on their own, without Calmas's guidance.

Bertolon is convinced that the sessions are having a positive impact on NECX's people and performance. When Calmas first began his work, Bertolon asked managers to rate, on a scale of 1 to 10, how much they agreed with statements such as "All the managers help one another" and "My staff finds it easy to talk to me about everything." The average score was 1.5. When the test was given again recently, the average score had jumped to 7.5. Bertolon also believes those results have driven other important numbers, such as revenues, which have jumped from $62 million in 1992 to almost $400 million in 1996. Employee turnover has dropped from 42 percent to 20 percent.

In a fast-growing business, Bertolon believes that getting people communicating in a way that builds common understanding is critical to success. The dialogue sessions create a safe environment for people to reveal their feelings, voice their opinions, and build common ground. It also keeps them loose, flexible, and open to new ideas—ready to respond to rapid changes taking place all around them.

www.necx.com

SOURCE: Scott Kirsner, "Want to Grow? Hire a Shrink!" *Fast Company,* December–January 1998, pp. 68, 70.

rapid change. In Leading the Revolution: The Learning Organization both dialogue and discussion can result in change. However, the result of discussion is limited to the topic being deliberated, whereas the result of dialogue is characterized by group unity, shared meaning, and transformed mindsets. As new and deeper solutions are developed, a trusting relationship is built among team members.[53]

■ MANAGING ORGANIZATIONAL COMMUNICATION

Many of the ideas described in this chapter pertain to barriers to communication and how to overcome them. Barriers can be categorized as those that exist at the individual level and those that exist at the organizational level. First we will examine communication barriers; then we will look at techniques for overcoming them. These barriers and techniques are summarized in Exhibit 14.8.

BARRIERS TO COMMUNICATION

Barriers to communication can exist within the individual or as part of the organization.

INDIVIDUAL BARRIERS *Interpersonal* barriers are problems that occur with emotions and perceptions held by employees. For example, rigid perceptual labeling or categorizing of others prevents modification or alteration of opinions. If a person's mind is made up before the communication starts, communication will fail. Moreover, people with different backgrounds or knowledge may interpret a communication in different ways.

Selecting the wrong channel or medium for sending a communication also can be a problem. For example, when a message is emotional, it is better to transmit it face-to-face rather than in writing. On the other hand, writing works best for routine messages but lacks the capacity for rapid feedback and multiple cues needed for difficult messages.

Barriers	How to Overcome
Individual	
Interpersonal dynamics	Active listening
Channels and media	Selection of appropriate channel
Semantics	Knowledge of other's perspective
Inconsistent cues	MBWA
Organizational	
Status and power differences	Climate of trust
Departmental needs and goals	Development and use of formal channels
Communication network unsuited to task	Changing organization or group structure to fit communication needs
Lack of formal channels	Encouragement of multiple channels, formal and informal

Semantics pertains to the meaning of words and the way they are used. A word such as *effectiveness* may mean achieving high production to a factory superintendent and employee satisfaction to a human resources staff specialist. Many common words have an average of 28 definitions; thus, communicators must take care to select the words that will accurately encode ideas.[54]

Sending inconsistent cues between verbal and nonverbal communications will confuse the receiver. If one's facial expression does not reflect one's words, the communication will contain noise and uncertainty. The tone of voice and body language should be consistent with the words, and actions should not contradict words.

ORGANIZATIONAL BARRIERS   Organizational barriers pertain to factors for the organization as a whole. First is the problem of *status and power differences*. Low-power people may be reluctant to pass bad news up the hierarchy, thus giving the wrong impression to upper levels.[55] High-power people may not pay attention or may feel that low-status people have little to contribute.

Second, *differences across departments* in terms of needs and goals interfere with communications. Each department perceives problems in its own terms. The production department is concerned with production efficiency and may not fully understand the marketing department's need to get the product to the customer in a hurry.

Third, the *communication flow may not fit* the team's or organization's task. If a centralized communication structure is used for non-routine tasks, there will not be enough information circulated to solve problems. The organization, department, or team is most efficient when the amount of communication flowing among employees fits the task.

Fourth, the *absence of formal channels* reduces communication effectiveness. Organizations must provide adequate upward, downward, and horizontal communication in the form of employee surveys, open-door policies, newsletters, memos, task forces, and liaison personnel. Without these formal channels, the organization cannot communicate as a whole.

OVERCOMING COMMUNICATION BARRIERS

Managers can design the organization so as to encourage positive, effective communication. Designing involves both individual skills and organizational actions.

INDIVIDUAL SKILLS   Perhaps the most important individual skill is active listening. Active listening means asking questions, showing interest, and occasionally paraphrasing what the speaker has said to ensure that one is interpreting accurately. Active listening also means providing feedback to the sender to complete the communication loop.

semantics
The meaning of words and the way they are used

FOCUS ON Diversity   HIGH TECH CONNECT L.L.C.

Rene Siegel works in her California home. Some years ago, that was considered odd, but now Siegel is part of a new trend. As cofounder of High Tech Connect, she brokers temporary marketing and public relations jobs for high-tech companies—all from her two-story, cul-de-sac house. Most of her "consultants" (the hired-out temps) are women in their 30s and 40s, who also work from their homes.

In only 16 months, the company has grown by 1,000 percent, from 30 consultants to more than 300 in 19 states and boasts a client base including Cisco, Oracle, and Novelle. The first year's revenue was $400,000.

One reason for her success is her understanding of the importance of communication. Siegel is a master networker, remembering names, doing favors. And she also knows the necessity of speaking the correct language. After 13 years in high-tech PR, she can talk about network integration or Unix software with anyone. Yet she knows not to get lost in tech-speak and can also take care of business in an understandable, down-to-earth manner.

High Tech is contacted by a client, which gives the specs they need. Siegel draws from her list of consultants, all of whom she has graded based on their résumés and former clients. Consultants earn $75 to $150 per hour and pay High Tech only a one-time $50 fee, as well as promising to work through the company with specific clients. Those clients pay High Tech for the consultants, plus a 20 percent brokerage fee.

At first, Siegel thought the best way to do business was pay the consultants within 30 days, even if High Tech hadn't gotten its check. It didn't take long to realize that was the road to cash-flow nightmares, so now consultants get paid only after High Tech does. And her networking pays off in assessing a new client's ability to pay. With 50 percent of her business coming from startups, she uses her connections to determine the viability of new ventures.

If you think working from home is a breeze, think again. Siegel typically works 60 hours per week, but she sets aside a "family no-work zone" from 5 to 9 P.M. every night in order to spend time with her husband and three children (ages one to six). Overworked, she recently took off five weeks, as a sabbatical.

Her business continues to grow. But she and her partner, Nancy Collins, have talked about moving to larger quarters, but decided against it. "Our goals haven't really changed since we started," says Siegel. "No matter how many consultants we help, we still believe in the virtual office."

SOURCES: Ilan Mochari, "Collect from the Worst," *Inc.*, Sept. 1999, p. 101; Rodney Ho, "Her Clients, Herself," *The Wall Street Journal*, May 21, 1998, p. R4

Second, individuals should select the appropriate channel for the message. A complicated message should be sent through a rich channel, such as face-to-face discussion or telephone. Routine messages and data can be sent through memos, letters, or electronic mail, because there is little chance of misunderstanding.

Third, senders and receivers should make a special effort to understand each other's perspective. Managers can sensitize themselves to the information receiver so that they will be better able to target the message, detect bias, and clarify missed interpretations. By communicators understanding the perspectives of others, semantics can be clarified, perceptions understood, and objectivity maintained. Entrepreneurs in high-tech companies need to know the basics of business and how to communicate to engineers and software designers, as well as nontechnical professionals—and they need to know which type of communication is appropriate for each situation (see Focus on Diversity).

The fourth individual skill is management by wandering around. Managers must be willing to get out of the office and check communications with others. For example, John McDonnell of McDonnell Douglas always eats in the employee cafeteria when he visits far-flung facilities. Through direct observation and face-to-face meetings, managers develop an understanding of the organization and are able to communicate important ideas and values directly to others.

ORGANIZATIONAL ACTIONS   Perhaps the most important thing managers can do for the organization is to create a climate of trust and openness. This will encourage people to communicate honestly with one another. Subordinates will feel free to transmit negative as well as positive messages without fear of retribution. Efforts to develop interpersonal skills among employees can be made to foster openness, honesty, and trust.

Second, managers should develop and use formal information channels in all directions. Scandinavian Design uses two newsletters to reach employees. GM's Packard Electric plant is designed to share all pertinent information—financial, future plans, quality, performance—with employees. Dana Corporation has developed innovative programs such as the "Here's a Thought" board—called a HAT rack—to get ideas and feedback from workers. Other techniques include direct mail, bulletin boards, and employee surveys.

Third, managers should encourage the use of multiple channels, including both formal and informal communications. Multiple communication channels include written directives, face-to-face discussions, MBWA, and the grapevine. For example, managers at GM's Packard Electric plant use multimedia, including a monthly newspaper, frequent meetings of employee teams, and an electronic news display in the cafeteria. Sending messages through multiple channels increases the likelihood that they will be properly received.

Fourth, the structure should fit communication needs. For example, Harrah's created the Communication Team as part of its structure at the Casino/Holiday Inn in Las Vegas. The team includes one member from each department. It deals with urgent company problems and helps people think beyond the scope of their own departments to communicate with anyone and everyone to solve those problems. An organization can be designed to use teams, task forces, project managers, or a matrix structure as needed to facilitate the horizontal flow of information for coordination and problem solving. Structure should also reflect information needs. When team or department tasks are difficult, a decentralized structure should be implemented to encourage discussion and participation. Dialogue can help team members arrive at collective solutions to complex problems.

Summary and Management Solution

This chapter described several important points about communicating in organizations. Communication takes up 80 percent of a manager's time. Communication is a process of encoding an idea into a message, which is sent through a channel and decoded by a receiver. Communication among people can be affected by communication channels, nonverbal communication, and listening skills. Important aspects of management communication include persuasion and influence. Managers use communication to sell people on the vision for the organization and to influence them to behave in such a way as to accomplish the vision. To influence others, managers connect with people on an emotional level by using symbols, metaphors, and stories to communicate their messages.

At the organizational level, managers are concerned with managing formal communications in a downward, upward, and horizontal direction. Informal communications also are important, especially management by wandering around and the grapevine. Moreover, research shows that communication structures in teams and departments should reflect the underlying tasks. Open communication and dialogue can develop a sense of trust and team spirit.

Finally, several barriers to communication were described. These barriers can be overcome by active listening, selecting appropriate channels, engaging in MBWA, developing a climate of trust, using formal channels, and designing the correct structure to fit communication needs.

In the beginning case, Umang Gupta's successful company crashed, leaving him a multimillionaire for only a few days. Gupta resigned as CEO and the company changed its name to Centura Software. He now realizes he made a number of mistakes. First, he was undercapitalized and could not withstand later competition. Then, he rode the company on one technology only, making it too vulnerable. But the root of these problems, he says, was his own ego, or the "hubris danger zone." He felt so certain of his own ideas, that he did not listen enough to others. One result of that was that he did not anticipate the importance of the Internet. "The company wasn't a company, but a cause. We were going to change the world." That attitude can motivate young employees, but it also can blind leaders and employees to market realities. In his new position as CEO of Keynote Systems, which measures performance of commercial Web sites, he is careful to con- struct the business around several technologies and techno- logical services. Plus he also delegates strategic information gathering to a number of employees, who keep their minds and eyes open to new developments outside. Rather than cramming meetings together like pieces of bread on a peanut butter sandwich, he now blocks out time to roam the halls and brainstorm with employees. And he regularly attends venture capital conferences. "I'm making sure my peripheral vision remains intact so I'm not blindsided again," he says.

Discussion Questions

1. ATI Medical, Inc., has a "no-memo" policy. The 300 employees must interact directly for all communica- tions. What impact do you think this policy would have on the organization?

2. Describe the elements of the communication process. Give an example of each part of the model as it exists in the classroom during communication between teacher and students.

3. Why do you think stories are more effective than hard facts and figures in persuading others?

4. Should the grapevine be eliminated? How might man- agers control information that is processed through the grapevine?

5. What do you think are the major barriers to upward communication in organizations? Discuss.

6. What is the relationship between group communication and group task? For example, how should communica- tions differ in a strategic planning group and a group of employees who stock shelves in a grocery store?

7. Some senior managers believe they should rely on writ- ten information and computer reports because these yield more accurate data than do face-to-face commu- nications. Do you agree?

8. Why is management by wandering around considered effective communication? Consider channel richness and nonverbal communications in formulating your answer.

9. Is speaking accurately or listening actively the more im- portant communication skill for managers? Discuss.

10. Assume that you have been asked to design a training program to help managers become better communica- tors. What would you include in the program?

Management Exercises

Manager's Workbook

Listening Self-Assessment

Instructions: Choose one response for each of the items be- low. Base your choice on what you usually do, not on what you think a person should do.

1. When you are going to lunch with a friend, you:
   a. Focus your attention on the menu and then on the service provided
   b. Ask about events in your friend's life and pay at- tention to what's said
   c. Exchange summaries of what is happening to each of you while focusing attention on the meal

2. When someone talks nonstop, you:
   a. Ask questions at an appropriate time in an attempt to help the person focus on the issue
   b. Make an excuse to end the conversation
   c. Try to be patient and understand what you are be- ing told

3. If a group member complains about a fellow employee who, you believe, is disrupting the group, you:
   a. Pay attention and withhold your opinions
   b. Share your own experiences and feelings about that employee
   c. Acknowledge the group member's feelings and ask the group member what options he or she has

4. If someone is critical of you, you:
   a. Try not to react or get upset
   b. Automatically become curious and attempt to learn more
   c. Listen attentively and then back up your position

5. You are having a very busy day and someone tells you to change the way you are completing a task. You believe the person is wrong, so you:
   a. Thank her or him for the input and keep doing what you were doing
   b. Try to find out why she or he thinks you should change
   c. Acknowledge that the other may be right, tell her or him you are very busy, and agree to follow up later

6. When you are ready to respond to someone else, you:
   a. Sometimes will interrupt the person if you believe it is necessary
   b. Almost always speak before the other is completely finished talking
   c. Rarely offer your response until you believe the other has finished

7. After a big argument with someone you have to work with every day, you:
   a. Settle yourself and then try to understand the other's point of view before stating your side again
   b. Just try to go forward and let bygones be bygones
   c. Continue to press your position

8. A colleague calls to tell you that he is upset about getting assigned to a new job. You decide to:
   a. Ask him if he can think of options to help him deal with the situation
   b. Assure him that he is good at what he does and that these things have a way of working out for the best
   c. Let him know you have heard how badly he feels

9. If a friend always complains about her problems but never asks about yours, you:
   a. Try to identify areas of common interest

   b. Remain understanding and attentive, even if it becomes tedious
   c. Support her complaints and mention your own complaints

10. The best way to remain calm in an argument is to:
    a. Continue to repeat your position in a firm but even manner
    b. Repeat what you believe is the other person's position
    c. Tell the other person that you are willing to discuss the matter again when you are both calmer

Score Each Item of Your Listening Self-Assessment

	(a)		(b)		(c)	
1.	(a)	0	(b)	10	(c)	5
2.	(a)	10	(b)	0	(c)	5
3.	(a)	5	(b)	0	(c)	5
4.	(a)	5	(b)	10	(c)	0
5.	(a)	0	(b)	10	(c)	5
6.	(a)	5	(b)	0	(c)	10
7.	(a)	10	(b)	5	(c)	0
8.	(a)	5	(b)	5	(c)	10
9.	(a)	0	(b)	10	(c)	5
10.	(a)	0	(b)	10	(c)	5

Add Up Your Total Score

80–100: You are an active, excellent listener. You achieve a good balance between listening and asking questions, and you strive to understand others.

50–75: You are an adequate-to-good listener. You listen well, although you may sometimes react too quickly to others before they are finished speaking.

25–45: You have some listening skills but need to improve them. You may often become impatient when trying to listen to others, hoping they will finish talking so you can talk.

0–20: You listen to others very infrequently. You may prefer to do all of the talking and experience extreme frustration while waiting for others to make their point.

SOURCE: Richard G. Weaver and John D. Farrell, *Managers As Facilitators: A Practical Guide to Getting Work Done in a Changing Workplace* (San Francisco: Berrett-Koehler Publishers, 1997), pp. 134–136. Used with permission.

Manager's Workshop

Evaluate This!

1. Form groups of five to eight members. Instructor will assign role of either Pat or Chris to each group. In other words, some groups will be "Pat" groups and some will be "Chris" groups. Only read the role you are assigned. *Do not* read the other role.

2. Fill in the box after each role, answering the questions. Role-play the next meeting between Pat and Chris. Be prepared to do your role-play in front of the class.

3. The instructor will call certain people to the front for the role-play.

4. Instructor picks a Chris from one of the Chris groups and a Pat from a Pat group and brings them up to role-play. After 5 to 10 minutes, the role-play is stopped and the class is asked to comment on what happened. Then the instructor chooses another Chris and Pat and has a second role-play, followed by class discussion.

5. Class discussion on communication in organizations.

Role for Pat to Read

It's time for annual performance evaluations at the Topflight Music Publishing Company. Pat, the new manager of the marketing department has one employee, Bob, who is not cutting it. Pat has convinced his/her boss, Chris, the vice president of marketing, to reassign Bob to a less client-oriented position. It was difficult for Chris to accept the fact that Bob was a nuisance in the department. After all Bob's wife, Veronica, executive vice president at Oldies Records, is an old friend and mentor of Chris's and helped Chris get the job with Topflight.

Bob has been very erratic in his behavior for the past two months. He comes in late to work three out of five days a week. He has become disruptive in the workplace and has thrown papers and files at coworkers. No one can explain his unpredictable behavior.

Pat meets with Bob on Thursday afternoon. Pat reviews Bob's past performance for the entire year with him. Near the end of the evaluation Pat explains to Bob that there is going to be a bit of a change in his workday. Pat demotes Bob. Bob is devastated. Suddenly he jumps up and begins yelling obscenities. He says to Pat, "With everything else going wrong in my life, I thought I could count on you for friendship and understanding. I'm going to talk to your boss Chris and I'll take you on later." He leaves Pat's office.

Thirty minutes later, Pat's phone rings. It's Chris saying, "I think we ought to give Bob another chance. I've told Bob that we want to meet with him tomorrow to discuss your meeting with him today."

	What concepts or principles are important in this interaction relevant to each player? What communication principles are important here?	What should have been done differently?	What should happen at the next meeting between Pat and Chris? What will you say?
Chris			
Pat			
Bob			

Role for Chris to Read

It's time for annual performance evaluations at the Topflight Music Publishing Company. Pat, the new manager of the marketing department has one employee, Bob, who is not cutting it. Pat has convinced his/her boss, Chris, the vice president of marketing, to reassign Bob to a less client-oriented position. It was difficult for Chris to accept the fact that Bob was a nuisance in the department. After all Bob's wife, Veronica, executive vice president at Oldies Records, is an old friend and mentor of Chris's and helped Chris get the job with Topflight.

Bob has been very erratic in his behavior for the past two months. He comes in late to work three out of five days a week. He has become disruptive in the workplace and has thrown papers and files at coworkers. No one can explain his unpredictable behavior.

Pat has just met with Bob to tell him that he is fired, after reviewing his performance for the year. Right after the meeting, Bob storms into Chris's office and sputters at Chris, as Bob leans menacingly over Chris's desk, "You better watch out. If you two fire me, I'll, why, well, my wife has friends in high places, at record companies and in the media, some who know where the bones are buried—if you get my drift." His eyes were wide and bulging as he came around the desk and poked his finger into Chris's face. "You better not mess with me, not if you want to... ." And then Bob stood staring hatefully at Chris, turned and stalked out of the office.

After a few minutes, Chris realized there could be a big mess if Bob was not appeased, so Chris telephoned Bob. Then Chris called Pat and said, "I think we ought to give Bob another chance. I've told Bob that we want to meet with him tomorrow to discuss your meeting with him today."

	What concepts or principles are important in this interaction relevant to each player? What communication principles are important here?	What should have been done differently?	What should happen at the next meeting between Pat and Chris? What will you say?
Chris			
Pat			
Bob			

SOURCE: Adapted by Dorothy Marcic from Lee Bolman's case. Used with permission.

Management in Practice: Ethical Dilemma

The Voice of Authority

When Gehan Rasinghe was hired as an account assistant at Werner and Thompson, a business and financial management firm, he was very relieved. He was overqualified for the job with his degree in accounting, but the combination of his accented English and his quiet manner had prevented him from securing any other position. Beatrice Werner, one of the managing partners of the firm, was impressed by his educational credentials and his courtly manner. She assured him he had advancement potential with the firm, but the account assistant position was the only one available. After months of rejections in his job hunt, Rasinghe accepted the position. He was committed to making his new job work at all costs.

Account Manager Cathy Putnam was Rasinghe's immediate superior. Putnam spoke with a heavy Boston accent, speaking at a lightning pace to match her enormous workload. She indicated to Rasinghe that he would need to get up to speed as quickly as possible to succeed in working with her. It was soon apparent that Putnam and Rasinghe were at odds. She resented having to repeat directions more than once to teach him his responsibilities. He also seemed resistant to making the many phone calls asking for copies of invoices, disputing charges on credit cards, and following up with a client's staff to get the information necessary to do his job. His accounting work was impeccable, but the public contact part of his job was in bad shape. Even his quiet answer of "No problem" to all her requests was starting to wear thin on Putnam. Before giving Rasinghe his three-month review, Putnam appealed to Beatrice Werner for help. Putnam was frustrated at their communication problems and didn't know what to do.

Werner had seen the problem coming. Although she had found Rasinghe's bank reconciliations and financial report preparations to be first-rate, she knew that phone work and client contact were a big part of any job in the firm. But as the daughter of German immigrants, Werner also knew that language and cultural barriers could be overcome with persistence and patience. Diversity was one of her ideals for her company, and it was not always easy to achieve. She felt sure that Rasinghe could become an asset to the firm in time. She worried that the time it would take was more than they could afford to give him.

What Do You Do?

1. Give Rasinghe his notice, with the understanding that a job that is primarily paperwork would be a better fit for him. Make the break now rather than later.

2. Place him with an account manager who has more time to help him develop his assertiveness and telephone skills and appreciates his knowledge of accounting.

3. Create a new position for him, where he could do the reports and reconciliations for several account managers, while their assistants concentrated on the public contact work. He would have little chance of future promotion, however.

Surf the Net

1. *e-mail.* e-mail is a common communication channel used in organizations. The Internet provides much advice on how to effectively use e-mail. Visit one of the sites below and prepare a two- to three-paragraph summary of the ideas that you found most helpful to you in improving your skill at using this communication channel.

   www.webfoot.com/advice/email.top.html

   www.augsburg.edu/library/aib/mailmanners.html

   www.cappyscove.com/bobf/e-mail/index.html

   www.ucc.ie/info/net/acronyms/acro.html

   http://netconference.miningco.com/msub6.htm

2. *Group Presentations.* Another common communication channel, particularly for managers, is speaking before groups both inside and outside the organization. Go to www.leaderx.com and test your presentation style. After completing and submitting your test for scoring, you

will get a customized report with valuable feedback on important presentation pointers. Print out and read your report, highlighting the most valuable idea you received from the report. Submit the printout to your instructor.

3. *Listening.* A communication skill development area from which nearly everyone can benefit is improving listening skills. Use your search engine to find helpful information on being a better listener (one example is provided below). After reading through the materials you locate, select one specific area that you will work to improve. Use every listening opportunity you have for the next 24 hours to apply what you have learned. Then write a two- to three-paragraph summary of what you practiced to become a better listener and the results you experienced.

   www.thepargroup.com/articles.html

4. Find five examples of what good communication is about in www.mgeneral.com.

Case for Critical Analysis

Inter-City Manufacturing, Inc.

The president of Inter-City Manufacturing Inc., Rich Langston, wanted to facilitate upward communication. He believed an open-door policy was a good place to start. He announced that his own door was open to all employees and encouraged senior managers to do the same. He felt this would give him a way to get early warning signals that would not be filtered or redirected through the formal chain of command. Langston found that many employees who used the open-door policy had been with the company for years and were comfortable talking to the president. Sometimes messages came through about inadequate policies and procedures. Langston would raise these issues and explain any changes at the next meeting of senior managers.

The most difficult complaints to handle were those from people who were not getting along with their bosses. One employee, Leroy, complained bitterly that his manager had overcommitted the department and put everyone under too much pressure. Leroy argued that long hours and low morale were major problems. But he would not allow Rich Langston to bring the manager into the discussion nor to seek out other employees to confirm the complaint. Although Langston suspected that Leroy might be right, he could not let the matter sit and blurted out, "Have you considered leaving the company?" This made Leroy realize that a meeting with his immediate boss was unavoidable.

Before the three-party meeting, Langston contacted Leroy's manager and explained what was going on. He insisted that the manager come to the meeting willing to listen and without hostility toward Leroy. During the meeting, Leroy's manager listened actively and displayed no ill will. He learned the problem from Leroy's perspective and realized he was over his head in his new job. After the meeting, the manager said he was relieved. He had been promoted into the job from a technical position just a few months earlier and had no management or planning experience. He welcomed Rich Langston's offer to help him do a better job of planning.

2. Do you think that an open-door policy was the right way to improve upward communications? What other techniques would you suggest?

3. What problems do you think an open-door policy creates? Do you think many employees are reluctant to use it? Why?

SOURCE: Based on Everett T. Suters, "Hazards of an Open-Door Policy," *Inc.,* January 1987, pp. 99–102.

Questions

1. What techniques increased Rich Langston's communication effectiveness? Discuss.

Endnotes

1 Hal Lancaster, "A Founder's Lesson: Market Reality Matters More Than a Mission," *Wall Street Journal*, Nov. 2, 1999, p. B1.

2 Jenny C. McCune, "That Elusive Thing Called Trust," *Management Review,* July–August 1998, pp. 10–16.

3 Henry Mintzberg, *The Nature of Managerial Work* (New York: Harper & Row, 1973).

4 D. K. Berlo, *The Process of Communication* (New York: Holt, Rinehart and Winston, 1960), p. 24.

5 Roberta Maynard, "Back to Basics, From the Top," *Nation's Business,* December 1996, pp. 38–39.

6 Bruce K. Blaylock, "Cognitive Style and the Usefulness of Information," *Decision Sciences,* 15 (Winter 1984), pp. 74–91.

7 Robert H. Lengel and Richard L. Daft, "The Selection of Communication Media as an Executive Skill," *Academy of Management Executive,* 2 (August 1988), pp. 225–232; Richard L. Daft and Robert H. Lengel, "Organizational Information Requirements, Media Richness and Structural Design," *Managerial Science,* 32 (May 1986), pp. 554–572.

8 Ford S. Worthy, "How CEOs Manage Their Time," *Fortune,* January 18, 1988, pp. 88–97.

9 M. Lynne Markus, "Electronic Mail as the Medium of Managerial Choice," *Organizational Science,* 5 (4) (November 1994), pp. 502–527.

10 Richard L. Daft, Robert H. Lengel, and Linda Klebe Trevino, "Message Equivocality, Media Selection and Manager Performance: Implication for Information Systems," *MIS Quarterly* 11 (1987), 355–368.

11 John A. Byrne, "Special Report: Jack," *Business Week,* June 8, 1998, pp. 91–106.

12 Jay A. Conger, "The Necessary Art of Persuasion," *Harvard Business Review,* May–June 1998, pp. 84–95.

13 David Armstrong, *Management by Storying Around: A New Method of Leadership* (New York: Doubleday Currency, 1992).

14 Nancy K. Austin, "Just Do It," *Working Woman,* April 1990, pp. 78–80, 126.

15 J. Martin and M. Powers, "Organizational Stories: More Vivid and Persuasive than Quantitative Data," in B. M. Staw, ed., *Psychological Foundations of Organizational Behavior* (Glenview, Illinois: Scott Foresman, 1982), pp. 161–168.

16 I. Thomas Sheppard, "Silent Signals," *Supervisory Management* (March 1986), pp. 31–33.

17 Albert Mehrabian, *Silent Messages* (Belmont, Calif.: Wadsworth, 1971); and Albert Mehrabian, "Communicating without Words," *Psychology Today,* September 1968, pp. 53–55.

18 Sheppard, "Silent Signals."

19 Arthur H. Bell, *The Complete Manager's Guide to Interviewing* (Homewood, Ill.: Richard D. Irwin, 1989).

20 Leigh Buchanan, "The Best of Small Business Web," *Inc. Tech 1999*, 4, pp. 64–112.

21 C. Glenn Pearce, "Doing Something about Your Listening Ability," *Supervisory Management* (March 1989), pp. 29–34.

22 Lt. General William G. Pagonis with Jeffrey L. Cruikshank, *Moving Mountains: Lessons in Leadership and Logistics from the Gulf War* (Boston, Mass.: Harvard Business School Press, 1992).

23 Gerald M. Goldhaber, *Organizational Communication,* 4th ed. (Dubuque, Iowa: Wm. C. Brown, 1980), p. 189.

24 Samantha Miller and Jamie Reno, "True Brew," *People*, Dec. 6, 1999, pp. 181–183.

25 Monci Jo Williams, "America's Best Salesman," *Fortune,* October 26, 1987, pp. 122–134; and David Carnoy, "Rick Pitino," *Success,* October 1998, pp. 68–71, 82.

26 Roberta Maynard, "Back to Basics, From the Top."

27 Nick Wingfield, "Rykodisc's Online Offering Could Rock the Music World," *The Wall Street Journal,* Feb. 4, 1999, p. 1; Hal Plotkin, "Spin Doctors," *Inc. Technology 2* (1995), 60–64.

28 Roberta Maynard, "It Can Pay to Show Employees the Big Picture," *Nation's Business,* December 1994, p. 10.

29 William R. Pape, "Relative Merits," *Inc. Technology,* 1 (1998), p. 23.

30 Geoff Williams, "Speed Freaks," *Entrepreneur*, Sept. 1999, pp. 118–122.

31 J. G. Miller, "Living Systems: The Organization," *Behavioral Science,* 17 (1972), p. 69.

32 Michael J. Glauser, "Upward Information Flow in Organizations: Review and Conceptual Analysis," *Human Relations,* 37 (1984), pp. 613–643.

33 "Wild Oats Markets to Buy 13 Stores from Competitors," *Los Angeles Times,* Nov. 1, 1999, p. 3.

34 Anne B. FIsher, "CEO's Think That Morale Is Dandy," *Fortune,* November 18, 1991, pp. 83–84.

35 Mary P. Rowe and Michael Baker, "Are You Hearing Enough Employee Concerns?" *Harvard Business Review,* 62 (May–June 1984), pp. 127–135.

36 Barbara Ettorre, "The Unvarnished Truth," *Management Review,* June 1997, pp. 54–57.

37 Thomas Petzinger, "A Hospital Applies Teamwork to Thwart An Insidious Enemy," *The Wall Street Journal,* May 8, 1998, p. B1.

38 William R. Pape, "Relative Merits," *Inc. Tech 1998*, No. 1, pp. 23–24.

39 Thomas J. Peters and Robert H. Waterman Jr., *In Search of Excellence* (New York: Harper & Row, 1982); and Tom Peters and Nancy Austin, *A Passion for Excellence: The Leadership Difference* (New York: Random House, 1985).

40 Lois Therrien, "How Ztel Went from Riches to Rags," *Business Week,* June 17, 1985, pp. 97–100.

41 Victor Wishna, "Guiding Lights," *Restaurant Business*, May 1, 1999, pp. 39–42.

42 Keith Davis and John W. Newstrom, *Human Behavior at Work: Organizational Behavior,* 7th ed. (New York: McGraw-Hill, 1985).

43 Donald B. Simmons, "The Nature of the Organizational Grapevine," *Supervisory Management* (November 1985), pp. 39–42; and Davis and Newstrom, *Human Behavior.*

44 Barbara Ettorre, "Hellooo. Anybody Listening?" *Management Review,* November 1997, p. 9.

45 "They Hear It Through the Grapevine," in Michael Warshaw, "The Good Guy's Guide to Office Politics," *Fast Company,* April–May 1998, pp. 157–178.

46 E. M. Rogers and R. A. Rogers, *Communication in Organizations* (New York: Free Press, 1976); and A. Bavelas and D. Barrett, "An Experimental Approach to Organization Communication," *Personnel,* 27 (1951), pp. 366–371.

47 This discussion is based on Daft and Steers, *Organizations.*

48 Bavelas and Barrett, "An Experimental Approach"; and M. E. Shaw, *Group Dynamics: The Psychology of Small Group Behavior* (New York: McGraw-Hill, 1976).

49 Richard L. Daft and Norman B. Macintosh, "A Tentative Exploration into the Amount and Equivocality of Information Processing in Organizational Work Units," *Administrative Science Quarterly* 26 (1981), 207–224.

50 Matt Goldberg, "Microsoft Knows How to Operate—Fast," *Fast Company,* April–May 1998, p. 76.

51 John Case, "Opening the Books," *Harvard Business Review,* March–April 1997, pp. 118–127.

52 David Bohm, *On Dialogue* (Ojai, Calif.: David Bohm Seminars, 1989).

53 The discussion is based on Glenna Gerard and Linda Teurfs, "Dialogue and Organizational Transformation," in *Community Building: Renewing Spirit and Learning in Business,* ed. Kazinierz Gozdz (New Leaders Press, 1995), 142–153; and Edgar H. Schein, "On Dialogue, Culture, and Organizational Learning," *Organizational Dynamics* (autumn 1993), 40–51.

54 James A. F. Stoner and R. Edward Freeman, *Management,* 4th ed. (Englewood Cliffs, N.J.: Prentice-Hall, 1989).

55 Janet Fulk and Sirish Mani, "Distortion of Communication in Hierarchical Relationships," in *Communication Yearbook,* vol. 9, ed. M. L. McLaughlin (Beverly Hills, Calif.: Sage, 1986), pp. 483–510.

15

Teamwork in Organizations

LEARNING OBJECTIVES

After studying this chapter, you should be able to:

- Identify the types of teams in organizations

- Discuss new applications of teams to facilitate employee involvement

- Identify roles within teams and the type of role you could play to help a team be effective

- Explain the general stages of team development

- Explain the concepts of team cohesiveness and team norms and their relationship to team performance

- Understand the causes of conflict within and among teams and how to reduce conflict

- Discuss the assets and liabilities of organizational teams

MANAGEMENT PROBLEM

Chapter 15

ROBERTS EXPRESS, the largest

expedited freight carrier in North America, has

done it all. They've moved lighting equipment for Oprah Winfrey's

show to the Texas town where she broadcast while battling cattle ranchers in a

lawsuit, taken equipment to the set of Titanic in Nova Scotia, and delivered Christmas

cards to the White House. Roberts picks up most shipments within 90 minutes of receiving an

order and delivers more than half of them on the *same day*. Most of Roberts's shipments have to get

there fast—or else. Joe Greulich, manager of management information systems, says the company is the

"ambulance service for industrial freight." Moving freight by truck more quickly and cheaply than air freight

• *What would you recommend to recapture the responsiveness and customer intimacy*

of the "old Roberts"? How might the formation of teams help solve this problem?

gave Roberts a competitive edge when the company started in the early 1980s. Roberts served customers in a

limited regional area, and agents and dispatchers knew most of their customers and drivers by name. The

company rapidly expanded nationwide and was eventually making more than 200,000 deliveries a year.

Success came at a price, however. Agents, unaware of which trucks or drivers were available, took orders

and then passed them on to dispatchers, who scrambled to cover the deliveries. Service began to

suffer. In addition, customers missed the intimacy of the old Roberts, where they could deal

with an agent who knew their names and their company's needs. Roberts needed a

way to serve each customer with the responsiveness and personal

attention that the company had started out with.[1]

The problems facing Roberts Express also confront many other companies. How can they be more flexible and responsive in an increasingly competitive environment? A quiet revolution has been taking place in organizations across the country and around the world as companies respond by using employee teams. From the assembly line to the executive office, from large corporations such as British Petroleum and 3M to government entities such as the United States Information Agency, teams are becoming the basic building block of organizations. One survey found that, within three years, the number of Fortune 1000 companies using work teams increased by almost 20 percent, and teamwork has become the most frequent topic taught in company training programs. Similarly, a study of 109 Canadian organizations found that 42 percent report "widespread team-based activity" and only 13 percent report little or no team activity.[2]

Teams are popping up in the most unexpected places. An electromechanical assembly plant found that both quality and productivity increased after it abandoned the traditional production line in favor of work teams.[3] At Mattel, a team of artists, toy designers, computer experts, and automobile designers slashed 13 months from the usual toy design process, creating Top Speed toy cars in only five months. Hecla Mining Company uses teams for company goal setting; a major telecommunications company uses teams of salespeople to deal with big customers with complex purchasing requirements; and Lassiter Middle School in Jefferson County, Kentucky, uses teams of teachers to prepare daily schedules and handle student discipline problems. Multinational corporations are now using international teams composed of managers from different countries. Ford uses teams to spot quality problems and improve efficiency, and other manufacturers use teams to master sophisticated new production technologies.[4] And as we saw in Chapter 6, teams often are used to make important decisions, and many organizations are now run by top management teams under the title of Office of the CEO.

As we will see in this chapter, teams have emerged as a powerful management tool, because they involve and empower employees.

Teams can cut across organizations in unusual ways, employing horizontal channels of communication. Hence workers are more satisfied, and the typical results are higher productivity and product quality. Moreover, managers discover a more flexible organization, and workers don't feel stuck in narrow jobs.

This chapter focuses on teams and their new applications within organizations. We will define various types of teams, explore their stages of development, and examine such characteristics as size, cohesiveness, and norms. We will discuss how individuals can make contributions to teams and review the benefits and costs associated with teamwork. Teams are an important aspect of organizational life, and the ability to manage them is an important component of manager and organization success.

■ TEAMS AT WORK

In this section, we will first define teams and then discuss a model of team effectiveness that summarizes the important concepts.

WHAT IS A TEAM?

A **team** is a unit of two or more people who interact and coordinate their work to accomplish a specific goal. This definition has three components. First, two or more people are required. Teams can be quite large, although most have fewer than 15 people. Second, people in a team have regular interaction. People who do not interact, such as when standing in line at a lunch counter or riding in an elevator, do not compose a team. Third, people in a team share a performance goal, whether it is to design a new handheld computer, build a car, or write a textbook. Students often are assigned to teams to do classwork assignments, in which case the purpose is to perform the assignment and receive an acceptable grade.

Although a team is a group of people, the two terms are not interchangeable. An employer, a teacher, or a coach can put together a *group* of people and never build a team. The team concept implies a sense of shared mission and collective responsibility. Here are the

team
A unit of two or more people who interact and coordinate their work to accomplish a specific goal

FOCUS ON Diversity SNOWBALL.COM

Two Harvard and Yale management-grad women with young children did not want to give up the idea of exciting jobs at an e-company. But even though the Internet is changing everything, some things stay the same; that is, demands of family life, where kids still have to be fed, bathed, and taken to school. And grueling 80-hour workweeks at a startup did not seem compatible with regular family dinners. So after consulting jobs at Snowball.com, an Internet media company targeting the Generation I 12- to 29-year-olds, they made a proposal to Mark Jung, a former colleague and current CEO of Snowball.

How about if they become a team? A job-sharing team, that is, of vice president. Jung was skeptical, because most successful job sharing he had seen was at the project level. But a vice president, someone with great line authority? That seemed kind of risky. "I had anxieties about giving a job share to an officer of the company," he said, "Though I would have hired either of them as vice president full time." As a compromise, he hired them to job share as director of affiliate services. The team, known as SKZ (for Sandra and

Kathleen, with nickname KZ) did so well that within four months they were promoted to vice presidents of affiliate development and marketing. Jung is now a true believer and sees that any job, given the right team, can become a job-share. It can be a real high to have someone to talk over all the issues of the job. But it also requires lots of organization, twice-weekly meetings, sharing of files and huge doses of trust.

Many mothers have forsaken ideas of startups because of the overwhelming demands. But SKZ has shown that people choosing flexible hours can still make important contributions to e-business. And because startups have no set rules, players can propose situations that suit their needs. Because of a vacuum of talent in the high-tech area, executive search consultant Lauren Benton tells her clients to be as creative as possible. "When CEOs find the perfect candidate," she says, "They do whatever they can to hire them."

SOURCE: Patricia Nakache, "One VP, Two Brains," *Fortune*, Dec. 20, 1999, pp. 327–329.

---

primary differences between groups and teams:

Groups have a designated strong *leader;* individual *accountability;* identical *purpose* for group and organization; *individual* work products; *efficient* meetings; effectiveness that is measured *indirectly* by influence on business (i.e., financial performance); and work that is discussed, decided on, and *delegated* to individuals.

Teams have leadership roles that are *shared* (or rotated); individual and *mutual* accountability; specific team *vision* or purpose; *collective* work products; meetings that encourage *open-ended discussion* and problem solving; effectiveness that is measured *directly* by assessing collective work; and work that is discussed, decided on, and *shared.*

When the University of Kentucky Wildcats won the 1998 national basketball championship, coaches and commentators noted that

the team had less individual talent and fewer stars than some other teams but achieved a high level of success through excellent teamwork— shared leadership, purpose, and responsibility by all members working toward a common goal. As we see in Focus on Diversity, Snowball.com has taken a new approach toward teamwork, and its risky method has paid off.

MODEL OF WORK TEAM EFFECTIVENESS

Factors associated with team effectiveness are illustrated in Exhibit 15.1. Work team effectiveness is based on two outcomes—productive output and personal satisfaction.[5] *Satisfaction* pertains to the team's ability to meet the personal needs of its members and hence maintain their membership and commitment. *Productive output* pertains to the quality and quantity of task outputs as defined by team goals.

The factors that influence team effectiveness begin with the organizational context,[6] which includes structure, strategy, environment,

Exhibit 15.1

WORK TEAM EFFECTIVENESS MODEL

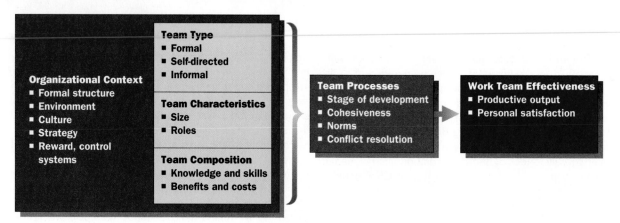

culture, and reward systems. Within that context, managers define teams. Important team characteristics are the type of team, the team structure, and team composition. Factors such as the diversity of the team in terms of gender and race, as well as knowledge, skills, and attitudes, can have a tremendous impact on team processes and effectiveness.[7] Managers must decide when to create permanent teams within the formal structure and when to use a temporary task team. Team size and roles also are important. Managers must also consider whether a team is the best way to do a task. If costs outweigh benefits, managers may wish to assign an individual employee to the task.

This chapter builds on the team performance model (Exhibit 15.1) and examines types of organizational teams, team structure, internal processes, and team benefits and costs. These team characteristics influence processes internal to the team, which in turn affect output and satisfaction. Leaders must understand and manage stages of development, cohesiveness, norms, and conflict in order to establish an effective team. These processes are continually influenced by the characteristics of the team and organization and by the ability of members and leaders to direct these processes in a positive manner.

■ TYPES OF TEAMS

Many types of teams can exist within organizations. The easiest way to classify teams is in terms of those created as part of the organization's formal structure and those created to increase employee participation.

FORMAL TEAMS

Formal teams are created by the organization as part of the formal organization structure. Two common types of formal teams are vertical and horizontal, which typically represent vertical and horizontal structural relationships, as described in Chapter 7. These two types of teams are illustrated in Exhibit 15.2. A third type of formal team is the special-purpose team.

VERTICAL TEAM A **vertical team** is composed of a manager and his or her subordinates in the formal chain of command. Sometimes called a *functional* team or a command team, the vertical team may in some cases include three or four levels of hierarchy within a functional department. Typically, the vertical team includes a single department in an organization. The third-shift nursing team on the second floor of St. Luke's Hospital is a vertical team that includes nurses and a supervisor. A financial analysis department, a quality control department, an accounting department, and a human resource department are all command teams. Each is created by the organization to attain specific goals through members' joint activities and interactions. Sometimes in small companies the vertical team becomes all the employees, as it is in Oregon Chai.

formal team
A team created by the organization as part of the formal organization structure

vertical team
A formal team composed of a manager and his or her subordinates in the organization's formal chain of command

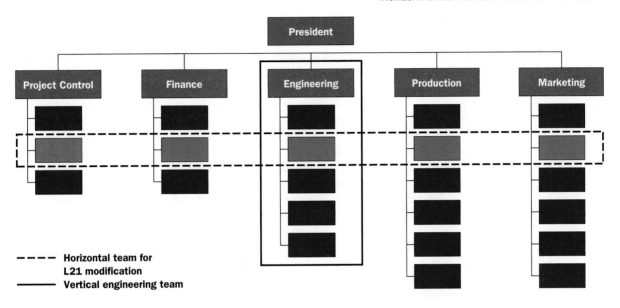

- - - - Horizontal team for
L21 modification
——— Vertical engineering team

OREGON CHAI

There are two types of entrepreneurs: those who know it all and those who seek out information. UC Santa Cruz grad Heather Howitt and her mother are the latter. They teamed up in 1994 to start Oregon Chai. "We know what we don't know," says Howitt of her current nine-person team. "And we're not afraid to ask for help."

They mean to learn a lot about one another, too, as a means of becoming a more effective team. They have periodic team-building sessions, where they learn the personality styles of one another and where they listen to Chairman Rex Bird talk about business, laced with quotations from F. Scott Fitzgerald and Bob Dylan.

Because they accept their relative lack of business experience, they are always on the lookout for fresh talent. In fact, that's how they snagged Bird, after reading a newspaper article about his departure from a food chain that he had taken public. Their board of directors is something most CEOs would salivate for and includes such top players as ad executive Joel Lewis, the person responsi-ble for putting Lipton Ice Tea in a can. Because they are not afraid to show their ignorance, they've gotten valuable advice from distributors and retailers. For example, their chai drink, which is unknown to most consumers, confused people on how to mix it with milk. Distributor Sunshine Dairy Foods suggested they show up in the mornings before the teamster drivers head out—typically between 1 and 5 A.M.—and give cups of chai to the drivers. Howitt's early morning samples meant that when accounts ask if Sunshine carries chai, the drivers know exactly how to answer.

Back in 1994 when Howitt and her mother started out, with little experience or know-how, Oregon Chai had revenues of $20,000. Now it makes over one-third of all prepared chai on the market and has annual revenues approaching $10 million.[8] ■

HORIZONTAL TEAM   A **horizontal team** is composed of employees from about the same hierarchical level but from different areas of expertise.[9] A horizontal team is drawn from several departments, is given a specific task, and may be disbanded after the task is completed.

horizontal team
A formal team composed of employees from about the same hierarchical level but from different areas of expertise

The two most common types of horizontal teams are task forces and committees.

As described in Chapter 7, a *task force* is a group of employees from different departments formed to deal with a specific activity and existing only until the task is completed. Sometimes called *a cross-functional team*, the task force might be used to create a new product in a manufacturing organization or a new history curriculum in a university. Several departments are involved, and many views have to be considered, so these tasks are best served with a horizontal team. US Airways set up a task force made up of mechanics, flight attendants, dispatchers, aircraft cleaners, ramp workers, luggage attendants, reservations agents, and others to design and start a low-fare airline to compete with the expansion of Southwest Airlines into the East. The task force spent several months pricing peanuts, conducting focus groups, studying the competition, and developing a plan to present to senior management for a new low-fare airline, MetroJet.[10] At Hallmark Cards, a cross-functional team made up of artists, writers, lithographers, designers, and photographers is set up to develop new greeting cards for each major holiday.

A **committee** sometimes will become a permanent part of the organization's structure. Membership on a committee usually is decided by a person's title or position rather than by personal expertise. A committee often needs official representation, compared with selection for a task force, which is based on personal qualifications for solving a problem. Committees typically are formed to deal with tasks that regularly recur. For example, a grievance committee handles employee grievances; an advisory committee makes recommendations in the areas of employee compensation and work practices; a worker-management committee may be concerned with work rules, job design changes, and suggestions for work improvement.[11]

As part of the horizontal structure of the organization, task forces and committees offer several advantages: (1) They allow organization members to exchange information; (2) They generate suggestions for coordinating the organizational units that are represented; (3) They develop new ideas and solutions for existing organizational problems; and (4) They assist in the development of new organizational practices and policies.

SPECIAL-PURPOSE TEAM   **Special-purpose teams** are created outside the formal organization structure to undertake a project of special importance or creativity. McDonald's created a special team to create the Chicken McNugget. E. J. (Bud) Sweeney was asked to head up a team to bring bits of batter-covered chicken to the marketplace. The McNugget team needed breathing room and was separated from the formal corporate structure to give it the autonomy to perform successfully. A special-purpose team still is part of the formal organization and has its own reporting structure, but members perceive themselves as a separate entity.[12]

SELF-DIRECTED TEAMS

Employee involvement through teams is designed to increase the participation of low-level workers in decision making and the conduct of their jobs, with the goal of improving performance. Employee involvement represents a revolution in business prompted by the success of teamwork in Japanese companies. Hundreds of companies, large and small, are jumping aboard the bandwagon, including DaimlerChrysler, Cummins Engine, Wilson Golf Ball, and Edy's Grand Ice Cream. Employee involvement started out simply with techniques such as information sharing with employees or asking employees for suggestions about improving the work. Gradually, companies moved toward greater autonomy for employees, which led first to problem-solving teams and then to self-directed teams.[13]

Problem-solving teams typically consist of 5 to 12 hourly employees from the same department who voluntarily meet to discuss ways of improving quality, efficiency, and the work environment. Recommendations are proposed to management for approval. Problem-solving teams usually are the first step in a company's move toward greater employee participation. The most widely known application is *quality circles,* initiated by the Japanese, in which

committee
A sometimes permanent team in the organization structure created to deal with tasks that regularly recur

special-purpose team
A team created outside the formal organization to undertake a project of special importance or creativity

problem-solving teams
Teams of 5 to 12 hourly employees from the same department who meet to discuss ways of improving quality, efficiency, and the work environment

employees focus on ways to improve quality in the production process. USX has adopted this approach in several of its steel mills, recognizing that quality takes a team effort. Under the title All Product Excellence program (APEX), USX set up 40 APEX teams of up to 12 employees at its plant in West Mifflin, Pennsylvania. These teams meet several times a month to solve quality problems. The APEX teams have since spread to mills in Indiana, Ohio, and California.[14]

As a company matures, problem-solving teams can gradually evolve into self-directed teams, which represent a fundamental change in how employee work is organized. Self-directed teams enable employees to feel challenged, find their work meaningful, and develop a strong sense of identity with the company.[15] **Self-directed teams** typically consist of 5 to 20 multiskilled workers who rotate jobs to produce an entire product or service or at least one complete aspect or portion of a product or service (e.g., engine assembly, insurance claim processing). The central idea is that the teams themselves, rather than managers or supervisors, take responsibility for their work, make decisions, monitor their own performance, and alter their work behavior as needed to solve problems, meet goals, and adapt to changing conditions.[16] Self-directed teams are permanent teams that typically include the following elements:

- The team includes employees with several skills and functions, and the combined skills are sufficient to perform a major organizational task. A team may include members from the foundry, machining, grinding, fabrication, and sales departments, with each member cross-trained to perform one another's jobs.

- The team eliminates barriers among departments, enabling excellent coordination to produce a product or service.

- The team is given access to resources such as information, equipment, machinery, and supplies needed to perform the complete task.

- The team is empowered with decision-making authority (i.e., members have the freedom to select new members, solve problems, spend money, monitor results, and plan for the future).[17]

In a self-directed team, members take over managerial duties such as scheduling work or vacations or ordering materials. They work with minimum supervision, perhaps electing one of their own as supervisor, who may change each year. Teams at Corning work without shift supervisors and work closely with other plant divisions to solve production-line problems and coordinate deadlines and deliveries. Teams have the authority to make and implement decisions, complete projects, and solve problems.[18]

Self-directed teams can be highly effective. Service companies such as Federal Express and IDS have boosted productivity up to 40 percent by adopting self-directed teams. Volvo uses self-directed teams of 7 to 10 hourly workers to assemble four cars per shift. However, there still is a reluctance among management to entrust workers with managerial responsibilities and duties. A survey conducted by the University of Southern California's Center for Effective Organizations found that although 68 percent of Fortune 1000 companies report using self-directed teams, only 10 percent of workers are involved.[19]

One type of self-directed team, the **virtual team,** has resulted from globalization and advances in technology. Virtual teams use computer technology and groupware to tie together geographically distant members working toward a common goal. Virtual teams can be formed within an organization whose plants and offices are scattered across the nation or around the world. A company may also use virtual teams in partnership with suppliers or, in many cases, with competitors to pull together the best minds to complete a project or speed a new product to market. Leadership among team members is shared or altered, depending on the area of expertise needed at each point in the project. The success of virtual teams is dependent upon several crucial elements, including careful selection of partners and team members, strong management support of the team and its goals, clear goals, utilization of the best communications tools and

self-directed teams
Teams of 5 to 20 multiskilled workers who rotate jobs to produce an entire product or service, often supervised by an elected member

virtual team
A team that uses computer technology and groupware so that geographically distant members can collaborate on projects and reach common goals

TECHNOLOGY FOR TOMORROW
VERIFONE'S VIRTUAL WORLD

VeriFone, an equipment supplier for credit card verification and automated payments, started out as a virtual company over 15 years ago and today uses virtual teams in every aspect of its business. Teams of facility managers work together to determine how to reduce toxins in their offices. Marketing and development groups brainstorm new products. Sales reps pool information and customer testimonials.

VeriFone's concept of virtual teams is highly flexible. Some teams may include only VeriFone employees while others include outsiders, such as the employees of a customer or partner. Some are permanent, such as operational teams that run their companies virtually, while others are temporary. Any employee can organize a temporary virtual team to work on a specific problem. For example, one sales rep sent out an SOS when he saw a major sales prospect in Greece falling apart. Overnight, a team made up of sales, marketing, and technical-support staff from around the world came together to provide data and testimonials that eventually helped the Greek representative make the sale.

Despite all this flexibility, VeriFone has some pretty strict "rules" to ensure that teams are not formed haphazardly. Employees complete a 40-hour training program in which they learn how to create a successful virtual team. In addition, leaders of virtual teams follow written procedures put together by the company's senior managers. VeriFone offers these guidelines for successful virtual teams:

1. DEFINE THE PURPOSE. A VeriFone team always starts by putting its purpose in writing. This keeps everyone on track and prevents misunderstandings.

2. RECRUIT TEAM MEMBERS. Most virtual teams should be between three and seven members. Also, the team should include people who represent a diversity of views and experiences. Selecting members in different time zones means productive work can be going on around the clock.

3. DETERMINE THE DURATION OF THE TEAM. Decide whether the purpose and goals call for a short-term task force or problem-solving team or for a long-term operational team.

4. SELECT THE COMMUNICATIONS TECHNOLOGY. All VeriFone staffers are not only well trained in how to use communications tools but also in when to use them. General guidelines are that for keeping in contact remotely, teams use beepers, cell phones, and voice mail; for disseminating information, fax, e-mail, and application sharing over the network. For brainstorming, discussion, and decision making, teams use e-mail, conference calls, and videoconferencing. Selecting the right tool is critical to the success of the virtual team.

VeriFone employees also are trained to understand the psychological pitfalls of communicating virtually. Some subtleties of meaning are always lost and misunderstandings are more common than when teams work face-to-face. E-mail in particular can lead to misunderstandings, so team members communicate by phone or videoconference on sensitive or complicated issues.

www.verifone.com

SOURCE: William R. Pape, "Group Insurance," *Inc. Technology*, 2 (1997), pp. 29, 31.

procedures, the development of trust among all members, and information sharing.[20] Technology for Tomorrow describes the use of virtual teams in every aspect of VeriFone's business.

Companies trying to integrate a variety of team approaches into their operations have turned teamwork into a highly profitable business model. Whole Foods Market, the largest natural foods grocer in the United States, had barely a dozen stores in three states. Today, it has the clout of a nationwide chain, with 100 stores nationwide and net profits that are typically double the national average.

The Whole Foods culture is based on decentralized teamwork. Each store is an autonomous profit center made up of an average of 10 self-directed teams—grocery, produce, and so forth. Teams (and only teams) have the power to approve new hires for full-time jobs. Store leaders screen candidates and recommend them for a job on a specific team, but it takes a two-thirds vote of the team to approve the hire.

The company believes the first prerequisite of teamwork is trust, which starts with the hiring vote. Whole Foods supports teamwork with wide-open information on financial and operations systems. Sensitive figures on store sales, team sales, profit margins, and even yearly salaries and bonuses are available to any employee. Executive salaries are limited to no more than eight times the average wage. According to CEO John Mackey, open information keeps everyone "aligned to the vision of shared fate. . . . If you're trying to create a high-trust organization, an organization where people are all-for-one and one-for-all, you can't have secrets."[21]

■ WORK TEAM CHARACTERISTICS

Teams in organizations take on characteristics that are important to internal processes and team performance. Two characteristics of concern to managers are team size and member roles.

SIZE

The ideal size of work teams often is thought to be seven, although variations of from 5 to 12 typically are associated with good team performance. These teams are large enough to take advantage of diverse skills, enable members to express good and bad feelings, and aggressively solve problems. They also are small enough to permit members to feel an intimate part of the group.

In general, as a team increases in size, it becomes harder for each member to interact with and influence the others. A summary of research on group size suggests the following:

1. Small teams (two to four members) show more agreement, ask more questions, and exchange more opinions. Members want to get along with one another. Small teams report more satisfaction and enter into more personal discussions. They tend to be informal and make few demands on team leaders.

2. Large teams (12 or more) tend to have more disagreements and differences of opinion. Subgroups often form, and conflicts among them occur, ranging from protection of "turf" to trivial matters such as the kind of coffee brewing in the pot. Demands on leaders are greater because there is more centralized decision making and less member participation. Large teams also tend to be less friendly. Turnover and absenteeism are higher in a large team, especially for

blue-collar workers. Because less satisfaction is associated with specialized tasks and poor communication, team members have fewer opportunities to participate and feel an intimate part of the group.

As a general rule, large teams make need satisfaction for individuals more difficult; thus, there is less reason for people to remain committed to their goals. Teams of from 5 to 12 seem to work best. If a team grows larger than 20, managers should divide it into subgroups, each with its own members and goals. The University of Michigan Housing Facilities Department experimented with a team structure, starting out with seven members and later enlarging it to twelve. But having definite structure, goals and values for the team has been one of the reasons for its success.

UNIVERSITY OF MICHIGAN HOUSING FACILITIES

Starting full-time work at age 16, George SanFacon was a jack of all trades—mechanic, painter, security guard, factory assembler, aerospace engineer—having worked his way up though the years. But everywhere he worked, it was always the same. "People were disfranchised from one another as a community in the workplace," he says. "They were typically treated as means rather than ends, thereby limiting what the organization and community could ultimately produce."

So when he took over as director of the University of Michigan Housing Facilities Department, he offered the staff a chance to be part of a bold experiment: Collapse the top three layers of administration in the 250 employees and $20 million yearly budget unit into a single self-governing council to operate solely on consensus-based decision making. This means that top-guy SanFacon was willing to give up his hierarchical position and become no greater than any of the other seven council members.

It took several years to transform the pyramidal structure into a circular one, eliminating the boss-subordinate relationship. Now all 12 (increased from the original seven) members report to the entire team, rather than one person. And rather than a midlevel layer of management, there are now four self-directed teams, three of which are responsible for day-to-day operations and one that takes care of architecture, engineering, and interior design. These changes also required a shift in emphasis from individual performance to the importance of good faith and community. The resulting framework evolved over time and came from a genuine effort to create the kind of workplace experience that "promotes the well-being and growth of both those involved and those affected."

Each of the four self-managed teams has a "first among equals" who is accountable to the entire council for performance of the team, as well as a peer member delegate of their choice, using the "linking pin" model of management. The council meets every two weeks and is committed to the spirit of good faith, defined as "demonstrating a sincere commitment to the mutual well-being of all affected parties" and encompasses working with good intentions, honesty, trust, and motivation above self-interest in order to accomplish common goals. In order to do this the staff attends seminars on dialogue, believing good conversation to be the foundation of their work. They have found skilled dialogue to bring greater understanding and acceptance to one another's individual differences, as well as promoting more creativity and increased effectiveness.

It was a difficult, but ultimately rewarding journey. Turnover is reduced, financial performance has improved, and customers satisfaction levels are up. Plus there is more joy, caring, and fun at work now. But this is not for everyone. SanFacon says if managers aren't really serious about sharing power—or learning—others will get the picture. "If the leader is not interested in growing as a person, forget it. You'll be found out and exposed; an open framework [of shared governance] like this makes it impossible to mask duplicity and dishonesty behind a veil of power and position."[22] ■

MEMBER ROLES

For a team to be successful over the long run, it must be structured so as to both maintain the social well-being of its members and accomplish its task. In successful teams, the requirements for task performance and social satisfaction are met by the emergence of two types of roles: task specialist and socioemotional.[23]

People who play the **task specialist role** spend time and energy helping the team reach its goal. They often display the following behaviors:

- *Initiation*. Propose new solutions to team problems.
- *Give opinions*. Offer opinions on task solutions; give candid feedback on other people's suggestions.
- *Seek information*. Ask for task-relevant facts.
- *Summarize*. Relate various ideas to the problem at hand; pull ideas together into a summary perspective.
- *Energize*. Stimulate the team into action when interest drops.[24]

People who adopt a **socioemotional role** support the team's emotional needs and help to strengthen the social entity. They display the following behaviors:

- *Encourage*. Are warm to others and receptive to their ideas; give praise and support to draw out their contributions
- *Harmonize*. Reconcile group conflicts; help disagreeing parties reach agreement
- *Reduce tension*. May tell jokes or in other ways diminish group tensions
- *Follow*. Go along with the team; agree to the ideas of other team members
- *Compromise*. Will shift own opinions to maintain team harmony[25]

Exhibit 15.3 illustrates task specialist and socioemotional roles in teams. When most in-

task specialist role
A role in which the individual devotes personal time and energy to helping the team accomplish its task

socioemotional role
A role in which the individual provides support for the emotional needs of team members and social unity

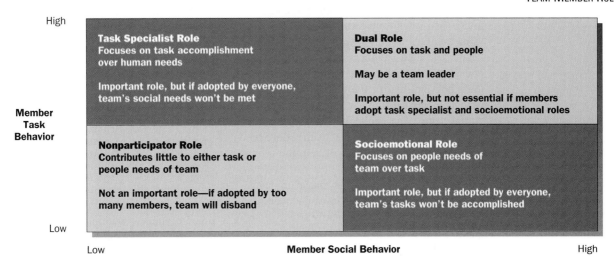

dividuals in a team play a social role, the team is socially oriented. Members do not criticize or disagree with one another and do not force-fully offer opinions or try to accomplish team tasks, because their primary interest is to keep the team happy. Teams with mostly socioemo-tional roles can be very satisfying, but they also can be unproductive. At the other extreme, a team made up primarily of task specialists will tend to have a singular concern for task accomplishment. This team will be effective for a short period of time but will not be satis-fying for members over the long run. Task spe-cialists convey little emotional concern for one another, are unsupportive, and ignore team members' social and emotional needs. The task-oriented team can be humorless and un-satisfying.

As Exhibit 15.3 illustrates, some team members may play a **dual role.** People with dual roles both contribute to the task and meet the emotional needs of members. Such people may become team leaders because they satisfy both types of needs and are looked up to by other members. The exhibit also shows the fi-nal type of role, called the *nonparticipator role*. People in the **nonparticipator role** con-tribute little to either the task or the social needs of team members and generally are held in low esteem by the team.

The important thing for managers to re-member is that effective teams must have peo-ple in both task specialist and socioemotional roles. Humor and social concern are as impor-tant to team effectiveness as are facts and problem solving. Managers also should re-member that some people perform better in one type of role; some are inclined toward so-cial concerns and others toward task concerns. A well-balanced team will do best over the long term because it will be personally satisfy-ing for team members and permit the accom-plishment of team tasks.

■ TEAM PROCESSES

Now we turn our attention to internal team processes. Team processes pertain to those dy-namics that change over time and can be influ-enced by team leaders. In this section, we will discuss the team processes of stages of devel-opment, cohesiveness, and norms. The fourth type of team process, conflict, will be covered in the next section.

STAGES OF TEAM DEVELOPMENT

After a team has been created, distinct stages of development occur.[26] New teams are

dual role
A role in which the individual both contributes to the team's task and supports the emotional needs of members

nonparticipator role
A role in which the individual contributes little to either the task or the socioemotional needs of members

different from mature teams. Recall a time when you were a member of a new team, such as a fraternity or sorority pledge class, a committee, or a small team formed to do a class assignment. Over time the team changed. In the beginning, team members had to get to know one another, establish roles and norms, divide the labor, and clarify the team's task. In this way, members became parts of a smoothly operating team. The challenge for leaders is to understand the stage of the team's development and take action that will help the group improve its functioning.

Research findings suggest that team development is not random but evolves over five definitive stages, which typically occur in sequence. In teams that are under time pressure or that will exist for only a few days, the stages may occur rapidly. Each stage confronts team leaders and members with unique problems and challenges.[27]

1. The **forming** stage is a period of orientation and getting acquainted. Members break the ice and test one another for friendship possibilities and task orientation. Team members find which behaviors are acceptable to others. Uncertainty is high during this stage, and members usually accept whatever power or authority is offered by either formal or informal leaders. Members are dependent on the team until they find out what the ground rules are and what is expected of them. During the forming stage, the team leader should provide time for members to get acquainted with one another and encourage them to engage in informal social discussions.

2. During the **storming** stage, individual personalities emerge. People become more assertive in clarifying their roles and what is expected of them. This stage is marked by conflict and disagreement, typically involving their perceptions of the team's mission. Members may jockey for positions, and coalitions or subgroups based on common interests may form. The team is not yet cohesive and may exhibit a general lack of unity. Unless teams can successfully move beyond this stage, they may get bogged down and never achieve high performance.

During the storming stage, the team leader should encourage participation by each team member. Members should propose ideas, disagree with one another, and work through the uncertainties and conflicting perceptions about team tasks and goals.

3. In the **norming** stage, conflict is resolved, and team harmony and unity emerge. Consensus develops on who has the power, who is the leader, and the roles of the members. Members come to accept and understand one another. Differences are resolved, and a sense of team cohesion grows. This stage typically is short in duration. During the norming stage, the team leader should emphasize oneness within the team and help clarify team norms and values.

4. During the **performing** stage, the major emphasis is on problem solving and accomplishing the assigned task. Members are committed to the team's mission. They are coordinated with one another and handle disagreements in a mature way. They confront and resolve problems in the interest of task accomplishment. They interact frequently and direct discussion and influence toward achieving team goals. During this stage, the leader should concentrate on managing high task performance. Both socioemotional and task specialists should contribute.

5. The **adjourning** stage occurs in committees, task forces, and teams that have a limited task to perform and are disbanded afterward. During this stage, the emphasis is on wrapping up and gearing down. Task performance is no longer a top priority. Members may feel heightened emotionality, strong cohesiveness, and depression or even regret over the team's disbanding. They may feel happy about mission accomplishment and sad about the loss of friendship and associations. At this point, the leader may wish to signify the team's disbanding with a ritual or ceremony, perhaps giving out plaques and awards to signify closure and completeness.

The formation of self-directed teams at BP Norge, the Norwegian arm of British Petroleum, illustrates the stages of team development.

forming
The stage of team development characterized by orientation and acquaintance

storming
The stage of team development in which individual personalities and roles, and resulting conflicts, emerge

norming
The stage of team development in which conflicts developed during the storming stage are resolved and team harmony and unity emerge

performing
The stage of team development in which members focus on problem solving and accomplishing the team's assigned task

adjourning
The stage of team development in which members prepare for the team's disbanding

Excite, the number two search engine company after Yahoo!, was founded through teamwork. The Excite team, made up of members whose nicknames are (from left to right), Okmo, Koenig, Foopee, Mister Swiss, Picklock, and Tsar, met at Stanford University. During their team's forming stage, they engaged in informal social discussions while developing a plan to protect themselves from injury. "Well, when we played at Cal, the students used to throw frozen fruit at us. It would really hurt if you got hit, so one year we got golf clubs—three woods, I think they were, and we whaled those oranges right back in the crowd. It was great." Genius comes in many forms, and today the company's revenues exceed $50.2 million dollars.

BP NORGE
www.bp.no

Early efforts to introduce self-directed teams at BP Norge failed, leaving employees disillusioned and skeptical. Managers needed a way to work through barriers of resistance and negativity, reenergize the work force, and help the existing work groups develop into true self-directed teams.

The solution was to hold a series of workshops and meetings to discuss the self-directed team concept and educate employees about the stages of team development. At BP Norge, the stages of team development were called denial, resistance, exploration, and commitment. In the denial stage (similar to forming), employees idealized the past, resisted mutual accountability, and gradually their skepticism, confusion, and uncertainty began to surface. Relationships were characterized by politeness as people explored what was expected of them in their new roles. The resistance stage (storming) was marked by anxiety, anger, depression, apathy, and conflict. BP Norge's exploration stage straddles the storming and the norming stages in our model. There still is some confusion, but teams are letting go of old values and ideas and incorporating new ones. Conflict is resolved and team roles and expectations are defined. The final stage, commitment, is analogous to the performing stage in our model. The focus here is on a common purpose and approach and the complete movement from "I" to "we." Team members accept the concept of mutual responsibility and accountability and are focused on performance and task accomplishment.

Because workers understood the stages of team development, they were able to recognize what was happening as normal and take a nonjudgmental "this is where we are in the process" attitude rather than a "this will never work" attitude. Thus, each member was able to approach the development of teams as a natural process that involved self-discovery, exploration of new ideas, and the opportunity to grow and develop.[28] ■

TEAM COHESIVENESS

Another important aspect of the team process is cohesiveness. **Team cohesiveness** is defined

team cohesiveness
The extent to which team members are attracted to the team and motivated to remain in it

as the extent to which members are attracted to the team and motivated to remain in it.[29] Members of highly cohesive teams are committed to team activities, attend meetings, and are happy when the team succeeds. Members of less cohesive teams are less concerned about the team's welfare. High cohesiveness is normally considered an attractive feature of teams.

DETERMINANTS OF TEAM COHESIVENESS

Characteristics of team structure and context influence cohesiveness. First is team interaction. The greater the amount of contact among team members and the more time spent together, the more cohesive the team. Through frequent interactions, members get to know one another and become more devoted to the team.[30] Second is the concept of *shared goals.* If team members agree on goals, they will be more cohesive. Agreeing on purpose and direction binds the team together. Third is *personal attraction to the team,* meaning that members have similar attitudes and values and enjoy being together.

Two factors in the team's context also influence group cohesiveness. The first is the presence of competition. When a team is in moderate competition with other teams, its cohesiveness increases as it strives to win. Whether competition is among sales teams to attain the top sales volume or among manufacturing departments to reduce rejects, competition increases team solidarity and cohesiveness.[31] Finally, team success and the favorable evaluation of the team by outsiders add to cohesiveness. When a team succeeds in its task and others in the organization recognize the success, members feel good, and their commitment to the team will be high.

CONSEQUENCES OF TEAM COHESIVENESS

The outcome of team cohesiveness can fall into two categories—morale and productivity. As a general rule, morale is higher in cohesive teams because of increased communication among members, a friendly team climate, maintenance of membership because of commitment to the team, loyalty, and member participation in team decisions and activities. High cohesiveness has almost uniformly good effects on the satisfaction and morale of team members.[32]

With respect to team performance, research findings are mixed, but cohesiveness may have several effects.[33] First, in a cohesive team, productivity of members tends to be more uniform. Productivity differences among members are small because the team exerts pressure toward conformity. Noncohesive teams do not have this control over member behavior and therefore tend to have wider variation in member productivity.

With respect to the productivity of the team as a whole, research findings suggest that cohesive teams have the potential to be productive, but the degree of productivity depends on the relationship between management and the working team. Thus, team cohesiveness does not necessarily lead to higher team productivity. One study surveyed more than 200 work teams and correlated job performance with their cohesiveness.[34] Highly cohesive teams were more productive when team members felt management support and less productive when they sensed management hostility and negativism. Management hostility led to team norms and goals of low performance, and the highly cohesive teams performed poorly, in accordance with their norms and goals.

This "trust fall" during a team-building session at Gilbane Building Company helps strengthen team cohesiveness by leading to increased communication, trust, and a friendly team atmosphere. High team cohesiveness has almost uniformly good effects on the satisfaction and morale of team members. Team building and project partnering are major components of Gilbane's culture, and the company is now extending the team concept to include clients, customers, and subcontractors.

The relationship between performance outcomes and cohesiveness is illustrated in Exhibit 15.4. The highest productivity occurs when the team is cohesive and also has a high performance norm, which is a result of its positive relationship with management. Moderate productivity occurs when cohesiveness is low, because team members are less committed to performance norms. The lowest productivity occurs when cohesiveness is high and the team's performance norm is low. Thus, cohesive teams are able to attain their goals and enforce their norms, which can lead to either very high or very low productivity. For an excellent example of team cohesiveness combined with a high performance norm, consider the "Rainbow Warriors," the pit crew that helped lead NASCAR driver Jeff Gordon from anonymity to unprecedented success.

THE RAINBOW WARRIORS
www.nascar.com

Jeff Gordon, at age 24 the youngest-ever winner of the Winston Cup Championship, has become a "superstar," showing up on late-night talk shows and *People* magazine's 50 Most Beautiful People list. But he gives much of the credit for his success to his pit crew, led by Ray Evernham, widely considered the premier pit crew chief in NASCAR (the National Association for Stock Car Auto Racing). Evernham has spoken to groups of executives from DuPont, Digital, and Ingersoll Rand on how to win in the game of business as well as auto racing. Both Evernham and Gordon sup-

port the pit crew and push them to be the best in the business. When Gordon's car wins, everybody shares in the prize money. In addition, Evernham puts a percentage of his own bonus into the team account. Whenever he gets a personal service contract and is paid to speak or sign autographs, the team gets a share of what he earns. Evernham and Gordon constantly strive to make sure team members know that every success belongs to the team.

Evernham promotes team cohesiveness in a number of ways. Crew members wear rainbow-striped jumpsuits and call themselves the Rainbow Warriors. When they meet, they put their chairs in a circle to symbolize the "circle of strength," that they are stronger as a team than on their own. Evernham even hired a coach to train and rehearse the crew with exercises to build trust and cohesiveness. "I'm sure that it all looked funny, but it worked," Evernham says. "Typically we pit in 17 seconds or less—about a second faster than other teams do. In one second, a car going 200 mph travels nearly 300 feet. So right there, we gain 300 feet on the competition."[35] ■

TEAM NORMS

A team **norm** is a standard of conduct shared by team members that guides their behavior.[36] Norms are informal. They are not written down as are rules and procedures. Norms are valuable because they define boundaries of

norm
An informal standard of conduct shared by team members that guides their behavior

Exhibit 15.5

FOUR WAYS TEAM NORMS DEVELOP

acceptable behavior. They make life easier for team members by providing a frame of reference for what is right and wrong. Norms identify key values, clarify role expectations, and facilitate team survival. For example, union members may develop a norm of not cooperating with management because they do not trust management's motives. In this way, norms protect the group and express key values.

Norms begin to develop in the first interactions among members of a new team.[37] Norms tell members what is acceptable and direct the actions of members toward acceptable productivity or performance. Four common ways in which norms develop for controlling and directing behavior are illustrated in Exhibit 15.5.[38]

Critical events in a team's history often can establish an important precedent. One example occurred when Arthur Schlesinger, despite his serious reservations about the Bay of Pigs invasion, was pressured by Attorney General Robert Kennedy not to raise his objections to President Kennedy. This critical incident helped create a norm in which team members refrained from expressing disagreement with the president.

Primacy refers to the first behaviors that set precedents for later team expectations. At

one company, a team leader began his first meeting by raising an issue and then "leading" team members until he got the solution he wanted. The pattern became ingrained so quickly into an unproductive team norm that team members dubbed meetings the "Guess What I Think" game.[39]

Carryover behaviors bring norms into the team from outside. One current example is the strong norm against smoking. Some team members sneak around, gargling with mouthwash, and fear expulsion because the team culture believes everyone should kick the habit. At such companies as Johnson & Johnson, Dow Chemical, and Aetna Life & Casualty, the norm is "If you want to advance, don't smoke."[40]

Explicit statements are statements leaders or team members articulate to the team to initiate norms. Explicit statements symbolize what counts and thus have considerable impact. Making explicit statements is probably the most effective way for managers to change norms in an established team. For example, Richard Boyle of Honeywell wrote a memo relaxing the company's excessive formality and creating a new norm. Called "Loosening Up the Tie," the memo said in part:

I wish to announce a relaxed wearing apparel policy, and loosen my tie for the summer. Let's try it starting on May 15th and tentatively ending on September 15th. Since departments vary in customer contact and, depending on location, may even vary slightly in temperature, Department Heads are hereby given authority to allow variations. . . .

This change requires each of us to use good judgment. On the one extreme it means you do not have to wear a tie; on the other, tennis shoes, shorts, and a T-shirt are too relaxed. Have a comfortable, enjoyable summer. I hope to.[41] ■

The tie memo helped demonstrate management's interest in developing a relaxed, more casual atmosphere at Honeywell.

Development of successful teams begins with development of confident team leaders; companies should not merely toss the ball to managers and expect them to automatically become experts in team leadership. Training can help managers define and learn how to be effective team leaders. There are a number of points team leaders should remember:

- Team leaders don't have to know everything. This can be especially daunting in leading cross-functional teams. The leader should determine his or her own strengths and how those strengths can benefit the entire group.
- Team leaders embrace the concept of teamwork in deeds as well as words. That means sharing power and information in order to empower team members and reach goals.
- Team leaders enable members to find answers for themselves by asking questions and encouraging balanced participation.
- Team leaders coordinate team activities and avoid wasting time on details that can be better handled through transfer of responsibility to the team.
- Team leaders accept the concept of continuous, on-the-job learning.

■ MANAGING TEAM CONFLICT

The final characteristic of team process is conflict, which refers to antagonistic interaction in which one party attempts to block the intentions or goals of another.[42] Of all the skills required for effective team management, none is more important than handling the conflicts that inevitably arise among members. Whenever people work together in teams, some degree of conflict is inevitable. Conflict can arise among members within a team or between one team and another. On the other hand, competition (or rivalry among individuals or teams) can have a healthy impact because it energizes people toward higher performance.[43] Also, conflict within teams can lead to better decision making when multiple viewpoints are considered. Some research suggests that low conflict in top management teams is associated with poor decision making (i.e., when team members just go along with the strongest opinion, which often is that of the CEO, rather than considering alternate ideas and solutions).[44] However, too much conflict can be destructive, tear relationships apart, and interfere with the healthy exchange of ideas and information.[45] In a fast-growing newer company, such as Clif Bar Inc., one scarce resource is often time. Results are burned-out employees, who don't have much energy to take advantage of company-offered stress reducers.

CLIF BAR INC.

Strapped with a harness and tight rubber boots, 25-year-old Clif Bar marketing coordinator Tom Richardson is spending his lunchtime scampering up the company's 22-foot-high artificial rock wall. "It's a relaxing way to separate myself from everything that's going on in the office," he says.

The 77-employee energy-bar maker has a gym that includes two climbing walls, three trainers, weightlifting, foot races, and other workouts, and it will pay for weekends at the spa, skiing, or camping. It's part of the reason the turnover is so low: since its inception in 1992, only five people have quit.

But the downside to their commitment and success is warp speed growth, quadrupling in 1998 and increasing another 40 percent in 1999 to $30 million. Twenty-five employees were hired in 1998.

It all began in cofounder Gary Erickson's mother's kitchen where he and his soon-to-be business partner Lisa Thomas perfected a recipe for a delicious energy bar that would not be gooey or hard, as PowerBars were. They rented after-hours facilities in a local bakery and named the bar after Erickson's father.

Now, though, they can hardly keep up with demand. "Its hard to get anything done," says customer service manager Alline Anderson. "It seems my department's staffed for where we were 9 or 10 months ago." Part of the reason they are doing so well is they anticipate the market, as evidenced by their innovative, inexpensive (cost to launch: $5,000), and interactive Web site (www.clifbar.com, which does not sell bars), where you can even concoct your dream bar.

All of which means most employees are too overloaded and stressed out to take advantage of the stress-reducing gym facilities. Yet the company is committed to keeping the culture and promoting the on-site workouts. "It's the most pressing issue on our minds right now," says Erickson. Thomas notes how many employees have shed body fat and added self-esteem in the gym. "You're more productive because you feel good about yourself," she says.

Business experts warn that the fast growth of Clif Bars dooms its "happy healthiness" theme. No way, says Thomas. "We've decided the corporate culture is more important than how big we want to be." To accommodate the growth, the company is moving to ever-larger facilities. "I'd like to see people back on the office wall," says Erickson. "That's why we put it there."[46] ■

CAUSES OF CONFLICT

Several factors can cause people to engage in conflict.[47]

- *Scarce resources.* Resources include money, information, and supplies. Whenever individuals or teams must compete for scarce or declining resources, conflict is almost inevitable. At the Levi Strauss blue jeans plant near Knoxville, Tennessee, a change in pay systems—in which employees were paid based on team output rather than on the old individual piecework system—led to severe conflict because some employees felt that slower team members hurt their pocketbooks. One worker says her hourly pay dropped nearly $2, while slower team members realized an increase over what they earned on the piecework system.[48]

- *Jurisdictional ambiguities.* Conflicts also emerge when job boundaries and responsibilities are unclear, which results in people disagreeing about who has responsibility for specific tasks or who has a claim on resources. A conflict emerged between the two sides of Andersen Worldwide because both sides were going after the same business. Jurisdictional ambiguities are threatening to tear apart the giant company.[49]

- *Communication breakdown.* Communication among humans can be a faulty process. The potential for communication breakdown is even greater with virtual teams and global teams made up of members from different countries and cultures. Poor communications result in misperceptions and misunderstandings about and among other people and teams. In some cases, information may be intentionally withheld, which can jeopardize trust among teams and lead to long-lasting conflict.

- *Personality clashes.* When people simply do not get along with one another and do not see eye-to-eye on any issue clashes will occur. Personality clashes are caused by basic differences in personality, values, and attitudes. Separating the parties so that they need not interact with one another is often the best answer.

- *Power and status differences.* These occur when one party has disputable influence over another. Low-prestige individuals or departments may resist their low status. People may engage in conflict to increase their power and influence in the team or organization.

- *Goal differences.* Conflict often occurs simply because people are pursuing conflicting goals. Goal differences are natural in organizations. Individual salespeople's targets may put them in conflict with one another or with the sales manager, or the sales department may have goals that conflict with those of manufacturing.

STYLES TO HANDLE CONFLICT

Teams as well as individuals develop specific styles for dealing with conflict, based on the desire to satisfy their own concern versus the other party's concern. Five styles of handling conflict can be seen in the model (Exhibit 15.6). The two major dimensions are the extent to which an individual is assertive versus cooperative in his or her approach to conflict.

Effective team members vary their style of handling conflict to fit a specific situation. Each style is appropriate in certain cases.

1. *Competing style.* Reflects assertiveness to get one's own way and should be used when quick, decisive action is vital on important issues or unpopular actions, such as during emergencies or urgent cost cutting.

2. *Avoiding style.* Reflects neither assertiveness nor cooperation and is appropriate when an issue is trivial, when there is no chance of winning, when a delay to gather more information is needed, or when a disruption would be very costly.

E x h i b i t   15.6

A MODEL OF STYLES TO HANDLE CONFLICT

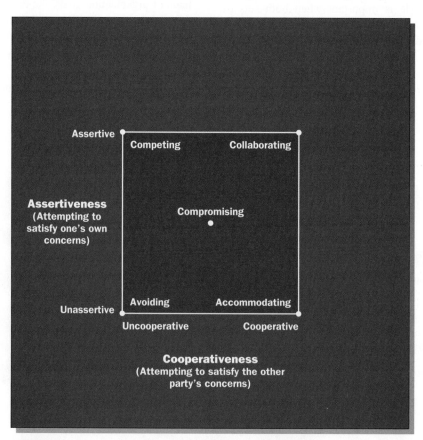

SOURCE: Adapted from Kenneth Thomas, "Conflict and Conflict Management," in *Handbook of Industrial and Organizational Behavior,* ed. M. D. Dunnette (New York: John Wiley, 1976), 900.

3. *Compromising style.* Reflects a moderate amount of both assertiveness and cooperation and is appropriate when the goals on both sides are equally important, when opponents have equal power and both sides want to split the difference, or when people need to arrive at temporary or expedient solutions under time pressure.

4. *Accommodating style.* Reflects a high degree of cooperation and works best when people realize they are wrong, when an issue is more important to others than to oneself, when building social credits for use in later discussions, and especially, when maintaining harmony is important.

5. *Collaborating style.* Reflects both a high degree of assertiveness and cooperation. The collaborating style enables both parties to win, although it may require substantial bargaining and negotiation. The collaborating style is important when both sets of concerns are too important to be compromised, when insights from different people need to be merged into an overall solution, and when the commitment of both sides is needed for a consensus.[50]

superordinate goal
A goal that cannot be reached by a single party

The various styles of handling conflict can be used when an individual disagrees with others. But what does a manager or team member do when a conflict erupts among others within a team or among teams for which the manager is responsible? Research suggests that several techniques can be used as strategies for resolving conflicts among people or departments. These techniques might also be used when conflict is formalized, such as between a union and management.

- *Superordinate goals.* A powerful vision or direction in which the organization wants to go often compels employees to overcome conflicts and cooperate for the greater good. Achieving this **superordinate goal,** one that cannot be achieved by any single party, requires the cooperation of conflicting team members. People must pull together. To the extent that employees can be focused on team or organization goals, the conflict will decrease because the big picture is accepted as important enough to work together for.

- *Bargaining/Negotiation.* Bargaining and negotiation mean that the parties engage one another in an attempt to systematically

Lloyd Ward is the head of Maytag Corporation's large appliance division, which is responsible for more than 50 percent of the company's approximately $4 billion in revenues. A former Michigan State basketball star, Ward has earned a reputation as a team builder who excels at revving up the troops. Using team strategy to focus employees on a superordinate goal, he has astounded skeptics and revived this once-faltering unit. His strategies helped Maytag shares to soar more than 60 percent in 1998. Profits have since increased 50 percent to $271 million.

reach a solution. They attempt logical problem solving to identify and correct the conflict. This approach works well if the individuals can set aside personal animosities and deal with the conflict in a businesslike way.

- *Mediation.* Using a disinterested third party to settle a dispute involves **mediation.** A mediator could be a supervisor, higher-level manager, or someone from the human resource department. The mediator can discuss the conflict with each party and work toward a solution. If a solution satisfactory to both sides cannot be reached, the parties may be willing to turn the conflict over to the mediator and abide by his or her solution.
- *Facilitating communication.* Managers can use this to ensure that conflicting parties hold accurate perceptions. Providing opportunities for the disputants to get together and exchange information reduces conflict. As the parties in conflict learn more about one another, suspicions diminish and improved teamwork becomes possible.

Facilitating communication is an important responsibility of a team leader. Four guidelines can help facilitate communication and keep teams focused on substantive issues rather than interpersonal conflicts.[51]

1. *Focus on facts.* Keep team discussions focused on issues, not personalities. Working with more data and information rather than less can help team members focus on important issues and keep meetings from degenerating into pointless debates.
2. *Develop multiple alternatives.* Teams that deliberately develop many alternatives, sometimes considering four or five options at once, have a lower incidence of interpersonal conflict. Having a multitude of options to consider concentrates team members' energy on solving problems. In addition, the process of generating multiple choices is more creative, which sets a positive tone for the meeting.
3. *Maintain a balance of power.* Managers and team leaders should accept the team's decision as fair, even if they do not agree with it. Fairness requires a balance of power within the team.
4. *Never force a consensus.* There will naturally be conflict over some issues, which managers find a way to resolve without forcing a consensus. When there are persistent differences of opinion, the team leader sometimes has to make a decision guided by input from other team members. At Andromeda Processing, the CEO insisted on consensus from his top management team, causing a debate to rage on for months. Eventually, most of the managers just wanted a decision, no matter whether it was the one they agreed with or not. Conflict and frustration mounted to the point where some top managers left the company. The group achieved consensus only at the price of losing several key managers.

■ BENEFITS AND COSTS OF TEAMS

In deciding whether to use teams to perform specific tasks, managers must consider benefits and costs. Teams may have positive impact on both the output productivity and satisfaction of members. On the other hand, teams may also create a situation in which motivation and performance actually are decreased.

POTENTIAL BENEFITS OF TEAMS

Teams come closest to achieving their full potential when they enhance individual productivity through increased member effort, personal satisfaction, integration of diverse abilities and skills, and increased organizational flexibility.

- *Level of effort.* Employee teams often unleash enormous energy and creativity from workers who like the idea of using their brains to learn and solve problems. Organizations are breaking down barriers, empowering workers, and encouraging their creativity, and research is backing it up: Working in a team increases an individual's motivation and performance. Simply being in the presence of other people has an energizing effect,[52] called **social facilitation,** or the tendency for the presence of others to enhance an individual's motivation and performance.

mediation
The process of using a disinterested third party to settle a dispute

social facilitation
The tendency for the presence of others to influence an individual's motivation and performance

• *Satisfaction of members.* Employees have needs for belongingness and affiliation (see page 413). Working in teams can help meet these needs. Participative teams reduce boredom and often increase employees' feeling of dignity and self-worth because the whole person is employed. People who have a satisfying team environment cope better with stress and enjoy their jobs.

• *Expanded job knowledge and skills.* Employee empowerment brings greater knowledge and abilities to the task, and teams gain the intellectual resources of several members who can suggest shortcuts and offer alternative points of view for team decisions.

• *Organizational flexibility.* Traditional organizations are structured so that each worker does only one specific job. But when employee teams are used, people work next to one another and are able to exchange jobs. Work can be reorganized and workers reallocated as needed to produce products and services with greater flexibility. The organization is able to be responsive to rapidly changing customer needs.

POTENTIAL COSTS OF TEAMS

When managers decide whether to use teams, they must assess certain costs or liabilities associated with teamwork. When teams do not work very well, the major reasons usually are power realignment, free riding, coordination costs, or legal hassles.

• *Power realignment.* Often, when companies form teams, the major losers are low- and middle-level managers. These managers are reluctant to give up power. Indeed, when teams are successful, fewer supervisors are needed. This is especially true for self-directed teams, because workers take over supervisory responsibility. The adjustment is difficult for managers who fear the loss of status or even their job and who have to learn new, people-oriented skills to survive.[53]

• *Free riding.* A **free rider** is a team member who attains benefit from team membership but does not do a proportionate share of the work.[54] Free riding sometimes is called social loafing, because members do not exert equal effort. In large teams, some people are likely to work less. For example, research found that the pull exerted on a rope was greater by individuals working alone than by individuals in a group. Similarly, people who were asked to clap and make noise made more noise on a per person basis when working alone or in small groups than they did in a large group.[55]

• *Coordination costs.* The time and energy required to coordinate the activities of a group to enable it to perform its task are called **coordination costs.** Groups must spend time getting ready to do work and lose productive time in deciding who is to do what and when.[56]

• *Legal hassles.* As more companies utilize teams, new questions of legality surface. A

free rider
A person who benefits from team membership but does not make a proportionate contribution to the team's work

coordination costs
The time and energy needed to coordinate the activities of a team to enable it to perform its task

The Bussman division of Cooper Industries has firsthand knowledge of the benefits of teams. Angelina Bernardi, Steve Goble, Ed Haworth, and Lynne Sanick worked on Bussman's first experimental team to develop the new line of Optima overcurrent protection modules, which combines a fuse and a fuse holder in a single, easy-to-use power protection system. The team introduced the line in 10 months compared to the average 24-month cycle time. The enhanced flexibility and rapid response to customer needs led Bussman to create Rapid Development Teams for each of its major market segments. The teams consistently cut new-product development times in half.

1990 National Labor Relations Board judgment against management's use of union-member teams at Electromation, Inc., set a confusing precedent. The Wagner Act of 1935 was enacted to prevent companies from forming organizations or employee committees to undercut legitimate unions. Union leaders today support the formation of problem-solving teams but may balk when management takes an active role in the formation and direction of such teams.

As union membership and power decline, increasingly vocal critics charge that the team concept is a management ploy to kill unions. Autoworkers especially are challenging team approaches because union jobs continue to disappear despite repeated concessions. Although few experts expect the courts to halt teams altogether, most believe that strict new guidelines will be implemented to control the formation and use of teams.[57]

Summary and Management Solution

Several important concepts about teams were described in this chapter. Organizations use teams both to achieve coordination as part of the formal structure and to encourage employee involvement. Formal teams include vertical teams along the chain of command and horizontal teams such as cross-functional task forces and committees. Special-purpose teams are used for special, large-scale, creative organization projects. Employee involvement via teams is designed to bring low-level employees into decision processes to improve quality, efficiency, and satisfaction. Companies typically start with problem-solving teams, which may evolve into self-directed teams that take on responsibility for management activities.

At Roberts Express, described at the beginning of this chapter, managers decided to reorganize into teams to help the growing company operate more quickly yet still serve customers as if it were a small, regional shipping service. Roberts "shrunk" itself by dividing into several self-directed Customer Assistance Teams (CATs). Each CAT is assigned to a specific geographic region, and the company's phone system automatically routes calls accordingly. To regular customers, Roberts seems no bigger than a particular CAT—when a call comes through from a customer in New Jersey, they hear the same familiar voices and are usually rerouted to the dispatcher or agent they worked with the previous time. In addition, having agents, dispatchers, and other employees all working together to serve a particular region increases both the quality and speed of service. The team approach, combined with new information technology that helps Roberts' employees always know where their drivers and trucks are located, guarantees that Roberts can continue its tradition of delivering hot, last-minute shipments right on time.

Most teams go through systematic stages of development: forming, storming, norming, performing, and adjourning. Team characteristics that can influence organizational effectiveness are size, cohesiveness, norms, and roles of members. All teams experience some conflict because of scarce resources, ambiguous responsibility, communication breakdown, personality clashes, power and status differences, and goal conflicts. Techniques for resolving these conflicts include superordinate goals, bargaining, mediation, and communication. Techniques for facilitating team communication to minimize conflict are to focus on facts, develop multiple alternatives, maintain a balance of power, and never force a consensus. Advantages of using teams include increased motivation, diverse knowledge and skills, satisfaction of team members, organizational flexibility, and learning. Potential costs of using teams are power realignment, free riding, coordination costs, and legal hassles.

Discussion Questions

1. Volvo went to self-directed teams to assemble cars because of the need to attract and keep workers in Sweden, where pay raises are not a motivator (high taxes) and many other jobs are available. Is this a good reason for using a team approach? Discuss.

2. During your own work experience, have you been part of a formal vertical team? A task force? A committee? An employee involvement team? How did your work experience differ in each type of team?

3. What are the five stages of team development? What happens during each stage?

4. How would you explain the emergence of problem-solving and self-directed teams in companies throughout North America? Do you think implementation of the team concept is difficult in these companies? Discuss.

5. Do you think a moderate level of conflict might be healthy for an organization? Discuss.

6. When you are a member of a team, do you adopt a task specialist or socioemotional role? Which role is more important for a team's effectiveness? Discuss.

7. What is the relationship between team cohesiveness and team performance?

8. Describe the advantages and disadvantages of teams. In what situations might the disadvantages outweigh the advantages?

9. What is a team norm? What norms have developed in teams to which you have belonged?

10. One company had 40 percent of its workers and 20 percent of its managers resign during the first year after reorganizing into teams. What might account for this dramatic turnover? How might managers ensure a smooth transition to teams?

Management Exercises

Manager's Workbook

Is Your Group a Cohesive Team?

Think about a student group with which you have worked. Answer the questions below as they pertain to the functioning of that group.

	Disagree Strongly				Agree Strongly
1. Group meetings were held regularly and everyone attended.	1	2	3	4	5
2. We talked about and shared the same goals for group work and grade.	1	2	3	4	5
3. We spent most of our meeting time talking business, but discussions were open-ended and active.	1	2	3	4	5
4. We talked through any conflicts and disagreements until they were resolved.	1	2	3	4	5
5. Group members listened carefully to one another.	1	2	3	4	5
6. We really trusted each other, speaking personally about what we really felt.	1	2	3	4	5

7. Leadership roles were rotated and shared, with people taking initiative at appropriate times for the good of the group.	1	2	3	4	5
8. Each member found a way to contribute to the final work product.	1	2	3	4	5
9. I was really satisfied being a member of the group.	1	2	3	4	5
10. We freely gave each other credit for jobs well done.	1	2	3	4	5
11. Group members gave and received feedback to help the group do even better.	1	2	3	4	5
12. We held each other accountable; each member was accountable to the group.	1	2	3	4	5
13. Group members really liked and respected each other.	1	2	3	4	5

Total Score

The questions here are about team cohesion. If you scored 52 or greater, your group experienced authentic teamwork. Congratulations. If you scored between 39 and 51, there was a positive group identity that might have been developed even further. If you scored between 26 and 38, group identity was weak and probably not very satisfying. If you scored below 26, it was hardly a group at all, resembling a loose collection of individuals.

Remember, teamwork doesn't happen by itself. Individuals like you have to understand what a team is and then work to make it happen. What can you do to make a student group more like a team? Do you have the courage to take the initiative?

Manager's Workshop

Team-Based Decision Processes

As organizations shift from traditional hierarchical designs to learning organizations, the reliance on team-based decision processes increases. During this transition, a shift occurs in problem solving. It is from

- *adaptive thinking,* where individuals follow established norms, "My way is the only way," to

- *generative thinking,* where teams examine the underlying structure of problems to determine cause and effect. Teams can increase their ability to use generative thinking by practice with looking at events or decisions and discussing what would be the impact of those events or decisions.

The purpose of this exercise is to help you to better understand this concept of generative thinking in teams.

1. Each student independently completes the immediate and long-term impact/effect for the events or situations described in the box on the following page. Optionally, think of two other events or situations with their impacts. Or you may think of a situation where you made an important decision and look at the possible impacts of that decision.

2. Divide into groups of four to six. The group discusses the three or four events/situations, coming to a consensus on the immediate and long-term impacts for each situation. If you have time, think of one or two other situations, events or decisions and discuss impacts of those.

3. The entire class shares impacts discussed in small groups and answers the following questions:
   a. How is adaptive thinking different from generative?
   b. What are some examples of adaptive and generative thinking you have seen or experienced?
   c. Why does understanding impacts help develop more generative thinking?

Situation	Immediate Impact/Effect	Long-Term Impact/Effect
(Example) Passed driving test	Could drive independently.	Increased self-esteem, greater self-reliance, responsible for safety of other drivers, began part-time employment to pay for auto, job expanded social circle outside of homogeneous surroundings.
Admission to graduate school		
Employed as research analyst with newly created e-commerce business		
Eight percent of the workforce in your company is retiring in three years		
Other		

SOURCE: Adapted by Dorothy Marcic from Marcia Salner, (1999). "The Learning Organization," *Journal of Management Education,* Vol. 23 (5), pp. 489–508.

Management in Practice: Ethical Dilemma

Consumer Safety or Team Commitment?

Nancy was part of a pharmaceutical team developing a product called loperamide, a liquid treatment for diarrhea for people unable to take solid medicine, namely infants, children, and the elderly. Loperamide contained 44 times the amount of saccharin allowed by the FDA in a 12-ounce soft drink, but there were no regulations governing saccharin content in medication.

Nancy was the only medical member of the seven-person project team. The team made a unanimous decision to reduce the saccharin content before marketing loperamide, so the team initiated a three-month effort for reformulation. In the meantime, management was pressuring the team to allow human testing with the original formula until the new formula became available. After a heated team debate, all the team members except Nancy voted to begin testing with the current formula.

Nancy believed it was unethical to test on old people and children a drug she considered potentially dangerous. As the only medical member of the team, she had to sign the forms allowing testing. She refused and was told that unless she signed, she would be removed from the project, demoted, and seen as a poor team player, nonpromotable, lacking in judgment, and unable to work with marketing people. Nancy was aware that no proof existed that high saccharin would be directly harmful to potential users of loperamide.

What Do You Do?

1. Refuse to sign. As a medical doctor, Nancy must stand up for what she believes is right.

2. Resign. There is no reason to stay in this company and be punished for ethically correct behavior. Testing the drug will become someone else's responsibility.

3. Sign the form. The judgment of other team members cannot be all wrong. The loperamide testing is not illegal and will move ahead anyway, so it would preserve team unity and company effectiveness to sign.

SOURCE: Based on Tom L. Beauchamp, *Ethical Theory and Business,* 2d ed. (Englewood Cliffs, N.J.: Prentice-Hall, 1983).

Surf the Net

1. *Self-Directed Work Teams.* Use your search engine to find a site such as www.oeg.net/tmb.html that will provide information on the team-building process. Another good site can be found at http://users.ids.net/~brim/ sdwth.html, where you can click on "Sites on Team Basics" and read several of the linked features (most of them are fairly short). Select three ideas that you could apply to improve the performance of a team that you are currently a member of—an employee group, an athletic team, a campus or community organization, etc. Report to your class the ideas you implemented and what impact they had on your team's performance.

2. *Team Meetings.* The communication process used frequently in the team environment is group meetings. Productive meetings don't just automatically happen. One Web site loaded with excellent links to information about improving the meeting process can be found at www.infoteam.com/nonprofit/nica/meeting.html. Find information on the following issues: (a) What can the team leader do to facilitate the meeting? (b) What common characteristics do the best meeting facilitators possess? (c) What are some techniques for managing conflicts that arise during meetings?

3. *Team Performance.* Something very evident among athletic teams is the importance of keeping the team members motivated to achieve their goal of winning the game. Assume the role of "chief motivator" for a work team and design a one-page flyer to be given to each team member in which you include the best advice you can find for enhancing team performance. A good starting point for finding information for your flyer is http://pw1.netcom.com/~spritex/frames.html (select the heading of "Teamwork"). You can copy and paste those items from this site or other sites into your word-processing program to create your flyer.

Case for Critical Analysis

Acme Minerals Extraction Company

Several years ago, Acme Minerals Extraction Company introduced teams in an effort to solve morale and productivity problems at its Wichita plant. Acme used highly sophisticated technology, employing geologists, geophysicists, and engineers on what was referred to as the "brains" side of the business, as well as skilled and semiskilled labor on the "brawn" side to run the company's underground extracting operations. The two sides regularly clashed, and when some engineers locked several operations workers out of the office in 100-degree heat, the local press had a field day. Suzanne Howard was hired to develop a program that would improve productivity and morale at the Wichita plant, with the idea that it would then be implemented at other Acme sites.

Howard had a stroke of luck in the form of Donald Peterson, a long-time Acme employee who was highly respected at the Wichita plant and was looking for one final, challenging project before he retired. Peterson had served in just about every possible line and staff position at Acme over his 39-year career, and he understood the problems workers faced on both the "brains" and the "brawn" sides of the business. Howard was pleased when Peterson agreed to serve as leader for the Wichita pilot project. There were three functional groups at the Wichita plant: operations, made up primarily of hourly workers who operated and maintained the extracting equipment; the "belowground" group, consisting of engineers, geologists, and geophysicists who determined where and how to drill; and the "aboveground" group of engineers in charge of cursory refinement and transportation of the minerals. Howard and Peterson decided the first step was to get these different groups talking to one another and sharing ideas. They instituted a monthly "problem chat," an optional meeting to which all employees were invited to discuss unresolved problems. At the first meeting, Howard and Peterson were the only two people who showed up. However, people gradually began to attend the meetings, and after about six months they had become lively problem-solving discussions that led to many improvements.

Next, Howard and Peterson introduced teams to "select a problem and implement a tailored solution," or SPITS. These were ad hoc groups made up of members from each of the three functional areas. They were formed to work on a specific problem identified in a chat meeting and were disbanded when the problem was solved. SPITS were given the authority to address problems without seeking management approval. There were some rocky moments, as engineers resented working with operations personnel and vice versa. However, over time, and with the strong leadership of Peterson, the groups began to come together and focus on the issues rather than spending most of their time arguing. Eventually, workers in Wichita were organized into permanent cross-functional teams that were empowered to make their own decisions and elect their own leaders. After a year and a half, things were really humming. The different groups weren't just working together; they had also started socializing together. At one of the problem chats, an operations worker jokingly suggested that the brains and the brawn should duke it out once a week to get rid of the tensions so they could focus all their energy on the job to be done. Several others joined in the joking, and eventually, the group decided to square off in a weekly softball game. Peterson had T-shirts printed up that said BRAINS AND BRAWN. The softball games were well attended, and both sides usually ended up having a few beers together at a local bar afterward. Productivity and morale soared at the Wichita plant, and costs continued to decline.

Top executives believed the lessons learned at Wichita should make implementing the program at other sites less costly and time-consuming. However, when Howard and her team attempted to implement the program at the Lubbock plant, things didn't go well. They felt under immense pressure from top management to get the team-based productivity project running smoothly at Lubbock. Because people weren't showing up for the problem chat meetings, attendance was made mandatory. However, the meetings still produced few valuable ideas or suggestions. Although a few of

the SPITS teams solved important problems, none of them showed the kind of commitment and enthusiasm Howard had seen in Wichita. In addition, the Lubbock workers refused to participate in the softball games and other team-building exercises that Howard's team developed for them. Howard finally convinced some workers to join in the softball games by bribing them with free food and beer. "If I just had a Donald Peterson in Lubbock, things would go a lot more smoothly," Howard thought. "These workers don't trust us the way workers in Wichita trusted him." It seemed that no matter how hard Howard and her team tried to make the project work in Lubbock, morale continued to decline and conflicts between the different groups of workers actually seemed to increase.

Questions

1. What types of teams described in the chapter are represented in this case?

2. Why do you think the team project succeeded at Wichita but isn't working in Lubbock?

3. What advice would you give Suzanne Howard and her team for improving the employee involvement climate at the Lubbock plant?

SOURCE: Based on Michael C. Beers, "The Strategy That Wouldn't Travel," *Harvard Business Review,* November–December 1996, pp. 18–31.

Endnotes

1 Chuck Salter, "Roberts Rules of the Road," *Fast Company,* September 1998, pp. 114–128.

2 Susan G. Cohen, Gerald E. Ledford, Jr., and Gretchen M. Spreitzer, "A Predictive Model of Self-Managing Work Team Effectiveness," *Human Relations,* 49 (5) (1996), pp. 643–676.

3 Rajiv D. Banker, Joy M. Field, Roger G. Schroeder, and Kingshuk K. Sinha, "Impact of Work Teams on Manufacturing Performance: A Longitudinal Field Study," *Academy of Management Journal,* 39 (4) (1996), pp. 867–890.

4 Eric Schine, "Mattel's Wild Race to Market," *Business Week,* February 21, 1994, pp. 62–63.

5 Eric Sundstrom, Kenneth P. De Meuse, and David Futrell, "Work Teams," *American Psychologist,* 45 (February 1990), pp. 120–133.

6 Deborah L. Gladstein, "Groups in Context: A Model of Task Group Effectiveness," *Administrative Science Quarterly,* 29 (1984), pp. 499–517.

7 Dora C. Lau and J. Keith Murnighan, "Demographic Diversity and Faultlines: The Compositional Dynamics of Organizational Groups," *Academy of Management Review,* 23 (2) (1998), pp. 325–340.

8 Esther Schrader, "Brewing a Trendier Cup of Tea," *Los Angeles Times*, Aug. 3, 1998, p. 1.

9 Thomas Owens, "Business Teams," *Small Business Report,* January 1989, pp. 50–58.

10 Susan Carey, "US Air 'Peon' Team Pilots Startup of Low-Fare Airline," *The Wall Street Journal,* March 24, 1998, p. B1.

11 "Participation Teams," *Small Business Report,* September 1987, pp. 38–41.

12 Larson and LaFasto, *TeamWork.*

13 James H. Shonk, *Team-Based Organizations* (Homewood, Ill.: Business One Irwin, 1992).

14 Gregory L. Miles, "Suddenly, USX Is Playing Mr. Nice Guy," *Business Week,* June 26, 1989, pp. 151–152.

15 Jeanne M. Wilson, Jill George, and Richard S. Wellings, with William C. Byham, *Leadership Trapeze: Strategies for Leadership in Team-Based Organizations* (San Francisco: Jossey-Bass, 1994).

16 Ruth Wageman, "Critical Success Factors for Creating Superb Self-Managing Teams," *Organizational Dynamics,* Summer 1997, pp. 49–61.

17 Thomas Owens, "The Self-Managing Work Team," *Small Business Report,* February 1991, pp. 53–65.

18 Mary Cianni and Donna Wnuck, "Individual Growth and Team Enhancement: Moving Toward a New Model of Career Development," *Academy of Management Executive,* 11 (1) (1997), pp. 105–115.

19 Brian Dumaine, "The Trouble with Teams," *Fortune,* September 5, 1994, pp. 86–92.

20 Dumaine, "The Trouble with Teams"; and Beverly Geber, "Virtual Teams," *Training,* April 1995, pp. 36–40.

21 Charles Fishman, "Whole Foods is All Teams," *Fast Company,* April–May 1996, pp. 102–109; "Wild Oats Markets to Buy 13 Stores from Competitors," *The Los Angeles Times,* Nov. 1, 1999; p. 3

22 Bernadette Malinoski, Janet Murray and George Sanfacon, "Shared Management—It Can Work," *At Work,* 7 (4), July/Aug. 1998, pp. 1–4.

23 George Prince, "Recognizing Genuine Teamwork," *Supervisory Management* (April 1989), pp. 25–36; R. F. Bales, *SYMLOG Case Study Kit* (New York: Free Press, 1980).

24 Robert A. Baron, *Behavior in Organizations,* 2d ed. (Boston: Allyn & Bacon, 1986).

25 Ibid.

26 Kenneth G. Koehler, "Effective Team Management," *Small Business Report,* July 19, 1989, pp. 14–16; and Connie J. G. Gersick, "Time and Transition in Work Teams: Toward a New Model of Group Development," *Academy of Management Journal,* 31 (1988), pp. 9–41.

27 Bruce W. Tuckman and Mary Ann C. Jensen, "Stages of Small-Group Development Revisited," *Group and Organizational Studies,* 2 (1977), pp. 419–427.

28 Milan Moravec, Odd Jan Johannessen, and Thor A. Hjelmas, "Thumbs Up for Self-Managed Teams," *Management Review,* July–August 1997, pp. 42–47.

29 M. E. Shaw, *Group Dynamics,* 3d ed. (New York: McGraw-Hill, 1981).

30 Daniel C. Feldman and Hugh J. Arnold, *Managing Individual and Group Behavior in Organizations* (New York: McGraw-Hill, 1983).

31 Dumaine, "Who Needs a Boss?"

32 Elliot Aronson, *The Social Animal* (San Francisco: W. H. Freeman, 1976).

33 Miriam Erez and Anit Somech, "Is Group Productivity Loss the Rule or the Exception? Effects of Culture and Group-Based Motivation," *Academy of Management Journal,* 39 (6) (1996), pp. 1513–1537.

34 Peter M. Mudrack, "Group Cohesiveness and Productivity: A Closer Look," *Human Relations* 42 (1989), 771–785. Also see Miriam Erez and Anit Somech, "Is Group Productivity Loss the Rule or the Exception? Effects of Culture and Group-Based Motivation," *Academy of Management Journal* 39, no. 6 (1996), 1513–1537.

35 Chuck Salter, "Life in the Fast Lane," *Fast Company,* October 1998, pp. 172–178.

36 J. Richard Hackman, "Group Influences on Individuals," in *Handbook of Industrial and Organizational Psychology,* ed. M. Dunnette (Chicago: Rand McNally, 1976).

37 Kenneth Bettenhausen and J. Keith Murnighan, "The Emergence of Norms in Competitive Decision-Making Groups," *Administrative Science Quarterly,* 30 (1985), pp. 350–372.

38 The following discussion is based on Daniel C. Feldman, "The Development and Enforcement of Group Norms," *Academy of Management Review,* 9 (1984), pp. 47–53.

39 Wilson, et al., *Leadership Trapeze,* 12.

40 Alix M. Freedman, "Cigarette Smoking Is Growing Hazardous to Career in Business," *The Wall Street Journal,* April 23, 1987, pp. 1, 14.

41 Reprinted by permission of the *Harvard Business Review.* Excerpts from "Wrestling with Jellyfish" by Richard J. Boyle (January–February 1984). Copyright © 1984 by the president and Fellows of Harvard College; all rights reserved.

42 Stephen P. Robbins, *Managing Organizational Conflict: A Nontraditional Approach* (Englewood Cliffs, N.J.: Prentice-Hall, 1974).

43 Daniel Robey, Dana L. Farrow, and Charles R. Franz, "Group Process and Conflict in System Development," *Management Science,* 35 (1989), pp. 1172–1191.

44 Kathleen M. Eisenhardt, Jean L. Kahwajy, and L. J. Bourgeois III, "Conflict and Strategic Choice: How Top Management Teams Disagree," *California Management Review,* 39 (2) (Winter 1997), pp. 42–62.

45 Koehler, "Effective Team Management"; and Dean Tjosvold, "Making Conflict Productive," *Personnel Administrator,* 29 (June 1984), p. 121.

46 Joann S. Lubin, "Climbing Walls on Company Time," *Wall Street Journal,* Dec. 1, 1998, pp. B1, B16.

47 This discussion is based in part on Richard L. Daft, *Organization Theory and Design* (St. Paul, Minn.: West, 1992), Chapter 13; and Paul M. Terry, "Conflict Management," *The Journal of Leadership Studies* 3, no. 2 (1996), 3–21.

48 Ralph T. King, Jr., "Levi's Factory Workers Are Assigned to Teams, and Morale Takes a Hit," *The Wall Street Journal,* May 20, 1998, p. A1.

49 Elizabeth MacDonald and Joseph B. White, "How Consulting Issue Is Threatening to Rend Andersen Worldwide," *The Wall Street Journal,* February 4, 1998, pp. A1, A10.

50 This discussion was based on K. W. Thomas, "Towards Multidimensional Values in Teaching: The Example of Conflict Behaviors," *Academy of Management Review,* 2 (1977), p. 487.

51 Based on Kathleen M. Eisenhardt, Jean L. Kahwajy, and L. J. Bourgeois III, "How Management Teams Can Have a Good Fight," *Harvard Business Review,* July–August 1997, pp. 77–85.

52 R. B. Zajonc, "Social Facilitation," *Science,* 149 (1965), pp. 269–274; and Erez and Somech, "Is Group Productivity Loss the Rule or the Exception?"

53 Aaron Bernstein, "Detroit vs. the UAW: At Odds over Teamwork," *Business Week,* August 24, 1987, pp. 54–55.

54 Robert Albanese and David D. Van Fleet, "Rational Behavior in Groups: The Free-Riding Tendency," *Academy of Management Review,* 10 (1985), pp. 244–255.

55 Baron, *Behavior in Organizations.*

56 Harvey J. Brightman, *Group Problem Solving: An Improved Managerial Approach* (Atlanta: Georgia State University, 1988).

57 Aaron Bernstein, "Putting a Damper on That Old Team Spirit," *Business Week,* May 4, 1992, p. 60; and Hoerr, "Is Teamwork a Management Plot? Mostly Not," p. 70.

PART

6

CONTROLLING

Innovative use of technology played a big part in the seventh Whitbread Round the World Race. For starters, the locations and speeds of the boats were relayed via satellite to the race office every six hours. And because the boats rely on wind currents for motion, world weather forecasts and satellite picture analysis of pressure systems were communicated to crews to help them plan and revise their strategies. Navigators used weather-routing software and databases to calculate the optimal routes to take and then refined them based on the crew's knowledge of the boat's general design and the speed it could achieve using various sail configurations. So, with all the technology available, did the crews put the boats on autopilot? No—the combination of technology and human know-how gave the race its thrills.

Crews used other high-tech equipment as well, like water desalinators, Kevlar sails, and laptop computers. Communication technologies kept race crews in 24-hour touch with their shore teams and the world—via the Internet. Through satellite transmitters, the boats were linked directly to the Whitbread Race Office, where a central server processed and delivered e-mail, images, and audio from the crews. The race was broadcast to a worldwide TV audience, and for the first time, couch sailors with an Internet hookup could track the race whenever they wanted. Today, technology plays a major role in controlling organizations.

In Part VI, we'll discuss the role of information systems technology and how operations and service management and managerial excellence play their part in quality control and productivity.

16

Productivity through Management and Quality Control

LEARNING OBJECTIVES

After studying this chapter, you should be able to:

- Define organizational control and explain why it is a key management function

- Describe differences in control focus, including feedforward, concurrent, and feedback control

- Explain the four steps in the control process

- Contrast the bureaucratic and decentralized control approaches

- Describe the concept of total quality management and major TQM techniques

- Discuss the use of and budgeting as a management control

- Identify current trends in control and discuss their impact on organizations

- Summarize the characteristics of an effective control system

MANAGEMENT PROBLEM

Chapter 16

MICHAEL DELL was 19 years old

when he started his computer company from his dorm room at the University of Texas. He had no way to push his computers through traditional distribution channels, so he took $1,000 of his personal savings and advertised in various publications that he was selling computer components through the mail. Dell's success is now legendary in selling made-to-order PCs directly to consumers. At the beginning, Dell focused on growth—wooing large corporate customers by offering an unprecedented level of service for the PC industry and taking its direct-sales model global. But within a few years, the company was in trouble because top management had failed to implement effective control systems. Most of Dell's managers did not have experience running a large company, and top executives

• If you were a consultant to Dell, what would you recommend to top managers? How can the company broaden its control strategies to strengthen its position in the computer industry?

soon learned that a single-minded focus on growth—and the failure to measure other performance indicators—was hurting profitability. For example, the company had expanded its product line to include notebook computers on the assumption that any growth was good, but it wound up with poorly designed, unreliable machines that had to be withdrawn from the market. Dell also experimented with selling through retail stores such as CompUSA and Wal-Mart. Although sales grew to $2.8 billion in one year, Dell actually suffered a net loss of $36 million. "Any one strength used to excess becomes a weakness," notes Thomas J. Meredith, Dell's chief financial officer, who joined the company from Sun Microsystems in 1993.

Meredith needed to work with Michael Dell to implement an effective overall control system that could keep Dell both growing and profitable.[1]

Control is an issue facing every manager in every organization today. Dell managers continually look for new ways to improve customer satisfaction, maintain relationships with suppliers, cut inventory costs, and develop the right products. Other businesses face similar challenges, such as minimizing the time needed to resupply merchandise in stores, the time that customers must wait in checkout lines, and the number of steps to process and package a roll of film. Control, including quality control, also involves office productivity, such as improved customer service, elimination of bottlenecks, and reduction in paperwork mistakes. In addition, every organization needs basic systems for allocating financial resources, developing human resources, analyzing financial performance, and evaluating overall profitability.

This chapter introduces basic mechanisms for controlling the organization. It begins by summarizing the basic structure and objectives of the control process. Then it discusses controlling financial performance through the use of budgets. Relatively recent perspectives on control, including a changing philosophy, the use of total quality management, and open-book management and international standards for quality control are examined. The chapter concludes by identifying the qualities of effective control systems.

management is complacent and slow to learn or to encourage employees to improve. North American managers were unnerved by this realization two decades ago, and they began to adopt a new control philosophy. As we saw in Part V on leadership (Chapter 12), motivation (Chapter 13), communicating (Chapter 14), and teams (Chapter 15), management began including low-level employees in the control and decision-making processes.

Organizational control is the systematic process of regulating organizational activities to make them consistent with the expectations established in plans, targets, and standards of performance. In a classic article on the control function, Douglas S. Sherwin summarizes this concept:

> The essence of control is action which adjusts operations to predetermined standards, and its basis is information in the hands of managers.[3] ■

Thus, effectively controlling an organization requires information about performance standards and actual performance, as well as actions taken to correct any deviations from the standards. Managers need to decide what information is essential, how they will obtain that information (and share it with employees), and how they can and should respond to it. Leading the Revolution: Leadership describes the importance of control in an organization's survival.

■ THE IMPORTANCE OF CONTROL

Ken Jones, president of the Ontario Centre for Advanced Manufacturing, said that once when IBM Canada Ltd. ordered some parts from a new supplier in Japan, it specified that acceptable quality would be 1.5 percent defects—a high standard in North America at that time. The Japanese supplier sent the parts, with a few packaged separately in plastic. An accompanying letter said, "We don't know why you want 1.5 percent defective parts, but for your convenience we have packaged them separately."[2]

These radically different perceptions of acceptable quality dramatize what happens when

■ ORGANIZATIONAL CONTROL FOCUS

Control can focus on events before, during, or after a process. For example, a local automobile dealer can focus on activities before, during, or after sales of new cars. Careful inspection of new cars and cautious selection of sales employees are ways to ensure high quality or profitable sales even before those sales take place. Monitoring how salespeople act with customers would be considered control during the sales task. Counting the number of new cars sold during the month or telephoning buyers about their satisfaction with sales transactions would constitute control after sales

organizational control
The systematic process through which managers regulate organizational activities to make them consistent with expectations established in plans, targets, and standards of performance

A TALE OF TWO LEADERS, ONE COMPANY

If a manager understands the best types of controls to implement in his or her company, the company can be successful, but if the controls don't fit the company, it can hit bottom. Both things happened to Viewpoint DataLabs International Inc. in the span of a few years.

John Wright started Viewpoint with a unique idea. While working at a previous job, he noticed that lawyers used customized, computer-generated renderings of auto accidents in courtroom cases involving car accidents. Instead of throwing away each model when the case was over, he thought, why not build a library of the computerized images and license them? Thus, Viewpoint was launched. Wright hired graphic artists, salespeople, and other staff. But soon, he had run through all the venture capital, as well as all of Viewpoint's revenues. When he had a new idea, he pulled artists off an existing project and assigned them immediately to the fledgling project. Once he sent engineers to the Indianapolis 500 just to measure cars, at a cost of several hundred thousand dollars, without investigating whether there was a market for the images. Another time he decided to completely restructure the company from a decentralized, egalitarian environment to one with a hierarchical bureaucracy, with layers of managers. To cut costs, he fired all his in-house artists and outsourced all the art, un-

til he was convinced by managers that his artists were his only source of revenue. There were no quantifiable standards of performance; people in the same job earned vastly different salaries for no apparent reason. "There were no rules," recalls one former employee. "No development plans." Although Wright was considered a visionary, his company was out of control.

Wright recognized that Viewpoint needed someone with the skills to develop and implement control systems, so in stepped Eliot Jacobsen, a young alumnus from Harvard Business School and Boston's Bain & Co. When he took the job as CFO of Viewpoint, Jacobsen had no clear idea of the state of the company. But he soon discovered how badly stretched Viewpoint's finances were and the tumultuous state of the employees. He had to turn things around. With a short-term infusion of cash from the outside, Jacobsen began to repair shop. First, he changed marketing and sales from a reactive force to a proactive force by initiating a product line called Collections and Libraries—bundles of models that could be sold as discrete entities "so we could proactively turn ourselves into a product business." Then he established standards of performance so that the work done by employees could be appraised fairly. Now each assignment that comes in to Viewpoint is evaluated in terms of

time and skill required; in-house artists bid for the job. Every model generates the same pay, but the artists who are more experienced or faster can move on to the next assignment more quickly, thus earning more money. This method of control has increased productivity tremendously because Jacobsen understands how artists want to work. "Our new meritocracy is a practice people trust. Creative people want to control their own destiny. It changed from a 40-hour week to a 55-hour week . . . ; you see them here at 2:00 in the morning." Finally, Viewpoint's prime source of revenue was truly invested in the success of the company.

Viewpoint is now a leader in the three-dimensional modeling market, with 90 happy employees, productivity up 60 percent, and revenue per employee leaping from $40,000 to $100,000. Its digitized models now appear in TV commercials for Oldsmobile and Dodge, Reebok and Nike, and other highly visible products. Jacobsen remains modest about his role. "I wouldn't call it a turnaround," he demurs. "It was more a restart, like a computer. If a business crashes, you load the programs in a different order and, sometimes, it works."

www.viewpoint.com

Source: Robert A. Mamis, "Change of Viewpoint," *CFO,* February 1998, pp. 54–58.

have occurred. These three types of control are formally called feedforward, concurrent, and feedback as illustrated in Exhibit 16.1.

FEEDFORWARD CONTROL

Control that attempts to identify and prevent deviations before they occur is called **feedforward control.** Sometimes called *preliminary* or *preventive* control, it focuses on human, material, and financial resources that flow into

the organization. Its purpose is to ensure that input quality is high enough to prevent problems when the organization performs its tasks.

Feedforward controls are evident in the selection and hiring of new employees. Organizations attempt to improve the likelihood that employees will perform up to standards by identifying the necessary skills and using tests and other screening devices to hire people who have those skills. Many organizations also conduct drug screening to ensure that job

feedforward control
Control that focuses on human, material, and financial resources flowing into the organization; also called *preliminary* or *preventive* control

For Netpreneurs like Matthew Glickman (left) and Mark Selcow, control means learning to strike a balance between their dual roles as chief technologists and CEOs. According to a recent study by Pricewaterhouse Coopers LLP, the main control issue of concern, as reported by two-thirds of the CEOs polled, was lack of qualified workers. Other control issues included control over market demand (43 percent), legislative and regulatory pressures (32 percent), competition from foreign markets (13 percent), and their own ability to manage or reorganize (26 percent).

Exhibit 16.1

ORGANIZATIONAL CONTROL FOCUS

Feedforward Control Anticipates Problems

Examples
- Pre-employment drug testing
- Inspect raw materials
- Hire only college graduates

Focus is on

Inputs

Concurrent Control Solves Problems as They Happen

Examples
- Adaptive culture
- Total quality management
- Employee self-control

Focus is on

Ongoing Processes

Feedback Control Solves Problems After They Occur

Examples
- Analyze sales per employee
- Final quality inspection
- Survey customers

Focus is on

Outputs

candidates or employees do not impair their ability to work safely and effectively. Another example is the requirement that professional football, basketball, and baseball players pass a physical exam before their contracts are validated. All of these kinds of testing are feedforward controls because they are intended to prevent deviations from acceptable performance.

Another type of feedforward control is to identify and manage risks. The large accounting firms have recognized that they can offer value to their clients by looking for risks the clients have knowingly or unknowingly taken on, rather than merely evaluating their financial performance after the fact. The firms have developed methods, such as Arthur Andersen's Business Audit, to study a client's industry, strategy, and operations to identify key business risks not shown on typical financial statements. In conducting such an audit for an Asian client, Arthur Andersen learned that the company was preparing to enter a contract to buy natural gas futures without sufficiently protecting itself against sudden shifts in the price of natural gas. A sudden change in gas prices could have forced the company to buy at an excessive price, costing it as much as a year's earnings. Because the problem was identified ahead of time, the client was able to protect itself from this potential loss.[4] High-technology feedforward controls were used in Hartford's and Beaton's farms to achieve maximum crop productivity.

PRECISION FARMING

Doug Hartford walks through his fields with a backpack on his back. Not so unusual for a farmer. But this year is different. In his backpack is a Geographic Information System (GIS) unit. Carrying a small computer with a blinking cursor for his field-position and data from the most recent planting serving as an overlay, the GIS software coordinates information and tells him, on the spot, what should be done. Coming up: A wireless modem will send the information to the local farm supply store, which will convert the data into an order.

Welcome to American farmland of the new millennium, no longer the bastion of the stereotyped "yokels" in bib overalls. Modern farms, losing their long-held price supports, are now subject to the same influences as other businesses—foreign competition, need for better marketing, restructuring, outsourcing.

A pioneer in "precision farming," the executive-looking Hartford works the 1,500-acre Illinois farm like his ancestors did as another kind of pioneer over 100 years ago. In 1992 he took his first laptop and a global positioning system (GPS) receiver, using 21 different satellites to ascertain the precise geographic coordinates of his combine or tractor from moment to moment and fixing that with a software-driven analysis of yield monitoring to know how every square meter of his farm performs. GPS was developed by the defense department to track missiles and has been available for civilian use since 1983.

In far-away Massachusetts cranberry farmers are learning similar lessons. Peter Beaton's grandfather and father used an "old reliable" system to determine the kinds of fertilizer that were needed each year, which depended on weather conditions and nutritional needs of each variety. They would walk around the bogs, jot down observations, and then return to the farm's office and make up a complicated color-coded map, with varying shades showing needs for 25 different kinds of fertilizer. Then they spent many hours hand delivering the maps to various suppliers. Mistakes or underestimates were made in the delivery and precious growing time was lost.

Peter Beaton's entomologist wife suggested he use computers, particularly the MapcoProfessional software, which helped her build a database on the particulars of every acre. When Benton returns from the bogs, he spends just a short time, using drop-down menus of fertilizers, to create a map that he faxes to the suppliers. Mistakes are greatly reduced, and much time is saved.

The cost is not as bad as it might seem. Hartford has spent only $20,000 since in four years on the technology and upgrades. Is it worth it? In just one year he saved $18,000 by using seed, fertilizer, and herbicides more wisely. However, the system has its limits. "We have the ability to control everything," says Hartford, "but the weather."[5] ∎

CONCURRENT CONTROL

Control that monitors ongoing employee activities to ensure they are consistent with quality standards is called **concurrent control.** Concurrent control assesses current work activities, relies on performance standards, and includes rules and regulations for guiding employee tasks and behaviors. Its intent is to ensure that work activities produce the correct results. It includes self-control, through which individuals impose concurrent controls on their own behavior.

Many manufacturing operations include devices that measure whether the items being produced meet quality standards. Employees monitor the measurements; if they see that standards are not met in some area, they make a correction themselves or signal the appropriate person that a problem is occurring.

An organization's cultural norms and values influence employee behavior, as do the norms of an employee's peers or work group. Total quality management (discussed later in this chapter) establishes the norm that employees will seek ways to continuously improve the organization's activities. Employees who accept that norm will look for ways to improve quality, and thus will contribute to the standard of continuous improvement.

FEEDBACK CONTROL

Sometimes called *postaction* or *output control*, **feedback control** focuses on the organization's outputs—in particular, the quality of an end product or service. An example of feedback control in a manufacturing department is an intensive final inspection of a refrigerator at a General Electric assembly plant. In Kentucky, school administrators conduct feedback control by evaluating each school's performance every other year. They review reports of student scores on an annual test featuring essay questions about core subjects, as well as the school's dropout and attendance rates. The state rewards schools with rising scores and brings in consultants to work with schools whose scores have fallen.[6]

Besides producing high-quality products and services, businesses need to earn a profit, and even nonprofit organizations need to operate efficiently to carry out their mission. Therefore, many feedback controls focus on financial measurements, and managers evaluate whether they have operated within their budget targets and whether they have generated sufficient sales and profits.

concurrent control
Control that consists of monitoring ongoing activities to ensure they are consistent with standards

feedback control
Control that focuses on the organization's outputs; also called *postaction* or *output control*

■ FEEDBACK CONTROL MODEL

All well-designed control systems involve the use of feedback to determine whether performance meets established standards. Managers set up control systems that consist of the four key steps illustrated in Exhibit 16.2.

1. *Establish standards of performance.* Within the organization's overall strategic plan, managers define goals for organizational departments in specific, operational terms that include a standard of performance against which to compare organizational activities.

Pyramidal systems, in which top managers control everything, are giving way to a new philosophy about organizational control that involves lower-level workers in management and control decisions. At the Honeywell Industrial Automation and Control facility in Phoenix, quality control decisions by employees cut defect rates by 70 percent, inventory by 46 percent, and customer lead time by an average of 75 percent. Their efforts were recognized when *Industry Week* magazine named the facility one of America's 10 best plants.

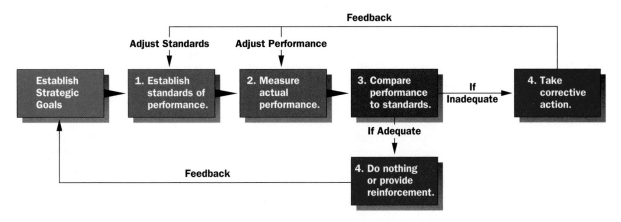

Managers should carefully assess what they will measure and how they will define it. Especially when the organization will reward employees for the achievement of standards, these standards should reflect activities that contribute to the organization's overall strategy in a significant way. Standards should be defined precisely so that managers and workers can determine whether activities are on target. In addition, the people responsible for achieving standards must be able to understand them. One organization that exercises this type of care in establishing performance standards is Texaco.

TEXACO INC.

www.texaco.com

Texaco's management has emphasized the careful defining of meaningful standards of performance. First, the company sought to avoid information overload by consolidating the categories of expenses that executives monitor, shrinking the number from 400 to fewer than 200; eventually, management hopes to simplify budgets to 75 or fewer line items. The objective is to state expenses in terms of a limited number of categories so that executives can really watch all the critical budget lines.

In addition to reducing the number of financial standards employees must monitor, Texaco has formally reviewed the terminology used in each of its business units and developed common terms for the entire range of company activities. That way, everyone understands exactly what is being measured. Simple as that sounds, few large companies take this basic step to ensure that everyone in the organization understands what a standard really means.

Finally, the company has identified financial measures that actually drive the company's long-term profitability, such as expenses per barrel of oil. The next step is to establish clear standards of performance for nonfinancial operational factors, such as worker safety, and tie them to employee compensation. Managers admit that establishing standards for these intangible factors is more difficult than the financial measures. However, they are committed to clearly defining meaningful standards that all employees can understand and work toward.[7] ∎

2. *Measure actual performance.* Most organizations prepare formal reports of quantitative performance measurements that managers review daily, weekly, or monthly. These measurements should be related to the standards set in the first step of the con-

trol process. For example, if sales growth is a target, the organization should have a means of gathering and reporting sales data. If the organization has identified appropriate measurements, regular review of these reports helps managers stay aware of whether the organization is doing what it should be.

In most companies, managers do not rely exclusively on quantitative measures. They go out into the organization to see how things are going, especially for such goals as increasing employee participation and learning. Managers have to observe for themselves whether employees are participating in decision making and have opportunities to add to and share their knowledge.

3. *Compare performance to standards.* The third step in the control process is comparing actual activities to performance standards. When managers read computer reports or walk through the plant, they identify whether actual performance meets, exceeds, or falls short of standards. Typically, performance reports simplify such comparisons by placing the performance standards for the reporting period alongside the actual performance for the same period and by computing the variance; that is, the difference between each actual amount and the associated standard.

When performance deviates from a standard, managers must interpret the deviation and find the cause of the problem. If the sales goal is to increase the number of sales calls by 10 percent and a salesperson achieved an increase of 8 percent, where did she fail to achieve her goal? Perhaps several businesses on her route closed, additional salespeople were assigned to her area by competitors, or she needs training in making her cold sales calls more effective. Managers should take an inquiring approach to deviations in order to gain a broad understanding of factors that influenced performance. Effective management control involves subjective judgment and employee discussions as well as objective analysis of performance data.

4. *Take corrective action.* When performance deviates from standards, managers must determine what changes, if any, are necessary and how they will be applied. In a traditional top-down approach to control, managers encourage employees to work harder, redesign the production process, or fire employees. In a participative control approach, managers collaborate with employees to determine the corrective action that is necessary.

Also, managers may wish to provide positive reinforcement when performance meets or exceeds targets. They may reward a department that has exceeded its planned goals or congratulate employees for a job well done. Managers should not ignore high-performing departments at the expense of taking corrective actions elsewhere.

In small startups, a frequent problem is too much success, which then requires some corrective action to avoid complete breakdown (see Leading the Revolution: The Learning Organization).

In some cases, managers may take corrective action to change performance standards. They may realize that standards are too high or too low if departments continually fail to meet or routinely exceed standards. When contingency factors that influence organizational performance change, performance standards may need to be altered to make them realistic and provide continued motivation for employees.

■ THE CHANGING PHILOSOPHY OF CONTROL

Bureaucratic control and decentralized control represent different philosophies of corporate culture, which was discussed in Chapter 1. Most organizations display some aspects of both bureaucratic and decentralized control, but managers generally emphasize one or the other, depending on the organizational culture and their own beliefs about control. In general, today's organizations are moving away from strict, hierarchical control toward greater decentralization, information sharing, and empowerment of employees.

The Learning Organization

BUCKEYE BEANS & HERBS

Doug and Jill Smith had more success than they could handle. Their small Spokane (Washington) Specialty food company was growing at an exponential rate for much of the 90s. In one year alone it grew 50 percent. But it was so intense they "got a hangover" from the rapid growth and started to see increased revenues, but declining profits.

Core customers were department stores, gourmet retailers, and upscale grocery stores, but then they started to sell to mass marketers and got big volumes but low margins. Plus there was increasing competition from the Big Guys—such as Quaker Oats and Hormel Foods. They refocused on core markets and let the big customers go. Revenues ultimately went down, but profits were up again.

Understanding the truth of the saying "You can have too much of a good thing," they knew they had expanded their market past its optimal growth. The growth was too rapid and chaos prevailed. It hit them

when they moved into a larger facility and found they were not running a little mom-and-pop business anymore. "We realized we needed people to fill the orders, to take the order, to package the product, and so on," says Doug. Needing more control and structure than they were used to providing, the company was in crisis. "We just couldn't do it all, as we had done in the past, and we didn't have the people in place yet."

The Smiths were smart enough to realize they were in over their head, so they hired a consultant, whom they refer to as a "pro-sultant," which Jill feels is not as negative as "consultant." (Some entrepreneurs use the free consulting service of SCORE—Service Corp of Retired Executives; see www.score.org.) So they now had an advisor who helped them look at strengths and weaknesses, as well as providing ideas to restructure the company and improve communications.

They resisted the advice, however, of hiring a Chief Financial Officer (CFO), because Doug was so

good with numbers. But finally they succumbed and now Jill says, "One of the smartest things we did was hire a CFO," who provided them even more useful financial information (after all, that is a CFO's business) and improved their cash-flow management.

Even so, Buckeye got a little too secure in its growth and forgot to innovate, causing slipping sales. In 1998, the Smiths sold out and the company lost its direction even further, with disastrous results.

It's some hard lessons for entrepreneurs to learn: keep the focus, innovate, hire to delegate, and say no to certain customers. But as one business founder said, "Growth manages you if you let it. The challenge is to manage the growth."

SOURCES: Kim Crompton, "Buckeye Beans Slashes Staff, Changes Direction," *Journal of Business*, March 11, 1999, p. A5; Sharon Nelton, "Coming to Grips with Growth," *Nation's Business*, Feb. 1998, pp. 26–32.

Bureaucratic control involves the use of rules, policies, hierarchy of authority, reward systems, and other formal devices to influence employee behavior and assess performance. In contrast, **decentralized control** relies on organizational culture, group norms, and a focus on goals, rather than rules and procedures, to foster compliance with organizational goals. Traditions and trust are seen as forces that help foster compliance with organizational goals. Managers operate on the assumption that employees are trustworthy and willing to perform effectively without extensive rules and close supervision.

Exhibit 16.3 contrasts the use of bureaucratic and decentralized methods of control. Technology often is used to control the flow and pace of work or to monitor employees, such as by measuring how long employees spend on phone calls or how many keystrokes they make at the computer.

Bureaucratic control techniques can enhance organizational efficiency and effectiveness. Many employees appreciate a system that clarifies what is expected of them, and they may be motivated by challenging, but achievable, goals.[8] However, though many managers effectively use bureaucratic control, too much control can backfire. Employees resent being watched too closely, and they may try to sabotage the control system. Veteran truck driver Clink Satterlund expressed his unhappiness with electronic monitoring to a *Wall Street Journal* reporter investigating the use of devices that monitor truck locations. According to Satterlund, "It's getting worse and worse all the time. Pretty soon they'll want to put a chip in the drivers' ears and make them robots." He added that he occasionally escapes the relentless monitoring by parking under an overpass to take a needed nap out of the range of the surveillance satellites.[9]

bureaucratic control
The use of rules, policies, hierarchy of authority, reward systems, and other formal devices to influence employee behavior and assess performance

decentralized control
The use of organizational culture, group norms, and a focus on goals, rather than rules and procedures, to foster compliance with organizational goals

Exhibit 16.3

BUREAUCRATIC VERSUS
DECENTRALIZED METHODS
OF CONTROL

Bureaucratic Control	**Decentralized Control**
Uses detailed rules and procedures; formal control systems	Limited use of rules; relies on values, group and self-control, selection and socialization
Top-down authority, formal hierarchy, position power, quality control inspectors	Flexible authority, flat structure, expert power, everyone monitors quality
Task-related job descriptions; measurable standards define minimum performance	Results-based job descriptions; emphasis on goals to be achieved
Emphasis on extrinsic rewards (pay, benefits, status)	Extrinsic and intrinsic rewards (meaningful work, opportunities for growth)
Rewards given for meeting individual performance standards	Rewards individual and team; emphasis on equity across employees
Limited, formalized employee participation (e.g., grievance procedures)	Broad employee participation, including quality control, system design, and organizational governance
Rigid organizational culture; distrust of cultural norms as means of control	Adaptive culture; culture recognized as means for uniting individual, team, and organizational goals for overall control

Decentralized control is based on values and assumptions that are almost opposite to those of bureaucratic control. Rules and procedures are used only when necessary. Managers rely instead on shared goals and values to control employee behavior. The organization places great emphasis on the selection and socialization of employees to ensure that workers have the appropriate values needed to influence behavior toward meeting company goals. No or-ganization can control employees 100 percent of the time, and self-discipline and self-control are what keep workers performing their jobs up to standard. Empowerment of employees, effective socialization, and training all can contribute to internal standards that provide self-control. Technology is used to empower employees by giving them the information they need to make effective decisions, work together, and solve problems. People are re-

For more than a decade, managers at General Electric have been dedicated to decentralized control through a program called "Work Out." Work Out is an ongoing effort to achieve what Jack Welch has called "boundaryless behavior"—behavior that, "ends all barriers of rank, function, geography, and bureaucracy in an endless pursuit of the best idea" (as stated in the GE Annual Report). With boundaries diminished, GE launched "Six Sigma," a disciplined methodology that focuses on quality for every process that affects the GE customer. Cindy Lee and S. Mani were part of a Six Sigma team at the color lab of the GE Plastics plant in Singapore. The team reduced the lead time for matching colors of GE resins to customer requirements by 85 percent, providing a distinct competitive advantage in the fast-paced global market for plastics.

warded for team and organizational success as well as their individual performance, and there is an emphasis on equity among employees.

With decentralized control, the culture is adaptive, and managers recognize the importance of organizational culture for uniting individual, team, and organizational goals for greater overall control. Ideally, with decentralized control, employees will pool their areas of expertise to arrive at procedures better than managers working alone. In this way, the decentralized approach to control supports efforts to build and maintain a learning organization; that is, an organization whose members continually add to and share their knowledge. One organization reaping the benefits of decentralized control is CompuWorks, a computer software company based in Pittsfield, Massachusetts.

CompuWorks
www.cwsite.com

Decentralized control is the rule at CompuWorks, which develops, installs, and trains people to use software that integrates a company's computer systems. Through a series of strategic planning sessions, the company created profit goals, specifying the revenues and profits that each department was to contribute to the company's overall goals. Each department then takes responsibility for determining how to meet its goals and how to track its progress.

The departments assembled teams of employees to identify what measurements were most significant and how to display those numbers. The group that develops custom software designed a scoreboard resembling the yellow brick road from the Wizard of Oz. A wizard in a balloon floats upward as sales dollars grow, and to track the source of those dollars, Dorothy moves along the chart to show the number of billable hours—preferably trailed, not led, by a witch representing internal (i.e., nonbillable) time. Similarly, the sales department designed its own chart to measure sales, profits, and expenses. The train-

ing department created a vase with paper flowers—when certain targets for billable hours or students trained are reached, the department adds a flower to the vase. Every department set targets by month, quarter, and year, and each department has a small budget for rewards if it reaches its goals. A big green scoreboard tracks the company's overall progress. President of CompuWorks, Alan Bauman, says, "People don't necessarily feel they can change the big board directly. What they do feel they can do is change their numbers."[10] ■

Although decentralized control utilizes methods different from those of bureaucratic control, it is a mistake to assume that decentralized control is weak or represents the absence of control simply because visible rules, procedures, and supervision are absent. Indeed, some people believe that the decentralized approach is the stronger form of control because it engages the commitment and involvement of employees. Spurred by this belief, a growing number of organizations are adopting decentralized control as part of a strong corporate culture that encourages employee involvement and commitment to quality.

■ MANAGING PRODUCTIVITY

During the 1980s, globalization and increased competition from Japan and Europe created a sense of urgency among Americans regarding U.S. growth and productivity. Productivity is significant because it influences the well-being of the entire society as well as of individual companies. The only way to increase the output of goods and services to society is to increase organizational productivity.

MEASURING PRODUCTIVITY

What is productivity, and how is it measured? In simple terms, productivity is the organization's output of goods and services divided by its inputs. This means that productivity can be improved by either increasing the amount of output using the same level of inputs or reducing the number of inputs required to produce the output. Sometimes a company can even do both. Ruggieri & Sons, for example, invested in mapping software to help it plan deliveries of heating fuel. The software plans the most efficient routes based on the locations of customers and fuel reloading terminals, as well as the amount of fuel each customer needs. When Ruggieri switched from planning routes by hand to using the software, its drivers began driving fewer miles but making 7 percent more stops each day—in others words, burning less fuel in order to sell more fuel.[11]

The accurate measure of productivity can be complex. Two approaches for measuring productivity are *total factor* productivity and *partial* productivity. Total factor productivity is the ratio of total outputs to the inputs from labor, capital, materials, and energy:

$$\text{Total factor productivity} = \frac{\text{Output}}{\text{Labor} + \text{Capital} + \text{Materials} + \text{Energy}}$$

Total factor productivity represents the best measure of how the organization is doing. Often, however, managers need to know about productivity with respect to certain inputs. Partial productivity is the ratio of total outputs to a major category of inputs. For example, many organizations are interested in labor productivity, which would be measured as:

$$\text{Productivity} = \frac{\text{Output}}{\text{Labor dollars}}$$

Calculating this formula for labor, capital, or materials provides information on whether improvements in each element are occurring. However, managers often are criticized for relying too heavily on partial productivity measures, especially direct labor.[12] Measuring direct labor misses the valuable improvements in materials, manufacturing processes, and work quality. Labor productivity is easily measured, but may show an increase as a result of capital improvements. Thus, managers will misinterpret the reason for productivity increases.

■ TOTAL QUALITY MANAGEMENT

Driven by stiff international competition and rising customer expectations, beginning in the 1980s U.S. organizations identified improvement of quality as the route to competitiveness. Many adopted an approach called **total quality management (TQM)**, an organizationwide effort to infuse quality into every activity in a company through continuous improvement. TQM was attractive because it had been successfully implemented by Japanese companies that were gaining market share—and an international reputation for high quality. The Japanese system was based on the work of such U.S. researchers and consultants as Deming, Juran, and Feigenbaum, whose ideas attracted U.S. executives after the methods were tested overseas.[13]

The TQM philosophy focuses on teamwork, increasing customer satisfaction, and lowering costs. Organizations implement TQM by encouraging managers and employees to collaborate across functions and departments, as well as with customers and suppliers, to identify areas for improvement, no matter how small. Teams of workers are trained and empowered to make decisions that help the organization achieve high standards of quality. Organizations shift responsibility for quality control from specialized departments to all employees. Thus, total quality management means a shift from a bureaucratic to a decentralized approach to control.

Companywide participation in quality control requires a major change from the Western notion of achieving an "acceptable quality level," which by definition allows a certain percentage of defects. Total quality management not only engages the participation of all employees to improve quality, it has a target of zero defects. Each quality improvement is a step toward perfection, and quality control is part of the day-to-day business of every employee.

The implementation of total quality management is similar to that of other decentralized control methods. Feedforward controls include training employees to think in terms of prevention, not detection, of problems and giving them the responsibility and power to correct errors, expose problems, and contribute to solutions. Concurrent controls include an organizational culture and employee commitment that favor total quality and employee participation. Feedback controls

total quality management (TQM)
A management approach that focuses organizationwide attention on delivering total quality to customers and includes (1) employee involvement, (2) focus on the customer, (3) benchmarking, and (4) continuous improvement

include targets for employee involvement and for zero defects.

TQM TECHNIQUES

The implementation of total quality management involves the use of many techniques. Most companies that have adopted TQM have incorporated quality circles, empowerment, benchmarking, outsourcing, standards for reduced cycle time, and continuous improvement.

QUALITY CIRCLES   One approach to implementing the decentralized approach of TQM is to use quality circles. A **quality circle** is a group of 6 to 12 volunteer employees who meet regularly to discuss and solve problems affecting the quality of their work.[14] At a set time during the workweek, the members of the quality circle meet, identify problems, and try to find solutions. Circle members are free to collect data and take surveys. Many companies train team members in team building, problem solving, and statistical quality control. The reason for using quality circles is to push decision making to an organization level at which recommendations can be made by the people who do the job and know it better than anyone else. The quality circle process as used in most U.S. companies is illustrated in Exhibit 16.4, which begins with a selected problem and ends with a decision given back to the team.

The quality circle concept spread to the United States and Canada from Japan, having been developed as a method of gaining employee commitment to high standards. The success of quality circles impressed executives visiting Japan from Lockheed, the first U.S. company to adopt this practice. Many other North American companies, including Westinghouse and Baltimore Gas & Electric Company, have since adopted quality circles. Managers consistently attest to the improved performance and cost savings.

EMPOWERMENT   TQM relies on the empowerment of employees, as well as the contributions of suppliers and customers in the decision-making process. Input from all these groups is essential to continuous improvement. Furthermore, as companies reduce staff and layers of management, or shift tasks to suppliers or outside organizations, managers need to share information and collaborate with customers and suppliers. As customers increase their product sophistication and demands for higher quality, organizations need to include them in the information loop by providing product and service information and developing relationships with them.

BENCHMARKING   Introduced by Xerox in 1979, benchmarking is now a major TQM component. **Benchmarking** is defined by

quality circle
A group of 6 to 12 volunteer employees who meet regularly to discuss and solve problems affecting the quality of their work

benchmarking
The continuous process of measuring products, services, and practices against major competitors or industry leaders

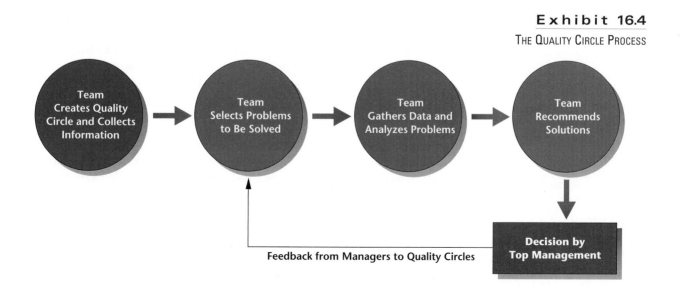

E x h i b i t   16.4
THE QUALITY CIRCLE PROCESS

Team Creates Quality Circle and Collects Information → Team Selects Problems to Be Solved → Team Gathers Data and Analyzes Problems → Team Recommends Solutions → Decision by Top Management

Feedback from Managers to Quality Circles

Xerox as "the continuous process of measuring products, services, and practices against the toughest competitors or those companies recognized as industry leaders."[15] The key to successful benchmarking lies in analysis. Starting with its own mission statement, a company should honestly analyze its current procedures and determine areas for improvement. As a second step, a company carefully selects competitors worthy of copying. For example, Xerox studied the order fulfillment techniques of L. L. Bean and learned ways to reduce warehouse costs by 10 percent. Companies can emulate internal processes and procedures of competitors, but must take care to select companies whose methods are compatible. Once a strong, compatible program is found and analyzed, the benchmarking company can then devise a strategy for implementing a new program.

OUTSOURCING   Although it is not inherently a part of TQM, an organization can improve quality through **outsourcing,** the contracting out of a company's in-house functions to a preferred vendor with a high-quality level in the particular task area. Outsourcing is one of the fastest-growing trends in U.S. business. Companies such as B. F. Goodrich and J. C. Penney have latched onto outsourcing as a route to almost immediate savings and quality improvement. By "farming out" activities in which they do not specialize, such as human resource or inventory management, organizations can save costs on employee benefits and free up existing personnel for other duties. Manufacturing companies have outsourced the designing of new plants, and service organizations have outsourced mailrooms, warehousing, and delivery services. Outsourcing also has become a viable option for city and state governments trying to slash costs and improve efficiency. In Scottsdale, Arizona, Rural/Metro Company contracts with the city to run fire departments and emergency medical services and is able to provide better service at a fraction of the cost of traditional government-run services.[16]

Outsourcing does not eliminate the need for control. Rather, managers must identify how they will ensure that the quality of the out-

sourced function meets their standards. Feedforward controls include carefully selecting the operations that can be accomplished with greater quality elsewhere and finding the best outsourcing partners. Concurrent controls include maintaining good relationships and communications with the partners. Feedback controls include regular reports on the outsourced activities and associated costs.

REDUCED CYCLE TIME   In the book *Quality Alone Is Not Enough,* the authors refer to cycle time as the "drivers of improvement." **Cycle time** refers to the steps taken to complete a company process, such as teaching a class, publishing a textbook, or designing a new car. The simplification of work cycles, including the dropping of barriers between work steps and among departments and the removal of worthless steps in the process, is what enables a TQM program to succeed. Even if an organization decides not to use quality circles, substantial improvement is possible by focusing on improved responsiveness and acceleration of activities into a shorter time. Reduction in cycle time improves overall company performance as well as quality.[17]

L. L. Bean, Inc., the Freeport, Maine, mail-order firm, is a recognized leader in cycle time control. Workers have used flowcharts to track their movements and pinpoint wasted motions. They also completely redesigned the order-fulfillment process. A computerized system breaks down an order based on the geographic area of the warehouse in which items are stored. Items are placed on conveyor belts, where electronic sensors re-sort the items for individual orders. After orders are packed, they are sent to a FedEx facility on site. Improvements such as these have enabled L. L. Bean to process most orders within two hours after the order is received.[18]

CONTINUOUS IMPROVEMENT   In North America, crash programs and designs have traditionally been the preferred method of innovation. Managers measure the expected benefits of a change and favor the ideas with the biggest payoffs. In contrast, Japanese companies have realized extraordinary success from making a series of mostly small improvements.

outsourcing
The contracting out of a company's in-house function to a preferred vendor

cycle time
The steps taken to complete a company process

Continuous innovation is what makes great companies and Silicon Valley has been the place for intense innovation. But until the 1950s the Santa Clara Valley was a lovely patchwork of orchards. After World War II Stanford University engineering professor Frederick Terman started encouraging promising students, such as William Hewlett and David Packard (who started Hewlett-Packard in a garage), to stay in the San Francisco Bay area rather than make their fortunes back east. By the end of the 1950s, the semiconductor industry took off and orchards started to disappear. Since then, Valley inventors and researchers have developed the microprocessor, the Ethernet, the computer mouse, and loads of software and e-commerce companies.

What makes Silicon Valley so unique among high-tech places in the world? Why has it arguably spurred the largest legal wealth creation in history? Researcher Anna Lee Saxenian believes it is the culture of the region—sometimes known as "Route 128"—which rewards innovation, risk taking, and mobility among engineers. Author Michael Lewis takes that a bit further, looking at the way engineers are seen. In the northeast, for example, engineers are seen as drones, while financiers are in charge. Boston would have been a more logical place for Silicon Valley, since it had a better infrastructure. Lewis argues that it took the lack of social stratification of Northern California for engineers to have enough respect to develop ideas. This led to a fixation with finding new ways, a process of "creative destruction"

of the old, and a collective obsession with not merely cutting edge, but "bleeding edge" technology. In order to maintain this culture, Silicon Valley seems to have no nostalgia for the way things were. Therefore anyone, even the creator of an idea, will easily tear it down if something more hopeful looms on the horizon.

Some worry that Silicon Valley is beginning to be warped by easy money, by the glitter of deals, rather than the promise of new technology. And the process of creative destruction that works so well in maintaining the bleeding edge wreaks havoc on families, relationships, and psyches. This creative destruction doesn't play well with the low-paid assembly-line workers who are more and more being priced out of affordable housing and are the first to feel the injustices in this whole process.

Alex Soojung-Kim Pang sees how Silicon Valley has already morphed itself several times and may do so again as a center for information technology and high finance. "But if it loses the ability to attract people fascinated with technology and willing to make great sacrifices in the belief that they'll be treated fairly," he says, "it will cease to be the valley of the heart's—and mind's delight."

SOURCES: Alex Soojung-Kim Pang, "Creative Destruction," *Los Angeles Times*, Oct. 31, 1999, p. 1; Michael Lewis, *The New New Thing* (New York: McGraw-Hill), 1999; Robert D. Hot, "No Satisfaction in Silicon Valley," *Business Week*, Nov. 8, 1999, p. 15.

This approach, called **continuous improvement,** is the implementation of a large number of small, incremental improvements in all areas of the organization on an ongoing basis. In a successful TQM program, all employees learn that they are expected to contribute by initiating changes in their own job activities. The basic philosophy is that improving things a little bit at a time, all the time, has the highest probability of success. Innovations can start simple, and employees can build on their success in this unending process. Silicon Valley is known for its never-ending innovation (as discussed in Focus on Innovation).

The continuous improvement concept applies to all departments, products, services, and activities throughout an organization. At South Carolina Baptist Hospital in Columbia, South Carolina, 2,500 employees have been trained in continuous improvement techniques. Managers learn a coaching role, empowering employees to recognize and act on their contributions. Baptist has learned that countless improvements require a long-term approach to building high quality into the very fiber of the organization. Over time, project by project, human activity by human activity, quality through continuous improvement has become the way the hospital's employees do their work.[19]

TQM AND OPERATIONS MANAGEMENT

When implemented properly, TQM can improve operations management. However, many

continuous improvement
The implementation of a large number of small, incremental improvements in all areas of the organization on an ongoing basis

Baldor Electric Company designs, manufactures, and markets a broad line of energy-efficient motors and adjustable-speed drives. AC motors from 20 to 300 HP (manufactured in Baldor's Columbus, Mississippi, plant) are one of the fastest growing segments of their motor business. Company managers credit the commitment by Columbus plant employees to continuous improvement as one of the reasons for that growth.

companies have not experienced success. One recent study tried to determine the factors that distinguish companies that enjoy operations improvements from those that see no reduction in defects. The researchers found that companies that experienced success were those in which management viewed TQM as a means to make their companies one of the best and to achieve growth by attracting new customers. Thus, these managers saw TQM not merely as a means to solve current problems but as a way to position the company for the future. These managers viewed the various TQM techniques as being interrelated, and they saw their customers as partners, rather than as adversaries.[20]

STATISTICAL QUALITY CONTROL

Quality is not just an abstract concept. It must be measured if a TQM system is to be successful. One operations management technique for improving quality and productivity is **statistical process control (SPC)**, which refers to the application of statistical techniques to the control of quality. But measurement is by workers, not top managers or formal control systems. Workers must be given the training and tools to use statistical techniques to evaluate their tasks and make improvements as needed. The use of statistical measurements is a powerful weapon in the drive to improve quality.

statistical process control (SPC)

An operations management technique involving the application of statistical techniques to improve control of quality

The best known SPC applies statistical techniques to the control of work processes to detect production of defective items. In addition, workers often are trained in traditional statistical concepts such as frequency distributions, regression and correlation, acceptance sampling, and tests of significance. These techniques are widely used in manufacturing departments, where production activities can be measured and analyzed.

For example, employees can be trained to use charts as graphic representations of work processes. A statistical process control chart measures a specific characteristic, as illustrated in Exhibit 16.5. In this particular chart, workers take a sample of five parts each hour, where the production rate is approximately 100 per hour. The diameters of the five parts are measured, and the sample mean is calculated and plotted on the chart. If the upper control limit or lower control limit is exceeded, the variation is too great and is not due to chance alone. If either limit is exceeded, the operation is stopped and the cause determined. In this particular case, the tool had become loose, and so it was reset.

Procedures have been developed for implementing statistical quality control, which include the following steps.

1. *Define the characteristics of a high-quality output.* The output can be a hamburger

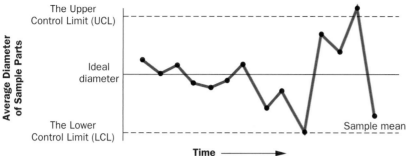

SOURCE: Ross Johnson and William O. Winchell, "Management and Quality," (Milwaukee, Wis.: American Society for Quality Control, 1989), p. 7.

produced by a Wendy's restaurant, a job description written by an employee in the human resource department of AT&T, or a radial tire produced at a Firestone plant. The supervisor must provide an exact definition of a high-quality output or service.

2. *Break down work activities into the separate elements required for producing a high-quality output.* For making a hamburger, one separate element is forming the raw hamburger patty, a second is cooking it, and a third is garnishing it. The quality associated with each element must be defined separately.

3. *Have current and reasonable standards for each work element.* If standards for work elements are not already available, they must be developed. The standard is the basis for comparison of worker performance.

4. *Discuss specific performance expectations for every job with workers.* Each worker must understand what is expected with respect to his or her work elements and quality outputs. Workers should participate in decisions about how their performances will be measured.

5. *Make checksheets and collect data for each task element.* Written documents must be developed that reflect performance, and machine operators must be taught to collect data and assess whether their performances are up to standard. Likewise, supervisors can monitor departmental performance by gathering data on team outputs.

6. *Evaluate employee progress at frequent intervals.* In some manufacturing situations,

the output records should be checked for every worker several times during the day. If employees are involved in running several different batches of material, different standards will apply. If planned quality standards are not met, adjustments can be made before the end of the work period.

TQM SUCCESS FACTORS

Despite TQM's promise, a few firms have had disappointing results. Many factors can influence the success of a TQM program (see Exhibit 16.6). For example, quality circles are most beneficial when employees have challenging jobs; participation in a quality circle can contribute to productivity because it enables employees to pool their knowledge and solve interesting problems. TQM also tends to be most successful when it enriches jobs and improves employee motivation. In addition, when participating in the program improves the problem-solving skills of workers, productivity is likely to increase. Finally, a quality program has the greatest chance of success in a corporate culture that values high quality and stresses continuous improvement as a way of life.

IMPROVING PRODUCTIVITY

When an organization decides that improving productivity is important, there are three indicators.

- *Increased technological productivity* refers to the use of more efficient computers, machines, robots, and other technologies to

Positive Factors	Negative Factors
• Tasks make high skill demands on employees.	• Management expectations are unrealistically high.
• TQM serves to enrich jobs and motivate employees.	• Middle managers are dissatisfied about loss of authority.
• Problem-solving skills are improved for all employees.	• Workers are dissatisfied with other aspects of organizational life.
• Participation and teamwork are used to tackle significant problems.	• Union leaders are left out of QC discussions.
• Continuous improvement is a way of life.	• Managers wait for big, dramatic innovations.

increase outputs. This may involve outsourcing. NationsBank, for example, arranged for Pitney Bowes Management Services (PBMS) to handle its mail services, in part because PBMS has the computer applications to handle the task. Now, NationsBank doesn't have to incur the cost of new technology to set up a modern mailing system for its 60 mail centers that are spread out over 16 states and the District of Columbia.[21]

• *Increased worker productivity* means workers are producing more output within the same time period. Companies can improve worker productivity by establishing the means for existing employees to do more by working harder or improving work processes. Employees may simply need more knowledge, more resources, or improved task or workplace design. The company may also decide to hire employees with greater expertise or to outsource certain operations to a firm with expertise in that area, as NationsBank did. Improving worker productivity can be a real challenge for American companies, because too often workers have an antagonistic relationship with management. Thus, increasing employee productivity often requires improving that relationship.

• *Increased managerial productivity* simply means that managers are doing a better job of running the business. Leading experts in productivity and quality have stated often that the real reason for productivity problems in the United States is poor manage-

ment.[22] One of these authorities, W. Edwards Deming, proposed specific points for how management can improve productivity (see Exhibit 16.7).

Management productivity improves when managers emphasize quality over quantity, break down barriers and empower their employees, and do not overmanage using numbers. Managers can learn to use reward systems, employee involvement, teamwork, and other management techniques that have been described throughout this book. However, it is important for managers to consider the linkage between these techniques and the company's strategy—not just to blindly insert a technique into the organization's activities. For example, although many managers have tried to create learning organizations by encouraging their employees to share knowledge, their efforts failed when employees saw no benefits and they lost interest. In contrast, creation of a learning organization tends to succeed when managers establish a strategy-related focus for what information is to be shared, then measure the results. At General Electric, for example, employees focused on learning about how to improve response time. Management had determined that improvements in this area would significantly improve the company's performance. When GE instituted its knowledge management program, managers looked for—and found—improvements in such performance measures as sales per employee.[23] The difference can be attributed to better management, not to specific techniques.

Exhibit 16.7

CONDENSATION OF THE 14
POINTS FOR MANAGEMENT

1. Create constancy of purpose toward improvement of product and service, with the aim to become competitive and to stay in business, and to provide jobs.

2. Adopt the new philosophy. We are in a new economic age. Western management must awaken to the challenge, must learn their responsibilities, and take on leadership for change.

3. Cease dependence on inspection to achieve quality. Eliminate the need for inspection on a mass basis by building quality into the product in the first place.

4. End the practice of awarding business on the basis of price tag. Instead, minimize total cost. Move toward a single supplier for any one item, on a long-term relationship of loyalty and trust.

5. Improve constantly and forever the system of production and service, to improve quality and productivity, and thus constantly decrease costs.

6. Institute training on the job.

7. Institute leadership (see Point 12). The aim of supervision should be to help people and machines and gadgets to do a better job. Supervision of management is in need of overhaul as well as supervision of production workers.

8. Drive out fear, so that everyone may work effectively for the company.

9. Break down barriers between departments. People in research, design, sales, and production must work as a team, to foresee problems of production and in use that may be encountered with the product or service.

10. Eliminate slogans, exhortations, and targets for the workforce asking for zero defects and new levels of productivity. Such exhortations only create adversarial relationships, as the bulk of the causes of low quality and low productivity belong to the system and thus lie beyond the power of the workforce.

11. a. Eliminate work standards (quotas) on the factory floor. Substitute leadership.
    b. Eliminate management by objective. Eliminate management by numbers, numerical goals. Substitute leadership.

12. a. Remove barriers that rob the hourly worker of his right to pride of workmanship. The responsibility of supervisors must be changed from sheer numbers to quality.
    b. Remove barriers that rob people in management and in engineering of their right to pride of workmanship. This means, *inter alia*, abolishment of the annual merit rating and of management by objective.

13. Institute a vigorous program of education and self-improvement.

14. Put everybody in the company to work to accomplish the transformation. The transformation is everybody's job.

SOURCE: Reprinted from *Out of the Crisis*, by W. Edwards Deming by permission of MIT and The W. Edwards Deming Institute. Published by MIT, Center for Advanced Educational Services, Cambridge, MA 02139. Copyright 1986 by The W. Edwards Deming Institute.

■ THE BUDGETING PROCESS

BUDGETING

Budgeting is used in planning an organization's expenditures. Budgeting is also a control technique. As such, budgets are reports that list planned and actual expenditures for cash, assets, raw materials, salaries, and other resources. In addition, budget reports usually list the variance between the budgeted and actual amounts for each item. Focus on Collaboration box lists tips for effective budgeting.

A budget is created for every division or department within an organization, no matter how small, so long as it performs a distinct project, program, or function. The fundamental unit of analysis for a budget control system is called a **responsibility center**, any organizational department or unit under the supervision of a single person who is responsible for its activity.[24] Top managers use budgets for the company as a whole, and middle managers traditionally focus on the budget performance of their department or division. Here are four types of budgets used by managers.

responsibility center
An organizational unit under the supervision of a single person who is responsible for its activity

FOCUS ON Collaboration

BUDGETING IS A PEOPLE THING

It's easy to think of budgeting as a money thing, a numbers thing—even a computer thing. And that's the problem with budgeting processes in many companies, say some experts. Lawrence B. Serven, a manager at Deloitte & Touche Consulting Group, notes that, while many managers may agree that their budgeting process needs an overhaul to be effective, all the time, money, and technology in the world won't help if people aren't involved in the budgeting process and if they can't make the connection between budgets and their own jobs. "The real issues are not process related or systems related; they are people related." Holly Snyder, director of planning and management reporting at Nationwide Financial Services (NFS) agrees. She says today's budgets often fail to be effective because they are designed simply to please corporate headquarters. "People don't take ownership of the process," she explains. Here is some advice from the experts for managers who want their budgets to be effective:

1. INVOLVE THE TEAM. In other words, make sure the budget has input from people in all divisions and functions within the company. If possible, establish a formal team to develop a budget.

2. LIMIT DATA REQUESTS TO THOSE THAT ARE NECESSARY TO STRATEGIC OBJECTIVES. Stick to the subject. Don't digress.

3. USE TECHNOLOGY AS A TOOL, BUT DON'T RELY ON IT TO RESOLVE EVERYTHING. Data must be well defined, and there must not be too much data, for the planning process to succeed.

4. LINK BUDGET FORECASTING TO ACTIVITY-BASED MANAGEMENT. Spell out clear definitions of processes and other factors that affect your projections. Be sure to take into account the expense side of sales and operations.

5. DON'T FALL PREY TO TRENDY PROCEDURES. Stick to proven procedures, or ones that you are reasonably certain will be effective and valuable. Otherwise, your time and effort may be wasted.

6. BE A BUSINESS PARTNER. Budgeting and other financial processes need to be linked in partnership to the overall business process.

SOURCE: Cathy Lazere, "All Together Now," *CFO*, February 1998, pp. 28–36.

---

expense budget
A budget that outlines the anticipated and actual expenses for a responsibility center

revenue budget
A budget that identifies the forecasted and actual revenues of the organization

cash budget
A budget that estimates and reports cash flows on a daily or weekly basis to ensure that the company has sufficient cash to meet its obligations

capital budget
A budget that plans and reports investments in major assets to be depreciated over several years

1. An **expense budget** includes anticipated and actual expenses for each responsibility center and for the total organization. It may show all types of expenses or may focus on a particular category, such as materials or research and development expenses. When actual expenses exceed budgeted amounts, the difference signals the need for managers to identify the reason. The difference may arise from inefficiency, or because the organization's sales are growing faster than anticipated. Conversely, expenses below budget may signal exceptional efficiency or failure to meet some other standards, such as a desired level of sales or quality of service.

2. A **revenue budget** lists forecasted and actual revenues of the organization. In general, revenues below the budgeted amount signal a need to ascertain whether the organization can improve revenues. In contrast, revenues above budget require determining whether the organization can obtain the necessary resources to meet the higher-than-expected demand for its products.

3. The **cash budget** estimates receipts and expenditures of money on a daily or weekly basis to ensure that the organization has sufficient cash to meet its obligations. The cash budget shows the level of funds flowing through the organization and the nature of cash disbursements. If the cash budget shows that the firm has more cash than necessary to meet short-term needs, the company can arrange to invest the excess to earn interest income. In contrast, if the cash budget shows a payroll expenditure of $20,000 coming at the end of the week but only $10,000 in the bank, the organization must borrow cash to meet the payroll.

4. The **capital budget** lists planned investments in major assets such as buildings, trucks, and heavy machinery, often involving expenditures over more than a year. Capital expenditures not only have a large

impact on future expenses, they are investments designed to enhance profits. Therefore, a capital budget is necessary to plan the impact of these expenditures on cash flow and profitability. Controlling involves not only monitoring the amount of capital expenditures but evaluating whether the assumptions made about the return on the investments are holding true. Managers should evaluate whether continuing investment in particular projects is advisable, as well as whether their procedures for making capital expenditure decisions are adequate.

Navistar, Scott Paper, Seagram & Sons, and other large companies assign financial analysts to work exclusively on developing capital budgets and monitoring whether actual capital expenditures and returns are going according to plan. These analysts can provide important expertise for assessing risks and forecasting returns, but their advice will not be worth as much if managers primarily view their analysis as a hurdle to cross to obtain approval for projects they wish to carry out. In contrast, if the people providing information for capital budgeting decisions view themselves as partners with those who analyze the information, the quality of information will be much higher.[25]

Many traditional companies use **top-down budgeting,** which means that the budgeted amounts for the coming year are literally imposed on middle- and lower-level managers. These managers set departmental budget targets in accordance with overall company revenues and expenditures specified by top executives. Although there are some advantages to the top-down process, the movement toward employee empowerment, participation, and learning means that many organizations are adopting **bottom-up budgeting,** a process in which lower-level managers anticipate their department's resource needs and pass them up to top management for approval.

■ TRENDS IN QUALITY AND FINANCIAL CONTROL

Changing organizational structures and the resulting management methods that emphasize in-

formation sharing, employee participation, and teamwork have required changes in organizational control. More stringent quality demands from customers, together with the need to cut costs while improving products and services, also require new approaches to financial control.

INTERNATIONAL QUALITY STANDARDS

One impetus for total quality management in the United States is the increasing significance of the global economy. Many countries have endorsed a universal framework for quality assurance called **ISO 9000,** a set of international standards for quality management adopted in the late 1980s by more than 50 nations, including the United States. These standards, established by the International Standards Organization (a federation of 130 national standards bodies based in Geneva, Switzerland), set uniform guidelines to define what manufacturing and service organizations should do to ensure that their products conform to high quality requirements.[26] These standards do not detail the inputs (such as materials) that will be used for particular products or the outputs (specifications for products) but rather assume that when a company has a quality management system, it can successfully negotiate and meet the desired specifications. For example, such a system would include subsystems for ensuring that testing is carried out and that employees have adequate training. Organizations whose facilities pass an independent audit may obtain a certificate showing they have complied with ISO 9000 standards.

By the mid-1990s, as international corporations increasingly required ISO registration from their suppliers, over 90,000 sites became registered worldwide. U.S. companies initially lagged behind as the world rushed to meet the rigid standards, but pressure to meet international competition prompted a surge of applications, to more than 8,000 by the mid-1990s. Ford, General Motors, and Chrysler (now DaimlerChrysler) together established their own QS9000 standard, which combines ISO 9000 standards with other criteria that are specific to the auto industry. Beginning in 1997, all parts suppliers to these three companies had to comply with QS9000.[27]

top-down budgeting
A budgeting process in which middle and lower-level managers set departmental budget targets in accordance with overall company revenues and expenditures specified by top management

bottom-up budgeting
A budgeting process in which lower-level managers budget the resource needs of departments and pass them up to top management for approval

ISO 9000
A set of international standards for quality management to ensure that products conform to customer requirements

OPEN-BOOK MANAGEMENT

When information sharing, teamwork, and manager/facilitators are present, financial data must not be hoarded. Executives must admit employees into the financial control and responsibility loop. A growing number of managers are opting for full disclosure in the form of open-book management. **Open-book management** allows employees to see for themselves—through charts, computer printouts, meetings, and so forth—the financial condition of the company. Open-book management shows the individual employee how his or her job fits into the big picture and affects the financial future of the organization. Also, open-book management ties employee rewards to the company's overall success. With training in interpreting the financial data, employees can see the interdependence and importance of each function. If they are rewarded according to performance, they become motivated to take responsibility for their entire team or function, rather than merely their individual jobs.[28] The result is enhanced cross-functional communication and cooperation.

ECONOMIC VALUE-ADDED (EVA) SYSTEMS

Hundreds of companies, including AT&T, Quaker Oats, the Coca-Cola Company, and Philips Petroleum Company, have set up **economic value-added systems (EVA)** as a new way to measure financial performance. EVA can be defined as a company's net (after-tax) operating profit minus the cost of capital invested in the company's tangible assets.[29] Measuring performance in terms of EVA is intended to capture all the things a company can do to add value from its activities, such as run the business more efficiently, satisfy customers, and reward shareholders. Each job, department, or process in the organization is measured by the value added.

ACTIVITY-BASED COSTING (ABC)

A basic objective of controlling is to ensure that the organization's activities are profitable. Managers measure the cost of producing goods and services so that they can be sure they are selling these products for more than the cost to produce them. The traditional approach to costing has assumed that most production costs involve the materials and labor used to manufacture the products. These costs are measured precisely, and other costs—such as selling and administrative expenses—are divided equally among the organization's products.

In many situations, however, the traditional approach to costing no longer reflects the modern realities of doing business. The relationship between labor and overhead has changed. Increased automation has resulted in less labor. Total product costs are driven to a degree by higher overhead costs for setup, distribution, and maintenance of sophisticated machinery and information systems. Furthermore, the traditional approach does not always show the results of efforts to improve quality. Reliable quality should reduce the time spent resolving problems and redoing work, but these changes often are buried in overhead figures. Managers therefore need a way to monitor the costs of everything the organization does to get high-quality products to satisfied customers.

The solution at a growing number of organizations has been **activity-based costing (ABC),** which identifies various activities needed to provide a product and determines the cost of each of those activities. For example, an ABC system might list the costs associated with processing orders for a particular product, scheduling production for that product, producing it, shipping it, and resolving problems with it. The manager might discover that the production cost is within budget but that problems with scheduling and quality control were making the product unprofitable. Therefore, the manager can work with employees to improve engineering and production planning. Managers can also evaluate whether most costs go to activities that add value for customers (meeting customer deadlines, achieving high quality) or to activities that do not add value (processing internal paperwork). The organization can focus on reducing or eliminating expenditures for non-value-added activities.[30]

open-book management
Sharing financial information and results with all employees throughout the organization

economic value-added system (EVA)
A control system that measures after-tax profits minus the cost of capital invested in tangible assets

activity-based costing (ABC)
A control system that identifies the various activities needed to provide a product and determines the cost of those activities

■ QUALITIES OF EFFECTIVE CONTROL SYSTEMS

Properly used, controls help managers respond to unforeseen developments and achieve strategic plans. Whether organizational control focuses on feedforward or feedback measurement or emphasizes the bureaucratic or decentralized approach, certain characteristics should be present. In general, for organizational controls to be effective, they should be tailored to the organization's needs and facilitate the accomplishment of its tasks. More specifically, effective controls share the following traits:

1. *Linkage to strategy.* The control system should not simply measure what was important in the past or be tailored to current operations. It should reflect where the organization is going and adapt to new strategies. Moreover, the organization should focus on activities that are relevant for strategic goals. If the dominant competitive issue facing a company is to reduce cycle time, the control system should not emphasize raw materials cost, which is unrelated.

2. *Understandable measures.* Organizations depend on employees to carry out work according to standards. An effective control system ensures that employees know and understand what is expected. In addition, managers must understand what is being measured—an obvious but important criterion in these days of new and sometimes complex control systems such as ABC and EVA. A highly sophisticated analysis of a department's performance is wasted if the manager cannot interpret whether, or where, problems exist.

3. *Acceptance by employees.* The more committed employees are to control standards, the more successful the control system will be. The control system should motivate, not demotivate, as when they do not perceive the measurement process to be overly intrusive.

4. *Balance of objective and subjective data.* Managers can be misled when control system data are either completely numeric or based solely on subjective opinion. Control should be perceived as objective, but quantitative information tells only part of the story. Managers should balance quantitative and qualitative performance indicators to provide a well-rounded picture of performance.

5. *Accuracy.* Upward communication, especially about performance, often is influenced by what employees believe management wants to hear. However, the control system should encourage accurate information in order to detect deviations.

6. *Flexibility.* Internal goals and strategies must be responsive to changes in the environment and the control system should be flexible enough to adapt as needed. Managers who rely too heavily on existing controls, especially feedback controls, will find themselves out of synchronization with changing events.

7. *Timeliness.* The control system should provide information soon enough to permit a management response. Corrective action is of no value if performed too late.

8. *Support of action.* Control goes beyond monitoring performance to taking corrective action. Managers therefore need a system that helps them focus on performance areas in which change is needed. The control system should highlight variances, and managers should focus on these variances, diagnosing the cause of each variance and using judgment to decide when intervention is required.

Summary and Management Solution

This chapter introduced a number of important concepts about organizational control. Organizational control is the systematic process through which managers regulate organizational activities to meet planned goals and standards of performance. The focus of the control system may include feedforward control to prevent problems, concurrent control to monitor ongoing activities, and feedback control to evaluate past performance. Well-designed control systems include four key steps: establish standards, measure performance, compare performance to standards, and make corrections as necessary. Budget and financial controls ensure that expenditures and sales are in line with the organization's objectives.

The philosophy of controlling has shifted to reflect changes in leadership methods. Traditional bureaucratic controls emphasized establishing rules and procedures, then monitoring employee behavior to make sure the rules and procedures have been followed. With decentralized control, employees assume responsibility for monitoring their own performance.

Besides monitoring financial results, organizations control the quality of their goods and services. They may do this by adopting total quality management (TQM) techniques such as quality circles, empowerment, benchmarking, outsourcing, reduced cycle time, and continuous improvement. Other trends in controlling include the use of international quality standards, open-book management, EVA systems, and activity-based costing.

Control systems generally succeed when they match an organization's strategy, have understandable and reasonable standards, use a variety of performance standards, provide accurate information, are flexible, and focus on areas in which action is required.

The story of Dell Computer Corporation at the beginning of the chapter demonstrates the importance of financial control, as well as the importance of aligning control systems with an organization's strategy. As we learned in this chapter, managers should carefully assess and define the indicators they will measure. Some years ago, Dell began to suffer because managers focused entirely on measuring growth and failed to look at other key factors that determine organizational success. Dell's top managers, including Michael Dell himself, knew they had to make some changes in management structure and financial controls in order for their company to survive. First, Dell refocused the company's financial control strategy on a cash conversion cycle, which is made up of inventory, payables, receivables, and cash flow from operations. The pay of the company's top managers also was adjusted to reflect the return on invested capital as well as growth. For the first time, managers were actually invested in the success of the company. Then Dell made sure that training videos, newsletters, and other information packages were distributed to all employees, so they became part of the financial information loop through open-book management. Dell also brought in experienced managers, including Morton L. Topfer, a 23-year veteran of Motorola, to implement the systems needed to control a large corporation. As vice chairman of Dell, Topfer pulled the company out of retail sales to allow managers to focus on improving their direct sales efforts. Topfer also reorganized the company from a centralized, functional structure to a decentralized structure based on geographic divisions. Topfer recognized the change in structure as one way to shift to a more decentralized approach to control. Kevin Rollins, senior vice president and general manager of Dell Americas, says the company's managers are expected to communicate constantly with each other, with employees, with customers—in fact, with everyone. "You have to talk, you have to listen, and all of a sudden, you'll realize you are in the loop," he explains. Ironically, by attacking its previous singular focus on growth, Dell is in fact growing. But it is growing in a stronger, more focused manner. Today, the company is known as one of the best in the industry at rapidly responding to changes in the volatile PC market.

Discussion Questions

1. Why is it important for managers to understand the process of organizational control?

2. How might a public school system use feedforward control to identify the best candidates for its teaching positions?

3. How might the manager of a family-style restaurant use concurrent controls to ensure that the restaurant is providing customers with the highest quality food and service? What feedback controls could be useful?

4. What standards of performance has your professor established for this class? How will your actual performance be measured? How will your performance be compared to the standards? Do you think the standards and methods of measurement are fair? Why or why not?

5. What is the difference between budgeting and financial analysis? Why is each type of control important to a company?

6. Imagine that you are going to be the manager of a new Wal-Mart being built in your area. What items might be listed in your capital budget? What items might be listed in your expense budget?

7. In what ways could a university benefit from bureaucratic control? In what ways might it benefit from decentralized control? Overall, which approach do you think would be best at your college or university? Why?

8. If you were managing a local video rental store, which company would you choose to benchmark one aspect of your store's performance against? Why?

9. Would you like to work for a company that uses open-book management? Would you like to be a manager in the company? Why or why not?

10. Why is it important for an organization's control system to be linked to its overall strategy?

Management Exercises

Manager's Workbook

Are You Fast Enough to Succeed in Internet Time?

Students: See the solutions section on p. 576 to check your responses.

Is your company, or idea of a company, ready to handle the kind of productivity and speed required to make it on the Internet? Do YOU have what it takes to be a successful and productive Netprenuer? Take the quiz below and find out.

Does Your Business Have What It Takes to Move at Internet Speed?

What is an Internet year? It's the time in which an e-company needs to accomplish the kind of business goals that once took a year. Conventional wisdom puts an Internet year anywhere from 60 to 90 days. Regardless, few will argue that companies need to move faster now than ever imagined.

Can you afford the luxury of in-depth analysis, full due diligence, building consensus, test marketing—all the cornerstones of responsible corporate management? Does their value change when you weigh it against the cost to your company's scarcest commodity—time?

Kelsey Biggers, executive vice president of Micro Modeling Associates (MMA), offers the following scenarios to help determine whether you are capable of operating at Internet speed. Choose the best course of action from the choices given.

1. You have met a company that can be a potential strategic partner for marketing your service to a new industry online. The vibes are good and you want to map out the potential relationship, but in order to do so you need to share client and billing information. A nondisclosure agreement is necessary, and the company hands you their standard agreement. What do you do?

   a. Get a copy of your company's standard nondisclosure agreement and submit it to your potential partner as an alternative to their NDA.

   b. Fax the agreement to your lawyer and ask her to get back to you ASAP with any amendments so you can continue the conversation.

   c. Look over the agreement and sign it right away.

2. You're looking for a creative director for your Web site, and you know the position will be critical to your whole look and feel online. You hope to have three or four excellent candidates to choose from and have considered doing a retained search for the position. Out of nowhere your old college roommate, whom you respect enormously, refers you to an associate of his for the position. Meeting the candidate for breakfast and reviewing his work, you are blown away. You have three choices:

   a. Offer the candidate the job before the check arrives.

   b. Give the candidate a strong "warm and fuzzy" that there is a job for him while you initiate a quick search for a couple alternate candidates.

   c. Schedule a round of interviews with your senior colleagues back in the office to confirm your positive instincts, while also identifying one or two alternative candidates for comparison.

3. Your online strategy calls for targeting two vertical markets for your service in the next nine months. Your service can be tailored to meet the buying needs of companies in several industries, so it's a matter of

picking the right industries to target. High-growth, dynamic industries are obviously preferred. Which approach would you select?

a. Hire an MBA with finance and marketing and ask her to create high-level screening criteria for target industries and identify the five best fits for your services.

b. Hire your neighbor, who happens to be a doctor and knows the health-care industry and can make several introductions into HMOs and pharmaceutical companies.

c. Ask an intern to research publicly available information from Gartner Group, Forrester Research, and other industry analyst organizations for online spending habits in different industries and make recommendations.

4. Your company has been looking to merge with a strategic partner for some time. You have identified three companies that would be good fits, but each has its advantages and disadvantages. Which would you choose?

a. Company A offers a service that is perfectly complementary to your own, and the price is right. However, the company has indicated that it doesn't feel it has enough scale to do a merger now and would rather wait nine months until after the holiday selling season to complete the transaction.

b. Company B is smaller and dynamic, but has grown too fast and has a bad balance sheet. They could be picked up immediately, but your company would have to assume some unwanted debt along with the merger.

c. Company C has a great off-line presence in their space, but has not yet executed their e-commerce plan. They feel the two companies would be a great fit once they had established their online presence by mid-summer.

5. Your e-commerce strategy requires a real-time fulfillment system that can process orders straight through and provide data on client buying patterns. You have looked outside your firm for technology support to help bring this capability online and have been presented with three alternative approaches from which you must choose one:

a. A senior programmer from your prior firm is now a freelance consultant. He can get started immediately and hire a dozen coders who promise to get a capability up and running in 60 days and grow out the functionality.

b. Your internal technology group can staff a team of a dozen people to build out the system in a year and will then have the ability to support and grow the service when it goes live.

c. An e-solutions consultancy can project, manage, and build the entire system, but would want to take 60 days to design the technical architecture before starting development. They insist this time is necessary to ensure a scaleable service.

SOURCE: Adapted by Dorothy Marcic from "Are You Fast Enough to Succeed in Internet Time? Does Your Business Have What It Takes to Move at Internet Speed?" *Entrepreneur Magazine,* September 1999.

Manager's Workshop

Organizational Control Mechanisms

1. Divide into groups of five or six members.

2. Each group examines the following university request form for a complimentary parking pass and identifies flaws with the design of the form.

3. After identifying basic design flaws, groups then answer the following questions:

a. *Is the control cost effective?* Are the costs associated with the control mechanism offset by the benefits derived?

b. *Is the control acceptable?* Do the people affected believe it is necessary?

c. *Is the control appropriate?* Are the steps involved commensurate with the activity?

d. *Is the process strategic?* Is it a critical activity in the operation of the university?

e. *Is the control reliable and effective?* Is it clear what criteria are necessary for the approval of the request and what will be construed as sufficient justification?

Request for Complimentary Campus Parking Permits

Requesting Department:	Person Requesting:
Phone:	Event:
Date(s):	Time(s):
Number of Persons for Event:	Number of Permits Requested:
Permits Mailed:	Justification for Waived Fee:
Dean Signature	Vice President Signature

Approve: _____   Approve: _____

Disapprove: _____   Disapprove: _____

SOURCE: Adapted by Dorothy Marcic from H. Eugene Baker III and Kenneth M. Jennings, (1994). "An Out of Control Organizational Control Mechanism." *Journal of Management Education*, Vol. 18 (3), pp. 380–384.

Management in Practice: Ethical Dilemma

Go Along to Get Along?

Rhonda Gilchrist became a nurse because she wanted to help people. As the home health care industry began to take off, she was presented with what she thought was a terrific opportunity: A startup home health care agency offered her a position managing its staff of visiting nurses. She supported home health care because patients were treated in the relaxed, comfortable atmosphere of their homes; home visits gave patients and nurses more independence; and home visits were intended to be much cheaper than hospital stays or doctor's office visits. Therefore, Rhonda eagerly accepted the job.

Most of the patients treated by Gilchrist's nurses were elderly, with a variety of complaints ranging from diabetes to hip injuries. At first, Gilchrist encouraged her staff to make their visits efficient and productive so that patients could be weaned from care in a timely manner. She assumed this was what the head of the agency wanted. However, when she reported that one patient had recovered enough from a heart attack that he no longer needed three visits a week, the agency owner replied, "You should be looking for ways to increase the number of visits, not decrease them!" Gilchrist was shocked, but she soon understood that the only way to keep her job—and the jobs of her nurses—was to go along with her company's wishes. Those extra visits, paid for by Medicare, were paying her salary.

Meanwhile, Gilchrist did some research on her own. She learned that the average home-care patient now gets 80 visits per year (nearly four times the number of a decade ago), for which Medicare pays up to $90 per visit. In 1995, Medicare spent $16 billion on home care. Although lawmakers eagerly embraced the idea of home health care in the 1980s, believing that the shift would save insurance companies, Medicare, and even average citizens a huge sum, the savings haven't materialized. In fact, the opposite has happened. Rhonda knows home health care is extremely important to many patients, but she also realizes it is being abused by others, as well as by the agencies. As she learned in her research, people who want to start up home health agencies don't even need any type of special training. One local doctor told her in confidence that the owner of her own agency, an engineer by training, simply wanted to open his own business, so he chose between retail clothing and home health care. The latter, with its guaranteed payments from Medicare, was a sure bet.

As she drove to the office, Rhonda considered her alternatives. She knew that some of her clients no longer needed care. But she also knew that she needed a job, and most patients were lonely and looked forward to the visits. She wondered if there was a better way to control costs and deliver the best care to her patients.

What Do You Do?

1. Go along with the status quo and forget about the abuses of the system—that's your boss's problem. Besides, Medicare has deep pockets.

2. Look for another job as soon as possible. You don't want to be associated with unethical, and potentially illegal, practices.

3. Approach the owner of the agency and suggest other ways the agency might make a profit and deliver high-quality care, such as innovative ways to attract new clients to replace those that leave the roster in better health.

SOURCE: Based on George Anders and Laurie McGinley, "Medical Morass: How Do You Tame a Wild U.S. Program?" *The Wall Street Journal*, March 6, 1997, pp. A1, A8.

Surf the Net

1. *Benchmarking.* Assume your boss is interested in adding benchmarking to your company's recently instituted TQM program and has asked you to locate benchmarking information on the Internet. He told you that at the conference he attended last week he heard about a Web site called "The Benchmark Exchange" (www.benchnet.com). Your job is to report back to your boss with a complete report on what the Web site is all about, what the benefits of subscribing are, how much it costs to join, and the reasons for or against your company subscribing.

2. *ISO 9000.* Visit a site such as www.connect.ab.ca/~praxiom/ or find another where you can locate the following information about ISO 9000, the international standards for quality management. (a) Briefly describe the kind of company that would use each of the three sets of standards: ISO 9001, ISO 9002, and ISO 9003. (b) Se-

lect one of the guidelines sections—ISO 9000, ISO 9004, ISO 10011, or ISO 10012—and tell how many sections it has and what the section titles are. (c) At the site listed above, go to page www.connect.ab.ca/~praxiom/concepts.htm, briefly read the "Theoretical Overview of ISO 9000," and describe your impressions of the process.

3. *EVA Systems.* Go to www.sternstewart.com to supplement the text information on EVA systems. At this site select one of the following activities: (a) View the video showing what corporate executives have to say about EVA and submit a summary of their comments. (b) Go to the "Performance Rankings" section and check out the United States and one other country of interest. Submit a comparison summary of what you learned about the two countries. (c) Choose another category of information available at the site and submit a summary of your findings.

Case for Critical Analysis

Lincoln Electric

Imagine having a management system that is so successful people refer to it with capital letters—the Lincoln Management System—and other businesses benchmark their own systems by it. That is the situation of Ohio-based Lincoln Electric. For a number of years, other companies have tried to figure out Lincoln Electric's secret—how management coaxes maximum productivity and quality from its workers, even during difficult financial times.

Lincoln Electric is a leading manufacturer of welding products, welding equipment, and electric motors, with more than $1 billion in sales and 6.000 workers worldwide. The company's products are used for cutting, manufacturing, and repairing other metal products. Although it is now a publicly traded company, members of the Lincoln family still own more than 60 percent of the stock.

Lincoln uses a diverse control approach. Tasks are rigidly defined, and individual employees must meet strict measurable standards of performance. However, the Lincoln system succeeds largely because of an organizational culture based on openness and trust, shared control, and an egalitarian spirit. Although the line between managers and workers at Lincoln is firmly drawn, managers respect the expertise of production workers and value their contributions to many aspects of the business. The company has an open-door pol-

icy for all top executives, middle managers, and production workers, and regular face-to-face communication is encouraged. Workers are expected to challenge management if they believe practices or compensation rates are unfair. Most workers are hired right out of high school, then trained and cross-trained to perform different jobs. Some eventually are promoted to executive positions, because Lincoln believes in promoting from within. Many Lincoln workers stay with the company for life.

One of Lincoln's founders felt that organizations should be based on certain values, including honesty, trustworthiness, openness, self-management, loyalty, accountability, and cooperativeness. These values continue to form the core of Lincoln's culture, and management regularly rewards employees who manifest them. Because Lincoln so effectively socializes employees, they exercise a great degree of self-control on the job. Production workers are paid on a piece-rate system, plus merit pay based on performance. Employees also are eligible for annual bonuses that fluctuate according to the company's fortunes, and they participate in stock purchase plans. Bonuses are based on a number of factors, such as productivity, quality, dependability, and cooperation with others. Factory workers at Lincoln have been known to earn more than $100,000 a year, and the average compensation in 1996 was $62,000. However, there also are other, less tangible rewards. Pride of workmanship and feelings of involvement, contribution, and esprit de corps are intrinsic rewards that flourish at Lincoln Electric. Cross-functional teams, empowered to make decisions, take responsibility for product planning, development, and marketing. Information about the company's operations and financial performance is openly shared with workers throughout the company.

Lincoln places emphasis on anticipating and solving customer problems. Sales representatives are given the technical training they need to understand customer needs, help customers understand and use Lincoln's products, and solve problems. This customer focus is backed up by attention to the production process through the use of strict accountability standards and formal measurements for productivity, quality, and innovation for all employees. In addition, a software program called Rhythm is used to streamline the flow of goods and materials in the production process.

Lincoln's system has worked extremely well in the United States. The cultural values, open communication, and formal control and reward systems interact to align the goals of managers, workers, and the organization as well as encourage learning and growth. Now Lincoln is discovering

whether its system can hold up overseas. Although most of Lincoln's profits come from domestic operations, and a foreign venture in the 1990s lost a lot of money for the company, top managers want to expand globally because foreign markets are growing much more rapidly than domestic markets. Thus far, Lincoln managers have not developed a strategic control plan for global operations, relying instead on duplicating the domestic Lincoln system.

Questions

1. What types of control—feedforward, concurrent, or feedback—are illustrated in this case? Explain.

2. Based on what you've just read, what do you think makes the Lincoln System so successful?

3. What changes might Lincoln managers have to make to adapt their management system to overseas operations?

SOURCE: Joseph Maciariello, "A Pattern of Success: Can This Company Be Duplicated?" *Drucker Management,* 1 (1) (Spring 1997), pp. 7–11.

Endnotes

1 Lawrence M. Fisher, "Inside Dell Computer Corporation," *Strategy and Business,* Issue 10, first quarter 1998, 68–75.

2 "Quality: The Soul of Productivity, the Key to Future Business Growth," Interview, Inter-City Gas Corporation, vol. 3 (autumn 1988), 3–5.

3 Douglas S. Sherwin, "The Meaning of Control," *Dunn's Business Review,* January 1956.

4 Jeannie Cameron, "Death of Traditional Accounting Will Prove to Be a Boon," *The Asian Wall Street Journal,* April 27, 1998, 16.

5 Anne Field, "Mapping Bears Fruit," *Inc.,* June 15, 1999, p. 93; Ronald E. Yates, "High-Tech Farming Sows Success," *Chicago Tribune,* May 12, 1996, pp. 5–6.

6 Steve Stecklow, "Kentucky's Teachers Get Bonuses, but Some Are Caught Cheating," *The Wall Street Journal,* September 2, 1997, p. A1, A5.

7 Cathy Lazere, "All Together Now," *CFO,* February 1998, pp 28–34, 36.

8 Sherwin, "The Meaning of Control."

9 Anna Wilde Mathews, "New Gadgets Trace Truckers' Every Move," *The Wall Street Journal,* July 14, 1997, p. B10.

10 John Case, "Keeping Score," *Inc.,* June 1998, p. 84.

11 Emily Esterson, "First-Class Delivery," *Inc.* Technology, September 15, 1998, p. 89.

12 W. Bouce Chew, "No-Nonsense Guide to Measuring Productivity," *Harvard Business Review* (January–February 1988), pp. 110–118.

13 John Lorinc, "Dr. Deming's Traveling Quality Show," *Canadian Business,* September 1990, 38–42.

14 Philip C. Thompson, *Quality Circles: How to Make Them Work in America* (New York: AMACOM, 1982).

15 Howard Rothman, "You Need Not Be Big to Benchmark," *Nation's Business,* December 1992, 64–65.

16 Christopher Farrell, "America's New Watchword: If It Moves, Privatize It," *Business Week,* December 12, 1994, 39.

17 Philip R. Thomas, Larry J. Gallace, and Kenneth R. Martin, *Quality Alone Is Not Enough* (AMA Management Briefing), New York: American Management Association, August 1992.

18 Kate Kane, "L. L. Bean Delivers the Goods," *Fast Company,* August/September 1997, 104–113.

19 Robert W. Haney and Charles D. Beaman, Jr., "Management Leadership Critical to CQI Success," *Hospitals,* July 20, 1992, 64.

20 Thomas Y. Choi and Orlando C. Behling, "Top Management and TQM Success: One More Look after All These Years," *Academy of Management Executive,* vol. 11 (1) (1997), pp. 37–47.

21 The Outsourcing Institute, "Outsourcing: The New Midas Touch," *Business Week,* Dec. 15, 1997, special advertising section.

22 W. E. Deming, *Quality, Productivity, and Competitive Position* (Cambridge, Mass.: Center for Advanced Engineering Study, MIT, 1982); and P. B. Crosby, Quality Is Free (New York: McGraw-Hill, 1979).

23 Charles E. Lucier and Janet D. Torsilieri, "Why Knowledge Programs Fail: A CEO's Guide to Managing Learning," *Strategy and Business,* Fourth Quarter 1997, pp. 143–146, 21–27.

24 Sumantra Ghoshal, *Strategic Control* (St. Paul, Minnesota: West, 1986), Chapter 4; and Robert N. Anthony, John Dearden, and Norton M. Bedford, *Management Control Systems,* 5th ed. (Homewood, Illinois: Irwin, 1984).

25 John A. Boquist, Todd T. Milbourn, and Anjan V. Thakor, "How Do You Win the Capital Allocation Game?" *Sloan Management Review,* winter 1998, pp. 59–71.

26 Web site of the International Organization for Standardization, www.iso.ch, accessed January 19, 1999.

27 Mustafa V. Uzumeri, "ISO 9000 and the Other Metastandards: Principles for Management Practice?" *Academy of Management Executive,* 11(no. 1) (1997), 21–36.

28 Perry Pascarella, "Open the Books to Unleash Your People," *Management Review,* May 1998, 58–60.

29 Don L. Bohl, Fred Luthans, John W. Slocum Jr., and Richard M. Hodgetts, "Ideas That Will Shape the Future of Management Practice," *Organizational Dynamics,* summer 1996, 7–14.

30 Bohl et al., "Ideas That Will Shape the Future of Management Practice."

THE NEW MANAGEMENT PARADIGM (PART 1, CHAPTER 1)

"I would much rather have a company that was bound by love than bound by fear," notes Herb Kelleher, president and CEO of Southwest Airlines. His simple statement speaks volumes about how his company, as well as others you see in this video, has adopted the new paradigm of management that emphasizes the values of change, technology, diversity, and employee empowerment, to name a few. As companies strive to remain competitive in the face of tough global competition, uncertain environments, cutbacks in personnel and resources, as well as economic and political shifts around the world, organizational leaders face a management revolution. Their ability to embrace these complex dynamics and skillfully guide and delegate authority to their managers and workers will impact the success of their companies. In this video, you will meet players who are fully engaged in the day-to-day aspects of this revolution, which has led to a new paradigm of management, the learning organization.

At Southwest, the "culture is designed to promote high spirit and avoid complacency," says Libby Sartain, vice president of the People Department. "We have little hierarchy here. Our employees are encouraged to be creative and innovative, to break the rules when they need to in order to provide good service to our customers." Southwest management focuses on customer satisfaction and empowerment of its 29,000 employees, rather than strictly on profits. For skeptics of Southwest's approach, the company is consistently named as one of the Top Ten Best Companies to Work For in America, is the recipient of the Triple Crown Award, and is the world's most profitable airline.

Dineh Mohajer, founder of super hip Hard Candy Cosmetics, agrees with the Southwest approach. "My motto is not to rule with fear, but to rule with empowerment, and to bring people in that are capable and that you can empower, and they can empower you. It's a very mutualistic relationship. That's the only way you can get anywhere." As a manager, Mohajer seems to have wisdom beyond her 27 years. The entrepreneur launched her company when she was a senior at the University of Southern California and sold her homemade sky blue nail polish to the Fred Segal boutique in Santa Monica.

Empowerment, a focus on people, is a recurring value in learning organizations. "Good people are very important, obviously, to the success of any company. They're the backbone," says Jeremy Hartley, former vice president of operations at La Madeleine French Bakery & Cafés. "We believe in taking care of our guests. But equally important are the people who work in the company, at any level." David Gatchel, former president and CEO of Paradigm Entertainment agrees: "In our business the real value of our company is in the employee base and maintaining good relationships with them."

Collaboration is part of employee empowerment in many of these organizations. Julie Cohn and Linda Finnell, two artists who became entrepreneurs, discovered this as they struggled through the first few years of their company, Two Women Boxing. Both Cohn and Finnell admit that early on they encountered some conflicts with employees. But they found ways to solve these conflicts as their company progressed toward the new paradigm of management. In one instance, they brought in an independent facilitator to help foster communication. They also learned the value of having employees contribute to design ideas. Rather than compete, employees and managers collaborate on designs.

A similar situation presented itself at a much larger, more established organization—Centex Corporation, one of the largest and most geographically diverse homebuilders in the United States. When top managers discovered that escalating land and construction costs were cutting into the company's profit margin, they turned to employees for help in coming up with innovative ideas. "We conducted a number of focus groups using our own employees to really start to get an idea of how the various trends we saw in society were affecting our own people. It brought people from all over our company together, who then saw they were important to the company—that they were participating in the strategic direction of the company," recalls chairman and CEO Larry Hirsch.

Fossil, like many companies facing the new millennium, is aggressively striving for a global presence, which is also part of the new paradigm of management. Richard Gundy, executive vice president of Fossil, explains, "We were started by a 23-year-old who had a vision, who is driven to be successful, who is driven to have a brand that is world dominant." Gundy believes that this global drive meshes well with the young work force at Fossil. "Having young people as management, young people throughout the corporation just gives us a new view on things all the time." Fossil capitalizes on this youth perspective, believing that it keeps the company forward looking all the time. In addition, Fossil leadership, rather than being autocratic as it would be in the old management paradigm, is dispersed and empowering. Tim Hale, vice president of Image notes, "Although there is a structure within the company, I feel like it's a loose structure. It is a tiered structure, but it is a structure that allows for a lot of interaction between very upper management and the very bottom guy who's working in the warehouse. And that openness, I think, is essential to the success of this company."

Finally, there's the issue of diversity, which is very much a part of the learning organization. Charles Brown, vice president and director of credit and consumer banking at J. C. Penney states, "The J. C. Penney company does place a tremendous value on diversity—understanding diversity, valuing diversity, and certainly embracing it. We see it as having a direct link with our associates, our workforce. We see the demographics. We see what's happening. We see the different consumer mix. We see the consumer becoming more diverse. There are more women in the workplace. There are more minorities in the workplace, more seniors. All those elements are part of our need to understand and value diversity." At Drew Pearson Marketing, Inc., partner and president Ken Shead agrees. "We have a multiethnic work force with one common goal. All of our employees are rewarded on an incentive-type basis. What that brings to our corporate culture is a quest to be the best."

As you progress through the text and video series, consider the ways in which each of these companies em-

braces the new paradigm of management, working toward becoming a learning organization. Note which are more advanced than others and why. Look for organizations where managers can say, as Susan Harmon, vice president of finance at North Texas Public Broadcasting, does, "I think you have a sense of mission that is very strong among people who work here. I think it means that they are willing often to work for less money than they could make on the commercial side."

Questions
1. Which of these companies would you like to work for as a manager? Why?
2. Choose one of the companies described here and explain how a manager's conceptual skills, human skills, and technical skills would benefit the company.
3. Choose one of the companies described here and write a memo predicting how you think a manager's role in that company may change in the next ten years.

HARD CANDY: BLUE TOENAILS TURN TO GREEN (PART 2, CHAPTER 2)

If you're going to start a company, it really helps if you are your own best customer. That way, you'll know the demographics of your market, and you'll have a jump on the competition. Chances are, your corporate culture will reflect your own personality and beliefs. You may even be a symbolic leader—providing a vision and helping it become reality. All of this has been true for Dineh Mohajer, the 20-something entrepreneur who started her own nail polish company when she couldn't find the exact shade of pale blue polish she wanted. Since then, Hard Candy has sweetened Mohajer's bank account, which sees $25 million a year in sales and is rapidly expanding.

Hard Candy's success isn't sugarcoated; it has come about for a number of solid reasons. First, its founder Dineh Mohajer understands the company's external environment and uses it to her advantage. And she has her well-polished nails in the demographics of her market. Her target customers are between the ages of 17 and 25, they like to shop in upscale department stores such as Bloomingdale's and Neiman Marcus; and they are willing and able to pay $12 for a bottle of their favorite nail polish in hip colors like Trailer Trash (metallic silver) and Sushi (aqua). If those two colors don't appeal to you, you can always try Tantrum, Jailbait, or the more subdued Mint or Sky. How does Mohajer know her customers so well? "I function like an average human being of my age," she explains. "I go to clubs, movies, and watch MTV." Mohajer knows not only to whom she can sell the polish, but also where to sell it. "I was approached by

many stores that were considered low-end, which didn't qualify." By selling her products in trendy shopping areas around Beverly Hills and Los Angeles, Mohajer attracts the type of customers she wants, including celebrities such as Madonna, Winona Ryder, and Alicia Silverstone.

Mohajer is keenly aware of her competitive environment—and the competition is certainly aware of her. Consumers can find $1-per-bottle knockoffs of Hard Candy polishes in drugstores everywhere. "We've been knocked off left and right by high-end and low-end cosmetic companies," says Mohajer. "It really says something when you're knocked off by Revlon." Being tuned in to the competitive environment is also part of understanding customers. "There's a benefit to being part of your market," explains Mohajer. "I know what I like. Revlon has to do market analysis."

Being head of a rapidly growing company like this means taking on the role of symbolic leader and developing a strong corporate culture, even though it may not seem to be a typical business corporate culture. "It is important to me that the environment I create for myself and for the people I employ is one that's creative and open and exciting and very, very much so, like, team spirited," says Mohajer. "You're only as good as your team is. You're only as good as the people you've empowered to do it for you. . . ." The atmosphere at Hard Candy is, as one employee puts it, "free flowing." Mohajer might conduct an interview with a journalist while sitting cross-legged on the office floor, and employees might be found singing in their offices. Mohajer often asks employees for their opinions on product colors, names, and so forth. "Dineh will ask everybody in the office for their opinions," says one staffer. "It's kind of like a collaborative brainstorm, and everybody gets involved, and I think everybody's input is valuable . . . not only with the creativity but also in terms of management and improving our operations and our systems." Hard Candy's management team is not entirely made up of people Mohajer's age, though. She has peppered it with a few seasoned marketing executives. Both Mohajer and her managers understand that the company and its culture are still constantly changing and growing; in fact, they embrace change as part of creativity. All of these factors, Mohajer believes, are what make Hard Candy such a sweet success.

Questions

1. Dineh Mohajer believes that she has an advantage over her competitors because she is "part of the market." Could this advantage ever turn into a disadvantage? Are there aspects of the organizational environment that she might not be tuned in to?

2. Do you think that Dineh Mohajer is an effective symbolic leader? Why or why not? Describe some specific actions she might take to reinforce her cultural vision for Hard Candy.

3. List some dimensions of Hard Candy's external environment that could contribute to uncertainty and threaten long-term success of the company. Consider sociocultural, economic, and technological dimensions in your analysis. What ways could Hard Candy help reduce the uncertainty?

4. Do you think you would be an effective manager at Hard Candy? Why or why not?

Sources: Jeffrey Zaslow, "Straight Talk: Dineh Mohajer," *Chicago Sun-Times,* June 26–28, 1998, accessed at www.usaweekend.com; "A Polished Kind of Girl," *Maxi* online magazine accessed March 18, 1999, at www.maximag.com; Ted Rall, "Marketing Madness," *Link, the College Magazine,* September 1997, accessed at www.linkmag.com; "The Best Entrepreneurs: Dineh Mohajer," *Business Week,* February 1998; Jeanne Whalen, "Dineh Mohajer" *Advertising Age's Marketing* 100 (1997), accessed March 18, 1999 at www.adage.com.

FOSSIL: KEEPING WATCH ON GLOBAL BUSINESS (PART 2, CHAPTER 3)

When Fossil watches first hit jewelry cases in American department stores in the mid-1980s, their appeal was distinctly American. Designed to bring back nostalgic memories of the 1950s, the watches became a fashion accessory instead of a purely functional item. Within a few years, Fossil founders Tom and Kosta Kartsotis had branched into other accessories, including leather goods and sunglasses. Then they decided to go international. Gary Bolinger, senior vice president of international sales and marketing recalls, "It was probably ten years ago Fossil became an international company. We made our first sell, I believe it was into Germany at the time. It was really just the last four to five years that we've concentrated on becoming a global company. And that's where you really take time to become a partner with a given, whether it be a distributor, a sales rep company, our own wholly owned subsidiaries. You're really involved in the community and the activities of a country, and you're part of the culture."

Clearly, Fossil has quickly come a long way from its initial domestic offerings toward becoming a truly global company, including entering into alliances with foreign organizations. Recently, the company announced a multi-year licensing agreement with Safilo USA, Inc., and Safint B.V. Safilo is one of the world's largest eyewear manufacturers and distributors, and it will design, manufacture, and sell Fossil brand optical frames and sunglasses in Italy. "Safilo provides us the opportunity to extend the Fossil brand into this market and to be represented by one of the largest companies in the eyewear business," says Fossil's Mark Quick.

Going international, then global, can be a complicated process for company managers. Fossil had to have market entry strategies for numerous markets, as well as strategies for dealing with competition. Bolinger explains, "It starts with product. You have to have the right product. Secondly, you have to have a marketing package that puts together your story. . . . That has to be uniform and cohesive worldwide. Third, and probably most important, is that [a] business system [must be] in place, the infrastructure, to deliver the product and the marketing to the proper channels and get it where you need it at the right time, the right place." Bolinger also notes the importance of finding the right partners to work with in each country, whether it is for manufacturing, distribution, marketing, or any other business function.

Part of Fossil's strategy for globalization is to acquire companies in the countries where it does business. "We own our own company in Japan," notes Richard Gundy, executive vice president of Fossil. "We own our own company in Italy. We own our own company in Germany, where we can get the management in there that has our vision, shares the passion for the brand, and can commit to the service that our customers demand in those markets."

In addition, despite the political and legal uncertainty, Fossil's strongest manufacturing and distribution partners are located in Hong Kong. Gary Bolinger explains that the reason for this is that Hong Kong has both the necessary infrastructure and the cultural attitude that "they can get anything done." After Britain returned Hong Kong to China, China agreed to leave Hong Kong's political system untouched for the next fifty years. Thus far, according to Bolinger, there have been few changes in the regulation of importing and exporting; and those changes have, in fact, been improvements.

The condition of the economic environment is, of course, vital to the success of a globalization effort. In Hong Kong, rents have decreased and salary increases have slowed, which benefits Fossil. In general, Bolinger says, "Currencies can devalue 30 percent in a day and bounce back 50 percent the next day. There's a constant change that goes on that you just have to monitor. . . . We talk with each of our distributors, if not daily, at least weekly with every country we're in around the world."

Fossil lies somewhere between a multinational and a global organization, having achieved this status in a relatively short period of time. Fossil sells over 500 watch styles, leather goods, and sunglasses in more than 70 countries worldwide. And that number continues to increase. When asked what the company's ultimate goal is, Bolinger's answer is direct. "We want world domination,"

he says. His company has no intention of becoming a relic of the past.

Questions

1. What characteristics do you think a Fossil manager would need to be successful in an international business environment?
2. Gary Bolinger notes the importance of infrastructure in doing business in Hong Kong. Name some specific features of infrastructure that you think would be important to Fossil's activities in Hong Kong and explain why.
3. How do you think the European Union might affect Fossil's efforts in Germany and other European countries?
4. What are the advantages to Fossil of having a licensing agreement with Safilo in Italy?
5. Based on what you know about Fossil's products, consider what types of cultural characteristics Fossil managers might want to consider as they enter new markets around the world, then list questions that managers might ask.

Sources: "Fossil Profile," Trade Media Ltd., accessed March 18, 1999, at www.asiansources.com; "The Fossil Story," and Fossil press release, "Fossil & Safilo Enter Licensing Agreement for Optical Frames," accessed at www.fossil.com, March 17, 1999.

LA MADELEINE: MERCI MARKETING (PART 2, CHAPTER 4)

"We understand the more we give, the more we receive. That's something we practice every day." Patrick Esquerré might sound like a kindergarten teacher or a preacher. But he's not. He's a successful entrepreneur who understands the importance of corporate responsibility.

Nearly twenty years ago, Esquerré, who spoke little English, opened up a charming little pastry shop on Mockingbird Lane in Dallas, Texas, where customers (whom he calls his "guests") could purchase fabulous French breads and pastries. Soon, La Madeleine, as it was called, became a gathering spot where neighbors could linger over freshly brewed coffee and daily baked treats. Within a few years, Esquerré had opened shops in Fort Worth, Austin, Houston, San Antonio, Atlanta, Chicago, Washington, D.C., New Orleans, and Phoenix. Now, La Madeleine is just as well known for its giving back, or "Merci marketing" as Esquerré calls it, as it is for its baked delicacies. "Merci marketing is something very natural to La Madeleine," explains Esquerré, who sold his stake in the company to his partners in 1998. "It is a way to say thank you even prior to receiving something."

How does La Madeleine accomplish this? Esquerré practiced leadership by example. More than a decade

ago, he began to donate food to the local food bank. Now, La Madeleine donates both food and money on a regular basis. "We help them by supplying them with fresh food. Not leftover food, but fresh food that is good for them," notes Esquerré. Fresh food includes bread, soup, quiche, and, of course, pastries. La Madeleine's annual contributions to community food banks total nearly $250,000. According to Robert Sank, director of the Dallas Food Bank, "The food bank serves 199 different agencies that operate food pantries, shelters, soup kitchens, programs like that. The on-site feeding programs would serve close to 500,000 meals a month. And without people like Patrick and La Madeleine, we wouldn't be able to supply the food to serve those people." In another demonstration of leadership by example, every Saturday morning Esquerré himself distributed breakfast to the homeless who would gather near Dallas City Hall.

Activities like supporting the food bank illustrate the discretionary responsibility that Esquerré feels his organization should take on. In addition, La Madeleine is a strong fundraiser for public broadcasting. Sank explains, "When public radio conducts their fundraising campaigns, Patrick offers to donate $1 worth of food to the food bank for every $2 donated to public radio." The pitch works. "We help PBS—radio and TV—everywhere we go to raise money for their pledge drive," says Esquerré. And I tell you, there's two weeks per year where every single day, or every single morning, where I'm on PBS just to help them raise money, and it does very, very well."

For an entire organization to be socially responsible, it is important for top leaders like Esquerré to foster the appropriate organizational values among managers and other employees. Esquerré does just that. Managers like Bill Buchanan, a regional manager for La Madeleine, note that Esquerré is key to the success of socially responsible activity within the organization. "Patrick Esquerré is unlike any man that I've ever met in my life. The environment that he provided for everyone to be successful and to care for others to give back to the community, in particular, has made an impact on my own management style, as well as how I conduct my life. With Patrick, the feeling that you get in your heart is tremendous when you have the freedom to take the food that you bake in your bakery and take it out and feed the homeless. To give it to the children that are sleeping on the sidewalks." Jeremy Hartley, former president of La Madeleine, builds on Buchanan's opinion about how socially responsible values are an integral part of the organization's culture. "Our sense of social responsibility, charitable work, all those things—I think it's driven a lot by being very guest oriented, first and foremost." A com-

pany that exists to serve its customers can just as easily extend that service to the surrounding community and those who are in need.

All of that service doesn't hurt the bottom line. In fact, it seems to enhance the company's success. Bill Buchanan says, "The most valuable thing for the management personnel who work with me is the fact that they have the special heart and ability to communicate with other people and to build sales."

Questions
1. Can you think of other ways that La Madeleine could practice "Merci marketing?" Describe them.
2. How does Patrick Esquerré's vision for La Madeleine illustrate the way he views stakeholders—customers, employees, and the local communities?
3. Describe a firm in your own community that is generally considered to be socially responsible. What types of socially responsible activities does it engage in? Do you think this behavior has increased the organization's success in your community? Why or why not?
4. Could social responsibility be taken too far? Explain why you do or don't think so.
5. Would you like to be a manager in the La Madeleine organization? Why or why not?

Sources: La Madeleine French Bakery and Café, at Web site www.lamadeleine.com; Company capsule for La Madeleine French Bakery & Café at www.hoovers.com, accessed April 3, 2000.

NORTH TEXAS PUBLIC BROADCASTING: BUILDING FISCAL STABILITY (PART 3, CHAPTER 5)

Nonprofit organizations exist in competitive environments just as commercial organizations do. In fact, in some ways a nonprofit organization faces even greater obstacles because it is competing with other nonprofits as well as companies for consumer, corporate, and government dollars, often without being able to promise commensurate products in return. But North Texas Public Broadcasting isn't daunted by this challenge. Instead, the nonprofit broadcasting organization, which operates television stations KERA Channel 13 and KDTN Channel 2, along with radio station KERA 90.1, simply incorporates the challenge into its planning process.

Planning, including effective goal setting, is critical to NTPB's survival. All three stations share the same mission, which is accessible not only to those who work at NTPB but also to the general public on the organization's Web site. The formal mission statement reads:

The mission of KERA 13, KERA 90.1, and KDTN 2 is to serve their communities by excelling in the production, presentation, and distribution of televi-

sion and radio programming and related activities that educate, inspire, enrich, inform, and entertain. One example is that KDTN 2 touches the lives of 300,000 Texas school children by providing education services to over 100 school districts, representing 700 schools and 28,000 teachers in North Texas. NTPB has many other programs as well that reach out into the surrounding communities and provide programs of the highest quality.

NTPB's mission statement influences the organization's strategic goals and plans. It takes money—lots of it—to produce and distribute high-quality programming to the public, and NTPB runs no paid advertising. The organization had an operating budget of $17,400,000 for fiscal year 2000, and must find a way to raise the money to meet that budget. Sylvia Komatsu, vice president of programming explains, "Our ability to raise funds has a direct impact on what we're able to do, on how we're able to meet our mission." Because NTPB serves local communities with thought-provoking, award-winning television and radio programs, a full 20 percent of the operating budget goes toward TV programming and educational services.

Although NTPB does sell a few promotional products, most of the money raised must come from noncommercial ventures such as several pledge drives for membership per year, as well as drives for corporate donations. (Individual memberships make up 50 percent of the annual operating budget.) Strategic, tactical, and operational planning are all connected to the organization's overall goals. "We work in a very competitive marketplace," notes Susan Harmon, vice president of finance and radio. "So when we're planning, even for the next week or the next year or the next three years, we really have to look strategically at what's going on in the marketplace."

Richard Meyer, NTPB's former president and CEO, explains further. "Planning goes on every single day. However, we have a budget cycle, and we know, from our records, how much money we raised through various pledge drives, which is only one source of revenue. We have direct mail, we have major gifts, we have underwriting, and so on. So, each year when we prepare the budget, we look at, for example, where the money came from in the past, what the factors are in the coming year, that we can absorb in our own minds to increase the revenue in each of the categories and then we plan how to do that."

Komatsu notes the importance of teamwork to all types of planning at NTPB, particularly strategic. "We work together as a team, because we have to know the big picture of the entire station in order to do our individual departmental budgets. . . . We all submit our projects to the business office, which then works with each of us and coordinates with each of us to make sure that we arrive at an overall budget that we think meets the needs of each of the departments that we have at our station."

In addition to ongoing budget planning, NTPB has developed single-use plans for major projects such as the new $8.6 million telecommunications center it opened. Overall goal setting and planning for the new facility started at the top, with senior management and a community-based board of directors. Harmon recalls, "We did a very careful year's worth of planning with the board about what the facility would look like, about the budget, and how we would go about raising the money. We paid for a feasibility study where somebody went out and interviewed leaders in the community to ask them what they thought about our need for a new facility and what they might give towards it. So, we had an idea going into the campaign that the committee . . . that the leaders in this community perceived we had a need, and that at some level they were going to participate." In the end, more than 1,600 foundations, corporations, and individual donors contributed to NTPB's first capital campaign, which raised complete funding for the facility in a matter of months.

North Texas Public Broadcasting has been one of the top public broadcasting systems in the nation for more than 35 years because of its ability to meet its mission and remain in the black financially. NTPB managers believe the organization's success is due to good planning, which has kept NTPB in good shape. "One of the things we've discovered is when we show our balance sheet to foundations, businesses, and wealthy individuals and they see that we operate in a fiscally sound manner, they're more likely to give us money," says Meyer. Proof positive that good planning pays.

Questions

1. In what ways is NTPB's strategic planning different from that of commercial corporations? In what ways is it similar?

2. Describe some operational plans that lower-level managers might make to reach goals at NTPB.

3. Does NTPB sound like a learning organization? Why or why not?

Source: North Texas Public Broadcasting Web site, "About KERA/KDTN," "Membership," and "Educational Resources," accessed at www.kera.org April 3, 2000, brochure provided by North Texas Public Broadcasting, April 7, 2000.

THE HOLIGAN GROUP: A SOLID FOUNDATION FOR BUSINESS (PART 3, CHAPTER 5)

In today's fast-paced, high-tech world, most Americans' dream is still very old-fashioned: to own their own home. With the current strong economy, there are now about 1.3 million housing starts each year, but the housing industry is fragmented and highly competitive. Michael Holigan and his father Harold, of Holigan Homes, have simple, old-fashioned goals in this competitive market: "Our ultimate goal is to become the most profitable home builder in the United States," says Michael. "We want to be on the cutting edge of technol-ogy. And we want to provide the best jobs for our people." Such grand goals calls for a grand strategy.

Michael and Harold have one—growth. "Mike and I like to expand home building as widely as possible," explains Harold. "Home building to us is creating magazines about home building, TV shows about homebuilding, Web sites about home building, retail centers to help people sell homes . . . unique advertising vehicles to help other people sell homes." In other words, home building to the Holigans is a lot more than sawing boards and banging nails.

The Holigans have already achieved both internal and external growth in a variety of ways. They began their business in land acquisition and manufactured home building, then moved into conventional home building in the early 1990s. Their core competence was a lot like other builders' who were already in conventional home building, so they had to come up with a competitive strategy that created greater value for their customers. They chose a differentiation strategy, focusing on quality, something that many consumers would complain is lacking in current home-building practices. "Mike and I have decided that quality is gonna be the difference between our company and other companies," comments Harold. Michael continues, "We would build our homes a little different. We would use 2-by-6 walls, more efficient insulation, more energy efficient heating and air conditioning units. We would protect them from tornadoes with hurricane straps and tying the frames down to the foundation, things that most builders, volume builders won't do." To get the word out about their superior product, the Holigans made a 30-minute infomercial that was so successful they were about to change their corporate-level strategy.

Michael came up with a novel idea: Create a television show that would educate home buyers about the process of buying and owning a home. Called *Your New House,* the weekly show debuted in Dallas in 1994, was picked up by Home & Garden Television for 13 episodes, and eventually landed on the Discovery Channel. Now, Michael and Harold were forced to ask themselves, "What business are we in?" Along with the show came a magazine, then a Web site, and the formation of the Holigan Group, whose "total focus was to produce national television shows about home building and expand into other media," says Michael. So father and son were no longer just building homes; they were creating television shows, publishing a magazine, updating a Web site. This change in corporate strategy, of course, influences business-level strategies, which includes the company's approach to advertising (Holigan not only advertises its own products, it also sells advertising on its Web site to vendors such as carpet manufacturers, paint, roof tiles, and so forth), its continued efforts to create value (customers can "design" their own homes right on the Web site), and the development of retail centers for home buyers.

Synergy is an important characteristic of the Holigan organization, between father and son as well as among the different company divisions. Harold notes, "Mike is, without any question, the best long-range planner we have. . . . I, on the other hand, run the day-to-day operations on the home building, the factories that we own and the land development side of the business." In addition, father and son rely on good managers. "We've been extremely fortunate in being able to attract extremely good managers," observes Harold. "Managers that I have a lot of confidence in." Good relations also exist between workers and management. "The structure of both companies is very, very flat," explains Michael. "My father is the chairman. I'm the president and, I mean, we talk to everybody. It doesn't matter what you do at Holigan, we're there."

Michael speaks specifically about synergy on the media side of the organization. "The media side is a stand-alone and will make millions of dollars on its own side from the home-building company. But again, they're very, very interrelated. Everyone talks about synergy but hardly anyone does anything about it. My role is to make sure that the focus of the show, the magazine, the Internet stays on the same idea, that's to teach people how to buy and build homes."

The Holigans have proved themselves skilled at recognizing opportunities and threats to their business. Indeed, it appears that Michael Holigan will let no opportunity pass his company by. Threats, of course, include changes in interest rates, changes in the economy in general, changes in cost and availability of building materials, changes in the demand for new housing (and thus a change in consumer interest in Holigan's television show, magazine, and Web site). But Michael Holigan isn't letting these threats slow him down. "I'm 33 years old and have a great opportunity right now, probably better than anybody in the home building industry. . . . I'm working on the TV show, building the brand through the different types of media. I'm working on the franchising unit, designing it for the next year or so to start selling Michael Holigan Home franchises, the Internet, you know, pushing that to the next level." Indeed, Michael Holigan gives a whole new meaning to home builder.

Questions

1. What business do you think the Holigan Group is in?
2. List what you think the Holigan Group's strengths and weaknesses are.
3. The Holigans have adopted cooperative strategies through franchising and accepting vendor advertising on its Web site. What other cooperative strategies might help the organization?

Source: Michael Holigan Homes, accessed at www.yournewhouse.com, March 26, 1999.

GOOD DECISIONS DEFINE SUCCESS (PART 3, CHAPTER 6)

Every day, managers make decisions that may mean life or death to their companies. The programmed decisions are easy: order more paper, renew the office cleaning contract. But the nonprogrammed decisions are the tough ones, and managers who can make them skillfully will help their companies not only survive, but thrive.

Managers at each of the companies in this case have been able to diagnose and analyze problems, recognize opportunities, and deal with risk and uncertainty. They may have different decision-making styles, but they all manage to make good decisions for their companies. Jerry Yang and David Filo were graduate students at Stanford University when they began compiling lists of their favorite Web pages and created a free directory called "David's Guide to the World Wide Web." Filo and Yang used a conceptual style of decision making, evaluating a broad amount of information, to come up with a product that eventually revolutionized use of the Internet. "We realized that there weren't really any good tools out there to help you find what you were looking for," recalls Filo. "There was no organization of the Web. And so just for ourselves, we started things." They built a list of sites, continued to classify them, and attracted more users. When their hobby grew bigger than they intended, they transformed it into a search engine called Yahoo! Filo and Yang's intuition, which was really based on recognition, paid off. Today, nearly 2 million users access the Yahoo! site every day, making it one of the most popular sites on the Internet.

Wes Hoffman, Mike Engledinger, and Ron Toupal turned a problem into an opportunity when they were laid off from their software engineering jobs and decided to form their own company, Paradigm Simulation (now MultiGen-Paradigm, Inc.). "Paradigm started out as a company doing very high end simulation for the defense industry," says David Gatchel, former president and CEO. But then another problem—and more uncertainty—arose. The defense industry took a slide downhill, and Paradigm was faced with the problem of finding new customers for its simulation software. The company's managers recognized that the price of their product was an obstacle—three-dimensional simulation software cost around $70,000 and the hardware as much as $300,000. They decided to take a risk—if they could reduce the price, they could sell quite a bit more. The move paid off, and Paradigm was already serving a solid client list when Nintendo approached them to create a 3-D game, Pilot Wings 64. The rest, as they say, is computer game history.

Patrick Esquerré faced ambiguity when he emigrated from France to Texas. He barely spoke English, and he vaguely thought he might export professional rodeo back to his homeland. He didn't know what his goals were, what his alternatives were, or what the possible outcomes were. Essentially, he had no idea what he was going to do. "When I came here, I was the 'no'-'no' guy," says Esquerré. "I was not a restaurateur. I was not a baker. I was not a Texan. I was not a lawyer. I was not a bunch of things. I was just a guy that I call the 'extra virgin' because I came not knowing anything." At some point, Esquerré thought that introducing French cuisine to Texas might be easier than exporting rodeo. So Esquerré decided to conduct his own, unique market research. Esquerré stopped pedestrians and told them there would be a bakery nearby. When they asked, "A bakery with a brick oven?" Esquerré said yes. When they asked, "With old beams from the farms in France?" Esquerré replied affirmatively. So it went. "This was in fact the way La Madeleine was built. We tried to tailor the concept of La Madeleine to the way that our guests told us they wanted it to be," explains Esquerré. In his own creative way, Esquerré reduced the uncertainty surrounding his business venture by talking with his future customers. Now, the chain of La Madeleine French Bakery and Cafés has a loyal following in several Texas cities, as well as Atlanta; Chicago; Washington, D.C.; New Orleans; and Phoenix.

Not every decision works out perfectly. Drew Pearson, former wide receiver with the Dallas Cowboys, now an entrepreneur, has fumbled a few. Pearson started a small company manufacturing sports caps and at first sold his products to a wide range of retailers—department stores, discounters, even 7-Eleven convenience stores. J. C. Penney, who was an early customer of Pearson's, was unhappy with Pearson's expanding distribution because the retailer needed to charge higher prices for its inventory than, say, 7-Eleven. Pearson and his managers needed to sell as many caps as possible, but they also needed to keep their best customers happy. They considered several alternatives, then decided to refine the company's distribution strategy to better serve their clients and obtain a greater market share. "We separate our brands with the more involved looks on our embroidery on our caps," explains Ken Shead, president of Drew Pearson Marketing, Inc. The more complex designs go to high-end customers; the simpler ones go to the low end of the marketplace. DPM's decision paid off. Today, it is the only headwear company with exclusive rights to market Disney characters worldwide.

The construction business is riddled with uncertainty. Larry Hirsch, chairman and CEO of Centex, the nation's largest and most geographically diverse home builder, is one manager who is undaunted by the uncertainty and risk inherent in his business. He practices a conceptual and participative style of decision making, relying on hard data as well as input from individuals who can help him make a decision. In one instance, "We conducted a number of focus groups using our own employees to really start to get an idea of how the various trends that we saw in society were affecting our own people. It brought people from all over the company together who saw that they were important to the company, that they were participating in the strategic direction of the company." Centex has been responsible for many major public and private building projects, including Disneyland, the Orlando International Airport, and Clorox Company Headquarters.

Questions

1. Choose one of the companies in this case and describe its decision-making process in light of the decision-making model in Chapter 6 that seems to fit most appropriately.

2. Choose one of the companies in this case and draw a diagram like the one in Exhibit 6.3, filling in each space with information pertinent to that company's decision-making process.

3. Which of these companies would you like to work for? Why?

HUMAN GENOME SCIENCES USE IT TO FIND CURES (PART 3, CHAPTER 6)

Half a millennium ago, Leonardo da Vinci sketched the human body in such detail that for centuries, scientists and artists relied on his interpretation of human anatomy for their work. Today, his drawings—as beautiful and complex as they are—have been replaced by computers. Human Genome Sciences is one company that is using state-of-the-art information technology to probe the mysteries of human genetic makeup in order to find cures for all kinds of diseases worldwide. Human Genome Sciences is a bio-pharmaceutical company based in Rockville, Maryland, that employs about 400 scientists, doctors, and other staff in nearly 178,000 square feet of research facilities. The thing that sets HGS apart from other, much larger and older pharmaceutical companies is its heavy reliance on information technology for drug discovery. In fact, while the organization is researching its own drugs, it is earning substantial revenues by offering other pharmaceutical companies access to its technology.

It's one thing to gather vast amounts of data—it's another thing to turn that data into information. That's what Human Genome Sciences is good at. "[It's] our ability to go from large numbers of experimental results—on the order of several million over the last five years—and be able to make inferences about those experiential results using computational methods," comments Mike Fannon, vice president and chief information officer of HGS. HGS technology is able to automate the process of identifying and characterizing genes, involving information systems at every level, according to Fannon. "We capture information about human tissues, the source of the tissue, the organ system that it came from. . . any diseases that are associated with that. That goes into the database. Then our scientists make extracts of the DNA that's in those cells. All of that information gets captured in the database, and we track these samples through a production process that involves a variety of biological and chemical processing steps." If this seems complicated, it's just the beginning. "This is a very demanding computational requirement as well as a rather demanding data

management requirement that's involved here," notes Fannon.

By now you may be wishing that you could just take a peek at da Vinci's sketches and be done with it; there's way too much data here. But the key to HGS's success with its IT is that it meets the criteria that determine how well the system is functioning. The system quality and information quality are high. "We have integrated things to the point where the instruments can talk directly to databases so that there's really very little chance that information is going to get entered incorrectly," explains Fannon. Scientists who work at HGS all use the system in some fashion. "In the downstream analysis we have our own scientists who are contributing to the database for helping us understand characterization of the genes, results of various experiments that they might perform," continues Fannon. From an organizational standpoint, the system allows HGS to achieve its mission of finding cures or preventing human disease, first by understanding how problems can occur. "We're helping our pharmaceutical partners and ourselves by characterizing these genes and filing for patents on the composition of the sequence, and we speculate about the possible utilities that that might be good for," says Fannon.

Human Genome Sciences conducts its highly sensitive research with strategic partners, who have access to certain information through a secure extranet. "All of the connections between us and our partners are typically dedicated connections with hardware encryption devices so that anyone snooping on the network wouldn't be able to, to get anything of use," Fannon explains. "We use Internet firewalls to drastically limit the number of circuits that come into HGS. So we enable our scientists to go out to the Internet for their own research purposes, but we've established a standard that none of our sequence data gets transmitted across the Net. We use cryptographic authentication devices." If this sounds extreme, it is also necessary in a very competitive industry in which companies routinely spend millions of dollars to research and develop new products. Companies like HGS live and die by the currency and quality of their information, so they tend to protect it any way they can.

Although many of HGS's processes have become automated through information systems, top management has not lost sight of the human factor in scientific research. "We view automation as a way to enhance the way people do the work, rather than to replace the way people work," claims Fannon. "And especially in a research environment where really our biggest asset is our scientists' intuition and their ability to make inferences about the results of these experiments. Our emphasis has been on delivering information systems that don't get in their way." It makes you wonder, if he had had access to

the same kind of information, how would da Vinci's drawings have been different.

Questions

1. Why is it so important for managers at HGS to maintain the distinction between data and information?
2. How might HGS use knowledge management to enhance its competitiveness?
3. In what ways other than those described might HGS make strategic use of information technology?

Source: Human Genome Sciences Web site, accessed March 30, 2000, at www.hgsi.com.

HARD CANDY: FROM COSMIC CHAOS TO COSMETIC ORDER (PART 4, CHAPTER 7)

Dineh Mohajer admits it herself: She had no intention of founding her own company. She just wanted a certain shade of pale blue nail polish that didn't exist, so she made her own. Several high-end department stores such as Bloomingdale's and Neiman Marcus picked up on it, and five years later she was running a multimillion dollar company with 40 employees producing 60 shades of nail polish with such catchy names as Tantrum and Sushi. Ben Einstein, Mohajer's boyfriend and co-founder recalls simply, "The idea started as a way to make a little bit of extra money over the summer." Mohajer echoes that memory, perhaps still in shock over how quickly it all happened: "Basically what happened in the beginning of Hard Candy was it turned into this company overnight."

Success is sweet, but it comes at a price. In this case, Mohajer and Einstein didn't have a chance to build their company slowly, from the ground up. So, even though they had some basic strategies, the company lacked organization. Of course, decision making was centralized— but there were only two people managing the company and responding to demands from customers. Problems stemming from lack of organizational structure arose almost immediately. For instance, Hard Candy simply couldn't produce enough bottles of polish, in enough shades, to satisfy customers because the polish had become so popular so quickly. "It just got bigger and worse and badder and more insane every day," recalls Mohajer. "Every day that went by as we grew and this monster, like, took over my house and took over my bathroom and took over my relationship . . . it was too much." In addition to explosive growth, Hard Candy, whose initial strategy had been to target certain types of high-end customers and stores, began to sell everywhere, which ultimately could have hurt its relationship with the customers it truly wanted to attract. Jeanne Chavez, who is now vice president of sales, explains that the polishes

were going to "salons and beauty supply stores, and that really doesn't mesh well with being in Neiman Marcus or Bloomingdale's in New York City. So we had to really clean it up." As Mohajer puts it, Hard Candy was being run by "crisis management."

Another entrepreneur might have given up, sold the company, or gone under. But Dineh Mohajer decided to get organized for the long haul. "It came to the point where if there's not formal structure implemented into this organization, there's no way that this company can get to the next level," says Pooneh Mohajer, Dineh's sister. "We decided that the company needed a seasoned businessperson to come in and help lead the growth." So the young entrepreneurs hired Ernst & Young to find them a temporary CEO who immediately helped implement accounting systems, began inventory tracking systems, and formed a management team. Now Hard Candy has an organizational chart that looks a little top heavy, but that's because Dineh, Pooneh, and Ben share the position of CEO. There is also a chief operating officer who, according to Dineh, is "primarily focused on financial information and inventory systems." At the next level, "some of the first steps we took in strategic planning were hiring department heads," explains Chavez. "We hired a marketing manager, a production manager, sales managers throughout the country and overseas. We hired some in-house PR people and basically each of us focus[ed] on our departments." The company also has an outside management consultant "for the likeness and image, and developing the brand and making strategic choices about what the right things are for the brand."

The company seems to have the organizational chart of a very traditional, departmentalized company. It does—except for those three CEOs at the top. The founders recognized that in order to move their strategy forward, they needed to organize the structure of the company. And they adapted a vertical structure to suit their own needs. They are glad they did. "Getting, you know, good people to help with different . . . parts of the operation definitely was a relief," admits Ben Einstein.

Dineh Mohajer is also sold on the effectiveness of teams, both cross-functional and permanent. She uses them at Hard Candy whenever she can. "What I have now is a team of people," she explains. "That's what I've always looked for . . . worked for . . . worked toward, was assembling the right team, a team that can work together and grow a company." With her co-CEOs, she even forms a team at the top. "There's a core team that drives the growth of the company," she says. "The three owners, I guess, I guess you could coin them as CEOs, but collectively." They each have different talents and perspectives—Ben is the strategist, Pooneh focuses on the bottom line, and Dineh is the creative force behind product development. "It's nice because we kind of really balance each other out," says Pooneh. And balance is, after all, the ideal of any organizational structure.

Questions

1. Describe a specific situation in which Dineh Mohajer might form a cross-functional team, including who might be on it (representatives from which departments), and what goal they might be striving to accomplish.
2. Do you think that Hard Candy places emphasis on work specialization? Why or why not?
3. Do you think that Hard Candy will become increasingly decentralized as the company grows? Why or why not?
4. Do you think that having a team of CEOs will be effective in the long run? Why or why not? If not, what might be some alternative solutions?

Sources: Jeffrey Zaslow, "Straight Talk: Dineh Mohajer," *Chicago Sun-Times*, June 26–28, 1998, accessed at www.usaweekend.com; "A Polished Kind of Girl," *Maxi* online magazine accessed March 18, 1999, at www.maximag.com; Ted Rall, "Marketing Madness," *Link, the College Magazine,* September 1997, accessed at www. linkmag.com; "The Best Entrepreneurs: Dineh Mohajer," *Business Week*, February 1998; Jeanne Whalen, "Dineh Mohajer," *Advertising Age's Marketing* 100 (1997), accessed March 18, 1999 at www.adage.com.

MULTIGEN-PARADIGM, INC.: REALITY BYTES IN VIRTUAL WORLD (PART 4, CHAPTER 8)

Change, for better or for worse, is inevitable for all organizations. All kinds of forces, environmental and internal, drive this change. Outside the organization, customers may demand new products or lower prices, regulations may tighten or loosen, new technology may develop, competition may increase. Inside the organization, top managers may set a goal of rapid growth, employees may request better benefits, production may increase or decline. A decade ago, three young software engineers who were laid off from their jobs responded to the change in their environment by forming their own company, Paradigm Simulation (now MultiGen-Paradigm, Inc. as a result of a 1998 merger). Mike Engledinger, Wes Hoffman, and Ron Toupal saw a coming change in computer technology that their former employer did not—and they bet their careers on it. "That company did simulation and training applications, but they didn't see the computer graphics side as being all that important," recalls Engledinger, former Paradigm vice president of engineering. "They didn't think there was much of a future in it. As it turns out, there is, and we knew there was."

The three partners figured out a way to develop and produce three-dimensional simulation software at a price that was accessible. (Before Paradigm came along, 3-D simulation software products cost upwards of $80,000

and the hardware could run as much as $300,000. Paradigm was able to drop the price to $5,000.) Their core product was a tool called Vega—software that enabled both programmers and nonprogrammers to build interactive, 3-D simulations and virtual reality applications, meaning that average managers could use the product without knowing how to write computer code. At first, Paradigm focused on developing high-end simulation products for the defense industry. Next, it began to develop a client list that included Chrysler, Silicon Graphics, and BMW. Then Nintendo came along.

Paradigm was founded as a creative organization, by creative people. Nintendo approached Paradigm about creating a 3-D game to launch their Nintendo 64 console system, and Paradigm accepted. It came up with Pilot Wings 64. When the game sold more than a million copies, Paradigm's founders decided to reevaluate its original vision, with an eye toward a possible change in direction. They knew technology changes would be continual. But they had to decide whether a product change would benefit the company. "Technology has always been a core strength for us," says David Gatchel, former executive vice president of entertainment. "That's how we've distinguished ourselves initially, and that's something we continue to try to emphasize. We have an R&D [research and development] staff that continues to try to come up with innovative technologies that we can use to develop our products and stay on the leading edge of what's currently out in the market, as far as hardware or delivery platforms."

All of the signs of successful new product development were there: Paradigm managers understood what their customers wanted. Software developers were working on state-of-the-art technology, and all key employees were on board with the new direction. So Paradigm shifted its focus from defense to entertainment. The company began conservatively. "We started off really doing technical production," says Gatchel. "And as we've learned more about the business, we've understood that there's a lot of opportunity there if we could begin to do full production and control the creative side. So we've adapted to that, and we've brought on new staff to try to accomplish those things."

Although Paradigm values its creative side, the company is systematic in the way it makes changes. Formal goals are set, and new product ideas are fully researched in an organization that illustrates the horizontal linkage model (even if its founders wouldn't call it that) by fully integrating research, manufacturing, and marketing. "Normally we try to come up with corporate objectives each year," explains Gatchel. "One [objective] that we wanted was to become stronger in character animation, and it was clearly a weakness we had. If we could improve on that, we'd become much more competitive and we would have increased opportunities."

In a single decade, Paradigm has become a leader in the race to develop 3-D, real-time software technology, but company managers are not content to rest on their laurels. In 1998, organization executives announced another major change: a merger agreement with MultiGen Inc., whose products are different from, but complementary to, Paradigm's. "The synergy represented by this merger is phenomenal," exclaims Ron Toupal, one of Paradigm's founders and a member of the board of directors. "While the benefits to both companies are obvious, the true beneficiaries will be our customers. Together we will find efficient and innovative ways to deliver groundbreaking solutions to customers in a wide variety of markets worldwide." The benefits were further increased when MPI became a wholly owned subsidiary of Computer Associates International, Inc. (CA) in February of 2000. Merging products and organizational cultures will be perhaps the biggest change—and challenge—the company has yet faced. But so far, these leaders of the virtual world have proved themselves up to the task.

Questions

1. Does Paradigm Simulation appear to be a learning organization? Why or why not?
2. The last change described, the merger with MultiGen and CA, may not be accomplished as easily as some of the others. Why not?
3. In what ways might MPI and CA managers use OD activities to complete a successful merger of the two organizations?

Sources: "Computer Associates to Strengthen a Business Solution Portfolio with Acquisition of MultiGen-Paradigm," press release, February 9, 2000; "MultiGen Inc. and Paradigm Simulation Inc. Sign Definitive Merger Agreement," press release, September 3, 1998, accessed at www.paradigmsim.com, March 30, 2000.

YAHOO! MANAGING HUMAN RESOURCES (PART 4, CHAPTER 9)

When Jerry Yang and David Filo, two engineering graduate students at Stanford University, first created their directory to Internet Web sites, they did it for themselves. But the directory soon became so popular that they formed a company called Yahoo! in 1995 to market and expand their search engine. Forming a company meant hiring people and managing them. The company grew so fast in the first five years that if human resource management had not been addressed, it could have fallen apart. But the two did address the issue, and although everyone who works for Yahoo! likes to think that the organization is nontraditional, funky, and maverick, it still has a management structure, and it has a human resource department. "I consider Yahoo! a flat organization," notes Beth Haba, human resource manager. "It's an organization where, you know, your executive management is a team of about four or five people, and functionally there's about three functional areas. You've got sales and marketing. You've got engineering and operation type roles, and then you've got finance administration." And, there is human resources.

At Yahoo! the link between human resource management and organizational strategic planning appears right in the job description. "As the position acts as an important pivot between the strategic objectives of the corporation and the outstanding professionals who work there, the HR manager must be capable of developing partnerships with management while also serving as a resource/ombudsman for the employee populations," says the description for the position of human resource manager. Human resource professionals at Yahoo! work directly with managers to accomplish the company's goals. "Must be effective at influencing management, exhibit superior communication skills, work well in a quickly changing environment, and be able to prioritize and demonstrate initiative. Experience in integrating employee growth through mergers and acquisitions desired," continues the job description for human resource manager. In addition, as Yahoo! expands from its Santa Clara, California, headquarters to worldwide operations, its human resource professionals must be familiar with legislative and societal trends overseas. "HR professionals working in the international arena will need to ensure compliance with local laws and regulations, as well as work with Manager of Worldwide Compensation and Benefits to establish and manage competitive compensation and benefits programs in these regions."

Yahoo! uses various methods of recruitment, from in-house human resource managers to its Web site, where potential candidates can review the company's job listings and learn a little more about the company's policies. What kind of employees does Yahoo! want to attract? "Our workforce is a very young workforce and that kind of lends toward the spontaneity and creativity that we have around here," says Haba. "We prefer to hire obviously people who have . . . business degrees or engineering degrees. It's not necessarily required for every position. We obviously feel that a college graduate carries a certain level of maturity within the organization. . . ." On the Yahoo! Web site, candidates will find these remarks: "We're always interested in intelligent, adventurous people with backgrounds in software engineering, marketing, sales, finance, and information systems. And, honestly, that's just the beginning. The way we're growing, we're constantly expanding in new directions."

As a young company, Yahoo! embraces the new social contract between company and employees in a variety of ways. Part of this is a flexible work schedule. Haba observes, "This really, truly is a flexible environment in the sense that for the most part people can come in to work anywhere between . . . 8:00 A.M. and about 11:30 or 12:00 noon, and some people choose to work a later hour because that's when they're creative." Haba notes that Yahoo! does have an employee handbook that spells out more of the contract, but "we tried to add a positive, fun spin on it." On its Web site, Yahoo! describes the work environment: "From our highly creative (and highly casual) work environment, to the fact that we celebrate just about every success with a party. . . . Not to mention our funky yellow and purple color scheme. . . . At Yahoo!, we have a corporate culture unlike any other. And that's a good thing." What does Yahoo! expect in return? People who are willing to contribute to the "behind the scenes" action

at the company; people who are willing to learn and to take responsibility for their contributions to the organization. "Show us what you're good at; we'll see if there's a place for you at Yahoo!" proclaims the company.

Part of the new social contract includes benefits. Yahoo! has some traditional benefits and some less traditional ones. "Compensation at Yahoo! and in startup environments is typically, you'll have a base salary and you'll have stock options," explains Haba. "In Yahoo!'s case now we're a public company and to some regards that is a big incentive because you know that the stock has value. . . . Stock options at Yahoo! are offered to every regular full-time hire that has benefits, which is a very, very neat thing." As for salaries, Haba notes that "basically, we base all of our salaries on market wages and internal equity to make sure that we're, you know, compensating people fairly internally so that you don't have problems from an internal standpoint." Other employee benefits include a 401(k) plan; vacation time; medical, dental, vision, and life insurance benefits; education reimbursement; domestic partner coverage; sick days and paid holidays; a catered lunch program; and membership at an upscale health club. "Everyone here puts their all into everything they do, and we reward them with a generous compensation package," claims the company on its Web site. According to the new contract, much is expected of every employee—but employees are valued and rewarded for their contributions to the organization. Yahoo! illustrates how a young, creative, aggressive company can use human resource management to help the organization grow and remain competitive in a rapidly changing, highly competitive environment.

Questions

1. What questions might Yahoo! human resource managers ask in order to forecast human resource needs for the next five years?
2. What types of selection devices would be most appropriate for design or engineering job candidates at Yahoo!? What types of selection devices would be most appropriate for marketing and sales candidates? For customer care candidates?
3. Would you call Yahoo! a learning organization? Why or why not?

Source: Yahoo! Web site, accessed March 30, 2000, at www.yahoo.com.

J. C. PENNEY: DOING DIVERSITY RIGHT (PART 4, CHAPTER 10)

When James Cash Penney opened his first retail store in Kemmerer, Wyoming, in 1902, he called it "The Golden Rule." Penney promised that he would treat his customers as he would wish to be treated—with courtesy and respect—and would offer high-quality merchandise and low prices. The golden rule also applied to employees, whom Penney referred to as associates. "If there is a secret of good management in the business of living, it lies in the partnerships we make," explained Penney in a speech before a gathering of associates to celebrate the company's 40th anniversary. "For no man is sufficient unto himself. I say partners because we believe that all our associates work together as partners. We make our selection of partners according to the character qualities that best fit into our business. That builds rapidly into the principles of our business. . . . Honor, Confidence, Service and Cooperation." Whether or not he realized it at the beginning, James Cash Penney had planted the seeds of a corporate culture that would nourish diversity in a changing population.

Nearly a century after its opening, the name of that original store has taken on more meaning, as the J. C. Penney organization strives to manage an increasingly diverse workforce and serve an increasingly diverse customer base. Today, there are nearly 1,150 J. C. Penney department stores in all 50 states, Puerto Rico, Mexico, and Chile. More than 272,000 Penney associates serve 98 million customers each year. Penney's may be the country's largest department store, but its founder's philosophy of partnership and the golden rule still lies at the core of the organization's culture. During the last decade, the company has launched an aggressive initiative to support diversity and nurture ethnorelativism throughout the organization. The initiative includes a formal diversity awareness training program. "We have in place at J. C. Penney a Valuing Cultural Differences program," says Mary Rostad, former vice president of human resources. "It is a one-and-a-half day workshop designed to develop and to create an awareness for each and every associate in our company." In another move to meet the needs of diverse employees, "We've instituted two internal advisory teams—a minority advisory team and a women's advisory team," continues Rostad.

Penney's supports its training programs with a formal policy statement that applies to the organization as a whole. "We participated in the development of a diversity positioning statement, which for the first time established the company's position relative to diversity," notes Charles Brown, former chair of the minority advisory team and current vice president and director of credit and consumer banking. "And more importantly, we took that position statement and we put it in the hands of every associate in the J. C. Penney Company, so that they clearly understand that it's a commitment that the company has made to diversity. They clearly understand that it is everyone's responsibility to embrace diversity in this company." When the policy was finalized, it was introduced to employees in a video message from then-company chairman W. R. Howell who retired in 1997. "I want to talk with you about a topic that is very important to me and to our company . . . valuing diversity," the message began. "Each of us is a one-of-a-kind combination of physical characteristics, personality, gender, race, religion, skills, and ethnic and cultural background. This uniqueness of individuals is what we call diversity. Valuing diversity means respecting individual differences and appreciating the advantages our diversity offers. The golden rule asks us to respect each other regardless of our differences and to look beyond the differences to see what we have in common."

To carry out the policy statement, the advisory teams continued their work, including establishing a mentor program to provide positive role models for minority employees. Charles Brown explains that the mentor program was designed to help minority employees understand the corporate culture and thus be most effective within it. In addition, the advisory teams assisted minority workers in developing career paths within the organization, making certain that employees had equal opportunities for career planning and advancement. The teams also assisted the human resources department in its recruitment of top minority job candidates. Finally, the teams addressed the problem of the glass ceiling that women have traditionally faced. With Howell's support, the organization established a formal policy of accelerating the representation of women at all levels of the company, but particularly at upper management levels, including the executive committee. Recognizing that policies and goals are ineffective without accountability and measurement, Penney's made sure to follow through. "I think the important thing to remember with any goal is that if it isn't measured, it doesn't matter," says Cathy Mills, vice president of corporate communications. "And so, measurements were established—accountability measurements—where all members of the organization were challenged and held accountable for their efforts, not only to women, but the minority population."

J. C. Penney recognizes that if it can meet some of the special needs of its diverse employees, the employees will be more productive and more likely to stick with the organization. Rostad notes, "Here in our home office we have on-site child care, and we also have flexible work arrangements throughout our company, part-time employment positions, telecommuting, and a fitness center here in the home office." Mills observes, "We're finding more and more that initiatives that began in response to the needs of women are serving the whole population phase."

All of these programs and policies are terrific for associates, but how do they benefit the J. C. Penney organization from a business standpoint? Howell answers very clearly. "Our diversity gives us a real competitive advantage. So we must use this tremendous resource to the fullest. . . . This way we will ensure our continued success." Rostad addresses the bottom line. "Certainly if we have a workforce that mirrors our customer base, that will bring in sales and profits."

Questions

1. In addition to those mentioned by W. R. Howell and Mary Rostad, in what other ways might the J. C. Penney organization benefit from its diversity programs?

2. Based on its corporate culture, do you think that J. C. Penney is properly positioned to expand globally? Why or why not? What further steps might the organization take to manage diversity overseas?

3. Do you think a formal affirmative action program is necessary in an organization like J. C. Penney? Why or why not?

Sources: "J. C. Penney Names Kapplinger President of J. C. Penney," press release, accessed at www.jcpenney.com, February 15, 2000; Company capsule accessed at www.hoovers.com, April 5, 2000; company web site at www.jcpenney.com accessed April 5, 2000.

SOUTHWEST AIRLINES: POSITIVELY OUTRAGEOUS LEADERSHIP (PART 5, CHAPTER 12)

Launching a new airline requires leadership from someone who's gutsy, determined, and a maverick. Herb Kelleher, CEO of Southwest Airlines, is all of those things—and more. Twenty-nine years ago, when the first Southwest Airlines plane taxied down the runway at Dallas's Love Field, industry experts were certain the company would skid out of control before it ever got off the ground. Company founder Herb Kelleher wasn't just trying to start up a conventional airline; he was trying to start up a whole new type: a short-haul, low-fare, high-frequency, point-to-point carrier. Today, Southwest Airlines is proud to be the most profitable commercial airline in the world.

Everyone, including business experts and Southwest employees, credit Kelleher with Southwest's success. A true leader rather than simply a good manager, Kelleher began with a vision and had the ability to use his position power as founder and head of the company to influence employees at all levels to do everything they could to attain the organization's goals. His own traits were reflected in the corporate culture. One business writer describes Kelleher as "commonsensical, down-to-earth and pragmatic, with an underpinning of zaniness." She continues by cataloging Kelleher's many roles at Southwest: "coach, quarterback, cheerleader, sage, father figure, huggy bear, entertainer, friend, and legend." Kelleher's zaniness is what gets most people's attention. He's not afraid to dress up as Elvis Presley in public to make a point; he rides a Harley-Davidson; he's known for giving employees big bear hugs when he meets them in the hallway. Kelleher is more reserved and modest in his description of necessary leadership traits. "Tolerance, patience, and respect are very important to leadership," he counsels.

Kelleher calls himself a charismatic leader, and no one would dispute that. When asked in an interview why Southwest Airlines employees treat their customers so well, he answers, "Well, I'll tell you, I could give you a short assessment of that: I think it's the charisma of the Chief Executive." By necessity, he has also been a transformational leader. Not only has he brought about change and innovation within his own organization, but he has done the same to the entire airline industry. Noticeably, he credits his workers as much as—or more than—himself. Inscribed on a lobby wall at corporate headquarters is this tribute: "Our people transformed an idea into a legend. That legend will continue to grow only so long as it is nourished by our people's indomitable spirit, boundless energy, immense goodwill, and burning desire to excel." This description of Southwest's workforce is indistinguishable from many people's description of Kelleher.

Kelleher is very achievement oriented and stresses high-quality performance and improvement. When Kelleher first became CEO, he realized that the information systems department was spinning its wheels. "There were no programs or applications coming out," he says. "Just constant demands for more people and more machines." So Kelleher took action, creating a new corporate services department and focusing the department on serving internal customers as well as the entire company focused on external ones. He also recognizes that, in many cases, achievement requires participative leadership behavior. Recently, Southwest employees were engaged in a training exercise in which they were required to work as a team to create a structure that could hold a raw egg intact when the egg was dropped. What looked like fun and games was really training in meeting goals with limited time and resources. When the exercise was over, the instructor announced to participants, "It didn't matter if your egg broke or stayed intact. . . . My goals were met when you guys took this seemingly impossible task with limited resources and limited time, and nobody threw up their hands and said it was impossible"—a lesson in determination that all could apply to daily work.

Kelleher's views on both participative and supportive leadership are evident in his comments. "Our employees are encouraged to be creative and innovative, to break rules when they need to, in order to provide good service to our customers." In other words, they are empowered to make decisions based on their knowledge and good judgment. Once, when Kelleher stumbled on a technological problem, he learned that a team of technical and business employees had already begun planning the solution—an improvement that was later proved to be revolutionary in the industry—ticketless reservations. "We don't view leaders as just being top leadership. And in fact, our culture allows no elitism at all. We feel like we're all one big team. We work together as a team. And so we start with employees from the minute they're hired in training them to be good leaders." Participative leadership dovetails

with supportive leadership. "If you create the type of environment that a person really feels valued and they felt that they make a difference, then they're going to be motivated," muses Kelleher. Those are high-flying words.

Questions

1. Do you think that referent power is a factor in Kelleher's success with his employees? Why or why not?
2. Is Kelleher an autocratic leader or a democratic leader? Explain your choice.
3. Where would you plot Southwest Airlines on the Blake and Mouton leadership grid? Why?
4. Would you describe each of the three elements of the Southwest leadership situation (leader-member relations, task structure, and leader position power) as favorable or unfavorable for Herb Kelleher? Why?

Sources: Kathleen Melymuka, "Sky King," *Computerworld,* September 28, 1998, accessed at www.computerworld.com; John Huey and Geoffrey Colvin, "Staying Smart," *Fortune,* January 11, 1999, accessed at cgi.pathfinder.com/fortune; company web site at www. iflyswa.com, accessed April 5, 2000.

MOTIVATING EMPLOYEES (PART 5, CHAPTER 13)

In the early 1900s, employers didn't think much about what motivated employees. They expected people to show up at work on time, do their jobs, and go home. Working conditions in many industrial environments were sometimes harsh and hours were long, but no one complained. In fact, it may never have occurred to them to complain. Employees were happy just to have a job. Early studies of motivation, such as scientific management, were really designed to find out how to get more out of workers in less time. Punishment was not unusual, and rewards were extrinsic rather than intrinsic. Today, things have changed radically in the work environment. Treating employees right has become an integral part of the way companies do business in order to remain competitive. The companies in this case illustrate a new order in the approach to motivation.

Both extrinsic and intrinsic rewards are used by these companies, but the extrinsic rewards have a distinctly different flavor than they did nearly a century ago. Southwest Airlines, a company that is well known for its focus on people, uses the extrinsic reward of stock purchases. "Because every employee who comes in is a stockholder, they do focus on costs. We're the low-cost airline. That relates to the bottom line for them as well as for the company because when Southwest makes money, all of our people make money," explains Sherry Phelps, director of employment. Michael Holigan, president of Holigan Companies, describes the extrinsic reward system at his

organization. "Motivation of employees really depends on which side you're talking to. When you're with the home building side and you're talking to the superintendents, the motivation is a bonus structure according to how quickly they get a home done, and how few callbacks they have on warranties. On the sales side, it's totally a money deal, and it's also some patting on the back—having Salesperson of the Month. Seeing how much money they made, and encouraging them to get to that next level. We want everyone to become rich, and we're going to give them the tools to help them do that."

Most of these companies also focus on intrinsic rewards, satisfaction in a job well done. These rewards dovetail with employees' needs for relatedness and growth. "I want to put a broadcast schedule together that literally can give somebody the opportunity to learn a little bit more about themselves or the world around them," says Michael Seymour, vice president of broadcasting at North Texas Public Broadcasting. Susan Harmon, vice president of finance for the same organization notes, "I think it means that [employees] are willing more often to work for less money than they could make on the commercial side. I think people want to work here primarily because they want to make a difference." Managers at Fossil Watch are clear that the company combines extrinsic and intrinsic rewards. "The way we motivate is to be very performance driven. We have a shipping goal every month," says Gary Bolinger, senior vice president of international sales and marketing. But Tim Hale, vice president of image, observes, "The thing that really keeps people motivated is when they see their idea put into play and make an impact. . . . When people see those kinds of rewards, it fuels an energy."

Reinforcement at these companies tends to be positive whenever possible. "I think it's important to recognize when people do well. To recognize them with words and appreciation financially," notes Dineh Mohajer, founder and president of Hard Candy. Promotion—also a reward—is perhaps the ultimate positive reinforcement. "Whenever possible, we believe in promoting from within," comments Patrick Esquerré, founder and former CEO of La Madeleine.

Meeting various types of employee needs is an important goal of human resource managers at these organizations. On Maslow's hierarchy, the physiological and safety needs (as they relate to employment) include good pay, job security, and fringe benefits. David Gatchel, former president and CEO of Paradigm Entertainment, talks about a corporate environment that mirrors the "safety" of home. "People can relax as far as they are dressed. The hours are flexible. We provide free soft drinks and snacks and distractions for people when they want to take a break . . . activities where the employees can relax a little bit, forget about a problem they're working on for a few minutes, and take a little bit of time off, and then refocus and get back to it." Yahoo! has a similar philosophy about meeting employees' needs by providing a flexible working environment that "lends toward people that do have obligations at home," explains Beth Haba, human resources manager. "You know, if they've got kids they need to be picking up later in the day, they'll come in earlier." In other words, these organizations strive to provide a worry-free environment so that workers can concentrate on their jobs. Other needs include those of belongingness and esteem. "We want people here at the Drew Pearson Marketing, Inc. to feel that they are a part of this team—that what they do on a daily basis is the reason why we're here," says Drew Pearson, founder and CEO of his own company. "And if we can continue to impress the importance of each and every individual to the organization, then I think we can have a chance to continue to be successful."

The issue of equity gained increasing importance among organizations during the last half of the twentieth century, particularly in regard to women and racial or ethnic minorities, as more and more members of these groups entered the workforce. Linda Finnell, co-founder of Two Women Boxing, notes, "We have an incredible number of women who have worked for us, who come back and talk to us about what it was like to work here, and they say it was one of the most wonderful work experiences they've ever had, as far as being able to flex their own hours and interject ideas into a design business." J. C. Penney, a much larger organization, has formal programs in place designed to promote equity. The move makes sense: since 80 percent of all purchases at the company's stores are made by women, the company has focused on moving women into higher positions within the company. Charles Brown, vice president and director of credit and consumer banking, describes the team set up to encourage advancement by minorities. "The team, early on, established really three priorities. One was to establish a mentor program. . . . The second priority we had was what we call career pathing. . . . And the third priority that we established was one of recruiting."

Questions

1. How do the issues of motivation discussed in the case relate to the concept of the learning organization?
2. Choose one of the companies discussed and describe how you would apply Herzberg's two-factor theory in order to motivate employees.
3. Assume the role of manager at one of these companies and describe how you would use empowerment to motivate your employees.

CENTEX: BUILDING COMMUNITY THROUGH COMMUNICATION (PART 5, CHAPTER 14)

Since its founding in 1950 in Dallas, Texas, Centex Corporation has become the largest builder of single-family, detached homes in the United States and was recently ranked number one in the Engineering and Construction category of *Fortune* Magazine's List of America's Most Admired Companies. A Fortune 500 company, Centex not only builds homes but provides customers with security monitoring, pest-control services, lawn care, financial services, and construction products. Managing all of these activities effectively requires superior communication throughout the organization. Recog-

nizing the importance of communication, Sheila Gallagher, vice president of corporate communications notes, "I think in any company, the communications philosophy has to come from the top."

Formal communication at Centex isn't just a phrase, and it isn't always that formal. Organization executives and managers look for all kinds of ways to use formal communication to disseminate as much information as possible to employees, customers, and stockholders. They also strive for channel richness in every communication event. For instance, when the organization went through a major restructuring, managers recognized that the change could create anxiety among employees and that information would help reduce that anxiety. "So what we have done is put together a slide show to tell everybody what the plan is . . . and we've gone around the country and met with each of [the] groups to try to answer any of their questions, tell them what the game plan is, help them understand why we needed to make the changes. . . . Our CEO of the parent company went with us on every one of these trips," explains Mike Albright, senior vice president. When the company acquired Vista Properties, "we also covered that in employee meetings and put out a press release to the media, which was received by . . . analysts, shareholders, and others," reports David Quinn, vice chairman and CFO of the Executive Committee.

Perhaps a company's most formal communication document is its annual report, which is usually distributed to top managers and stockholders. But Centex executives believe that everyone in the company should have access to this information. So a copy is mailed to each Centex employee at home. "We want it to go to the homes so that the families of the people who work here have a sense of what the company's about and how important our employees are to us," explains Gallagher.

Centex understands the value of stories and other informal ways of communicating—even if they appear in formal disguise. The company has put together a video called *The Movie,* "which gives a very good picture of the company and our operations," says Gallagher. "Another means of communicating here is the corporate newsletter called *Some Times* . . . so named because it only comes out sometimes. And in that publication, we capture all kinds of information about the company, what's going on financially, new products we may be building, new markets we may be going into."

Because of the organization's large size, much communication is decentralized, conducted face to face. "We get together in a very casual and relaxed atmosphere and have a lot of green light discussion, and it can be very energetic," comments John Lile, vice president of Centex Homes. Face-to-face communication also takes place between top managers and employees. "Centex executives get together with the employees several times a year," remarks Albright. "We generally try to do it for one of two

reasons. We either try to impart information to them or we try to solicit their views on various topics."

The importance of listening is hard to overstate. Although Centex seems to be continually finding ways to disseminate information, managers go to great lengths to listen. "We went out in the field and met with 20 different offices throughout the United States and asked them what they wanted from their healthcare benefits, what was important to them," recalls Albright. "We also have a very successful series of meetings called fishbowl luncheons where one of the executives . . . has luncheon with 10 or 15 of the employees who just put their names in a hat and are selected on a random basis, and [the executive] tells something about himself or herself and has an opportunity to answer questions," says Larry Hirsch, chairman and CEO of Centex Corporation.

The Centex organization's commitment to communication with and among its 13,000 employees in nearly 1,000 offices and job sites has paid off in its ability to continue growing in an extremely uncertain business environment. Centex now has annual revenues exceeding $5 billion. "We're very fortunate that our senior management is very committed to internal communication because of the way we feel about our employees," notes Gallagher. "We do feel like they're the heart and soul of the company." Centex management has learned how to listen—and make it count.

Questions

1. If you were an entry-level employee at Centex, would you feel comfortable approaching one of the top managers with an idea? Why or why not?
2. How might managers at Centex make positive use of the grapevine?
3. Do you think Centex senior managers chose the best channel and medium for informing employees about the company restructuring? Why or why not?

Sources: "Centex Ranked Tops In Its Industries on *Fortune* Magazine's 'Most Admired' List," press release, February 7, 2000; Trish Brennan, "Centex Homes Building Intelligent Homes in Houston," Centex press release, *Business Wire,* March 11, 1999; "Centex Homes and Its Chief Executive Named National Builder of the Year," Centex press release, *PR Newswire,* January 26, 1999; "About Centex Corp," accessed March 26, 1999, at www.centex.com.

SOUTHWEST AIRLINES: RANK & FILE TEAMWORK (PART 5, CHAPTER 15)

Teamwork is part of the organizational culture at Southwest Airlines, which is the most profitable commercial airline in the world. Employees even sing and dance about teams as part of a company video. "What a team," they exclaim. "What a family. From the top to the bottom, we're a fun factory."

If singing and dancing about teamwork is hard to imagine, then imagine this. At a Southwest orientation seminar, an instructor stands before a group of new employees and outlines their assignment. They will break into teams and work together to create a device (using straws and tape) that will protect a raw egg from cracking when the contraption (containing the egg) is dropped from a height of eight feet. How important is the assignment? Very. These employees are learning how to function as special-purpose teams within the organization, brought together to undertake a particularly important or creative new project. In another teamwork training exercise, employees work together to create an airline report card, discussing qualities of an excellent airline. At the conclusion of the assignment the orientation instructor explains, "No matter how impossible the task is, if you put your mind to it, and if you put your collective minds to it, you can do whatever it takes to keep this airline on top." Collaboration and creative problem solving are the keys to Southwest's success—what it calls "positively outrageous service."

Training employees to become effective team members is a vital part of Southwest's organizational strategy. "We feel like we're all one big team," notes Libby Sartain, vice president of people. "We work together as a team. And so we start with employees from the minute they're hired in training them to be good leaders." The company also recruits and hires people who show potential as good team members. "We hire people who show a high degree of commitment to team work," continues Sartain, "and a high interest in being part of the company. When someone joins the company, we have a continuous learning process, and they go to training."

How does teamwork training translate to results at Southwest? One special-purpose team consisting of technical and business employees identified problems in the reservations system and began immediately to plan a new innovation—ticketless reservations—without the nod from CEO Herb Kelleher. They simply recognized a problem and went to work. Ticketless reservations quickly became a revolution in the airline industry. "We were really forced into it," Kelleher now recalls. "It grew out of necessity, and our people did a fabulous job. All of a sudden, the whole U.S. airline industry had to go ticketless because people liked it so much." One reason the team was so effective was that it was able to move quickly as a special-purpose team—something like entrepreneurs within the larger organization. Satisfaction and productive output were high. "I tell our people to try

to preserve that entrepreneurial quickness and alertness," says Kelleher. Still another team developed Southwest's Web site, complete with company home page (the first in the airline industry). "It was done all inside by our own people," boasts Kelleher. "No consultants whatsoever. And everybody loves the Web page." Joyce Rogge, vice president of marketing, describes how Kelleher empowers his teams. "He sets the blueprint and clears the decks and makes room [for the group] to let this explode. But we don't sit around waiting for Herb to tell us what to do. He hires good people and gives them the freedom to do their job."

Formal horizontal teams also exist at Southwest. Joint steering committees identify technology projects and prioritize them based on potential business benefits to the company. Kelleher allows these committees to function autonomously. "It's much too labyrinthine and complex a process to go through," he objects, with a hint of humor. "But I have seen them taking claw hammers into their meetings."

If a family is an example of a successfully functioning team, Kelleher views his company as family—and he says so. "Southwest Airlines is not a company in my opinion. It is a family with everybody well loved, well regarded, well thought of, and very important, likes each other personally." Of course, it doesn't hurt that this team-family is considered by many to be the best in the world.

Questions

1. Based on what you've read about Southwest's teams, what might be some of the norms for teamwork at Southwest?

2. Assume the role of a Southwest manager and describe how you would set up a self-directed team to improve productivity in your department.

3. All Southwest employees own stock in the company. How does this help form teamwork? What factors other than financial reward seem to be the key to Southwest teamwork success?

Source: Kathleen Melymuka, "Sky King," *Computerworld,* September 28, 1998, accessed at www.computerworld.com; company web site at www.iflyswa.com, accessed April 5, 2000.

PIER 1 IMPORTS: MAINTAINING QUALITY AROUND THE WORLD (PART 6, CHAPTER 16)

It seems like a manager's nightmare, when everything is out of control: 800 stores, 12,600 associates, 5,000 merchandise items, vendors from 60 countries. In a way, it is. But that's the way Pier 1 Imports conducts its business, and so far, the nightmare has actually been a dream come true. The huge retailer achieved

$1.1 billion in sales during 1999 by selling decorative home furnishings, dinnerware, casual clothing, and unique gift items.

A retailer that purchases 85 percent of its merchandise, much of it handmade, from international vendors located in developing countries around the world needs to have a variety of controls in place for its processes and its products. Pier 1 employs a kind of cafeteria-style control focus, using a combination of feedforward, concurrent, and feedback controls whenever they suit the situation. The company also relies on both bureaucratic and decentralized controls. In short, Pier 1 chooses control methods the way it selects merchandise for its customers. "Our corporate values have really been based on relationships," observes Jim Prucha, former vice president of merchandise shelf goods. "Since we have this tremendous network of agents and manufacturers throughout the world, we depend on their continuity to give us great product year after year." Thus, Pier 1 practices feedforward control by hiring the best agents and contracting with the best manufacturers and uses decentralized control by empowering these agents and manufacturers, who are located around the world, to make decisions. "Our buyers may come and go," notes Prucha, "but our manufacturers and agents stay the same. They in turn help educate the buyer and help keep the buyers from making mistakes. . . . Normally we've got an agent for each major country that we buy from, and that person is pretty much in charge of representing us in each of these countries, whether it be quality control or facilitating a buy or actually going out and finding product for us."

Control actually comes home to a more bureaucratic approach when merchandise samples are transported back to Pier 1's corporate headquarters in Fort Worth, Texas, to be evaluated for quality. "One of the things that we need to do when we're evaluating quality standards for products at Pier 1 is first set what the standards will be," notes Steve Woodward, vice president of merchandise furniture. "We do that here in the sample room by first bringing the goods in from around the world and having the buyer set the standards here in the sample room. . . . After we sign off on the final standard, that standard becomes the rule." Then control becomes decentralized once again, returned to the agent and manufacturer, who engage in concurrent controls. "We constantly compare [the standard] with the production that's coming off the line," remarks Woodward.

"Once the order is placed, it is up to the agent and his staff to actually monitor the manufacturing of this product to make sure that all the quality standards are maintained, that the colors are exactly the same colors that we buy, that the size is correct, that there's no issue of poor quality," notes Prucha. Practicing concurrent controls

over processes is easier said than done because most of Pier 1's products are handmade, and raw materials may be passing through several factories before a finished product emerges. So Pier 1 managers adapt. Woodward explains, "We've got one factory in China, for example, that has over 15,000 employees, and it is a logistical nightmare for them to have all the goods come together like we expect them. So we have to sit down with them on a constant basis reevaluating the flow of goods and what's coming and pushing back orders and moving up orders to help them with their production."

Feedforward and concurrent controls aren't enough to maintain Pier 1's high quality standards, so feedback controls are in place as well, with employees trained and empowered to identify problems and resolve them. "Sometimes we don't catch all the issues and we can catch it at our distribution center as merchandise arrives," says Prucha. "If it's not caught at the distribution center, certainly it will be caught at a store level as our store employees are unpacking merchandise." When that happens, Pier 1 notifies all company stores within 24 hours. Of course, if all else fails, customers will inform Pier 1 of any quality problems. When this happens, explains Prucha, "Our manufacturers do a very good job in reimbursing us. And we, of course, reimburse the customer for any quality problems." Because Pier 1 believes in monitoring quality every step of the way, the organization is able to control not only the quality of its products, but the quality of its processes as well. In this way, the store can offer shoppers high-quality, crafted pieces that look as though they are one of a kind.

Questions

1. Pier 1 produces low-tech products—handcrafted items made one at a time. How might company managers use high technology to implement process controls?
2. Why doesn't feedforward control completely prevent quality problems at Pier 1?
3. Why is it especially important for Pier 1 managers to establish standards of performance when products are brought to the sampling room in Texas?
4. Would you describe Pier 1 as a learning organization? Why or why not?

Source: "Welcome to Pier 1," accessed April 5, 2000, at www.pier1.com; 1999 Annual report accessed April 5, 2000 at www.pier1.com; Company capsule accessed at www.hoovers.com, April 5, 2000.

TWO WOMEN BOXING: THE ART OF BUSINESS (APPENDIX C)

Linda Finnell and Julie Cohn aren't experts in martial arts; they are experts in design arts who became, almost by accident, entrepreneurs. In 1983, artist Linda Finnell was commissioned by a nonprofit photography gallery to make boxes to be used as artists' portfolios. She asked her best friend and fellow artist, Julie Cohn, to help her fill the order. The two handmade each box in Finnell's living room, then went on to make and sell more boxes, cards, and small books. Julie Cohn recalls sitting on the floor among stacked boxes and joking, "You know, Linda, if we ever have a business, we should call it Two Women Boxing." Thus, Two Women Boxing was born—a new business idea, but without a formal business plan or venture capital (unless you count $400 in startup cash).

Both Finnell and Cohn had the energy and self-confidence that it takes for entrepreneurs to get their businesses off the ground. Tolerance for ambiguity was also necessary, particularly as their own self-images had to change somewhat as the business took shape. "The transition from artist to businessperson, I think, is an ongoing transformation," observes Julie Cohn. "There's never been a point in 13 years where I've thought, 'OK, now I'm a businessperson.'" In addition, there was no way of knowing what direction the business would take, or how things would work out.

During the first few years, the two entrepreneurs concentrated on selling their products as well as hiring sales representatives who could handle larger geographic regions and go to the trade shows where the company's new products were displayed. "I think a big turning point was when we took our rep on; in terms of our wholesale manufacturing, that was a point in which we had a showroom in the Dallas Trade Center," recalls Cohn. "Probably the next turning point after that was when we took a booth at the New York Stationery Show, and that really, for the first time, put us in sort of a national arena and [we] started taking orders—could we actually accommodate those orders?" In addition, Cohn and Finnell had begun to hire employees to help with production, which meant shaping, gluing, and sewing each item by hand, and eventually a part-time office manager. Two Women Boxing was now moving from the existence stage of growth to the survival stage.

By the early 1990s, the company was grossing nearly half a million dollars each year. Now there was a production manager, but because items were (and still are) made by hand, by about a dozen employees, there was a limit to how much the company could grow. That is still the case. "We are still so primitive in our technique and what we're doing that we again have to look at mechanizing to a certain extent or mechanizing to a certain extent even what

we do, because we just can't—and you can't—compete efficiently and effectively with what's being done overseas if you continue to manufacture by hand, especially in the United States," explains Cohn. So, Cohn and Finnell have developed what Finnell calls "a real global awareness that is essential to the business. . . . It's having to be aware of everything else that's going on from the flow of retail sales to the price of products that we import, to how we get things in from the Orient in between monsoon seasons. . . ."

Another strategy for growth is the licensing of designs to other companies, including fine china and accessories to manufacturer Fitz and Floyd and specialty publisher Chronicle Books. "It was very exciting to have the opportunities come to us to do the china that we did with Fitz and Floyd, for instance," says Finnell. "Where our designs could be taken completely out of the realm that we had for making things. The work with Chronicle Books has been wonderful in a different way, in that what it's done is really expanded our audience." Of course, not every such venture is without glitches. Cohn explains, "There's been some frustration with the outcome of the product. With Fitz and Floyd there were more compromises to be made because of pricing. And I think that is something that we've actually confronted in all of our licensing situations, is the price of the product. . . . We've overdesigned for the market. We've overdesigned for the price point."

But there have been artistic triumphs that hopefully outshine other problems. "I think probably the biggest high was when the Japanese department store Takashimaya opened in New York, and we were in Takashimaya. That, to me, was the Museum of Modern Art of retailing," says Cohn with pride. "It's one of the most exquisite stores I've ever been in my life, and to have the small selection of product that they do in that store, and to have us be a part of that, it was the equivalent of finally getting in a really good gallery." Proof positive, perhaps, that art and business do mix successfully.

Questions

1. What stage of growth do you think Two Women Boxing is at now? What steps might the company take to reach the next stage?
2. Two Women Boxing managed to start up without a formal business plan. But what kind of planning might now help the company succeed as it enters the new millennium?
3. In what ways might Finnell and Cohn promote intrapreneurship in their small company?

IN THE BEGINNING: A BITE TAKEN FROM THE APPLE (PART 1)

On April Fool's Day 1976, Apple Computer was founded by two guys who had been friends in high school, who liked to tinker with electronics, and who had dropped out of college to pursue jobs in the new computer industry in what would later be called the Silicon Valley of California. Apple was no April Fool's joke, although not many people took it seriously at first. Consumers hadn't yet grasped the idea that they could use computers for anything themselves. They saw large mainframes in secluded, air-conditioned rooms at work. But personal computers were still unheard of. Even businesses were reluctant to invest in computers for their employees; after all, they had typewriters, and calculators were available for number crunching. But Steve Jobs and Steve Wozniak had a product they thought they could sell: the Apple I computer, created in Steve Jobs's garage. The face of business, and daily life, has never been the same.

The Apple computer did sell—especially the second model, the Apple II. According to Jobs, it was the first really user-friendly PC, for three reasons. It was the first PC in a molded plastic case, rather than a forbidding metal box, and the first PC to offer color graphics. Most importantly, the Apple II was the first PC to come fully assembled to perform its applications, thereby establishing Apple as the computer of choice for nontechnical users. Within three years, the Apple II had earned $139 million, representing a 700 percent growth. Consumers were snapping up Apple IIs for writing and calculating as quickly as the company could produce them.

With success came further company growth, and the necessity for management. Through the first few years of Apple's existence, Steve Jobs controlled the business side of the company, taking on all of the management functions: planning, organizing, leading, and controlling. He hired a succession of presidents, financial officers, public relations people, and marketing people to handle the company's expanding business. Then there were the product design teams, midlevel managers, and ultimately, more and more investors. Although the atmosphere during the early days was radical—both employees and management liked to foster the counterculture image—as new investors began to take their seats on the board of directors, things changed. These older, more conservative directors insisted that the company be managed in a more traditional fashion. Many of the original employees became disenchanted with what replaced the pioneering company they had helped found, and some began to leave. Meanwhile, only five years into the venture, Steve Wozniak was injured in a plane crash and forced to take a leave of absence. Steve Jobs became chairman of Apple at only 26 years old.

As a young manager, Jobs certainly had technical skills. After all, the Apple computer was his brainchild.

Although some critics might disagree, he also had conceptual skills: he understood where his organization was and had a vision of where he wanted it to go. But Jobs has never been known for his human skills. Driven toward perfection himself, he expected perfection from his managers and employees. One former employee recalls that Jobs rejected anyone's work the first time he saw it, just on principle. (Employees eventually caught on to this, and deliberately showed him their undeveloped work first, saving their best work for later.) He earned himself a notorious reputation as a manager, one that has followed him to this day.

In 1981, a competitor of Goliath proportions emerged: IBM—the powerhouse of mainframe computing—introduced its first personal computer to the marketplace. Jobs, who was essentially an engineer, recognized that he did not have the business or management skills necessary to take his company to the next level. So, he began to pursue John Sculley, who was then president of Pepsi-Cola. He lured Sculley to Apple with the language of a visionary: "If you stay at Pepsi, five years from now all you'll have accomplished is selling a lot more sugar water to kids . . . If you come to Apple you can change the world." Sculley accepted the challenge.

As the company went public and began to compete with larger organizations like IBM, the people who had originally gone to work for Apple found themselves in a changing environment. Despite Jobs's iron grip, they viewed themselves as a young, hip, innovative group who did things their own way. Even though both Apple founders had dropped out of college, Apple workers were highly educated, creative, and technically skilled. They valued their independence, and most likely chafed under the new "business" orientation. On a larger scale, Apple was charged with changing the way the general public viewed—and ultimately valued—computers. As they introduced new products, it was crucial for consumers to make the connection between the computer and the way it could change their daily work and home environments. Apple was lauded for its product innovations and creativity, and its users became devoted followers.

The economic environment, both inside and outside Apple, was ripe for success. The economic boom of the 1980s meant that people had money to spend. But it also meant that competition, from IBM and other fledgling computer companies, followed closely on Apple's heels. By the early 1980s, Apple management, including new CEO John Sculley (who was a sharp businessman, but who didn't know much about computers), made some costly mistakes. For instance, the Lisa, which was the first mouse-controlled personal computer, was priced at $10,000, far above what the public would accept. No one bought it. And the Apple III was so filled with design flaws that the first 14,000 computers had to be recalled. That computer's image never recovered. Still, many more ups and downs lay ahead for the company as Apple continued to grow and change as an organization.

Questions

1. In what ways did Apple fit the old paradigm of management? In what ways did it fit the new paradigm?
2. From the overview presented in this case, what features of Apple's culture are similar to learning organizations? To bureaucratic organizations? What steps might Apple managers take toward creating—or strengthening—a learning organization?
3. Of the four management functions, which do you think Jobs excelled at? Which was his weakest? Why?
4. What types of roles does a person in Jobs's position at Apple need to perform? List as many informational, interpersonal, and decisional roles that you think apply and explain why you think so.
5. Do you think that you would have liked to be a manager at Apple during its early days? Why or why not?

Sources: Michael Krantz, "Steve Jobs at 44," *Time.com,* October 18, 1999, accessed February 14, 2000, at www.pathfinder.com; Apple Computer Inc. Web site, "Business Summary," "History," and "Steve Paul Jobs," accessed March 23, 1999, at www.apple.com; Brent Schlender and Michael Martin, "Paradise Lost," *Fortune,* February 19, 1996, accessed at www.pathfinder.com.

iMac photo: Courtesy of Apple Computer, Inc.

FROM MACINTOSH TO MICROSOFT (PART 2)

When they founded Apple Computer, Steve Jobs and Steve Wozniak were the kind of entrepreneurs everyone loves to read about. Both college dropouts in their twenties, they developed and built their first product in a family garage in Cupertino, California. When the Apple II took off, so did the personal computing industry. Not only had these two young men changed an industry, but some would argue that they changed history. If indeed they did, it was a fulfillment of Jobs's ambitions. Years later, Jobs told a reporter for *Fortune* magazine that his role models in the 1970s were "the semiconductor guys like Robert Noyce and Andy Grove of Intel, and of course Bill Hewlett and David Packard. They were out not so much to make money as to change the world and to build companies that could keep growing and changing."

As the company progressed through its early stages of growth, Jobs and Wozniak diverged in their managerial focus. Whereas Jobs became market driven, Wozniak remained more interested in the technical design of the computers the company built. Eventually, Wozniak left Apple to teach computer science in the Los Gatos, California, school system, another of his career goals.

At Apple, Jobs was about to launch the company's most revolutionary product: the Macintosh. The development of the Macintosh during the early 1980s was a direct response to Apple's competitive and technological environment. IBM had fought back vigorously after Apple's release of its first several computers, coming out with its own PC and surpassing Apple in sales only two years after doing so. In addition, engineers at the Xerox Palo Alto Research Center (known as PARC) were working on a product called Alto, which had a graphical user interface—with elements such as windows, menus, and icons. (Ironically, Xerox never brought the Alto to market because Xerox executives believed that it was too new and probably not usable. But Jobs and his team were allowed to visit PARC and were impressed by what they saw.) Jobs knew that his organization had to adapt quickly to this opportunity in an uncertain environment, so he made two major moves: he hired as president of Apple John Sculley, who was an experienced businessman from Pepsi Cola, and he began development of the new Macintosh product. During this time, to revitalize what was once a pioneering corporate culture, Jobs made efforts to create an environment in which the intelligent, talented, quirky, creative hardware and software designers could thrive. Jobs described his Macintosh team as "well grounded in the philosophical traditions of the last 100 years and the sociological traditions of the '60s." But Jobs drove the team through long hours against impossible deadlines. A reporter who interviewed the team wrote, "The machine's development was, in turn, traumatic, joyful, grueling, lunatic, rewarding, and ultimately the major event in the lives of almost everyone involved." Jobs spoke of the team in public and private as brilliant and committed gladiators. But while he thought he was fostering a spirited, revolutionary culture, in fact workers were exhausted and burned out.

In 1984, the Macintosh was introduced to the world in a dramatic 60-second commercial spot during the Super Bowl. At first, the computer didn't sell well because potential customers perceived it as an expensive toy. But once such products as laser printers and the Pagemaker desktop paging program hit the market, people began to understand how the Macintosh could improve many aspects of the jobs they did. So the Macintosh finally took off about a year after its initial launch. As Macintosh sales increased, so did the size of Apple Computer. Since the computer put more computing power into individual employees' hands, it had mass appeal. The industry was a natural for "boundaryless" corporations, and Apple began to expand around the world until it had an operating territory that included Canada, western and eastern Europe, Asia, South America, Central America, the Caribbean, Scandinavia, South Africa, and the British Isles. Interestingly enough, however, Apple is not yet a truly global organization. Although it has customers, partners, and developers around the world and offers products such as an operating system using high-quality type fonts for Japanese characters, Apple remains a multinational corporation, headquartered in Cupertino, California.

As difficult and driven a manager as Jobs often was, he didn't forget his company's social responsibility. During his tenure, he established several educational projects including Kids Can't Wait, the Apple Education Foundation, and the Apple University Consortium. Currently, Apple encourages employees to volunteer in support of its partnership with the Second Harvest Food Bank and Cupertino's Nimitz Elementary School. In addition, during the war in Kosovo, Apple donated computers to the Internet Center at Fort Dix, New Jersey, so that refugees could search online for information about loved ones.

With all the initiatives Jobs undertook to make Apple a formidable force in the computer industry, his position would seem secure in the company. But eventually, the intense personality of this original entrepreneur became his downfall. In a power struggle with Apple president John Sculley, Steve Jobs was voted out of the company by the board of directors in 1985.

A heated competitive environment can also produce some unsavory results, including companies accusing each other of unethical behaviors such as stealing or hoarding technology. In 1985, John Sculley became im-mersed in combat with Microsoft's Bill Gates over the introduction of Windows 1.0, whose graphical operating system had technological similarities to Apple's Macintosh operating system. Sculley finally got Gates to agree that Microsoft wouldn't use Mac technology in Windows 1.0, but the signed statement did not include future versions of the Windows interface. Thus, the stage was set for future lawsuits between Apple and Microsoft, which would continue well into the 1990s. More than a decade after the initial tussle, Apple and Microsoft were back in court, with Microsoft being accused of trying to sabotage Apple's multimedia software, Quicktime.

Questions

1. Based on what you've read so far, how do you think Steve Jobs viewed Apple stakeholders?
2. Jobs referred to the Mac team as gladiators. How did this image relate to the Apple corporate culture?
3. What steps might Apple take to become a global corporation?
4. In what ways do you think Steve Jobs, Steve Wozniak, and the company they founded have been important to the American economy?

Sources: Brent Schlender, "Apple's One-Dollar-a-Year Man," *Fortune*, January 24, 2000, accessed February 15, 2000, at www.pathfinder.com; Apple Computer, "Mac OS X to Ship with Highest-Quality Japanese Fonts and Expanded Character Set," news release, February 16, 2000, accessed at Apple Web site, www.apple.com, February 22, 2000; "Apple in the Community," Web page, Apple Web site, www.apple.com, accessed March 14, 2000; Ryan J. Fass, "Happy 15th Birthday Macintosh," miningco.com, January 25, 1999; Brent Schlender and Michael H. Martin, "Paradise Lost," *Fortune*, February 19, 1996, accessed online at www.pathfinder.com; "Apple in Higher Education," "History," "Steve Paul Jobs," and "Area List," accessed March 23, 1999, at the Apple Web site, www.apple.com.

APPLE MANAGERS DECIDE TO KICK, BUT MISS THE GOAL (PART 3)

The journey of Apple Computer is one of paths taken and not taken—goals, strategies, and decisions. Some decisions proved to be good moves, others not so great. With both of Apple's founders out of the picture, CEO John Sculley decided to capitalize on one of his company's strengths by pursuing refinement of the Macintosh, one of Apple's most successful products. In 1987, Apple introduced the Mac II, which was designed to be expandable, adapting to the market as technology changed. Customers seemed to fall in love with the Mac all over again, and soon the company was shipping 50,000 computers a month. By 1989, competitor Microsoft's software for PCs looked like it would be a flop in the marketplace, so instead of developing strategies to deal with this potential threat, Apple managers decided to ignore it and concentrate on goals and plans that involved only their own view of personal computing. Meanwhile, the IBM hardware manufacturers were gaining ground.

Within a year, the market was glutted with PC clones, and Apple was the single company selling its Macs. Microsoft then launched Windows 3.0, which was a graphical operating system (like the Mac OS) capable of running on almost all PC clones worldwide. Microsoft had taken a big bite out of Apple's share of the software market. Apple's managers were forced to reevaluate the company's goals, plans, and strategies or risk losing everything. Apple management seemed to be rife with conflicting goals and inconsistent viewpoints. The industry environment itself was filled with uncertainty and ambiguity, making decisions difficult—even risky—at every step. But managers came up with the idea to license the Mac OS. Some managers thought that doing so would actually reduce the quality of the Mac and perhaps create even more threats in the form of competition in its own system, but they agreed that Apple simply couldn't design and manufacture both the hardware and the software necessary to control the computer industry. Some managers even proposed the idea of licensing the operating system to run on the new Intel-based machines. But Michael Spindler, Apple's new chief operating officer, vetoed the whole plan. He said it was "too late to license." The strategy was dead, or so it seemed.

Meanwhile, new products were being developed. In 1991, Apple introduced the first generation of Power-Books, the first laptop computer to offer the kind of power saving and management features we now take for granted; it was an instant success. Backstage, designers were working on the Newton palm computer, which John Sculley took on as his pet project and personal goal. But the first Newtons, which relied on handwriting recognition and did not function well at it, sold poorly. Sculley was losing interest in the company, and within the next couple of years he was phased out.

Michael Spindler became the new Apple CEO. With a directive decision-making style, he drove the company to new achievements, which were desperately needed. Personally, he was not approachable and was most likely not keen on participative decision making. But he was extremely goal driven. Spindler entered an alliance with two competitors, Motorola and IBM, to produce the PowerPC chip, which allowed Macs to compete with Intel's speedy new processors. Spindler then reversed his earlier opinion and pursued a licensing strategy, licensing the Mac OS to several companies. But on later evaluation, it appeared that Apple was actually too strict in its licensing agreements, and only a few companies actually licensed the system. In the meantime, the alliance with IBM fell apart.

The mid-1990s were perhaps Apple's lowest point. Although corporate-level strategy continued to include building computers, business-level strategy failed in getting the machines to customers. During one year, Apple had $1 billion in back orders but lacked the parts needed to build the computers. Apple managers continued to fail in their competitive strategies against unrelenting Microsoft, which launched the powerful Windows 95 operating system in the summer of that year. Finally, Apple made a further strategic mistake by putting more marketing muscle behind its cheaper Performa than the mid-priced PowerMac (containing the PowerPC chip), and consumers weren't interested. The company posted a huge loss that year, and Michael Spindler was asked to resign.

Mike Markkula, a long-time Apple insider and chairman of the board of directors, proposed examining potential alliances with other companies, and at that time, in 1996, a big one was on the table: a potential merger with Sun Microsystems. "This isn't anything new," Markkula claimed. "Since 1986, we held serious discussions with DEC, Kodak, Sony, Sun, Compaq, IBM, and other companies I'd rather not name now. We considered everything from 'Let's trade technology' to 'Let's put the companies together' with each of them." But the merger never went through.

Gil Amelio, former head of National Semiconductor, took Spindler's place as CEO. His biggest and most surprising move was to acquire Next, the innovative but unprofitable company that Steve Jobs founded when he left Apple in 1985, and to arrange for Jobs to serve as a consultant to Apple. But under Amelio, Apple continued to post huge losses, and Amelio was out the door in a year. Critics complained that Apple was the only computer company to persist with the apparently foolish strategy of vertical integration—developing everything from the hardware to the operating system to the applications software. Surely, said the critics, this strategy was doomed.

Unclear goals and inadequately conceived strategies had pushed Apple from the height of success to the depths of disaster. The company had gone through four top managers, launched several flops, and seemed to be floundering, all because of poor decision making in an admittedly ambiguous environment. But all was not lost. The Macintosh would prove itself to be one of the most innovative, reliable computers available in the marketplace over the years—with a host of loyal followers. Apple was still alive.

Questions

1. It seems that Apple did not have a clear organizational mission during this period of its history. Assume the role of CEO and write a mission statement that you think would have helped the company clarify its goals and plans.

2. Based on what you've read about Apple so far, create a chart showing a SWOT analysis of the company, using one column for each of the following characteristics: strengths, weaknesses, opportunities, threats.

3. Do you think that John Sculley and Michael Spindler were effective managers during their tenure at Apple? Why or why not?

Sources: Brent Schlender, "Steve Jobs' Apple Gets Way Cooler," *Fortune*, January 24, 2000, accessed February 15, 2000, at www.pathfinder.com; Michael Krantz, "Steve Jobs at 44," *Time.com*, October 18, 1999, accessed February 14, 2000, at www.pathfinder.com; Michael Krantz, "Steve's Two Jobs," *Time.com*, October 18, 1999, accessed February 14, 2000, at www.pathfinder.com; Ryan J. Fass, "Happy 15th Birthday Macintosh," miningco.com, January 25, 1999; Brent Schlender and Michael H. Martin, "Paradise Lost," *Fortune*, February 19, 1996, accessed online at www.pathfinder.com; "History," accessed at the Apple Web site, www.apple.com.

THE APPLE MOTTO—THINK DIFFERENT (PART 4)

Think Different. The new Apple motto implies—and invites—change. "'Think different' isn't just advice we dispense to our customers: it's the ethic that guides everything we do," said the Apple Web site in 1999. By the mid-1990s, it seemed that Apple had been through as much organizational change as it could stand, most from the top down. Even changes that were designed to solve problems or increase the company's competitiveness caused more chaos, leading to more changes. Gil Amelio, Apple CEO for a little more than a year, instituted grand changes in the organizational structure, breaking Apple into seven separate divisions, each responsible for its own profits and losses. In late 1997, another major change shook the company: Apple's board of directors asked Amelio to step down and persuaded then-consultant Jobs to take his place, at least as "interim" chief executive.

Jobs quickly determined that Apple's cumbersome structure was ill-suited for what he saw as building on Apple's strength: innovating to offer computers that meet the needs of consumers. A simpler organizational structure and streamlined product mix would better position Apple to innovate. Jobs cut the number of product lines from 15 ("You couldn't figure out what to buy") down to four: the iMac desktop computer and iBook laptop for consumers and the G-line of desktops and PowerBook laptop for professionals. Jobs also replaced about three-quarters of Apple's top management, creating a simple structure with a few main divisions: design, software, engineering, manufacturing, and sales. One thing that did not change was Apple's strategy of vertical integration—developing and making computer hardware as well as software and operating systems. According to Jobs, this approach, when it was coupled with a lean, flexible organizational structure and a clear sense of mission, would enable Apple to take the lead in innovation. Innovations in its computers would extend the usability of its software, and vice versa.

But the most shocking change was yet to come: Jobs's announcement of an alliance with Microsoft, in which Microsoft invested $150 million in Apple. With the infusion of cash from Microsoft, Jobs turned to even more structural changes designed to achieve new strategic goals. In late 1997, Apple began selling its computers directly to consumers, both over the Web and by phone. The Web site, called The Apple Store, was an instant success. Within its first week, it had become the third largest e-commerce site on the Web. Apple began to show profits again. Over the next few years, as Apple shifted back to its beginnings and focused again on its core competencies, its organizational structure began to reflect clear strategic goals. Besides laying off employees, Apple created new types of jobs that were better "aligned with our new technical directions, customer needs and in identifying new markets." This meant restoring the spirit of a startup company that values innovation and change. Not only did Jobs simplify Apple's structure, he shifted executive compensation from cash bonuses to company stock, so that their rewards grow as the company does—just as at a Silicon Valley startup.

Steve Jobs began to call the new Apple "a really well-funded startup." As at a successful startup, the environment is lively, creative, hectic, and pioneering. "We've gone back to our roots," explained a recent edition of the company's Web site. "And though we're proud of our past, we live in the future."

This spirit infuses the way Apple manages human resources. Apple began actively recruiting employees via its Web site, where potential job candidates can learn about job openings, have basic employment questions answered, review company benefits, and e-mail résumés directly to the human resource department. Apple is a prime example of the new social contract with workers, who are expected to be employable, take personal responsibility for their performance, continue to learn, and act as partners in business improvement. In return, Apple offers creative development opportunities, continuous learning (including an education reimbursement program), challenging assignments, and necessary resources. Apple also offers intrinsic rewards: "the opportunity to work on great projects with some of the finest minds in the computer industry," according to its Web site.

Benefits at Apple are both tangible and intangible, designed to attract and keep the best workers. Compensation includes salaries, bonuses, stock purchases (at less than the market price), and a 401(k) plan. A program called FlexBenefits is designed to allow employees to choose the benefits package that best suits them. The company allocates what it calls "FlexDollars," which employees use to purchase basic insurance benefits such as medical, dental, vision care, and life insurance for themselves and eligible family members. If employees do not use up their full allotment of FlexDollars by purchasing these benefits, they increase their take-home pay or deposit the remaining FlexDollars in their 401(k) account. In addition, Apple has a health and fitness program that includes exercise programs, health education, and preventive care.

Apple relies heavily on training to continue to develop an effective workforce. Training programs not only provide workers with new knowledge and skills but also help reduce environmental uncertainty in an industry that is based almost entirely on cutting-edge knowledge and technology. The company has a number of formal training programs, including the Apple Learn & Earn

Program, which is available to employees in the United States, Canada, and Asia/Pacific region and is designed to help employees stay abreast of the many developments in Apple strategies, products, technologies, and solutions. In other words, Apple wants its workers to continue to "think different."

Questions

1. Do you think that the number of structural changes presented a unique challenge to human resource managers at Apple over the years? If so, what types of challenges can you think of?
2. How are culture/people changes related to technology/product changes at Apple?
3. Do you think the functional, divisional, or matrix approach to structure would work best for Apple as it faces the future?

Sources: Apple Web site accessed April 27, 1999, and March 14, 2000, at www.apple.com; Matt Beer, "Apple's 'iCEO' to Stay On," *San Francisco Examiner,* January 5, 2000, accessed February 22, 2000, at http://eXaminer.com; Michael Krantz, "Steve's Two Jobs," *Time .com,* October 18, 1999, accessed February 14, 2000, at www. pathfinder.com; Michael Krantz, "Steve Jobs at 44," *Time.com,* October 18, 1999, accessed February 14, 2000, at www.pathfinder .com; Brent Schlender, "Apple's One-Dollar-a-Year Man," *Fortune,* January 24, 2000, accessed February 15, 2000, at www.pathfinder .com; Guy Kawasaki, "Steve Jobs to Return as Apple CEO," *Macworld,* November 1994, accessed March 9, 1999, at macworld.zd-net.com; Sean Silverthorne, "Steve Jobs, Interim CEO—Now and Forever?" *ZDNet news,* September 16, 1997, accessed March 9, 1999, at www.zdnet.com.

THE LEADER RETURNS (PART 5)

Perhaps Steve Jobs is forever destined to be linked with Apple. Even though he already had a job—CEO at Pixar Animation Studios—Jobs continued to serve as Apple's interim CEO through the late 1990s. By 1999, industry observers began to predict that Jobs's interim status would become permanent, and they were right. At the MacWorld Exposition held in January 2000 in San Francisco, Jobs announced he was no longer "interim." (He did, however, like the title "iCEO," so he decided to keep the *i* to remind him of the company's plans to focus on the Internet over the next decade.) With both position power as top executive and personal power (as co-founder of the company and an expert in the field), Jobs couldn't lose. He appeared to be at the top of his game.

Jobs has always exhibited strong leadership traits—self-confidence, intelligence, energy, creativity, and achievement drive to name a few. Many people also consider him to be charismatic. "Steve's a pied piper," says Wes Richards, a managing partner at the executive recruitment firm Heidrick & Struggles. "People want to work for him. One of the great attributes that few executives have is that ability to recruit—which is usually dependent on the name of the company or on its brand." Jean-Louis Gassee, a former chief technology officer at Apple and now CEO at Be Inc., credits Jobs with using his leadership personality to turn the company around. "Steve is the ultimate salesman. And, he commands a level of respect that keeps his people focused and keeps them on target. This was critical to Apple's turnaround."

Jobs has not always received such high praise as a leader. In fact, his achievement drive actually caused him to alienate employees during earlier days with the com-

pany. A *Time* reporter describes the stereotype of Jobs as "a brilliant, driven man-child in sandals and shorts, screaming at underlings while trying to build the perfect digital machine." That stereotype, adds the reporter, "remains more or less correct." However, Apple employees have conceded that Jobs has matured, has been trying harder to become a consensus manager, and knows how to keep the company focused on its mission.

Even though Apple is now considered to be back on track (the return of Jobs and the introduction of the popular iMac personal computer have probably been the two greatest contributing factors), management continues to seek ways to attract and motivate employees. One way it does this is by recognizing and meeting employees' needs, at several levels. A progressive compensation and benefits package, including competitive salaries, stock purchase opportunities, and retirement plans, as well as a variety of insurances and a health and fitness program, takes care of existence needs. An environment that fosters teamwork and good relationships among employees (including informal opportunities to play basketball, volleyball, and billiards on site) addresses relatedness needs. And opportunities to take part in innovative projects with talented people drawn to Apple's culture cover growth needs. Informal communication is encouraged at Apple and is actually used as a motivational tool. At the headquarters alone, there are places to play games, cafes where employees can eat and chat, and a fitness center where staffers can socialize as they work out. Thus, the grapevine flourishes at Apple.

Apple products are almost always developed and marketed by teams, so the company recruits people who are team players. The company relies on all kinds of teams, from self-directed to special projects. Jobs himself recognizes the importance of teams at all levels in the company. He put together a strong management team to carry out the company's objectives, and industry writers have noticed that teamwork is now a priority among top executives, rather than the "intrigue and back stabbing" that characterized the management of earlier years. However, Jobs is well known for making life difficult for executives who disagree with him, and it may be that some managers go along with the team spirit in order to get along.

In two decades, Apple has enjoyed the highest highs and survived the lowest lows. And while the media have focused on the company's products, stock prices, and management upheaval, not much attention has been paid to the stresses that Apple employees have undergone. Long hours, nearly impossible deadlines, and uncertainty about the future are just a few of the stresses that workers have endured. Recognizing this, and the fact that employees need ways to manage their stress, Apple has put a number of programs in place that function as stress management techniques, including the fitness center, the open areas on campus where colleagues are encouraged to relax and chat with each other, and the various on-site informal eateries. In addition, the company tries to emphasize having fun in the workplace as a way to reduce stress. The formula of leadership, motivation, teamwork, and stress management seems to be working as Apple faces the challenges of the new millennium. "I love coming to work in the morning, and when I leave, I know that I helped contribute to our success," says employee Tammy Taylor. "There is strong leadership at every organizational level."

Questions

1. How will work-related attitudes among employees be important to Apple as it faces new challenges?
2. Do you think that Steve Jobs's leadership style has helped or hindered Apple's progression toward becoming a learning organization? Explain your answer.
3. Do you think that empowerment is a key to employee motivation at Apple? Why or why not?
5. What might be some barriers to organizational communication at Apple?

Sources: Matt Beer, "Apple's 'iCEO' to Stay On," *San Francisco Examiner*, January 5, 2000, accessed February 22, 2000, at http://eXaminer.com; Michael Krantz, "Steve's Two Jobs," *Time.com*, October 18, 1999, accessed February 14, 2000, at www.pathfinder.com; Charles Cooper, "Steve Jobs' Job for Life (or the Interim)," *ZDNN Tech News Now*, April 27, 1999, accessed at www.zdnet.com; Sean Silverthorne, "Steve Jobs, Interim CEO—Now and Forever?" *ZDNN*, September 16, 1997, accessed at www.zdnet.com; "About Apple—Employment," accessed March 1999 at www.apple.com.

APPLE IS BACK IN THE BLACK (PART 6)

Few companies have survived as much upheaval in the first two decades of their existence and come back on top as Apple has. But, by 1999, the company was again rolling out hot new products, some of which were winning industry awards. Sales of the iMac restored profitability, even in a niche market (worldwide market share remains in the single digits). Apple's portable model for consumers, the iBook, became the top-selling U.S. laptop in the last quarter of 1999.

How did the company manage to make such a comeback? The media seem to love crediting the return of Steve Jobs as CEO—it makes a great story—but Jobs himself, though generally considered modest, objects. "This is not a one-man show," he explains. It's much more complicated, involving more people. First was the issue of quality control and productivity. For several years, Apple products had failed in the marketplace. Their technology didn't meet customers' needs, they were too expensive, or they didn't live up to expectations. Much of the feedback that Apple received from customers, industry reviewers, and others, was negative. Apple also seemed to lose its confidence and focus on innovation. With profits down and layoffs looming, productivity declined as employees lost confidence in themselves and the company. Still, the visionary Jobs saw opportunity even in this bleak situation. He observed in an interview that "if Apple sold $7 billion worth of stuff, and it lost a billion, that means it spent $8 billion. That's a huge amount of money." In other words, Apple could spend $5 or $6 billion at the same level of sales and still earn a profit. As Jobs put it, "If you could eliminate waste and work to come up with a focused strategy, you have enormous resources to do good work."

So Jobs provided the vision for a more focused approach. Just as one product launched the company twenty years ago, one product helped turn it around—the iMac. Apple managers used their information system to obtain customer feedback about Apple products as they began to develop the iMac. "We have a lot of customers, and we have a lot of research into our installed base," says Jobs. "We also watch industry trends pretty carefully. But in the end, for something this complicated, it's really hard to design products by focus groups." So Apple designers had to implement feedforward controls to minimize the risks of failure and maximize the likelihood of delighting customers by offering more than they imagined asking for. "A lot of times people don't know what they want until you show it to them," notes Jobs. "That's why a lot of people at Apple get paid a lot of money, because they're supposed to be on top of these things." The result is that the iMac is a competitively priced computer that gives customers what they want. It is easy to set up and operate, comes Internet ready, is speedy and powerful, and most of all fun—with its rounded translucent case and rainbow of colors. This is more than concern with cosmetics; it is all part of a commitment to creating what Jobs has called "insanely great products"—an effort that results in continuous improvement. For example, Jobs insisted that designers figure out how to eliminate the fan from later models of the iMac. His rationale was simply that it would be more pleasant to use a computer that doesn't hum. Keeping a computer cool enough without a fan was a feat of engineering, but Apple's talented people seem to have pulled it off.

In addition to addressing issues of product quality, Apple managers have addressed quality within their processes, starting with feedback from software developers. "The real problem is that a lot of [software] developers have had a really tough time dealing with Apple over the last few years," admits Jobs. "I talked to these folks. It wasn't even about the volume of Mac sales declining—it was problems in dealing with Apple. We fixed almost all of that. The developers are coming back, and it feels really good. We haven't brought everybody back yet, but a lot of them." Improvement in product and process quality has led Apple to innovate again. "Apple is back to its roots, starting to innovate again, and people are sensing that, seeing it concretely, and really feeling good about it," says Jobs proudly. In addition, Jobs says that streamlining the organization has helped improve company processes. "The organization is clean and simple to understand and very accountable. Everything just got simpler. That's been one of my mantras—focus and simplicity. Simple can be harder than complex: You have to work hard to get your thinking clean to make it simple. But it's worth it in the end because once you get there, you can move mountains."

The world is taking notice of Apple's turnaround. The company has received praise for its G3 line of computers and its QuickTime media software, which allows multi-

media presentations to play as they are downloaded from the Internet. More recently, the company has generated excitement with the introduction of the iMac DV, which can be connected to a video camera to edit and enhance home movies. *Network Computing* designated Apple's WebObjects 4.0 its Software Product of the Year. WebObjects is a network product that simplifies development of Internet, intranet, and extranet applications. *Network Computing*, which reviews IT and networking products each year, said, "WebObjects makes development of Internet and e-commerce applications fast, efficient and scalable. . . . Along with substantial power and flexibility, WebObjects brings an ease of development rarely seen in industrial-strength development environments." High praise in a competitive industry. But for Steve Jobs, the highest praise comes from competitors' reactions: "Every PC manufacturer is trying to copy the iMac in one way or another. And you can bet they'll be cloning iBook next year. The same goes for our software. . . . And I don't mind." After all, as the saying goes, imitation is the sincerest form of flattery.

In some respects, Jobs and his company have come full circle—the winner's circle. Jobs is pleased. He likes to win.

Questions

1. In what ways might Jobs's leadership and values influence product and service design at Apple?
2. Do you think Jobs's decision to stay on as CEO of Apple will benefit the company? Why or why not?
3. Would you want to work at Apple as a manager now? Why or why not?

Sources: James Coates, "Apple Looks to Shine in Digital Video Market," *Chicago Tribune*, January 31, 2000, accessed February 15, 2000, at http://chicagotribune.com; Apple Computer, "PC Data Ranks iBook Number One Portable in U.S.," news release, January 25, 2000, accessed February 22, 2000, at Apple Web site, www.apple.com; Brent Schlender, "Steve Jobs' Apple Gets Way Cooler," *Fortune*, January 24, 2000, accessed February 15, 2000, at www.pathfinder.com; Brent Schlender, "Apple's One-Dollar-a-Year Man," *Fortune*, January 24, 2000, accessed February 15, 2000, at www.pathfinder.com; Michael Krantz, "Steve Jobs at 44," *Time.com*, October 18, 1999, accessed February 14, 2000, at www.pathfinder.com; Art Wittmann, "The 50 Best Products of the Year," *Network Computing*, May 17, 1999, accessed at www.networkcomputing.com; "Steve Jobs: 'There's Sanity Returning,'" *Business Week*, May 25, 1998, accessed at www.businessweek.com.

ENTREPRENEURSHIP AND SMALL BUSINESS MANAGEMENT

Entrepreneurship achieved cult status in the 1980s, and interest continues to grow. At college campuses across the nation, ambitious courses, new programs, and centers devoted to entrepreneurship spring up constantly. In the local bookstore, more and more shelf space is being given over to titles like *How to Run a Small Business* and *Entrepreneurial Life: How to Go for It and How to Get It. Rolling Stone, Time,* and other popular magazines always seem to have something on the subject. Computer technology and the Internet have given big-business power to even the smallest of companies. In addition, the enormous growth of franchising gives beginners an escorted route into a new business.

But, running a small business is difficult and risky. Two out of three fail within the first five years. Those that survive this period continue to face tremendous challenges. Despite the risks, Americans are entering the world of entrepreneurship at an unprecedented rate. Small business is booming, and most analysts see the trend continuing.

Becoming an entrepreneur means initiating a business venture, organizing the necessary resources, and assuming the associated risks and rewards. An entrepreneur recognizes a viable idea for a business product or service and carries it out. He or she finds and assembles the necessary resources—money, people, machinery, and location. The entrepreneur assumes the risks and reaps the rewards of the effort. The risks involve the financial and legal ramifications of ownership, and the rewards include receiving the profits from the business. Mark Moore experienced three business failures by age 22, but then found success doing criminal background checks for employers. With $800 and a leased laptop, Moore started Tenant Information Services (now TIS) to provide landlords with up-to-date eviction information on prospective tenants. When he expanded into criminal background checks on job applicants, his business really took off, and Moore is now doing $3 and $4 million in business a year. When Nancy Friedman started the Telephone Doctor, a company that trains employees in good telephone manners, her first seminar generated a 38-cent profit. Today, the company earns $3 million a year and serves clients on five continents. Moore and Friedman took the risks and are now reaping the rewards of entrepreneurship.

The Entrepreneurship Option

We've all heard stories about individuals who left corporate America and went it alone, or with a few partners, and with a dream—if not squashed in its infancy by worried parents, friends, and spouses—found success and happiness. Downsizing in the 1980s forced millions of people to look around and consider their options. Now,

entrepreneurship is considered by many to be a better use of their time and skills. They generally make more money when on their own, they have more time, more freedom, and a better quality of life. In a global economy, opportunity is greater than ever before, and technology has made it easier for small companies to compete. Candace Kendle Bryan and Christopher C. Bergen founded Kendle International, Inc., now a $44.2 million Cincinnati drug-testing company, when they grew "tired of office politics." In addition, more and more executives are voluntarily leaving big-company pay and perks at AT&T, IBM, American Express, and others to work for small startup companies, citing the opportunity to do something new, creative, and exciting.

Women and minorities, who find opportunities limited in the corporate world, often see entrepreneurship as the only way to go. Victoria Bondoc, the daughter of Philippine immigrants, is legally blind, but she didn't let that stop her at age 26 from using $1,500 in personal savings to start an information services and facilities management firm. Today, Bondoc's Gemini Industries employs 100 people and operates out of six offices in Massachusetts, New York, Virginia, and the Philippines. William Davis, who was downsized out of Occidental Petroleum, started Pulsar Data Systems, the largest black-owned computer firm. In partnership with IBM, Pulsar also helps incubate other black-owned, high-tech companies.

Women are starting businesses today at twice the rate of men. According to the National Foundation for Women Business Owners, women-owned businesses in the United States comprise 36 percent of the business population and are a growing economic force throughout the world. Women own almost one-third of all businesses in Australia, Canada, Germany, and Japan. Moreover, businesses owned by minority women are expanding at three times the rate of U.S. business.

Entrepreneurship and the Environment

Not so long ago, scholars and policymakers were worrying about the potential of small business to survive. Today, there are approximately 23 million small businesses in the United States, which account for nearly half the sales of all goods and services. More than 20 million Americans work out of their homes, providing financial services, high-tech marketing, political consultation, and software development skills to companies. These "solo professionals" began the millennium as the fastest growing market for phones, fax machines, and computers, and one-person offices constitute a $7.5 billion market for office and computer equipment. As companies continue to downsize, decentralize operations, and outsource more functions, the opportunities for solo professionals will increase. The economic reason for the boon in entrepreneurialism include:

- *Economic changes.* Today's economy is changing constantly and providing new opportunities for new businesses. Ninety-seven percent of service firms are small, with fewer than 100 employees.

- *Globalization and Increased Competition.* Globalization demands entrepreneurial behavior. Companies have to find ways to do things faster, better, and cheaper. Large companies with economies of scale are cutting substantial costs by outsourcing to smaller businesses or freelancers, which provides more flexibility and allows them to respond faster to consumer demands.

- *Technology.* Rapid advances and dropping prices in computer technology and the explosive growth of the Internet has created tremendous opportunities for entrepreneurs. From printing services and publishing to pharmaceutical and equipment sales to just about everything else, the Internet has made it possible for small businesses to achieve success. Rosalind Resnick runs a popular Web site, LoveSearch.com, out of her Brooklyn brownstone, aimed at capturing some of the millions that people spend on personals ads and dating services.

- *New Opportunities and Market Niches.* Entrepreneurs perceive and then meet the changing needs of the marketplace. John Erickson founded Senior Campus Living, Inc. to build and manage communities for middle-income retirees. SCL promotes a sense of community, making the sunset years of its residences socially stimulating. Anna Maria Arias founded Latina Style, a spicy mix of Hispanic cultural, business, and entertainment news after recognizing the need for a magazine to serve the 3 million educated, affluent Latina professionals in the United States.

Definition of Small Business

Most people think of a small business as any organization that has fewer than 500 employees. This general definition works fine, but the Small Business Administration further defines it by industry and describes "small business" in a detailed, complex, 37-page list of SBA regulations (see Exhibit C.1).

Impact of Entrepreneurial Companies

Approximately 600,000 new businesses are incorporated in the United States each year, and in 1995 alone, 807,000 new small firms were established, setting an all-time record. According to the Internal Revenue Service, approximately 21 million businesses exist, with only 15,000 of those employing more than 500 people. Further, most U.S. businesses employ fewer than five people and almost 90 percent employ fewer than 20 people. Clearly, entrepreneurs and their small businesses are driving the U.S. economy. The SBA reports that U.S. small businesses employ the majority of the private workforce, generate most of the nation's gross domestic product, and are responsible for 55 percent of all business innovations.

Exhibit C.1

EXAMPLES OF SBA DEFINITIONS OF SMALL BUSINESSES

Manufacturing

Computer terminals and peripheral equipment	Number of employees does not exceed 1,000
Motor vehicle parts and accessories	Number of employees does not exceed 750
Apparel and footwear	Number of employees does not exceed 500

Retail

Department stores	Average annual receipts do not exceed 20.0 million
Computer and software stores	Average annual receipts do not exceed 6.5 million
Sporting goods stores and bicycle shops	Average annual receipts do not exceed 5.0 million

Services

Business consulting services	Average annual receipts do not exceed 5.0 million
Architectural services	Average annual receipts do not exceed 2.5 million
Building cleaning and maintenance	Average annual receipts do not exceed 12.0 million

Miscellaneous

Book, magazine, or newspaper publishing	Number of employees does not exceed 1,000
Banks and credit unions	Has no more than $100 million in assets

Historically, entrepreneurs tended to start in business service industries and restaurants. But, the Internet has changed things considerably. Now, environmental services, children's services, fitness, and home health care have replaced them. The entrepreneurship miracle in the United States has become an engine for U.S. job creation, innovation, and diversity. Let's examine these benefits:

- *Job Creation.* One dramatic estimate indicates that, from 1986 to 1990, large firms created no new jobs, but the smallest businesses—20 employees or fewer—provided a 170 percent increase in new jobs. During 1996—the most recent year for which statistics are available—small, business-dominated industries produced about 64 percent of the 2.5 million new jobs, according to the U.S. Department of Labor. These jobs statistics give the United States an economic vitality that no other country can claim.

- *Innovation.* Cognetics, Inc., a research firm run by David Birch, traces the employment and sales records of some nine million companies and found that new and smaller firms have been responsible for 55 percent of the innovations—and 95 percent of all radical innovations—in 362 different industries. The "gazelles," or fast-growing businesses according to Birch, produce twice as many product innovations per employee than larger firms. Notable products developed by small businesses are cellophane, the jet engine, and the ballpoint pen. Virtually every new business represents an innovation of some sort, whether a new product or service, how the product is delivered, or how it is made. Small-business innovation keeps U.S. companies competitive, which is especially important in today's global marketplace.

- *Diversity.* Women-owned and minority-owned businesses are emerging as the next big-growth companies. In 1997 there were 6.4 million women-owned businesses providing jobs for about 18.5 million people. Women now own 34 percent of all U.S. businesses. Statistics for minorities also are impressive. Minority-owned businesses now represent 8.9 percent of all businesses, and the number is growing. Between 1982 and 1987, the number of businesses owned by African-Americans businesses increased 38 percent, Hispanic-owned businesses rose over 80 percent, and Asian/Pacific Islander-owned businesses jumped nearly 90 percent. Verle Hammond, the African-American founder of Innolog, a logistics engineering firm leads a workforce of different races, nationalities, and ages, as well as a growing number of women in what is still considered a male-populated industry. Exhibit C.2 shows how U.S. small businesses compare to the largest world economies, based on total output.

Who Are Entrepreneurs?

Ray Kroc, Spike Lee, Henry Ford, Sam Walton, Mary Kay Ash, Bill Gates, Michael Dell—are the entrepreneurial heroes of American business. Each one started with a vision and saw an opportunity to bring together or

Exhibit C.2

TOTAL OUTPUT OF U.S. SMALL BUSINESSES COMPARED TO WORLD'S LARGEST ECONOMIES

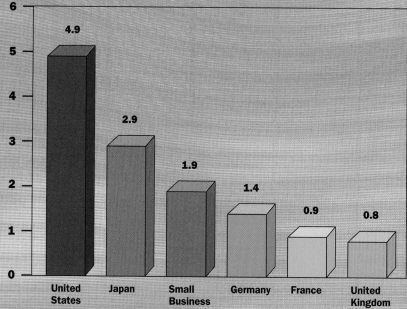

$ Trillion

United States	4.9
Japan	2.9
Small Business	1.9
Germany	1.4
France	0.9
United Kingdom	0.8

SOURCE: John Case, "The Wonderful Economy," *The State of Small Business,* 1995, p. 27.

create the resources needed for a new venture. A survey among CEOs of the nation's fastest-growing small firms found that these entrepreneurs are best characterized as hardworking and practical, with great familiarity with their market and industry. Entrepreneurs generally want different things out of life than do traditional managers. Entrepreneurs seem to place high importance on being free to achieve and maximize their potential. Mark Bozzini of Pete's Brewing Company traded in his plush office at Seagram Company for a corner office in a barn—his desk was an old door—all because he wanted "control of my own destiny."

Some 40 traits have become associated with entrepreneurs, and six have special importance, as illustrated in Exhibit C.3.

1. *Locus of Control.* The entrepreneur functions on the belief that he can make things come out the way he wants. He or she not only has a vision but also a plan to achieve that vision and believe it will happen. An internal locus of control is the belief by individuals that their future is within their control and that other external forces will have little influence. For entrepreneurs, reaching the future is seen as being in the hands of the individual. Others, in contrast, feel that the world is highly uncertain and that they are unable to bring about the results they want. An external locus of control is the belief by individuals that their future is not within their control but rather is influenced by external forces. Entrepreneurs are convinced they can make the difference between success and failure and are therefore motivated to achieve the goal of setting up and running a new business.

2. *Energy Level.* Most entrepreneurs report struggle and hardship, yet they persist and work incredibly hard despite traumas and obstacles. Sixty hours of working, or more, per week is typical, although one study showed that going beyond 70 hours produced little benefit.

3. *Need to Achieve.* Entrepreneurs are motivated to excel, and they choose situations in which success is likely. As high achievers, they like to set their own goals; ones with a moderate degree of difficulty. Entrepreneurs understand that easy goals present no challenge, and unrealistic goals cannot be achieved. Intermediate goals, however, offer both challenge and satisfaction when achieved. These achievers also tend to pursue goals for which they will obtain feedback about their success.

4. *Self-confidence.* Running a business means acting decisively, so entrepreneurs tend to have great confidence in their ability to master the tasks of their business. They also believe that they can deal with anything the future brings, no matter the complexity, ambiguity, or unpredictability; these can be handled as they arise.

5. *Awareness of Passing Time.* Entrepreneurs are impatient people with a strong sense of urgency that motivates them to want things moving immediately. There is little room for procrastination.

6. *Tolerance for Ambiguity.* Clear structure, specific instructions, and complete information in the workplace are not typical entrepreneurial environments. Entrepreneurs exhibit a high tolerance for ambiguity. This psychological characteristic allows a person to be untroubled by disorder and uncertainty. This is an important trait, because few situations present more uncertainty than starting a new business, where decisions are often made without a clear grasp of options, and there tends to be a great deal of uncertainty about which path should be taken.

To these six personality traits should be added *demographic factors;* entrepreneurs often have a background and demographic characteristics that distinguish them from others. Entrepreneurs are more likely to be firstborn children. Their parents are more likely to have been entrepreneurs themselves. And they tend to come from families in which their father was absent for at least part of their childhood.

Some research suggests that there are particular times during a person's career life cycle when the opportunities for entrepreneurship are particularly favorable. When an individual is just beginning a career and when one is retiring from a career are the two most obvious "windows of opportunity." The entrepreneurial continuum develops as a person grows in experience, industry knowledge, understanding of the marketplace, or financial ability. Other "windows of necessity" include unplanned events (i.e., loss of job, gain of inheritance, or break up of marriage or family). Entrepreneurship, however, is a much greater

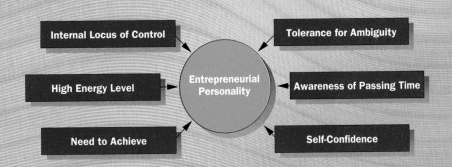

Exhibit C.3

CHARACTERISTICS OF ENTREPRENEURS

sum than its parts; it should be viewed as an opportunity throughout one's life—to take when it presents itself—not as something that can only be done at a certain time or age.

In the past, between ages 25 and 40 was the time to start a business. Today, older entrepreneurs—due to early retirement programs or corporate downsizing—with high-level skills and years of experience are creating an entirely new class of active entrepreneurs. Many decided that their chances were better being entrepreneurs than trying to reenter an overcrowded job market. The point is, successful entrepreneurs come in all ages and will have a combination of personality traits.

Starting an Entrepreneurial Firm

Pursuing your entrepreneurial dream requires a viable idea and careful planning. Once the idea is in mind for the venture, next comes the business plan, a document in which decisions are made about legal structure, financing, and basic tactics, such as whether to pursue international opportunities from the start or begin a little closer to home.

The new idea for the business is the easy part, at least for some. While a few do not even consider entrepreneurship until they are inspired by an exciting idea, others decide to start and set about looking for an idea or opportunity. Exhibit C.4 shows the most important reasons people start a new business and the source of new-business ideas (based on a survey of 500 fast-growing firms in the United States). Note that 37 percent of business founders got their idea from an in-depth understanding of the industry, primarily because of past job experience. Interestingly, almost as many—36 percent—spotted a market niche that wasn't being filled. When Michael Kares was doing construction work just out of

college, he saw a need for a national, standardized contracting firm to install steel storage systems in warehouses, stores, and factories from coast to coast. He turned his idea into a $10 million-a-year business, Coast-To-Coast Installations.

The business plan, the entrepreneur's initial tool for effective planning, specifies the business details prior to opening the business. Preparing this document forces the entrepreneur to carefully think through all of the issues and problems associated with starting, developing, funding, and running the business. Because most entrepreneurs have to borrow money, a good business plan can persuade lenders and investors to participate in the startup. Studies have shown that small businesses with a carefully thought out, written business plan are much more likely to succeed than those without one.

The details of a business plan may vary, but successful business plans generally share these characteristics:

- Demonstrates a clear, compelling vision that creates an air of excitement
- Provides clear and realistic financial projections
- Gives detailed information about the target market
- Includes detailed information about the industry and competitors
- Provides evidence of an effective entrepreneurial management team
- Pays attention to good formatting and clear writing
- Keeps the plan brief (no more than 50 pages in length)
- Highlights critical risks that may threaten business success

Exhibit C.4

SOURCES OF ENTREPRENEURIAL MOTIVATION AND NEW BUSINESS IDEAS

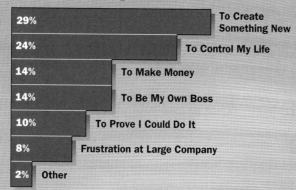

Reasons for Starting a Business

- 29% To Create Something New
- 24% To Control My Life
- 14% To Make Money
- 14% To Be My Own Boss
- 10% To Prove I Could Do It
- 8% Frustration at Large Company
- 2% Other

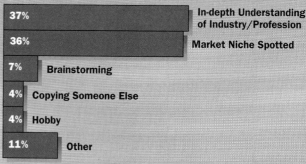

Source of New-Business Ideas

- 37% In-depth Understanding of Industry/Profession
- 36% Market Niche Spotted
- 7% Brainstorming
- 4% Copying Someone Else
- 4% Hobby
- 11% Other

Here are the major elements of a typical business plan.

- *The Summary.* This introduction should not be longer than three pages. It is the most crucial part of your plan because it must immediately capture the reader's interest. The what, how, why, where, etc., must be concisely summarized. It is best to complete this part *after* the finished business plan has been written.
- *The Business Description Segment.* State the name of the business, followed by a background of the industry with relevant history of the new company (if any). The potential of the new venture should be described clearly. Definitely spell out any unique or distinctive features of the venture.
- *The Marketing Segment.* Convince investors that sales projections and competition can be met with real data, not inaccurate, inflated numbers. Use and disclose market studies and any other material used for this section, and identify the target market, market position, and market share. Evaluate *all* competition and specifically cover why and how you will be better than the competitors. Demonstrate pricing strategy to show how the price will penetrate and maintain a market share that *produces profits*. Remember, the lowest price is *not* necessarily the "best" price.

  Describe a plan for advertising and cost estimates to validate the proposed strategy.
- *The Research, Design, and Development Segment.* Cover the *extent* of and *costs* involved in needed research, testing, or development. Explain carefully what has been accomplished *already,* such as whether a prototype has been made, any lab testing results, and early development performed. Be sure to mention any research or technical assistance used in conducting the tests.
- *The Manufacturing Segment.* Describe the advantages of your location (zoning, tax laws, wage rates). List the production needs in terms of facilities (plant, storage, office space) and equipment (machinery, furnishings, supplies). Define the transportation needed and what is needed for shipping and receiving. Provide details on the location of suppliers (whether they are conveniently accessible), the availability of labor in your location, and estimates of manufacturing costs (be careful; too many entrepreneurs underestimate these costs).
- *The Management Segment.* Provide the résumés of all key people involved in the management of the venture. Carefully describe the legal structure of the venture (sole proprietorship, partnership, or corporation) and the assistance (if any) that will be needed from advisers, consultants, and directors. Provide information on how everyone is to be compensated (specific information on salaries; not ranges, but real pay).
- *The Critical Risks Segment.* Discuss the risks *before* potential investors point them out (and they will). These include price cutting by competitors, potentially unfavorable industrywide trends, design or manufacturing costs in excess of estimates, sales projections not achieved, product development schedule not met, difficulties or long lead times encountered in the procurement of parts or raw materials, and larger-than-expected innovation and development costs needed to stay competitive. Then describe the plan for alternative courses of action.
- *The Financial Segment.* Provide financial statements and describe the needed sources for funds and intended uses for the money. Provide a budget and show the stages of financing (to allow evaluation by investors at various points).
- *The Milestone Schedule Segment.* Provide a timetable or chart to demonstrate when each phase of the venture is to be completed. This shows the relationship of events and provides a deadline for accomplishment.

- Spells out the sources and uses of startup funds and operating funds
- Captures the reader's interest with a persuasive, "killer" summary

The business plan should indicate where the product or service fits in the overall industry and should draw on concepts discussed throughout this book. Here are a few detailed suggestions for writing a business plan:

Legal Form

Before founding a business, and perhaps again as it expands, an appropriate legal structure for the company must be chosen. The three basic choices are:

- *Proprietorship.* A proprietorship is an unincorporated, for-profit business owned by an individual. Proprietorships make up 70 percent of the 16 million businesses in the United States. This form is popular because it is easy to start and has few legal requirements.

A proprietor has total ownership and control of the company and can make all decisions without consulting anyone. However, this type of organization also has drawbacks. The owner has unlimited liability for the business, meaning that if someone sues, the owner's personal (as well as business assets) are at risk. Also, financing can be harder to obtain because business success rests on one person's shoulders.

- *Partnership.* A partnership is also an unincorporated business and is relatively easy to start, but ownership is shared by two or more people. Two friends, for instance, agree to start a pet store. To avoid misunderstandings and to make sure the business is well planned, they draw up and sign a formal partnership agreement with the help of an attorney. The agreement specifies how the partners are to share responsibility and resources and how they will contribute their expertise. The disadvantages of partnerships are the unlimited liability of the partners and the disagreements that almost always occur among strong-minded people. A poll by *Inc.* magazine illustrated the volatility of partnerships. Fifty-nine percent of respondents considered partnerships a bad business move, citing reasons such as partner problems and conflicts. Partnerships often dissolve within five years. Respondents who liked partnerships pointed to the equality of partners (e.g., sharing of workload, emotional and financial burdens) as the key to a successful partnership.

- *Corporation.* A considerable departure from the informality of proprietorships and partnerships is the corporation, which is an artificial entity created by the state. It exists apart from its owners. As a separate legal entity, the corporation is liable for its actions and must pay taxes on its income. Unlike other forms of ownership, the corporation has a legal life of its own; it continues to exist regardless of whether the owners live or die. And the corporation, not the owners, is responsible when sued in cases of liability. Thus continuity and limits on owners' liability are two principal advantages of forming a corporation. For example, a physician can form a corporation so that liability for malpractice will not affect his or her personal assets. The major disadvantage of the corporation is that it is expensive and complex to do the paperwork required to incorporate the business and to keep the records required by law. When proprietorships and partnerships are successful and grow large, they often incorporate to limit liability and to raise funds through the sale of stock to investors.

Financial Resources

Of crucial concern when starting a business is the financing. An investment usually is required to acquire labor and raw materials and perhaps a building and equipment (overhead). The financing decision initially involves two options—whether to obtain loans that must be repaid (debt financing) or whether to share ownership (equity financing). A survey of successful growth businesses asked, "How much money was needed to launch the company?" Approximately one-third were started on less than $10,000, one-third needed from $10,000 to $50,000, and one-third needed more than $50,000. The primary source of this money was the entrepreneur's own resources, but they often had to mortgage their home, borrow money from the bank, or give part of the business to a venture capitalist. The two primary sources of financing are:

- *Debt Financing.* Borrowing money that has to be repaid at a later date in order to start a business is called debt financing. Common sources of debt financing for a startup include borrowing from family and friends, getting a bank loan—which makes up approximately 25 percent of all small business financing—or acquiring funds from a finance company, wealthy individuals, or potential customers.

    Loan financing is also provided by the Small Business Administration (SBA). The SBA often supplies direct loans to entrepreneurs who are unable to get bank financing because they are considered high-risk. The SBA is especially helpful for people without substantial assets and provides an opportunity for single parents, minority group members, and others who happen to have a good idea.

- *Equity Financing.* All monies invested by owners or by those who purchase stock in a corporation are considered equity funds. Equity financing consists of funds that are invested in exchange for ownership in the company.

    Venture capitalists are companies or individuals that invest money in new or expanding businesses in exchange for ownership and potential profits. This is a potential form of capital for businesses with high earning and growth possibilities. For example, San Francisco research firm VentureOne reports that in 1997 alone, venture capitalists invested more than $6 billion in about 1,100 "Point-Casts," small firms founded by engineers and software gurus that have the potential for rapid growth and high earnings. Venture capital firms want new businesses with an extremely high rate of return, but in return the venture capitalist will provide assistance, advice, and information to help the entrepreneur prosper. Advice and information from venture capitalists can include any of the following:

- *Original ideas are good, but marketable ones are even better.* Also, variations on existing ideas that make them cheaper, simpler, or better are good, too.

- *Find a garage.* Venture capital startup stories just have to have a garage in order to build the right amount of drama. We've all heard the stories: "We were just two women working in my garage when the big venture capital money arrived." They inspire people.

- *Develop the idea* only to the level that you can hint at the huge potential it has, once you have enough capital to "do it right."

- *Make room for all the money that's coming,* so you'll be ready.

If it all sounds murky and melodramatic, it is. The world of venture capitalism is thrilling, mysterious, and high risk, as well as often misunderstood. It surprises many entrepreneurs when their venture capitalists become almost as emotionally involved with the effort and tied to the operations that they fund as themselves. Call it daring, insanity, or just a good old-fashioned need for speed, but venture capitalists gravitate toward companies that innovate, have an early lead, possess a workable plan, and are operated by talented, trustworthy people.

One person who lives in the world of venture capitalism as often, if not more so, than perhaps anyone else is Neil Weintraut, of Hambrecht & Quist, who is very selective.

> We get approached by startups all the time, [but when I ask them to state the problem they are trying to solve], you'd be amazed at how many startups cannot tell you [and don't have a clue about what the customer wants]. People like us are not about money. Silicon Valley is awash in money. [It's the idea, the excitement of being at the starting gate, the thrill of taking the lead.] If all we were was a broker of money, our role in life would be more at risk than any stockbroker's. When you launch a startup, what you have done is created the opportunity to get out in front and run like hell.

Venture capitalism these days is more like parenting than investing. Take the case of eBay's founder Pierre Omidyar, who started part-time until he was making enough money to quit his day job. Then he went looking for venture partners and found Benchmark Capital, whose money went in the bank and stayed there. Unlike so many other struggling startups, they didn't need the money. What they were really looking for was a real partner, who ended up giving valuable advice in strategy and business understanding. Money is sometimes the *least* valuable tool venture-capital partners provide.

Minnesotan Ann Winblad, entrepreneur turned venture capitalist, has certain things she looks for when deciding to fund a company:

1. Is the proposed market large enough to absorb this idea?
2. Is there a decent opportunity for a dramatic change in the market or a new entrant?
3. Can the team actually do it? (She spends a lot of time on this one, including checking references.)
4. If the startup team can't do it, are they willing to accept another leader, and can find this person themselves?

Her team can only spend a couple of days going through this process for each company, because "We fund fewer than 20 new companies a year," she says, "and review close to 3,000 submissions." Every three months, they do a one-day stint at the Software Development Forum, where every 30 minutes, someone new gives a pitch, like "I can control networks with brain waves." It's a cross between *The Gong Show* and *Ed Sullivan*.

They like to fund the typical company—the proverbial two engineers in a garage—and they work with them on everything from acquiring real estate agents so they can have a roof over their heads to helping develop strategic alliances with companies like Yahoo! Lately, about $12 billion per year, more than half of all venture capital dollars, have been going to Internet ventures. But the core principles remain consistent: a belief in the company and a commitment to its ideas and to the people running it.

Tactics

Starting a new business from scratch, buying an existing business, or starting a franchise are the most common ways for an aspiring entrepreneur to begin. Other entrepreneurial tactics include participating in a business incubator, being a spin-off of a large corporation, or pursuing international markets from the beginning. These are briefly described here:

- *Starting a New Business.* This is arguably the most exciting because, out of nothing, the entrepreneur sees a need, fills it, and gets to see the dream become reality. When Cuban-American Leopoldo Fernández Pujals noticed a growing appetite for fast food in Spain, he invested $80,000 to start a pizza delivery service. Today, TelePizza boasts $260 million in sales and employs some 6,000 workers. The advantage of starting a business is the prospect of developing and designing the business in the entrepreneur's own way. A potential disadvantage is the long time it can take to get the business off the ground and make it profitable, and all the while, the entrepreneur is responsible for every aspect of its success. The uphill battle is typically caused by a lack of established clientele and the mistakes made by inexperienced new-business owners. Moreover, no matter how much planning is done, a startup is risky; there is no guarantee that the new idea will work.

- *Buy an Existing Business.* Because of the long startup time and the inevitable mistakes, some entrepreneurs prefer to reduce risk by purchasing an existing business. This offers the advantage of a shorter time to get started and an existing track record. The entrepreneur may get a bargain price if the owner wishes to retire or has other family considerations. Moreover, a new business may overwhelm an entrepreneur with the amount of work to be done and procedures to be determined. An established business already has filing systems, a payroll tax system, and other operating procedures. Potential disadvantages are the need to pay for goodwill that the owner believes exists and the possible existence of ill will toward the business. In addition, the company may have bad habits and procedures or outdated technology, which may be why the business is for sale. Although it is high risk, gutsy entrepreneurs sometimes can achieve great success by taking over a troubled company. Eric Close and Chris Farls, fresh out of graduate school, bought a company that specialized in cleaning, painting, repairing, and inspecting railroad cars. The company (now named ProLine Services, Inc.) had the potential to be a big moneymaker but was in deep trouble, with heavy debt, a load of uncollected accounts receivable, and major operational problems. The two twenty-somethings purchased the company, promptly turned it around, and are getting very rich. "Sales just walk through the door," says Close.

- *Buy a Franchise.* Franchising is perhaps the most rapidly growing path to entrepreneurship nowadays.

Currently, one out of every 12 businesses in the United States is franchised, and a new franchise business opens every eight minutes of every business day. Today, franchising employs more than eight million people. Franchising is an arrangement by which the owner of a product or service allows others to purchase the right to distribute the product or service with the owner's help. The franchisee invests his or her money and owns the business, but does not have to develop a new product, create a new company, or test the market. The franchisee typically pays a flat fee plus a percentage of gross sales. Franchises exist for fast-food eateries, weight-loss clinics, pet-sitting services, sports photography, bakeries, janitorial services, auto repair shops, real estate offices, and many other types of businesses. Exhibit C.5 shows examples of some of today's fastest growing franchises in four investment categories. Startup costs for a franchise range from less than $5,000, for a business that doesn't require extensive facilities or equipment, to more than $500,000, for a franchise like McDonald's or Econo Lodge. The powerful advantage of a franchise is that management leadership is provided by the owner. For example, Burger King does not want a franchisee to fail and will provide the studies necessary to find a good location. The franchisor also provides an established name and national advertising to stimulate demand for the product or service. Poten-

Exhibit C.5

TODAY'S WINNING FRANCHISES

	Company	Product Category	Number of Units
$75,000 or Under	Coldwell Banker Residential Affiliates	Real Estate	2,066
	Money Mailer, Inc.	Business Services	675
	Merry Maids	Maintenance Services	810
$75,001 to $150,000	Blimpie International	Fast Food	966
	GNC Franchising	Retail	2,246
	Snap-On Inc.	Automotive Services	4,963
	Mail Boxes Etc.	Business Services	2,676
$150,001 to $250,000	Glamour Shots Licensing Inc.	Retail	323
	Sir Speedy, Inc.	Printing	887
	ExecuTrain Corp.	Computer-Related Services	135
$250,001 or More	Choice Hotels International	Lodging	3,384
	Dunkin' Donuts	Bakery Goods	3,632
	Hardee's Food Systems	Fast Food	4,060
	Ben Franklin Stores	Retail	912

tial disadvantages are the lack of control that occurs when franchisors want every business managed in exactly the same way. In some cases, franchisors require that franchise owners use certain contractors or suppliers that may be more expensive than others. In addition, franchises can be very expensive, and the high startup costs are followed with monthly payments to the franchisor that can run from 2 percent to 12 percent of sales.

Entrepreneurs who are considering buying a franchise should investigate the company thoroughly. The prospective franchisee is legally entitled to a copy of franchisor disclosure statements, which include information on 20 topics, including litigation and bankruptcy history, identities of the directors and executive officers, financial information, identification of any products the franchisee is required to buy, and from whom those purchases must be made. The entrepreneur also should consult other franchise owners, who are often the best sources of information about how the franchisor really operates. Here are a few specific questions entrepreneurs should ask about themselves and the franchising company when considering the franchise option.

1. *Questions about the Entrepreneur:* Will I enjoy the day-to-day work of this business? Do my background, experience, and goals make this a good choice for me? Am I willing to work within the rules and guidelines established by the franchisor?

2. *Questions about the Franchisor:* What assistance does the company provide in terms of selecting a location, getting set-up costs, securing credit, providing marketing advice and assistance, and training and developing staff?

3. *Before Signing on the Dotted Line:* Do I understand the risks associated with this business and am I willing to assume them? Has an adviser reviewed the disclosure documents and franchise agreement? Do I understand all the terms of the contract?

- *Participate in a Business Incubator.* An attractive innovation for entrepreneurs who want to start a business from scratch is to join a business incubator. The business incubator provides shared office space, management support services, and management advice. By sharing office space with other entrepreneurs, managers share information about local business, financial aid, and market opportunities.

This innovation arose nearly two decades ago to nurture startup companies and has become a significant segment of the small business economy, jumping from 385 in 1990 to more than 800 by March 1997, with new ones opening at a rate of one every week. Nearly 90 percent of incubators are operated by not-for-profit organizations (i.e., government agencies and universities) to boost

creation of small businesses and jobs. The in-house mentor—serving as adviser, role model, and cheerleader—gives the incubator concept an edge. This nurturing can be particularly helpful to low-income and minority entrepreneurs. Before she entered the Philadelphia Enterprise Center, Donna DuBose Miller needed food stamps even after she started DuBose Business Services, which she ran out of her home. Della Clark, president of the Enterprise Center, paired DuBose Miller with a graphic artist to share the $100 rent for a space and coached her in marketing and other business basics. Now, DuBose Miller has put welfare behind her, has hired a part-time employee, and is making enough money to send one of her children to a private school.

- *Be a Spin-Off.* A unique form of entrepreneurial company, spin-offs are already associated with, and owe their startup to, another organization. A spin-off is an independent company producing a product or service similar to that produced by the entrepreneur's former employer. Spin-offs occur when entrepreneurs with a desire to produce a similar product quit their employers; or in some cases they produce a related product that is purchased by the former employer. The former employer may recognize that it can profit from the idea by selling patents to the spin-off and by investing in it. Employer approval is often the basis for a spin-off, although in some cases entrepreneurs start a new business because they disagree with former employers. Disagreement usually concerns the failure of the employer to try a new idea from the employee, so when the possibility of a spin-off begins, it is best to reduce future risk by getting the support of the current employer for the spin-off. With this approval may come a source of management advice and experience and a guaranteed customer, ways to further reduce the risk of failure.

- *Try Globalization.* In today's global economy, no small business can afford to ignore overseas markets. Multiplex Co., a Ballwin, Missouri, maker of beverage-dispensing equipment, now has offices in Germany, France, Taiwan, England, and Canada, with overseas business accounting for about 30 percent of sales. Many small businesses never reach their potential because they are focused domestically. Former chief economist for the Small Business Administration, Tom Gray, has estimated that for every dollar of growth in the United States during the next decade, there will be five dollars of growth elsewhere. New technology, better air travel, and higher-quality electronic communications are helping companies do business on a global scale in ways that were previously limited. Telephone interpreters, software kits, and translation services help bypass language difficulties and make it easier to do business internationally.

Getting Help

Unlike large corporations, small businesses don't have in-house specialists to help them develop a global presence. Fortunately, assistance is available from a number of sources. The Service Corps of Retired Executives (SCORE) works with the Small Business Administration to match small businesses with mentors who have experience in international business. The Bankers' Association for Foreign Trade, a trade group, runs a program to help small exporters find financing. A good place for small companies to start is the U.S. Commerce Department's hot line, which can provide guidesheets on tricky exporting problems and details about the variety of federal programs designed to help new exporters tap foreign markets. Many government departments offer counseling; research; assistance in finding overseas agents and sales leads; and help with export licensing, loans, export credit insurance, and other services. The Commerce Department has also set up 19 U.S. Export Assistance Centers, or USEACs, around the country. These are one-stop shops designed to help companies get into or expand their exporting operations.

Perhaps the first piece of advice for entrepreneurs is to find a good accountant and attorney to help with the financial and legal aspects of the business. For incorporated businesses, a board of directors also can be a good source of knowledge and advice. The SBA has a Web site (www.sbaonline.sba.gov) offering information, and the Directory for Small Business Management lists all SBA publications and videotapes on management issues. The Service Corps of Retired Executives is an excellent resource for small businesses. These experienced managers can provide advice and assistance on a wide range of issues.

Managing a Growing Business

Once an entrepreneurial business is up and running, how does the owner manage it? Often the traits of self-confidence, creativity, and internal locus of control lead to financial and personal grief as the enterprise grows. A hands-on entrepreneur who gives birth to the organization loves perfecting every detail. But after the startup, continued growth requires a shift in management style. Those who fail to adjust to a growing business can be the cause of the problems rather than the solution. Let's now look at important entrepreneurial stages and how managers should carry out their planning, organizing, leading, and controlling.

Entrepreneurial businesses go through five distinct stages of growth, with each stage requiring different management skills.

1. *Existence.* In this stage, the main problems are producing the product or service and obtaining customers. Key issues facing managers are: Can we get enough customers? Will we survive? Do we have enough money?
2. *Survival.* At this stage, the business has demonstrated that it is a workable business entity. It is producing a product or service and has sufficient customers. Concerns here have to do with finances—generating sufficient cash flow to run the business and making sure revenues exceed expenses. The organization will grow in size and profitability during this period.
3. *Success.* At this point, the company is solidly based and profitable. Systems and procedures are in place to allow the owner to slow down if desired. The owner can stay involved or consider turning the business over to professional managers.
4. *Takeoff.* Here the key problem is how to grow rapidly and wisely finance that growth. The owner must learn to delegate, and the company must find sufficient capital to invest in major growth. This is a pivotal period in an entrepreneurial company's life. Properly managed, the company can become a big business. However, another problem for companies at this stage is how to maintain the advantages of "smallness" as the company grows.
5. *Resource maturity.* At this stage, the company has made substantial financial gains, but it may start to lose the advantages of small size, including flexibility and the entrepreneurial spirit. A company in this stage has the staff and financial resources to begin acting like a mature company with detailed planning and control systems.

Planning

In the early stage of existence, formal planning tends to rest solely in the business plan, which entrepreneurs must view as a living document that should evolve as the company grows or the market changes.

Organizing

In the first two stages of growth, the organization's structure is very informal with all employees reporting to the owner. At about the success stage, functional managers often are hired to assume the duties of the owner, such as finance, manufacturing, and marketing. During the latter stages of entrepreneurial growth, managers must learn to delegate and decentralize authority. If the business has multiple product lines, the owner may consider creating teams or divisions responsible for each line. The organization must hire competent managers and have sufficient management talent to handle fast growth and eliminate problems caused by increasing size. The latter growth stages also are characterized by greater use of rules, procedures, and written job descriptions.

Some of today's small companies are finding creative ways to stay small but still grow. Barbara Bobo, who turned a stove-top operation making all-natural herbal and floral soaps into a $500,000 company and created a network of independent contractors when demand outpaced the company's capabilities. Today, her company, Woodspirits, produces and distributes 300,000 bars of soap annually with just three employees.

Leading

The driving force in the early stages of development is the leader's vision. This vision combined with the leader's personality shapes the corporate culture. The leader can signal cultural values of service, efficiency, quality, or ethics. Often entrepreneurs do not have good people skills but do have excellent task skills in either manufacturing or marketing. By the success stage of growth, the owner must either learn to motivate employees or bring in managers who can. Rapid takeoff is not likely to happen without employee cooperation.

Stepping from the self-absorption of the early days of a company to the more active communication necessary for growth can be tricky for entrepreneurs. Charles Barnard, the owner of Foot Traffic, a chain of eight specialty sock stores based in Kansas City, Missouri, believes leaders should focus on communication as a company grows.

A lot of the time, you get to running real fast, and you don't think about the people around you. But you can never get anywhere if you're pulling your staff around behind you all the time.

Small companies that grow rapidly often have a hard time hiring qualified employees. A healthy corporate culture can help attract and retain good people.

Controlling

Financial control is important in each stage of small business growth. By the success stage, operational budgets are in place, and the owner starts implementing more structured control systems. During the takeoff stage, the company will need to make greater use of budgets and standard cost systems and perhaps acquire computers to provide statistical reports. These control techniques will become more sophisticated during the resource maturity stage.

Sophisticated accounting software has helped Jay Shrager maintain control at Somerset Farms, a Spring House, Pennsylvania, distributor of food products. Since 1988, when the company entered the profitable niche of providing food products to prisons throughout the country, revenues have grown at the dizzying rate of 40 percent a year. Shrager quickly realized things were moving so fast he couldn't keep up with them. The software program he selected not only keeps the books but also ties accounting to other facets of the business such as ordering, manufacturing, and distribution.

Coping with Chaotic Times

Small businesses operate in the same environment as larger, well-established firms and are affected by the same dramatic changes of (1) increasingly tougher global competition, (2) rapid technological change, (3) uncertain environments, (4) the need to do more with less, and (5) new challenges brought on by demographic shifts in the population and workforce. Small companies sometimes are in a better position to weather the chaos because of the speed and flexibility that comes with being small.

If a small business does not evolve, it risks failure. Burns & Russell, a family-owned business started in Baltimore in 1775, supplied the bricks for many of the structures around town, including the wharves, the B & O railroad tunnels, and Johns Hopkins Hospital. But Burns & Russell hasn't made a brick for 45 years; today the company has evolved into a high-tech manufacturer of specialty glazes for concrete blocks, along with other specialty chemicals.

Stephen Harper, author of *The McGraw-Hill Guide to Managing Growth in Your Emerging Business*, emphasizes that small businesses can be learning organizations, which in large part means paying attention to signals from the marketplace and changing and adapting to meet customer needs. Harper believes missing those signals is one of the biggest sins of entrepreneurs. "Too many people don't evolve, and the market just passes them by."

The way to keep innovation within the organization is to create conditions in which intrapreneurs can flourish. Intrapreneurship is the process whereby an individual sees the need for innovation and promotes it within an organization. The goal for managers, who at one time were innovators themselves, is to create a climate that encourages intrapreneurs. Companies such as 3M are known for intrapreneurship. 3M intrapreneur Art Frey invented the Post-it Note as the result of personal frustration when his page markers repeatedly fell out of his church hymnal. Even the best ideas need nurturing, support, and financing in a large corporation.

The following rules provide an approach for developing the necessary atmosphere:

1. Encourage action by stripping away rigid procedures and when red tape gets in the way, encourage people to go around it.
2. Use informal meetings whenever possible; even plan the firm's physical layout to encourage informal communication.
3. Tolerate failure and use it as a learning experience.

4. Be persistent in getting an idea to market.
5. Reward innovation for its own sake and encourage clever bootlegging of ideas. Reward and/or promote the people who do.
6. Organize people into small teams for future-oriented projects.

As with any strategy, intrapreneurship is only as successful as the planning and support it receives throughout a company.

Summary and Management Solution

Entrepreneurship and small-business management plays important roles in the economy by stimulating job creation, innovation, and opportunities for minorities and women. An entrepreneurial personality includes the traits of internal locus of control, high energy level, need to achieve, tolerance for ambiguity, awareness of passing time, and self-confidence.

Starting an entrepreneurial firm requires a new-business idea. At that point a comprehensive business plan should be developed and decisions made about legal structure and financing. Tactical decisions for the new venture include whether to start new, buy old, franchise, participate in a business incubator, be a company spin-off, and go global from the start. After the business is started, it will typically proceed through five stages of growth—existence, survival, success, takeoff, and resource maturity. The management functions of planning, organizing, leading, and controlling should be tailored to each stage of growth. Finally, intrapreneurship, a variation of entrepreneurship, is a mechanism for encouraging innovation within a larger firm. Small businesses must continually evolve to cope with changes in the environment of chaos that characterizes today's business world.

Questions

1. Dan McKinnon started an airline with one airplane. To do so required filing more than 10,000 pages of manuals, ordering 50,000 luggage tags, buying more than $500 million in insurance, and spending more than $300,000 to train employees. A single inspection test cost $18,000. Evaluate whether you think this is a good entrepreneurial opportunity and discuss why you think Dan McKinnon undertook it.
2. Why would small-business ownership have great appeal to immigrants, women, and minorities?
3. Consider the six personality characteristics of entrepreneurs. Which two traits do you think are most like those of managers in large companies? Which two are least like those of managers in large companies?
4. Why is purchasing an existing business or franchise less risky than starting a new business?
5. What is the difference between debt financing and equity financing? What are common sources of each type?

Are you right for a startup? Lots of people think about starting a business. Should you stay in your more secure job, or go for it as an entrepreneur? Answer the questions below and see.

1. Do you have the right personality to run your own company?
2. Are you a self-starter?
3. Do you enjoy competition?
4. Do you get intimidated easily?
5. Can you adapt quickly to changes?
6. Are you at ease when taking advice from others?
7. Do you have a realistic awareness of your strengths and weaknesses?
8. Can you assess risk and make decisions quickly?
9. Are you self-disciplined?
10. Do you see mistakes as opportunities to learn or useless failures?
11. Are you ready to do a lot of everything?
12. Does "sell" seem like a four-letter word to you?
13. Can you handle nonstop networking all day and night, even after business hours?
14. Is your family completely and 100 percent behind you?
15. Can you wait for success?

It takes the right kind of person, who has lots of support from family and friends, to make it as a successful entrepreneur. In fact, collaboration and networking are far more important than most novices realize. The more "Yes" answers you have, the more suited you are to being an entrepreneur. Not everyone should be self-employed, so be honest with yourself.

References

Ballon, Marc, "Startup Mambos to Beat of Booming Market," *Inc.*, September 1997, p. 23.

Barrier, Michael, "The Changing Face of Leadership," *Nation's Business,* January 1995, pp. 41–42.

Bateman, Thomas S., and Carl P. Zeithaml, *Management Function and Strategy* (Homewood, Ill.: Irwin, 1990).

Bobo, Barbara, "Building a Business Using Contractors," *Nation's Business,* June 1995, p. 6.

Branch, Shelly, "The New Black Power: The Players," *Fortune,* August 4, 1997, p. 73.

Brown, Carolyn M., "The Do's and Don'ts of Writing a Winning Business Plan," *Black Enterprise,* April 1996, pp. 114–116.

Buss, Dale D., "Coping with Faster Change," *Nation's Business,* March 1995, pp. 27–29.

Buss, Dale, "Bringing New Firms Out of Their Shell," *Nation's Business,* March 1997, pp. 48–50.

Case, John, "The Origins of Entrepreneurship," *Inc.*, June 1989, pp. 51–63.

Case, John, "The Wonderland Economy," *The State of Small Business,* 1995, pp. 14–29.

Coleberd, R. E., "The Business Economist at Work: The Economist as Entrepreneur," *Business Economics,* October 1994, pp. 54–57.

Costa, Shu shu, "100 Years and Counting," *American Management Association,* December 1994, pp. 32–34.

Daft, Richard L., *Management,* 3d ed. (Fort Worth, Texas: The Dryden Press, 1992).

Dolan, Carrie, "Entrepreneurs Often Fail as Managers," *The Wall Street Journal,* May 15, 1989, p. B1.

Dunlap Godsey, Kristin, "Terminal Velocity," *Success,* October 1997, p. 12.

Elkins, Linda, "Tips for Preparing a Business Plan," *Nation's Business,* June 1996, pp. 60R–61R.

Fagenson, Ellen A., "Personal Value Systems of Men and Women Entrepreneurs versus Managers," *Journal of Business Venturing,* 8 (5) (September 1993), pp. 409–430.

Flynn, Julia, with Heidi Dawley, Stephen Baker, and Gail Edmondson, "Startups to the Rescue," *Business Week,* March 23, 1998, pp. 50–52.

Galuskza, Peter, "The $44 Million Mom-and-Pop," *Business Week,* June 1, 1998, pp. 74, 76.

Garrett, Echo Montgomery, "The Twenty-First-Century Franchise," *Inc.,* January 1995, pp. 79–88.

Gruner, Stephanie, "Death by Unnatural Causes," *Inc.* 500, 1997, pp. 60–65.

Gunn, Eileen P., "Is It Time to Bail from Big-Company Life?" *Fortune,* March 2, 1998, pp. 217–218.

Gupta, Udayan, and Jeffrey A. Tannenbaum, "Labor Shortages Force Changes at Small Firms," *The Wall Street Journal,* May 22, 1989, pp. B1, B2.

"Harnessing Employee Productivity," *Small Business Report,* November 1987, pp. 46–49.

Harvey, Michael, and Rodney Evans, "Strategic Windows in the Entrepreneurial Process," *Journal of Business Venturing* 10 (1995), pp. 331–347.

Hirsch, James S., "Kodak Effort at 'Intrapreneurship' Fails," *The Wall Street Journal,* August 17, 1990, p. B1.

Hisrich, Robert D., "Entrepreneurship-Intrapreneurship," *American Psychologist,* February 1990, pp. 209–222.

Hodgetts, Richard M., and Donald F. Kuratko, *Effective Small Business Management,* 5th ed. (Fort Worth, Texas: The Dryden Press, 1995), pp. 96–97.

Klimas, Molly, "How to Recruit a Smart Team," *Nation's Business,* May 1995, pp. 26–27.

Kuehl, Charles R., and Peggy A. Lambing, *Small Business: Planning and Management,* 3d ed. (Chicago: The Dryden Press, 1994).

Kuratko, Donald F., and Richard M. Hodgetts, "100 Ideas for New Businesses," *Venture,* November 1988, pp. 35–74.

Kuratko, Donald F., and Richard M. Hodgetts, "Black Entrepreneurship: By the Numbers," *The Wall Street Journal,* April 3, 1992, p. R4.

Kuratko, Donald F., and Richard M. Hodgetts, *Entrepreneurship: A Contemporary Approach,* 4th ed. (Fort Worth: The Dryden Press, 1998), pp. 7–8, 61, 295–297.

Kuratko, Donald F., Ray V. Montagno, and Frank J. Sabatine, *The Entrepreneurial Decision* (Muncie, IN: The Midwest Entrepreneurial Education Center, Ball State University, 1997), pp. 45–46.

Kurson, Ken, "Diamonds in the Rough," *Esquire,* Nov. 1999, pp. 52–58.

Love, Thomas, "The Perfect Franchise," *Nation's Business,* April 1998, pp. 59–65.

Margoshes, Pamela, "Basic Training," *Success,* August 1998, p. 44.

Maynard, Roberta, "Choosing a Franchise," *Nation's Business,* October 1996, pp. 56–63.

Maynard, Roberta, "A Simplified Route to Markets Abroad," *Nation's Business,* November 1997, pp. 46–48.

McCollum, Tim, "Making the Internet Work for You," *Nation's Business,* March 1997, pp. 6–20.

McCollum, Tim, "More Than Just Number Crunchers," *Nation's Business,* April 1998, pp. 46–48.

McCone, Jenny C., "The Entrepreneur Express," *Management Review,* March 1995, pp. 13–19.

O'Reilly, Brian, "The New Face of Small Business," *Fortune,* May 2, 1994, pp. 82–88.

Petzinger Jr., Thomas, "The Front Lines: The Rise of the Small and Other Trends to Watch This Year," *The Wall Street Journal,* January 9, 1998, p. B1.

Pinchot III, Gifford, *Intrapreneuring* (New York: Harper & Row, 1985).

Reynolds, Paul, "The Truth about Startups," *Inc.,* February 1995, p. 23.

Richman, "Creators of the New Economy."

Anonymous, Scared to Be Great," *Success,* August 1998, vol. 45 (8), p. 88.

Sprout, Alison L., "Looking for Love in All the Web Places," *Fortune,* March 3, 1997, p. 186.

The INC. FAXPOLL, *Inc.,* February 1992, p. 24.

The State of Small Business: A Report of the President (Washington, D.C.: Government Printing Office, 1995), p. 13.

Anonymous, "Two Men and a Bottle," *Inc.: The State of Small Business* 1998, vol 20 (7), pp. 60–63.

Useem, Jerry, "The New Entrepreneurial Elite," *Inc.,* December 1997, pp. 50–68.

"Venture Capitalists' Criteria," *Management Review,* November 1985, pp. 7–8.

"Want to Go Global? Here's Where to Find Help," *Business Week,* April 17, 1995, p. 101.

Webster, Harriet, "The 'Expert' Beginner," *Nation's Business,* January 1995, p. 16.

Whitford, David, "Taking It to the Street," *Fortune,* August 4, 1997, pp. 48–51.

"Women Entrepreneurs," *Management Review,* May 1997, p. 6.

"Women-Owned Businesses Outpace All U.S. Firms," *Self-Employed America,* July–August 1995, p. 7.

Zetlin, Minda, "Off the Beaten Path," *American Management Association,* December 1994, pp. 28–31.

Answers to Manager's Workbook Exercises

Answers to Chapter 3

1. China (1.3 b)
   India (982 m)
   US (256 m)
   Indonesia (206 m)
   Brazil (166)
   Russia (147 m)

2.
1. Pakistan (148 m)	11. Italy (58)
2. Japan (126 m)	12. United Kingdom (58)
3. Bangladesh (124 m)	13. France (59)
4. Nigeria (106 m)	14. Thailand (60)
5. Mexico (88 m)	15. Egypt (66)
6. Germany (82 m)	16. Ethiopia (60)
7. Vietnam (69)	17. Ukraine (51)
8. Phillipines (73)	18. South Korea (44)
9. Iran (66)	19. Myanmar (Burma) (44)
10. Turkey (64)	

3.
1. Mandarin (885)	6. Arabic (202)
2. English (450)	7. Bengali (187)
3. Hindi (367)	8. Portugese (174)
4. Spanish (353)	9. Malay-Portuguese (145)
5. Russian (294)	10. Japanese (126)

4. *c.* 223

5. *b.* 188

6. Japan

7. United States

8. *e.* increased substantially (by about 35 percent, although since then changes have been more erratic due to a number of political, economic, and climatic factors)

9. *c.* increased (from 5 to 15 percent, and has continued to increase since 1985)

10. *c.* 6,000

11. *c.* $17 trillion

12. *c.* 2/3

13. 1/10

14. *b.* 20 percent

15. 35 percent

Answers to Chapter 4

Compare your answers with other Americans who were surveyed.

1. 34 percent said personal e-mail on company computers is wrong

2. 37 percent said using office equipment for schoolwork is wrong

3. 49 percent said playing computer games at work is wrong

4. 54 percent said Internet shopping at work is wrong

5. 61 percent said it's unethical to blame your error on technology

6. 87 percent said it's unethical to visit pornographic sites at work

7. 33 percent said $25 is the amount at which a gift from a supplier or client becomes troubling, while 33 percent said $50, and 33 percent said $100

8. 35 percent said a $50 gift to the boss is unacceptable

9. 12 percent said a $50 gift from the boss is unacceptable

10. 70 percent said it's unacceptable to take the $200 football tickets

11. 70 percent said it's unacceptable to take the $120 theater tickets

12. 35 percent said it's unacceptable to take the $100 food basket

13. 45 percent said it's unacceptable to take the $25 gift certificate

14. 40 percent said it's unacceptable to take the $75 raffle prize

15. 11 percent reported they lie about sick days

16. 4 percent reported they take credit for the work or ideas of others

Answers to Chapter 16

Answers: (each correct answer is worth one point)

1. *c.* The objective is to make a decision quickly and to move the process forward without a great deal of red tape and delay. The legal process can often slow decision making—whether by three weeks or three months—and time is of the essence in the online world. Moreover, when was the last time an NDA about client information materially impacted your business? Better to spend your time building trust than protecting against an unlikely downside.

2. *a.* Give the candidate a job while waiting for the check. If he has been vouched for by someone you trust and you love his work, grab him while he's available and put him to work. If you think he's a great hire, chances are so will your competitors.

3. *b.* Hire your neighbor. Any list of dynamic industries you put together is bound to include health care, and your biggest challenge is to find a credible person with industry know-how and contacts who can take you into the industry. Your neighbor can do that. Now start looking for the other industries you want to focus on.

4. *b.* Buy Company B. Company B has proven itself to be fast moving and dynamic, and their balance sheet issues make them open to a favorable price. Company A and C are both tying their success to future events—a strong holiday selling season or a successful online launch—either of which may not happen and are in the distant Internet future.

5. *c.* The one area a company cannot afford to get wrong is its technical architecture. It must scale and be reliable, or your whole business will be at risk. Programmers without a blueprint cannot ensure a successful online environment, and staffing internally is time-consuming and uncertain. Better to outsource the project immediately while building an internal team to take it over after its launch.

accommodative response A response to social demands in which the organization accepts—often under pressure—social responsibility for its actions to comply with the public interest

accountability The degree to which people with authority and responsibility are subject to reporting and justifying task outcomes to those above them in the chain of command

activity-based costing (ABC) A control system that identifies the various activities needed to provide a product and determines the cost of those activities

adjourning The stage of team development in which members prepare for the team's disbanding

administrative model A decision-making model that focuses on organizational factors and describes how managers actually make decisions in difficult, nonprogrammed situations

administrative principles A subfield of the classical management perspective that focused on the total organization rather than the individual worker, delineating the management functions of planning, organizing, commanding, coordinating, and controlling

affirmative action A policy requiring employers to take positive steps to guarantee equal employment opportunities for people within protected groups

ambiguity Occurs when unclear goals or unsolved problems prevail and alternatives are difficult to define and information about outcomes is unavailable, unstable, or unpredictable

application form A device for collecting information about an applicant's education, previous job experience, and other background characteristics

assessment center An approach for selecting individuals with high managerial potential based on their performance on a series of simulated managerial tasks

attitude A cognitive and affective evaluation that predisposes a person to act in a certain way

attributions Judgments about what caused a person's behavior—either characteristics of the person or of the situation

authoritarianism The belief that differences in power and status should exist within the organization

authority The formal and legitimate right of a manager to make decisions, issue orders, and allocate resources to achieve organizationally desired outcomes

autocratic leader A leader who tends to centralize authority and rely on legitimate, reward, and coercive power to manage subordinates

behavior modification Reinforcement techniques used to modify human behavior

behavioral sciences approach A subfield of the humanistic management perspective that applies social science to an organizational context, drawing from economics, psychology, sociology, and other disciplines

behaviorally anchored rating scale (BARS) A rating technique that relates an employee's performance to specific job-related incidents

benchmarking The continuous process of measuring products, services, and practices against major competitors or industry leaders

biculturalism The sociocultural skills and attitudes used by racial minorities to move back and forth between the dominant culture and their own ethnic or racial culture

Big Five personality factors Traits that describe the degrees of extroversion, agreeableness, conscientiousness, emotional stability, and openness to experience individuals display

bottom-up budgeting A budgeting process in which lower-level managers budget the resource needs of departments and pass them up to top management for approval

bounded rationality The concept that people have limits, or boundaries, on their cognitive abilities and on how rational they can be in a given situation

brainstorming A decision-making technique in which group members present spontaneous, problem-solving suggestions to promote free, flexible, and creative thinking

bureaucracy An organization managed on an impersonal, rational basis that depends on the legal power invested in the managerial position

bureaucratic control The use of rules, policies, hierarchy of authority, reward systems, and other formal devices to influence employee behavior and assess performance

bureaucratic organizations A subfield of the classical management perspective that emphasized management on an impersonal, rational basis through such elements as clearly defined authority and responsibility, formal record keeping, and separation of management and ownership

capital budget A budget that plans and reports investments in major assets to be depreciated over several years

cash budget A budget that estimates and reports cash flows on a daily or weekly basis to ensure that the company has sufficient cash to meet its obligations

centralization Refers to decision authority located near the top of organizational levels

centralized network A communication structure in which team members must communicate through one individual to solve problems or make decisions

ceremony A planned activity or a special event conducted for the benefit of an audience to reinforce principles, create bonds, and celebrate heroes

certainty Accompanies situations in which all the information the decision maker needs is fully available and accessible

chain of command An unbroken line of authority that links all individuals in the organization and defines who reports to whom

change agent OD specialist who performs a systematic diagnosis of the organization and identifies work-related problems

changing OD intervention in which individuals experiment with new workplace behavior and learn new skills

channel The carrier of a communication

channel richness The amount of information that can be transmitted during a communication episode

chaos theory A theory suggesting that the world is characterized by randomness and uncertainty and that small events can have massive and far-reaching consequences

charismatic leader A leader who has the ability to motivate subordinates to transcend their expected performance

classical model A decision-making model based on economic assumptions in which managers make logical decisions based on the organization's economic interests

classical perspective A management perspective that emerged during the nineteenth and early-twentieth centuries that emphasized a rational, scientific approach to the study of management and sought to make organizations efficient operating machines

coalition An informal alliance among managers who support a specific goal

code of ethics A formal statement of the organization's values regarding ethics and social issues

coercive power Power that stems from the authority to punish or recommend punishment

cognitive dissonance A condition in which two attitudes or a behavior and an attitude conflict

collectivism A preference for a tightly knit social framework in which individuals look after one another and organizations protect their members' interests

committee A sometimes permanent team in the organization structure created to deal with tasks that regularly recur

communication The process by which information is exchanged and understood by two or more people, usually with the intent to motivate or influence behavior

compensation Monetary payments (wages, salaries) and nonmonetary goods/commodities (benefits, vacations) used to reward employees

compensatory justice The concept that individuals should be compensated for the cost of their injuries by the party responsible and also that individuals should not be held responsible for matters over which they have no control

competitors Other organizations in the same industry or type of business that provide goods or services to the same set of customers

conceptual skill The cognitive ability to see the organization as a whole and the relationship among its parts

concurrent control Control that consists of monitoring ongoing activities to ensure they are consistent with standards

consideration The extent to which the leader is mindful of subordinates, respects other's ideas and feelings, and establishes mutual trust

content theories Motivation theories emphasizing the needs that motivate people

contingency approaches Models of leadership that describe the relationship between leadership styles and specific organizational situations

contingency plans Plans that define company responses to specific situations, such as emergencies, setbacks, or unexpected conditions; also called *scenarios*

continuous improvement The implementation of a large number of small, incremental improvements in all areas of the organization on an ongoing basis

continuous reinforcement schedule A schedule in which every occurrence of the desired behavior is reinforced

coordination costs The time and energy needed to coordinate the activities of a team to enable it to perform its task

countertrade The barter of products for other products rather than their sale for currency

creativity Generating novel ideas that have the potential to meet perceived needs or respond to opportunities

cross-functional teams Groups of employees from functional departments responsible for resolving mutual problems mutually

culture The set of key values, assumptions, beliefs, and norms shared by members of an organization

culture gap The difference between an organization's desired cultural norms and values and actual norms and values

culture/people change A change in employees' values, norms, attitudes, beliefs, and behavior

culture shock The frustration, anxiety, and stress that result from being subjected to new and unfamiliar cues about what to do and how to do it

customers Individuals and organizations in the environment that acquire goods or services from the organization

cycle time The steps taken to complete a company process

decentralization Refers to decision authority located at lower organizational levels

decentralized control The use of organizational culture, group norms, and a focus on goals, rather than rules and procedures, to foster compliance with organizational goals

decentralized network A communication structure in which individuals can communicate freely with other team members

decentralized planning staff A group of planning specialists assigned to major departments and divisions to help managers develop their own strategic plans

decision A determination made from available choices and alternatives

decision making The process of identifying problems and opportunities and then resolving them

decision style Differences among people with respect to how they perceive problems and make decisions

decode To translate the symbols used in a message for the purpose of interpreting its meaning

defensive response A response to social demands in which the organization admits to some errors of commission or omission but does not act in an obstructive manner

delegation The means by which managers transfer authority and responsibility to positions below them in the hierarchy

democratic leader A leader who delegates authority to others, encourages participation, and relies on expert and referent power to manage subordinates

departmentalization The fundamental principle by which individuals are grouped into departments and departments into total organizations

descriptive An approach that describes how managers actually make complex decisions and does not impose a theoretical ideal on their decision making

devil's advocate A decision-making technique in which an individual is assigned to challenge the assumptions and assertions made by the group and prevent premature consensus

diagnosis The step in the decision-making process in which managers analyze underlying causal factors

dialogue A communication process in which groups create a stream of shared meaning about each other and their views of the world

discretionary responsibility Organizational responsibility that is voluntary and guided by the organization's desire to make social contributions not mandated by economics, law, or ethics

discrimination The hiring or promoting of applicants based on criteria that are not job relevant

distributive justice The concept that different treatment of people should not be based on arbitrary characteristics; in cases of substantive differences, people can be treated differently in proportion to the differences among them

diversity awareness training Special training designed to provide awareness of personal prejudices and stereotypes

divisional structure An organization structure in which departments are grouped based on similar organizational outputs

downward communication The flow of communication from top management downward to subordinates

dual role A role in which the individual both contributes to the team's task and supports the emotional needs of members

economic dimension The dimension of the general environment representing the overall economic health of the country or region in which the organization functions

economic forces The availability, production, and distribution of resources in a society that affect its competitiveness

economic value-added system (EVA) A control system that measures after-tax profits minus the cost of capital invested in tangible assets

effectiveness The degree to which an organization achieves a stated goal

empowerment The delegation of decision-making authority, freedom, knowledge, autonomy, and skills to subordinates; a fundamental principle of learning organizations

encode To select symbols with which to compose a message

equity theory A process theory that focuses on individuals' perceptions of how fairly they are treated relative to others

E→P expectancy The degree of expectation that putting effort into a given task will lead to high performance

ERG theory A simplification of Maslow's hierarchy that proposes three categories of needs: existence, relatedness, and growth

ethical dilemma A situation that arises when all alternative choices or behaviors have been deemed undesirable because of potentially negative ethical consequences, making it difficult to distinguish right from wrong

ethics The code of moral principles and values that govern the behaviors of a person or group with respect to what is right or wrong

ethics committee A group of executives assigned to oversee the organization's ethics by ruling on questionable issues and disciplining violators

ethics ombudsman An official given the responsibility of corporate conscience who hears and investigates ethics complaints and points out potential ethical failures to top management

ethnocentrism The tendency to regard one's own group or culture as superior to those of others

ethnorelativism The acceptance of groups and subcultures as being inherently equal

euro The single European currency that will replace 15 national currencies

exchange rate The rate at which one country's currency is exchanged for another country's

exit interview An interview conducted with departing employees to determine the reasons for their leaving/termination

expatriates Employees who live and work in a country other than their own

expectancy theory A process theory proposing that motivation depends on individuals' expectations about their ability to perform tasks and receive desired rewards

expense budget A budget that outlines the anticipated and actual expenses for a responsibility center

expert power Power that stems from special knowledge or skills regarding the tasks performed by subordinates

exporting An entry strategy in which the organization maintains its production facilities within its home country and transfers its products for sale in foreign markets

extranet A network that uses Internet technology to link authorized users inside the company with certain outsiders, including international ones, such as customers or vendors

extrinsic reward Rewards given by another person for performing an action

feedback A response by the receiver to the sender's communication

feedback control Control that focuses on the organization's outputs; also called *postaction* or *output* control

feedforward control Control that focuses on human, material, and financial resources flowing into the organization; also called *preliminary* or *preventive* control

femininity A cultural preference for cooperation, group decision making, and quality of life

firewall Software that limits access by unauthorized users

flat structure A management structure characterized by an overall broad span of control and relatively few hierarchical levels

force field analysis The process of determining which forces drive and which resist a proposed change

formal communication channels Channels of communication that flow within the chain of command or task responsibility defined by the organization; traditional approach is upward/downward versus newer horizontal approach

formal team A team created by the organization as part of the formal organization structure

formalization The written documentation used to direct and control employees

forming The stage of team development characterized by orientation and acquaintance

franchising A form of licensing in which an organization provides its foreign franchisees with a complete assortment of materials and services

free rider A person who benefits from team membership but does not make a proportionate contribution to the team's work

frustration-regression principle The idea that failure to meet a high-order need may cause a regression to an already satisfied lower-order need

functional structure An organization structure in which positions are grouped into departments based on similar skills, expertise, and resource use

fundamental attribution error The tendency to underestimate the influence of external factors on another's behavior and to overestimate the influence of internal factors

General Adaptation Syndrome (GAS) A physiological response to a stressor that begins with an alarm response, continues to resistance, and will end in exhaustion when the stressor continues beyond a person's ability to cope

general environment The layer of the external environment that indirectly affects the organization

glass ceiling Invisible barrier that separates women and minorities from top management positions

global outsourcing Engaging in the international division of labor so as to obtain the cheapest sources of labor and supplies regardless of country; also called global sourcing

goal A desired future state that the organization attempts to realize

grapevine Informal, person-to-person communication network of employees that is not officially sanctioned by the organization

groupthink A phenomenon in which members of a group are reluctant to express contrary opinions

halo effect An overall impression of a person or situation based on one attribute, either favorable or unfavorable

halo error A type of rating error that occurs when an employee receives the same rating on all dimensions regardless of his or her performance on individual ones

Hawthorne studies A series of experiments on worker productivity begun in 1924 at the Hawthorne plant of Western Electric Company in Illinois; attributed employees' increased output to managers' better treatment of them during the study

hero A figure, real or not, that exemplifies the deeds, character, and attributes of a strong corporate culture

hierarchy of needs theory A content theory that proposes a hierarchy of five categories of needs that motivate people—physiological, safety, belongingness, esteem, and self-actualization

high-context culture A culture in which communication is used to enhance personal relationships

historical forces The effect of the past on the present and the future; the study of how learning from past mistakes and past successes can promote understanding of why things happen and how they can improve

homogeneity A type of rating error that occurs when a rater gives all employees a similar rating regardless of their individual performances

horizontal communication The flow of communication laterally or diagonally among peers or coworkers

horizontal linkage model An approach to product change that emphasizes shared development of innovations among several departments

horizontal team A formal team composed of employees from about the same hierarchical level but from different areas of expertise

human relations movement A movement in management thinking and practice that emphasized satisfaction of employees' basic needs as the key to increased worker productivity

human resource management (HRM) Activities undertaken to attract, develop, and maintain an effective workforce within an organization

human resource planning The forecasting of human resource needs and the projected matching of individuals with expected job vacancies

human resources perspective A management perspective that suggests jobs should be designed to meet higher-level needs by allowing workers to use their full potential

humanistic perspective A management perspective that emerged around the late nineteenth century that emphasized understanding human behavior, needs, and attitudes in the workplace

hygiene factors Factors that involve the presence or absence of job dissatisfiers, including working conditions, pay, company policies, and interpersonal relationships

idea champion A person who sees the need for productive change and champions it within the organization

implementation The step in the decision-making process that involves using managerial, administrative, and persuasive abilities to ensure that a chosen alternative is carried out

individualism A preference for a loosely knit social framework in which individuals are expected to take care of themselves

individualism approach The ethical concept that acts are moral when they promote the individual's best long-term interests, which ultimately leads to the greater good

informal communication channels Channels of communication that exist outside the formally authorized channels and often cut across vertical chains of command

infrastructure A country's physical facilities, such as highways and airports, that support economic activities

initiating structure The extent to which a leader is task oriented and directs a subordinate's work activities toward goal achievement

internal environment The environment within the organization's boundaries

international dimension The portion of the external environment that represents events originating in foreign countries as well as opportunities for American companies in other countries

international management The management of business operations conducted in more than one country

intranet A network that uses Internet technology to provide access to some or all of the organization's employees

intrinsic reward The satisfactions received in the process of performing an action

intuition The quick apprehension of a situation using past experience, not conscious planning or thought

ISO 9000 A set of international standards for quality management to ensure that products conform to customer requirements

job characteristics model A model of job design that comprises core job dimensions, critical psychological states, and employee growth-need strength

job description A listing of duties as well as desirable qualifications for a particular job

job design The application of motivational theories to the structure of work for improving productivity and satisfaction

job enlargement A job design that combines a series of tasks into one new, broader job to give employees variety and challenge

job enrichment A job design that incorporates achievement, recognition, and other high-level motivators into the work

job evaluation The process of determining the value of jobs within an organization through an examination of job content

job rotation A job design that systematically moves employees from one job to another to provide them with variety and stimulation

job satisfaction A positive attitude toward one's job

job simplification A job design whose purpose is to improve task efficiency by reducing the number of tasks a single person must perform

joint venture A currently popular risk- and cost-sharing approach that many companies are taking to expand in a global market

justice approach The ethical concept that moral decisions must be based on standards of equity, fairness, and impartiality

labor market The people in the environment who can be hired by the organization

large-group intervention OD approach that brings together participants from all parts of the organization, who often are key stakeholders from outside the organization, to discuss problems or opportunities and make plans for change

law of effect The assumption that positively reinforced behavior tends to be repeated and unreinforced or negatively reinforced behavior tends to be inhibited

leadership The ability to influence people toward the attainment of goals

learning A change in behavior or performance as a result of experience

learning organization An organization in which everyone is engaged in identifying and solving problems, enabling the company to continuously experiment, improve, and increase its ability to grow, learn, and achieve its goals

legal-political dimension The dimension of the general environment that includes federal, state, and local government regulations and political activities designed to control company behavior

legitimate power Power that stems from a formal management position in an organization and the authority granted to it

licensing An entry strategy in which an organization in one country makes certain resources available to companies in another in order to participate in the production and sale of its products abroad

line authority Authority in which individuals in management positions have the formal power to direct and control immediate subordinates

listening The skill of grasping facts and feelings to interpret a message's genuine meaning

locus of control The tendency to place the primary responsibility for one's success or failure either within oneself (internally) or on outside forces (externally)

low-context culture A culture in which communication is used to exchange facts and information

LPC scale The "least preferred coworker" questionnaire designed to measure relationship-oriented leadership versus task-oriented leadership

machiavellianism The tendency to focus one's attention on acquiring power and manipulating others for purely personal gain

management The attainment of organizational goals in an effective and efficient manner through planning, organizing, leading, and controlling organizational resources

management by objectives (MBO) A method of management whereby managers and employees define goals for every department, project, and person and use them to monitor subsequent performance

management by wandering around (MBWA) Informal communication channel in which management "wanders around" to describe key ideas and values and to learn about problems

management information systems (MIS) A recent subfield of the management science perspective that seeks to provide relevant information to managers in a timely and cost-efficient manner

management science perspective A management perspective that emerged after World War II and applied mathematics, statistics, and other quantitative techniques to managerial problems

market entry strategy An organizational strategy for entering a foreign market

masculinity A cultural preference for achievement, heroism, assertiveness, work centrality, and material success

mechanistic structure An organizational structure characterized by rigidly defined tasks, many rules and regulations, little teamwork, and centralized decision making

mediation The process of using a disinterested third party to settle a dispute

message The tangible formulation of an idea to be sent to a receiver

middle manager A manager who works at the middle levels of the organization and is responsible for major departments

mission The organization's reason for existence

mission statement A broadly stated definition of the organization's basic business scope and operations that distinguishes it from similar types of organizations

monoculture A culture that accepts only one way of doing things and one set of values and beliefs

moral-rights approach The ethical concept that moral decisions are those that best maintain the rights of those people affected by them

most favored nation A term describing a GATT clause that calls for member countries to grant other member countries the most favorable treatment they accord any country concerning imports and exports

motivation Internal and external forces that arouse enthusiasm, desire, purpose, and persistence; affects productivity and the company's ability to meet its organizational goals

motivators Factors that influence job satisfaction based on fulfillment of high-level needs such as achievement, recognition, responsibility, and opportunity for growth

multiple advocacy A decision-making technique that involves several advocates and presentation of multiple points of view, including minority and unpopular opinions

network structure An organization structure in which major functions are outsourced to discrete organizations and activities are coordinated by a central headquarters

neutralizer A situational variable that counteracts a leadership style and prevents the leader from displaying directive behaviors

new-venture fund A fund that provides resources from which individuals and groups draw to develop new ideas, products, or businesses

new-venture team A unit separate from the mainstream of the organization that is responsible for developing and initiating innovations

nonparticipator role A role in which the individual contributes little to either the task or the socioemotional needs of members

nonprogrammed decision A decision made in response to a situation that is unique, poorly defined, largely unstructured, or involve important consequences for the organization

nonverbal communication Messages sent through human actions and behaviors rather than through words

norm An informal standard of conduct shared by team members that guides their behavior

normative Norms and guidelines on how to reach an ideal outcome

norming The stage of team development in which conflicts developed during the storming stage are resolved and team harmony and unity emerge

obstructive response A response to social demands in which the organization denies responsibility, claims that evidence of misconduct is misleading or distorted, and attempts to obstruct investigation

on-the-job training (OJT) Training in which an experienced employee "adopts" a new employee to teach him or her how to perform job duties

open-book management Sharing financial information and results with all employees throughout the organization

open communication A communication structure that allows sharing of all types of information throughout the company, across functional and hierarchical levels

operational goals Specific, measurable results expected from departments, work groups, and individuals within the organization

operational plans Plans developed at the organization's lower levels that specify action steps toward achieving operational goals and that support tactical planning activities

opportunity A situation in which managers recognize the possibility of enhancing performance beyond current levels

organic structure An organizational structure that is free flowing, has few rules and regulations, encourages employee teamwork, and decentralizes decision making to employees doing the job

organization A social entity that is goal-directed and deliberately structured

organization chart The visual representation of an organization's structure

organization structure A management tool used to define how tasks are divided, deploy resources, and coordinate departments

organizational behavior An interdisciplinary field dedicated to the study of how individuals and groups tend to act in organizations

organizational change The adoption of a new idea or behavior by an organization

organizational citizenship Work behavior that goes beyond job requirements and contributes as needed to the organization's success

organizational commitment Loyalty to, and heavy involvement in, one's organization

organizational control The systematic process through which managers regulate organizational activities to make them consistent with expectations established in plans, targets, and standards of performance

organizational development (OD) The application of behavioral science knowledge to improve an organization's health and effectiveness by coping with environmental changes, improving internal relationships, and increasing problem-solving capabilities

organizational environment All elements existing outside the organization's boundaries that have the potential to affect the organization

organizing The deployment of organizational resources to achieve strategic goals

outsourcing The contracting out of a company's in-house function to a preferred vendor

paper-and-pencil test A written test designed to measure a particular attribute such as intelligence or aptitude

paradigm A shared mind-set that represents a fundamental way of thinking about, perceiving, and understanding the world

path-goal theory A contingency approach to leadership specifying that the leader's responsibility is to increase a subordinate's motivation by clarifying the behaviors necessary for task accomplishment and rewards

partial reinforcement schedule A schedule in which only some occurrences of the desired behavior are reinforced

pay surveys Studies of what other companies pay employees in jobs that correspond to a sample of key positions selected by the organization

pay-trend line A graph that shows the relationship between pay and total job point values for determining the worth of a given job

perception The process people use to make sense of the environment by selecting, organizing, and interpreting information from the environment

perceptual defense The tendency of perceivers to protect themselves by disregarding threatening ideas, objects, or people

perceptual distortions Errors in perceptual judgment that arise from inaccuracies in any part of the perception process

perceptual selectivity The process by which individuals screen and select various environmental stimuli

performance The attainment of organizational goals by using resources in an efficient and effective manner

performance appraisal The process of observing and evaluating an employee's performance, recording the assessment, and providing feedback to the employee

performance gap A disparity between existing and desired performance levels

performing The stage of team development in which members focus on problem solving and accomplishing the team's assigned task

permanent teams Groups of employees who are permanently assigned to solve ongoing, mutual problems

personality The set of characteristics supporting a relatively stable pattern of behavior in response to ideas, objects, or people in the environment

person-job fit The extent to which a person's ability and personality match the requirements of a job

plan A blueprint specifying the resource allocations, schedules, and other actions necessary for attaining goals

planning The act of determining the organization's goals and the means for achieving them

planning task force A temporary group consisting of line managers responsible for developing strategic plans

pluralism The organization accommodates several subcultures, including employees who would otherwise feel isolated and ignored

P→O expectancy The degree of expectation that successful performance of a task will lead to the desired outcome

point system A job evaluation system that assigns a predetermined point value to each compensable job factor in order to determine the worth of a given job

political activity Organizational attempts, such as lobbying, to influence government legislation and regulation

political forces The influence of political and legal institutions on people and organizations

political risk A company's risk of loss of assets, earning power, or managerial control due to politically based events or actions by host governments

power The potential ability to influence the behavior of others

power distance The degree to which people accept inequality in power among institutions, organizations, and people

pressure group An interest group that works within the legal-political framework to influence companies to behave in socially responsible ways

proactive response A response to social demands in which the organization seeks to learn what is in its constituencies' interest and to respond without pressure from them

problem A situation in which organizational accomplishment falls below established goals

problem-solving teams Teams of 5 to 12 hourly employees from the same department who meet to discuss ways of improving quality, efficiency, and the work environment

procedural justice The concept that rules should be clearly stated and consistently and impartially enforced

process theories Motivation theories emphasizing the thought processes that influence behavior

product change A change in the organization's product or service output

programmed decision A decision made in response to a situation that has occurred often enough to enable decision rules to be developed and applied in the future

project manager A person responsible for coordinating the activities of several departments for the completion of a specific project

projection The tendency to see one's own personal traits in other people and to allow these traits to affect one's judgment of others

quality circle A group of 6 to 12 volunteer employees who meet regularly to discuss and solve problems affecting the quality of their work

realistic job preview (RJP) A recruiting approach that gives applicants all pertinent and realistic information about the job and the organization

recruiting The activities or practices involved in seeking out applicants and applying selection procedures to determine qualifications for specific positions

reengineering Radically redesigning business processes to achieve dramatic improvements in cost, quality, service, and speed

referent power Power that results from leadership characteristics that command identification, respect, and admiration from subordinates who then desire to emulate the leader

refreezing OD reinforcement in which individuals acquire a desired new skill or attitude for which they are rewarded by the organization

reinforcement The appropriate application of rewards and punishments meant to modify on-the-job behaviors and cause certain behaviors to be repeated or inhibited

reinforcement theory A motivation theory emphasizing the relationship between behavior and its consequences for the purpose of teaching desired work behaviors

responsibility The duty to perform the task or activity an employee has been assigned

responsibility center An organizational unit under the supervision of a single person who is responsible for its activity

revenue budget A budget that identifies the forecasted and actual revenues of the organization

reward power Power that stems from the authority to reward others

risk Accompanies situations in which outcomes are subject to chance

risk propensity The willingness to undertake risk with the opportunity of gaining a positive result

role A set of expectations for a manager's behavior

role ambiguity A stressor created by uncertainty about the behaviors expected of a person in a particular role

role conflict A stressor created by incompatible demands of different roles

satisfice To choose the first alternative that satisfies criteria minimums, even when better solutions are presumed to exist

schedules of reinforcement The frequency of reinforcement; that is, the frequency of the occurrence and the intervals between the occurrences

scientific management A subfield of the classical management perspective that emphasized scientifically-determined changes in management practices as the solution to improving labor productivity

search The process of learning about current developments inside or outside the organization that can be used to meet a perceived need for change

selection The process of determining the skills, abilities, and other attributes a person needs to perform a particular job

self-directed teams Teams of 5 to 20 multiskilled workers who rotate jobs to produce an entire product or service, often supervised by an elected member

self-serving bias The tendency to overestimate the contribution of internal factors to one's successes and the contribution of external factors to one's failures

semantics The meaning of words and the way they are used

servant leaders Leaders who work to fulfill the needs and goals of subordinates, as well as to achieve the organization's larger mission

shared vision A picture of an ideal future for the organization that includes what the organization will look like, performance outcomes, and underlying values

Shewhart cycle A planning cycle used in companies that have instituted quality management; also called the PDCA Cycle—plan, do, check, act

single-use plans Plans that are developed to achieve a set of goals that are unlikely to be repeated in the future

situational theory A contingency approach to leadership that links the leader's behavioral style with the task readiness of subordinates

slogan A phrase or sentence that succinctly expresses a key corporate value

social contract The unwritten, common rules and perceptions about relationships among people and between employees and management

social facilitation The tendency for the presence of others to influence an individual's motivation and performance

social forces Those aspects of a culture that guide and influence relationships among people and their values, needs, and standards of behavior

social responsibility The obligation of organization management to make decisions and take actions that will enhance the welfare and interests of society as well as the organization

sociocultural dimension The dimension of the general environment representing the demographic characteristics, norms, customs, and values of the population within which the organization operates

socioemotional role A role in which the individual provides support for the emotional needs of team members and social unity

span of management The number of employees who report to a supervisor; also called *span of control*

special-purpose team A team created outside the formal organization to undertake a project of special importance or creativity

staff authority Authority granted to staff specialists in their areas of expertise

stakeholder Any group within or outside the organization that has a stake in the organization's performance

standing plans Ongoing plans used to provide guidance for tasks performed repeatedly within the organization

statistical process control (SPC) An operations management technique involving the application of statistical techniques to improve control of quality

state of equity A situation that exists when the ratio of one person's outcomes to inputs equals that of another's

stereotyping The tendency to assign an individual to a group or broad category and then attribute generalizations about the group to the individual

storming The stage of team development in which individual personalities and roles, and resulting conflicts, emerge

story In organizations, a narrative based on true events that is repeated frequently and shared by organizational employees

strategic goals Broad statements about the organization's direction and future that pertain to the organization as a whole rather than to specific divisions or departments

strategic plans The action steps by which an organization intends to attain its strategic goals

stress A physiological/emotional response to physical or psychological demands in which uncertainty and a lack of personal control become evident and important outcomes are at stake

structural change Any change in the way the organization is designed and managed

substitute A situational variable that makes a leadership style redundant or unnecessary

superordinate goal A goal that cannot be reached by a single party

suppliers People and organizations who provide the raw materials the organization uses to produce its output

survey-feedback activities OD interventions in which questionnaires on organizational climate and other factors are distributed among employees and the results reported back to them

symbol An object, act, or event that conveys significant meaning

symbolic leader A manager who defines and uses signals and symbols to influence corporate culture

tactical goals Goals that define the outcomes that major divisions and departments must achieve in order for the organization to reach its overall goals

tactical plans Plans designed to help execute major strategic plans and to accomplish a specific part of the company's strategy

tall structure A management structure characterized by an overall narrow span of management and a relatively large number of hierarchical levels

task specialist role A role in which the individual devotes personal time and energy to helping the team accomplish its task

team A unit of two or more people who interact and coordinate their work to accomplish a specific goal

team building activities OD interventions that enhance the cohesiveness of departments by helping members learn to function as a team

team cohesiveness The extent to which team members are attracted to the team and motivated to remain in it

task environment The layer of the external environment that directly influences the organization

technical complexity The degree to which machinery is involved in the production to the exclusion of people

technological dimension The dimension of the general environment that includes scientific and technological advancements in the industry and society at large

technology change A change that pertains to the organization's production process

telecommuting Using computers and telecommunications equipment to perform work from home or another remote location

Theory Z A hybrid form of management that incorporates techniques from both Japanese and North American management practices

360-degree feedback A process that uses multiple raters, including self-rating, to appraise employee performance and guide development

time-based competition A strategy of competition based on the ability to deliver products and services faster than competitors

top manager A manager who is at the top of the organizational hierarchy and is responsible for the entire organization

top-down budgeting A budgeting process in which middle and lower-level managers set departmental budget targets in accordance with overall company revenues and expenditures specified by top management

total quality management (TQM) A management approach that focuses organizationwide attention on delivering total quality to customers and includes (1) employee involvement, (2) focus on the customer, (3) benchmarking, and (4) continuous improvement

trade association An association made up of organizations with similar interests for the purpose of influencing the environment

traits Distinguishing personal characteristics such as intelligence, values, and appearance

transactional leader A leader who clarifies a subordinate's role and task requirements, initiates structure, provides rewards, and displays consideration for subordinates

transformational leader A leader distinguished by a special ability to bring about innovation and change

Type A behavior Behavior pattern characterized by extreme competitiveness, impatience, aggressiveness, and devotion to work

Type B behavior Behavior pattern that lacks every Type A characteristic and includes a more balanced, relaxed lifestyle

uncertainty Accompanies situations in which managers know the goals they wish to achieve, but information about alternatives and future events is incomplete or unpredictable

uncertainty avoidance A value characterized by people's intolerance for uncertainty and ambiguity and resulting support for beliefs that promise certainty and conformity

unfreezing OD diagnosis in which participants become aware of problems and increase their willingness to change

upward communication The flow of messages from the lower to the higher levels in the organization's hierarchy

utilitarian approach The ethical concept that moral behaviors produce the greatest good for the greatest number

valence The value or attraction an individual has for an outcome

validity The relationship between an applicant's score on a selection device and his or her future job performance

value The combined benefit to the customer of cost and quality

vertical team A formal team composed of a manager and his or her subordinates in the organization's formal chain of command

virtual team A team that uses computer technology and groupware so that geographically distant members can collaborate on projects and reach common goals

Vroom-Jago model A model designed to help managers gauge the appropriate amount of subordinate participation in decision making

whistle-blowing The disclosure by an employee of illegal, immoral, or illegitimate practices by the organization

wholly owned foreign affiliate A foreign subsidiary over which an organization has complete control

work redesign The altering of jobs to increase both the quality of employees' work experience and their productivity

work specialization The degree to which organizational tasks are subdivided into individual jobs; also called *division of labor*

workforce diversity Hiring and being inclusive with people who have different human qualities and/or belong to different cultural groups

CREDITS

PHOTO

LITERARY

York: Wiley, 1987), pp. 176-177. Reprinted by permission of John Wiley & Sons, Inc.

Page 91 Leading the Revolution, from "A Passage to India Eases a Worker Scarcity in Ohio," by Timothy Aeppel from *The Wall Street Journal,* October 5, 1999, pp. B1, B20. Copyright © 1999 by Dow Jones, Inc. Reprinted by permission of Dow Jones, Inc., via Copyright Clearance Center.

Page 97 Leading the Revolution, from "Power to the People," by Alex Markels, *Fast Company,* February-March 1998, pp. 155-165.

Pages 98-99 Summary and Management Solution, from "Van @ttack," *The Economist,* September 18, 1999, pp. 69-70, www.economist.com. Copyright © 1999 by The Economist Newspaper Group, Inc. Further reproduction prohibited. Reprinted with permission.

Pages 99-100 Manager's Workbook, from United Nations Web site, 1999 and *State-of-the-World Test,* by Jan Drum, Steve Hughes, and George Otere, Global Winners (Yarmouth, ME: Intercultural Press), 1994, pp. 9-12.

Pages 102-104 Case for Critical Analysis: Unocal Corporation, from "Unocal Corporation," *International Management: Text and Cases* by David H. Holt. Copyright © 1998 by Harcourt, Inc. Reprinted by permission of the publisher.

Page 110 Technology for Tomorrow, from firstuse.com, from "First to Mark It," by Jamie Beckett, *CIO Web Business,* May 1, 1999, pp. 24-25. Reprinted by permission of the publisher.

Exhibit 4.3 From "A Cultural Perspective on Changing and Developing Organizational Ethics," by Linda Klebe Trevino, *Research in Organizational Change and Development,* edited by R. Woodman and W. Pasmore. Copyright © 1990 by JAI Press Inc. Reprinted by permission of the publisher.

Page 130 Summary and Management Solution, from "In E/Town We Trust," by Charles Pappas, *Success,* May 1999, pp. 22-25. Reprinted by permission.

Page 151 Focus on Ethics, from "When the Devil Is In the Emails," by Marcia Stepanek, with Steve Hamm, *Business Week,* June 8, 1998, pp. 72-74. Copyright © 1998 by Business Week.

Reprinted by permission of the publisher.

Page 161 Leading the Revolution, from "The Perfect Internet Business," by Edward O. Welles, *Inc.,* August 1999, pp. 71-78. Copyright © 1999 by Inc. Reprinted by permission of the publisher.

Page 164 Technology for Tomorrow, from "Choose Your Medicine," by Sari Kalin, *CIO Web Business,* June 1, 1999, pp. 30-38. Reprinted by permission of the publisher.

Pages 166-167 Cisco Systems, from "Computing's Next Superpower," by Brent Schlender, *Fortune,* May 12, 1997, pp. 88-101. Copyright © by Time Inc. Reprinted by permission.

Page 180 Gospelcom.net and iBelieve, from "As Religion Spreads on the Web, Will Ideal or Mammon Prevail?" by Thomas A. Weber, *The Wall Street Journal,* November 29, 1999, p. B1. Copyright © 1999 by Dow Jones, Inc. Reprinted by permission of Dow Jones, Inc., via Copyright Clearance Center.

Exhibit 6.4 From *The New Leadership: Managing Participation in Organizations,* (Englewood Cliffs, NJ: Prentice-Hall, 1988) by Victor H. Vroom and Arthur G. Jago. Copyright © 1987 by V. H. Vroom and A. G. Jago. Used by permission of the authors.

Exhibit 6.5 From *The New Leadership: Managing Participation in Organizations,* (Englewood Cliffs, NJ: Prentice-Hall, 1988) by Victor H. Vroom and Arthur G. Jago. Copyright © 1987 by V. H. Vroom and A. G. Jago. Used by permission of the authors.

Page 203 Focus on Collaboration, from "Making the Internet Work for You," by Tim McCollum, *Nation's Business,* March 1997, pp. 6-13. Reprinted with permission.

Pages 202-204 Puck Pages, from "A Fine and Private Page," by Jim Sterne, *Inc. Technology,* 1999, No. 4, pp. 144-145. Copyright © 1999 by Inc. Reprinted by permission of the publisher.

Exhibit 6.8 Output from ArcView® GIS Software reprinted courtesy of Environmental Systems Research Institute, Inc. Copyright © 1995 by Environmental Systems Research Institute, Inc. All rights reserved. ArcView® is a registered trademark of ESRI.

Exhibit 12.4   The Leadership Grid® Figure from Robert R. Blake and Anne Adams McCanse, *Leadership Dilemmas—Grid Solutions* (Houston: Gulf, 1991), 29. Copyright © 1991 by Scientific Methods, Inc. Reproduced by permission of the owners.

Exhibit 12.5   From Paul Hersey, *Situational Selling* (Escondido, CA: Center for Leadership Studies, Inc., 1985). Copyrighted material. All rights reserved. Used by permission.

Page 401   Summary & Management Solution, from "Silicon Valley Hybrid: A Boss Who Makes Others," by Hal Lancaster, *The Wall Street Journal,* October 26, 1999, p. B1. Copyright © 1999 by Dow Jones, Inc. Reprinted by permission of Dow Jones, Inc., via Copyright Clearance Center.

Page 418   Technology for Tomorrow, from "Changing Internet Opening New Doors to Women Entrepreneurs," by Vicki Torres, *Los Angeles Times,* October 27, 1999, p. 8. Copyright © 1998 by the *Los Angeles Times*. Reprinted by permission of the publisher.

Page 432   Manager's Workshop, adapted from "Must See TV: The Timelessness of Television as a Teaching Tool," presented by Courtney Hunt at Academy of Management, August 2000. Reprinted by permission of the author.

Page 458   The Learning Organization, from "Want to Grow? Hire a Shrink!" by Scott Kirsner, *Fast Company,* December-January 1998, p. 68, 70. Reprinted by permission.

Pages 461-462   Summary and Management Solution, from "A Founder's Lesson: Market Reality Matters More Than a Mission," by Hal Lancaster, *The Wall Street Journal,* November 2, 1999, p. B1. Copyright © 1999 by Dow Jones, Inc. Reprinted by permission of Dow Jones, Inc., via Copyright Clearance Center.

Page 462-463   Manager's Workbook, from *Managers As Facilitators,* by Richard G. Weaver and John D. Farrell. Copyright © 1997 by Richard G. Weaver and John D. Farrell. All rights reserved. Reprinted by permission of Berrett-Koehler Publishers, Inc., San Francisco, CA.

Page 473   Focus on Diversity, from "One VP, Two Brains," by Patricia Nakache, *Fortune,* December 20, 1999, pp. 327-329. Copyright © 1999 by Time Inc. Reprinted by permission.

Page 478   Technology for Tomorrow, from "Group Insurance," by William R. Pape, *Inc. Technology,* 1997, no. 2, 29, 31. Copyright © 1997 by Inc. Reprinted by permission of the publisher.

Page 505   Leading the Revolution, from "Change of Viewpoint," by Robert A. Mamis, *CFO,* February 1998, pp. 54-58. Reprinted by permission of the publisher.

Exhibit 16.5   From Ross Johnson and William O. Winchell, *Management and Quality*, (Milwaukee, WI: American Society for Quality Control, 1989), 7.

Exhibit 16.7   From *Out of the Crisis* by W. Edwards Deming. Copyright © 1986 by The W. Edwards Deming Institute®. Reprinted by permission of the publisher.

Page 522   Focus on Collaboration, from "All Together Now," by Cathy Lazere, *CFO,* February 1998, p. 28-36. Reprinted by permission of the publisher.

Pages 527-528   Manager's Workbook, adapted from "Are You Fast Enough to Succeed in Internet Time? Does Your Business Have What it Takes to Move at Internet Speed?" *Entrepreneur Magazine*, September 1999.

Pages 528-529   Manager's Workbook, adapted from "An Out of Control Organizational Control Mechanism," by Eugene H. Baker, III and Kenneth M. Jennings, *Journal of Management Education*, Vol. 18 (3), 1994, 380-384.

Pages 530-531   Case for Critical Analysis, from "A Pattern of Success: Can This Company Be Duplicated?" by Joseph Maciariello, *Drucker Management,* No. 1, Spring 1997, p. 7-11. Reprinted by permission of the author.

Pages 537-538   Video Case, from brochure, *North Texas Public Broadcasting*. Published by KERA, 1999. Reprinted by permission of KERA/KDTN

Pages 547-548   Video Case, from "Sky King," by Kathleen Melymuka from *Computerworld,* September 28, 1998, www.computerworld.com. Reprinted by permission of Computerworld, Inc.

Pages 550-551   Video Case, from "Sky King," by Kathleen Melymuka from *Computerworld,* September 28, 1998, www.computerworld.com. Reprinted by permission of Computerworld, Inc.